# Microsoft®
# Windows Server 2012
# Inside Out

William R. Stanek

PUBLISHED BY
Microsoft Press
A Division of Microsoft Corporation
One Microsoft Way
Redmond, Washington 98052-6399

Library of Congress Control Number: 2012955900
ISBN: 978-0-7356-6631-3

Printed and bound in the United States of America.

Fourth Printing: April 2014

Microsoft Press books are available through booksellers and distributors worldwide. If you need support related to this book, email Microsoft Press Book Support at mspinput@microsoft.com. Please tell us what you think of this book at http://www.microsoft.com/learning/booksurvey.

Microsoft and the trademarks listed at http://www.microsoft.com/about/legal/en/us/IntellectualProperty/Trademarks/EN-US.aspx are trademarks of the Microsoft group of companies. All other marks are property of their respective owners.

The example companies, organizations, products, domain names, email addresses, logos, people, places, and events depicted herein are fictitious. No association with any real company, organization, product, domain name, email address, logo, person, place, or event is intended or should be inferred.

**Acquisitions Editor:** Anne Hamilton
**Developmental Editor:** Karen Szall
**Project Editor:** Karen Szall
**Editorial Production:** Waypoint Press
**Technical Reviewer:** Mitch Tulloch; Technical Review services provided by Content Master, a member of CM Group, Ltd.
**Copyeditor:** Roger LeBlanc
**Indexer:** Christina Yeager
**Cover:** Microsoft Press Brand Team

[2013-09-27]

*To my readers*—Windows Server 2012 Inside Out *is my 40th book for Microsoft Press. Thank you for being there with me through many books and many years.*

*To my wife—for many years, through many books, many millions of words, and many thousands of pages she's been there, providing support and encouragement and making every place we've lived a home.*

*To my kids—for helping me see the world in new ways, for having exceptional patience and boundless love, and for making every day an adventure.*

*To Anne, Karen, Martin, Lucinda, Juliana, and many others who've helped out in ways both large and small.*

—WILLIAM R. STANEK

# Contents at a Glance

# Table of Contents

## Part 1: Windows Server 2012 Overview

---

**What do you think of this book? We want to hear from you!**

Microsoft is interested in hearing your feedback so we can continually improve our books and learning resources for you. To participate in a brief online survey, please visit:

**microsoft.com/learning/booksurvey**

## Part 2:  Managing Windows Server 2012 Systems

## Part 3 Managing Windows Server 2012 Storage and File Systems

## Part 4: Managing Windows Server 2012 Networking and Domain Services

# Part 5:  Managing Active Directory and Security

---

**What do you think of this book? We want to hear from you!**

Microsoft is interested in hearing your feedback so we can continually improve our books and learning resources for you. To participate in a brief online survey, please visit:

**microsoft.com/learning/booksurvey**

# Introduction

**W**elcome to *Windows Server 2012 Inside Out*. As the author of many popular technology books, I've been writing professionally about Windows and Windows Server since 1994. Over the years, I've gained a unique perspective—the kind of perspective you can gain only after working with technologies for many years. The advantage for you, the reader, is that my solid understanding of these technologies allowed me to dig into the Windows Server 2012 architecture, internals, and configuration to see how things really work under the hood and then pass this information on to you throughout this book.

From top to bottom, Windows Server 2012 is substantially different from earlier versions of Window Server. Not only are there major changes throughout the operating system, but this just might be the first version of Windows Server that you manage using a touch-based user interface. If you do end up managing it this way, mastering the touch-based UI and the revised interface options will be essential for your success. For this reason, I discuss both the touch UI and the traditional mouse and keyboard techniques throughout this book.

When you are working with touch UI–enabled computers, you can manipulate onscreen elements in ways that weren't possible previously. You can enter text using the onscreen keyboard and manipulate onscreen elements in the following ways:

- **Tap**   Tap an item by touching it with your finger. A tap or double-tap of elements on the screen generally is the equivalent of a mouse click or double-click.

- **Press and hold**   Press your finger down, and leave it there for a few seconds. Pressing and holding elements on the screen generally is the equivalent of a right-click.

- **Swipe to select**   Slide an item a short distance in the opposite direction of how the page scrolls. This selects the items and also might bring up related commands. If pressing and holding doesn't display commands and options for an item, try swiping to select instead.

- **Swipe from edge (slide in from edge)**   Starting from the edge of the screen, swipe or slide in. Sliding in from the right edge opens the Charms panel. Sliding in from the left edge shows open apps and allows you to easily switch between them. Sliding in from the top or bottom edge shows commands for the active element.

- **Pinch**   Touch an item with two or more fingers, and then move those fingers toward each other. Pinching zooms in or shows less information.

- **Stretch**   Touch an item with two or more fingers, and then move those fingers away from each other. Stretching zooms out or shows more information.

In this book, I teach you how server roles, role services, and features work; why they work the way they do; and how to customize them to meet your needs. Regardless of your job title, if you're deploying, configuring, managing, or maintaining Windows Server 2012, this book is for you. To pack in as much information as possible, I had to assume that you have basic networking skills and a basic understanding of Windows Server, and that you are familiar with Windows commands and procedures. With this in mind, I don't devote entire chapters to basic skills or why you want to use Windows Server. Instead, I focus on configuration, security, auditing, storage management, performance analysis, performance tuning, troubleshooting, and much more.

# Conventions

The following conventions are used in this book:

- **Abbreviated menu commands**   For your convenience, this book uses abbreviated menu commands. For example, "Tap or click Tools, Track Changes, Highlight Changes" means that you should tap or click the Tools menu, select Track Changes, and then tap or click the Highlight Changes command.

- **Boldface type**   **Boldface** type is used to indicate text that you enter or type.

- **Initial Capital Letters**   The first letters of the names of menus, dialog boxes, dialog box elements, and commands are capitalized. Example: the Save As dialog box.

- **Italicized type**   *Italicized* type is used to indicate new terms.

- **Plus sign (+) in text**   Keyboard shortcuts are indicated by a plus sign (+) separating two key names. For example, Ctrl+Alt+Delete means that you press the Ctrl, Alt, and Delete keys at the same time.

# How to reach the author

**Email**: williamstanek@aol.com

**Web**: *http://www.williamrstanek.com/*

**Facebook**: *https://www.facebook.com/William.Stanek.Author*

**Twitter**: *http://twitter.com/williamstanek*

# Errata & book support

We've made every effort to ensure the accuracy of this book and its companion content. Any errors that have been reported since this book was published are listed on our Microsoft Press site:

*http://go.microsoft.com/FWLink/?Linkid=275534*

If you find an error that is not already listed, you can report it to us through the same page.

If you need additional support, email Microsoft Press Book Support at *mspinput@microsoft.com*.

Please note that product support for Microsoft software is not offered through the addresses above.

# We want to hear from you

At Microsoft Press, your satisfaction is our top priority, and your feedback our most valuable asset. Please tell us what you think of this book at:

*http://www.microsoft.com/learning/booksurvey*

The survey is short, and we read every one of your comments and ideas. Thanks in advance for your input!

# Stay in touch

Let's keep the conversation going! We're on Twitter: *http://twitter.com/MicrosoftPress*.

# Introducing Windows Server 2012

WINDOWS Server 2012 is Microsoft's most powerful, versatile, and fully featured server operating system yet. If you've been using Windows Server operating systems for a while, I think you'll be impressed. Why? For starters, Windows Server 2012 includes a significantly enhanced operating system kernel, the NT 6.2 kernel. Because this kernel is also used by Windows 8, the two operating systems share a common code base and many common features, enabling you to readily apply what you know about Windows 8 to Windows Server 2012.

In Windows Server 2012, Microsoft delivers a server operating system that is something more than the sum of its parts. Windows Server 2012 isn't just a server operating system or a network operating system. It is a best-of-class operating system with the foundation technologies necessary to provide networking, application, web, and cloud-based services that can be used anywhere within your organization. From top to bottom, Windows Server 2012 is dramatically different from earlier releases of Windows Server operating systems—so much so that it has an entirely new interface as well.

The way you approach Windows Server 2012 will depend on your background and your implementation plans. If you are moving to Windows Server 2012 from an early Windows server operating system or switching from UNIX, you'll find that Windows Server 2012 is a significant change that requires a whole new way of thinking about the networking, application services, and interoperations between clients and servers. The learning curve will be steep, but you will find clear transition paths to Windows Server 2012. You will also find that Windows Server 2012 has an extensive command-line interface that makes it easier to manage servers, workstations, and, indeed, the entire network, using both graphical and command-line administration tools.

If you are moving from Windows Server 2008 or Windows Server 2008 R2 to Windows Server 2012, you'll find the changes are no less significant but easier to understand. You are already familiar with the core technologies and administration techniques. Your learning curve might still be steep, but in only some areas, not all of them.

You can adopt Windows Server 2012 incrementally as well. For example, you might add Windows Server 2012 Print And Document Services and Windows Server 2012 File And Storage Services to allow the organization to take advantage of the latest enhancements and capabilities without having to implement a full transition of existing servers. In most, but not all, cases, incremental adoption has little or no impact on the network, while allowing the organization to test new technologies and incrementally roll out features to users as part of a standard continuance or upgrade process.

Regardless of your deployment plans and whether you are reading this book to prepare for implementation of Windows Server 2012 or to manage existing implementations, my mission in this book is to help you take full advantage of all the features in Windows Server 2012. You will find the detailed inside information you need to get up to speed quickly with Windows Server 2012 changes and technologies, to make the right setup and configuration choices the first time, and to work around the rough edges, annoyances, and faults of this complex operating system. If the default settings are less than optimal, I'll show you how to fix them so that things work the way you want them to work. If something doesn't function like it should, I'll let you know and I'll also show you the fastest, surest way to work around the issue. You'll find plenty of hacks and secrets, too.

To pack as much information as possible into the 1500-plus pages of this book, I am assuming that you have basic networking skills and some experience managing Windows-based networks but that you don't need me to explain the basic structure and architecture of an operating system. So, I'm not going to waste your time answering such questions as, "What's the point of networks?", "Why use Windows Server 2012?", or "What's the difference between the GUI and the command line?" Instead, I'll start with a discussion of what Windows Server 2012 has to offer so that you can learn about changes that will most affect you, and then I'll follow this discussion with a comprehensive, informative look at Windows Server 2012 planning and installation.

# Getting to know Windows Server 2012

A primary purpose of Windows Server 2012 is to ensure that the operating system can be optimized for use in small, medium, and large enterprises. An edition of the server operating system is available to meet your organization's needs whether you want to deploy a basic server for hosting applications, a network server for hosting domain services, a robust enterprise server for hosting essential applications, or a highly available datacenter server for hosting critical business solutions.

Windows Server 2012 is available for production use only on 64-bit hardware. 64-bit computing has changed substantially since it was first introduced for Windows operating systems. Not only do computers running 64-bit versions of Windows perform better and run faster than their 32-bit counterparts, they are also more scalable because they can process more data per clock cycle, address more memory, and perform numeric calculations faster. The primary 64-bit architecture supported by Windows Server 2012 is based on 64-bit extensions to the x86 instructions set, which is implemented in AMD64 processors, Intel Xeon processors with 64-bit extension technology, and other processors. This architecture offers native 32-bit processing and 64-bit extension processing, allowing simultaneous 32-bit and 64-bit computing.

# INSIDE OUT   Running 32-bit applications on 64-bit hardware

In most cases, 64-bit hardware is compatible with 32-bit applications; however, 32-bit applications typically perform better on 32-bit hardware. Windows Server 2012 64-bit editions support both 64-bit and 32-bit applications using the Windows on Windows 64 (WOW64) x86 emulation layer. The WOW64 subsystem isolates 32-bit applications from 64-bit applications. This prevents file system and registry problems. The operating system provides interoperability across the 32-bit/64-bit boundary for Component Object Model (COM) and basic operations, such as cut, copy, and paste from the clipboard. However, 32-bit processes cannot load 64-bit dynamic-link libraries (DLLs), and 64-bit processes cannot load 32-bit DLLs.

64-bit computing is designed for performing operations that are memory-intensive and that require extensive numeric calculations. With 64-bit processing, applications can load large data sets entirely into physical memory (that is, RAM), which reduces the need to page to disk and increases performance substantially.

## Note

In this text, I typically refer to 32-bit systems designed for x86 architecture as *32-bit systems* and 64-bit systems designed for x64 architecture as *64-bit systems*. Support for Itanium 64-bit (IA-64) processors is no longer standard in Windows operating systems.

Running instances of Windows Server 2012 can either be in a physical operating system environment or a virtual operating system environment. To better support mixed environments, Microsoft introduced a new licensing model, based on the number of processors, users, and virtual operating system environments. Thus, the four main product editions can be used as follows:

- **Windows Server 2012 Foundation**   Has limited features and is available only from original equipment manufacturers (OEMs). This edition supports one physical processor, up to 15 users, and one physical environment, but it does not support virtualized environments. Although there is a specific user limit, a separate client access license (CAL) is not required for every user or device accessing the server.

- **Windows Server 2012 Essentials**   Has limited features. This edition supports up to two physical processors, up to 25 users, and one physical environment, but it does not support virtualized environments. Although there is a specific user limit, a separate CAL is not required for every user or device accessing the server.

- **Windows Server 2012 Standard**   Has all the key features. It supports up to 64 physical processors, one physical environment, and up to two virtual instances. Two incremental virtual instances and two incremental physical processors are added for each Standard license. Thus, a server with four processors, one physical environment, and four virtual instances would need two Standard licenses, but the same server with eight virtual environments would need four Standard licenses. CALs are required for every user or device accessing the server.

- **Windows Server 2012 Datacenter**   Has all the key features. It supports up to 64 physical processors, one physical environment, and unlimited virtual instances. Two incremental physical processors are added for each Datacenter license. Thus, a server with two processors, one physical environment, and 32 virtual instances would need only one Datacenter license, but the same server with four processors would need two Datacenter licenses. CALs are required for every user or device accessing the server.

> **Note**
>
> Windows Server 2012 Datacenter is not available for retail purchase. If you want to use the Datacenter edition, you need to purchase it through Volume Licensing, an OEM, or a Services Provider Licensing Agreement (SPLA).

You implement virtual operating system environments using Hyper-V. Hyper-V is a virtual-machine technology that allows multiple guest operating systems to run concurrently on one computer and provide separate applications and services to client computers, as shown in Figure 1-1. As part of the Hyper-V role, which can be installed on servers with x64-based processors that implement hardware-assisted virtualization and hardware data execution protection, the Windows hypervisor acts as the virtual machine engine, providing the necessary layer of software for installing guest operating systems. You can, for example, use this technology to concurrently run Ubuntu, Linux, and Windows Server 2012 on the same computer.

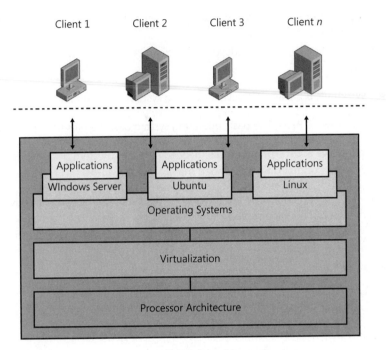

**Figure 1-1** A conceptual view of virtual machine technology.

> **Note**
> With Hyper-V enabled, Windows Server 2012 Standard and Datacenter support up to 320 logical processors. Otherwise, these operating systems support up to 640 logical processors.

Hyper-V also is included as a feature of Windows 8 Pro and Windows 8 Enterprise. The number of virtual machines you can run on any individual computer depends on the computer's hardware configuration and workload. During setup, you specify the amount of memory available to a virtual machine. Although that memory allocation can be changed, the amount of memory actively allocated to a virtual machine cannot be otherwise used. Virtualization can offer performance improvements, reduce the number of servers, and reduce the Total Cost of Ownership (TCO).

# Windows 8 and Windows Server 2012

Like Windows Server 2012, Windows 8 has several main editions. These editions include the following:

- **Windows 8**   The entry-level operating system designed for home users

- **Windows 8 Pro**   The basic operating system designed for use in Windows domains

- **Windows 8 Enterprise**   The enhanced operating system designed for use in Windows domains with extended management features

Windows 8 Pro and Enterprise are the only editions intended for use in Active Directory domains. You can manage servers running Windows Server 2012 from a computer running Windows 8 Pro or Windows 8 Enterprise using the Remote Server Administration Tools for Windows 8. Download the tools from the Microsoft Download Center (*http://download .microsoft.com*).

Windows 8 uses the NT 6.2 kernel, the same kernel that Windows Server 2012 uses. Sharing the same kernel means that Windows 8 and Windows Server 2012 share the following components as well as others:

- **Automatic Updates**   Responsible for performing automatic updates to the operating system. This ensures that the operating system is up to date and has the most recent security updates. If you update a server from the standard Windows Update to Microsoft Update, you can get updates for additional products. By default, automatic updates are installed but not enabled on servers running Windows Server 2012. You can configure automatic updates using the Windows Update utility in Control Panel.

- **BitLocker Drive Encryption**   Provides an extra layer of security for a server's hard disks. This protects the disks from attackers who have physical access to the server. BitLocker encryption can be used on servers with or without a Trusted Platform Module (TPM). When you add this feature to a server using the Add Roles And Features Wizard, you can manage it using the BitLocker Drive Encryption utility in Control Panel.

- **Remote Assistance**   Provides an assistance feature that allows an administrator to send a remote assistance invitation to a more senior administrator. The senior administrator can then accept the invitation to view the user's desktop and temporarily take control of the computer to resolve a problem. When you add this feature to a server using the Add Roles And Features Wizard, you can manage it using options on the Remote tab of the System Properties dialog box.

- **Remote Desktop**   Provides a remote connectivity feature that allows you to remotely connect to and manage a server from another computer. By default, Remote Desktop is installed but not enabled on servers running Windows Server 2012. You can manage the Remote Desktop configuration using options on the Remote tab of the System Properties dialog box. You can establish remote connections using the Remote Desktop Connection utility.

- **Task Scheduler**   Allows you to schedule execution of one-time and recurring tasks, such as tasks used for performing routine maintenance. Like Windows 8, Windows Server 2012 makes extensive use of the scheduled task facilities. You can view and work with scheduled tasks in Computer Management.

- **Desktop Experience**   Installs additional Windows 8 desktop functionality on a server. You can use this feature when you use Windows Server 2012 as your desktop operating system. When you add this feature using the Add Roles And Features Wizard, the server's desktop functionality is enhanced and these programs are installed as well: Windows Media Player, desktop themes, Video for Windows (AVI support), Disk Cleanup, Sync Center, Sound Recorder, Character Map, and Snipping Tool.

- **Windows Firewall**   Helps protect a computer from attack by unauthorized users. Windows Server 2012 includes a basic firewall called Windows Firewall and an advanced firewall called Windows Firewall With Advanced Security. By default, the firewalls are not enabled on server installations.

- **Windows Time**   Synchronizes the system time with world time to ensure that the system time is accurate. You can configure computers to synchronize with a specific time server. The way Windows Time works depends on whether a computer is a member of a domain or a workgroup. In a domain, domain controllers are used for time synchronization and you can manage this feature through Group Policy. In a workgroup, you use Internet time servers for time synchronization and you can manage this feature through the Date And Time utility.

- **Wireless LAN Service**   Installs the Wireless LAN Service feature to enable wireless connections. Wireless networking with Windows Server 2012 works the same as it does with Windows 8. If a server has a wireless adapter, you can enable this feature using the Add Roles And Features Wizard.

In most instances, you can configure and manage these core components in exactly the same way on both Windows 8 and Windows Server 2012.

# Planning for Windows Server 2012

Deploying Windows Server 2012 is a substantial undertaking, even on a small network. Just the task of planning a Windows Server 2012 deployment can be a daunting process, especially in a large enterprise. The larger the business, however, the more important it is that the planning process be thorough and fully account for the proposed project's goals, as well as lay out exactly how those goals will be accomplished.

Accommodating the goals of all the business units in a company can be difficult, and it is best accomplished with a well-planned series of steps that includes checkpoints and plenty of opportunity for management participation. The organization as a whole will benefit from your thorough preparation and so will the Information Technology (IT) department. Careful planning can also help you avoid common obstacles by helping you identify potential pitfalls and then determine how best to avoid them, or at least be ready for any unavoidable complications.

## Your plan: The big picture

A clear road map can help with any complex project, and deploying Windows Server 2012 in the enterprise is certainly a complex project. A number of firms have developed models to describe IT processes such as planning and systems management. For our purposes, I'll break down the deployment process into a roughly sequential set of tasks:

- **Identify the team** For all but the smallest rollouts of a new operating system, a team of people will be involved in both the planning and deployment processes. The actual size and composition of this team will be different in each situation. Collecting the right mixture of skills and expertise will help ensure the success of your project.

- **Assess your goals** Any business undertaking the move to Windows Server 2012 has many reasons for doing so, only some of which are obvious to the IT department. You need to carefully identify the goals of the entire company before determining the scope of the project to ensure that all critical goals are met.

- **Analyze the existing environment** Examine the current network environment, even if you think that you know *exactly* how everything works—you will often find you are only partially correct. Gather hardware and software inventories, network maps, and lists of which servers are providing which services. Also, identify critical business processes, and examine the administrative and security approaches that are currently in place. Windows Server 2012 offers a number of improvements, and you'll find it useful to know which ones are particularly important in your environment.

- **Define the project scope**   Project scope is often one of the more difficult areas to pin down, and one that deserves particular attention in the planning process. Defining scope requires prioritizing the goals of the various groups within the organization and then realistically assessing what can be accomplished within an acceptable budget and time frame. It's not often that the wish list of features and capabilities from the entire company can be fulfilled in the initial, or even later, deployment.

- **Design the new network environment**   After you have pinned down the project scope, you must develop a detailed design for the new operating system deployment and the affected portions of the network. During this time, you should create documentation describing the end state of the network, as well as the process of getting there. This design document serves as a road map for the people building the testing environment and, with refinements during the testing process, for the IT department later on.

- **Test the design**   Thorough testing in the lab is an often overlooked, but critically important, phase of deploying a new network operating system. By building a test lab and putting a prototype environment through its paces, you can identify and solve many problems in a controlled environment rather than in the field.

- **Install Windows Server 2012**   After you have validated your design in the lab and management has approved the deployment, you can begin to install Windows Server 2012 in your production environment. The installation process has two phases:

  - **Pilot phase**   During the pilot phase, you deploy and test a small group of servers running Windows Server 2012 (and perhaps clients running Microsoft Windows 8) in a production environment. You should pick a pilot group that is comfortable working with new technology, and for whom minor interruptions will not pose significant problems. In other words, this is not a good thing to do to the president of the company or the finance department just before taxes are due.

  - **Rollout**   After you have determined that the pilot phase was a success, you can begin the rollout to the rest of the company. Make sure you schedule adequate downtime, and allow for ongoing minor interruptions and increased support demands as users encounter changed functionality.

As mentioned, these steps are generally sequential, but not exclusively so. You are likely to find that as you work through one phase of planning, you must return to activities that are technically part of an earlier phase. This is actually a good thing, because it means you are refining your plan dynamically as you discover new factors and contingencies.

## INSIDE OUT Getting off to a quick start

People need not be assigned to all these tasks at the beginning of the planning process. If you have people who can take on the needs analysis and research on the current and new network environment, you can get the project under way while recruiting the rest of the project team.

## Identifying your organizational teams

A project like this requires a lot of time and effort as well as a broad range of knowledge, expertise, and experience. Unless you are managing a very small network, this project is likely to require more than one person to plan and implement. Team members are assigned to various roles, each of which is concerned with a different aspect of the project.

Each of these roles can be filled by one or more persons, devoting all or part of their workday—and beyond in some cases—to the project. No direct correlation exists between a team role and a single individual who performs it. In a large organization, a team of individuals might fulfill each of these roles, while in a small organization one person can fill more than one role.

As with IT processes, a number of vendors and consultants have put together team models, which you can use in designing your own team. Specific teams you might want to use include

- **Architecture team** In increasingly complex IT environments, there needs to be someone responsible for overall project architecture and providing guidance for integrating the project into existing architecture. This role is filled by the architecture team. Specific deliverables include the architecture design and guidance for the integration solution.

- **Program management team** Program management's primary responsibility is ensuring that project goals are met within the constraints set forth at the beginning of the project. Program management handles the functional design, budget, schedule, and reporting. Specific deliverables include a vision or scope document, functional specifications, a master project plan, a master project schedule, and status reports.

- **Product management team** This team is responsible for identifying the business and user needs of the project and ensuring that the final plan meets those needs.

Specific deliverables include the project charter and team orientation guidance as well as documents for project structure documents and initial risk assessment.

- **User experience team**  This team manages the transition of users to the new environment. This includes developing and delivering user training, as well as conducting an analysis of user feedback during testing and the pilot deployment. Specific deliverables include user reference manuals, usability test scenarios, and user interface graphical elements.

- **Development team**  The development team is responsible for defining the physical design and feature set of the project and estimating the budget and time needed for project completion. Specific deliverables include any necessary source code or binaries as well as necessary integrated-solution components.

- **Testing team**  The testing team is critical in ensuring that the final deployment is successful. It designs and builds the test environment, develops a testing plan, and then performs the tests and resolves any issues it discovers before the pilot deployment occurs. Specific deliverables include test specifications, test cases with expected results, test metrics, test scripts, test data, and test reports.

- **Release management team**  The release management team designs the test deployment and then performs that deployment as a means of verifying the reliability of the deployment before widespread adoption. Specific deliverables include deployment processes and procedures, installation scripts and configuration settings for deployment, operations guides, help desk and support procedures, knowledge base, help and training materials, operations documentation, and troubleshooting documentation.

Working together, these teams cover the various aspects of a significant project, such as rolling out Windows Server 2012. Although all IT projects share some things in common, and therefore need someone to handle those areas of the project, that's where the commonality stops. Each company has IT needs related to its specific business activities. This might mean additional team members are needed to manage those aspects of the project. For example, if external clients, the public, or both also access some of your IT systems as users, you have a set of user acceptance and testing requirements different from many other businesses.

The project team needs business managers who understand, and who can represent, the needs of the various business units. This requires knowledge of both the business operations and a clear picture of the daily tasks performed by staff.

Representatives of the IT department bring their technical expertise to the table not only to detail the inner workings of the network, but also to help business managers realistically assess how technology can help their departments and sort out the impractical goals from the realistic ones.

Make sure that all critical aspects of business operations are covered—include representatives from all departments that have critical IT needs, and be sure the team takes the needs of the entire company into account. This means that people on the project team must collect information from line-of-business managers and the people actually doing the work. (Surprisingly enough, the latter escapes many a project team.)

After you have a team together, management must ensure that team members have adequate time and resources to fulfill the tasks required of them for the project. This can mean shifting all or part of their usual workload to others for the project duration or providing resources such as Internet access, project-related software, and so on. Any project is easier, and more likely to be successful, with this critical real-time support from management.

# INSIDE OUT  Hiring talent

Sometimes you don't have people available in-house with all the needed skills and must look to consultants or contracted workers. Examine which tasks should be outsourced and exactly what you must receive from the relationship. Pay particular attention to highly specialized or complex areas—the Active Directory Domain Services architecture, for example—and those with a high rate of change.

One-time tasks, such as creating user training programs and documentation, are also good candidates for outsourcing. For areas in which there will be an ongoing need for the lacking expertise, such as security, it might be a better idea to send a staff member to get additional training instead.

## Assessing project goals

Carefully identifying the goals behind moving to Windows Server 2012 is an important part of the planning process. Without a clear list of objectives, you are unlikely to achieve them. Even with a clear set of goals in mind, it is unlikely you will accomplish them all. Most large business projects involve some compromises, and the process of deploying Windows Server 2012 is unlikely to be an exception.

Although deploying a new operating system is ultimately an IT task, most of the reasons behind the deployment won't be coming from the IT department. Computers are, after all, tools used by business to increase productivity, enhance communications, facilitate business tasks, and so on; the IT department is concerned with making sure that the computer environment needed by the business is implemented.

# INSIDE OUT Creating documentation almost painlessly

During the planning process, and as you begin to use the new network environment, you'll be creating numerous documents describing the current state of the network, the planned changes, IT standards, administrative procedures, and the like. It's a good idea to take advantage of all of this up-to-date information to create policies and procedures documents, which will help ensure that the network stays in compliance with your new standards and administration is accomplished as intended.

The same set of documents can also serve as a basis for user guides, as well as administrator and user training, and can be made available through the corporate intranet. If the people working on the project, especially those performing testing, take notes about any error conditions they encounter and the resolutions to them, you'll also have a good start on frequently asked questions (FAQs) and other technical support data.

## The business perspective

Many discussions of the business reasons for new software deployments echo common themes: enhance productivity, eliminate downtime, reduce costs, and the like. Translating these often somewhat vague (and occasionally lofty) aspirations into concrete goals sometimes takes a bit of effort. It is well worth taking the time, however, to refine the big picture into specific objectives before moving on. An IT department should serve the needs of the business, not the other way around; if you don't understand those needs clearly, you'll have a hard time fulfilling them.

Be sure to ask for the input of people close to where the work is being done—department managers from each business area should be asked about what they need from IT, what works now, and what doesn't. These people care about the day-to-day operations of their computing environment. Will the changes help their staff do their work? Ask about work patterns, both static and burst—the finance department's workflow is not the same in July as it is in April. Make sure to include all departments, as well as any significant subsets—human resources (HR), finance, sales, business units, executive management, and so on.

You should also identify risks that lie at the business level, such as resistance to change, lack of commitment (frequently expressed as inadequate resources: budget, staff, time, and so on), or even the occasional bit of overt opposition. At the same time, look for positives to exploit—enthusiastic staff can help energize others, and having a manager in your corner can smooth many bumps along the way. By getting people involved, you can gain allies who are vested in the success of the project.

# INSIDE OUT Talk to the people who will use the technology

Not to put too fine a point on it, but make sure that the team members who will be handling aspects of the user experience actually talk with users. The only way to adequately assess what the people doing the work need in critical areas such as usability, training, and support is to get in the trenches and see what they are doing. If possible, have meetings at the user's workstation because it can provide additional insight into daily operations. If passwords are visible on sticky notes stuck to monitors—a far too common practice—you know you have security issues.

## Identifying IT goals

IT goals are often obvious: improve network reliability, provide better security, deliver enhanced administration, and maybe even implement a particular new feature. They are also easier to identify than those of other departments—after all, they are directly related to technology.

When you define your goals, make sure that you are specific. It is easy to say you will improve security, but how will you know when you have done so? What's improved, and by how much? In many cases, IT goals map to the implementation of features or procedures; for example, to improve security you will implement Internet Protocol Security (IPsec) and encrypt all traffic to remote networks.

Don't overpromise either—eliminating downtime is a laudable goal, but not one you are likely to achieve on your network, and certainly not one on which you want your next review based.

## Get to know each other

Business units often seem to have little idea of the IT department's capabilities and operations—or worse, they have an idea, but it is an extremely unrealistic one. This can lead to expectations ranging from improbable to absurd, which is bad for everyone involved.

A major project like this brings together people from all over the company, some from departments that seldom cross paths. This is a great opportunity for members of the various areas of the company to become familiar with IT operations, and vice versa. A clearer understanding of both the big picture of the business and the workings of other departments will help smooth the interactions of IT and the rest of the company.

## Examining the interaction between IT and business units

A number of aspects of your organization's business should be considered when evaluating your overall IT requirements and the business environment in which you operate. Consider things such as the following:

- **Business organization**   How large is the business? Are there offices in more than one location? Does the business operate across international, legal, or other boundaries? What sorts of departmental or functional boundaries exist?

- **Stability**   Does the business undergo a lot of change? Are there frequent reorganizations, acquisitions, changes, and the like in business partnerships? What is the expected growth rate of the organization? Conversely, are substantial downsizings planned in the future?

- **External relationships**   Do you need to provide access to vendors, partners, and so on? Are there external networks that people operating on your network must access?

- **Impact of Windows Server 2012 deployment**   How will this deployment affect the various departments in your company? Are there any areas of the company that are particularly intolerant of disruption? Are there upcoming events that must be taken into consideration in scheduling?

- **Adaptability**   Is management easily adaptable to change? If not, make sure you get every aspect of your plan right the first time. Having an idea of how staff might respond to new technologies and processes can help you plan for education and support.

## Predicting network change

Part of planning is projecting into the future and predicting how future business needs will influence the activities of the IT department. Managing complicated systems is easier when it's done from a proactive stance rather than a reactive one. Predicting network change is an art, not a science, but it will behoove you to hone your skills at it.

This is primarily a business assessment, based on things such as expected growth, changes in business focus, or possible downsizing and outsourcing—each of which provides its own challenges to the IT department. Being able to predict what will happen in the business and what those changes will mean to the IT department allows you to build in room for expansion in your network design.

When attempting to predict what will happen, look at the history of the company. Are mergers, acquisitions, spin-offs, and so on common? If so, this indicates a considerable need for flexibility from the IT department, as well as the need to keep in close contact with people on the business side to avoid being blindsided by a change in the future.

As people meet to discuss the deployment, talk about what is coming up for the business units. Cultivate contacts in other parts of the company, and talk with those people regularly about what's going on in their departments, such as upcoming projects, as well as what's happening with other companies in the same business sector. Reading the company's news releases and articles in outside sources can also provide valuable hints of what's to come. By keeping your ear to the ground, doing a little research, and thinking through the potential impact of what you learn, you can be much better prepared for whatever is coming up next.

## The impact of growth on management

Many networks start out with a single administrator (or a small team), which only makes sense because many networks are small when first implemented. As those networks grow, it is not uncommon for a few administrative tasks to be delegated to others in the company who, although it is not their job, know how to assist the highly limited IT staff. This can lead to a haphazard approach to management, where who is doing what isn't always clear, and the methods for basics (such as data backups) vary from one department to the next, leading to potential problems as time goes by and staff moves on. If this sounds familiar to you, this is a good time to remedy the situation.

## Analyzing the existing network

Before you can determine the path to your new network environment, you must determine where you are right now in terms of your existing network infrastructure. This requires determining a baseline for network and system hardware, software installation and configuration, operations, management, and security. Don't rely on what you think is the case; actually verify what is in place.

## Project worksheets consolidate information

A large network environment, with a lot of architectural and configuration information to be collected, can require juggling enormous amounts of data. If this is the case, you might find it useful to use project worksheets of some sort. If your company has not created customized worksheets, you can use those created by Microsoft to aid in the upgrade process. Typically, these are available in the operating system deployment kit.

## Evaluating the network infrastructure

You should get an idea of what the current network looks like before moving to a new operating system. You will require configuration information while designing the modifications to the network and deploying the servers. In addition, some aspects of Windows Server 2012, such as the sites used in Active Directory replication, are based on your physical network configuration. (A *site* is a segment of the network with good connectivity, consisting of one or more Internet Protocol [IP] subnets.)

For reasons such as this, you'll want to assess a number of aspects related to your physical network environment. Consider such characteristics as the following:

- **Network topology**   Document the systems and devices on your network, including link speeds, wide area network (WAN) connections, sites using dial-up connections, and so on. Include devices such as routers, switches, servers, and clients, noting all forms of addressing, such as both computer names and IP addresses for Windows systems.

- **Network addressing**   Are you currently employing Internet Protocol version 4 (IPv4) and Internet Protocol version 6 (IPv6)? What parts of the address space are private or public? Which IP subnets are in use at each location?

- **Remote locations**   How many physical locations does the organization have? Are they all using broadband connections, or are there remote offices that connect sporadically by dial-up? What is the speed of those links?

- **Traffic patterns**   Monitoring network traffic can provide insights into current performance, as well as help you to identify potential bottlenecks and other problems before they occur. Examine utilization statistics, paying attention to both regularly occurring patterns and anomalous spikes or lulls, which might indicate a problem.

- **Special cases**   Are there any portions of the network that have out-of-the-ordinary configuration needs, such as test labs that are isolated from the rest of the network?

## INSIDE OUT   Mapping the territory

Create a network map illustrating the location of all your current resources—this is easier by using tools such as Microsoft Visio. Collect as much detailed information as possible about those resources, starting with basics, such as what is installed on each server, the services it's providing, and so on. Additional information, such as critical workflow processes and traffic patterns between servers, can also be very useful when it comes time to consolidate servers or deploy new ones. The easier it is to cross-reference all of this information, the better.

## Assessing systems

As part of planning, you should inventory the existing network servers, identifying each system's operating system version, IP address, Domain Name System (DNS) names, as well as the services provided by that system. Collect such information by performing the following tasks:

- **Inventory hardware**   Conduct a hardware inventory of the servers on your network, noting central processing unit (CPU), random access memory (RAM), disk space, and so on. Pay particular attention to older machines that might present compatibility issues if upgraded. You can use the Microsoft Assessment and Planning (MAP) toolkit, Microsoft System Center Configuration Manager (SCCM), or other tools to help you with the hardware inventory.

- **Identify operating systems**   Determine the current operating system on each computer, including the entire version number (even if it runs to many digits), as well as service packs, hot fixes, and other post-release additions.

- **Assess your current Microsoft Windows domains**   Do you have only Windows domains on the network? Are all domains using Active Directory? Do you have multiple Active Directory forests? If you have multiple forests, detail the trust relationships. List the name of each domain, what it contains (users, resources, or both), and which servers are acting as domain controllers.

- **Identify localization factors**   If your organization crosses international boundaries, language boundaries, or both, identify the localized versions of Windows Server in use and the locations in which they are used. This is critical when upgrading to Windows Server 2012 because attempting an upgrade using a different localized version of Windows Server 2012 might fail.

- **Assess software licenses**   Evaluate licenses for servers and client access. This will help you select the most appropriate licensing program.

- **Identify file storage**   Review the contents and configuration of existing file servers, identifying partitions and volumes on each system. Identify existing distributed file system (DFS) servers and the contents of DFS shares. Don't forget shares used to store user data.

# INSIDE OUT   Where is the data?

Locating file shares that are maintained at a departmental, team, or even individual level can take a little bit of investigation. However, the effort to do so can well be worth it because it allows you to centralize the management of data that is important to individual groups, while providing valuable services such as ensuring that regular data backups are performed.

You can gather hardware and software inventories of computers that run the Windows operating system by using a tool such as System Center Configuration Manager. Review the types of clients that must be supported so that you can configure servers appropriately. This is also a good time to determine any client systems that must be upgraded (or replaced) to use Windows Server 2012 functionality.

> **Note**
>
> You can also gather this information with scripts. To find more information on scripting, I recommend *Microsoft Windows PowerShell 2.0 Administrator's Pocket Consultant* by William R. Stanek (Microsoft Press, 2009).

## Identify network services and applications

Look at your current network services, noting which services are running on which servers, and the dependencies of these services. Do this for all domain controllers and member servers that you'll be upgrading. You'll use this information later to plan for server placement and service hosting on the upgraded network configuration. Some examples of services to document are as follows:

- **DNS services**   You must assess your current DNS configuration. If you're currently using a non–Microsoft DNS server, you'll want to carefully plan DNS support because Active Directory relies on Windows Server 2012 DNS. See Chapter 21, "Architecting DNS infrastructure," for guidance, and be sure to review "Deploying global names zones" in Chapter 22, "Implementing and managing DNS."

- **WINS services**   You should assess the use of Network Basic Input/Output System (NetBIOS) by legacy applications and computers running early versions of the

Windows operating system to determine whether NetBIOS support (such as Windows Internet Naming Service [WINS]) will be needed in the new network configuration. See "Understanding name resolution" in Chapter 18, "Networking with TCP/IP," to review important changes, including Link-Local Multicast Name Resolution (LLMNR).

- **Print services**   List printers and the print server assigned to each one. Consider who is assigned to the various administrative tasks and whether the printer will be published in Active Directory. Also determine whether all of the print servers will be upgraded in place or whether some will be consolidated.

- **Network applications**   Inventory your applications, creating a list of the applications that are currently on the network, including the version number (as well as post-release patches and such), which server hosts it, and how important each application is to your business. Use this information to determine whether upgrades or modifications are needed. Also watch for software that is never used and thus need not be purchased or supported—every unneeded application you can remove represents savings of both time and money.

This list is only the beginning. Your network will undoubtedly have many more services that you must take into account.

**CAUTION**

Make sure that you determine any dependencies in your network configuration. Discovering after the fact that a critical process relied on the server that you just decommissioned is not going to make your job any easier. You can find out which Microsoft and third-party applications are certified to be compatible with Windows Server 2012 in the Windows Server Catalog (*http://www.windowsservercatalog.com/*).

## Identifying security infrastructure

When you document your network infrastructure, you will need to review many aspects of your network security. In addition to security concerns that are specific to your network environment, the following factors should be addressed:

- Consider exactly who has access to what and why. Identify network resources, security groups, and assignment of access permissions.

- Determine which security protocols and services are in place. Are adequate virus protection, firewall protection, email filtering, and so on in place? Do any applications or services require legacy NTLM authentication? Have you implemented a public key infrastructure (PKI) on your network?

- Examine auditing methods, and identify the range of tracked access and objects.

- Determine which staff members have access to the Internet and which sorts of access they have. Look at the business case for access that crosses the corporate firewall—does everyone who has Internet access actually need it, or has it been provided across the board because it was easier to provide blanket access than to provide access selectively? Such access might be simpler to implement, but when you look at Internet access from the security perspective, it presents many potential problems.

- Consider inbound access as well; for example, can employees access their information from home? If so, examine the security that is in place for this type of access.

> **Important**
>
> Security is one area in which well-established methods matter—pay particular attention to all established policies and procedures, what has been officially documented, and what isn't documented as well.

Depending on your existing network security mechanisms, the underlying security methods can change upon deployment of Windows Server 2012. Windows Server 2003 is the minimum forest and domain functional level supported by Windows Server 2012. When the forest and domain functional levels are raised to this level or higher from a lower level, Kerberos is the default authentication mechanism used between computer systems. This also means that although the Windows NT 4 security model (using NTLM authentication) continues to be supported, it is no longer the default authentication mechanism.

## Reviewing network administration

Examining the administrative methods currently in use on your network provides you with a lot of information about what you are doing right, as well as identifying areas that could use some improvement. Using this information, you can tweak network procedures where needed to optimize the administration of the new environment.

## How did you get here?

Some networks are entirely designed—actually considered, discussed, planned, and so forth—while other networks grow. At one extreme is a formally designed and carefully implemented administration scheme, complete with its supporting documentation set, training, and ongoing compliance monitoring. At the other end of the spectrum is the network for which administrative methods just sort of happen organically—someone did it that way once, it worked, that person kept doing it that way and maybe even taught others to do it that way. Not surprisingly, this occurs most often on small networks. In the middle, and perhaps more typically, is a looser amalgamation of policies and procedures, some of which were formally implemented, while others were created ad hoc.

Depending on the path that led to your current administrative methods, you might have more or less in the way of documentation, or an actual idea, of the detailed workings of day-to-day administration. Even if you have fully documented policies and procedures, you should still assess how management tasks are actually performed—you might be surprised at what you learn.

**Network administrative model**   Each company has its own sort of approach to network administration—some are very centralized, with even the smallest changes being made by the IT department, while others are partially managed by the business units, which control aspects such as user management. Administrative models fit into these categories:

- **Centralized**   Administration of the entire network is handled by one group, perhaps in one location, although not necessarily. This provides a high degree of control at the cost of requiring IT staff for every change to the network, no matter how small.

- **Decentralized**   This administrative model delegates more of the control of day-to-day operations to local administrators of some sort, often departmental. Certain aspects of network management might still be managed by a central IT department, in that a network with decentralized administration often has well-defined procedures controlling exactly how each administrative task is performed.

- **Hybrid**   On many networks, a blend of these two methods is used. A centralized IT department performs many tasks (generally, the more difficult, delicate operations, and those with the broadest impact on the network), while delegating simpler tasks (such as user management) to departmental or group administrators.

**Disaster recovery**   The costs of downtime caused by service interruption or data loss can be substantial, especially in large enterprise networks. As part of your overall planning, determine whether a comprehensive IT disaster recovery plan is in place. If one is in place, this is the time to determine its scope and effectiveness, as well as to verify that it is being followed. If one isn't in place, this is the time to create and implement one.

Document the various data sets being archived, schedules, backup validation routine, staff assignments, and so on. Make sure there are provisions for offsite data storage to protect your data in the case of a catastrophic event, such as a fire, earthquake, or flood.

Examine the following:

- **Systems and servers**   Are all critical servers backed up regularly? Are secondary servers, backup servers, or both available in case of system failure?

- **Enterprise data**   Are regular backups made of core enterprise data stores such as databases, Active Directory, and the like?

- **User information**   Where is user data stored? Is it routinely archived? Does the backup routine get all of the information that is important to individuals, or is some of it stored on users' personal machines and thus not archived?

**CAUTION**

> Whatever your current disaster recovery plan is, make sure that it is being followed before you start making major changes to your network. Although moving to Windows Server 2012 should not present any major problems on the network, it's always better to have your backups and not need them than the other way around.

**Network management tools**   This is an excellent time to assess your current suite of network management tools. Pay particular attention to those that are unnecessary, incompatible, redundant, inefficient, or otherwise not terribly useful. You might find that some of the functionality of those tools is present natively in Windows Server 2012. Assess the following aspects of your management tools:

- Identify the tools currently in use, which tasks they perform, who uses them, and so on. Make note of administrative tasks that could be eased with additional tools.

- Decide whether the tools you identified are actually used. A lot of software ends up sitting on a shelf (or on your hard disk drive) and never being used. Identifying which tools are truly needed and eliminating those that aren't can save you money and simplify the learning curve for network administrators.

- Disk-management and backup tools deserve special attention because of file-system changes in Windows Server 2012. These tools are likely to require upgrading to function correctly under Windows Server 2012.

# INSIDE OUT    Think about compatibility issues early

Dealing with compatibility issues can take a lot of time, so examine them early in the process. The time needed to determine whether your current hardware and software will work and what changes must be made to allow them to work with Windows Server 2012 can be lengthy. When you add to that the time necessary to requisition, obtain, install, and configure new software—especially if you must write custom code—you can see why you don't want to leave this until the end of the project.

## Defining objectives and scope

A key aspect of planning any large-scale IT deployment of an operating system is determining the overall objectives for the deployment and the scope of users, computers, networks, and organization divisions that are affected. The fundamental question of scope is this: What can you realistically expect to accomplish in the given time within existing project constraints, such as staffing and budget?

Some of the objectives that you identified in the early stages of the project are likely to change as constraints become more apparent and new needs and requirements emerge. To start with, you must identify who will be affected—which organizational subdivisions and which personnel—as well as who will be doing what. These are questions that map to the business goals that must be accomplished.

You also must identify the systems that will be affected—which WANs, local area networks (LANs), subnets, servers, and client systems? In addition, you must determine the software that will be changed—which server software, client software, and applications?

# INSIDE OUT    Planning for scope creep

Projects grow—it's inevitable—and although the scope of some projects creep, others gallop. Here are a few tips to help you keep the project scope to a manageable level:

- When an addition to the project is proposed, never say yes right away. Think through the consequences thoroughly, examining the impact on the rest of the project and the project team, before agreeing to any proposed changes.

- Insist on management buyoff on changes to the plan. In at least some cases, you won't get approval, automatically deferring the requested changes.

- Argue for trade-offs in the project when possible—so that adding one objective means removing another—rather than just adding tasks to your to-do list.

- Try to defer any noncritical proposed changes to a future project.

## Specifying organizational objectives

Many goals of the various business units and IT are only loosely related, while others are universal—everyone wants security, for example. Take advantage of the places where goals converge to engage others in the project. If people can see that their needs are met, they are more likely to be supportive of others' goals and the project in general.

You have business objectives at this point; now they must be prioritized. You should make lists of various critical aspects of projects, as well as dependencies within the project plan, as part of the process of winnowing the big picture into a set of realistic objectives. Determine what you can reasonably accomplish within the constraints of the current project. Also, decide what is outside the practical scope of this Windows Server 2012 deployment but is still important to implement at some later date.

The objectives that are directly related to the IT department will probably be clearer, and more numerous, after completing the analysis of the current network. These objectives should be organized to conform to existing change-management procedures within your enterprise network.

When setting goals, be careful not to promise too much. Although it's tempting and sometimes easier in the short run to try to do everything, you can't. It's unlikely that you will implement every single item on every person's wish list during the first stage of this project, if at all. Knowing what you can't do is as important as knowing what you can.

# INSIDE OUT    Gauging deployment success

You'll find it difficult to gauge the success of a project without having clearly defined goals. Make sure that you define specific, measurable goals you can use to determine when each portion of the project is complete. Everyone on the project team, particularly management, should agree on these milestones *before* the rollout gets under way.

Some goals should map to user functionality (for example, "The XYZ department is able to do ABC"), while others will correspond to administrative tasks. Be granular in your goals. For example, "Security policies will be followed" is difficult to quantify; however, "Virus definition files are updated daily" or "Operating system patches will be installed within 48 hours of release" is easy.

## Setting the schedule

You should create a project schedule, laying out the timeline, tasks, and staff assignments. Including projected completion dates for milestones helps you keep on top of significant portions of the project and ensure that dependencies are managed.

You must be realistic when considering timelines—not just a little bit realistic, but *really realistic*. This is, after all, your time you are allocating. Estimate too short a time and you are likely to spend evenings and weekends at the office with some of your closest coworkers.

A number of tasks will be repeated many times during the rollout of Windows Server 2012, which should make estimating the time needed for some things fairly simple: a 1-hour process repeated 25 times takes 25 hours (unless it's automated). If, for example, you are building 25 new servers in-house, determine the actual time needed to build one and then do the math.

When you have a rough idea of the time required, do the following:

- Assign staff members to the various tasks to make sure you have adequate staff assistance to complete the project.

- Add some time to your estimates—IT projects always seem to take more time than you thought they would. This is the only buffer you are likely to get, so make sure you build in some "extra" time from the start.

- As much as possible, verify how long individual tasks take. You might be surprised at how much time you spend doing a seemingly simple task, and if your initial estimate is significantly off, you could end up running significantly short on time.

- Develop a schedule that clearly shows who is doing what and when they are doing it.

- Get drop-dead dates, which should be later than the initial target date.

- Post the schedule in a place where the team, and perhaps other staff, can view it. Keep this schedule updated with milestones reached, changes to deliverable dates, and so on.

> **Note**
> You might want to use a project-management tool, such as Microsoft Project, to develop the schedule. This sort of tool is especially useful when managing a project with a number of staff members working on a set of interdependent tasks.

## Shaping the budget

Determining the budget is a process constrained by many factors, including, but not limited to, IT-related costs for hardware and licensing. In addition to fixed IT costs, you also must consider the project scope and the non-IT costs that can come from the requirements of other departments within the organization. Thus, to come up with the budget, you need information and assistance from all departments within the organization and you must consider all aspects of the project.

Many projects end up costing more than is initially budgeted. Sometimes this is predictable and preventable with proper research and a bit of attention to ongoing expenses. As with timelines, pad your estimates a little bit to allow for the unexpected. Even so, it helps if you can find out how much of a buffer you have for any cost overruns.

In planning the budget, also keep in mind fiscal periods. If your project is crossing budget periods, find out if next year's budget for the project is allocated and approved.

### Budget for project changes

Keep in mind there are likely to be changes as the project is under way. Each change probably has a cost associated with it, and you might have to fight to have additional funds budgeted or go back to the department or individuals who want the change and ask them to allocate money from their budget to cover the requested change.

## Allowing for contingencies

No matter how carefully you plan any project, it is unlikely that everything will go exactly as planned. Accordingly, you should plan for contingencies that might present themselves. By having a number of possible responses to unforeseen events ready, you can better manage the vagaries of the project.

Start with perhaps the most common issue encountered during projects: problems in getting the assigned people to do the work. This all-too-common problem can derail any project, or at least cause the project manager a great deal of stress. After all, the ultimate success of any project depends on people doing their assigned tasks. Many of these people are already stretched pretty thin, however, and you might encounter times when they aren't quite getting everything done. Your plan should include what to do in this circumstance—is the person's manager brought in, or is a backup person automatically assigned to complete the job?

Another possibility to plan for is a change in the feature set being implemented. Should such shifts occur, you must decide how to adjust to compensate for the reallocated time and money required. To make this easier, identify and prioritize the following:

- Objectives that could slip off this project and be placed onto a later one should the need arise

- Objectives that you want to slip into the project if the opportunity presents itself

Items on both of these lists should be relatively small and independent of other processes and services. Avoid incurring additional expenses; you are more likely to be given extra time than extra funding during your deployment.

In general, ask yourself what could happen to cause significant problems along the way. Then, more important, consider what you would do in response. By thinking through potential problems ahead of time and planning what you might do in response, you can be prepared for many of the inevitable bumps along the way.

## INSIDE OUT Padding project estimates

Many consultants pad their project estimates, primarily as a means of ensuring that the inevitable project scope creep isn't problematic later on. After all, it's preferable to have a client who is happy that the project came in early and under budget than one who is unhappy at the cost and time overruns. You might want to use this approach by adding in a little extra time and not allocating quite all of the available money. If you come in early and under budget, so much the better—but you probably won't.

## Finalizing project scope

You have goals, know the timeline, and have a budget pinned down—now it's time to get serious. Starting with the highest-priority aspects of the project, estimate the time and budget needed to complete each portion. Work your way through the planned scope, assessing the time and costs associated with each portion of the project. This will help ensure that you have enough time and budget to successfully complete the project as designed.

As you finalize the project plan, each team member should review the final project scope, noting any concerns or questions he or she has about the proposal. Encourage the team to look for weak spots, unmet dependencies, and other places where the plan might break down. Although it is tempting to ignore potential problems that are noted this late in the game, you do so at your own peril. Avoiding known risks is much easier than recovering from unforeseen ones.

## Change management

Formalized change-management processes are very useful, especially for large organizations and those with distributed administrative models. By creating structured change-control processes and implementing appropriate auditing, you can control the ongoing management of critical IT processes. This makes it easier to manage the network and reduces the opportunity for error.

Although this is particularly important when dealing with big-picture issues such as domain creation or Group Policy implementation, some organizations define change-control mechanisms for every possible change, no matter how small. You'll have to determine for which IT processes you must define change-management processes, finding a balance between managing changes effectively and over-regulating network management.

Even if you're not planning on implementing a formal change-control process, make sure that the information about the initial configuration is collected in one spot. By doing this, and collecting brief notes about any changes that are made, you will at least have data about the configuration and the changes that have been made to it. This will also help later on, if you decide to put more stringent change-control mechanisms in place, by providing at least rudimentary documentation of the current network state.

# Final considerations for planning and deployment

If you are doing a new installation—perhaps, for a new business or a new location of an existing one—you have a substantial amount of additional planning to do. This extends well beyond your Windows Server 2012 systems to additional computers (clients, for a start), devices, services, applications, and so on.

The details of such a project are far beyond the scope of this book; indeed, entire books have been written on the topic. If you have to implement a network from the ground up, you might want to pick one up.

You must plan the entire network, including areas such as the following:

- Infrastructure architecture (including network topology, addressing, DNS, and so on)

- Active Directory design

- Servers and services

- Administration methods

- Network applications

- Clients

- Client applications

- Client devices (printers, scanners, and the like)

This is a considerable undertaking and requires educated, dedicated staff, as well as adequate time and other resources.

## INSIDE OUT Good news, bad news

Having the responsibility for deploying a new Windows-based network is both a good thing and a not-so-good thing:

- The not-so-good part is straightforward: It can be a staggering amount of work.

- The good thing—and it is a very good thing—is that you are starting with a clean slate and you have a chance to get it (at least mostly) right the first time. Many a network administrator would envy the chance to do a clean deployment, to start fresh with no existing problems, no legacy hardware or applications to maintain, and no kludges or workarounds.

If you are faced with creating a new network, take advantage of this opportunity and do lots of research before you touch the first computer. With the abundance of technical information available, you should be able to avoid most problems and quickly resolve the few you encounter.

# Thinking about server roles and Active Directory

When planning for server usage, consider the workload of each server: which services it is providing, the expected user load, and so on. In small network environments, it is common for a single server to act as a domain controller and to provide DNS and Dynamic Host Configuration Protocol (DHCP) services and possibly even additional services. In larger network environments, one or more standalone servers might provide each of these services rather than them being aggregated on a single system.

Active Directory is an extremely complicated, and critical, portion of Windows Server 2012, and you should plan for it with appropriate care. This book goes into detail on doing this in Part 5, "Managing Active Directory and security." You should read this information if you are going to be designing a new Active Directory tree.

The following section discusses, in abbreviated form, some high-level aspects of server usage and Active Directory that you must consider. It is meant to offer a perspective on how various server roles, including domain controllers, fit in the overall planning picture, not to explain how to plan for a new Active Directory installation.

## Planning for server usage

Windows Server 2012 employs a number of server roles, each of which corresponds to one or more services. Your plan should detail which roles (and additional services) are needed and the number and placement of servers, as well as define the configuration for each service. When planning server usage, be sure to keep the expected client load in mind and account for remote sites that might require additional servers to support local operations.

Key Windows Server 2012 server roles are as follows:

- **Domain controller**   Active Directory domain controllers are perhaps the most important type of network server on a Windows network. Domain controllers are also one of the most intensively used servers on a Windows network, so it is important to realistically assess the operational requirements and server performance for each one. Remember to take into account any secondary Active Directory–related roles the server will be performing (such as global catalog, operations master, and so on). Keep the following questions in mind:

    - How many domain controllers are required, and which ones will fulfill which roles?

    - Which domains must be present at which sites?

    - Where should global catalogs be placed?

    - What remote offices (if any) will use RODCs?

- **DNS server**   DNS is an integral part of a Windows network, with many important features (such as Active Directory) relying on it. Accordingly, DNS servers are now a required element of your suite of network services. Plan for enough DNS servers to service client requests, with adequate redundancy for fault tolerance and performance, and plan to have them distributed throughout your network to be available to all clients. Factor in remote sites with slow links to the main corporate network and those that might be only intermittently connected by dial-up. Be sure to do the following:

    - Define both internal and external namespaces.

    - Plan the name-resolution path (forwarders and so on).

    - Determine the storage of DNS information (zone files, Active Directory–integrated, application partitions).

○ Determine whether you need read-only DNS services at remote offices with RODCs.

○ Determine whether you need secure DNS (DNSSEC).

> ### Note
> Microsoft DNS is the recommended method of providing domain name services on a network with Active Directory deployed, although some other DNS servers provide the required functionality. In practice, however, the intertwining of Active Directory and DNS, along with the complexity of the DNS records used by Active Directory, has meant that Microsoft DNS is the one most often used with Active Directory.

> ### Note
> DNS information can be stored in traditional zone files, Active Directory-integrated zones, or application partitions. An application partition contains a subset of directory information used by a single application. In the case of DNS, this partition is replicated only to domain controllers that are also providing DNS services, minimizing network traffic for DNS replication. There is one application partition for the forest (ForestDnsZones) and another for each domain (DomainDnsZones).

- **DHCP server**   DHCP simplifies the management of the IP address pool used by both server and client systems. A number of operational factors regarding the use of DHCP should be considered:

  ○ Determine whether DNS servers are going to act as DHCP servers also and, if so, will all of them or only a subset of them be used in this way?

  ○ Define server configuration factors such as DHCP scopes and the assignment of scopes to servers, as well as client settings such as the DHCP lease length.

  ○ Determine whether failover scopes are needed to increase fault tolerance and provide redundancy.

- **WINS server**　First, determine whether you still need WINS on your network. If you have legacy applications in your network environment, WINS might be required to translate NetBIOS names to IP addresses. If so, consider the following:

  - Which clients need to access the WINS servers?

  - What WINS replication configuration is required?

- **Network Policy and Access Services**　Network Policy and Access Services provides integrated protection, routing, and remote-access services that facilitate secure, protected access by remote users. Consider the following:

  - Do you need protection policies?

  - Do you need to provide routing between networks?

  - Do you want to replace existing routers?

  - Do you have external users who need access to the internal network?

- **Hyper-V server**　Hyper-V provides infrastructure for virtualizing applications and workloads. Use Hyper-V to

  - Consolidate servers and workloads onto fewer, more powerful servers and reduce requirements for power and space.

  - Implement a centralized desktop strategy by combining Hyper-V technology with Remote Desktop Virtualization Host technology.

  - Create a private cloud for shared resources that you can adjust as demand changes.

- **Application server**　A Windows Server 2012 application server hosts distributed applications built using ASP.NET, Enterprise Services, and .NET Framework. It includes more than a dozen role services, which are discussed in detail in *Internet Information Services (IIS) 7.0 Administrator's Pocket Consultant* (Microsoft Press, 2007).

- **File and storage services**　The File And Storage Services role provides essential services for managing files and the way they are made available and replicated on the network. A number of server roles require some type of file service.

- **Print and document services**　The Print And Document Services role fulfills the needed role of managing printer operations on the network. Windows Server 2012 enables publishing printers in Active Directory, connecting to network printers using a Uniform Resource Locator (URL), and enhanced printer control through Group Policy.

- **Remote Desktop Services**  The Remote Desktop Services role supports virtual desktops, enabling a single server to pool virtual desktops centrally and, in this way, host network access for many users. A client with a web browser, a Windows thin client, or a Remote Desktop client can access the Remote Desktop server to gain access to network resources.

- **Web server**  Web servers host websites and web-based applications. Websites hosted on a web server can have both static content and dynamic content. You can build web applications hosted on a web server using ASP.NET and .NET Framework.

## INSIDE OUT  Servers with multiple roles

It is common for a single server to fill more than one role, especially on smaller networks. When selecting which roles to put on a single server, try to select ones with different needs. For instance, putting one processor-intensive role (for example, an application server) and a role (such as a file server) that does a lot of network input/output (I/O) on a single system makes more sense than putting two roles that stress the same subsystem on the same machine.

## Designing the Active Directory namespace

The Active Directory tree is based on a DNS domain structure, which must be implemented prior to, or as part of, installing the first Active Directory server in the forest. Each domain in the Active Directory tree is both a DNS and Windows domain, with the associated security and administrative functionality. DNS is thoroughly integrated with Active Directory, providing location services (also called *name resolution services*) for domains, servers, sites, and services, as well as constraining the structure of the Active Directory tree. It is wise to keep Active Directory in mind as you are designing the DNS namespace, and vice versa, because they are immutably linked.

### Note

Active Directory trees exist within a *forest*, which is a collection of one or more domain trees. The first domain installed in an Active Directory forest functions as the *forest root*.

The interdependence of Active Directory and DNS brings some special factors into play. For example, if your organization has outward-facing DNS servers, you must decide whether you will be using your external DNS name or another DNS domain name for Active Directory. Many organizations choose not to use their external DNS name for Active Directory, unless they want to expose the directory to the Internet for a business reason, such as an Internet service provider (ISP) that uses Active Directory logon servers.

Within a domain, another sort of hierarchy exists in the form of container objects called *organizational units* (OUs), which are used to organize and manage users, network resources, and security. An OU can contain related users, groups, or computers, as well as other OUs.

> ## Important
> Designing the Active Directory namespace requires the participation of multiple levels of business and IT management, so be sure to provide adequate time for a comprehensive review and sign-off on domain architecture.

## Managing domain trusts

Domain trusts allow automatic authentication and access to resources across domains. Active Directory automatically configures trust relationships such that each domain in an Active Directory forest trusts every other domain within that forest.

Active Directory domains are linked by a series of such transitive trust relationships between all domains in a domain tree, and between all domain trees in the forest. By using Windows Server 2012, you can also configure transitive trust relationships between forests.

> ## Understand explicit trust relationships
> Explicit trusts between domains can speed up authentication requests. An explicit trust relationship allows authentication queries to go directly to the domain in question rather than having to search the domain tree, forest, or both to locate the domain in which to authenticate a user.

## Identifying the domain and forest functional level

Active Directory now has multiple domain and forest functional levels, each constraining the types of domain controllers that can be in use and the available feature set.

The domain functional levels are as follows:

- **Windows Server 2003 mode**   When the domain is operating in Windows Server 2003 mode, the directory supports domain controllers running Windows Server 2003 and later. A domain operating in Windows Server 2003 mode can use universal groups, group nesting, group type conversion, easy domain controller renaming, update logon time stamps, and Kerberos KDC key version numbers. This functional level also supports passwords for InetOrgPerson users. InetOrgPersons are a special type of user, discussed in Chapter 30, "Managing users, groups, and computers."

- **Windows Server 2008 mode**   When the domain is operating in Windows Server 2008 mode, the directory supports Windows Server 2008 and later domain controllers. Windows Server 2003 domain controllers are no longer supported. A domain operating in Windows Server 2008 mode can use additional Active Directory features, including the DFS replication service for enhanced intersite and intrasite replication, and Advanced Encryption Services (AES) 128-bit or AES 256-bit encryption for the Kerberos protocol. This level also supports the display of the last interactive logon details for users and fine-grained password policies for applying separate password and account lockout policies to users and groups.

- **Windows Server 2008 R2 mode**   When the domain is operating in Windows Server 2008 R2 mode, the directory supports Windows Server 2008 R2 and later domain controllers. Windows Server 2003 and Windows Server 2008 domain controllers are no longer supported. A domain operating in Windows Server 2008 R2 mode can use Active Directory Recycle Bin, managed service accounts, Authentication Mechanism Assurance, and other important Active Directory enhancements.

- **Windows Server 2012 mode**   When the domain is operating in Windows Server 2012 mode, the directory supports only Windows Server 2012 domain controllers. Windows Server 2003, Windows Server 2008, and Windows Server 2008 R2 domain controllers are no longer supported. Active Directory schema for Windows Server 2012 includes many enhancements, but only the Kerberos with Armoring feature requires this mode.

The forest functional levels are as follows:

- **Windows Server 2003**   Supports domain controllers running Windows Server 2003 and later

- **Windows Server 2008**   Supports domain controllers running Windows Server 2008 and later

- **Windows Server 2008 R2**   Supports domain controllers running Windows Server 2008 R2 and Windows Server 2012

- **Windows Server 2012**    Supports domain controllers running Windows Server 2012

When a forest is operating at the Windows Server 2003 or higher functional level, key Active Directory features, including the following, are enabled:

- **Replication enhancements**    Each changed value of a multivalued attribute is now replicated separately—eliminating the possibility for data conflict and reducing replication traffic. Additional changes include enhanced global catalog replication and application partitions (which segregate data, and thus the replication of that data).

- **Schema**    Schema objects can be deactivated, and dynamic auxiliary classes are supported.

- **Management**    Forest trusts allow multiple forests to easily share resources. Active Directory domains can be renamed, and thus the Active Directory tree can be reorganized.

- **User management**    Last logon time is now tracked, and enhancements to InetOrgPerson password handling are enabled.

However, to take advantage of the latest Active Directory features, your forests must operate at the Windows Server 2008 R2 or higher function level. Selecting your domain and forest functional levels is generally a straightforward choice. Ultimately, the decision regarding the domain and forest functional levels at which to operate mostly comes down to choosing the one that supports the domain controllers you have in place now and expect to have in the future. In most circumstances, you will want to operate at the highest possible level because it enables more functionality. Also, keep in mind that all changes to the functional level are one-way and cannot be reversed.

## Defining Active Directory server roles

In addition to serving as domain controllers, a number of domain controllers fulfill special roles within Active Directory. Some of these roles provide a service to the entire forest, although others are specific to a domain or site. The Active Directory setup routine assigns and configures these roles, although you can change them later.

The Active Directory server roles are as follows:

- **Operations masters**    A number of Active Directory operations must be carefully controlled to maintain the integrity of the directory structure and data. A specific domain controller serves as the operations master for each of these functions. That server is the only one that can perform certain operations related to that area. For example, you can make schema changes only on the domain controller serving as the

Chapter 1

schema master; if that server is unavailable, no changes can be made to the schema. There are two categories of operations masters:

○ **Forest-level operations masters** The schema master manages the schema and enforces schema consistency throughout the directory.

The domain-naming master controls domain creation and deletion, guaranteeing that each domain is unique within the forest.

○ **Domain-level operations masters** The RID master manages the pool of *relative identifiers* (RIDs). (A RID is a numeric string used to construct SIDs for security principals.)

The infrastructure master handles user-to-group mappings, changes in group membership, and replication of those changes to other domain controllers.

The PDC emulator is responsible for processing password changes and replicating password changes to other domain controllers. The PDC emulator must be available to reset and verify external trusts.

- **Global catalogs** A global catalog server provides a quick index of Active Directory objects, which is used by a variety of network clients and processes to locate directory objects. Global catalog servers can be heavily used, yet they must be highly available to clients, especially for user logons because the global catalog provides membership information for universal groups. Accordingly, each site in the network should have at least one global catalog server, or you should have a Windows Server 2003 or later domain controller with universal group caching enabled.

- **Bridgehead servers** Bridgehead servers manage intersite replication over low-bandwidth WAN links. Each site replicating with other sites usually has at least one bridgehead server, although a single site can have more than one if that's required for performance reasons.

> **Note**
> Active Directory replication depends on the concept of *sites*, which are defined as a collected set of subnets with good interconnectivity. Replication differs depending on whether it is within a site or between sites; intrasite replication occurs automatically every 15 seconds, while intersite replication is scheduled and usually quite a bit slower.

# Planning for availability, scalability, and manageability

The enterprise depends on highly available, scalable, and manageable systems. *High availability* refers to the ability of the system to withstand hardware, application, or service outages while maintaining system availability. *High scalability* refers to the ability of the system to expand processor and memory capacity, as business needs demand. *High manageability* refers to the ability of the system to be managed locally and remotely and the ease with which components, services, and applications can be administered.

Planning for high availability, scalability, and manageability is critical to the success of using Windows Server 2012 in the enterprise, and you need a solid understanding of the recommendations and operating principles for deploying and maintaining high-availability servers before you deploy servers running these editions. You should also understand the types of hardware, software, and support facilities needed for enterprise computing. These concepts are all covered in this chapter.

> ### Note
> The discussion that follows focuses on achieving high availability, scalability, and manageability in the enterprise. Smaller organizations or business units can adopt similar approaches to meet business objectives, but they should determine the scope appropriately with budgets and available resources in mind.

## Planning for software needs

Software should be chosen for its ability to support the high-availability needs of the business system. Not all software is compatible with high-availability solutions like clustering or load balancing. Not all software must be compatible, either. Instead of making an arbitrary decision, you should let the uptime needs of the application determine the level of availability required.

An availability goal of 99 percent uptime is usual for most noncritical business systems. If an application must have 99 percent uptime, the application might not need to support clustering or load balancing. To achieve 99 percent uptime means that the application can have about 88 hours of downtime in an entire year, or 100 minutes of downtime a week.

To have 99.9 percent uptime is the availability goal for highly available business systems. If an application must have 99.9 percent uptime, the application must support some type of high-availability solution, such as clustering or load balancing. To achieve 99.9 percent uptime means that the application has less than 9 hours of downtime in an entire year or, put another way, less than 10 minutes of downtime a week.

# INSIDE OUT Clustering support alone isn't enough

Applications that support clustering are said to be *cluster aware*. Microsoft SQL Server and Microsoft Exchange Server are examples of applications that are cluster aware. Although both applications can be configured to provide high availability in the enterprise, they don't achieve high availability through cluster support alone. High-availability applications must support online backups and be tested for compatibility with Windows Server 2012. Support for online backups ensures that you don't have to take the application offline to back up critical data. Compatibility testing ensures that the software has been thoroughly evaluated for operation with Windows Server 2012.

To evaluate the real-world environment prior to deployment, you should perform integration testing on applications that will be used together. The purpose of integration testing is to ensure that disparate applications interact as expected and to uncover problem areas if they don't. During integration testing, testers should look at system performance and overall system utilization, as well as compatibility. Testing should be repeated prior to releasing system or application changes to a production environment.

You should standardize the software components needed to provide system services. The goal of standardization is to set guidelines for software components and technologies that will be used in the enterprise. Standardization accomplishes the following:

- Reduces the total cost of maintaining and updating software

- Reduces the amount of integration and compatibility testing needed for upgrades

- Improves recovery time because problems are easier to troubleshoot

- Reduces the amount of training needed for administration support

Software standardization isn't meant to limit the organization to a single specification. Over the life of a data center, new application versions, software components, and technologies will be introduced, and the organization can implement new standards and specifications as necessary. The key to success lies in ensuring that there is a standard process for deploying software updates and new technologies. The standard process must include the following:

- Software compatibility and integration testing

- Software support training for personnel

- Predeployment planning

- Step-by-step software deployment checklists

- Postdeployment monitoring and maintenance

The following checklist summarizes the recommendations for designing and planning software for high availability:

- Choose software that meets the availability needs of the solution or service.

- Choose software that supports online backups.

- Test software for compatibility with other applications.

- Test software integration with other applications.

- Repeat testing prior to releasing updates.

- Create and enforce software standards.

- Define a standard process for deploying software updates.

## Planning for hardware needs

Sound hardware strategy helps increase system availability while reducing total cost of ownership and improving recovery times. Windows Server 2012 is designed and tested for use with high-performance hardware, applications, and services. To ensure that hardware components are compatible, choose only components that are certified as compatible, such as those that are listed as certified for Windows Server 2012 in the Windows Server Catalog (*http://www.windowsservercatalog.com/*).

> **Note**
>
> All certified components undergo rigorous testing, with a retest for firmware revisions, service pack updates, and other minor revisions. After a component is certified through testing, hardware vendors must maintain the configuration through updates and resubmit the component for testing and certification. The program requirements and the tight coordination with vendors greatly improve the reliability and availability of Windows Server 2012. All hardware certified for Windows Server 2012 also is fully supported in Hyper-V environments.

You should standardize on a hardware platform, and this platform should have standardized components. Standardization accomplishes the following:

- Reduces the amount of training needed for support

- Reduces the amount of testing needed for upgrades

- Requires fewer spare parts because subcomponents are the same

- Improves recovery time because problems are easier to troubleshoot

Standardization isn't meant to restrict a data center to a single type of server. In an *n*-tier environment, standardization typically means choosing a standard server configuration for the front-end servers, a standard server configuration for middle-tier business logic, and a standard server configuration for back-end data services. The reason for this is that web servers, application servers, and database servers all have different resource needs. For example, although a web server might need to run on a dual-processor system with limited hardware RAID control and 4 gigabytes (GBs) of random access memory (RAM), a database server might need to run on an eight-way system with dual-channel RAID control and 64 GBs of RAM.

Standardization isn't meant to limit the organization to a single hardware specification either. Over the life of a data center, new equipment will be introduced and old equipment likely will become unavailable. To keep up with the pace of change, new standards and specifications should be implemented when necessary. These standards and specifications, as with the previous standards and specifications, should be published and made available to you.

Redundancy and fault tolerance must be built into the hardware design at all levels to improve availability. You can improve hardware redundancy by using the following components:

- **Clusters**    Clusters provide failover support for critical applications and services.

- **Standby systems**    Standby systems provide backup systems in case of total failure of a primary system.

- **Spare parts**    Spare parts ensure replacement parts are available in case of failure.

- **Fault-tolerant components**    Fault-tolerant components improve the internal redundancy of the system.

Storage devices, network components, cooling fans, and power supplies all can be configured for fault tolerance. For storage devices, you should be sure to use multiple disk controllers, hot-swappable drives, and redundant drive arrays. For network components, you should look well beyond the network adapter and also consider whether fault tolerance is needed for routers, switches, firewalls, load balancers, and other network equipment.

A standard process for deploying hardware must be defined and distributed to all support personnel. The standard process must include the following:

- Hardware compatibility and integration testing

- Hardware support training for personnel

- Predeployment planning

- Step-by-step hardware deployment checklists

- Postdeployment monitoring and maintenance

The following checklist summarizes the recommendations for designing and planning hardware for high availability:

- Choose hardware that is listed on the Hardware Compatibility List (HCL).

- Create and enforce hardware standards.

- Use redundant hardware whenever possible.

- Use fault-tolerant hardware whenever possible.

- Provide a secure physical environment for hardware.

- Define a standard process for deploying hardware.

If possible, add these recommendations to the preceding checklist:

- Use fully redundant internal networks, from servers to border routers.

- Use direct peering to major tier-1 telecommunications carriers.

- Use redundant external connections for data and telephony.

- Use a direct connection with high-speed lines.

## Planning for support structures and facilities

The physical structures and facilities supporting your server room are critically important. Without adequate support structures and facilities, you will have problems. The primary considerations for support structures and facilities have to do with the physical environment of the servers. These considerations also extend to the physical security of the server environment.

Just as hardware and software have availability requirements so should support structures and facilities. Factors that affect the physical environment are as follows:

- Temperature and humidity

- Dust and other contaminants

- Physical wiring

- Power supplies

- Natural disasters

- Physical security

Temperature and humidity should be carefully controlled at all times. Processors, memory, hard drives, and other pieces of physical equipment operate most efficiently when they are kept cool; between 65 and 70 degrees Fahrenheit is the ideal temperature in most situations. Equipment that overheats can malfunction or cease to operate altogether. Servers should have multiple redundant internal fans to ensure that these and other internal hardware devices are kept cool.

> **Important**
> You should pay particular attention to fast-running processors and hard drives. Typically, fast processors and hard drives can become overheated and need additional cooling fans—even if the surrounding environment is cool.

Humidity should be kept low to prevent condensation, but the environment shouldn't be dry. A dry climate can contribute to static electricity problems. Antistatic devices and static guards should be used in most environments.

Dust and other contaminants can cause hardware components to overheat or short out. Servers should be protected from these contaminants whenever possible. You should ensure that an air-filtration system is in place in the server room or hosting facility that is used. The regular preventive maintenance cycle on the servers should include checking servers and their cabinets for dust and other contaminants. If dust is found, the servers and cabinets should be carefully cleaned.

Few things affect the physical environment more than wiring and cabling. All electrical wires and network cables should be tested and certified by qualified technicians. Electrical wiring should be configured to ensure that servers and other equipment have adequate power available for peak usage times. Ideally, multiple dedicated circuits should be used to provide power.

Improperly installed network cables are the cause of most communications problems. Network cables should be tested to ensure that their operation meets manufacturer specifications. Redundant cables should be installed to ensure the availability of the network. All wiring and cabling should be labeled and well maintained. Whenever possible, use cable management systems and tie wraps to prevent physical damage to wiring.

Ensuring that servers and their components have power is also important. Servers should have hot-swappable, redundant power supplies. Being hot-swappable ensures that the power supply can be replaced without having to turn off the server. Redundancy ensures that one power supply can malfunction and the other will still deliver power to the server. You should be aware that having multiple power supplies doesn't mean that a server or hardware component has redundancy. Some hardware components require multiple power supplies to operate. In this case, an additional (third or fourth) power supply is needed to provide redundancy.

The redundant power supplies should be plugged into separate power strips, and these power strips should be plugged into separate local uninterruptible power supply (UPS) units if other backup power sources aren't available. Some facilities have enterprise UPS units that provide power for an entire room or facility. If this is the case, redundant UPS systems should be installed. To protect against long-term outages, gas-powered or diesel-powered generators should be installed. Most hosting and colocation facilities have generators. But having a generator isn't enough; the generator must be rated to support the peak power needs of all installed equipment. If the generator cannot support the installed equipment, brownouts (temporary outages) will occur.

## Protect equipment against earthquakes

To protect against earthquakes, server racks should have seismic protection. Seismic protection should be extended to other components and to wiring. All cables should be securely attached at both ends and, whenever possible, should be latched to something other than the server, such as a server rack.

## CAUTION

A fire-suppression system should be installed to protect against fire. Dual gas-based systems are preferred because these systems do not harm hardware when they go off. Water-based sprinkler systems, on the other hand, can destroy hardware.

In addition, access controls should be used to restrict physical access to the server room or facility. Use locks, key cards, access codes, or biometric scanners to ensure that only designated individuals can gain entry to the secure area. If possible, use surveillance cameras and maintain recorded tapes for at least a week. When the servers are deployed in a hosting or colocation facility, ensure that locked cages are used and that fencing extends from the floor to the ceiling.

The following checklist summarizes the recommendations for designing and planning structures and facilities:

- Maintain the temperature at 65 to 70 degrees Fahrenheit.

- Maintain low humidity (but not dry).

- Install redundant internal cooling fans.

- Use an air-filtration system.

- Check for dust and other contaminants periodically.

- Install hot-swappable, redundant power supplies.

- Test and certify wiring and cabling.

- Use wire management to protect cables from damage.

- Label hardware and cables.

- Install backup power sources, such as UPS and generators.

- Install seismic protection and bracing.

- Install dual, gas-based, fire-suppression systems.

- Restrict physical access by using locks, key cards, access codes, and so forth.

- Use surveillance cameras, and maintain recorded tapes (if possible).

- Use locked cages, cabinets, and racks at offsite facilities.

- Use floor-to-ceiling fencing with cages at offsite facilities.

## Planning for day-to-day operations

Day-to-day operations and support procedures must be in place before you deploy mission-critical systems. The most critical procedures for day-to-day operations involve the following activities:

- Monitoring and analysis

- Resources, training, and documentation

- Change control

- Problem escalation procedures

- Backup and recovery procedures

- Postmortem after recovery

- Auditing and intrusion detection

Monitoring is critical to the success of business system deployments. You must have the necessary equipment to monitor the status of the business system. Monitoring allows you to be proactive in system support rather than reactive. Monitoring should extend to the hardware, software, and network components but shouldn't interfere with normal systems operations—that is, the monitoring tools chosen should require limited system and network resources to operate.

> **Note**
> Keep in mind that having too much data is just as bad as not collecting any data. The monitoring tools should gather only the data required for meaningful analysis.

Without careful analysis, the data collected from monitoring is useless. Procedures should be put in place to ensure that personnel know how to analyze the data they collect. The network infrastructure is a support area that is often overlooked. Be sure you allocate the appropriate resources for network monitoring.

# INSIDE OUT   Use monitoring to ensure availability

A well-run and well-maintained network should have 99.99 percent availability. There should be less than 1 percent packet loss and a packet turnaround of 80 milliseconds or less. To achieve this level of availability and performance, the network must be monitored. Any time business systems extend to the Internet or to wide area networks (WANs), internal network monitoring must be supplemented with outside-in monitoring that checks the availability of the network and business systems. With outside-in monitoring, you use external systems for your checks, rather than internal systems.

Resources, training, and documentation are essential to ensuring that you can manage and maintain mission-critical systems. Many organizations cripple the operations team by staffing minimally. Minimally staffed teams will have marginal response times and nominal effectiveness. The organization must take the following steps:

- Staff for success to be successful.

- Conduct training before deploying new technologies.

- Keep the training up to date with what's deployed.

- Document essential operations procedures.

Every change to hardware, software, and the network must be planned and executed deliberately. To do this, you must have established change-control procedures and well-documented execution plans. Change-control procedures should be designed to ensure that everyone knows what changes have been made. Execution plans should be designed to ensure that everyone knows the exact steps that were or should be performed to make a change.

Change logs are a key part of change control. Each piece of physical hardware deployed in the operational environment should have a change log. The change log should be stored in a text document or spreadsheet that is readily accessible to support personnel. The change log should show the following information:

- Who changed the hardware

- What change was made

- When the change was made

- Why the change was made

## Establish and follow change-control procedures

Change-control procedures must take into account the need for both planned changes and emergency changes. All team members involved in a planned change should meet regularly and follow a specific implementation schedule. No one should make changes that aren't discussed with the entire implementation team.

You should have well-defined backup and recovery plans. The backup plan should specifically state the following information:

- When full, incremental, differential, and log backups are used

- How often and at what time backups are performed

- Whether the backups must be conducted online or offline

- The amount of data being backed up, as well as how critical the data is

- The tools used to perform the backups

- The maximum time allowed for backup and restore

- How backup media is labeled, recorded, and rotated

Backups should be monitored daily to ensure that they are running correctly and that the media is good. Any problems with backups should be corrected immediately. Multiple media sets should be used for backups, and these media sets should be rotated on a specific schedule. With a four-set rotation, there is one set for daily, weekly, monthly, and quarterly backups. By rotating one media set offsite, support staff can help ensure that the organization is protected in case of a disaster.

The recovery plan should provide detailed step-by-step procedures for recovering the system under various conditions, such as procedures for recovering from hard disk drive failure or troubleshooting problems with connectivity to the back-end database. The recovery plan should also include system design and architecture documentation that details the configuration of physical hardware, application-logic components, and back-end data. Along with this information, support staff should provide a media set containing all software, drivers, and operating system files needed to recover the system.

> **Note**
>
> One thing administrators often forget about is spare parts. Spare parts for key components—such as processors, drives, and memory—should also be maintained as part of the recovery plan.

You should practice restoring critical business systems using the recovery plan. Practice shouldn't be conducted on the production servers. Instead, the team should practice on test equipment with a configuration similar to the real production servers. Practicing once a quarter or semiannually is highly recommended.

You should have well-defined, problem-escalation procedures that document how to handle problems and emergency changes that might be needed. Some organizations use a three-tiered help desk structure for handling problems:

- Level 1 support staff forms the front line for handling basic problems. They typically have hands-on access to the hardware, software, and network components they manage. Their main job is to clarify and prioritize a problem. If the problem has occurred before and there is a documented resolution procedure, they can resolve the problem without escalation. If the problem is new or not recognized, they must understand how, when, and to whom to escalate it.

- Level 2 support staff includes more specialized personnel who can diagnose a particular type of problem and work with others to resolve a problem, such as system administrators and network engineers. They usually have remote access to the hardware, software, and network components they manage. This allows them to troubleshoot problems remotely and to send out technicians after they've pinpointed the problem.

- Level 3 support staff includes highly technical personnel who are subject matter experts, team leaders, or team supervisors. The level 3 team can include support personnel from vendors as well as representatives from the user community. Together, they form the emergency-response or crisis-resolution team that is responsible for resolving crisis situations and planning emergency changes.

All crisis situations and emergencies should be responded to decisively and resolved methodically. A single person on the emergency response team should be responsible for coordinating all changes and executing the recovery plan. This same person should be responsible for writing an after-action report that details the emergency response and resolution process used. The after-action report should analyze how the emergency was resolved and what the root cause of the problem was.

In addition, you should establish procedures for auditing system usage and detecting intrusion. In Windows Server 2012, auditing policies are used to track the successful or failed execution of the following activities:

- **Account logon events**    Tracks events related to user logon and logoff

- **Account management**    Tracks tasks involved with handling user accounts, such as creating or deleting accounts and resetting passwords

- **Directory service access**    Tracks access to the Active Directory Domain Service (AD DS)

- **Object access**    Tracks system resource usage for files, directories, and objects

- **Policy change**    Tracks changes to user rights, auditing, and trust relationships

- **Privilege use**    Tracks the use of user rights and privileges

- **Process tracking**    Tracks system processes and resource usage

- **System events**    Tracks system startup, shutdown, restart, and actions that affect system security or the security log

You should have an incident-response plan that includes priority escalation of suspected intrusion to senior team members and provides step-by-step details on how to handle the intrusion. The incident-response team should gather information from all network systems that might be affected. The information should include event logs, application logs, database logs, and any other pertinent files and data. The incident-response team should take immediate action to lock out accounts, change passwords, and physically disconnect the system if necessary. All team members participating in the response should write a postmortem report that details the following information:

- What date and time they were notified and what immediate actions they took

- Who they notified and what the response was from the notified individual

- What their assessment of the issue is and the actions necessary to resolve and prevent similar incidents

The team leader should write an executive summary of the incident and forward this to senior management.

The following checklist summarizes the recommendations for operational support of high-availability systems:

- Monitor hardware, software, and network components 24/7.

- Ensure that monitoring doesn't interfere with normal systems operations.

- Gather only the data required for meaningful analysis.

- Establish procedures that let personnel know what to look for in the data.

- Use outside-in monitoring any time systems are externally accessible.

- Provide adequate resources, training, and documentation.

- Establish change-control procedures that include change logs.

- Establish execution plans that detail the change implementation.

- Create a solid backup plan that includes onsite and offsite tape rotation.

- Monitor backups, and test backup media.

- Create a recovery plan for all critical systems.

- Test the recovery plan on a routine basis.

- Document how to handle problems and make emergency changes.

- Use a three-tier support structure to coordinate problem escalation.

- Form an emergency-response or crisis-resolution team.

- Write after-action reports that detail the process used.

- Establish procedures for auditing system usage and detecting intrusion.

- Create an intrusion response plan with priority escalation.

- Take immediate action to handle suspected or actual intrusion.

- Write postmortem reports detailing team reactions to the intrusion.

## Planning for deploying highly available servers

You should always create a plan before deploying a business system. The plan should show everything that must be done before the system is transitioned into the production environment. After a system is in the production environment, the system is deemed operational and should be handled as outlined in "Planning for day-to-day operations" earlier in this chapter.

The deployment plan should include the following items:

- Checklists

- Contact lists

- Test plans

- Deployment schedules

Checklists are a key part of the deployment plan. The purpose of a checklist is to ensure that the entire deployment team understands the steps they need to perform. Checklists should list the tasks that must be performed and designate individuals to handle the tasks during each phase of the deployment—from planning to testing to installation. Prior to executing a checklist, the deployment team should meet to ensure that all items are covered and that the necessary interactions among team members are clearly understood. After deployment, the preliminary checklists should become a part of the system documentation and new checklists should be created any time the system is updated.

The deployment plan should include a contact list. The contact list should provide the name, role, telephone number, and email address of all team members, vendors, and solution-provider representatives. Alternative numbers for cell phones and pagers should be provided as well.

The deployment plan should include a test plan. An ideal test plan has several phases. In Phase I, the deployment team builds the business system and support structures in a test lab. Building the system means accomplishing the following tasks:

- Creating a test network on which to run the system

- Putting together the hardware and storage components

- Installing the operating system and application software

- Adjusting basic system settings to suit the test environment

- Configuring clustering, network load balancing, or another high-availability solution, if necessary

The deployment team can conduct any necessary testing and troubleshooting in the isolated lab environment. The entire system should undergo burn-in testing to guard against faulty components. If a component is flawed, it usually fails in the first few days of operation. Testing doesn't stop with burn-in. Web and application servers should be stress tested. Database servers should be load tested. The results of the stress and load tests should be analyzed to ensure that the system meets the performance requirements and expectations of the customer. Adjustments to the configuration should be made to improve performance and optimize the configuration for the expected load.

In Phase II, the deployment team tests the business system and support equipment in the deployment location. They conduct similar tests as before, but in the real-world environment. Again, the results of these tests should be analyzed to ensure that the system meets the performance requirements and expectations of the customer. Afterward, adjustments should be made to improve performance and optimize as necessary. The team can then deploy the business system.

After deployment of the server or servers, the team should perform limited, nonintrusive testing to ensure that the system is operating normally. After Phase III testing is completed, the team can use the operational plans for monitoring and maintenance.

The following checklist summarizes the recommendations for predeployment planning of mission-critical systems:

- Create a plan that covers the entire testing-to-operations cycle.

- Use checklists to ensure that the deployment team understands the procedures.

- Provide a contact list for the team, vendors, and solution providers.

- Conduct burn-in testing in the lab.

- Conduct stress and load testing in the lab.

- Use the test data to optimize and adjust the configuration.

- Provide follow-on testing in the deployment location.

- Follow a specific deployment schedule.

- Use operational plans once final tests are completed.

# CHAPTER 2

# Deploying Windows Server 2012

**M**ICROSOFT Windows Server 2012 supports only 64-bit architecture. You can install the operating system only on computers with 64-bit processors. You are likely to find yourself installing Windows Server 2012 in various circumstances—a new installation for a new system, an upgrade of an existing Microsoft Windows installation, or perhaps even a new installation into a multiboot environment. You might need to install just a few systems, or you might need to deploy hundreds—or even thousands—in a diverse network environment.

In this chapter, I discuss the things you should know to help you prepare for and perform installations. The way you deploy Windows servers will depend on your objectives and requirements. Windows Server 2012 supports both interactive and automated setup processes, providing flexibility in how you install and configure the operating system. You can even fully automate the installation of a basic or fully configured operating system onto a brand new computer to ease the administrative burden in large deployments, and an automation tool like System Center Configuration Manager 2012 can help you do that.

## Getting a quick start

To install Windows Server 2012, you can boot from the Windows distribution media, run Setup from within your current Windows operating system, perform a command-line installation, or use one of the automated installation options.

In performing the installation, there are two basic approaches to setting up Windows Server 2012: interactively or as an automated process. An interactive installation is what many people regard as the regular Windows installation—the kind where you walk through the setup process and enter a lot of information during setup. It can be performed from distribution media (by booting from the distribution media or running Windows Setup from a command line). The default Windows setup process when booting from the retail Windows Server 2012 DVD is interactive, prompting you for configuration information throughout the process.

There are several types of automated setup, which actually have administrator-configurable amounts of user interaction. The most basic form of unattended setup you can perform is an unattended installation using only answer files. To take unattended setup a step further, you can use your unattended answer files with Windows Deployment Services. In either case, the answer file contains all or part of the configuration information usually prompted for during a standard installation process. You can author unattended answer files using Windows System Image Manager. For full automation, you can use System Center Configuration Manager 2012.

The standard setup program for Windows Server 2012 is Setup.exe. You can run Setup.exe from within the Windows operating system to upgrade the existing operating system or to install Windows Server 2012 to a different partition. The command-line switches on the Windows Setup programs offer you additional options for configuring the installation process. The general installation parameters include the following:

- **Setup /addbootmgrlast**   The */addbootmgrlast* option adds the Windows Boot Manager as the last entry in the Unified Extensible Firmware Interface (UEFI) firmware boot order. This option is supported only on computers with UEFI running Windows Preinstallation Environment 4.0 or later.

- **Setup /m:folder_name**   The */m:*folder_name option sets an alternate location for files to be used by Setup during the installation process—during setup, the alternate location is searched first, and files in the default location are used only if the installation files are not found in the specified alternate location.

- **Setup /noreboot**   The */noreboot* parameter prevents the rebooting of the system upon completion of the file copy phase. This option is used to allow other commands or operations to be performed after the files have been copied, but it's used prior to further Setup phases.

- **Setup /tempdrive:*drive_letter***   The */tempdrive:*drive_letter parameter designates the hard disk drive location where the temporary installation files will be placed.

- **Setup /unattend:*answer_file***   The */unattend:*answer_file parameter, when used with an answer file, instructs Setup to do an unattended new installation (a fresh installation as opposed to an upgrade) based on the values specified in the answer file. The answer file can contain all or part of the configuration information for which the installation process normally prompts the user.

# Product licensing

As discussed in Chapter 1, "Introducing Windows Server 2012," in the section "Getting to know Windows Server 2012," there are four main editions of Windows Server 2012: Foundation, Essentials, Standard, and Datacenter. While the Foundation and Essentials editions are for small businesses, the Standard and Datacenter are for any organization that needs a full-featured server.

Licensing for Windows Server 2012 has two aspects: server licenses and client access licenses (CALs). Each installation of Windows Server 2012 on a computer requires appropriate server licensing.

Each server license can be assigned to only a single physical server, and licensing requirements are based on the number of physical processors installed and the number of virtual instances the server runs. All of the physical processors on a server must be licensed with the same version and edition of Windows Server 2012.

Foundation can be used only with a server that has a single physical processor and allows up to 15 users without a need for separate CALs. Essentials can be used on servers with up to 2 physical processors and allows up to 25 users without a need for separate CALs.

Each Standard or Datacenter license covers up to two physical processors. While each Standard license covers up to two virtual instances, a Datacenter license covers an unlimited number of virtual instances. Thus, a server with 4 physical processors would require either two Standard licenses or two Datacenter licenses.

In addition to ensuring that you have the required licenses for Windows Server 2012, you must decide on the client access licensing scheme you will use before installing Windows Server 2012. With the Standard and Datacenter editions, your choices are as follows:

- **Per server**   One CAL is required for each concurrent connection to the server. This usually means one CAL for every connection to that server.

- **Per device or per user**   A CAL is purchased for each user or device connecting to the server—this usually corresponds to one CAL for every user or computer that will access the server.

Your licensing program determines how you handle both the product key and product activation. Table 2-1 describes how each type of licensing affects installation.

**TABLE 2-1** Overview of Windows Server 2012 product keys and activation

| Product License | Product Key | Product Activation |
|---|---|---|
| Retail Product License | Unique product key needed | Windows Product Activation (WPA) |
| Open License program | Reusable product key | No WPA |
| Select License | On volume license media | No WPA |
| Enterprise Agreement License | On volume license media | No WPA |

**TROUBLESHOOTING**

Matching product keys to products

The product ID used during the installation of a retail version is for a specific Windows Server 2012 edition and can be used only with the retail DVD. Likewise, Open License keys are usable only with the media issued by Microsoft as part of obtaining the volume license. In enterprises using both types of software, knowing which keys go with which software makes the installation process easier.

# Preparing for a Windows Server 2012 installation

Installing a server operating system requires some assessment and preparation before you actually do the work. You'll want to review the server hardware and installation details, check the latest technical notes, verify backups, and have more than a few discussions with other Information Technology (IT) staff and managers.

Most editions of Windows Server 2012 share baseline requirements, such as a minimum of a 1.4-gigahertz (GHz) 64-bit CPU, 512 megabytes (MBs) of random access memory (RAM), and 32 gigabytes (GBs) of hard disk drive space.

## Understanding installation options

Before you start an installation, you need to consider whether you want to manage the computer's drives and partitions during the setup process. If you want to use the advanced drive setup options that Setup provides for creating and formatting partitions, you need to boot the computer using the distribution media. If you don't boot using the distribution media, these options won't be available, and you'll be able to manage disk partitions only at a command prompt using the DiskPart utility.

You have two installation options: a clean installation or an upgrade. When you install Windows Server 2012, the Setup program automatically makes recovery options available on the server as an advanced boot option. In addition to a command line for troubleshooting and options for changing the startup behavior, you can use System Image Recovery to perform a full recovery of the computer using a system image created previously. If other troubleshooting techniques fail to restore the computer and you have a system image for recovery, you can use this feature to restore the computer from the backup image.

If you have existing servers running the Windows operating system, you must decide which servers, if any, you will upgrade. The major differences between a clean installation and an upgrade are the following:

- **Upgrade**   With an upgrade, the Windows Server 2012 Setup program transitions the older operating system to the new operating system using a phased approach. Here, the new operating system is installed side by side with the old operating system, which allows rollbacks if necessary. Setup parses the old operating system for executable files, settings, registry entries, and data files and converts as appropriate. This data parsing ensures that the operating system state, applications, user data, drivers, and operating system binary files are migrated. Prior to deleting the old operating system, files not listed in upgrade manifests and other unrecognized files are moved to temporary storage (%SystemRoot%\$Windows.~Q). Finally, Setup migrates the parsed data and settings into a clean installation of the new operating system.

- **Clean installation**   In contrast, a clean installation does not retain any user or system settings or knowledge of any installed applications, and you must configure all aspects of the hardware and software. You should use a clean installation when the operating system cannot be upgraded, the system must boot to multiple operating systems, a standardized configuration is required, or (obviously) when no operating system is currently installed.

Before performing an upgrade, you should make sure the server's installed software and hardware support Windows Server 2012. You can download tools for testing compatibility and documentation at the Windows Server Catalog website (*http://www.windowsservercatalog.com/*).

Microsoft server operating systems from Windows Server 2008 and later can be upgraded to Windows Server 2012. In general, servers can be upgraded to a similar or higher edition of the product.

You cannot perform an upgrade installation of Windows Server 2012 on a computer with a 32-bit operating system, even if the computer has 64-bit processors. You cannot upgrade Windows Server 2003 to Windows Server 2012. In either case, you need to migrate the services being provided by the computer to other servers and then perform a clean installation. The Windows Server Migration tools might be able to help you migrate your server. These tools are available on computers running Windows Server 2012.

Chapter 2

# Determining which installation type to use

Windows Server 2012 supports three installation types:

- **Full Server**   Full Server installations, also referred to as Server With A GUI Installations, have the Graphical Management Tools And Infrastructure and Server Graphical Shell features (which are part of the User Interfaces And Infrastructure feature) and the WOW64 Support framework installed.

- **Minimal Server Interface**   Minimal Server Interface installations, also referred to as Server With Minimal Interface Installations, are Full Server installations with the Server Graphical Shell removed. Although this option is not available when installing Windows Server 2012, you can convert to a Minimal Server Interface later.

- **Server Core**   Server Core installations have a limited user interface and do not include any of the User Interfaces And Infrastructure features or the WOW64 Support framework. This is the default installation option.

## TROUBLESHOOTING

**Server Core limits installable roles and role services**

With a Full Server installation, you have a complete working version of Windows Server 2012 you can deploy with any permitted combination of roles, role services, and features. With a Minimal Server Interface installation, you also can deploy any permitted combination of roles, role services, and features. However, with a Server Core installation, you have a minimal installation of Windows Server 2012 that supports a limited set of roles and role combinations. The supported roles include AD CS, AD DS, AD LDS, DHCP Server, DNS Server, File Services, Hyper-V, Media Services, Print And Document Services, Routing And Remote Access Server, Streaming Media Services, Web Server (IIS), and Windows Server Update Services. In its current implementation, a Server Core installation is not a platform for running server applications. That said, you can run Hyper-V on Server Core and use it to host virtual machines that run server applications, such as SQL Server, Exchange Server, and SharePoint.

Whereas all three installation types use the same licensing rules and can be managed remotely using any available and permitted remote-administration technique, Full Server, Minimal Server Interface, and Server Core installations are completely different when it comes to local console administration. With a Full Server installation, you're provided with a user interface that includes a full desktop environment for local console management of the server. With a Minimal Server Interface installation, you have only Microsoft Management Consoles, Server Manager, and a subset of Control Panel available for management tasks. Missing from both a Minimal Server Interface installation and a Server Core installation are File Explorer, taskbar, notification area, Internet Explorer, built-in help system, themes, desktop apps, and Windows Media Player.

Unlike earlier releases of Windows Server, you can change the installation type of any server running Windows Server 2012. This is possible because a key difference among the installation types relates to whether the installation has the following User Interfaces And Infrastructure features:

- Graphical Management Tools And Infrastructure

- Desktop Experience

- Server Graphical Shell

Server Core installations have none of these features. Minimal Server Interface installations have only the Graphical Management Tools And Infrastructure feature and Full Server installations have both the Graphical Management Tools And Infrastructure feature and the Server Graphical Shell feature.

Full Server installations also might have Desktop Experience, which provides Windows desktop functionality on the server. Windows features added include Windows Media Player, desktop themes, Video for Windows (AVI support), Disk Cleanup, Sync Center, Sound Recorder, Character Map, and Snipping Tool. These features allow a server to be used like a desktop computer, but they also can reduce the server's overall performance.

Knowing that Windows also automatically installs or uninstalls dependent features, server roles, and management tools to match the installation type, you can convert from one installation type to another simply by adding or removing the appropriate User Interfaces And Infrastructure features. For more information on converting the installation type, see "Postinstallation tasks" later in the chapter.

## Using Windows Update

Windows Update is a convenient way of ensuring that the most recently updated driver and system files are always used during server installation. Windows Update connects to a distribution server containing updated files used during Windows installation. The files in Windows Update include setup information files, dynamic libraries used during setup, file assemblies, device drivers, and system files.

Chapter 2

**Note**

During setup of the operating system, the Windows Update process does not provide new installation files, but rather it supplies only updated files that replace existing files used during setup. Windows Update might, however, provide device drivers that are not a replacement for device drivers existing on the distribution media (in-box device drivers) but that are new device drivers supplying additional support for devices or system hardware.

The Windows Update files can be obtained by using two methods:

- Windows Update files can be obtained directly from the Windows Update site during setup, ensuring that the absolute latest setup files are used during the installation.

- Windows Update files can be downloaded to a server on your local network and then shared to provide clients with access to a consistent local copy of the files.

Getting Windows Updates from the update site online is recommended for consumers and small businesses that do not have a full-time Windows administrator. Otherwise, your organization probably should centralize the functionality locally using Windows Server Update Services (WSUS) in a client/server configuration. WSUS is available as an optional download for Windows Server 2012. Hosting Windows Update files on a local network provides you with additional security and the advantage of being able to ensure that important operating system updates are applied to all systems within your network environment.

# INSIDE OUT  Using Windows Server Update Services

WSUS is available as an installable role in Window Server 2012. WSUS has both a server component and a client component. The client component is built into Windows client operating systems. Each managed client requires a Windows Server CAL. The WSUS server component uses a data store that runs with Microsoft SQL Server Desktop Engine (MSDE), Microsoft SQL Server Desktop Engine for Windows (WMSDE), or Microsoft SQL Server. With SQL Server, every device managed by WSUS requires a SQL Server CAL or a per-processor license.

WSUS requires Internet Information Services (IIS). The WSUS server component uses IIS to obtain updates over the Internet using HTTP port 80 and HTTPS port 443. WSUS can also use IIS to automatically update client computers with the necessary client software for WSUS.

For performance and network load balancing, large enterprises might want to have an extended WSUS environment with multiple WSUS servers. In a multiple WSUS server environment configuration, one WSUS server can be used as the central server for downloading updates and other WSUS servers can connect to this server to obtain settings and updates to distribute to clients.

## Preinstallation tasks

You will want to assess the specifics of an installation and identify any tasks that must be done prior to the installation taking place. The following is a partial list—a general set of pointers to the installation-related tasks that must be performed:

- Check for firmware updates.

- Check requirements for the operating system version.

- Review the release notes on the operating system media.

- Determine whether to upgrade or perform a clean installation.

- Check your system hardware compatibility.

- Configure how the target computer boots.

- Determine the installation type: interactive or automated.

- Determine the license mode.

- Choose the installation partition.

- Determine the network connectivity and settings.

- Identify domain or workgroup membership account information.

- Disconnect the uninterruptible power supply (UPS).

- Disable virus scanning.

Chapter 2

> **Note**
>
> When doing a clean installation on old hardware, check to see whether an operating system exists. If one does exist, check the event or system logs for hardware errors, consider using multiboot, uncompress the drives, and resolve any partition upgrade issues.

## Plan for Windows Update

Hosting Windows Update on a local network server—as opposed to downloading updates directly from Microsoft each time you install the operating system—can speed up the updates and ensure the consistency of driver versions across the network environment.

You must also assess your installation requirements and plan the configuration of the drives and partitions on the target computers. If you must create a new partition, modify the system partition, or format the system partition before installation, you can use configuration tools such as the DiskPart, Format, and Convert commands to manage partitions (prior to beginning the automated installation).

# Installing Windows Server 2012

For many situations in which you're about to install Windows Server 2012 onto a new computer system—a bare-metal or a clean installation to a computer you can sit in front of—booting from the Windows Server 2012 distribution media is certainly the simplest approach. You need only configure the server to boot from the DVD-ROM by setting the boot device order in the firmware and provide information when prompted. The exception to this is when you must specify command-line switches or run the command line from within Setup. Alternatively, if you work in an environment that maintains standing images of operating systems in use, you can do an interactive installation from a deployment share on the network.

The way you install a server depends somewhat on its firmware interface. As discussed in detail in Chapter 3, "Boot configuration," computers can be either Basic Input Output System (BIOS) based or Extensible Firmware Interface (EFI) based. While BIOS-based computers normally use the master boot record (MBR) disk type for boot and system volumes, EFI-based computers normally use the GUID partition table (GPT) disk type for boot and system volumes. These two disk types are very different.

## Installation on BIOS-based systems

When you are working with Windows Server 2012 on BIOS-based systems, you should be aware of the special types of drive sections used by the operating system:

- **Active**   The active partition or volume is the drive section for system cache and startup. Some devices with removable storage might be listed as having an active partition.

- **Boot**   The boot partition or volume contains the operating system and its support files. The system and boot partition or volume can be the same.

- **Crash Dump**   This is the partition to which the computer attempts to write dump files in the event of a system crash. By default, dump files are written to the %SystemRoot% folder, but they can be located on any partition or volume you choose.

- **Page File**   This is a partition containing a paging file used by the operating system. Because a computer can page memory to multiple disks, according to the way you configure virtual memory, a computer can have multiple page-file partitions or volumes.

- **System**   The system partition or volume contains the hardware-specific files needed to load the operating system. As part of software configuration, the system partition or volume can't be part of a striped or spanned volume.

> **Note**
>
> Partitions and volumes are essentially the same thing. The term used varies at times, however, because you create partitions on basic disks and you create volumes on dynamic disks. Keep in mind, however, that a primary partition on a basic disk is a volume, and a logical drive in an extended partition is also a volume. On a BIOS-based computer, you can mark a partition as active using Disk Management.
>
> Yes, the definitions of *boot partition* and *system partition* are backward from what you'd expect. The boot partition, in fact, does contain the \Windows directory—that's just the way it is.

Although these volumes or partitions can be the same, they are required nonetheless. When you install Windows Server 2012, the Setup program assesses all hard-disk-drive resources available. Typically, Windows Server 2012 puts the boot and system volumes on the same drive and partition and marks this partition as the active partition. The advantage

Chapter 2

of this configuration is that you don't need multiple drives for the operating system and can use an additional drive as a mirror of the operating system partitions.

## Installation on EFI-based systems

A GUID partition table (GPT)–based disk has two required partitions and one or more optional (original equipment manufacturer [OEM] or data) partitions (up to 128 total):

- EFI system partition (ESP)

- Microsoft Reserved (MSR) partition

- At least one data partition

Although EFI-based computers can have both GPT and MBR disks, the computer must have at least one GPT disk for booting.

## Planning partitions

Now that you know how Windows Server 2012 uses disks on both BIOS-based and EFI-based computers, consider carefully how you want to partition the hard disk drives. The boot and system files require about 10 GBs of space. To allow for flexibility, you should create a partition for the operating system with at least 40 GBs. This allows for the addition of service packs and other system files later. Don't forget that you should also have enough disk space for the pagefile and crash dump; I recommend reserving additional disk space equivalent to twice the installed RAM for this purpose.

Although a server could have a single hard disk with a single partition, it sometimes is better to have multiple partitions, even if the computer has only one drive. By using multiple partitions, you can separate operating system files from application data as might be a recommended best practice for the application. Although this permits the use of services that require installation on nonsystem partitions, it could make migrating to a future operating system more difficult.

### Create additional partitions

If you plan to create multiple partitions, you don't have to worry about doing it when installing the operating system. You can configure the Windows operating system to use a partition of the correct size, such as 40 GBs or more, and then create the other partitions that you want to use after the installation is finished.

For systems with multiple disks, this is a good time to think about whether you want to use a redundant array of independent disks (RAID) to add fault tolerance for the operating system. RAID can be performed at the hardware level or at the operating system level. You will find that the hardware-based RAID provides the best performance and is the easiest solution.

Increasingly, enterprises are using storage arrays. If your servers are allocated storage from storage arrays, keep in mind that each logical unit number, or LUN, assigned is a virtual disk and that the virtual disk likely is spread across multiple physical disks (also called *spindles*). Here, hardware RAID is configured within the storage array and you might not need additional software-based RAID. That said, several software RAID options are available and administrators often will want to implement one of these options as an additional safeguard, including

- **Traditional software RAID**   This is the software-based RAID technology built into the operating system and available in earlier releases of Windows.

- **Storage Spaces**   This is a new resilient storage solution available for Windows 8 and Windows Server 2012 that uses virtual disk technology. Storage Spaces are preferred over traditional software RAID.

RAID options are discussed in Chapter 12, "Storage management," and include the following:

- Disk striping (RAID 0)

- Disk mirroring or duplexing (RAID 1)

- Disk striping with parity (RAID 5)

Software-based RAID is implemented by using dynamic disks. For a bare-metal installation, the disks on the computer should be formatted as basic disks, and then after installation, you could upgrade to dynamic disks so that you can implement software-based RAID. On existing installations, the computer might already have dynamic disks, which could be the case if a computer is currently using Microsoft Windows Server and you are performing a new installation of Windows Server 2012. Keep in mind, however, that dynamic disks are deprecated for all usages except mirrored boot volumes. If you want to mirror the volume that hosts the operating system, you might want to use dynamic disks because this is one of the best approaches.

> **Important**
>
> Deprecated means that dynamic disks might not be supported in future releases of Windows and that you might not want to use dynamic disks on new Windows deployments. It doesn't mean that you can't use dynamic disks. Dynamic disks continue to be available in Windows 8 and Windows Server 2012.

For resilience, virtual disks that you create as part of a server's Storage Spaces can use mirroring or parity as well. As part of software configuration, you cannot use RAID 0 with system or boot volumes. More typically, operating system files are mirrored, and application data is striped with parity. If you plan to mirror the operating system, you will need two disks. If you plan to create a RAID-5 volume for your data, you'll need at least three disks.

## Naming computers

It is surprising how few organizations take the time to plan out the names they're going to use for their computers. Sure, it is fun to have servers named Lefty, Curly, Moe, Ducky, Ruddy, and Aardvark, but just what do the names say about the role and location of those servers? You guessed it—nothing, which can make it difficult for users and even other administrators to find resources they need. Not to mention the management nightmare that happens when your six cutely named servers grow to number 50 or 500.

Rather than using names that are cute or arbitrary, decide on a naming scheme that is meaningful to both administrators and users—and this doesn't mean naming servers after the seven dwarfs or *Lord of the Rings* characters. OK, it might be cool—way cool—to have servers named Bilbo, Gandalf, Frodo, and Gollum. But pretty soon you'd have Galadriel, Boromir, Theoden, Eowyn, and all the rest of the cast. And at that point, you'd better be ready to field lots of questions, such as, "How do you spell Aeyowin, anyway?" or "What's Thedding, and where is it again?"

To help users and ease the administrative burden, you might decide to use a naming scheme that helps identify what the computer does and where it is located. For example, you could name the first server in the Engineering department EngServer01 and the first server in the Technical Services department TechServer01. These names identify the computers as servers and specify the departments in which they are located. You might also have servers named CorpMail01 and CorpIntranet01, which identify the corporate mail and intranet servers, respectively.

Although naming conventions can be helpful, don't go overboard. The names EngServer01, TechServer01, CorpMail01, and CorpIntranet01 help identify computers by role and location, but they aren't overly complex. Keeping things simple should help ensure that the computer names are easy to remember and easy to work with. Stay away from overly complex names, such as SeattleSrvBldg48DC17 or SvrSeaB48F15-05, if at all possible. Overly complex names are unnecessary in most instances and probably contain information that most users don't need. For example, users won't care that a server is in building 48 or that it is on floor 15. In fact, that information might be too specific and could actually help someone who wants to break into or sabotage the corporate network. Instead of putting exact mapping information in the computer name, keep a spreadsheet that maps computer locations for administrative use, and include only general information about the location or department in the computer name.

While we're talking about security, keep in mind that some organizations use server names with arbitrary character strings on purpose. They want to make the network infrastructure difficult to discover and navigate for anyone trying to gain unauthorized access. Thus, they might use computer names like Srv4Wg8th3kb12a or Tkl82jeb4j2e9pz. Here, the organization is using random 15-character strings as computer names but giving up ease of use and reference with the goal of enhancing overall security.

Finally, keep in mind that computer names must be unique in the domain and must be 64 characters or less in length. The first 15 characters of the computer name are used as the pre–Windows 2000 computer name for Network Basic Input/Output System (NetBIOS) communications and must be unique in the domain as well. Further, for Domain Name System (DNS) compatibility, the name should consist of only alphanumeric characters (A–Z, a–z, and 0–9) and the hyphen.

## Network and domain membership options

During installation, you must decide on several important network and domain membership options, such as the following:

- Which protocols the server will use

- Whether the server will be a member of the domain

- What networking components will be installed

### Protocols

The primary networking protocols that Windows Server 2012 installs by default are Transmission Control Protocol/Internet Protocol version 4 (TCP/IPv4) and Transmission Control Protocol/Internet Protocol version 6 (TCP/IPv6). Throughout this book, I'll refer to TCP/IPv4 and TCP/IPv6 collectively as TCP/IP. To correctly install TCP/IP, you must decide whether you want to use static IP addressing or dynamic IP addressing. For static IP addresses, you need the following information:

- IP address

- Subnet mask/subnet prefix length

- Default gateway

- Preferred DNS server

For dynamic IP addressing, the IP information is assigned automatically by an available Dynamic Host Configuration Protocol (DHCP) server. If no DHCP server is available, the server will autoconfigure itself. Autoconfigured addressing is typically nonroutable, so you must correct this issue after installation.

## Domain membership

Just about every server you install will be a member of a domain rather than a member of a workgroup (with some exceptions, of course). You can join a computer to a domain after installation. If you want to do that, you should have a computer account created in the domain (or create one while joining the domain using an account with Administrator or Account Operator rights). A computer account is similar to a user account in that it resides in the accounts database held in Active Directory Domain Services and is maintained by domain controllers.

If a server is a member of a domain, users with domain memberships or permissions can access the server and its resources based on, of course, their individual rights and permissions without having to have a separate logon. This means that users can log on once to the domain and work with resources for which they have permissions to access, and they won't be prompted to log on separately for each server they work with. In contrast, however, if a server is a member of a workgroup, users must log on each time they want to work with a server and its resources.

## Networking components

During installation, you have the opportunity to install networking components. The common networking components for servers are selected automatically. They include the following:

- **Client for Microsoft Networks**    Allows the computer to access resources on Windows-based networks

- **File and Printer Sharing for Microsoft Networks**    Allows other Windows-based computers to access resources on the computer (required for remote logon)

- **Internet Protocol version 4 (TCP/IPv4)**    Allows the computer to communicate over the network by using TCP/IPv4

- **Internet Protocol version 6 (TCP/IPv6)**   Allows the computer to communicate over the network by using TCP/IPv6

- **QoS Packet Scheduler**   Helps the computer manage the flow of network traffic and prioritize services

- **Link-Layer Topology Discovery Mapper I/O Driver**   Allows the computer to discover and locate other computers, devices, and networking components on the network

- **Link-Layer Topology Discovery Responder**   Allows the computer to be discovered and located on the network by other computers

You can install additional clients, services, and protocols as well, including Microsoft LLDP Protocol Driver and Reliable Multicast Protocol. However, try to keep additional component installation to a minimum. Install the components that you know must be installed. Don't install components you think you might need because they might use system resources that would otherwise be available for others services to use.

## Performing a clean installation

To perform a clean installation of Windows Server 2012, complete the following steps:

1.  Start the Setup program using one of the following techniques:

    ○ For a new installation, turn on the computer with the Windows Server 2012 distribution media in the computer's disc drive, and then press any key when prompted to start Setup from your media. If you are not prompted to boot from the disc drive, you might need to select advanced boot options and then boot from media rather than hard disk, or you might need to change the computer's firmware settings to allow booting from media.

    ○ For a clean installation over an existing installation, you can boot from the distribution media, or you can start the computer and log on using an account with administrator privileges. When you insert the Windows Server 2012 distribution media into the computer's disc drive, Setup should start automatically. If Setup doesn't start automatically, use File Explorer to access the distribution media and then double-tap or double-click Setup.exe.

> **Note**
>
> When you try to install Windows Server 2012 using a DVD, you might find that your computer doesn't recognize the installation media. If the media is damaged, you'll need to obtain replacement media. Otherwise, make sure that the DVD drive is configured as a startup device and that you are inserting the media into the appropriate DVD drive.

Chapter 2

**TROUBLESHOOTING**

**Using the Rollback Wizard during setup**

If Windows Setup encounters a problem during installation, you can select the Rollback option on the boot menu to start the Rollback Wizard (x:\sources\rollback.exe). You can use this wizard to subsequently attempt to restore the previous version of Windows. If the Rollback Wizard is successful, the previous version of Windows is completely restored. If the Rollback Wizard is unsuccessful, the server typically is left in an unbootable state and you must either perform a full restore of the previous installation or a clean installation of Windows Server 2012.

**2.** If you started the computer using the distribution media, choose your language, time, and currency formats and keyboard layout when prompted. Only one keyboard layout is available during installation. If your keyboard language and the language edition of Windows Server 2012 you are installing are different, you might see unexpected characters as you type. Be sure that you select the correct keyboard language to avoid this. When you are ready to continue with the installation, tap or click Next.

**3.** On the next Setup page, note that you have several options:

   ○ **Install Now**   By tapping or clicking Install Now, you can start the installation.

   ○ **What To Know Before Installing Windows Server 2012**   By tapping or clicking What To Know Before Installing Windows Server 2012, you can review helpful information about installing Windows Server 2012.

**4.** If you are starting the installation from an existing operating system and are connected to a network or the Internet, choose whether to get updates during the installation. Tap or click either Go Online To Get The Latest Updates For Setup or Do Not Get The Latest Updates For Setup.

**5.** With volume and enterprise licensed editions of Windows Server 2012, you might not need to provide a product key during installation of the operating system. With retail editions, however, you'll be prompted to enter a product key, and then tap or click Next to continue. Keep the following in mind:

   ○ When entering the product key, be sure to enter a key for the server edition you want to install. You don't need to worry about using the correct letter case or entering dashes. Setup enters all letters you type in uppercase. When a dash is needed, Setup enters the dash automatically.

○ On the Type Your Product Key For Activation page, the Next button is available for tapping or clicking only when the Product Key box is empty or when you've entered all 25 of the required characters. If you want to enter a product key, you must type the full product key before the Next button is available for tapping or clicking. If you don't want to enter a product key at this time, leave the Product Key box blank and then tap or click Next.

○ The Activate Windows When I'm Online check box is selected by default to automatically activate the operating system the next time you connect to the Internet. Windows Server 2012 must be activated within the first 30 days after installation. If you don't activate Windows Server 2012 in the allotted time, you see an error stating "Your activation period has expired" or that you have a "non-genuine version of Windows Server 2012 installed." Windows Server 2012 will then run in a reduced functionality mode. You need to activate and validate Windows Server 2012 as necessary to resume full functionality mode.

6. If you enter an invalid product key, Setup will continue to display the Type Your Product Key For Activation page. To let you know there's a problem with the product key, Setup displays the following warning in the lower portion of the page: "Your product key cannot be validated. Review your product key and make sure you have entered it correctly." Before you can continue, you need to change the product key so that it exactly matches the product key sticker. If you don't see the discrepancy causing the problem, you might want to delete the previously entered product key and then retype the product key. After you re-enter the product key, tap or click Next to continue. As long as you enter a valid product key, you'll continue to the next page. Otherwise, you have to repeat this step.

7. If you did not enter a product key, you'll then see the warning prompt, asking whether you want to enter a product key at this time. If you tap or click Yes, you'll return to the Type Your Product Key For Activation page. If you tap or click No, you'll be allowed to continue with the installation without entering a product key.

8. You need to choose whether to perform a Server With A GUI installation or a Server Core installation. If you selected to continue without entering a product key, you'll next need to select the edition of Windows Server 2012 to install as well. Although Setup will allow you to choose any edition, it is important to choose the edition that you purchased. If you choose the wrong edition, you will need to purchase that edition or reinstall the correct edition.

Chapter 2

> **Note**
>
> If you enter a product key and the server edition you want to install is not listed, tap or click the Back arrow and enter the correct product key for that server edition. Keep in mind that you can continue without entering a product key and this will allow you to choose any available edition. However, if you choose the wrong edition, you will need to purchase that edition, reinstall the correct edition, or upgrade to the correct edition.

9.  The license terms for Windows Server 2012 have changed from previous releases of Windows. When prompted, review the license terms. Select the I Accept The License Terms check box, and then tap or click Next.

10. On the Which Type Of Installation Do You Want page, you need to select the type of installation you want Setup to perform. Because you are performing a clean installation to completely replace an existing installation or configure a new computer, select Custom (Advanced) as the installation type. If you started Setup from the boot prompt rather than from within Windows itself, the upgrade option is disabled. To upgrade rather than perform a clean install, you need to restart the computer and boot the currently installed operating system. After you log on, you then need to start the installation.

11. On the Where Do You Want To Install Windows page, you need to select the disk or disk and partition on which you want to install the operating system. Windows Server 2012 requires between 10 and 40 GBs of disk space for installation. Keep the following in mind:

    ❍ When a computer has a single hard disk with a single partition encompassing the whole disk, the whole disk partition is selected by default and you can tap or click Next to choose this as the install location. With a disk that is completely unallocated, you need to create the necessary partition for installing the operating system as discussed in "Creating, deleting, and extending disk partitions during installation" later in this chapter.

    ❍ When a computer has multiple disks or a single disk with multiple partitions, you need to either select an existing partition to use for installing the operating system or create one. You can create and manage partitions as discussed in "Creating, deleting, and extending disk partitions during installation" later in this chapter.

    ❍ You might see a warning message stating "This computer's hardware may not support booting to this disk." This can occur if the disk has not been initialized for use or if the firmware of the computer does not support starting the operating system from the selected disk. To resolve this problem, create one or more partitions on all the hard disks that are not initialized.

○ You cannot select or format a hard-disk partition that uses FAT or FAT32 or has other incompatible settings. To work around this issue, you might want to convert the partition to NTFS. Because the inability to select a disk or partition could also be due to a problem with the drivers for the hard disk, you might need to install the device drivers required by a hard disk.

○ When working with this page, you can access a command prompt to perform any necessary preinstallation tasks, to forcibly remove a disk partition that is locked, or to load device drivers to support hard disks that aren't listed as available but should be available. To learn more see "Performing additional administration tasks during installations" later in this chapter.

**12.** If the partition you selected contains a previous Windows installation, Setup provides a prompt stating that existing user and application settings will be moved to a folder named Windows.old and that you must copy these settings to the new installation to use them. Tap or click OK.

**13.** Tap or click Next. Setup starts the installation of the operating system. During this procedure, Setup copies the full disk image of Windows Server 2012 to the location you selected and then expands it. Afterward, Setup installs features based on the computer's configuration and detected hardware. This process requires several automatic restarts. When Setup finishes the installation, the operating system will be loaded and you'll see the logon screen. After you enter and confirm a password for the administrator account, you can log on.

**14.** Perform initial configuration tasks using Server Manager, such as setting the computer name and administrator password.

## Use a strong password for the Administrator account

A strong password uses a combination of uppercase letters, lowercase letters, numbers, and special characters. If your administrator password does not meet the Windows Server criteria for strong passwords, a dialog box explaining the criteria for the administrator password appears and you are given the opportunity to change the password or continue with it as is. The use of a strong password for the Administrator account is a security step well worth taking. Weak passwords remain one of the more significant ways that the security of a Windows network is compromised, yet they are one of the easiest problems to fix.

Chapter 2

## Performing an upgrade installation

Although Windows Server 2012 provides an upgrade option during installation, an upgrade with Windows Server 2012 might not be your best option. Why? Not every Windows role, role service, feature, or application can be upgraded. When you start an upgrade, Setup performs compatibility checks to verify that all of the components and applications installed on the computer can be upgraded. Identified issues are shown in a compatibility report.

The compatibility report will notify you about identified problems and might include guidance on what you need to do before upgrading the server. If there are incompatible components and applications installed, you should stop the upgrade and take any required, corrective actions before continuing with the upgrade. Keep in mind that Setup might not identify every compatibility issue and there might still be unidentified issues that need to be resolved. Additionally, keep in mind that any files that an application cannot locate after the upgrade process might have been moved to the temporary storage directory (%SystemDrive%\$WINDOWS.~Q). Because of the challenges presented with upgrading a server, it often is more efficient to migrate services and applications a server is hosting to other servers and then perform a clean installation.

The steps you perform for an upgrade installation of Windows Server 2012 are nearly identical to those you follow for a clean installation. The key difference is that in step 10, you need to select the installation type as Upgrade. If you started Setup from the boot prompt rather than from within Windows itself, the upgrade option is disabled. To upgrade rather than perform a clean install, you need to restart the computer and boot the currently installed operating system. After you log on, you then need to start the installation.

Because you are upgrading the operating system, you do not need to choose an installation location. During this process, Setup copies the full disk image of Windows Server 2012 to the system disk. Afterward, Setup installs features based on the computer's configuration and detected hardware. When Setup finishes the installation, the operating system will be loaded and you can complete the installation.

When Setup finishes the installation, the operating system will be loaded and you'll see the logon screen. After you log on, you can perform initial configuration tasks.

## Activation sequence

After you install Windows Server 2012, you should configure TCP/IP networking as discussed in Chapter 19, "Managing TCP/IP networking." If the type of licensing you are using requires product activation after installation, you have 10 days to complete online activation. If you don't, the evaluation period begins and runs for 180 days. During the evaluation period, a notification is displayed on the desktop telling you the number of days remaining in the evaluation period (except in Windows Server 2012 Essentials). You can also run **slmgr.vbs /dlv** from an elevated command prompt to see the time remaining.

You have several activation options, including activating over the Internet, by telephones, and various automated activation techniques.

## TROUBLESHOOTING

### Identifying an elapsed evaluation period

During the evaluation period, the server is fully functional but cannot be booted to Safe Mode. When the evaluation period elapses, a warning appears on the desktop stating the Windows license is expired. When you log on to Windows, you are prompted to activate Windows. If you don't activate Windows, the server will shut itself down every hour and the only updates that will be applied are security updates.

## INSIDE OUT    Converting an evaluation license to a retail license

The evaluation period is different from installing an evaluation version of Windows. When you install an evaluation version of Windows, you also have an evaluation period of 180 days. When that time elapses, you must re-install the server with another evaluation product or convert the license to a retail license. You can convert Windows Server 2012 Essentials to the full retail version by entering a retail, volume license, or OEM key using the command **slmgr.vbs**.

For other editions, note the current edition or type the following command at an elevated prompt to determine the edition name: **DISM /online /Get-CurrentEdition**. Next, at an elevated prompt, type **DISM /online /Set-Edition:** *EditionId* **/ProductKey:***ProdKey* **/AcceptEula**, where *EditionId* is either ServerStandard or ServerDataCenter and *ProdKey* is the full product key including any dashes. The server will restart twice. Although you cannot convert a domain controller to a retail license, you can install an additional domain controller and assign any roles to this server and then demote the server so that it can be converted.

## Activate Windows over the Internet

Although volume-licensed versions of Windows Server 2012 might not require activation or product keys, retail versions of Windows Server 2012 require both activation and product keys. You can determine whether Windows Server 2012 has been activated in Control Panel. To do this, perform the following steps:

1. In Control Panel, tap or click System And Security, and then tap or click System.

2. On the System page, read the Windows Activation entry. This entry specifies whether you have activated the operating system.

3. If Windows Server 2012 has not been activated and you are connected to the Internet, select View Details In Windows Activation and then tap or click Activate.

The computer then checks its Internet connection and attempts to activate the operating system. If this process fails, you need to resolve any issues that are preventing your computer from connecting to the Internet and then tap or click Activate again.

## Activate Windows by telephone

With activation over the telephone, you can go straight to product activation by performing the following steps:

1. In Control Panel, tap or click System And Security, and then tap or click System.

2. If Windows Server 2012 has not been activated, select View Details In Windows Activation.

3. In the Windows Activation dialog box, tap or click Show Me Other Ways To Activate and then tap or click Use The Automated Phone System.

4. Select a geographic or country/region location and then tap or click Next to obtain a telephone number for your area. You will also get an installation ID, which is a very long string of numbers that you will need to enter into the automated customer service phone system.

5. After you call the phone number and give the installation ID, you will get an activation code, which is another long string of numbers that you have to enter on the Activate Windows page before you can continue with the activation.

6. Tap or click Next and follow the prompts to complete activation.

## Using Managed Activation

You also can perform volume activation using Key Management Service (KMS) or Active Directory. Both technologies use a client/server architecture and require that you install the Volume Activation Services role on a server running Windows Server 2012 and then use Volume Activation Tools to enable and configure the technology.

With KMS, you use Volume Activation Tools to install Generic Volume License Keys or KMS client product keys, and you must specifically configure computers for KMS activation. On the other hand, Active Directory–based activation allows you to automatically activate computers using only their domain connection. Any computer running Windows 8 or Windows Server 2012, whether offsite or onsite, can be activated if the computer can join a domain. Activation is performed automatically when a user joins the computer to the domain.

# Performing additional administration tasks during installations

Sometimes, you forget to perform a preinstallation task prior to starting the installation. Rather than restarting the operating system, you can access a command prompt from within Setup or use advanced drive options to perform the necessary administrative tasks.

## Accessing a command prompt during installation

When you access a command prompt from within Setup, you access the Windows Preinstallation Environment (Windows PE) used by Setup to install the operating system. During installation, you can access a command prompt at any time by pressing Shift+F10. As Table 2-2 shows, Windows PE gives you access to many of the same command-line tools that are available in a standard installation of Windows Server 2012.

**TABLE 2-2  Commands available in the Windows PE environment**

| Command | Description |
|---------|-------------|
| Arp | Displays and modifies the IP-to-physical address translation tables used by the Address Resolution Protocol (ARP). |
| Assoc | Displays and modifies file-extension associations. |
| Attrib | Displays and changes file attributes. |
| Cacls | Displays or modifies access control lists of files. |
| Call | Calls a script or script label as a procedure. |
| CD/Chdir | Displays the name of the current directory or changes its name. |
| Chcp | Displays or sets the active code page number. |
| Chkdsk | Checks a disk for errors, and displays a report. |
| Chkntfs | Displays the status of volumes. It sets or excludes volumes from automatic system checking when the computer is started. |
| Choice | Creates a selection list from which users can select a choice in batch scripts. |
| Cls | Clears the console window. |
| Cmd | Starts a new instance of the Windows command shell. |

Chapter 2

| Command | Description |
|---|---|
| Color | Sets the colors of the command-shell window. |
| Comp | Compares the contents of two files or sets of files. |
| Compact | Displays or modifies the compression of files or sets of files. |
| Convert | Converts FAT volumes to NTFS. |
| Copy | Copies or combines files. |
| Date | Displays or sets the system date. |
| Del | Deletes one or more files. |
| Dir | Displays a list of files and subdirectories within a directory. |
| Diskcomp | Compares the contents of two floppy disks. |
| Diskcopy | Copies the contents of one floppy disk to another. |
| Diskpart | Invokes a text-mode command interpreter so that you can manage disks, partitions, and volumes using a separate command prompt and commands that are internal to Diskpart. |
| DISM | Services and manages Windows images. |
| Doskey | Edits command lines, recalls Windows commands, and creates macros. |
| Echo | Displays messages, or turns command echoing on or off. |
| Endlocal | Ends localization of environment changes in a batch file. |
| Erase | See the entry for Del. |
| Exit | Exits the command interpreter. |
| Expand | Uncompresses files. |
| FC | Compares two files, and displays the differences between them. |
| Find/Findstr | Searches for a text string in files. |
| For | Runs a specified command for each file in a set of files. |
| Format | Formats a floppy disk or hard drive. |
| Ftp | Transfers files. |
| Ftype | Displays or modifies file types used in file-extension associations. |
| Goto | Directs the Windows command interpreter to a labeled line in a script. |
| Graftabl | Enables Windows to display extended character sets in graphics mode. |
| Hostname | Prints the computer's name. |
| IF | Performs conditional processing in batch programs. |
| Ipconfig | Displays TCP/IP configuration. |
| Label | Creates, changes, or deletes the volume label of a disk. |
| Md/Mkdir | Creates a directory or subdirectory. |
| Mode | Configures a system device. |

| Command | Description |
| --- | --- |
| More | Displays output one screen at a time. |
| Mountvol | Manages the volume mount point. |
| Move | Moves files from one directory to another directory on the same drive. |
| Nbtstat | Displays status of NetBIOS. |
| Net Accounts | Manages user account and password policies. |
| Net Computer | Adds or removes computers from a domain. |
| Net Config Server | Displays or modifies the configuration of the Server service. |
| Net Config Workstation | Displays or modifies the configuration of the Workstation service. |
| Net Continue | Resumes a paused service. |
| Net File | Displays or manages open files on a server. |
| Net Group | Displays or manages global groups. |
| Net Localgroup | Displays or manages local group accounts. |
| Net Pause | Suspends a service. |
| Net Print | Displays or manages print jobs and shared queues. |
| Net Session | Lists or disconnects sessions. |
| Net Share | Displays or manages shared printers and directories. |
| Net Start | Lists or starts network services. |
| Net Statistics | Displays workstation and server statistics. |
| Net Stop | Stops services. |
| Net Time | Displays or synchronizes network time. |
| Net Use | Displays or manages remote connections. |
| Net User | Displays or manages local user accounts. |
| Net View | Displays network resources or computers. |
| Netsh | Invokes a separate command prompt that allows you to manage the configuration of various network services on local and remote computers. |
| Netstat | Displays the status of network connections. |
| Path | Displays or sets a search path for executable files in the current command window. |
| Pathping | Traces routes, and provides packet loss information. |
| Pause | Suspends processing of a script, and waits for keyboard input. |
| Ping | Determines if a network connection can be established. |
| Popd | Changes to the directory stored by Pushd. |

Chapter 2

| Command | Description |
| --- | --- |
| Print | Prints a text file. |
| Prompt | Changes the Windows command prompt. |
| Pushd | Saves the current directory and then changes to a new directory. |
| Rd/Rmdir | Removes a directory. |
| Recover | Recovers readable information from a bad or defective disk. |
| Reg Add | Adds a new subkey or entry to the registry. |
| Reg Compare | Compares registry subkeys or entries. |
| Reg Copy | Copies a registry entry to a specified key path on a local or remote system. |
| Reg Delete | Deletes a subkey or entries from the registry. |
| Reg Query | Lists the entries under a key and the names of subkeys (if any). |
| Reg Restore | Writes saved subkeys and entries back to the registry. |
| Reg Save | Saves a copy of specified subkeys, entries, and values to a file. |
| Regsvr32 | Registers and un-registers dynamic-link libraries (DLLs). |
| Rem | Adds comments to scripts. |
| Ren | Renames a file. |
| Replace | Replaces a file. |
| Route | Manages network routing tables. |
| Set | Displays or modifies Windows environment variables. It's also used to evaluate numeric expressions at the command line. |
| Setlocal | Begins the localization of environment changes in a batch file. |
| Sfc | Scans and verifies protected operating system files. |
| Shift | Shifts the position of replaceable parameters in scripts. |
| Start | Starts a new command-shell window to run a specified program or command. |
| Subst | Maps a path to a drive letter. |
| Time | Displays or sets the system time. |
| Title | Sets the title for the command-shell window. |
| Tracert | Displays the path between computers. |
| Tree | Graphically displays the directory structure of a drive or path. |
| Type | Displays the contents of a text file. |
| Ver | Displays the Windows version. |
| Verify | Tells Windows whether to verify that your files are written correctly to a disk. |
| Vol | Displays a disk volume label and serial number. |
| Xcopy | Copies files and directories. |

## Forcing disk-partition removal during installation

During installation, you might be unable to select the hard disk you want to use. This issue can occur if the hard-disk partition contains an invalid byte-offset value. To resolve this issue, you need to remove the partitions on the hard disk (which destroys all associated data) and then create the necessary partitions using the advanced options in the Setup program. During installation on the Where Do You Want To Install Windows page, you can remove unrecognized hard-disk partitions by following these steps:

1.  Press Shift+F10 to start a command prompt. At the command prompt, type **diskpart**. This starts the DiskPart utility.

2.  To view a list of disks on the computer, type **list disk**. Select a disk by typing **select disk *DiskNumber***, where *DiskNumber* is the number of the disk you want to work with.

3.  To permanently remove the partitions on the selected disk, type **clean**. When the cleaning process finishes, type **create partition primary size=*N***, where *N* is the size of the space you want to allocate to the partition in megabytes.

4.  When the create-partition process finishes, tap or click the back arrow button in the Install Windows dialog box. This will return you to the previous window.

5.  On the Which Type Of Installation Do You Want? page, tap or click Custom (Advanced) to start a custom install.

6.  On the Where Do You Want To Install Windows? page, tap or click the disk you previously cleaned to select it as the install partition. You can then continue with the installation as discussed previously.

## Loading mass storage drivers during installation

During installation on the Where Do You Want To Install Windows? page, you can use the Load Drivers option to load the device drivers for a hard disk drive. Typically, you use this option when a disk drive you want to use for installing the operating system isn't available for selection because the device drivers aren't available.

To load the device drivers and make the hard disk available for use during installation, follow these steps:

1.  During installation on the Where Do You Want To Install Windows? page, tap or click Load Driver.

2. When prompted, insert the installation media, or USB flash drive, and then tap or click OK. Setup will then search the computer's removable media drives for the device drivers.

   a. If Setup finds multiple device drivers, select the driver to install and then tap or click Next.

   b. If Setup doesn't find the device driver, tap or click Browse to use the Browse For Folder dialog box to select the device driver to load, tap or click OK, and then tap or click Next.

You can use the Rescan button to have Setup rescan the computer's removable media drives for the device drivers. If you are unable to successfully install a device driver, tap or click the back arrow button in the upper left corner of the Install Windows dialog box to go back to the previous page.

## Creating, deleting, and extending disk partitions during installation

When you are performing a clean installation and have started the computer from the distribution media, the Where Do You Want To Install Windows? page has additional options. You can display these options by tapping or clicking Drive Options (Advanced). These additional options are used as follows:

- **New**   Creates a partition. You must then format the partition.

- **Format**   Formats a new partition so that you can use it for installing the operating system.

- **Delete**   Deletes a partition that is no longer wanted.

- **Extend**   Extends a partition to increase its size.

Creating a partition is the key task you need to perform, but you can also delete and extend partitions as necessary. You generally don't need to format partitions because Setup will handle this for you. If the advanced options aren't available, you can still work with the computer's disks by following these steps:

1. Press Shift+F10 to open a command prompt. At the command prompt, type **diskpart**. This starts the DiskPart utility.

2. To view a list of disks on the computer, type **list disk**.

3. Select a disk by typing **select disk *DiskNumber***, where *DiskNumber* is the number of the disk you want to work with.

4.  List the existing partitions on the disk by typing **list partition**. You can now do the following:

    ○  **Create a partition**   Use available space to create a partition by typing **create partition primary size=N**, where *N* is the size of the space to allocate in megabytes.

    ○  **Delete a partition**   Select the partition to delete by typing **select partition** followed by the partition number, and then delete it by typing **delete partition**.

    ○  **Extend a partition**   Select the partition to extend by typing **select partition** followed by the partition number, and then extend it by typing **extend size=N**, where *N* is the size of the additional space to allocate in megabytes.

5.  When you are finished working with disks, tap or click the back arrow button in the Install Windows dialog box. This will return you to the previous window.

6.  On the Which Type Of Installation Do You Want? page, tap or click Custom (Advanced) to start a custom install.

7.  On the Where Do You Want To Install Windows? page, tap or click the disk you previously cleaned to select it as the install partition. You can then continue with the installation as discussed previously.

# Troubleshooting installation

Most of the time, installation completes normally and the Windows operating system starts without any problems. Some of the time, however, installation won't complete or, after installation, the server won't start up, and you must troubleshoot to figure out what's happening. The good news is that installation problems are usually the result of something simple. The bad news is that simple problems are sometimes the hardest to find.

> ### Note
> For more information about troubleshooting and recovery, see Chapter 17, "Backup and recovery." Beyond that, you'll also find troubleshooters in the Help And Support console and in the Microsoft Knowledge Base, which is available online at *http://support.microsoft.com/*. Both are good resources for troubleshooting.

Chapter 2

# Start with the potential points of failure

Setup can fail for a variety of reasons, but more often than not it's because of incompatible hardware components or the failure of the system to meet the minimum requirements for a Windows Server 2012 installation. With this in mind, start troubleshooting by looking at the potential points of failure and how these failure points can be resolved.

## Setup refuses to install or start

If a hardware component is incompatible with Windows Server 2012, this could cause the failure of the installation or a failure to start up after installation. Make sure that Windows Server 2012 is detecting the system hardware and that the hardware is in the Windows Server Catalog or on the Hardware Compatibility List (HCL). As discussed previously, you can perform a compatibility check prior to installing Windows Server 2012.

After you start the installation, however, it's too late. At this point, you have several choices. You can reboot to a working operating system and then restart the installation from the command prompt using Setup and one of the following debugging options:

- **/1394debug:<*channel*>**    Enables kernel debugging over a FireWire (IEEE 1394) port on a specific channel

- **/debug:<*port*>**    Enables kernel debugging over a COM1 or COM2 port

- **/usbdebug:<*target*>**    Enables kernel debugging over a USB port to a specific target device

These options put Setup in debug mode, which can help you identify what is going wrong. If Setup determines you have hardware conflicts, you can try to configure the hardware and server firmware to eliminate the conflicts. Troubleshooting firmware involves booting the server to the firmware and then completing the following steps:

- **Examine the boot order of disk devices**    You might want to configure the system so that it boots first from DVD-ROM. Watch out, though; after installation, don't keep booting to DVD-ROM thinking you are booting to the operating system—hey, we all get tired and sometimes we just have to stop and think for a moment. If the installation problem is that you keep going back to the installation screen after installing the operating system, you are probably inadvertently booting from DVD-ROM—and you're probably way too tired by now to realize it.

- **Check Plug and Play device configuration and interrupt reservations**    If a system has older components or components that aren't Plug and Play compatible, you might have a device conflict for a hard-coded interrupt. For example, a non–Plug and Play sound card could be hard-coded to use interrupt 13, which is already in use by a Plug and Play device. To work around this, you must configure interrupt 13 under your Plug and Play BIOS settings to be reserved for a non–Plug and Play device. This ensures that Plug and Play does not attempt to use that interrupt and resolves the issue in most cases.

> **Note**
> The only sure way to avoid problems with non–Plug and Play devices is to avoid using them altogether.

Rather than spending time—which could run into several hours—trying to troubleshoot a hardware conflict, you might consider removing the hardware component if it's nonessential—and you might be surprised at what I consider nonessential at this stage. By nonessential, I mean most anything that isn't needed to start up and give you a display for logon. You probably don't need a network card, a sound card, a multimedia controller card, a video coder/decoder (codec), or a removable media drive. If these items are incompatible, you might resolve the problem simply by removing them. You can always try to install the components again after installation is complete.

### Setup reports a media or DVD-ROM error

When you install directly from the Windows Server 2012 DVD-ROM or perform a network install from a distribution share, you might encounter a media error that causes Setup to fail. With an actual DVD-ROM, you might need to clean the DVD-ROM so that it can be read or use a different DVD drive. If a computer's sole DVD-ROM drive is the problem, you must replace the drive or install from a distribution share. If you are working with a distribution share, the share might not have all the necessary files, or you might encounter problems connecting to the share. Try using an actual DVD-ROM.

### Setup reports insufficient system resources

Windows Server 2012 requires a minimum of 512 MBs of RAM and about 32 GBs of disk space. If the system doesn't have enough memory, Setup won't start. If Setup starts and detects that there isn't enough space, it might not continue or you might need to create a new partition or delete an existing partition to get enough free space to install the operating system.

## Continue past lockups and freezes

If you can get past the potential points of failure, you still might find that the installation locks up or freezes. In this case, you might get a stop error; then again, you might not.

Most stop errors have cryptic error codes rather than clear messages telling you what's wrong. If you get a stop error, write down the error number or code, and then refer to the Microsoft Knowledge Base (available online at *http://support.microsoft.com/*) for help troubleshooting the problem. To break out of the stop, you most likely will have to press Ctrl+Alt+Delete (sometimes several times) to get the server to restart. If this doesn't break out of the stop, press and hold the power button on the server until it reboots. Alternatively, disconnect the system power, wait a few seconds, and then connect it again.

The Windows operating system should start up and go directly back to Setup. In some cases, you will see a boot menu. If so, choose the Windows Setup option to allow the Setup program to attempt to continue the installation. Setup could freeze again. If it does, stay with it, and repeat this process—sometimes it takes several tries to get completely through the installation process.

RAM and CPUs can also be the source of problems. Issues to watch out for include the following:

- **Incompatible RAM**   Not all RAM is compatible, and you can't mix and match RAM of different speeds and types. Ensure that all RAM modules are the same type and speed. Further, RAM modules from different manufacturers, in some cases, can perform differently (read incompatibly). In such a case, try changing the RAM so that all modules have the same manufacturer.

- **Malfunctioning RAM**   Static discharges can ruin RAM faster than anything else. If you didn't ground yourself and use a static discharge wire before working with the RAM modules, you could have inadvertently fried the RAM so that the modules don't work at all or are malfunctioning. RAM could have also arrived in this condition from the manufacturer or distributor. There are several troubleshooting techniques for determining this. You could update firmware to add a wait state to the RAM so that if the RAM is partially faulty the system will still boot (but you still must replace the RAM eventually). You can also try removing some RAM modules or changing their order.

- **Incompatible processors**   Not all processors are created equal, and I'm not just talking about their speed in megahertz (which you generally want to be the same for all processors on a server). Some processors might have a cache or configuration that is incompatible with the server hardware or other processors. Check the processor speed and type to ensure that they are compatible with the server. In some cases, you might need to change hardware jumpers, depending on the speed and type of your processors.

- **Misconfigured processors**   Adding additional processors to a server isn't a simple matter of inserting them. Often, you must change jumpers on the hardware, remove several terminators (one for a power subcomponent and one for the processor—and save them because, trust me, you might find that you need them), and then insert the new components. Check the hardware jumpers (even if you think there aren't any), and ensure that the processors and the power subcomponents you added are seated properly. If you can't get the installation to continue or the server to start up, you might need to remove the components you added. Watch out, though; you probably don't want to continue the installation until the processor issue is resolved—single-processor systems have a different threading and default configuration than multi-processor systems, meaning this situation might not be a simple matter of adding the processor after installation and making it all work properly.

- **System processor cache problems**   Sometimes there can be an issue with the system processor cache and its compatibility with Windows Server 2012. Consult the server documentation to determine the correct configuration settings and how the cache can be disabled. If you suspect a problem with this, boot to firmware and temporarily disable the system processor cache, following the server documentation. After the installation is complete, you should be able to enable the cache to avoid a performance hit. Be sure to check both the hardware vendor support site and the Microsoft Knowledge Base to see whether any known issues with your server's processor cache exist.

## TROUBLESHOOTING

### RAM and CPUs are incompatible

You might be surprised at how common it is for incompatible RAM or CPUs to present problems, especially when installing enterprise-class servers. We had a problem once when we ordered all the components from a single hardware vendor that had verified the compatibility of every element down to the last detail, only to find that the wrong processors and RAM were shipped for the systems ordered. The result was that every time we added the additional processors and RAM modules, the server wouldn't start up. The only recourse was to continue installation with the minimum processor and RAM configurations shipped or wait until replacements arrived. Electing to wait for replacements added time to the project but ultimately proved to be the right decision. You can bet that we were glad that we padded the project schedule to allow for the unexpected—because the unexpected usually happens.

Most of the time, the installation or setup problem is caused by a compatibility issue with the Windows operating system, and that problem can be fixed by making changes to firmware settings. Sometimes, however, the problem is the firmware, and you'll find that you must upgrade the firmware to resolve the problem.

Chapter 2

Check with the hardware vendor to see whether a firmware upgrade is available. If so, install it as the hardware vendor directs. If a new firmware version isn't available, you might be able to disable the incompatible option prior to setup. If this doesn't work, the option you changed wasn't the source of the problem and you should re-enable it before continuing.

> **Note**
>
> Re-enabling the option might be necessary because some hardware-specific firmware settings cannot be changed after the installation. Thus, the only way to enable the option would be to reinstall the operating system.

Finally, hard-disk-drive settings could also cause lockups or freezes, particularly if you are using Integrated Device Electronics (IDE) drives. When using IDE drives and controllers, you want to ensure that the system recognizes both the drives and the controllers and that both are enabled and configured properly in firmware. You might have to check jumper settings on the drives and the cables that connect the drives. As discussed previously, check for conflicts between the drives, controllers, and other system components. You might need to temporarily remove unnecessary components, such as the sound card, to see whether this resolves a conflict. If a DVD drive is on the same channel as the disk drives, try moving it to the secondary channel and configuring it as a master device. You can also try lowering the data transfer rate for the IDE drives.

# Postinstallation tasks

After you've installed a server and logged on, you might be ready to call it a day. Don't do this yet because you should first perform a few final postinstallation procedures. The Tools menu in Server Manager gives you quick access to tools for administration. Using Server Manager as your starting point, you can do the following:

- **Check devices**  Select Device Manager on the Tools menu, and then use Device Manager, as discussed in Chapter 7 "Managing and troubleshooting hardware" under "Viewing device and driver details," to look for undetected or malfunctioning hardware components. If you find problems, you might need to download and install updated drivers for the computer—you can download from another system and then transfer the files to the new server using a USB key or by burning the files to a CD/DVD-ROM. If you removed any system hardware prior to installation, you might want to add it back in and then check again for conflicts and issues that must be corrected. You aren't finished with Device Manager until every piece of hardware is working properly.

- **Check the TCP/IP configuration**   When you select the Local Server node in Server Manager, you'll see the server's basic configuration settings. Tap or click the links for the Ethernet settings to open the Network Connections dialog box. Ensure that the TCP/IP configuration is correct and that any additional settings are applied as necessary for the network. Test TCP/IP networking from the command line using Ping or Tracert and in the Windows operating system by trying to browse the network. See Chapter 19 for details.

- **Check event logs**   When you select the Dashboard node, you'll see an entry for the Local Server. If there are errors or critical events, you can tap or click Events to review them. You also can use the Events panel under Local Server and the Event Viewer to check the Windows event logs. Any startup warnings or errors will be written to the logs. See Chapter 10, "Performance monitoring and tuning," for details.

- **Check disk partitioning**   Select Computer Management on the Tools menu, and then use the Computer Management console to check and finalize the disk partitions. Often, you must create the server's application partition or configure software RAID. See Chapter 12 for details.

- **Optimize system configuration**   Follow the techniques discussed in Chapter 4, "Managing Windows Server 2012," for tuning the operating system. For example, you might need to change the display settings, virtual memory pagefile usage, or the Server service configuration. You might also need to add local group and user accounts to the server per standard IT procedures.

- **Update the server**   Use Windows Update or Windows Server Update Services to ensure that the operating system is up to date and has the most recent updates for stability and security. When Windows Update is configured properly, you can tap or click the Windows Update link on the Local Server node and then tap or click Check For Updates to get updates for the server.

- **Reboot for good measure**   After you configure the server and optimize its settings, perform a final reboot to ensure that (1) the server starts, (2) all the server services start, and (3) no other errors occur. You should reboot even if the changes you made don't require it—it's better to find out about problems now rather than at 3 A.M. on a Saturday night.

- **Prepare backup and recovery**   You're almost done, but not quite. Don't forget about creating an automated recovery disk for the server. You might also want to perform a full backup. For details on backing up servers and creating recovery disks, see Chapter 17.

These postinstallation procedures are not only important, they're essential to ensuring that the server performs as well as can be expected. After these procedures are completed, you

Chapter 2

should have a server that is nearly ready for its role in a production environment. Don't make the server available to users just yet. To finish the job, you need to install and configure any necessary roles, role services, features, and applications. For certain, configuring these components requires quite a bit of extra work beyond installing the operating system. The installation of these additional components and applications could require one or more reboots or might require several time periods in which users are blocked from accessing the server or in which they are requested not to connect to it as well. Remember, from the users' perspective, it's usually better to not have a resource than to be given one and then have it taken away (even temporarily). Finalize the server, and then deploy it, and you'll have happier users.

As discussed earlier in the chapter, you can convert the installation type. To convert a Full Server installation to a Minimal Server Interface installation, you remove the Server Graphical Shell. Although you can use the Remove Roles And Features Wizard to do this, you also can do this at a Windows PowerShell prompt by typing the following command:

```
uninstall-windowsfeature server-gui-shell -restart
```

This command instructs Windows Server to uninstall the Server Graphical Shell and restart the server to finalize the removal. If Desktop Experience also is installed, this feature will be removed as well.

To convert a Minimal Server Interface installation to a Server With A GUI installation, you add the Server Graphical Shell. You can use the Add Roles And Features Wizard to do this, or you can type the following command at a PowerShell prompt:

```
install-windowsfeature server-gui-shell -restart
```

This command instructs Windows Server to install the Server Graphical Shell and restart the server to finalize the installation. If you also want to install the Desktop Experience, you can use this command instead:

```
install-windowsfeature server-gui-shell, desktop-experience -restart
```

To convert a Full Server or Minimal Server Interface installation to a Server Core installation, you remove the user interfaces for Graphical Management Tools And Infrastructure. If you remove the WOW64 Support framework, you also convert the server to a Server Core installation. Although you can use the Remove Roles And Features Wizard to remove the user interfaces, you also can do this at a PowerShell prompt by typing the following command:

```
uninstall-windowsfeature server-gui-mgmt-infra -restart
```

This command instructs Windows Server to uninstall the user interfaces for Graphical Management Tools And Infrastructure and restart the server to finalize the removal. Because many dependent roles, role services, and features might be uninstalled along with the user interfaces, run the command with the *–Whatif* parameter first to get details on what exactly will be uninstalled.

If you installed the server with the user interfaces and converted it to a Server Core installation, you can revert back to a Full Server installation with the following command:

```
install-windowsfeature server-gui-mgmt-infra -restart
```

As long as the binaries for this feature and any dependent features haven't been removed, the command should succeed. If the binaries were removed, however, or Server Core was the original installation type, you need to specify a source for the required binaries. If you don't do this, the required feature will be downloaded from Windows Update, which could take a long time for some features.

You use the *–Source* parameter to restore required binaries from a Windows Imaging (WIM) mount point. For example, if your enterprise has a mounted Windows Image for the edition of Windows Server 2012 you are working with available at the network path \\ImServer18\ WinS12EE, you could specify the source as follows:

```
install-windowsfeature server-gui-mgmt-infra -source \\imserver18\wins12ee
```

Although many large enterprises might have standard images that can be mounted using network paths, you also can mount the Windows Server 2012 distribution media and then use the Windows\WinSXS folder from the installation image as your source. To do this, follow these steps:

1.  Insert the installation disc into the server's disc drive, and then create a folder to mount the Installation image by typing the following command: **mkdir c:\mountdir**.

2.  Locate the index number of the image you want to use by typing the following command at an elevated prompt: **dism /get-wiminfo /wimfile:e:\sources\ install.wim**, where *e:* is the drive designator of the server's disc drive.

3.  Mount the installation image by typing the following command at an elevated prompt: **dism /mount-wim /wimfile:e:\sources\install.wim /index:2 /mountdir:c:\mountdir /readonly**, where *e:* is the drive designator of the server's disc drive, *2* is the index of the image to use, and *c:\mountdir* is the mount directory. Mounting the image might take several minutes.

4.  Use Install-WindowsFeature at a PowerShell prompt with the source specified as **c:\mountdir\windows\winsxs**, as shown in this example:

    ```
    install-windowsfeature server-gui-mgmt-infra
    -source c:\mountdir\windows\winsxs
    ```

# Boot configuration

U NLIKE early releases of server operating systems for Microsoft Windows, Windows Server 2012 doesn't boot from an initialization file. Instead, the operating system uses the Windows Boot Manager to initialize and start the operating system. The boot environment dramatically changes the way the operating system starts, and it is designed to resolve issues related to boot integrity, operating system integrity, and firmware abstraction. The boot environment is loaded prior to the operating system, making it a pre-operating system environment. This ensures that the boot environment can be used to validate the integrity of the startup process and the operating system itself before actually starting the operating system.

## Boot from hardware and firmware

At first glance, startup and shutdown seem to be the most basic features of an operating system, but as you get a better understanding of how computers work, you quickly see that there's nothing simple or basic about startup, shutdown, or related processes and procedures. In fact, anyone who's worked with computers probably has had a problem with startup or shutdown at one time or another. Problems with startup and shutdown can be compounded in modern computers because of their extended frameworks for advanced configuration and power management in firmware and hardware.

> ### Note
> Many administrators install Windows Server 2012 on desktop-class systems without giving careful consideration to how this could affect the operation of the computer. When you install Windows Server 2012 on a desktop-class system, it is critically important for you to understand how computers designed for desktop operating systems handle advanced configuration and power management in hardware and firmware. This will enable you to modify the hardware and firmware settings so that they work better with Windows Server 2012.

# Hardware and firmware power states

Before the boot environment is loaded, computers start up from hardware and firmware. Windows desktop operating systems do things a bit differently from Windows Server operating systems when it comes to power-state management features. In Windows desktops, turning off a computer and shutting down a computer are separate tasks. By default, when you turn off a computer running a Windows desktop operating system, the computer enters standby mode. When entering standby mode, the operating system automatically saves all work, turns off the display, and enters a low power-consumption mode with the computer's fans and hard disks stopped. The state of the computer is maintained in the computer's memory. When the computer wakes from standby mode, its state is exactly as it was when you turned off your computer.

You can turn off a computer running a Windows desktop operating system and enter standby mode by tapping or clicking the Settings charm, tapping or clicking Power, and then tapping or clicking Sleep. To wake the computer from the standby state, you can press the power button on the computer's case or a key on the computer's keyboard. Moving the mouse also wakes the computer.

If you install Windows 8 or Windows Server 2012 on a mobile computer, the computer's power state can be changed by closing the lid. By default with Windows 8, the computer enters the standby state when you close the lid. By default with Windows Server 2012, the computer doesn't change its power state when you close or open the lid, but you can configure the server to shut down when you close the lid.

There are, however, a few "gotchas" with the power button and the standby state in Windows desktop operating systems. The way the power button works depends on the following:

- **System hardware**   For the power button to work, the computer hardware must support the standby state. If the computer hardware doesn't support the standby state, the computer can't use the standby state and turning off the computer powers it down completely.

- **System state**   For the power button to work, the system must be in a valid state. If the computer has installed updates that require a reboot or you've installed programs that require a reboot, the computer can't enter the standby state and turning off the computer powers it down completely.

- **System configuration**   For the power button to work, sleep mode must be enabled. If you reconfigured the power options on the computer and set the power button to the Shut Down action, the computer can't use the standby state and turning off the computer powers it down completely.

You can determine exactly how the power options are configured on a Windows computer by tapping or clicking the Settings charm, tapping or clicking Control Panel, and tapping or clicking Power Options. The options available depend on the type of computing device.

## Diagnosing hardware and firmware startup problems

Whether you are working with a Windows desktop operating system or a Windows Server operating system and trying to diagnose and resolve startup problems, be sure to keep in mind that power-state management capabilities are provided by the hardware but are enabled by the operating system. Because of this, to fully diagnose and resolve boot issues, you must look at the computer's hardware and software, including the following items:

● Motherboard/chipset

● Firmware

● Operating system

To better understand the hardware aspects of boot issues, let's dig in and take a look at Advanced Configuration and Power Interface (ACPI). A computer's motherboard/chipset, firmware, and operating system must support ACPI for the advanced power-state features to work. There are many types of motherboards/chipsets. Although older motherboards/chipsets might not be updateable, most of the newer ones have updateable firmware. Chipset firmware is separate from and different from the computer's underlying firmware interface.

Currently, there are three prevalent firmware interfaces:

● Basic Input Output System (BIOS)

● Extensible Firmware Interface (EFI)

● Unified Extensible Firmware Interface (UEFI)

A computer's BIOS, EFI, or UEFI programming provides the hardware-level interface between hardware components and software. Like chipsets themselves, BIOS, EFI, and UEFI can be updated. ACPI-aware components track the power state of the computer. An ACPI-aware operating system can generate a request that the system be switched into a different ACPI mode. BIOS, EFI, or UEFI responds to enable the requested ACPI mode.

ACPI 4.0 was finalized in June 2009 and ACPI 5.0 was finalized in December 2011. Computers manufactured prior to this time will likely not have firmware that is fully compliant, and you will probably need to update the firmware when a compatible revision becomes available. In some cases, and especially with older hardware, you might not be able to update a computer's firmware to make it fully compliant with ACPI 4.0 or ACPI 5.0.

Chapter 3

For example, if you are configuring the power options and you don't have minimum and maximum processor-state options, the computer's firmware isn't fully compatible with ACPI 3.0 and likely will not fully support ACPI 4.0 or ACPI 5.0 either. Still, you should check the hardware manufacturer's website for firmware updates.

ACPI defines active and passive cooling modes. These cooling modes are inversely related to each other:

- Passive cooling reduces system performance but is quieter because there's less fan noise. With passive cooling, Windows lessens power consumption to reduce the operating temperature of the computer but at the cost of system performance. Here, Windows reduces the processor speed in an attempt to cool the computer before increasing fan speed, which would increase power consumption.

- Active cooling allows maximum system performance. With active cooling, Windows increases power consumption to reduce the temperature of the machine. Here, Windows increases fan speed to cool the computer before attempting to reduce processor speed.

Power policy includes upper and lower limits for the processor state, referred to as the *maximum processor state* and the *minimum processor state*, respectively. These states are implemented by making use of a feature of ACPI 3.0 and later versions called *processor throttling*, and they determine the range of currently available processor performance states that Windows can use. By setting the maximum and minimum values, you define the bounds for the allowed performance states, or you can use the same value for each to force the system to remain in a specific performance state. Windows reduces power consumption by throttling the processor speed. For example, if the upper bound is 100 percent and the lower bound is 5 percent, Windows can throttle the processor within this range as workloads permit to reduce power consumption. In a computer with a 3-GHz processor, Windows would adjust the operating frequency of the processor between 0.15 GHz and 3.0 GHz.

Processor throttling and related performance states were introduced with Windows XP and Windows Server 2003, but these early implementations were designed for computers with discrete-socketed processors and not for computers with processor cores. As a result, they are not effective in reducing the power consumption of computers with logical processors. Beginning with Windows 7 and Windows Server 2008 R2, Windows reduces power consumption in computers with multicore processors by using a feature of ACPI 4.0 called *logical processor idling* and by updating processor-throttling features to work with processor cores.

Logical processor idling is designed to ensure that Windows uses the fewest number of processor cores for a given workload. Windows accomplishes this by consolidating workloads onto the fewest cores possible and suspending inactive processor cores. As additional processing power is required, Windows activates inactive processor cores. This idling functionality works in conjunction with the management of process performance states at the core level.

ACPI defines processor performance states, referred to as *p-states*, and processor idle sleep states, referred to as *c-states*. Processor performance states include P0 (the processor or core uses its maximum performance capability and can consume maximum power), P1 (the processor or core is limited below its maximum and consumes less than maximum power), and P*n* (where state *n* is a maximum number that is processor dependent, and the processor or core is at its minimal level and consumes minimal power while remaining in an active state).

Processor idle sleep states include C0 (the processor or core can execute instructions), C1 (the processor or core has the lowest latency and is in a nonexecuting power state), C2 (the processor or core has longer latency to improve power savings over the C1 state), and C3 (the processor or core has the longest latency to improve power savings over the C1 and C2 states).

> **Note**
> Windows switches processors or cores between any p-state and from the C1 state to the C0 state nearly instantaneously (fractions of milliseconds) and tends not to use the deep sleep states, so you don't need to worry about the performance impact of throttling or waking up processors or cores. The processors or cores are available when they are needed. That said, the easiest way to limit processor power management is to modify the active power plan and set the minimum and maximum processor states to 100 percent.

Windows saves power by putting processor cores in and out of appropriate p-states and c-states. On a computer with four logical processors, Windows might use p-states 0 to 5, where P0 allows 100 percent usage, P1 allows 90 percent usage, P2 allows 80 percent usage, P3 allows 70 percent usage, P4 allows 60 percent usage, and P5 allows 50 percent usage. When the computer is active, logical processor 0 would likely be active with a p-state of 0 to 5, and the other processors would likely be at an appropriate p-state or in a sleep state.

# INSIDE OUT

### Processor Idling

Logical processor idling is used to reduce power consumption by removing a logical processor from the operating system's list of non-processor-affinitized work. However, because processor-affinitized work reduces the effectiveness of this feature, you'll want to plan carefully prior to configuring processing-affinity settings for applications. You can use Windows System Resource Manager to manage processor resources through percent-processor-usage targets and processor-affinity rules. However, both techniques reduce the effectiveness of logical processor idling. Note also that Windows System Resource Manager is deprecated for Windows Server 2012 and will be phased out in future releases of Windows Server.

ACPI 4.0 and ACPI 5.0 define four global power states. In G0, the working state in which software runs, power consumption is at its highest and latency is at its lowest. In G1, the sleeping state (in which software doesn't run), latency varies with the sleep state and power consumption is less than the G0 state. In G2 (also referred to as *S5 sleep state*), the soft off state where the operating system doesn't run, latency is long and power consumption is very near zero. In G3, the mechanical off state (in which the operating system doesn't run), latency is long and power consumption is zero. There's also a special global state, known as *S4 nonvolatile sleep*, in which the operating system writes all system context to a file on nonvolatile storage media, allowing the system context to be saved and restored.

Within the global sleeping state, G1, are the sleep-state variations summarized in Table 3-1. S1 is a sleeping state in which the entire system context is maintained. S2 is a sleeping state similar to S1 except that the CPU and system-cache contexts are lost and control starts from a reset. S3 is a sleeping state in which all CPU, cache, and chipset contexts are lost and hardware maintains the memory context and restores some CPU and L2 cache configuration context. S4 is a sleeping state in which it is assumed that the hardware has powered off all devices to reduce power usage to a minimum and only the platform context is maintained. S5 is a sleeping state in which it is assumed that the hardware is in a soft off state, where no context is maintained and a complete boot is required when the system wakes.

**TABLE 3-1** Power states for ACPI in firmware and hardware

| State | Type | Description |
|-------|------|-------------|
| S0 | ON state | The system is completely operational, is fully powered, and completely retains the context (such as the volatile registers, memory caches, and RAM). |
| S1 | Sleep state | The system consumes less power in this state than in the S0 state. All hardware and processor contexts are maintained. |

| State | Type | Description |
|-------|------|-------------|
| S2 | Sleep state | The system consumes less power in this state than in the S1 state. The processor loses power, and the processor context and contents of the cache are lost. |
| S3 | Sleep state | The system consumes less power in this state than in the S2 state. The processor and hardware contexts, cache contents, and chipset context are lost. The system memory is retained. |
| S4 | Hibernate state | The system consumes the least power in this state compared to all other sleep states. The system is almost at an OFF state. The context data is written to hard disk, and there is no context retained. The system can restart from the context data stored on the disk. |
| S5 | OFF state | The system is in a shutdown state, and the system retains no context. The system requires a full reboot to start. |

Motherboard chipsets support specific power states. For example, a motherboard might support S0, S1, S4, and S5 states, but it might not support the S2 or S3 states. In Windows operating systems, the *sleep power transition* refers to switching off the system to a Sleep or Hibernate mode, and the *wake power transition* refers to switching on the system from a Sleep or Hibernate mode. The Sleep and Hibernate modes allow users to switch off and switch on systems much faster than the regular shutdown and startup processes.

Thus, a computer is waking up when the computer is transitioning from the OFF state (S5) or any sleep state (S1–S4) to the ON state (S0), and the computer is going to sleep when the computer is transitioning from ON state (S0) to OFF state (S5) or sleep state (S1–S4). A computer cannot enter one sleep state directly from another because it must enter the ON state before entering any other sleep state. Sleep and hibernate are disabled in Windows Server.

## Resolving hardware and firmware startup problems

On most computers, you can enter BIOS, EFI, or UEFI during boot by pressing F2 or another function key. When you are in firmware, you can go to the Power screen or a similar screen to manage ACPI and related settings.

Power settings you might see include the following:

- **Restore AC Power Loss or AC Recovery**   Determines the mode of operation if a power loss occurs and for which you'll see settings such as Stay Off/Off, Last State/ Last, Power On/On. Stay Off means the system remains off after power is restored. Last State restores the system to the state it was in before power failed. Power On means the system will turn on after power is restored.

- **Wake On LAN From S4/S5 or Auto Power On**   Determines the action taken when the system power is off and a PCI Power Management wake event occurs. You'll see settings such as Stay Off or Power On.

- **ACPI Suspend State or Suspend Mode**   Sets the suspend mode. Typically, you'll be able to set S1 state or S3 state as the suspend mode.

> ### Note
> I provide two standard labels for each setting because your computer hardware might not have these exact labels. The firmware variant you are working with determines the actual labels that are associated with boot, power, and other settings.

Because Intel and AMD also have other technologies to help reduce startup and resume times, you might also see the following power settings:

- Enhanced Intel SpeedStep Technology (EIST), which can be either Disabled or Enabled

- Intel Quick Resume Technology, which can be either Disabled or Enabled

Enhanced Intel SpeedStep Technology (EIST or SpeedStep) allows the system to dynamically adjust processor voltage and core frequency, which can result in decreased average power consumption and decreased average heat production. When EIST or a similar technology is enabled and in use, you'll see two different processor speeds on the System page in Control Panel. The first speed listed is the specified speed of the processor. The second speed is the current operating speed, which should be less than the first speed. If Enhanced Intel Speed-Step Technology is off, both processor speeds will be equal. Advanced Settings for Power Options under Processor Power Management can also affect how this technology works. Generally speaking, although you might want to use this technology with a Windows desktop operating system, you won't want to use this technology with a Windows Server operating system.

Intel Quick Resume Technology Driver (QRTD) allows an Intel Viiv technology–based computer to behave like a consumer electronic device with instant on/off after an initial boot. Intel QRTD manages this behavior through the Quick Resume mode function of the Intel Viiv chipset. Pressing the power button on the computer or a remote control is what puts the computer in the Quick Sleep state, and the computer can Quick Resume from sleep by moving the mouse, pressing an on/off key on the keyboard (if available), or pressing the sleep button on the remote control. Quick Sleep mode is different from standard sleep mode. In Quick Sleep mode, the computer's video card stops sending data to the display, the sound is muted, and the monitor LED indicates a lowered power state on the monitor, but the power continues to be supplied to vital components on the system, such as the processor, fans, and so on. Because this technology was originally designed for Windows XP Media Center Edition, it does not work in many cases with later Windows desktop operating systems and generally should not be used with Windows Server operating systems. You might need to disable this feature in firmware to allow a Windows desktop operating system to properly sleep and resume.

After you look at the computer's power settings in firmware, you should also review the computer's boot settings in firmware. Typically, you have a list of bootable devices and can select which one to boot. You also might be able to configure the following boot settings:

- **Boot Drive Order**   Determines the boot order for fixed disks

- **Boot To Hard Disk Drive**   Determines whether the computer can boot to fixed disks, and can be set to Disabled or Enabled

- **Boot To Removable Devices**   Determines whether the computer can boot to removable media, and can be set to Disabled or Enabled

- **Boot To Network**   Determines whether the computer can perform a network boot, and can be set to Disabled or Enabled

- **USB Boot**   Determines whether the computer can boot to USB flash devices, and can be set to Disabled or Enabled

As with power settings, your computer might not have these exact labels, but the labels should be similar. You need to optimize these settings for the way you plan to use the computer. In most cases, with server hardware, you'll only want to enable Boot To Hard Disk Drive. The exception is for when you use BitLocker Drive Encryption. With BitLocker, you'll want to enable Boot To Removable Devices, USB Boot, or both to ensure that the computer can detect the USB flash drive with the encryption key during the boot process.

# Boot environment essentials

Windows Server 2012 supports several different processor architectures and several different disk partitioning styles. EFI was originally developed for Itanium-based computers. Computers with EFI use the GUID partition table (GPT) disk type for boot and system volumes. Computers based on x86 use BIOS and the master boot record (MBR) disk type for boot and system volumes. Computers based on x64 use UEFI wrapped around BIOS or EFI.

With the increasing acceptance and use of UEFI and the ability of Windows to use both MBR and GPT disks regardless of firmware type, the underlying chip architecture won't necessarily determine which firmware type and disk type a computer uses for boot and startup. That said, generally, BIOS-based computers use MBR for booting or for data disks and GPT only for data disks. EFI-based computers can have both GPT and MBR disks, but you typically must have at least one GPT disk that contains the EFI system partition (ESP) and a primary partition or simple volume that contains the operating system for booting.

With early releases of the server operating system for Windows, BIOS-based computers use Ntldr and Boot.ini to boot into the operating system. Ntldr handles the task of loading the operating system, while Boot.ini contains the parameters that enable startup, including the identity of the boot partitions. Through Boot.ini parameters, you can add options that control the way the operating system starts, the way computer components are used, and the way operating system features are used.

On the other hand, with early releases of the server operating system for Windows, EFI-based computers use Ia64ldr.efi, Diskpart.efi, and Nvrboot.efi to boot into the operating system. Ia64ldr.efi handles the task of loading the operating system, while Diskpart.efi identifies the boot partitions. Through Nvrboot.efi, you set the parameters that enable startup.

Windows Server 2008 and later don't use these boot facilities. Instead, they use a pre-operating system boot environment. Figure 3-1 provides a conceptual overview of how the boot environment fits into the overall computer architecture.

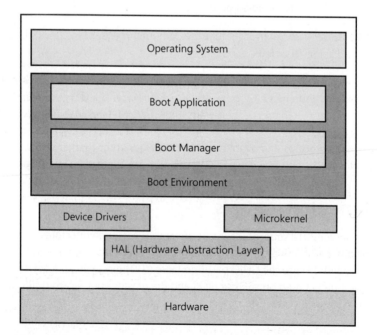

**Figure 3-1** A conceptual view of how the boot environment works.

The boot environment is an extensible abstraction layer that allows the operating system to work with multiple types of firmware interfaces without requiring the operating system to be specifically written to work with these firmware interfaces. Within the boot environment, startup is controlled using the parameters in the BCD data store.

The BCD store is contained in a file called the *BCD registry*. The location of this registry depends on the computer's firmware:

- On BIOS-based operating systems, the BCD registry file is stored in the \Boot\Bcd directory of the active partition.

- On EFI-based operating systems, the BCD registry file is stored on the EFI system partition.

Entries in the BCD data store identify the boot manager to use during startup and the specific boot applications available. The default boot manager is the Windows Boot Manager. Windows Boot Manager controls the boot experience, and you can use it to choose which boot application is run. Boot applications load a specific operating system or operating system version. For example, a Windows Boot Loader application loads Windows Server 2012. Because of this, you can boot BIOS-based and EFI-based computers in much the same way.

# Managing startup and boot configuration

As discussed in "Troubleshooting startup and shutdown" in Chapter 17, "Backup and recovery," you can press F8 during startup of the operating system to access the Advanced Boot Options menu and then use this menu to select one of several advanced startup modes, including Safe Mode, Enable Boot Logging, and Disable Driver Signature Enforcement. Although these advanced modes temporarily modify the way the operating system starts to help you diagnose and resolve problems, they don't make permanent changes to the boot configuration or to the BCD store. Other tools you can use to modify the boot configuration and manage the BCD store include the Startup And Recovery dialog box, the System Configuration utility, and BCD Editor. The sections that follow discuss how these tools are used.

## Managing startup and recovery options

The Startup And Recovery dialog box controls the basic options for the operating system during startup. You can use these options to set the default operating system, the time to display the list of available operating systems, and the time to display recovery options when needed. Whether you start a computer to different operating systems or not, you'll want to optimize these settings to reduce the wait time during startup and, in this way, speed up the startup process.

You can access the Startup And Recovery dialog box by completing the following steps:

1. In Control Panel\System and Security, tap or click System to access the System window.

2. In the System window, tap or click Advanced System Settings under Tasks in the left pane. This displays the System Properties dialog box.

3. On the Advanced tab of the System Properties dialog box, tap or click Settings under Startup And Recovery. This displays the Startup And Recovery dialog box, as shown in Figure 3-2.

> **Note**
> Open the Advanced tab of the System Properties dialog box directly by typing **SystemPropertiesAdvanced.exe** in the Apps Search box and pressing Enter.

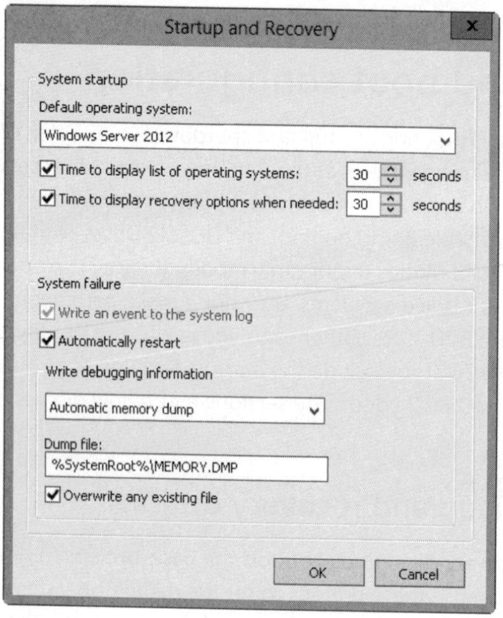

Figure 3-2 Configure system startup options.

4.  On a computer with multiple operating systems, use the Default Operating System list to specify the operating system you want to start by default.

5.  Set the timeout interval for the operating system list by selecting the Time To Display List Of Operating Systems check box and specifying a timeout in seconds in the field provided. To speed up the startup process, you might want to use a value of five seconds.

6.  Set the timeout interval for the recovery options list by selecting the Time To Display Recovery Options When Needed check box and specifying a timeout in seconds in the field provided. Again, to speed up the startup process, you might want to use a value of five seconds.

7.  Tap or click OK to save your settings.

## Managing System Boot Configuration

You can use the System Configuration utility (Msconfig.exe) to fine-tune the way a computer starts. Typically, you use this utility during troubleshooting and diagnostics. For example, as part of troubleshooting, you can configure the computer to use a diagnostic startup where only basic devices and services are loaded.

The System Configuration utility is available on the Tools menu in Server Manager. You can also start the System Configuration utility by pressing the Windows key, typing **msconfig.exe** in the Apps Search box, and pressing Enter. As shown in Figure 3-3, this utility has a series of tabs with options.

Use the General tab options to configure the way startup works. This tab is where you should start your troubleshooting and diagnostics efforts. Using these options, you can choose to perform a normal startup, diagnostic startup, or selective startup. After you restart the computer and resolve any problems, access the System Configuration utility again, select Normal Startup on the General tab, and then tap or click OK.

Chapter 3

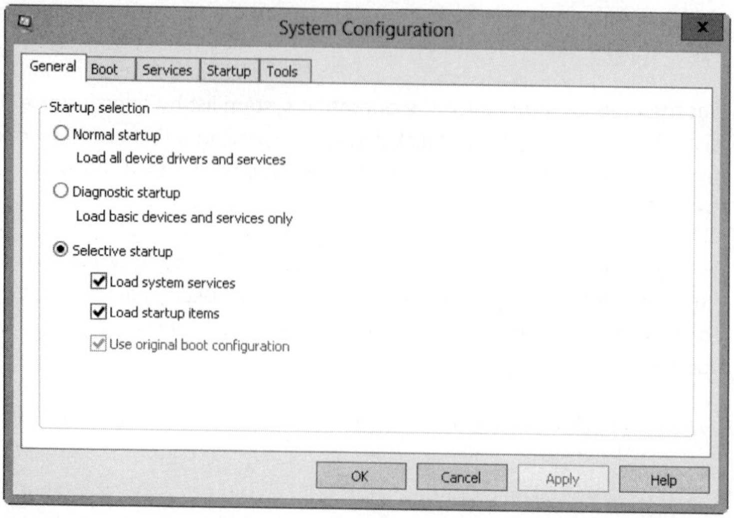

**Figure 3-3**  Perform a diagnostic or selective startup as part of troubleshooting.

Use the Boot tab options, shown in Figure 3-4, to control the way the individual startup-related processes work. You can configure the computer to start in one of various Safe Boot modes and set additional options, such as No GUI Boot. If after troubleshooting you find that you want to keep these settings, you can select the Make All Boot Settings Permanent check box to save the settings to the boot configuration startup entry.

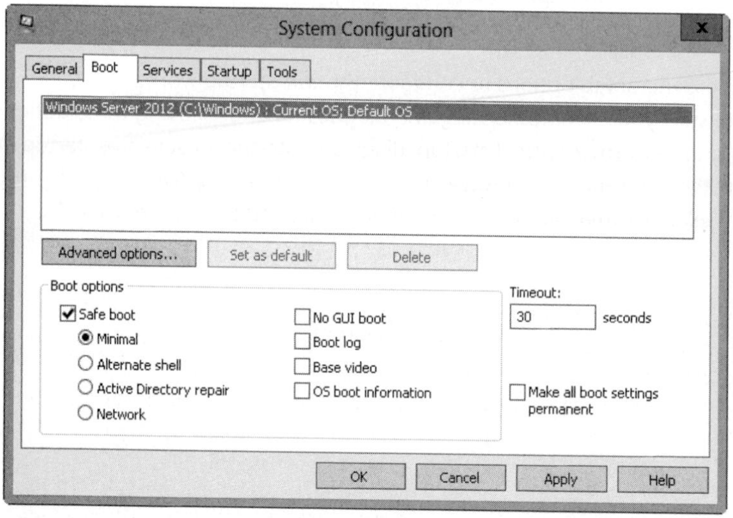

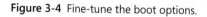

**Figure 3-4**  Fine-tune the boot options.

Tapping or clicking the Advanced Options button on the Boot tab displays the BOOT Advanced Options dialog box shown in Figure 3-5. In addition to being able to lock PCI, detect the correct HAL, and enable debugging, you can use the advanced options to do the following:

- Specify the number of processors the operating system should use. You should use this option when you suspect there is a problem with additional processors you installed in a server and you want to pinpoint which processors are possibly causing startup problems. Consider the following scenario: A server shipped with two processors, and you installed two additional processors. Later, you find that you cannot start the server. You could eliminate the new processors as the potential cause by limiting the computer to two processors.

- Specify the maximum amount of memory the operating system should use. You should use this option when you suspect there is a problem with additional memory you installed in a server. Consider the following scenario: A server shipped with 4 GB of RAM, and you installed 4 additional GB of RAM. Later, you find that you cannot start the server. You could eliminate the new RAM as the potential cause by limiting the computer to 4096 MB of memory.

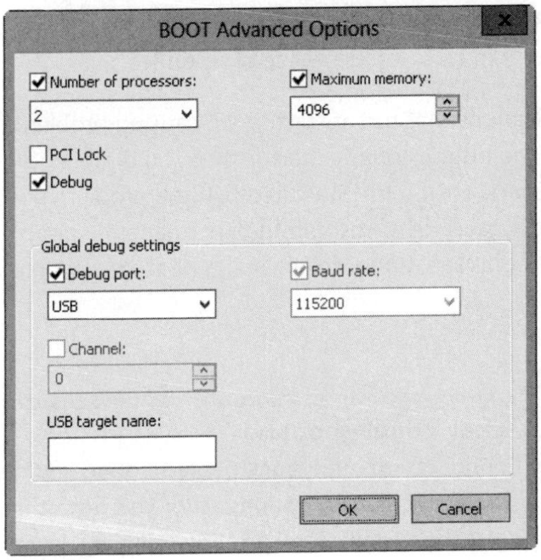

**Figure 3-5** Set advanced boot options as necessary to help troubleshoot specific types of problems.

If you suspect services installed on a computer are causing startup problems, you can quickly determine this by choosing a diagnostic or selective startup on the General tab. After you identify that services are indeed causing startup problems, you can temporarily disable services using the Services tab options and then reboot to see if the problem goes away. If the problem no longer appears, you might have pinpointed it. You can then permanently disable the service or check with the service vendor to see if an updated executable is available for the service. As shown in Figure 3-6, you disable a service by clearing the related check box on the Services tab.

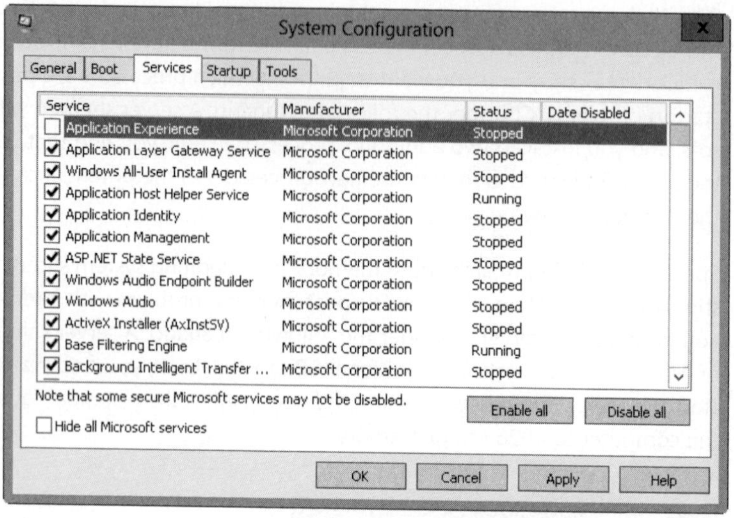

**Figure 3-6**  Disable services to try to pinpoint the source of a problem.

Similarly, if you suspect applications that run at startup are causing problems, you can quickly determine this using the options on the Startup tab. You disable a startup application by clearing the related check box on the Startup tab. If the problem no longer appears, you might have pinpointed the cause of it. You can then permanently disable the startup application or check with the software vendor to see if an updated version is available.

## TROUBLESHOOTING

### Remove selective startup after troubleshooting

If you are using the System Configuration utility for troubleshooting and diagnostics, you should later remove your selective startup options. After you restart the computer and resolve any problems, access the System Configuration utility again, restore the original settings, and then tap or click OK.

# Working with BCD Editor

The BCD store contains multiple entries. On a BIOS-based computer, you'll see the following entries:

- One Windows Boot Manager entry. There is only one boot manager, so there is only one boot manager entry.

- One or more Windows Boot Loader application entries, with one for each Windows Server 2008 operating system, Windows Vista operating system, or later versions of Windows installed on the computer.

- One legacy operating system entry. The legacy entry is not for a boot application. This entry is used to initiate Ntldr and Boot.ini so that you can boot into Windows XP or an earlier release of Windows. If the computer has more than one Windows XP or earlier operating system, you'll be able to select the operating system to start after selecting the legacy operating system entry.

Windows Boot Manager is itself a boot loader application. There are other boot loader applications, including

- Legacy OS Loader, identified as NTLDR

- Windows Vista or later operating system loader, identified as OSLOADER

- Windows Boot Sector Application, identified as BOOTSECTOR

- Firmware Boot Manager, identified as FWBOOTMGR

- Windows Resume Loader, identified as RESUME

You can directly view and manage the BCD data store using BCD Editor (BCDEdit.exe). BCD Editor is a command-line utility. You can use BCD Editor to view the entries in the BCD store by following these steps:

1. Press and hold or right-click the lower-left corner of the Start screen or the desktop. This displays a shortcut menu.

2. Select the Command Prompt (Admin) to open an elevated command prompt.

3. Enter **bcdedit** at the elevated command prompt.

Table 3-2 summarizes commands you can use when you are working with the BCD data store. These commands allow you to

- Create, import, export, and identify the entire BCD data store.

- Create, delete, and copy individual entries in the BCD data store.

- Set or delete entry option values in the BCD data store.

- Control the boot sequence and the boot manager.

- Configure and control Emergency Management Services (EMS).

- Configure and control boot debugging as well as hypervisor debugging.

**TABLE 3-2  Commands for BCD Editor**

| Commands | Description |
| --- | --- |
| /bootdebug | Enables or disables boot debugging for a boot application. |
| /bootems | Enables or disables Emergency Management Services for a boot application. |
| /bootsequence | Sets the one-time boot sequence for the boot manager. |
| /copy | Makes copies of entries in the store. |
| /create | Creates new entries in the store. |
| /createstore | Creates a new (empty) boot configuration data store. |
| /dbgsettings | Sets the global debugger parameters. |
| /debug | Enables or disables kernel debugging for an operating system entry. |
| /default | Sets the default entry that the boot manager will use. |
| /delete | Deletes entries from the store. |
| /deletevalue | Deletes entry options from the store. |
| /displayorder | Sets the order in which the boot manager displays the multiboot menu. |
| /ems | Enables or disables Emergency Management Services for an operating system entry. |
| /emssettings | Sets the global Emergency Management Services parameters. |
| /enum | Lists entries in the store. |
| /export | Exports the contents of the system store to a file. This file can be used later to restore the state of the system store. |
| /hypervisorsettings | Sets the hypervisor parameters. |
| /import | Restores the state of the system store using a backup file created with the /export command. |
| /mirror | Duplicates a specified entry by mirroring it in the data store. |
| /set | Sets entry option values in the store. |
| /store | Sets the BCD store to use. If not specified, the system store is used. |

| Commands | Description |
|---|---|
| */sysstore* | Sets the system store device. Note that this affects only EFI systems. |
| */timeout* | Sets the boot manager timeout value. |
| */toolsdisplayorder* | Sets the order in which the boot manager displays the tools menu. |
| */v* | Sets output to verbose mode. |

# Managing the Boot Configuration Data store and its entries

BCD Editor (BCDEdit.exe) is an advanced command-line tool for viewing and manipulating the configuration of the pre-operating system boot environment. Although I discuss tasks related to modifying the BCD data store in the sections that follow, you should attempt to modify the BCD store only if you are an experienced IT pro. As a safeguard, you should make a full backup of the computer prior to making any changes to the BCD store. Why? If you make a mistake, your computer might end up in a nonbootable state and you would then need to initiate recovery.

## Viewing BCD entries

Computers can have system and nonsystem BCD stores. The system BCD store contains the operating system boot entries and related boot settings. Whenever you work with the BCD Editor, you will be working with the system BCD store.

On a computer with only one operating system, the BCD entries for your computer will look similar to those in Listing 3-1. As the listing shows, the BCD store for this computer has two entries: one for the Windows Boot Manager and one for the Windows Boot Loader. Here, the Windows Boot Manager calls the boot loader and the boot loader uses Winload.exe to boot Windows Server 2012.

**Listing 3-1** Entries in the BCD store on a single boot computer

```
Windows Boot Manager
--------------------
identifier              {bootmgr}
device                  partition=F:
description             Windows Boot Manager
locale                  en-US
inherit                 {globalsettings}
bootshutdowndisabled    Yes
default                 {current}
resumeobject            {5824ba7d-acee-11e1-ba52-cfa3fef36259}
displayorder            {current}
```

```
toolsdisplayorder         {memdiag}
timeout                   30

Windows Boot Loader
-------------------
device                    partition=C:identifier            {current}
path                      \Windows\system32\winload.exe
description               Windows Server 2012
locale                    en-US
inherit                   {bootloadersettings}
recoverysequence          {5824ba7f-acee-11e1-ba52-cfa3fef36259}
recoveryenabled           Yes
allowedinmemorysettings   0x15000075
osdevice                  partition=C:
systemroot                \Windows
resumeobject              {5824ba7d-acee-11e1-ba52-cfa3fef36259}
nx                        OptOut
```

BCD entries for Windows Boot Manager and Windows Boot Loader have similar properties. These properties include those summarized in Table 3-3.

**TABLE 3-3  BCD entry properties**

| Property | Description |
| --- | --- |
| *Description* | Shows descriptive information to help identify the type of entry. |
| *Device* | Shows the physical device path. For a partition on a physical disk, you'll see an entry such as partition=C:. |
| *FileDevice* | Shows the path to a file device, such as partition=C:. |
| *FilePath* | Shows the file path to a necessary file, such as \hiberfil.sys. |
| *Identifier* | Shows a descriptor for the entry. This can be a boot loader application type, such as BOOTMGR or NTLDR. Or it can be a reference to the current operating system entry or the GUID of a specific object. |
| *Inherit* | Shows the list of entries to be inherited. |
| *Locale* | Shows the computer's locale setting, such as en-us. The locale setting determines the UI language shown. In the \Boot folder, there are locale subfolders for each locale supported, and each of these subfolders has language-specific UI details for the Windows Boot Manager (BootMgr.exe) and the Memory Diagnostics Utility (MemDiag.exe). |
| *OSDevice* | Shows the path to the operating system device, such as partition=C:. |
| *Path* | Shows the actual file path to the boot loader application, such as \Windows\System32\winresume.exe. |

When you are working with the BCD store and BCD Editor, you'll see references to well-known identifiers, summarized in Table 3-4, as well as globally unique identifiers (GUIDs).

When a GUID is used, the GUID has the following format where each N represents a hexadecimal value:

{NNNNNNNN-NNNN-NNNN-NNNN-NNNNNNNNNNNN}

Such as:

{5824ba7d-acee-11e1-ba52-cfa3fef36259}

The dashes that separate the parts of the GUID must be entered in the positions shown.

**TABLE 3-4 Well-known identifiers**

| Identifier | Description |
| --- | --- |
| {badmemory} | Contains the global RAM defect list that can be inherited by any boot application entry. |
| {bootloadersettings} | Contains the collection of global settings that should be inherited by all Windows boot loader application entries. |
| {bootmgr} | Indicates the Windows boot manager entry. |
| {current} | Represents a virtual identifier that corresponds to the operating system boot entry for the operating system that is currently running. |
| {dbgsettings} | Contains the global debugger settings that can be inherited by any boot application entry. |
| {default} | Represents a virtual identifier that corresponds to the boot manager default application entry. |
| {emssettings} | Contains the global Emergency Management Services settings that can be inherited by any boot application entry. |
| {fwbootmgr} | Indicates the firmware boot manager entry. This entry is used on EFI systems. |
| {globalsettings} | Contains the collection of global settings that should be inherited by all boot application entries. |
| {hypervisorsettings} | Contains the hypervisor settings that can be inherited by any operating system loader entry. |
| {legacy} | Indicates the Windows Legacy OS Loader (Ntldr) that can be used to start operating systems earlier than Windows Vista. |
| {memdiag} | Indicates the memory diagnostic application entry. |
| {ntldr} | Indicates the Windows Legacy OS Loader (Ntldr) that can be used to start operating systems earlier than Windows Vista. |
| {ramdiskoptions} | Contains the additional options required by the boot manager for RAM disk devices. |
| {resumeloadersettings} | Contains the collection of global settings that should be inherited by all Windows resume from hibernation application entries. |

Chapter 3

When a computer has additional Windows Vista, Windows Server 2008, or later operating systems installed, the BCD store for it has additional entries for each additional operating system. For example, the BCD store might have one entry for the Windows Boot Manager and one Windows Boot Loader for each operating system.

When a computer has a legacy operating system installed, the BCD store has three entries: one for the Windows Boot Manager, one for the Windows Legacy OS Loader, and one for the Windows Boot Loader. Generally, the entry for the Windows Legacy OS Loader will look similar to Listing 3-2.

**Listing 3-2** Sample Legacy OS Loader entry

```
Windows Legacy OS Loader
------------------------
identifier:             {ntldr}
device:                 partition=C:
path:                   \ntldr
description:            Earlier version of Windows
```

Although the Windows Boot Manager, Windows Legacy OS Loader, and Windows Boot Loader are the primary types of entries that control startup, the BCD also stores information about boot settings and boot utilities. The Windows Boot Loader entry can have parameters that track the status of boot settings, such as whether No Execute (NX) policy is set for Opt In or Opt Out. The Windows Boot Loader entry also can provide information about available boot utilities, such as the Memory Diagnostics utility.

To view the actual value of the GUIDs needed to manipulate entries in the BCD data store, type **bcdedit /v** at an elevated command prompt.

## Creating and identifying the BCD data store

Using BCD Editor, you can create a new, nonsystem BCD data store by using the following command:

```
bcdedit /createstore StorePath
```

Here *StorePath* is the actual folder path to the location where you want to create the nonsystem store, such as:

```
bcdedit /createstore c:\non-sys\bcd
```

On an EFI system, you can temporarily set the system store device using the */sysstore* command. Use the following syntax:

```
bcdedit /sysstore StoreDevice
```

Here *StoreDevice* is the actual device identifier store, such as:

```
bcdedit /sysstore C:
```

> **Note**
> The device must be a system partition. Note this setting does not persist across reboots and is used only in cases where the system store device is ambiguous.

## Importing and exporting the BCD data store

BCD Editor provides separate commands for importing and exporting the BCD store. You can use the */export* command to export a copy of the system BCD store's contents to a specified folder. Use the following command syntax:

```
bcdedit /export StorePath
```

Here *StorePath* is the actual folder path to which you want to export a copy of the system store, such as:

```
bcdedit /export c:\backup\bcd.dat
```

To restore an exported copy of the system store, you can use the */import* command. Use the following command syntax:

```
bcdedit /import ImportPath
```

Here *ImportPath* is the actual folder path from which you want to import a copy of the system store, such as:

```
bcdedit /import c:\backup\bcd.dat
```

On an EFI system, you can add */clean* to the import to specify that all existing firmware boot entries should be deleted. Here is an example:

```
bcdedit /import c:\backup\bcd.dat /clean
```

## Creating, copying, and deleting BCD entries

BCD Editor provides separate commands for creating, copying, and deleting entries in the BCD store. You can use the */create* command to create identifier, application, and inherit entries in the BCD store.

As shown previously in Table 3-4, BCD Editor recognizes many well-known identifiers, including {dbgsettings} used to create a debugger settings entry, {ntldr} used to create a Windows Legacy OS entry, and {ramdiskoptions} used to create a RAM disk additional options entry. To create identifier entries, you use the following syntax:

```
bcdedit /create Identifier /d "Description"
```

Here *Identifier* is a well-known identifier for the entry you want to create, such as:

```
bcdedit /create {ntldr} /d "Earlier Windows OS Loader"
```

You can create the following entries for specific boot-loader applications as well:

- **Bootsector**    A real-mode, boot-sector application, used to set the boot sector for a real-mode application

- **OSLoader**    An operating-system loader application, used to load a Windows Vista or later operating system

- **Resume**    A Windows Resume Loader application, used to resume the operating system from hibernation

- **Startup**    A real-mode application, used to identify a real-mode application

Use the following command syntax:

```
bcdedit /create /application AppType /d "Description"
```

Here *AppType* is one of the previously listed application types, such as:

```
bcdedit /create /application osloader /d "Windows 8"
```

You can delete entries in the system store using the */delete* command and the following syntax:

```
bcdedit /delete Identifier
```

If you are trying to delete a well-known identifier, you must use the */f* command to force deletion, such as:

```
bcdedit /delete {ntldr} /f
```

By default, when using the */delete* command, the */cleanup* option is implied, and this means BCD Editor cleans up any other references to the entry being deleted. This ensures that the data store doesn't have invalid references to the identifier you removed. Because entries are removed from the display order as well, this can result in a different default operating system being set. If you want to delete the entry and clean up all other references except the display order entry, you can use the */nocleanup* command.

## Setting BCD entry values

After you create an entry, you then need to set additional entry option values as necessary. Here is the basic syntax for setting values:

```
bcdedit /set Identifier Option Value
```

Here *Identifier* is the identifier of the entry to be modified, *Option* is the option you want to set, and *Value* is the option value, such as:

```
bcdedit /set {current} device partition=d:
```

To delete options and their values, use the */deletevalue* command with the following syntax:

```
bcdedit /deletevalue Identifier Option
```

Here *Identifier* is the identifier of the entry to be modified and *Option* is the option you want to delete, such as:

```
bcdedit /deletevalue {current} badmemorylist
```

> **Note**
> When you are working with options, Boolean values can be entered in several different ways. For *true*, you can use 1, ON, YES, or TRUE. For *false*, you can use 0, OFF, NO, or FALSE.

To view the BCD entries for all boot utilities and values for settings, type **bcdedit /enum all /v** at an elevated command prompt. This command enumerates all BCD entries regardless of their current state and lists them in Verbose Mode. The additional entries will look similar to those in Listing 3-3 (shown later in the chapter). Each additional entry has a specific purpose and lists values that you can set, including the following:

- **Resume From Hibernate**    The Resume From Hibernate entry shows the current configuration for the resume feature. The pre-operating system boot utility that controls resume is Winresume.exe, which in this example is stored in the C:\Windows\system32 folder. The hibernation data, as specified in the *filepath* parameter, is stored in the Hiberfil.sys file in the root folder on the *osdevice* (c: in this example). Because the resume feature works differently if the computer has Physical Address Extension (PAE) and debugging enabled, these options are tracked by the *PAE* and *Debugoptionenabled* parameters.

- **Windows Memory Tester**    The Windows Memory Tester entry shows the current configuration for the Windows Memory Diagnostics utility. The pre-operating system boot utility that controls memory diagnostics is Memtest.exe, which in this example is stored in the C:\Boot folder. Because the Memory Diagnostics utility is designed to detect bad memory by default, the *badmemoryaccess* parameter is set to *yes* by default. You can turn this feature off by entering **bcdedit /set {memdiag} badmemoryaccess NO**. With memory diagnostics, you can configure the number of passes using *Passcount* and configure the test mix as BASIC or EXTENDED using *Testmix*. Here is an example: **bcdedit /set {memdiag} passcount 2**.

- **Windows Legacy OS Loader**   The Windows Legacy OS Loader entry shows the current configuration for the loading of earlier versions of Windows. The *Device* parameter sets the default partition to use, such as C:, and the *Path* parameter sets the default path to the loader utility, such as Ntldr.

- **EMS Settings**   The EMS Settings entry shows the configuration used when booting with Emergency Management Services. Individual Windows Boot Loader entries control whether EMS is enabled. If EMS is provided by BIOS and you want to use the BIOS settings, you can enter **bcdedit /emssettings bios**. With EMS, you can set an EMS port and an EMS baud rate as well. Here is an example: **bcdedit /emssettings EMSPORT:2 EMSBAUDRATE:115200**. You can enable or disable EMS for a boot application by typing **/bootems** followed by the identity of the boot application with the desired state, such as ON or OFF.

- **Debugger Settings**   The Debugger Settings entry shows the configuration used when booting with the debugger turned on. Individual Windows Boot Loader entries control whether the debugger is enabled. You can view the hypervisor debug settings by entering **bcdedit /dbgsettings**. When debug booting is turned on, *DebugType* sets the type of debugger as SERIAL, 1394, or USB. With SERIAL debugging, *DebugPort* specifies the serial port being used as the debugger port and *BaudRate* specifies the baud rate to be used for debugging. With 1394 debugging, you can use *Channel* to set the debugging channel. With Universal Serial Bus (USB) debugging, you can use *TargetName* to set the USB target name to be used for debugging. With any debug type, you can use the */Noumex* flag to specify that user-mode exceptions should be ignored. Here are examples of setting the debugging mode: **bcdedit /dbgsettings SERIAL DEBUGPORT:1 BAUDRATE:115200, bcdedit /dbgsettings 1394 CHANNEL:23**, and **bcdedit /dbgsettings USB TARGETNAME:DEBUGGING**.

- **Hypervisor Settings**   The Hypervisor Settings entry shows the configuration used when working with the Hypervisor with the debugger turned on. Individual Windows Boot Loader entries control whether the debugger is enabled. You can view the hypervisor debug settings by entering **bcdedit /hypervisorsettings**. When hypervisor debug booting is turned on, *HypervisorDebugType* sets the type of debugger, *HypervisorDebugPort* specifies the serial port being used as the debugger port, and *HypervisorBaudRate* specifies the baud rate to be used for debugging.

These parameters work the same as with Debugger Settings. Here is an example: **bcdedit /hypervisorsettings SERIAL DEBUGPORT:1 BAUDRATE:115200**. You can also use FireWire for hypervisor debugging. When you do, you must set the debug channel, such as shown in this example: **bcdedit /hypervisorsettings 1394 CHANNEL:23**.

**Listing 3-3** Additional entries in the BCD data store on a single boot computer

```
Resume from Hibernate
---------------------
identifier                 {5824ba7d-acee-11e1-ba52-cfa3fef36259}
device                     partition=C:
path                       \Windows\system32\winresume.exe
description                Windows Resume Application
locale                     en-US
inherit                    {1afa9c49-16ab-4a5c-901b-212802da9460}
recoverysequence           {5824ba7f-acee-11e1-ba52-cfa3fef36259}
recoveryenabled            Yes
allowedinmemorysettings    0x15000075
filedevice                 partition=C:
filepath                   \hiberfil.sys
debugoptionenabled         No

Windows Memory Tester
---------------------
identifier                 {b2721d73-1db4-4c62-bf78-c548a880142d}
device                     partition=F:
path                       \boot\memtest.exe
description                Windows Memory Diagnostic
locale                     en-US
inherit                    {7ea2e1ac-2e61-4728-aaa3-896d9d0a9f0e}
badmemoryaccess            Yes

EMS Settings
------------
identifier                 {0ce4991b-e6b3-4b16-b23c-5e0d9250e5d9}
bootems                    Yes

Debugger Settings
-----------------
identifier                 {4636856e-540f-4170-a130-a84776f4c654}
debugtype                  Serial
debugport                  1
baudrate                   115200

RAM Defects
-----------
identifier                 {5189b25c-5558-4bf2-bca4-289b11bd29e2}
```

Chapter 3

```
Global Settings
---------------
identifier              {7ea2e1ac-2e61-4728-aaa3-896d9d0a9f0e}
inherit                 {4636856e-540f-4170-a130-a84776f4c654}
                        {0ce4991b-e6b3-4b16-b23c-5e0d9250e5d9}
                        {5189b25c-5558-4bf2-bca4-289b11bd29e2}

Boot Loader Settings
--------------------
identifier              {6efb52bf-1766-41db-a6b3-0ee5eff72bd7}
inherit                 {7ea2e1ac-2e61-4728-aaa3-896d9d0a9f0e}
                        {7ff607e0-4395-11db-b0de-0800200c9a66}

Hypervisor Settings
-------------------
identifier              {7ff607e0-4395-11db-b0de-0800200c9a66}
hypervisordebugtype     Serial
hypervisordebugport     1
hypervisorbaudrate      115200

Resume Loader Settings
----------------------
identifier              {1afa9c49-16ab-4a5c-901b-212802da9460}
inherit                 {7ea2e1ac-2e61-4728-aaa3-896d9d0a9f0e}

Device options
--------------
identifier              {5824ba7c-acee-11e1-ba52-cfa3fef36259}
description             Windows Recovery
ramdisksdidevice        partition=C:
ramdisksdipath          \Recovery\5824ba7b-acee-11e1-ba52-cfa3fef36259\boot.sdi
```

Table 3-5 summarizes key options that apply to entries for boot applications (BOOTAPP). Because Windows Boot Manager, Windows Memory Diagnostics, Windows OS Loader, and Windows Resume Loader are boot applications, these options apply to them as well.

**TABLE 3-5  Key options for boot application entries**

| Option | Value Description |
|---|---|
| *BadMemoryAccess* | When *true*, allows an application to use the memory on the bad memory list. When *false*, applications are prevented from using memory on the bad memory list. |
| *BadMemoryList* | An integer list that defines the list of Page Frame Numbers of faulty memory in the system. |
| *BaudRate* | Sets an integer value that defines the baud rate for the serial debugger. |
| *BootDebug* | Sets a Boolean value that enables or disables the boot debugger. |

| Option | Value Description |
|---|---|
| *BootEMS* | Sets a Boolean value that enables or disables Emergency Management Services. |
| *Channel* | Sets an integer value that defines the channel for the 1394 debugger. |
| *DebugAddress* | Sets an integer value that defines the address of a serial port for the debugger. |
| *DebugPort* | Sets an integer value that defines the serial port number for the serial debugger. |
| *DebugStart* | Can be set to ACTIVE, AUTOENABLE, or DISABLE. |
| *DebugType* | Can be set to SERIAL, 1394, or USB. |
| *EMSBaudRate* | Defines the baud rate for Emergency Management Services. |
| *EMSPort* | Defines the serial port number for Emergency Management Services. |
| *GraphicsModeDisabled* | Sets a Boolean value that enables or disables graphics mode. |
| *GraphicsResolution* | Defines the graphics resolution, such as 1024 by 768 or 800 by 600. |
| *Locale* | Sets the locale of the boot application. |
| *Noumex* | When set to TRUE, user-mode exceptions are ignored. When set to FALSE, user-mode exceptions are not ignored. |
| *NoVESA* | Sets a Boolean value that enables or disables the use of Video Electronics Standards Association (VESA) display modes. |
| *RelocatePhysical* | Sets the physical address to which an automatically selected Non-Uniform Memory Access (NUMA) node's physical memory should be relocated. |
| *TargetName* | Defines the target name for the USB debugger as a string. |
| *TruncateMemory* | Sets a physical memory address at or above which all memory is disregarded. |

Table 3-6 summarizes key options that apply to entries for Windows OS Loader (OSLOADER) applications.

**TABLE 3-6  Key options for Windows OS Loader applications**

| Option | Value Description |
|---|---|
| *AdvancedOptions* | Sets a Boolean value that enables or disables advanced options. |
| *BootLog* | Sets a Boolean value that enables or disables the boot initialization log. |
| *BootStatusPolicy* | Sets the boot status policy. It can be *DisplayAllFailures*, *IgnoreAllFailures*, *IgnoreShutdownFailures*, or *IgnoreBootFailures*. |

Chapter 3

| Option | Value Description |
|---|---|
| ClusterModeAddressing | Sets the maximum number of processors to include in a single Advanced Programmable Interrupt Controller (APIC) cluster. |
| ConfigFlags | Sets processor-specific configuration flags. |
| DbgTransport | Sets the file name for a private debugger transport. |
| Debug | Sets a Boolean value that enables or disables kernel debugging. |
| DetectHal | Sets a Boolean value that enables or disables hardware abstraction layer (HAL) and kernel detection. |
| DriverLoadFailurePolicy | Sets the driver load failure policy. It can be *Fatal* or *UseErrorControl*. |
| Ems | Sets a Boolean value that enables or disables kernel Emergency Management Services. |
| Hal | Sets the file name for a private HAL. |
| HalBreakPoint | Sets a Boolean value that enables or disables the special HAL breakpoint. |
| HypervisorLaunchType | Configures the hypervisor launch type. It can be *Off* or *Auto*. |
| IncreaseUserVA | Sets an integer value that increases the amount of virtual address space that the user-mode processes can use. |
| Kernel | Sets the file name for a private kernel. |
| LastKnownGood | Sets a Boolean value that enables or disables boot to last known good configuration. |
| MaxProc | Sets a Boolean value that enables or disables the display of the maximum number of processors in the system. |
| Msi | Sets the MSI to use. It can be *Default* or *ForceDisable*. |
| NoCrashAutoReboot | Sets a Boolean value that enables or disables automatic restart on crash. |
| NoLowMem | Sets a Boolean value that enables or disables the use of low memory. |
| NumProc | Sets the number of processors to use on startup. |
| Nx | Controls No Execute protection. It can be *OptIn*, *OptOut*, *AlwaysOn*, or *AlwaysOff*. |
| OneCPU | Sets a Boolean value that forces only the boot CPU to be used. |
| OptionsEdit | Sets a Boolean value that enables or disables the options editor. |
| OSDdevice | Defines the device that contains the system root. |
| Pae | Controls PAE. It can be *Default*, *ForceEnable*, or *ForceDisable*. |
| PerfMem | Sets the size (in megabytes) of the buffer to allocate for performance data logging. |

| Option | Value Description |
|--------|-------------------|
| *RemoveMemory* | Sets an integer value that removes memory from the total available memory that the operating system can use. |
| *RestrictAPICCluster* | Sets the largest APIC cluster number to be used by the system. |
| *SafeBoot* | Sets the computer to use a Safe boot mode. It can be *Minimal*, *Network*, or *DsRepair*. |
| *SafeBootAlternateShell* | Sets a Boolean value that enables or disables the use of the alternate shell when booted into Safe mode. |
| *Sos* | Sets a Boolean value that enables or disables the display of additional boot information. |
| *SystemRoot* | Defines the path to the system root. |
| *UseFirmwarePCISettings* | Sets a Boolean value that enables or disables the use of BIOS-configured Peripheral Component Interconnect (PCI) resources. |
| *UsePhysicalDestination* | Sets a Boolean value that forces the use of the physical APIC. |
| *Vga* | Sets a Boolean value that forces the use of the VGA display driver. |
| *WinPE* | Sets a Boolean value that enables or disables boot to Windows Preinstallation Environment (Windows PE). |

## Changing Data Execution Prevention and physical address extension options

Data Execution Prevention (DEP) is a memory-protection technology. With DEP enabled, the computer's processor marks all memory locations in an application as nonexecutable unless the location explicitly contains executable code. If code is executed from a memory page marked as nonexecutable, the processor can raise an exception and prevent the code from executing. This behavior prevents malicious application code, such as virus code, from inserting itself into most areas of memory.

For computers with processors that support the nonexecute page protection (NX) feature, you can configure the operating system to opt in to NX protection by setting the *nx* parameter to *OptIn* or opt out of NX protection by setting the *nx* parameter to *OptOut*. Here is an example:

```
bcdedit /set {current} nx optout
```

When you configure NX protection to *OptIn*, DEP is turned on only for essential Windows programs and services. This is the default. When you configure NX protection to *OptOut*, all programs and services—not just standard Windows programs and services—use DEP.

Chapter 3

Programs that shouldn't use DEP must be specifically opted out. You can also configure NX protection to be always on or always off using *AlwaysOn* or *AlwaysOff*, such as:

```
bcdedit /set {current} nx alwayson
```

Processors that support and opt in to NX protection must be running in PAE mode. You can configure PAE by setting the *PAE* parameter to *Default*, *ForceEnable*, or *ForceDisable*. When you set *paeState* to *Default*, the operating system will use the default configuration for PAE. When you set *paeState* to *ForceEnable*, the operating system will use PAE. When you set *paeState* to *ForceDisable*, the operating system will not use PAE. You can set *DebugOptionEnabled* to *true* or *false*. Here is an example:

```
bcdedit /set {current} pae default
```

## Changing the operating system display order

You can change the display order of boot managers associated with a particular Windows Vista, Windows Server 2008, or later operating system using the */Displayorder* command. The syntax is

```
bcdedit /displayorder id1 id2 … idn
```

Here *id1* is the operating system identifier of the first operating system in the display order, *id2* is the identifier of the second, and so on. Thus, you could change the display order of the operating systems identified in these BCD entries:

```
Windows Boot Loader
-------------------
identifier              {5824ba7f-acee-11e1-ba52-cfa3fef36259}

Windows Boot Loader
-------------------
identifier              {16b857b4-9e02-11e0-9c17-b7d085eb0682}
```

You can do this by using the following command:

```
bcdedit /displayorder {16b857b4-9e02-11e0-9c17-b7d085eb0682}
{5824ba7f-acee-11e1-ba52-cfa3fef36259}
```

You can set a particular operating system as the first entry using */addfirst* with */displayorder*, such as:

```
bcdedit /displayorder {5824ba7f-acee-11e1-ba52-cfa3fef36259} /addfirst
```

4. On the Server Selection page, you can choose to install roles and features on running servers or virtual hard disks. Either select a server from the server pool or select a server from the server pool on which to mount a virtual hard disk (VHD). Keep in mind that only servers that have been added for management in Server Manager are listed. If you are adding roles and features to a VHD, tap or click Browse and then use the Browse For Virtual Hard Disks dialog box to locate the VHD. When you are ready to continue, tap or click Next twice. This skips the Server Roles page.

5. On the Features page, expand Remote Server Administration Tools and the related subnodes to view the available feature and role administration tools. Select the tool or tools to install. If additional features are required to install a tool you selected, you'll see an additional dialog box. Tap or click Add Features to close the dialog box and add the required features to the server installation. When you are ready to continue, tap or click Next.

6. If the server on which you want to install the administrative tools doesn't have all the required binary source files, the server gets the files via Windows Update by default or from a location specified in Group Policy. You also can specify an alternate path for the source files. To do this, tap or click the Specify An Alternate Source Path link, type that alternate path in the box provided, and then tap or click OK. For network shares, enter the UNC path to the share, such as \\CorpServer41\WS12\. For mounted Windows images, enter the WIM path prefixed with WIM: and including the index of the image to use, such as WIM:\\CorpServer41\WS12\install.wim:4. For a locally mounted image, enter the alternate path for the mounted WIM file, such as c:\mountdir\windows\winsxs.

7. Tap or click Install to begin the installation process. The Installation Progress page tracks the progress of the installation. If you close the wizard, tap or click the Notifications icon in Server Manager and then tap or click the link provided to re-open the wizard.

8. When Setup finishes installing the administration tools you selected, the Installation Progress page will be updated to reflect this. Review the installation details to ensure that all phases of the installation were completed successfully.

## Using command-line utilities

Many command-line utilities are included with Windows Server 2012. Most of the utilities you'll work with as an administrator rely on TCP/IP. Because of this, you should install TCP/IP networking before you experiment with these tools.

Chapter 4

## Utilities to know

As an administrator, you should familiarize yourself with the following command-line utilities:

- **Appcmd**   Displays and manages the configuration of IIS.

- **Arp**   Displays and manages the IP-to-physical address mappings used by Windows Server 2012 to send data on the TCP/IP network.

- **Bcdedit**   Displays and manages Boot Configuration Data on the local system.

- **DiskPart**   Displays and manages disk partitions on local and remote systems.

> **Note**
>
> Windows 8 and Windows Server 2012 might be the last versions of Windows to support Disk Management, DiskPart, and DiskRaid. The Virtual Disk Service (VDS) COM interface is being superseded by the Storage Management API. You can continue to use Disk Management and DiskPart to manage storage. These tools cannot be used to manage Storage Spaces, nor can the cmdlets in the Storage module for PowerShell be used to manage dynamic disks. Dynamic disks also are being phased out in favor of Storage Spaces and might not be available in future versions of Windows.

- **Dnscmd**   Displays and manages the configuration of DNS services.

- **Ftp**   Starts the built-in FTP client.

- **Hostname**   Displays the computer name of the local system.

- **Ipconfig**   Displays the TCP/IP properties for network adapters installed on the system. You can also use it to renew and release DHCP information.

- **Nbtstat**   Displays statistics and current connections for NetBIOS over TCP/IP.

- **Net**   Displays a family of useful networking commands.

- **Netsh**   Displays and manages the network configuration of local and remote computers.

- **Netstat**   Displays current TCP/IP connections and protocol statistics.

- **Nslookup**   Checks the status of a host or IP address when used with DNS.

- **Pathping**    Traces network paths, and displays packet loss information.

- **Ping**    Tests the connection to a remote host.

- **Route**    Manages the routing tables on the system.

- **Schtasks**    Displays and manages scheduled tasks on local and remote systems.

- **Tracert**    During testing, determines the network path taken to a remote system.

- **Wbadmin**    Performs backup and recovery operations, including system state recovery and recovery of any type of disk to an alternate location. Also gets disk details, including name, GUID, available space, and related volumes.

- **Wevtutil**    Displays and manages event logs on local and remote systems.

To learn how to use these command-line tools, type the name at a command prompt followed by /?. Windows Server 2012 then provides an overview of how the command is used (in most cases).

## Using Net tools

You can more easily manage most of the tasks performed with the Net commands by using graphical administrative tools and Control Panel utilities. However, some of the Net tools are very useful for performing tasks quickly or for obtaining information, especially during telnet sessions to remote systems. These commands include the following:

- **Net Start**    Starts a service on the system.

- **Net Stop**    Stops a service on the system.

- **Net Time**    Displays the current system time, or synchronizes the system time with another computer.

- **Net Use**    Connects and disconnects from a shared resource.

- **Net View**    Displays a list of network resources available to the system.

To learn how to use any of the Net command-line tools, type **net help** at a command prompt followed by the command name, such as **net help start**. Windows Server 2012 then provides an overview of how the command is used.

## Using Windows PowerShell

Windows PowerShell is installed by default with Windows Server 2012. PowerShell is a full-featured command shell that can use built-in commands called *cmdlets* and built-in

**Chapter 4**

programming features, as well as standard command-line utilities. Normally, PowerShell is installed by default on Windows Server 2012 and on Windows 8 Pro and Windows 8 Enterprise. If so, you can run Windows PowerShell, using the following techniques:

- From Start, a quick way to open Windows PowerShell is to type **powershell** and press Enter.

- From Desktop, PowerShell is normally pinned to the taskbar, enabling you to run PowerShell simply by tapping or clicking the related taskbar button.

> **Note**
>
> If Windows PowerShell is not installed, you can install it as a feature of the operating system. In Windows Server 2012, use the Add Features And Roles Wizard. In Windows 8, use Control Panel to turn on Windows PowerShell as a feature.

After starting Windows PowerShell, you can enter the name of a cmdlet at the prompt and it will run in much the same way as a command-line command. You can also execute cmdlets from within scripts. Cmdlets are named using verb-noun pairs. The verb tells you what the cmdlet does in general. The noun tells you what specifically the cmdlet works with. For example, the get-variable cmdlet either gets all Windows PowerShell environment variables and returns their values or gets a specifically named environment variable and returns its values. These are the common verbs associated with cmdlets:

- **Get-**  Queries a specific object or a subset of a type of object, such as a specified mailbox or all mailbox users.

- **Set-**  Modifies specific settings of an object.

- **Enable-**  Enables a setting or mail-enables a recipient.

- **Disable-**  Disables an enabled setting or mail-disables a recipient.

- **New-**  Creates a new instance of an item, such as a new mailbox.

- **Remove-**  Removes an instance of an item, such as a mailbox.

At the Windows PowerShell prompt, you can get a complete list of cmdlets available by typing **help \*-\***. To get help documentation on a specific cmdlet, type **help** followed by the cmdlet name, such as **help get-variable**.

All cmdlets have configurable aliases as well, which act as shortcuts for executing cmdlets. To list all aliases available, type **get-item –path alias:** at the PowerShell prompt. You can create an alias that invokes any command using the following syntax:

```
new-item –path alias:AliasName –value:FullCommandPath
```

Here, *AliasName* is the name of the alias to create, and *FullCommandPath* is the full path to the command to run, such as:

```
new-item –path alias:sm –value:c:\windows\system32\compmgmtlauncher.exe
```

This example creates the alias *sm* for starting Server Manager. To use this alias, you simply type **sm** and then press Enter when you are working with PowerShell.

# INSIDE OUT  Running Windows commands at the PowerShell prompt

Increasingly administrators are using Windows PowerShell as their go-to prompt for entering both standard Windows commands and Windows PowerShell commands. Although it is true that anything you can type at a command prompt can be typed at the Windows PowerShell prompt, you need to understand the caveats that apply. Windows PowerShell looks for external commands and utilities as part of its normal processing. As long as the external command or utility is found in a directory specified by the PATH environment variable, the command or utility is run as appropriate. However, keep in mind Windows PowerShell execution order could affect whether a command runs as expected. For Windows PowerShell, the execution order is as follows:

1. Alternate built-in or profile-defined aliases
2. Built-in or profile-defined functions
3. Cmdlets or language keywords
4. Scripts with the .ps1 extension
5. External commands, utilities, and files

Thus, when you run a Windows command from the PowerShell prompt, you have to ensure that no element in 1 to 4 of the execution order has the same name as the Windows command you want to run. If an element has the same name, that element will run instead of the expected command.

Chapter 4

**TROUBLESHOOTING**

**Resolving passthrough problems**

When you are working with the PowerShell prompt, arguments you pass in with commands won't be handled as expected. The reason for this is that PowerShell doesn't pass the arguments through in the same way as the command prompt expects them. To resolve this and make it possible to pass in arguments with Windows commands run at the PowerShell prompt, you must enclose the arguments in single quotation marks.

# Working with Server Manager

Server Manager is your central management console. You can use it for the initial setup and configuration of roles and features and much, much more. Not only can Server Manager help you quickly set up a new server, the console also can help you quickly set up and maintain your server environment.

## Getting to know Server Manager

Normally, Windows Server 2012 starts Server Manager whenever you log on and you can access Server Manager on the desktop. If you don't want the console to start each time you log on, tap or click Manage and then tap or click Server Manager Properties. In the Server Manager Properties dialog box, select Do Not Start Server Manager Automatically At Logon and then tap or click OK.

> **Note**
>
> Group Policy can be used to control the automatic start of Server Manager as well. Enable or disable the Do Not Display Server Manager Automatically At Logon policy setting within Computer Configuration\Administrative Templates\System\Server Manager.

As Figure 4-2 shows, the default view of Server Manager is the Dashboard. The Dashboard has quick links for adding roles and features to local and remote servers, adding servers to manage, and creating server groups. You'll find similar options are on the Manage menu:

- **Add Roles And Features** Starts the Add Roles And Features Wizard, which you can use to install roles, role services, and features on the server.

- **Add Other Servers To Manage**   Opens the Add Servers dialog box, which you can use to add servers you want to manage. Added servers are listed when you select the All Servers node. Press and hold or right-click a server in the Servers pane of the All Servers node to display a list of management options, including Restart Server, Manage As, and Remove Server.

- **Create A Server Group**   Opens the Create A Server Group dialog box, which you can use to add servers to server groups for easier management. Server Manager creates role-based groups automatically. For example, domain controllers are listed under AD DS, and you can quickly find information about any domain controllers by selecting the related node.

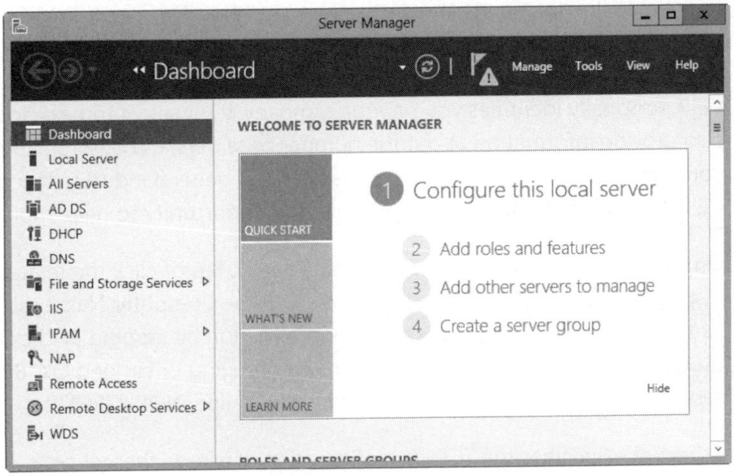

**Figure 4-2** Use the Dashboard for general administration.

In the left pane of Server Manager (also sometimes referred to as the *console tree*), you'll find options for accessing the Dashboard, the local server, all servers added for management, and server groups. When you need to connect to a server using alternate credentials, press and hold or right-click a server in the All Servers node and then select Manage As. In the Windows Security dialog box, enter your alternate credentials and then tap or click OK. Credentials you provide are cleared when you exit Server Manager. To save the credentials and use them each time you log on, select Remember My Credentials in the Windows Security dialog box. You need to repeat this procedure any time you change the password associated with the alternate credentials.

Chapter 4

When you are logged on to a server and select Local Server, you can manage the basic configuration of the server. The Properties panel is where you perform much of your initial server configuration. Properties available for quick management include the following:

- **Computer Name**    Lists the computer name. Tap or click the related link to display the System Properties dialog box with the Computer Name tab selected. You can then change a computer's name by tapping or clicking Change, providing the computer name, and then tapping or clicking OK. By default, servers are assigned a randomly generated name.

- **Customer Experience Improvement Program**    Specifies whether the server is participating in the Customer Experience Improvement Program (CEIP). Tap or click the related link to change the participation settings. Participation in CEIP allows Microsoft to collect information about the way you use the server. Microsoft collects this data to help improve future releases of Windows. No data collected as part of CEIP personally identifies you or your company. If you elect to participate, you can also provide information about the number of servers and desktop computers in your organization, as well as your organization's general industry. If you opt out of CEIP by turning this feature off, you miss the opportunity to help improve Windows.

- **Domain**    Lists the domain membership (if any). Tap or click the related link to display the System Properties dialog box with the Computer Name tab selected. You can then change a computer's domain information by tapping or clicking Change, providing the domain information, and then tapping or clicking OK. By default, servers are configured as part of a workgroup called WORKGROUP.

- **Ethernet**    Specifies the TCP/IP configuration of wired Ethernet connections. Tap or click the related link to display the Network Connections console. You can then configure network connections by double-tapping or double-clicking the connection you want to work with and then tapping or clicking Properties to open the Properties dialog box. By default, servers are configured to use dynamic addressing for both Internet Protocol version 4 (IPv4) and Internet Protocol version 6 (IPv6). You can also display the Network Connections console by tapping or clicking Change Adapter Settings under Tasks in Network And Sharing Center.

- **IE Enhanced Security Configuration**    Specifies the status of Internet Explorer Enhanced Security Configuration (IE ESC). Tap or click the related link to enable or disable IE ESC. If you tap or click the link for this option, you can turn this feature on or off for administrators, users, or both. IE ESC is a security feature that reduces the exposure of a server to potential attacks by raising the default security levels in Internet Explorer security zones and changing default Internet Explorer settings. By default, IE ESC is enabled for both administrators and users.

INSIDE OUT  Understanding Enhanced Security Configuration

Enabling IE ESC reduces the functionality of Internet Explorer but is recommended for both users and administrators. When IE ESC is enabled, security zones are configured as follows: The Internet zone is set to Medium-High, the Trusted Sites zone is set to Medium, the Local Intranet zone is set to Medium-Low, and the Restricted zone is set to High. Additionally, the following Internet settings are changed: The Enhanced Security Configuration dialog box is on, third-party browser extensions are off, sounds in webpages are off, animations in webpages are off, signature checking for downloaded programs is on, server certificate revocation is on, encrypted pages are not saved, temporary Internet files are deleted when the browser is closed, warnings for secure and nonsecure mode changes are on, and memory protection is on.

- **NIC Teaming**   Shows the status and configuration of network interface card (NIC) teaming. Tap or click the related link to add or remove teamed interfaces and to manage related options.

- **Product ID**   Shows the product identifier for Windows Server. Tap or click the related link to enter a product key and activate the operating system over the Internet.

- **Remote Desktop**   Opens the System Properties dialog box with the Remote tab selected. You can then configure Remote Desktop by selecting the configuration option you want to use and tapping or clicking OK. By default, no remote connections to a server are allowed. In the Small Icons or Large Icons view of Control Panel, you can display the System Properties dialog box with the Remote tab selected by double-tapping or double-clicking System and then tapping or clicking Remote Settings in the left pane.

- **Remote Management**   Specifies whether remote management of this server from other servers is enabled. Tap or click the related link to enable or disable remote management.

- **Time Zone**   Lists the current time zone for the server. Tap or click the related link to display the Date And Time dialog box. You can then configure the server's time zone by tapping or clicking Change Time Zone, selecting the appropriate time zone, and then tapping or clicking OK twice. You can also display the Date And Time dialog box by pressing and holding or right-clicking the clock on the taskbar and then selecting Adjust Date/Time. Although all servers are configured to synchronize time automatically with an Internet time server, the time synchronization process does not change a computer's time zone.

Chapter 4

- **Windows Error Reporting**   Specifies the status of Windows Error Reporting (WER). Tap or click the related link to change the participation settings for WER. In most cases, you'll want to enable WER for at least the first 60 days following the installation of the operating system. With WER enabled, your server sends descriptions of problems to Microsoft, and Windows notifies you of possible solutions to those problems. You can view problem reports and possible solutions using Action Center. To open Action Center, tap or click the Action Center icon in the notification area of the taskbar and then select Open Action Center.

- **Windows Firewall**   Lists the status of Windows Firewall. If Windows Firewall is active, this property displays the name of the firewall profile that currently applies and the firewall status. Tap or click the related link to display the Windows Firewall utility. By default, Windows Firewall is enabled. In the Small Icons or Large Icons view of Control Panel, you can display Windows Firewall by tapping or clicking the Windows Firewall option.

- **Windows Update**   Specifies the current configuration of Windows Update. Tap or click the related link to display the Windows Update utility in Control Panel, which you can then use to enable automatic updating (if Windows Update is disabled) or to check for updates (if Windows Update is enabled). In the Small Icons or Large Icons view of Control Panel, you can display Windows Update by selecting the Windows Update option.

Other information about the local server is organized into several main headings, each with an associated management panel. The available management panels include

- **Best Practices Analyzer**   Allows you to run the Best Practices Analyzer on the server and review the results. To start a scan, tap or click Tasks and then tap or click Start BPA Scan.

- **Events**   Provides summary information about warning and error events from the server's event logs. Tap or click an event to display more information about the event.

- **Performance**   Allows you to configure and view the status of performance alerts for CPU and memory usage. To configure performance alerts, tap or click Tasks and then tap or click Configure Performance Alerts.

- **Properties**   Shows the computer name, domain, network IP configuration, time zone, and more. Each property can be tapped or clicked to quickly display a related management interface.

- **Roles And Features**   Lists the roles and features installed on the server, in the approximate order of installation.

- **Services**    Lists the services running on the server by name, status, and start type. Press and hold or right-click a service to manage its run status.

When you press and hold or right-click a server name in the Servers pane of a server group or in the All Servers view, you open an extended list of management options. These options perform the corresponding task or open the corresponding management tool with the selected server in focus. For example, if you right-click CorpServer53 and then select Computer Management, Computer Management connects to CorpServer53 and then opens.

## Adding servers for management

Before you can use Server Manager to manage remote servers, you must add the servers for management. Any server running Windows Server 2012 can be easily added. Servers running Windows Server 2008 with Service Pack 2 or later and Windows Server 2008 Release 2 with Service Pack 1 or later can be added as well, as long as each server has .NET Framework 4.0 and Windows Management Framework 3.0 and has been enabled for remote management.

You can add a single server to Server Manager by completing these steps:

1. Open Server Manager. In the left pane, select All Servers to view the servers that have been added for management already. If the server you want to work with isn't listed, select Add Servers on the Manage menu to display the Add Servers dialog box.

2. In the Add Servers dialog box, the Active Directory panel is selected by default. Use the options on the Active Directory panel to enter the computer name or fully qualified domain name (FQDN) of the remote server that is running Windows Server. After you enter a name, tap or click Find Now. Alternatively, use the options on the DNS panel to specify a server by computer name or IP address and then tap or click the Search button.

3. In the Name list, double-tap or double-click the server to add it to the Selected list.

4. Repeat steps 2 and 3 to add others servers. Tap or click OK.

Rather than add servers one by one, you can use the Import process to add multiple servers. To do this, follow these steps:

1. Create a text file that has one host name, fully qualified domain name, or IP address per line.

2. In Server Manager, select Add Servers on the Manage menu. In the Add Servers dialog box, select the Import panel.

3. Tap or click the options button to the right of the File box, and then use the Open dialog box to locate and open the server list.

4. In the Computer list, double-tap or double-click each server you want to add to the Selected list. Tap or click OK.

Server Manager tracks the services, events, and more for each added server. Servers are listed in the All Servers view by server name, IP address, and manageability status. Server Manager always resolves IP addresses to host names. If a server is listed as Not Accessible, you typically need to log on locally and take corrective action as necessary. For example, you might need to use a console logon to enable remote management.

## Creating server groups

When you add servers to Server Management, the servers are added to the appropriate server groups automatically based on the roles and features installed. Automatically created server groups make it easier to manage the various roles and features that are installed on your servers. If you select the AD DS group, as an example, you see a list of the domain controllers you added for management as well as any critical or warning events for these servers and the status of services the role depends on.

You can create your own server groups as well to group servers by department, geographic location, or other characteristic. When you create groups, the servers you want to work with don't have to be added to Server Manager already. You can add servers to a group at any time and those servers are added automatically for management as well.

You can create a server group by completing these steps:

1. Open Server Manager. Select Create Server Group on the Manage menu to display the Create Server Group dialog box.

   Enter a descriptive name for the group. Use the panels and options provided to add servers to the group with the following in mind:

   ○ The Active Directory panel allows you to enter the computer name or fully qualified domain name of the remote server that is running Windows Server. After you enter a name, tap or click Find Now. In the Name list, double-tap or double-click a server to add it to the Selected list.

   ○ The DNS panel allows you to add servers by computer name or IP address. After you enter the name or IP address, tap or click the Search button. In the Name list, double-tap or double-click a server to add it to the Selected list.

   ○ The Import panel allows you to import a list of servers. Tap or click the options button to the right of the File box, and then use the Open dialog box to locate and open the server list. In the Computer list, double-tap or double-click a server to add it to the Selected list.

○ The Server Pool panel, selected by default, lists servers that have been added for management already. If a server you want to add to your group is listed here, add it to the group by double-tapping or double-clicking it.

**2.** Tap or click OK to create the server group.

## Enabling remote management

You can use Server Manager and other Microsoft Management Consoles (MMCs) to perform some management tasks on remote computers, as long as the computers are in the same domain or you are working in a workgroup and have added the remote computers in a domain as trusted hosts. You can connect to servers running Full Server, Minimal Server Interface, and Server Core installations. On the computer you want to use for managing remote computers, you should be running either Windows Server 2012 or Windows 8 and you need to install the Remote Server Administration Tools.

With Windows Server 2012, remote management is enabled by default for applications and commands that use the following:

- Windows Remote Management (WinRM) and Windows PowerShell remote access for management

- Windows Management Instrumentation (WMI) and Distributed Component Object Model (DCOM) remote access for management

You'll find that these types of applications and commands are enabled for remote management because related inbound rules and exceptions for Windows Firewall are enabled. For remote management, Windows Firewall has specific exceptions for Windows Management Instrumentation, Windows Remote Management, and Windows Remote Management (Compatibility). In Windows Firewall With Advanced Security, there are inbound rules that correspond to the standard firewall-allowed applications. For WMI, the inbound rules are Windows Management Instrumentation (WMI-In), Windows Management Instrumentation (DCOM-In), and Windows Management Instrumentation (ASync-In). For WinRM, the matching inbound rule is Windows Remote Management (HTTP-In). For WinRM compatibility, the matching inbound rule is Windows Remote Management - Compatibility Mode (HTTP-In).

You manage these exceptions or rules in either the standard Windows Firewall or in Windows Firewall With Advanced Security, not both. Generally, if you want to allow remote management using Server Manager, MMCs, and Windows PowerShell, you should permit WMI, WinRM, and WinRM compatibility exceptions in Windows Firewall.

When you are working with Server Manager, you can select Local Server in the console tree to view the status of the remote management property. If you don't want to allow remote management of the local server, tap or click the related link. Next, in the Configure Remote Management dialog box, clear Enable Remote Management Of This Server From Other Computers and then tap or click OK.

When you clear the Enable Remote Management Of This Server From Other Computers check box and then tap or click OK, Server Manager performs several background tasks that disable Windows Remote Management (WinRM) and Windows PowerShell remote access for management on the local server. One of these tasks is to turn off the related exception that allows applications to communicate through Windows Firewall using Windows Remote Management. The exceptions for Windows Management Instrumentation and Windows Remote Management (Compatibility) aren't affected.

You must be a member of the Administrators group on computers you want to manage by using Server Manager. For remote connections in a workgroup-to-workgroup or workgroup-to-domain configuration, you should be logged on using the built-in Administrator account or configure the LocalAccountTokenFilterPolicy registry key to allow remote access from your computer. To set this key, enter the following command at an elevated, administrator command prompt:

```
reg add HKLM\SOFTWARE\Microsoft\Windows\CurrentVersion\Policies\System /v
LocalAccountTokenFilterPolicy /t REG_DWORD /d 1 /f
```

Another way to enable remote management is to type **Configure-SMRemoting.exe –Enable** at an elevated, administrator prompt.

Although these techniques enable basic remote management of computers, you also need to enable rules for these specific management areas:

- **Disks and volumes**   Remote Volume Management must be allowed in Windows Firewall to remotely manage a computer's disks and volumes in Computer Management or Disk Management. In the advanced firewall, there are several related rules that allow management of the Virtual Disk Service and Virtual Disk Service Loader.

> **Note**
> You don't need to enable Virtual Disk Service–related rules to remotely manage Storage Spaces. You manage Storage Spaces in Server Manager using the options available when you are working with File And Storage Services.

- **Event Log**    Remote Event Log Management must be allowed in Windows Firewall to remotely manage a computer's event logs. In the advanced firewall, there are several related rules that allow management via named pipes (NP) and remote procedure calls (RPCs).

- **Remote Desktop**    Remote Desktop must be enabled to allow someone to connect to a server using Remote Desktop. You also must configure access as discussed later in this chapter in "Remote Desktop essentials."

- **Scheduled Tasks**    Remote Scheduled Task Management must be allowed in Windows Firewall to remotely manage a computer's scheduled tasks. In the advanced firewall, there are several related rules that allow management of scheduled tasks via RPC.

- **Services**    Remote Service Management must be allowed in Windows Firewall to remotely manage a computer's services. In the advanced firewall, there are several related rules that allow management via named pipes and RPCs.

Only Remote Service Management is enabled by default. Remote management is enabled by default on Server Core. You can configure remote management on a Server Core installation of Windows Server 2012 using sconfig. Start the Server Configuration utility by typing **sconfig**.

# INSIDE OUT    Using Windows PowerShell for remote management

Windows PowerShell provides several ways for you to work with remote computers. One way is to use an interactive remote session. To do this, open an elevated, administrator Windows PowerShell prompt. Type **enter-pssession** *ComputerName* **–credential** *UserName*, where *ComputerName* is the name of the remote computer and *UserName* is the name of a user who is a member of the Administrators group on the remote computer or in the domain of which the remote computer is a member. When prompted to enter the authorized user's password, type the password and then press Enter. You can now enter commands in the session as you would if you were using Windows PowerShell locally. To exit the session, type **exit-pssession**.

Chapter 4

# Working with Computer Management

Computer Management, shown in Figure 4-3, provides tools for managing local and remote systems. The tools available through the console tree provide the core functionality and are divided into the following three categories, as shown in the accompanying screen:

- System Tools

- Storage

- Services And Applications

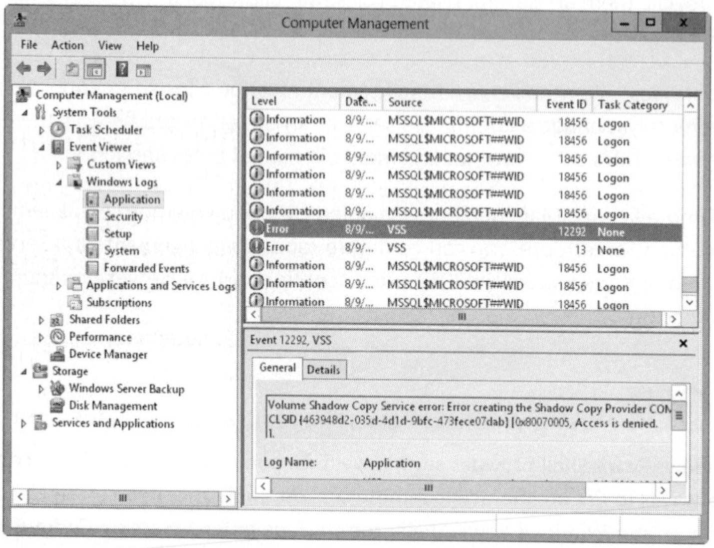

**Figure 4-3**  Computer Management provides several tools for managing systems.

## Computer Management system tools

The system tools are designed to manage systems and view system information. The available system tools are these:

- **Task Scheduler**   Used to view the Task Scheduler Library as well as to create and manage tasks.

- **Event Viewer**   Used to view the event logs on the selected computer. Event logs are covered in Chapter 10, "Performance monitoring and tuning."

- **Shared Folders**   Used to manage the properties of shared folders as well as sessions for users working with shared folders and the files the users are working with. Managing shared folders is covered in Chapter 15, "File sharing and security."

- **Local Users And Groups**   On non–domain controller (DC) computers, used to manage local users and local user groups on the currently selected computer. Local users and local user groups aren't a part of Active Directory and are managed instead through the Local Users And Groups view. Domain controllers don't have local users or groups, and because of this there isn't a Local Users And Groups view. Local users and groups are discussed in Chapter 30, "Managing users, groups, and computers."

- **Performance**   Used to monitor system reliability and performance through charts and logs. You can also use this tool to alert users of adverse performance conditions. For more information about performance logging and alerting, see "Performance logging" in Chapter 11, "Comprehensive performance analysis and logging."

- **Device Manager**   Used as a central location for checking the status of any device installed on a computer and for updating the associated device drivers. You can also use it to troubleshoot device problems. Managing devices is covered in Chapter 7, "Managing and troubleshooting hardware."

## Computer Management storage tools

The Computer Management storage tools display drive information and provide access to drive-management tools. The available storage tools include the following:

- **Windows Server Backup**   Used to manage backups for server data. As discussed in Chapter 17, "Backup and recovery," you enable backups by adding the Windows Server Backup feature.

- **Disk Management**   Used to manage hard disks and the way they are partitioned. You can also use it to manage volume sets and software-based redundant array of independent disks (RAID) arrays. Disk Management is discussed in "Configuring storage" in Chapter 12, "Storage management."

> **Note**
> Storage Spaces are preferred to software-based RAID and traditional disk-partitioning techniques. Before you implement software-based RAID or partition disks with Disk Management, you might want to review the options for creating Storage Spaces and allocating storage using Storage Spaces. See "Managing Storage Spaces" in Chapter 14.

Chapter 4

## Computer Management Services And Applications tools

The Computer Management Services And Applications tools help you manage services and applications installed on the server. Any application or service-related task that can be performed in a separate tool can be performed through the Services And Applications node as well. For example, if the currently selected system has DHCP installed, you can manage DHCP through the server Applications And Services node. You could also use the DHCP tool, which can be accessed on the Tools menu in Server Manager, and either way, you can perform the same tasks.

# Using Control Panel

From Start, you access Control Panel by tapping or clicking the Control Panel tile. From the desktop, you can display Control Panel by accessing the Charms bar, tapping or clicking Settings, and then tapping or clicking Control Panel. The Control Panel in Windows Server 2012 has two views:

- Category Control Panel, shown in Figure 4-4, is the default view that provides access to system utilities by category, utility, and key tasks. Category Control Panel view is also referred to simply as Control Panel.

- Standard Control Panel is an alternate view in which each Control Panel utility is listed separately by name.

**Figure 4-4** Access system utilities and change operating system settings using Control Panel.

You use the View By option to specify the view you want to use. Select Category on the View By list to use Category Control Panel. Select Large Icons or Small Icons on the View By list to use Standard Control Panel.

Because Category Control Panel provides quick access to frequent tasks, it is the view you typically will use most often. With this view, Control Panel opens as a console on which categories of utilities are listed. For each category, there's a top-level link and under this are several of the most frequently performed tasks for the category.

Tap or clicking a category link provides a list of utilities in that category. For each utility listed within a category, there's a link to open the utility, and under this are several of the most frequently performed tasks for the utility.

In Category Control Panel view, all utilities and tasks run with a single tap or click. The left pane of the console has a link to take you to the Control Panel Home page, links for each category, and links for recently performed tasks. Not only is this very efficient, but it's very easy to use.

As you might already know, some Control Panel utilities offer a simple interface and are easy to work with, while others are fairly complex. Utilities that require little or no explanation are not discussed in this text; you will find a discussion of some of the more complex utilities later in this section.

> ### Tip
>
> When you are working with Category Control Panel view, you'll see a Search box in the upper right corner. To quickly find what you are looking for, type in part of the tool or task name. Consider the following example: Normally, you access the Change The Display Setting task under Control Panel\Appearance\Display (or Control Panel\ Appearance And Personalization\Personalization if Desktop Experience is installed), which requires you to navigate through several Control Panel pages. If you type **display** in the Search box instead, you can quickly display this task and tap or click it.
>
> Keep in mind that you don't have to open Control Panel to search for and find its settings. By accessing the Charms bar, tapping or clicking Search, and then tapping or clicking Settings, you can quickly search for and find settings in Control Panel.

## Using the Folder Options utility

The Folder Options utility, shown in Figure 4-5, is used to control how File Explorer displays files and folders and to set a wide variety of folder and file options, including the type of desktop used, the folder views used, whether offline files are used, and whether you must single-click/single-tap or double-click/double-tap to open items.

**Figure 4-5**  Change how folders are viewed and opened.

In Control Panel, you can access the Folder Options utility by tapping or clicking Appearance (or Appearance And Personalization if Desktop Experience is installed), and then tapping or clicking Folder Options. As an administrator, you will probably want to manage the following options:

- **Single-Click To Open An Item (Point To Select)**   Select this option on the General tab to enable single-click/single-tap to open and point to select.

> **Note**
>
> Because menu options and Control Panel options open with a single click/single tap by default, you might want to configure your computer to use single-click to open items such as documents as well. This might help you avoid confusion as to whether you need to tap or click once or tap or click twice. When you have the single-click option configured, pointing to an item selects it.

- **Show Hidden Files, Folders, And Drives**   Select this option on the View tab to see hidden files, folders, and drives.

- **Hide Extensions For Known File Types**   Clear this check box on the View tab to see file names as well as file extensions.

- **Hide Protected Operating System Files**   Clear this check box on the View tab so that you can see and work with operating system files, which are otherwise hidden.

# Using the System console

You use the System console to view system information and perform basic configuration tasks. To access the System console, tap or click System And Security and then System in Control Panel. As Figure 4-6 shows, the System console is divided into four basic areas that provide links for performing common tasks and a system overview:

- **Windows Edition**   Shows the operating system edition and version. In addition, it lists any service packs that you've applied.

- **System**   Lists the processor, memory, and type of operating system installed on the computer.

- **Computer Name, Domain, And Workgroup Settings**   Provides the computer name, description, domain, and workgroup details. If you want to change any of this information, tap or click Change Settings and then tap or click Change in the System Properties dialog box.

- **Windows Activation**   Shows whether you have activated the operating system and the product key. If Windows Server 2012 isn't activated yet, tap or click the link provided to start the activation process and then follow the prompts.

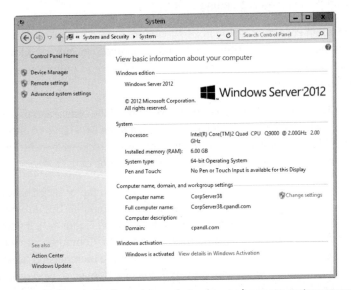

**Figure 4-6** Use the System console to view and manage system properties.

When you're working in the System console, links in the left pane provide quick access to key support tools, including the following:

- Device Manager

- Remote Settings

- Advanced System Settings

Although volume-licensed versions of Windows Server 2012 might not require activation or product keys, retail versions of Windows Server 2012 require both activation and product keys. If Windows Server 2012 has not been activated, you can activate the operating system by selecting Activate Windows Now under Windows Activation. You can also activate Windows by typing **slmgr –ato** at a command prompt. You can change the product key provided during installation of Windows Server 2012 to stay in compliance with your licensing plan. At a command prompt, type **slmgr –ipk** followed by the product key you want to use, and then press Enter.

When Windows finishes validating the product key, you need to reactivate the operating system. The Windows Software Management Licensing tool has many other options, including options for offline activation using a confirmation identifier. To view this and other options, type **slmgr** at a command prompt.

From within the System console, you can access the System Properties dialog box and use this dialog box to manage system properties. Tap or click Change Settings under Computer Name, Domain, And Workgroup Settings.

You use the System Properties dialog box to configure system properties, including properties for managing the operating system configuration, startup, shutdown, environment variables, and user profiles. System is the most advanced Control Panel utility, and its options are organized into several tabs.

The Computer Name tab displays the full computer name of the system and the domain membership, if applicable. The full computer name is essentially the DNS name of the computer, which also identifies the computer's place within the Active Directory hierarchy. To change the computer name or move a computer to a new domain, use one of the following procedures:

- For member servers (not domain controllers), you can tap or click Change to change the system name and domain associated with the computer. This displays the Computer Name/Domain Changes dialog box (as shown in Figure 4-7). If you want to change the computer's name, type a new name in the Computer Name field. If you want to change the computer's domain or workgroup membership, select Domain or Workgroup as appropriate, and then enter the new domain or workgroup name. Tap or click OK. If you change the computer's domain, the computer will be moved to that domain and, in which case, you might be prompted to provide the appropriate credentials for joining the computer to that domain.

**Figure 4-7**  Change the computer name and domain or workgroup membership.

- For domain controllers, you can tap or click Change to modify the name of the computer, but doing so will make the domain controller temporarily unavailable to other computers in the domain. You cannot use this feature to change the domain in which the domain controller is running. To change the domain, you must demote the domain controller to make it a member server, change the computer's network ID by using the System utility, and then promote the server so that it is once again a domain controller.

The other System utility tabs are as follows:

- **Hardware**  Used to configure a computer's Device Installation Settings. If you enable these settings, Windows Server 2012 checks for driver updates as part of the normal update process. On the Hardware tab, tap or click the Device Installation Settings button. Select the desired update setting. By default, Windows Server 2012 is set to never install driver software from Windows Update. Typically, this is the best setting because you'll want to test all driver updates before deploying them to production servers. In a test or development lab, however, you might want to configure Windows Server 2012 to automatically install the best driver software from Windows Update.

- **Advanced**  Used to control many of the key features of the Windows operating system, including application performance, user profiles, startup and recovery, environment variables, and virtual memory. User profiles are discussed in Chapter 30, and application performance is discussed in Chapter 10.

- **Remote**  Used to control Remote Assistance invitations and Remote Desktop connections. Remote Assistance invitations are primarily used with workstations and not servers. Remote Desktop is discussed later in this chapter.

Chapter 4

# Customizing the desktop and the taskbar

By default, the only items on the Windows Server 2012 desktop are the Recycle Bin and the taskbar. That's it. Everything else has been cleared away to allow you to customize the desktop anyway you want. The problem is that some of the missing items—such as Computer, Network, and Internet Explorer—were pretty useful, or at least most of us have grown so accustomed to having the items on the desktop that we expect them to be there. So, if you're like me, the first thing you'll want to do to customize the desktop is to add frequently accessed programs, files, and folders and to restore the missing items. Another thing you might want to do is customize the taskbar so that it works the way you want it to. By default, the taskbar doesn't automatically hide or lock, and it might include items that you don't want.

## Configuring desktop items

Windows Server 2012 allows you to drag program shortcuts, files, and folders from a File Explorer window onto the desktop. Simply tap or click the item you want to move, hold down the mouse button, and drag the item to a location on the desktop. When you release the mouse button, the item is moved from its original location to the desktop. If you want to copy the item instead of moving it, press Ctrl, tap or click the item, and then hold the mouse button while dragging the item to the new location. On the desktop, release the mouse button and then release the Ctrl key.

You can, in fact, use the copy and move techniques to add shortcuts for your personal folder, Computer, Network, and Control Panel to the desktop. If you installed the Desktop Experience feature, there's another way to add these items to the desktop so that they appear as standard desktop icons instead of shortcuts. Press and hold or right-click an empty area of the desktop, and choose Personalize. In the left pane of the Personalization window, tap or click Change Desktop Icons under the Tasks heading. This opens the Desktop Icon Settings dialog box, shown in Figure 4-8.

In the Desktop Icon Settings dialog box, select the items that you want to display on the desktop—for instance, Computer, Network, and Control Panel. Several uses for Computer and Network aren't obvious but are great time-savers.

Use Computer in the following ways:

- Press and hold or right-click and choose Manage to start Server Manager.

- Press and hold or right-click and choose Properties to display the System console in Control Panel.

- Press and hold or right-click and choose Map Network Drive or Disconnect Network Drive to manage network shares.

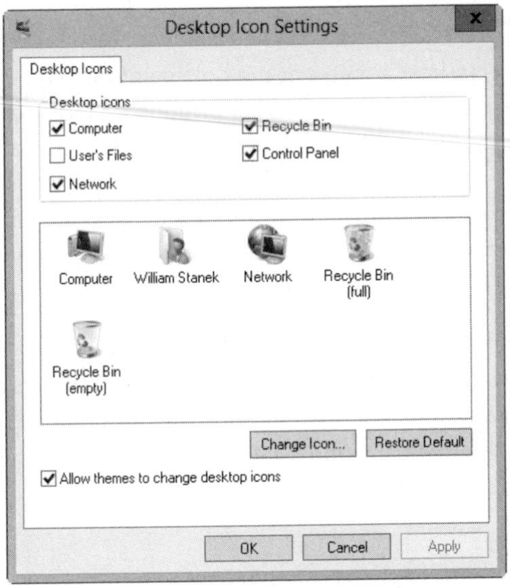

**Figure 4-8** Add or remove desktop icons.

Use Network as follows:

- Press and hold or right-click and choose Open to find computers on the network.

- Press and hold or right-click and choose Properties to display the Network And Sharing Center.

- Press and hold or right-click and choose Map Network Drive or Disconnect Network Drive to manage network shares.

## Configuring the taskbar

The taskbar is one of those areas of the desktop that most people take for granted. It's sort of like people think, "Hey, there's the taskbar. What can I open?" when they should be thinking, "Hey, there's a taskbar. It tracks all the running programs for quick access, and I can customize it to work the way I want it to." Beyond the hidden buttons on the left and right, the taskbar has two main areas:

- **Programs/Toolbars**  Shows icons for pinned and running programs, which can be grouped according to type, as well as the toolbars that are selected for display.

- **Notification**  Shows the system clock and programs that were loaded automatically at startup and that are running in the background.

You can change the behavior and properties of these taskbar areas in many ways.

## Changing the taskbar size and position

In the default configuration, the taskbar appears at the bottom of the screen and is sized so that one row of options is visible. As long as the taskbar position isn't locked, you can move it to any edge of the Windows desktop and resize it as necessary. To move the taskbar, simply tap or click it and hold the mouse button while dragging it to a different edge of the desktop. When you move the mouse toward the left, right, top, or bottom edge of the desktop, you'll see a gray outline that shows you where the taskbar will appear. When you release the mouse button, the taskbar will appear in the new location.

With a left-docked or right-docked taskbar, you'll often have to resize the taskbar somewhat to ensure that you can easily access all its features. I've found this approach useful when I am troubleshooting a system and I have lots of programs running and want to be able to switch quickly between them. In contrast, a top-docked taskbar seems to remove the clutter from the desktop, and I've found it useful when I don't want to use the Auto Hide feature.

To resize the taskbar, move the mouse pointer over the taskbar edge and then drag it up or down, left or right, as appropriate.

> **Note**
> If the taskbar appears to get stuck in one location when you are trying to move it, simply log off and then log back on. As long as the taskbar isn't locked, you should then be able to move the taskbar.

## Using Auto Hide and locking

Windows Server 2012 has several features that control the visibility of the taskbar. You can enable the Auto Hide feature to hide the taskbar from view when it is not in use. You can lock the taskbar so that it cannot be resized or repositioned. After the taskbar is positioned and sized the way you want it, I recommend enabling both of these options. In this way, the taskbar has a fixed location and is visible when it is pointed to but otherwise hidden.

You can enable these options as shown in Figure 4-9 by pressing and holding or right-clicking the taskbar and then choosing Properties from the shortcut menu. Afterward, select the Lock The Taskbar and Auto-Hide The Taskbar check boxes as appropriate. Then tap or click OK.

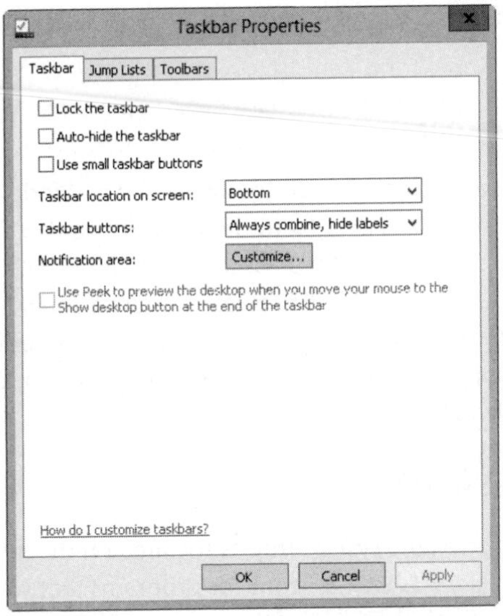

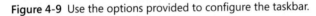

**Figure 4-9** Use the options provided to configure the taskbar.

---

**Note**

Locking the taskbar doesn't prevent you from changing the taskbar in the future. If you want to change the taskbar, all you must do is press and hold or right-click the taskbar and then clear the Lock The Taskbar check box. You can then make any necessary changes and, if desired, relock the taskbar to ensure that the settings are protected from being accidentally changed.

---

## Combining similar taskbar items

By default, Windows groups similar taskbar items together to reduce taskbar clutter. For example, if you open multiple MMCs, these consoles are grouped under a single button and are then accessible by tapping or clicking the button and selecting the individual MMC you want to use. In some ways, this is a good thing, but it can be confusing.

You can control whether similar items are grouped together by pressing and holding or right-clicking the taskbar and then choosing Properties from the shortcut menu. Afterward, use the Taskbar Buttons list to specify whether and how similar items are grouped. Instead of the default Always Combine, Hide Labels option, which combines similar items by default and hides item labels, you can specify that Windows Server does the following:

- **Combine When Taskbar Is Full**    Combines similar items only when the taskbar is full. Also, it displays labels for items on the taskbar.

- **Never Combine**    Ensures items are never combined and that labels for items are always displayed.

## Pinning shortcuts to the taskbar

Windows Server 2012 does not have a Quick Launch toolbar. Instead, Windows Server 2012 allows you to pin commonly used programs directly to the taskbar. You can do this whenever you are working with the Start screen. Simply press and hold or right-click an item you want to add to the taskbar, and then tap or click Pin To Taskbar. Once you pin an item to the taskbar, you can change the item's position on the taskbar by tapping or clicking and dragging the program's icon. To unpin an item, press and hold or right-click the item on the taskbar, and then tap or click Unpin This Program From Taskbar.

## Controlling programs in the notification area

The notification area, also referred to as the *system tray*, is the area on the far right side of the taskbar. It shows the system clock as well as icons for programs that were loaded automatically by the operating system at startup and that are running in the background. Notifications for the operating system and programs behave in different ways:

- If you move the pointer over a system notification icon, you'll see a status window that provides information about the notification.

- If you move the pointer over a system notification icon and tap or click, you'll see a control window that provides information about the notification and that you can use to configure the related feature.

- If you move the pointer over a program notification icon and then tap or click, you'll see a shortcut menu (if one is available).

- If you press and hold or right-click a system or program notification icon, you'll see a shortcut menu (if one is available).

User-specified programs that run in the background are managed through the Startup folder. The Startup folder is configured at two levels. Under the %SystemDrive%\ProgramData\Microsoft\Windows\Start Menu\Programs folder, there is a Startup folder for all users of a given system. Any program referenced in this folder is run in the background regardless of which user logs on. Within the profile data for individual users, there is a

Startup folder specific to each user's logon under %SystemDrive%\Users\%UserName%\AppData\Roaming\Microsoft\Windows\Start Menu\Programs. Programs referenced in a personal Startup folder are run only when that user logs on.

You can add or remove startup programs for all users by opening File Explorer and navigating to the %SystemDrive%\ProgramData\Microsoft\Windows\Start Menu\Programs\Startup folder. Add or remove startup programs for all users as follows:

- To add startup programs, create a shortcut to the program that you want to run.

- To remove a startup program, delete its shortcut from the Startup folder.

You can add or remove startup programs for individual users as well, such as the administrator. To do this, open File Explorer and navigate to the %SystemDrive%\Users\%UserName%\AppData\Roaming\Microsoft\Windows\Start Menu\Programs\Startup folder, where *%UserName%* is the name of the user you want to work with. Finally, add or remove startup programs for this user as discussed previously.

User-specified programs that run in the background are only one type of program that is displayed in the notification area. Some programs, such as Windows Update, are managed by the Windows operating system. For example, Windows Update runs periodically to check for updates to the operating system. When an update is detected, the user can be notified and given the opportunity to apply the update. Other types of programs are configured during installation to run in the background at startup, such as an antivirus program. You can typically enable or disable the display of notification area icons related to these programs through the setup options in the related applications. Windows Server 2012 also provides a common interface for controlling whether the icons for these programs are displayed in the notification area. This allows you to specify whether and how icons are displayed on a per-program basis.

To control the display of icons in the notification area, press and hold or right-click the taskbar, and then choose Properties from the shortcut menu. In the Taskbar Properties dialog box, tap or click Customize under Notification Area. This opens the Notification Area Icons page in Control Panel as shown in Figure 4-10.

Chapter 4

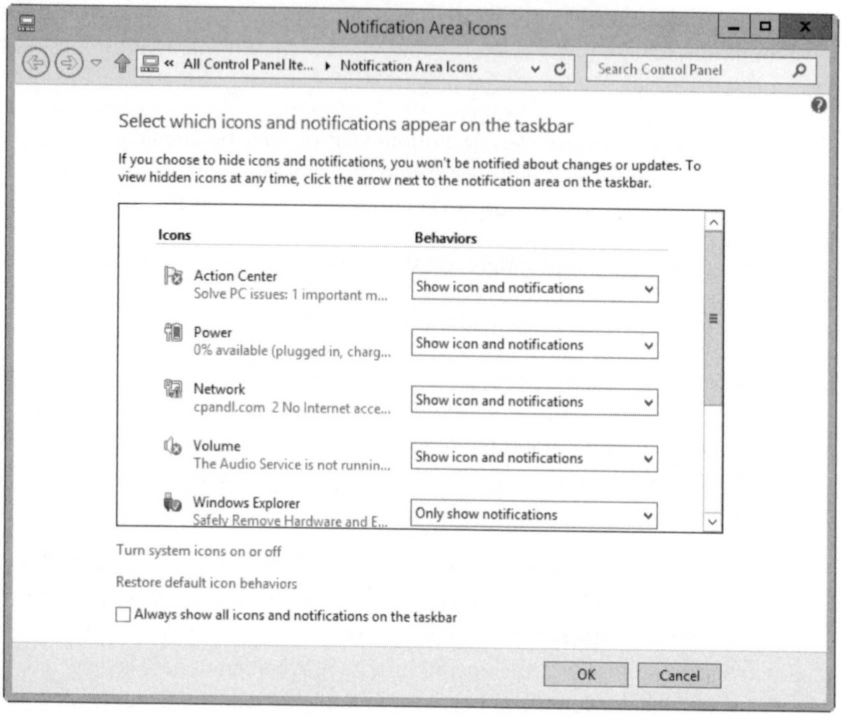

**Figure 4-10**  You can customize notifications for notification area items.

You can now optimize the notification behavior for current items displayed in the notification area as well as items that were displayed in the past but aren't currently active. The Icons column shows the name of the program. The Behaviors column shows the currently selected notification behavior. To change the notification behavior, tap or click the related list in the Behaviors column and then select one of the following options:

- **Show Icon And Notifications**   The default. This option shows the program's icon and notifications when active, and it hides the icon otherwise.

- **Hide Icons And Notifications**   Hides the program's icon and notifications, whether they are active or inactive.

- **Only Show Notifications**   Shows notifications for the program, but doesn't show the program's icon.

By default, inactive icons are shown only when they are active and are otherwise hidden to reduce clutter. If you want all icons to be always displayed, select Always Show All Icons And Notifications On The Taskbar.

# Optimizing toolbars

Several custom toolbars are available for the taskbar. You can create your own toolbars as well. For example, if your organization has custom applications or a preferred suite of applications, you can add buttons for these applications to the toolbar. If applications are no longer used, you can later remove the additional buttons.

## Displaying custom toolbars

Toolbars available for the taskbar include the following:

- **Address**    Provides an Address text box into which you can type Uniform Resource Locators (URLs) and other addresses that you want to access, either on the World Wide Web, on the local network, or on the local computer. When full file paths are specified, the default application for the file is launched automatically to display the specified file, such as Internet Explorer or Microsoft Office Word. One of the things you might not realize about the Address toolbar is that it retains the same URL history as the Address bar in Internet Explorer, meaning if you previously opened a document on a network share, you could quickly access it again through the history.

- **Desktop**    Provides access to all the shortcuts on the local desktop so that you don't have to minimize windows to access them.

- **Links**    Provides access to the Links folder on the Favorites menu of Internet Explorer. To add links to files, webpages, or other resources, drag shortcuts onto the Links toolbar. To remove links, press and hold or right-click the link and select Delete. When prompted, confirm the action by tapping or clicking Yes.

- **Touch Keyboard**    Provides quick access to the touch keyboard.

You can display or hide individual toolbars by pressing and holding or right-clicking the taskbar to display the shortcut menu, pointing to Toolbars, and then selecting the toolbar you want to use. This toggles the toolbar on and off.

> ## Have toolbars use less space by turning off the title
>
> **B**y default, a name label is displayed for all toolbars except the touch keyboard. This label wastes taskbar space, and you can turn it off. Press and hold or right-click the toolbar and then choose Show Title to clear the option. The option is a toggle; if you want to see the title again, repeat this procedure.

Chapter 4

## Creating personal toolbars

In addition to using the custom toolbars that are available, you can create personal toolbars as well. Personal toolbars are based on existing folders, and their buttons are based on the folder contents. The most common toolbars you might create are ones that point to folders on the computer or shared folders on the network. For example, if you routinely access the C:\Windist, C:\Windows\System32\LogFiles, and C:\Windows\System32\Inetsvr folders, you could add a toolbar to the taskbar that provides quick access buttons to these resources. Then you could access one of the folders simply by tapping or clicking the corresponding toolbar button.

You can create personal toolbars by pressing and holding or right-clicking the taskbar to display the shortcut menu, pointing to Toolbars, and then choosing New Toolbar. This displays the New Toolbar – Choose A Folder dialog box.

Next use the Choose A Folder list box to choose the folder you want to make into a toolbar. When you tap or click OK, the folder is displayed as a new toolbar on the taskbar. If you add shortcuts to the folder, the shortcuts automatically appear on the toolbar as buttons that can be selected. Keep in mind that if you decide that you don't want to use the toolbar anymore and close it, you must reselect the folder before it can be viewed on the taskbar again.

# Using Remote Desktop

Remote support is an important part of administration. Although Server Manager and related MMCs allow you to perform remote management, sometimes you might prefer to connect and work with remote systems as if you were logged on locally, and Remote Desktop allows you to do this.

## Remote Desktop essentials

Using Remote Desktop, you can use a local area network (LAN), wide area network (WAN), or Internet connection to manage computers remotely with the Windows graphical interface. Because all the application processing is performed on the remote system, only the data from devices such as the display, keyboard, and mouse are transmitted over the network.

Remote Desktop is part of Remote Desktop Services. Microsoft has separated Remote Desktop Services into two operating modes:

- Remote Desktop mode
- Remote Desktop Server mode

You enable and configure Remote Desktop using the System utility in Control Panel. You set up a Remote Desktop Server by installing and configuring the appropriate role services for the Remote Desktop Services role.

To be operational, the Remote Desktop and Remote Desktop Server modes both depend on the Remote Desktop Services service being installed and running on the server. By default, the Remote Desktop Services service is installed and configured to run automatically. Both features use the same client, Remote Desktop Connection (RDC), for connecting to remote systems.

> **Note**
> Remote Desktop isn't designed for application serving. Most productivity applications such as Microsoft Office Word, Outlook, and Excel require specific environment settings that are not available through this feature. If you want to work with these types of applications (rather than server applications), you should install and use the Remote Desktop Services role.

No Remote Desktop Client Access License (RD CAL) is required to use Remote Desktop. Windows Server 2012 allows two active administration sessions:

- One administrator can be logged on locally, and another administrator can be logged on remotely.

- Or two administrators can be logged on remotely.

Most remote sessions run in admin mode. The reason for this is that the admin session provides full functionality for administration. Standard Remote Desktop Services connections are created as virtual sessions.

Why is this important? Using admin mode, you can interact with the server just as if you were sitting at the keyboard. This means all notification area messages directed to the console are visible remotely. For security, only two sessions are allowed. If a third administrator tries to log on, the administrator will be prompted to end an existing session so that she can log on.

Although it is recommended that administrators use admin sessions, you can use virtual sessions—hey, that's what they're there for. When working with a virtual session, you can perform most administration tasks, and your key limitation is in your ability to interact with the console session itself. This means users logged on using a virtual session do not see console messages or notifications, cannot install some programs, and cannot perform tasks that require console access.

You'll want to formalize a general policy on how Remote Desktop should be used in your organization. You don't want multiple administrators trying to perform administration tasks on a system because this could cause serious problems. For example, if two administrators are both working with Disk Management, this could cause serious problems with the volumes on the remote system. Because of this, you'll want to coordinate administration tasks with other administrators.

# Configuring Remote Desktop

The two components of Remote Desktop you need to support and configure are Remote Desktop Services for the server portion and the Remote Desktop Connection (RDC) for the client portion.

## Enabling Remote Desktop on servers

Enabling the Remote Desktop mode on all servers on your network is recommended, especially for servers in remote sites that have no local administrators. To view the current status of Remote Desktop on the server, select Local Server in Server Manager and then check the enabled or disabled status for the Remote Desktop entry. Just because Remote Desktop is enabled, doesn't mean the feature is fully configured. With that in mind, tap or click the Enabled or Disabled link for the Remote Desktop entry. This opens the System Properties dialog box to the Remote tab, as shown in Figure 4-11.

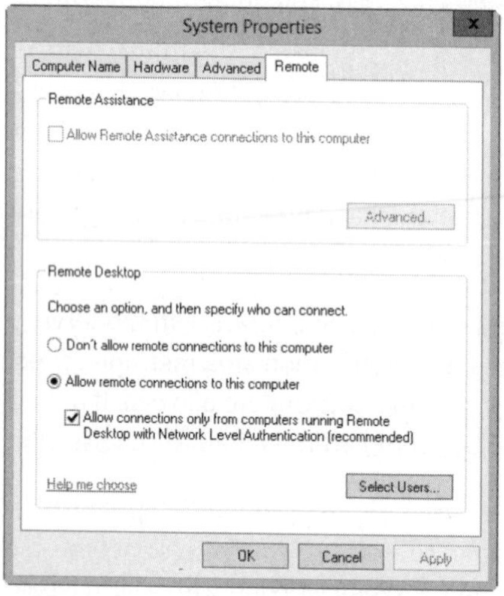

**Figure 4-11**  Enabling Remote Desktop.

You have two configuration options for enabling Remote Desktop. You can do either of the following:

- Select Allow Remote Connections To This Computer, which allows connections from any version of Windows.

- Select Allow Remote Connections To This Computer and also select the Allow Connections Only From Computers Running Remote Desktop With Network Level Authentication check box to allow connections only from Windows Vista or later, as well as other computers with secure network authentication.

Keep the following details about using Remote Desktop in mind:

- All remote connections must be established using accounts that have passwords. If a local account on the system doesn't have a password, you can't use the account to connect to the system remotely.

- If the computer is running Windows Firewall, the operating system automatically creates an exception that allows Remote Desktop Protocol (RDP) connections to be established. The default port used is TCP port 3389. The registry value HKEY_LOCAL_MACHINE\System\CurrentControlSet\Control\TerminalServer\WinStations\RDP-Tcp\PortNumber controls the actual setting.

- If you are running a different firewall on the computer, you must open a port on the firewall to allow incoming Remote Desktop Protocol (RDP) connections to be established. Again, the default port used is TCP port 3389.

# INSIDE OUT   Authentication certificate validation

Prior to establishing an RDP connection, your computer will validate the remote computer's identify by default. If the remote computer's authentication certificate is invalid or has expired, you will not be allowed to connect and will see a warning prompt stating the following: "The authentication certificate received from the remote computer has expired or is not valid." Because a date/time disparity between the two computers can make it appear that the authentication certificate is invalid, you should check the current date and time on both computers. If you don't want your computer to authenticate the remote computer's identity, you can disable this feature by setting the Server Authentication option to Connect And Don't Warn Me. To set the Server Authentication option, tap or click Options to display the additional configuration tabs, tap or click the Advanced tab, and then use the selection list on the Server Authentication panel to set the option as desired.

Chapter 4

## Permitting and restricting remote logon

By default, all members of the Administrators group can log on remotely. The Remote Desktop User group has been added to Active Directory to ease managing Remote Desktop Services users. Members of this group are allowed to log on remotely.

If you want to add a member to this group, select Local Server in Server Manager and then tap or click the Enabled or Disabled link for the Remote Desktop entry. This opens the System Properties dialog box to the Remote tab. On the Remote tab, tap or click Select Users. As shown in Figure 4-12, any current members of the Remote Desktop Users group are listed in the Remote Desktop Users dialog box. To add users or groups to the list, tap or click Add. This opens the Select Users Or Groups dialog box.

**Figure 4-12** Configuring Remote Desktop users.

In the Select Users Or Groups dialog box, type the name of a user in the selected or default domain, and then tap or click Check Names. If multiple matches are found, select the name or names you want to use and then tap or click OK. If no matches are found, you either entered an incorrect name part or you're working with an incorrect location. Modify the name and try again, or tap or click Locations to select a new location. To add additional users or groups, type a semicolon (;) and then repeat this process. When you tap or click OK, the users and groups are added to the list in the Remote Desktop Users dialog box.

In Group Policy, members of the Administrators and Remote Desktop Users groups have the user right Allow Log On Through Remote Desktop Services by default. If you modified Group Policy, you might need to double-check to ensure that this user right is still granted to these groups. Typically, you will want to do this through local policy on a per-machine basis. You can also do this through site, domain, and organizational policy. Access the appropriate Group Policy Object and select Computer Configuration, Windows Settings, Security Settings, Local Policies, and User Rights Assignments. Double-tap or double-click Allow Log On Through Remote Desktop Services to see a list of users and groups currently granted this right.

# INSIDE OUT    Restrict remote logon through Group Policy

If you want to restrict users or groups from remotely administering a server, access the appropriate Group Policy Object and expand Computer Configuration\Windows Settings\Security Settings\Local Policies\User Rights Assignments. Double-tap or double-click Deny Log On Through Remote Desktop Services. In the policy Properties dialog box, select Define These Policy Settings and then tap or click Add User Or Group. In the Add User Or Group dialog box, tap or click Browse. This displays the Select Users, Computers, Or Groups dialog box. Type the name of the user or group for which you want to deny logon through Remote Desktop Services, and then tap or click OK. You can also change the default permissions for groups in the Remote Desktop Services Configuration tool. For instance, you could remove Administrators from having Full Control of the Remote Desktop Services objects.

## Configuring Remote Desktop through Group Policy

Remote Desktop is part of Remote Desktop Services, and you can use Group Policy to configure Remote Desktop Services. Microsoft recommends using Group Policy as the first choice when you are when configuring Remote Desktop Services for use with Remote Desktop. The precedence hierarchy for Remote Desktop Services configuration is as follows:

- Computer-level Group Policy

- User-level Group Policy

- Local computer policy using the Remote Desktop Services Configuration tool

- User policy on the Local User And Group level

- Local client settings

You can configure local policy on individual computers or on an organizational unit (OU) in a domain. You can use Group Policy to configure Remote Desktop Services settings per connection, per user, per computer, or for groups of computers in an OU of a domain. The Group Policy settings for Remote Desktop Services are modified using the Group Policy Object Editor and are located in Computer Configuration\Administrative Templates\ Windows Components\Remote Desktop Services and in User Configuration\Administrative Templates\Windows Components\Remote Desktop Services.

Chapter 4

> ## Create a separate OU for Remote Desktop Services
>
> Typically, Remote Desktop is used throughout an organization, but Remote Desktop Services servers are isolated to a particular group of servers operating in a separate OU. So, if you plan to use Remote Desktop Services servers as well in the organization, you should consider creating a separate OU for the Remote Desktop Services servers. In this way, you can manage Remote Desktop Services servers separately from Remote Desktop.

## Supporting Remote Desktop Connection clients

The Remote Desktop Connection client is the Remote Desktop Services client. It uses the Microsoft Remote Desktop Protocol (RDP) version 6.0 or later. Clients can use the Remote Desktop Connection client to connect to a remote server or workstation that has been set up to be administered remotely.

### Remote Desktop Connection client

Most current versions of Windows include the Remote Desktop Connection client. The features you should be aware of when supporting RDC are the following:

- Custom display resolutions allow for high-color and full-screen viewing. Resolutions of 1680 x 1920, 1920 x 1200, and higher are fully supported. To set the resolution from a command prompt or the Search box, add the /w and /h options, such as **mstsc /w:1920 /h:1200**. In an RDP file, you can set the screen size using desktop-width and desktopheight, such as **desktopwidth:i:1920** or **desktopheight:i:1200**.

- Monitor spanning settings allow you to display remote sessions across multiple monitors. All monitors must be horizontally aligned and use the same resolution. The maximum resolution across all monitors shouldn't exceed 4096 x 2048. To enable monitor spanning from a command prompt or the Search box, add the /span option, such as **mstsc /span**. In an RDP file, you can enable spanning by typing **Span:i:1**.

- By default, data sent between the client and the server is encrypted at the maximum key strength supported by the client. If you configure RDP on your Remote Desktop Services server to require high encryption, a client can make a connection only if it supports 128-bit or higher encryption.

- If a connection is interrupted or lost while you are performing a task, the client software attempts to reconnect to the session and, in the interim, processing continues on the server so that any running processes can be finished without interruption.

If for some reason you are unable to log on remotely after you are disconnected, your logon session can be accessed by logging on locally.

Enhanced experience settings include font smoothing and display data prioritization. Font smoothing ensures that computer fonts appear clear and smooth (as long as the desktop has ClearType enabled). Display data prioritization gives priority to display, keyboard, and mouse data over other types of data, such as printing or file transfers. The default bandwidth ratio is 70:30. This means that display and input data will be allocated 70 percent of the bandwidth, and all other traffic, such as file transfers or print jobs, will be allocated 30 percent of the bandwidth.

You can adjust the data prioritization settings by making changes to the registry of the Remote Desktop Services server. Change the value of the following entries under the HKEY_LOCAL_MACHINE\SYSTEM\CurrentControlSet\Services\TermDD subkey:

- FlowControlDisable

- FlowControlDisplayBandwidth

- FlowControlChannelBandwidth

- FlowControlChargePostCompression

When working with flow control, keep the following in mind:

- If these entries do not appear, you can create them. To do this, press and hold or right-click TermDD, point to New, and then tap or click DWORD (32-bit) Value.

- You can disable display data prioritization completely by setting the value of FlowControlDisable to 1. If you do this, all requests are handled on a first-in-first-out basis and other registry settings are ignored.

- You can set the relative bandwidth priority for display and input data by setting the FlowControlDisplayBandwidth value. The default value is 70. The maximum allowed value is 255.

- You can set the relative bandwidth priority for other data, such as file transfers or print jobs by setting the FlowControlChannelBandwidth value. The default value is 30. The maximum allowed value is 255.

- The bandwidth ratio for display data prioritization is based on the values you set. For example, if you set FlowControlDisplayBandwidth 200 and FlowControlChannelBandwidth to 50, the ratio is 200:50 (or 4:1), so display and input data will be allocated 80 percent of the bandwidth.

Chapter 4

- The FlowControlChargePostCompression value determines whether the bandwidth allocation is based on the precompression or postcompression data size. The default value is 0, which means that the calculation will be made on the size of the data before it is compressed. In most cases, this is the value you'll want to use. This setting ensures the client doesn't have to wait or perform compression calculations prior to sending data.

- If you make any changes to the registry values, you need to restart the Remote Desktop Services server for the changes to take effect.

Resource redirection allows audio, mapped drives, ports, printers, and certain keyboard combinations to be handled by the client computer. If an application generates audio feedback, such as an error notification, this can be redirected to the client. Key combinations that perform application functions are passed to the remote server except for Ctrl+Alt+Delete, which is handled by the client computer. In addition, local devices such as drives, printers, and serial ports are also available. Because both local and network drives are available on the client, users can easily access local drives and transfer files between the client and the server.

Plug and Play device redirection extends the resource redirection features to allow locally connected and supported Plug and Play devices to be installed on and used with a remote computer. You can now redirect media players that support Media Transfer Protocol (MTP) and digital cameras that support Picture Transfer Protocol (PTP). Plug and Play notifications will appear in the taskbar on the remote computer. When you start a remote session for the first time after connecting a supported device locally, you should see the device get installed automatically on the remote computer. After the redirected device is installed on the remote computer, the device is available for use in your session with the remote computer. For example, if you are redirecting a Windows Portable Device (WPD) such as a digital camera, you can access the device directly from a remote application.

You can control Plug and Play device redirection on the Client Settings tab in the Remote Desktop Services Configuration tool (tsconfig.msc). Use the Supported Plug And Play Devices options. You can also control Plug and Play device redirection by using Group Policy. To do this, you can use the Do Not Allow Supported Plug And Play Device Redirection policy setting in the Administrative Templates for Computer Configuration under Windows Components\Remote Desktop Services\Remote Desktop Session Host\ Device and Resource Redirection. Several related policy settings are found under Computer Configuration\Administrative Templates\System\Device Installation\Device Installation Restrictions.

## Running the Remote Desktop Connection client

As discussed previously, you now can open two administrator sessions on computers that run Windows Server 2012 without needing an RD CAL. The use of an admin or console session greatly enhances your capabilities as an administrator to successfully execute programs, applications, and processes that will not run in a virtual session.

There are several ways to start the Remote Desktop Connection client:

- **Run in admin mode**   Admin mode is used by administrators to enable full interaction with the console of the remote system. To run the client in admin mode, type **mstsc /admin** at the command prompt or in the Apps Search box.

- **Run in virtual session mode**   Virtual session mode is used by administrators as well as users to start a virtual session on a remote system. To run the client in virtual session mode, type **mstsc** at the command prompt or in the Apps Search box.

After the client is started, enter the name or Internet Protocol (IP) address of the computer to which you want to connect, as shown in Figure 4-13. If you don't know the name of the computer, use the drop-down list provided to choose an available computer, or select Browse For More on the drop-down list to display a list of domains and computers in those domains.

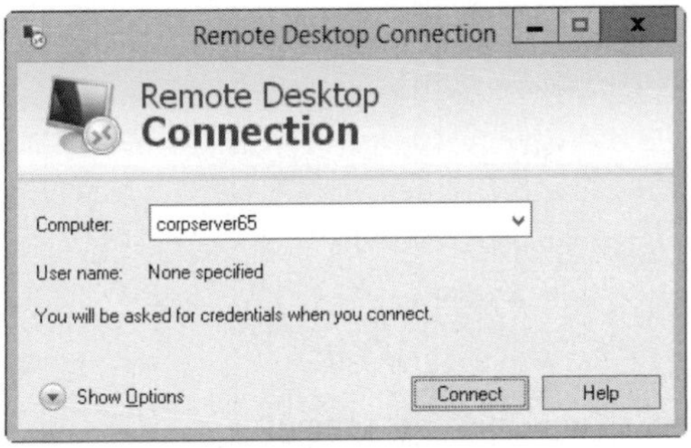

**Figure 4-13** Specifying the remote computer with which to establish a connection.

By default, Windows uses your current user name and domain to log on to the remote computer. If you want to use different account information, tap or click Options and then enter your user name in the field provided. (See Figure 4-14.) To set the domain, you can

Chapter 4

enter your user name in the DOMAIN\USERNAME format, such as ADATUM\WILLIAMS. Select the Allow Me To Save Credentials check box to enable automatic logon if desired.

> ## Note
> Even if you select the Allow Me To Save Credentials check box, you might be prompted to enter your password during the logon process depending on your network's policies and the configuration of the Remote Desktop Services server.

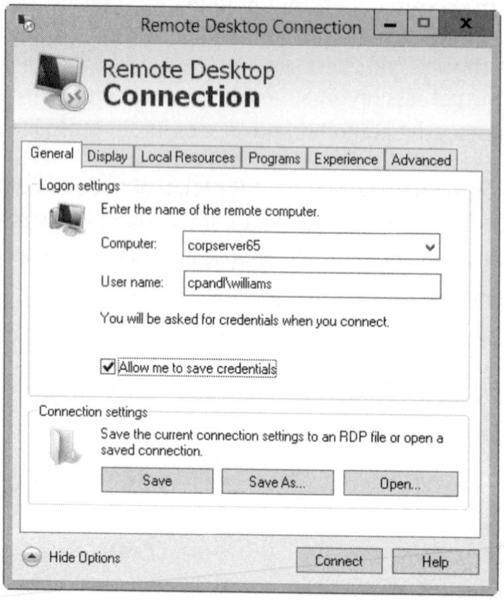

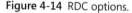

**Figure 4-14**  RDC options.

There are six tabs you can use to change the client settings:

- **General**  You might want to use these options to save keystrokes by adding logon information. Rather than typing in your settings each time, you can save the connection settings and load them when you want to make a connection.

   To save the current connection settings, tap or click Save As and then use the Save As dialog box to save the .rdp file for the connection.

   To load previously saved connection settings, tap or click Open and then use the Open dialog box to find and open the previously saved connection settings.

- **Display**   The default settings for RDC are full-screen and high-color. You can modify these settings here.

  Use the Display Configuration option to set the screen size. The size options available depend on the display size on the local computer.

  Use the Colors option to choose the preferred color depth. The default is 32-bit highest quality color, but settings on the remote computer might override this setting.

- **Local Resources**   You can modify the way the resource and device redirection work, including audio redirection, keystroke combination redirection, and local device and resource redirection.

  By default, remote computer sound is redirected to the local computer. Using the Remote Audio option, you can change the default setting by selecting Do Not Play or Play On Remote Computer.

  By default, when you are working in full-screen mode, key combinations such as Alt+Tab and Ctrl+Esc are redirected to the remote system, and Ctrl+Alt+Delete is handled locally. Using Apply Windows Key Combinations, you change this behavior so that key combinations are sent to the local computer or the remote computer only. However, if you send key combinations to the remote computer only, you could get in a situation where you cannot log on locally.

  By default, local printers are connected automatically when users are logged on to the remote computer. This makes it easy to print to your currently configured printers when you are working with a remote system.

  By default, anything you copy to the remote computer's clipboard is copied to the local computer's clipboard. This makes it easy to copy from a remote source and paste into a local source.

  Tap or click More on the Local Devices And Resource panel to see additional options. By default, the additional options ensure that smart cards connected to a remote computer are available for use in your remote session. You can also connect serial ports, local disk drives, and supported Plug and Play devices to make them available for use. Drives and supported devices can be selected by name, or you can simply select the Drives and Supported Plug And Play Devices options to make all drives and devices available for use. Selecting drives allows you to easily transfer files between the local and remote computer. Selecting Plug And Play devices allows you to work with supported devices, including media players and digital cameras.

Chapter 4

- **Programs**   You can configure the execution of programs when a session starts from this dialog box. Select the Start The Following Program On Connection check box, and then set the program path or file name and the start folder for the program.

- **Experience**   You can select the connection speed and other network performance settings. For optimal performance, choose the connection speed you are using, such as Modem (56 Kbps) or LAN (10 Mbps or higher), and allow only bitmap caching.

  Other options you can allow include Desktop Background, Font Smoothing, Desktop Composition, Show Window Contents While Dragging, Menu And Window Animation, and Visual Styles. If you select these additional check boxes, you cause additional processing on the remote system and additional network traffic, which can slow down performance. Desktop composition creates an enhanced desktop, as long as you installed the Desktop Experience feature on the Remote Desktop Services servers and clients that are using Windows Vista or later. Font Smoothing allows the client to pass through ClearType fonts, as long as Clear Type is enabled (which is the default setting).

  By default, Reconnect If Connection Is Dropped is selected. If the session is interrupted, the RDC will try to reconnect it automatically. Getting disconnected from a connection doesn't stop processing. The session will go into a disconnected state and continue executing whatever processes the session was running.

- **Advanced**   You can select these options to control the use of server authentication and the Remote Desktop Gateway feature. By default, the RDP client is configured to warn you if the authentication protocols fail and automatically detect RD Gateway settings.

When you tap or click Connect, you are connected to the remote system. Enter your account password if prompted, and then tap or click OK. If the connection is successful, you'll see the Remote Desktop window on the selected computer and you'll be able to work with resources on the computer. In the case of a failed connection, check the information you provided and then try to connect again.

When you are working in full-screen mode, a connection bar is displayed at the top of the screen. On the left side of the connection bar is a push pin. If you tap or click the push pin, it unpins the connection bar so that the bar disappears when you move the mouse away. To make the bar appear again, you then need to point the mouse to the top part of the screen. On the right side of the connection bar are several other buttons. The first button switches you to the local desktop. The second button switches between full mode and tile display mode. The third button disconnects the remote session.

Disconnecting from a session does not end a session. The session continues to run on the server, which uses resources and can prevent other users from connecting because only one console session and two virtual sessions are allowed. The proper way to end a session is to log off the remote computer just as you would a local computer. In the Remote Desktop Connection window, tap or click Start and then tap or click the Shutdown Options button. In the shortcut menu, tap or click Logoff.

> **CAUTION !**
>
> Don't try to log off the remote session by pressing Ctrl+Alt+Delete and tapping or clicking Logoff. Doing this will log you off the console session on your local client but still leave the remote session running on the Remote Desktop Server.

# Tracking who's logged on

When you deploy Remote Desktop Services, you can use the Remote Desktop Services Manager to view and manage logon sessions. With Remote Desktop, you can use this as well, but you typically don't need all the additional options and details. A more basic way to keep track of who is logged on to a server is to use the QUSER command. Type **quser** to see who is logged on to the system on which you are running the command prompt, or type **quser /server:*ServerName*** to see who is logged on to a remote server. Consider the following example:

```
USERNAME        SESSIONNAME      ID      STATE     IDLE TIME  LOGON TIME
tedg            rdp-tcp#1        1       Active    .          5/04/2014 11:42 AM
Wrstanek        console          2       Active    2:27       5/04/2014 09:43 AM
```

Here, there are two active sessions:

- TEDG is logged on to an active RDP session. The session ID is 1, meaning it is Session 1.

- WRSTANEK is logged on locally to the console. The session ID is 2, meaning it is Session 2.

You can also use the Task Manager to view user sessions. Press Ctrl+Alt+Delete, and then tap or click Task Manager. In the Task Manager dialog box, tap or click the Users tab. Here, each user connection is listed with user name, status, CPU utilization, and memory usage by default. Other columns can be added by pressing and holding or right-clicking any column header and then tapping or clicking the columns to add. If you double-tap or double-click a user's name, there's an entry for each running process. Processes are listed by name, CPU usage, and memory usage.

Chapter 4

You can also use Task Manager to manage remote user sessions:

- To disconnect a user session, select the user entry, tap or click Disconnect, and then tap or click Disconnect User when prompted to confirm the action.

- To log off a user, select the user entry, tap or click Logoff, and then tap or click Log Off User when prompted to confirm the action.

The difference between disconnecting a session and logging off a session is important. When you disconnect a session, the session goes into a disconnected state and continues executing current processes. If you log off a user, you end that user's session, closing any applications the user was running and ending any foreground processes the person was running as well. A foreground process is a process being run by an active application as opposed to a background or batch process being run independently from the user session.

# Windows Server 2012 MMC administration

T HE Microsoft Management Console (MMC), and the prepackaged administration tools that use it, help you more readily manage computers, users, and other aspects of the network environment. Not only does the MMC simplify administration, it also helps to integrate the many disparate tools in the Windows operating system.

The advantages of having a unified interface are significant because after you learn the structure of one MMC tool, you can apply what you've learned to all the other MMC tools. Equally significant is the capability to build your own consoles and customize existing consoles. You can, in fact, combine administrative components to build your own console configuration and then store this console for future use. You would then have quick access to the tools you use the most through a single console.

In this chapter, you'll learn how to work with and customize the MMC. You'll also find a discussion of administration tools that use the MMC. You can learn many techniques to help you better understand Windows Server 2012, and indeed, as mentioned in the previous chapter, you must master the MMC before you can truly master Windows Server 2012.

## Using the MMC

The MMC is a framework for management applications that offers a unified interface for administration. It is not designed to replace management applications; rather, it is designed to be their central interface. As such, the MMC doesn't have any inherent management functions. It uses add-in components, called *snap-ins*, to provide the necessary administrative functionality.

Keep in mind that the MMC isn't a one-size-fits-all approach to administration. Some administrative functions aren't implemented for use with the MMC. You configure many system and operating system properties using Control Panel utilities. Many other system and administrative functions are accessed using wizards. Most administrative tools, regardless of type, have command-line counterparts that run as separate executables from the command line.

The really good news, however, is that you can integrate all non-MMC tools and even command-line utilities into a custom console by creating links to them. In this way, your custom console remains the central interface for administration, and you can use it to access quickly any type of tool with which you routinely work. For more information, see the section "Building custom MMCs" later in this chapter.

For selected snap-ins, the MMC supports the following capabilities:

- **Multiple-item selecting and editing**   These features allow you to select multiple objects and perform the same operations on them, including editing.

- **Drag-and-drop functionality**   This allows you to perform such tasks as dragging a user, computer, or group from one organizational unit (OU) to another in Active Directory Users And Computers.

For the Active Directory Users And Computers snap-in, you can do the following:

- Reset access permissions to the default values for objects, show the effective permission for an object, and show the parent of an inherited permission.

- Save Active Directory queries, and reuse them so that you can easily perform common or complex queries.

MMC 3.0 is designed to support snap-ins created for MMC 2.0 and MMC 1.2. You can add these snap-ins to an MMC 3.0 console, and they will run as they do in the versions of MMC for which they were designed. You can use MMC 3.0 to open a console created using MMC 2.0 or 1.2. If you then save the console, you will be prompted to save the console in MMC 3.0 format. Doing so will update the console so that it uses the MMC 3.0 framework. However, you will not be able to open the console on computers running previous versions of MMC. The reason for this is that MMC 2.0 and 1.2 do not support MMC 3.0 snap-ins or consoles.

## MMC snap-ins

To take advantage of what the MMC framework has to offer, you add any of the available standalone snap-ins to a console. A console is simply a container for snap-ins that uses the MMC framework. Dozens of preconfigured snap-ins are available from Microsoft, and they provide the functionality necessary for administration. Third-party tools from independent software vendors now use MMC snap-ins as well.

> **Note**
> The terms *console* and *tool* are often used interchangeably. For example, in the text, I often refer to something as a tool when technically it is a preconfigured console containing a snap-in. For example, Active Directory Users And Computers is a tool for managing users, groups, and computers. Not all tools are consoles, however. The System tool in Control Panel is a tool for managing system properties, but it is not a console.

Although you can load multiple snap-ins into a single console, most of the preconfigured consoles have only a single snap-in. For example, most of the tools on the Tools menu in Server Manager consist of a preconfigured console with a single snap-in—even the Computer Management tool, as shown in Figure 5-1, consists of a preconfigured console with the Computer Management snap-in added to it.

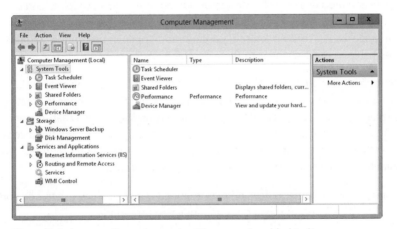

**Figure 5-1**  A preconfigured console with a snap-in added to it.

The many features of the Computer Management snap-in are good examples of how snap-ins can have nodes and extension components. A node defines a level within the console or within a snap-in. Computer Management has a root node, which is labeled Computer Management, and three top-level nodes, which are labeled System Tools, Storage, and Services And Applications. An *extension component* is a type of snap-in that is used to extend the functionality of an existing snap-in. Computer Management has many extensions. In fact, each entry under the top-level nodes is an extension—and many of these extensions can themselves have extensions.

These particular extensions are also implemented as standalone snap-ins, and when you use them in your own console, they add the same functionality as they do in the preconfigured administration tools. You'll find that many extensions are implemented as both extensions and standalone snap-ins. *Many* doesn't mean *all*: Some extensions are meant only to add functionality to an existing snap-in, and they are not also implemented as standalone snap-ins.

Keep in mind extensions are optional and can be included or excluded from a snap-in by changing options within the console when you are authoring it. For example, if you didn't want someone to be able to use Disk Management from within Computer Management, you could edit the extension options for Computer Management on that user's computer to remove the entry for Disk Management. The user would then be unable to manage disks from within Computer Management. The user would still, however, be able to manage disks using other tools.

## MMC modes

An MMC has two operating modes: author mode and user mode. In author mode, you can create and modify a console's design by adding or removing snap-ins and setting console options. In user mode, the console design is frozen, and you cannot change it. By default, the prepackaged console tools for administration open in user mode, and this is why you are unable to make changes to these console tools.

When you open a console that is in author mode, you have additional options on the File menu that help you design the interface. You can use these options to create new consoles, open existing consoles, save the current console, add or remove snap-ins, and set console options. In contrast, when you are working with one of the preconfigured console tools or any other tool in user mode, you have a limited File menu. With user mode, you can access a limited set of console options or exit the console—that's it.

In author mode, you also have a Favorites menu, which you can use to add and organize favorites. The Favorites menu does not appear in user mode.

When you are finished designing a console tool, you should change to user mode. Console tools should be run in user mode, and author mode should be used only for configuring console tools. Three user-mode levels are defined:

- **User mode—full access**   Users can access all window-management commands in the MMC but can't add or remove snap-ins or change console properties.

- **User mode—limited access, multiple window**   Users can access only the areas of the console tree that were visible when the console was saved. Users can create new windows but cannot close existing windows.

- **User mode—limited access, single window**   Users can access only the areas of the console tree that were visible when the console was saved and are prevented from opening new windows.

A console's mode is stored when you save the console and is applied when you open the console. In author mode, you can change the console mode by using the Options dialog box, which you display by selecting Options from the File menu. You cannot change the mode when a console is running in user mode. That doesn't mean you can't change back to author mode, however, and then make further changes as necessary.

To open any existing console tool in author mode, press and hold or right-click the tool's icon and choose Author. This works for the preconfigured administration tools as well. Simply navigate to the %SystemRoot%\ProgramData\Microsoft\Windows\Start Menu\ Programs\Administrative Tools folder, press and hold or right-click the related shortcut, and then choose Author. You will then have full design control over the console, but remember that if you make changes, you probably don't want to overwrite the existing .msc file for the console. So, instead of choosing Save from the File menu after you make changes, choose Save As, and save the console with a different name. For best results and easy access to the modified console, be sure to follow the techniques discussed later in the chapter in the section "Saving the console tool."

# INSIDE OUT   Group Policy settings control authoring and snap-in availability

Remember that at any time, a user with appropriate permissions can enter author mode by pressing and holding or right-clicking the console's shortcut and selecting Author, or by running the console tool from the command line with the /A switch. In author mode, users could change the configuration of the tool. One way to prevent this is to restrict authoring in Group Policy.

You can restrict all authoring by users at the local machine, OU, or domain level by enabling the Restrict The User From Entering Author Mode policy setting in User Configuration\Administrative Templates\Windows Components\Microsoft Management Console within Group Policy.

You can set specific restricted and permitted snap-ins and extensions as well. One way to do this is first to prohibit the use of all snap-ins by enabling the Restrict Users To The Explicitly Permitted List Of Snap-Ins policy setting in User Configuration\Administrative Templates\Windows Components\Microsoft Management Console within Group Policy. Then specifically enable the snap-ins and extensions that are permitted using the additional policy settings in the same location. All other snap-ins and extensions would then be prohibited.

Alternatively, you can disable Restrict Users To The Explicitly Permitted List Of Snap-Ins and then explicitly prohibit snap-ins by disabling them using the policy settings under User Configuration\Administrative Templates\Windows Components\Microsoft Management Console within Group Policy. All other snap-ins and extensions would then be permitted.

Chapter 5

**TROUBLESHOOTING**

**Group Policy settings can be reset**

Be sure to read Chapter 31, "Managing Group Policy," before you try to implement Group Policy or make changes to Group Policy objects. If you get into trouble, such as could happen if you prohibit all snap-ins but neglect to enable snap-ins needed for management, you'll need edit or delete the GPO. You can reset a default policy to its default configuration by using the Dcgpofix command-line utility as discussed in "Fixing default Group Policy," in Chapter 31.

## MMC window and startup

As Figure 5-2 shows, the MMC window consists of the console tree, the main pane, and an optional actions pane. The left pane is the console tree. It provides a hierarchical list of nodes available in the console. At the top of the tree is the console root, which could be specifically labeled Console Root or, as with the preconfigured tools, it is simply the snap-in name. Generally, snap-ins appear as nodes below the console root. Snap-ins can also have nodes, as is the case with Computer Management. In any case, if there are nodes below the console root, you can expand them by tapping or clicking the plus sign to the left of the node label or by double-tapping or double-clicking the node.

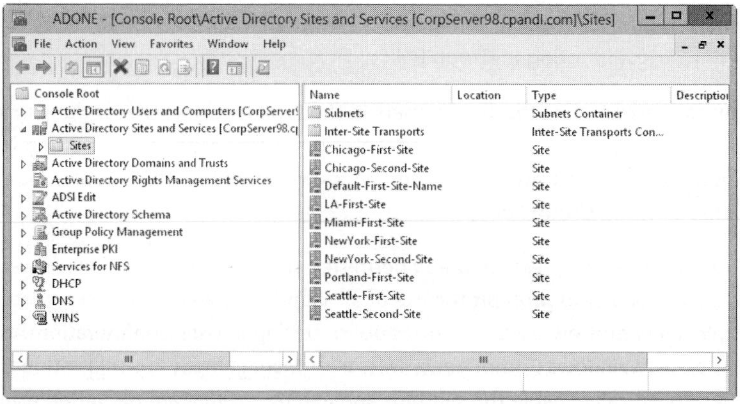

**Figure 5-2**  MMC windows are customizable.

The main pane is also referred to as the details pane, and its contents change depending on the item you've selected in the console tree. When you are working with one of the lowest-level nodes in the console tree, you'll sometimes have two views to choose from in the details pane: standard or extended view. The difference between the two is that the extended view typically provides quick access links to related, frequently performed tasks and a detailed description of the selected item. These are not displayed in the standard view.

One way to start a console tool is to select it on the Tools menu in Server Manager or double-tap or double-click its icon on the desktop or in File Explorer. You can also start console tools from the Search box, the command prompt, and the Windows PowerShell prompt. The executable for the MMC is Mmc.exe, so you can open the MMC by typing **mmc** in the Search box and then pressing Enter or by entering **mmc** at a command prompt. Either way, you'll end up with a blank (empty) console you can use to design your custom administration tool.

To use an existing console, you can specify the console file to open when the MMC runs. This is, in fact, how the preconfigured tools and any other tools that you create are started. For example, if you press and hold or right-click the shortcut for Computer Management in the %SystemRoot%\ProgramData\Microsoft\Windows\Start Menu\Programs\Administrative Tools folder and then select Properties, you'll see that the target (the command that is run) for the menu item is as follows:

```
%windir%\System32\Compmgmt.msc /s
```

The first part of the target (%windir%\System32\Compmgmt.msc) is the file path to the associated Microsoft Saved Console (.msc) file. The second part of the target (/S) is a command parameter to use when running the MMC. It follows that you can run the MMC by specifying the file path to the .msc file to use and any necessary command parameters as well using the following syntax:

```
mmc FilePath Parameter(s)
```

Here *FilePath* is the file path to the .msc file to use and *Parameter(s)* can include any of the following parameters:

- **/A**   Enables author mode, which lets you make changes to preconfigured consoles as well as other consoles previously set in user mode.

- **/S**   Prevents the console from displaying the splash screen that normally appears when the MMC starts in earlier versions of the Windows operating system. This parameter isn't needed when running on Windows Server 2008 or later.

- **/32**   Starts the 32-bit version of the MMC, which is needed only if you explicitly want to run the 32-bit version of the MMC on a 64-bit Windows system.

- **/64**   Starts the 64-bit version of the MMC, which is available only on 64-bit versions of Windows.

Chapter 5

# INSIDE OUT  Using 32-bit and 64-bit versions of the MMC

The */32* and */64* parameters for the *mmc* command are meaningful only on 64-bit Windows versions. The 64-bit versions of the Windows operating system can run both 32-bit and 64-bit versions of the MMC. For 32-bit versions of the MMC, you use 32-bit snap-ins. For 64-bit versions of the MMC, you use 64-bit snap-ins. You can't mix and match MMC and snap-in versions, though. The 32-bit version of the MMC can be used only to work with 32-bit snap-ins. Similarly, the 64-bit version of the MMC can be used only to work with 64-bit snap-ins. In most cases, if you aren't sure which version to use, don't use the */32* or */64* parameter. This lets the Windows operating system decide which version to use based on the snap-ins contained in the .msc file you are opening.

When a console contains both 32-bit and 64-bit snap-ins and you don't specify the */32* or */64* parameter, Windows will open a subset of the configured snap-ins. If the console contains more 32-bit snap-ins, Windows will open the 32-bit snap-ins. If the console contains more 64-bit snap-ins, Windows will open the 64-bit snap-ins. If you explicitly use */32* or */64* with a console that contains both 32-bit and 64-bit snap-ins, Windows will open only the snap-ins for that bitness. On 64-bit systems, 32-bit versions of snap-ins are stored in the %SystemRoot%\SysWow64 folder and 64-bit versions of snap-ins are stored in the %SystemRoot%\System32 folder. By examining the contents of these folders, you can determine when 32-bit and 64-bit versions of snap-ins are available.

Most console tools are found in the %SystemRoot%\System32 directory. This puts them in the default search path for executables. Because there is a file type association for .msc files, specified files of this type are opened using Mmc.exe; you can open any of the preconfigured tools stored in %SystemRoot%\System32 by specifying the file name followed by the .msc extension. For example, you can start Event Viewer by typing **eventvwr.msc**.

This works because of the file association that specifies .msc files are executed using Mmc .exe. (You can examine file associations using the ASSOC and FTYPE commands at the command prompt.)

Some console tools aren't in the %SystemRoot%\System32 directory, or the search path for that matter. For these tools, you must type the complete file path.

## MMC tool availability

Generally, the preconfigured MMC consoles available on a server depend on the roles, role services, and features that are installed. As you install additional roles, role services, and features, additional tools for administration are installed, and these tools can be both console tools and standard tools. You don't have to rely on roles, role services, and features installation for tool availability, however. You can, in fact, install the complete administrative tool set on any Full-server installation regardless of the roles, role services, or features being used.

Follow these steps to install the complete administrative tool set:

1. In Server Manager, the local server is added automatically for management. If you want to install the admin tools on another server, you need to add the server for management using the Add Servers option. Using Server Manager for remote management requires the configuration discussed in Chapter 4, "Managing Windows Server 2012," and a minimum set of permissions.

2. In Server Manager, tap or click Manage and then tap or click Add Roles And Features. This starts the Add Roles And Features Wizard. If the wizard displays the Before You Begin page, read the Welcome message, and then tap or click Next.

3. On the Select Installation Type page, select Role-Based Or Feature-Based Installation and then tap or click Next.

4. On the Select Destination Server page, the server pool shows servers you've added for management. Tap or click the server you are configuring and then tap or click Next twice.

5. On the Select Features page, select the Remote Server Administration Tools check box. This selects key tools under the Role Administration Tools and Feature Administration Tools nodes. If you want to select additional tools, expand the tools node and select tools to install as appropriate. Tap or click Next.

6. Tap or click Install. When the wizard finishes installing the administration tools, tap or click Close.

These tools are then available on the Tools menu in Server Manager and can also be started quickly in the Search box or at the command prompt by typing only their file name (in most cases). At times, you might find it quicker to open consoles from the command line. For example, on a server optimized for handling background services and not programs being run by users, you might find that navigating the menu is too slow. To help you in these instances, Table 5-1 provides a list of the key console tools and their .msc file names. Note that some of the MMCs won't be available even if you install all of the Remote Server Administration Tools. Tools for certain server roles and features are only available when those roles and features are installed.

Chapter 5

**TABLE 5-1** Key console tools and their .msc file names

| Tool Name | .msc File Name |
|---|---|
| Active Directory Administrative Center | dsac.exe |
| Active Directory Domains And Trusts | domain.msc |
| Active Directory Rights Management Services | AdRmsAdmin.msc |
| Active Directory Sites And Services | dssite.msc |
| Active Directory Users And Computers | dsa.msc |
| ADSI Edit | adsiedit.msc |
| Certificate Templates Console | certtmpl.msc |
| Certificates - Current User | certmgr.msc |
| Certificates - Local Computer | certlm.msc |
| Certification Authority | certsrv.msc |
| Computer Management | compmgmt.msc |
| Device Manager | devmgmt.msc |
| DFS Management | dfsmgmt.msc |
| DHCP Manager | dhcpmgmt.msc |
| Disk Management | diskmgmt.msc |
| DNS Manager | dnsmgmt.msc |
| Event Viewer | eventvwr.msc |
| Failover Cluster Management | cluadmin.msc |
| Fax Service Manager | fxsadmin.msc |
| File Server Resource Manager | fsrm.msc |
| Group Policy Management | gpmc.msc |
| Health Registration Authority | hcscfg.msc |
| Hyper-V Manager | virtmgmt.msc |
| Local Group Policy Editor | gpedit.msc |
| Local Security Policy | secpol.msc |
| Local Users And Groups | lusrmgr.msc |
| NAP Client Configuration | napclcfg.msc |
| Network Policy Server | nps.msc |
| Online Responder Manager | ocsp.msc |
| Performance Monitor | perfmon.msc |
| Print Management | printmanagement.msc |
| RD Gateway Manager | tsgateway.msc |
| RD Remote App Manager | remoteprograms.msc |

| Tool Name | .msc File Name |
|---|---|
| Reliability And Performance Monitor | perfmon.msc |
| Remote Desktop Services Configuration | tsconfig.msc |
| Remote Desktop Services Manager | tsadmin.msc |
| Remote Desktops | tsmmc.msc |
| Resultant Set of Policy | rsop.msc |
| Routing And Remote Access | rrasmgmt.msc |
| Services | services.msc |
| Services For Network File System | nfsmgmt.msc |
| Share And Storage Management | storagemgmt.msc |
| Storage Explorer | storexpl.msc |
| Storage Manager For SANs | sanmmc.msc |
| Task Scheduler | taskschd.msc |
| Trusted Platform Module Management | tpm.msc |
| UDDI Services | uddi.msc |
| Windows Deployment Services | wdsmgmt.msc |
| Windows Firewall With Advanced Security | wf.msc |
| Windows Server Backup | wbadmin.msc |
| Windows System Resource Manager | wsrm.msc |
| WINS Manager | winsmgmt.msc |

## MMC and remote computers

Some snap-ins can be set to work with local or remote systems. If this is the case, you'll see the name of the computer with focus in parentheses after the snap-in name in the console tree. When the snap-in is working with the local computer, you'll see (Local) after the snap-in name. When the snap-in is working with a remote computer, you'll see the remote computer name in parentheses after the snap-in name, such as (CORPSERVER01).

Generally, regardless of which type of snap-in you are using, you can specify the computer you want to work with in one of two ways. Within the MMC, you can press and hold or right-click the snap-in node in the console tree and then select Connect To Another Computer. This displays the Select Computer dialog box, as shown in Figure 5-3.

Chapter 5

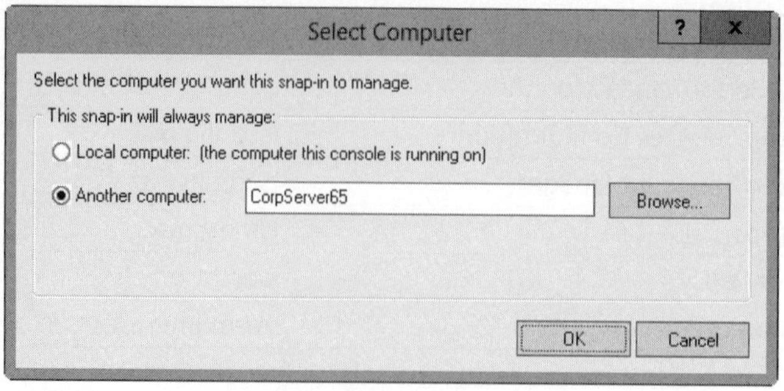

**Figure 5-3** Specify the computer you want to work with.

If you want the snap-in to work with the computer the console is running on, select Local Computer. Otherwise, select Another Computer and then type the computer name or Internet Protocol (IP) address of the computer you want to use. If you don't know the computer name or IP address, tap or click Browse to search for the computer you want to work with.

Some snap-ins that can be set to work with local and remote systems can be started from the command line with the focus set on a specific computer. This is a hidden feature that many people don't know about or don't understand. Simply set the focus when you start a console from the command line using the following parameter:

```
/computer=RemoteComputer
```

Here *RemoteComputer* is the name or IP address of the remote computer you want the snap-in to work with, such as

```
compmgmt.msc /computer=corpserver01
```

or

```
services.msc /computer=corpserver32
```

> **Note**
>
> For remote management, the appropriate Windows Firewall rules must be enabled on the target computer. Specifically, the inbound rule for COM+ Network Access (DCOM-In) must be enabled, as well as any appropriate rules related to the snap-in you want to work with. For more information, see Chapter 4.

Several hidden options are available with the Active Directory–related snap-ins. For Active Directory Users And Computers, Active Directory Sites And Services, and Active Directory

Domains And Trusts, you can use the */Server* parameter to open the snap-in and connect to a specified domain controller. For example, if you want to start Active Directory Users And Computers and connect to the CorpSvr02 domain controller, you could do this by typing the following:

```
dsa.msc /server=CorpSvr02
```

For Active Directory Users And Computers and Active Directory Sites And Services, you can use the */Domain* parameter to open the snap-in and connect to a domain controller in the specified domain. For example, if you want to start Active Directory Users And Computers and connect to the cpandl.com domain, you could do this by typing the following:

```
dsa.msc /domain=cpandl.com
```

# Building custom MMCs

If you find that the existing console tools don't meet your needs or you want to create your own administration tool with the features you choose, you can build your own custom console tools. This allows you to determine which features the console includes, which snap-ins it uses, and which additional commands are available.

The steps for creating custom console tools are as follows:

1. Create the console for the tool.

2. Add snap-ins to the console. Snap-ins you use can include Microsoft console tools as well as console tools from third-party vendors.

3. When you are finished with the design, save the console in user mode so that it is ready for use.

Each step is examined in detail in the sections that follow. Optionally, you can create one or more taskpad views containing shortcuts to menu commands, shell commands, and navigation components you want to include in your custom tool. Techniques for creating taskpad views are discussed in "Designing custom taskpads for the MMC" later in this chapter.

## Step 1: Creating the console

The first step in building a custom console tool is to create the console you'll use as the framework. To get started, open a blank MMC in author mode. Type **mmc** in the Search box, and then press Enter. This opens a blank console titled Console1 that has a default console root, as shown in Figure 5-4.

Chapter 5

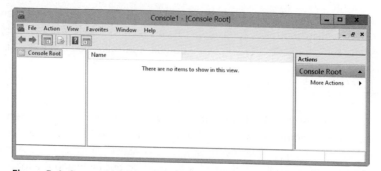

**Figure 5-4** Open a blank console with the default console root.

If you want your custom tool to be based on an existing console, you can open its .msc file and add it to the new console. Select Open on the File menu, and then use the Open dialog box to find the .msc file you want to work with. As discussed previously, most .msc files are in the %SystemRoot%\System32 directory. Any existing console you choose will open in author mode automatically. Keep in mind that you generally don't want to overwrite the existing .msc file with the new .msc file you are creating. Because of this, when you save the custom console, be sure to choose Save As rather than Save on the File menu.

If you want to start from scratch, work with the blank console you just opened. The first thing you'll want to do is rename the console root to give it and the related window a more meaningful name. For example, if you are creating a console tool to help you manage the Active Directory Domain Services, you could rename the console root Active Directory Management. To rename the console root and the related window, press and hold or right-click the console root, and select Rename. Type the name you want to use, and then press Enter.

Next consider how many windows the console tool must have. Most console tools have a single window, but as shown in Figure 5-5, a console can have multiple windows, each with its own view of the console root. You add windows to the console by using the New Window option on the Window menu. After you add a window, you'll probably want the MMC to automatically tile the windows as shown in the figure. You can tile windows by selecting Tile Horizontally on the Window menu. You don't have to do this, however; any-time there are multiple windows, you can use the options on the Window menu to switch between them.

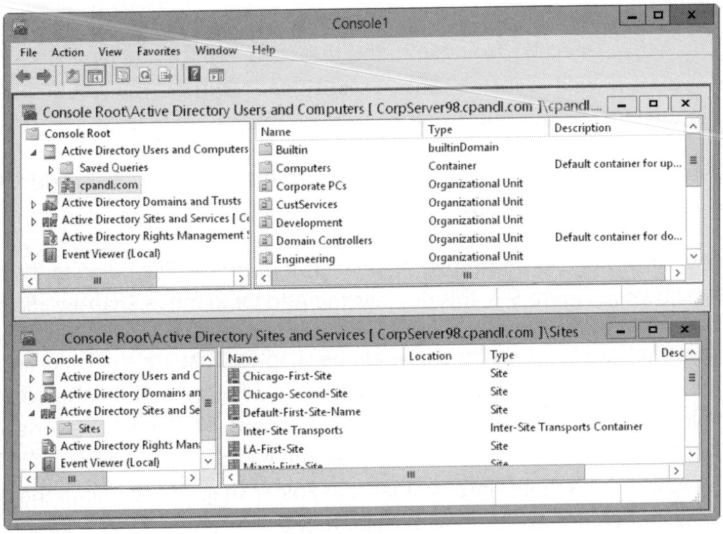

**Figure 5-5**  Although consoles can have multiple windows, most consoles have a single window.

# INSIDE OUT  Using multiple windows in consoles

Most console tools have a single window for a good reason: The tool creators wanted to keep the interface as simple as possible. When you introduce multiple windows, you create additional views of the console root, making the interface more complex, and often unnecessarily so. Still, there are times when a console tool with multiple windows could come in handy. For example, you might want to have multiple views of the console root where different areas of the tool are featured, and you could do this by using multiple windows.

## Step 2: Adding snap-ins to the console

While you are thinking about the organization of the tool and the possibility of using additional views of the console root, you should also consider the types of snap-ins that you want to add to the console. Each of the tools listed in Table 5-1 is available as a stand-alone snap-in you can add to the console. If you've installed any third-party tools on the computer, these tools might have standalone snap-ins you can use. Many other snap-ins are available from Microsoft as well.

Again, think of snap-in types or categories, not necessarily specific snap-ins you want to use. You might want to organize the snap-ins into groups by creating folders for storing snap-ins of a specific type or category. For example, if you are creating a console tool for managing Active Directory, you might find that there are four general types of snap-ins you want to work with: General, Policy, Security, and Support. You would then create four folders in the console with these names.

Folders are implemented as a snap-in you add to the console root. To add folders to the console root, follow these steps:

1. In your MMC, choose Add/Remove Snap-In from the File menu in the main window. As shown in Figure 5-6, this displays the Add Or Remove Snap-Ins dialog box.

2. The Available Snap-ins list shows all the snap-ins that are available. Scroll through the list until you see the Folder snap-in. Select Folder, and then tap or click Add. The Folder snap-in is added to the Selected Snap-ins list. Repeat this for each folder you want to use. If you are following the example and want to use four folders, you tap or click Add three more times so that four Folder snap-ins appear in the Add Or Remove Snap-Ins dialog box, as shown in Figure 5-6.

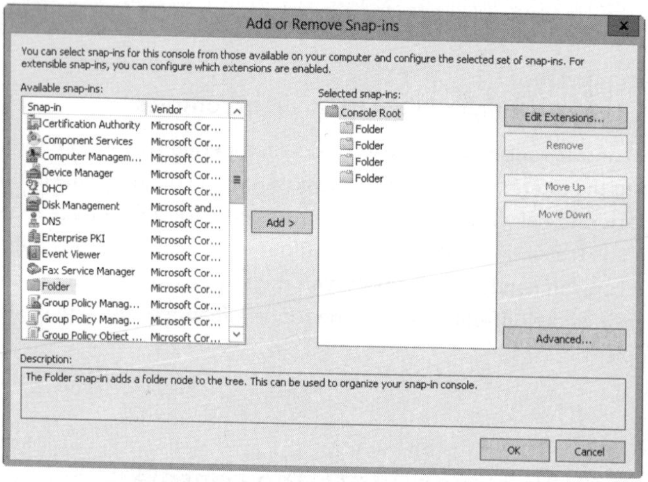

**Figure 5-6** Added snap-ins are listed in the Selected Snap-ins list.

3. Now close the Add Or Remove Snap-ins dialog box by tapping or clicking OK and return to the console you are creating.

After you add folders, you must rename them. Press and hold or right-click the first folder, and choose Rename. Type a new name, and then press Enter. If you are following the example, rename the folders: General, Policy, Security, and Support. When you are finished renaming the folders, follow a similar process to add the appropriate snap-ins to your console:

1. Choose Add/Remove Snap-in on the File menu in the main window. This displays the Add Or Remove Snap-ins dialog box shown previously in Figure 5-6.

2. Tap or click Advanced. Select the Allow Changing The Parent Snap-in check box. When you tap or click OK, the Add Or Remove Snap-ins dialog box is updated to include a Parent Snap-in drop-down list.

3. In the Parent Snap-in drop-down list, choose the folder to use. In the Available Snap-ins list, choose a snap-in to add as a subnode of the selected folder and then tap or click Add. When you are finished adding snap-ins to the selected folder, repeat this step to add snap-ins to other folders.

4. When you are finished adding snap-ins to folders, tap or click OK to close the Add Or Remove Snap-ins dialog box and return to the console you are creating.

Some snap-ins prompt you to select a computer to manage, as shown in Figure 5-7.

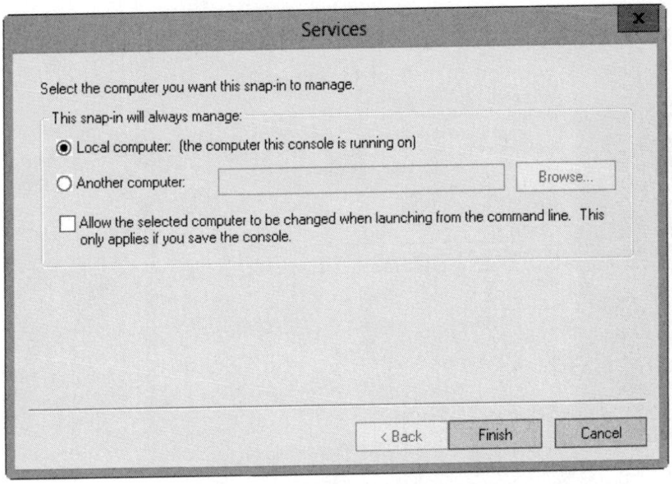

**Figure 5-7** This Services dialog box is where you specify which computer a snap-in will manage.

If you want the snap-in to work with whichever computer the console is running on, select Local Computer. Otherwise, select Another Computer and then type the computer name or IP address of the computer you want to use. If you don't know the computer name or IP address, tap or click Browse to search for the computer you want to work with.

Chapter 5

## Specify which computer to manage

To ensure you can specify which computer to manage when running the console from the command line, you must select the Allow The Selected Computer To Be Changed When Launching From The Command Line check box. When you select this option and save the console, you can set the computer to manage using the /Computer=RemoteComputer parameter.

Some snap-ins are added by using wizards with several configuration pages, so when you select these snap-ins you start the associated wizard and the wizard helps you configure how the snap-in is used. One snap-in in particular that uses a wizard is Link To Web Address. When you add this snap-in, you start the Link To Web Address Wizard, as shown in Figure 5-8, and the wizard prompts you to create an Internet shortcut. Here, you type the Uniform Resource Locator (URL) you want to use, tap or click Next, enter a descriptive name for the URL, and then tap or click Finish. Then, when you select the related snap-in in the console tree, the designated webpage appears in the details pane.

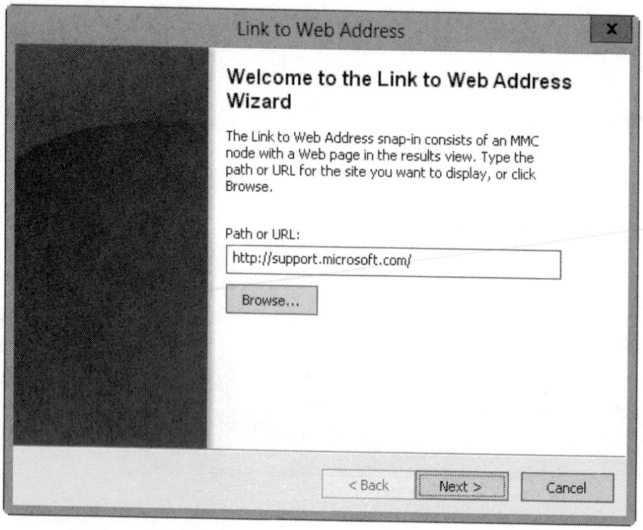

**Figure 5-8**  You add snap-ins with multiple configuration pages by using a wizard.

While you are adding snap-ins, you can also examine the available extensions for snap-ins. In the Add Or Remove Snap-ins dialog box, choose a previously selected snap-in and then tap or click Edit Extensions. In the Extensions For dialog box, all available extensions are enabled by default, as shown in Figure 5-9. So, if you want to change this behavior, you can select the Enable Only Selected Extensions option and then clear the individual check boxes for extensions you want to exclude.

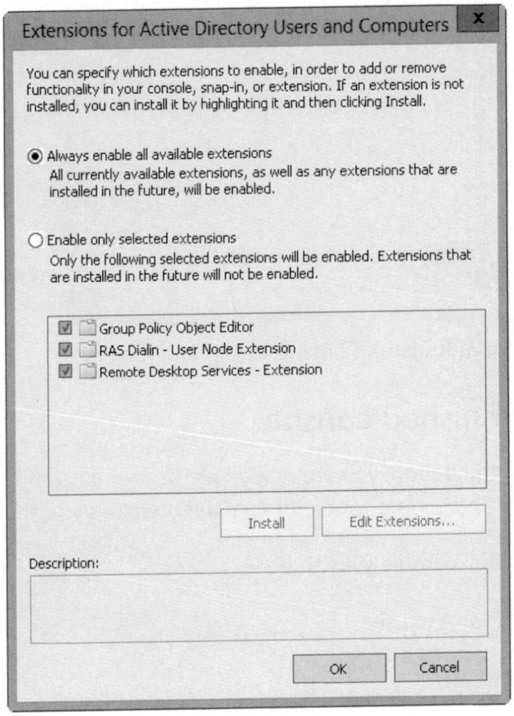

**Figure 5-9**  You can enable all extensions or selected extensions.

Figure 5-10 shows the example console with snap-ins organized using the previously discussed folders:

- **General**   Contains Active Directory Users And Computers, Active Directory Sites And Services, and Active Directory Rights Management Services

- **Policy**   Contains Group Policy Management and Resultant Set of Policy

- **Security**   Contains Security Templates and Security Configuration And Analysis

- **Support**   Contains links to Microsoft Knowledge Base, Microsoft Tech Support, and Windows Server Home Page

Chapter 5

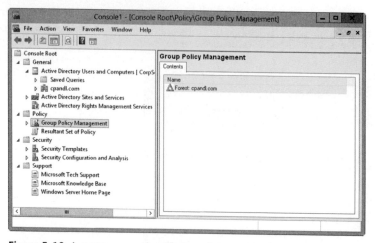

**Figure 5-10** A custom console with snap-ins organized into four folders.

# Step 3: Saving the finished console

When you are finished with the design, you are ready to save your custom console tool. Before you do this, however, there are a couple of final design issues you should consider:

- What you want the initial console view to be

- Which user mode you want to use

- Which icon you want to use

- What you want to name the console tool and where you want it to be located

## Setting the initial console view before saving

By default, the MMC remembers the last selected node or snap-in and saves this as the initial view for the console. In the example tool created, if you expand the General folder, select Active Directory Users And Computers, and then save the console, this selection is saved when the console is next opened.

Keep in mind that subsequent views depend on user selections.

> **Note**
> Only the folder with the selected snap-in is expanded in the saved view. If you use folders and select a snap-in within a folder, the expanded view of the folder is saved with the snap-in selected. If you expand other folders, the console is not saved with these folders expanded.

## Setting the console mode before saving

When you are finished authoring the console tool, select Options on the File menu. In the Options dialog box, as shown in Figure 5-11, you can change the console mode so that it is ready for use.

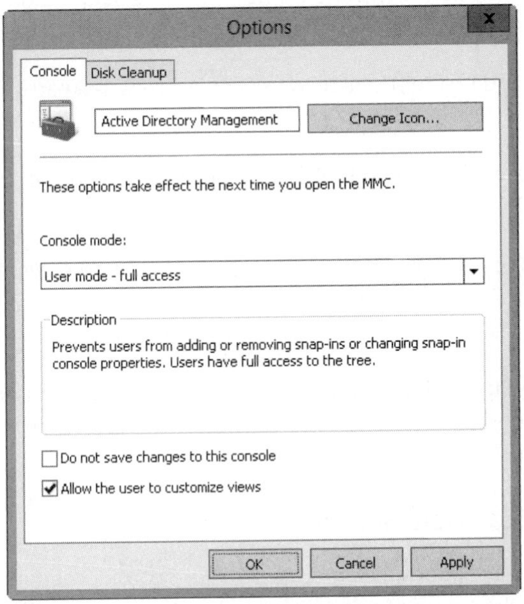

**Figure 5-11** On the Console tab of the Options dialog box, you select a console mode and determine whether users can change the console.

In most cases, you'll want to use User Mode—Full Access. Full access has the following characteristics:

- Users have a Window menu that allows them to open new windows, and they can also press and hold or right-click a node or snap-in and choose New Window From Here to open a new window.

- Users can press and hold or right-click and choose New Taskpad View to create a new taskpad view.

With user mode set to Limited Access, Multiple Window, the console has the following characteristics:

- Users have a Window menu that allows them to arrange windows, and they can also press and hold or right-click a node or snap-in and choose New Window From Here to open a new window.

- Users cannot press and hold or right-click and choose New Taskpad View to create a new taskpad view.

User mode set to Limited Access, Single Window has the following characteristics:

- Users do not have a Window menu and cannot press and hold or right-click a node or snap-in and choose New Window From Here to open a new window.

- Users cannot press and hold or right-click and choose New Taskpad View to create a new taskpad view.

To prevent user selections from changing the view, you'll find two handy options when you select Options from the File menu:

- **Do Not Save Changes To This Console**   Select this option to prevent the user from saving changes to the console. Clear this option to change the view automatically based on the user's last selection in the console before exiting.

- **Allow The User To Customize Views**   Select this option to allow users to add windows focused on a selected item in the console. Clear this option to prevent users from adding customized views.

## Setting the console icon before saving

While you are working in the Options dialog box, you might consider setting custom icons for your console tools. All the console tools developed by Microsoft have their own icons. You can use these icons for your console tools as well, or you could use icons from other Microsoft programs quite easily. In the Options dialog box (which is displayed when you select Options on the File menu), tap or click Change Icon. This displays the Change Icon dialog box, as shown in Figure 5-12.

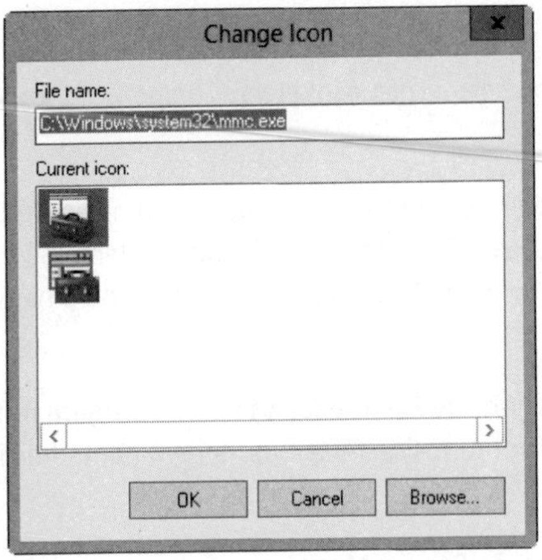

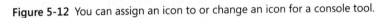

**Figure 5-12** You can assign an icon to or change an icon for a console tool.

In the Change Icon dialog box, tap or click Browse. By default, the Open dialog box should open with the directory set to %SystemRoot%\System32. In this case, type **shell32.dll** as the File Name, and tap or click Open. You should now see the Change Icon dialog box with the Shell32.dll selected, which will allow you to choose one of several hundred icons registered for use with the operating system shell. (See Figure 5-13.) Choose an icon, tap or click OK, and then tap or click OK to close the Options dialog box. From then on, the icon will be associated with your custom console tool.

**Figure 5-13** There are many icons to choose from.

## Saving the console tool

After you set the user mode, you can save the console tool. The console tool can appear as one of the following:

- **A desktop icon**    Select Save As on the File menu, and then navigate the folder structure to %SystemDrive%\Users\%UserName%\Desktop. Here, *%UserName%* is the name of the user who will work with the tool. After you type a name for the console, tap or click Save.

- **A folder icon**    Select Save As on the File menu, and then navigate to the folder where you want the console tool to reside. After you type a name for the console, tap or click Save.

- **An option on the Tools menu in Server Manager**    Select Save As on the File menu, and then navigate to the %SystemDrive%\Windows\System32 folder. After you type a name for the console, tap or click Save. Tap and hold or right-click the MMC and then select Create Shortcut. By default, you are prompted to save the shortcut on the desktop and tap or click Yes to confirm. Tap and hold or right-click the shortcut and then select Cut. In File Explorer, navigate the folder structure to %SystemDrive%\ProgramData\Microsoft\Windows\Start Menu\Programs\Administrative Tools. In the right pane of File Explorer, tap and hold or right-click and then select Paste.

- **An option on the Tools menu in Server Manager for a specific user**    Select Save As on the File menu, and then navigate to the %SystemDrive%\Windows\System32 folder. After you type a name for the console, tap or click Save. Tap and hold or right-click the MMC and then select Create Shortcut. By default, you are prompted to save the shortcut on the desktop and tap or click Yes to confirm. Tap and hold or right-click the shortcut and then select Cut. In File Explorer, navigate the folder structure to %SystemDrive%\Users\%UserName%\AppData\Roaming\Microsoft\Windows\Start Menu\Programs\Administrative Tools. In the right pane of File Explorer, tap and hold or right-click and then select Paste. Here, *%UserName%* is the name of the user who will work with the tool.

### Change tool names using the Options dialog box

By default, the name shown on the console tool's title bar is set to the file name you designate when saving it. As long as you are in author mode, you can change the console tool name using the Options dialog box. Select Options on the File menu, and then type the name in the box provided at the top of the Console tab.

# Designing custom taskpads for the MMC

When you want to simplify administration or limit the available tasks for junior administrators or Power Users, you might want to consider adding a taskpad to a console tool. By using taskpads, you can create custom views of your console tools that contain shortcuts to menu commands, shell commands, and navigation components.

## Getting started with taskpads

Basically, taskpads let you create a page of tasks you can perform quickly by tapping or clicking the associated shortcut links rather than using the existing menu or interface provided by snap-ins. You can create multiple taskpads in a console, each of which is accessed as a taskpad view. The revised Control Panel introduced with Windows XP features a taskpad view of the Control Panel. As with most taskpads, the Control Panel has two purposes: It provides direct access to the commands or tasks so that you don't have to navigate menus, and it limits your options to a set of predefined tasks you can perform.

You create taskpads when you are working with a console tool in author mode. Taskpads can contain the following items:

- **Menu commands**   Menu commands are used to run the standard menu options of included snap-ins.

- **Shell commands**   Shell commands are used to run scripts or programs or to open webpages.

- **Navigation components**   Navigation components are used to navigate to a saved view on the Favorites menu.

Taskpad commands are also called *tasks*. You run tasks simply by tapping or tapping or clicking their links. In the case of menu commands, tapping or clicking the links runs the menu commands. For shell commands, tapping or clicking the links runs the associated scripts or programs. For navigation components, tapping or clicking the links displays the designated navigation views. If you have multiple levels of taskpads, you must include navigation components to allow users to get back to the top-level taskpad. The concept is similar to having to create a home link on webpages.

Figure 5-14 shows a taskpad created for the Active Directory Users And Computers snap-in that has been added to the custom tool created earlier in the chapter.

Chapter 5

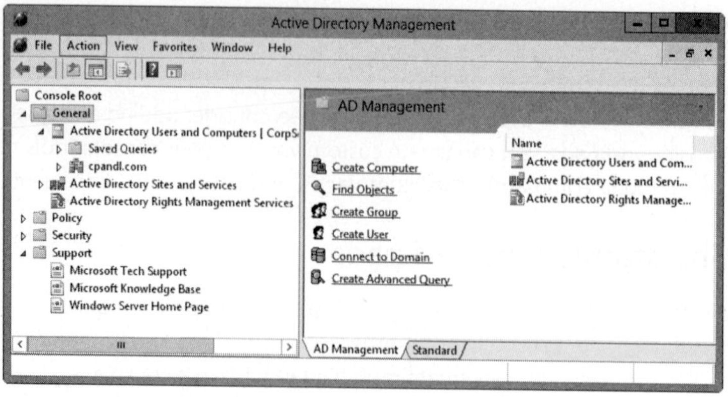

**Figure 5-14** A custom console with a taskpad that uses a vertical list.

As you can see, the task page view is labeled AD Management, and it provides the following commands:

- **Create Computer** Used to start the New Object—Computer Wizard

- **Find Objects** Used to open the Find Users, Contacts, And Groups dialog box

- **Create Group** Used to start the New Object—Group Wizard

- **Create User** Used to start the New Object—User Wizard

- **Connect To Domain** Used to select the domain to work with

- **Create Advanced Query** Used to define an Active Directory query and save it so that it can be reused

> **Note**
>
> You could also add a Connect To Domain Forest option that would be used to select the domain forest to work with. We haven't used the taskpad to limit the options; rather, we've simply provided quick access shortcuts to commonly run tasks. In the next section, you'll learn how to limit user options.

## Understanding taskpad view styles

Taskpads can be organized in several ways. By default, they will have two views: an extended taskpad view and a standard view. The extended view contains the list of tasks you've defined and can also contain the console items being managed. The standard view contains only the console items being managed. When you create the taskpad, you have the option of hiding the standard view simply by selecting the Hide Standard Tab check box.

The extended view of the taskpad can be organized using a vertical list, a horizontal list, or no list. In a vertical list, as shown previously in Figure 5-14, taskpad commands are listed to the left of the console items they are used to manage. This organization approach works well when you have a long list of tasks and you still want users to be able to work with the related snap-ins.

With a horizontal list, as shown in Figure 5-15, the console items managed by the taskpad are listed above the taskpad commands. This organization style is best when you want to display multiple columns of taskpad commands and still be able to work with the related snap-ins.

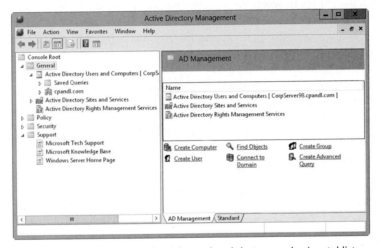

**Figure 5-15** A custom console with a taskpad that uses a horizontal list.

In some cases, you might not want to show the console items being managed by the taskpad on the same view as the tasks. In this case, you can specify that no list should be used. When you choose the No List option, the taskpad commands are shown by themselves in the taskpad tab (AD Management in the example), and users can tap or click the Standard tab to access the related console items.

# INSIDE OUT Limiting user options in taskpads

As discussed, you can limit the options users have in console tools by selecting both the No List option and the Hide Standard Tab check box. Keep in mind that if the console tool doesn't include a taskpad for a snap-in, users will still be able to manage the snap-in in the usual way. For example, the taskpad shown in Figure 5-15 doesn't define any tasks that manage policy or security, so the snap-ins in these folders will be fully accessible. To make it so that users can't work with these snap-ins directly, you must define taskpads for those snap-ins or add tasks that use menu commands from those snap-ins to the current taskpad or another taskpad.

When you select the No List option, you can limit users' options to the tasks you've defined and not allow users to access the console items being managed. To do this, you specify that the Standard tab should be hidden. From then on, when working with the console items being managed, users can perform only the tasks defined on the taskpad, such as shown in Figure 5-16.

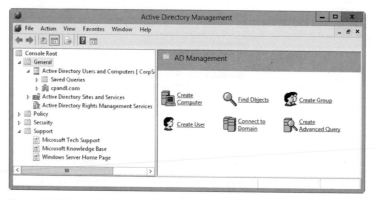

**Figure 5-16** By using the No List style and hiding the Standard tab, you can limit user options.

## Creating and managing taskpads

Any console tool that has at least one snap-in can have an associated taskpad. To create a taskpad, you must open the console in author mode, and then follow these steps:

1.  In your custom MMC, press and hold or right-click the folder or console item you want to work with, choose Action, and then choose New Taskpad View to start the New Taskpad View Wizard. Keep in mind that a single taskpad can be used to manage multiple console items.

2. In the New Taskpad View Wizard, tap or click Next, and then configure the taskpad display. (See Figure 5-17 for an example.) Select the style for the details page as Vertical List, Horizontal List, or No List, and set the task description style as Text or InfoTip. You can also choose to hide the Standard tab (which only limits the tasks that can be performed if you also select the No List style). As you make selections, the wizard provides a depiction of what the results will look like as a finished taskpad. Tap or click Next to continue.

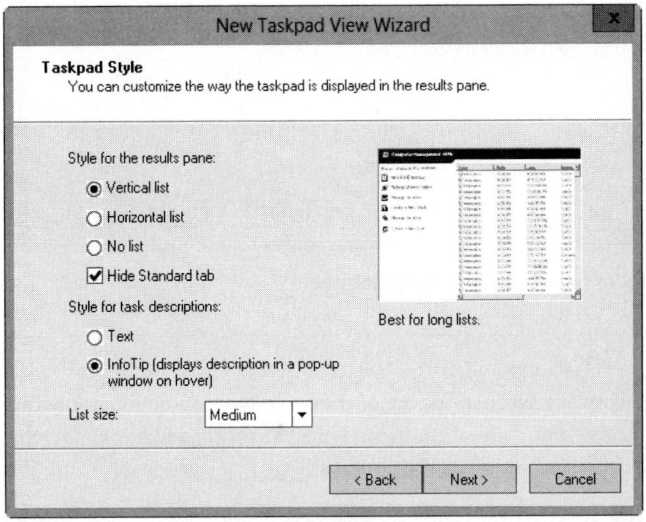

**Figure 5-17** Configure the taskpad display in the New Taskpad View Wizard.

3. On the Taskpad Reuse page (shown in Figure 5-18), you must decide whether to apply the taskpad view to the selected tree item only (the item you press and hold or right-click) or to any other tree item of the same type. If you choose the latter option, you also have the option to change the default display for any items used in the taskpad to the taskpad view. Typically, you'll want to do this to standardize the view, especially if you've hidden the Standard tab and don't want users to have other options. Tap or click Next.

Chapter 5

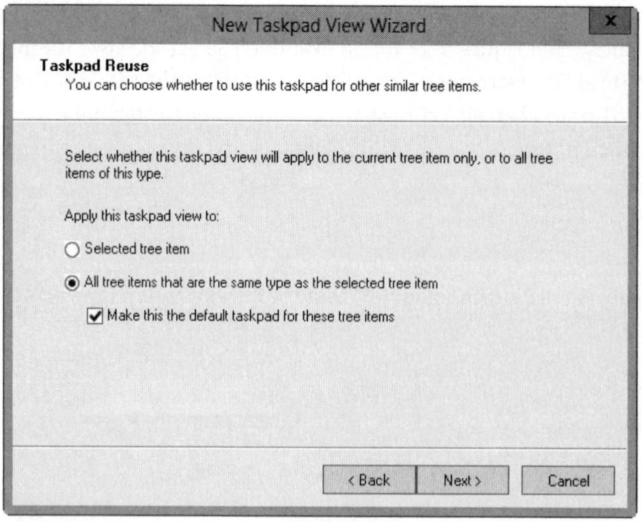

**Figure 5-18** Specify a taskpad target.

> **Note**
>
> Basically, all snap-ins are of the same type. So, if you apply the taskpad to any other tree item of the same type, the taskpad view can include any snap-in that you have added to the console.

4. Next, you set the name and description for the taskpad. The name appears at the top of the taskpad and on the tab at the bottom of the taskpad. The description appears at the top of the taskpad under the taskpad name. Tap or click Next.

5. On the final wizard page, you can tap or click Finish to create the taskpad. The Add New Tasks To This Taskpad After The Wizard Closes check box is selected by default, so if you tap or click Finish without clearing this option, the New Task Wizard starts and helps you create tasks for the taskpad.

If you want to create multiple taskpads, you can repeat this procedure. For the example console, you might want to have a taskpad for each folder; in that case, you would create three additional taskpads. Any additional taskpads you create can be placed at the same place in the console tree or at a different part of the console tree. You access multiple taskpads placed at the same part of the console tree by using the tabs provided in the details pane.

As long as you are in author mode, any taskpad you created can easily be edited or removed. To edit a taskpad view, press and hold or right-click the item where you defined the taskpad, and then select Edit Taskpad View from the shortcut menu. This opens a Properties dialog box containing two tabs:

- **General**   Use the options in the General tab, shown in Figure 5-19, to control the taskpad style as well as to display or hide the Standard tab. Tap or click Options to specify to which items the taskpad view is applied.

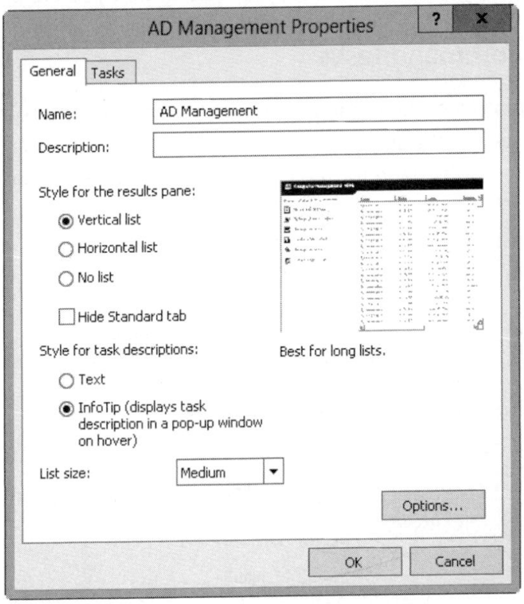

**Figure 5-19**  Change view options of a custom taskpad.

- **Tasks**   Use the Tasks tab to list current tasks defined for the taskpad. Use the related options to create new tasks or manage the existing tasks.

## Creating and managing tasks

You create tasks by using the New Task Wizard. By default, this wizard starts automatically when you finish creating a taskpad view. You can start the wizard using the taskpad Properties dialog box as well. In the Tasks tab, tap or click New. Alternatively, in your MMC, press and hold or right-click the folder or console item where you defined the taskpad, and then select Edit Taskpad View from the shortcut menu.

Chapter 5

After the New Task Wizard is started, tap or click Next, and then select the command type as follows:

- Choose Menu Command to run the standard menu options of included snap-ins.

- Choose Shell Command to run scripts or programs or to open webpages.

- Choose Navigation to navigate to a saved view on the Favorites menu.

The subsequent screens you see depend on the type of task you are creating.

## Creating menu command tasks

After choosing to create a menu command, select a source for the command, as shown in Figure 5-20. You specify the source of the command as a node from the console tree or from the list in the results pane for the item selected when you started the wizard. If you choose Node In The Tree as the source, select a snap-in in the console tree, and then choose one of the available commands for that snap-in. The commands available change based on the snap-in you've selected.

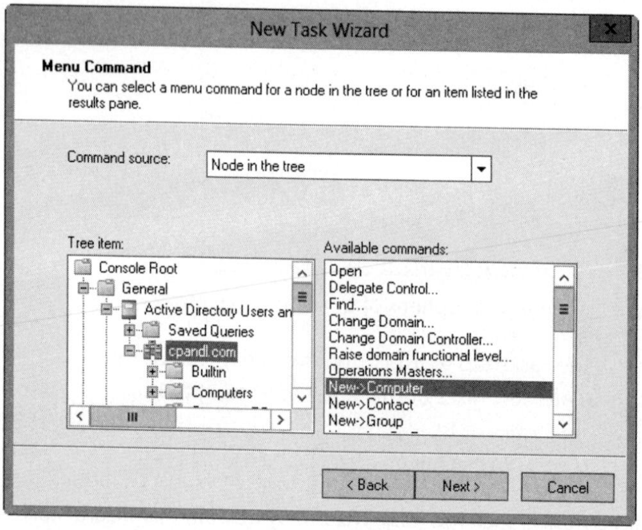

**Figure 5-20** Select a command source and then choose a command from the list of available commands.

Next, you set the name and description for the task. The name is used as the shortcut link designator for the task. The description is displayed as text under the shortcut link or as an InfoTip, depending on the way you configured the taskpad.

On the Task Icon page, you can choose an icon for the task. Select Icons Provided By MMC to choose any of the icons provided by the MMC. Tap or click an icon to select it and to display what the icon symbolizes and its alternate meanings. If you want to use a different set of icons, select Custom Icon and then tap or click Browse. This displays the Change Icon dialog box. Tap or click Browse to display the Open dialog box. By default, the Open dialog box should open with the directory set to %SystemRoot%\System32. In this case, type **shell32.dll** as the File Name and tap or click Open. You should now see the Change Icon dialog box with the Shell32.dll selected, which will allow you to choose one of several hundred icons registered for use with the operating system shell.

When you tap or click Next again, the wizard confirms the task creation and shows a current list of tasks on the taskpad if you tap or click Finish to finalize the creation of the current task. If you want to create another task, select the When I Click Finish, Run This Wizard Again check box and then repeat this process. Otherwise, just tap or click Finish.

## Creating shell command tasks

After choosing to create a shell command, specify the command line for the task, as shown in Figure 5-21.

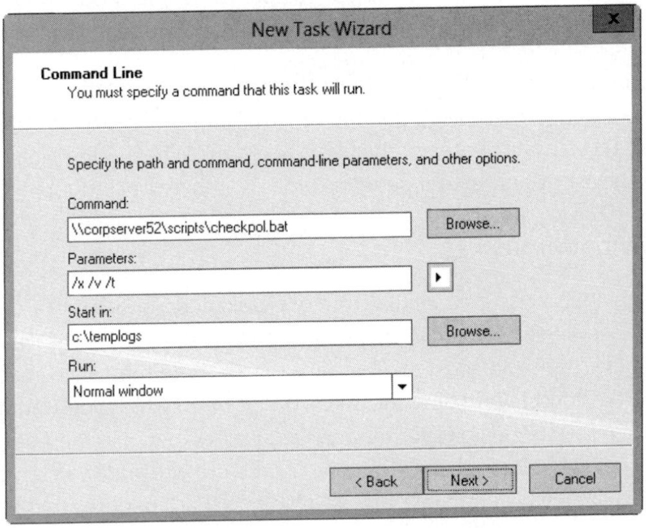

**Figure 5-21** Set the command line for the script or program you want to run.

The options are as follows:

- **Command**   The full file or Universal Naming Convention (UNC) path to the command you've chosen to run, such as C:\Scripts\Checkpol.bat or \\Corpserver01\Scripts\Checkpol.bat. The command can be a shell or batch script or a program. If you don't know the path to use, tap or click Browse and then use the Open dialog box to find the program you want to run.

- **Parameters**   The command-line parameters you want to pass to the script or program. Tap or click the right arrow beside the parameters field to display variables you can use. (These are related to the snap-in you selected originally when creating the taskpad.) Select a variable to add it to the list of command-line parameters.

- **Start In**   The startup (or base) directory for the script or program you've chosen, such as C:\Temp.

- **Run**   The type of window the script or program should run within, either a normal, minimized, or maximized window.

Next, you set the name and description for the task. The name is used as the shortcut link designator for the task. The description is displayed as text under the shortcut link or as an InfoTip, depending on the way you configured the taskpad.

Next, you can choose an icon for the task. As discussed previously, you can select Icons Provided By MMC or Custom Icon. If you use custom icons, you probably want to use the Shell32.dll in the %SystemRoot%\System32 directory to provide the custom icon.

When you tap or click Next again, the wizard confirms the task creation and shows a current list of tasks on the taskpad if you tap or click Finish to finalize the creation of the current task. If you want to create another task, select the When I Click Finish, Run This Wizard Again check box and then repeat this process. Otherwise, just tap or click Finish.

## Creating navigation tasks

Navigation tasks are used to create links from one taskpad to another or from a taskpad to a saved console view. Before you can create navigation tasks, you must save a console view or a view of a particular taskpad to the Favorites menu. To do this, while in author mode, navigate down the console tree until the taskpad or item to which you want to navigate is selected and then select Add To Favorites on the Favorites menu. In the Add To Favorites dialog box, shown in Figure 5-22, type a name for the favorite and then tap or click OK. Then you can create a navigation task on a selected taskpad that uses that favorite.

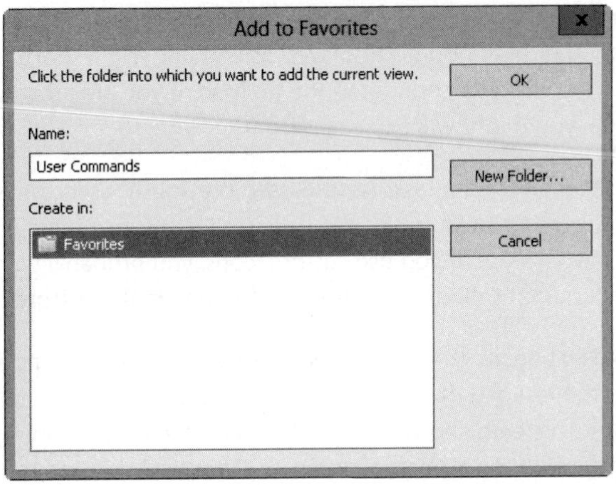

**Figure 5-22** Save the current view of the console tool to the Favorites menu.

You create the navigation task using the New Task Wizard. In the New Task Wizard, choose Navigation as the task type. Next, select the favorite to which you want users to navigate when they tap or click the related link. As shown in Figure 5-23, the only favorites available are the ones you've created as discussed previously.

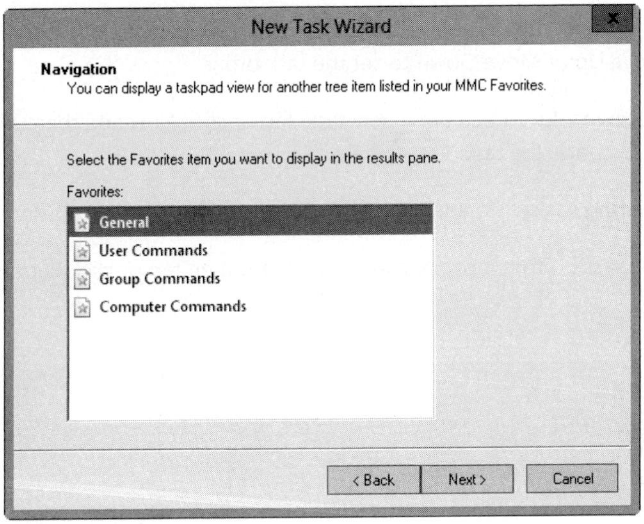

**Figure 5-23** Select the previously defined favorite you want to use.

Next, you set the name and description for the task. The name is used as the shortcut link designator for the task. The description is displayed as text under the shortcut link or as an InfoTip, depending on the way you configured the taskpad. If you are creating a link to the main console tool page, you might want to call it Home.

Next, you can choose an icon for the task. As discussed previously, you can select Icons Provided By MMC or Custom Icon. If you created a link called Home, there is a Home icon provided by the MMC to use. If you use custom icons, you probably want to use the Shell32.dll in the %SystemRoot%\System32 directory to provide the custom icon.

When you tap or click Next again, the wizard confirms the task creation and shows a current list of tasks on the taskpad if you tap or click Finish to finalize the creation of the current task. If you want to create another task, select the When I Click Finish, Run This Wizard Again check box and then repeat this process. Otherwise, just tap or click Finish.

## Arranging, editing, and removing tasks

As long as you are in author mode, you can edit tasks and their properties by using the taskpad Properties dialog box. To display this dialog box, press and hold or right-click the folder or item where you defined the taskpad and then select Edit Taskpad View from the shortcut menu. In the Tasks tab shown in Figure 5-24, you can do the following:

- **Arrange tasks**   To arrange tasks in a specific order, select a task and then tap or click Move Up or Move Down to set the task order.

- **Create new tasks**   To create a new task, tap or click New and then use the New Task Wizard to define the task.

- **Edit existing tasks**   To edit a task, select it and then tap or click Modify.

- **Remove tasks**   To remove a task, select it and then tap or click Remove.

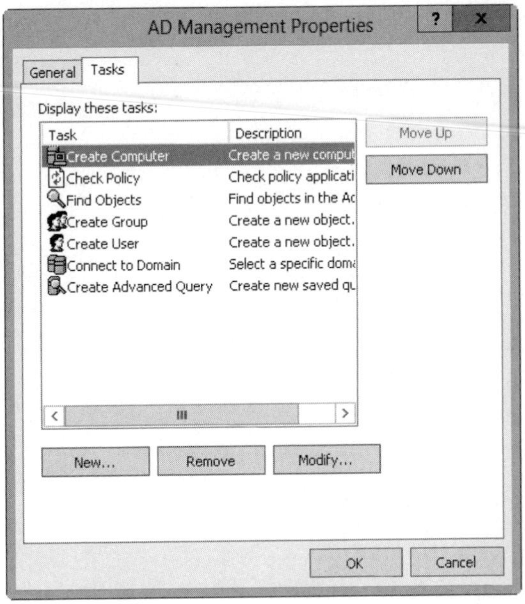

**Figure 5-24** Use the Tasks tab in the taskpad Properties dialog box to arrange, create, edit, and remove tasks.

# Publishing and distributing your custom tools

As you've seen, the MMC provides a complete framework for creating custom tools that can be tailored to the needs of a wide range of users. For administrators, you could create custom consoles tailored for each individual specialty, such as security administration, network administration, or user administration. For junior administrators or advanced users with delegated privileges, you could create custom consoles that include taskpads that help guide them by providing lists of common commands, and you can even restrict this list so that these individuals can perform only these commands.

Because custom consoles are saved as regular files, you can publish and distribute them as you would any other file. You could put the consoles on a network file server in a shared folder. You could email the consoles directly to those who will use them. You could use Active Directory to publish the tools. You could even copy them directly to the Start menu on the appropriate computer, as discussed previously.

In any case, users need appropriate access permissions to run the tasks and access the snap-ins. These permissions must be granted for a particular computer or the network.

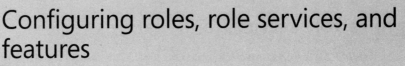

You prepare servers for use by installing and configuring the following components:

- **Server roles**   Server roles are related sets of software components that allow servers to perform a specific function for users and other computers on networks. A computer can be dedicated to a single role, such as Active Directory Domain Services (AD DS), or a computer can provide multiple roles.

- **Role services**   Role services are software components that provide the functionality of server roles. Each server role has one or more related role services. Some server roles, such as Domain Name Service (DNS) and Dynamic Host Configuration Protocol (DHCP), have a single function, and installing the role installs this function. Other roles, such as Network Policy And Access Services and Active Directory Certificate Services, have multiple role services that you can install. With these server roles, you can choose which role services to install.

- **Features**   Features are software components that provide additional functionality. Features, such as Windows Internet Naming Service (WINS) and Windows Server Backup, are installed and removed separately from roles and role services. A computer can have multiple features installed or none, depending on its configuration.

You configure roles, role services, and features using the Server Manager console. Server Manager's command-line counterpart is the ServerManager module for Windows PowerShell.

> **Note**
> Although Server Manager allows you to work with a local server, other servers must be added for management, as discussed in "Adding servers for management" in Chapter 4, "Managing Windows Server 2012." For ease of reference in this chapter, I will refer to servers added for management in Server Manager as *managed servers*.

# Using roles, role services, and features

Before modifying a server's configuration, you should carefully plan how adding or removing a role, role service, or feature will affect a server's overall performance. Although you typically want to combine complementary roles, doing so increases the workload on the server, so you need to optimize the server hardware accordingly. Also, keep in mind that roles, role services, and features can be dependent on other roles, role services, and features. When you install roles, role services, and features, Server Manager prompts you to install any additional roles, role services, or features that are required. If you try to remove a required component of an installed role, role service, or feature, Server Manager warns that you cannot remove the component unless you also remove the other role, role service, or feature.

Table 6-1 provides an overview of the primary roles and the related role services that you can deploy on a server running Windows Server 2012. In addition to roles and features that are included with Windows Server 2012 by default, Server Manager enables integration of additional roles and features that might become available on the Microsoft Download Center as optional updates to Windows Server 2012.

**TABLE 6-1**  **Primary roles and related role services for Windows Server 2012**

| Role | Description |
| --- | --- |
| Active Directory Certificate Services (AD CS) | AD CS provides functions necessary for issuing and revoking digital certificates for users, client computers, and servers. It includes these role services: Certification Authority, Certification Authority Web Enrollment, Online Responder, Network Device Enrollment Service, Certificate Enrollment Web Service, and Certificate Enrollment Policy Web Service. |
| Active Directory Domain Services (AD DS) | AD DS provides functions necessary for storing information about users, groups, computers, and other objects on the network and makes this information available to users and computers. Active Directory domain controllers give network users and computers access to permitted resources on the network. |
| Active Directory Federation Services (AD FS) | AD FS complements the authentication and access-management features of AD DS by extending them to the World Wide Web. It includes these role services and subservices: Federation Service, Federation Service Proxy, AD FS Web Agents, Claims-Aware Agent, and Windows Token-Based Agent. |
| Active Directory Lightweight Directory Services (AD LDS) | AD LDS provides a data store for directory-enabled applications that do not require AD DS and do not need to be deployed on domain controllers. It does not include additional role services. |
| Active Directory Rights Management Services (AD RMS) | AD RMS provides controlled access to protected email messages, documents, intranet pages, and other types of files. It includes these role services: Active Directory Rights Management Server and Identity Federation Support. |

| Role | Description |
| --- | --- |
| Application Server | Application Server allows a server to host distributed applications built using ASP.NET, Enterprise Services, and Microsoft .NET Framework 4.5. It includes more than a dozen role services. |
| DHCP Server | DHCP Server provides centralized control over IP addressing. DHCP servers can assign dynamic IP addresses and essential TCP/IP settings to other computers on a network. It does not include additional role services. |
| DNS Server | DNS Server is a name-resolution system that resolves computer names to IP addresses. DNS servers are essential for name resolution in Active Directory domains. It does not include additional role services. |
| Fax Server | Fax Server provides centralized control over sending and receiving faxes in the enterprise. A fax server can act as a gateway for faxing and allows you to manage fax resources, such as jobs, reports, and fax devices on the server or on the network. It does not include additional role services. |
| File And Storage Services | File And Storage Services provides essential services for managing files and storage, and the way they are made available and replicated on the network. A number of server roles require some type of file service. It includes these role services and subservices: BranchCache for Network Files, Data Deduplication, Distributed File System, DFS Namespaces, DFS Replication, File Server, File Server Resource Manager, Services for Network File System (NFS), File Server VSS Agent Service, iSCSI Target Server, iSCSI Target Storage Provider, and Storage Services. |
| Hyper-V | Hyper-V provides services for creating and managing virtual machines that emulate physical computers. Virtual machines have separate operating system environments from the host server. |
| Network Policy and Access Services (NPAS) | NPAS provides essential services for managing network access policies. It includes these role services: Network Policy Server (NPS), Health Registration Authority (HRA), and Host Credential Authorization Protocol (HCAP). |
| Print and Document Services | Print and Document Services provides essential services for managing network printers, network scanners, and related drivers. It includes these role services: Print Server, LPD Service, Internet Printing, and Distributed Scan Server. |
| Remote Access | Remote Access provides services for managing routing and remote access to networks. Use this role if you need to configure virtual private networks (VPNs), Network Address Translation (NAT), and other routing services. It includes these role services: DirectAccess and VPN (RAS) And Routing. |

| Role | Description |
|---|---|
| Remote Desktop Services | Remote Desktop Services provides services that allow users to run Windows-based applications that are installed on a remote server. When users run an application on a terminal server, the execution and processing occur on the server and only the data from the application is transmitted over the network. |
| Volume Activation Services | Volume Activation Services provides services for automating the management of volume license keys and volume key activation. |
| Web Server (IIS) | Internet Information Services (IIS) is used to host websites and web-based applications. Websites hosted on a web server can have both static content and dynamic content. You can build web applications hosted on a web server by using ASP.NET and .NET Framework 4.5. When you deploy a web server, you can manage the server configuration using IIS 8 modules and administration tools. It includes several dozen role services. |
| Windows Deployment Services (WDS) | WDS provides services for deploying Windows computers in the enterprise. It includes these role services: Deployment Server and Transport Server. |
| Windows Server Update Services (WSUS) | WSUS provides services for Microsoft Update, allowing you to distribute updates from designated servers. |

Table 6-2 provides an overview of the primary features that you can deploy on a server running Windows Server 2012. Unlike early releases of Windows, some important server features are not installed automatically. For example, you must add Windows Server Backup to use the built-in backup and restore features of the operating system.

**TABLE 6-2  Primary features for Windows Server 2012**

| Feature | Description |
|---|---|
| .NET Framework 3.5 | .NET Framework 3.5 provides APIs for application development, including .NET 2.0 and .NET 3.0 for backward compatibility. |
| .NET Framework 4.5 | .NET Framework 4.5 provides APIs for application development. Additional subfeatures include .NET Framework 4.5, ASP.NET 4.5, and Windows Communication Foundation (WCF) Activation Components. |
| Background Intelligent Transfer Service (BITS) | BITS provides intelligent background transfers. When this feature is installed, the server can act as a BITS server that can receive file uploads from clients. This feature isn't necessary for downloads to clients using BITS. Additional subfeatures include BITS IIS Server Extension and BITS Compact Server. |

| Feature | Description |
|---------|-------------|
| BitLocker Drive Encryption | BitLocker Drive Encryption provides hardware-based security to protect data through full-volume encryption that prevents disk tampering while the operating system is offline. Computers that have Trusted Platform Module (TPM) can use BitLocker Drive Encryption in Startup Key or TPM-Only mode. Both modes provide early integrity validation. |
| BitLocker Network Unlock | BitLocker Network Unlock provides support for network-based key protectors that automatically unlock BitLocker-protected operating system drives when a domain-joined computer is restarted. |
| BranchCache | BranchCache provides services needed for BranchCache client and server functionality. It includes HTTP protocol, Hosted Cache, and related services. |
| Client for NFS | Client for NFS provides functionality for accessing files on UNIX-based NFS servers. |
| Data Center Bridging | Data Center Bridging supports a suite of Institute of Electrical and Electronics Engineers (IEEE) standards for enhancing LANs and enforcing bandwidth allocation. |
| Enhanced Storage | Enhanced Storage provides support for Enhanced Storage Devices. |
| Failover Clustering | Failover Clustering provides clustering functionality that allows multiple servers to work together to provide high availability for services and applications. Many types of services can be clustered, including file and print services. Messaging and database servers are ideal candidates for clustering. |
| Group Policy Management | Group Policy Management installs the Group Policy Management Console (GPMC), which provides centralized administration of Group Policy. |
| Ink and Handwriting Services | Ink and Handwriting Services provides support for use of a pen or stylus and handwriting recognition. |
| Internet Printing Client | Internet Printing Client provides functionality that allows clients to use HTTP to connect to printers on web print servers. |
| IP Address Management Server | IP Address Management Server provides support for central management of the enterprise's IP address space and the related infrastructure servers. |
| iSNS Server Service | iSNS Server Service provides management and server functions for Internet SCSI (iSCSI) devices, allowing the server to process registration requests, deregistration requests, and queries from iSCSI devices. |
| LPR Port Monitor | LPR Port Monitor installs the LPR Port Monitor, which allows printing to devices attached to UNIX-based computers. |

Chapter 6

| Feature | Description |
| --- | --- |
| Media Foundation | Media Foundation provides essential functionality for Windows Media Foundation. |
| Message Queuing | Message Queuing provides management and server functions for distributed message queuing. A group of related subfeatures is available as well. |
| Multipath I/O (MPIO) | MPIO provides the functionality necessary for using multiple data paths to a storage device. |
| Network Load Balancing (NLB) | NLB provides failover support and load balancing for IP-based applications and services by distributing incoming application requests among a group of participating servers. Web servers are ideal candidates for load balancing. |
| Peer Name Resolution Protocol (PNRP) | PNRP provides Link-Local Multicast Name Resolution (LLMNR) functionality that allows peer-to-peer, name-resolution services. When you install this feature, applications running on the server can use LLMNR to register and resolve names. |
| Quality Windows Audio Video Experience | Quality Windows Audio Video Experience is a networking platform for audio video (AV) streaming applications on IP home networks. |
| RAS Connection Manager Administration Kit | RAS Connection Manager Administration Kit provides the framework for creating profiles for connecting to remote servers and networks. |
| Remote Assistance | Remote Assistance allows a remote user to connect to the server to provide or receive Remote Assistance. |
| Remote Differential Compression | Remote Differential Compression provides support for differential compression by determining which parts of a file have changed and replicating only the changes. |
| Remote Procedure Call (RPC) over HTTP Proxy | RPC over HTTP Proxy installs a proxy for relaying RPC messages from client applications to the server over HTTP. RPC over HTTP is an alternative to having clients access the server over a VPN connection. |
| Remote Server Administration Tools (RSAT) | RSAT installs role-management and feature-management tools that can be used for remote administration of other Windows Server systems. Options for individual tools are provided, or you can install tools by top-level category or subcategory. |
| Simple Mail Transfer Protocol (SMTP) Server | SMTP Server is a network protocol for controlling the transfer and routing of email messages. When this feature is installed, the server can act as a basic SMTP server. For a full-featured solution, you need to install a messaging server, such as Microsoft Exchange Server. |
| Simple Network Management Protocol (SNMP) Services | SNMP Services is a protocol used to simplify management of TCP/IP networks. You can use SNMP for centralized network management if your network has SNMP-compliant devices. You can also use SNMP for network monitoring via network-management software. |

| Feature | Description |
|---|---|
| Simple TCP/IP Services | Simple TCP/IP Services installs additional TCP/IP services, including Character Generator, Daytime, Discard, Echo, and Quote of the Day. |
| Subsystem for UNIX-Based Applications (SUA) | SUA provides functionality for running UNIX-based programs. You can download additional management utilities from the Microsoft website. (Deprecated) |
| Telnet Client | Telnet Client allows a computer to connect to a remote Telnet server and run applications on that server. |
| Telnet Server | Telnet Server hosts the remote sessions for Telnet clients. When Telnet Server is running on a computer, users can connect to the server with a Telnet client from a remote computer. |
| User Interfaces And Infrastructure | User Interfaces And Infrastructure allows you to control the user experience and infrastructure options (Graphical Management Tools And Infrastructure, Desktop Experience, or Server Graphical Shell). Desktop Experience provides Windows desktop functionality on the server (but these functions can reduce the server's overall performance). |
| Windows Biometric Framework | Windows Biometric Framework provides the functionality required for using fingerprint devices. |
| Windows Internal Database | Windows Internal Database allows the server to use relational databases with Windows roles and features that require an internal database, such as AD RMS, UDDI Services, Windows Server Update Services (WSUS), Windows SharePoint Services, and Windows System Resource Manager. |
| Windows PowerShell | Windows PowerShell allows you to manage the Windows PowerShell features of the server. Windows PowerShell 3.0 and the PowerShell ISE are installed by default. |
| Windows PowerShell Web Access | Windows PowerShell Web Access allows the server to act as a web gateway for remotely managing servers in a web browser. |
| Windows Process Activation Service | Windows Process Activation Service provides support for distributed, web-based applications that use HTTP and non-HTTP protocols. |
| Windows Server Backup | Windows Server Backup allows you to back up and restore the operating system, system state, and any data stored on a server. |
| Windows Standards-Based Storage Management | Windows Standards-Based Storage Management provides support for managing standards-based storage and includes management interfaces as well as extensions for Windows Management Instrumentation (WMI) and Windows PowerShell. |
| Windows System Resource Manager (WSRM) | WSRM allows you to manage resource usage on a per-processor basis. (Deprecated) |

Chapter 6

| Feature | Description |
|---|---|
| Windows TIFF IFilter | Windows TIFF IFilter focuses on text-based documents, which means that searching is more successful for documents that contain clearly identifiable text (for example, black text on a white background). |
| WinRM IIS Extension | WinRM IIS Extension provides an Internet Information Services (IIS)–based hosting model. WinRM IIS Extension can be enabled at either the website or virtual-directory level. |
| WINS Server | WINS Server is a name-resolution service that resolves computer names to IP addresses. Installing this feature allows the computer to act as a WINS server. |
| Wireless LAN Service | Wireless LAN Service allows the server to use wireless networking connections and profiles. |
| WOW64 Support | WOW64 Support supports WOW64, which is required on a Full Server installation. Removing this feature converts a Full Server installation to a Server Core installation. |
| XPS Viewer | XPS Viewer is a program you can use to view, search, set permissions for, and digitally sign XPS documents. |

# Making supplemental components available

Microsoft designed Server Manager and the underlying framework for managing components to be extensible. This makes it easier to provide supplemental roles, role services, and features for the operating system.

You can make these components available for installation and configuration by completing the following steps:

1. Download the installer package or packages from the Microsoft website. Typically, these are provided as a set of Microsoft Update Standalone Packages (.msu) files.

2. Double-tap or double-click each installer package to register it for use.

3. If Server Manager is running on the server, restart or refresh Server Manager to make the new components available.

4. In Server Manager, use the appropriate wizard to install and configure the supplemental role, role service, or feature.

# Installing components with Server Manager

Server Manager is the primary tool you'll use to manage roles, role services, and features. Not only can you use Server Manager to add or remove roles, role services, and features, but you can also use Server Manager to view the configuration details and status for these software components.

By default, Server Manager is started automatically. If you closed the console or disabled automatic startup, you can open the console by tapping or clicking the related option on the taskbar. Another way to do this is by pressing the Windows key, typing **ServerManager.exe** in the Apps Search box, and then pressing Enter.

## Viewing configured roles and role services

Server Manager automatically creates server groups based on the roles of managed servers. When you select a role-based group in the left pane, the Servers panel shows the managed servers that have this role. As shown in Figure 6-1, the details for the selected server group provide the following information for all servers in the group:

- The status of related system services. You can manage a service (and its dependent services) by pressing and holding or right-clicking and then selecting Stop Services, Start Services, or Restart Services. In many cases, if a service isn't running as you think it should, you can tap or click Restart Services to resolve the issue by stopping and then starting the service.

- Error and warning events the related services and components have generated recently. If you tap or click an event, you get additional information about the event (if available).

- Summary information about the related role services and features, including the number of related role services and features installed as well as the name and sub-path of the related role, role service, or feature in the UI. For example, with Storage Services, the component type is listed as Role Services and the path is listed as File And Storage Services\Storage Services.

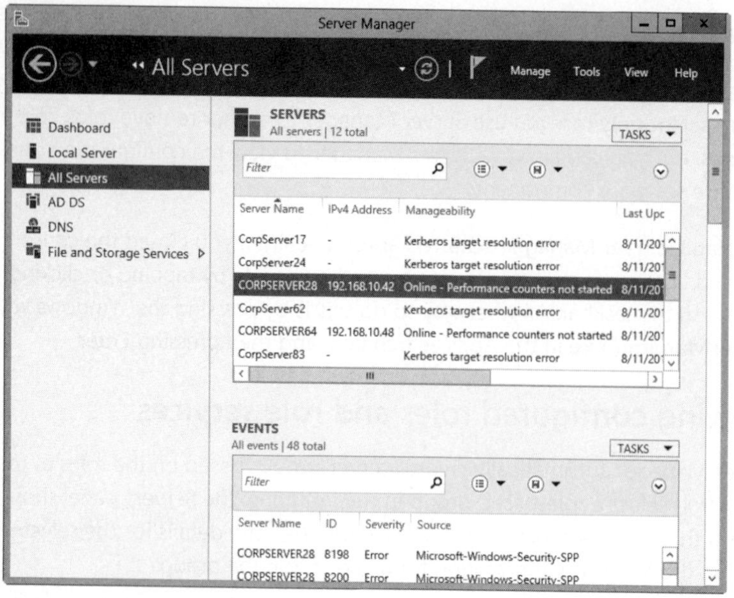

**Figure 6-1** View the status details for installed roles.

You can refresh the server details manually by tapping or clicking the Refresh Servers button on the toolbar. Otherwise, Server Manager refreshes the details periodically for you. If you want to set a different default refresh interval, tap or click Manage and then tap or click Server Manager Properties. Next, set the new refresh interval in minutes and then tap or click OK.

## Managing server roles and features

When you select All Servers in Server Manager, the Roles And Features pane provides details on the current roles and features that are installed on all managed servers. As you set out to add roles to a server, keep in mind that some roles cannot be added at the same time as other roles, and you'll have to install each role separately. Other roles cannot be combined with existing roles, and you'll see warning prompts about this.

### Adding server roles and features

You can add a server role or feature by following these steps:

1.  In Server Manager, select Add Roles And Features on the Manage menu. This starts the Add Roles And Features Wizard.

> **Note**
>
> If the wizard displays the Before You Begin page, read the introductory text and then tap or click Next. You can avoid seeing the Before You Begin page the next time you start this wizard by selecting the Skip This Page By Default check box before tapping or clicking Next.

2. On the Installation Type page, Role-Based Or Feature-Based Installation is selected by default. Tap or click Next.

3. On the Server Selection page, shown in Figure 6-2, you can choose to install roles and features on running servers or virtual hard disks. Only servers running Windows Server 2012 and that have been added for management are listed. Either select a server from the server pool or select a server from the server pool on which to mount a virtual hard disk (VHD). If you are adding roles and features to a VHD, tap or click Browse and then use the Browse For Virtual Hard Disks dialog box to locate the VHD. When you are ready to continue, tap or click Next.

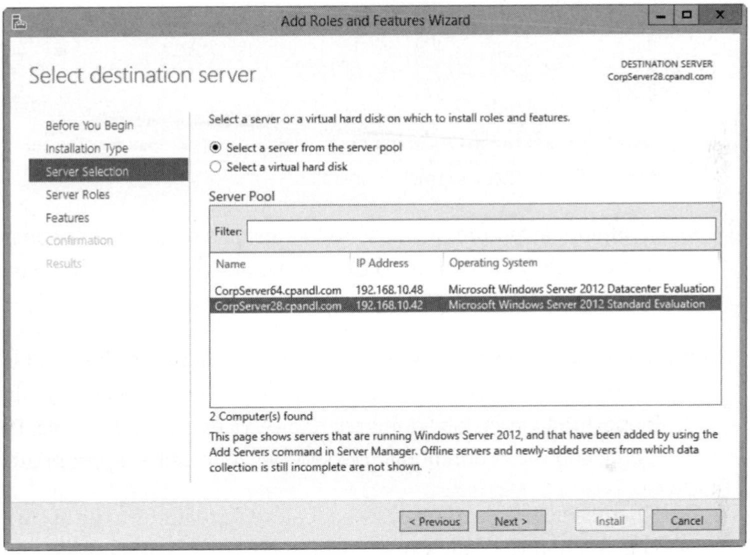

Figure 6-2 Select the server or virtual hard disk to use for the installation.

4. On the Server Roles page, shown in Figure 6-3, select the role or roles to install. Some roles cannot be added at the same time as other roles. You have to install each role separately. Other roles cannot be combined with existing roles, and you'll see warning prompts about this. A server running a Server Core installation can act as a domain controller and can also hold any of the flexible single-master operations (FSMOs) roles for Active Directory.

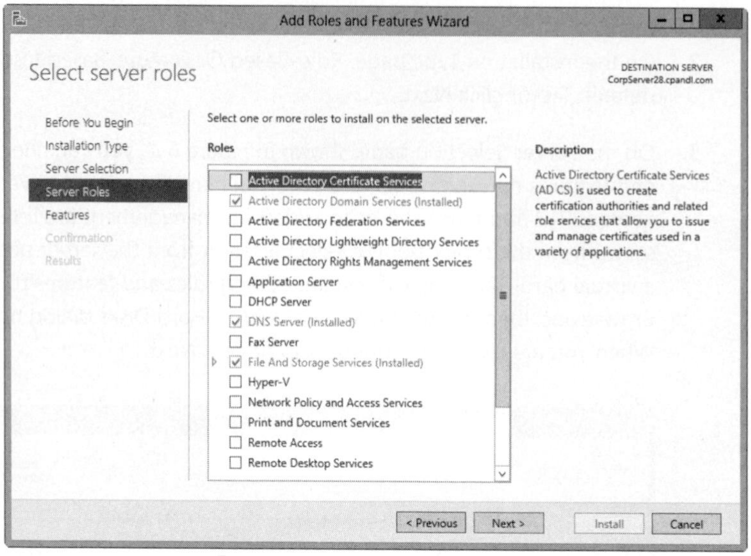

**Figure 6-3** Select the roles to install.

5. If additional features are required to install a role, you'll see an additional dialog box. Tap or click Add Features to close the dialog box and add the required features to the server installation. Tap or click Next to continue.

6. With some roles, you'll see an extra wizard page, which provides additional information about using and configuring the role. You might also have the opportunity to install additional role services as part of a role. Read the information page, and select additional role services to install as appropriate.

7. On the Features page, select the feature or features to install. If additional features are required to install a feature you selected, you'll see an additional dialog box. Tap or click Add Features to close the dialog box and add the required features to the server installation. When you are ready to continue, tap or click Next.

8. On the Confirmation page, tap or click the Export Configuration Settings link to generate an installation report that can be displayed in Internet Explorer.

## TROUBLESHOOTING

**Accessing binary source files**

Access to binary source files is required to successfully install server roles, role services, and features. If the server on which you want to install roles or features doesn't have all the required binary source files, the server gets the files via Windows Update by default or from a location specified in Group Policy.

You also can specify an alternate path for the source files. To do this, click the Specify An Alternate Source Path link, type that alternate path in the box provided, and then tap or click OK. If you mount a Windows image and make it available on the local server, you can enter the alternate path as **c:\mountdir\windows\winsxs**. For network shares, enter the UNC path to the share, such as **\\CorpServer36\WS12\**. For mounted Windows images, enter the WIM path prefixed with WIM: and including the index of the image to use, such as **WIM:\\CorpServer36\WS12\install.wim:4**.

For information on managing binary source files, see "Managing server binaries" later in this chapter.

9. Restarting the destination server might be required to complete the installation of some roles and features. To automatically restart the destination server if required, select the related check box. If you do not select this check box and a restart is required, you will need to manually restart the server to complete the installation.

10. After you review the installation options and save them as necessary, tap or click Install to begin the installation process. The Installation Progress page tracks the progress of the installation. If you close the wizard, tap or click the Notifications icon in Server Manager and then tap or click the link provided to re-open the wizard.

11. When Setup finishes installing the server with the roles and features you selected, the Installation Progress page will be updated to reflect this. Review the installation details to ensure that all phases of the installation were completed successfully. If any portion of the installation failed, note the reason for the failure. Review the Server Manager entries for installation problems, and take corrective actions as appropriate.

Chapter 6

# INSIDE OUT   Completing additional installation tasks

Any additional actions that might be required to complete the installation are listed when Setup finishes installing the roles and features you selected. Typically, you'll have a link you can click to begin these additional tasks. For example, installing a domain controller is a multipart process that begins with installing the components required for the role. After this, you must promote the server and configure directory services—all of which can be done in Server Manager.

If you close the Add Roles And Features Wizard, tap or click the Notifications icon in Server Manager to display a list of recent notifications, as shown in the graphic that follows:

In this example, there are several important notifications:

- The first notification tells you that the automatic refresh of server information failed. This can happen for several reasons, with the most common reason being that one or more of the servers added for management is offline or otherwise inaccessible.

- The second notification tells you that CorpServer64 must be restarted to complete the installation of an added feature. You also could confirm that a restart was required by selecting the All Servers node in Server Manager, where you'd see a status of Online - Restart Pending for CorpServer64 (as long as the server was online and accessible). Finally, tapping or clicking the Add Roles And Features link, opens the Add Roles And Features Wizard, where you'd see the Installation Progress page and could note exactly what had been installed to require the restart.

- The third notification tells you that CorpServer64 has a post-deployment configuration task that needs to be performed for DHCP. Tapping or clicking Complete DHCP Configuration opens the DHCP Post-Install Configuration Wizard.

## Removing server roles and features

You can remove a server role by following these steps:

1. In Server Manager, select Remove Roles And Features on the Manage menu. This starts the Remove Roles And Features Wizard.

> **Note**
>
> If the wizard displays the Before You Begin page, read the introductory text and then tap or click Next. You can avoid seeing the Before You Begin page the next time you start this wizard by selecting the Skip This Page By Default check box before tapping or clicking Next.

2. On the Server Selection page, you can choose to remove roles and features from running servers or virtual hard disks. Only servers running Windows Server 2012 and that have been added for management are listed. Either select a server from the server pool or select a server from the server pool on which to mount a virtual hard disk (VHD). If you are removing roles and features from a VHD, tap or click Browse and then use the Browse For Virtual Hard Disks dialog box to locate the VHD. When you are ready to continue, tap or click Next.

3. On the Server Roles page, shown in Figure 6-4, clear the check box for the role you want to remove. If you try to remove a role that another role or feature depends on, a warning prompt appears stating that you cannot remove the role unless you remove the other role as well. If you tap or click the Remove Features button, Setup removes the dependent roles and features as well. Note that if you want to keep related management tools, you should clear the Remove Management Tools check box prior to tapping or clicking the Remove Features button and then click Continue. Tap or click Next.

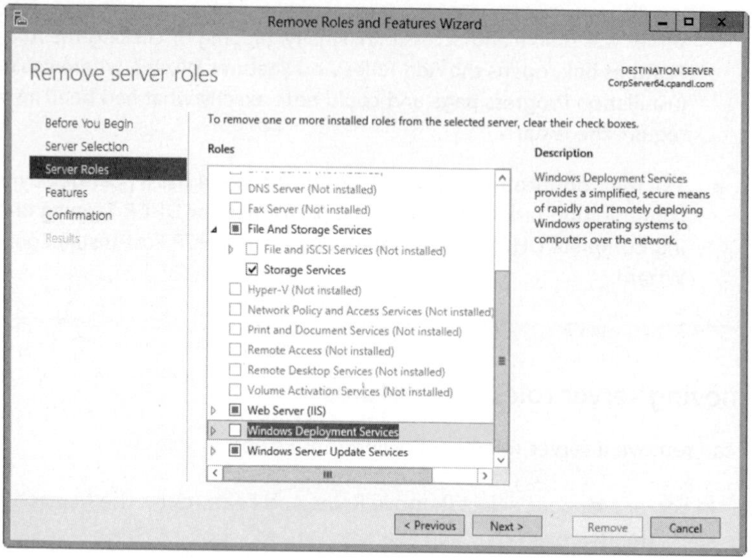

**Figure 6-4** Clear selected roles to remove them.

**4.** On the Features page, the currently installed features are selected. To remove a feature, clear the related check box. If you try to remove a feature that another feature or role depends on, you'll see a warning prompt stating that you cannot remove the feature unless you also remove the other feature or role. If you tap or click the Remove Features button, Setup removes the dependent roles and features as well. Note that if you want to keep related management tools, you should clear the Remove Management Tools check box and then click Continue prior to tapping or clicking the Remove Features button. Tap or click Next.

**5.** On the Confirmation page, review the components that Setup will remove based on your previous selections. Restarting the destination server might be required to complete the removal of some roles and features. To automatically restart the destination server if required, select the related check box. If you don't select this check box and a restart is required, you will need to manually restart the server to complete the removal.

**6.** Tap or click Remove. The Removal Progress page tracks the progress of the removal. If you close the wizard, tap or click the Notifications icon in Server Manager and then tap or click the link provided to re-open the wizard.

When Setup finishes modifying the server configuration, you'll see the Removal Progress page. Review the modification details to ensure that all phases of the removal process were completed successfully. As necessary, note any additional actions that might be required to complete the removal, such as restarting the server or performing additional removal tasks. If any portion of the removal failed, review the Server Manager entries for removal problems and take corrective actions as appropriate.

## Managing server binaries

Binaries needed to install roles and features are referred to as *payloads*. With Windows Server 2012, payloads normally are stored in subfolders of the Windows Side-by-Side folder (%SystemDrive%\Windows\WinSXS). However, to enhance security, you can disable roles and features and remove the payload used to install these roles and features. When you remove a payload, servers try to get the required binary files via Windows Update by default. In Group Policy, you can configure an alternative to Windows Update. You do this by specifying an alternative download location.

If you want to remove binaries, you use Windows PowerShell to do this and not Server Manager. The ServerManager module for Windows PowerShell is the command-line counterpart of Server Manager.

# INSIDE OUT   Importing the ServerManager module

Generally, when you are logged on to a server running Windows Server 2012, this module is imported into Windows PowerShell by default. If you are working from your management computer running a different operating system, however, you might need to import the module before you can use the ServerManager module's cmdlets. You import the Server Manager module by entering the following command at the Windows PowerShell prompt:

```
import-module servermanager
```

Once the module is imported, you can use it with the currently running instance of Windows PowerShell. If the module is not automatically imported, you will need to import the module again the next time you start Windows PowerShell. Note also that if the module isn't being imported automatically for you when you start Windows PowerShell, you can add an import statement to your profile and scripts to ensure the ServerManager module is available, as shown in this example:

```
import-module servermanager
```

The Get-WindowsFeature cmdlet returns a detailed list of a server's current state with regard to roles, role services, and features. When you type **get-windowsfeature** at a PowerShell prompt, you'll see the state of each role, role service, and feature listed as one of the following:

- **Available**    Meaning the component is available for installation

- **Installed**    Meaning the component is already installed

- **Removed**    Meaning the payload for the component has been removed

As shown in the partial listing that follows, each role, role service, or feature is listed by display name and then by its management naming component:

```
[ ] Active Directory Certificate Services      AD-Certificate          Removed
    [ ] Certification Authority                 ADCS-Cert-Authority     Removed
    [ ] Certificate Enrollment Policy Web Serv... ADCS-Enroll-Web-Pol   Removed
    [ ] Certificate Enrollment Web Service      ADCS-Enroll-Web-Svc     Removed
    [ ] Certification Authority Web Enrollment  ADCS-Web-Enrollment     Removed
    [ ] Network Device Enrollment Service       ADCS-Device-Enrollment  Removed
    [ ] Online Responder                        ADCS-Online-Cert        Removed
[X] Active Directory Domain Services            AD-Domain-Services      Installed
[ ] Active Directory Federation Services        AD-Federation-Services  Available
    [ ] Federation Service                      ADFS-Federation         Available
    [ ] AD FS 1.1 Web Agents                    ADFS-Web-Agents         Available
        [ ] AD FS 1.1 Claims-aware Agent        ADFS-Claims             Available
        [ ] AD FS 1.1 Windows Token-based Agent ADFS-Windows-Token      Available
    [ ] Federation Service Proxy                ADFS-Proxy              Available
[X] Active Directory Rights Management Se...     ADRMS                   Installed
```

By using Install-WindowsFeature followed by the management name, you can install a role, role service, or feature and get its binaries if necessary. Use –*includeallsubfeature* when adding components to add all subordinate components. Use –*includemanagementtools* when adding components to add the related management tools.

You can uninstall a role, role service, or feature using Uninstall-WindowsFeature. If you specify a top-level role with role service and feature subcomponents, the subcomponents are uninstalled as well.

To uninstall a role, role service, or feature and then remove the related binaries from the Windows Side-By-Side folder, you use the –*Remove* parameter with Uninstall-WindowsFeature. If you specify a top-level role with role service and feature subcomponents, the binaries for the subcomponents are removed as well.

Use –*includemanagementtools* when removing components to remove the related management tools.

In the previous example, Active Directory Certificate Services and its subcomponents were removed. Knowing this, you could retrieve the binaries for the role, subordinate role services, and features and then install these components as well as the related management tools by entering the following command:

```
install-windowsfeature ad-certificate –includeallsubfeature –includemanagementtools
```

Because adding or removing components requires administrator privileges, you must run this command at an elevated PowerShell prompt.

## TROUBLESHOOTING

**Performing administrator tasks at a prompt**
Whether you are working with the command prompt or the Windows PowerShell prompt, you must open an elevated prompt to perform administration tasks. To open an elevated prompt, press and hold or right-click the shortcut for the prompt on Start, Desktop, or the taskbar and then tap or click Run As Administrator.

If you forget to elevate the prompt and try to perform administration, you typically will see an error stating you don't have adequate user rights to make changes. Sometimes, however, the error message won't be as explicit and command execution will simply fail.

By default, when you use Install-WindowsFeature, payloads are restored via Windows Update. You can use the –*Source* parameter to restore a payload from a Windows Imaging (WIM) mount point. For example, if an image for Windows Server 2012 is available at the network path \\ImageServer32\WinServer12EE, you could specify the source as follows:

```
install-windowsfeature -name ad-certificate –includeallsubfeature
-source \\imageserver18\winserver12ee
```

The path you specify is used only if the required binaries are not found in the Windows Side-By-Side folder on the destination server. You also can mount the Windows Server 2012 distribution media and use the Windows\WinSXS folder from the installation image as your source. To do this, follow these steps:

1. Log on to the server using an account with administrator privileges. Insert the installation disc into the server's disc drive.

2. Open an elevated command prompt. Create a folder to mount the Installation image by typing the following command: **mkdir c:\mountdir**.

3.  Locate the index number of the image you want to use by typing the following command at the elevated prompt: **dism /get-wiminfo /wimfile:e:\sources\ install.wim**, where *e:* is the drive designator of the server's disc drive.

4.  Mount the installation image by typing the following command at the elevated prompt: **dism /mount-wim /wimfile:e:\sources\install.wim /index:2 /mountdir:c:\mountdir /readonly**, where *e:* is the drive designator of the server's disc drive, *2* is the index of the image to use, and *c:\mountdir* is the mount directory. Mounting the image might take several minutes.

5.  Open an elevated PowerShell prompt. Use Install-WindowsFeature with the source specified as c:\mountdir\windows\winsxs, as shown in this example:

```
install-windowsfeature -name ad-domain-services -includeallsubfeature
-source c:\mountdir\windows\winsxs
```

You can use Group Policy to control whether Windows Update is used to restore payloads and to provide alternate source paths for restoring payloads. The policy you want to work with is Specify Settings For Optional Component Installation And Component Repair, which is under Computer Configuration\Administrative Templates\System. This policy also is used for obtaining payloads needed to repair components.

If you enable Specify Settings For Optional Component Installation And Component Repair (as shown in Figure 6-5), you can do the following:

*   Set at alternate source file path for payloads as a network location. For network shares, type the UNC path to the share, such as **\\CorpServer82\WinServer2012\**. For mounted Windows images, type the WIM path prefixed with WIM: and including the index of the image to use, such as **WIM:\\CorpServer82\WinServer2012\ install.wim:4**.

*   Restrict downloading payloads from Windows Update. If you enable the policy and use this option, you do not have to specify an alternate path. In this case, payloads cannot be obtained automatically and administrators will need to explicitly specify the alternate source path.

*   Designate Windows Update as the source for repairing components rather than Windows Server Update Services.

## TROUBLESHOOTING

### Resolving blocked downloads of binaries

Disabling or not configuring Specify Settings For Optional Component Installation And Component Repair doesn't disable component installation and repair. In fact, if you disable or do not configure this policy, Windows uses the standard approach for installing and repairing components, which is to do so via Windows Update. However, if you enable this policy and then specify to never attempt to download payloads from Windows Update, you prevent computers from using Windows Update and require them to get the payload from a designated alternate source. If you don't specify an alternate source (or the alternate source is inaccessible), computers are blocked from getting payloads for removed components as well as payloads for components that need to be repaired. To re-enable automatic component installation and repair, you will need to change the policy state to either Not Configured or Disabled and then refresh the policy (or wait for the policy to refresh automatically).

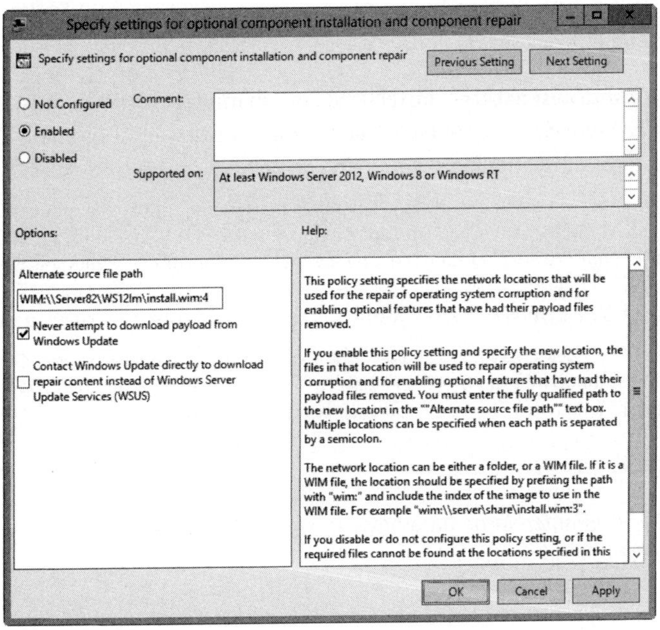

**Figure 6-5** Configuring component installation and repair through Group Policy.

# Installing components at the prompt

Earlier in the chapter, in the section "Managing server binaries," I discussed using the ServerManager module and its cmdlets. Now it's time to take a closer look at the module and its cmdlets and provide additional examples.

When you want to manage server configuration at a prompt or in a script, you'll use Windows PowerShell and the ServerManager module. Not only can you use this module's cmdlets to add or remove roles, role services, and features, but you can use them to view the configuration details and status for these software components.

## Going to the prompt for Server Management

You manage roles, role services, and features using the following cmdlets, which are part of the ServerManager module:

- **Get-WindowsFeature**   Lists the server's current state with regard to roles, role services, and features.

  ```
  Get-WindowsFeature [[-Name] ComponentNames] [-ComputerName Computer]
  [-Credential Credential] [-LogPath LogFile.txt] [-Vhd VhdPath] [-WhatIf]
  ```

- **Install-WindowsFeature**   Installs the named role, role service, or feature. The *-IncludeAllSubFeature* parameter allows you to install all subordinate role services and features of the named component.

  ```
  Install-WindowsFeature [-Name] ComponentNames [-ComputerName Computer]
  [-IncludeAllSubFeature] [-IncludeManagementTools] [-Credential Credential]
  -LogPath LogFile.txt] [-Source SourcePath] [-Restart | -Vhd VhdPath] [-WhatIf]
  ```

- **Uninstall-WindowsFeature**   Removes the named role, role service, or feature.

  ```
  Uninstall-WindowsFeature [-Name] ComponentNames [-ComputerName Computer]
  [-IncludeManagementTools] [-Credential Credential] [-LogPath LogFile.txt]
  [-Remove] [-Restart | -Vhd VhdPath] [-WhatIf]
  ```

When applicable, you can

- Use the *-ComputerName* parameter to specify the name or IP address of a remote computer to work with. Only one computer can be specified.

- Use the *-Credential* parameter to pass in a credential for authentication. Credential objects are returned by the Get-Credential cmdlet.

> **Note**
> You can specify a user name as the credential using the format: "UserName"
> or "Domain\UserName" where the quotes are required, such as –Credential
> "CPANDL\Williams". If you enter a user name, you will be prompted for a
> password.

- Use the –*LogPath* parameter to log error details to a named log file as an alternative to the default logging used. The value you specify sets the path and the name of the log file.

- Use the –*Restart* parameter to restart the computer automatically (if restarting is necessary to complete the operation).

- Use the –*Vhd* parameter to specify the path to an offline VHD, which can be a relative local path on the target computer, such as C:\virt\server12b.vhd, or a network share specified by the UNC path, such as \\server42\curr\server12b.vhd.

- Use the –*WhatIf* parameter to display the operations that would be performed if the command were executed.

Installable roles, role services, and features have a corresponding component name that identifies the component so that you can manipulate it from the PowerShell prompt. This also is true for supplemental components you've made available by downloading and installing their installer packages from the Microsoft website. You specify the list of components to install using the –*Name* parameter. This parameter matches actual component names and not display names. With Get-WindowsFeature, you can use wildcard characters. With Install-WindowsFeature and Uninstall-WindowsFeature, you cannot use wildcards but can use pipelining to get the required input names from another command, such as Get-WindowsFeature.

## Understanding component names

Every installable role, role service, and feature has a component name. This name identifies the component so that it can be manipulated from the prompt. Remember, supplemental components are made available by downloading and installing their installer packages from the Microsoft website.

Table 6-3 provides a hierarchical listing of the component names associated with roles, related role services, and related subcomponents. When you are installing a role, you can use the –*IncludeAllSubFeature* parameter to install all the subordinate role services and features listed under the role and the *–IncludeManagementTools* parameter to install the related management tools.

**TABLE 6-3 Component names for key roles and role services**

| Component Name | Role | Role Service | Subcomponent |
| --- | --- | --- | --- |
| AD-Certificate | Active Directory Certificate Services[1] | | |
| AD-Domain-Services | Active Directory Domain Services | | |
| AD-Federation-Services | Active Directory Federation Services[1] | | |
| ADLDS | Active Directory Lightweight Directory Services | | |
| ADRMS | Active Directory Rights Management Services | | |
| ADRMS-Server | | Active Directory Rights Management Server | |
| ADRMS-Identity | | Identity Federation Support | |
| Application-Server | Application Server[1] | | |
| DHCP | DHCP Server | | |
| DNS | DNS Server | | |
| Fax | Fax Server | | |
| FileAndStorage-Services | File And Storage Services | | |
| File-Services | | File and iSCSI Services | |
| FS-FileServer | | | File Server |
| FS-BranchCache | | | BranchCache for Network Files |
| FS-Data-Deduplication | | | Data Deduplication |
| FS-DFS-Namespace | | | DFS Namespaces |
| FS-DFS-Replication | | | DFS Replication |
| FS-Resource-Manager | | | File Server Resource Manager |
| FS-VSS-Agent | | File Server VSS Agent Service | |
| FS-iSCSITarget-Server | | iSCSI Target Server | |

| Component Name | Role | Role Service | Subcomponent |
|---|---|---|---|
| iSCSITarget-VSS-VDS | | iSCSI Target Storage Provider | |
| FS-NFS-Service | | Server for NFS | |
| Storage-Services | | Storage Services | |
| Hyper-V | Hyper-V | | |
| NPAS | Network Policy and Access Services | | |
| NPAS-Policy-Server | | Network Policy Server | |
| NPAS-Health | | Health Registration Authority | |
| NPAS-Host-Cred | | Host Credential Authorization Protocol | |
| Print-Services | Print and Document Services | | |
| Print-Server | | Print Server | |
| Print-Scan-Server | | Distributed Scan Server | |
| Print-Internet | | Internet Printing | |
| Print-LPD-Service | | LPD Service | |
| RemoteAccess | Remote Access | | |
| DirectAccess-VPN | | DirectAccess and VPN (RAS) | |
| Routing | | Routing | |
| Remote-Desktop-Services | Remote Desktop Services[1] | | |
| VolumeActivation | Volume Activation Services | | |
| Web-Server | Web Server (IIS)[1] | | |
| WDS | Windows Deployment Services | | |
| WDS-Deployment | | Deployment Server | |
| WDS-Transport | | Transport Server | |
| UpdateServices | Windows Server Update Services | | |
| UpdateServices-WidDB | | WID Database | |
| UpdateServices-Services | | WSUS Services | |
| UpdateServices-DB | | Database | |

[1] Indicates the component has unlisted subordinate components that generally are installed together by adding the -IncludeAllSubFeature parameter.

Chapter 6

Table 6-4 provides a hierarchical listing of the component names associated with features and related subfeatures. When you are installing a feature, you can use the *–IncludeAllSubFeature* parameter to install all the subordinate second-level and third-level features listed under the feature and the *–IncludeManagementTools* parameter to install the related management tools.

**TABLE 6-4** **Component names for features and subfeatures**

| Component Name | Feature | Subcomponent |
|---|---|---|
| NET-Framework-Features | .NET Framework 3.5 Features[1] | |
| NET-Framework-45-Features | .NET Framework 4.5 Features | |
| NET-Framework-45-Core | | .NET Framework 4.5 |
| NET-Framework-45-ASPNET | | ASP.NET 4.5 |
| NET-WCF-Services45 | | WCF Services[1] |
| BITS | Background Intelligent Transfer Service (BITS)[1] | |
| BitLocker | BitLocker Drive Encryption | |
| BitLocker-NetworkUnlock | BitLocker Network Unlock | |
| BranchCache | BranchCache | |
| NFS-Client | Client for NFS | |
| Data-Center-Bridging | Data Center Bridging | |
| EnhancedStorage | Enhanced Storage | |
| Failover-Clustering | Failover Clustering | |
| GPMC | Group Policy Management | |
| InkAndHandwritingServices | Ink and Handwriting Services | |
| Internet-Print-Client | Internet Printing Client | |
| IPAM | IP Address Management (IPAM) Server | |
| ISNS | iSNS Server service | |
| LPR-Port-Monitor | LPR Port Monitor | |
| ManagementOdata | Management OData IIS Extension | |
| Server-Media-Foundation | Media Foundation | |
| MSMQ | Message Queuing[1] | |
| Multipath-IO | Multipath I/O | |
| NLB | Network Load Balancing | |
| PNRP | Peer Name Resolution Protocol | |
| qWave | Quality Windows Audio Video Experience | |

| Component Name | Feature | Subcomponent |
|---|---|---|
| CMAK | RAS Connection Manager Administration Kit (CMAK) | |
| Remote-Assistance | Remote Assistance | |
| RDC | Remote Differential Compression | |
| RSAT | Remote Server Administration Tools | |
| RSAT-Feature-Tools | | Feature Administration Tools[1] |
| RSAT-Role-Tools | | Role Administration Tools[1] |
| RPC-over-HTTP-Proxy | RPC over HTTP Proxy | |
| Simple-TCPIP | Simple TCP/IP Services | |
| SMTP-Server | SMTP Server | |
| SNMP-Service | SNMP Service[1] | |
| User-Interfaces-Infra | User Interfaces and Infrastructure | |
| Server-Gui-Mgmt-Infra | | Graphical Management Tools and Infrastructure |
| Desktop-Experience | | Desktop Experience |
| Server-Gui-Shell | | Server Graphical Shell |
| Biometric-Framework | Windows Biometric Framework | |
| PowerShellRoot | Windows PowerShell | |
| PowerShell | | Windows PowerShell 3.0 |
| PowerShell-V2 | | Windows PowerShell 2.0 Engine |
| PowerShell-ISE | | Windows PowerShell ISE |
| WindowsPowerShellWebAccess | | Windows PowerShell Web Access |
| WAS | Windows Process Activation Service[1] | |
| Search-Service | Windows Search Service | |
| Windows-Server-Backup | Windows Server Backup | |
| Migration | Windows Server Migration Tools | |
| WINS | WINS Server | |
| Wireless-Networking | Wireless LAN Service | |

| Component Name | Feature | Subcomponent |
|---|---|---|
| WoW64-Support | WoW64 Support | |
| XPS-Viewer | XPS Viewer | |

[1] Indicates the component has unlisted subordinate components that generally are installed together by adding the -IncludeAllSubFeature parameter.

# Tracking installed roles, role services, and features

As discussed previously, you can determine the roles, roles services, and features that are installed on a server by typing **get-windowsfeature** at a PowerShell prompt. Each installed role, role service, and feature is highlighted and marked as such, with roles and role services listed in the output before features as shown in the following example:

```
Display Name                                        Name                      Install State
------------                                        ----                      -------------
[ ] Active Directory Certificate Services           AD-Certificate            Available
   [ ] Certification Authority                       ADCS-Cert-Authority       Available
   [ ] Certificate Enrollment Policy Web Service     ADCS-Enroll-Web-Pol       Available
   [ ] Certificate Enrollment Web Service            ADCS-Enroll-Web-Svc       Available
   [ ] Certification Authority Web Enrollment        ADCS-Web-Enrollment       Available
   [ ] Network Device Enrollment Service             ADCS-Device-Enrollment    Available
   [ ] Online Responder                              ADCS-Online-Cert          Available
[X] Active Directory Domain Services                 AD-Domain-Services        Installed

...

[X] .NET Framework 4.5 Features                      NET-Framework-45-Fea...   Installed
   [X] .NET Framework 4.5                             NET-Framework-45-Core     Installed
   [X] ASP.NET 4.5                                    NET-Framework-45-ASPNET   Installed
   [X] WCF Services                                   NET-WCF-Services45        Installed
      [ ] HTTP Activation                             NET-WCF-HTTP-Activat...   Available
      [ ] Message Queuing (MSMQ) Activation           NET-WCF-MSMQ-Activat...   Available
      [ ] Named Pipe Activation                       NET-WCF-Pipe-Activat...   Available
      [X] TCP Activation                              NET-WCF-TCP-Activati...   Installed
      [X] TCP Port Sharing                            NET-WCF-TCP-PortShar...   Installed
[ ] Background Intelligent Transfer Service (B...    BITS                      Available
   [ ] IIS Server Extension                           BITS-IIS-Ext              Available
   [ ] Compact Server                                 BITS-Compact-Server       Available
[ ] BitLocker Drive Encryption                       BitLocker                 Available
```

Because the *–Name* parameter, which allows you to look for components with a specific name, accepts wildcards, you can easily check the installation status and availability of related components. This example returns a list of components with a management name that starts with *NET* or *web*:

```
get-windowsfeature –name net*, web*
```

Technically, you don't need to include *–Name*. The *–Name* parameter is the first expected parameter. Thus, you could perform the previous search by entering the following as well:

```
get-windowsfeature net*, web*
```

Because you won't always be working with a local computer at the prompt, you can use the *–ComputerName* parameter to specify the name or IP address of the remote computer you want to work with. In this example, you get the status of components on CorpServer18:

```
get-windowsfeature –computername corpserver18
```

For the purposes of documenting a server's configuration, you can save the output in a file as standard text using the redirection symbol (>) as shown in this example:

```
get-windowsfeature > MySavedResults.txt
```

Here, you save the output to a file named MySavedResults.txt in the current (working) directory.

## Installing components at the prompt

You can install roles, role services, and features by typing **Install-WindowsFeature ComponentName** at an elevated prompt, where *ComponentName* is the management name of the component to install as listed in Table 6-3 or Table 6-4. In the following example, you install DHCP Server and the DHCP console for managing DHCP Server on CorpServer15:

```
Install-windowsfeature dhcp –ComputerName corpserver15 –includemanagementtools
```

Here, you don't need to include the *–IncludeAllSubFeature* parameter because DHCP Server doesn't have any subordinate role services or features. As PowerShell works, you see a Start Installation progress bar. When the installation is complete, you see the result. The output for a successful installation should look similar to the following:

```
Success Restart Needed Exit Code      Feature Result
------- -------------- ---------      --------------

True    No             Success        {DHCP Server}
```

As you can see, the output specifies whether the installation was successful, whether a restart is needed, an exit code, and a list of the exact change or changes made. The exit code can be different from the Success status. For example, if the components you specify are already installed, the exit code is NoChangeNeeded, as shown in this example and sample output:

```
Success Restart Needed Exit Code         Feature Result
------- -------------- ---------         --------------

True    No             NoChangeNeeded    {}
```

Here, you see that Install-WindowsFeature was successful but didn't actually make any changes. The Feature Result shows no changes as well.

You don't have to explicitly name the component or components you want to install. Install-WindowsFeature accepts redirected output for component names, allowing you to use another command to get the name or names of the components you want to work with. For example, if you want to install multiple components, such as all .NET components across the multiple .NET Frameworks that are available, you could use Get-WindowsFeature to help you do this, as shown in the following example:

```
get-windowsfeature -name NET-* | install-windowsfeature
```

Here, you use Get-WindowsFeature to obtain a list of components with names that start with NET– and then pipe that list to Install-WindowsFeature. The result is that you install all .NET components across all available .NET frameworks.

Component installation doesn't always succeed, and that's a common reason that the server cannot be accessed, as shown in this example, with accompanying error text:

```
Success Restart Needed Exit Code         Feature Result
------- -------------- ---------         --------------
False   Maybe          Failed            {}
```

```
install-windowsfeature : WinRM cannot process the request. The following error
occurred while using Kerberos authentication: Cannot find the computer
corpserver15. Verify that the computer exists on the network and that the
name provided is spelled correctly.
```

Here, Windows Remote Management (WinRM) couldn't connect to the remote computer. Typically, this occurs because the server is offline or otherwise unavailable. This also could occur if you entered an incorrect server name.

## TROUBLESHOOTING

### Resolving authentication failure

Less common reasons for authentication failure include improper WinRM configuration or a Kerberos authentication issue:

- Regarding WinRM, the server might not be enabled for remote management in Server Manager. To resolve this, log on to the server console (either locally or via Remote Desktop), open Server Manager, and then select the Local Server Node. If Remote Management is listed as Disabled, click the related link, select Enable Remote Management, and then tap or click OK. For more advanced troubleshooting of WinRm, see "Enabling remote management" in Chapter 4, "Managing Windows Server 2012."

- Regarding Kerberos, the authentication failure could be related to a disparity between the local computer's date and time and the remote computer's date and time. With Kerberos, authentication fails if the message time stamp is off by more than the allowable time difference. To learn more about Kerberos authentication, see "NTLM and Kerberos authentication" in Chapter 25, "Designing and managing the domain environment."

Inadequate user rights is another common reason for component installation to fail, as shown in this example, with accompanying error text:

```
install-windowsfeature : You do not have adequate user rights to make changes to
the target computer. If you are already a member of the Administrators group on
the target computer, the changes might have failed because of security restrictions
imposed by User Account Control. Try running Install-WindowsFeature in a Windows
PowerShell session that has been opened with elevated rights (Run as administrator).

Success Restart Needed Exit Code    Feature Result
------- -------------- ---------    --------------
False   No             Failed       {}
```

Normally, when you are using Windows PowerShell for administration, you'll use an elevated, administrator prompt and your current credentials will pass through to remote computers you work with. However, if your account doesn't have appropriate user rights, you need to provide different credentials and you can do this using the *–Credential* parameter. You'll be prompted for the user's password if you follow the *–Credential* parameter with a user name, as shown in this example:

```
Install-windowsfeature dns -credential "CPANDL\wrstanek" -includemanagementtools
```

Here, you simply type the password and press Enter when prompted to run the command with the named account's permissions. Rather than enter credentials for an account each time you want to perform administration, you can store credentials and then refer to the stored credential, as shown in this example:

```
$cred = get-credential
install-windowsfeature dns -credential $cred -includemanagementtools
```

Here, you use Get-Credential to prompt for a user name and password, and then store those credentials in the *$cred* variable. Next, you refer to the stored credentials to install DNS. Because the credentials are stored for the duration of your current PowerShell session, you can refer to them as needed for additional administration as well.

## TROUBLESHOOTING

**Understanding stored credentials**

Stored credentials are available only in the current PowerShell session. The stored credentials are cleared when you close the PowerShell window. If you have multiple PowerShell windows open, the credentials stored in one window aren't available in another window's session.

To test the installation prior to performing that actual operation, you can use the *–Whatif* parameter, as shown in the following example:

```
get-windowsfeature -name BIT* | install-windowsfeature -whatif
```

If you run this command, you might be surprised to see that BitLocker components are included along with BITS components. To resolve this, you need to be more specific when specifying the component name to match. If you intend to install BitLocker and BitLocker Network Unlock, you can use the following command instead:

```
get-windowsfeature -name bitlock* | install-windowsfeature -whatif
```

If a restart is required to complete an installation, you can have Install-WindowsFeature restart the computer by including the *–Restart* parameter. For planning purposes, especially on highly active production servers, keep in mind that both successful and failed installations could require a restart.

# Removing components at the prompt

You can uninstall roles, role services, and features by typing **Uninstall-ServerManager** **ComponentName** at an elevated command prompt, where *ComponentName* is the name of the component to uninstall as listed in Table 6-3 or Table 6-4. Because Uninstall-ServerManager automatically uninstalls any subordinate role services and features of the specified component, you normally want to test the uninstallation prior to performing that actual operation. To do this, you can use the *–Whatif* parameter, as shown in the following example:

```
uninstall-windowsfeature net-framework-45-features -whatif
```

Here, you want to uninstall .NET Framework 4.5 and related features, which include .NET Framework 4.5 (NET-Framework-45-Core), ASP.NET 4.5 (NET-Framework-45-ASPNET), and multiple subcomponents of WCF Services (NET-WCF-Services45). However, if you want to uninstall only the WCF Services, you enter the following instead:

```
uninstall-windowsfeature net-wcf-services45
```

As with Install-WindowsFeature, you don't have to explicitly name the component or components you want to uninstall. Uninstall-WindowsFeature accepts redirected output for component names, allowing you to use another command to get the name or names of the components you want to work with. For example, if you want to uninstall multiple components, such as all .NET components across the multiple .NET Frameworks that are available, you could use Get-WindowsFeature to help you do this, as shown in the following example:

```
get-windowsfeature -name NET-* | uninstall-windowsfeature
```

To ensure that the command works exactly as expected, you should test the command first using the *–Whatif* parameter, as shown in the following example:

```
get-windowsfeature -name NET-* | uninstall-windowsfeature -whatif
```

As with installing components, the command output specifies if a restart is required to complete the task. If a restart is required to complete a removal, you can have Uninstall-WindowsFeature restart the computer by including the *–Restart* parameter.

If an error occurs and Uninstall-WindowsFeature is not able to perform the operation specified, you'll see an error. Tips and techniques for resolving common errors were discussed in the previous section, "Installing components at the prompt."

Chapter 6

# Managing and troubleshooting hardware

U NLESS you've standardized on a particular hardware platform, most servers that you'll work with will have different hardware components. This means different servers will probably have different motherboards, disk controllers, graphics cards, and network adapters. Fortunately, Windows Server 2012 is designed to work with an extensive list of hardware devices. When you install new hardware, Windows tries to detect the device automatically and then install the correct driver software so that you can use the device. If Windows has a problem with a device, you must troubleshoot the installation, which usually means finding the correct device drivers for the hardware component and installing them.

One thing to keep in mind when working with devices is that, like other software, driver software can contain bugs. These bugs can cause a variety of problems on your servers, and not only could the hardware stop working, but the server could freeze as well. Because of this, you'll want to monitor routinely for hardware problems and take corrective actions as necessary. You'll also find it helpful to maintain a hardware inventory for servers so that you know which devices are installed and who the manufacturers are.

# Understanding hardware installation changes

Hardware installation for Windows Server 2012 hasn't changed much. What has changed significantly, however, are the available options when it comes to hardware devices. All computers can use internal and external hardware devices.

## Choosing internal devices

Internal hardware devices are devices you install inside your computer. Typically, you'll need to power down and unplug your computer, and then remove the computer case before you can install an internal device.

Hard drives are the most commonly installed internal devices and, in this area, there are many options. Windows Server 2012 supports both Standard Format and Advanced Format hard drives. Standard Format drives have 512 bytes per physical sector and are also referred to as *512b drives*. Advanced Format drives have 4096 bytes per physical sector and are also referred to as *512e drives*. 512e represents a significant shift for the hard drive industry, and it allows for large, multiterabyte drives.

> # INSIDE OUT   Working with advanced-format hard drives
>
> Hard drives perform physical media updates in the granularity of their physical sector size. 512b drives work with data 512 bytes at a time; 512e drives work with data 4096 bytes at a time. Having a larger physical sector size is what allows 512e drive capacities to jump well beyond previous physical capacity limits of 512b drives.
>
> Keep in mind, however, that enterprise applications might need to be updated to work efficiently with 512e drives. When there is only a 512-byte write, hard disks must perform additional work to complete the 4096-byte sector write. For optimal perfor-mance, applications must read and write data properly in this new level of granularity (4096 bytes).
>
> With 512b and 512e, it's not an all-or-nothing proposition. Drive manufacturers have released drives with technology that allows them to transition from 512b to 512e. Seagate drives with SmartAlign technology are one example.
>
> If you don't know whether a drive is standard format or advanced format, you can easily determine bytes per physical sector by typing the following at an elevated command prompt:
>
> ```
> Fsutil fsinfo ntfsinfo DriveDesignator
> ```
>
> Here *DriveDesignator* is the designator of the drive to check, such as
>
> ```
> Fsutil fsinfo sectorinfo c:
> ```

Small Computer System Interface (SCSI) is one of the most commonly used interfaces, and there are multiple bus designs for SCSI and multiple interface types. Parallel SCSI (also called SPI), though popular, is giving way to Serial Attached SCSI (SAS). Internet SCSI (iSCSI) uses the SCSI architectural model, but it uses TCP/IP as the transport rather than the traditional physical implementation.

Although many workgroup and enterprise-class server systems continue to use serial attached SCSI devices, servers aren't always built using such robust disk systems. Increas-ingly, for general use, desktop-class computers are being configured with server operating systems, and most of these computers use internal devices with Serial ATA (SATA). That said, for many years, enhanced integrated drive electronics (EIDE), also called Parallel ATA (PATA), was used with desktop class computers.

EIDE is still in use as of the time this book was written. However, you might find that most newer computers use SATA devices instead. Because SATA cables are significantly smaller than EIDE cables, this results in less clutter inside your computer and improved airflow for better cooling.

# INSIDE OUT   Understanding solid-state drives

Solid-state drives (SSDs) are increasingly being used in computers throughout the enterprise. Although they can be higher in cost than traditional hard disks, they make up for this with high performance, reliability, and low power consumption. Because SSDs have no moving parts, they also run quiet and cool. How do they do this? SSDs use flash memory modules rather than platters, and there are no disk heads that need to travel over platters to read data. Instead, data is accessed directly from the flash memory over multiple internal flash buses. Typically, SSDs use NAND flash memory modules that have either multilevel cells (MLCs) storing two bits per cell or single-level cells (SLCs) storing one bit per cell.

In data centers where reducing power and cooling requirements is extremely important, you might want to use SSDs. Indeed, a typical SSD uses around 400 to 700 milliwatts of power and runs cool as opposed to the typical SCSI hard drive, which uses 4 to 7 watts of power and requires cooling. Before you deploy SSDs, however, keep in mind that a SATA SSD is not the same as a SATA hard drive. Most SSDs require specialized hard disk controllers to operate whether they are SATA compliant or not.

SSDs are ideal for high random read, low write workloads. For enterprise use, you should keep in mind that SSDs have duty-cycle and lifespan limitations. Check the warranty and specifications to determine an SSD's specific duty-cycle and lifespan limitations. Duty-cycle limitations, often listed in Total Bytes Written or Bytes Per Day, directly affect how many times the flash memory can be written to. Lifespan limitations directly affect how long the SSD will be viable. Often SSDs are optimized for durability to extend their lifespan, but doing so might require significant overhead. As an example, one current enterprise SSD had a 7 percent provisioning overhead, meaning 7 percent of the raw drive capacity was reserved for code storage and wear leveling. With a 400-GB SSD, this means that approximately 28 GB of the raw capacity is dedicated to provisioning overhead, leaving 372 GB of raw capacity for data storage.

SATA was designed to replace IDE. SATA drives are increasingly popular as a low-cost alternative to SCSI. SATA II and SATA III, the most common SATA interfaces, are designed to operate at 3 gigabits per second and 6 gigabits per second, respectively. Windows Server 2012 provides improved support for SATA drives by reducing metadata inconsistencies and allowing SATA drives to cache data more efficiently. Improved disk caching helps to protect cached data in the event of an unexpected power loss.

Although Windows Server 2012 can be used with SCSI, EIDE, and SATA hardware devices, your computer must be configured specifically to work with these devices. For example, your computer needs a SCSI controller card to use SCSI devices. Although some older computer system motherboards don't have SATA input ports, you can install a SATA controller card to add support for SATA drives.

## Choosing external devices

External hardware devices are devices you connect to your computer. Because you don't have to open your computer's case to connect external devices, you typically don't need to power down or unplug your computer before installing an external device. This makes external devices easier to install and also means you can attach most external devices without having to restart your computer.

Most current computers use external devices with USB, FireWire, external SATA (eSATA), or a combination of these interfaces. An example of each interface is shown in Figure 7-1.

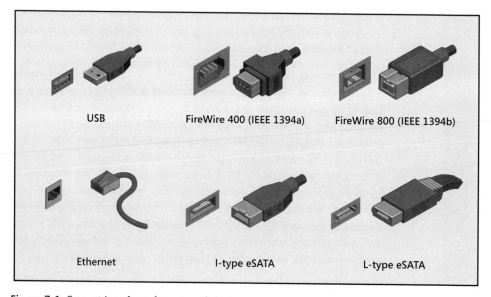

**Figure 7-1**  Current interfaces for external devices.

USB 2.0 is the industry standard, while the world transitions to USB 3.0. USB 2.0 devices can be rated as either full speed (up to 12 Mbps) or high speed (up to 480 Mbps). High-speed USB 2.0 supports data transfers at a maximum rate of 480 megabits per second, with sustained data transfer rates usually from 10 to 30 megabits per second. The actual sustainable transfer rate depends on many factors, including the type of device, the data you are transferring, and the speed of your computer. Each USB controller on your computer has a fixed amount of bandwidth, which all devices attached to the controller must share. If your computer's USB port is an earlier version, USB 1.0 or 1.1, you can use USB 2.0 and USB 3.0 devices, but the transfer rates will be significantly slower. The same is true when using a USB 2.0 device in a USB 3.0 port. Figure 7-2 compares connectors for USB 2.0 and USB 3.0.

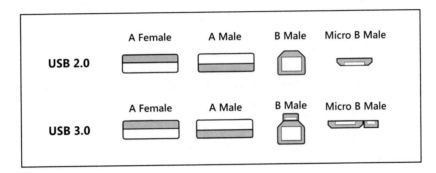

**Figure 7-2** Comparing USB 2.0 and USB 3.0 connectors.

# INSIDE OUT  Using USB 3.0

USB 3.0 has transfer rates up to 4.8 Gbps, which is 10 times faster than the maximum transfer rate of USB 2.0. To use USB 3.0, a computer must have USB 3.0–compliant ports and buses, and you must connect USB 3.0–compatible devices to computers using USB 3.0–compatible cables. Often, USB 3.0 ports and cables can be easily differentiated from USB 2.0 ports and cables. This is because USB 3.0 ports and cables normally have a blue color coding on the inside.

The blue coding is only one of several physical differences between USB 2.0 and USB 3.0 ports and cables. USB 2.0 cables have four wires within the cable and provide power up to 500 milliamps (mA). USB 3.0 cables have eight wires within the cable and provide power up to 900 mA. While USB 2.0 ports have four internal connectors, USB 3.0 ports have eight internal connectors.

Additionally, although USB 3.0 is capable of transfer rates up to 4.8 Gbps, the sustained data transfer rate is much lower. The bus type also might be a limiting factor because older buses might not be capable of reaching the maximum rate. For example, PCIe 1.0a and ExpressCard 1.0 buses have a maximum transfer rate of 2.5 Gbps.

## TROUBLESHOOTING

### Connecting USB 3.0 to USB 2.0 and vice versa

USB 3.0 cables and ports have different connectors than USB 2.0 cables and ports. To operate properly, USB 3.0 devices require USB 3.0 cables. USB 3.0 cables with standard connectors (A-type connectors), like the connector shown in Figure 7-1, can be used with USB 2.0 devices and plugged into USB 2.0 ports, but they are subject to the USB 2.0 transfer rate and power limitations. USB 2.0 devices and cables with standard connectors can be plugged into USB 3.0 ports and will work properly. USB 2.0 devices and cables with other connector types (B-type or micro B-type connectors) will not work properly with USB 3.0 ports. That said, although you might be able to fit a USB 2.0 cable with a B-type connector into a USB 3.0 B port, data will not transfer properly because of the different wiring configuration.

When you have USB devices connected to a monitor, the monitor acts like a USB hub device. As with any USB hub device, all devices attached to the hub share the same bandwidth and the total available bandwidth is determined by the speed of the USB input to which the hub is connected on your computer. Generally speaking, never connect devices through a server's monitor when end-user performance is a concern.

FireWire, also called IEEE 1394, is a high-performance connection standard for most Windows-based computers. This interface uses a peer-to-peer architecture in which peripherals negotiate bus conflicts to determine which device can best control a data transfer. FireWire has several configurations, including FireWire 400, FireWire 800, and FireWire 1600. FireWire 400 (IEEE 1394a) has maximum sustained transfer rates of up to 400 Mbps. IEEE 1394b allows 400 Mbps (S400), 800 Mbps (S800), and 1600 Mbps (S1600). As with USB devices, if you connect an IEEE 1394b device to an IEEE 1394a port or vice versa, the device operates at the significantly reduced FireWire 400 transfer speed.

eSATA is an ultra-high-performance connection standard, primarily used with high-performance external devices. With external hard drives, eSATA provides a secure, reliable, and ultra-fast connection. eSATA has maximum sustained transfer rates of up to 3 Gbps. Note that there are several types of eSATA connectors and cables, and that eSATA and internal SATA cables and connectors cannot be used interchangeably.

Chapter 7

# INSIDE OUT    Using FireWire devices

Although Windows Server 2012 can be used with FireWire hardware devices, your computer must be configured specifically to work with these devices. Specifically, a computer needs a FireWire controller card.

When working with FireWire, keep in mind FireWire ports and cables have different shapes and connectors, making it easy to tell the difference between them—if you know what you're looking for. Early FireWire implementations, which I'll call standard FireWire (as opposed to FireWire 400 or FireWire 800), have a different number of pins on their connector cables and a different number of connectors on their ports. Because of this, you can tell standard FireWire and FireWire 400 apart by looking closely at the cables and ports.

If you look closely at standard FireWire cables and ports, you'll see 4 pins or 4 connectors. If you look closely at FireWire 400 cables and ports, you'll see 6 pins or 6 connectors. Although standard FireWire and FireWire 400 cables have rectangular-shaped connectors with one short flat end and the other rounded, FireWire 800 cables are square with one of the long sides having a notch.

When you are purchasing external devices, you might want to get a device with multiple interfaces. A device with multiple interfaces will give you more configuration options.

# Installing devices

Every hardware component installed on a system has an associated device driver. Drivers are used to handle the low-level communications tasks between the operating system and hardware components. When you install a hardware component through the operating system, you tell the operating system about the device driver it uses. From then on, the device driver loads automatically and runs as part of the operating system.

## Understanding device installation

Unlike early versions of Windows, Windows Server 2012 is very good at detecting devices that were not installed after upgrading or installing the operating system. If a device wasn't installed because Windows Server didn't include the driver, the built-in hardware diagnostics will, in many cases, detect the hardware and then use the automatic update framework to retrieve the required driver the next time Windows Update runs, provided that Windows Update is enabled and you've allowed driver updating as well as operating system updating. Windows can also check for device software and device info. Device software, if available from the device manufacturers, typically includes a custom app for working with the device and a device driver. Device info provides additional information about the device and can include the product name, model number, and manufacturer name.

After upgrading or installing the operating system, you should check for driver updates and apply them as appropriate before trying other techniques to install device drivers. Device Installation Settings control whether Windows Server checks for drivers automatically. The settings also control whether Windows Server checks for driver updates, device software, and device info. To access these settings, open the System Properties dialog box, tap or click the Hardware tab, and then tap or click Device Installation Settings. You now have several options:

- **Yes, Do This Automatically (Recommended)**    When selected, Windows Server checks for and downloads drivers for new devices and driver updates automatically as part of the Windows Update process. Windows Server also checks for and downloads device software and device info.

- **Always Install The Best Driver Software From Windows Update**    When selected, Windows Server checks for and downloads drivers for new devices and driver updates automatically as part of the Windows Update process. You control whether you want to check for and download device software and device info by either selecting or clearing the Automatically Get The Device App And Info check box.

- **Never Install Driver Software From Windows Update**    When selected, Windows Server does not check for or download drivers for new devices or driver updates automatically as part of the Windows Update process. You control whether you want to check for and download device software and device info by either selecting or clearing the Automatically Get The Device App And Info check box.

Typically, device driver updates are seen as optional updates. The exceptions are for essential drivers, such as those for video, network adapters, and hard disk controllers.

When looking for driver updates, you'll want to view all available updates on a computer, rather than only the important updates, to determine whether device driver updates are available. To install available driver updates, follow these steps:

1. In Control Panel\System And Security, tap or click Windows Update. In Windows Update, tap or click View Available Updates. If the computer has installed the updates it last downloaded, the View Available Updates option isn't available. In this case, you can tap or click Check For Updates to see if there are new updates for the computer and then view the available updates (if any).

# INSIDE OUT  Controlling how Windows Update works with devices

Although driver updates can be downloaded automatically through Windows Update, they are not installed automatically. The only drivers that are installed automatically are those required for new hardware and newly connected devices. Here, Windows Server checks the driver cache for drivers when you connect the device. If the driver is available in the cache, Windows Server installs the device.

In Group Policy, the Specify Search Order For Device Driver Source Locations policy can override this default behavior. This policy is found under Computer Configuration\Administrative templates\System\Device Installation. If you set this policy to Always Search Windows Update, the operating system will search Windows Update for drivers rather than the driver cache doing so by default and this search occurs only once. If the computer isn't connected to the Internet, the search will occur the next time the computer is connected to the Internet. The policy also can be set to search Windows Update only if needed or to never search Windows Update.

In Group Policy, the Turn Off Access To All Windows Update Features policy controls whether Windows Update can be used. This policy is under Computer Configuration\Administrative Templates\System\Internet Communication Management\Internet Communication Settings. If you enable this policy, all Windows Update features are blocked and not available to users. Users will also be unable to access the Windows Update website. In early releases of the Windows operating system, other policies could be used to control driver search locations and driver search prompts. However, these policies do not apply to current Windows operating systems.

2. When Windows finishes checking for updates, you might find that there are important updates as well as optional updates available. If the computer is set to automatically install updates, important updates will be installed as part of automatic maintenance. You can install important updates immediately by clicking the related link and then clicking Install.

3. Most driver updates are listed as optional updates, and optional updates are not installed automatically. If optional updates are available, tap or click the related link and review the available optional updates. Select the check boxes for the optional updates that you want to install and then tap or click Install.

The relative priority of your servers as well as your organization's IT policies will determine whether you install driver updates as they become available—for example:

- On mission-critical production servers, you might not want to install drivers without extensive testing beforehand. If you don't need driver apps to configure a device, you probably don't want to download or install driver apps.

- On noncritical servers, you might want to install updated drivers as they become available. Again, if you don't need driver apps to configure a device, you probably don't want to download or install driver apps. If you install driver apps, you might want to analyze their resource usage to ensure that the apps work as expected and do not degrade overall system performance.

After you've installed the device driver, Windows Server 2012 should both detect the hardware and install the device automatically. If Windows Server detects the device but isn't able to install the device automatically, the installation silently fails and you might find a related solution in Action Center. You will then be able to view the problem response and attempt to solve the problem.

## TROUBLESHOOTING

### Solving problems with Windows Update

By default, computers check for and download updates from the Windows Update website. If you configure Windows Server Update Services (WSUS) on the network, computers can use WSUS to obtain updates. When using WSUS, don't forget that you also need to enable and configure the Specify Intranet Microsoft Update Service Location policy in a Group Policy Object (GPO) that will be processed by the client computer. This policy is found under Computer Configuration\Administrative Templates\Windows Components\Windows Update.

After you enable and configure the Specify Intranet Microsoft Update Service Location policy, you can use the Specify The Search Server For Device Driver Updates policy to specify the search server used for driver installation and updates. This policy is found under Computer Configuration\Administrative templates\System\Device Installation. If you enable this policy, you can specify whether the operating system searches Windows Update, a managed server, or a managed server and then Windows Update.

Keep in mind that if connection issues or the Windows Firewall are causing update problems, you need to resolve the problem before you can obtain updates for the computer. Note also that some updates might require accepting license terms before they install and that you might also need to restart a computer to complete the installation of some updates. With driver updates for video, network adapters, and hard disk controllers, you might find that a driver update causes unexpected behavior or instability. If so, roll back the update as discussed later in this chapter under "Rolling back drivers."

# Installing new devices

After you install or connect a new hardware device, you must set up the device so that it is available for use. Most available new devices are Plug and Play compatible. Plug and Play is optimized to support USB, FireWire, eSATA, PCIe, and ExpressCard devices. When you connect a Plug and Play device for the first time, Windows Server 2012 reads the Plug and Play identification tag contained in the device's firmware and then searches its master list of identification tags (which is created from the Setup Information files in the Inf folder). If the operating system finds a signed driver with a matching identification tag, it installs the driver and makes the device available for use automatically. Notifications are displayed only if there's a problem. Otherwise, the installation process just happens in the background.

This means you should be able to install new devices easily by using one of the following techniques:

- For an internal device, simply shut down the computer, insert the card into the appropriate slot or connect the device as appropriate, start the computer, and then let Windows Server 2012 automatically detect the new device.

- For a USB, FireWire, or eSATA device, simply insert the device into the appropriate slot or connect it to the computer and then let Windows Server 2012 automatically detect the new device.

Depending on the device, Windows Server 2012 should automatically install a built-in driver to support the new device as discussed previously. The device should then function immediately without any problems. Well, that's the idea, but it doesn't always work out that way. The success of an automatic detection and installation depends on the device being Plug and Play compatible and a device driver being available.

Windows Server 2012 includes many device drivers in a standard installation, and in this case, it should install the device automatically. If driver updating is allowed through Windows Update, Windows Server 2012 checks for drivers automatically using Windows Update either when you connect a new device or when it first detects the device. Because Windows Update does not automatically install device drivers, you need to check for available updates to install the driver.

# INSIDE OUT   Testing new drivers

All device drivers provided through Windows Update have been thoroughly tested in the Windows Hardware Quality Labs (WHQL), and you should be able to count on them not to cause your system to crash or become unstable. However, just because driver updates are available doesn't mean you should install them. In a production environment, you'll rarely want to download and install new device drivers without thoroughly testing them yourself first. Better safe than sorry—always. Typically, you install new device drivers because you are experiencing problems with the old drivers or looking for new functionality. If you aren't experiencing problems or don't require the additional functionality, you might not want to update the drivers.

You'll know a new device installed because it will be available for you to use. You also can confirm device availability in either Devices And Printers or Device Manager:

- From Control Panel, you can open Devices And Printers by tapping or clicking View Devices And Printers under the Hardware heading.

- From Server Manager, you can open Device Manager by selecting Computer Management on the Tools menu and then selecting Device Manager in the left pane of Computer Management.

Keep in mind that Windows Server might automatically detect the new device, but the Driver Software Installation component might run into problems installing the device. If this happens, the installation silently fails. You'll know installation failed because the device will not be available for you to use. In Devices And Printers, you should see warning icons for both the computer and the device. In this case, if you touch or move the mouse pointer over the computer device, you should see error status messages, such as the following:

```
Status: Driver is unavailable
```

```
Status: Driver Error
```

When you tap or click the computer device, the details pane should show the Needs Troubleshooting status. After a failed installation, you can attempt to install the device by following these steps:

1. In Devices And Printers, press and hold or right-click the device and then select Properties.

2. In the Properties dialog box, on the Hardware tab, tap or click the Properties button.

3.  Tap or click Change Settings and then tap or click Update Driver. This starts the
    Update Driver Software Wizard.

4.  Specify whether you want to install the drivers automatically or manually by selecting
    the driver from a list or specific location. (See Figure 7-3.)

> **Note**
>
> Updated drivers can add functionality to a device, improve performance, and
> resolve device problems. However, you should rarely install the latest drivers on a
> computer without first testing them in a test environment. Test first, then install.

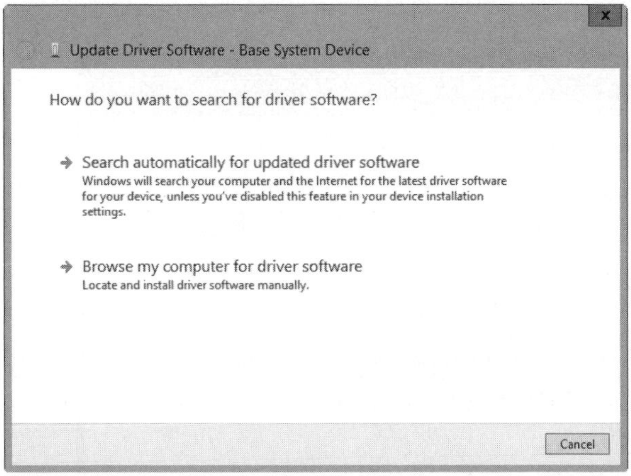

**Figure 7-3**  Choose to install drivers automatically or manually.

5.  If you elect to search automatically for the driver and Device Installation Settings
    allow this, Windows Server checks for the device driver using either Windows Update
    or WSUS. Then, if a driver is available, Windows Server downloads it and installs it
    automatically. In this case, tap or click Close to complete the process and then skip
    the remaining steps.

6.  If you chose to install the driver manually, you'll have the opportunity to do one of
    the following, as shown in Figure 7-4:

    ○  **Search for the driver**    If you want to search for drivers, tap or click Browse to
       select a search location. Use the Browse For Folder dialog box to select the start
       folder for the search, and then tap or click OK. Because all subfolders of the
       selected folder are searched automatically, you can select the drive root path,
       such as C, to search an entire drive.

Chapter 7

○ **Choose a driver to install**    If you want to choose the driver to install, tap or click Let Me Pick From A List Of Device Drives On My Computer. The wizard then displays a list of common hardware types. Select the appropriate hardware type, such as Storage Controllers or Network Adapters, and then tap or click Next. Scroll through the list of manufacturers to find the manufacturer of the device, and then choose the appropriate device in the right pane.

> **Note**
>
> If the manufacturer or device you want to use isn't listed, insert the media containing the device driver disc or USB flash drive, and then tap or click Have Disk. Follow the prompts. Afterward, select the appropriate device.

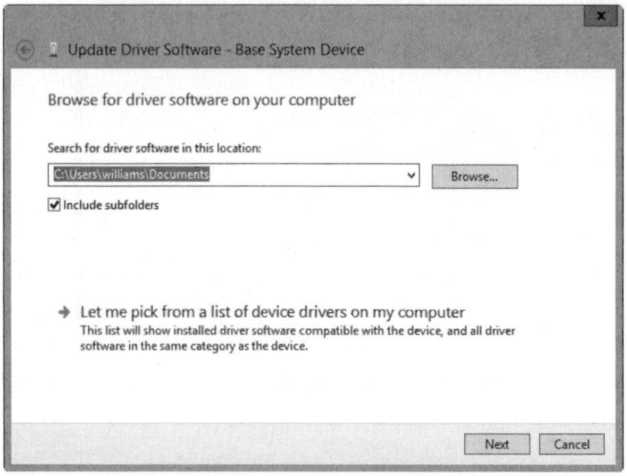

**Figure 7-4**  Search for or select a driver to install.

7. After selecting a device driver through a search or a manual selection, continue through the installation process by tapping or clicking Next. Tap or click Close when the driver installation is completed. If the wizard can't find an appropriate driver, you need to obtain one and then repeat this procedure. Keep in mind that in some cases you'll need to restart the system to activate the newly installed device driver.

> **Important**
>
> If the wizard fails to install the device, there might be a problem with the device itself or the driver, or a conflict with existing hardware. For additional details on troubleshooting and resolving conflicts, see "Managing hardware" later in this chapter.

After you successfully install a device, you need to perform maintenance tasks periodically for the device and its drivers. When new drivers for a device are released, you might want to test them in a development or support environment to see whether the drivers resolve problems that users have been experiencing or include the new functionality you are looking for. If the drivers install without problems and resolve outstanding issues, you might then want to install the updated drivers on computers that use this device. On a server operating system, you can implement the driver update procedure as follows:

1. Check the device and driver information on each system prior to installing the new driver. Note the location, version, and file name of the existing driver.

2. Install the updated driver. If the computer and the device function normally, consider the update a success.

3. If the computer or the device malfunctions after the driver installation, roll back to the previously installed driver using the standard Device Manager utilities. If you cannot restart the computer and restore the driver, you might need to start the computer in Safe Mode or use Startup Repair to restore the system.

**TROUBLESHOOTING**

**Configuring the device installation timeout**
By default, Windows Server waits 300 seconds for device installation tasks to complete and then terminates the installation. Using the Configure Device Installation Time-out policy, you can override the default setting and specify a different timeout value. This policy is found under Computer Configuration\Administrative Templates\System\ Device Installation.

## Viewing device and driver details

You use Device Manager to view and configure hardware devices. You'll spend a lot of time working with this tool, so you should get to know it before working with devices.

To open Device Manager and obtain a detailed list of all the hardware devices installed on a system, follow these steps:

1. In Server Manager, select Computer Management on the Tools menu.

2. Select the Device Manager node. As shown in Figure 7-5, you should now see a complete list of devices installed on the system. By default, this list is organized by device type.

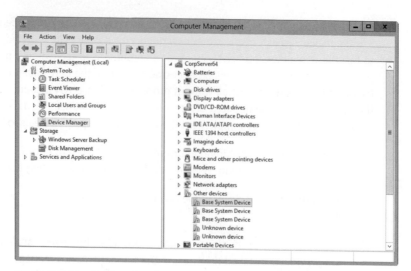

**Figure 7-5** Use Device Manager to work with hardware devices.

**3.** Expand a device type to see a list of the specific instances of that device type.

After you access Device Manager, you can work with any of the installed devices. If you press and hold or right-click a device entry, a shortcut menu is displayed. The available options depend on the device type, but they include the following:

- **Properties**  Displays the Properties dialog box for the device

- **Uninstall**  Uninstalls the device and its drivers

- **Disable**  Disables the device but doesn't uninstall it

- **Enable**  Enables a device if it's disabled

- **Update Driver Software**  Starts the Update Driver Software Wizard, which you can use to update the device driver

- **Scan For Hardware Changes**  Tells Windows Server 2012 to check the hardware configuration and determine whether there are any changes

> **Note**
>
> The device list shows warning symbols if there are problems with a device. A yellow warning symbol with an exclamation point indicates a problem with a device. A red X indicates a device that was improperly installed or disabled by the user or the administrator for some reason.

You can use the options on the View menu in Server Manager to change the defaults for which types of devices are displayed and how the devices are listed. The options are as follows:

- **Devices By Type**   Displays devices by the type of device installed, such as disk drive or printer. The connection name is listed below the type. This is the default view.

- **Devices By Connection**   Displays devices by the connection type, such as audio and video codecs.

- **Resources By Type**   Displays the status of allocated resources by the type of device using the resource. Resource types are direct memory access (DMA) channels, input/output (I/O) ports, interrupt requests (IRQs), and memory addresses.

- **Resources By Connection**   Displays the status of all allocated resources by connection type rather than device type.

- **Show Hidden Devices**   Displays non–Plug and Play devices as well as devices that have been physically removed from the computer but haven't had their drivers uninstalled.

# INSIDE OUT   View and save device settings for local and remote computers

You can use Computer Management to view and work with settings on remote computers. Press and hold or right-click Computer Management in the console tree, and then select Connect To Another Computer on the shortcut menu. In the Select Computer dialog box, choose Another Computer and then type the fully qualified name of the computer you want to work with, such as **entdc01.microsoft.com**, where *entdc01* is the computer name and *microsoft.com* is the domain name. If you don't know the computer name, tap or click Browse to search for the computer you want to work with.

If you want detailed driver lists for multiple computers, you can get this using the Driverquery command-line utility. Use the /V parameter to get verbose output about all drivers or the /SI parameter to display properties only for signed drivers, such as **driverquery /v** or **driverquery /si**. If you want to write the information to a file, use the output redirection symbol (>) followed by the name of the file, such as **driverquery /si > system-devices.txt**.

To list devices on remote computers, use the /S parameter followed by a computer name or Internet Protocol (IP) address to specify a remote computer to query. You can also specify the Run As permissions by using /U followed by the user name and /P followed by the user's password. Here's an example: **driverquery /v /s corpserver01 /u wrstanek /p 49iners**.

# Working with device drivers

Each hardware component installed on a computer has an associated device driver. The job of the device driver is to describe how the operating system uses the hardware abstraction layer (HAL) to work with a hardware component. The HAL handles the low-level communication tasks between the operating system and a hardware component. By installing a hardware component through the operating system, you are telling the operating system about the device driver it uses. From then on, the device driver loads automatically and runs as part of the operating system.

## Device driver essentials

Windows Server 2012 includes an extensive library of device drivers. In the base installation of the operating system, these drivers are maintained in the file repository of the driver store. Some service packs you install will also include updates to the driver store. You can find drivers in the FileRepository folder under %SystemRoot%\System32\DriverStore. The DriverStore folder also contains subfolders for localized driver information. You'll find a subfolder for each language component configured on the system. For example, for localized U.S. English driver information, you'll find a subfolder called en-US.

Every device driver in the driver store is certified to be fully compatible with Windows Server 2012 and is also digitally signed by Microsoft to assure the operating system of its authenticity. When you install a new Plug and Play–compatible device, Windows Server 2012 checks the driver store for a compatible device driver. If one is found, the operating system automatically installs the device.

Every device driver has an associated Setup Information file. This file, which ends with the .inf extension, is a text file containing detailed configuration information about the device being installed. The information file identifies any source files used by the driver as well. Source files have the .sys extension. Drivers are also associated with a component manifest (component.man) file. The manifest file is written in extensible markup language (XML), includes details on the driver's digital signature, and might also include Plug and Play information used by the device to configure itself automatically.

Every driver installed on a system has a source (.sys) file in the %SystemRoot%\System32\Drivers folder. When you install a new device driver, the driver is written to a subfolder of %SystemRoot%\System32\Drivers, and configuration settings are stored in the registry. The driver's .inf file is used to control the installation and write the registry settings. If the driver doesn't already exist in the driver store, it does not already have an .inf file or other related files on the system. In this case, the driver's .inf file and other related files are written to a subfolder of %SystemRoot%\System32\DriverStore\FileRepository when you install the device.

## Understanding and troubleshooting driver signing

Speaking of new device drivers, Microsoft requires that you use signed device drivers. Every device driver in the driver cache is digitally signed, which certifies the driver as having passed extensive testing by the Windows Hardware Quality Labs (WHQL). A device driver with a digital signature signed by Microsoft should not cause your system to crash or become unstable. The presence of a digital signature signed by Microsoft also ensures that the device driver hasn't been tampered with. If a device driver doesn't have a digital signature signed by Microsoft, it hasn't been approved for use through testing, or its files might have been modified from the original installation by another program. This means that unsigned drivers are much more likely than any other program you've installed to cause the operating system to freeze or the computer to crash.

The assurances you get with digitally signed drivers aren't applicable to unsigned device drivers. With an unsigned driver, there is no guarantee that it has been tested thoroughly, and if the driver is poorly written, it is much more likely to cause the operating system to freeze or the server to crash than any other program you've installed. Because of this, Windows Server will not let you install unsigned drivers.

That said, an invalid or missing digital signature on a driver for an important device could prevent a server from starting. There are several ways you can work around this, allowing you to boot the server and fix the problem. The two key options require that you start the server in safe mode.

If the computer won't start normally, the Recovery screen is displayed during startup. On the Recovery screen, tap or click Troubleshoot. On the Advanced Options screen, tap or click Startup Settings. Next, on the Windows Startup Settings screen, tap or click Restart. When the server restarts, you need to select the safe mode you want to use.

With the standard safe modes, the basic drivers loaded include the mouse, monitor, keyboard, mass storage, and base video. If one of the basic drivers is the source of the problem though, you won't be able to use one of the standard safe modes. Because of this, select Disable Driver Signature Enforcement as the start mode.

## Viewing driver Information

To view detailed information about a device, press and hold or right-click the device and select Properties or simply double-tap or double-click the related entry in Device Manager. This opens the device's Properties dialog box, as shown in Figure 7-6. Most devices have at least two tabs, either General and Properties or General and Driver.

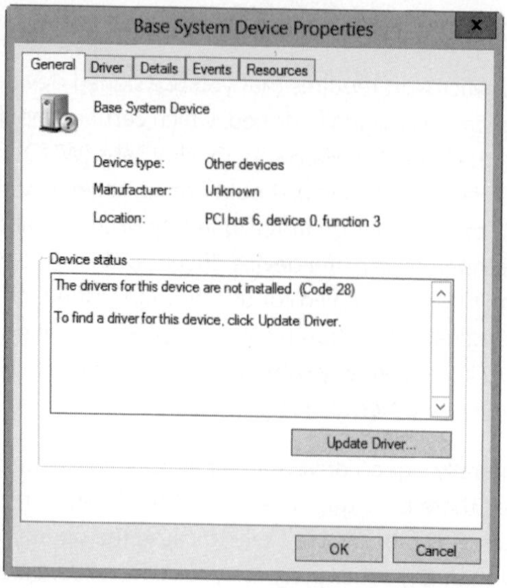

**Figure 7-6**  Use the device's Properties dialog box to obtain essential information about a device, including whether it is functioning properly.

The most important information in the General tab is the device status. If the device is working properly, this is specifically stated. Otherwise, the error status of the device is shown. If the device is disabled, you have an option to enable the device instead (as shown in Figure 7-7).

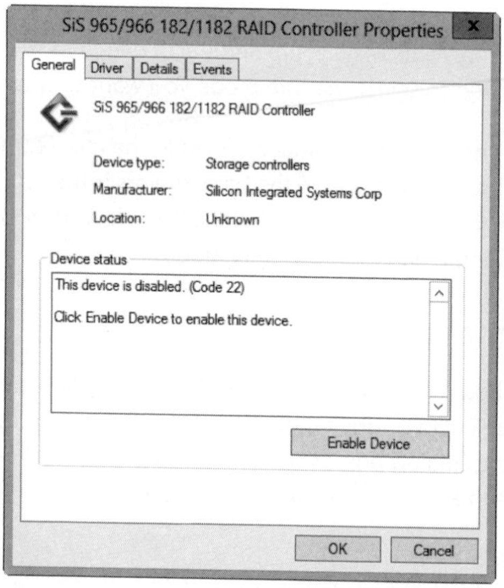

**Figure 7-7**  Disabled devices are listed with an error status because they aren't functioning; you can enable them by tapping or clicking Enable Device.

You can temporarily disable a device by selecting Disable on the Driver tab. If you later want to enable the device, tap or click the Enable Device button on the General tab and then, when the Troubleshooting Wizard starts, tap or click Next and then tap or click Finish.

The Driver tab, shown in Figure 7-8, provides basic information about the driver provider, creation date, version, and digital signature. You should be wary of any drivers that list the provider as Unknown as well as drivers that are listed as Not Digitally Signed. Drivers signed by Microsoft are listed as being signed by Microsoft Windows or Microsoft Windows Hardware Compatibility Publisher.

**Figure 7-8**  Use the Driver tab to determine the driver provider, creation date, version, and digital signature.

You can view additional information about the driver by tapping or clicking Driver Details. If no driver files are required or none have been loaded for the device, you'll see a message stating this. Otherwise, you'll see the names and locations of all associated files, including an icon that indicates the signing status of each individual file. Selecting a file in this list displays details for that file in the lower section of the dialog box, as shown in Figure 7-9.

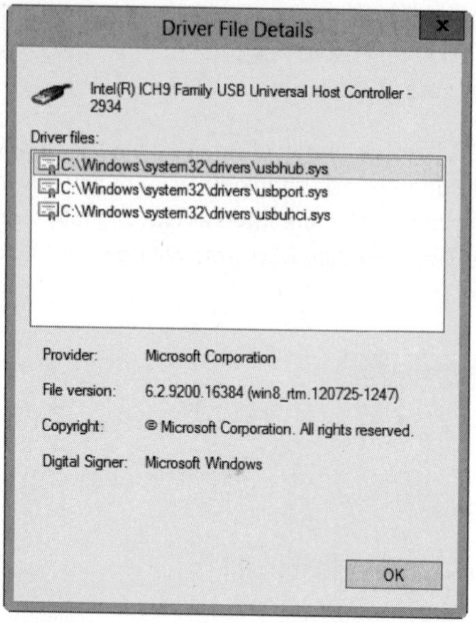

**Figure 7-9** The Driver File Details dialog box displays information on the driver file locations, the provider, and the file versions.

## Viewing Advanced, Resources, and other settings

Devices often have other tabs, such as Advanced, Resources, and Power Management. Most network adapters have an Advanced tab. As shown in Figure 7-10, these options can control transmission preferences. You should change these options only if you are trying to resolve specific performance or connectivity issues as directed by the device manufacturer or a Microsoft Knowledge Base article. The setting that causes the most problems is Speed & Duplex. Most of the time, you'll want this set to Auto Detect or Auto Negotiation. Sometimes, however, to correct a specific problem, you must use a preset speed and duplex setting, such as 100 Mbps Half Duplex or 1000 Mbps Full Duplex. You should do this, however, only when this setting is recommended based on your network configuration or the issue you are trying to troubleshoot.

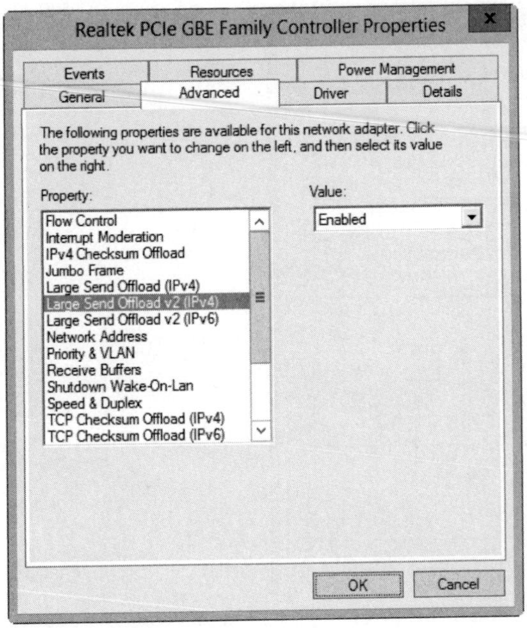

**Figure 7-10**  You'll find that most network adapters have an Advanced tab for setting transmission preferences.

Any device that uses system resources will have a Resources tab like the one shown in Figure 7-11.

The Resources tab options show the device resources that are currently assigned and their settings. There are four types of device resources:

- **DMA**  The DMA channel used by the device. Values are shown as integers, such as 02.

- **Memory Range**  The range of memory addresses used by the device. Values are shown in hexadecimal format, such as E8206000–E8206FFF.

- **I/O Range**  The range of I/O ports used by the device. Values are shown in hexadecimal format, such as 5400–543F.

- **IRQ Line**  IRQ line used by the device. Values are shown as hexadecimal, such as 0xFFFFFFD8 (-40).

Chapter 7

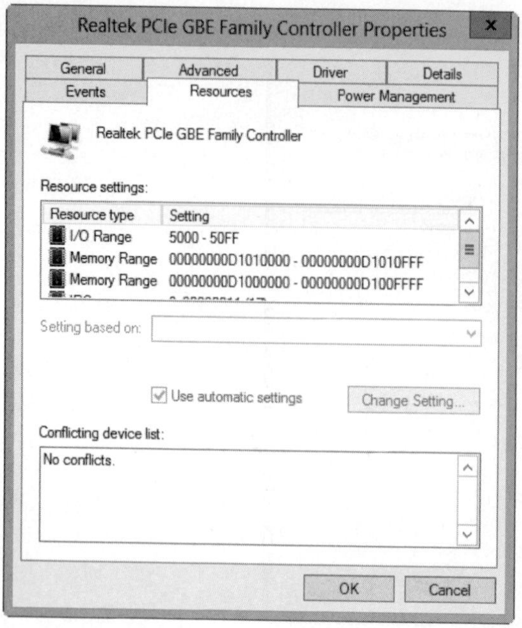

**Figure 7-11**  Any device that uses system resources has a Resources tab.

Devices can use multiple I/O and memory ranges. For example, the Video Graphics Adapter (VGA) adapter on one of our computers used three I/O ranges and three memory ranges. Additionally, multiple PCIe devices can share the same IRQs when using Advanced Configuration and Power Interface (ACPI) BIOS. This is because ACPI BIOS allows IRQ sharing. To learn more about resource sharing and configuration options, see "Resolving resource conflicts" later in this chapter.

## Installing and updating device drivers

Device drivers are essential to the proper operation of Windows Server 2012. A faulty device driver can cause many problems on your systems—everything from unexpected restarts to application hangs to blue screens. To make it easier to detect and diagnose problems, you should maintain an inventory of all installed device drivers on systems you manage. Previously, I talked about using the Driverquery command to obtain a list of drivers for computers throughout the network. Ideally, the driver information should be stored on a centralized network share rather than on individual computers, or it could be printed out and placed in a binder where it is easily accessible. You should then periodically check manufacturer websites for known problems with related device drivers and for updated drivers. Windows Update can also help you because driver updates are made available through this service and can be installed automatically.

Although you can be fairly certain drivers obtained through Windows Update are newer than installed versions, this isn't the case for drivers you download yourself, and you should always double-check the driver version information before installation. As discussed previously, the current driver version is displayed in the driver's Properties dialog box, as shown in Figure 7-12. Double-tap or double-click the device in Device Manager to display the driver's Properties dialog box, and then select the Driver tab, as shown in Figure 7-12. Be sure to check the driver date as well as the driver version.

**Figure 7-12**  Check the current driver version and date.

Next, check the driver version information for the driver you downloaded. To do this, extract the downloaded driver files to a folder. In the folder, you should find .dll or .sys files. Press and hold or right-click one of these files, and choose Properties. Then, in the Properties dialog box, tap or click the Version tab to find the version information.

To continue with the installation of downloaded drivers, check to see whether the driver download includes a Setup program. If it does, run this program so that the proper files are copied to your system. If the drivers aren't installed as part of setup, you can install and update the drivers using the Update Driver Software Wizard. The wizard can search for updated device drivers in the following locations:

- On the local computer

- On a hardware installation disc

- On the Windows Update site or your organization's Windows Update server

In Group Policy, the main policy that controls access to Windows Update is Turn Off Access To All Windows Update Features. This policy is under Computer Configuration\Administrative Templates\System\Internet Communication Management\Internet Communication Settings. If you enable this policy setting, all Windows Update features are blocked and not available to users. Users will also be unable to access the Windows Update website. In early releases of the Windows operating system, other policies could be used to control driver search locations and driver search prompts. However, these policies do not apply to current Windows operating systems.

You can install and update device drivers by following these steps:

1. In Computer Management, select the Device Manager node. You should now see a complete list of devices installed on the system. By default, this list is organized by device type.

2. Press and hold or right-click the device you want to manage, and then select Update Driver Software. This starts the Update Driver Software Wizard.

3. You can specify whether you want to install the drivers automatically or manually by selecting the driver from a list or specific location.

> **Note**
> Updated drivers can add functionality to a device, improve performance, and resolve device problems. However, you should rarely install the latest drivers on a user's computer without first testing them in a test environment. Test first, then install.

4. If you elect to install the driver automatically, Windows Server 2012 looks for a more recent version of the device driver and installs the driver if found. If a more recent version of the driver is not found, Windows Server 2012 keeps the current driver. In either case, tap or click Close to complete the process and then skip the remaining steps.

5. If you chose to install the driver manually, you'll next have the opportunity to do one of the following:

   ○ **Search for the driver**   If you want to search for drivers, tap or click Browse to select a search location. Use the Browse For Folder dialog box to select the start folder for the search, and then tap or click OK. Because all subfolders of the selected folder are searched automatically, you can select the drive root path, such as C, to search an entire drive.

○ **Choose the driver to install**    If you want to choose the driver to install, tap or click Let Me Pick From A List Of Device Drivers On My Computer. The wizard then displays a list of common hardware types. Select the appropriate hardware type, such as Modems or Network Adapters, and then tap or click Next. Scroll through the list of manufacturers to find the manufacturer of the device, and then choose the appropriate device in the right pane.

> **Note**
>
> If the manufacturer or device you want to use isn't listed, insert the media containing the device driver disc or USB flash drive, and then tap or click Have Disk. Follow the prompts. Afterward, select the appropriate device.

6. After selecting a device driver through a search or a manual selection, continue through the installation process by tapping or clicking Next. Tap or click Close when the driver installation is completed. If the wizard can't find an appropriate driver, you need to obtain one and then repeat this procedure. Keep in mind that in some cases you'll need to restart the computer to activate the newly installed or updated device driver.

## Restricting device installation using Group Policy

In addition to specifying driver installation and search restrictions, you can use Group Policy settings to allow or prevent installation of devices based on the device type. The related policy settings are found under Computer Configuration\Administrative Templates\System\Device Installation\Device Installation Restrictions and include the following:

- Allow Administrators To Override Device Installation Restriction Policies

- Allow Installation Of Devices Using Drivers That Match These Device Setup Classes

- Prevent Installation Of Drivers That Match These Device Setup Classes

- Allow Installation Of Devices That Match Any Of These Device IDs

- Prevent Installation Of Devices That Match Any Of These Device IDs

- Prevent Installation Of Removable Devices

- Prevent Installation Of Devices Not Described By Other Policy Settings

- Time (In Seconds) To Force Reboot When Required

You can configure these policies by following these steps:

1. Access the policy for the appropriate site, domain, or organizational unit (OU).

2. Expand Computer Configuration, then Administrative Templates, then System, then Device Installation, and then Device Installation Restrictions.

3. Double-tap or double-click the appropriate policy to view its Properties dialog box.

4. Set the state of the policy as Not Configured if you don't want the policy to be applied, Enabled if you want the policy to be applied, or Disabled if you want to block the policy from being used (all as permitted by the Group Policy configuration).

5. If you are enabling the policy and it has a Show option, tap or click Show to use the Show Contents dialog box to specify which device IDs should be matched to this policy. Tap or click OK twice.

Device installation restrictions will not take effect until computers are restarted. To force computers to restart when device installation restrictions are changed, you can enable and configure the Time (In Seconds) To Force Reboot When Required policy. For example, you might want to force computers to restart within 60 minutes of the policy change. If so, you'd enter 3600 in the Reboot Timeout (In Seconds) box.

## Rolling back drivers

Occasionally, you'll find that an updated driver doesn't work as expected. It could cause problems, such as device failure or system instability. Generally, this shouldn't occur when you've installed signed device drivers. However, it can sometimes occur with any device driver—even those published through Windows Update.

If you suspect that an updated driver is causing the system or device problems you are experiencing, you can attempt to recover the system to the previously installed device driver. To do this, follow these steps:

1. If you are having problems starting the system, you need to start the system in safe mode.

2. In Computer Management, select the Device Manager node. You should now see a complete list of devices installed on the system. By default, this list is organized by device type.

3. Press and hold or right-click the device you want to manage, and then select Properties. This opens the Properties dialog box for the device.

4.  Tap or click the Driver tab, and then tap or click Roll Back Driver. When prompted to confirm the action, tap or click Yes.

5.  Tap or click Close to close the driver's Properties dialog box.

> **Important**
> If the driver file hasn't been updated, a backup drive file won't be available. In this case, the Roll Back Driver button will be disabled and you will not be able to tap or click it. In this case, you should check the manufacturer's website for available versions of the driver for the device.

## Removing device drivers for removed devices

Windows device drivers for Plug and Play devices are loaded and unloaded dynamically. You can remove the driver for a device only when the device is plugged in. This means the proper way to remove a device from a system is first to uninstall its related device driver and then remove the device from the system.

One reason for uninstalling a device is to remove a device that you no longer use or need. Start by uninstalling the related device driver. Open Computer Management, and then select the Device Manager node. Press and hold or right-click the device you want to remove, and then select Uninstall. When prompted, tap or click OK to confirm that you want to remove the driver. Windows Server 2012 will then remove the related files and registry settings.

At this point, you can shut down the system and remove the related hardware component if you want to. However, you might first want to check to see how the computer operates without the device in case some unforeseen problem or error occurs. So, rather than removing the device, you'll want to disable it. Disabling the device prevents Windows from reinstalling the device automatically the next time you restart the system. You disable a device by pressing and holding or right-clicking it in Device Manager and then selecting Disable.

Sometimes when you are troubleshooting and trying to get a device to work properly, you might want to uninstall or unplug the device temporarily. Here, you could disable the device and then monitor the system to see whether problems previously experienced reoccur, or you could reinstall the device to see whether normal operations are restored. Uninstalling and then reinstalling the device forces Windows to go back to the device's original device and registry settings, which can sometimes recover the device.

Chapter 7

After you uninstall a device driver, one way to get Windows Server 2012 to reinstall the device is to restart the computer. You can also try to rescan for devices using Device Manager by selecting the computer node in the main pane and then selecting Scan For Hardware Changes on the Action menu. Either way, the operating system should detect the uninstalled device as new hardware and then automatically reinstall the necessary device driver. If this doesn't happen, you must reinstall the device manually using the Add Hardware Wizard as discussed later in this chapter.

## Uninstalling, reinstalling, and disabling device drivers

Uninstalling a device driver uninstalls the related device. When a device isn't working properly, sometimes you can completely uninstall the device, restart the system, and then reinstall the device driver to restore normal operations. You can uninstall and then reinstall a device by following these steps:

1. Open Computer Management, and then select the Device Manager node. You should now see a complete list of devices installed on the system. By default, this list is organized by device type.

2. Press and hold or right-click the device you want to manage, and then select Uninstall. When prompted to confirm the action, tap or click OK.

3. Restart the system. Windows Server 2012 should detect the presence of the device and automatically reinstall the necessary device driver. If the device isn't automatically reinstalled, reinstall it manually as discussed in the section "Installing and updating device drivers."

To prevent a device from being reinstalled automatically, disable the device instead of uninstalling it. You disable a device by pressing and holding or right-clicking it in Device Manager and then selecting Disable.

# Managing hardware

Windows Plug and Play technology does a good job of detecting and automatically configuring new hardware. However, if the hardware doesn't support Plug and Play or it isn't automatically detected, you need to enter information about the new hardware into the Windows Server 2012 system. You do this by using the Add Hardware Wizard to install the hardware device and its related drivers on the system. You can also use this wizard to troubleshoot problems with existing hardware.

# Adding non–Plug and Play, legacy hardware

Although Windows Server 2012 doesn't detect or set up non–Plug and Play devices automatically, it does maintain a driver cache for these devices. You might also be able to use an older driver if a Windows Server 2012 device driver isn't available. In either case, you install the device using the Add Hardware Wizard. Follow these steps:

1. If the device has installation media or a downloadable Setup program, run it to copy the driver files to your hard disk.

2. Connect the device to the computer. For internal devices, you must shut down the computer, add the device, and then restart the computer.

3. Open Computer Management, and then select the Device Manager node.

4. Select the computer node in the main pane, and then choose Add Legacy Hardware on the Action menu.

5. In the Add Hardware Wizard, read the introductory message and then tap or click Next.

6. Determine whether the wizard should search for new hardware or whether you want to select the hardware from a list (as shown in Figure 7-13):

   o If you choose the search option, the wizard searches for and attempts to automatically detect the new hardware. The process can take several minutes to go through all the device types and options. When the search is complete, any new devices found are displayed, and you can select one.

   o If you choose the manual option, or if no new devices are found in the automatic search, you have to select the hardware type yourself. Select the type of hardware, such as Storage Controllers or Network Adapters, and then tap or click Next. Scroll through the list of manufacturers to find the manufacturer of the device, and then choose the appropriate device in the right pane.

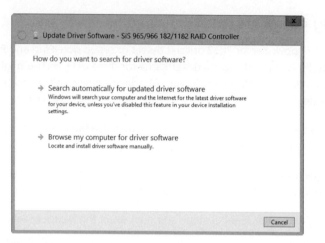

**Figure 7-13**  Search for or select the new hardware to install.

7. After you complete the selection and installation process, tap or click Next, and then tap or click Next again to confirm that you want to install the hardware.

8. After the wizard installs the drivers for the hardware device, tap or click Finish. The new hardware should now be available.

## Enabling and disabling hardware

When a device isn't working properly, sometimes you'll want to uninstall or disable it. Uninstalling a device removes the driver association for the device so that it temporarily appears that the device has been removed from the system. The next time you restart the system, Windows Server 2012 might try to reinstall the device. Typically, Windows Server 2012 reinstalls Plug and Play devices automatically, but it does not automatically reinstall non–Plug and Play devices.

Disabling a device turns it off and prevents Windows Server 2012 from using it. Because a disabled device doesn't use system resources, you can be sure that it isn't causing a conflict on the system.

You can uninstall or disable a device by following these steps:

1. Open Computer Management, and then select the Device Manager node. You should now see a complete list of devices installed on the system. By default, this list is organized by device type.

2. Press and hold or right-click the device you want to manage, and then select Enable, Uninstall, or Disable, depending on what you want to do with the device.

3. If prompted to confirm the action, tap or click Yes or OK as appropriate.

# Troubleshooting hardware

Windows Server 2012 built-in hardware diagnostics can detect many types of problems with hardware devices. If a problem is detected, you might see a Problem Reporting balloon telling you there is a problem. Tapping or clicking this balloon opens Action Center. Action Center can also be accessed in Control Panel by tapping or clicking the System And Security link and then selecting Action Center. To open Action Center, tap or click the Action Center icon in the notification area of the taskbar and then select Open Action Center.

## INSIDE OUT  Using Action Center for hardware troubleshooting

Action Center might have a solution for the hardware problem the computer is experiencing. If so, you can apply the solution or get more information about the problem using the options provided. To check for solutions to known problems, click the Check For Solutions link on the Maintenance panel.

While you are working with Action Center, click the View Reliability History link to open Reliability Monitor, which allows you to review the computer's reliability history. If hardware devices are causing reliability problems, the problem history will depict this. Select an item in the history to review its details. Additional options are available for saving the reliability history, viewing all problem reports, and checking for solutions to all known problems.

Events related to malfunctioning hardware often will be written to the system logs. You can quickly find events related to a specific device by following these steps:

1. Open Computer Management, and then select the Device Manager node.

2. Press and hold or right-click the device that you want to troubleshoot, and then select Properties.

3. If there's a problem with a device, there'll be an error status and a related error code on the General tab.

4. On the Events tab, you'll see the most recent events related to the device, as shown in Figure 7-14. Select an event to view its details in the Information panel. Tap or click View All Events to open a custom view for the device in Event Viewer. The custom view will show all available events for the device, allowing you to review them for troubleshooting.

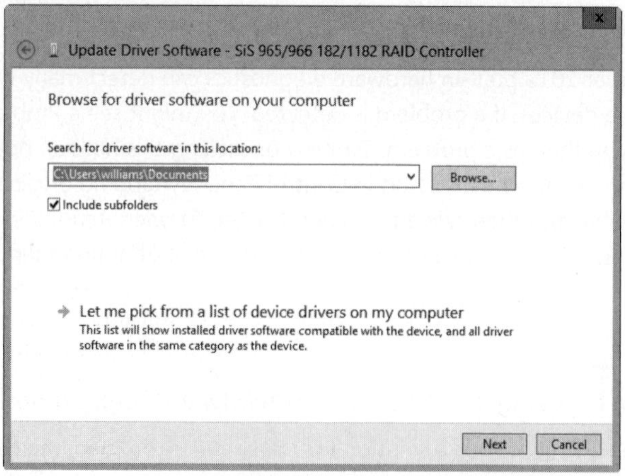

**Figure 7-14** Review events to troubleshoot the device.

Whenever a device is installed incorrectly or has another problem, Device Manager displays a warning icon indicating that the device has a problem. If you double-tap or double-click the device, an error code displays on the General tab of the device's Properties dialog box. As Table 7-1 shows, this error code can be helpful when trying to solve device problems as well. Most of the correction actions assume that you selected the General tab from the device's Properties dialog box.

**TABLE 7-1 Common device errors and techniques to resolve them**

| Error Message | Correction Action |
| --- | --- |
| This device is not configured correctly. (Code 1) | Obtain a compatible driver for the device and tap or click Update Driver on the Driver tab to start the Update Driver Software Wizard. |
| The driver for this device might be corrupted, or your system might be running low on memory or other resources. (Code 3) | Tap or click Update Driver on the Driver tab to run the Update Driver Software Wizard. You might see an "Out of Memory" message at startup because of this. |
| This device cannot start. (Code 10) | Tap or click Update Driver on the Driver tab to run the Update Driver Software Wizard. Don't try to find a driver automatically. Instead, choose the manual install option, and select the device driver you want to use. |
| This device cannot find enough free resources that it can use. (Code 12) | Resources assigned to this device conflict with another device, or the BIOS is incorrectly configured. Check the BIOS, and check for resource conflicts on the Resources tab of the device's Properties dialog box. |
| This device cannot work properly until you restart your computer. (Code 14) | Typically, the driver is installed correctly but will not be started until you restart the computer. |

| Error Message | Correction Action |
|---|---|
| Windows cannot identify all the resources this device uses. (Code 16) | Check whether a signed driver is available for the device. If one is available and you already installed it, you might need to manage the resources for the device. Check the Resources tab of the device's Properties dialog box. |
| This device is asking for an unknown resource type. (Code 17) | Reinstall or update the driver using a valid, signed driver. |
| Reinstall the drivers for this device. (Code 18) | After an upgrade, you might need to log on as an administrator to complete device installation. If this is not the case, tap or click Update Driver on the Driver tab to reinstall the driver. |
| Your registry might be corrupted. (Code 19) | Remove and reinstall the device. This should clear out incorrect or conflicting registry settings. |
| Windows is removing this device. (Code 21) | The system will remove the device. The registry might be corrupted. If the device continues to display this message, restart the computer. |
| This device is disabled. (Code 22) | This device has been disabled using Device Manager. To enable it, select Use This Device (Enable) under Device Usage on the General tab of the device's Properties dialog box. |
| This device is not present, is not working properly, or does not have all its drivers installed. (Code 24) | This might indicate a bad device or bad hardware. This error code can also occur with legacy ISA devices; upgrade the driver to resolve the issue. |
| The drivers for this device are not installed. (Code 28) | Obtain a compatible driver for the device and then tap or click Update Driver to start the Update Driver Software Wizard. |
| This device is disabled because the firmware of the device did not give it the required resources. (Code 29) | Check the device documentation on how to assign resources. You might need to upgrade the BIOS or enable the device in the system BIOS. |
| This device is not working properly because Windows cannot load the drivers required for this device. (Code 31) | The device driver might be incompatible with Windows Server. Obtain a compatible driver for the device and tap or click Update Driver to start the Update Driver Software Wizard. |
| A driver for this device was not required and has been disabled. (Code 32) | A dependent service for this device has been set to Disabled. Check the event logs to determine which services should be enabled and started. |
| Windows cannot determine which resources are required for this device. (Code 33) | This might indicate a bad device or bad hardware. This error code can also occur with legacy ISA devices; upgrade the driver, refer to the device documentation on how to set resource usage, or do both. |

Chapter 7

| Error Message | Correction Action |
|---|---|
| Windows cannot determine the settings for this device. (Code 34) | The legacy device must be manually configured. Verify the device jumpers or BIOS settings, and then configure the device resource usage using the Resources tab of the device's Properties dialog box. |
| Your computer's system firmware does not include enough information to properly configure and use this device. (Code 35) | This error occurs on multiprocessor systems. Update the BIOS; check for a BIOS option to use MPS 1.1 or MPS 1.4. Usually, you want MPS 1.4. |
| This device is requesting a Peripheral Component Interconnect (PCI) interrupt but is configured for an ISA interrupt (or vice versa). (Code 36) | ISA interrupts are nonshareable. If a device is in a PCI slot but the slot is configured in BIOS as "reserved for ISA," the error might be displayed. Change the BIOS settings. |
| Windows cannot initialize the device driver for this hardware. (Code 37) | Run the Update Driver Software Wizard by tapping or clicking Update Driver on the Driver tab. |
| Windows cannot load the device driver for this hardware because a previous instance of the device driver is still in memory. (Code 38) | A device driver in memory is causing a conflict. Restart the computer. |
| Windows cannot load the device driver for this hardware. The driver might be corrupted or missing. (Code 39) | Check to ensure that the hardware device is properly installed and connected and that it has power. If it is properly installed and connected, look for an updated driver or reinstall the current driver. |
| Windows cannot access this hardware because its service key information in the registry is missing or recorded incorrectly. (Code 40) | The registry entry for the device driver is invalid. Reinstall the driver. |
| Windows has stopped this device because it has reported problems. (Code 43) | The device was stopped by the operating system. You might need to uninstall and then reinstall the device. The device might have problems with the no-execute processor feature. In this case, check for a new driver. |
| An application or service has shut down this hardware device. (Code 44) | The device was stopped by an application or service. Restart the computer. The device might have problems with the no-execute processor feature. In this case, check for a new driver. |

## Resolving resource conflicts

Anyone who remembers IRQ conflicts will be thankful that current computers support ACPI BIOS. With ACPI BIOS, resources are allocated automatically by the operating system at startup, and multiple devices can share the same IRQ settings. These changes mean IRQ conflicts are largely a thing of the past. However, ACPI depends on Plug and Play, and devices that are not fully compatible can sometimes cause problems, particularly legacy ISA devices.

## TROUBLESHOOTING

### Check the device slot configuration

Some conflicts occur because PCI interrupts are shareable, while ISA interrupts are nonshareable. Typically, this is a BIOS problem. If a device is in a PCI slot but the slot is configured in BIOS as "reserved for ISA," a conflict can occur. You must change the BIOS settings rather than the resource configuration to resolve the problem.

If you suspect a device conflict is causing a problem with the current device, check the Conflicting Device list in the lower portion of the Resources tab. It will either list No Conflicts or the specific source of a known conflict. In Device Manager, you can quickly check resource allocations by choosing Resources By Type or Resources By Connection on the View menu.

In Figure 7-15, both ISA and PCI devices are using IRQ settings. You'll note each ISA device has a separate IRQ setting, while multiple PCI devices share the same IRQ settings. This is very typical. Note also that the PCI Modem device has a question mark as an icon. This is because the device isn't configured properly, not because there's a conflict. In this example, there are no conflicts.

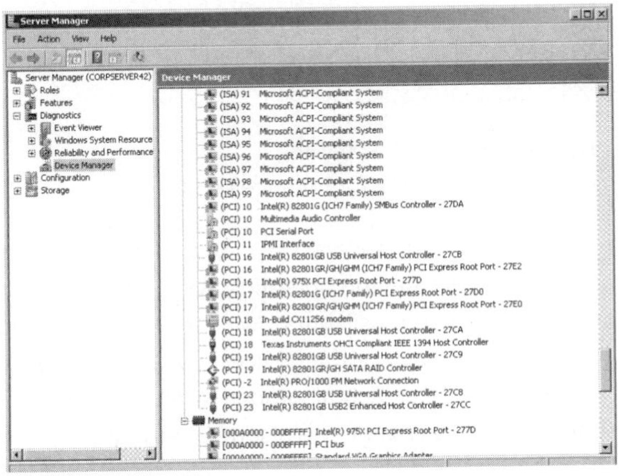

**Figure 7-15** View resources by type or resources by connection to check resource settings in Device Manager.

Another way to check for conflicts is to use the System Information utility (Msinfo32.exe). In Server Manager, select System Information on the Tools menu. In System Information, expand Hardware Resources, and then select Conflicts/Sharing.

As shown in Figure 7-16, a list of all resources that are in use is displayed. Again, keep in mind that devices can share IRQ settings thanks to ACPI, so what you are looking for are two unrelated devices sharing the same memory addresses or I/O ports, which would cause a conflict. Keep in mind related devices can share memory addresses and I/O ports. In the example, the PCI Express Root Complex shares the same I/O port as the Direct Memory Access Controller and the Mobile Express Root Port shares the same memory addresses as the Basic Display Adapter resources. That's okay because this is typical and not causing an issue.

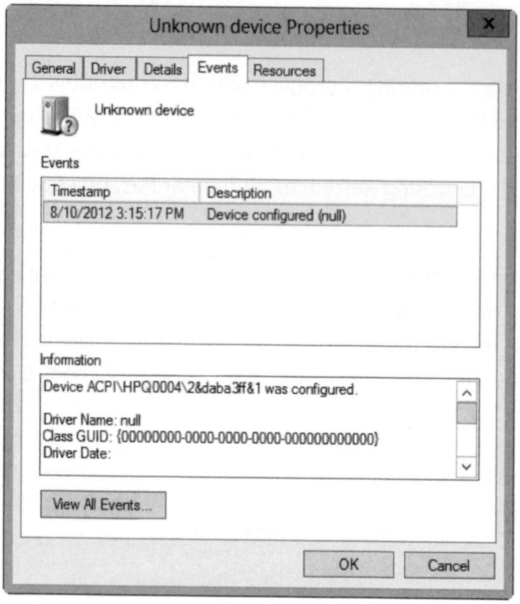

**Figure 7-16** Use System Information to check for resource conflicts.

You can try to resolve resource conflicts in several ways. Some devices use jumpers to manage resource settings, and in this case, the operating system cannot control the resource settings. To make changes, you must shut down the computer, remove the device, change the jumper settings, and then replace the device. In some cases, the jumpers are managed through software rather than an actual jumper switch. Here, you would use the device setup or configuration utility to change the resource settings.

For PCI devices, you can try swapping the cards between PCI slots. This will help if the IRQ or other resource settings are assigned on a per-slot basis, as is the case with some motherboards. You might be able to check the motherboard documentation to see which IRQ interrupts are assigned to which slots. In any case, you need to experiment to see which card configuration works.

For PCI devices, a conflict could also be caused by the device driver and the way it works with the ACPI BIOS. You should check to see whether an updated device driver and a BIOS update are available. Installing one or both should resolve the conflict.

As a last resort, you can change the resource settings manually for some devices in Device Manager. In the Resources tab, select the resource type that you want to work with. If you can make a change, you should be able to clear the Use Automatic Settings check box and then see whether any of the alternate configurations in the Setting Based On box resolve the conflict. Keep in mind that you are now manually managing the resource settings. To allow the Windows operating system again to manage the settings automatically, you must select the Use Automatic Settings check box.

Chapter 7

# Managing the registry

E VERYONE who accesses a computer, whether in a workgroup or on a domain, at one time or another has worked with the Microsoft Windows registry whether the person realizes it or not. Whenever you log on, your user preferences are read from the registry. Whenever you make changes to the system configuration, install applications or hardware, or make other changes to the working environment, the changes are stored in the registry. Whenever you uninstall hardware, applications, or system components, these changes are recorded in the registry as well.

The registry is the central repository for configuration information in Microsoft Windows. Applications, system components, device drivers, and the operating system kernel all use the registry to store settings and to obtain information about user preferences, system hardware configuration, and system defaults. The registry also stores information about security settings, user rights, local accounts, and much more. In domains, Windows does not store information about domain accounts or network objects in the registry; these settings are managed by Active Directory Domain Services as discussed in Part 5, "Managing Active Directory and Security."

With so much information being read from and written to the registry, it is not only important for administrators to understand its structures and uses, it is essential. You should know the types of data the registry works with, what type of data is stored where, and how to make changes if necessary. This is important because often when you must fine-tune the system configuration or correct errors to stabilize systems, you might be instructed to access the registry and make a particular change. Generally, the instructions assume you know what you're doing. Unfortunately, if you attempt such a change and really don't know what you're doing, you could make it so the system won't boot at all. So, with this in mind, let's look at how the registry works and how you can work with it.

# Introducing the registry

The registry is written as a binary database with the information organized in a hierarchy. This hierarchy has a structure much like that used by a file system and is an inverted tree with the root at the top of the tree. Any time the Windows operating system must obtain system default values or information about your preferences, it obtains this information from the registry. Any time you install programs or make changes in Control Panel, these changes usually are written to the registry.

> **Note**
>
> I say "usually" because in Windows domains some configuration information is written to the Active Directory directory service. For example, beginning with Microsoft Windows 2000, information about user accounts and network objects is stored in Active Directory. In addition, when you promote a member server to a domain controller, key registry settings that apply to the server, such as the default configuration values, are transferred to Active Directory and thereafter managed through Active Directory. If you were later to demote the domain controller, the original registry settings would not be restored either. Instead, the default settings are restored as they would appear on a newly installed server.

The registry's importance is that it stores most of a system's state. If you make preference and settings changes to a system, these changes are stored in the registry. If a system dies and cannot be recovered, you don't have to install a new system and then configure it to look like the old one. You could instead install Microsoft Windows Server 2012 and then restore a backup of the failed system's registry. This restores all the preferences and settings of the failed system on the new system.

Although it's great that the registry can store settings you've made, you might be wondering what else the registry is good for. Well, in addition to storing settings you've made, the registry stores settings that the operating system makes as well. For example, the operating system kernel stores information needed by device drivers in the registry, including the driver initialization parameters, which allows the device drivers to configure themselves to work with the system's hardware.

Many other system components make use of the registry as well. When you install Windows Server, the setup choices you make are used to build the initial registry database.

Setup modifies the registry whenever you add or remove hardware from a system. Similarly, application setup programs modify the registry to store the application installation settings and to determine whether components of the application are already installed. Then, when you run applications, the applications make use of the registry settings.

Unlike Windows XP and early releases of Windows, current Windows operating systems don't always store application settings directly in the registry and might, in fact, read some settings from a user's profile. This behavior occurs because of User Account Control (UAC). Of the many features UAC implements, there are two key features that change the way Windows installs and runs applications: application run levels and application virtualization.

To support run levels and virtualization, all applications that run on current Windows operating systems have a security token. The security token reflects the level of privileges required to run the application. Applications written for Windows Vista and later can have either an *administrator* token or a *standard user* token. Applications with administrator tokens require elevated privileges to run and perform core tasks. After it's started in elevated mode, an application with an administrator token can perform tasks that require administrator privileges and can also write to system locations of the registry and the file system.

On the other hand, applications with "standard user" tokens do not require elevated privileges to run and perform core tasks. After it's started in standard user mode, an application with a standard user token must request elevated privileges to perform administration tasks. For all other tasks, the application should not run using elevated privileges. Further, the application should write data only to nonsystem locations of the registry and the file system.

Standard user applications run in a special compatibility mode and use file system and registry virtualization to provide virtualized views of resources. When an application attempts to write to a system location, Windows Vista and later give the application a private copy of the file or registry value. Any changes are then written to the private copy, and this private copy, in turn, is stored in the user's profile data. If the application attempts to read or write to this system location again, it is given the private copy from the user's profile to work with. By default, if an error occurs when working with virtualized data, the error notification and logging information shows the virtualized location rather than the actual location the application was trying to work with.

Chapter 8

# INSIDE OUT  The Transactional Registry

Windows Server 2012 implements transactional technology in the kernel to preserve data integrity and handle error conditions when writing to the NTFS file system and the registry. Applications that are written to take advantage of the Transactional Registry can use transactions to manage registry changes as discrete operations that can be committed if successful or rolled back if unsuccessful. While a transaction is active, registry changes are not visible to users or other applications—it is only when Windows Server 2012 commits the transaction that the changes are applied fully and become visible. Transactions used with the registry can be coordinated with any other transactional resource, such as Microsoft Message Queuing (MSMQ). If the operating system fails during a transaction, work that has started to commit is written to the disk and incomplete transactional work is rolled back.

The registry provider built into Windows PowerShell is designed to be used with transactions as well. In fact, when you manage the registry using Windows PowerShell, you script your changes within a transaction. Here, you use Start-Transaction to start a transaction before you modify the registry. Next, you make and verify your changes. Finally, you either finalize your changes using Stop-Transaction or you roll back your changes using Undo-Transaction. You can learn more about scripting the registry with Windows PowerShell in Chapter 12, "Managing and Securing the Registry," of *Windows PowerShell 2.0 Administrator's Pocket Consultant* (Microsoft Press, 2009).

# Understanding the registry structure

Many administrative tools are little more than friendly user interfaces for managing the registry, especially when it comes to Control Panel. So, rather than having you work directly with a particular area of the registry, Microsoft provides tools you can use to make the necessary changes safely and securely. Use these tools—that's what they are for.

## CAUTION !

The importance of using the proper tools to make registry changes cannot be overstated. If there's a tool that lets you manage an area of the registry, you should use it. Don't fool around with the registry just because you can. Making improper changes to the registry can cause a system to become unstable, and in some cases, it could even make it so that the system won't boot.

# INSIDE OUT     Controlling virtualization

In Local Security Policy, Security Options can enable or disable registry virtualization. With Windows Vista and later, User Account Control: Virtualize File And Registry Write Failures To Per-User Locations enables the redirection of legacy application write failures to defined locations in the registry and file system. This feature is designed to allow legacy programs that require administrator privileges to run. When enabled as per the default setting, this setting allows the redirection of application write failures to defined user locations for both the file system and the registry. When you disable this setting, applications that write data to protected locations silently fail.

To view or modify this setting in the Local Security Settings console, open the Local Security Policy console, expand the Local Policies node in the left pane, and then select the Security Options node. In the main pane, you should now see a list of policy settings. Scroll down through the list of security settings. Double-tap or double-click User Account Control: Virtualize File And Registry Write Failures To Per-User Locations. On the Local Policy Setting tab of the dialog box, you'll see the current enabled or disabled state of the setting. To change the state of the setting, select Enabled or Disabled as appropriate and then tap or click OK.

As you can see, nearly everything you do with the operating system affects the registry in one way or another. That's why it's so important to understand what the registry is used for, how you can work with it, how you can secure it, and how you can maintain it.

The registry is first a database. Like any other database, the registry is designed for information storage and retrieval. Any registry value entry can be identified by specifying the path to its location. For example, the path HKEY_LOCAL_MACHINE\SOFTWARE\Microsoft\ServerManager\DoNotOpenServerManagerAtLogon specifies a registry value you can use to enable or disable the automatic display of Server Manager at log on.

Figure 8-1 shows this value in the registry. Because of its hierarchical structure, the registry appears to be organized much like a file system. In fact, its structure is often compared to that of a file system. However, this is a bit misleading because there is no actual folder/file representation on a system's hard disk to match the structure used by the registry. The registry's actual physical structure is separate from the way registry information is represented. Locations in the registry are represented by a logical structure that has little correlation to how value entries are stored.

Windows Server doesn't keep the entire registry in paged pool memory. Instead, 256-kilobyte (KB) views of the registry are mapped into system cache as needed. This is an important change from the original architecture of the registry, which effectively limited the registry to about 80 percent of the total size of paged pool memory. Now registry implementation is limited only by available space in the paging file.

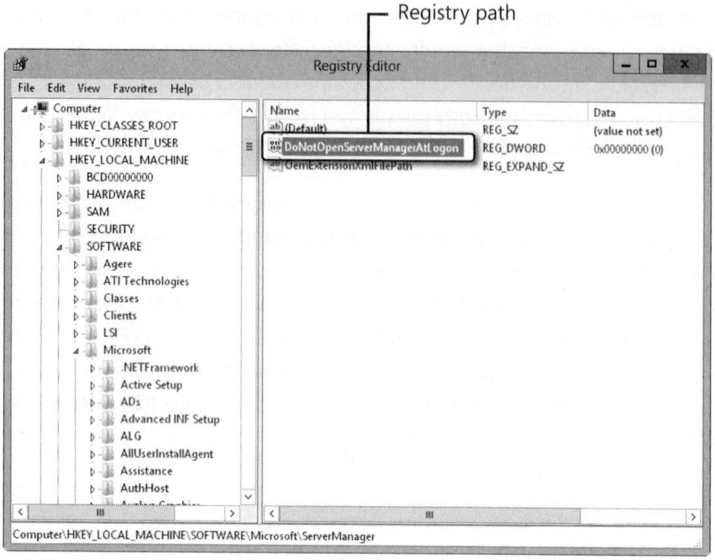

Figure 8-1  Accessing a value according to its path in the registry.

At startup, 256-KB mapped views of the registry are loaded into system cache so that Windows Server 2012 can quickly retrieve configuration information. Some of the registry's information is created dynamically based on the system hardware configuration at startup and doesn't exist until it is created. For the most part, however, the registry is stored in persistent form on disk and read from a set of files called *hives*. Hives are binary files that represent a grouping of keys and values. You'll find the hive files in the %SystemRoot%\System32\Config directory. Within this directory, you'll also find .sav and .log files, which serve as backup files for the registry.

# INSIDE OUT   Windows Server manages the registry size and memory use

Early releases of Windows Server stored the entire registry in paged, pooled memory. For 32-bit systems, this limited the registry to approximately 160 megabytes (MBs) because of the layout of the virtual address space in the operating system kernel. Unfortunately, in this configuration as the registry grows in size it uses a considerable amount of paged, pooled memory and can leave too little memory for other kernel-mode components.

Current releases of Windows Server resolve this problem by changing the way the registry is stored in memory. Here, 256-KB mapped views of the registry are loaded into the system cache as necessary by Cache Manager. The rest of the registry is stored in the paging file on disk. Because the registry is written to system cache, it can exist in system random access memory (RAM) and be paged to and from disk as needed. In previous versions of the Windows operating system, the operating system allowed you to control the maximum amount of memory and disk space that could be used by the registry. With the improved memory management features, the operating system has now taken over control of managing how much memory the registry uses. Most member servers use between 24 and 32 MBs of memory for the registry. Domain controllers or servers that have many configuration components, services, and applications can use considerably more. That said, however, one of my key domain controllers uses only 28 to 42 MBs of memory for the registry. This represents quite a change from the old architecture, when the in-memory requirements of the registry could be up to 160 MBs.

To read the registry, you need a special editor. The editor provided in Windows Server is Registry Editor. By using Registry Editor, you can navigate the registry's logical structure from the top of the database to the bottom. From the top down, the levels of the database are defined as root keys, subkeys, and value entries.

At the top of the registry hierarchy are the root keys. Each root key contains several subkeys, which contain other subkeys and value entries. The names of value entries must be unique within the associated subkey, and the value entries correspond to specific configuration parameters. The settings of those configuration parameters are the values stored in the value entry. Each value has an associated data type that controls the type of data it can store. For example, some value entries are used to store only binary data, while others are used to store only strings of characters, and the value's data type controls this.

Chapter 8

# INSIDE OUT Regedit replaces Regedt32

Unlike early versions of the Windows operating system that included two versions of Registry Editor, current releases of Windows Server ship with a single version. This version, Regedit.exe, integrates all of the features of both the previous registry editors. From the original Regedit.exe, it gets its core features. From Regedt32.exe, which is no longer available, it gets its security and favorites features. By using the Permissions feature, you can view and manage permissions for registry values. By using the Favorites feature, you can create and use favorites to quickly access stored locations within the registry.

Regedt32 *really* is gone—although I, like many administrators, still refer to it. It is, after all, the editor administrators used because it gave us the ability to manage registry security, and it is the one that was recommended for administrators over Regedit. Because old habits die hard, Windows Server 2012 still has a stub file for Regedt32. However, if you run Regedt32, the operating system, in fact, starts Regedit.

We can now break down the registry path HKEY_LOCAL_MACHINE\SOFTWARE\Microsoft\Windows NT\CurrentVersion\Winlogon\AllowMultipleTSSessions so that it is more meaningful. Here, HKEY_LOCAL_MACHINE is the root key. Each entry below the root key until we get to *AllowMultipleTSSessions* represents a subkey level within the registry hierarchy. Finally, *AllowMultipleTSSessions* is the actual value entry.

The registry is very complex, and it is often made more confusing because documentation on the subject uses a variety of terms beyond those already discussed. When reading about the registry in various sources, you might see references to the following:

- **Subtrees**  A *subtree* is the name for the tree of keys and values stemming from a root key down the registry hierarchy. In documentation, you often see root keys referred to as subtrees. What the documentation means when it refers to a subtree is the branch of keys and values contained within a specified root key.

- **Keys**  Technically, root keys are the top of the registry hierarchy, and everything below a root key is either a subkey or a value entry. In practice, subkeys are often referred to as keys. It's just easier to refer to such and such a key—sort of like when we refer to "such and such a folder" rather than saying "subfolder."

- **Values**  A value is the lowest level of the registry hierarchy. For ease of reference, value entries are often simply referred to as values. Technically, however, a value entry comprises three parts: a name, data type, and value. The name identifies the configuration setting. The data type identifies the format for the data. The value is the actual data within the entry.

Now that you know the basics of the registry's structure, let's dig deeper, taking a closer look at the root keys, major subkeys, and data types.

# Registry root keys

The registry is organized into a hierarchy of keys, subkeys, and value entries. The root keys are at the top of the hierarchy and form the primary branches, or subtrees, of registry information. There are two physical root keys: HKEY_LOCAL_MACHINE and HKEY_USERS. These physical root keys are associated with actual files stored on the disk and are divided into additional logical groupings of registry information. As shown in Table 8-1, the logical groupings are simply subsets of information gathered from HKEY_LOCAL_MACHINE and HKEY_USERS.

**TABLE 8-1  Registry subtrees**

| Subtree | Description |
| --- | --- |
| **Physical Subtree** | |
| HKEY_LOCAL_MACHINE (HKLM) | Stores all the settings that pertain to the hardware currently installed on the machine. |
| HKEY_USERS (HKU) | Stores user profile data for each user who has previously logged on to the computer locally as well as a default user profile. |
| **Logical Subtree** | |
| HKEY_CLASSES_ROOT (HKCR) | Stores all file associations and object linking and embedding (OLE) class identifiers. This subtree is built from HKEY_LOCAL_MACHINE\SOFTWARE\ Classes and HKEY_CURRENT_USER\SOFTWARE\ Classes. |
| HKEY_CURRENT_CONFIG (HKCC) | Stores information about the hardware configuration with which you started the system. This subtree is built from HKEY_LOCAL_MACHINE\ SYSTEM\CurrentControlSet\Hardware Profiles\ Current, which in turn is a pointer to a numbered subkey that has the current hardware profile. |
| HKEY_CURRENT_USER (HKCU) | Stores information about the user currently logged on. This key has a pointer to HKEY_USERS\ UserSID, where *UserSID* is the security identifier for the current user as well as for the default profile discussed previously. |

# INSIDE OUT The registry on 64-bit Windows systems

The registry on 64-bit Windows systems is divided into 32-bit and 64-bit keys. Many keys are created in both 32-bit and 64-bit versions, and although the keys belong to different branches of the registry, they have the same name. On these systems, Registry Editor (Regedit.exe) is designed to work with both 32-bit and 64-bit keys.

Registry keys are either shared or redirected for use under WOW64. With shared keys, a physical copy of each key is mapped into each logical view of the registry and applications make calls into these logical views. With redirected keys, the registry redirector intercepts calls to the redirected keys and maps them to the actual physical location in the registry.

## HKEY_LOCAL_MACHINE

HKEY_LOCAL_MACHINE, abbreviated as HKLM, contains all the settings that pertain to the hardware currently installed on a system. It includes settings for memory, device drivers, installed hardware, and startup. Applications are supposed to store settings in HKLM only if the related data pertains to everyone who uses the computer.

As Figure 8-2 shows, HKLM contains the following major subkeys:

- BCD00000000

- HARDWARE

- SAM

- SECURITY

- SOFTWARE

- SYSTEM

These subkeys are discussed in the sections that follow.

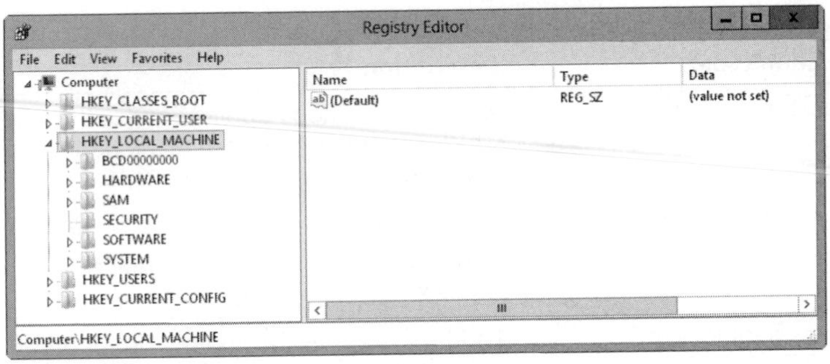

**Figure 8-2** Accessing HKEY_LOCAL_MACHINE in the registry.

## HKLM\BCD00000000

The HKLM\BCD00000000 key stores information regarding the configuration and state of the computer's Boot Configuration Data (BCD). BCD provides a firmware-independent approach for managing the boot environment for Windows systems. As discussed in Chapter 3, "Boot configuration," you manage the BCD store using the BCDEdit tool (and not via the related registry keys).

The BCD architecture has three main components: stores, objects, and elements. A store is a top-level component that establishes the namespace and acts as a container for BCD objects and elements. There are three general types of BCD objects:

- **Application objects**   Describe boot environment objects, such as Windows Boot Manager or Windows Boot Loader.

- **Inheritable objects**   Act as containers for elements that are shared across multiple object instances.

- **Device objects**   Act as containers for elements that describe complex devices, such as a RAM disk that was created from a Windows Imaging file.

Application objects have an image type and an application type associated with them. The image type specifies how the executable for the application is loaded, such as through the firmware or by a boot application. The application type specifies what the application does and the standard application types are listed in Table 8-2.

Chapter 8

**TABLE 8-2 BCD application types**

| Application type | Description |
| --- | --- |
| Boot sector | A 16-bit real-mode application for BIOS-based systems, which can be used to restart the boot process and load a non-Windows operating system. |
| Firmware boot manager | Manages the firmware boot for EFI systems. |
| Ntldr | Loads versions of Windows earlier than Windows Vista on BIOS-based systems. |
| Windows boot loader | Loads a particular version or configuration of Windows. |
| Windows boot manager | Controls boot of the system. In a multi-boot system, displays a boot selection menu to the user. |
| Windows memory tester | An application for performing memory diagnostics. |
| Windows resume application | Restores Windows to its running state when a computer resumes from hibernation. |

Each BCD object has a globally unique identifier or GUID. For example, the GUID of the Windows resume application is 5824ba7d-acee-11e1-ba52-cfa3fef36259. In the registry, the GUID sets the key path and each object has a description entry and associated elements entries.

## HKLM\HARDWARE

HKLM\HARDWARE stores information about the hardware configuration for the computer. This key is re-created by the operating system each time you start Windows Server 2012, and it exists only in memory, not on disk. To build this key, the operating system enumerates every device it can find by scanning the system buses and by searching for specific classes of devices, such as serial ports, keyboards, and pointer devices.

Under HKLM\HARDWARE, you'll find four standard subkeys that are dynamically created at startup and contain the information gathered by the operating system. These subkeys are as follows:

- **ACPI** Contains information about the Advanced Configuration and Power Interface (ACPI), which is a part of system BIOS that supports Plug and Play and advanced power management. This subkey doesn't exist on non-ACPI-compliant computers.

- **DESCRIPTION** Contains hardware descriptions, including those for the system's central processor, floating-point processor, and multifunction adapters. For portable computers, one of the multifunction devices lists information about the docking state. For any computer with multipurpose chip sets, one of the multifunction devices lists information about the controllers for disks, keyboards, parallel ports, serial ports, and pointer devices. There's also a catchall category for other controllers, such as when a computer has a PC Card controller.

- **DEVICEMAP**   Contains information that maps devices to device drivers. You'll find device mappings for keyboards, pointer devices, parallel ports, Small Computer System Interface (SCSI) ports, serial ports, and video devices. Of particular note is that within the VIDEO subkey is a value entry for the VGA–compatible video device installed on the computer. This device is used when the computer must start in VGA display mode.

- **RESOURCEMAP**   Contains mappings for the hardware abstraction layer (HAL), for the Plug and Play Manager, and for available system resources. Of particular note is the Plug and Play Manager. It uses this subkey to record information about devices it knows how to handle.

Additional nonstandard subkeys can exist under HKLM\HARDWARE. The subkeys are specific to the hardware used by the computer.

## HKLM\SAM

HKLM\SAM stores the Security Accounts Manager (SAM) database. When you create local users and groups on member servers and workstations, the accounts are stored in HKLM\SAM. This key is also used to store information about built-in user and group accounts, as well as group membership and aliases for accounts.

By default, the information stored in HKLM\SAM is inaccessible through Registry Editor. This is a security feature designed to help protect the security and integrity of the system.

## HKLM\SECURITY

HKLM\SECURITY stores security information for the local machine. It contains information about cached logon credentials, policy settings, service-related security settings, and default security values. It also has a copy of the HKLM\SAM. As with the HKLM\SAM subkey, this subkey is inaccessible through Registry Editor. This is a security feature designed to help protect the security and integrity of the system.

## HKLM\SOFTWARE

HKLM\SOFTWARE stores machine-wide settings for every application and system component installed on the system. This includes setup information, executable paths, default configuration settings, and registration information. Because this subkey resides under HKLM, the information here is applied globally. This is different from the HKCU\SOFTWARE configuration settings, which are applied on a per-user basis.

As Figure 8-3 shows, you'll find many important subkeys within HKLM\SOFTWARE, including the following:

- **Classes**    Contains all file associations and OLE class identifiers. This is also the key from which HKEY_CLASSES_ROOT is built.

- **Clients**    Stores information about protocols and shells used by every client application installed on the system. This includes the calendar, contacts, mail, media, and news clients.

- **Microsoft**    Contains information about every Microsoft application and component installed on the system. This includes their complete configuration settings, defaults, registration information, and much more. You'll find most of the graphical user interface (GUI) preferences in HKLM\SOFTWARE\Microsoft\Windows\CurrentVersion. You'll find the configuration settings for most system components, language packs, hot fixes, and more under HKLM\SOFTWARE\Microsoft\Windows NT\CurrentVersion.

- **ODBC**    Contains information about the Open Database Connectivity (ODBC) configuration on the system. It includes information about all ODBC drives and ODBC file Data Source Names (DSNs).

- **Policies**    Contains information about local policies for applications and components installed on the system.

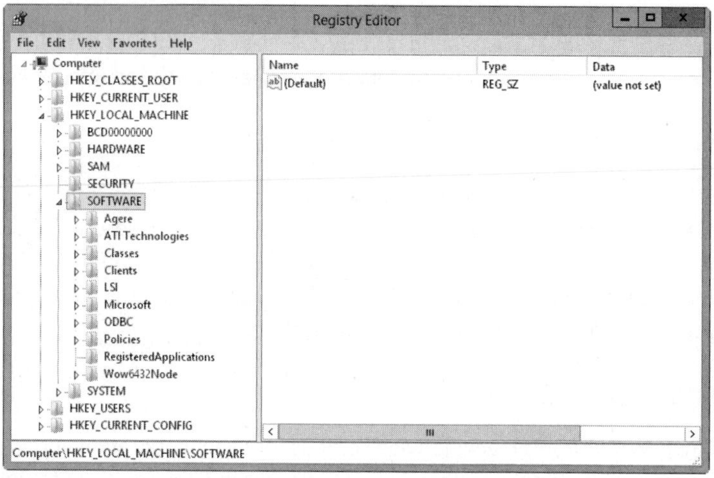

**Figure 8-3**  Accessing HKEY_LOCAL_MACHINE\SOFTWARE in the registry.

# HKLM\SYSTEM

HKLM\SYSTEM stores information about device drivers, services, startup parameters, and other machine-wide settings. You'll find several important subkeys within HKLM\SYSTEM. One of the most important is HKLM\SYSTEM\CurrentControlSet, as shown in Figure 8-4.

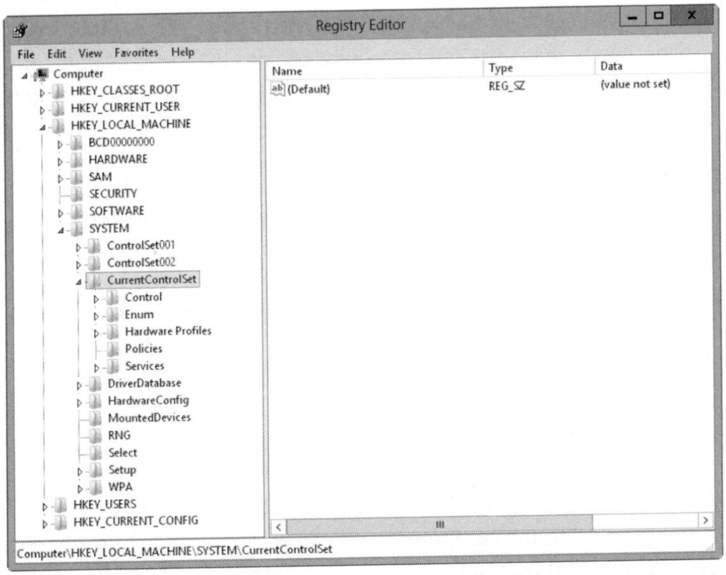

**Figure 8-4** Accessing HKEY_LOCAL_MACHINE\SYSTEM\CurrentControlSet in the registry.

CurrentControlSet contains information about the set of controls and services used for the last successful boot of the system. This subkey always contains information on the set of controls actually in use and represents the most recent successful boot. The operating system writes the control set as the final part of the boot process so that it updates the registry as appropriate to reflect which set of controls and services was last used for a successful boot. This is, in fact, how you can boot a system to the Last Known Good Configuration after it crashes or experiences a Stop error.

HKLM\SYSTEM also contains previously created control sets. These are saved under the subkeys named ControlSet001, ControlSet002, and so forth. Within the control sets, you'll find four important subkeys:

- **Control**   Contains control information about key operating system settings, tools, and subcomponents, including the HAL, keyboard layouts, system devices, interfaces, and device classes. Under BackupRestore, you'll find the saved settings for Backup, which include lists of Automated System Recovery (ASR) keys, files, and registry settings not to restore. Under the SafeBoot subkey, you'll find the control sets used for minimal and network-only boots of the system.

- **Enum**   Contains the complete enumeration of devices found on the computer when the operating system scans the system buses and searches for specific classes of devices. This represents the complete list of devices present during startup of the operating system.

- **Hardware Profiles**   Contains a subkey for each hardware profile available on the system. The first hardware profile, 0000, is an empty profile. The other numbered profiles, beginning with 0001, represent profiles that are available for use on the system. The profile named Current always points to the profile being used currently by the operating system.

- **Services**   Contains a subkey for each service installed on the system. These subkeys store the necessary configuration information for their related services, which can include startup parameters as well as security and performance settings.

Another interesting subkey is HKLM\SYSTEM\MountedDevices. The operating system creates this key and uses it to store the list of mounted and available disk devices. Disk devices are listed according to logical volume configuration and drive-letter designator.

# HKEY_USERS

HKEY_USERS, abbreviated as HKU, contains user-profile data for every user who has previously logged on to the computer locally, as well as a default user profile. Each user's profile is owned by that user unless you change permissions or move profiles. Profile settings include the user's desktop configuration, environment variables, folder options, menu options, printers, and network connections.

User profiles are saved in subkeys of HKEY_USERS according to their security identifiers (SIDs). There is also a *SecurityID_Classes* subkey that represents file associations that are specific to a particular user. For example, if a user sets Adobe Photoshop as the default program for .jpeg and .jpg files and this is different from the system default, there are entries within this subkey that show this association.

When you use Group Policy as discussed in Part 5, the policy settings are applied to the individual user profiles stored in this key. The default profile specifies how the machine behaves when no one is logged on and is also used as the base profile for new users who log on to the computer. For example, if you want to ensure that the computer uses a password-protected screen saver when no one is logged on, you modify the default profile accordingly. The subkey for the default user profile is easy to pick out because it is named HKEY_USERS\.DEFAULT.

> **Note**
> The profile information stored in HKU is loaded from the profile data stored on disk. The default location for profiles is %SystemDrive%\Users\*UserName*, where *UserName* is the user's pre–Windows 2000 logon name.

# HKEY_CLASSES_ROOT

HKEY_CLASSES_ROOT, abbreviated as HKCR, stores all file associations that tell the computer which document file types are associated with which applications, as well as which action to take for various tasks—such as open, edit, close, or play—based on a specified document type. For example, if you double-tap or double-click a .doc file, the document typically is opened for editing in Microsoft Word. This file association is added to HKCR when you install Microsoft Office or Microsoft Word. If Microsoft Office or Microsoft Word isn't installed, a .doc file is opened instead in WordPad because of a default file association created when the operating system is installed.

HKCR is built from HKEY_LOCAL_MACHINE\SOFTWARE\Classes and HKEY_CURRENT_USER\ SOFTWARE\Classes. The former provides computer-specific class registration, and the latter provides user-specific class registration. Because the user-specific class registrations have precedence, this allows for different class registrations for each user of the machine. This is different from previous versions of the Windows operating system for which the same class registration information was provided for all users of a particular machine.

# HKEY_CURRENT_CONFIG

HKEY_CURRENT_CONFIG, abbreviated as HKCC, contains information about the hardware configuration with which you started the system, which is also referred to as the machine's boot configuration. This key contains information about the current device assignments, device drivers, and system services that were present at boot time.

HKCC is built from HKEY_LOCAL_MACHINE \SYSTEM\CurrentControlSet\Hardware Profiles\ Current, which in turn is a pointer to a numbered subkey that contains the current hardware profile. If a system has multiple hardware profiles, the key points to a different hardware profile, depending on the boot state or the hardware profile selection made at startup.

# HKEY_CURRENT_USER

HKEY_CURRENT_USER, abbreviated as HKCU, contains information about the user currently logged on. This key has a pointer to HKEY_USERS\\*UserSID*, where *UserSID* is the security identifier for the current user as well as for the default profile discussed previously. Microsoft requires that applications store user-specific preferences under this key. For example, Microsoft Office settings for individual users are stored under this key. Additionally, as discussed previously, HKEY_CURRENT_USER\\SOFTWARE\\Classes stores the user-specific settings for file associations.

> **Tip**
>
> If you don't want users to be able to set their own file associations, you could change the permissions on HKLM\\SOFTWARE\\Classes so that users can't alter the global settings you want them to have. For more information about registry permissions, see the section "Securing the registry" later in this chapter.

# Registry data: How it is stored and used

Now that you know more about the registry's structure, let's take a look at the actual data within the registry. Understanding how registry data is stored and used is just as important as understanding the registry structure.

## Where registry data comes from

As mentioned previously, some registry data is created dynamically during the startup of the operating system and some is stored on disk so that it can be used each time you boot a computer. The dynamically created data is volatile, meaning that when you shut down the system, it is gone. For example, as part of the startup process, the operating system scans for system devices and uses the results to build the HKEY_LOCAL_MACHINE\\HARDWARE subkey. The information stored in this key exists only in memory and isn't stored anywhere on disk.

On the other hand, registry data stored on disk is persistent. When you shut down a system, this registry data remains on disk and is available the next time you boot the system. Some of this stored information is very important, especially when it comes to recovering from boot failure. For example, by using the information stored in HKEY_LOCAL_MACHINE\\SYSTEM\\CurrentControlSet, you can boot using the Last Known Good Configuration. If the registry data was corrupted, however, this information might not be available and the only way to recover the system is to try repairing the installation or reinstalling the operating system.

To help safeguard the system and ensure that one section of bad data doesn't cause the whole registry to fail to load, Windows Server 2012 has several built-in redundancies and fail-safe processes. For starters, the registry isn't written to a single file. Instead, it is written to a set of files called hives. There are six main types of hives, each representing a group of keys and values. Most of the hives are written to disk in the %SystemRoot%\System32\Config directory. Within this directory, you'll find these hive files:

- DEFAULT, which corresponds to the HKEY_USERS\.DEFAULT subkey

- DRIVERS, which corresponds to the HKLM\Drivers subkey

- SAM, which corresponds to the HKEY_LOCAL_MACHINE\SAM subkey

- SECURITY, which corresponds to the HKEY_LOCAL_MACHINE\SECURITY subkey

- SOFTWARE, which corresponds to the HKEY_LOCAL_MACHINE\SOFTWARE subkey

- SYSTEM, which corresponds to the HKEY_LOCAL_MACHINE\SYSTEM subkey

The remaining hive files are stored in individual user-profile directories with the default name of Ntuser.dat. These files are, in fact, hive files that are loaded into the registry and used to set the pointer for the HKEY_CURRENT_USER root key. When no user is logged on to a system, the user profile for the default user is loaded into the registry. When an actual user logs on, this user's profile is loaded into the registry.

> **Note**
> The root keys not mentioned are HKEY_CURRENT_CONFIG and HKEY_CLASSES_ROOT. The on-disk data for HKEY_CURRENT_CONFIG comes from the subkey from which it is built: HKEY_LOCAL_MACHINE \SYSTEM\CurrentControlSet\Hardware Profiles\ Current. Similarly, the on-disk data for HKEY_CLASSES_ROOT comes from HKEY_LOCAL_ MACHINE \SOFTWARE\Classes and HKEY_CURRENT_USER\SOFTWARE\Classes.

Every hive file has associated log files—even Ntuser.dat. Windows Server 2012 uses the log files to help protect the registry during updates. When a hive file is to be changed, the operating system writes the change to a log file and stores this log file on disk. The operating system then uses the change log to write the changes to the actual hive file. If the operating system were to crash while a change is being written to a hive file, the change log could later be used by the operating system to roll back the change, resetting the hive to its previous configuration.

**INSIDE OUT**   How Windows Server 2012 starts over with a clean registry

Ever wonder how Windows Server 2012 can reset the registry to that of a clean install after you demote a domain controller? Examine %SystemRoot%\System32\Config\ RegBack on a domain controller and you'll see backup files. These files represent the backed-up state of the registry created by Windows Server prior to promoting a member server to a domain controller. By loading these files into the registry and then writing them to disk as the original hive files, a demoted server is returned to its original state.

## Types of registry data available

When you work your way down to the lowest level of the registry, you see the actual value entries. Each value entry has a name, data type, and value associated with it. Although value entries have a theoretical size limit of 1024 KBs, most value entries are less than 1 KB in size. In fact, many value entries contain only a few bits of data. The type of information stored in these bits depends on the data type of the value entry.

The data types defined include the following:

- **REG_BINARY**   Raw binary data without any formatting or parsing. You can view binary data in several forms, including standard binary and hexadecimal. In some cases, if you view the binary data, you will see the hexadecimal values as well as the text characters these values define.

- **REG_DWORD**   A binary data type in which 32-bit integer values are stored as 4-byte-length values in hexadecimal. REG_DWORD is often used to track values that can be incremented, 4-byte status codes, or Boolean flags. With Boolean flags, a value of 0 means the flag is off (false) and a value of 1 means the flag is on (true).

- **REG_LINK**   A Unicode string specifying a symbolic link to another registry value.

- **REG_NONE**   Data without a particular type that is displayed in Registry Editor in hexadecimal format as a binary value.

- **REG_QWORD**   A binary data type in which 64-bit integer values are stored as 8-byte-length values in hexadecimal. REG_QWORD is often used to track large values that can be incremented, 8-byte status codes, or Boolean flags. With Boolean flags, a value of 0 means the flag is off (false) and a value of 1 means the flag is on (true).

- **REG_SZ**   A fixed-length string of Unicode characters. REG_SZ is used to store values that are meant to be read by users and can include names, descriptions, and so on, as well as stored file system paths.

- **REG_EXPAND_SZ**   A variable-length string that can include environment variables that are to be expanded when the data is read by the operating system, its components, or services, as well as installed applications. Environment variables are enclosed in percentage signs (%) to set them off from other values in the string. For example, %SystemDrive% refers to the SystemDrive environment variable. A REG_EXPAND_SZ value that defines a path to use could include this environment variable, such as %SystemDrive%\Program Files\Common Files.

- **REG_MULTI_SZ**   A multiple-parameter string that can be used to store multiple string values in a single entry. Each value is separated by a standard delimiter so that the individual values can be picked out as necessary.

- **REG_RESOURCE_LIST**   A value that stores a series of nested arrays and that was designed to store a resource list for hardware device drivers or a physical device a driver controls. The value is displayed in Registry Editor in hexadecimal format as a binary value.

- **REG_RESOURCE_REQUIREMENTS_LIST**   A value that stores a series of nested arrays and that was designed to store a list of hardware resources for device drivers or a physical device a driver controls. The value is displayed in Registry Editor in hexadecimal format as a binary value.

- **REG_FULL_RESOURCE_DESCRIPTOR**   A value with an encoded resource descriptor, such as a list of resources used by a device driver or a hardware component. REG_FULL_RESOURCE_DESCRIPTOR values are associated with hardware components, such as a system's central processors, floating-point processors, or multifunction adapters.

The most common data types you'll see in the registry are REG_SZ and REG_DWORD. The vast majority of value entries have this data type. The most important thing to know about these data types is that one is used with strings of characters and the other is used with binary data that is normally represented in hexadecimal format. And don't worry, if you have to create a value entry—typically, you do so because you are directed to by a Microsoft Knowledge Base article in an attempt to resolve an issue—you are usually told which data type to use. Again, more often than not, this data type is either REG_SZ or REG_DWORD.

Chapter 8

# Registry administration

Windows Server 2012 provides several tools for working with the registry. The main tool, of course, is Registry Editor, which you start by typing **regedit** or **regedt32** at the command line or in the Run dialog box. Another tool for working with the registry is the REG command. Both tools can be used to view and manage the registry. Keep in mind that although both tools are considered editors, Windows Server 2012 applies any changes you make immediately. Thus, any change you make is applied automatically to the registry without you having to save the change.

> **CAUTION**
>
> As an administrator, you have permission to make changes to most areas of the registry. This allows you to make additions, changes, and deletions as necessary. However, before you do this, you should always make a backup of the system state along with the registry first, as discussed in "Backing up and restoring the registry" later in this chapter. This helps ensure that you can recover the registry in case something goes wrong when you are making your modifications.

## Searching the registry

One of the common tasks you'll want to perform in Registry Editor is to search for a particular key. You can search for keys, values, and data entries using the Find option on the Edit menu.

Don't let the simplicity of the Find dialog box, shown in Figure 8-5, fool you—there is a bit more to searching the registry than you might think. So, if you want to find what you're looking for, do the following:

- The Find function in Registry Editor searches from the current node forward to the last value in the final root key branch. So, if you want to search the complete registry, you must select the Computer node in the left pane before you select Find on the Edit menu or press Ctrl+F.

- Type the text you want to find in the Find What box. You can search only for standard American Standard Code for Information Interchange (ASCII) text. So, if you're searching for data entries, Registry Editor searches only string values (REG_SZ, REG_EXPAND_SZ, and REG_MULTI_SZ) for the specified text.

- Use the Look At options to control where Registry Editor looks for the text you want to find. You can search on key names, value names, and text within data entries. If you want to match only whole strings instead of searching for text within longer strings, select the Match Whole String Only check box.

**Figure 8-5**  Searching the registry.

After you make your selections, tap or click Find Next to begin the search. If Registry Editor finds a match before reaching the end of the registry, it selects and displays the matching item. If the match isn't what you're looking for, press F3 to search again from the current position in the registry.

## Modifying the registry

When you want to work with keys and values in the registry, you typically are working with subkeys of a particular key. This allows you to add a subkey and define its values and to remove subkeys and their values. You cannot, however, add or remove root keys or insert keys at the root node of the registry. Default security settings within some subkeys might also prohibit you from working with their keys and values. For example, by default you cannot create, modify, or remove keys or values within HKLM\SAM and HKLM\SECURITY.

### Modifying values

The most common change you'll make to the registry is to modify an existing value. For example, a Knowledge Base article might recommend that you change a value from 0 to 1 to enable a certain feature in Windows Server 2012 or from 1 to 0 to disable it. To change a value, locate the value in Registry Editor, and then in the right pane double-tap or double-click the value name. This opens an Edit dialog box, the style of which depends on the type of data you are modifying.

The most common values you'll modify are REG_SZ, REG_MULTI_SZ, and REG_DWORD. Figure 8-6 shows the Edit String dialog box, which is displayed when you modify REG_SZ values. In the dialog box, you typically replace the existing value shown in the Value Data box with the value you need to enter.

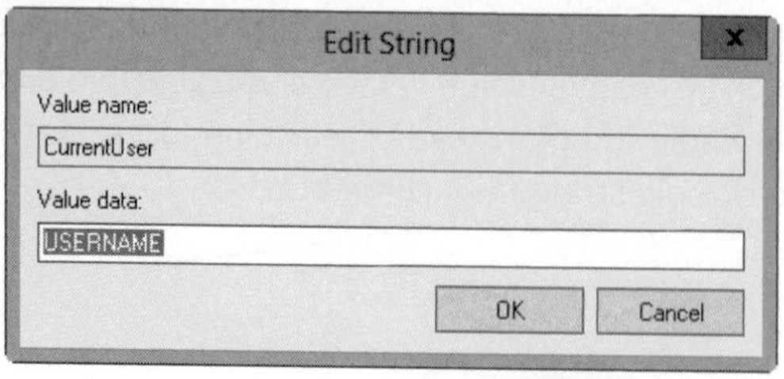

**Figure 8-6**  Using the Edit String dialog box.

Figure 8-7 shows the Edit Multi-String dialog box, which is displayed when you modify REG_MULTI_SZ values. In this example, there are three separate string values. In the dialog box, each value is separated by a new line to make the values easier to work with. If directed to change a value, you typically need to replace an existing value, making sure you don't accidentally modify the entry before or after the entry you are working with. If directed to add a value, you begin typing on a new line following the last value.

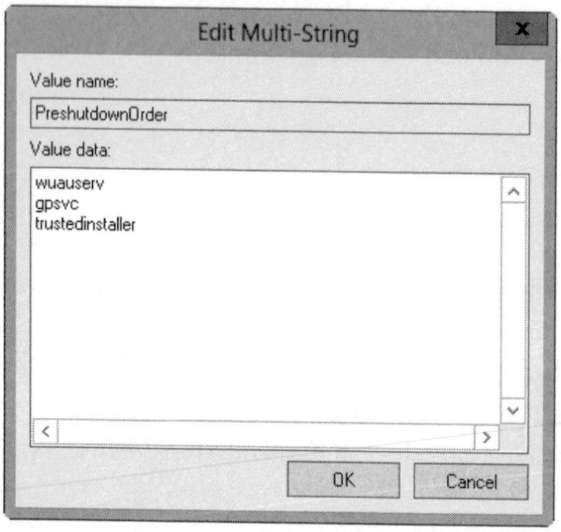

**Figure 8-7**  Using the Edit Multi-String dialog box.

Figure 8-8 shows the Edit DWORD Value dialog box, which is displayed when you modify REG_DWORD values. In this example, the value is displayed in hexadecimal format. Typically, you won't need to worry about the data format. You simply enter a new value as you've been directed. For example, if the Current value entry represents a flag, the data entry of 1 indicates the flag is on (or true). To turn off the flag (switch it to false), you replace the 1 with a 0.

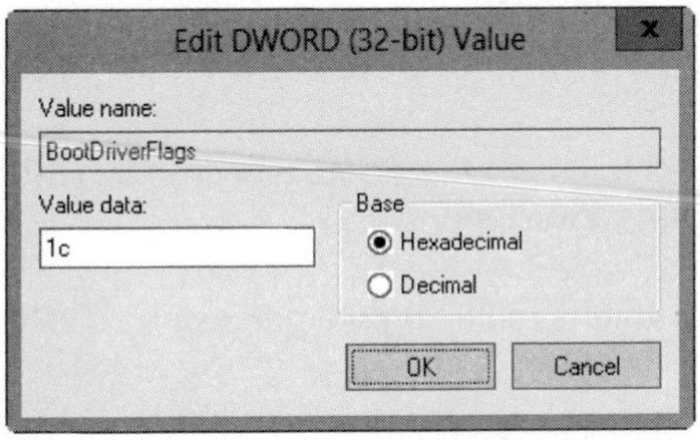

**Figure 8-8** Using the Edit DWORD Value dialog box.

> **Note**
> The Windows Clipboard is available when you are working with Registry Editor. This means you can use the Copy, Cut, and Paste commands just as you do with other Windows programs. If there is a value in a Knowledge Base article that's difficult to type, you might want to copy it to the Clipboard and then paste it into the Value Data box of the Edit dialog box.

## Adding keys and values

As noted previously, you can add or remove keys in most areas of the registry. The exceptions pertain to the root node, root keys, and areas of the registry where permissions prohibit modifications.

You add new keys as subkeys of a selected key. Access the key with which you want to work, and then add the subkey by pressing and holding or right-clicking the key and selecting Edit, New, and then Key. Registry Editor creates a new key and selects its name so that you can set it as appropriate. The default name is New Key #1.

The new key has a default value entry associated with it automatically. The data type for this default value is REG_SZ. Just about every key in the registry has a similarly named and typed value entry, so don't delete this value entry. Either set its value by double-tapping or double-clicking it to display the Edit String dialog box, or create additional value entries under the selected key.

To create additional value entries under a key, press and hold or right-click the key, and then select New followed by one of these menu options:

- **String Value**   Used to enter a fixed-length string of Unicode characters. The type is REG_SZ.

- **Binary Value**   Used to enter raw binary data without any formatting or parsing. The type is REG_BINARY.

- **DWORD (32-bit) Value**   Used to enter binary data type in which 4-byte integer values are stored. The type is REG_DWORD.

- **QWORD (64-bit) Value**   Used to enter binary data type in which 8-byte integer values are stored. The type is REG_QWORD.

- **Multi-String Value**   Used to enter a multiple-parameter string. The type is REG_MULTI_SZ.

- **Expandable String Value**   Used to enter a variable-length string that can include environment variables that are to be expanded when the data is read. The type is REG_EXPAND_SZ.

Creating a new value adds it to the selected key and gives it a default name of New Value #1, New Value #2, and so on. The name of the value is selected for editing so that you can change it immediately. After you change the value name, double-tap or double-click the value name to edit the value data.

## Removing keys and values

Removing keys and values from the registry is easy but should never be done without careful forethought to the possible consequences. That said, you delete a key or value by selecting it and then pressing the Delete key. Registry Editor will ask you to confirm the deletion. After you do this, the key or value is permanently removed from the registry. Keep in mind that when you remove a key, Registry Editor removes all subkeys and values associated with the key.

# Modifying the registry of a remote machine

You can modify the registry of remote computers without having to log on locally. To do this, select Connect Network Registry on the File menu in Registry Editor, and then use the Select Computer dialog box to specify the computer with which you want to work. In most cases, all you must do is type the name of the remote computer and then tap or click OK. If prompted, you might need to enter the user name and password of a user account that is authorized to access the remote computer.

After you connect, you get a new icon for the remote computer under your Computer icon in the left pane of Registry Editor. Double-tap or double-click this icon to access the physical root keys on the remote computer (HKEY_LOCAL_MACHINE and HKEY_USERS). The logical root keys aren't available because they are either dynamically created or simply pointers to subsets of information from within HKEY_LOCAL_MACHINE and HKEY_USERS. You can then edit the computer's registry as necessary. When you are done, you can select Disconnect Network Registry on the File menu and then choose the computer from which you want to disconnect. Registry Editor then closes the registry on the remote computer and breaks the connection.

When working with remote computers, you can also load or unload hives as discussed in "Loading and unloading hive files" later in this chapter. If you're wondering why you would do this, the primary reason is to work with a specific hive, such as the hive that points to Dianne Prescott's user profile because she inadvertently changed the display mode to an invalid setting and can no longer access the computer locally. With her user-profile data loaded, you could then edit the registry to correct the problem and then save the changes so that she can once again log on to the system.

# INSIDE OUT  Managing the registry using preferences

Rather than managing the registry on individual computers, you can use Group Policy preference items to configure the registry on any computer that processes a particular Group Policy Object (GPO). As when you configure the registry manually, you can use Group Policy preferences to create, modify, and delete registry keys and their values. Group Policy then writes the registry preferences during its normal refresh cycle and in this way, your registry preferences are deployed automatically. For more information on Group Policy, see Chapter 31, "Managing Group Policy."

## Importing and exporting registry data

Sometimes you might find that it is necessary or useful to copy all or part of the registry to a file. For example, if you've installed a service or component that requires extensive configuration, you might want to use it on another computer without having to go through the whole configuration process again. So, instead, you could install the service or component baseline on the new computer, export the application's registry settings from the previous computer, copy them over to the other computer, and then import the registry settings so that the service or component is properly configured. Of course, this technique works only if the complete configuration of the service or component is stored in the registry, but you can probably see how useful being able to import and export registry data can be.

By using Registry Editor, it is easy to import and export registry data. This includes the entire registry, branches of data stemming from a particular root key, and individual subkeys and the values they contain. When you export data, you create a .reg file that contains the designated registry data. This registry file is a script that can then be loaded back into the registry of this or any other computer by importing it.

> ## Note
>
> Because the registry script is written as standard text, you can view it and, if necessary, modify it in any standard text editor as well. Be aware, however, that double-tapping or double-clicking the .reg file starts Registry Editor, which prompts you as to whether you want to import the data into the registry. If you are concerned about this, save the data to a file with the .hiv extension because double-tapping or double-clicking files with this extension won't start Registry Editor. Files with the .hiv extension must be manually imported (or you could simply change the file extension to .reg when it is time to use the data).

To export registry data, press and hold or right-click the branch or key you want to export and then select Export. You can also press and hold or right-click the root node for the computer you are working with, such as Computer for a local computer, to export the entire registry. Either way, you'll see the Export Registry File dialog box as shown in Figure 8-9. Use the Save In selection list to choose a save location for the .reg file, and then type a file name. The Export Range panel shows you the selected branch within the registry that will be exported. You can change this as necessary or select All to export the entire registry. Then tap or click Save to create the .reg file.

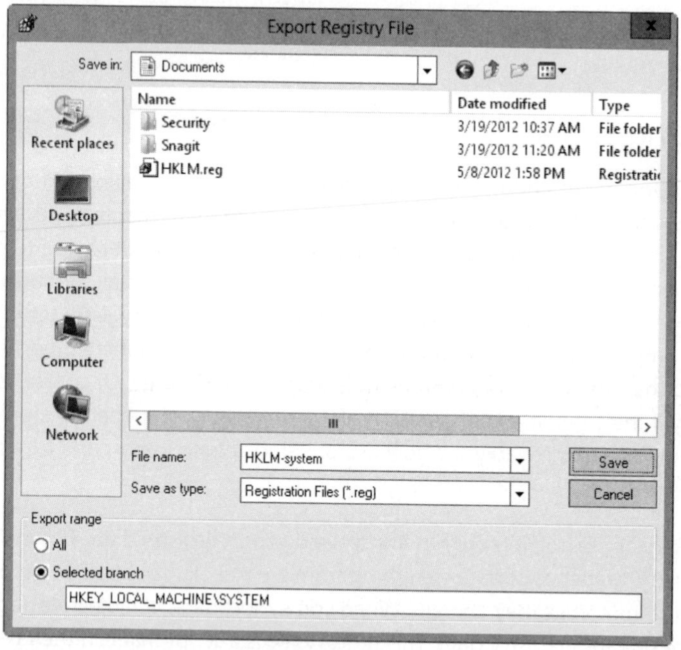

**Figure 8-9** Exporting registry data to a .reg file so that it can be saved and, if necessary, imported on this or another computer.

# INSIDE OUT  Want to export the entire registry quickly?

You can export the entire registry at the command line by typing **regedit /e SaveFile**, where *SaveFile* is the complete file path to the location where you want to save the copy of the registry. For example, if you want to save a copy of the registry to C:\Corpsvr06-regdata.reg, you type **regedit /e C:\corpsvr06-regdata.reg**.

You can also extend this technique to rapidly determine the exact registry values the operating system modifies when you make a change to a system or application setting. Start by opening the application of the System utility you want to work with as well as a command prompt window. Next, export the registry prior to making the change you want to track. Then immediately and without doing anything else, make the change you want to track and export the registry to a different file using the command-prompt window you opened previously. Finally, use the file comparison tool (fc.exe) to compare the two files. For example, if you saved the original registry to orig.reg and then changed registry to new.reg, you could type the following command at a command prompt to write the changes to a file called changes.txt: **fc /u orig.reg new.reg > changes.txt**. When you examine the changes.txt file in a text editor, you'll see a comparison of the registry files and the exact differences between the files.

Importing registry data adds the contents of the registry script file to the registry of the computer you are working with, either creating new keys and values if they don't already exist or overwriting keys and values if they do exist. You can import registry data in one of two ways. You can double-tap or double-click the .reg file, which starts Registry Editor and prompts you as to whether you want to import the data. Or you can select Import on the File menu, and then use the Import Registry File dialog box to select and open the registry data file you want to import.

# INSIDE OUT  Using export or import processes to distribute registry changes

The export and import processes provide a convenient way to distribute registry changes to users. You could, for example, export a subkey with an important configuration change and then mail the associated .reg file to users so that they could import it simply by double-tapping or double-clicking it. Alternatively, you could copy the .reg file to a network share where users could access and load it. Either way, you have a quick and easy way to distribute registry changes. Officially, however, distributing registry changes in this manner is frowned upon because of the potential security problems associated with doing so. The preferred technique is to distribute registry changes through Group Policy as discussed in Part 5.

Chapter 8

# Loading and unloading hive files

Just as you sometimes must import or export registry data, you'll sometimes need to work with individual hive files. The most common reason for doing this, as discussed previously, is when you must modify a user's profile to correct an issue that prevents the user from accessing or using a system. Here, you would load the user's Ntuser.dat file into Registry Editor and then make the necessary changes. Another reason for doing this is to change a particular part of the registry on a remote system. For example, if you need to repair an area of the registry, you could load the related hive file into the registry of another machine and then repair the problem on the remote machine.

Loading and unloading hives affects only HKEY_LOCAL_MACHINE and HKEY_USERS, and you can perform these actions only when you select one of these root keys. Rather than replacing the selected root key, the hive you are loading then becomes a subkey of that root key. HKEY_LOCAL_MACHINE and HKEY_USERS are, of course, used to build all the logical root keys used on a system, so you could work with any area of the registry.

After you select either HKEY_LOCAL_MACHINE or HKEY_USERS in Registry Editor, you can load a hive for the current machine or another machine by selecting Load Hive on the File menu. Registry Editor then prompts you for the location and name of the previously saved hive file. Select the file, and then tap or click Open. Afterward, enter a name for the key under which you want the hive to reside while it is loaded into the current system's registry, and then tap or click OK.

> **Note**
>
> You can't work with hive files that are already being used by the operating system or another process. You could, however, make a copy of the hive and then work with it. At the command line, type **reg save** followed by the abbreviated name of the root key to save and the file name to use for the hive file. For example, you could type **reg save hkcu c:\curr-hkcu.hiv** to save HKEY_LOCAL_MACHINE to a file called Curr-hkcu.hiv on drive C. Although you can save the logical root keys (HKCC, HKCR, HKCU) in this manner, you can save only subkeys of HKLM and HKU using this technique.

When you are finished working with a hive, you should unload it to clear it out of memory. Unloading the hive doesn't save the changes you've made—as with any modifications to the registry, your changes are applied automatically without the need to save them. To unload a hive, select it and choose Unload Hive on the File menu. When prompted to confirm, tap or click Yes.

# Working with the registry from the command line

If you want to work with the registry from the command line, you can do so using the REG command. REG is run using the permissions of the current user and can be used to access the registry on both local and remote systems. As with Registry Editor, you can work only with HKEY_LOCAL_MACHINE and HKEY_USERS on remote computers. These keys are, of course, used to build all the logical root keys used on a system, so you can work with any area of the registry on a remote computer.

REG has different subcommands for performing various registry tasks. These commands include the following:

- **REG ADD**   Adds a new subkey or value entry to the registry.

- **REG COMPARE**   Compares registry subkeys or value entries.

- **REG COPY**   Copies a registry entry to a specified key path on a local or remote system.

- **REG DELETE**   Deletes a subkey or value entry from the registry.

- **REG EXPORT**   Exports registry data and writes it to a file.

> **Note**
> These files have the same format as files you export from Registry Editor. Typically, however, they are saved with the .hiv extension, so double-tapping or double-clicking files with this extension won't start Registry Editor.

- **REG FLAGS**   Sets or queries the flags on a registry key. Flags that can be associated with keys include DONT_VIRTUALIZE, DONT_SILENT_FAIL, and RECURSE_FLAG.

- **REG IMPORT**   Imports registry data, and either creates new keys and value entries or overwrites existing keys and value entries.

- **REG LOAD**   Loads a registry hive file.

- **REG QUERY**   Lists the value entries under a key and the names of subkeys (if any).

- **REG RESTORE**   Writes saved subkeys and entries back to the registry.

- **REG SAVE**   Saves a copy of specified subkeys and value entries to a file.

- **REG UNLOAD**   Unloads a registry hive file.

You can learn the syntax for using each of these commands by typing **reg** followed by the name of the subcommand you want to learn about and then **/?**. For example, if you want to learn more about REG ADD, you type **reg add /?** at the command line.

## INSIDE OUT   Accessing the Registry in Windows PowerShell

Using Windows PowerShell to work with the registry is a bit more complicated. With Windows PowerShell, you work with registry keys in much the same was as you work with files and folders. You access keys and values in a registry location using Set-Location. Because the HKLM and HKCU root keys are available by default, you can access HKLM using:

```
set-location hklm:
```

You would then be able to work with registry keys and values in HKLM. For example, to view the available keys, you'd type get-childitem. To work with root keys other than HKLM and HKCU, you must register them as new PowerShell drives. Once you do that, you can work with these root keys and set them as locations you want to access. For more information on using Windows PowerShell to work with the registry, see Chapter 12 in *Window PowerShell 2.0 Administrator's Pocket Consultant* (Microsoft, 2009).

# Backing up and restoring the registry

By now, it should be clear how important the registry is and that it should be protected. I'll go so far as to say that part of every backup and recovery plan should include the registry. Backing up and restoring the registry normally isn't done from within Registry Editor, however. It is handled through the Windows Server Backup utility or through your preferred third-party backup software. Either way, you have an effective means to minimize downtime and ensure that the system can be recovered if the registry becomes corrupted.

You can make a backup of the entire registry very easily at the command line. Simply type **regedit /e *SaveFile***, where *SaveFile* is the complete file path to the save location for the registry data. Following this, you could save a copy of the registry to C:\Backups\Regdata .reg by typing **regedit /e c:\backups\regdata.reg**. You would then have a complete backup of the registry.

You can also easily make backups of individual root keys. To do this, you use REG SAVE. Type **reg save** followed by the abbreviated name of the root key you want to save and the file name to use. For example, you could type **reg save hkcu c:\backups\hkcu.hiv** to save HKEY_CURRENT_USER to a file in the C:\Backups directory. Again, although you can save the logical root keys (HKCC, HKCR, HKCU) in this manner, you can save only subkeys of HKLM and HKU using this technique.

OK, so now you have your fast and easy backups of registry data. What you do not have, however, is a sure way to recover a system in the event the registry becomes corrupted and the system cannot be booted. Partly, this is because you have no way to boot the system to get at the registry data.

You create a system state backup to help you recover the registry and get a system to a bootable state. The system state backup includes essential system files needed to recover the local system as well as registry data. All computers have system state data, which must be backed up in addition to other files to restore a complete working system.

Normally, you back up the system state data when you perform a normal (full) backup of the rest of the data on the system. Thus, if you are performing a full recovery of a server rather than a repair, you use the complete system backup as well as system state data to recover the server completely. Techniques for performing full system backups and recovery are discussed in Chapter 17, "Backup and recovery."

That said, you can create separate system state backups. The fastest and easiest way to do so is to use Wbadmin, the command-line counterpart to Windows Server Backup. You create a system state backup using Wbadmin by entering the following command at an elevated command prompt:

```
wbadmin start systemstatebackup –backuptarget:StorageDrive
```

Here *StorageDrive* is the drive letter for the storage location, such as:

```
wbadmin start systemstatebackup –backuptarget:d:
```

# Maintaining the registry

The registry is a database, and like any other database it works best when it is optimized. Optimize the registry by reducing the amount of clutter and information it contains. This means uninstalling unnecessary system components, services, and applications. One way to uninstall components, services, and applications is to use the Uninstall Or Change A Program utility in Control Panel. This utility allows you to remove Windows components and their related services safely, as well as applications installed using the Windows Installer. In Control Panel, tap or click the Uninstall A Program link under the Programs heading to access the Uninstall Or Change A Program utility.

Most applications include uninstall utilities that attempt to remove the application, its data, and its registry settings safely and effectively as well. Sometimes, however, applications either do not include an uninstall utility or, for one reason or another, do not fully remove their registry settings. This is where registry maintenance utilities come in handy.

At the Microsoft Download Center on the web, you'll find a download package for the Microsoft Fix It Portable. This download package includes several files as well as a helper application designed to be installed on removable media so that you can easily use Fix It Portable on any computer that has a problem. Learn more about this program and get the downloadable executable at *http://support.microsoft.com/mats/Program_Install_and_Uninstall/*. At the Microsoft website, instead of choosing Run Now, click the advanced options and then click the download option to save the executable file. After downloading, run the executable file and follow the prompts to create the Fix It Portable folder. Then copy this folder to the computer with a problem and run the Launch Fix It application.

In addition to being able to clear out registry settings for programs you've installed and then uninstalled, you can use this utility to recover the registry to the state it was in prior to a failed or inadvertently terminated application installation. This works as long as the application used the Windows Installer.

> **Note**
>
> Fix It Portable replaces the Windows Installer Clean Up Utility and Windows Installer Zapper. The program requires Windows PowerShell and the Microsoft .NET Framework 3.5 to be installed. Fix It Portable uses the Windows Diagnostics and Troubleshooting framework to resolve problems.

## Using the Microsoft Fix It Utility

Fix It Portable can remove registry settings for applications that were installed using the Windows Installer. It is most useful for cleaning up registry remnants of applications that were partially uninstalled or whose uninstall failed. It is also useful for cleaning up applications that can't be uninstalled or reinstalled because of partial or damaged settings in the registry. It isn't, however, intended to be used as an uninstaller. Use it when the normal uninstallation process fails.

> **Note**
>
> Keep in mind that the profile of the current user is part of the registry. Because of this, Fix It Portable will remove user-specific installation data from this profile. It won't, however, remove this information from other profiles.

To use Microsoft Fix It to uninstall and clean up a program, complete the following steps:

1.  If you've already run the installer package for Microsoft Fix It, you can start this utility by running the Launch Fix It executable. The utility can run from removable media.

2.  Locate the Fix Problems With Programs That Can't Be Installed Or Uninstalled troubleshooter and then click the related Run Now option.

3.  When the troubleshooter starts, select the option that allows you to select the fixes to apply.

4.  Next, specify that you are having a problem uninstalling a program. Windows will then diagnose the problem by checking the update information in the registry.

5.  Select the program you want to uninstall from a list of installed programs and then click Next.

6.  When prompted whether you want to uninstall and cleanup, click Yes, Try Uninstall. At the end of the uninstall process, you are able to view and save a troubleshooting report.

## Removing registry settings for active installations that have failed

Application installations can fail during installation or after installation. When applications are being installed, an *InProgress* key is created in the registry under the HKLM\SOFTWARE\Microsoft\Windows\CurrentVersion\Installer subkey. In cases when installation fails, the system might not be able to edit or remove this key, which could cause the application's setup program to fail the next time you try to run it. Running the Program Install And Uninstall Troubleshooter for Microsoft Fix It clears out the *InProgress* key, which should allow you to run the application's setup program.

After installation, applications rely on their registry settings to configure themselves properly. If these settings become damaged or the installation becomes damaged, the application won't run. Some programs have a repair utility that can be accessed simply by rerunning the installation. During the repair process, the Windows Installer might attempt to write changes to the registry to repair the installation or roll it back to get back to the original state. If this process fails for any reason, the registry can contain unwanted settings for the application. Running the Program Install And Uninstall Troubleshooter for Microsoft Fix It clears out the rollback data for the active installation as well. Rollback data is stored in the HKLM\SOFTWARE\Microsoft\Windows\CurrentVersion\Installer\Rollback key.

Any running installation also has rollback data.

Chapter 8

## Removing partial or damaged settings for individual applications

When an application can't be successfully uninstalled, you can attempt to clean up its settings from the registry using the Program Install And Uninstall Troubleshooter for Microsoft Fix It. Because the current user's profile is a part of the registry, user-specific settings for the application will be removed from this profile.

# Securing the registry

The registry is a critical area of the operating system. It has some limited built-in security to reduce the risk of settings being inadvertently changed or deleted. Additionally, some areas of the registry are available only to certain users. For example, HKLM\SAM and HKLM\SECURITY are available only to the LocalSystem user. This security, in some cases, might not be enough, however, to prevent unauthorized access to the registry. Because of this, you might want to set tighter access controls than the default permissions, and you can do this from within the registry. You can also control remote access to the registry and configure access auditing.

## Preventing access to the registry utilities

One of the best ways to protect the registry from unauthorized access is to make it so that users can't access the registry in the first place. For a server, this means tightly controlling physical security and allowing only administrators the right to log on locally. For other systems or when it isn't practical to prevent users from logging on locally to a server, you can configure the permissions on Regedit.exe and Reg.exe so that they are more secure. You could also remove Registry Editor and the REG command from a system, but this can introduce other problems and make managing the system more difficult, especially if you also prevent remote access to the registry.

To modify permissions on Registry Editor, access the %SystemRoot% folder, press and hold or right-click Regedit.exe, and then select Properties. In the Regedit Properties dialog box, tap or click the Security tab, as shown in Figure 8-10. Add and remove users and groups as necessary, and then set permissions as appropriate. Permissions work the same as with other types of files. You select an object and then allow or deny specific permissions. See Chapter 15, "File sharing and security," for details.

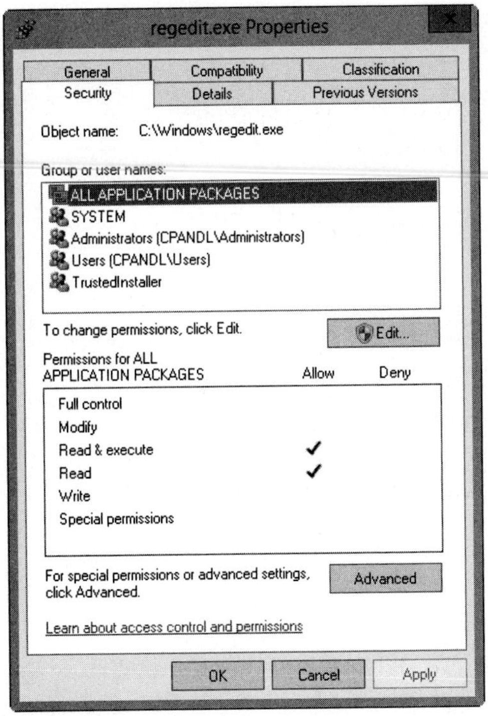

**Figure 8-10** Tighten controls on Registry Editor to limit access to it.

To modify permissions on the REG command, access the %SystemRoot%\System32 folder, press and hold or right-click Reg.exe, and then select Properties. In the Reg Properties dialog box, tap or click the Security tab. As Figure 8-11 shows, this command, by default, can be used by users as well as administrators. Add and remove users and groups as necessary, and then set permissions as appropriate.

> **Note**
>
> I'm not forgetting about Regedt32. It's only a link to Regedit.exe, so you don't really need to set its access permissions. The permissions on Regedit.exe will apply regardless of whether users attempt to run Regedt32 or Regedit.exe.

Chapter 8

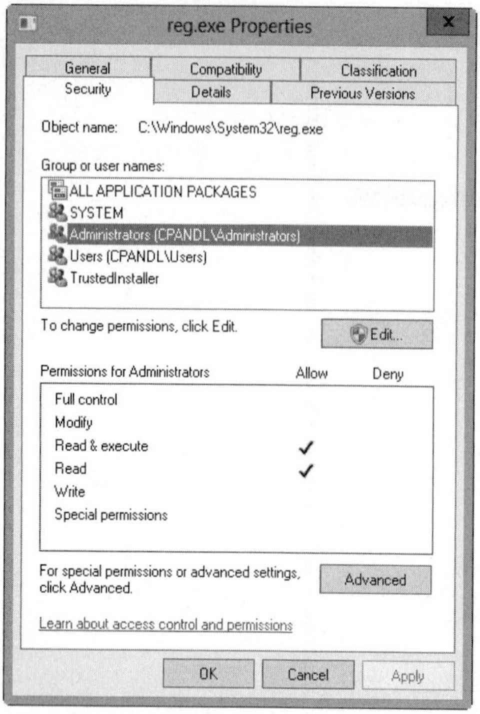

**Figure 8-11** Reg.exe is designed to be used by users as well as administrators and to be run from the command line; its permissions reflect this.

## Applying permissions to registry keys

Keys within the registry have access permissions as well. Rather than editing these permissions directly, I recommend you use an appropriate security template as discussed in Chapter 31. Using the right security template locks down access to the registry for you, and you won't have to worry about making inadvertent changes that will prevent systems from booting or applications from running.

That said, in some limited situations you might want to or have to change permissions on individual keys in the registry. To do this, start Registry Editor and then navigate to the key you want to work with. When you find the key, press and hold or right-click it, and select Permissions, or select the key, and then choose Permissions on the Edit menu. This displays a Permissions For dialog box similar to the one shown in Figure 8-12. Permissions work the same as for files. You can add and remove users and groups as necessary. You can select an object and then allow or deny specific permissions.

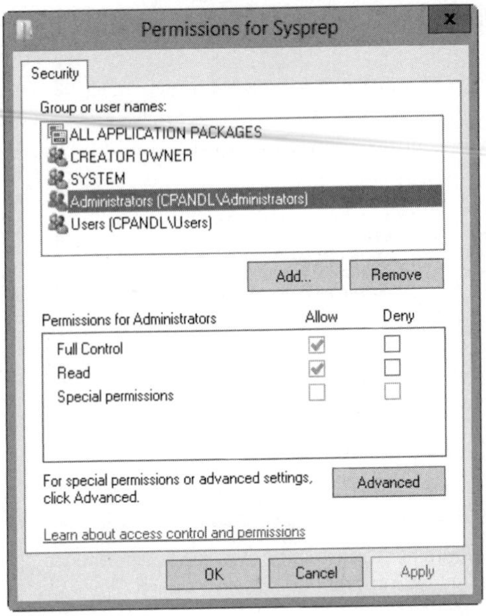

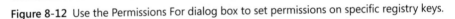

**Figure 8-12** Use the Permissions For dialog box to set permissions on specific registry keys.

Many permissions are inherited from higher-level keys and are unavailable. To edit these permissions, you must access the Advanced Security Settings dialog box by tapping or clicking the Advanced button. As Figure 8-13 shows, the Advanced Security Settings dialog box shows the current owner of the selected key and allows you to reassign ownership. By default, when you reassign ownership, only the selected key is affected, but if you want the change to apply to all subkeys of the currently selected key, choose Replace Owner On Subcontainers And Objects.

**CAUTION**

Be sure you understand the implications of taking ownership of registry keys. Changing ownership could inadvertently prevent the operating system or other users from running applications, services, or application components.

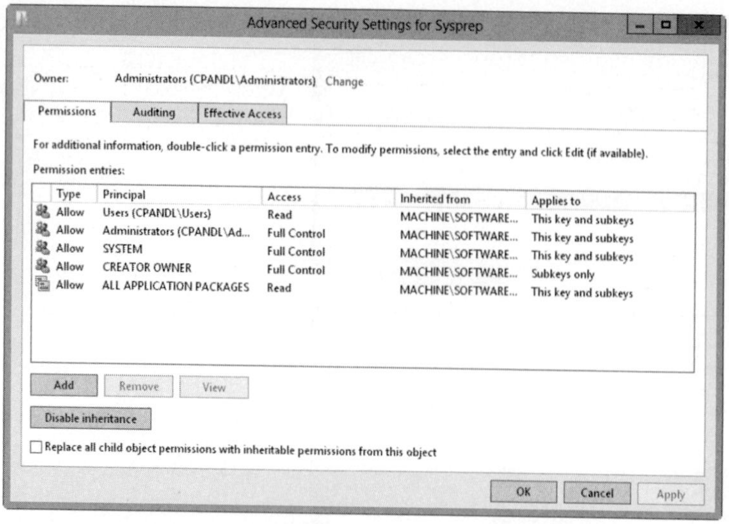

**Figure 8-13** Use the Advanced Security Settings dialog box to change the way permissions are inherited or set and to view auditing settings, ownership, and effective permissions.

The dialog box also has three tabs:

- **Permissions**   The Inherited From column in the Permissions tab shows where the permissions are inherited from. Usually, this is the root key for the key branch you are working with, such as CURRENT_USER. You can use the Add and Edit buttons in the Permissions tab to set access permissions for individual users and groups. Table 8-3 shows the individual permissions you can assign.

- **Auditing**   Allows you to configure auditing for the selected key. The actions you can audit are the same as the permissions listed in Table 8-3. See the section "Registry root keys" earlier in this chapter.

- **Effective Access**   Lets you see which permissions would be given to a particular user or group based on the current settings. This is helpful because permission changes you make in the Permissions tab aren't applied until you tap or click OK or Apply.

**TABLE 8-3** Registry permissions and their meanings

| Permission | Meaning |
|---|---|
| Full Control | Allows user or group to perform any of the actions related to any other permission |
| Query Value | Allows querying the registry for a subkey value |
| Set Value | Allows creating new values or modifying existing values below the specified key |
| Create Subkey | Allows creating a new subkey below the specified key |
| Enumerate Subkeys | Allows getting a list of all subkeys of a particular key |
| Notify | Allows registering a callback function that is triggered when the select value changes |
| Create Link | Allows creating a link to a specified key |
| Delete | Allows deleting a key or value |
| Write DAC | Allows writing access controls on the specified key |
| Write Owner | Allows taking ownership of the specified key |
| Read Control | Allows reading the discretionary access control list (DACL) for the specified key |

## Controlling remote registry access

Hackers and unauthorized users can attempt to access a system's registry remotely just like you do. If you want to be sure they are kept out of the registry, you can prevent remote registry access. One way that remote access to a system's registry can be controlled is through the registry key HKLM\SYSTEM\CurrentControlSet\Control\SecurePipeServers\Winreg. If you want to limit remote access to the registry, you can start by changing the permissions on this key.

If this key exists, then the following occurs:

1.  Windows Server 2012 uses the permissions on the key to determine who can access the registry remotely, and by default any authenticated user can do so. In fact, authenticated users have Query Value, Enumerate Subkeys, Notify, and Read Control permissions on this key.

2.  Windows Server 2012 then uses the permissions on the keys to determine access to individual keys.

If this key doesn't exist, Windows Server 2012 allows all users to access the registry remotely and uses the permissions on the keys only to determine which keys can be accessed.

Chapter 8

# INSIDE OUT
## Services might need remote access to the registry

Some services require remote access to the registry to function correctly. This includes the Directory Replicator service and the Spooler service. If you restrict remote access to the registry, you must bypass the access restrictions. Either add the account name of the service to the access list on the *Winreg* key or list the keys to which services need access in the *Machine* or *Users* value under the *AllowedPaths* key. Both values are REG_MULTI_SZ strings. Paths entered in the *Machine* value allow machine (LocalSystem) access to the locations listed. Paths entered in the *Users* value allow users access to the locations listed. As long as there are no explicit access restrictions on these keys, remote access is granted. After you make changes, you must restart the computer so that registry access can be reconfigured on startup.

Windows Vista and later Windows versions disable remote access to all registry paths by default. As a result, the only registry paths remotely accessible are those explicitly permitted as part of the default configuration or by an administrator. In Local Security Policy, you can use Security Options to enable or disable remote registry access. With Windows Vista and later Windows versions, the following additional security settings are provided for this purpose:

- Network Access: Remotely Accessible Registry Paths

- Network Access: Remotely Accessible Registry Paths And Subpaths

These security settings determine which registry paths and subpaths can be accessed over the network, regardless of the users or groups listed in the access control list (ACL) of the *Winreg* registry key. A number of default paths are set, and you should not modify these default paths without carefully considering the damage that changing this setting might cause.

You can follow these steps to access and modify these settings in the Local Security Settings console:

1. Open Local Security Policy. If you enabled Show Administrative Tools as a Start setting, you'll see a related tile on the Start screen. Another way to do this is by pressing the Windows key, typing **secpol.msc** into the Apps Search box, and then pressing Enter.

2. Expand the Local Policies node in the left pane and then select the Security Options node.

3.  In the main pane, you should now see a list of policy settings. Scroll down through the list of security settings. As appropriate, double-tap or double-click Network Access: Remotely Accessible Registry Paths or Network Access: Remotely Accessible Registry Paths And Subpaths.

4.  On the Local Policy Setting tab of the Properties dialog box, you'll see a list of remotely accessible registry paths or a list of remotely accessible registry paths and subpaths, depending on which security setting you are working with. You can now add or remove paths or subpaths as necessary. Note that the default settings are listed on the Explain tab.

> **Note**
>
> Windows Server 2012 has an actual service called the Remote Registry service. This service does, in fact, control remote access to the registry. You want to disable this service only if you are trying to protect isolated systems from unauthorized access, such as when the system is in a perimeter network and is accessible from the Internet. If you disable the Remote Registry service before starting the Routing and Remote Access service, you cannot view or change the Routing and Remote Access configuration. Routing and Remote Access reads and writes configuration information to the registry, and any action that requires access to configuration information could cause Routing and Remote Access to stop functioning. To resolve this, stop the Routing and Remote Access service, start the Remote Registry service, and then restart the Routing and Remote Access service.

## Auditing registry access

Access to the registry can be audited, as can access to files and other areas of the operating system. Auditing allows you to track which users access the registry and what they're doing. All the permissions listed previously in Table 8-3 can be audited. However, you usually limit what you audit to only the essentials to reduce the amount of data that is written to the security logs and to reduce the resource burden on the affected server.

Before you can enable auditing of the registry, you must enable the auditing function on the system you are working with. You can do this either through the server's local policy or through the appropriate Group Policy Object. The policy that controls auditing is Computer Configuration\Windows Settings\Security Settings\Local Policies\Audit Policy. For more information on auditing and Group Policy, see Chapter 16, "Managing file screening and storage reporting," and Chapter 31, respectively.

After auditing is enabled for a system, you can configure how you want auditing to work for the registry. This means configuring auditing for each key you want to track. Thanks to inheritance, this doesn't mean you have to go through every key in the registry and enable auditing for it. Instead, you can select a root key or any subkey to designate the start of the branch for which you want to track access and then ensure the auditing settings are inherited for all subkeys below it. (This is the default setting.)

Say, for example, you want to audit access to HKLM\SAM and its subkeys. To do this, you follow these steps:

1.  After you locate the key in Registry Editor, press and hold or right-click it, and select Permissions, or select the key, and then choose Permissions on the Edit menu. This displays the Permissions For SAM dialog box.

2.  In the Permissions For SAM dialog box, tap or click the Advanced button.

3.  In the Advanced Security Settings dialog box, tap or click the Auditing tab.

4.  Tap or click Add to display the Auditing Entry For dialog box. Click Select A Principal to display the Select User, Computer, Service Account, Or Group dialog box.

5.  Type the name of a user or a group account. Be sure to reference the user account name rather than the user's full name. Only one name can be entered at a time.

6.  Tap or click Check Names. If a single match is found for each entry, the dialog box is automatically updated and the entry is underlined. Otherwise, you'll see an additional dialog box. If no matches are found, you've either entered the name incorrectly or you're working with an incorrect location. Modify the name in the Name Not Found dialog box and try again, or tap or click Locations to select a new location. When multiple matches are found, in the Multiple Names Found dialog box, select the name or names you want to use and then tap or click OK.

7.  Tap or click OK. The user or group is added as the Principal, and the Auditing Entry For dialog box is updated to show this. Only basic permissions are listed by default. Click Show Advanced Permissions to display the special permissions, as shown in Figure 8-14.

8.  Use the Applies To list to specify how the auditing entry is to be applied. The options include the following:

    ○  **This Key Only**   The auditing entries apply only to the currently selected key.

    ○  **This Key And Subkeys**   The auditing entries apply to this key and any subkeys of this key.

○  **Subkeys Only**   The auditing entries apply to any subkeys of this key but not to the key itself.

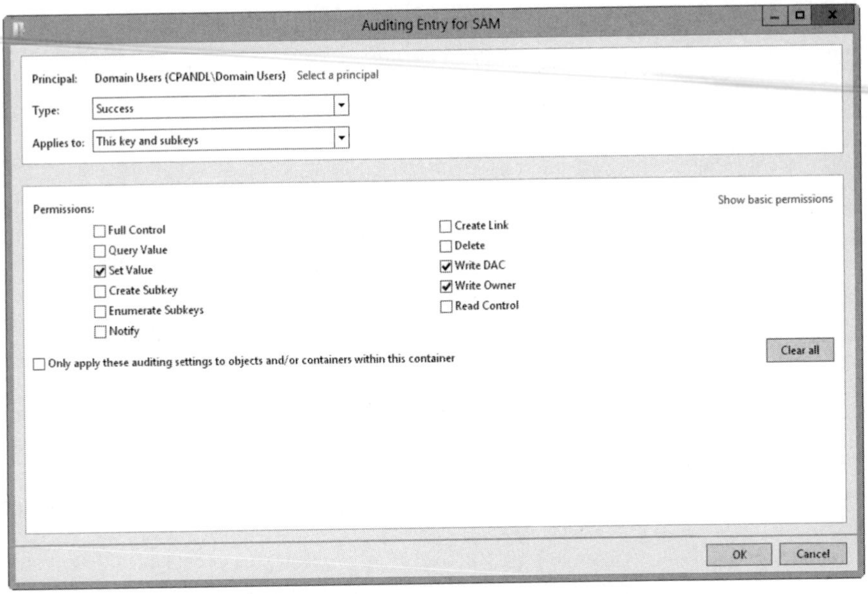

**Figure 8-14** Use the Auditing Entry For dialog box to specify the permissions you want to track.

9.  Use the Type list to specify whether you are configuring auditing for successful access, failed access, or both, and then specify which actions should be audited. The events you can audit are the same as the special permissions listed in Table 8-3.

10. Repeat steps 4–9 to configure auditing for other users or groups.

11. The auditing entries are applied to subkeys by default through inheritance. If you want to replace the auditing entries on all child objects of this key with this key's auditing entries, select Replace All Child Object Auditing Entries With Inheritable Auditing Entries From This Object.

12. Tap or click OK twice.

# CHAPTER 9

# Software and User Account Control administration

T HE security architecture in Microsoft Windows Server 2012 and Windows 8 controls the way accounts are used and the way applications are installed and run. Windows Server 2012 has two general types of user accounts: standard user accounts and administrator user accounts. Standard users can perform any general computing tasks, such as starting programs, opening documents, and creating folders, and any support tasks that do not affect other users or the security of the computer. Administrators, on the other hand, have complete access to the computer and can make changes that affect other users and the security of the computer. Windows 8 adds a special type of local account called a *Microsoft account*, which can be thought of as a synchronized local account and is not available on earlier releases of Windows.

When it comes to applications, Windows 8 behaves differently from how Windows Server 2012 does as well. Whereas Windows Server 2012 runs programs, some of which are designed specifically for client-server environments, Windows 8 also runs desktop apps. An app is a program in the most general sense. However, apps are new to Windows 8 and have many distinct characteristics, as I discuss in Chapter 8 of my book *Windows 8 Administration Pocket Consultant* (Microsoft Press, 2012). With that in mind, this chapter focuses specifically on software applications that are installed as programs rather than as apps.

## Software installation essentials

Software installation, configuration, and maintenance are processes that require elevated privileges. As discussed later in this chapter under "Mastering User Account Control," elevation is a feature of User Account Control (UAC). Because of User Account Control, the operating system is able to detect the installation of software. When the operating system detects a software installation–related process, it prompts for permission or consent prior to allowing you to install, configure, or maintain software on your computer. This means you must either install software using an account with administrator privileges or provide administrator permissions when prompted. It also means administrator privileges are required to perform the following software maintenance tasks:

- Change/Update

- Repair/Reinstall

- Uninstall/Remove

Windows does not include an Add/Remove Programs utility. Instead, Windows relies completely on the software itself to provide the necessary installation features through a related setup program. As discussed later in this chapter under "Maintaining application integrity," Windows also provides the architecture for software access tokens and restrictions that require software programs to write to specific system locations. Software applications not specifically designed to support this architecture are considered legacy applications. Thus, software is either compliant or legacy.

Part of the installation process involves validating your credentials and checking the software's compatibility. Most software applications have a setup program that uses Windows Installer, InstallShield, or Wise Install. The job of the installer program is to track the installation process and make sure the installation completes successfully. If the installation fails, the installer is also responsible for restoring a computer to its original state by reversing all the changes made by the setup program. Although this works great in theory, you can encounter problems, particularly when you are installing older programs. Older programs won't have and won't be able to use the features of the latest versions of installer programs, and as a result, they sometimes are unable to uninstall a program completely.

Because a partially uninstalled program can spell disaster for a computer, you should protect yourself by backing up a server prior to installing any software. By backing up a server as discussed in Chapter 17, "Backup and recovery," you can be sure that you can fully recover the server to the state it was in prior to installing the software. This way, if you run into problems, you'll have an effective recovery strategy.

Before installing any software, you should do the following:

- Check to see whether it is compatible. You can determine compatibility in several ways. You can check the software packaging, which should specify whether the program is compatible. Alternatively, you can check the software developer's website for a list of compatible operating systems.

- Check the software developer's website for updates for the program. If available, download the updates prior to installing the software and then install them immediately after completing the software installation. Some software programs have automated update processes that you can use to check for updates after installing the software. In this case, after installation, run the software and then use the built-in update feature to check for updates.

Diagnosing a problem you are having as a compatibility issue isn't always easy. For deeper compatibility issues, you might need to contact the software developer's technical support staff. To avoid known compatibility issues with legacy applications, Windows Server includes an automated detection feature known as the Program Compatibility Assistant.

If the Program Compatibility Assistant detects a known compatibility issue when you run a legacy application, it notifies you about the problem and provides possible solutions for resolving the problem automatically. You can then allow the Program Compatibility Assistant to reconfigure the application for you. Although the Program Compatibility Assistant is helpful, it can't detect or avoid all compatibility issues. You might have to configure compatibility manually. One way to do this is to press and hold or right-click the software shortcut, select Properties, and then use the options on the Compatibility tab to configure software compatibility options.

> **Important**
> Don't use the Program Compatibility Assistant or similar compatibility features to install older virus detection, backup, or system programs. These programs might attempt to modify your computer's file systems in a way that is incompatible with Windows Server, and this could prevent Windows Server from starting.

Installation using software application media is straightforward. Not all programs have distribution media on a disc or flash drive. If you download a program from the Internet, it'll probably be in a .zip or self-extracting executable file and you can install the program by following these steps:

1.  Start File Explorer. Extract the program's setup files using one of the following techniques:

    ○   If the program is distributed in a .zip file, press and hold or right-click the file and select Extract All. This displays the Extract Compressed (Zipped) Folders dialog box. Tap or click Browse, select a destination folder, and then tap or click OK. Tap or click Extract.

    ○   If the program is distributed in a self-extracting executable file, double-tap or double-click the .exe file to extract the setup files. You'll see one of several types of prompts. If prompted to run the file, tap or click Run. If prompted to extract the program files or select a destination folder, tap or click Browse, select a destination folder, and then tap or click OK. Tap or click Extract or OK as appropriate.

2. In File Explorer, browse the setup folders and find the necessary setup program file. Double-tap or double-click the setup file to start the installation process.

3. When Setup starts, follow the prompts to install the software.

If software installation fails and the software used an installer, follow the prompts to allow the installer to restore your computer to its original state. Otherwise, exit Setup and then try re-running Setup to either complete the installation or uninstall the program. If this doesn't work, you can use the techniques discussed in "Maintaining the registry" in Chapter 8, "Managing the registry," to clean up the installer settings.

Installing software is only one part of software management. Often after you install software, you need to make configuration changes to your computer or the software itself. You might need to reconfigure, repair, or uninstall the software, or you might need to resolve problems with the way the software starts or runs.

After you install software, you can manage its installation using the Programs And Features page in Control Panel. Windows Server takes advantage of the features of the installer program used with your software. This means you'll have more configuration options than you otherwise would. For example, previously, most software allowed you to re-run Setup to uninstall the program but didn't necessarily allow you to re-run Setup to change or repair the software. Windows Server provides these features to make it easier to manage your software.

You can use the Programs And Features page to reconfigure, repair, or uninstall software by following these steps:

1. In Control Panel, tap or click Uninstall A Program under Programs.

2. In the Name list, select the program you want to work with and then select one of the following options on the toolbar:

   ○ **Change** Modifies the program's configuration

   ○ **Repair** Repairs the program's installation

   ○ **Uninstall** Uninstalls the program

   ○ **Uninstall/Change** Uninstalls or changes a program with an older installer program

You can use Task Manager to work with running programs. To access Task Manager, press and hold or right-click the lower-left corner of the Start screen or the desktop and then tap or click Task Manager. Alternatively, press Ctrl+Alt+Delete and then click Task Manager. If the Summary view is displayed when you open Task Manager, tap or click More Details.

Use the information and options provided on the Processes, Performance, and Details tabs to get more information about running programs. When you select a program or process on the Processes tab, you can terminate the process by tapping or clicking End Task. You'll learn more about Task Manager in Chapter 10, "Performance monitoring and tuning."

# Mastering User Account Control

User Account Control seeks to improve usability while at the same time enhancing security by controlling how standard user and administrator user accounts are used. User Account Control does this by limiting the scope of administrator-level access privileges and requiring all applications to run in a specific user mode. In this way, UAC prevents users from making inadvertent changes to system settings and locks down the computer to prevent unauthorized applications from installing or performing malicious actions.

## Elevation, prompts, and the secure desktop

Unlike Windows XP and early releases of Windows, current releases of Windows make it easy to determine which tasks standard users can perform and which tasks administrators can perform. You might have noticed the multicolored shield icon next to certain options in windows, wizards, and dialog boxes. This is the Permissions icon. It indicates that the related option requires administrator permissions to run. That doesn't mean you'll see a prompt, though. The way the prompt works depends on the following:

- Whether UAC allows changing Windows settings without prompting

- Whether the computer is a member of a workgroup or a domain

- Whether you are logged on as a standard user or an administrator

> **Note**
> UAC is disabled in Server Core installations. With other Windows Server installations, the best way to configure the UAC prompt is to use Group Policy settings. In Control Panel, tap or click System And Security. Under the Action Center heading, tap or click Change User Account Control Settings. On the User Account Control Settings page, use the slider to choose when to be notified about changes to the computer.

By default, when you are logged on to a computer as a standard user, you see a User Account Control (UAC) prompt when programs try to make changes to the computer that require administrator permissions and when programs try to change Windows settings. In a workgroup, the prompt shows the accounts of administrators. If you tap or click an account, you must then enter the password for that account and then tap or click Yes.

In a domain, as shown in Figure 9-1, the prompt shows the logon domain and provides user name and password boxes. To proceed, you must enter the name of an administrator account, type the account's password, and then tap or click Yes. The task or application will then run with administrator permissions.

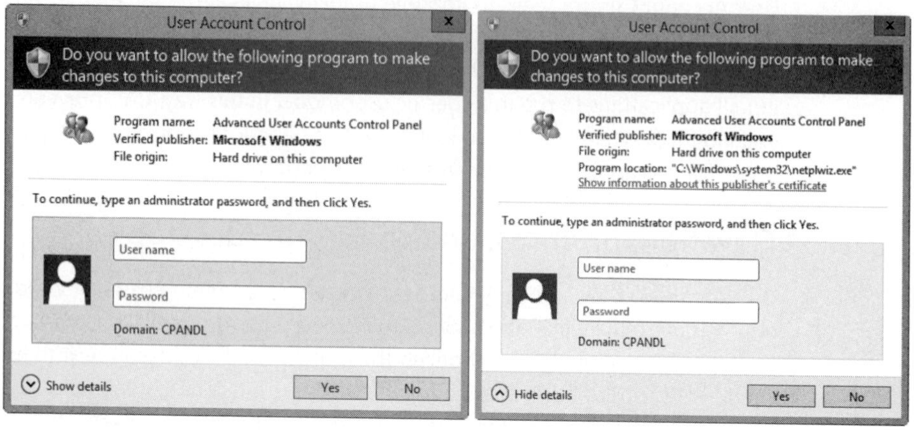

**Figure 9-1**  User Account Control requires a password to run certain applications when the user is not on an administrator account.

> **Note**
> The first screen capture shows the UAC prompt without details. The second screen capture shows the UAC prompt with details.

Whether the computer is in a workgroup or domain, the prompt shows the name of the program requesting elevation, the publisher of that program, and the file origin. If you have any question about the authenticity of the request, tap or click Show Details. You'll then see the program location, which shows the full path to the program's executable. For verified publishers, display their verification certificate by clicking the link provided.

The prompt works differently when you are logged on with an administrator account. Here, it doesn't matter whether the computer is in a workgroup or a domain and the prompt doesn't require an account selection or a password. Instead, your current credentials are used and you are simply prompted to confirm that you want to allow the task or program to make changes to the computer. If you click Yes, the task or application will then run with administrator permissions. (See Figure 9-2.)

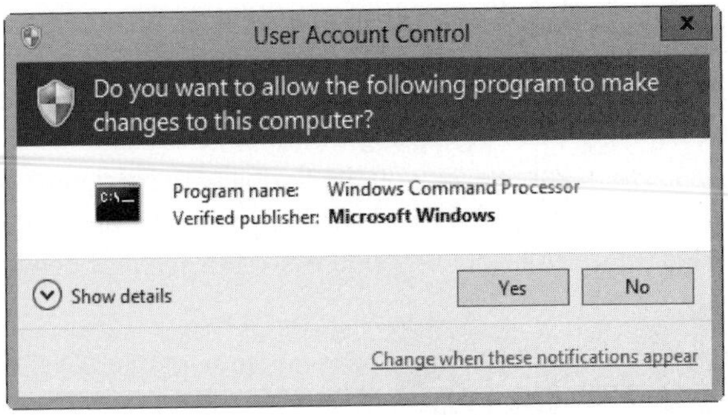

**Figure 9-2** User Account Control prompts users when they are already logged on to an administrator account.

The process of getting approval prior to running an application in administrator mode and prior to performing actions that change systemwide settings is known as *elevation*. Elevation enhances security by reducing the exposure and attack surface of the operating system. It does this by providing notification when you are about to perform an action that could affect system settings, such as installing an application, and it eliminates the ability of malicious programs to invoke administrator privileges without your knowledge and consent.

Prior to the elevation and display of the User Account Control (UAC) prompt, Windows Server performs several background tasks. The key task you need to know about is that Windows Server switches to a secure, isolated desktop prior to displaying the prompt. The purpose of switching to the secure desktop is to prevent other processes or applications from providing the required permissions or consent. All other running programs and processes continue to run on the interactive user desktop, and only the prompt itself runs on the secure desktop.

Elevation, prompts, and the secure desktop are aspects of User Account Control that affect you the most. Although they seem restrictive at first, these features prevent users from making inadvertent changes to system settings and they lock down the computer to prevent unauthorized applications from installing or performing malicious actions.

The key component of UAC that determines whether and how administrators are prompted is Admin Approval Mode. By default, all administrators, except the built-in local administrator account, run in and are subject to Admin Approval Mode. Because they are running in and subject to Admin Approval Mode, all administrators, except the built-in local administrator account, see the elevation prompt whenever they run administrator applications.

Chapter 9

# Configuring UAC and Admin Approval Mode

In Group Policy under Local Policies\Security Options, five security settings determine how Admin Approval Mode and elevation prompting works. Table 9-1 summarizes these security settings. Remember, Group Policy gives you the flexibility to configure UAC as needed for specific environments. For example, if servers at a remote office are in a separate GPO from workstations at that office, you could configure UAC for servers one way and UAC for workstations another way.

**TABLE 9-1  Security settings related to Admin Approval Mode**

| Security Setting | Description |
| --- | --- |
| User Account Control: Admin Approval Mode For The Built-in Administrator Account | Determines whether users and processes running as the built-in local administrator account are subject to Admin Approval Mode. By default, this feature is disabled, which means the built-in local administrator account is not subject to Admin Approval Mode or to the elevation-prompt behavior stipulated for other administrators in Admin Approval Mode. If you enable this setting, users and processes running as the built-in local administrator will be subject to Admin Approval and also subject to the elevation-prompt behavior stipulated for other administrators in Admin Approval Mode. |
| User Account Control: Behavior Of The Elevation Prompt For Administrators In Admin Approval Mode | Determines whether administrators subject to Admin Approval Mode see an elevation prompt when running administrator applications, and also determines how the elevation prompt works. By default, administrators are prompted for consent when running administrator applications. You can configure this option so that administrators are prompted for credentials, as is the case with standard users. You can also configure this option so that administrators are not prompted at all—in which case, the administrator will not be able to elevate privileges. This doesn't prevent administrators from pressing and holding or right-clicking an application shortcut and selecting Run As Administrator. |
| User Account Control: Behavior Of The Elevation Prompt For Standard Users | Determines whether users logged on with a standard user account see an elevation prompt when running administrator applications. By default, users logged on with a standard user account are prompted for the credentials of an administrator when running administrator applications. You can also configure this option so that users are not prompted—in which case, the users will not be able to elevate privileges by supplying administrator credentials. This doesn't prevent users from pressing and holding or right-clicking an application shortcut and selecting Run As Administrator. |

| Security Setting | Description |
| --- | --- |
| User Account Control: Run All Administrators In Admin Approval Mode | Determines whether users logged on with an administrator account are subject to Admin Approval Mode. By default, this feature is enabled, which means administrators are subject to Admin Approval Mode and further subject to the elevation-prompt behavior stipulated for administrators in Admin Approval Mode. If you disable this setting, users logged on with an administrator account are not subject to Admin Approval and therefore are not subject to the elevation-prompt behavior stipulated for administrators in Admin Approval Mode. |
| User Account Control: Switch To The Secure Desktop When Prompting For Elevation | Determines whether Windows Server switches to the secure desktop before prompting for elevation. As the name implies, the secure desktop restricts the programs and processes that have access to the desktop environment. In this way, it reduces the possibility that a malicious program or user could gain access to the process being elevated. By default, this security option is enabled. If you don't want Windows Server to switch to the secure desktop prior to prompting for elevation, you can disable this setting. However, if you do this, you'll make the computer more susceptible to malware and attack. |

In a domain environment, you can use Microsoft Active Directory–based Group Policy to apply the desired security configuration to a particular set of computers. Simply configure the desired settings to a Group Policy Object (GPO) that applies to those computers.

For workgroup configurations or for a special case, you can configure these security settings on a per-computer basis using local security policy. To access local security policy and configure UAC settings, follow these steps:

1.  Select Local Security Policy on the Tools menu in Server Manager. This starts the Local Security Policy console.

2.  In the console tree, under Security Settings, expand Local Policies and then select Security Options, as shown in Figure 9-3.

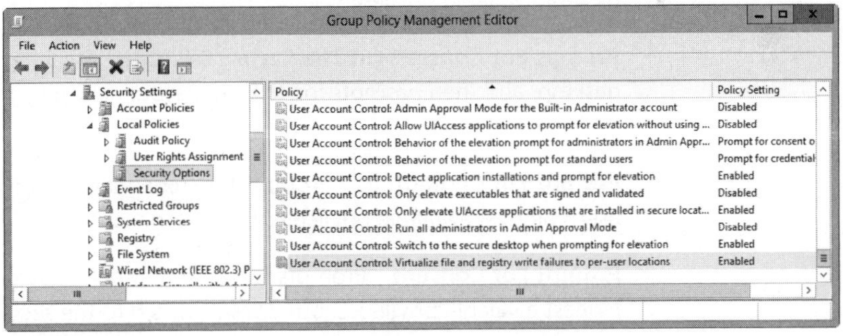

**Figure 9-3** Configure UAC options through local security policy.

3. Double-tap or double-click User Account Control: Admin Approval Mode For The Built-in Administrator Account. This opens the related properties dialog box shown in Figure 9-4. Select Enabled to turn on this setting or Disabled to turn off this setting. Tap or click OK.

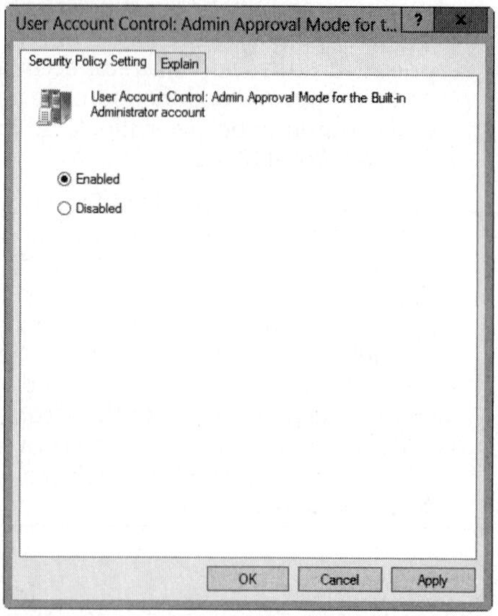

**Figure 9-4** Configure Admin Approval Mode for the built-in Administrator account.

4. Double-tap or double-click User Account Control: Behavior Of The Elevation Prompt For Administrators In Admin Approval Mode. The available options are used as follows:

- ○ **Elevate Without Prompting**  Enters Admin Approval Mode, and elevates to the user's highest available privileges without prompting for consent or credentials.

- ○ **Prompt For Credentials On The Secure Desktop**  Switches to the secure desktop, and then prompts for credentials before elevating to the user's highest available privileges.

- ○ **Prompt For Consent On The Secure Desktop**  Switches to the secure desktop, and then prompts for consent before elevating to the user's highest available privileges.

- ○ **Prompt For Credentials**  Prompts for credentials before elevating to the user's highest available privileges, but doesn't switch to the secure desktop.

- ○ **Prompt For Consent**  Prompts for consent before elevating to the user's highest available privileges, but doesn't switch to the secure desktop.

○ **Prompt For Consent For Non-Windows Binaries**   When running non-Windows applications that require elevation, prompts for consent on the secure desktop before elevating to the user's highest available privileges. This is the default.

5. Double-tap or double-click User Account Control: Behavior Of The Elevation Prompt For Standard Users. The available options are Automatically Deny Elevation Requests, Prompt For Credentials On The Secure Desktop, and Prompt For Credentials.

> **Important**
> If you deny elevation requests, elevation prompts will not be presented to users. This includes Remote Assistance users who might be trying to assist a user remotely.

6. Double-tap or double-click User Account Control: Run All Administrators In Admin Approval Mode. Select Enabled to turn on this setting or Disabled to turn off this setting. Tap or click OK.

7. Double-tap or double-click User Account Control: Switch To The Secure Desktop When Prompting For Elevation. Select Enabled to turn on this setting or Disabled to turn off this setting. Tap or click OK.

# Maintaining application integrity

To help maintain internal consistency and application integrity, Windows Server defines two run levels for applications: standard and administrator. Windows Server determines whether a user needs elevated privileges to run a program by supplying most applications and processes with a security token. If an application has a standard token, or an application cannot be identified as an administrator application, elevated privileges are not required to run the application, and Windows Server starts it as a standard application by default. If an application has an administrator token, elevated privileges are required to run the application, and Windows Server prompts the user for permission or confirmation prior to running the application.

## Application access tokens

Applications are said to be either compliant or legacy. Any application written specifically for Windows Server 2008 or later is considered to be a compliant application. Any application written for an earlier version of Microsoft Windows or not certified as compliant is considered to be a legacy application.

Distinguishing between compliant and legacy applications is important because of the architecture changes required to support UAC. Compliant applications use UAC to reduce the attack surface of the operating system. They do this by preventing unauthorized programs from installing or running without the user's consent and by restricting the default privileges granted to applications. This, in turn, makes it harder for malicious programs to take over a computer.

The Application Information service facilitates the running of interactive applications with an "administrator" access token. By default, this service is stopped and configured for manual start up. When this service is stopped, you will be unable to start interactive applications with the additional administrator privileges you might require to perform tasks.

# INSIDE OUT   Examining administrator and standard user access tokens

You can see the difference between the administrator user and standard user access tokens by opening two Command Prompt windows. Run the first command prompt with elevation by right tapping or clicking and selecting Run As Administrator. Run the other command prompt as a standard user.

In the administrator Command Prompt window, type the following:

1.   **cd %UserProfile%**

2.   **whoami /all > admin.txt**

In the standard Command Prompt window, type the following:

1.   **whoami /all > user.txt**

2.   **fc user.txt admin.txt**

The resulting output is a comparison of the differences between your administrator access token and your standard access token. Both access tokens will have the same security identifiers (SIDs), but the elevated administrator access token will have more privileges than the standard user access token.

Applications derive their security context from the current user's access token. By default, the Local Security Authority (LSA) turns all users into standard users even if they are members of the Administrators group. When a member of an administrator group logs on to a computer where UAC is enabled, the LSA creates two access tokens for two different logon sessions: one with administrator rights and one with administrator rights filtered out. The filtered access token is used to start the user's desktop. The other logon session runs as an administrator and is accessed when tasks are elevated. Thus, if an administrator user has consented to the use of her administrator privileges, the unfiltered access token (which contains all of the user's privileges) is used to start the application or process rather than the user's standard access token. Also note that the access tokens contain separate logon IDs because they are related to different logon sessions.

Most applications can run using a standard user access token. Whether applications need to run with standard or administrator privileges depends on the actions the applications perform. Applications that require administrator privileges, referred to as *administrator applications*, differ in several ways from user applications that require standard user privileges, referred to as *user applications*.

Administrator applications require elevated privileges to run and perform core tasks. When started in elevated mode, an application with a user's administrator access token can perform tasks that require administrator privileges and also can write to system locations of the registry and the file system.

Standard user applications do not require elevated privileges to run and perform core tasks. When started in standard user mode, an application with a user's standard access token must request elevated privileges to perform administration tasks. For all other tasks, the application should not run using elevated privileges. Further, the application should write data only to nonsystem locations of the registry and the file system.

## INSIDE OUT   Virtualization for legacy applications

You configure any applications not specifically written for or certified as compatible as legacy applications. Legacy applications run using a user's standard access token by default. To prevent legacy applications from making changes to the operating system that could cause problems, legacy applications run in a special compatibility mode. In this mode, the operating system uses file system and registry virtualization to provide "virtualized" views of file and registry locations.

When a legacy application attempts to write to a system location, the operating system gives the application a private copy of the file or registry value. Any changes the application makes are then written to the private copy, and this private copy, in turn, is stored in the user's profile data. If the application attempts to read or write to this system location again, the operating system gives it the private copy from the user's profile to work with.

By default, if an error occurs when the application is working with virtualized data, the error notification and logging information show the virtualized location rather than the actual location that the application is trying to work with. This ensures that there is consistency between how virtualization is used and how related errors are reported.

If you are an application developer and are debugging an application, you can use options on Task Manager's Details tab to put an application you are testing in "virtualized" mode. Press and hold or right-click the application's primary process and then tap or click UAC Virtualization. Repeat this process to exit "virtualized" mode.

Chapter 9

## TROUBLESHOOTING

### Virtualization exceptions

Some application tasks always require administrative privileges. If so, these tasks cannot be performed with a standard access token. Virtualization is designed for applications that are not UAC-compliant but require a full administrator access token to work properly. Virtualization doesn't apply to applications that are elevated and run with a full administrator access token. Virtualization is not supported for native Windows 64-bit applications and is disabled for applications that have a requested execution-level attribute in their application manifest.

You can verify that an application that won't work properly has a problem running as a standard user simply by pressing and holding or right-clicking the application icon and then tapping or clicking Run As Administrator. There's a problem if the application works when running with a full administrator access token but doesn't run when using a standard access token. However, because the application might write to areas of the file system or registry that cause problems with stability or startup, you should test this theory only on nonproduction computers. You can try to resolve the problem using one of the compatibility databases in the current version of the Microsoft Application Compatibility Toolkit, or you can use the toolkit to create your own compatibility databases.

## Application run levels

Because of UAC, the processes related to installing and running applications have also changed. In earlier versions of Windows, the Power Users group gave users specific administrator privileges to perform basic system tasks when installing and running applications. Compliant applications do not require the use of the Power Users group; this group is maintained only for legacy-application compatibility.

Windows Server detects application installations and prompts users for elevation to continue the installation by default. Installation packages for Windows Server–compliant applications use application manifests that contain run-level designations to help track required privileges. Application manifests define the application's desired privileges as one of the following:

- **RunAsInvoker**   Runs the application with the same privileges as the user. Any user can run the application. For a standard user or a user who is a member of the Administrators group, the application runs with a standard access token. The application runs with higher privileges only if the parent process from which it is started has an administrator access token. For example, if you start an elevated Command Prompt window and then start an application from this window, the application runs with an administrator access token.

- **RunAsHighest**    Runs the application with the highest privileges of the user. The application can be run by both administrator users and standard users. The tasks that can be performed by the application depend on the user's privileges. For a standard user, the application runs with a standard access token. For a user who is a member of a group with additional privileges—such as the Backup Operators, Server Operators, or Account Operators groups—the application runs with a partial administrator access token that contains only the privileges the user has been granted. For a user who is a member of the Administrators group, the application runs with a full administrator access token.

- **RunAsAdmin**    Runs the application with administrator privileges. Only administrators can run the application. For a standard user or a user who is a member of a group with additional privileges, the application runs only if the user can be prompted for credentials required to run in elevated mode or if the application is started from within an elevated process, such as an elevated Command Prompt window. For a user who is a member of the Administrators group, the application runs with an administrator access token.

Windows Server protects application processes by labeling them with integrity levels ranging from high to low. Applications that modify system data, such as Disk Management, are considered "high" integrity, while those performing tasks that could compromise the operating system, such as Microsoft Internet Explorer, are considered "low" integrity. Applications with lower integrity levels cannot modify data in applications with higher integrity levels.

Windows Server identifies the publisher of any application that attempts to run with an administrator's full access token. Then, depending on that publisher, Windows Server marks the application as being a compliant application, a publisher verified (signed) application, or a publisher not verified (unsigned) application. When you are installing or running an application, the elevation prompt is designed to help identify the potential security risk of installing or running the application. First of all, the prompt is color-coded. Second, the elevation prompt displays a unique message depending on the category to which the application belongs.

When working with the elevation prompt, keep the following in mind:

- Red is a strong warning, representing likely danger. If the application is from a blocked publisher or is blocked by Group Policy, the elevation prompt has a red background and displays the message "The application is blocked from running."

- Yellow is a general warning, indicating potential danger. If the application is unsigned (or is signed but not yet trusted), the elevation prompt has a yellow background and red shield icon and displays the message "An unidentified program wants access to your computer."

- Blue/green is for administrative elevation. If the application is administrative (such as Server Manager), the elevation prompt has a blue/green background and displays the message "Windows needs your permission to continue."

- Gray is for general elevation. If the application has been signed by Authenticode and is trusted by the local computer, the elevation prompt has a gray background and displays the message "A program needs your permission to continue."

Only core Windows processes can access the secure desktop prompt. This serves to further secure the elevation process by preventing spoofing of the elevation prompt. The secure desktop is enabled by default in Group Policy.

## Configuring run levels

By default, only applications running with a user's administrator access token run in elevated mode. Sometimes, you'll want an application running with a user's standard access token to be in elevated mode. For example, you might want to start the Command Prompt window in elevated mode so that you can perform administrator tasks.

In addition to application manifests discussed previously, Windows Server provides three different ways to set the run level for applications. You can choose to perform one of the following:

- **Running an application once as an administrator**   You can run an application once as an administrator by pressing and holding or right-clicking the application's shortcut or menu item and then selecting Run As Administrator, as shown in Figure 9-5. If you are using a standard account and prompting is enabled, you are prompted for consent before the application is started. If you are using a standard account and prompting is disabled, the application will fail to run. If you are using an administrator account and prompting for consent is enabled, you are prompted for consent before the application is started.

# INSIDE OUT
### Consider the RAID configuration of disks when setting the paging file location

You should always consider the RAID configuration of disks when setting the paging file location. RAID configurations can slow down read/write performance for the paging file. By using RAID 1, you typically get better write performance than you do with RAID 5. By using RAID 5, you typically get better read performance than with RAID 1. So, there's a trade-off to be made with either RAID configuration.

In most cases for computers with 8 gigabytes (GBs) or less of RAM, I recommend setting the total paging file size so that it's twice the physical RAM size on the system. For instance, on a computer with 2048 MBs of RAM, you would ensure that the Total Paging File Size For All Drives setting is at least 4096 MBs. On systems with more than 8 GBs of RAM, you should follow the hardware manufacturer's guidelines for configuring the paging file. Typically, this means setting the paging file to be the same size as physical memory.

When you're trying to fine-tune the paging file size, look closely at the actual workload of the server in typical and peak conditions. Applications and their processes can reserve large blocks of virtual memory and then commit it as needed. Applications do this to try to ensure that committed memory is contiguously allocated by the operating system. This reserved virtual memory doesn't count toward the total, combined amount of physical and virtual memory that can be committed at any one time, also referred to as the *commit limit*.

If you want to try to optimize the paging file size, focus on the actual amount of committed physical and virtual memory for all active processes, the *current commit charge*, and compare this to the commit limit. The current commit charge cannot exceed the commit limit. Ideally, you'll want to size the paging file to accommodate the maximum total commit charge for the applications, services, and processes you want to run simultaneously, while allowing some overhead for unexpected usage peaks beyond this and also testing the usage under typical-load and peak-load conditions.

Keep in mind, the commit limit will increase as the commit charge approaches it when a server has a system-managed paging file (until either exhausting its address space or reaching the 64-bit application-accessible address space limit). As the operating system approaches the maximum commit limit that is possible or explicitly configured, performance will be degraded. You might see application failures or even a system failure.

Chapter 10

# INSIDE OUT  Types of virtual memory

Virtual memory can be divided into several broad types, including reserved, file-mapping view, private, and page file–backed. Reserved virtual memory doesn't count toward the commit limit until it's actually allocated and committed. File-mapping views, which represent files on disk, don't count toward the limit either, except when an application requests copy-on-write. Private virtual memory counts toward the limit because it's for the garbage-collection heap, native heap, and language allocators. It's called "private" because it can't be shared between processes. Page file–backed virtual memory includes sections of virtual memory used by applications.

# INSIDE OUT  Paging file and address space limits

Windows Server 2012 can have paging files that are up to 16 terabytes (TBs) in size and support up to 16 paging files, with each on a separate volume. Sixty-four-bit processes use 64-bit pointers and have a theoretical maximum address space of 16 exabytes ($2^{64}$ bytes). Windows Server defines regions in the address space for processes and various resources. The process address space for user-mode applications is 8192 GBs (8 TBs). Resource address spaces for nonpaged pool, paged pool, and system page table entries are 128 GBs each. The resource address space for the file cache is 1024 GBs (1 TB).

Following this, you want to set the minimum size of the paging file to the greater of (1) the maximum total commit charge you determined minus the amount of physical RAM on the server or (2) the size needed to accommodate the type of crash dump the server is configured for. Then, set the maximum size of the paging file to accommodate unexpected usage peaks beyond this. Here are some examples:

- If you determine the maximum total commit charge for the expected typical workload to be 5796 MBs, you could set this as the minimum paging file size and then set the maximum to 8694 MBs, which is 1.5 times the minimum, or you could simply set a fixed paging file size of 8694 MBs by using this value for the minimum and maximum sizes.

- If you determine the maximum total commit charge for the peak observed workload to be 9184 MBs, you could set this as the minimum paging file size and then set the maximum to 11,480 MBs, which is 1.25 times the minimum, or you could simply set a fixed paging file size of 11,480 MBs by using this value for the minimum and maximum sizes. You also might want to look at creating multiple paging files. If so, you might want to evaluate the performance of a single paging file compared to multiple, smaller paging files in a test environment before using this approach on production servers.

You can track the total commit charge and commit limit in Task Manager. Open Task Manager by pressing and holding or right-clicking the taskbar, and then tapping or clicking Task Manager on the shortcut menu. Alternatively, press Ctrl+Shift+Esc.

When you are working with the expanded view in Task Manager, you'll find details about system resources on the Performance tab. Tap or click Memory in the left pane to see detailed information about memory usage in the main pane, as shown in Figure 10-3. The first value listed under the Committed heading is the current commit charge. The second value is the current commit limit. The total physical memory (RAM) on the server is shown in the upper right corner of the main pane.

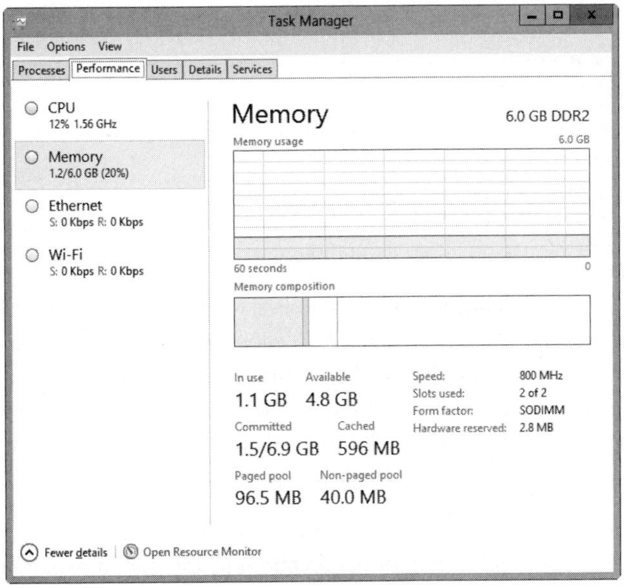

**Figure 10-3**  Viewing memory usage on the server.

## Other important tuning, memory, and data considerations

You can manage the paging file configuration by using the Virtual Memory dialog box, shown in Figure 10-4. To access this dialog box, tap or click the Advanced tab in the System Properties dialog box, and then tap or click the Settings button in the Performance panel to display the Performance Options dialog box. Finally, select the Advanced tab in the Performance Options dialog box, and then tap or click Change in the Virtual Memory panel. Alternatively, type **SystemPropertiesPerformance** in the Apps Search box and then press Enter.

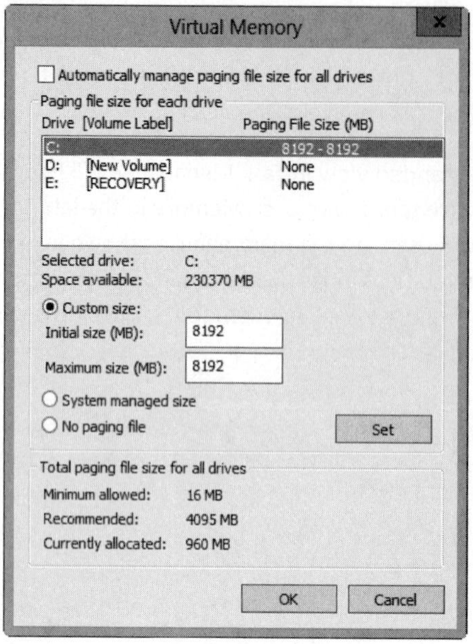

**Figure 10-4** Manage the paging file configuration.

Windows Server 2012 automatically manages virtual memory much better than its predecessors do. Typically, Windows Server 2012 allocates virtual memory at least as large as the total physical memory installed on the computer. You control whether Windows automatically manages virtual memory using the Automatically Manage Paging File Size For All Drives check box. When this check box is selected, Windows automatically manages virtual memory. When this check box is cleared, you can manually manage memory.

The upper section of the Virtual Memory dialog box shows the current paging file location and size. Each volume is listed with information about its associated paging file (if any). When a volume has a page-file managed by the operating system, the paging file is listed as System Managed. When a volume has a paging file, the initial and maximum size values set for the paging file are shown. If the paging file has a size that can be incremented, the initial and maximum sizes will be different, such as 768–9216 MB. If the paging file has a fixed size (recommended), the initial and maximum sizes will be the same, such as 8704–8704 MB.

By selecting a disk drive in the top portion of the Virtual Memory dialog box, you can configure whether and how the paging file is used. Usually, you'll want to select Custom Size and then set the Initial Size and Maximum Size options. Then, tap or click Set to apply the changes before you configure another disk drive. When you are finished configuring paging file usage, tap or click OK. You then will be prompted to restart the server for the changes to take effect. Tap or click OK. When you close the System utility, you will be prompted to restart the system for the changes to take effect. Tap or click Yes to restart the computer now, or tap or click No if you plan to restart the server later.

## TROUBLESHOOTING

**Be careful when setting or moving the paging file**

Some documentation recommends that you move the paging file from the system drive to a different drive to improve performance. Don't do this without understanding the implications of doing so. The paging file is also used for debugging purposes when a Stop error occurs. On the system volume, the initial size of the paging file must be as large as the current physical RAM. If it isn't, Windows Server won't be able to write Stop information to the system drive when fatal errors occur. Because of this, my recommendation is to leave the paging file on the system drive.

## CAUTION !

As you set the paging file for individual drives, pay particular attention to the Total Paging File Size For All Drives information. Generally, you don't want to configure a server so that the Currently Allocated value is 0 MB. This means no paging file is configured, and this will make it harder for you to troubleshoot STOP messages because no dump file will be generated. Keep in mind that a lack of a paging file won't necessarily affect performance. Enterprise server hardware tends to have a lot of RAM. If the server was sized correctly for its workload and has a lot of RAM, it might rarely page to disk.

Chapter 10

# Tracking a system's general health

The fastest, easiest way to track a system's general health is to use Task Manager or Process Resource Monitor. Unlike some of the other performance tools that require some preparation before you can use them, you can start and use these tools without any preparation. This makes them very useful when you want to see what's going on with a system right away.

## Monitoring essentials

By using Task Manager, you can track running applications and processes and determine resource usage. This can help you understand how a server is performing and whether there are any problems, such as applications that aren't running or processes that are hogging system resources. You can open Task Manager by pressing Ctrl+Shift+Esc or by typing **taskmgr** in the Apps Search box and then pressing Enter.

The first time you open Task Manager you'll see the summary view, which shows a quick summary of applications running in the foreground. To get more information about running tasks, tap or click More Details. You'll then see the expanded view, which has multiple tabs that you can use to get information about all running processes, system performance, connected users, and configured services. When you next open Task Manager, you'll see the view that you last used because the last-used view is displayed initially.

To work with the expanded view in Task Manager, the key issue you must understand is the distinction between an application and a process. Basically, the executable name of an application, such as Taskmgr.exe, is known to the operating system as its image name, and any time that you start an application the operating system starts one or more processes to support it. As Figure 10-5 shows, Task Manager has five tabs:

- **Processes** Shows apps, background processes, and Windows processes that were run on the system, and displays whether they're running, suspended, or not responding. It also allows you to interact with applications and halt their execution.

- **Performance** Displays current processor, memory, and network usage. It includes graphs as well as detailed statistics. Enabled network connections are listed by their display name.

- **Users** Details the users currently logged on to the system. It includes local users as well as users connected through Remote Desktop sessions. You can use this tab to disconnect, log off, and send console messages to these users. You also can use it to see the processes users are running.

- **Details** Lists the image name of the processes running on the system, including those run by the operating system and users. It includes usage statistics for system resources allocated to each process, and you can use it to interact with and stop processes.

- **Services**   Shows the system services configured on the server. It includes their status, such as running or stopped.

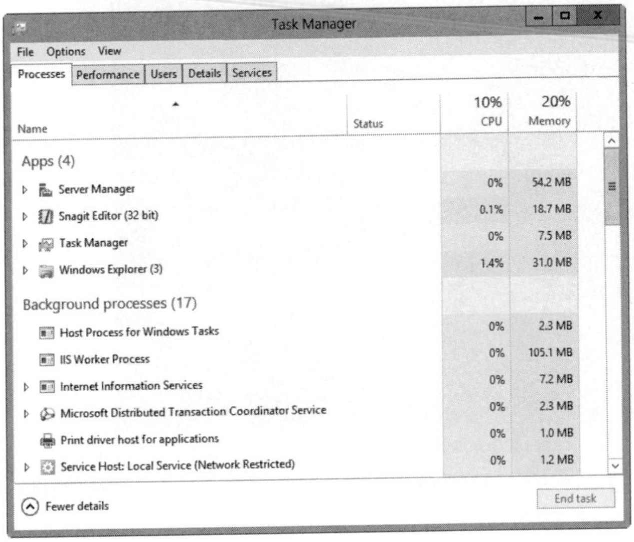

**Figure 10-5**  Use the Task Manager to track resource usage.

## CAUTION

Task Manager uses system resources while it's running. Because of this, you should run it only while you are tracking performance.

No single command-line tool performs all the same functions as Task Manager. The closest tools in functionality are the Windows PowerShell cmdlets get-process and get-service. You obtain detailed information about running processes using get-process and detailed information about configured services using get-service.

As Figure 10-6 shows, the standard output of get-process is much more detailed than the default Task Manager view, especially when it comes to current per-process resource usage and activity. To run get-process, access a PowerShell prompt and then type **get-process**.

Chapter 10

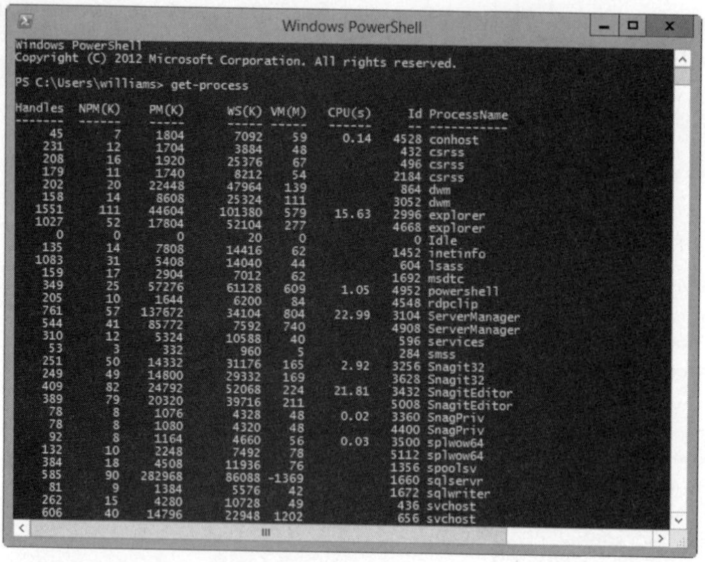

**Figure 10-6** Use get-process to track running applications and processes and to determine resource usage.

## Use get-process to reduce resource usage

Because get-process is text-based rather than a graphical utility, it will, in most cases, use fewer system resources than Task Manager. On systems for which you are very concerned about resource usage and the possibility of bogging down a system by tracking performance information, you might initially want to start tracking performance by using get-process.

As Figure 10-7 shows, the standard output for get-service shows the status of each configured service along with its internal name and display name. To run get-service, access a PowerShell prompt and then type **get-service**.

**Figure 10-7** Use get-service to track the status of configured services.

The sections that follow discuss how to use these tools to gather information about systems and resolve problems. The focus of the discussion is on Task Manager, get-process, and get-service, which should be your primary tools for tracking a system's general health.

# Getting processor and memory usage for troubleshooting

The Performance tab in Task Manager, shown in Figure 10-8, should be the first tab you check if you suspect there is a performance issue with a system. It allows you to quickly determine current processor, memory, and network usage, and it also graphs some historical usage statistics based on data collected since you started Task Manager.

Chapter 10

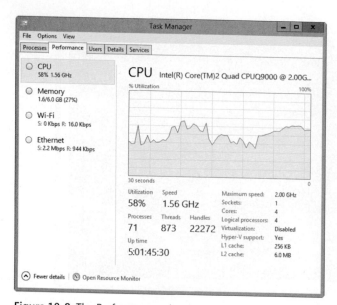

**Figure 10-8** The Performance tab provides a summary of current processor, memory, and network usage, as well as some historical usage statistics based on data collected since you started Task Manager.

## TROUBLESHOOTING

### Using performance views and graphs

When you are troubleshooting performance issues, you'll often want to refer to the graphs or summary details regarding CPU, memory, and network usage. The full view, however, can sometimes get in the way of your work, especially if you have several other windows open. Here, you might want to switch to the summary view of the Performance tab.

To do this, press and hold or right-click in the left pane of the Performance tab and then select Summary View. This reduces the Task Manager window so that it shows only a summary view of the performance statistics. If you also want to see summary graphs, press and hold or right-click the summary view and then select Show Graphs. Now you'll see the summary statistics and the summary graphs. This combined summary view is what I use when I'm monitoring performance issues.

When you are working with the summary view of the Performance tab and want to switch back to the expanded view, simply press and hold or right-click the summary view and then select Summary View. This clears the Summary View selection.

**Note**

Another handy view is the graph summary view, which shows only the currently selected graph. When you are working with the expanded view of the Performance tab, you can switch to the graph summary view simply by double-tapping or double-clicking the graph in the main pane. While you are working with the graph summary view, you can switch between graph categories as well. For example, if you are viewing the CPU graph, you can switch to the memory graph. To do this, press and hold or right-click in the graph summary view, select View, and then choose the type of graph. Switch back to the expanded view at any time by pressing and holding or right-clicking the summary view and then selecting Graph Summary View. This clears the Graph Summary View selection.

Some of the performance data is self-explanatory. When you select CPU in the left pane, the main window shows the CPU usage. The Overall Utilization graph shows the overall percentage of processor resources being used and is the default graph. If a system has multiple discrete sockets containing CPUs, you'll see a history graph for each CPU by default as well. If a system has multiple logical processors, you also can view the workload on each logical processor in separate graphs. To change the graph view, press and hold or right-click in the main pane, select Change Graph To, and then choose a viewing style.

In Figure 10-8, note the additional information about CPU usage. This information, which is shown below the graph, includes the following:

- **Utilization**   Shows the percentage of CPU utilization.

- **Speed**   Shows the (average) current speed of processor.

- **Maximum Speed**   Shows the maximum speed the process is capable of.

**Note**

If a server's processor or processors are throttled—to save power or for some other reason—the (average) current speed and the maximum speed will be different.

- **Sockets**   Shows the number of discrete sockets containing processors.

- **Cores**   Shows the total number of processor cores.

- **Logical Processors**   Shows the total number of active logical processors. If this value is less than the total number of processor cores, some portion of functionality has been disabled.

- **Virtualization**   Shows whether virtualization is enabled or disabled.

- **L1 Cache**   Shows the size of the L1 cache if the computer's processor or processors have L1 cache.

- **L2 Cache**   Shows the size of the L2 cache if the computer's processor or processors have L2 cache.

Also shown are summary statistics for handles, threads, processes, and uptime. The Processes area shows the number of processes in use. Threads shows the number of threads in use. Threads allow concurrent execution of process requests. Handles shows the number of input/output (I/O) file handles in use. Because each handle requires system memory to maintain, this is important to note. Up Time shows you the total amount of time the system has been up since it was last started.

In Figure 10-8, you see an example of a system with moderate CPU usage but with very little ongoing paging file or networking activity. A system with CPU usage consistently at these levels might warrant some additional monitoring to determine whether you should add resources to the system. Basically, you want to determine whether these are typical usage conditions and whether actual peak usage was significantly higher.

If these are average usage conditions and peak usage was significantly higher, increasing the processor speed or adding processors could improve performance and allow for better handling of peak usage situations. If these statistics represent peak usage conditions and typical usage conditions were much less, the system probably wouldn't need additional resources. Sometimes the CPU usage can be high if the system has too little memory as well. A quick check of the memory usage of the server (including its current and peak usage) shows, however, that this isn't the case for this particular system.

> **Important**
> When CPU throttling is being used, don't just look at the percentage of utilization—also look at the current CPU speed. In Figure 10-8, not only is the server only running at 58 percent CPU utilization, the average current CPU speed is 1.56 gigahertz (GHz), which is 36 percent below the server's maximum speed of 2.00 GHz.

Figure 10-9 shows performance data for the same system. In this example, the system has high CPU usage. In many cases, CPU usage is at 99 percent and the CPU speed is nearly at its maximum. If CPU usage was consistent at this level, I might suspect a runaway process and look for a process that is causing the problem. Here, however, there are times when CPU usage isn't maxed out, and you'd definitely want to take a closer look at what's going on, starting with memory usage.

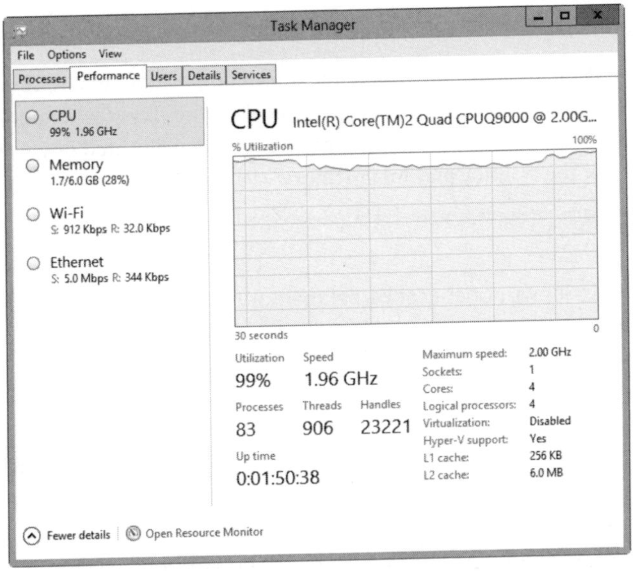

**Figure 10-9** Heavy activity on the system is causing CPU usage to soar and, in many cases, to max out.

Figure 10-10 shows the server's memory usage, which is displayed by selecting Memory in the left pane. Note that the total physical memory (RAM) on the server is shown in the upper-right corner of the main pane. Note also the following:

- **Cached**   Shows the physical memory used for system caching. This value represents the total amount of modified memory (needing to be written to disk before being available) and standby memory (containing cached data and code not actively being used).

- **In Use**   Shows the currently allocated physical memory. Use this value to help you determine the current paging file size. The size of the paging file is the difference between the current commit charge and the in-use memory.

- **Available**   Shows the nonallocated (available) physical memory. Use this value to help you determine whether the server is running out of available physical memory.

- **Committed**   Shows the current commit charge as the first value and the commit limit as the second value.

- **Memory Composition** Depicts in-use and available memory graphically, according to its status as in use (allocated), modified (needing to be written to disk before being available), standby (containing cached data and code not actively being used), and free (nonallocated).

> ### Note
> Tap or rest the mouse pointer on a memory-composition item to see a precise numeric value. Keep in mind that the total allocated physical memory is the sum of the in-use and modified values, and the total nonallocated physical memory is the sum of the standby and free memory.

- **Paged Pool** Shows noncritical kernel memory used by the operating system kernel. Noncritical portions of kernel memory can be paged to disk and don't have to reside in physical memory (RAM).

- **Non-paged Pool** Shows critical kernel memory used by the operating system kernel. Critical portions of kernel memory must operate in physical memory (RAM) and cannot be paged to disk.

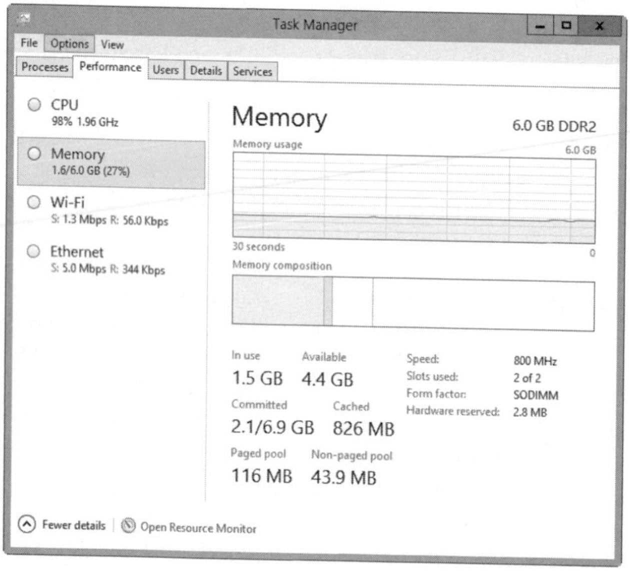

**Figure 10-10** Use the Memory graphs to check memory usage and composition.

# INSIDE OUT    Physical configuration of memory

The physical configuration of the memory is shown along with other memory information. This is handy because otherwise you would have to get this information from the System Information utility or elsewhere. Note the speed, slots used, and form factor. Generally, when adding memory to a server, you need to use memory that has the same speed and form factor as existing memory—and as required by the system bus. If you want to add memory and no additional slots are available, you need to replace the existing memory.

When you are reviewing Figure 10-10, one thing to note right away is that the system has quite a bit of available RAM—around 4.4 GBs. In checking the paging, you can see the current commit charge isn't very large either. It is only 2.1 GBs, and the difference between the commit charge and in-use RAM is only 0.6 GBs, meaning only 0.6 GBs is being paged to disk.

Such a large amount of available RAM and such little use of the paging file tells me that processes, disk I/O, or both activities are using up CPU resources. If this level of usage is consistent, you have a problem that needs investigating. Here, increasing the server's RAM or virtual memory will not solve the problem. Instead, you need to start by checking for system processes that have high CPU usage time, which tells you what activities are causing the strain on the server's processors. If the high CPU usage activities are related to installed applications, roles, or role services, you might want to consider adding CPUs to the server. Generally, you add CPUs to a server in matched pairs. In this example, the server has two CPUs, so you want to consider upgrading to four CPUs. You might also consider offloading some of the system's load. For example, you could move one of its roles or applications to a different server.

Another scenario you might encounter is one where the server has little available RAM and a large paging file. A small amount of available RAM is a concern, and if this level of usage is consistent, you might consider changing the way applications use RAM, adding RAM, or both. A large amount of virtual memory being used (relative to available physical RAM) is also an area of possible concern that might make you consider adding physical RAM. Although increasing the amount of RAM could offer some relief to the CPU, it might not be enough, so you could consider increasing the processor speed or adding processors. You might also consider offloading some of the system's load. For example, you could move one of its roles or applications to a different server.

**TROUBLESHOOTING**

### Resolving problems with RAM modules

Physical memory is installed on a server using available memory slots. Typically, memory is installed in matched pairs and according to the number of memory channels. When you boot a server with invalid or improperly configured memory, the server generates errors, which typically are written to the console window. Related events might also be written to the hardware event logs in firmware, the system event logs in the operating system, or both. You can use these error messages and events to help you diagnose and resolve memory problems. For pinpointing physical failures within the memory chips themselves, you can use the Windows Memory Diagnostic Tool (Memdiag.exe), which is discussed in Chapter 17, "Backup and recovery."

That said, some problems with RAM modules are less obvious than one might think and a missing RAM module is one problem you might not recognize immediately. RAM modules don't really go missing. They can, however, be improperly seated (meaning not fully pushed into their slot and connected), incompatible (meaning not the correct speed, form factor, or both), or bad (meaning failed or broken). One quick way to identify this type of problem is to note the total physical memory and the total number of memory slots being used. If either or both don't match up to what you expect, there's a problem—for example, if the server has 16 GBs of RAM and the current total is shown as 8 GBs, or if the server has memory in four slots and only three are shown as being used.

## Getting information on running applications

The Processes tab in Task Manager, shown in Figure 10-11, lists applications being run by users and the operating system, along with status details that show whether the applications are running, suspended, or not responding. If an application has an open file, such as a Microsoft Word document, the name of the file is shown as well. By default, applications are grouped into three general categories:

- **Apps**  Programs running in the foreground

- **Background processes**  Programs running in the background

- **Windows processes**  Processes run by the operating system

> **Important**
> Generally, foreground processes are processes being run by a user logged on to a computer's local console. In contrast, background processes include any processes run by the operating system, local services, network services, and remote users. Thus, if you are trying to track processes for remote users on the Processes tab, you'll look under the Background Processes group rather than the Apps group. However, the Users tab provides a better approach for identifying the specific processes being run by local and remote users, where each process a particular user is running is listed under the user's logon name.

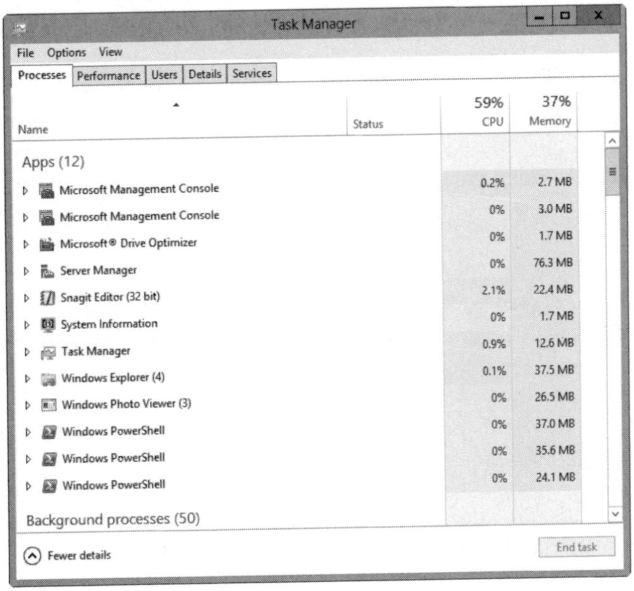

**Figure 10-11** The Processes tab in Task Manager tracks applications users are running.

You can use the Group By Type option on the View menu to control whether grouping is used. If you clear this option, processes are listed alphabetically without grouping by type. If a process has related subprocesses, you'll be able to tap or click a process to view the subprocesses.

To work with an application, select it by tapping or clicking it in the Task list. You can then press and hold or right-click the application name to select the End Task, Create Dump File, Go To Details, Open File Location, Search Online, and Properties options. Don't over-look the usefulness of the Go To Details option when you press and hold or right-click: Use this when you're trying to find the primary process for a particular application because selecting this option highlights the related process in the Details tab. Select Create Dump File to create a dump file for debugging an application. Select Search Online to start a search with your default search provider in your default browser. The search keywords are the image name and descriptive name of the process.

The Status column shows abnormal process statuses, if any. If you see an application with a status of Not Responding, that's an indicator that the application might be frozen, and you might want to select it and then tap or click End Task. Keep in mind that the Not Responding message can also be an indicator that an application is busy and should be left alone until it finishes. Generally, when an application is running without errors and might have unsaved data, don't use End Task to stop the application. Instead, try to gracefully exit the program. You can do this by expanding the related entry for the application, pressing and holding or right-clicking the related subprocess, selecting the Switch To option to switch to the application, and then exiting the application as you normally would.

Other columns on the Processes tab provide additional information about running processes. Use the values shown in the CPU and Memory columns to determine which processes are overconsuming these system resources. You can add other columns by pressing and holding or right-clicking any column header and then selecting options for the additional columns to display. In addition to Name and Status, the available columns are as follows:

- **CPU** Lists the percentage of CPU utilization for the process (across all physical and logical processors). The bold value in the column header represents the total CPU utilization for the server (across all physical and logical processors).

- **Memory** Lists the total physical memory reserved for the process. The bold value in the column header represents the total physical memory utilization for the server.

- **Command Line** Provides the full file path to the executable running the process, as well as any command-line arguments passed in when the process was started.

- **PID** Provides the numeric identifier for the process.

- **Process Name** Provides the name of the process or executable running the process.

- **Publisher** Shows the publisher of the process, such as Microsoft Corporation.

- **Type** Provides the general process type as app, background process, or Windows process, which is useful if you clear the Group By Type option on the View menu.

# Monitoring and troubleshooting processes

You can view information about processes running on a system by using the Details tab of Task Manager or by running get-process. The Task Manager display differs greatly from the output provided by get-process. The Details tab shows all processes that are running, including those run by the operating system, local services, network services, a user account logged on to the local console, and remote users.

The default view of the Details tab shows each running process by image name and user name. Here, the image name is the name of the executable for the process and the user name is the name of the user or service running the process.

The CPU column shows the percentage of processor utilization for each process. The Memory column shows the amount of memory the process is currently using. By default, processes are sorted by image name, but you can change this by tapping or clicking any of the available column headers to sort the information based on that column. Tapping or clicking again on the same column reverses the sort order. For example, tap or click User Name to alphabetically sort the user names. Tap or click User Name again to reverse sort the user names.

As you might recall from Figure 10-6, get-process shows much more detailed information for each process. This information is useful for troubleshooting. If you press and hold or right-click any column header and then choose Select Columns, you'll see a dialog box that allows you to add columns to the Details tab. To get the additional information shown by get-process, the following columns should be selected:

- PID

- CPU

- CPU Time

- Working Set (Memory)

- Memory (Private Working Set)

- Memory (Shared Working Set)

- Commit Size

- Handles

You will then have a process display like the one shown in Figure 10-12.

Chapter 10

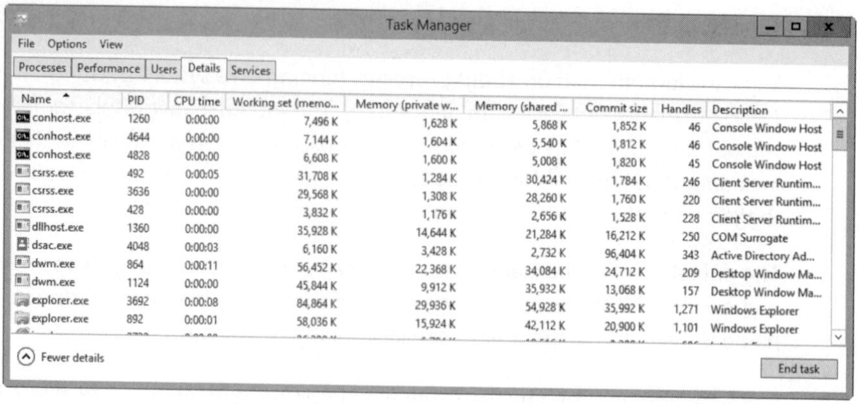

**Figure 10-12**  The Details tab provides detailed information on running processes according to image name and user name.

## TROUBLESHOOTING

### Isolate 32-bit or 64-bit processes

Sixty-four-bit Windows operating systems can only run 32-bit or 64-bit processes. If you want to isolate 32-bit or 64-bit processes, add the Platform column to the Details tab. You can then quickly determine whether a process is 32-bit or 64-bit.

For deeper troubleshooting, however, I recommend adding a few more columns, such as the following:

- Base Priority

- Image Path Name

- Page Faults

- PF Delta

- Threads

- Working Set Delta (Memory)

OK, so now that you've added all these extra columns of information, you are probably wondering what it all means and why you want to track it. As stated previously, you primarily use this information for troubleshooting. It helps you pinpoint which processes are hogging system resources and the type of resources the resource hogs are using. When you know what's going on with processes, you can modify the system or its applications accordingly to resolve a performance problem.

Table 10-1 summarizes the information provided by these and other process-related statistics. The value in parentheses following the Task Manager column name is the name of the corresponding get-process property (if available). If by monitoring processes you notice what looks like a problem, you will probably want to start more detailed monitoring of the system. One tool to consider is System Monitor, which is discussed in Chapter 11, "Comprehensive performance analysis and logging."

> **Note**
> For formatting purposes, the get-process property names are shown with brackets where necessary. The actual property names do not contain hyphens.

**TABLE 10-1** Process statistics and how they can be used

| Column Name | Description |
| --- | --- |
| Base Priority [BasePriority] | Shows the priority of the process. Priority determines how much of the system resources are allocated to a process. The standard priorities are Low (4), Below Normal (6), Normal (8), Above Normal (10), High (13), and Real-Time (24). Most processes have a Normal priority by default, and the highest priority is given to real-time processes. |
| Commit Size [VirtualMemorySize] | Shows the amount of virtual memory allocated to and reserved for a process. Virtual memory is memory on disk and is slower to access than pooled memory. By configuring an application to use more physical RAM, you might be able to increase performance. To do this, however, the system must have available RAM. If it doesn't, other processes running on the system might slow down. |
| CPU [CPU] | Shows the percentage of CPU utilization for the process. The System Idle Process shows what percentage of CPU power is idle. A 99 in the CPU column for the System Idle Process means 99 percent of the system resources currently aren't being used. If the system has low idle time (meaning high CPU usage) during peak or average usage, you might consider upgrading to faster processors or adding processors. |
| CPU Time [TotalProcessorTime] | Shows the total amount of CPU time used by the process since it was started. Tap or click the column header to quickly see the processes that are using the most CPU time. If a process is using a lot of CPU time, the related application might have a configuration problem. This could also indicate a runaway or nonresponsive process that is unnecessarily tying up the CPU. |

| Column Name | Description |
|---|---|
| Handles [HandleCount] | Shows the number of file handles maintained by the process. The number of handles used is an indicator of how dependent the process is on the file system. Some processes have thousands of open file handles. Each file handle requires system memory to maintain. |
| Image Path Name [Path] | Shows the full path to the executable for the process. |
| Name [ProcessName] | Shows the name of the process. |
| NP Pool [Nonpaged SystemMemorySize] | Shows the amount of virtual memory for a process that cannot be written to disk. The nonpaged pool is an area of RAM for objects that can't be written to disk. You should note processes that require a high amount of nonpaged pool memory. If there isn't enough free memory on the server, these processes might be the reason for a high level of page faults. |
| Page Faults | Shows page faults caused by the process. Page faults occur when a process requests a page in memory and the system can't find it at the requested location. If the requested page is elsewhere in memory, the fault is called a *soft page fault*. If the requested page must be retrieved from disk, the fault is called a *hard page fault*. Most processors can handle large numbers of soft faults. Hard faults, on the other hand, can cause significant delays. If there are a lot of hard faults, you might need to increase the amount of memory or reduce the system cache size. |
| Paged Pool [PagedSystemMemorySize] | Shows the amount of committed virtual memory for a process that can be written to disk. The paged pool is an area of RAM for objects that can be written to disk when they aren't used. As process activity increases, so does the amount of pool memory the process uses. Most processes have more paged pool than nonpaged pool requirements. |
| Peak Working Set (Memory) [PeakWorkingSet] | Shows the maximum amount of memory the process used, including both the private working set and the nonprivate working set. If peak memory is exceptionally large, this can be an indicator of a memory leak. |
| PF Delta | Shows the change in the number of page faults for the process recorded since the last update. As with memory usage, you might see an increase in page faults when a process is active and then a decrease as activity slows. |
| PID [Id] | Shows the run-time identification number of the process. |
| Session ID [SessionId] | Shows the identification number user (session) within which the process is running. This corresponds to the ID value listed on the Users tab. |

Chapter 10

| Column Name | Description |
|---|---|
| Threads [Threads] | Shows the number of threads that the process is using. Most server applications are multithreaded, which allows concurrent execution of process requests. Some applications can dynamically control the number of concurrently executing threads to improve application performance. Too many threads, however, can actually reduce performance because the operating system has to switch thread contexts too frequently. |
| Working Set (Memory) [WorkingSet] | Shows the amount of memory the process is currently using, including both the private working set and the non-private working set. The private working set is memory the process is using that cannot be shared with other processes. The nonprivate working set is memory the process is using that can be shared with other processes. If memory usage for a process slowly grows over time and doesn't go back to the baseline value, this can be an indicator of a memory leak. |
| Working Set Delta (Memory) | Shows the change in memory usage for the process recorded since the last update. A constantly changing memory delta can be an indicator that a process is in use, but it could also indicate a problem. Generally, the memory delta might show increasing memory usage when a process is being used and then show a negative delta (indicated by parentheses in Task Manager) as activity slows. |

At a PowerShell Prompt, you can get key stats for all processes by following these steps:

1. Get all the processes running on the server and store them in the $a variable by entering

   ```
   $a = get-process
   ```

2. Use the *InputObject* parameter to pass the process objects stored in $a to get-process, and then pass the objects to the format-table cmdlet along with the list of properties you want to see by entering

   ```
   get-process -inputobject $a | format-table –property ProcessName,
   BasePriority, HandleCount, Id, NonpagedSystemMemorySize,
   PagedSystemMemorySize, PeakPagedMemorySize, PeakVirtualMemorySize,
   PeakWorkingSet, SessionId, Threads, TotalProcessorTime,
   VirtualMemorySize, WorkingSet, CPU, Path
   ```

> **Note**
> The order of the properties in the comma-separated list determines the display order. If you want to change the display order, simply move the property to a different position in the list.

When you know the process you want to examine, you don't need to use this multistep procedure. Simply enter the name of the process without the .exe or .dll instead of using –*inputobject $a*. In this example, you list details about the Explorer process:

```
get-process explorer | format-list –property ProcessName, BasePriority,
HandleCount, Id, NonpagedSystemMemorySize, PagedSystemMemorySize,
PeakPagedMemorySize, PeakVirtualMemorySize, PeakWorkingSet, SessionId,
Threads, TotalProcessorTime, VirtualMemorySize, WorkingSet, CPU, Path
```

You can enter part of a process name as well use an asterisk as a wildcard to match a partial name. In this example, get-process lists any process with a name that starts with *exp*:

```
get-process exp* | format-list –property ProcessName, BasePriority,
HandleCount, Id, NonpagedSystemMemorySize, PagedSystemMemorySize,
PeakPagedMemorySize, PeakVirtualMemorySize, PeakWorkingSet, SessionId,
Threads, TotalProcessorTime, VirtualMemorySize, WorkingSet, CPU, Path
```

Some interesting additional properties you can use with get-process include

- **MinWorkingSet**   The minimum amount of working set memory used by the process

- **Modules**   The executables and dynamically linked libraries used by the process

- **PeakVirtualMemorySize**   The peak amount of virtual memory used by the process

- **PriorityBoostEnabled**   A Boolean value that indicates whether the process has the PriorityBoost feature enabled

- **PriorityClass**   The priority class of the process

- **PrivilegedProcessorTime**   The amount of kernel-mode usage time for the process

- **ProcessorAffinity**   The processor affinity setting for the process

- **Responding**   A Boolean value that indicates whether the process responded when tested

- **StartTime**   The date and time the process was started

- **UserProcessorTime**   The amount of user-mode usage time for the process

- **Description**   A description of the process

- **FileVersion**   The file version of the executable of the process

In Task Manager, you can stop processes that you suspect aren't running properly. To do this, press and hold or right-click the process, and choose End Process to stop the process or End Process Tree to stop the process as well as any other processes it started. To stop a process at the PowerShell prompt, you can use stop-process. The best way to use stop-process is to identity the process ID of the process that you want to stop rather than a process name. This ensures that you stop only the intended process rather than all instances of processes with a particular process name. By using the –*confirm* parameter, you should also have stop-process prompt you to confirm how you want to proceed. In the following example, you stop the process with the process ID 4524:

```
stop-process –id 4524 –confirm
```

As you are confirming this action and passing through the output, you'll see a prompt asking you to confirm. You can then

- Press Y to answer Yes and confirm that you want to perform the action and continue.

- Press A to answer Yes to all prompts and confirm that you want to perform all actions without further prompting.

- Press N to answer No and skip the action and continue to the next action.

- Press L to answer No to all prompts and confirm that you do not want to perform any actions.

- Press S to suspend the pipeline and return to the command prompt. To later return to the pipeline, type **exit**.

## Monitoring and troubleshooting services

You can view information about services running on a system by using the Services tab of Task Manager or by running get-service. By default, the Services tab shows all services configured on the system whether they are running, stopped, or in a different state. As shown in Figure 10-13, services are listed by name, process ID (PID), description, status, and group.

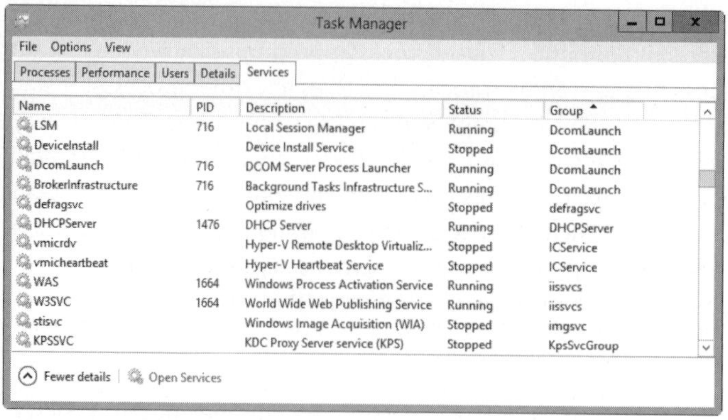

**Figure 10-13** The Services tab provides detailed information on configured services.

> **Note**
>
> You also can work with services using the Services pane in Server Manager, the Services node in Computer Management, or the Services console.

Because multiple services typically run under the same process ID, you can quickly sort services by their associated process ID by tapping or clicking the related column heading. You can tap or click the Status column heading to sort services according to their status as Running or Stopped. If you press and hold or right-click a service's listing in Task Manager, you display a shortcut menu that allows you to start a stopped service, stop a started service, or go to the related process on the Details tab.

The Group column provides additional information about related identities or service host contexts under which a service runs. Services running an identity with a restriction have the restriction appended. For example, a service running under the Local Service identity might be listed as *LocalServiceNoNetwork* to indicate that the service has no network access, or as *LocalSystemNetworkRestricted* to indicate that the service has restricted access to the network.

Services that have svchost.exe list their associated context for the –*k* parameter. For example, the *RemoteRegistry* service runs with the command line *svchost.exe –k regsvc* and you'll see an entry of regsvc in the Group column for this service.

At a PowerShell prompt, you can get the status of configured services simply by entering get-service. By default, only the service status, internal name, and display name are shown. Additional properties that you can display include

- **CanPauseAndContinue**   Indicates whether the service can be paused and resumed

- **CanStop**   Indicates whether you can stop the service

- **DependentServices**   Lists the services that depend on this service

- **ServicesDependedOn**   Lists the services on which this service depends

At a PowerShell prompt, you can get the available details for all services by following these steps:

1. Get all the services running on the server and store them in the *$a* variable by entering

   ```
   $a = get-service
   ```

2. Use the *InputObject* parameter to pass the service objects stored in *$a* to get-service and then pass the objects to the format-table cmdlet along with the list of properties you want to see by entering

   ```
   get-service -inputobject $a | format-table -property Name, DisplayName,
   CanPauseAndContinue, CanStop, DependentServices, ServicesDependedOn, Status
   ```

When you know the service you want to examine, you don't need to use this multistep procedure. Simply enter the internal name of the process instead of using *–inputobject $a*. In this example, you list details about the *TermService* process:

```
get-service TermService | format-list -property Name, DisplayName,
CanPauseAndContinue, CanStop, DependentServices, ServicesDependedOn, Status
```

You can enter part of a service name as well using an asterisk as a wildcard to match a partial name. In this example, get-service lists any service with a name that starts with *term*:

```
get-service Term* | format-list -property Name, DisplayName,
CanPauseAndContinue, CanStop, DependentServices, ServicesDependedOn, Status
```

To list services by display name, use the *–displayname* parameter and enclose the display name in quotation marks, as shown here:

```
get-service -displayname "Remote Desktop Services" | format-list -property Name,
DisplayName, CanPauseAndContinue, CanStop, DependentServices,
ServicesDependedOn, Status
```

Chapter 10

You can use the following cmdlets to manage services:

- **Suspend-Service**    Pauses a service

- **Resume-Service**    Resumes a paused service

- **Start-Service**    Starts a stopped service

- **Stop-Service**    Stops a started service

- **Restart-Service**    Stops and then starts a service

Typically, you'll use Restart-Service when you suspect a service is having a problem and you want to reset it.

## Getting network usage information

On the Performance tab, you can view the current usage of a computer's network connections. When you select the Performance tab, each enabled network connection is listed by name in the left pane, along with either a summary view or a summary graph view of current activity. If you select a network connection in the left pane, as shown in Figure 10-14, the main window provides more detailed information about the connection's current usage.

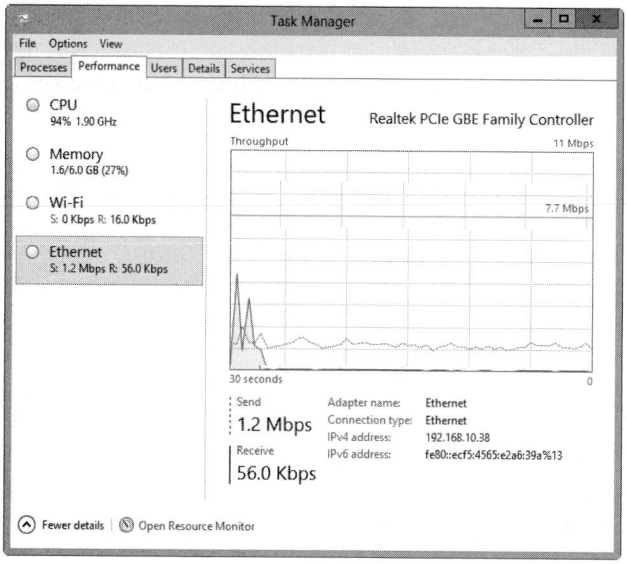

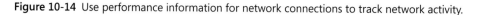

**Figure 10-14**  Use performance information for network connections to track network activity.

The adapter name is listed above the graph, as is the manufacturer name and model. The graph shows the selected network connection's throughput, with send and receive activity plotted separately over time. As the legend below the graph shows, send activity is plotted with a dashed line and receive activity is plotted with a solid line. Also shown are the current send and receive throughput, scaled according to current activity levels. With this in mind, if there is little current activity, you'll see activity plotted in Kbps. As activity increases, you might see activity plotted in Mbps or even Gbps.

You can also get more detailed information for a network connection. This information is useful for troubleshooting. If you tap or click the graph and choose View Network Details, you'll see a dialog box you can use to add columns for summary statistics to the Networking tab. Table 10-2 summarizes the key network statistics available.

**TABLE 10-2 Network statistics and how they can be used**

| Column Name | Description |
| --- | --- |
| Bytes Sent Throughput | Shows the percentage of the current connection bandwidth used by traffic sent from the system. |
| Bytes Received Throughput | Shows the percentage of the current connection bandwidth used by traffic received by the system. |
| Bytes Throughput | Shows the percentage of the current connection bandwidth used for all traffic on the network adapter. If this shows 50 percent or more utilization consistently, you'll want to monitor the system more closely and consider adding network adapters. |
| Bytes Sent | Shows the cumulative total bytes sent on the connection since the system booted. |
| Bytes Received | Shows the cumulative total bytes received on the connection since the system booted. |
| Bytes | Shows the cumulative total bytes on the connection since the system booted. |
| Unicasts | Shows the cumulative number of unicast packets received or sent since the system booted. |
| Unicasts Sent | Shows the total packets sent by unicast since the system booted. |
| Unicasts Received | Shows the total packets received by unicast since the system booted. |
| Nonunicasts | Shows the total number of broadcast packets sent or received since the system booted. Too much broadcast traffic on the network can be an indicator of networking problems. If you see a lot of nonunicast traffic, monitor the amount received during the refresh interval. |
| Nonunicasts Sent | Shows the total broadcast packets sent since the system booted. |
| Nonunicasts Received | Shows the total broadcast packets received since the system booted. |

Chapter 10

# Getting information on user and remote user sessions

Members of the Administrators group and any users to whom you specifically grant remote access can connect to systems using Remote Desktop Services or a Remote Desktop Connection. Both techniques allow users to access systems remotely and use the systems as if they were sitting at the keyboard. In the standard configuration, however, remote access is disabled. You can enable and configure the remote access feature by using Server Manager. In Server Manager, select Local Server in the left pane and then tap or click the Enabled or Disabled link for Remote Desktop. This opens the System Properties dialog box to the Remote tab, as shown in Figure 10-15.

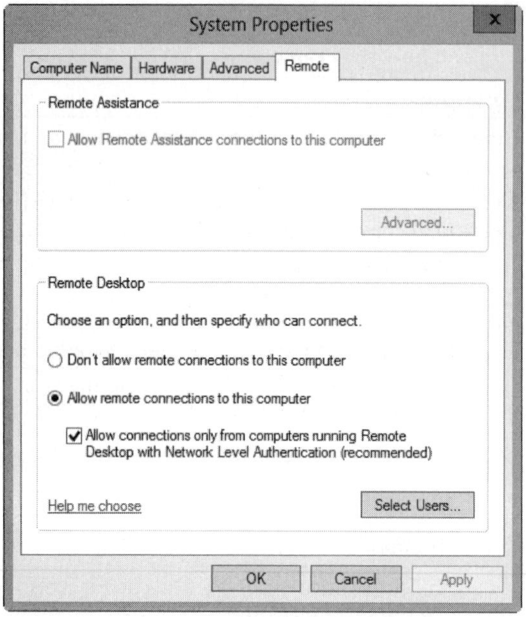

**Figure 10-15**  Configure Remote Desktop connections.

In the Remote Desktop panel, select Allow Remote Connections To This Computer. Before you tap or click OK, select the Allow Connections Only From Computers Running Remote Desktop With Network Level Authentication check box if you want to ensure that only more secure connections using Network Level Authentication are permitted. Windows Vista, Windows Server 2008, and later releases of Windows have Network Level Authentication. Most earlier releases of Windows do not.

With Remote Desktop, Windows Server 2012 allows two active console sessions at one time. Console sessions provide full functionality for administration. If you try to log on with a new console session and two others are already logged on to the console, the following happens:

1. You will see a prompt stating too many users are logged on. You can then select a user session to disconnect, or you can tap or click Cancel to exit the session. If you select the Force Disconnect Of This User check box prior to selecting a user, the user is forcibly disconnected. A user with a Remote Desktop Connection sees a prompt stating the following: Your Remote Desktop Services session has ended. A user with a local logon is logged off.

2. If you elect to disconnect a user, that user will see a prompt from Remote Desktop Connection stating that you have requested to disconnect her session. The user will have 30 seconds to respond by either tapping or clicking OK to disconnect immediately or tapping or clicking Cancel to deny the request.

3. If 30 seconds elapses without a response, the user is disconnected automatically. A user with a Remote Desktop Connection sees a prompt stating the following: Your Remote Desktop Services session has ended. A user with a local logon is logged off.

4. If the user selects Cancel when prompted to disconnect her session, she will see a prompt stating her request has been denied.

As shown in Figure 10-16, the Users tab lists user connections according to the following factors:

- **User**   The logon name of the user account, such as Wrstanek or Administrator. If you want to see the logon domain as well as the logon name, select Show Full Account Name on the Options menu.

- **Status**   The status of the connection. This can be either Blank for active connections or Disconnected for connections that have been disconnected.

- **CPU**   Lists the percentage of CPU utilization for the user (across all physical and logical processors). The bold value in the column header represents the total CPU utilization for the server (across all physical and logical processors).

- **Memory**   Lists the total physical memory reserved for the user. The bold value in the column header represents the total physical memory utilization for the server.

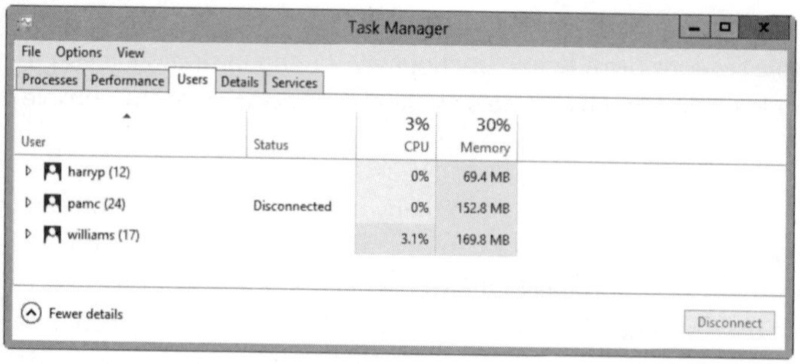

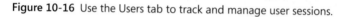

**Figure 10-16** Use the Users tab to track and manage user sessions.

CPU and memory utilization details are new for Windows Server 2012 and are helpful for troubleshooting performance issues related to logged-on users. The total utilization value is listed above the column heading, and individual utilization values for each logged-on user are listed below it.

You can add other columns by pressing and holding or right-clicking any column header and then selecting options for the additional columns to display. Other available columns are as follows:

- **ID**   The session ID. All user connections have a unique session ID.

- **Client Name**   The name of the computer from which an active user is connecting. This field is blank for console sessions (and for disconnected sessions).

- **Session**   The type of session. Console is used for users logged on locally. The value is blank for disconnected sessions. Otherwise, this column indicates the connection type and protocol, such as RDP-TCP for a connection using the Remote Desktop Protocol (RDP) with Transmission Control Protocol (TCP) as the transport protocol.

The Users tab can help you determine who is logged on and whether that user's status is either active or disconnected. Press and hold or right-click an active session and you can choose Send Message to send a console message to the user. This message is displayed on the screen of that user's session.

If you must end a user session, you can do this in one of two ways. Pressing and holding or right-clicking the session and choosing Sign Off logs the user off using the normal logoff process. This allows application data and system state information to be saved as it would be during a normal logoff. Pressing and holding or right-clicking the session and choosing Disconnect disconnects a user, but the user's session isn't affected.

You can also connect to or sign off an inactive session. To connect to the session, press and hold or right-click the inactive session and then choose Connect. When prompted, provide the user's password. To log off the user, press and hold or right-click the inactive session and then choose Sign Off. When prompted, confirm that you want to sign out the user, which might cause the user's unsaved data to be lost.

# Tracking events and troubleshooting by using Event Viewer

The Windows operating system defines an *event* as any significant occurrence in the operating system or an application that should be recorded for tracking purposes. Informational events can be tracked as well as events that record warnings, errors, and auditing. Critical errors that deserve immediate attention, such as when the server has run out of disk space or memory, are recorded in the logs and displayed on screen.

## Understanding the event logs

The Windows service that controls event logging is the Event Log service. When this service is started, events are recorded in one of the available event logs. To work with event logs remotely, remote management and inbound exceptions for Remote Event Log Management must be enabled. For more information, see "Enabling Remote Management" in Chapter 4, "Managing Windows Server 2012."

Two general types of log files are used:

- **Windows logs**   Logs that the operating system uses to record general system events related to applications, security, setup, and system components

- **Applications and services logs**   Logs that specific applications and services use to record application-specific or service-specific events

Windows logs you'll see include

- **Application**   Contains events logged by applications. You'll find events in this log for Microsoft Exchange Server, SQL Server, Internet Information Services (IIS), and other installed applications. It is also used to record events from printers and, if you configured alert logging, alerts. The default location is %SystemRoot%\System32\Winevt\Logs\Application.Evtx. The default log size is 20,480 KBs.

- **Forwarded Events**   When you configure event forwarding, this log records forwarded events from other servers. The default location is %SystemRoot%\System32\Config\ForwardedEvents.Evtx. The default log size is 20,480 KBs.

Chapter 10

- **Security** Contains events you set for auditing with local or global group policies. Depending on the auditing configuration, you'll find events for logon, logoff, privilege use, and shutdown, as well as general system events, such as the loading of the authentication package by the Local Security Authority (LSA). The default location is %SystemRoot%\System32\Winevt\Logs\Security.Evtx. The default log size is 131,072 KBs on domain controllers and 20,480 KBs on member servers.

> **Note**
>
> Only administrators are granted access to the Security log by default. If other users need to access the Security log, you must specifically grant them the Manage Auditing And The Security Log user rights. You can learn more about assigning user rights in Chapter 30, "Managing users, groups, and computers."

- **Setup** This log records events logged by the operating system or its components during setup and installation. The default location is %SystemRoot%\System32\Winevt\Logs\Setup.Evtx. The default log size is 1028 KBs.

- **System** Contains events logged by Windows Server and its components. You should routinely check this log for warnings and errors, especially those related to the failure of a service to start at bootup or the improper configuration of a service. The default location is %SystemRoot%\System32\Winevt\Logs\System.Evtx. The default log size is 20,480 KBs.

Applications and services logs you'll see include

- **DFS Replication** This log records distributed file system (DFS) replication activities. The default location is %SystemRoot%\System32\Winevt\Logs\DfsReplication.Evtx. The default log size is 15,168 KBs.

- **Directory Service** Contains events logged by Active Directory. The primary events relate to the Active Directory database and global catalogs. You'll find details on database consistency checks, online defragmentation, and updates. The default location is %SystemRoot%\System32\Winevt\Logs\Directory Service.Evtx.

- **DNS Server** Contains Domain Name System (DNS) queries, responses, and other DNS activities. You might also find details on activities that relate to DNS integration with Active Directory. The default location is %SystemRoot%\System32\Winevt\Logs\DNS Server.Evtx. The default log size is 16,384 KBs.

- **File Replication Service**    Contains events logged by the File Replication Service, a service used to replicate Active Directory changes to other domain controllers. You'll find details on any important events that took place while a domain controller attempted to update other domain controllers. The default location is %SystemRoot%\System32\Winevt\Logs\File Replication Service.Evtx. The default log size is 20,480 KBs.

- **Hardware Events**    When hardware subsystem event reporting is configured, this log records hardware events reported to the operating system. The default location is %SystemRoot%\System32\Config\HardwareEvents.Evtx. The default log size is 20,480 KBs.

- **Microsoft\Windows**    Logs that track events related to specific Windows services and features. Logs are organized by component type and event category. Operational logs track events generated by the standard operations of the related component. In some cases, you'll see supplemental logs for analysis, debugging, and recording administration-related tasks. Most of the related logs have a fixed default log size of 1028 KBs.

By default, the logs are sized as appropriate for the type of system you are working with and its configuration. In a standard configuration of Windows Server 2012, most logs are sized as listed previously. As shown, most logs have a fairly large maximum size. This includes the DNS Server, System, and Application logs. Because they are less critical, the Directory Service and File Replication Service logs on domain controllers have a maximum size of 1028 KBs. Because the Security log is so important, it is usually configured with a maximum size of 131,072 KBs on domain controllers and 20,480 KBs on member servers. Primarily, this is to allow the server to record a complete security audit trail for situations in which the server is under attack and a large number of security events are generated.

Windows Server 2012 logs are configured to overwrite old events as needed by default. So, when the log reaches its maximum size, the operating system overwrites old events with new events. If desired, you can have Windows automatically archive logs. In this configuration, when the maximum file size is reached, Windows archives the events by saving a copy of the current log in the default directory. Windows then creates a new log for storing current events.

You can also configure logs so that Windows never overwrites events. However, the problem with doing it that way is, when the maximum size is reached, events can't be overwritten and the system will generate an error message telling you that such and such an event log is full each time it tries to write an event—and you can quickly get to where there are dozens of these errors being displayed.

Chapter 10

> **Note**
>
> You can control the log configuration through Group Policy as well. This means changes you make in Group Policy, in turn, could change the maximum log size and which action to take when the maximum log size is reached. For more information about Group Policy, see Chapter 31, "Managing Group Policy."

## Accessing the event logs and viewing events

You can work with event logs in several ways. When you are working with Server Manager and select the Local Server node, the All Servers node, or a server group node, the right pane will have an Events panel. When you select the server you want to work with in the Servers panel, its events are listed in the Events panel, as shown in Figure 10-17. You can use this panel as follows:

- For a server you are logged on to locally, you can use the Events panel in the Local Server node or the All Servers node to view recent warning and error events in the application and system logs.

- Automatically created server group nodes are organized by server roles, such as AD DS or DNS, and you'll be able to view recent error and warning events in logs related to the server role, if applicable. Not all roles have associated logs, but some roles, like AD DS, have multiple associated logs.

- For custom server groups created by you or other administrators, you'll be able to use the related Events panel to view recent warning and error events in the application and system logs.

**EVENTS**
All events | 14 total

| Server Name | ID | Severity | Source |
|---|---|---|---|
| CORPSERVER28 | 10020 | Warning | Microsoft-Windows-DHCP-Server |
| CORPSERVER28 | 1056 | Warning | Microsoft-Windows-DHCP-Server |
| CORPSERVER28 | 1014 | Warning | Microsoft-Windows-DNS Client Events |
| CORPSERVER28 | 6038 | Warning | Microsoft-Windows-LSA |
| CORPSERVER28 | 12 | Warning | Microsoft-Windows-Time-Service |
| CORPSERVER28 | 1530 | Warning | Microsoft-Windows-User Profile Service |

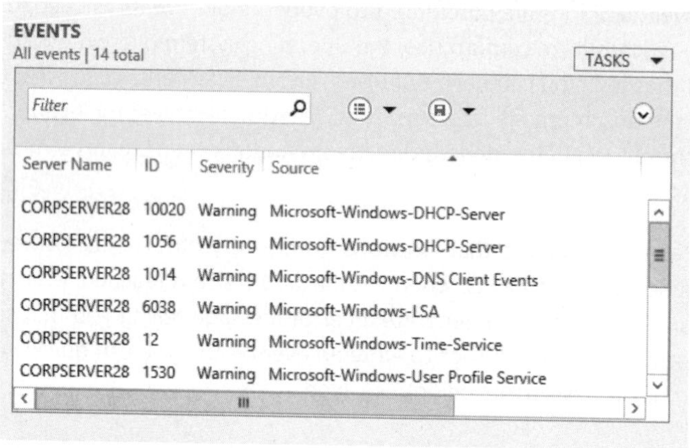

**Figure 10-17** Track errors and warnings for servers that have been added for management in Server Manager.

When you want to review all tracked events, you'll use Event Viewer, shown in Figure 10-18. Event Viewer is available from the Tools menu in Server Manager as a preconfigured console of the same name or as a standard add-in for the Computer Management console. To open Computer Management and access its Event Viewer add-in, select Computer Management from the Tools menu in Server Manager and then select Event Viewer under System Tools.

Event Viewer has custom views as well as standard views of logs. Using the custom Administrative Events view, you can view all errors and warnings for all logs. Using your own custom views, you can create views to surface particular types and categories of events from any logs you want to track. You can also access event logs directly to view all the events they contain.

You can use the following techniques to work with logs and custom views:

- To view all errors and warnings for all logs, expand Custom Views and then select Administrative Events. In the main pane, you should see a list of all warning and error events for the server.

- To view all errors and warnings for a specific server role, expand Custom Views, expand Server Roles, and then select the role to view. In the main pane, you should now see a list of all events for the selected role.

- To view summary information for Windows logs, select the Windows Logs node. You'll then see a list of available logs by name and type along with the number of events and log size.

- To view summary information for Applications and Services logs, select the Applications And Services Logs node. You'll then see a list of available logs by name and type along with the number of events and log size.

- To view events in a specific log, expand the Windows Logs node, the Applications And Services Logs node, or both nodes. Select the log you want to view, such as Application or System.

Chapter 10

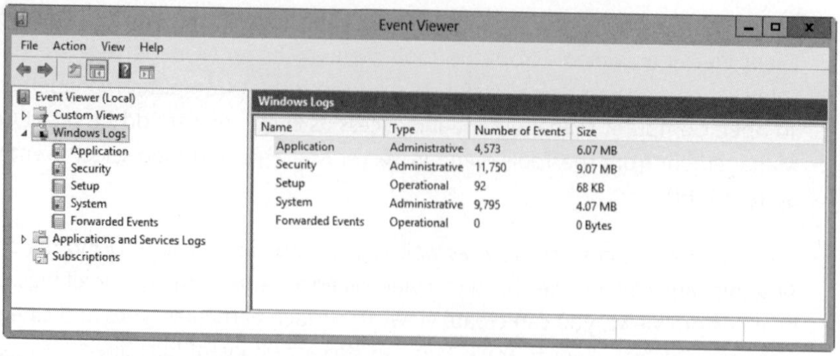

**Figure 10-18** The main view in Event Viewer lists the available logs and shows their current size.

As Figure 10-19 shows, individual event entries provide an overview of the event that took place. Each event is recorded according to the date and time the event took place as well as the event level. For all the logs except Security, the event levels are classified as Information, Warning, or Error. For the Security log, the event levels are classified as Audit Success or Audit Failure. These event levels have the following meanings:

- **Information**  Generally relates to a successful action, such as the success of a service starting up. If you configured Alert logging, the alerts are also recorded with this event type to show they've been triggered.

- **Warning**  Describes events that aren't critical but could be useful in preventing future system problems. Most warnings should be examined to determine whether a preventative measure should be taken.

- **Error**  Indicates a noncritical error or significant problem occurred, such as the failure of a service to start. All errors should be examined to determine what corrective measure should be taken to prevent the error from reoccurring.

- **Critical**  Indicates a critical error or highly significant problem occurred, such as the Cluster service shutting down because a quorum was lost. All critical errors should be examined to determine what corrective measure should be taken to prevent the critical error from reoccurring.

- **Audit Success**  Describes an audited security event that completed as requested, such as when a user logs on or logs off successfully.

- **Audit Failure**  Describes an audited security event that didn't complete as requested, such as when a user tries to log on and fails. Audit failure events can be useful in tracking down security issues.

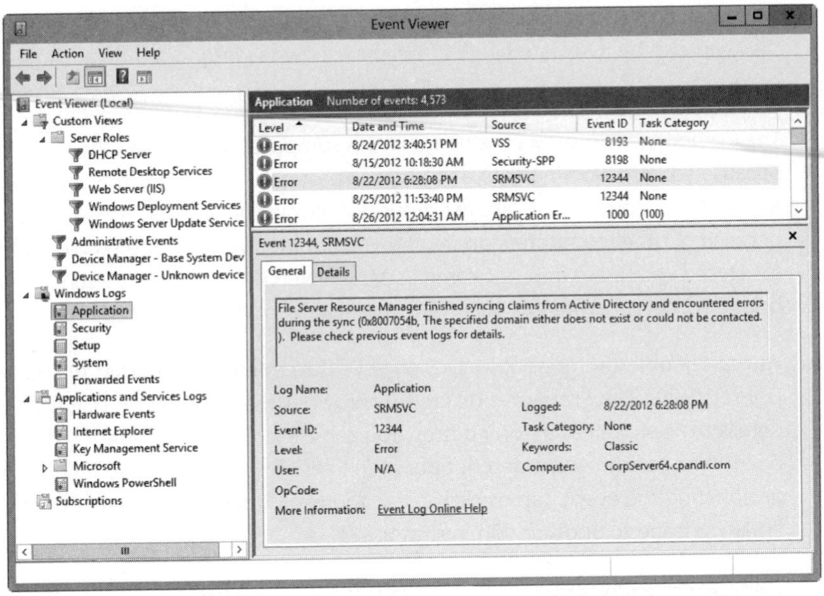

**Figure 10-19** Events are logged according to the date and time they occurred as well as by type.

> **Note**
> Any attempt by users, services, or applications to perform a task for which they don't have appropriate permissions can be recorded as an audit failure. If someone is trying to break into a system, you might see a large number of audit failure events. If a service or application doesn't have the permissions it needs to perform certain tasks, you might also see a large number of audit failure events.

Other pertinent information recorded with an event includes the event source, event ID, task category, user, and computer. The Source column lists the application, service, or component that logged the event. The Task Category column details the category of the event and is sometimes used to further describe the event. The Event ID column provides an identifier for the specific event that occurred. You can sometimes look up events in the Microsoft Knowledge Base to get more detailed information.

When you select an event, Event Viewer shows additional details in the lower pane, including a general description of the event and other fields of information. The User field shows the name of the user who was logged on when the event occurred (if applicable). If a server process triggered the event, the user name usually is that of the special identity that caused the event. This includes the special identities Anonymous Logon, Local Service,

Network Service, and System. Although events can have no user associated with them, they can also be associated with a specific user who was logged on at the time the event occurred.

The Computer field shows the name of the computer that caused the event to occur. Because you are working with a log from a particular computer, this is usually the account name of that computer. However, this is not always the case. Some events can be triggered because of other computers on the network. Some events triggered by the local machine are stored with the computer name as MACHINENAME. For some events, any binary data or error code generated by the event is available on the Details tab.

You can double-tap or double-click any event to open its Properties dialog box. (See Figure 10-20.) The Properties dialog box provides the information that is available in the details pane as well as a Copy button you can click to copy the event data to the clipboard. Most of the event descriptions aren't easy to understand, so if you need a little help deciphering the event, tap or click Copy. You can then paste the event description into an email message to another administrator.

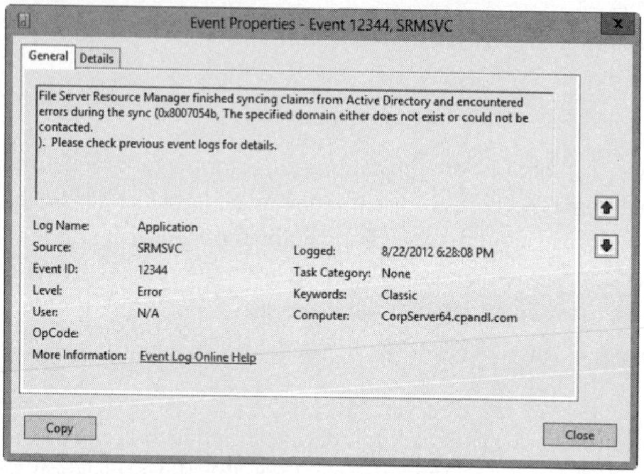

**Figure 10-20** Event details include a description of the event and, in some cases, binary data generated by the event.

> **Note**
>
> Within every event description is a Help And Support Center link that you can click. This link provides access to the Microsoft website where you can query for any additional information that might be available on the event.

## Viewing event logs on remote systems

You can use Event Viewer to view events on other computers on your network. Start Event Viewer, press and hold or right-click Event Viewer (Local) in the left pane, and then choose Connect To Another Computer. In the Select Computer dialog box, shown in Figure 10-21, type the domain name or Internet Protocol (IP) address of the computer for which you want to view the event log and then tap or click OK. Or you can tap or click Browse to search for the computer you want to use. If you need to specify logon credentials, select the Connect As Another User check box and then tap or click the Set User button. Afterward, type the user name and password to use for logon, and then tap or click OK.

> **Note**
> Keep in mind that you must be logged on as an administrator or be a member of the Administrators group to view events on a remote computer. You must also configure Windows Firewall on the local computer to allow your outbound connection and the remote computer to allow your inbound connection.

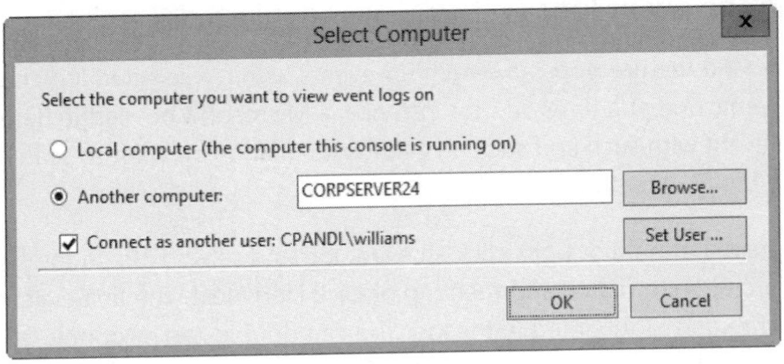

Figure 10-21  Connect to a remote computer.

# INSIDE OUT  Setting a remote computer as the focus for a management tool

By default, Microsoft Management Consoles (MMCs) connect to the local computer. By pressing and holding or right-clicking the console root in either the Computer Management console or the Event Viewer console and selecting Connect To Another Computer, you can use the options provided in the Select Computer dialog box to connect to a remote computer. Server Manager provides a shortcut for remote management as well. Here, select All Servers in the left pane, and then press and hold or right-click the remote server to which you want to connect in the Servers panel. You'll then see a list of tools you can open and connect automatically to the selected remote computer.

# Sorting, finding, and filtering events

Event Viewer provides several ways for you to organize and search for events in the logs. You can sort events based on date or other stored information. You can search a particular event log for specific events and view events one at a time. You can also filter events so that only the specific events you want to see are shown.

## Sorting the event logs

By default, logs are sorted so that the newest events are listed first. If you'd rather see the oldest events first, you can do this by tapping or clicking View, pointing to Sort By, and then selecting Date And Time. Or you can simply tap or click the Date And Time column header. This change must be made for each log in which you want to see the oldest events first.

You can also sort events based on information in other columns. For example, if you wanted to sort the events based on the event level, you would tap or click the Level column header.

## Searching the event logs

By using the Find feature, you can search for events within a selected log and view matching events one at a time. Say, for instance, a Microsoft Knowledge Base article says to look for an event with such and such an event source and you want to search for it quickly. You can use the Find feature to do this.

To search, press and hold or right-click an event log and select Find. In the Find dialog box, type the search text to match and then tap or click Find Next. The first event that matches the search criteria is highlighted in the log. You can double-tap or double-click the event to get more detailed information or tap or click Find Next to find the next match.

## Filtering the event logs

The Find option works well if you want to perform quick searches, such as for a single event of a specific type. If you want to perform an extended search, however, such as when you want to review all events of a particular type, there's a better way to do it and that's to create a filtered view so that only the specific events you want to see are shown.

Windows creates several filtered views of the event logs for you automatically. In Event Viewer, filtered views are listed under the Custom Views node. When you select the Administrative Events node, you'll see a list of all errors and warnings for all logs. When you expand the Server Roles node and then select a role-specific view, you'll see a list of all events for the selected role.

You can create and work with filtered views in several different ways:

- Create a custom view by filtering the events in a specific log, and save this filtered view for later use. Simply press and hold or right-click the log and select Create Custom View. This displays the Create Custom View dialog box, as shown in Figure 10-22. Choose the filter options you want to use, as described in Table 10-3, and then tap or click OK. If you are trying to create a filter for more than 10 logs (and really want to do this), tap or click Yes when warned about the possible performance impact. In the Save Filter To Custom View dialog box, type a name and description for the view. Select where to save the custom view. By default, custom views are saved under the Custom view node. You can create a new node by tapping or clicking New Folder, entering the name of the new folder, and then tapping or clicking OK. Tap or click OK to close the Save Filter To Custom View dialog box.

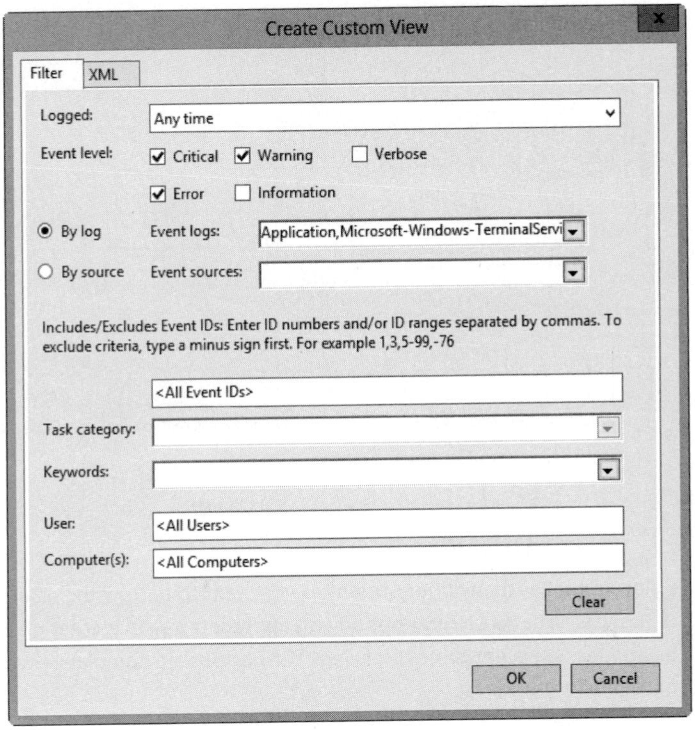

**Figure 10-22** Create a custom view for an events log.

- Create a temporary view by filtering the events in a specific log. Simply select the log, and then press and hold or right-click and select Filter Current Log. This displays the Filter Current Log dialog box, as shown in Figure 10-23. Choose the filter options you want to use, as described in Table 10-3, and then tap or click OK. After you apply the filter, only events with the options you specify are displayed in the selected event log. For the rest of the current Event Viewer session, the filter is applied to the selected log and you know this because the upper portion of the main pane shows you are working with a filtered log.

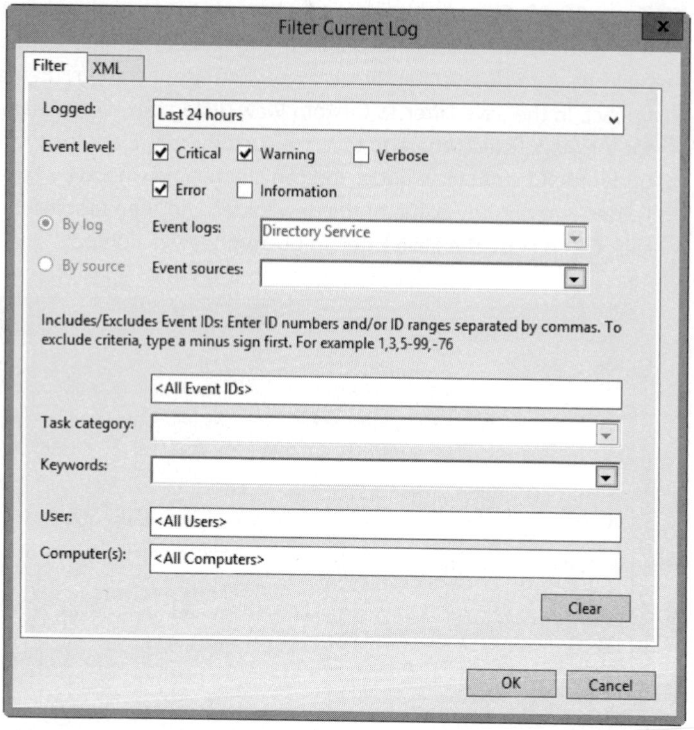

**Figure 10-23**  Create a temporary view.

## Set filter options

You can set as many filter options as you want to narrow the results. Keep in mind, however, that each filter option you apply sets a search criterion that must be matched for an event to be displayed. The options are cumulative, so an event must match all filter options.

**TABLE 10-3** Find and filter options for event logging

| Option | Description |
|--------|-------------|
| Computer | Includes all events associated with a particular computer. Usually, this is the name of the computer whose logs you are working with. |
| Event ID | Includes or excludes events with the event IDs you specify. Enter ID numbers or ID ranges separated by commas. To exclude an event, enter a minus sign before the event ID. |
| Event Level | Allows you to include or exclude events by level. The most important event levels are warnings, which indicate that something might pose a future problem and might need to be examined, and errors, which indicate a fatal error or significant problem occurred. |
| Event Sources | Includes events only from specified sources, such as an application, service, or component that logged the event. |
| Event Logs | Includes events only from specified logs. When working with a custom log view, the log you press and hold or right-click is selected automatically and you can't choose additional logs. |
| Logged | With filters, all events from the first to the last are displayed by default. You can choose to include events from the Last Hour, Last 12 Hours, Last 24 Hours, Last 7 Days, Last 30 Days, or a custom range. |
| Task Category | Includes events only within a given category. The categories available change based on the event source you choose. |
| User | Includes events associated with a particular user account that was logged on when the event was triggered. Server processes can log events with the special identities Anonymous Logon, Local Service, Network Service, and System. Not all events have a user associated with them. |

You can apply a filter to a custom view as well as to a log. To filter a custom view, press and hold or right-click the view and then select Filter Current Custom View. Choose the filter options you want to use and then tap or click OK. For the rest of the current Event Viewer session, the filter is applied to the selected view and you know this because the upper portion of the main pane shows you are working with a filtered view.

If you later want to clear a filter that is applied to a view or log, press and hold or right-click the log and select Clear Filter. Another option is to save the filtered view as a custom view so that you can access it the next time you open Event Viewer. To do this, press and hold or right-click the filtered log or custom view and select Save Filter To Custom View. Afterward, type a name and description for the view. Select where to save the custom view. By default, custom views are saved under the Custom view node. You can create a new node by tapping or clicking New Folder, entering the name of the new folder, and then tapping or clicking OK. Tap or click OK to close the Save Filter To Custom View dialog box.

# Archiving event logs

In most cases, you'll want to have several months' worth of log data available in case you must go back through the logs to troubleshoot a problem. One way to do this, of course, is to set the log size so that it is large enough to accommodate this. However, this usually isn't practical because individual logs can grow quite large. So, as part of your routine, you might want to archive the log files on critical systems periodically, such as for domain controllers or application servers.

To archive logs automatically, press and hold or right-click the log and select Properties. In the Properties dialog box, select Archive The Log When Full, Do Not Overwrite Events. To create a log archive manually, press and hold or right-click the log in the left pane of Event Viewer, and then select Save All Events As. In the Save As dialog box, select a directory and a log file name. Event Log (*.evtx) is the default file type. This saves the file in event log format for access in Event Viewer, but it can be used only when saving logs from the local computer. You can also select .txt to save the log in tab-delimited text format, such as for accessing it in a text editor. For importing the log data into a spreadsheet or database, select .csv to save the log in comma-delimited text format. Select .xml to save the log in extensible markup language (XML) format. After you select a log format, tap or click Save.

Logs saved in Event Log format (.evtx) can be reopened in Event Viewer at any time. To do this, press and hold or right-click the Event Viewer node in the left pane of Event Viewer and choose Open Saved Log. Use the Open Saved Log dialog box to select a directory and a log file. By default, the Event Log Files format is selected on the File Name list. This ensures that logs saved as .evtx, .evt, and .etl are listed. You can also filter the list by selecting a specific file type. When you tap or click Open, Windows displays the Open Saved Log dialog box. Type a name and description for the saved log. Select where to open the log in Event View. By default, saved logs are listed under Saved Logs. You can create a new node by tapping or clicking New Folder, entering the name of the new folder, and then tapping or clicking OK. Tap or click Open to close the Open Saved Log dialog box. Windows loads the saved event log into Event Viewer and adds a related entry to the list of available logs in the left pane, as shown in Figure 10-24.

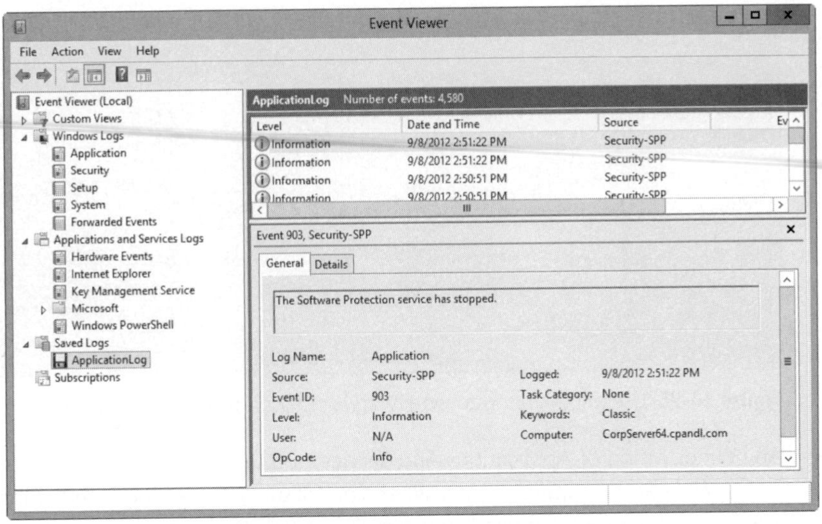

Figure 10-24  Archived logs can be reopened in Event Viewer.

If you later want to remove the saved log from Event Viewer, press and hold or right-click the log and select Delete. When prompted to confirm, tap or click Yes. The saved log file still exists in its original location on the hard disk but no longer is displayed in Event Viewer.

## Tracking events using Windows PowerShell

When you are working with a specific system or trying to track down issues, Event Viewer is an excellent tool to use and should be your tool of choice. As you've seen, Event Viewer can also be used to access logs on remote systems. No single command-line tool included with Windows Server 2012 provides the same level of functionality, though the Power-Shell cmdlet get-eventlog does come close. You can use get-eventlog to obtain detailed information from the event logs.

Because get-eventlog is a text-based rather than a graphical utility, it will, in most cases, use fewer system resources than Event Viewer. On systems for which you are very concerned about resource usage and the possibility of bogging down a system through your interactive logon, you might initially want to track events by using get-eventlog.

As Figure 10-25 shows, get-eventlog's standard output provides the essential information about events. To run get-eventlog, access a PowerShell prompt, and then type **get-eventlog** followed by the name of the event log you want to examine, such as **application**. If the log name contains spaces, you must enclose the log name in quotation marks, such as **get-eventlog "directory service"**.

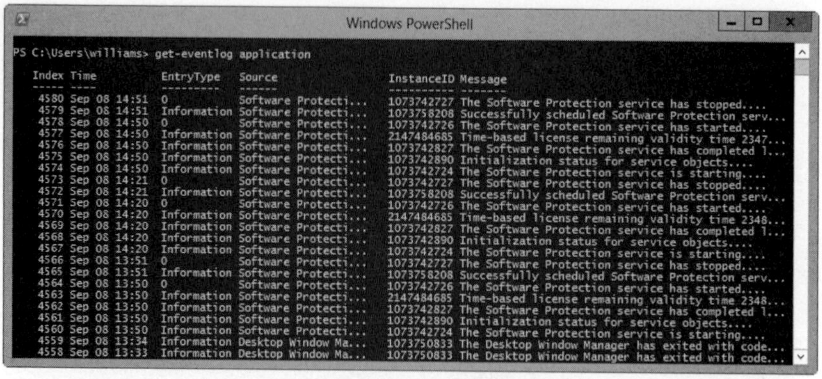

**Figure 10-25**  Use get-eventlog to work with event logs at the command line.

Any Windows log or Applications And Services log that you can work with in Event Viewer is accessible at the command line. When you follow get-eventlog with the log name, the *–logname* parameter is implied. You can also specify the *–logname* parameter directly as shown in this example:

```
get-eventlog –logname security
```

By default, get-eventlog returns every event in the specified event log from the newest to the oldest. In most cases, this is simply too much information and you'll need to filter the events to get a usable amount of data. One way to filter the event logs is to specify that you want to see details about only the newest events. For example, you might want to see only the 50 or 500 newest events in a log.

Using the *–newest* parameter, you can return only the newest events. The following example lists the 50 newest events in the security log:

```
get-eventlog security -newest 50
```

As shown in Figure 10-25, get-eventlog displays several properties in column format, including Index, TimeGenerated (listed with the column heading Time), Source, InstanceID, EntryType (listed with the column heading Type), and Message. To help make sense of the logs, you might want to group events by type, source, or event ID. When you group events by type, you can more easily separate informational events from critical, warning, and error events. When you group by source, you can more easily track events from specific sources. When you group by event ID, you can more easily correlate the recurrence of specific events.

You can group events by *source, eventid, entrytype,* and *timegenerated* using the following technique:

1. Get the events you want to work with and store them in the *$e* variable by entering

   ```
   $e = get-eventlog -newest 500 -logname application
   ```

2. Use the group-object cmdlet to group the event objects stored in *$e* by a specified property. In this example, you group by *eventid*:

   ```
   $e | group-object -property eventid
   ```

Another way to work with events is to sort them according to a specific property. You can sort by *source, eventid, entrytype,* or *timegenerated* using the following technique:

1. Get the events you want to work with and store them in the *$e* variable by entering

   ```
   $e = get-eventlog -newest 100 -logname application
   ```

2. Use the sort-object cmdlet to sort the event objects stored in *$e* by a specified property. In this example, you sort by *eventtype*:

   ```
   $e | sort-object -property entrytype
   ```

Finally, you might also want to match specific text in a specified property. For example, you might want to return only error events. To do this, you would search the *EntryType* property for occurrences of the word *error*. Here is an example:

1. Get the events you want to work with and store them in the *$e* variable by entering

   ```
   $e = get-eventlog -newest 500 -logname application
   ```

2. Use the where-object cmdlet to search for specific text in a named property of the event objects stored in *$e*. In this example, you match events with the *error* entry type:

   ```
   $e | where-object {$_.EntryType -match "error"}
   ```

The where-object cmdlet uses a search algorithm that is not case sensitive, meaning you could enter Error, error, or ERROR to match error events. You can also search for warning, critical, and information events. Because where-object considers partial text matches to be valid, you don't want to enter the full event type. You could also search for warn, crit, or info, as shown here:

```
$e = get-eventlog -newest 500 -logname application
$e | where-object {$_.EntryType -match "warn"}
```

Chapter 10

You can use where-object with other event object properties as well. The following example searches for event sources containing the text *.NET*:

```
$e = get-eventlog -newest 500 -logname application
$e | where-object {$_.Source -match ".NET"}
```

The following example searches for event ID 1101:

```
$e = get-eventlog -newest 500 -logname application
$e | where-object {$_.Source -match "1101"}
```

## Using subscriptions and forwarded events

In an enterprise, you might also want servers to forward specific events to central event-logging servers. To do this, you configure and enable event forwarding on the applicable servers and then you create subscriptions to the forwarded events on your central event logging server or servers.

In a domain, you can configure forwarding and collection of forwarded events by following these steps:

1. To configure forwarding, log on to all source computers and type **winrm quickconfig** at an elevated command prompt. This creates a WinRM listener on HTTP://* to accept WS-Man requests to any IP address on the source computer. When prompted to confirm, press **Y**.

2. To configure collection, type **wecutil qc** at an elevated command prompt and then press **Y** when prompted. This starts the Windows Event Collector Service and configures this service to use the delayed-start mode.

3. Add the computer account of the collector computer to the local Administrators group on each of the source computers. In Local Users And Computers, press and hold or right-click Administrators and select Add To Group. In the Properties dialog box, tap or click Add. In the Select Users, Computers, Or Groups dialog box, tap or click Object Types. In the Object Types dialog box, select Computers and then tap or click OK. In the Select Users, Computers, Or Groups dialog box, type the account name of the collector computer and then tap or click OK twice. Repeat this process as necessary.

You can create a subscription on the central logging server to collect forwarded events by following these steps:

1. Open Event Viewer, and connect to the central event-logging server. Afterward, press and hold or right-click the Subscriptions node and select Create Subscription.

2. In the Subscription Properties dialog box, shown in Figure 10-26, type a name for the subscription, such as **All File Servers**. Optionally, enter a description.

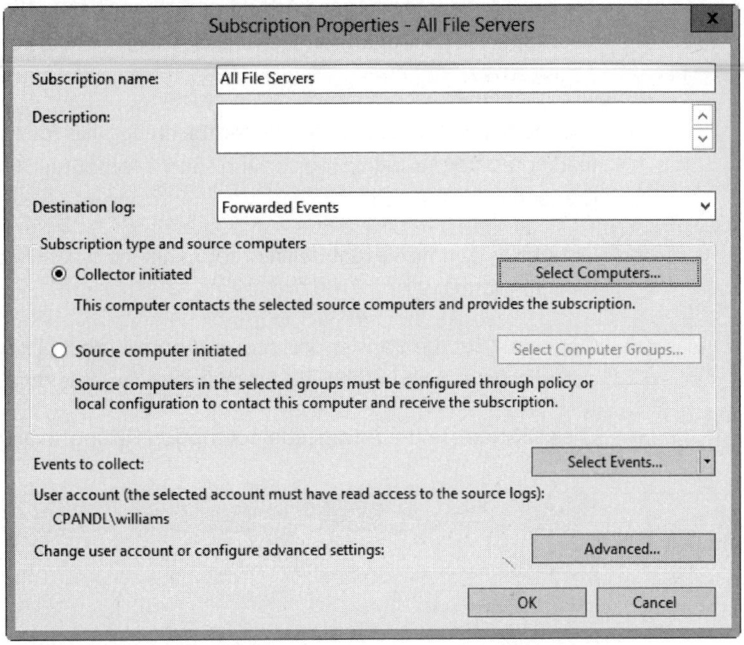

**Figure 10-26** Create a subscription to collect forwarded events.

3. The Forwarded Events log is selected as the destination log by default. Generally, this is the log you'll want to use.

4. Collector-initiated event forwarding is the easiest to configure and is the default setting. To specify the computers that forward events to the server, tap or click Select Computers. In the Computers dialog box, tap or click Add Domain Computers. In the Select Computer dialog box, type the account name of a computer that is forwarding events and then tap or click OK twice. Repeat this process as necessary.

5. Tap or click Select Events. In the Query Filter dialog box, select the filter options and logs to use and then tap or click OK.

6. If you added the computer account of the collector computer to the local Administrators group on each of the source computers, you can use this machine

account to collect events. Alternatively, you can use the permissions of a specific user account by doing the following:

a. Tap or click Advanced. In the Advanced Subscription Settings dialog box, select Specific User and then tap or click User And Password, as shown in Figure 10-27.

b. Use the dialog box provided to enter the credentials for an account that has read access to the source logs on the source computers. Click OK to close the Credentials dialog box.

c. Optionally, optimize event delivery for minimizing bandwidth usage or to minimize latency.

d. Optionally, set the transfer protocol and port. With HTTP, which is unsecure, the default port is 5985. With HTTPS, which is secure, the default port is 5986.

e. Click OK to close the Advanced Subscription Settings dialog box.

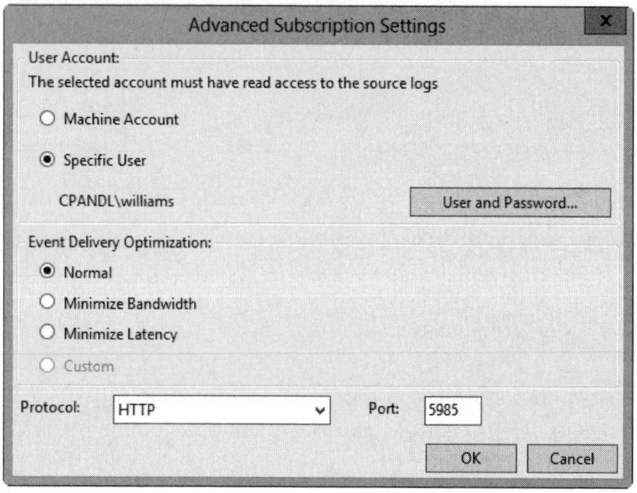

**Figure 10-27** Configuring a specific user for collection.

f. Tap or click OK to create the subscription. Now when you access the destination log, you'll see the forwarded events.

# CHAPTER 11

# Comprehensive performance analysis and logging

MICROSOFT Windows Server 2012 provides many tools to help you track performance. In the previous chapter, we looked at tuning performance through configuration settings; using Task Manager to track running processes, users, and network utilization; and using the event logs to track important occurrences recorded by the operating system. Although these tools are excellent and do their jobs well, you might need to dig deeper to establish comprehensive performance baselines, diagnose complex system problems, and optimize system performance.

The key comprehensive monitoring and optimization tools and features available include the following:

- **Performance Monitor**   Performance Monitor can be used to track and display performance information in real time. It gathers information on any performance parameters you configured for monitoring and presents it using a graphical display.

- **Reliability Monitor**   Tracks changes to the system and compares them to changes in system stability, thus giving you a graphical representation of the relationship between changes in the system configuration and changes in system stability.

- **Resource Monitor**   Displays detailed information about resource usage for the server, allowing you to isolate resources used by specific processes.

- **Data Collector Sets and Reports**   Data collector sets can be considered to be the logging counterpart to Performance Monitor. By using data collector sets, you can record performance information in real time and store it in a log so that it can be analyzed in a report later.

- **Performance Counter Alerts**   Performance counter alerts can be used to notify users when certain events occur or when certain performance thresholds are reached. For example, you could configure a performance alert that lets you know when the C drive is running low on free space or the central processing unit (CPU) is operating at 95 percent or more of capacity.

Before discussing each of these tools in turn, let's look at how you can establish performance baselines.

# Establishing performance baselines

Resource Monitor, Reliability Monitor, and Performance Monitor are the tools of choice for monitoring a system's reliability and performance. One of the key reasons for tracking performance information is to establish a baseline for a computer that allows you to compare past performance with current performance. There are several types of baselines you can use, including the following:

- **Postinstallation baselines**   A postinstallation baseline is a performance level that is meant to represent the way a computer performs after installing all the roles, role services, features, and applications that will be used on the system.

- **Typical usage baselines**   A typical usage baseline is a performance level that is meant to represent average usage conditions and serve as a starting point against which you can measure future performance.

- **Test baselines**   A test baseline is a performance level that you use during testing of a system. In the test lab, you might want to simulate peak usage loads and test how the system performs under these conditions.

Although it is important to obtain postinstallation and typical usage baseline values, the more important of the two is the typical usage baseline. This is the baseline you get when you simulate user loads or when users actually start working with a server. Ideally, it represents typical or average loads. After you have a typical usage baseline, you can gather information in the future to try to determine how resource usage has changed and how the computer is performing comparatively.

To be able to establish a baseline, you must collect a representative set of performance statistics. By that, I mean collect the data that you actually need to determine resource usage and performance in future scenarios. If possible, you should also collect several data samples at the same time each day over a period of several days. This will give you a more meaningful data sample.

You must work to keep the baseline in sync with how the server is used. As you install new roles, role services, features, and applications, you must establish new baselines. This ensures that future comparisons with the baseline are accurate and that they use the most current system configuration to determine how resource usage has changed and how the computer is performing comparatively.

## Tracking per-process resource usage

As discussed in Chapter 10, "Performance monitoring and tuning," you can use Task Manager to determine the overall utilization of system resources. The Processes and Details tabs in Task Manager provide information about resources being used by running processes. What's missing from Task Manager, however, is the ability to take a deep look at how processes are using resources, and this deep-look capability is exactly what Resource Monitor provides.

You can start Resource Monitor by selecting the related option on the Tools menu in Server Manager. Alternatively, type **Resource Monitor** in the Apps Search box and press Enter.

When you start Resource Monitor, shown in Figure 11-1, you'll see that the statistics provided are organized into five general categories:

- Overview

- CPU

- Memory

- Disk

- Network

Each of these categories can be used for comprehensive performance analysis, and in the sections that follow, I'll show you how.

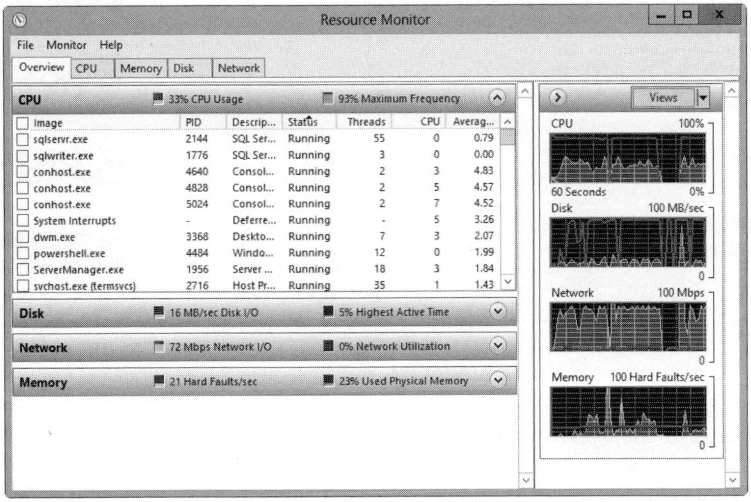

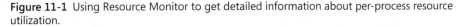

**Figure 11-1** Using Resource Monitor to get detailed information about per-process resource utilization.

## Getting an overview of resource utilization

The Overview tab in Resource Monitor, shown in Figure 11-2, provides a detailed overview of resource utilization. Top-level utilization statistics are tracked in the graphs and on the panel bars. As per the legend shown on the panel bars, the values are plotted in either green or blue on the corresponding graph. The statistics tracked include the following:

- % CPU usage

- CPU maximum frequency

- Disk I/O bytes per second

- Disk % highest active time

- Network I/O bytes per second

- % Network utilization

- Memory hard faults per second

- % Physical memory used

**Figure 11-2**  The Overview tab in Resource Monitor provides an overview of the resource usage.

At first glance, the information provided seems similar to that available in Task Manager. What's different, however, is that when you select one or more processes on the CPU panel, you see related utilization statistics for the processes on the Disk panel, Network panel, and Memory panel. You also see related activity plotted in orange on the CPU, Disk, Network, and Memory graphs.

> **Note**
> The CPU, Disk, Network, and Memory panels show a subset of the information available on the related tabs. Your process selections are applied globally so that you can determine exactly how the selected processes are using CPU, disk, network, and memory resources.

In the example, I selected three processes for tracking: sqlservr.exe, System, and sqlwriter.exe. I chose these processes because I already determined in Task Manager that these were some of the most active processes on the server and I wanted to determine how these processes were affecting the server. I quickly learned that these processes weren't affecting the CPU nearly as much as I thought. Although the processor utilization on the server was performing well at about 70 percent, these processes seemed to be using few actual CPU resources. On the other hand, they were high consumers of disk and network resources (and, in fact, accounted for nearly all of the disk and network activity).

By examining the disk and network activity, I was able to identify exactly which activities were using these resources. Although some of the disk I/O activity was related to SQL Server, the bulk of the activity was related to large data transfers. One data transfer in particular involved a large data set that was being moved from another file server to the server I was analyzing. You can see this in the three entries under Disk and the first entry under Network. Under Disk, a large write is in progress for the C:\Shares folder. Under Network, a large data set is being received from another server.

## Tracking per-process CPU utilization

The CPU tab in Resource Monitor shows the current CPU utilization and the maximum CPU frequency. If you expand the Processes panel (by tapping or clicking the options button), as shown in Figure 11-3, you'll see a list of currently running executables. Each process is listed according to the following categories:

- **Average CPU**  The average percentage of CPU utilization for the process in the last minute

- **CPU**  The percentage of CPU utilization for the process (across all physical and logical processors)

- **Description**  The name of the process (and sometimes other information as well)

- **Image**   The name of the process or executable running the process

- **PID**   The numeric identifier for the process

- **Status**   The execution status of the process

- **Threads**   The number of threads that the process is using

**Figure 11-3** The CPU tab in Resource Monitor provides detailed per-process information about CPU utilization.

If you press and hold or right-click any column header and then choose Select Columns, you'll see a dialog box that allows you to add columns to the CPU panel. The additional columns that are available include the following:

- **Average Cycle**   The average percentage of CPU cycle time for the process (over a 60-second interval).

- **Cycle**   The current percentage of CPU cycle time being used by the process.

- **Elevated**   The elevation status of the process. An entry of Yes indicates an elevated process.

- **Operating System Context**   The operating system context in which the process is running, such as Windows Server 2012 or Windows Vista.

- **Platform**   The platform on which the process is running, either 32-bit or 64-bit.

- **User Name**   The name of the user or service that is running the process.

Select one or more processes on the Processes panel to get more detailed information about how those processes are using CPU resources. As you select processes for tracking, keep in mind your selections are global. The same selections will appear in the other tabs in Resource Monitor.

When you select one or more processes for tracking, you'll see additional details on these panels:

- **Services**   Shows the name of the service running a process or processes, along with process identifiers, the status, descriptions of the services, percentage of CPU utilization, and the average percentage of CPU utilization.

- **Associated Handles**   Shows the names of the handles associated with the selected processes, listed by the executable name of the process, the process identifier, the handle type, and the handle file path.

- **Associated Modules**   Shows the names of modules loaded by the selected processes, listed by the executable name of the process, the process identifier, the module name, the module version, and the module file path.

Use this information to help you identify which services are running processes, as well as which handles and modules a process is using. No additional details can be added to the Services, Associated Handles, or Associated Modules panels.

**TROUBLESHOOTING**

**Resolve the CPU performance issue**

For troubleshooting performance issues related to a server's processors, you might want to evaluate whether it makes sense to move applications and services from an overutilized server to another, less-utilized server. You also might want to evaluate whether additional processing power is needed to ensure adequate performance. Faster or additional processors might resolve a performance issue related to high CPU utilization.

## Tracking per-process memory utilization

The Memory tab in Resource Monitor shows how processes are using memory, focused primarily on physical memory. As shown in Figure 11-4, the percent utilization of physical

Chapter 11

memory, the current commit charge, and the hard memory faults are graphed over time. On the Processes panel, individual processes are listed by the following categories:

- **Image**    The name of the process or executable running the process.

- **PID**    The numeric identifier for the process.

- **Hard Faults/Sec**    The average number of hard memory faults per second in the last minute.

- **Commit**    The commit charge for the process, measured in kilobytes (KB). The commit charge represents the amount of virtual memory reserved by the operating system for the process.

- **Working Set**    The amount of physical memory the process is currently using.

- **Shareable**    The nonprivate working set for the process, representing the amount of physical memory in use by the process that can be shared with other processes.

- **Private**    The private working set for the process, representing the amount of physical memory in use by the process that cannot be shared with other processes.

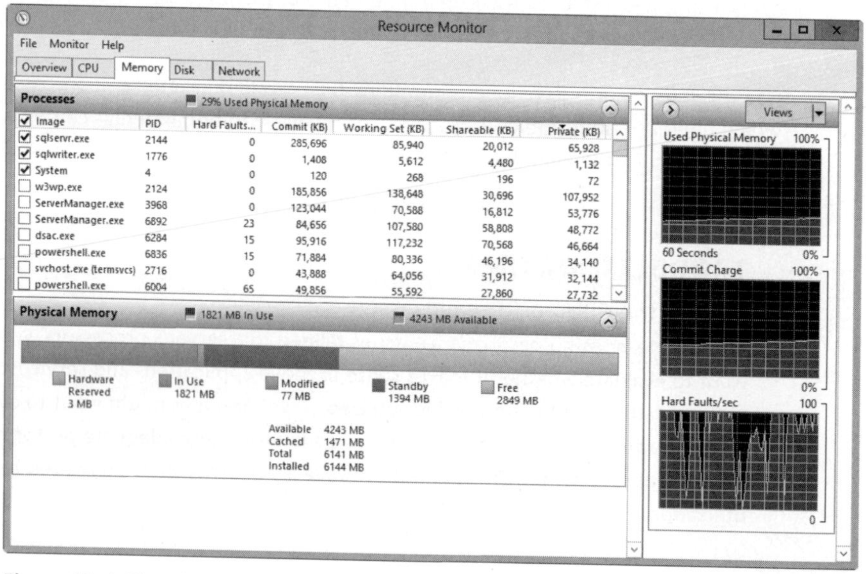

**Figure 11-4** The Memory tab in Resource Monitor provides detailed per-process information about CPU utilization.

On the Physical Memory panel, you'll see a graph showing the composition of in-use and available memory and related usage statistics. Although the details provided are similar to those provided in the Task Manager Performance tab, they are more precise and you'll see specific values listed for the following:

- **Available Memory**   The nonallocated physical memory (which includes the system's standby memory and free memory).

- **Cached Memory**   Part of the available physical memory. This memory is used for system caching (and includes the system's modified memory and standby memory).

- **Free Memory**   Nonallocated memory and part of the available memory. This memory doesn't contain any valuable data and will be used first whenever more memory is needed.

- **Hardware Reserved Memory**   Memory reserved for BIOS and some drivers for other peripherals.

- **In-Use Memory**   Currently allocated physical memory. The size of the paging file is the difference between the current commit charge and the in-use memory.

- **Installed Memory**   The total amount of physical memory installed on the system, inclusive of the hardware-reserved memory.

- **Modified Memory**   Part of the cached memory. This memory needs to be written to disk before becoming available.

- **Standby Memory**   Part of the cached memory. This memory contains cached data and code not actively being used.

- **Total Memory**   The total amount of physical memory installed on the system, not including hardware-reserved memory.

Use this information to help you identify how processes are using memory and whether there are performance issues related to memory. No additional details can be added regarding memory usage.

## TROUBLESHOOTING

### Resolve the memory performance issue

For troubleshooting performance issues related to memory, you might want to evaluate whether it makes sense to move applications and services from a highly utilized server to another, less-utilized server. You also might want to evaluate whether additional physical or virtual memory is needed to ensure adequate performance. Additional memory might resolve a performance issue related to high memory utilization.

# Tracking per-process disk utilization

The Disk tab in Resource Monitor shows the number of kilobytes per second being read from or written to disk and the highest percentage usage. As shown in Figure 11-5, processes with disk activity are listed by name, process ID, number of bytes being read per minute, number of bytes being written per minute, and total read/write bytes per second.

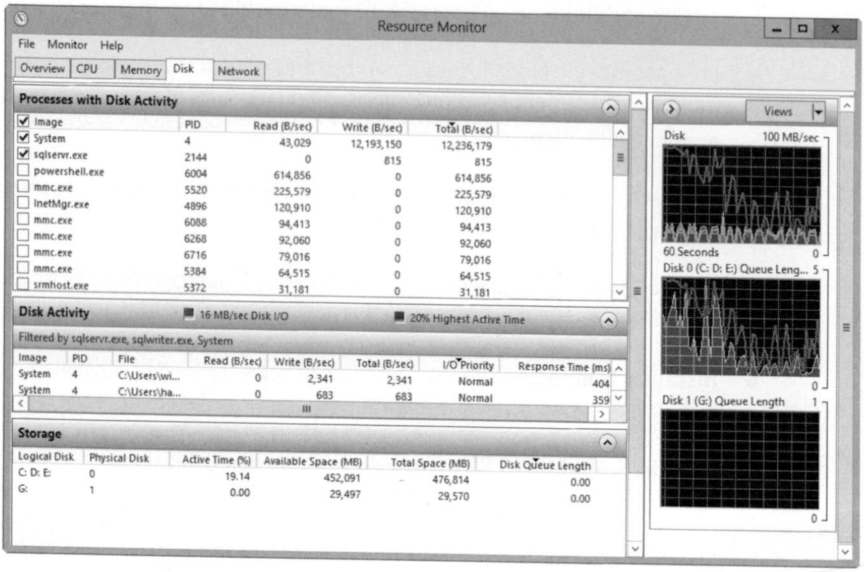

**Figure 11-5** The Disk tab in Resource Monitor provides detailed per-process information about CPU utilization.

Select one or more processes on the Processes With Disk Activity panel to get more detailed information about how those processes are using disk resources. As you select processes for tracking, keep in mind your selections are global. The same selections will appear in the other tabs of Resource Monitor.

When you select one or more processes for tracking, you'll see additional details on the Disk Activity and Storage panels. To help you quickly identify disk-related performance issues, the Disk Activity panel identifies the files a particular process is reading or writing along with the bytes read per second, bytes written per second, and total read/write bytes per second for each file. Also shown are the I/O priority and the response time.

The Storage panel provides information about the underlying logical and physical disks. The Logical Disk column shows the drive letters of logical disks with I/O activity. The Physical Disk column identifies the specific physical disk where the logical disks were created. If there are performance issues with a server's disks and files are being read from and written to multiple logical disks residing on the same physical disk (or a relative few physical disks as compared to the number of available physical disks), you might be able to improve performance by changing the storage configuration so that I/O activity is spread more evenly across the server's physical disks. You also can try to balance the workload by moving applications and services from an overutilized server to another, less-utilized server.

## Tracking per-process network utilization

The Network tab in Resource Monitor shows the current network bandwidth utilization in kilobytes and the percentage of total bandwidth utilization. As shown in Figure 11-6, processes that are transferring or have transferred data on the network are listed by name, process ID, number of bytes being sent per minute, number of bytes received per minute, and total bytes sent or received per minute.

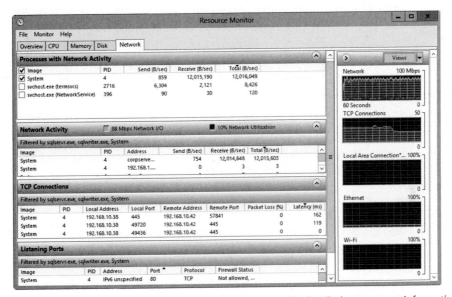

**Figure 11-6** The Network tab in Resource Monitor provides detailed per-process information about network utilization.

Select one or more processes on the Processes With Network Activity panel to get more detailed information about how those processes are using network resources. As you select processes for tracking, keep in mind your selections are global. The same selections will appear in the other tabs of Resource Monitor.

When you select one or more processes for tracking, you'll see additional details on these panels:

- **Network Activity**    Identifies the name or IP address of the computer to which a process is connected, along with the average number of bytes sent per second in the last minute, the average number of bytes received per second in the last minute, and the total number of bytes transferred per second in the last minute.

- **TCP Connections** Shows the TCP connections for processes with network activity according to the local addresses, local ports, remote addresses, and remote ports being used. Also shown are the percentage of packets lost during the connection and the roundtrip latency in milliseconds.

- **Listening Ports** Shows the specific listening ports being used by processes with network activity, along with the firewall status.

If there are performance issues with a server's network connections, you might be able to improve performance by installing multiple network adapters in the server and teaming the network cards. You configure network interface card (NIC) teaming using Server Manager, either through a local logon or using a remote desktop connection. Either way, once you are logged on to the server, you can configure NIC teaming by selecting Local Server in the left pane of Server Manager and then tapping or clicking the link provided for NIC teaming. Next, tap or click Tasks under Teams and then select New Team. Enter a name for the teamed network adapters, such as Team Set 1, select the member adapters, and then tap or click OK.

If you can't add or team network adapters, you can try to reduce the server's network activity by moving applications and services from an overutilized server to another, less-utilized server.

## Tracking the overall reliability of the server

You can use Performance Monitor and Reliability Monitor to track the overall reliability of a server. Performance Monitor graphically displays statistics for the set of performance parameters you selected for display. These performance parameters are referred to as *counters*. When you install additional roles, role services, and features on a system, Performance Monitor might be updated with a set of counters for tracking performance of the related components. You can update counters when you install additional services and applications as well.

Performance Monitor, shown in Figure 11-7, creates a graph depicting the counters you're tracking. The update interval for this graph is configurable but is set to one second by default. Tracking information is most valuable when you record performance information in a log file so that it can be played back. When you create alerts, you can notify yourself or others anytime specific performance criteria are met.

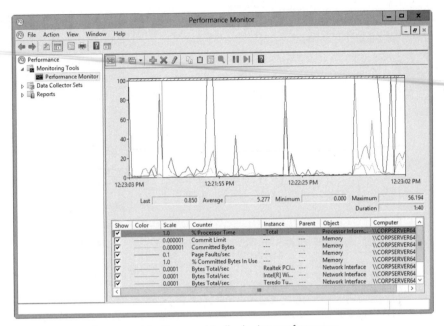

**Figure 11-7** Performance Monitor graphically depicts performance.

You can start Performance Monitor by selecting the related option on the Server Manager Tools menu. Alternatively, type **Performance Monitor** in the Apps Search box and press Enter.

Reliability Monitor, shown in Figure 11-8, tracks changes to the server and compares them to changes in system stability. In this way, you can see a graphical representation of the relationship between changes in the system configuration and changes in system stability. By recording software installation, software removal, application failure, hardware failure, and Windows failure events, as well as key events regarding the configuration of the server, you can see a timeline of changes in both the server and its reliability and then use this information to pinpoint changes that are causing problems with stability. For example, if you see a sudden drop in stability, you can tap or click a data point and then expand the related data set, such as Application Failure or Windows Failure, to find the specific event that caused the drop in stability.

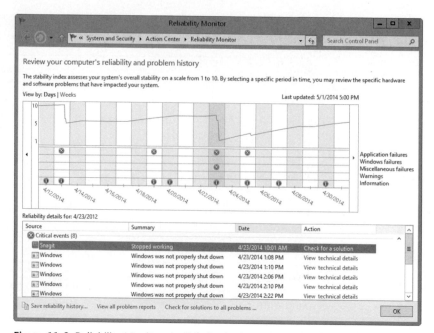

**Figure 11-8** Reliability Monitor graphically depicts overall reliability.

> **Important**
>
> Use the Save Reliability History option to save complete details about the server's stability for future reference. The information is saved as a Reliability Monitor report and is formatted as XML. Tap or click Save Reliability History, and then use the dialog box provided to select a save location and file name for the report. You can view the report in Windows Internet Explorer by double-tapping or double-clicking the file.

You can access Reliability Monitor from Action Center. On the desktop, tap or click the Action Center icon and then tap or click Open Action Center. In Action Center, expand the Maintenance panel, and then tap or click View Reliability History. Alternatively, you can open Reliability Monitor by entering **perfmon /rel** at a command prompt or in the Apps Search box.

Although reliability monitoring is enabled by default for Windows clients, it might be disabled for Windows servers. When you open Reliability Monitor on a server where reliability monitoring is disabled, you'll see that no reliability updates or history details are available. To enable reliability tracking, you must allow the Microsoft Reliability Analysis task, RacTask, to process system reliability data.

RacTask is a scheduled task that runs in the background to collect reliability data. You'll find RacTask in the Task Scheduler library under Microsoft, Windows, RAC. On servers, this task is best used as part of troubleshooting. If you enable the task for troubleshooting, review and modify the default triggers as appropriate for your environment. By default, the task is triggered at startup, once a day at 5:00 PM, and whenever event 1007 is written to the application log. Event 1007 tracks Custer Experience Improvement Program events, which Microsoft tracks to help improve the overall stability of Windows and Windows Server. Don't enable RacTask without considering the possible performance impact.

# Comprehensive performance monitoring

Performance Monitor is a tool designed to track and display performance information in real time. It gathers information on any performance parameters you configured for monitoring and presents it using a graphical display.

## Using Performance Monitor

When you are working with Performance Monitor, the main pane graphs any performance items you configured for monitoring, as shown previously in Figure 11-7. Each performance item you want to monitor is defined by the following three components:

- **Performance objects**   Represent any system component that has a set of measurable properties. A performance object can be a physical part of the operating system, such as the memory, the processor, or the paging file; a logical component, such as a logical disk or print queue; or a software element, such as a process or a thread.

- **Performance object instances**   Represent single occurrences of performance objects. If a particular object has multiple instances, such as when a computer has multiple processors, you can use an object instance to track a specific occurrence of that object. You could also elect to track all instances of an object, such as whether you want to monitor all processors on a system.

- **Performance counters**   Represent measurable properties of performance objects. For example, with a processor, you can measure the percentage of processor utilization using the % Processor Time counter.

In a standard installation of Windows Server 2012, many performance objects are available for monitoring. As you add services, applications, and components, additional performance objects can become available. For example, when you install the Domain Name System (DNS), the DNS object becomes available for monitoring on that computer.

Chapter 11

The most common performance objects you'll want to monitor are summarized in Table 11-1. Like all performance objects, each performance object listed here has a set of counters that can be tracked.

**TABLE 11-1 Commonly tracked performance objects**

| Performance Object | Description |
| --- | --- |
| Cache | Monitors the file system cache, which is an area of physical memory that indicates application I/O activity |
| Database ==> Instances | Monitors performance for instances of the embedded database management system used by Windows Server 2012 |
| DFS Replicated Folders | Monitors conflicts, deletions, replication, and other performance factors related to DFS replication folders |
| DFS Replication Connections | Monitors the data sent and received and other performance statistics for DFS replication connections |
| DHCPv6 Server | Monitors DHCPv6 message broadcasts and other types of DHCPv6 activities |
| DirectoryServices | Monitors performance statistics related to Active Directory Domain Services |
| DNS | Monitors DNS message traffic and other types of DNS activities |
| IPv4 | Monitors IPv4 communications and related activities |
| IPv6 | Monitors IPv6 communications and related activities |
| LogicalDisk | Monitors the logical volumes on a computer |
| Memory | Monitors memory performance for system cache (including pooled, paged memory, and pooled, non-paged memory), physical memory, and virtual memory |
| Network Interface | Monitors the network adapters configured on the computer |
| Objects | Monitors the number of events, mutexes, processes, sections, semaphores, and threads on the computer |
| Paging File | Monitors page file current and peak usage |
| PhysicalDisk | Monitors hard disk read/write activity as well as data transfers, hard faults, and soft faults |
| Print Queue | Monitors print jobs, spooling, and print queue activity |
| Process | Monitors all processes running on a computer |
| Processor | Monitors processor idle time, idle states, usage, deferred procedure calls, and interrupts |
| Server | Monitors current server activity and important server usage statistics, including logon errors, access errors, and sessions |

| Performance Object | Description |
|---|---|
| Server Work Queues | Monitors server threading and client requests |
| System | Monitors system-level counters, including processes, threads, context switching of threads, file system control operations, system calls, and system uptime |
| TCPv4 | Monitors TCPv4 communications and related activities |
| TCPv6 | Monitors TCPv6 communications and related activities |
| Thread | Monitors all running threads, and allows you to examine usage statistics for individual threads by process ID |
| UDPv4 | Monitors UDPv4 communications and related activities |
| UDPv6 | Monitors UDPv6 communications and related activities |

## Selecting performance objects and counters to monitor

The most commonly tracked performance objects are Memory, PhysicalDisk, and Processor. When you first open Performance Monitor, Performance Monitor is configured to graph only the % Processor Time counter. Many other performance counters are available for tracking. To track additional counters, you use the Add Counters dialog box, as shown in Figure 11-9. With the Performance Monitor node selected in the Performance console or Computer Management, you open this dialog box by pressing Ctrl+I or tapping or clicking the Add Counters button on the toolbar.

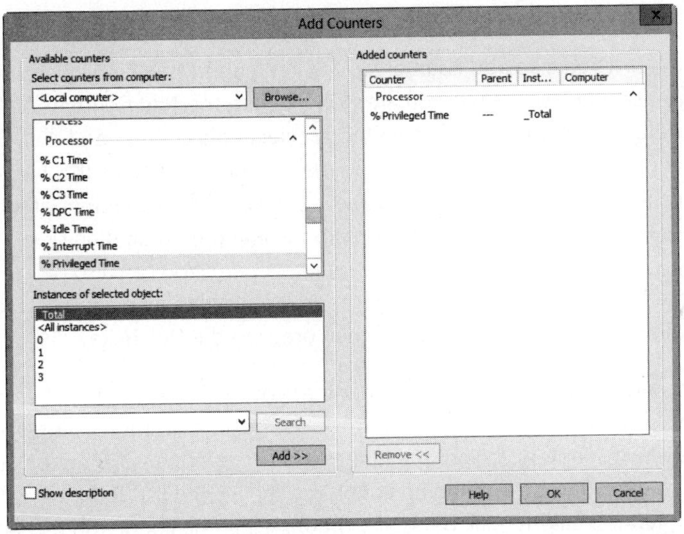

**Figure 11-9** Select the objects and the counters that you want to track.

Chapter 11

After you open the Add Counters dialog box, you can select objects and counters to track by completing these steps:

1. In the Select Counters From Computer box, enter the Universal Naming Convention (UNC) name of the server you want to work with, such as \\CorpServer62, or choose <Local computer> to work with the local computer. You need to be at least a member of the Performance Monitor Users group in the domain or the local computer to perform remote monitoring.

2. Adding counters to track is easy. Select the type of object you want to work with, such as Memory. When you select an object entry by tapping or clicking it, all related counters are selected. If you expand an object entry, you can see all the related counters and then select individual counters by tapping or clicking them. With a keyboard, use Ctrl+click or Shift+click to select multiple counters.

3. When you select an object or any of its counters, in most cases you will see the related instances. Choose _Total to work with a summary view of all counter instances. Choose All Instances to select all counter instances for monitoring. Or select one or more individual counter instances to monitor.

4. When you select an object or a group of counters for an object as well as the object instances, tap or click Add to add the counters to the graph. Repeat steps 2 and 3 to add other performance parameters. You can then repeat this process, as necessary, to add counters for other performance objects. Tap or click OK when you're finished adding counters.

As you've seen, it's easy to add counters to track. What isn't so easy is determining which counters you should track. While you are working with the Add Counters dialog box, you can get a detailed explanation of a counter by selecting a counter and then selecting the Show Description check box. If you add too many counters or track the wrong counters, don't worry. In the Performance Monitor view, you can delete counters later by selecting their entries in the lower portion of the details pane and then tapping or clicking Delete on the toolbar or pressing the Delete key on your keyboard. You can also delete all counters being tracked and start over with a clean graph by selecting an entry in the lower portion of the details pane, pressing Ctrl+A, and then pressing the Delete key.

Performance Monitor displays each counter that you are tracking in a different color and line thickness. You can use the legend in the lower portion of the details pane to help you determine which counter is being graphed where. If you are unsure, tap or click a line in the graph to select the corresponding counter in the legend list. To highlight a specific counter so that it is easy to pick out in the graph, select the counter in the legend list and then press Ctrl+H.

# Choosing views and controlling the display

Performance Monitor can present counter statistics in several ways. By default, it graphs the statistics. A graph is useful when you are tracking a limited number of counters because you can view historical data for each counter that you are working with. By default, Performance Monitor samples the counters once every second and updates the graph over a 100-second duration. This means at any given time there can be up to 100 seconds' worth of data on the graph. If you change the sample interval and duration, you can get more information into the chart. For example, if you set the sample interval to once every 10 seconds and the duration to 1000 seconds, you can get up to 1000 seconds' (or about 17 minutes') worth of data on the graph.

You can set the sample interval by using the General tab of the Performance Monitor Properties dialog box, as shown in Figure 11-10. To open this dialog box, press and hold or right-click the Performance Monitor node and select Properties. Then set the sample interval and duration using the Sample Every and Duration text boxes.

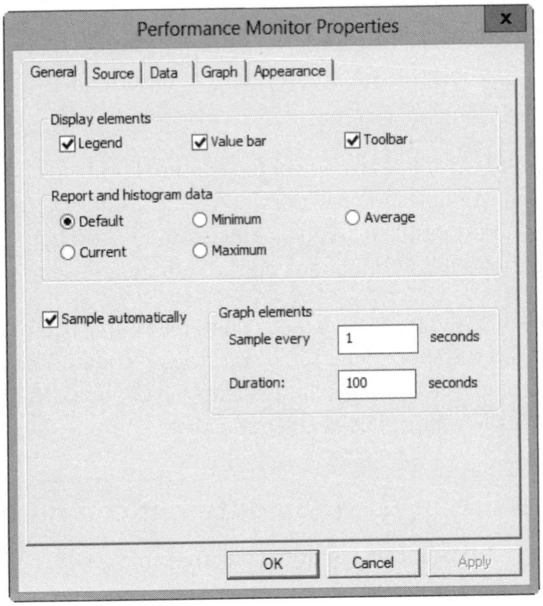

**Figure 11-10**  Configure the display properties.

The options on the Display Elements panel on the General tab of the Performance Monitor Properties dialog box control the availability of the Legend, Value Bar, and Toolbar. The Legend is displayed at the bottom of the details pane, and it shows the color and line style that are used for each counter. The Value Bar is displayed between the graph and the legend. It shows values related to the counter you selected in the graph or in the legend. The

Toolbar is displayed above the graph and provides the basic toolbar functions for working with Performance Monitor. You might find that it is much easier to use the shortcut keys than to tap or click the Toolbar buttons. The Toolbar buttons and their shortcut keys are as follows:

- **View Current Activity**   Ctrl+T; switches the view so that current activity being logged is displayed.

- **View Log Data**   Ctrl+L; switches the view so that data from a performance log can be replayed.

- **Change Graph Type**   Ctrl+G; switches the view to toggle among bar graph, report list, and graph format.

- **Add**   Ctrl+I; displays the Add Counter dialog box, which lets you add counters to track.

- **Delete**   Delete key; removes the counter so that it is no longer tracked.

- **Highlight**   Ctrl+H; highlights the counter using a white line so that it is easier to see. Highlighting works best with graphs. If you want to turn the Highlight function off, press Ctrl+H again.

- **Copy Properties**   Ctrl+C; creates a copy of the counter list along with the individual configuration of each counter, and puts it on the Windows Clipboard. The information is formatted as an extensible markup language (XML) file. If you open a text editor, you could paste in this information and save it for later use.

- **Paste Counter List**   Ctrl+V; pastes a copied counter list into Performance Monitor so that it is used as the current counter set. If you saved a counter list to a file, you simply open the file, copy the contents of the file to the Clipboard, and then press Ctrl+V in Performance Monitor to use that counter list.

## Save the counter list, or use it on different computers

You can use the Copy and Paste commands to track the same set of counters quickly and easily at a later date or to use the set on other computers. Press Ctrl+C to copy the counter list and save it to a file. Then you or someone else could access the counter list when you want to use the same setup again. You could also paste the counter list into an email message so that it could be sent to someone who wants to use the same counter list.

- **Properties**   Ctrl+Q; displays the Properties dialog box for a select item.

- **Freeze Display**   Ctrl+F; freezes the display so that Performance Monitor no longer updates the performance information. Press Ctrl+F a second time to resume sampling.

- **Update Data**   Ctrl+U; updates the display by one sampling interval. When you freeze the display, Performance Monitor still gathers performance information; it just doesn't update the display using the new information. If you want to update the display while it is frozen, use this option.

- **Help**   F1; displays the Performance Monitor Help information.

The Histogram Bar and Report views deserve a bit of additional discussion. In the Histogram Bar view, Performance Monitor represents the performance information by using a bar graph with the last sampling value for each counter displayed on an individual bar within the graph. The sizes of the bars within the graph are adjusted automatically based on the number of performance counters being tracked and can be adjusted to accommodate hundreds of counters. That is, in fact, the biggest advantage of the histogram—it allows you to track a lot of counters more easily. In Figure 11-11, approximately 100 counters are being tracked, and it is easy to pick out which counter is which.

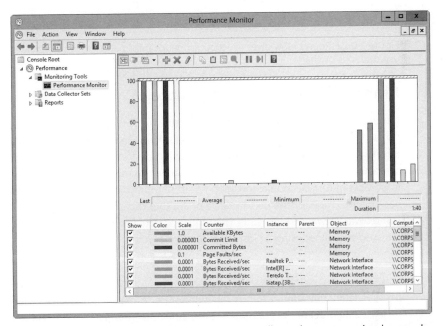

**Figure 11-11** The histogram view enables you to easily track counters using bar graphs.

Chapter 11

In the Report view, shown in Figure 11-12, Performance Monitor represents the performance information by using a report list format. In this view, objects and their counters are listed in alphabetical order. Current values are displayed rather than being graphed. If you are trying to determine specific performance values for many different counters, this is the best view to use because the actual values are always shown.

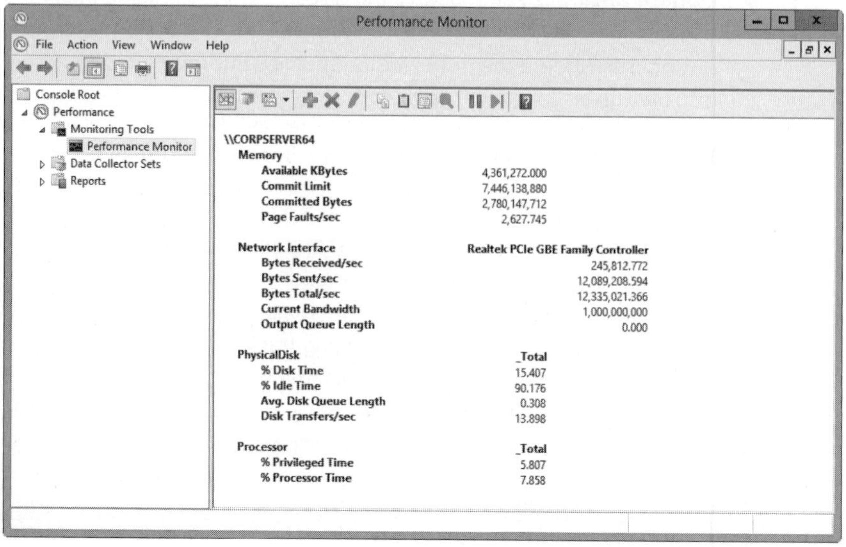

**Figure 11-12** Report view gives users performance information as specific values rather than using graphs or charts.

## Monitoring performance remotely

Monitoring performance on the computer for which you are trying to establish a baseline can skew the results. The reason for this is that Performance Monitor uses resources when it is running, particularly when you are graphing performance information, taking frequent samples, or tracking many performance counters. To remove the resource burden (or at least most of it), you should consider monitoring performance remotely. Here, you use one computer to monitor the performance of another computer. Although this does generate some extra network traffic, you'll get more accurate results for the monitored computer because you're not using its resources for monitoring.

> **Note**
>
> By default, only administrators can monitor performance remotely. You need to be at least a member of the Performance Monitor Users group in the domain or the local computer to perform remote monitoring. When you use performance logging, you need to be at least a member of the Performance Log Users group in the domain or the local computer to work with performance logs on remote computers.

## Configure remote monitoring

You can use any computer running current editions of Windows or Windows Server to perform remote monitoring, and that computer can monitor any other computer running current editions of Windows or Windows Server. The only exceptions are for nonbusiness editions of Windows. The computer you are using for monitoring can even monitor multiple computers.

To begin remote monitoring, select the Performance Monitor node in the Performance Monitor console or in Computer Management. To start with a new counter set and clear out any existing counters, select a counter entry in the lower portion of the details pane, press Ctrl+A and press the Delete key. Press Ctrl+I to open the Add Counters dialog box. In the Add Counters dialog box, type the Universal Naming Code (UNC) name or Internet Protocol (IP) address of the computer you want to monitor remotely in the Select Counters From Computer text box. A UNC computer name or IP address begins with two back slashes (\\). So, for instance, you could type **\\CorpServer03** or **\\192.168.1.56**.

After you type the UNC computer name or IP address, press Tab or tap or click the Performance Object list. When you do this, Performance Monitor will attempt to connect to the remote computer and retrieve a list of available performance objects to monitor. You can then choose performance objects and counters to track just as you would for a local computer.

## TROUBLESHOOTING

**Try the IP address if you can't connect**

Performance Monitor should be able to find any computer in any trusted domain of your organization's forest. Sometimes, however, it isn't able to do this and returns an error. If this happens, ensure that you entered the correct computer name. If you did and you still get an error, try entering the UNC path with the computer's IP address. Using an IP address saves Performance Monitor from having to perform a DNS lookup to resolve the computer's name to its IP address.

## Compare performance of multiple systems

The Legend area shows the associated UNC computer name or IP address for each performance counter you are tracking. If you want to see how performance compares on different computers, use your monitoring computer to track the same performance counters on these computers. You can then make direct comparisons of how these computers perform relative to each other.

Chapter 11

# Resolving performance bottlenecks

Generally, a *bottleneck* is any condition that keeps a computer from performing at its best. Bottlenecks can also apply to situations in which one resource is preventing another resource from performing optimally. For example, if a system doesn't have enough physical memory, it doesn't matter whether it has a fast processor or a slow processor. The system will still perform poorly because it doesn't have enough physical memory available and must rely heavily on the paging file, reading and writing to disk frequently.

Memory is usually the main bottleneck on both workstations and servers. It is the resource you should examine first to try to determine why a system isn't performing as expected. But memory isn't the only bottleneck. The processor, disk subsystem, and networking components are also sources of potential performance bottlenecks.

## Resolving memory bottlenecks

Windows applications use a lot of memory. If you install a server with the minimum amount of memory required, it isn't going to perform at its optimal level. The reason for this is that a server's memory requirements depend on many factors, including the services, components, and applications that are installed on the server, as well as the server's configuration.

Computers use both physical and virtual memory. Physical memory is represented by the amount of random access memory (RAM) installed. Virtual memory is memory written to a paging file on disk. Reading from and writing to the paging file involve the disk subsystem, and it is much slower than accessing physical memory. Because of this, you don't want a system to have to use the paging file too frequently.

Before you set out to monitor memory usage, you should check to ensure that the computer has the recommended amount of memory for the operating system and the applications it is running. After you've done this, you can determine how the system is using memory and check for problems. Look closely at the amount of memory available and the amount of virtual memory being used. If the server has very little available memory, you might need to add memory to the system. In general, you want the available memory to be no less than 5 percent of the total physical memory on the server. If the server has a high ratio of virtual memory being used to total physical memory on the system, you might need to add physical memory as well.

Look at the way the system is using the paged pool and nonpaged pool memory. The paged pool is an area of system memory for objects that can be written to disk when they aren't used. The nonpaged pool is an area of system memory for objects that can't be written to disk. If the size of the paged pool is large relative to the total amount of physical memory on the system, you might need to add memory to the system. If the size of the nonpaged pool is large relative to the total amount of virtual memory allocated to the server, you might want to increase the virtual memory size.

Look at the way the system is using the paging file. A page fault occurs when a process requests a page in memory and the system can't find it at the requested location. If the requested page is elsewhere in memory, the fault is called a *soft page fault*. If the requested page must be retrieved from the paging file on disk, the fault is called a *hard page fault*. Most processors can handle large numbers of soft faults. Hard faults, however, can cause significant delays. If there are a high number of hard page faults, you might need to increase the amount of memory or reduce the size of the system cache.

Counters you can use to check for memory bottlenecks include the following:

- **Memory\Available Bytes**   Records the number of bytes of physical memory available to processes running on the server. When there is less than 5 percent of memory free, the system is low on memory and performance can suffer. The server might page excessively to disk to try to keep up with resource demands. Memory is critically short if there is 128 megabytes (MBs) or less of memory free; in this case, the system might page excessively to disk and try to borrow memory from running processes to keep up with resource demands. If the system is very low on memory, it could also point to a possible memory leak.

- **Memory\Committed Bytes**   Records the number of bytes of committed virtual memory. This represents memory that has been paged to disk and is in use. If a server is using too much virtual memory relative to the total physical memory on the system, you might need to add physical memory.

- **Memory\Commit Limit**   Shows the total physical and virtual memory available. As the number of committed bytes grows, the paging file is allowed to grow up to its maximum size, which can be determined by subtracting the total physical memory on the system from the commit limit. If you set the initial paging file size too small, the system will repeatedly extend the paging file, and this requires system resources. It is better to set the initial page size as appropriate for typical usage or simply use a fixed paging file size. For a fixed paging file, set the size to at least two times the size of RAM.

- **Memory\Page Faults/Sec**   Records the average number of page faults per second. It includes both hard and soft page faults. Soft faults result in memory lookups. Hard faults require access to disk.

- **Memory\Pages/Sec**   Records the number of memory pages that are read from disk or written to disk to resolve hard page faults. It is the sum of Memory\Pages Input/Sec and Memory\Pages Output/Sec.

Chapter 11

- **Memory\Pages Input/Sec** Records the rate at which pages are read from disk to resolve hard page faults. Hard page faults occur when a requested page isn't in memory and the computer has to go to disk to get it. Too many hard faults can cause significant delays and hurt performance.

- **Memory\Pages Output/Sec** Records the rate at which pages are written to disk to free up space in physical memory. If the server has to free up memory too often, this is an indicator that there isn't enough physical memory (RAM) on the system.

- **Memory\Pool Paged Bytes** Represents the size in bytes of the paged pool. The paged pool is an area of system memory for objects that can be written to disk when they aren't used. If the size of the paged pool is large relative to the total amount of physical memory on the system, you might need to add memory to the system. If this value slowly increases in size over time, a kernel-mode process might have a memory leak.

- **Memory\Pool Nonpaged Bytes** Represents the size in bytes of the nonpaged pool. The nonpaged pool is an area of system memory for objects that can't be written to disk. If the size of the nonpaged pool is large relative to the total amount of virtual memory allocated to the server, you might want to increase the virtual memory size. If this value slowly increases in size over time, a kernel-mode process might have a memory leak.

- **Paging File\%Usage** Records the percentage of the paging file currently in use. If this value approaches 100 percent for all instances, you should consider either increasing the virtual memory size or adding physical memory to the system. This will ensure that the server has additional memory if it needs it, such as when the server load grows.

- **Paging File\%Usage Peak** Records the peak size of the paging file as a percentage of the total paging file size available. A high value can mean that the paging file isn't large enough to handle increased load conditions.

- **Physical Disk\%Disk Time** Records the percentage of time that the selected disk spent servicing read and write requests. Keep track of this value for the physical disks that have paging files. If you see this value increasing over several monitoring periods, you should more closely monitor paging-file usage and you might consider adding physical memory to the system.

- **Physical Disk\Avg Disk Queue Length** Records the average number of read and write requests that were waiting for the selected disk during the sample interval. Keep track of this value for the physical disks that have paging files. If you see this value increasing over time and the Memory\Page Reads/Sec is also increasing, the system is having to perform a lot of paging-file reads.

- **Physical Disk\Avg Disk Sec/Transfer** Records the length in seconds of the average disk transfer. Track this value for the physical disks that have paging files in conjunction with Memory\Pages/Sec. Memory\Pages/Sec tracks the number of reads and writes for the paging file. If you multiply the Physical Disk\Avg Disk Sec/Transfer by the Memory\Pages/Sec value, you have an excellent indicator of how much of the disk access time is being used by paging. Use the result to help you decide whether to move the paging files to faster disks or add physical memory to the system.

## Resolving processor bottlenecks

After you've eliminated memory as a potential bottleneck, you should examine the system's processor usage to determine whether there are any potential bottlenecks. Processor bottlenecks can occur if a process's threads need more processing time than is available. This, in turn, causes the processor queue to grow because threads have to wait to get processing time. As a result, the system response suffers and the system appears sluggish or nonresponsive.

Excess interrupts are another common reason for processor bottlenecks. Each time drivers or disk subsystem components, such as hard disk drives or network components, generate an interrupt, the processor has to stop what it is doing to handle the request because requests from hardware take priority. However, poorly designed drivers and components can generate false interrupts, which tie up the processor for no reason. System boards or components that are failing can generate false interrupts as well.

**TROUBLESHOOTING**

**Rule out processor affinity as an issue on multiprocessor systems**
On multiprocessor systems, you might need to rule out processor affinity as a cause of a processor bottleneck. By using processor affinity, you can set a program or process to use a specific processor to improve its performance. Assigning processor affinity, however, can block access to the processor for other programs and processes.

If a system's processors are the performance bottleneck, adding memory, drives, or network connections won't overcome the problem. Instead, you might need to upgrade the processors to faster clock speeds or add processors to increase the server's upper capacity. You could also move processor-intensive applications, such as Microsoft Exchange Server, to another server.

Chapter 11

Counters you can use to check for processor bottlenecks include the following:

- **System\Processor Queue Length**   Records the number of threads waiting to be executed. These threads are queued in an area shared by all processors on the system. If this counter has a sustained value of 10 or more threads, you might need to upgrade the processors to faster clock speeds or add processors to increase the server's upper capacity.

- **Processor\%Processor Time**   Records the percentage of time the selected processor is executing a nonidle thread. You should track this counter separately for all processor instances on the server. If the %Processor Time values for all instances are high (above 75 percent) while the network interface and disk input/output (I/O) throughput rates are relatively low, you might need to upgrade the processors to faster clock speeds or add processors to increase the server's upper capacity.

- **Processor\%User Time**   Records the percentage of time the selected processor is executing a nonidle thread in User mode. *User mode* is a processing mode for applications and user-level subsystems. A high value for all process instances might indicate that you need to upgrade the processors to faster clock speeds or add processors to increase the server's upper capacity.

- **Processor\%Privileged Time**   Records the percentage of time the selected processor is executing a nonidle thread in Privileged mode. *Privileged mode* is a processing mode for operating system components and services, allowing direct access to hardware and memory. A high value for all processor instances might indicate that you need to upgrade the processors to faster clock speeds or add processors to increase the server's upper capacity.

- **Processor\Interrupts/Sec**   Records the average rate, in incidents per second, that the processor received and serviced hardware interrupts. Compare this value to your baselines. If this value changes substantially (I mean by thousands of interrupts) without a corresponding increase in activity, the system might have a hardware problem. To resolve this problem, you must identify the device or component that is causing the problem. Start with devices that have drivers you've updated recently.

## Resolving disk I/O bottlenecks

With the high-speed disks available today, a system's hard disks are rarely the primary reason for a bottleneck. It is more likely that a system is having to do a lot of disk reads and writes because there isn't enough physical memory available and the system has to page to disk. Because reading from and writing to disk is much slower than reading and writing memory, excessive paging can degrade the server's overall performance. To reduce the amount of disk activity, you want the system to manage memory as efficiently as possible and page to disk only when necessary.

That said, you can do several things with a system's hard disks to improve performance. If the system has faster drives than the ones used for the paging file, you might consider moving the paging file to those disks. If the system has one or more drives that are doing most of the work and other drives that are mostly idle, you might be able to improve performance by balancing the load across the drives more efficiently.

To help you better gauge disk I/O activity, use the following counters:

- **PhysicalDisk\%Disk Time**    Records the percentage of time the physical disk is busy. Track this value for all hard disk drives on the system in conjunction with Processor\%Processor Time and Network Interface Connection\Bytes Total/Sec. If the %Disk Time value is high and the processor and network connection values aren't high, the system's hard disk drives might be creating a bottleneck. You might be able to improve performance by balancing the load across the drives more efficiently or by adding drives and configuring the system so that they are used.

> **Note**
> Redundant array of independent disks (RAID) devices can cause the PhysicalDisk\%Disk Time value to exceed 100 percent. For this reason, don't rely on PhysicalDisk\%Disk Time for RAID devices. Instead, use PhysicalDisk\Current Disk Queue Length.

- **PhysicalDisk\Current Disk Queue Length**    Records the number of system requests that are waiting for disk access. A high value indicates that the disk waits are affecting system performance. In general, you want there to be very few waiting requests.

> **Note**
> Physical disk queue lengths are relative to the number of physical disks on the system and proportional to the length of the queue minus the number of drives. For example, if a system has two drives and there are 6 waiting requests, that could be considered a proportionally large number of queued requests; but if a system has eight drives and there are 10 waiting requests, that is considered a proportionally small number of queued requests.

Chapter 11

- **PhysicalDisk\Avg. Disk Write Queue Length**   Records the number of write requests that are waiting to be processed.

- **PhysicalDisk\Avg. Disk Read Queue Length**   Records the number of read requests that are waiting to be processed.

- **PhysicalDisk\Disk Writes/Sec**   Records the number of disk writes per second. It is an indicator of how much disk I/O activity there is. By tracking the number of writes per second and the size of the write queue, you can determine how write operations are affecting disk performance. If lots of write operations are queuing and you are using RAID 5, it could be an indicator that you would get better performance by using RAID 1. Remember that by using RAID 5 you typically get better read performance than with RAID 1. So, there's a tradeoff to be made by using either RAID configuration.

- **PhysicalDisk\Disk Reads/Sec**   Records the number of disk reads per second. It is an indicator of how much disk I/O activity there is. By tracking the number of reads per second and the size of the read queue, you can determine how read operations are affecting disk performance. If lots of read operations are queuing and you are using RAID 1, it could be an indicator that you would get better performance by using RAID 5. Remember that by using RAID 1 you typically get better write performance than RAID 5. So, as mentioned, there's a tradeoff to be made by using either RAID configuration.

## Resolving network bottlenecks

The network that connects your computers is critically important. Its responsiveness, or lack thereof, weighs heavily on the way users perceive the responsiveness of their computers and any computers to which they connect. It doesn't matter how fast their computers are or how fast your servers are. If there's a big delay (and big network delays are measured in tens of milliseconds) between when a request is made and the time it's received, users might think systems are slow or nonresponsive.

Unfortunately, in most cases, the delay (latency) users experience is beyond your control. It's a function of the type of connection the user has and the route the request takes to your server. The total capacity of your server to handle requests and the amount of bandwidth available to your servers are factors you can control, however. Network capacity is a function of the network cards and interfaces configured on the servers. Network bandwidth availability is a function of your organization's network infrastructure and how much traffic is on it when a request is made.

Counters you can use to check network activity and look for bottlenecks include the following:

- **Network Interface\Bytes Total/Sec**   Records the rate at which bytes are sent and received over a network adapter. Track this value separately for each network adapter configured on the system. If the Bytes Total/Sec for a particular adapter is substantially slower than what you'd expect given the speed of the network and the speed of the network card, you might want to check the network card configuration. Check to see whether the link speed is set for half duplex or full duplex. In most cases, you'll want to use full duplex.

- **Network Interface\Current Bandwidth**   Estimates the current bandwidth for the selected network adapter in bits per second. Track this value separately for each network adapter configured on the system. Most servers use 100-Mbps, 1-Gbps, or 10-Gbps network cards, which can be configured in many ways. Someone might have configured a 1-Gbps card for 100 megabits per second (Mbps). If that is the case, the current bandwidth might be off by a factor of 10.

- **Network Interface\Bytes Received/Sec**   Records the rate at which bytes are received over a network adapter. Track this value separately for each network adapter configured on the system.

- **Network Interface\Bytes Sent/Sec**   Records the rate at which bytes are sent over a network adapter. Track this value separately for each network adapter configured on the system.

## TROUBLESHOOTING

**Compare network activity to disk time and processor time**

Compare these values in conjunction with PhysicalDisk\%Disk Time and Processor\%Processor Time. If the disk time and processor time values are low but the network values are very high, a capacity problem might exist. Solve the problem by optimizing the network card settings or by adding an additional network card.

You might be able to improve network performance by installing multiple network adapters and teaming the network cards. You configure NIC teaming using Server Manager by selecting Local Server in the left pane and then tapping or clicking the link provided for NIC teaming. You can then create and configure NIC teams.

Chapter 11

# INSIDE OUT    NIC teaming

NIC teaming allows multiple network adapters to have their bandwidth aggregated for the purposes of load balancing and failover protection. Windows Server 2012 supports up to 32 network adapters aggregated into a team. In turn, these aggregated adapters then present one or more virtual adapters, referred to as *team network adapters*, to the operating system. Each team network adapter organizes network traffic by virtual LAN (VLAN), allowing applications to simultaneously connect to different VLANs.

When you are configuring NIC teaming, you can tap or click Additional Properties to configure the teaming mode, load-balancing mode, and standby-adapter mode. By default, team network adapters use the switch independent team mode, which doesn't require the network switch to participate in the teaming, and this allows the team network adapters to be connected to different switches. Alternatively, you can configure

- Static teaming as the teaming mode, which requires you to configure the switch and the server to work with NIC teaming. Here, you typically use a server-class switch and identify which links form the team. Because there is no error detection and correction, you must be certain the network cables are properly connected.

- Link Aggregation Control Protocol (LACP) as the teaming mode, which uses Institute of Electrical and Electronics Engineers (IEEE) 802.1ax LACP to automatically create the NIC team by dynamically identifying links between the server and the switch. Here, you typically use a server-class switch and enable LACP on the appropriate switch ports.

If you have a server-class switch, the switch likely supports IEEE 802.1ax (also referred to as IEEE 802.3ad) and you can gain some additional performance benefits by having the switch participate in the teaming.

For load balancing, the default mode (Address Hash) creates a simple hash for packets and then assigns packets that have a particular hash to one of the available team network adapters. This can help to balance the workload across the team network adapters. Alternatively, if a server has virtual machines, you can use the MAC address of each virtual machine to determine how traffic is balanced. Load balancing by MAC address works best when virtual machines have similar workloads. Keep in mind that failover between network adapters in a virtual machine might result in traffic being sent with the MAC address of a different network adapter. If so, to prevent this from being blocked automatically, NIC teaming must be set to allow MAC spoofing or must have the *"AllowTeaming=On"* parameter set using the Set-VmNetworkAdapter cmdlet in Windows PowerShell.

Finally, the Standby Adapter setting allows you to specify whether all network adapters are active. Typically, for optimal performance, you'll want all network adapters in a team to be active. However, you can designate one or more network adapters in a team as standby adapters. Exactly as its name suggests, a *standby adapter* is inactive until another active adapter fails and is then activated as part of failover. Keep in mind that, technically, you can place a single network adapter in a team. However, you need two or more network adapters for fault protection through failover.

# Performance logging

Windows Server 2012 uses data collector sets and reports. Data collector sets allow you to specify sets of performance objects and counters that you want to track. When you create a data collector set, you can easily start or stop monitoring the performance objects and counters included in the set. In a way, this makes data collector sets similar to the performance logs used in earlier releases of Windows. However, data collector sets are much more sophisticated. You can use them in the following ways:

- Use a single data set to generate multiple performance counter and trace logs.

- Assign access controls to manage who can access collected data.

- Create multiple run schedules and stop conditions for monitoring.

- Use data managers to control the size of collected data and reporting.

- Generate reports based on collected data.

In Performance Monitor, you can review currently configured data collector sets and reports under the Data Collector Sets and Reports nodes, respectively. As shown in Figure 11-13, you'll find data sets and reports that are user defined and system defined. User-defined data sets are created by users for general monitoring and performance tuning. System-defined data sets are created by the operating system to aid in automated diagnostics.

Chapter 11

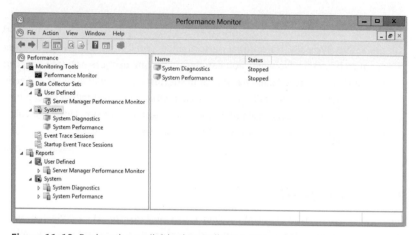

**Figure 11-13** Review the available data collector sets and reports.

## Creating and managing data collector sets

In Performance Monitor, you can view the currently configured data collector sets by expanding the Data Collector Sets node and then expanding the User Defined and System nodes. When you select a data collector set in the left pane, you'll see a list of the related data collectors in the main pane listed by name and type.

Data collector set types include the following:

- **Configuration**  The Configuration type is for data collectors that record changes to particular registry paths.

- **Trace**  The Trace type is for data collectors that record performance data whenever related events occur.

- **Performance Counter**  The Performance Counter type is for data collectors that record data on selected counters when a predetermined interval has elapsed.

Windows Server 2012 uses event traces to track a wide variety of performance statistics. You can view running event traces by selecting Event Trace Sessions. You can then stop a data collector running a trace by pressing and holding or right-clicking it and selecting Stop.

Some event traces are configured to start automatically with the operating system. These event traces are called *Startup Event Traces*. You can view the enabled or disabled status of event traces configured to run automatically when you start the computer by selecting Startup Event Trace Sessions. You can start a trace by pressing and holding or right-clicking a startup data collector and selecting Start As Event Trace Session. You can delete a startup data collector by pressing and holding or right-clicking it and then selecting Delete.

You can save a data collector as a template that can be used as the basis of other data collectors by pressing and holding or right-clicking the data collector and selecting Save Template. In the Save As dialog box, select a directory, type a name for the template, and then tap or click Save. The data collector template is saved as an XML file that can be copied to other systems.

You can delete a user-defined data collector by pressing and holding or right-clicking it and then selecting Delete. If a data collector is running, you need to stop collecting data first and then delete the collector. Deleting a collector deletes the related reports as well.

## Using data collector templates

Performance Monitor includes several preconfigured templates for gathering general diagnostics information, which can include information about the system configuration and performance:

- **Basic**    Generates a report that will include basic information about the computer, CPU and disk utilization, and active network adapters. After you create a data collector set based on this template, you can add or remove counters and change the scheduling by editing the properties of the data collector set. When you are reviewing the data, be sure to drill down into the details. For example, under disks, examine the *hot files*, which are the files causing the most disk I/O activity. Also, be sure to closely examine the resource overview, which provides a summary analysis of CPU, network, disk, and memory usage. Note that this basic data is included in the reports for the other predefined collector sets. Default run time: 60 seconds.

- **Active Directory Diagnostics**    Generates a report that provides detailed diagnostics data for Active Directory, which includes registry keys, performance counters, and trace events. On domain controllers, you can use this data to help troubleshoot Active Directory performance issues. Pay particular attention to the Active Directory diagnostics and tuning data provided in the report. For example, with searches, be sure to examine the detailed data provided for unique searches, directory search by object, search status codes, searches with the most CPU utilization, and clients with the most CPU usage. Also, don't overlook the tuning parameters for the registry. Default run time: 300 seconds.

- **System Performance**    Generates a report that provides detailed performance data regarding local hardware resources, system response times, and processes on the local computer. Use this information to identify the possible causes of performance issues. Note that the system performance data is included in the report for system diagnostics. Default run time: 60 seconds.

- **System Diagnostics**    Generates a report that provides detailed diagnostics data, which includes the status of local hardware resources, system response times, and processes on the local computer along with system information and configuration data. Suggests ways to maximize performance and streamline system operation. Be sure to closely examine the entries under basic system checks, particularly those for hardware devices and drivers. Default run time: 60 seconds.

On member servers, system data collector sets are created automatically for system diagnostics and system performance. On domain controllers, a system data collector set for Active Directory diagnostics is also created. If you press and hold or right-click the related entry under Data Collector Sets and then select Start, Performance Monitor will generate a report that you can review to evaluate performance and begin diagnostics for troubleshooting.

Although you can't modify the system data collector sets that were created automatically, you can create new collector sets based on the predefined templates and then modify their settings. To do this, follow these steps:

1. In Performance Monitor, under the Data Collector Sets node, press and hold or right-click the User Defined node in the left pane, point to New, and then choose Data Collector Set.

2. In the Create New Data Collector Set Wizard, type a name for the data collector, such as **Custom System Diagnostics**. The Create From A Template (Recommended) option is selected by default, as shown in Figure 11-14. Tap or click Next.

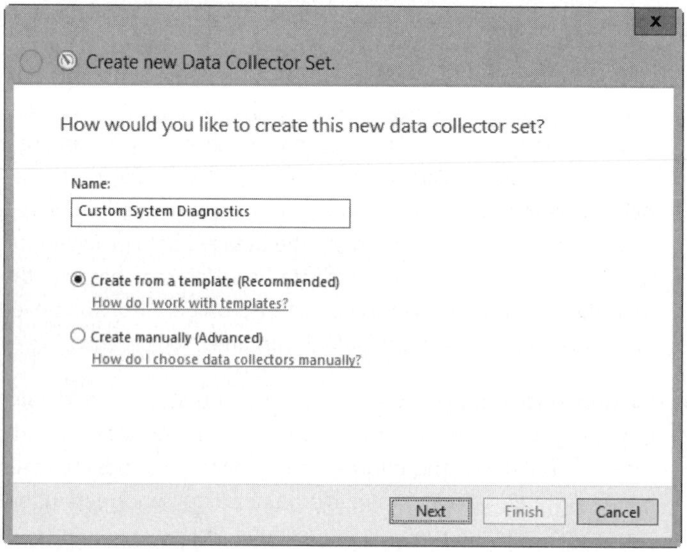

Figure 11-14 Specify the name of the collector set and base the set on a template.

3. On the Which Template Would You Like To Use page, shown in Figure 11-15, select the template to use or click Browse to search for a saved template. When you are ready to continue, tap or click Next.

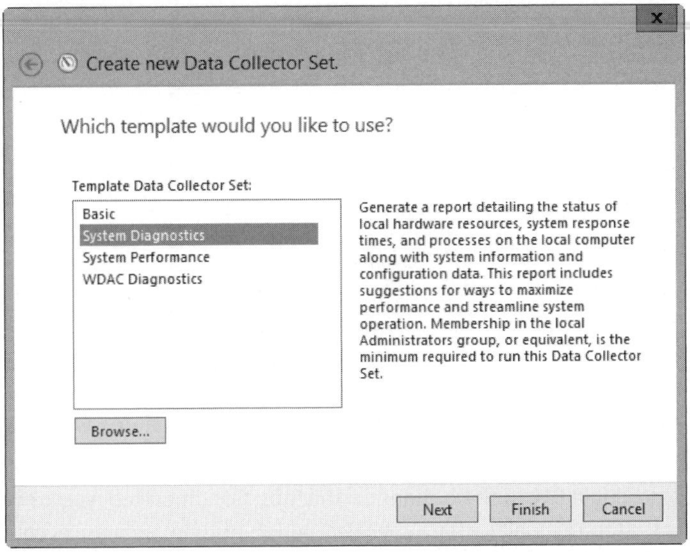

**Figure 11-15** Select a predefined template to use or browse for a saved template.

4. On the Where Would You Like The Data To Be Saved page, type the root path to use for logging collected data. Alternatively, tap or click Browse and then use the Browse For Folder dialog box to select the logging directory. Tap or click Next when you are ready to continue.

5. On the Create New Data Collector Set page, the Run As box lists <Default> as the user to indicate that the log will run under the privileges and permissions of the default system account. To run the log with the privileges and permissions of another user, tap or click Change. Type the user name and password for the desired account, and then tap or click OK. User names can be entered in DOMAIN\USERNAME format, such as CPANDL\WilliamS for the WilliamS account in the CPANDL domain.

6. Select the Open Properties For This Data Collector Set option, and then tap or click Finish. This saves the data collector set, closes the wizard, and then opens the related Properties dialog box.

7. By default, logging is configured to start manually. To configure a logging schedule, tap or click on the Schedule tab and then tap or click Add. You can now set the active range, start time, and run days for data collection. Figure 11-16 shows an example.

Chapter 11

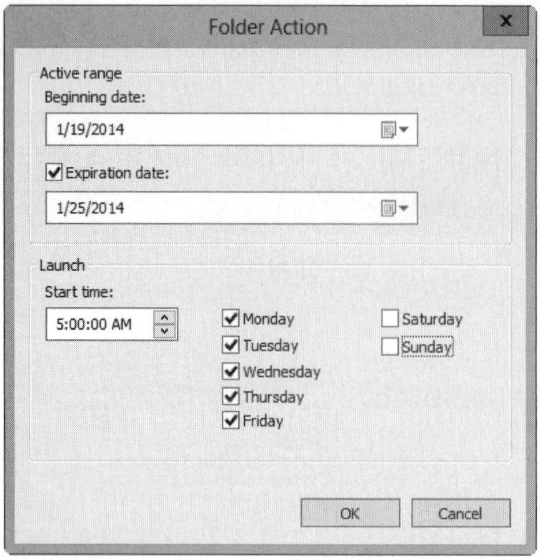

**Figure 11-16** Set the run schedule for the collector set.

8. By default, logging stops only if you set an expiration date as part of the logging schedule. Using the options on the Stop Condition tab, you can configure the log file to stop manually after a specified period of time, such as seven days, or when the log file is full (if you set a maximum size limit).

9. Tap or click OK when you finish setting the logging schedule and stop conditions. You can manage the data collector as explained in "Creating and managing data collector sets" earlier in this chapter. If you want Windows to run a scheduled task when data collection stops, configure the tasks on the Task tab in the Properties dialog box.

## Collecting performance counter data

Data collectors can be used to record performance data on the selected counters at a specific sampling interval. For example, you could sample performance data for the CPU every 15 minutes. The default location for logging is %SystemDrive%\PerfLogs\Admin. Log files can grow in size very quickly. If you plan to log data for an extended period, be sure to place the log file on a drive with lots of free space. Remember, the more frequently you update the log file, the greater the drive space and CPU resource usage on the system.

To collect performance counter data, follow these steps:

1. In Performance Monitor, under the Data Collector Sets node, press and hold or right-click the User Defined node in the left pane, point to New, and then choose Data Collector Set.

2.  In the Create New Data Collector Set Wizard, shown in Figure 11-17, type a name for the data collector, such as **Memory Monitor** or **Physical Disk Monitor**. Afterward, select the Create Manually (Advanced) option and then tap or click Next.

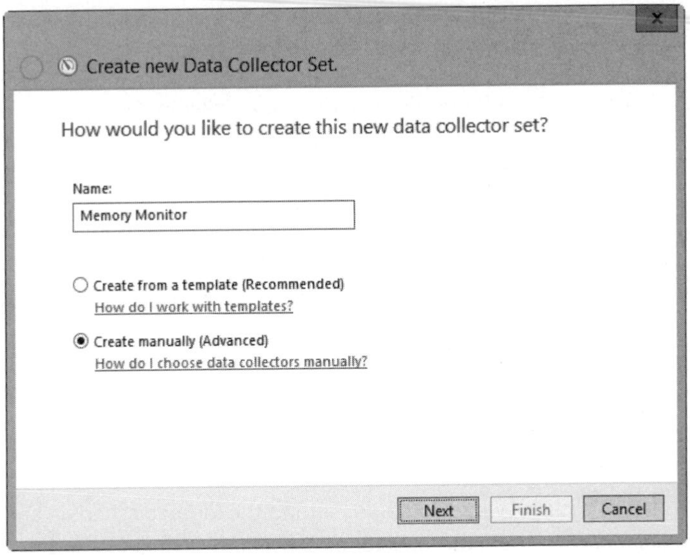

**Figure 11-17** Specify the name of the collector set.

3.  On the What Type Of Data Do You Want To Include page, the Create Data Logs option is selected by default. Select the Performance Counter check box, and then tap or click Next.

4.  On the Which Performance Counters Would You Like To Log page, tap or click Add. This displays the Add Counters dialog box, which you can use as previously discussed to select the performance counters to track. When you are finished selecting counters, tap or click OK.

5.  On the Which Performance Counters Would You Like To Log page, type in a sample interval and select a time unit in seconds, minutes, hours, days, or weeks. The sample interval specifies when new data is collected. For example, if you sample every 15 minutes, the data log is updated every 15 minutes. Tap or click Next when you are ready to continue.

6.  On the Where Would You Like The Data To Be Saved page, type the root path to use for logging collected data. Alternatively, tap or click Browse and then use the Browse For Folder dialog box to select the logging directory. Tap or click Next when you are ready to continue.

Chapter 11

7. On the Create New Data Collector Set page, the Run As box lists <Default> as the user to indicate that the log will run under the privileges and permissions of the default system account. To run the log with the privileges and permissions of another user, tap or click Change. Type the user name and password for the desired account, and then tap or click OK. User names can be entered in DOMAIN\USERNAME format, such as CPANDL\WilliamS for the WilliamS account in the CPANDL domain.

8. Select the Open Properties For This Data Collector Set option, and then tap or click Finish. This saves the data collector set, closes the wizard, and then opens the related Properties dialog box.

9. By default, logging is configured to start manually. To configure a logging schedule, tap or click the Schedule tab and then tap or click Add. You can now set the active range, start time, and run days for data collection.

10. By default, logging stops only if you set an expiration date as part of the logging schedule. Using the options on the Stop Condition tab, you can configure the log file to stop manually after a specified period of time, such as seven days, or when the log file is full (if you set a maximum size limit).

11. Tap or click OK when you finish setting the logging schedule and stop conditions. You can manage the data collector as explained in "Creating and managing data collector sets" earlier in this chapter. If you want Windows to run a scheduled task when data collection stops, configure the tasks on the Task tab in the Properties dialog box.

## Collecting performance trace data

You can use data collectors to record performance trace data whenever events related to their source providers occur. A source provider is an application or operating system service that has traceable events.

To collect performance trace data, follow these steps:

1. In Performance Monitor, under the Data Collector Sets node, press and hold or right-click the User-Defined node in the left pane, point to New, and then choose Data Collector Set.

2. In the Create New Data Collector Set Wizard, type a name for the data collector, such as **Disk IO Trace** or **Logon Trace**. Afterward, select the Create Manually (Advanced) option and then tap or click Next.

3. On the What Type Of Data Do You Want To Include page, the Create Data Logs option is selected by default. Select the Event Trace Data check box, and then tap or click Next.

4. On the Which Event Trace Providers Would You Like To Enable page, tap or click Add.

5. In the Event Trace Providers dialog box, shown in Figure 11-18, select an event trace provider to track, such as Active Directory: NetLogon, and then tap or click OK.

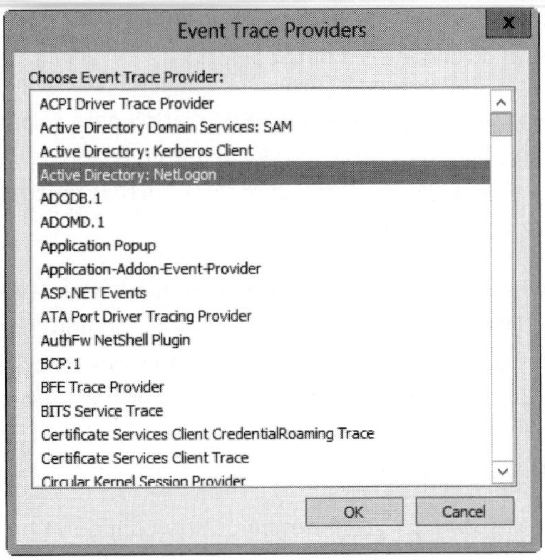

**Figure 11-18** Select a provider to trace.

6. On the Which Event Trace Providers Would You Like To Enable page, you can configure property values to track. By selecting individual properties in the Properties list and tapping or clicking Edit, you can track particular property values rather than all values for the provider. Repeat this process to select other event trace providers to track. Tap or click Next when you are ready to continue.

7. On the Where Would You Like The Data To Be Saved page, type the root path to use for logging collected data. Alternatively, tap or click Browse and then use the Browse For Folder dialog box to select the logging directory. Tap or click Next when you are ready to continue.

8. On the Create New Data Collector Set page, the Run As box lists <Default> as the user to indicate that the log will run under the privileges and permissions of the default system account. To run the log with the privileges and permissions of another user, tap or click Change. Type the user name and password for the desired account, and then tap or click OK. User names can be entered in DOMAIN\USERNAME format, such as CPANDL\WilliamS for the WilliamS account in the CPANDL domain.

9.  Select the Open Properties For This Data Collector Set option, and then tap or click Finish. This saves the data collector set, closes the wizard, and then opens the related Properties dialog box.

10. By default, logging is configured to start manually. To configure a logging schedule, tap or click the Schedule tab and then tap or click Add. You can now set the active range, start time, and run days for data collection.

11. By default, logging stops only if you set an expiration date as part of the logging schedule. Using the options on the Stop Condition tab, you can configure the log file to stop manually after a specified period of time, such as seven days, or when the log file is full (if you set a maximum size limit).

12. Tap or click OK when you finish setting the logging schedule and stop conditions. You can manage the data collector as explained in "Creating and managing data collector sets" earlier in this chapter. If you want Windows to run a scheduled task when data collection stops, configure the tasks on the Task tab in the Properties dialog box.

## Collecting configuration data

You can use data collectors to record changes in registry configuration. To collect configuration data, follow these steps:

1.  In Performance Monitor, under the Data Collector Sets node, press and hold or right-click the User-Defined node in the left pane, point to New, and then choose Data Collector Set.

2.  In the Create New Data Collector Set Wizard, type a name for the data collector, such as **System Registry Info** or **Current User Registry Info**. Afterward, select the Create Manually (Advanced) option and then tap or click Next.

3.  On the What Type Of Data Do You Want To Include page, the Create Data Logs option is selected by default. Select the System Configuration Information check box and then tap or click Next.

4.  On the Which Registry Keys Would You Like To Record page, tap or click Add. Type the registry path to track. Repeat this process to add other registry paths to track. Tap or click Next when you are ready to continue.

5.  On the Where Would You Like The Data To Be Saved page, type the root path to use for logging collected data. Alternatively, tap or click Browse and then use the Browse For Folder dialog box to select the logging directory. Tap or click Next when you are ready to continue.

6. On the Create New Data Collector Set page, the Run As box lists <Default> as the user to indicate that the log will run under the privileges and permissions of the default system account. To run the log with the privileges and permissions of another user, tap or click Change. Type the user name and password for the desired account, and then tap or click OK. User names can be entered in DOMAIN\USERNAME format, such as CPANDL\WilliamS for the WilliamS account in the CPANDL domain.

7. Select the Open Properties For This Data Collector Set option, and then tap or click Finish. This saves the data collector set, closes the wizard, and then opens the related Properties dialog box.

8. By default, logging is configured to start manually. To configure a logging schedule, tap or click on the Schedule tab and then tap or click Add. You can now set the active range, start time, and run days for data collection.

9. By default, logging stops only if you set an expiration date as part of the logging schedule. Using the options on the Stop Condition tab, you can configure the log file to stop manually after a specified period of time, such as seven days, or when the log file is full (if you set a maximum size limit).

10. Tap or click OK when you finish setting the logging schedule and stop conditions. You can manage the data collector as explained in "Creating and managing data collector sets" earlier in this chapter. If you want Windows to run a scheduled task when data collection stops, configure the tasks on the Task tab in the Properties dialog box.

## Viewing data collector reports

When you're troubleshooting problems, you'll often want to log performance data over an extended period of time and then review the data to analyze the results. For each data collector that has been or is currently active, you'll find related data collector reports. As with data collector sets themselves, data collector reports are usually organized into two general categories: user-defined and system.

To view data collector reports in Performance Monitor, expand the Reports node and then expand the individual report node for the data collector you want to analyze. Under the data collector's report node, you'll find individual reports for each logging session, as shown in Figure 11-19. A logging session begins when logging starts and ends when logging is stopped.

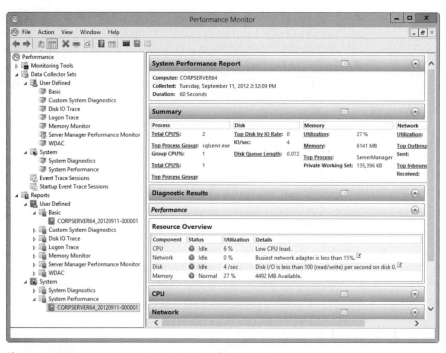

**Figure 11-19** Access a report to view the collected data.

The most recent log is the one with the highest log number. To view a log and analyze its related data graphically, double-tap or double-click it. Keep in mind that if a data collector is actively logging, you won't be able to view the most recent log. You can stop collecting data by pressing and holding or right-clicking a data collector set and selecting Stop. Collected data is shown by default in a graph view from the start of data collection to the end of data collection. Only counters that you selected for logging will be available. If a report doesn't have a counter that you want to work with, you need to modify the data collector properties, restart the logging process, and then check the logs again.

---

**Note**

Open the most recent report for a data collector set directly by pressing and holding or right-clicking a data collector set and then selecting Latest Report. This shortcut works only if reports are available.

Save a data collector set as a template that can be used on the current server as well as other servers by pressing and holding or right-clicking a data collector set and then selecting Save Template. Next, in the Save As dialog box, select a save location, type a name for the template, and then tap or click Save.

You can modify the report details using the following techniques:

1. In Performance Monitor, press and hold or right-click the Performance Monitor node and then select Properties. In the Performance Monitor Properties dialog box, tap or click the Source tab.

2. Specify data sources to analyze. Under Data Source, select Log Files and then tap or click Add to open the Select Log File dialog box. You can now select an additional log file to analyze.

3. Specify the time window that you want to analyze. Tap or click Time Range, and then drag the Total Range bar to specify the appropriate starting and ending times. Drag the left edge to the right to move up the start time. Drag the right edge to the left to move down the end time.

4. Tap or click the Data tab. You can now select counters to view. Select a counter, and then tap or click Remove to remove it from the graph view. Tap or click Add to display the Add Counter dialog box, which you can use to select the counters that you want to analyze.

5. Tap or click OK. In the monitor pane, tap or click the Change Graph Type button to select the type of graphing.

# INSIDE OUT  Use the Data Manager to automate report cleanup

Use the Data Manager to determine how much data can be generated and stored for each user-defined data collector set. To open the Data Manager, press and hold or right-click a user-defined data set and then select Data Manager.

Settings on the Data Manager tab allow you to ensure that a minimum amount of free space is available before generating reports, control the maximum number of sub-folders that can be created during report generation, configure whether the oldest or largest existing data set is cleaned up either before or after a report is generated, and much more.

Settings on the Actions tab allow you to specify cleanup actions. For example, reports based on the predefined templates are cleaned up in several ways by default. After one day, a .Cab file is created containing the report data and then the report data itself is deleted. After eight weeks, the .Cab file is deleted. After 24 weeks, any remaining data is deleted, including the report itself.

Chapter 11

# Configuring performance counter alerts

You can configure alerts to notify you when certain events occur or when certain performance thresholds are reached. You can send these alerts as network messages and as events that are logged in the application event log. You can also configure alerts to start applications and performance logs.

To configure an alert, follow these steps:

1.  In Performance Monitor, under the Data Collector Sets node, press and hold or right-click the User-Defined node in the left pane, point to New, and then choose Data Collector Set.

2.  In the Create New Data Collector Set Wizard, type a name for the data collector, such as **Memory Alert** or **Full Disk Alert**. Afterward, select the Create Manually (Advanced) option and then tap or click Next.

3.  On the What Type Of Data Do You Want To Include page, select the Performance Counter Alert option and then tap or click Next.

4.  On the Which Performance Counters Would You Like To Monitor page, shown in Figure 11-20, tap or click Add to open the Add Counters dialog box. This dialog box is identical to the Add Counters dialog box discussed previously. Use the Add Counters dialog box to add counters that trigger the alert. Tap or click OK when you're finished.

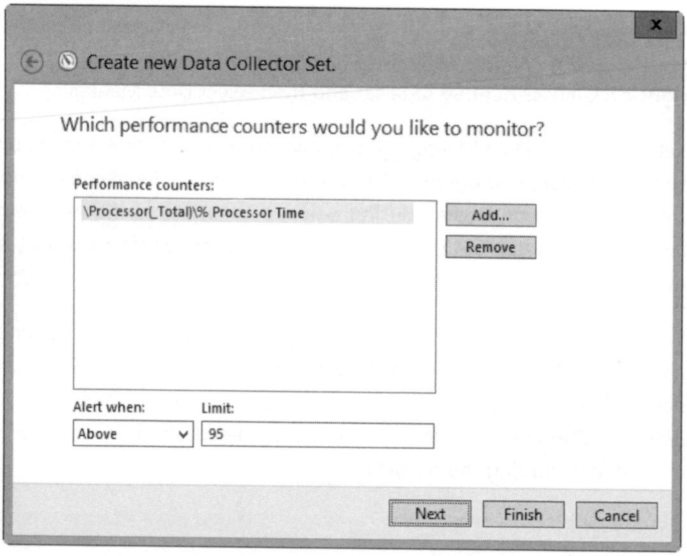

**Figure 11-20**  Select the performance counters for the alerts.

5. In the Performance Counters panel, select the first counter and then use the Alert When text box to set the occasion when an alert for this counter is triggered. Alerts can be triggered when the counter is above or below a specific value. Select Above or Below, and then set the trigger value. The unit of measurement is whatever makes sense for the currently selected counter or counters. For example, to alert if processor time is over 95 percent, you select Above and then type **95**. Repeat this process to configure other counters you've selected and then tap or click Next.

6. On the Create New Data Collector Set page, the Run As box lists <Default> as the user to indicate that the log will run under the privileges and permissions of the default system account. To run the log with the privileges and permissions of another user, tap or click Change. Type the user name and password for the desired account, and then tap or click OK. User names can be entered in DOMAIN\USERNAME format, such as CPANDL\WilliamS for the WilliamS account in the CPANDL domain.

7. Select the Open Properties For This Data Collector Set option, and then tap or click Finish. This saves the data collector set, closes the wizard, and then opens the related Properties dialog box.

8. By default, logging is configured to start manually. To configure a logging schedule, tap or click the Schedule tab and then tap or click Add. You can now set the active range, start time, and run days for data collection.

9. By default, logging stops only if you set an expiration date as part of the logging schedule. Using the options on the Stop Condition tab, you can configure the log file to stop manually after a specified period of time, such as seven days, or when the log file is full (if you set a maximum size limit).

10. Tap or click OK when you finish setting the logging schedule and stop conditions. You can manage the data collector as explained in "Creating and managing data collector sets" earlier in this chapter. If you want Windows to run a scheduled task when data collection stops, configure the tasks on the Task tab in the Properties dialog box.

## Monitoring performance from the command line

Windows Server 2012 includes a command-line utility called Typeperf for writing performance data to the command line. You can use it to monitor the performance of both local and remote computers. The available parameters for Typeperf are summarized in Table 11-2.

Chapter 11

**TABLE 11-2  Parameters for Typeperf**

| Parameter | Description |
|---|---|
| –cf <*filename*> | Specifies a file containing a list of performance counters to monitor. |
| –config <*filename*> | Specifies the settings file containing command options. |
| –f <CSV\|TSV\|BIN\|SQL> | Sets the output file format. The default is .csv for comma-separated values. |
| –o <*filename*> | Sets the path of an output file or SQL database. |
| –q [*object*] | Lists installed counters for the specified object. |
| –qx [*object*] | Lists installed counters with instances. |
| –s <*ComputerName*> | Sets the server to monitor if no server is specified in the counter path. |
| –sc <*samples*> | Sets the number of samples to collect. |
| –si <[[*hh:*]*mm:*]ss> | Sets the time between samples. The default is 1 second. |
| –y | Answers Yes to all questions without prompting. |

It looks complicated, I know, but Typeperf is fairly easy to use after you get started. In fact, all you really need to provide to get basic monitoring information is the path to the performance counter you want to track. The performance counter path has the following syntax:

```
\\ComputerName\ObjectName\ObjectCounter
```

Here, the path starts with the UNC computer name or IP address of the local or remote computer you are working with and includes the object name and the object counter to use. If you want to track System\Processor Queue Length on CORPSVR02, you type

```
typeperf "\\corpsvr02\System\Processor Queue Length"
```

> **Note**
> You might have noticed that I enclosed the counter path in double quotation marks. Although this is good form for all counter paths, it is required in this example because the counter path includes spaces.

You can also easily track all counters for an object by using an asterisk (*) as the counter name, such as in the following:

```
typeperf "\\corpsvr02\Memory\*"
```

Here, you track all counters for the *Memory* object.

A slight problem is introduced for objects that have multiple instances. For these objects, such as the *Processor* object, you must specify the object instance you want to work with. The syntax for this is as follows:

```
\\ComputerName\ObjectName(ObjectInstance)\ObjectCounter
```

Here, you follow the object name with the object instance in parentheses. To work with all instances of an object that has multiple instances, you use _Total as the instance name. To work with a specific instance of an object, use its instance identifier. For example, if you want to examine the Processor\%Processor Time counter, you must use either the following to work with all processor instances:

```
typeperf "\\corpsvr02\Processor(_Total)\%Processor Time"
```

or the code shown next to work with a specific processor instance:

```
typeperf "\\corpsvr02\Processor(0)\%Processor Time"
```

In this case, that is the first processor on the system.

By default, Typeperf writes its output to the command line in a comma-delimited list. You can redirect the output to a file using the *–o* parameter and set the output format using the *–f* parameter. The output format indicators are CSV for a comma-delimited text file, TSV for a tab-delimited text file, BIN for a binary file, and SQL for a SQL binary file. Consider the following example:

```
typeperf "\\corpsvr02\Memory\*" -o perf.bin -f bin
```

Here, you track all counters for the *Memory* object and write the output to a binary file called Perf.bin in the current directory.

If you need help determining the available counters, type **typeperf –q** followed by the object name for which you want to view counters, such as in the following:

```
typeperf -q Memory
```

If an object has multiple instances, you can list the installed counters with instances by using the *–qx* parameter, such as in the following:

```
typeperf -qx PhysicalDisk
```

You can use this counter information as input to Typeperf as well. Add the *–o* parameter, and write the output to a text file, such as in the following:

```
typeperf -qx PhysicalDisk -o perf.txt
```

Chapter 11

Then, edit the text file so that only the counters you want to track are included. You can then use the file to determine which performance counters are tracked by specifying the –*cf* parameter followed by the file path to this counter file. Consider the following example:

```
typeperf -cf perf.txt -o c:\perflogs\perf.bin -f bin
```

Here, Typeperf reads the list of counters to track from Perf.txt and then writes the performance data in binary format to a file in the C:\PerfLogs directory.

The one problem with Typeperf is that it will sample data once every second until you tell it to stop by pressing Ctrl+C. This is fine when you are working at the command line and monitoring the output. It doesn't work so well, however, if you have other things to do—and most administrators do. To control the sampling interval and set how long to sample, you can use the –*si* and –*sc* parameters, respectively. For example, if you want Typeperf to sample every 60 seconds and stop logging after 120 samples, you could type this:

```
typeperf -cf perf.txt -o C:\perf\logs\perf.bin -f bin -si 60 -sc 120
```

# INSIDE OUT   Use Windows PowerShell for performance monitoring

Windows PowerShell includes several cmdlets for performance monitoring. The one you'll use the most is Get-Counter. You use Get-Counter to get objects representing real-time performance counter data. The paths you work with when specifying counters are similar to those used with Typeperf. For example, you track all counters for the *Memory* object on CorpSvr35 by entering the following command:

```
get-counter "\\corpsvr35\Memory\*"
```

If you want to examine the Processor\%Processor Time counter, you either work with all processor instances:

```
get-counter "\\corpsvr35\Processor(_Total)\%Processor Time"
```

or with a specific processor instance:

```
get-counter "\\corpsvr35\Processor(0)\%Processor Time"
```

Need to know which counters are available for an object? Simply type **get-counter -listset** followed by the object name, such as:

```
get-counter -listset Memory
```

Here, you list all the counters for the *Memory* object.

# Analyzing trace logs at the command line

You can examine trace log data by using the Tracerpt command-line utility. Tracerpt processes trace logs, and you can use it to generate trace analysis reports and dump files for the events generated. Commonly used parameters for Tracerpt are summarized in Table 11-3.

**TABLE 11-3 Parameters for Tracerpt**

| Parameter | Description |
|---|---|
| –o [*filename*] | Sets the text output file to which the parsed data should be written. The default is Dumpfile.xml. |
| –summary [*filename*] | Sets the name of the text file to which a summary report of the data should be written. The default is Summary.txt. |
| –report [*filename*] | Sets the name of the text file to which a detailed report of the data should be written. The default is Workload.xml. |
| –rt <*session_name* [*session_name* ...]> | Sets the real-time event trace session data source to use instead of a converted log file. |
| –config <*filename*> | Specifies a settings file containing command options. |
| –y | Answers Yes to all questions without prompting. |
| -of <CSV\|EVTX\|XML> | Sets the dump file format. |
| -f <XML\|HTML> | Sets the report file format. |
| –export <*filename*> | Sets the name of the event schema export file. The default is schema.man. |

The most basic way to use Tracerpt is to specify the name of the trace log to use. By default, trace logs are written to C:\PerfLogs. So, if a log in this directory was named SysP_000002.etl, you could analyze it by typing the following:

```
tracerpt C:\Perflogs\SysP_000002.etl
```

Here, four files are created in the current directory. The parsed output is written to Dumpfile.xml, a summary report is written to Summary.txt, a detailed report is written to Workload.xml, and an event schema report file is written to schema.man.

You could also specify the exact files to use for output as shown in the following example:

```
tracerpt C:\Perflogs\ SysP_000002.etl -o c:\sysp.csv
 -summary c:\sysp-summary.txt -report sysp-report-.txt
```

Chapter 11

# PART 3

# Managing Windows Server 2012 Storage and File Systems

# Storage management

Tнıs chapter introduces Microsoft Windows Server 2012 storage management. Data is stored throughout the enterprise on a variety of systems and storage devices, the most common of which are hard disk drives but also can include storage-management devices and removable media devices. Managing and maintaining the myriad systems and storage devices are the responsibilities of administrators. If a storage device fails, runs out of space, or encounters other problems, serious negative consequences can result. Servers could crash, applications could stop working, and users could lose data, all of which affects the productivity of users and the organization's bottom line. You can help prevent such problems and losses by implementing sound storage-management procedures that enable you to evaluate your current and future storage needs and also help you meet current and future performance, capacity, and availability requirements. You then must configure storage appropriately for the requirements you've defined.

## Essential storage technologies

One of the few constants in Microsoft Windows operating system administration is that data storage needs are ever increasing. It seems that only a few years ago a 1-terabyte (TB) hard disk was huge and something primarily reserved for Windows servers rather than Windows workstations. Now Windows workstations ship with large hard disks as standard equipment, and some even ship with striped drives that allow workstations to have spanned drives that have multi-terabyte volumes—and all of that data must be backed up and stored somewhere other than on the workstations to protect it. This has meant that back-end storage solutions have had to scale dramatically as well. Server solutions that were once used for enterprise-wide implementations are now being used increasingly at the departmental level, and the underlying architecture for the related storage solutions has had to change dramatically to keep up.

# INSIDE OUT  Storage technologies are in transition

Storage technologies are in transition from traditional approaches to standards-based approaches. As a result, several popular tools and favored features are being phased out. Officially, a tool or feature that is being phased out is referred to as *deprecated*. When Microsoft deprecates a tool or feature that means it might not be in future releases of the operating system. Rather than not cover popular tools and features, I've chosen to discuss what is actually available in the operating system right now. That means I discuss both favored standbys and new options.

Like other Windows operating systems before them, Windows 8 and Windows Server 2012 will have long product life cycles. For most people deploying these operating systems today, what's in the box right now is what matters most and not what might or might not be in the box in a future release. My recommendation is to continue to use your favorite tools and features for servers you've already deployed and then transitioned to Windows Server 2012. Before you deploy new servers on new hardware, however, you should review the available storage options and then make informed decisions as to the tools and features to use on those new servers.

## Using internal and external storage devices

To help meet the increasing demand for data storage and changing requirements, organizations are deploying servers with a mix of internal and external storage. In internal-storage configurations, drives are connected inside the server chassis to a local disk controller and are said to be directly attached. You'll sometimes see an internal storage device referred to as *direct-attached storage (DAS)*.

In external-storage configurations, servers connect to external, separately managed collections of storage devices that are either network-attached or part of a storage area network. Although the terms *network-attached storage (NAS)* and *storage area network (SAN)* are sometimes used as if they are one and the same, the technologies differ in how servers communicate with the external drives.

NAS devices are connected through a regular Transmission Control Protocol/Internet Protocol (TCP/IP) network. All server-storage communications go across the organization's local area network (LAN), as shown in Figure 12-1, and typically use file-based protocols for communications, which can include Server Message Block (SMB), Distributed File System

(DFS), and Network File System (NFS). This means the available bandwidth on the network can be shared by clients, servers, and NAS devices. For best performance, the network should be running at 1 gigabit per second (Gbps) or higher. Networks operating at slower speeds can experience a serious decrease in performance as clients, services, and storage devices try to communicate using the limited bandwidth.

# INSIDE OUT   Working with NFS

You add support for NFS by adding the Server For NFS feature to a file server. Windows Server 2012 supports NFS 3 and NFS 4.1. NFS 3 brings with it support for continuous availability. NFS 4.1 adds supports for stateful connections with improved security and lower bandwidth utilization. Support for NFS 3 and NFS 4.1 also enables you to reliably deploy and run VMware ESX and VMware ESXi on virtual machines from file-based storage access over NFS. You also can deploy Server For NFS reliably in a clustered configuration.

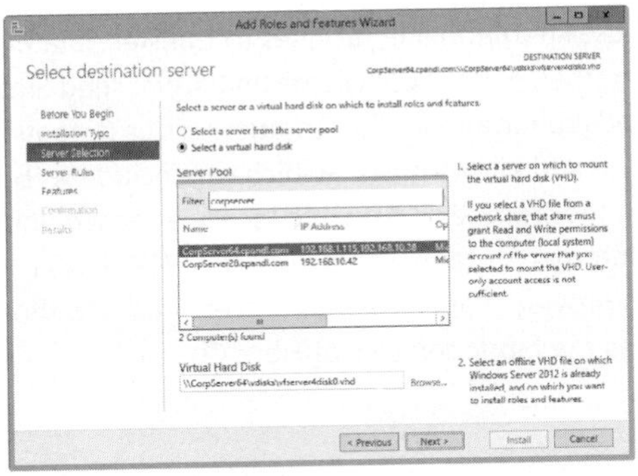

**Figure 12-1**  In a NAS, server-storage communications are on the LAN.

A SAN typically is physically separate from the LAN and is independently managed. As shown in Figure 12-2, this isolates the server-to-storage communications so that traffic doesn't affect communications between clients and servers. Several SAN technologies are implemented, including Fibre Channel Protocol (FCP), a more traditional SAN technology that delivers high reliability and performance, and Internet SCSI (iSCSI), which delivers good reliability and performance at a lower cost than Fibre Channel. As the name implies, iSCSI uses TCP/IP networking technologies on the SAN so that servers can communicate with storage devices using IP. The SAN is still isolated from the organization's LAN.

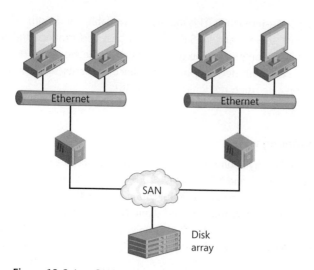

**Figure 12-2** In a SAN, server-storage communications don't affect communications between clients and servers.

You should be aware that iSCSI uses traditional IP facilities to transfer data over LANs, wide area networks (WANs), or the Internet. Here, iSCSI clients (initiators) send Small Computer System Interface (SCSI) commands to targeted iSCSI storage devices (targets) on remote servers. iSCSI consolidates storage and allows hosts—which can include web, application, and database servers—to access the storage as if it were locally attached. Initiators can locate storage resources using Internet Storage Name Service (iSNS). iSNS isn't required for communications, but it does provide management services similar to those for Fibre Channel networks. iSNS emulates the fabric services of Fibre Channel and can manage both Fibre Channel and iSCSI devices.

Although Fibre Channel requires special cabling, iSCSI uses standard Ethernet cabling and technically can operate over the same network as standard IP traffic. However, if iSCSI isn't operated on a dedicated network or subnet, performance can be severely degraded.

With TCP/IP, TCP is the transport protocol for IP networks. With Fibre Channel, FCP is a transport protocol used to transport SCSI commands over the Fibre Channel network. Fibre Channel networks can use a variety of topologies, including the following:

- Point-to-point (FC-PTP), where two devices are connected directly.

- Arbitrated loop (FC-AL), where all devices are in a ring, similar to token ring networking.

- Switched fabric (FC-SW), where all devices or device rings are connected to switches, similar to Ethernet.

The standard model for Fibre Channel has five layers:

- FC0, the physical layer, which includes cables and connectors

- FC1, the data-link layer

- FC2, the network layer

- FC3, the common services layer

- FC4, the protocol-mapping layer

Windows Server 2012 includes support for Fibre Channel over Ethernet (FCoE), a technology that allows IP network and SAN data traffic to be consolidated on a single network. FCoE encapsulates Fibre Channel frames over Ethernet and supports 10-Gbps and higher networks. With FCoE, the FC0 and FC1 layers of the Fibre Channel model are replaced with Ethernet and FCoE operates in the FC2, or network, layer. This is different from iSCSI, which runs on top of TCP and IP. Additionally, while iSCSI is routable across IP networks, FCoE isn't routable in the IP layer and won't work across routed IP networks.

You should also note that although Fibre Channel has priority-based flow controls, these controls aren't part of standard Ethernet. As a result, both FCoE and iSCSI needed enhancements to support priority-based flow controls and prevent the frame loss that might occur otherwise. These enhancements, provided in the Data Center Bridging suite of Institute of Electrical and Electronics Engineers (IEEE) standards, include the encapsulation of native frames, extensions to Ethernet to prevent frame loss, and mapping between ports/IDs and Ethernet media access control (MAC) addresses.

Several competing network protocols are available to provide fabric functionality to Fibre Channel devices over an IP network and to make the technology work over long distances. One is called Internet Fibre Channel Protocol (iFCP). iFCP uses gateways and routing to enable connectivity and TCP for error detection and correction as well as congestion control. A similar technology called Fibre Channel over IP (FCIP) also is available. FCIP uses storage tunneling, where Fibre Channel frames are encapsulated and then forwarded over an IP network using TCP.

## Storage-management features and tools

Windows Server 2012 includes many features for working with SANs and handling storage management in general. Volume Shadow Copy Service (VSS) allows administrators to create point-in-time copies of volumes and individual files called *snapshots*. This makes it possible to back up these items while files are open and applications are running and to restore them to a specific point in time. You also can use VSS to create point-in-time copies of documents on shared folders. These copies are called *shadow copies*.

Chapter 12

> **Note**
>
> Users can recover their own files when VSS is enabled. After you configure shadow copy, point-in-time backups of documents contained in the designated shared folders are created automatically, and users can quickly recover files that have been deleted or unintentionally altered as long as the Shadow Copy Client has been installed on their computer. For more information about VSS and the Shadow Copy Client, see Chapter 15, "File sharing and security."

The basic VSS functionality is built into the file and storage services and accessed through the File Server VSS provider. You can extend the basic functions in several ways. One of these ways is to add the File Server VSS Agent Service. You use this role service to create consistent snapshots of server application data, such as virtual machine files from Hyper-V. You install the agent service on a file server when you want to back up applications that are storing data files on the file server. Here, you are backing up application data stored on file shares, which is different from user data stored on file shares (which is managed using the standard File Server VSS provider).

Windows Server 2012 also includes storage providers. Storage providers make it possible for storage devices from multiple vendors to interoperate. To do this, Microsoft provides Storage Management application programming interfaces (APIs) that management tools and storage hardware can use, allowing for a unified interface for managing storage devices from multiple vendors and making it easier for administrators to manage a mixed-storage environment. Standard storage providers are built into the file and storage services.

Windows Server 2012 also supports the Storage Management Initiative (SMI-S) standard and storage providers that are compliant with this standard. Add this support by adding the Windows Standards-Based Storage Management feature. This feature enables the discovery, management, and monitoring of storage devices using management tools that support the SMI-S standard. It does this by installing related Windows Management Instrumentation (WMI) classes and cmdlets.

When your file servers are using iSCSI, Fibre Channel, or both storage device types, you might also want to install Multipath IO, iSNS Server service, and Data Center Bridging—all of which are installable features.

Multipath I/O supports SAN connectivity by establishing multiple sessions or connections to storage devices. Using Multipath I/O, you can configure as many as 32 separate physical paths to external storage devices that can be used simultaneously and load balanced if necessary. The purpose of having multiple paths is to have redundancy and possibly increased throughput. If you have multiple host bus adapters as well, you improve the chances of recovery from a path failure. However, if a path failure occurs, there might be a short period of time when the drives on the SAN aren't accessible. Microsoft Multipath I/O (MPIO) supports iSCSI, Fibre Channel, and Serial Attached SCSI (SAS).

iSNS Server service helps iSNS clients discover iSCSI storage devices on an Ethernet network and also automates the management and configuration of iSCSI and Fibre Channel storage devices (as long as Fibre Channel devices use iFCP gateways). Data Center Bridging helps manage bandwidth allocation for offloaded storage traffic on converged network adapters, which is useful with iSCSI and FCoE.

Other file and storage features you might want to install on file servers include the following:

- **Enhanced Storage**  Supports additional functions made available by devices that support hardware encryption and enhanced storage. Enhanced storage devices support IEEE standard 1667 to provide enhanced security, which can include authentication at the hardware level of the storage device.

- **Windows Search Service**  Allows for faster file searches for resources on the server from clients that are compatible with this service. Keep in mind, however, this feature is designed primarily for desktop and small office implementations (and not for large enterprises).

- **Windows Server Backup**  The standard backup utility included with Windows Server 2012.

Server Manager is your primary tool for managing storage. Windows Server 2012 also has several command-line tools for managing local storage and storage-replication services. These tools include the following:

- **DiskPart**  Used to manage basic and dynamic disks as well as the partitions and volumes on those disks. It is the command-line counterpart to the Disk Management tool and also includes features not found in the graphical user interface (GUI) tool, such as the capability to extend partitions on basic disks.

> **Note**
>
> DiskPart cannot be used to manage Storage Spaces. Windows 8 and Windows Server 2012 might be the last versions of Windows to support Disk Management, DiskPart, and DiskRaid. The Virtual Disk Service (VDS) COM interface is being superseded by the Storage Management API. You can continue to use Disk Management and DiskPart to manage basic and dynamic disks.

- **Dfsdiag**   Used to perform troubleshooting and diagnostics for DFS.

- **Dfsradmin**   Used to manage and monitor DFS replication throughout the enterprise. You'll use this tool for troubleshooting and diagnosing problems as well. This tool replaces Health_Chk and the other tools it worked with.

- **Dfsutil**   Used to configure DFS, back up and restore DFS directory trees (namespaces), copy directory trees, and troubleshoot DFS.

- **Fsutil**   Used to get detailed drive information and perform advanced file system maintenance. You can manage sparse files, reparse points, disk quotas, and other advanced features of NTFS.

- **Mountvol**   Used to manage volume automounting. By using volume mount points, administrators can mount volumes to empty NTFS folders, giving the volumes a drive path rather than a drive letter. This means it is easier to mount and unmount volumes, particularly with SANs.

- **Vssadmin**   Used to view and manage the Volume Shadow Copy Service and its configuration.

Many Windows PowerShell cmdlets are available for managing storage as well. These cmdlets are module-specific and correspond to the storage component you want to manage. Available modules include

- **BitsTransfer**   Used to manage the Background Intelligent Transfer Service (BITS).

- **BranchCache**   Used to configure and check the status of Windows BranchCache.

- **DFSN**   Used to manage DFS Namespaces.

- **FileServerResourceManager**   Used to manage File Server Resource Manager.

- **iSCSI**   Used to manage iSCSI connections, sessions, targets, and ports.

- **IscsiTarget**   Used to mount and manage iSCSI virtual disks.

- **SmbShare**   Used to configure and check the status of standard file sharing.

- **Storage**   Used to manage disks, partitions, and volumes, as well as storage pools and Storage Spaces. It cannot be used to manage dynamic disks.

You'll learn more about the technologies behind these modules later in this chapter. The easiest way to learn more about these PowerShell modules is to import a particular module, determine which cmdlets are associated with it, and then examine how the cmdlets are used. You import a module using the following syntax:

```
Import-module ModuleName
```

Here, *ModuleName* is the name of the module to import, such as the following:

```
Import-module iscsi
```

You list the cmdlets associated with an imported module using

```
get-command -module ModuleName
```

Here, *ModuleName* is the name of the module you want to examine, such as the following:

```
get-command -module iscsi
```

After you list the cmdlets associated with an imported module, you can get more information about a particular cmdlet using

```
get-help CmdletName -detailed
```

Here, *CmdletName* is the name of the cmdlet to examine in detail, such as the following:

```
get-help connect-iscsitarget -detailed
```

## Storage-management role services

You use File And Storage Services to configure your file servers. Several file and storage services are installed by default with any installation of Windows Server 2012. These include File Server, which you use to manage file shares that users can access over the network, and Storage Services, which you use to manage various types of storage, including storage pools and storage spaces. Storage pools group disks so that you can create virtual disks from the available capacity. Each virtual disk you create is a storage space. You'll learn how to work with storage pools and Storage Spaces in Chapter 14, "Managing file systems and storage."

Windows Server 2012 also supports thin provisioning of your storage spaces. With *thin provisioning*, you can create large virtual disks without having the actual space available. This allows you to provision storage to meet future needs and grow storage as needed. You also can reclaim storage that is no longer needed by trimming storage. To see how thin provisioning works, consider the following scenarios:

- Your file server is connected to a storage array with 2 TBs of actual storage, but with the capability to grow to 10 TBs as needed (by installing additional hard disks). When you set up storage, you provision it as if additional storage was already available.

One way to do this is to create a storage pool that has a total size of 10 TBs and then create 5 thin disks with 2 TBs of storage each.

- Your eight file servers are connected to a SAN with 10 TBs of actual storage, but with the capability to grow to 80 TBs as needed (by installing additional hard disks). When you set up storage, you provision it as if additional storage was already available. One way to do this is to create a storage pool on each file server that has a total size of 10 TBs. Next, within each storage pool, you create 5 thin disks with 2 TBs of storage each.

With thin-disk provisioning, volumes use space from the storage pool as needed, up to the volume size. Here, the actual storage utilization for a volume is based on the total size of the data stored on the volume. If a volume doesn't grow, the storage space is never allocated and isn't wasted.

Contrast this to fixed-disk provisioning, where a volume has a fixed size and uses space from the storage pool equal to its volume size. Here, the storage utilization for a volume is fixed and based on the total size of the volume itself. Because the storage is pre-allocated with a fixed size, any unused space isn't available for other volumes.

You can enhance file storage in many ways using the additional role services that are available for File And Storage Services. One of the first role services you might consider using is BranchCache For Network Files. You add the BranchCache For Network Files role service to enable enhanced support for Windows BranchCache on your file servers and to optimize data transfer over the WAN for caching.

Windows BranchCache is a file-caching feature that works in conjunction with BITS. By enabling branch caching in Group Policy, you allow computers to retrieve documents and other types of files from a local cache rather than retrieving files from servers over the network. This improves response times and reduces transfer times.

Branch caching can be used in either a distributed cache mode or a hosted cache mode. With the distributed cache mode, desktop computers running compatible versions of Windows host and send distributed file caches, and caching servers running at remote offices are not needed. With the hosted cache mode, compatible file servers at remote offices host local file caches and send them to clients. Generally, whether distributed or hosted, the caches at one office location are separate from caches at other office locations. That said, the Active Directory configuration and the way Group Policy is applied ultimately determine whether computers are considered to be part of one office location or another.

Branch caching is designed as a WAN solution. It optimizes bandwidth usage for files transferred with either SMB or Hypertext Transfer Protocol (HTTP). Your content servers can be located anywhere on your network, as well as in public or private cloud datacenters. You enable branch caching on web servers and BITS-based application servers by adding the

BranchCache feature. If you are deploying hosted cache servers, you add the BranchCache feature to these servers as well. You don't install this feature on your file servers, however. Instead, you add the BranchCache For Network Files role service.

# INSIDE OUT    Enhancing BranchCache

BranchCache For Network Files can take advantage of data deduplication techniques to optimize data transfers. Because of this, it is recommended that you also install the Data Deduplication role service on your file servers, but don't do this without a firm understanding of what data deduplication is and how it works. If you have multiple file servers, you might also want to enable hash publication per share to improve per-formance. For file servers that aren't domain members, you enable hash publication in local policy. For file servers that are domain members, you typically want to isolate your BranchCache-enabled file servers in their own organizational units (OUs) and then enable hash publication in the appropriate GPO (Group Policy Object) or GPOs that are applied to these OUs. Either way, the Hash Publication For BranchCache policy is what you want to work with. This policy is found under Computer Configuration\Administrative Templates\Network Lanman Server.

The Data Deduplication service can be installed with or without the BranchCache For Network Files role service. Data Deduplication uses subfile, variable-size chunking and compression to achieve higher storage efficiency. The service does this by segmenting files into 32-KB to 128-KB chunks, identifying duplicate chunks, and replacing the duplicates with references to a single copy. Because optimized files are stored as reparse points, files on the volume are no longer stored as data streams. Instead, they are replaced with stubs that point to data blocks within a common chunk store.

Previously, I mentioned the File Server VSS Agent Service, which you install on file servers when you want to ensure that you can make consistent backups of server application data using VSS-aware backup applications. When working with iSCSI, you also must install the iSCSI target VSS hardware provider on the initiator server you use to perform backups of iSCSI virtual disks. This ensures that the snapshots are application-consistent and can be restored at the logical unit number (LUN) level. If you don't use the iSCSI target VSS hard-ware provider on the initiator, server backups might not be consistent and you might not be able to completely recover your iSCSI virtual disks. On management computers running storage-management applications, you must install the iSCSI target Virtual Disk Service (VDS) hardware provider. The iSCSI target VSS hardware provider and the iSCSI target VDS hardware provider are part of the iSCSI Target Storage Provider role service.

Chapter 12

Another role service you might want to use with iSCSI is the iSCSI Target Server service. This role service turns any computer running Windows Server into a network-accessible block storage device. You can use this continuously available block storage to support network/diskless boot, shared storage on non-Windows iSCSI initiators, and development environments where you need to test applications prior to deploying them to SAN storage. Because the service uses standard Ethernet for its transport, no additional hardware is needed.

Although SMB is the default file-sharing protocol, other file-sharing solutions are available, including Network File System (NFS) and Distributed File System (DFS). To enable NFS on your file servers, you add the Server For NFS service. This service provides a file-sharing solution for enterprises with mixed Windows and UNIX environments. When you install Server For NFS, users can transfer files between Windows Server and UNIX operating systems using the NFS protocol. DFS, on the other hand, isn't an interoperability solution. Instead, DFS is a robust, enterprise solution for file sharing that you can use to create a single directory tree that includes multiple file servers and their file shares.

The DFS tree can contain more than 5000 shared folders in a domain environment (or 50,000 shared folders on a standalone server), located on different servers, enabling users to find files or folders distributed across the enterprise easily. DFS directory trees can also be published in the Active Directory directory service so that they are easy to search.

DFS has two key components:

- **DFS Namespaces**   You can use DFS Namespaces to group shared folders located on different servers into one or more logically structured namespaces. Each namespace appears as a single shared folder with a series of subfolders. However, the underlying structure of the namespace can come from shared folders on multiple servers in different sites.

- **DFS Replication**   You can use DFS Replication to synchronize folders on multiple servers across local or wide area network connections using a multimaster replication engine. The replication engine uses the Remote Differential Compression (RDC) protocol to synchronize only the portions of files that have changed since the last replication.

You can use DFS Replication with DFS Namespaces or by itself. When a domain is running in a Windows 2008 domain functional level or higher, domain controllers use DFS Replication to replicate the SYSVOL directory.

## DFS supports multiple roots and closest-site selection

Windows Server 2012 supports multiple DFS roots and closest-site selection. The capability to host multiple DFS roots allows you to consolidate and reduce the number of servers needed to maintain DFS. By using closest-site selection, DFS uses Active Directory site metrics to route a client to the closest available DFS server.

File Server Resource Manager (FSRM) installs a suite of tools that administrators can use to better manage data stored on servers. Using FSRM, you can do the following:

- **Define file-screening policies**   You use file-screening policies to block unauthorized, potentially malicious types of content. You can configure active screening, which does not allow users to save unauthorized files, or passive screening, which allows users to save unauthorized files but monitors or warns about usage (or you can configure both).

- **Configure Resource Manager disk quotas**   Using Resource Manager disk quotas, you can manage disk space usage by folder and by volume. You can configure quotas with a specific limit as a hard limit (meaning a limit can't be exceeded) or a soft limit (meaning a limit can be exceeded).

- **Generate storage reports**   You can generate storage reports as part of disk-quota and file-screening management. Storage reports identify file usage by owner, type, and other parameters. They also help identify users and applications that violate screening policies.

You'll learn more about FRSM in Chapter 16, "Managing file screening and storage reporting."

## INSIDE OUT   Windows Storage Server 2012

Windows Storage Server 2012 is a platform for NAS appliances. Several editions are available, including a rather limited Workgroup edition and a full-featured Standard edition. If you purchase a NAS that uses Windows Storage Server 2012 Workgroup or Standard, you can manage it using many of the techniques I discuss in this book. In fact, you'll be able to manage storage provisioning, pooling, virtual disks, volumes, and much more using Server Manager and PowerShell if you want to. You'll also be able to open the storage-provisioning wizards I discuss directly within the original equipment manufacturer (OEM) appliance. Also supported are central access policies, NIC teaming, DFS Namespaces, DFS Replication, Server For NFS, iSCSI targets, FSRM, folder redirection, offline files, offloaded data transfers, and the Resilient File System (ReFS).

Chapter 12

# Booting from SANs, and using SANs with clusters

Windows Server 2012 supports booting from a SAN, having multiple clusters attached to the same SAN, and having a mix of clusters and standalone servers attached to the same SAN. To boot from a SAN, the external storage devices and the host bus adapters of each server must be configured appropriately to allow booting from the SAN.

When multiple servers must boot from the same external storage device, you must either configure the SAN in a switched environment or you must directly attach it from each host to one of the storage subsystem's Fibre Channel ports. A switched or direct-to-port environment allows the servers to be separate from each other, which is essential for booting from a SAN.

## Fibre Channel–Arbitrated Loop isn't allowed

The use of a Fibre Channel–Arbitrated Loop (FC-AL) configuration is not supported because hubs typically don't allow the servers on the SAN to be isolated properly from each other—and the same is true when you have multiple clusters attached to the same SAN or a mix of clusters and standalone servers attached to the same SAN.

Each server on the SAN must have exclusive access to the logical disk from which it is booting, and no other server on the SAN should be able to detect or access that logical disk. For multiple-cluster installations, the SAN must be configured so that a set of cluster disks is accessible only by one cluster and is completely hidden from the rest of the clusters. By default, Windows Server 2012 will attach and mount every logical disk that it detects when the host bus adapter driver loads, and if multiple servers mount the same disk, the file system can be damaged.

To prevent file system damage, the SAN must be configured in such a way that only one server can access a particular logical disk at a time. You can configure disks for exclusive access using a type of logical unit number (LUN) management such as LUN masking, LUN zoning, or a preferred combination of these techniques. You can use the File And Storage Services node in the Server Manager console to manage Fibre Channel and iSCSI SANs that support Storage Management APIs and have a configured storage provider.

## TROUBLESHOOTING

### Detecting SAN configuration problems

On an improperly configured SAN, multiple hosts are able to access the same logical disks. This isn't what you want to happen, but it does happen and you might be able to detect this configuration problem when you are working with the logical disks. Try using File Explorer from multiple hosts to access the logical disks on the SAN. If you try to access a logical disk and receive an Access Denied, Device Not Ready, or similar error message, this can be an indicator that another server has access to the logical disk you are attempting to use. You might see another indicator of an improperly configured SAN when you add or configure logical disks. If you notice that multiple servers report that they've found new hardware when adding or configuring logical disks, there is a configuration problem with the SAN. If there is a configuration problem with clusters, you can see the following error events in the System logs:

- Warning event ID 11 with event source %HBADriverName%, "The driver detected a controller error on Device\ScsiPort*N*."

- Warning event ID 50 with event source Disk, "The system was attempting to transfer file data from buffers to \Device\HarddiskVolume*N*. The write operation failed, and only some of the data may have been written to the file."

- Warning event ID 51 with event source FTDISK, "An error was detected on device during a paging operation."

- Warning event ID 9 with event source %HBADriverName%, "Lost Delayed Write Data: The device, \Device\ScsiPort*N*, did not respond within the timeout period."

- Warning event ID 26 with event source Application Popup, "Windows—Delayed Write Failed: Windows was unable to save all the data for the file \Device\ HarddiskVolume*N*\MFT$. The data has been lost. This error may be caused by a failure of your computer hardware or network connection. Please try to save this file elsewhere."

# Working with SMB 3.0

Sever Message Block (SMB) is the standard technology used for file sharing. SMB 3.0 was released as part of Windows 8 and Windows Server 2012. Earlier releases of Windows support different versions of SMB. Windows 7 and Windows Server 2008 R2 support SMB 2.1. Windows Vista and Windows Server 2008 support SMB 2.0.

SMB 2.1 was an incremental improvement over SMB 2.0, which brought several important changes for file sharing, including support for BranchCache and large maximum transmission units (MTUs). SMB 3.0 has the following important improvements:

- **SMB Direct**   Provides support for network adapters that have Remote Direct Memory Access (RDMA) capability, allowing fast, offloaded data transfers and helping achieve high speeds and low latency while using few CPU resources. Previously, this capability was one of the key advantages of Fibre Channel block storage.

- **SMB encryption**   Provides secure data transfer by encrypting data automatically and without having to deploy Internet Protocol security (IPsec) or another encryption solution. SMB encryption can be enabled for an entire server (meaning for all its file shares) or for individual file shares as needed.

- **SMB Multichannel**   Allows servers to simultaneously use multiple connections and network interfaces, increasing fault tolerance and throughput. Configure network interface card (NIC) teaming to take advantage of this feature.

- **SMB scale-out**   Allows clustered file servers in an active-active configuration to aggregate bandwidth across the cluster. This provides simultaneous access to data files through all nodes in the cluster and allows administrators to load balance across cluster nodes simply by moving file server clients.

- **SMB signing**   Introduces AES-CCM and AES-CMAC for signing. Typically, signing with Advanced Encryption Standard (AES) is dramatically faster than signing with HMAC-SHA256 (which was used by SMB 2/SMB 2.1).

- **SMB Transparent Failover**   Allows administrators to perform maintenance on nodes in a clustered file server without affecting applications storing data on the server's file shares. If a failure occurs, SMB clients transparently reconnect to another cluster node. This provides the benefits of a multicontroller storage array without having to purchase one.

> **Note**
> Not only can you use the SMB Direct, SMB Multichannel, and SMB scale-out features to implement manageable, scalable active-active file shares, you also can use these features to take an existing Fibre Channel SAN and share its storage over SMB 3.0. This gives you a gateway to a SAN and extends your storage options.

Keep in mind that SMB is a client/server technology. For backward compatibility, newer clients continue to support older versions of the technology. While establishing a connection to a file share, an SMB client negotiates the SMB version to use for that connection based on the highest commonly supported SMB version. This process is referred to as *dialect negotiation*.

During dialect negotiation, the version downgrade is automatic, such that an SMB 3.0 client connecting to a SMB 2.1 server will use SMB 2.1 for that connection. Because older versions of SMB are less secure, forcing a client to downgrade the version used is one way someone might try to gain unauthorized access.

SMB 3.0 includes a security feature that attempts to detect forced downgrade attempts. If such an attempt is detected, the connection is disconnected and Event ID 1005 is logged in the Microsoft-Windows-SmbServer/Operational log. This security feature works only when a client tries to force a downgrade from SMB 3.0 to SMB 2.0/SMB 2.1. It doesn't work if a client attempts to downgrade to SMB 1.0. For this reason, Microsoft recommends that you disable support for SMB 1.0.

## INSIDE OUT  Checking for and disabling SMB 1.0

Before you disable SMB 1.0, you should determine whether any clients are using SMB 1.0. SMB 1.0 is used by Windows 2000, Windows XP, and Windows Server 2003. Computer Browser functionality also relies on SMB 1.0. To determine whether any SMB clients are currently using SMB 1.0, you can run the following command on each file server:

```
Get-SmbSession | Select ClientUserName,ClientComputerName,Dialect |
Where-Object {$_.Dialect -lt 2.00}
```

Keep in mind this command must be run with elevated privileges and returns information only about active connections to SMB shares. To disable SMB 1.0 support, you can run the following command at an elevated PowerShell prompt on each file server:

```
Set-SmbServerConfiguration -EnableSMB1Protocol $false
```

You can easily run this command on multiple file servers. One technique is to invoke a remote command, as shown in this example:

```
Invoke-command -computername fileserver12, fileserver23, fileserver45
-scriptblock {Set-SmbServerConfiguration -EnableSMB1Protocol $false}
```

Here, you run the code block on FileServer12, FileServer23, and FileServer45.

If you want to ensure that SMB encryption is used whenever possible, you can enable SMB encryption on either a per-server or per–file share basis. To enable encryption for an entire server and all its SMB file shares, run the following command at an elevated PowerShell prompt on the server:

```
Set-SmbServerConfiguration -EncryptData $true
```

To enable encryption for a specific file share rather than an entire server, run the following command at an elevated PowerShell prompt on the server:

```
Set-SmbShare -Name ShareName -EncryptData $true
```

Here, *ShareName* is the name of the share for which encryption should be used when possible, such as the following:

```
Set-SmbShare -Name CorpData -EncryptData $true
```

You can turn on encryption when you create a share as well. To do this, run the following command at an elevated PowerShell prompt on the server:

```
New-SmbShare -Name ShareName -Path PathName -EncryptData $true
```

Here, *ShareName* is the name of the share for which encryption should be used when possible and *PathName* is the path to an existing folder to share, such as the following:

```
New-SmbShare -Name CorpData -Path D:\Data -EncryptData $true
```

When you want to enable encryption support on multiple file servers, you can invoke remote commands. Consider the following example:

```
$servers = get-content c:\files\server-list.txt
Invoke-command -computername $servers -scriptblock {Set-SmbServerConfiguration
-EnableSMB1Protocol $false}
```

Here, C:\Files\Server-list.txt is the path to a text file containing a list of the file servers to configure. In this file, each file server should be listed on a separate line, as shown here:

```
FileServer12
FileServer23
FileServer45
```

The command will then be invoked on each of the file servers.

# Installing and configuring file services

File servers are central repositories for an organization's data. As you seek to manage and distribute the data stored on your organization's file servers, you might find that you need to optimize file and storage services. Although basic file and storage services are installed by default on servers running Windows Server 2012, you must specifically configure other services and features as they're needed. Use the Add Roles And Features Wizard in Server Manager to add the appropriate role services and features, and then use the related management tools to configure the role services and features as needed.

## Configuring the File And Storage Services role

You can add role services and features to a file server by following these steps:

1.  In Server Manager, tap or click Manage and then tap or click Add Roles And Features, or select Add Roles And Features in the Quick Start pane. This starts the Add Roles And Features Wizard. If the wizard displays the Before You Begin page, read the Welcome text and then tap or click Next.

> **Note**
>
> Beginning with Windows Server 2012, binary source files for roles, role services, and features can be removed to enhance security. If the binaries for the tools you want to use have been removed, you need to install the tools by specifying a source. For more information about role and feature binaries, see Chapter 6, "Configuring roles, role services, and features."

2.  On the Installation Type page, Role-Based Or Feature-Based Installation is selected by default. Tap or click Next.

3.  On the Server Selection page, you can choose to install roles and features on running servers or virtual hard disks. After you make your selection, do one of the following and then tap or click Next:

    a.  Select the server that you want to configure. Keep in mind that only servers running Windows Server 2012 and that have been added for management in Server Manager are listed.

    b.  Select the server host to use, and then type the UNC path to the offline virtual hard disk (VHD) file on that server, as shown in Figure 12-3. Keep in mind that Windows Server 2012 must already be installed on the VHD. Alternatively, tap or click Browse and then use the Browse For Virtual Hard Disks dialog box to locate the offline VHD.

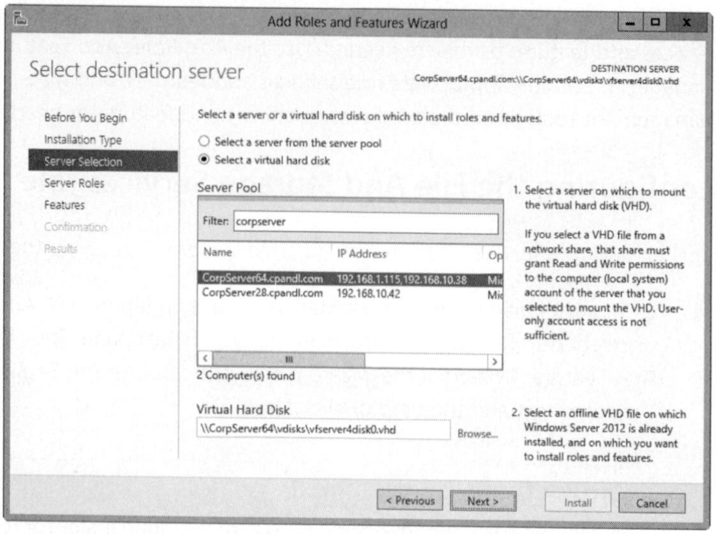

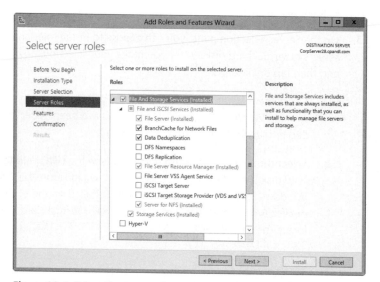

**Figure 12-3** If you are adding roles and features to a VHD, specify the UNC path to the VHD.

4. On the Server Roles page, select File And Storage Services. Expand the related node, and select the additional role services to install, as shown in Figure 12-4. If additional features are required to install a role, you'll see an additional dialog box. Tap or click Add Features to close the dialog box and add the required features to the server installation. When you are ready to continue, tap or click Next.

**Figure 12-4** Select the appropriate role services for the file server.

5. On the Features page, shown in Figure 12-5, select any features you want to install. If additional features are required to install a feature you selected, you'll see an additional dialog box. Tap or click Add Features to close the dialog box and add the required features to the server installation. When you are ready to continue, tap or click Next.

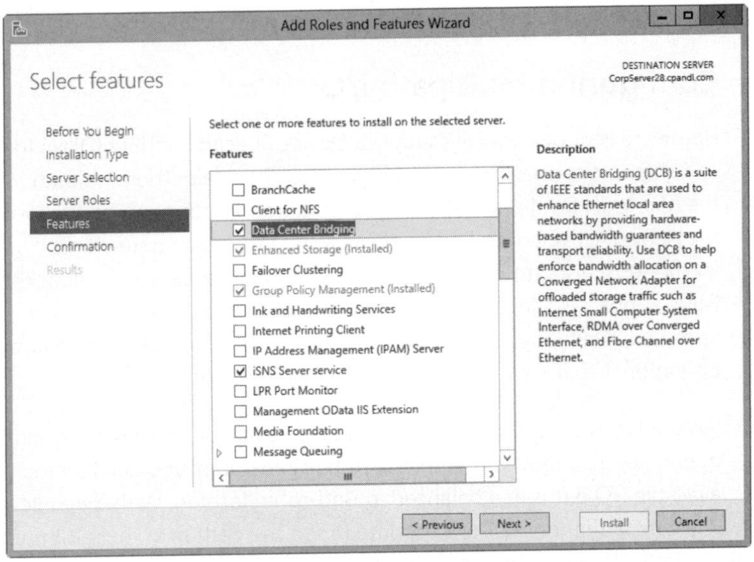

**Figure 12-5** Select the additional features for the file server.

6. On the Confirm page, tap or click the Export Configuration Settings link to generate an installation report that can be displayed in Internet Explorer.

7. If the server on which you want to install roles or features doesn't have all the required binary source files, the server gets the files via Windows Update by default or from a location specified in Group Policy. You also can specify an alternate path for the required source files. To do this, click the Specify An Alternate Source Path link, type that alternate path in the box provided, and then tap or click OK. For network shares, enter the UNC path to the share, such as \\CorpServer14\WinServer2012\. For mounted Windows images, enter the WIM path prefixed with WIM: and including the index of the image to use, such as WIM:\\CorpServer14\WinServer2012\install.wim:4.

8. After you review the installation options and save them as necessary, tap or click Install to begin the installation process. The Installation Progress page tracks the progress of the installation. If you close the wizard, tap or click the Notifications icon in Server Manager and then tap or click the link provided to re-open the wizard.

Chapter 12

9.   When Setup finishes installing the server with the roles and features you selected, the Installation Progress page will be updated to reflect this. Review the installation details to ensure that all phases of the installation were completed successfully. Note any additional actions that might be required to complete the installation, such as restarting the server or performing additional installation tasks. If any portion of the installation failed, note the reason for the failure. Review the Server Manager entries for installation problems, and take corrective actions as appropriate.

## Configuring multipath I/O

Hardware vendors typically supply a Device Specific Module (DSM) for SAN hardware and software for configuring multipath I/O. That said, the Multipath I/O feature includes the Microsoft DSM and some basic configuration options. The Microsoft DSM supports the Active/Active controller model as well as the asymmetric logical unit access controller model. It also implements path selection policies failover, failback, and load balancing. Failover policies allow you to configure a secondary path that should be used if a preferred path fails. If you want the preferred path to be used automatically when it becomes operational again, you can configure a failback policy.

Several types of load-balancing policies are available, including round-robin, dynamic least queue depth, and weighted path. With round-robin, you can configure the DSM to use all available I/O paths in a balanced, round-robin fashion. With dynamic least queue depth, you can configure the DSM to route I/O to the path with the least number of outstanding requests. With weighted path, you assign each path a weight to indicate its relative priority with regard to a particular application, and the DSM selects the path with the least weight among the available paths.

Devices that support the Active/Active controller model are referred to as *Active/Active devices* and, by default, are configured to use round-robin. Generally, devices that support the asymmetric logical unit access (ALUA) controller model are compliant with the SCSI Primary Commands-3 (SPC-3) standard or later and, by default, are configured to use failover.

You manage the multipath I/O (MPIO) configuration using the MPIO Properties dialog box, the Mpclaim command-line tool, or the cmdlets of the MPIO module in PowerShell. After you install the Multipath I/O feature using the Add Roles And Features Wizard, these tools are available on the server. You open the MPIO Properties dialog box, shown in Figure 12-6, by selecting MPIO on the Tools menu in Server Manager.

> **Note**
> You can get a list of the available cmdlets for working with MPIO by typing
> **get-command -module mpio** at a PowerShell prompt.

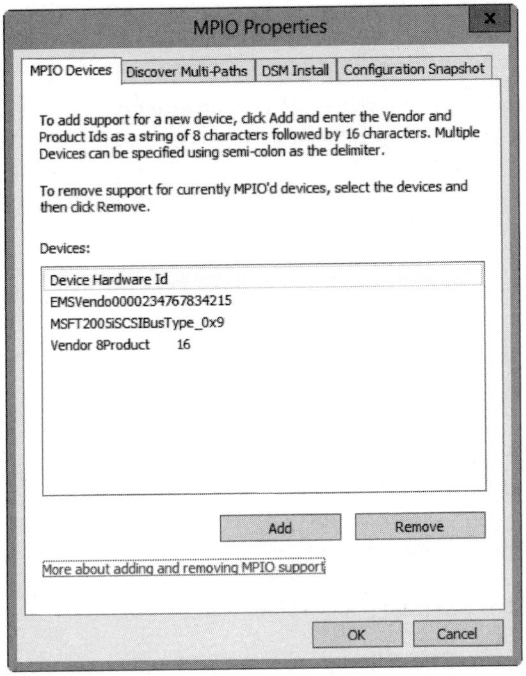

**Figure 12-6** Manage the multipath I/O configuration.

After you enable MPIO, you might also want to do the following:

- Enable automatic claiming of iSCSI devices for MPIO.

- Set the default load-balance policy.

- Set the Windows disk timeout.

For MPIO to manage a device, you must first add the hardware ID for the device to MPIO. You can add devices either manually or automatically.

Chapter 12

Automatic claiming of iSCSI devices allows MPIO to configure available iSCSI devices with multiple paths automatically. Enable this feature by entering the following at an elevated, PowerShell prompt:

```
Enable-MSDSMAutomaticClaim -BusType iSCSI
```

Load balancing and fault tolerance are core features of MPIO. You set the default load-balancing policy using Get-MSDSMGlobalDefaultLoadBalancePolicy. The default policies available are

- Fail over only, which allows one active path, with all other paths designated as standby paths for failover. Use the value FOO.

- Round robin, which sets all available paths to be load-balanced using a round-robin technique. Use the value RR.

- Least queue path, which load-balances by sending I/O to the path with the fewest I/O requests. Use the value LQD.

- Least blocks, which load-balances by sending I/O to the path with the least number of data blocks currently being processed. Use the value LB.

Set the default load-balancing policy by entering the following command at an elevated PowerShell prompt:

```
Get-MSDSMGlobalDefaultLoadBalancePolicy -Policy PolicyValue
```

Here, *PolicyValue* is one of the accepted policy values—either FOO, RR, LQD, LB, or NONE.

You set the timeout value for new disks using Set-MPIOSetting. The basic syntax is

```
Set-MPIOSetting -NewDiskTimeout NumSeconds
```

Here, *NumSeconds* is the number of seconds to wait before reaching the timeout.

Set-MPIOSetting accepts other parameters as well:

- **–PathVerifyEnabled**    When set to –*PathVerifyEnabled $true*, path verification by MPIO is enabled on all paths according to –*PathVerificationPeriod*. By default, this feature is disabled.

- **–PathVerificationPeriod**    When –*PathVerifyEnabled* is set to *$true*, this parameter sets the interval for path verification. For example, use –*PathVerificationPeriod* to verify MPIO on all paths every 60 seconds. The default value is every 30 seconds.

- **–PDORemovePeriod**    Controls the amount of time (in seconds) that a multipath pseudo-LUN will remain in system memory, even after losing all paths to the device.

When the removal period is exceeded, all pending I/O operations are stopped and set as failed, and the failure is passed on to applications. The default value is 20 seconds.

- **–RetryCount**  Controls the number of times a failed I/O is retried. The default value is 3.

- **–RetryInterval**  Sets the number of seconds to wait before retrying a failed I/O. The default is 1 second.

Before you change MPIO settings, you should determine what the current settings are. You can do this by entering Get-MPIOSetting at the PowerShell prompt.

## Adding and removing multipath hardware devices

You manually add devices to MPIO using the MPIO Properties dialog box, which is opened by selecting MPIO on the Tools menu in Server Manager. To manually configure a device to use multipath I/O, follow these steps:

1. Open the MPIO Properties dialog box. On the MPIO Devices tab, you'll see a list of currently configured multipath devices. If the device you want to work with is not listed, tap or click Add.

2. In the Add MPIO Support dialog box, type the vendor ID as an eight-character string followed by the product ID for the device as a 16-character string. Tap or click OK.

3. You are prompted to restart the server to complete the operation. Tap or click Yes to restart the server.

At an elevated command prompt, you can use Mpclaim to configure devices to use multipath I/O as well. The basic syntax for installing a device follows:

```
Mpclaim -r -i [-a | -c | -d DeviceId]
```

The *–r* parameter indicates that you want to restart the server to allow the device installation to be completed. Although you can suppress the restart using the *–n* parameter instead of *–r*, the device will not be installed and available for use until you restart the server. Use the *–a* parameter to configure multipath I/O support for all compatible devices. Use the *–c* parameter to configure multipath I/O support for all SPC-3-compliant devices. Use the *–d* parameter followed by a device's hardware ID to install a specific hardware device. The hardware ID of a device includes the vendor ID as an eight-character string followed by the product ID for the device as a 16-character string. In the following example, you install a device with EMSVendo0000234767834215 as the hardware ID:

```
Mpclaim -r -i -d EMSVendo0000234767834215
```

Chapter 12

Alternatively, you can use Get-MSDSMSupportedHw to list available devices by their hardware ID and New-MSDSMSupportedHw to add a device to MPIO.

Using the MPIO Properties dialog box, you can remove a device from MPIO by following these steps:

1. Open the MPIO Properties dialog box. On the MPIO Devices tab, you'll see a list of currently configured multipath devices.

2. Select the device that should no longer use multiple path IO and then tap or click Remove.

3. You are prompted to restart the server to complete the operation. Tap or click Yes to restart the server.

At an elevated command prompt, you can use Mpclaim to uninstall multipath I/O for a device as well. The basic syntax for installing a device follows:

```
Mpclaim -r -u [-a | -c | -d DeviceId]
```

Except for the *-u* parameter for uninstalling a device, the other parameters are the same as when you are installing MPIO for a device. The following example uninstalls the previously installed device:

```
Mpclaim -r -u -d EMSVendo0000234767834215
```

Alternatively, you can use Get-MSDSMSupportedHw to list available devices by their hardware ID and Remove-MSDSMSupportedHw to remove a device from MPIO.

## Managing and maintaining MPIO

The MPIO Properties dialog box has several other tabs that you can use for general management of MPIO:

- **Discover Multi-Paths**   When you select the Discover Multi-Paths tab, Windows runs a discovery algorithm to examine added device instances and determine if multiple instances represent the same LUN through different paths. Available multipath devices are then listed by their hardware ID. The hardware ID combines a vendor's name and a product string that matches a device ID that is maintained by MPIO. Tap or click Add to add hardware IDs for Fibre Channel devices that use Microsoft DSM.

- **DSM Install**   Use the options on this tab to install DSMs provided by independent hardware vendors (IHVs). Keep in mind that many SPC-3-compliant storage arrays can use the Microsoft DSM and you might not need to install an IHV DSM.

- **Configure Snapshot**    Use the options on this tab to save the current MPIO configuration to a log file. Because the log includes details about the DSM, paths, and path states, you can use this information for troubleshooting.

# INSIDE OUT    Discover iSCSI and SAS devices

On the Discover Multi-Paths tab, you also can discover iSCSI devices and SAS devices and add MPIO support for the discovered devices automatically. To discover iSCSI devices, select the Add Support For iSCSI Devices check box. To discover SAS devices, select the Add Support For SAS Devices check box. Adding support for iSCSI, SAS, or both allows the Microsoft Device Specific Module (MSDSM) to claim all iSCSI, SAS, or both devices for MPIO.

You configure the load-balancing policy for LUNs using their disk properties. In Computer Management, select Disk Management and then press and hold or right-click the disk you want to work with. In the Properties dialog box, click on the MPIO tab. Use the Select MPIO Policy list to choose the load-balancing policy for the selected disk. If you use Failover Only as the load-balancing policy, you can configure a preferred path to the storage. This path is used for automatic failback.

## Meeting performance, capacity, and availability requirements

Whether you are working with internal or external disks, you should follow the same basic principles to help ensure that the chosen storage solutions meet your performance, capacity, and availability requirements. Storage performance is primarily a factor of the disk's access time (how long it takes to register a request and scan the disk), seek time (how long it takes to find the requested data), and transfer rate (how long it takes to read and write data). Storage capacity relates to how much information you can store on a volume or logical disk.

Although early NTFS implementations limited the maximum volume size and file size limit to 32 GBs, later implementations extended these limits. This means you can have a maximum NTFS volume size of 256 TBs minus 64 KBs when you are using 64-KB clusters, and 16 TBs minus 4 KBs when you are using 4-KB clusters. The maximum file size on an NTFS volume is 16 TBs minus 64 KBs. Further, a maximum of 4,294,967,294 files can be created on each volume, and a single server can manage hundreds of volumes (theoretically, around 2000).

Storage availability relates to fault tolerance. You ensure availability for essential applications and services by using availability technologies. If a server has a problem or a

Chapter 12

particular application or service fails, you have a way to continue operations by failing over to another server. In addition to clusters, you can help ensure availability by saving redundant copies of data, keeping spare parts, and if possible making standby servers available. At the disk and data levels, availability is enhanced by using redundant array of independent disks (RAID) technologies. RAID allows you to combine disks and to improve fault tolerance.

RAID can be implemented in hardware or software. When servers have hardware RAID controllers installed, the internal controller can be used to implement RAID on the server's internal disks. When a server is allocated storage from a storage array, one or more logical unit numbers, or LUNs, are assigned. Each LUN is a virtual disk. Typically, hardware RAID configured within the storage array is used to spread the LUN across multiple physical disks (also called *spindles*).

Windows Server 2012 supports several software RAID options, including traditional software-based RAID and Storage Spaces. Traditional software RAID is the software-based RAID technology built into the operating system and available in earlier releases of Windows. Storage Spaces provide resilient storage using new technologies and are preferred over traditional software RAID. However, each of these software-implemented RAID levels requires processing power and memory resources to maintain. By using hardware RAID, you use separate hardware controllers (RAID controllers) to maintain the disk arrays. Although this requires the purchase of additional hardware, it takes the burden off the server and can improve performance. Why? In a hardware-implemented RAID system, a server's processing power and memory aren't used to maintain the disk arrays. Instead, the hardware RAID controller (which is installed internally or in a storage array) handles all the necessary processing tasks.

The RAID levels available with a hardware implementation depend on the hardware controller/storage array and the vendor's implementation of RAID technologies. Some hardware RAID configurations include RAID 0 (disk striping), RAID 1 (disk mirroring), RAID 0+1 (disk striping with mirroring), RAID 5 (disk striping with parity), and RAID 5+1 (disk striping with parity plus mirroring). Table 12-1 provides a summary of these RAID technologies. The table entries are organized listing the highest RAID level to the lowest.

**TABLE 12-1 Hardware RAID configurations for clusters**

| RAID Level | RAID Type | RAID Description | Advantages and Disadvantages |
|---|---|---|---|
| 5+1 | Disk striping with parity plus mirroring | Uses at least six volumes, with each one on a separate drive. Each volume is configured identically as a mirrored striped set with parity error checking. | Provides a high level of fault tolerance, but has a lot of overhead. |

| RAID Level | RAID Type | RAID Description | Advantages and Disadvantages |
|---|---|---|---|
| 5 | Disk striping with parity | Uses at least three volumes, with each one on a separate drive. Each volume is configured as a striped set with parity error checking. In the case of failure, data can be recovered. | Provides fault tolerance with less overhead than mirroring. It has better read performance than disk mirroring. |
| 1 | Disk mirroring | Uses two volumes on two drives. The drives are configured identically, and data is written to both drives. If one drive fails, there is no data loss because the other drive contains the data. This approach does not include disk striping. | Provides redundancy with better write performance than disk striping with parity. |
| 0+1 | Disk striping with mirroring | Uses two or more volumes, with each one on a separate drive. The volumes are striped and mirrored. Data is written sequentially to drives that are identically configured. | Provides redundancy with good read and write performance. |
| 0 | Disk striping | Uses two or more volumes, with each one on a separate drive. Volumes are configured as a striped set. Data is broken into blocks, called stripes, and then written sequentially to all drives in the striped set. | Provides speed and performance without data protection. |

# Configuring Hyper-V

Microsoft's virtualization technology is Hyper-V. Hyper-V is a virtual machine technology that allows multiple guest operating systems to run concurrently on one computer and provide separate applications and services to client computers. When you deploy Hyper-V, the Windows hypervisor acts as the virtual machine engine, providing the necessary layer of software for installing guest operating systems.

## Understanding Hyper-V

Hyper-V can be installed only on computers with 64-bit processors that implement hardware-assisted virtualization and hardware-enforced data execution protection. Specifically, you must enable virtualization support in firmware and also enable either Intel XD bit (execute disable bit) or AMD NX bit (no execute bit) as appropriate.

Chapter 12

Virtualization can offer performance improvements, reduce the number of servers, and reduce the total cost of ownership (TCO). Although you can use both Windows 8 and Windows Server 2012 to deploy virtualized computers, Hyper-V for Windows Server is very different from Client Hyper-V for Windows 8. The focus in this section is on Hyper-V for Windows Server 2012.

Windows Server 2012 supports AMD Virtualization (AMD-V) and Intel Virtualization Technology (Intel VT). AMD-V is included in second-generation and later AMD Opteron processors as well as other AMD processors. Third-generation AMD Opteron processors feature Rapid Virtualization Indexing (RVI) to accelerate the performance of virtualized applications. Intel VT is included in most current Intel Xeon processors as well as Intel vPro and some other Intel processors. Keep in mind that older processors with virtualization might have different features from newer processors, and these differences can present special challenges when you are migrating from one hardware platform to another.

## Important

Windows Server 2012 also supports second-level address translation (SLAT) as implemented by Intel and AMD processors. SLAT adds a second level of paging below the architectural paging tables in the server's processors. This improves performance by providing an indirection layer from virtual machine memory access to physical memory access. On Intel-based processors, this feature is called *extended page tables (EPTs)*, and on AMD-based processors, this feature is called *nested page tables (NPTs)*.

## TROUBLESHOOTING

### Hyper-V compatibility issues

Just as different processors have different sets of supported virtualization features, Windows itself has different implementations of Hyper-V. Because of this, the Hyper-V management tools in Windows Server 2012 can be used to manage only the current version of Hyper-V. The tools cannot be used to manage earlier versions of Hyper-V.

Windows Server 2012 supports many virtualization features, including live migration and dynamic virtual machine storage. You can use live migration to transparently move running virtual machines either from one node of a cluster to another or from one nonclustered server to another. You also can perform multiple live migrations simultaneously. With dynamic virtual machine storage, you can add or remove virtual hard disks and physical disks while a virtual machine is running. You also can move the virtual disks of running virtual machines from one storage location to another without downtime.

Virtual machines also can be stored on SMB 3.0 file shares. Typically, you use this feature by creating the virtual machine and a virtual hard disk on the SMB 3.0 file share. Initially, the virtual machine will think it is using local storage. You then change the storage type by migrating the virtual machine storage from a local configuration to a file-share configuration. Hyper-V also supports connections to Fibre Channel storage using virtual Fibre Channel.

## Installing Hyper-V

Virtual machines require virtual networks to communicate with other computers. When you install Hyper-V, you can create one virtual network for each adapter available. After installing Hyper-V, you can create and manage virtual networks by using Virtual Network Manager. Microsoft recommends that you reserve one network adapter for remote access to the server. You do this by not designating the adapter for use with a virtual network.

You can install Hyper-V on a server with a virtualization-enabled processor by completing these steps:

1. In Server Manager, tap or click Manage and then tap or click Add Roles And Features. If the wizard displays the Before You Begin page, read the Welcome text and then tap or click Next.

2. On the Installation Type page, Role-Based Or Feature-Based Installation is selected by default. Tap or click Next.

3. On the Server Selection page, select the server on which you want to install Hyper-V and then tap or click Next. Keep in mind that only servers running Windows Server 2012 and that have been added for management in Server Manager are listed.

4. On the Server Roles page, select Hyper-V as the role to install. If additional features are required to install a role, you'll see an additional dialog box. Tap or click Add Features to close the dialog box, and add the required features to the server installation. When you are ready to continue, tap or click Next three times, skipping the Features page and the Hyper-V page.

5. On the Create Virtual Switches page, shown in Figure 12-7, select a network adapter on which to create a virtual switch. A virtual switch is needed so that virtual machines can communicate with other computers. The virtual switch allows virtual machines to connect to the physical network. When you are ready to continue, tap or click Next.

Chapter 12

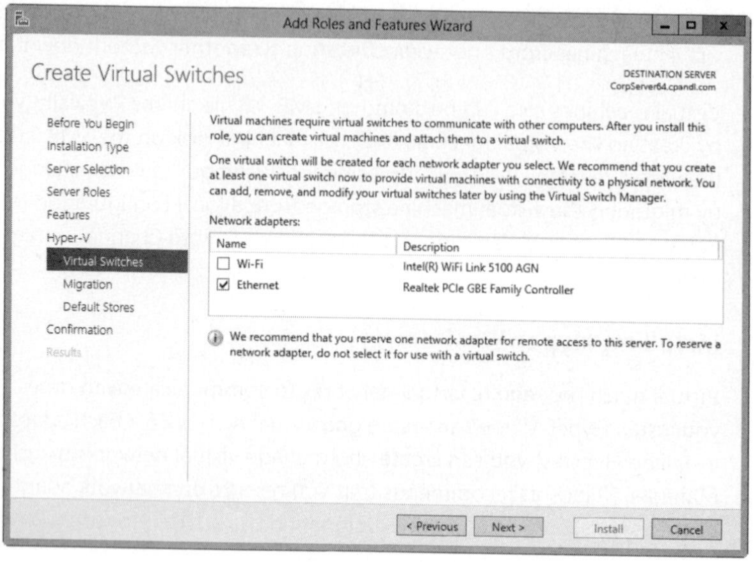

**Figure 12-7** Select the network adapter to use as a virtual switch.

6. On the Virtual Machine Migration page, you can enable live migrations of virtual machines on this server by selecting the check box provided. You don't have to enable this feature now; instead, you can enable this feature later by modifying the Hyper-V settings. However, if you enable live migrations, you also must choose the Credential Security Support Provider (CredSSP) protocol or Kerberos for authentication. Kerberos is the most secure, but you also must configure constrained delegation. CredSSP is less secure but doesn't require you to configure constrained delegation. When you are ready to continue, tap or click Next.

7. On the Default Stores page, you can accept the current default locations for virtual hard disk files and virtual machine configuration files or enter new default locations. Regardless of your choices, you can modify the defaults later using the Hyper-V settings. When you are ready to continue, tap or click Next.

8. On the Confirm page, tap or click the Export Configuration Settings link to generate an installation report that can be displayed in Internet Explorer. If the server on which you want to install Hyper-V doesn't have all the required binary source files, the server gets the files via Windows Update by default or from a location specified in Group Policy. You also can specify an alternate path for the required source files. To do this, click the Specify An Alternate Source Path link, type the alternate path in the box provided, and then tap or click OK.

9. Because a restart is required to complete the installation of Hyper-V, you might want to select the Restart The Destination Server check box. Tap or click Install to

begin the installation process. The Installation Progress page tracks the progress of the installation. If you close the wizard, tap or click the Notifications icon in Server Manager and then tap or click the link provided to re-open the wizard.

**10.** When Setup finishes installing Hyper-V, the Installation Progress page will be updated to reflect this. Review the installation details to ensure that all phases of the installation were completed successfully. If you didn't restart the server, a restart will be pending and required to complete the installation.

## Creating virtual machines

Installing Hyper-V on a server establishes the server as a virtualization server. Each virtual machine you install on the server must be assigned resources to use and then be configured. The number of virtual machines you can run on any individual server depends on the server's hardware configuration and workload. During setup, you specify the amount of memory available to a virtual machine. Although you can change that memory allocation, the amount of memory actively allocated to a virtual machine cannot be used in other ways.

You create and manage virtual machines using Hyper-V Manager, shown in Figure 12-8. Start Hyper-V Manager by selecting Hyper-V Manager on the Tools menu in Server Manager.

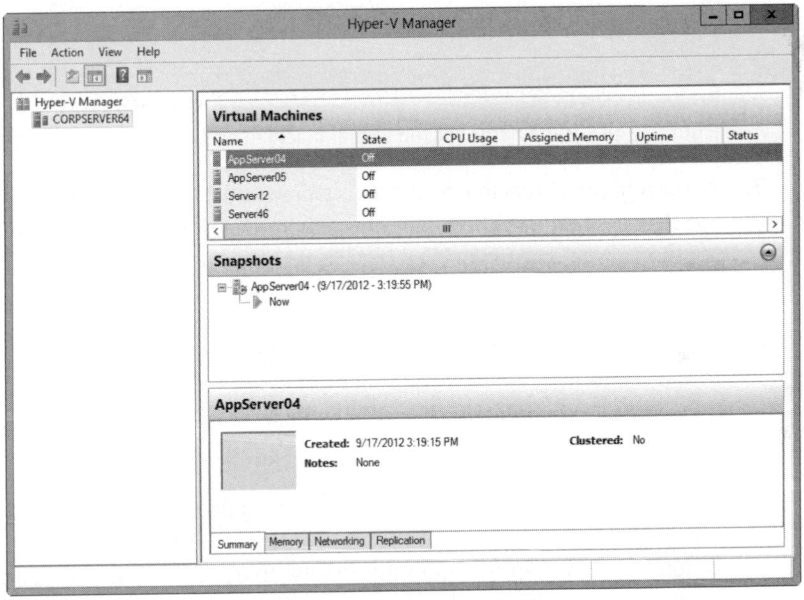

**Figure 12-8** Use Hyper-V Manager to install and manage virtual machines.

Chapter 12

To install and configure a virtual machine, complete the following steps:

1.  In Hyper-V Manager, press and hold or right-click the server node in the left pane, point to New, and then select Virtual Machine. This starts the New Virtual Machine Wizard.

2.  Tap or click Next to display the Specify Name And Location page, shown in Figure 12-9. In the Name text box, enter a name for the virtual machine, such as AppServer02.

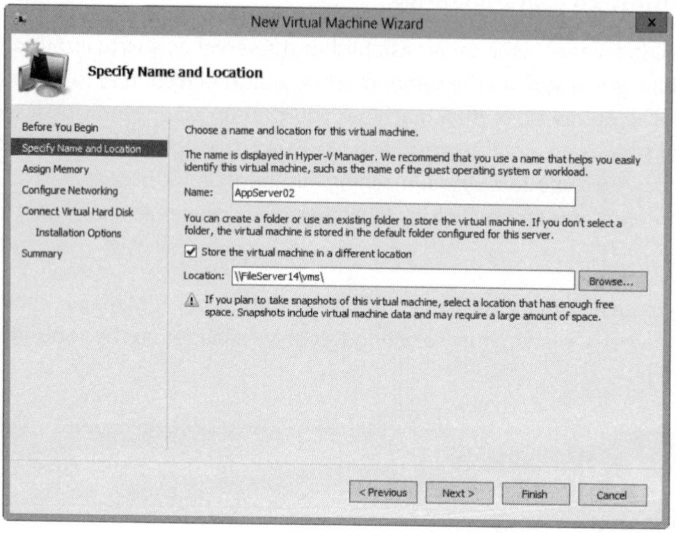

**Figure 12-9**  Set the name for the virtual machine and, optionally, its storage location.

3.  By default, the virtual machine data is stored in the default location for the server. To select a different location, select the Store The Virtual Machine In A Different Location check box, tap or click Browse, and then use the Select Folder dialog box to select a save location.

4.  Tap or click Next. On the Assign Memory page, specify the amount of memory to allocate to the virtual machine. In most cases, you should reserve at least the minimum amount of memory recommended for the operating system you plan to install. You might also want to enable dynamic memory allocation.

5.  Tap or click Next. On the Configure Networking page, use the Connection list to select a network adapter to use. Each new virtual machine includes a network adapter, and you can configure the adapter to use an available virtual switch for communicating with other computers.

6.  Tap or click Next. On the Connect Virtual Hard Disk page, use the options provided to name and set the location of a virtual hard disk for the virtual machine. Each virtual machine requires a virtual hard disk so that you can install an operating system and required applications.

7.  Tap or click Next. On the Installation Options page, select Install An Operating System From A Boot CD/DVD-ROM. If you have physical distribution media, insert the distribution media, and then specify the CD/DVD drive to use. If you want to install from an .iso image, select Image File, tap or click Browse, and then use the Open dialog box to select the image file to use.

8.  Tap or click Next, and then tap or click Finish.

9.  In Hyper-V Manager, press and hold or right-click the name of the virtual machine and then tap or click Connect.

10. In the Virtual Machine Connection window, tap or click Start. After the virtual machine is initialized, the operating system installation should start automatically. Continue with the operating system installation as you normally would.

When the installation is complete, log on to the virtual machine and configure it as you would any other server. From then on, you manage the virtual machine much as you would any other computer, except that you can externally control its state, available resources, and hardware devices using Hyper-V Manager. Additionally, when it comes to backups, several approaches are available:

- Back up the host server and all virtual machine data.

- Back up the host server and only the configuration data for virtual machines.

- Log on to virtual machines and perform normal backups as you would with any other server.

- Use Hyper-V manager to create point-in-time snapshots of virtual machines.

Ideally, you should use a combination of these approaches to ensure that your host server and virtual machines are protected. In some cases, you might want to back up the host server and configuration data and then log on to each virtual machine and use normal backups. Other times, you might want to back up the host machine and all virtual machine data. You will likely want to supplement your backup strategy by creating point-in-time snapshots of virtual machines.

Chapter 12

# Configuring storage

When you install disks, you must configure them for use by choosing a partition style and a storage type to use. After you configure drives, you prepare them to store data by partitioning them and creating file systems in the partitions. *Partitions* are sections of physical drives that function as if they are separate units. This allows you to configure multiple logical disk units even if a system has only one physical drive and to apportion disks appropriately to meet the needs of your organization.

## Using the Disk Management tools

When you want to manage basic or dynamic disks, one of the tools you can use is Disk Management, which is shown in Figure 12-10. Disk Management also is a snap-in included in Computer Management and can be added to any custom Microsoft Management Console (MMC) you create as well.

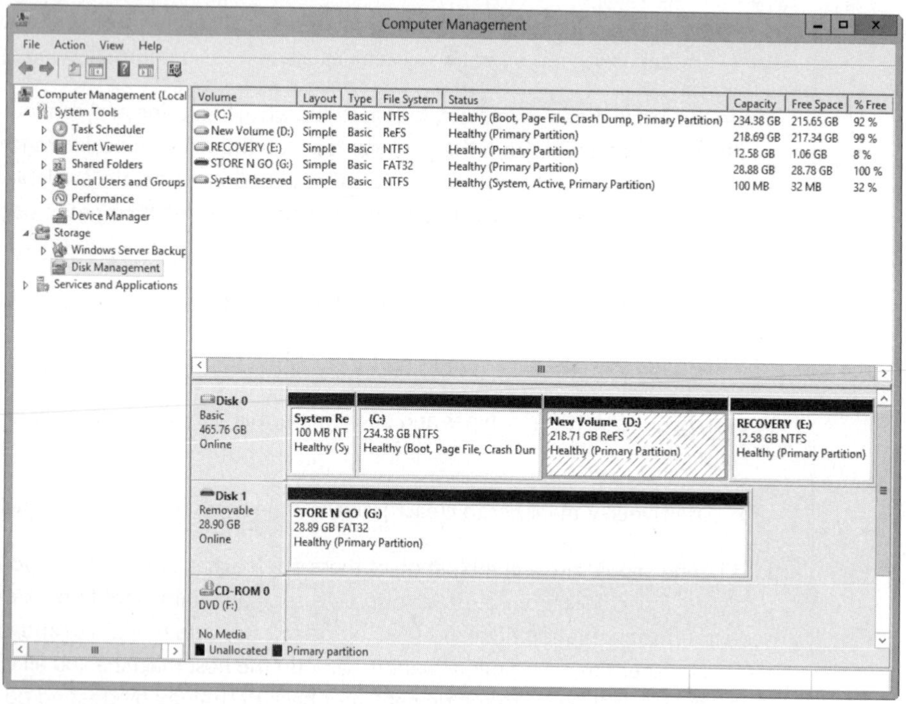

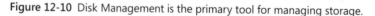

**Figure 12-10**  Disk Management is the primary tool for managing storage.

> **Important**
> Although Disk Management is a trusty favorite for working with disks, it might not be available in future releases of Windows and cannot be used to manage Storage Spaces. Dynamic disks also are being phased out in favor of Storage Spaces and might not be available in future versions of Windows.

Disk Management makes it easy to work with any available internal and external drives on both local and remote systems. When you start Disk Management by tapping or clicking the related option on the Tools menu in Server Manager, you're automatically connected to the local computer on which you're running Computer Management. In Computer Management, expand Storage and then select Disk Management. You can now manage the drives on the local system.

To work with a remote system, press and hold or right-click the Computer Management entry in the left pane, and select Connect To Another Computer on the shortcut menu. This opens the Select Computer dialog box (shown in Figure 12-11). Type the domain name or IP address of the system whose drives you want to view, and then tap or click OK.

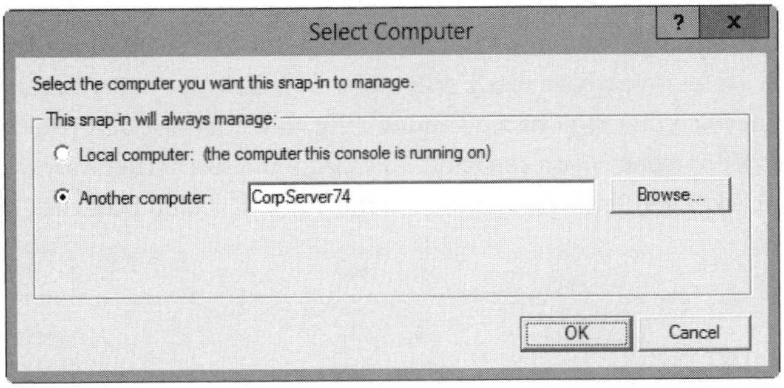

**Figure 12-11** Select the remote system to manage with Computer Management.

> **Important**
> Server Manager provides a shortcut for remote management as well. Select All Servers in the left pane, press and hold or right-click the remote server to which you want to connect in the Servers panel, and then select Computer Management. This opens Computer Management and connects to the remote server automatically. Keep in mind that the remote management of computers is a feature that must be enabled. As discussed in Chapter 4, "Managing Windows Server 2012," you need to enable inbound rules on the Windows Firewall for each management area you want to work with.

Disk Management has three views:

- **Disk List**  Shows a list of physical disks on, or attached to, the selected system. It includes details on type, capacity, unallocated space, and status. It is the only disk view that shows the device type, such as Small Computer System Interface (SCSI) or Integrated Device Electronics (IDE), and the partition style, such as Master Boot Record (MBR) or GUID Partition Table (GPT).

- **Graphical View**  Displays summary information for disks graphically according to disk capacity and the size of disk regions. By default, disk and disk-region capacity are shown on a logarithmic scale, meaning the disks and disk regions are displayed proportionally.

- **Volume List**  Shows all volumes on the selected computer (including hard-disk partitions and logical drives). It includes details on volume layout, type, file system, status, capacity, and free space. It also shows whether the volume has fault tolerance and the related disk usage overhead. The fault-tolerance information is for software RAID only.

---

### Change the scaling options to get different disk views

You can also specify that you want all disks to be the same size regardless of capacity (which is useful if you have many disk regions on disks) or that you want to use a linear scale in which disk regions are sized relative to the largest disk (which is useful if you want to get perspective on capacity). To change the size settings for the Graphical View, tap or click View, Settings, and then in the Settings dialog box, click the Scaling tab.

---

Volume List and Graphical View are the default views. In Figure 12-10, the Volume List view is in the top right corner, and the Graphical View is in the bottom right corner. To change the top view, select View, choose Top, and then select the view you want to use. To change the bottom view, select View, choose Bottom, and then select the view you want to use.

The command-line counterpart to Disk Management is the DiskPart utility. You can use DiskPart to perform all Disk Management tasks. DiskPart is a text-mode command interpreter that you invoke so that you can manage disks, partitions, and volumes. As such, DiskPart has a separate command prompt and its own internal commands. Although earlier releases of DiskPart did not allow you to format partitions, logical drives, and volumes, the version that ships with Windows Server 2012 allows you to do this using the internal format command.

You invoke the DiskPart interpreter by typing **diskpart** at the command prompt. DiskPart is designed to work with physical hard disks installed on a computer, which can be internal, external, or a mix of both. Although it will list other types of disks—such as CD/DVD drives, removable media, and universal serial bus (USB)–connected flash random access memory (RAM) devices—and allow you to perform some minimal tasks, such as assigning a drive letter, these devices are not supported.

After you invoke DiskPart, you can list available disks, partitions, and volumes by using the following list commands:

- **List Disk**   Lists all internal and external hard disks on the computer

- **List Volume**   Lists all volumes on the computer (including hard-disk partitions and logical drives)

- **List Partition**   Lists partitions, but only on the disk you selected

Then you must give focus to the disk, partition, or volume you want to work with by selecting it. Giving a disk, partition, or volume focus ensures that any commands you type will act only on that disk, partition, or volume. To select a disk, type **select disk *N***, where *N* is the number of the disk you want to work with. To select a volume, type **select volume *N***, where *N* is the number of the volume you want to work with. To select a partition, first select its related disk by typing **select disk *N***, and then select the partition you want to work with by typing **select partition *N***.

If you use the list commands again after selecting a disk, partition, or volume, you'll see an asterisk (*) next to the item with focus. When you are finished working with DiskPart, type **exit** at the DiskPart prompt to return to the standard command line.

Listing 12-1 shows a sample DiskPart session. As you can see, when you first invoke DiskPart, it shows the operating system and DiskPart version you are using as well as the name of the computer you are working with. When you list available disks, the output shows you the disk number, status, size, and free space. It also shows the disk-partition style and type. If there's an asterisk in the Dyn column, the disk is a dynamic disk. Otherwise, it is a basic disk. If there's an asterisk in the Gpt column, the disk uses the GPT partition style. Otherwise, it is an MBR disk. You'll find more information on partition styles in "Using the MBR and GPT partition styles" later in this chapter.

**Listing 12-1** Using DiskPart: An example

```
C:\> diskpart

Microsoft DiskPart version 6.2.9200
Copyright (C) 1999-2012 Microsoft Corporation.
On computer: CORPSVR02

DISKPART> list disk

  Disk ###  Status      Size     Free   Dyn  Gpt
  --------  ----------  -------  ------  ---  ---
  Disk 0    Online      465 GB   0 B     *    *
  Disk 1    Online      292 GB   27 GB
  Disk 2    Online      378 GB   90 GB

DISKPART> list volume

  Volume ###  Ltr  Label        Fs     Type      Size     Status   Info
  ----------  ---  ----------   -----  -------   -------  ------   ------
  Volume 0    F    HRM_SSS_X64  UDF    DVD-ROM   3525 MB  Healthy
  Volume 1         System Rese  NTFS   Partition 100 MB   Healthy  System
  Volume 2    C                 NTFS   Partition 234 GB   Healthy  Boot
  Volume 3    D    New Volume   REFS   Partition 218 GB   Healthy
  Volume 4    E    Recovery     NTFS   Partition 12 GB    Healthy
  Volume 5    G    Store n Go   FAT32  Removable 28 GB    Healthy

DISKPART> select disk 0

Disk 0 is now the selected disk.

DISKPART> list partition

  Partition ###  Type              Size     Offset
  -------------  ----------------  ------   -------
  Partition 1    Primary           100 MB   1024 KB

  Partition 2    Primary           234 GB   101 MB

  Partition 3    Primary           218 GB   234 GB

  Partition 4    Primary           12 GB    453 GB


DISKPART> select partition 2

Partition 2 is now the selected partition.
```

```
DISKPART> list partition

  Partition ###    Type              Size      Offset
  -------------    ----------------  -------   -------
  Partition 1      Primary           100 MB    1024 KB

* Partition 2      Primary           234 GB    101 MB

  Partition 3      Primary           218 GB    234 GB

  Partition 4      Primary            12 GB    453 GB


DISKPART> exit

Leaving DiskPart...

C:\>
```

## Adding new disks

Windows Server 2012 supports both Standard Format and Advanced Format hard drives. Standard Format drives have 512 bytes per physical sector and are also referred to as *512b drives*. Advanced Format drives have 4096 bytes per physical sector and are also referred to as *512e drives*. 512e represents a significant shift for the hard-drive industry, and it allows for large, multiterabyte drives.

When working with physical disks, keep in mind that disks perform physical media updates in the granularity of their physical sector size. 512b disks work with data 512 bytes at a time; 512e disks work with data 4096 bytes at a time. Having a larger physical sector size is what allows drive capacities to jump well beyond previous physical capacity limits.

# INSIDE OUT  Deploying 512e disks

512e disks might require some architecture changes in your applications. For best performance, applications must be updated to read and write data properly in this new level of granularity (4096 bytes). Otherwise, when there is only a 512-byte write, 512e hard disks must perform additional work to complete the sector write.

Wondering how to determine whether a disk is 512b or 512e? Use Fsutil to determine bytes per physical sector by typing the following at an elevated prompt:

```
Fsutil fsinfo ntfsinfo DriveDesignator
```

Here, *DriveDesignator* is the designator of the drive to check, such as

```
Fsutil fsinfo sectorinfo c:
```

Chapter 12

Thanks to hot-swapping and Plug and Play technologies, the process of adding new internal disks is much easier than in the past. If a computer supports hot swapping of disks, you can install new internal disks without having to shut down the computer. Simply insert the hard disk drives you want to use. If the computer doesn't support hot swapping, you need to shut down the computer, insert the drives, and restart the computer.

Either way, after you insert the drives you want to use, log on and access Disk Management in the Computer Management tool or in Server Manager. If the new drives have already been initialized, meaning they have disk signatures, they should be brought online automatically when you select Rescan Disks from the Action menu. If you are working with new drives that haven't been initialized, meaning they lack a disk signature, when you choose to initialize the new disk, Windows Server 2012 opens the Initialize Disk dialog box. In the Initialize Disk dialog box, select either the MBR or GPT partitioning style. When you tap or click OK, Windows writes a disk signature to the disks and initializes the disks with the basic disk type.

If you don't want to use the Initialize Disk dialog box, you can close it and use Disk Management instead to view and work with the disk. In the Disk List view, the disk is marked with a red downward-pointing arrow icon, the disk's type is listed as Unknown, and the disk's status is listed as Not Initialized. You can then press and hold or right-click the disk's icon and select Online. Press and hold or right-click the disk's icon again, and select Initialize Disk. You can then initialize the disk. In the Initialize Disk dialog box, select either the MBR or GPT partitioning style. Next tap or click OK so that Windows can write a disk signature and initialize the disk with the basic disk type.

# INSIDE OUT Windows Server 2012 can use disk write caching

As discussed previously, storage performance is primarily a factor of a disk's access time (how long it takes to register a request and scan the disk), seek time (how long it takes to find the requested data), and transfer rate (how long it takes to read and write data). By enabling disk write caching, you can reduce the number of times the operating system accesses the disk by caching disk writes and then performing several writes at once. In this way, disk performance is primarily influenced by seek time and transfer rate.

The drawback of disk write caching is that in the event of a power or system failure, the cached writes might not be written to disk, and this can result in data loss. Windows Server 2012 disables disk write caching by default, but you can enable it on a per-disk basis. Keep in mind that some server applications require disk write caching to be enabled or disabled, and if these applications use a particular set of disks, these disks must use the required setting for disk write caching.

To configure disk write caching, start Computer Management, expand the System Tools node, and select Device Manager. In the details pane, expand Disk Drives, press and hold or right-click the disk drive you want to work with, and then select Properties. In the Device Properties dialog box, click the Policies tab. Select or clear Enable Write Caching On The Disk as appropriate. If the drive has a separate power supply that allows it to flush its buffer in case of power failure, also select Turn Off Windows Write-Cache Buffer Flushing On The Device. Tap or click OK.

## Using the MBR and GPT partition styles

The term *partition style* refers to the method that Windows Server uses to organize partitions on a disk. Two partition styles are available: MBR and GPT. Originally, only x86-based computers used the MBR partition style, and only Itanium-based computers running 64-bit versions of Windows used the GPT partition style. With current Windows and Windows Server operating systems, both 32-bit and 64-bit editions support both MBR and GPT. However, the GPT partition style is not recognized by any early releases of Windows or Windows Server.

GPT is recommended for disks larger than 2 TBs on x86 and x64 systems or any disks used on Itanium-based computers. The key difference between the GPT partition style and the MBR partition style has to do with how partition data is stored.

### Note

For this discussion, I focus on the basic storage type and won't get into the details of the dynamic storage type. That's covered in the next section. Note also that for virtual machines and Hyper-V specifically, you should use GPT only for data disks and not for boot disks. The reason for this is that Hyper-V emulates a BIOS firmware environment and won't recognize the Extensible Firmware Interface (EFI).

## Working with MBR disks

MBR uses a partition table that describes where the partitions are located on the disk. The first sector on a hard disk contains the MBR and a master boot code that's used to boot the system. The MBR resides outside of partitioned space.

> **Note**
>
> It's easy to confuse *Master Boot Record* with *boot sector*. These are two different structures on the hard drive. The Master Boot Record contains the disk signature and partition table and is the first sector of the hard drive. A boot sector contains the BIOS parameter block and marks the first sector of the file system.

MBR disks support a maximum volume size of up to 4 TBs unless they're dynamic disks and use RAID. MBR disks have two special types of partitions associated with them. The first partition type, called a *primary partition*, is used with drive sections that you want to access directly for file storage. You make a primary partition accessible to users by creating a file system on it and assigning it a drive letter or mount point. The second partition type, called an *extended partition*, is used when you want to divide a section of a disk into one or more logical units called *logical drives*. Here, you create the extended partition first, and then create the logical drives within it. You then create a file system on each logical drive and assign a drive letter or mount point.

Each MBR drive can have up to four primary partitions or three primary partitions and one extended partition. It is the extended partition that allows you to divide a drive into more than four parts.

> **Note**
>
> These rules apply to MBR disks that use the basic storage type. There's also a storage type called *dynamic*. I discuss basic and dynamic storage types in "Working with basic and dynamic disks" later in this chapter.

## Working with GPT disks

GPT disks don't have a single MBR. With GPT disks, critical partition data is stored in the individual partitions, and there are redundant primary and backup partition tables. Further, checksum fields are maintained to allow for error correction and to improve partition structure integrity.

# INSIDE OUT    GPT headers and error checking

GPT disks use a primary and backup partition table. Each partition table has a header that defines the range of logical block addresses on the disk that can be used by partition entries. The GPT header also defines its location on the disk, its globally unique identifier (GUID), and a 32-bit cyclic redundancy check (CRC32) checksum that is used to verify the integrity of the GPT header. The primary GPT header is created directly after the protected boot sector on the disk. The backup GPT header is located in the last sector on the disk.

Firmware acts as the interface between a computer's hardware and its operating system. Although most computers use the basic input/output system (BIOS) as their firmware, the Extensible Firmware Interface (EFI) also is available. Generally, only systems that use EFI will be able to boot directly to a GPT disk, but all current Windows and Windows Server operating systems can use GPT disks for data.

A computer's firmware verifies the integrity of the GPT headers by using the CRC32 checksum. The checksum is a calculated value used to determine whether there are errors in a GPT header. If the primary GPT header is damaged, firmware checks the backup header. If the backup header's checksum is valid, the backup GPT header is used to restore the primary GPT header. The process of restoring the GPT header works much the same way if it is determined that the backup header is damaged—only in reverse. If both the primary and backup GPT headers are damaged, the Windows operating system won't be able to access the disk.

GPT disks support partitions of up to 18 exabytes (EBs) in size and up to 128 partitions per disk. EFI-based computers using GPT disks for boot have two required partitions and one or more optional original equipment manufacturer (OEM) or data partitions. The required partitions are the EFI system partition (ESP) and the Microsoft Reserved (MSR) partition. Although the optional partitions that you see depend on the system configuration, the optional partition type you see the most is the primary partition. Primary partitions are used to store user data on GPT disks.

Keep in mind that additional GPT disks (data disks) do not require an ESP. Further, a basic GPT disk might not contain primary partitions. For example, when you install a new disk and configure it as a GPT disk, the Windows operating system automatically creates the ESP and MSR partitions, but it does not create primary partitions.

Chapter 12

Although GPT offers a significant improvement over MBR, it does have limitations. You cannot use GPT with removable disks, disks that are direct-attached using USB or FireWire interfaces, or disks attached to shared storage devices on server clusters.

> **CAUTION**!
>
> To make changes to GPT disks, you should use only Disk Management or DiskPart. If you are working in the EFI firmware environment, you'll find there's a version of DiskPart available as well—DiskPart.efi.

## Using and converting MBR and GPT disks

Tasks for using MBR and GPT disks are similar but not necessarily identical. Partitions and volumes on MBR and GPT disks can be formatted using FAT, FAT32, exFAT, NTFS, and ReFS. When you create partitions or volumes in Disk Management, you have the opportunity to format the disk and assign it a drive letter or mount point as part of the volume creation process. Although Disk Management lets you format the partitions and volumes on MBR disks using FAT, FAT32, exFAT, NTFS, and ReFS, you can format partitions and volumes on GPT disks using only NTFS or ReFS. If you want to format GPT disks by using FAT or FAT32, you must use the FORMAT command at the command prompt. Further, keep in mind that you can use Windows Server Backup to back up MBR and GPT disks and their volumes whether they are formatted with FAT, FAT32, exFAT, NTFS, or ReFS.

You can change partition table styles from MBR to GPT or from GPT to MBR. Changing partition table styles can be useful when you want to move disks between computers or you receive new disks that are formatted for the wrong partition table style. You can convert partition table styles only on empty disks, however. This means the disks must either be new or newly formatted. You could, of course, empty a disk by removing its partitions or volumes.

You can use both Disk Management and DiskPart to change the partition table style. To use Disk Management to change the partition style of an empty disk, start Computer Management from the Administrative Tools menu or by typing **compmgmt.msc** at the command line, expand the Storage node, and then select Disk Management. All available disks are displayed. Press and hold or right-click the disk to convert in the Graphical View, and then tap or click Convert To GPT Disk or Convert To MBR Disk as appropriate.

To use DiskPart to change the partition style of an empty disk, invoke DiskPart by typing **diskpart** and then selecting the disk you want to convert. For example, if you want to convert disk 3, type **select disk 3**. After you select the disk, you can convert it from MBR to GPT by typing **convert gpt**. To convert a disk from GPT to MBR, type **convert mbr**.

## Using the disk storage types

The term *storage type* refers to the method that Windows Server uses to structure disks and their contents. Windows Server offers several storage types, including basic disk, dynamic disk, removable disk, and virtual disk. The storage type you use doesn't depend on the processor architecture—it can depend, however, on whether you are working with fixed or nonfixed disks. When you are working with fixed disks, you can use basic, dynamic, or both storage types on any edition of Windows Server and also have the option of creating virtual disks. When you are working with nonfixed disks, the disk has the removable storage type automatically and you generally do not have the option of creating a virtual disk.

### Working with basic and dynamic disks

Basic disks use the same disk structure as early versions of the Windows operating system. When using basic disks, you are limited to creating four primary partitions per disk, or three primary partitions and one extended partition. Within an extended partition, you can create one or more logical drives. For ease of reference, primary partitions and logical drives on basic disks are known as *basic volumes*. Dynamic disks were introduced with early Windows operating systems as a way to improve disk support by requiring fewer restarts after disk configuration changes, improved support for combining disks, and enhanced fault tolerance using RAID configurations. All volumes on dynamic disks are known as *dynamic volumes*.

Windows Server 2012 systems can use both basic and dynamic disks. You cannot, however, mix disk types when working with volume sets. Note also that although you can continue to use dynamic disks with Windows 8 and Windows Server 2012, dynamic disks are being phased out in favor of Storage Spaces. If you want to mirror the volume that hosts the operating system, you might want to use dynamic disks because this is one of the best approaches. Otherwise, Microsoft recommends that you use Storage Spaces instead of dynamic disks.

All disks, regardless of whether they are basic or dynamic, have five special types of drive sections:

- **Active**  The active partition or volume is the drive section for system cache and startup. Some devices with removable storage might be listed as having an active partition (though they don't actually have the active partition).

- **Boot**  The boot partition or volume contains the operating system and its support files. The system and boot partition or volume can be the same.

- **Crash Dump**   The partition to which the computer attempts to write dump files in the event of a system crash. By default, dump files are written to the %SystemRoot% folder, but they can be located on any desired partition or volume.

- **Page File**   A partition containing a paging file used by the operating system. Because a computer can page memory to multiple disks, according to the way virtual memory is configured, a computer can have multiple page-file partitions or volumes.

- **System**   The system partition or volume contains the hardware-specific files needed to load the operating system. The system partition or volume can't be part of a striped or spanned volume.

The volume types are set when you install the operating system. You can mark a partition as active to ensure that it is the one from which the computer starts. You can do this only for partitions on basic disks. You can't mark an existing dynamic volume as the active volume, but you can convert a basic disk containing the active partition to a dynamic disk. After the update is complete, the partition becomes a simple volume that's active.

## Using and converting basic and dynamic disks

Basic disks and dynamic disks are managed in different ways. For basic disks, you use primary and extended partitions. Extended partitions can contain logical drives. Dynamic disks allow you to combine disks to create spanned volumes, to mirror disks to create mirrored volumes, and to stripe disks using RAID 0 to create striped volumes. You can also create RAID-5 volumes for high reliability on dynamic disks.

You can change storage types from basic to dynamic and from dynamic to basic. When you convert a basic disk to a dynamic disk, existing partitions are changed to volumes of the appropriate type automatically and existing data is not lost. Converting a dynamic disk to a basic disk isn't so easy and can't be done without taking some drastic measures. You must delete the volumes on the dynamic disk before you can change the disk back to a basic disk. Deleting the volumes destroys all the information they contain, and the only way to get it back is to restore the data from backup.

You should consider a number of things when you want to change the storage type from basic to dynamic. To be converted successfully, an MBR disk must have 1 megabyte (MB) of free space at the end of the disk. This space is used for the dynamic disk database, which tracks volume information. Without this free space at the end of the disk, the conversion will fail. Because both Disk Management and DiskPart reserve this space automatically, primarily only if you used third-party disk management utilities will you need to be concerned about whether this space is available. However, if the disk was formatted using another version of the Windows operating system, this space might not be available either.

A GPT disk must have contiguous, recognized data partitions to be converted successfully. If the GPT disk contains partitions that the Windows operating system doesn't recognize, such as those created by another operating system, you won't be able to convert a basic disk to a dynamic disk. When you convert a GPT disk, the Windows operating system creates LDM Metadata and LDM Data partitions as discussed in "LDM metadata and LDM data partitions" later in this chapter. GPT disks that are dynamic will store the dynamic disk database in the LDM partitions instead of out at the end of the drive like on an MBR disk.

You can't convert a disk if the system or boot partition uses software RAID. You must stop using the software RAID before you convert the disk.

Both Disk Management and DiskPart can be used to change the storage type.

**Using Disk Management to convert a basic disk to a dynamic disk**    To use Disk Management to convert a basic disk to a dynamic disk, start Computer Management from the Administrative Tools menu or by typing **compmgmt.msc** at the command line, expand the Storage node, and then select Disk Management. In Disk Management, press and hold or right-click a basic disk that you want to convert, either in Disk List view or in the left pane of Graphical View, and select Convert To Dynamic Disk.

In the Convert To Dynamic Disk dialog box (shown in Figure 12-12), select the disks you want to convert. If you're converting a RAID volume, be sure to select all the basic disks in the set because they must be converted together. Tap or click OK when you're ready to continue.

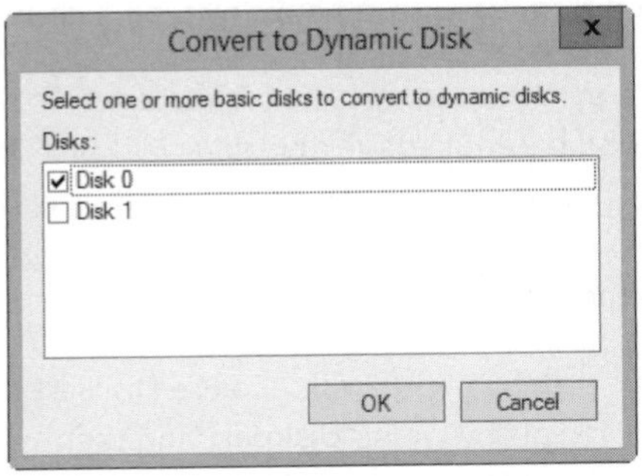

**Figure 12-12**  Select the disk to convert.

Next, as shown in Figure 12-13, the Disks To Convert dialog box shows the disks you're converting along with details of the disk contents. To see the drive letters and mount points that are associated with a disk, select the disk in the Disks list and then tap or click Details. If a disk cannot be converted for some reason, the Will Convert column will show No and the Disk Contents column will provide a reason. You must correct whatever problem is noted before you can convert the disk.

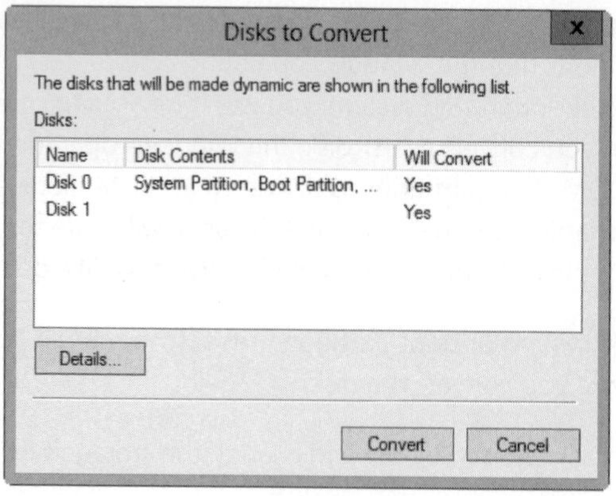

**Figure 12-13** Confirm that the disk can be converted.

When you're ready to start the conversion, tap or click Convert. Disk Management will then warn you that after you finish the conversion you won't be able to boot previous versions of the Windows operating system from volumes on the selected disks. Tap or click Yes to continue. If a selected drive contains the boot partition, system partition, or a partition in use, you'll see another warning telling you that the computer will need to be rebooted to complete the conversion process.

**Using DiskPart to Convert a basic disk to a dynamic disk**   To use DiskPart to convert a basic disk to a dynamic disk, invoke DiskPart by typing **diskpart** and then select the disk you want to convert. For example, if you want to convert disk 2, type **select disk 2**. After the disk is selected, you can convert it from basic to dynamic by typing **convert dynamic**.

Using Disk Management to change a dynamic disk back to a basic disk   To use Disk Management to change a dynamic disk back to a basic disk, you must first delete all dynamic volumes on the disk. Then press and hold or right-click the disk, and select Convert To Basic Disk. This changes the dynamic disk to a basic disk, and you can then create new partitions and logical drives on the disk.

**Using DiskPart to convert a dynamic disk to a basic disk**   To use DiskPart to convert a dynamic disk to a basic disk, invoke DiskPart by typing **diskpart** and then select the disk you want to convert. For example, if you want to convert disk 2, type **select disk 2**. If there are any existing volumes on the disk, you must delete them. You can do this by typing **clean**. However, be sure to move any data the disk contains to another disk prior to deleting the disk volumes.

After you delete all the volumes on the disk, you can convert the disk from dynamic to basic by typing **convert basic**. This changes the dynamic disk to a basic disk, and you can then create new partitions and logical drives on the disk.

# Creating and managing virtual hard disks for Hyper-V

You can use Disk Management to create, attach, and detach virtual hard disks. To create a virtual hard disk, choose Create VHD from the Action menu. In the Create And Attach Virtual Hard Disk dialog box, shown in Figure 12-14, tap or click Browse. Use the Browse Virtual Disk Files dialog box to select the location where you want to create the .vhd file for the virtual hard disk. Next type a name for the virtual hard disk, and then tap or click Save.

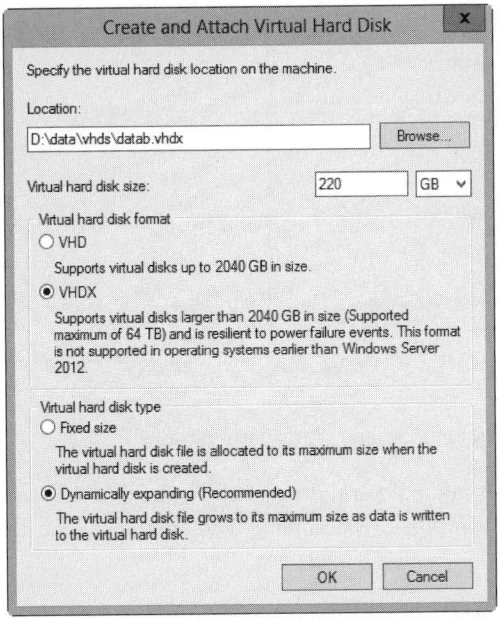

**Figure 12-14**  Specify the location, format, and type for the virtual hard disk.

In the Virtual Hard Disk Size list, enter the size of the disk in MB, GB, or TB. Keep in mind disk sizes aren't necessarily fixed.

Next, chose a virtual hard disk format. Two virtual hard disk formats are available:

- Standard virtual disks with the .vhd extension, which are backward compatible with earlier releases of Windows Server and support a maximum disk size of 2040 GBs.

- Enhanced virtual disks with the .vhdx extension, which are compatible only with Windows Server 2012 and support enhanced features, including a maximum size of 64 TBs and improved handling of power failures.

Use the Virtual Hard Disk Type options to specify whether the size of the VHD dynamically expands to its fixed maximum size as data is saved to it or uses a fixed amount of space regardless of the amount of data stored on it. When you tap or click OK, Disk Management creates the virtual hard disk.

The VHD is attached automatically and added as a new disk. To initialize the disk for use, press and hold or right-click the disk entry in Graphical View and then tap or click Initialize Disk. In the Initialize Disk dialog box, shown in Figure 12-15, the disk is selected for initialization. Specify the disk type as MBR or GPT, and then tap or click OK.

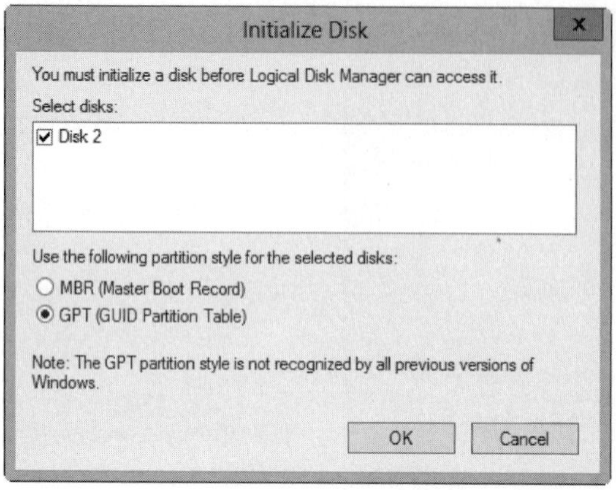

**Figure 12-15** Specify the disk to initialize, and set its partition style.

After initializing the disk, press and hold or right-click the unpartitioned space on the disk and create a volume of the appropriate type. After you create the volume, the VHD is available for use.

After you create, attach, initialize, and format a VHD, you can work with a virtual disk in much the same way as you work with other disks. You can write data to and read data from a VHD. You can boot the computer from a VHD. You are able to take a VHD offline or put a VHD online by pressing and holding or right-clicking the disk entry in Graphical View and selecting Offline or Online, respectively. If you no longer want to use a VHD, you can detach it by pressing and holding or right-clicking the disk entry in Graphical View, selecting Detach VHD, and then tapping or clicking OK in the Detach Virtual Hard Disk dialog box.

You can use VHDs created with other programs as well. If you created a VHD using another program or have a detached VHD you want to attach, you can work with the VHD by completing the following steps:

1. In Disk Management, tap or click the Attach VHD option on the Action menu.

2. In the Attach Virtual Hard Disk dialog box, tap or click Browse. Use the Browse Virtual Disk Files dialog box to select the .vhd or .vhdx file for the virtual hard disk, and then tap or click Open.

3. If you want to attach the VHD in read-only mode, select Read-Only. Otherwise, the VHD will open in read-write mode. Tap or click OK to attach the VHD.

## Converting FAT or FAT32 to NTFS

On both MBR and GPT disks, you can convert FAT or FAT32 partitions, logical drives, and volumes to NTFS by using the Convert command. This preserves the file and directory structure without the need to reformat. Before you use Convert, you should check to see whether the volume is being used as the active boot volume or is a system volume containing the operating system. If it is a system volume, Convert must have exclusive access to the volume before it can begin the conversion. Because exclusive access to boot or system volumes can be obtained only during startup, you will see a prompt asking if you want to schedule the drive to be converted the next time the system starts.

As part of the preparation for conversion, you should check to see if there's enough free space to perform the conversion. You'll need a block of free space that's about 25 percent of the total space used by the volume. For example, if the volume stores 12 GBs of data, you should have about 3 GBs of free space. Convert checks for this free space before running, and if there isn't enough, it won't convert the volume.

> **CAUTION** Conversion is one-way only. You can convert only from FAT or FAT32 to NTFS. You can't convert from NTFS to FAT or NTFS to FAT32 without deleting the volume and re-creating it using FAT or FAT32. You can't convert exFAT or ReFS volumes to NTFS.

You run Convert at the command line. Its syntax is as follows:

```
convert volume /FS:NTFS
```

Here, *volume* is the drive letter followed by a colon, drive path, or volume name. So, for instance, if you want to convert the E drive to NTFS, type **convert e: /fs:ntfs**. This starts Convert. As shown in the following example, Convert checks the current file-system type and then prompts you to enter the volume label for the drive:

```
The type of the file system is FAT32.
Enter current volume label for drive E:
```

As long as you enter the correct volume label, Convert will continue as shown in the following example:

```
Volume CORPDATA created 4/10/2014 12:53 PM
Volume Serial Number is AA6B-CEDE
Windows is verifying files and folders...
File and folder verification is complete.
Windows has checked the file system and found no problems.
   91,827,680 KB total disk space.
   91,827,672 KB are available.

   8,192 bytes in each allocation unit.
   11,478,460 total allocation units on disk.
   11,478,459 allocation units available on disk.

Determining disk space required for file system conversion...
Total disk space:              91927860 KB
Free space on volume:          91929680 KB
Space required for conversion:    12080460 KB
Converting file system
Conversion complete
```

Here, Convert examines the file and folder structure and then determines how much disk space is needed for the conversion. If there is enough free space, Convert performs the conversion. Otherwise, it exits with an error, stating there isn't enough free space to complete the conversion.

Several additional parameters are available as well, including /v, which tells Convert to display detailed information during the conversion, and /x, which tells Convert to force the partition or volume to dismount before the conversion if necessary. You can't dismount a boot or system drive—these drives can be converted only when the system is restarted.

On converted boot and system volumes, Convert applies the same default security as that applied during Windows setup. On other volumes, Convert sets security so that the Users group has access but doesn't give access to the special group Everyone. If you don't want security to be set, you can use the /Nosecurity parameter. This parameter tells Convert to remove all security attributes and make all files and directories on the disk accessible to the group Everyone. In addition, you can use the /Cvtarea parameter to set the name of a contiguous file in the root directory to be a placeholder for NTFS system files.

- **Remove a drive letter**   If you want to remove the drive letter, tap or click Remove and then confirm the action when prompted by tapping or clicking Yes.

> **Note**
>
> When you change or remove a drive letter, the volume or partition will no longer be accessible using the old drive letter, and this can cause programs using the volume to not work properly or it can cause the partition to stop running.

After you make a change, the new drive letter or mount point assignment is made automatically as long as the volume or partition is not in use. If the partition or volume is in use, Windows Server 2012 displays the warning shown in Figure 12-21.

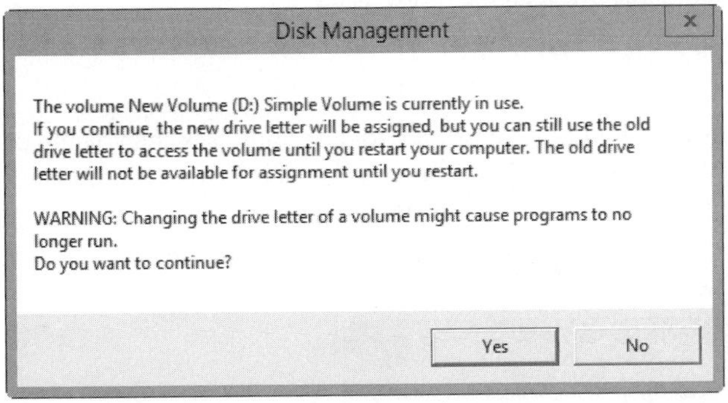

**Figure 12-21**  New drive letters are not assigned to in-use drives until you restart the computer.

This prompt tells you the drive is in use and the new drive letter won't be assigned until you restart the computer. At this point, you can tap or click No to cancel the change or tap or click Yes to accept the change and continue. If you cancel the change, the new drive letter is not assigned. If you accept the change and continue, the old drive letter remains available for use by users and programs until you restart the computer. When you restart the computer, the new drive letter is applied.

## Configuring mount points

Any volume or partition can be mounted to an empty NTFS folder as long as the folder is on a fixed disk drive rather than a removable media drive. A volume or partition mounted in such a way is called a *mount point*. Each volume or partition can have multiple mount points associated with it. For example, you could mount a volume to the root folder of the C drive as both C:\EngData and C:\DevData, giving the appearance that these are separate folders.

The real value of mount points, however, lies in how they give you the capability to create the appearance of a single file system from multiple hard-disk drives without having to use spanned volumes. Consider the following scenario: A department file server has four data drives—drive 1, drive 2, drive 3, and drive 4. Rather than mount the drives as D, E, F, and G, you decide it would be easier for users to work with the drives if they were all mounted as folders of the system drive, which is C:\Data. You mount drive 1 to C:\Data\UserData, drive 2 to C:\Data\CorpData, drive 3 to C:\Data\Projects, and drive 4 to C:\Data\History. If you then shared the C:\Data folder, users could access all the drives using a single share.

> **Note**
> Wondering why I mounted the drives under C:\Data rather than C:\, as is recommended in some documentation? The primary reason I did this is to help safeguard system security. I didn't want users to have access to other directories, which includes the operating system directories, on the C drive.

To add or remove a mount point, press and hold or right-click the volume or partition in Disk Management and choose Change Drive Letter And Paths. This displays the Change Drive Letter And Paths For dialog box (as shown in Figure 12-22), which shows any current mount point and mount points associated with the selected drive.

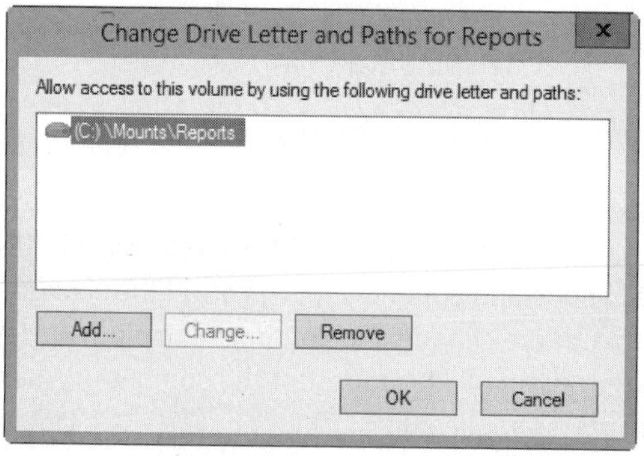

**Figure 12-22** Add or remove a mount point.

You now have the following options:

- **Add a mount point**   Tap or click Add. Then in the Add Drive Letter Or Path dialog box, select Mount In The Following Empty NTFS Folder, as shown in Figure 12-23. Type the path to an existing folder or tap or click Browse to search for or create a folder. Tap or click OK to mount the volume or partition.

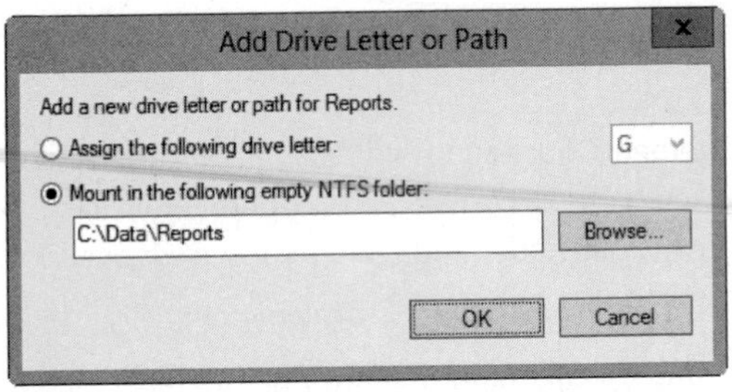

**Figure 12-23** Select the path for the new mount point.

- **Remove a mount point**  If you want to remove a mount point, select the mount point and then tap or click Remove. When prompted to confirm the action, tap or click Yes.

> **Note**
>
> You can't change a mount-point assignment after making it. However, you can simply remove the mount point you want to change and then add a new mount point so that the volume or partition is mounted as appropriate.

## Extending partitions

You can extend volumes on both basic and dynamic disks using either Disk Management or DiskPart. This is handy if you create a partition that's too small and you want to extend it so that you have more space for programs and data. In extending a volume, you convert areas of unallocated space and add them to the existing volume. For spanned volumes on dynamic disks, the space can come from any available dynamic disk, not only those on which the volume was originally created. Thus, you can combine areas of free space on multiple dynamic disks and use those areas to increase the size of an existing volume.

Before you try to extend a volume, be aware of several limitations. First, you can extend simple and spanned volumes only if they are formatted and the file system is NTFS (and in some instances, ReFS). You can't extend striped volumes. You can't extend volumes that aren't formatted or that are formatted with FAT, FAT32, or exFAT. You can extend NTFS (and in some instances, ReFS) volumes on both basic and dynamic disks using either Disk Management or DiskPart.

Using Disk Management, you can extend a simple or spanned volume by following these steps:

1. Open Disk Management. Press and hold or right-click the volume that you want to extend, and then select Extend Volume. This option is available only if the volume meets the previously discussed criteria and free space is available on one or more of the system's dynamic disks.

2. In the Extend Volume Wizard, read the introductory message and then tap or click Next.

3. On the Select Disks page, shown in Figure 12-24, select the disk or disks from which you want to allocate free space. Any disks currently being used by the volume are selected automatically. By default, all remaining free space on those disks will be selected for use.

4. With dynamic disks, you can specify the additional space that you want to use on other disks. Select the disk and then tap or click Add to add the disk to the Selected list box. In the Selected list box, select each disk that you want to use, and in the Select The Amount Of Space In MB list box, specify the amount of unallocated space to use on the selected disk.

5. Tap or click Next, confirm your options, and then tap or click Finish.

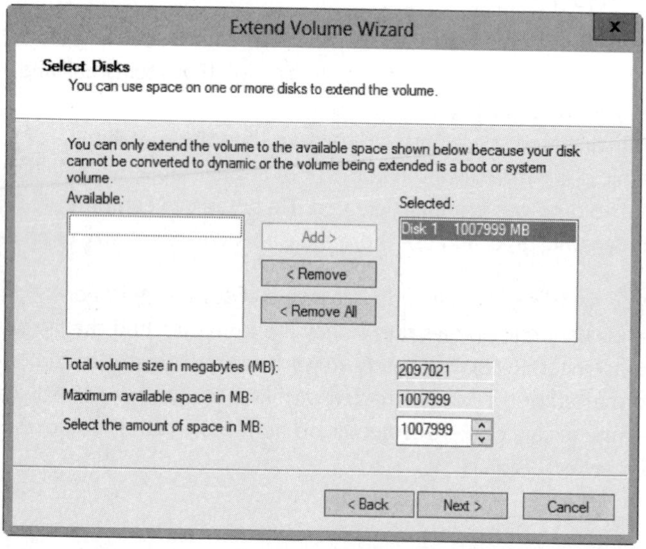

**Figure 12-24** Specify the amount of space to add to the volume.

By using DiskPart, you can extend partitions using the command line. To extend a partition, invoke DiskPart by typing **diskpart** at the command prompt. List the disks on the computer by typing **list disk**. After you check the free space of each disk, select the disk by typing select **disk *N***, where *N* is the disk you want to work with. Next, list the partitions on the selected disk by typing **list partition**. Select the last partition in the list by typing **select partition *N***, where *N* is the disk you want to work with.

Now that you've selected a partition, you can extend it. To extend the partition to the end of the disk, type **extend**. To extend the partition by a set amount, type **extend size=*N***, where *N* is the amount of space to add in megabytes. For example, if you want to add 90 GBs to the partition, type **extend size=90000**.

Listing 12-2 shows an actual DiskPart session in which a disk is extended. You can use this as an example to help you understand the process of extending disks. Here, disk 2 has 119 GBs of free space, and its primary partition is extended so that it fills the disk.

**Listing 12-2** Extending disks

```
C:\> diskpart

    Microsoft DiskPart version 6.2.9200
    Copyright (C) 1999-2012 Microsoft Corporation.
    On computer: CORPSVR02

DISKPART> list disk

    Disk ###  Status    Size      Free    Dyn   Gpt
    --------  --------  -----     -----   ---   ---
    Disk 0    Online    1560 GB   504 GB   *     *
    Disk 1    Online    1290 GB   0 B
    Disk 2    Online    370 GB    119 GB

DISKPART> select disk 2

Disk 2 is now the selected disk.

DISKPART> list partition

    Partition ###   Type       Size     Offset
    -------------   ---------  -------   -------
    Partition 1     Primary    370 GB    32 KB

DISKPART> select partition 1

Partition 1 is now the selected partition.

DISKPART> extend

DiskPart successfully extended the partition.
```

```
DISKPART> exit

Leaving DiskPart...

C:\>
```

To extend a partition on a dynamic disk to free space on another disk, you use the following syntax:

```
extend size=X disk=Y
```

Here, *size=X* sets the amount of space to use in megabytes and disk=*Y* sets the number of the disk from which to allocate the space. Following this, you could allocate 50 GBs of free space from disk 0 to the selected disk in the previous example (disk 2) using the following command:

```
extend size=50000 disk=0
```

## Shrinking partitions

You can shrink volumes on both basic and dynamic disks using either Disk Management or DiskPart. This is handy if you create a partition that's too large and you want to shrink it so that you have more space for other partitions. In shrinking a volume, you convert areas of allocated but unused space to free space by removing them from an existing volume.

As with extending volumes, several limitations apply to shrinking volumes. First, you can shrink simple and spanned volumes only if they are formatted and the file system is NTFS. You can't shrink striped volumes. You can't shrink volumes that are formatted with FAT, FAT32, exFAT, or ReFS. However, you can shrink volumes that have not been formatted. If a volume is heavily fragmented, you might have to defragment the volume to free up additional space before shrinking.

Using Disk Management, you can shrink a simple or spanned volume by following these steps:

1. Open Disk Management. Press and hold or right-click the volume that you want to shrink, and then select Shrink Volume. This option is available only if the volume meets the previously discussed criteria.

2. In the field provided in the Shrink dialog box shown in Figure 12-25, enter the amount of space to shrink. The Shrink dialog box provides the following information:

   - **Total Size Before Shrink In MB**   Lists the total capacity of the volume in megabytes. This is the formatted size of the volume.

- ○ **Size Of Available Shrink Space In MB**    Lists the maximum amount by which the volume can be shrunk. This doesn't represent the total amount of free space on the volume; rather, it represents the amount of space that can be removed, not including any data reserved for the master file table, volume snapshots, page files, and temporary files.

- ○ **Enter The Amount Of Space To Shrink In MB**    Lists the total amount of space that will be removed from the volume. The initial value defaults to the maximum amount of space that can be removed from the volume. For optimal drive performance, you'll want to ensure that the drive has at least 10 percent of free space after the shrink operation.

- ○ **Total Size After Shrink In MB**    Lists what the total capacity of the volume in megabytes will be after the shrink. This is the new formatted size of the volume.

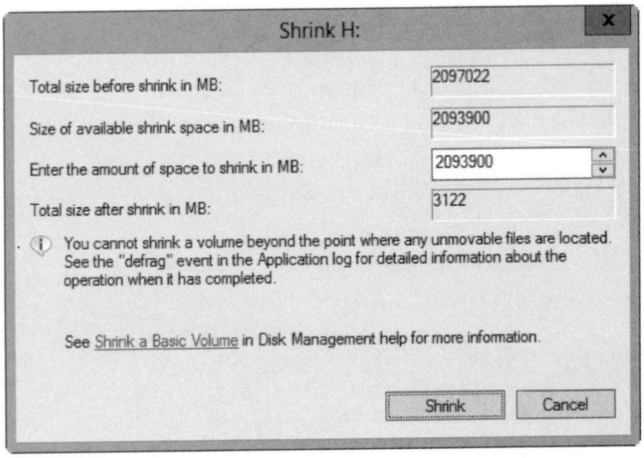

**Figure 12-25**  Specify the amount of space to shrink from the volume.

3.   Tap or click Shrink to shrink the volume.

By using DiskPart, you can shrink partitions using the command line. To shrink an NTFS-formatted partition, invoke DiskPart by typing **diskpart** at the command prompt. List the disks on the computer by typing **list disk**. After you check the free space of each disk, select the disk by typing **select disk N**, where N is the disk you want to work with. Next, list the partitions on the selected disk by typing **list partition**. Select the last partition in the list by typing **select partition N**, where N is the disk you want to work with.

Now that you've selected a partition, you can shrink it. To determine the maximum amount of space by which you can shrink the disk, type **shrink querymax**. To shrink the partition by the maximum amount, type **shrink**. To shrink the partition by a set amount, type **shrink**

Chapter 12

**desired=N**, where *N* is the amount of space to remove in megabytes. For example, if you want to remove 225 GBs from the partition, type **shrink desired=225000**.

Listing 12-3 shows an actual DiskPart session in which you shrink a disk. You can use this as an example to help you understand the process of shrinking disks. Here you determine that there are 40 GBs of space available for shrinking on the selected partition and then shrink the partition by 32 GBs.

**Listing 12-3** Shrinking disks

```
C:\> diskpart

    Microsoft DiskPart version 6.2.9200
    Copyright (C) 1999-2012 Microsoft Corporation.
      On computer: CORPSVR02

    DISKPART> list disk

      Disk ###  Status    Size   Free  Dyn   Gpt
      --------  --------  -----  -----  ---   ---
      Disk 0    Online    1560 GB 504 GB   *     *
      Disk 1    Online    1290 GB   0 B
      Disk 2    Online    489 GB    0 B

    DISKPART> select disk 2

    Disk 2 is now the selected disk.

    DISKPART> list partition

      Partition ###   Type      Size    Offset
      -------------   --------- -------  -------
      Partition 1     Primary   489 GB   32 KB

    DISKPART> select partition 1

    Partition 1 is now the selected partition.

    DISKPART> shrink querymax

    The maximum number of reclaimable bytes is: 40 GB

    DISKPART> shrink desired=32000

    DiskPart successfully shrunk the partition by: 32000 MB

    DISKPART> exit

    Leaving DiskPart...

    C:\>
```

## Deleting a partition, logical drive, or volume

Deleting a partition, logical drive, or volume removes the associated file system and all associated data. When you delete a logical drive, the logical drive is removed from the associated extended partition and its space is marked as free. When you delete a partition or volume, the entire partition or volume is deleted and its space is marked as Unallocated. If you want to delete an extended partition that contains logical drives, however, you must delete the logical drives before trying to delete the extended partition.

In Disk Management, you can delete a partition, logical drive, or volume by pressing and holding or right-clicking it and then choosing Delete Partition, Delete Logical Drive, or Delete Volume, as appropriate. When prompted to confirm the action, tap or click Yes.

# Managing GPT disk partitions on basic disks

GPT disks can have the following types of partitions:

- ESP

- MSR partition

- Primary partition

- Logical Disk Manager (LDM) Metadata partition

- LDM Data partition

- OEM or Unknown partition

Each of these partition types is used and managed in different ways.

## ESP

EFI-based computers must have one GPT disk that contains an ESP. This partition is similar to the system volume on a computer with an MBR boot disk in that it contains the files that are required to start the operating system. Windows Server 2012 creates the ESP during setup and formats it by using FAT. Normally, the partition is sized so that it is at least 100 MBs in size or 1 percent of the disk, up to a maximum size of 1000 MBs.

The ESP is shown in Disk Management but isn't assigned a drive letter or mount point. All Disk Management commands associated with the ESP are disabled, however, and you cannot store data on it, assign a drive letter to it, or delete it by using Disk Management or DiskPart. The ESP has several directories that contain the operating system boot loader, such as Ia64ldr.efi, and other files that are necessary to start the operating system as well as utilities such as Diskpart.efi and Nvrboot.efi. Other directories are created as necessary by the operating system.

The only way to access these directories is to use the EFI firmware's Boot Manager or the MountVol command. If you access the ESP, don't make changes, additions, or deletions unless you've been specifically directed to by a Microsoft Knowledge Base article or other official documentation by an OEM vendor. Any changes you make could prevent the system from starting.

## INSIDE OUT You can create an ESP if necessary—but do so only if directed to

Although the ESP is normally created for you automatically when you install Windows Server 2012, there are some limited instances when you might be directed to create an ESP after installing an additional GPT disk on a server, such as when you want to use the new disk as a boot device rather than the existing boot device. You can create the necessary ESP by using DiskPart. Select the disk you want to work with, and then type the following command: **create partition efi size=N**, where *N* is at least 100 MBs or 1 percent of the disk, up to a maximum size of 1000 MBs. After you create the partition, follow the vendor-directed or Microsoft-directed guidelines for preparing the partition for use. Never create an ESP unless you are directed to do so, however. One instance in which you must create an ESP is when you want to establish and boot to mirrored GPT disks. Here, you must prepare the second disk of the mirror so that it can be booted, and you do this by creating the necessary ESP and MSR partitions.

## MSR partitions

EFI-based computers that use GPT for boot must have an MSR partition on every GPT disk. The MSR partition contains additional space that might be needed by the operating system to perform disk operations. For example, when you convert a basic GPT disk to a dynamic GPT disk, the Windows operating system takes 1 MB of the MSR partition space and uses it to create the LDM Metadata partition, which is required for the conversion.

The MSR partition is not shown in Disk Management and does not receive a drive letter or mount point. The Windows operating system creates the MSR partition automatically. For the boot disk, it is created along with the ESP when you install the operating system. An MSR partition is also created automatically when a disk is converted from MBR to GPT and any time you access a GPT disk that doesn't already have an MSR partition in Disk Management or DiskPart.

If a GPT disk contains an ESP as the first partition on the disk, the MSR partition is usually the second partition on the disk. If a GPT disk does not contain an ESP, the MSR partition is typically the first partition on the disk. However, if a disk already has a primary partition at the beginning of the disk, the MSR partition is placed at the end of the disk.

The MSR partition is sized according to the size of the associated disk. For disks up to 16 GBs in size, it normally is 32 MBs in size. For all other disks, it normally is 128 MBs in size.

## INSIDE OUT    You can create an MSR partition if necessary—but do so only if directed to

The MSR partition is normally created for you automatically when you install Windows Server 2012. It can also be created automatically when you access a secondary GPT disk that doesn't already have an MSR partition in Disk Management or DiskPart. You shouldn't attempt to create a Microsoft Reserved partition unless you are directed to by vendor-specific or Microsoft-specific documentation. In this case, you can use Disk Part to create the partition. Select the disk you want to work with, and then type the following command: **create partition msr size=N**, where *N* is 32 for disks up to 16 GBs in size and 128 for all other disks.

## Primary partitions

You create primary partitions on basic disks to store data. GPT disks support up to 128 partitions, which can be a mix of required and optional partitions. Every primary partition you create appears in the GUID partition entry array within the GPT header. If you convert a basic disk that contains primary partitions to a dynamic disk, the primary partitions become simple volumes, and information about them is then stored in the dynamic disk database and not in the GUID partition entry array.

To create a primary partition, complete the following steps:

1. In Disk Management Graphical View, press and hold or right-click an area marked Unallocated on a basic disk, and then choose New Simple Volume. This starts the New Simple Volume Wizard. Tap or click Next.

2. The partition is created as a primary partition automatically. Use the Assign Drive Letter Or Path page to assign a drive letter or path. You can also choose Do Not Assign A Drive Letter Or Drive Path if you want to create the partition without assigning a drive letter or path. Tap or click Next.

3. Use the Format Partition page to set the formatting options. If you opt not to format the partition at this time, you can format the partition later as discussed in "Formatting a partition, logical drive, or volume" earlier in this chapter.

4. Tap or click Next. The final page shows you the options you've selected. If the options are correct, tap or click Finish. The wizard then creates the partition and configures it.

## LDM Metadata and LDM Data partitions

Windows Server 2012 creates LDM Metadata and LDM Data partitions when you convert a basic GPT disk to a dynamic GPT disk. The LDM Metadata partition is 1 MB in size and is used to store the partitioning information needed for the conversion. The LDM Data partition is the partition in which the actual dynamic volumes are created.

The LDM Data partition is used to represent sections of unallocated space on the converted disk as well as sections that had basic partitions that are now dynamic volumes. For example, if a disk had a primary boot partition that spanned the whole disk, the converted disk will have a single LDM Data partition. If a disk had a boot partition and other primary partitions, it will have two LDM Data partitions after the conversion: one for the boot volume, and one for all the rest of the partitions. Although the LDM Metadata and LDM Data partitions are not shown in Disk Management and do not receive drive letters or mount points, you are able to use this space by creating primary partitions as discussed in the previous section.

## OEM or unknown partitions

GPT disks can have partitions that are specific to OEM implementations, and your vendor documentation should describe what they are used for. The Windows operating system might display these partitions in Disk Management as Healthy (Unknown Partition). You cannot, however, manipulate these partitions in Disk Management or DiskPart. Additionally, if an unknown partition lies between two known partitions on a GPT disk, you typically can't convert the disk from the basic disk type to the dynamic disk type.

# Managing volumes on dynamic disks

Any disk using the MBR or GPT partition style can be configured as a dynamic disk. Unlike basic disks, which have basic volumes that can be created as primary partitions, extended partitions, and logical drives, dynamic disks have dynamic volumes that can be created as the following types:

- **Simple volumes**  A simple volume is a volume that's on a single drive and has the same purpose as a primary partition.

- **Spanned volumes**   A spanned volume is a volume that spans multiple drives.

- **Striped volumes**   A striped volume is a volume that uses RAID 0 to combine multiple disks into a striped set.

- **Mirrored volumes**   A mirrored volume is a volume that uses RAID 1 to mirror a primary disk onto a secondary disk that is available for disaster recovery.

- **RAID-5 volumes**   A RAID-5 volume is a volume that uses RAID 5 to create a fault-tolerant striped set on three or more disks.

Techniques for creating and managing these volume types are discussed in the sections that follow. Keep in mind that the RAID technology built into the operating system is software-based and is being phased out. Standards-based storage also has software RAID options, and they're preferred for new server deployments. See "Managing Storages Spaces" in Chapter 14 for complete details on Storage Spaces.

## Creating a simple or spanned volume

You create simple and spanned volumes in much the same way. The differences between these volume types are subtle:

- A simple volume uses free space from a single disk to create a volume. Windows is able to write to the selected disk until there is no more free space available within the volume.

- A spanned volume is used to combine the disk space on multiple disks to create the appearance of a single volume. Windows always writes to the first disk in the spanned set first and then when this disk fills, Windows writes to the second disk, and so on.

If you later need more space, you can extend a simple or spanned volume type by using Disk Management. Here, you select an area of free space on any available disk and add it to the volume. When you extend a simple volume onto other disks, it becomes a spanned volume. Any volume that you want to extend should be formatted using NTFS because only NTFS volumes can be extended.

Simple and spanned volumes aren't fault tolerant. If you create a volume that spans disks and one of those disks fails, you won't be able to access the volume. Any data on the volume will be lost. You must restore the data from backup after you replace the failed drive and re-create the volume.

To create a simple or spanned volume, complete the following steps:

1.  In Disk Management Graphical View, press and hold or right-click an area marked Unallocated on a dynamic disk, and then choose New Simple Volume or New Spanned Volume as appropriate. Read the Welcome page and then tap or click Next.

2.  If you select New Spanned Volume, you next see the Select Disks page shown in Figure 12-26. Use this page to select disks that should be part of the volume and to size the volume segments on the designated disks. Select one or more disks from the list of disks that are available and have unallocated space. Tap or click Add to add the disk or disks to the Selected list box. Next, select each of the disks in turn, and then specify the amount of space you want to use on the selected disk. Tap or click Next when you are ready to continue.

> **Note**
>
> If you started with a dynamic disk, the disk wizard shows both basic and dynamic disks with available disk space. If you add space from a basic disk that is not a system or boot volume, the wizard will attempt to convert the disk to a dynamic disk before creating the volume set. Before tapping or clicking Yes to continue, make sure you really want to do this because this can affect how the disk is used by the operating system.

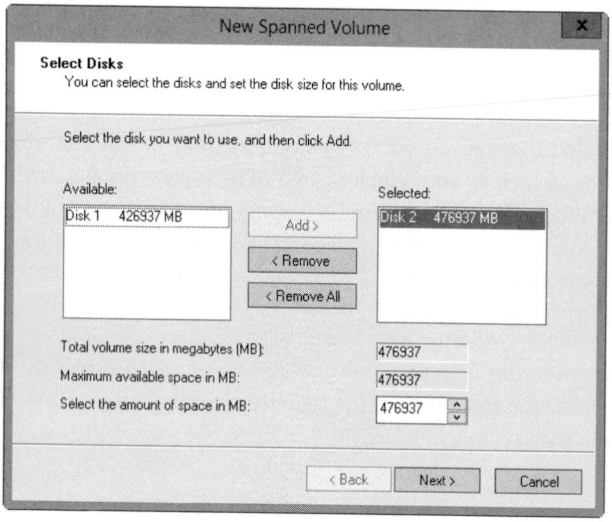

**Figure 12-26**  Select the disks that should be part of the volume, and then specify how much space to use on each disk.

3. Use the Assign Drive Letter Or Path page to assign a drive letter or path. You can also choose Do Not Assign A Drive Letter Or Drive Path if you want to create the partition without assigning a drive letter or path. Tap or click Next.

4. Use the Format Volume page, to set the formatting options. Simple and spanned volumes can be formatted by using FAT, FAT32, exFAT, NTFS, or ReFS. If you think you might need to extend the volume at a later date, you might want to use NTFS because NTFS can be easily extended. If you opt not to format the partition at this time, you can format the partition later as discussed in "Formatting a partition, logical drive, or volume" earlier in this chapter.

5. Tap or click Next. The final page shows you the options you selected. If the options are correct, tap or click Finish. The wizard then creates the volume and configures it.

## Configuring RAID 0: Striping

RAID level 0 is disk striping. With disk striping, two or more volumes—each on a separate drive—are configured as a striped set. Unlike spanning, Windows breaks the data to be written into blocks called *stripes* and then writes the stripes sequentially to all disks in the set. So, if there are three disks in the set, Windows writes part of the data to the first disk, part of the data to the second disk, and part of the data to the third disk—this process of alternating between the disks is called *striping*.

Although the boot and system volumes shouldn't be part of a striped set, you can place volumes for a striped set on up to 32 drives, but in most circumstances sets with 2 to 5 volumes offer the best performance improvements. When 3 to 32 drives are used, the major advantage of disk striping is speed. Data can be accessed on multiple disks using multiple drive heads, which improves performance considerably. When you try to use more than 32 drives, the performance improvement decreases significantly.

When you create striped sets, you'll want to use volumes that are approximately the same size. Disk Management bases the overall size of the striped set on the smallest volume size. Specifically, the maximum size of the striped set is a multiple of the smallest volume size. For example, if the smallest volume is 100 GBs, the maximum size for a three-disk striped set is 300 GBs.

You can maximize performance using disks that are on separate disk controllers. This allows the system to simultaneously access the drives. Keep in mind that this configuration offers no fault tolerance. If any hard disk drive in the striped set fails, the striped set can no longer be used, which essentially means that all data in the striped set is lost. You'll need to re-create the striped set and restore the data from backups. Data backup and recovery are discussed in Chapter 17, "Backup and recovery."

Chapter 12

You can create a striped set by following these steps:

1. In the Disk Management Graphical View, press and hold or right-click an area marked Unallocated on a dynamic disk and then choose New Striped Volume. This starts the New Striped Volume Wizard. Read the Welcome page, and then tap or click Next.

2. Create the volume as described previously in "Creating a simple or spanned volume" earlier in this chapter. The key difference is that you need at least two dynamic disks to create a striped volume.

After you create a striped volume, you can use the volume just like any other volume. You can't extend a striped set after it's created. Therefore, you should carefully consider the setup before you implement it.

## Recovering a failed simple, spanned, or striped disk

Simple disks are the easiest to troubleshoot and recover because there is only one disk involved. Spanned or striped disks, on the other hand, have multiple disks and the failure of any one disk makes the entire volume unusable. The drive status might show as Missing, Failed, Online (Errors), Offline, or Unreadable.

The Missing (and sometimes Offline) status usually happens if drives have been disconnected or powered off. If the drives are part of an external storage device, check the storage device to ensure that it is connected properly and has power. Reconnecting the storage device or turning on the power should make it so that the drives can be accessed. You then must start Disk Management and rescan the disks by selecting Rescan Disks from the Action menu. When Disk Management finishes, press and hold or right-click the drive that was missing, and then choose Reactivate.

The Failed, Online (Errors), and Unreadable statuses indicate input/output (I/O) problems with the drive. As before, try rescanning the drive, and then try to reactivate the drive. If the drive doesn't come back to the Healthy state, you might need to replace it.

## Moving dynamic disks

One of the advantages that dynamic disks have over basic disks is that you can easily move them from one computer to another. For example, if after setting up a server, you decide that you don't really need its two additional hard disk drives, you could move them to another server where they could be better used. Before you move disks, you should access Disk Management on the server where the dynamic disks are currently installed and check their status. The status should be Healthy. If it isn't, you should fix any problems before moving the disks.

## Moving system disks requires additional planning

**B**efore you move a system disk from one computer to another, you must ensure that the computers have identically configured hard disk subsystems. If they don't, the Plug and Play ID on the system disk from the original computer won't match what the new computer is expecting. As a result, the new computer won't be able to load the right drivers and boot will fail.

You cannot move drives with BitLocker Drive Encryption using this technique. BitLocker Drive Encryption wraps drives in a protected seal so that any offline tampering is detected and results in the disk being unavailable until an administrator unlocks it. Before you can move a BitLocker encrypted drive, you must remove BitLocker Drive Encryption.

Next check to see whether any dynamic disks that you want to move are part of a spanned, extended, mirrored, striped, or RAID-5 set. If they are, you should make a note of which disks are part of which set and plan on moving all disks in a set together. If you are moving only part of a disk set, you should be aware of the consequences. For spanned, extended, or striped volumes, moving only part of the set will make the related volumes unusable on the current computer and on the computer to which you are planning to move the disks. If you plan to move only one disk of a mirrored volume, you should break the mirror before you move it. This ensures that you can keep using the disks on both computers. For RAID-5 volumes, you should move all of the disks in the set if possible. If you move only part of the RAID-5 set, you might find that you can't use the set on either computer.

To move the disks, open Computer Management and then, in the left pane, select Device Manager. In the Device List, expand Disk Drives. This shows a list of all the physical disk drives on the computer. Press and hold or right-click each disk that you want to move, and then select Uninstall. If you are unsure which disks to uninstall, press and hold or right-click each disk and select Properties. In the Properties dialog box, click the Volumes tab and then choose Populate. This shows you the volumes on the selected disk. In Computer Management, select Disk Management. Press and hold or right-click each disk that you want to move, and then select Remove Disk.

After you perform these procedures, you can move the dynamic disks. If the disks are hot swappable and this feature is supported on both computers, remove the disks from the original computer and then install them on the destination computer. Otherwise, turn off both computers, remove the drives from the original computer, and then install them on the destination computer. When you're finished, restart the computers. On the destination computer, access Disk Management, and then select Rescan Disks on the Action menu. When Disk Management finishes scanning the disks, press and hold or right-click any disk marked Foreign and tap or click Import. You should now be able to access the disks and their volumes on the destination computer.

> **Note**
>
> When you move dynamic disks, the volumes on those disks should retain the drive letters they had on the previous computer. If a drive letter is already used on the destination computer, a volume receives the next available drive letter. If a dynamic volume previously did not have a drive letter, it does not receive a drive letter when moved to another computer. Additionally, if automounting is disabled, the volumes aren't automatically mounted and you must manually mount volumes and assign drive letters.

## Configuring RAID 1: Disk mirroring

For RAID 1, disk mirroring, you configure two volumes on two drives identically. Data is written to both drives. If one drive fails, there is no data loss because the other drive contains the data. After you repair or replace the failed drive, you can restore full mirroring so that the volume is once again fault tolerant.

By using disk mirroring, you gain the advantage of redundancy. Because disk mirroring doesn't write parity information, mirrored volumes can usually offer better write performance than disk striping with parity. The key drawback, however, is that disk mirroring has a 50 percent overhead, meaning it effectively cuts the amount of storage space in half. For example, to mirror a 750-GB drive, you need another 750-GB drive. That means you use 1500 GBs of space to store 750 GBs of information.

As with disk striping, you'll often want the mirrored disks to be on separate disk controllers. This provides redundancy for the disk controllers. If one of the disk controllers fails, the disk on the other controller is still available. When you use two separate disk controllers to duplicate data, you're using a technique known as *disk duplexing* rather than disk mirroring—but why mince words?

You can create a mirrored set either by using two new disks or by adding a mirror to an existing volume. As with other RAID techniques, mirroring is transparent to users. Users see the mirrored set as a single volume that they can access and use like any other drive.

### Creating a mirrored set using two new disks

To create a mirrored set using two new disks, start Disk Management. In Graphical View, press and hold or right-click an area marked Unallocated on a dynamic disk and then choose New Mirrored Volume. This starts the New Mirrored Volume Wizard. Tap or click Next. Create the volume as described in "Creating a simple or spanned volume" earlier in this chapter. The key difference is that you must create two identically sized volumes and these volumes must be on separate dynamic drives. The volumes can be formatted as FAT, FAT32, exFAT, NTFS, or ReFS. You won't be able to continue past the Selected Disks page until you select the two disks that you want to work with.

When you tap or click Finish, you'll return to the main Disk Management window, and Disk Management will create the mirrored set. During the creation of the mirror, you'll see a status of Resynching. This tells you that Disk Management is creating the mirror. When this process finishes, you'll have two identical volumes. Both volumes will show the same drive letter in Disk Management, but the separation of volumes is transparent to users. Users see the mirror set as a single volume. The volume status should be listed as Healthy. This is the normal status for volumes. If the status changes, you might need to repair or resync the mirrored set, as discussed in "Resolving problems with mirrored sets" later in this chapter.

### Adding a mirror to an existing volume

You can also use an existing volume to create a mirrored set. For this to work, the volume you want to mirror must be a simple volume and you must have an area of unallocated space on a second dynamic drive with an equal or larger amount of space than the existing volume. When you add a mirror onto this unallocated space, Disk Management creates a volume that is the same size and file-system type as the simple volume you are mirroring. It then copies the data from the simple volume to the new volume using a process called *resynching*.

To add a mirror to an existing volume, start Disk Management. In Graphical View, press and hold or right-click the simple volume you want to mirror and then select Add Mirror. This displays the Add Mirror dialog box. Use the Disks list to select a location for the mirror, and then tap or click Add Mirror. Windows Server 2012 begins the mirror creation process, and you'll see a status of Resynching on both volumes.

When the resynching is complete, you have two identical copies of the original volume. Although both volumes show the same drive letter in Disk Management, the separation of volumes is transparent to users. Users see the mirror set as a single volume.

## Mirroring boot and system volumes

Disk mirroring is often used to mirror boot and system volumes. Mirroring these volumes ensures that you'll be able to boot the server in case of a single drive failure.

### Mirroring boot and system volumes on MBR disks

When you want to mirror boot or system volumes on MBR disks, the process is straightforward. You start with two disks, which I'll call Disk 0 and Disk 1, where Disk 0 has the system files and Disk 1 is a new disk. The system disk is typically a basic disk that must be upgraded to a dynamic disk before you can mirror it—mirroring is possible only on dynamic disks.

To begin, upgrade Disk 0 to a dynamic disk and then upgrade Disk 1 as discussed in "Using and converting basic and dynamic disks" earlier in this chapter. In Disk Management, press and hold or right-click the boot or system volume that you want to mirror and then select Add Mirror. This displays the Add Mirror dialog box. Select the disk onto which you want to add the mirror (Disk 1 in the example), and then tap or click Add Mirror. Windows Server 2012 begins the mirror creation process, and you'll see a status of Resynching on both volumes. When the resynching is complete, the status should change to Healthy.

During the creation of the mirror, the operating system should add an entry to the system's Boot Manager that allows you to boot to the secondary mirror. Resolving a primary mirror failure is much easier with this entry in the Boot Manager file than without it because all you need to do is select the entry to boot to the secondary mirror. If you mirror the boot volume and a secondary mirror entry is not created for you, you could modify the boot entries in the Boot Manager to create one using the BCD Editor (bcdedit.exe).

If a system fails to boot to the primary system volume, restart the system and select the Boot Mirror - Secondary Plex option for the operating system you want to start. The system should start up normally. After you successfully boot the system to the secondary drive, you can schedule the maintenance necessary to rebuild the mirror if desired.

## Mirroring boot and system volumes on GPT disks

Mirroring boot and system volumes on GPT disks isn't the same as for MBR disks. Primarily, this is because GPT disks used to boot the operating system have an ESP and an MSR partition that must be created on the disk in a certain order. Thus, to mirror boot and system volumes on GPT disks, you must create the necessary partitions on the second disk of the mirrored set and tell the operating system that these partitions can be used for booting.

> **Note**
> As stated previously, not all computers are capable of booting to GPT disks. Only EFI-based computers can boot to GPT disks.

To get started, you need two disks that use the GPT partition style and the basic storage type. One of the disks should already be designated as the boot volume. I'll refer to this volume as Disk 0. The other disk should be identical in size or larger than the boot volume. I'll refer to this volume as Disk 1. Disk 1 should be a clean disk, meaning it can't already have partitions on it; so, if necessary, copy any data on the disk to another disk or make a backup of the data and then delete any existing partitions. You can use DiskPart to do this by completing the following steps:

1.  At the command prompt, invoke DiskPart by typing **diskpart**. List the disks available on the system by typing **list disk**.

2.  Select the disk you are going to use as the secondary boot disk. Following the example, this is Disk 1, so you type **select disk 1**.

3.  List the partitions on this disk by typing **list partition**.

4.  If there are any existing partitions, select and delete each partition in turn. For example, if the disk has Partition 1, you type **select partition 1**, and then type **delete partition override**. The *Override* parameter ensures that you can delete nonuser partitions.

After you make sure the second disk doesn't contain any partitions, list the available disks again by typing **list disk**, and then select the disk you are going to use as the current boot disk. Following the example, this is Disk 0, so you type **select disk 0**. List the partitions on this disk by typing **list partition**. The output you'll see will be similar to the following:

```
Partition ###    Type             Size        Offset
-------------    ------------------------    -------
Partition 1      System           316 MB      32 KB
Partition 2      Primary          9992 MB     312 MB
Partition 3      Reserved         32 MB       9 GB
```

The output shows you which partitions are being used as the ESP and MSR partitions. The ESP is listed with the partition type System. The MSR partition is listed with the partition type Reserved. Note the size of each partition. Here, System is 316 MBs and Reserved is 32 MBs.

You now must create the ESP and MSR partitions on the second disk by completing the following steps:

1.  In DiskPart, select this disk to give it focus. Following the example, you type **select disk 1**.

2.  Afterward, you create the ESP first by typing **create partition efi size=N**, where *N* is the size previously noted, such as **size=316**.

> **Note**
> The target disk must still be basic at this point. If you already converted the disk to dynamic, steps 2 and 3 will result in errors.

3.  Create the MSR partition by typing **create partition msr size=N**, where *N* is the size previously noted, such as **size=32**.

4.  If you type **list partition**, you should see that both partitions have been created and are sized appropriately, such as follows:

```
Partition ###      Type                    Size        Offset
-------------      -----------------       --------    -------
Partition 1        System                  316 MB      32 KB
Partition 2        Reserved                32 MB       316 MB
```

Next you must prepare the ESP for use by assigning it a drive letter, formatting it, and copying over the necessary startup files from the current boot volume. To do this, follow these steps:

1.  In DiskPart, select the partition by typing **select partition 1**.

2.  Assign a drive letter by typing **assign letter=X**, where *X* is the drive letter, such as **letter=H**.

3.  Format the ESP as FAT. Following the example, you type **format /fs=fat quick**.

4.  After formatting is complete, select the current boot volume. Following the example, you type **select disk 0**.

5.  Type **select partition 1** to select the ESP on the current boot volume.

6.  Assign this partition a drive letter by typing **assign letter=X**, where *X* is the drive letter to assign, such as **letter=I**.

7.  Exit DiskPart by typing **exit**.

8.  Use the XCOPY command to copy all the files from the ESP on the current boot volume to the ESP on the second disk. Following the example, you type **xcopy i:\\*.* h: /s /h**. The */S* and */H* parameters ensure that hidden system files are copied.

You now must convert both drives to the dynamic storage type. Start with the second disk, and then convert the current boot disk. Follow these steps:

1.  Invoke DiskPart by typing **diskpart**.

2.  Select the disk you are going to use as the secondary boot disk. Following the example, this is Disk 1, so you type **select disk 1**.

3.  Convert the disk by typing **convert dynamic**.

4.  Select the current boot disk. Following the example, this is Disk 0, so you type **select disk 0**.

5.  Convert the disk by typing **convert dynamic**.

6.  Exit DiskPart by typing **exit**.

7.  You must shut down and restart the computer to complete the conversion process for the current boot disk. In some cases, this process takes several reboots to complete.

> **Note**
> You don't have to delete the drive letters assigned in the previous procedure. These drive letters will not be reassigned after the restart.

When the conversion process is complete, log on to the system, and then follow these steps to mirror the boot drive:

1.  Invoke DiskPart by typing **diskpart**.

2.  Select the current boot disk. Following the example, this is Disk 1, so you type **select disk 0**.

3.  Add the disk to use as the second drive to this volume to create the mirrored set. Following the example, you type **add disk=1**.

    DiskPart will then begin the mirror creation process by synchronizing the data on both volumes.

During the creation of the mirror, the operating system should add an entry to the system's Boot Manager that allows you to boot to the secondary mirror. Resolving a primary mirror failure is much easier with this entry in the Boot Manager file than without it because all you need to do is select the entry to boot to the secondary mirror. If you mirror the boot volume and a secondary mirror entry is not created for you, you could modify the boot entries in the Boot Manager to create one using the BCD Editor (bcdedit.exe).

If a system fails to boot to the primary system volume, restart the system and select the Boot Mirror - Secondary Plex option for the operating system you want to start. The system should start up normally. After you successfully boot the system to the secondary drive, you can schedule the maintenance necessary to rebuild the mirror if desired.

Now if you shut down the system and restart it, you should be able to boot successfully to either the primary or secondary boot disk.

Chapter 12

# Configuring RAID 5: Disk striping with parity

RAID 5, disk striping with parity, offers fault tolerance with less overhead and better read performance than disk mirroring. To configure RAID 5, you use three or more volumes, each on a separate drive, as a striped set, similar to RAID 0. Unlike RAID 0, however, RAID 5 adds parity error checking to ensure that the failure of a single drive won't bring down the entire drive set. In the event of a single drive failure, the set continues to function with disk operations directed at the remaining disks in the set. The parity information can also be used to recover the data using a process called *regeneration*.

RAID 5 works like this: Each time the operating system writes to a RAID-5 volume, the data is written across all the disks in the set. Parity information for the data, used for error checking and correction, is written to disk as well, but it's always written on a separate disk from the one used to write the data. For example, if you are using a three-volume RAID-5 set and save a file, the individual data bytes of the file are written to each of the disks in the set. Parity information is written as well, but not to the same disk as one of the individual data bytes. Thus, a disk in the set could have a chunk of the data or the corresponding parity information, but not both. This, in turn, means that the loss of one disk from the set doesn't cause the entire set to fail.

Like any type of RAID, RAID 5 has its drawbacks as well. First, if multiple drives in the set fail, the entire set will fail and you won't be able to regenerate the set from the parity information. Why? If multiple drives fail, there won't be enough parity information to use to recover the set. Second, having to generate and write parity information every time data is written to disk slows down the write process (and, in the case of software RAID, reduces processing power). To compensate for the performance hit, hardware RAID controllers have their own processors that handle the necessary processing—and this is why hardware RAID is preferred over software RAID.

OK, so RAID 5 gives you fault tolerance at some cost to performance. It does, however, have less overhead than RAID 1. By using RAID 1, you have 50 percent overhead, which effectively cuts the amount of storage space in half. By using RAID 5, the overhead depends on the number of disks in the RAID set. With three disks, the overhead is about one-third. If you have three 750-GB drives using RAID 5, you use 2250 GBs of space to store about 1500 GBs of information. If you have additional disks, the overhead is reduced incrementally, but not significantly.

To create a RAID-5 set, start Disk Management. In Graphical View, press and hold or right-click an area marked Unallocated on a dynamic disk and then choose New RAID-5 Volume. This starts the New RAID-5 Volume Wizard. Tap or click Next. Create the volume as described in "Creating a simple or spanned volume" earlier in this chapter. The key difference is that you must select free space on three or more separate dynamic drives.

When you tap or click Finish, you'll return to the main Disk Management window and Disk Management will create the RAID-5 set. During the creation of the mirror, you'll see a status of Resynching. This tells you that Disk Management is creating the RAID-5 set. When this process finishes, you'll have three or more identical volumes, all of which will show the same drive letter in Disk Management. Users, however, will see the RAID-5 set as a single volume. The volume status should be listed as Healthy. This is the normal status for volumes. If the status changes, you might need to repair or regenerate the RAID-5 set as discussed in "Resolving problems with RAID-5 sets" later in this chapter.

## Breaking or removing a mirrored set

Windows Server 2012 provides two ways to stop mirroring. You can break a mirrored set, creating two separate but identical volumes. Or you can remove a mirror, which deletes all the data on the removed mirror.

To break a mirrored set, follow these steps:

1.  In Disk Management, press and hold or right-click one of the volumes in the mirrored set and then choose Break Mirrored Volume.

2.  Confirm that you want to break the mirrored set by tapping or clicking Yes. If the volume is currently in use, you'll see another warning dialog box. Confirm that it's OK to continue by tapping or clicking Yes.

    Windows Server 2012 will then break the mirrored set, creating two independent volumes.

To remove a mirror, follow these steps:

1.  In Disk Management, press and hold or right-click one of the volumes in the mirrored set and then choose Remove Mirror. This opens the Remove Mirror dialog box.

2.  In the Remove Mirror dialog box, select the disk from which to remove the mirror. If the mirror contains a boot or system volume, you should remove the mirror from the secondary drive rather than the primary. For example, if Drive 0 and Drive 1 are mirrored, remove Drive 1 rather than Drive 0.

3.  Confirm the action when prompted. All data on the removed mirror is deleted.

## Resolving problems with mirrored sets

Occasionally, data on mirrored volumes can get out of sync. Typically, this happens if one of the drives in the set goes offline or experiences temporary I/O problems and, as a result, data can be written only to the drive that's online. To reestablish mirroring, you must get both drives online and then resynchronize the mirror, but you must rebuild the set using

Chapter 12

a disk with the same partition style—either MBR or GPT. The corrective action you take depends on the drive status.

> **Note**
>
> When mirroring boot volumes, Windows requires you to use the same partition style. With data volumes, you can mirror between MBR and GPT.

The Missing or Offline status usually happens if drives have been disconnected or powered off. If the drives are part of an external storage device, check the storage device to ensure that it is connected properly and has power. Reconnecting the storage device or turning on the power should make it so that the drives can be accessed. You then must start Disk Management and rescan the missing drive by selecting Rescan Disks on the Action menu. When Disk Management finishes, press and hold or right-click the drive and choose Reactivate Volume. The drive status should change to Regenerating and then to Healthy. If the volume doesn't return to the Healthy status, press and hold or right-click the volume and then choose Resynchronize Mirror.

A status of Failed, Online (Errors), or Unreadable indicates I/O problems with the drive. As before, try rescanning the drive, and then try to reactivate the drive. The drive status should change to Regenerating and then to Healthy. If the volume doesn't return to the Healthy status, press and hold or right-click the volume and then choose Resynchronize Mirror.

If these actions don't work, you must remove the failed mirror, replace the bad drive, and then rebuild the mirror. To do this, follow these steps:

1. Press and hold or right-click the failed volume, and then select Remove Mirror.

2. You now must mirror the volume on an Unallocated area of free space on a different disk. If you don't have free space, you must create space by shrinking a volume, deleting other volumes, or replacing the failed drive.

3. When you are ready to continue, press and hold or right-click the remaining volume in the original mirror and then select Add Mirror. This opens the Add Mirror dialog box.

4. Use the Disks list to select a location for the mirror, and then tap or click Add Mirror. Windows Server 2012 begins the mirror creation process, and you'll see a status of Resynching on both volumes.

# Repairing a mirrored system volume

When you mirror a system volume, an entry that allows you to boot to the secondary mirror is added to the system's boot configuration data. So, if a system fails to boot to the primary system volume, restart the system, and select the Boot Mirror—Secondary Plex option for the operating system you want to start. The system should start up normally. After you successfully boot the system to the secondary drive, you can schedule the maintenance necessary to rebuild the mirror if desired.

## Rebuilding mirrored system volumes on MBR disks

To rebuild the mirror, you must complete the following steps:

1. Shut down the system, and replace the failed drive. Then restart the system using the secondary drive.

2. In Disk Management, press and hold or right-click the remaining volume in the mirrored set and choose Break Mirrored Volume. Tap or click Yes at the prompts to confirm the action.

3. Next, press and hold or right-click the volume again, and choose Add Mirror. Use the Add Mirror dialog box to select the second disk to use for the mirror, and then tap or click Add Mirror.

If you want the primary mirror to be on the drive you added or replaced, perform these additional steps:

1. Use Disk Management to break the mirrored set again.

2. Make sure that the primary drive in the original mirror set has the drive letter that was previously assigned to the complete mirror. If it doesn't, assign the appropriate drive letter.

3. Press and hold or right-click the original system volume, select Add Mirror, and then re-create the mirror.

## Rebuilding mirrored system volumes on GPT disks

For GPT disks, rebuilding mirrored system volumes is a bit different. To rebuild the mirror, shut down the system and replace the failed drive, and then restart the system using the secondary drive. In Disk Management, press and hold or right-click the remaining volume in the mirrored set and choose Break Mirrored Volume. Tap or click Yes at the prompts to confirm the action. After this, you can use the secondary boot disk as your primary boot

Chapter 12

disk and follow the procedures outlined in "Mirroring boot and system volumes on MBR disks" earlier in this chapter to re-enable mirroring properly using the secondary disk as the primary.

## Resolving problems with RAID-5 sets

Most problems with RAID-5 sets have to do with the intermittent or permanent failure of a drive. If one of the drives in the set goes offline or experiences temporary I/O problems, parity data cannot be properly written to the set and, as a result, the set's status will show as Failed Redundancy and the failed volume's status changes to Missing, Offline, or Online (Errors).

You must get all drives in the RAID-5 set online. If the status of the problem volume is Missing or Offline, make sure that the drive has power and is connected properly. You then must start Disk Management and rescan the missing drive by choosing Rescan Disks from the Action menu. When Disk Management finishes, press and hold or right-click the drive and choose Reactivate. The drive status should change to Regenerating and then to Healthy. If the volume doesn't return to the Healthy status, press and hold or right-click the volume and then tap or click Regenerate Parity.

A status of Failed, Online (Errors), or Unreadable indicates I/O problems with the drive. As before, try rescanning the drive, and then try to reactivate the drive. The drive status should change to Regenerating and then to Healthy. If the volume doesn't return to the Healthy status, press and hold or right-click the volume and then tap or click Regenerate Parity.

If one of the drives still won't come back online, you must repair the failed region of the RAID-5 set. Press and hold or right-click the failed volume, and then select Remove Volume. You now must press and hold or right-click an unallocated space on a separate dynamic disk with the same partition style—either MBR or GPT—and choose Repair Volume. This space must be at least as large as the region to repair, and it can't be on a drive that's already being used by the RAID-5 set. If you don't have enough space, the Repair Volume option is unavailable and you must free space by shrinking a volume, deleting other volumes, or replacing the failed drive.

# TPM and BitLocker Drive Encryption

**M**ANY of the security features built into the Microsoft Windows operating system are designed to protect a computer from attacks by individuals accessing the computer over the network or from the Internet. But what about when individuals have direct physical access to a computer? When someone has direct physical access to a computer, many of Windows security safeguards don't apply. For example, if someone can boot a computer—even if it is to another operating system that person has installed—he or she could gain access to any data stored on the computer, perhaps even your organization's most sensitive data. To protect a computer from individuals who have direct access to it, current Windows and Windows Server operating systems include the Trusted Platform Module Services architecture and BitLocker Drive Encryption. Together these features help protect a computer from many types of attacks by individuals who have direct access to it.

## Working with trusted platforms

Current Windows and Windows Server operating systems include the Encrypting File System (EFS) for encrypting files and folders. Using EFS, users can protect sensitive data so that it can be accessed only by using their public key certificate. Encryption certificates are stored as part of the data in a user's profile. As long as users have access to their profiles and the encryption keys they contain, they can access their encrypted files.

Although EFS offers excellent protection for your data, it doesn't necessarily safeguard the computer from attack by someone who has direct physical access. In a situation where a user loses a computer, a computer has been stolen, or the attacker is logging on to a computer, EFS might not protect the data because the attacker might be able to gain access to the computer before it boots. He could then access the computer from another operating system and change the computer's configuration. He might then be able to hack into a logon account on the original operating system so that he can log on as the user or configure the computer so that he can log on as a local administrator. If

Chapter 13

he can do this without having to reset the password of the user who encrypted the files or the administrator, the attacker could eventually gain full access to a computer and its encrypted data.

To seal a computer from physical attack and wrap it in an additional layer of protection, current Windows and Windows Server operating systems include the Trusted Platform Module (TPM) Services architecture. TPM Services protect a computer using a dedicated hardware component called a TPM. A TPM is a microchip that is usually installed on the motherboard of a computer where it communicates with the rest of the system using a hardware bus. Computers can use a TPM to provide enhanced protection for data, to ensure early validation of the boot file's integrity, and to guarantee that a disk has not been tampered with while the operating system was offline.

A TPM has the ability to create cryptographic keys and encrypt them so that they can be decrypted only by the TPM. This process, referred to as *wrapping* or *binding*, protects the key from disclosure. A TPM has a master "wrapping" key called the Storage Root Key (SRK). The SRK is stored within the TPM itself to ensure that the private portion of the key is secure.

Computers that have a TPM can create a key that has not only been wrapped but also sealed. The process of sealing the key ensures the key is tied to specific platform measurements and can be unwrapped only when those platform measurements have the same values that they had when the key was created. This is what gives TPM-equipped computers increased resistance to attack.

Because TPM stores private portions of key pairs separately from memory controlled by the operating system, keys can be sealed to the TPM to provide absolute assurances about the state of a system and its trustworthiness. TPM keys are unsealed only when the integrity of the system is intact. Further, because the TPM uses its own internal firmware and logical circuits for processing instructions, it does not rely upon the operating system and is not subject to external software vulnerabilities.

The TPM can also be used to seal and unseal data that is generated outside of the TPM, and this is where the true power of the TPM lies. In current Windows and Windows Server operating systems, the feature that accesses the TPM and uses it to seal a computer is called BitLocker Drive Encryption. Although BitLocker Drive Encryption can be used in both TPM or non-TPM configurations, the most secure method is to use TPM.

When you use BitLocker Drive Encryption and a TPM to seal the boot manager and boot files of a computer, the boot manager and boot files can be unsealed only if they are unchanged since they were last sealed. This means you can use the TPM to validate a computer's boot files in the pre-operating system environment. When you seal a hard disk using TPM, the hard disk can be unsealed only if the data on the disk is unchanged since it was last sealed. This guarantees that a disk has not been tampered with while the operating system was offline.

When you use BitLocker Drive Encryption and do not use TPM to seal the boot manager and boot files of a computer, TPM cannot be used to validate a computer's boot files in the pre-operating system environment. This means there is no way to guarantee the integrity of the boot manager and boot files of a computer.

# Managing TPM

A computer must be equipped with a compatible TPM and compatible firmware to take advantage of TPM. Current Windows and Windows Server operating systems support TPM version 1.2 and require Trusted Computing Group (TCG)–compliant firmware. Firmware that is TCG-compliant is firmware that supports the Static Root of Trust Measurement as defined by the Trusted Computing Group. In some configurations of TPM and BitLocker Drive Encryption, you also need to make sure the firmware supports reading USB flash drives at startup.

## Understanding TPM states and tools

The TPM Services architecture provides the basic features required to configure and deploy TPM-equipped computers. This architecture can be extended with a feature called BitLocker Drive Encryption, which is discussed in "Introducing BitLocker Drive Encryption" later in this chapter.

Before you can use TPM, you must turn on TPM in firmware and initialize the TPM for first use in software. As part of the initialization process, you set the owner password on the TPM. After TPM is enabled, you can manage the TPM configuration.

In some cases, computers that have TPM might ship with TPM turned off. If so, you must turn on TPM in firmware. With one of my computers, I needed to do the following:

1.  Start the computer, and then press F2 during startup to access the firmware. In the firmware, I accessed the Advanced screen and then the Peripheral Configuration screen.

2.  On the Peripheral Configuration screen, Trusted Platform Module was listed as an option. After scrolling down to highlight this option, I pressed Enter to display an options menu. From the menu, I chose Enable and then pressed Enter.

3.  To save the changes to the setting and exit the firmware, I pressed F10. When prompted to confirm that I wanted to exit, I pressed Y, and the computer then rebooted.

Next, you need to initialize and prepare the TPM for first use in software. As part of this process, you take ownership of the TPM, which sets the owner password on the TPM. After TPM is enabled, you can manage the TPM configuration. Several tools for working with TPM are available:

- **Trusted Platform Module Management**   An MMC console for configuring and managing TPM. You can access this tool by typing **tpm.msc** in the Apps Search box and then pressing Enter.

- **Manage The TPM Security Hardware**   A wizard for creating the required TPM owner password. You can access this tool by typing **tpminit** in the Apps Search box and then pressing Enter.

When you are working with the Trusted Platform Module Management, you'll be able to determine the exact state of the TPM. If you try to start Trusted Platform Module Management without turning on TPM, you'll see an error like the one shown in Figure 13-1.

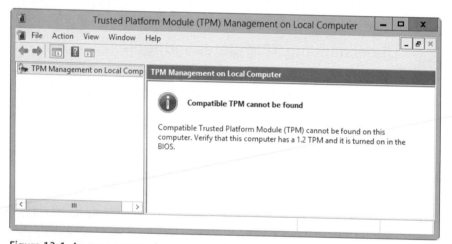

**Figure 13-1** An error occurs when you start the Trusted Platform Module Management without turning on TPM.

Similarly, if you try to run Manage The TPM Security Hardware without turning on TPM, you'll see an error like the one shown in Figure 13-2.

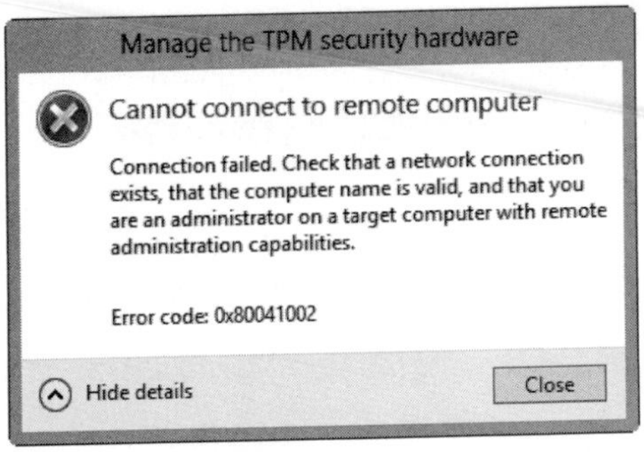

**Figure 13-2** An error occurs when you try to run Manage The TPM Security Hardware without turning on TPM.

> **Important**
>
> To perform TPM management tasks on a local computer, you must be a member of the local computer's Administrators group or be logged on as the local computer administrator. Additionally, access to the Trusted Platform Module Management console can be restricted in Group Policy. If you are unable to open the console, check to see if a Group Policy Object (GPO) being processed includes Management Console restrictions. Related policies are found in the Administrative Templates for User Configuration under Windows Components\Microsoft Management Console.

Only when you've turned on TPM in firmware will you be able to access and work with the TPM tools. When you are working with the Trusted Platform Module Management console, shown in Figure 13-3, you should note the TPM status and the TPM manufacturer information. The TPM status indicates the state of the TPM. The TPM manufacturer information shows whether the TPM supports specification version 1.2 or 2.0. Support for TPM version 1.2 or later is required.

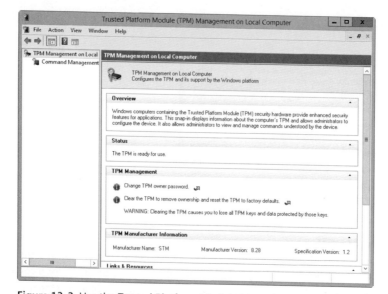

**Figure 13-3** Use the Trusted Platform Module Management console to initialize and manage TPM.

Although earlier releases of Windows showed the exact TPM state as listed in Table 13-1, Windows 8 and Windows Server 2012 normally show either a status of "The TPM is ready for use" or "The TPM is not ready for use." If the TPM is ready for use, the TPM is on and ownership has been taken.

**TABLE 13-1** TPM status indicators and their meaning

| Status Indicator | Meaning |
| --- | --- |
| The TPM is on, and ownership has not been taken. | The TPM is turned on in firmware, but it hasn't been initialized yet. |
| The TPM is on, and ownership has been taken. | The TPM is turned on in firmware and has been initialized. |
| The TPM is off, and ownership has not been taken. | The TPM is turned off in software, but it hasn't been initialized yet. |

## Managing TPM owner authorization information

Windows 8 and Windows Server 2012 include important fundamental changes in the way TPM is used. One of these changes is the ability to set the level of authorization information stored in the registry as any of the following:

- **Full**   The full TPM owner authorization, the TPM administrative delegation blob, and the TPM user delegation blob are stored in the registry. This setting allows a TPM to be used without requiring remote or external storage of the TPM owner authorization. Note that TPM-based applications designed for earlier versions of Windows or that rely on TPM antihammering logic might not support full TPM owner authorization in the registry.

- **Delegated**   Only the TPM administrative delegation blob and the TPM user delegation blob are stored in the registry. This level is appropriate for TPM-based applications that rely on TPM antihammering logic. When you use this setting, Microsoft recommends that you remotely or externally store the TPM owner authorization.

- **None**   No TPM owner authorization information is stored in the registry. Use this setting for compatibility with earlier releases of Windows and for applications that require external or remote storage of the TPM owner authorization. When you use this setting, remote or external storage of the TPM owner authorization is required, just as it was in earlier releases of Windows.

You set the level of authorization information stored in the registry using the Configure The Level Of TPM Owner Authorization Information Available To The Operating System policy. This policy is found in the Administrative Templates policies for Computer Configuration under System\Trusted Platform Module Services. Keep in mind that if you change the policy setting from Full to Delegated or vice versa, the full TPM owner authorization value is regenerated and any copies of the original TPM value will be invalid. Note also that when this policy is set to Delegated or None, you'll be prompted for the TPM owner password before you are able to perform most TPM administration tasks. Figure 13-4 shows an example.

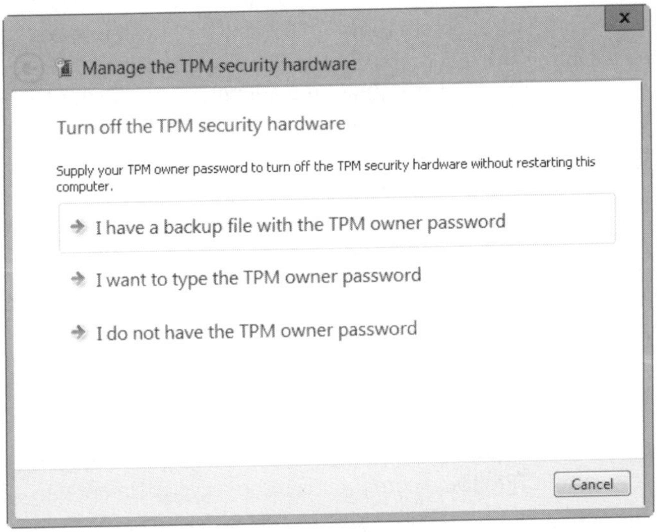

**Figure 13-4** Supply the TPM owner password, if prompted for one.

With earlier releases of Windows, Microsoft recommended remotely storing the TPM owner authorization in Active Directory for domain-joined computers, which could be accomplished by enabling the Turn On TPM Backup To Active Directory Domain Services policy, extending the schema for the directory, and setting the appropriate access controls.

Enabling backup to Active Directory changes the default way TPM owner information is stored. Specifically, when Turn On TPM Backup To Active Directory Domain Services is enabled and Configure The Level Of TPM Owner Authorization Information Available To The Operating System is disabled or not configured, only the TPM administrative delegation blob and the TPM user delegation blob are stored in the registry. Here, to store the full TPM owner information, you must use the Enabled setting of Full (or disable the Active Directory backup of the TPM owner authorization).

Under System\Trusted Platform Module Services, you'll find the following related policies:

- Ignore The Default List Of Blocked TPM Commands

- Ignore The Local List Of Blocked TPM Commands

- Standard User Lockout Duration

- Standard User Individual Lockout Threshold

- Standard User Total Lockout Threshold

- Configure the List of Blocked TPM Commands

These policies control the way command block lists are used and when lockout is triggered after multiple failed authorization attempts. An administrator can fully reset all lockout-related parameters in the Trusted Platform Module Management console. On the Action menu, tap or click Reset TPM Lockout. When the full TPM owner authorization is stored in the registry, you don't need to provide the TPM owner password. Otherwise, follow the prompts to provide the owner password or select the file containing the TPM owner password.

## Preparing and initializing a TPM for first use

Initializing a TPM prepares it for use on a computer so that you can use the TPM to secure volumes on the computer's hard drives. The initialization process involves turning on the TPM and then setting ownership of the TPM. By setting ownership of the TPM, you are assigning a password that helps ensure only the authorized TPM owner can access and manage the TPM. The TPM password is required to turn off the TPM if you no longer want to use it and to clear the TPM if the computer is to be recycled. In an Active Directory domain, you can configure Group Policy to save TPM passwords.

To initialize the TPM and create the owner password, complete the following steps:

1.  Open the Trusted Platform Module Management console. On the Action menu, choose Prepare The TPM to start the Manage the TPM Security Hardware Wizard (tpminit). If a TPM was previously initialized and then cleared, you are prompted to restart the computer and follow on-screen instructions during startup to reset TPM in firmware. Here, when I clicked Restart, I needed to enter firmware by pressing F2 during startup. I then needed to disable TPM, save the changes, and exit firmware. This triggered an automatic reset. After this, I needed to enter firmware by pressing F2, which let me enable TPM, save changes, and then exit firmware. This triggered another automatic reset. When the operating system loaded, I logged on and then needed to restart the Manage The TPM Security Hardware Wizard.

> **Note**
> You must have administrator privileges to manage the TPM configuration. Additionally, if the Manage The TPM Security Hardware Wizard detects firmware that does not meet Windows requirements or no TPM is found, you will not be able to continue and should ensure that the TPM has been turned on in firmware. Otherwise, you'll see the Create The TPM Owner Password page.

2.  When the wizard finishes its initial tasks, you'll see a prompt similar to the one shown in Figure 13-5. Tap or click Restart to restart the computer.

**Figure 13-5**  Restart the computer after the TPM is initialized.

3. Typically, hardware designed for Windows 8 and Windows Server 2012 can automatically complete the initialization process. On other hardware, you need physical access to the computer to respond to the manufacturer's firmware confirmation prompt. Figure 13-6 shows an example. Here, you must press F10 to enable and activate the TPM and allow a user to take ownership of the TPM.

> A configuration change was requested to enable, activate, and allow a user to take ownership of this computer's TPM (Trusted Platform Module)
>
> NOTE: This action will turn on the TPM
> Press F10 to enable, activate, and allow a user to take ownership of the TPM
> Press ESC to reject this change request and continue

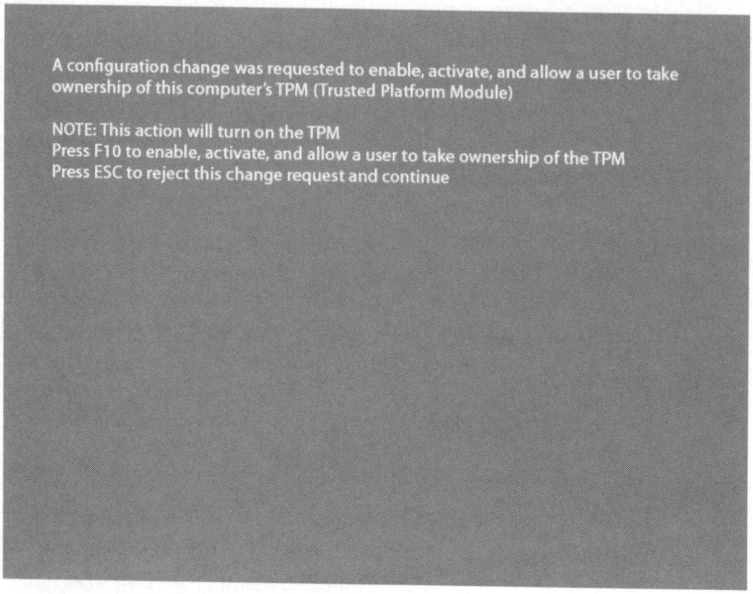

**Figure 13-6** Confirm that you want to enable and activate the TPM and allow a user to take ownership of it.

4. When Windows starts and you log on, the Manage The TPM Security Hardware Wizard continues running. Windows will take ownership of the TPM. Setting ownership on the TPM prepares it for use with the operating system. Once ownership is set, TPM is ready for use and you'll see confirmation of this, as shown in Figure 13-7.

5. Before tapping or clicking Close, save the TPM owner password. Tap or click Remember My TPM Owner Password. In the Save As dialog box, select a location to save the password backup file, and then tap or click Save. By default, the password backup file is saved as *ComputerName*.tpm.

6. In the TPM Management console, the status should be listed as "The TPM is ready for use."

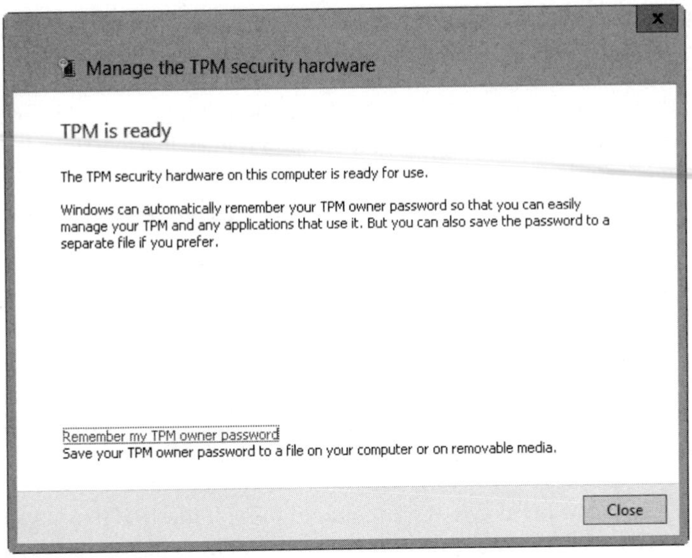

**Figure 13-7** With ownership set, the TPM is ready for use.

# INSIDE OUT  Backing up the TPM owner password

Typically, you'll want to save the TPM ownership password to removable media, such as a USB flash drive, and store the media in a secure location. In a domain where the TPM Backup To Active Directory Domain Services policy is applied, you won't have the option to save the TPM password. Here, the password is saved to Active Directory automatically.

The password backup file is an unencrypted XML file that can be opened in any text editor to confirm the name of the computer the password belongs to. In the following example, the password was created for CorpServer15:

```
<?xml version="1.0" encoding="UTF-8"?>
<tpmOwnerData version="1.0" softwareAuthor="Microsoft Windows
[Version 6.2.9200]" creationDate="2015-02-12T12:23:32-07:32"
creationUser="CORPSERVER15\Administrator" machineName="CORPSERVER15">
        <tpmInfo manufacturerId="1335342671"/>
        <ownerAuth>cEBACDgNV8Z2EBJbERTSD87KICB=
</ownerAuth>
</tpmOwnerData>
```

## Turning an initialized TPM on or off

Computers that have TPM might ship with TPM turned on. If you decide not to use TPM, you should take ownership of the TPM and then turn off the TPM. This ensures that the operating system owns the TPM but the TPM is in an inactive state. If you want to reconfigure or recycle a computer, you should clear the TPM. Clearing the TPM invalidates any stored keys, and data encrypted by these keys can no longer be accessed.

You must have administrator privileges to manage the TPM state. Turn off TPM by opening the Trusted Platform Module Management console and then tapping or clicking Turn TPM Off on the Action menu.

When the full TPM owner authorization is stored in the registry, you don't need to provide the TPM owner password. Otherwise, follow the prompts to provide the owner password or select the file containing the TPM owner password.

After you follow the previous procedure to turn off the TPM in software, you can turn on the TPM in software at any time following the steps in the "Preparing and initializing a TPM for first use" section.

## Clearing the TPM

Clearing the TPM erases information stored on the TPM and cancels the related ownership of the TPM. You should clear the TPM when a TPM-equipped computer is to be recycled. Clearing the TPM invalidates any stored keys, and data encrypted by these keys can no longer be accessed.

After clearing the TPM, you should take ownership of the TPM. This will write new information to the TPM. You might then want to turn off the TPM so that it isn't available for use.

You must have administrator privileges to clear the TPM. Clear the TPM, take ownership, and then turn off the TPM by completing the following steps:

1.  Start the Trusted Platform Module Management console. On the Action menu, tap or click Clear TPM. This starts the Manage The TPM Security Hardware Wizard.

> **Important**
> When you clear the TPM, the TPM is reset to factory defaults. Because of this, you lose all keys and the data protected by those keys. You do not need the TPM owner password to clear the TPM.

2. Read the warning on the Clear The TPM Security Hardware page, shown in Figure 13-8, and then tap or click Restart. Tap or click Cancel to exit without clearing the TPM.

```
[ x ]

▣ Manage the TPM security hardware

Clear the TPM security hardware

You must restart your computer to configure your TPM security hardware settings so that
your TPM can be cleared. To do so:

    Click the Restart button below.

    Be Physically present at the computer to follow the instructions that appear during the
    startup process.

    Log on to Windows to continue the wizard automatically.

                                            [ Restart ]   [ Cancel ]
```

**Figure 13-8** Confirm that you want to clear the TPM by tapping or clicking Restart.

3. Typically, hardware designed for Windows 8 and Windows Server 2012 can automatically complete the re-initialization process. On other hardware, you need physical access to the computer to respond to the manufacturer's firmware confirmation prompt. Figure 13-9 shows an example. Here, you must press F12 to clear, enable, and activate the TPM, or press Esc to cancel and continue loading the operating system.

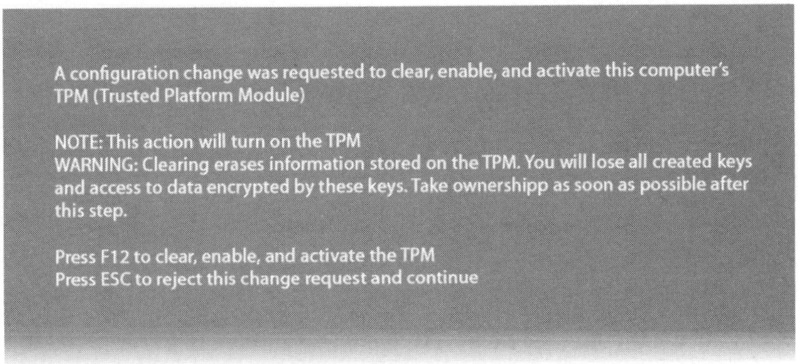

```
A configuration change was requested to clear, enable, and activate this computer's
TPM (Trusted Platform Module)

NOTE: This action will turn on the TPM
WARNING: Clearing erases information stored on the TPM. You will lose all created keys
and access to data encrypted by these keys. Take ownershipp as soon as possible after
this step.

Press F12 to clear, enable, and activate the TPM
Press ESC to reject this change request and continue
```

**Figure 13-9** Confirm the configuration change when prompted.

4. When Windows starts and you log on, the Manage The TPM Security Hardware Wizard continues running. Windows will take ownership of the TPM. Setting

ownership on the TPM prepares it for use with the operating system. Once ownership is set, the status should be listed as "The TPM is ready for use."

## Changing the TPM owner password

You can change the TPM password at any time. Generally, you do this if you suspect that the TPM owner password has been compromised. Your company's security policy also might require TPM owner password changes in certain situations.

You must have administrator privileges to change the TPM owner password. To change the TPM owner password, complete the following steps:

1. Start the Trusted Platform Module Management console. On the Action menu, tap or click Change Owner Password. This starts the Manage The TPM Security Hardware Wizard.

2. When the full TPM owner authorization is stored in the registry, you don't need to provide the TPM owner password. Otherwise, follow the prompts to provide the owner password or select the file containing the TPM owner password.

3. On the Create The TPM Owner Password page, shown in Figure 13-10, you can elect to create the password automatically or manually:

- If you want the wizard to create the password for you, select Automatically Create The Password (Recommended). The new TPM owner password is displayed. Tap or click Change Password.

- If you want to create the password, select Manually Create The Password. Type and confirm a password of at least eight characters, and then tap or click Change Password.

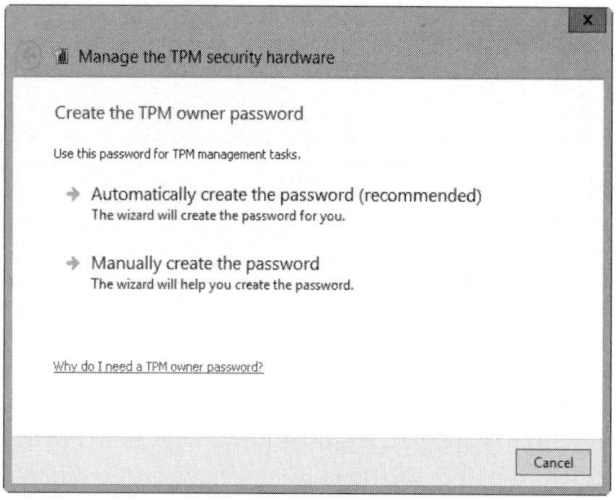

**Figure 13-10** Create a new password.

4. Before tapping or clicking Close, you might want to save the TPM owner password. Tap or click Remember My TPM Owner Password. In the Save As dialog box, select a location to save the password backup file and then tap or click Save.

# Introducing BitLocker Drive Encryption

BitLocker Drive Encryption is designed to protect the data on lost, stolen, or inappropriately decommissioned computers. Without BitLocker Drive Encryption, there is a variety of ways a user with direct physical access to a computer could gain full control and then access the computer's data whether that data was encrypted with EFS or not. For example, a user could use a boot disk to boot the computer and reset the administrator password. A user could also install and then boot to a different operating system, and then use this operating system to unlock the other installation.

## INSIDE OUT    Understanding BitLocker To Go

Although BitLocker Drive Encryption and BitLocker To Go are often referred to simply as *BitLocker*, they are separate but similar features. BitLocker Drive Encryption is designed to protect the data on the internal hard drives and is a volume-level encryption technology. BitLocker To Go is designed to protect the data on removable data drives, such as external hard drives and USB flash drives, and is a virtual-volume encryption technology. Standard BitLocker encrypts by wrapping the entire volume or only the used portion of the volume in protected encryption. BitLocker To Go, on the other hand, creates a virtual volume on a USB flash drive. This virtual volume is encrypted by using an encryption key stored on the USB flash drive.

## BitLocker essentials

BitLocker Drive Encryption prevents all access to a computer's drives except by authorized personnel by wrapping entire drives or only the used portions of volumes in tamper-proof encryption. If a user tries to access a BitLocker encrypted drive, the encryption prevents the user from viewing or manipulating the data in any way. This dramatically reduces the risk of an unauthorized person gaining access to confidential data using offline attacks.

**CAUTION**

BitLocker Drive Encryption reduces disk throughput. Because of this, you might want to use this technology on an enterprise server only if the server is not in a physically secure location and requires additional protection.

BitLocker Drive Encryption can use a TPM to validate the integrity of a computer's boot manager and boot files at startup, and to guarantee that a computer's hard disk has not been tampered with while the operating system was offline. BitLocker Drive Encryption also stores measurements of core operating system files in the TPM.

Every time the computer is started, Windows validates the boot files, the operating system files, and any encrypted volumes to ensure they have not been modified while the computer is offline. If the files have been modified, Windows alerts the user and refuses to release the key required to access Windows. The computer then goes into Recovery mode, prompting the user to provide a recovery key before allowing access to the boot volume. The Recovery mode is also used if a BitLocker encrypted disk drive is transferred to another system.

BitLocker Drive Encryption can be used in both TPM and non-TPM computers. If a computer has a TPM, BitLocker Drive Encryption uses the TPM to provide enhanced protection for your data and to ensure early boot file integrity. These features together help prevent unauthorized viewing and accessing of data by encrypting the entire Windows volume and by safeguarding the boot files from tampering. If a computer doesn't have a TPM or its TPM isn't compatible with Windows, BitLocker Drive Encryption can be used to encrypt entire volumes and, in this way, protect the volumes from being tampered with. This configuration, however, doesn't allow the added security of early boot file integrity validation.

## BitLocker modes

On computers with a compatible TPM that is initialized, BitLocker Drive Encryption typically uses one of the following TPM modes:

- **TPM-Only** In this mode, only TPM is used for validation. When the computer boots, TPM is used to validate the boot files, the operating system files, and any encrypted volumes. Because the user doesn't need to provide an additional startup key, this mode is transparent to the user, and the user logon experience is unchanged. However, if the TPM is missing or the integrity of files or volumes has changed, BitLocker enters Recovery mode and requires a recovery key or password to regain access to the boot volume.

- **TPM and PIN**    In this mode, both TPM and a user-entered numeric key are used for validation. When the computer boots, TPM is used to validate the boot files, the operating system files, and any encrypted volumes. The user must enter a PIN when prompted to continue startup. If the user doesn't have the PIN or is unable to provide the correct PIN, BitLocker enters Recovery mode instead of booting to the operating system. As before, BitLocker also enters Recovery mode if the TPM is missing or the integrity of boot files or encrypted volumes has changed.

- **TPM and Startup Key**    In this mode, both TPM and a startup key are used for validation. When the computer boots, TPM is used to validate the boot files, the operating system files, and any encrypted volumes. The user must have a USB flash drive with a startup key to log on to the computer. If the user doesn't have the startup key or is unable to provide the correct startup key, BitLocker enters Recovery mode. As before, BitLocker also enters Recovery mode if the TPM is missing or the integrity of boot files or encrypted volumes has changed.

- **TPM and Smart Card Certificate**    In this mode, both TPM and a smart card certificate are used for validation. When the computer boots, TPM is used to validate the boot files, the operating system files, and any encrypted volumes. The user must have a smart card with a valid certificate to log on to the computer. If the user doesn't have a smart card with a valid certificate and is unable to provide one, BitLocker enters Recovery mode. As before, BitLocker also enters Recovery mode if the TPM is missing or the integrity of boot files or encrypted volumes has changed.

# INSIDE OUT    Using TPM when three-factor authentication is required

A less commonly used TPM mode requires a TPM, PIN, and startup key. Use this mode when the highest security is required or when your organization has a requirement for three-factor authentication. This mode can be configured only by using the Manage-bde command-line utility. Here, when the computer boots, TPM is used to validate the boot files, the operating system files, and any encrypted volumes. The user must insert the startup key prior to startup and then enter a PIN when prompted to continue startup. If the user doesn't have the startup key, PIN, or both, BitLocker enters Recovery mode instead of booting to the operating system. As before, BitLocker also enters Recovery mode if the TPM is missing or the integrity of boot files or encrypted volumes has changed.

When working with BitLocker Drive Encryption and TPM, don't overlook the importance of Network Unlock. The Network Unlock feature allows the system volume on a computer with TPM to be automatically unlocked on startup, as long as the computer is joined and connected to a domain. When the computer is not joined and connected to a domain, other means of validation can be used, such as a startup PIN.

On computers without a TPM or on computers that have incompatible TPMs, the operating system can be configured to use an unlock password for the system drive. To configure this, you must enable the Configure Use Of Passwords For Operating System Drives policy in the Administrative Templates policies for Computer Configuration under Windows Components\BitLocker Drive Encryption\Operating System Drives. As with logon passwords, the unlock password can be configured with minimum-length and complexity requirements. The default minimum password length is eight characters, meaning the password must be at least eight characters long. Complexity requirements can be any of the following:

- Always validated using the Require Password Complexity setting

- Not validated using the Do Now Allow Password Complexity setting

- Validated if possible using the Allow Password Complexity setting

The unlock password is validated when you enable BitLocker Drive Encryption and set the password, as well as whenever the password is changed by a user. With required complexity, you can only set a password (and enable encryption) when the computer can connect to a domain controller and validate the complexity of the password. With allowed complexity, the computer will attempt to validate the complexity of the password when you set it but will allow you to continue and enable encryption if no domain controllers are available.

On computers without a TPM or on computers that have incompatible TPMs, BitLocker Drive Encryption also can use

- **Startup Key Only mode**   This mode requires a USB flash drive containing a startup key. The user inserts the USB flash drive in the computer before turning it on. The key stored on the flash drive unlocks the computer.

- **Smart Card Certificate Only mode**   This mode requires a smart card with a valid certificate. The user validates the smart card certificate after turning on the computer. The certificate unlocks the computer.

> ## Important
> Standard users can reset the BitLocker PIN and password on operating system drives, fixed data drives, and removable data drives. This is an important change for Windows 8 and Windows Serer 2012. If you don't want standard users to be able to perform these tasks, enable the Disallow Standard Users From Changing The PIN Or Password policy. This Computer Configuration policy is found under Windows Components\BitLocker Drive Encryption\Operating System Drives.

## BitLocker changes

BitLocker Drive Encryption has changed substantially since it was first implemented on Windows Vista and Windows Server 2008. With Windows 7 and later, as well as Windows Server 2008 R2 and later, you can

- Allow a data-recovery agent to be used with BitLocker Drive Encryption. This option is configured through Group Policy. The data-recovery agent allows an encrypted volume to be unlocked and recovered by using a recovery agent's personal certificate or a 48-digit recovery password. You can optionally save the recovery information in Active Directory. In the Administrative Templates policies for Computer Configuration, there are separate policies for operating-system volumes, other fixed drives, and removable drives.

- Deny write access to removable data drives not protected with BitLocker. This option is configured through Group Policy. If you enable this option, users have read-only access to unencrypted removable data drives and read/write access to encrypted removable data drives.

- Encrypt FAT volumes as well as NTFS and Resilient File System (ReFS) volumes. When you encrypt FAT volumes, you have the option of specifying whether encrypted volumes can be unlocked and viewed on computers running Windows Vista or later. This option is configured through Group Policy and is enabled when you turn on BitLocker. In the Administrative Templates policies for Computer Configuration under Windows Components\BitLocker Drive Encryption, there are separate policies for earlier versions of Windows that allow FAT-formatted fixed drives and FAT-formatted removable drives to be unlocked and viewed.

In a domain, domain administrators are the default data-recovery agents. A homegroup or workgroup has no default data-recovery agent, but you can designate one. Any user you want to designate as a data-recovery agent needs a personal encryption certificate. You can generate a certificate by using the Cipher utility and then using the certificate to assign the data-recovery agent in Local Security Policy under Public Key Policies\BitLocker Drive Encryption.

Although earlier implementations of BitLocker Drive Encryption supported Advanced Encryption Standard (AES) encryption with a diffuser, Windows 8 and Windows Server 2012 move away from this approach to support standard AES with 128-bit encryption by default. Additionally, if you enable the Choose Drive Encryption Method And Cipher Strength policy, you can set the AES cipher strength to 256-bit encryption. Keep in mind that the cipher strength must be set prior to turning on BitLocker Drive Encryption. Changing the cipher strength has no effect if a drive is already encrypted or encryption is in progress.

# Using hardware encryption, secure boot, and Network Unlock

BitLocker Drive Encryption has other enhancements for Windows 8 and Windows Server 2012 as well. You can manage most of these enhancements using the Administrative Templates policies for Computer Configuration under Windows Components\BitLocker Drive Encryption.

## Hardware encrypted drives

Windows 8 and Windows Server 2012 add support for disk drives with hardware encryption (referred to as *encrypted hard drives*). Encryption in hardware is faster and moves the processing burden from the computer's processor to the hardware processor on the hard disk. By default, if a computer has hardware encryption, Windows 8 will use it with BitLocker. To use encrypted hard drives with Windows Server 2012, you must add the Enhanced Storage feature.

When the operating system initializes an encrypted hard drive, it activates a security mode that allows the drive controller to generate a media key for every volume created on the encrypted hard drive. This media key set is used to encrypt every byte of data written to the drive and decrypt every byte of data read from the drive. The key set consists of the following:

- **A data-encryption key** This key is used to encrypt all data on the drive. The key is stored in an encrypted format in a random location on the drive.

- **An authentication key** This key is used to unlock data on the drive. A hash of the authentication key is stored on the drive and used to decrypt the data-encryption key.

An encrypted drive is locked and inaccessible when it is in a powered-off state. When the drive is powered on (as part of the computer startup), the drive remains locked until the authentication key is used to decrypt the data-encryption key. All data read from or written to the drive passes through the encryption engine. If the data-encryption key needs to be changed or erased, the drive doesn't need to be re-encrypted. Instead, the encryption engine creates a new authentication key and then re-encrypts the data-encryption key. Afterward, the data-encryption key can be unlocked with the new authentication key and data can be read from and written to the drive as before.

Before you enable hardware encryption there are some important caveats. With data drives, the drive must be in an uninitialized state and in a security-inactive state. With system drives, the drive must be in an uninitialized state and in a security-inactive state, and the computer must always boot natively from Unified Extensible Firmware Interface (UEFI). Further, neither data drives nor system drives can be attached to RAID controllers. Although future updates or service packs could change or remove these restrictions, these are the restrictions as of the time I wrote this.

> **Important**
> System drives must boot natively from UEFI 2.3.1 or later and have a defined EFI_STORAGE_SECURITY_COMMAND_PROTOCOL. System drives must also have the Compatibility Support Module (CSM) disabled in UEFI.

## Optimizing encryption

In Group Policy, you can precisely control whether to permit software-based encryption when hardware encryption is not available and whether to restrict encryption to those algorithms and cipher strengths supported by hardware. To do this, use Group Policy to enable hardware-based encryption for system drives, data drives, or both.

You can enable hardware-based encryption for data drives using the Configure Use Of Hardware-Based Encryption For Fixed Data Drives policy, shown in Figure 13-11. When the policy is enabled, you must specifically allow software-based encryption when hardware-based encryption isn't available. You also have the option of restricting the encryption algorithms used to a specific subset. Keep in mind that the encryption algorithm is set when a drive is partitioned and that the Choose Drive Encryption Method And Cipher Strength policy doesn't apply to hardware-based encryption.

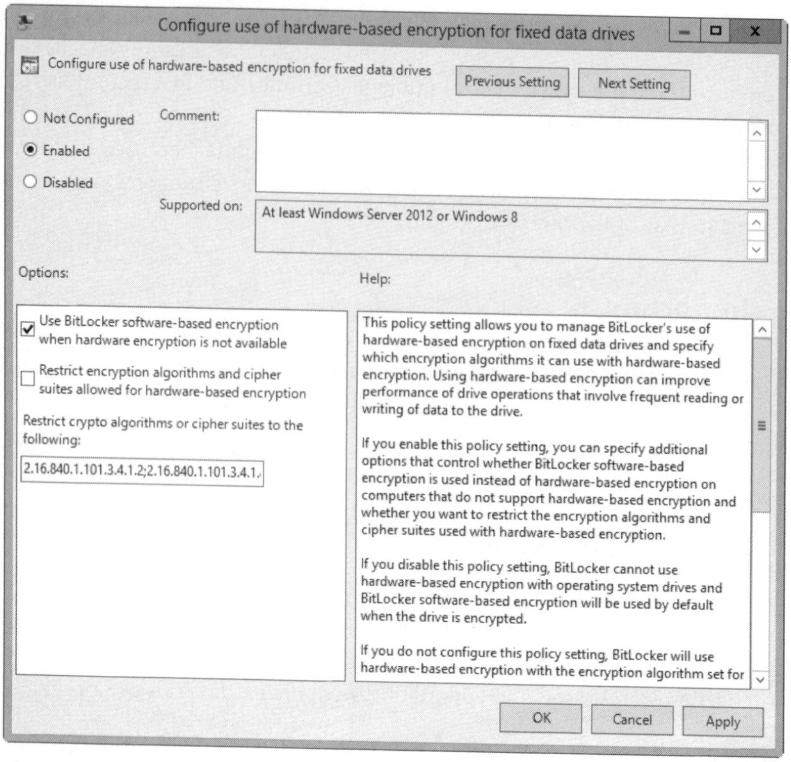

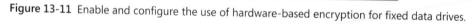

**Figure 13-11** Enable and configure the use of hardware-based encryption for fixed data drives.

You can enable hardware-based encryption for system drives using the Configure Use Of Hardware-Based Encryption For Operating System Drives policy, shown in Figure 13-12. As with data drives, when the policy is enabled, you must keep in mind the following:

- You must specifically allow software-based encryption when hardware-based encryption isn't available.

- You have the option of restricting the encryption algorithms used to a specific subset.

- You know the Choose Drive Encryption Method And Cipher Strength policy doesn't apply to hardware-based encryption.

Finally, as necessary, use the Configure Use Of Hardware-Based Encryption For Removable Data Drives policy to control whether software-based encryption is permitted when hardware encryption is not available and whether to restrict encryption to those algorithms and cipher strengths supported by hardware.

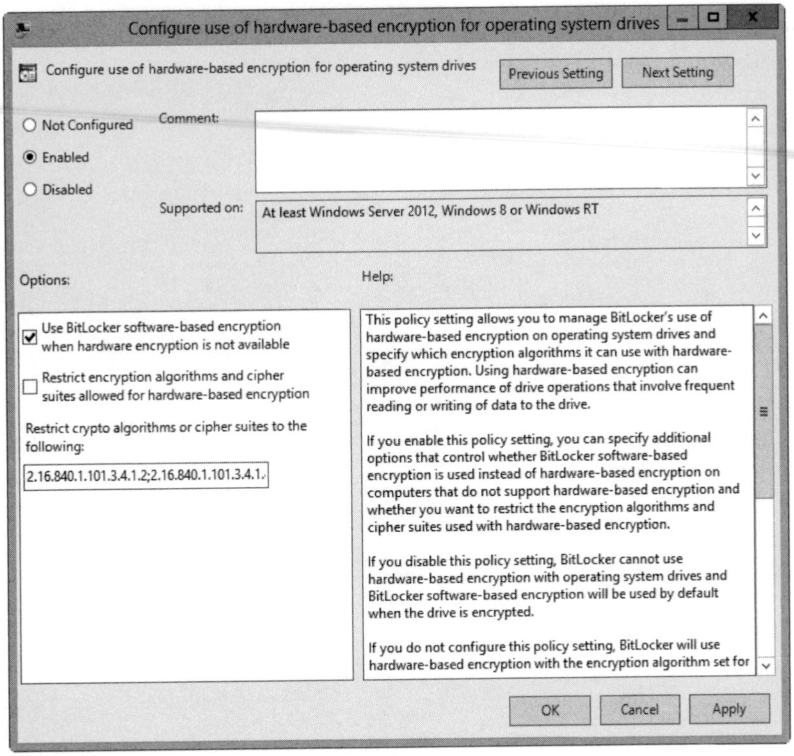

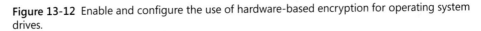

**Figure 13-12** Enable and configure the use of hardware-based encryption for operating system drives.

## Setting permitted encryption types

Windows Server allows users to encrypt full volumes or used space only. Encrypting full volumes takes longer, but it is more secure because the entire volume is protected. Encrypting used space protects only the portion of the drive used to store data. By default, either option can be used. To allow only one type or the other, you can enable and con-figure the related Enforce Drive Encryption Type policy for BitLocker. There are separate Enforce Drive Encryption Type policies for the operating system, fixed data, and remov-able data drives. Figure 13-13 shows the policy for operating system drives. Here, after you select Enabled to enable the policy, you set the encryption type to either Full Encryption or Used Space Only Encryption.

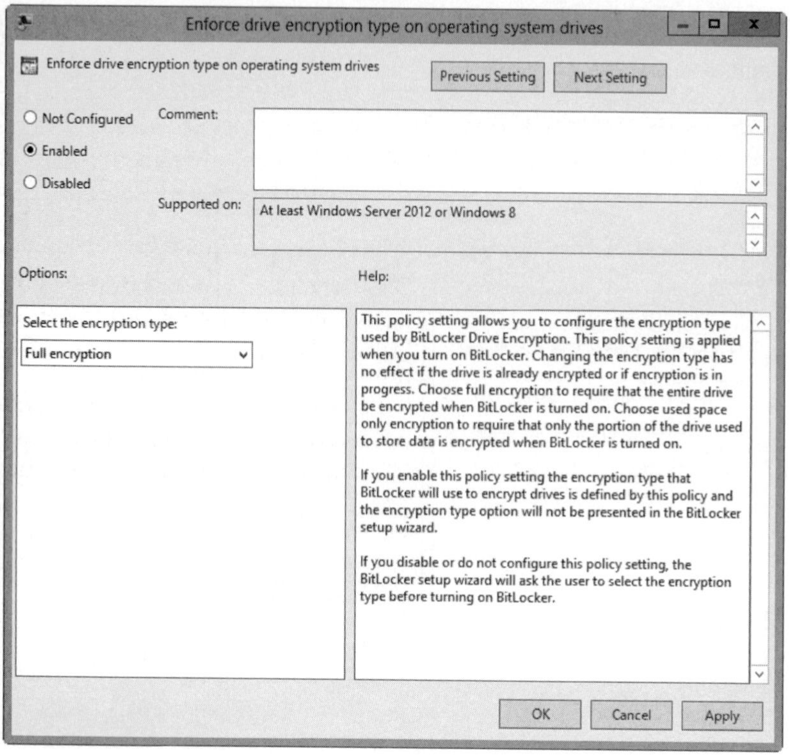

**Figure 13-13**  Restrict the encryption type, if desired.

> **Important**
>
> In high-security environments, you will want to encrypt entire volumes. At the time of this writing, and unless fixed with a future update or service pack, deleted files appear as free space when you encrypt used space only. As a result, until the files are wiped or overwritten, information in the files could be recovered with certain tools.

# Preparing BitLocker for startup authentication and secure boot

Windows allows you to pre-provision BitLocker so that you can turn on encryption prior to installation. Windows also can be configured to do the following:

- Require additional authentication at startup. If you enable and configure the related policy Require Additional Authentication At Startup, user input is required, even if the platform lacks a preboot input capability. To allow a USB keyboard to be used on such a platform in the preboot environment, you should set the Enable Use Of BitLocker Authentication Requiring Preboot Keyboard Input On Slates policy to Enabled.

- Allow secure boot for integrity validation. Secure boot is used by default to verify Boot Configuration Data (BCD) settings according to the TPM validation-profile settings (also referred to as Secure Boot policy). When you use secure boot, the settings of the Use Enhanced Boot Configuration Data Validation Profile policy are ignored (unless you specifically disable secure-boot support by setting Allow Secure Boot For Integrity Validation to Disabled).

You set TPM validation-profile settings by platform. For BIOS-based firmware, you use the Configure TPM Platform Validation Profile For BIOS-Based Firmware Configurations policy. For UEFI-based firmware, you use the Configure TPM Platform Validation Profile For Native UEFI Firmware Configurations policy. When you enable these policies, you specify exactly which platform configuration registers to validate during boot.

For BIOS-based firmware, Microsoft recommends validating Platform Configuration Registers (PCRs) 0, 2, 4, 8, 9, 10, and 11. For UEFI firmware, Microsoft recommends validating PCRs 0, 2, 4, 7, and 11. In both instances, PCR 11 validation is required for BitLocker protection to be enforced. PCR 7 validation is required to support secure boot with UEFI (and you need to enable this by selecting the related option). Figure 13-14 shows an example platform validation-profile configuration.

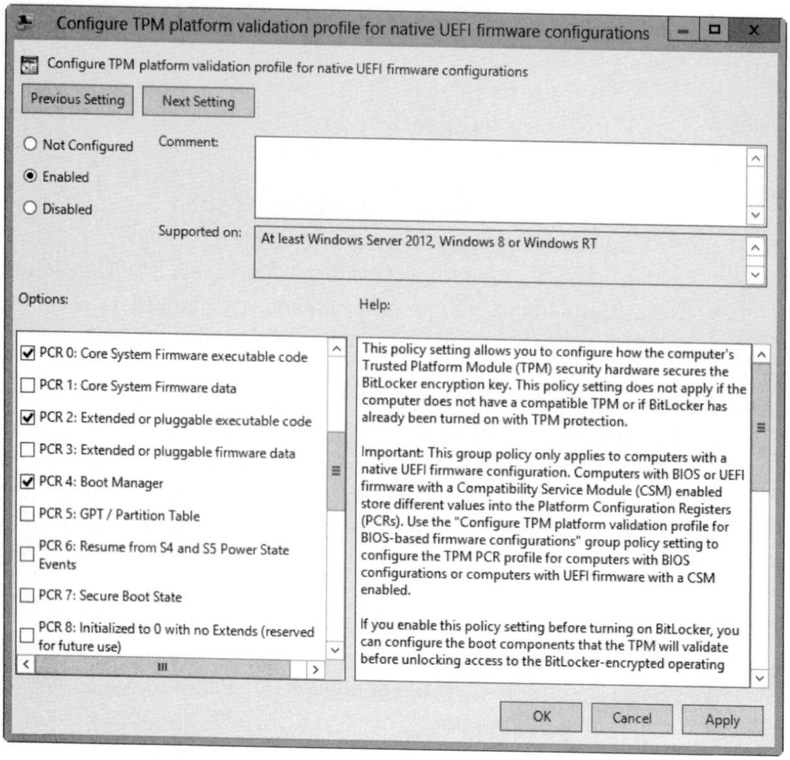

**Figure 13-14**  Specify the PCRs to validate.

## Using Network Unlock

When you protect a computer with BitLocker, you can require additional authentication at startup. Normally, this means a user is required to have a startup key on a USB flash drive, a startup PIN, or both. The Network Unlock feature provides this additional layer of protection without requiring the startup key, startup PIN, or both by automatically unlocking the operating system drive when a computer is started. It does this as long as the following conditions are met:

- The BitLocker-protected computer has an enabled TPM.

- The computer is on a trusted, wired network.

- The computer is joined to and connected to a domain.

- A Network Unlock server with an appropriate Network Unlock certificate is available.

Because the computer must be joined to and connected to the domain for Network Unlock to work, user authentication is still required when a computer is not connected to the domain. When connected to the domain, the client computer (whether it's a Windows desktop or a Windows server) connects to a Network Unlock server to unlock the system drive. You allow Network Unlock to be used by enabling the Allow Network Unlock At Startup policy, as shown in Figure 13-15.

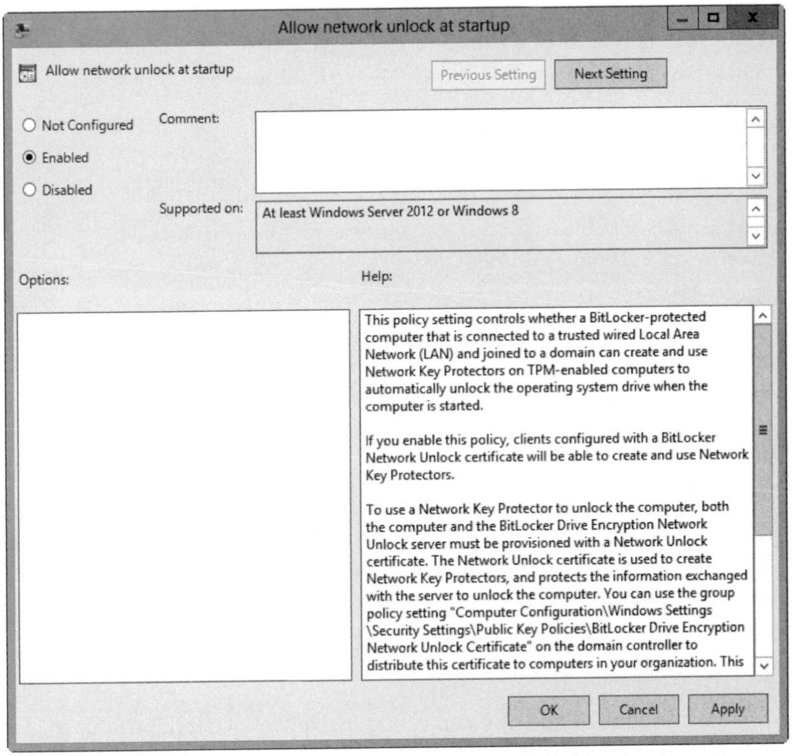

**Figure 13-15** Enable Network Unlock at startup, if desired.

Typically, the Network Unlock server is a domain controller configured to use and distribute Network Unlock certificates to clients. The Network Unlock certificates, in turn, are used to create the Network Unlock keys.

You can configure a domain controller to distribute this certificate to clients. To do this, create an X.509 certificate for the server—for example, by using Certmsg.mc and then using the BitLocker Driver Encryption Network Unlock Certificate setting to add this certificate to a GPO applied to the domain controller. You'll find this Computer Configuration setting under Windows Settings\Security Settings\Public Key Policies.

## Provisioning BitLocker prior to deployment

Windows allows you to provision BitLocker during operating system deployment. You can do this from the Windows Pre-Installation Environment (WinPE). It's important to point out that Windows PowerShell includes a Deployment Image Servicing and Management (DISM) module that you can import. Because this module doesn't support wildcards when searching for feature names, you can use the Get-WindowsOptionalFeatures cmdlet to list feature names, as shown in this example:

```
get-windowsoptionalfeature -online | ft
```

To completely install BitLocker and related management tools, use the following command:

```
enable-windowsoptionalfeature -online -featurename bitlocker,
bitlocker-utilities, bitlocker-networkunlock -all
```

# Deploying BitLocker Drive Encryption

Deploying BitLocker Drive Encryption in an enterprise changes the way both administrators and users work with computers. A computer with BitLocker Drive Encryption normally requires user intervention to boot to the operating system—a user must enter a PIN, insert a USB flash drive containing a startup key, or use a smart card with a valid certificate. Because of this, after you deploy BitLocker Drive Encryption, you can no longer be assured that you can perform remote administration that requires a computer to be restarted without having physical access to the computer—someone will need to be available to type in the required PIN, insert the USB flash drive with the startup key, or use a smart card with a valid certificate.

To work around this issue, you can configure Network Unlock on your trusted, wired networks. Before you use BitLocker Drive Encryption, you should perform a thorough evaluation of your organization's computers. You need to develop plans and procedures for the following:

- Evaluating the various BitLocker authentication methods and applying them as appropriate

- Determining whether computers support TPM, and thus whether you must use TPM or non-TPM BitLocker configurations

- Storing, using, and periodically changing encryption keys, recovery passwords, and other validators used with BitLocker

You also need to develop procedures for the following activities:

- Working with BitLocker-encrypted drives

- Supporting BitLocker-encrypted drives

- Recovering computers with BitLocker-encrypted drives

When developing these procedures, you need to take into account the way BitLocker encryption works and the requirements to have PINs, startup keys, and recovery keys available whenever you work with BitLocker-encrypted computers. After you evaluate your organization's computers and develop basic plans and procedures, you need to develop a configuration plan for implementing BitLocker Drive Encryption.

## TROUBLESHOOTING

**Several versions of BitLocker**
**Several implementations of BitLocker Drive Encryption are available: the original as released with Windows Vista, an update for Windows Server 2008 and Windows 7, and an update for Windows 8 and Windows Server 2012. Although computers running Windows 8 and Windows Server 2012 can work with any of the available versions, earlier versions of Windows can't necessarily work with the latest version of BitLocker. With this in mind, you might need to configure Group Policy to allow access from earlier versions of Windows.**

BitLocker Drive Encryption requires a specific disk configuration. To turn on BitLocker Drive Encryption on the drive containing the Windows operating system, the drive must have at least two partitions:

- The first partition is for BitLocker Drive Encryption. This partition, designated as the active partition, holds the files required to start the operating system and is not encrypted.

- The second is the primary partition for the operating system and your data. This partition is encrypted when you turn on BitLocker.

With implementations of BitLocker prior to Windows 7 and Windows Server 2008, you need to create the partitions in a certain way to ensure compatibility. This is no longer the case. When you install Windows 7 and later or Windows Server 2008 and later, an additional partition is created automatically during setup. By default, this additional partition is used by the Windows Recovery Environment (Windows RE). However, if you enable BitLocker on the system volume, Windows usually moves Windows RE to the system volume and then uses the additional partition for BitLocker.

Using BitLocker on a hard disk is easy. On a computer with a compatible TPM, you must create or make available a BitLocker Drive Encryption partition on your hard drive and then initialize the TPM as discussed previously under "Preparing and initializing a TPM for first use" earlier in this chapter. On a computer without a compatible TPM, you only need to create or make available a BitLocker Drive Encryption partition on your hard drive.

You can use local Group Policy and Active Directory–based Group Policy to help manage and maintain TPM and BitLocker configurations. Group Policy settings for TPM Services are found in Administrative Templates policies for Computer Configuration under System\Trusted Platform Module Services. Group Policy settings for BitLocker are found in Administrative Templates policies for Computer Configuration under Windows Components\BitLocker Drive Encryption. There are separate subfolders for fixed data drives, operating system drives, and removable data drives.

Policies you might want to configure include the following:

- Trusted Platform Module Services policies

    ○ Configure The Level Of TPM Owner Authorization Information Available To The Operating System

    ○ Configure The List Of Blocked TPM Commands

    ○ Ignore The Default List Of Blocked TPM Commands

    ○ Ignore The Local List Of Blocked TPM Commands

    ○ Standard User Individual Lockout Threshold

    ○ Standard User Lockout Duration

    ○ Standard User Total Lockout Threshold

    ○ Turn On TPM Backup To Active Directory Domain Services

- BitLocker Drive Encryption policies

    ○ Choose Default Folder For Recovery Password

    ○ Choose Drive Encryption Method And Cipher Strength

    ○ Prevent Memory Overwrite On Restart

    ○ Provide The Unique Identifiers For Your Organization

    ○ Validate Smart Card Certificate Usage Rule Compliance

- Fixed Drive policies

  - Allow Access To BitLocker-Protected Fixed Data Drives From Earlier Versions Of Windows

  - Choose How BitLocker-Protected Fixed Drives Can Be Recovered

  - Configure Use Of Hardware-Based Encryption For Fixed Data Drives

  - Configure Use Of Passwords For Fixed Data Drives

  - Configure Use Of Smart Cards On Fixed Data Drives

  - Deny Write Access To Fixed Drives Not Protected By BitLocker

  - Enforce Drive Encryption Type On Fixed Data Drives

- Operating System Drive policies

  - Allow Enhanced PINs For Startup

  - Allow Network Unlock At Startup

  - Allow Secure Boot For Integrity Validation

  - Choose How BitLocker-Protected Operating System Drives Can Be Recovered

  - Configure Minimum PIN Length For Startup

  - Configure TPM Platform Validation Profile For BIOS-Based Firmware Configurations

  - Configure TPM Platform Validation Profile For Native UEFI Firmware Configurations

  - Configure TPM Platform Validation Profile (Windows Vista, Windows 7, Windows Server 2008, Windows Server 2008 R2)

  - Configure Use Of Hardware-Based Encryption For Operating System Drives

  - Configure Use Of Passwords For Operating System Drives

  - Disallow Standard Users From Changing The PIN Or Password

  - Enable User Of BitLocker Authentication Requiring Preboot Keyboard Input On Slates

  - Enforce Drive Encryption Type On Operating System Drives

  - Require Additional Authentication At Startup

- ○ Reset Platform Validation Data After BitLocker Recovery

- ○ Use Enhanced Boot Configuration Data Validation Profile

- Removable Data Drive policies

  - ○ Allow Access To BitLocker-Protected Removable Data Drives From Earlier Versions Of Windows

  - ○ Choose How BitLocker-Protected Removable Drives Can Be Recovered

  - ○ Configure Use Of Hardware-Based Encryption For Removable Data Drives

  - ○ Configure Use Of Passwords For Removable Data Drives

  - ○ Configure Use Of Smart Cards On Removable Data Drives

  - ○ Control Use Of BitLocker On Removable Drives

  - ○ Deny Write Access To Removable Drives Not Protected By BitLocker

  - ○ Enforce Drive Encryption Type On Removable Data Drives

Active Directory includes TPM and BitLocker recovery extensions for *Computer* objects. For TPM, the extensions define a single property of the *Computer* object, called *ms-TPM-OwnerInformation*. When the TPM is initialized or when the owner password is changed, the hash of the TPM ownership password can be stored as a value of the *ms-TPM-OwnerInformation* attribute on the related *Computer* object. For BitLocker, these extensions define *Recovery* objects as child objects of *Computer* objects and are used to store recovery passwords and associate them with specific BitLocker-encrypted volumes.

By default, Windows stores the full TPM owner authorization, the TPM administrative delegation blob, and the TPM user delegation in the registry. Because of this change, you no longer have to save this information separately to Active Directory for backup and recovery purposes. For more information, see the "Managing TPM owner authorization information" section earlier in this chapter.

Generally, you want to ensure that BitLocker recovery information is always available if it's needed. You can configure Group Policy to save recovery information in Active Directory using the following techniques:

- With Choose How BitLocker-Protected Fixed Drives Can Be Recovered, enable the policy, accept the default options to allow data-recovery agents, and then save the recovery information in Active Directory.

- With Choose How BitLocker-Protected Operating System Drives Can Be Recovered, enable the policy, accept the default options to allow data-recovery agents, and then save the recovery information in Active Directory.

- With Choose How BitLocker-Protected Removable Drives Can Be Recovered, enable the policy, accept the default options to allow data-recovery agents, and then save the recovery information in Active Directory.

## INSIDE OUT    Ensuring FIPS compliance

For Federal Information Processing Standard (FIPS) compliance, you cannot create or save a BitLocker recovery password. Instead, you need to configure Windows to create recovery keys. The FIPS setting is located in the Security Policy Editor at Local Policies\ Security Options\System Cryptography.

Use FIPS-compliant algorithms for encryption, hashing, and signing. To do this, enable the security option System Cryptography: Use FIPS Compliant Algorithms For Encryption, Hashing, And Signing in Local Group Policy or Active Directory Group Policy as appropriate. With this setting enabled, users can save only a recovery key to a USB flash drive. Users will not be able to save a recovery password to Active Directory Domain Services (AD DS), local folders, or network folders, and they also will not be able to use the BitLocker Drive Encryption Wizard or other methods to create a recovery password. Because recovery passwords cannot be saved to AD DS when FIPS is enabled, Windows will display an error if AD DS backup is required by Group Policy.

# Setting up and managing BitLocker Drive Encryption

You can configure and enable BitLocker Drive Encryption on both system volumes and data volumes. When you encrypt system volumes, you must unlock the computer at startup, typically by using a TPM and Network Unlock when connected to the domain as well as a TPM, a startup key, a startup PIN, or any required or optional combination of these. To enforce the strictest and highest security possible, use all three authentication methods.

In the current implementation of BitLocker, you do not have to encrypt a computer's system volume prior to encrypting a computer's data volumes. When you use encrypted data volumes, the operating system mounts BitLocker data volumes as it would any other volume, but it requires either a password or a smart card with a valid certificate to unlock the drive.

The encryption key for a protected data volume is created and stored independently from the system volume and all other protected data volumes. To allow the operating system to mount encrypted volumes, the key chain protecting the data volume is stored in an encrypted state on the operating-system volume. If the operating system enters Recovery mode, the data volumes are not unlocked until the operating system is out of Recovery mode.

Setting up BitLocker Drive Encryption is a multistep process that involves the following:

1. Partitioning a computer's hard disks appropriately, and installing the operating system (if you are configuring a new computer). Windows Setup partitions the drives for you automatically. However, the volume where BitLocker data is stored must always be the active, system volume.

2. Initializing and configuring a computer's TPM (if applicable).

3. Turning on the BitLocker Drive Encryption feature (as necessary).

4. Checking firmware to ensure that the computer is set to start first from the disk containing the active, system partition and the boot partition, not from USB or CD/DVD drives (which is applicable only when you encrypt system volumes).

5. Turning on and configuring BitLocker Drive Encryption.

After you turn on and configure BitLocker encryption, you can use several techniques to maintain the environment and perform recovery. When you are using a Microsoft account on a non-domain-joined computer, you have an additional save option. You can save the recovery key to the Windows Live SkyDrive. The user's SkyDrive account will then contain a BitLocker folder with a separate file for each saved recovery key.

## Configuring and enabling BitLocker Drive Encryption

As discussed previously, BitLocker Drive Encryption can be used in a TPM or non-TPM configuration. Both configurations require some preliminary work before you can turn on and configure BitLocker Drive Encryption.

With Windows Vista, Windows 7, and Windows 8 editions designed for business, BitLocker Drive Encryption and BitLocker Network Unlock should be installed by default.

With Windows Server 2008 and later, you can install BitLocker Drive Encryption, BitLocker Network Unlock, or both as features using the Add Roles And Features Wizard. Alternatively, on a server, you can install BitLocker Drive Encryption by entering the following command at an elevated PowerShell prompt:

```
add-windowsfeature -name bitlocker, bitlocker-networkunlock -includemanagementtools
```

With either approach, you need to restart the computer to complete the installation process.

After you install BitLocker, you can determine the readiness status of a computer by accessing the BitLocker Drive Encryption console. In Control Panel, tap or click System And Security, and then tap or click BitLocker Drive Encryption. If the system isn't properly configured yet, you'll see an error message either when you open BitLocker Drive Encryption or when you try to encrypt a drive.

If you see this message on a computer with a compatible TPM, refer to "Understanding TPM states and tools" earlier in this chapter to learn more about TPM states and enabling TPM in firmware. If you see this message on a computer with an incompatible TPM or no TPM, you need to change the computer's Group Policy settings so that you can turn on BitLocker Drive Encryption without a TPM.

You can configure policy settings for BitLocker encryption in Local Group Policy or in Active Directory Group Policy. For local policy, you apply the desired settings to the computer's Local Group Policy Object. For domain policy, you apply the desired settings to a Group Policy Object processed by the computer. While you are working with domain policy, you can also specify requirements for computers with a TPM.

To configure the way BitLocker can be used with or without a TPM, follow these steps:

1. Open the appropriate Group Policy Object for editing in the Group Policy Management Editor.

2. Double-tap or double-click the setting Require Additional Authentication At Startup in the Administrative Templates for Computer Configuration under Windows Components\BitLocker Drive Encryption folder\Operating System Drives.

3. In the Require Additional Authentication At Startup dialog box, shown in Figure 13-16, define the policy setting by selecting Enabled. Note that there are several versions of this policy and they are operating-system specific. Configure the version or versions of this policy that are appropriate for your working environment and the computers to which the policy will be applied. The options for each related policy are slightly different because the TPM features supported are slightly different for each operating system.

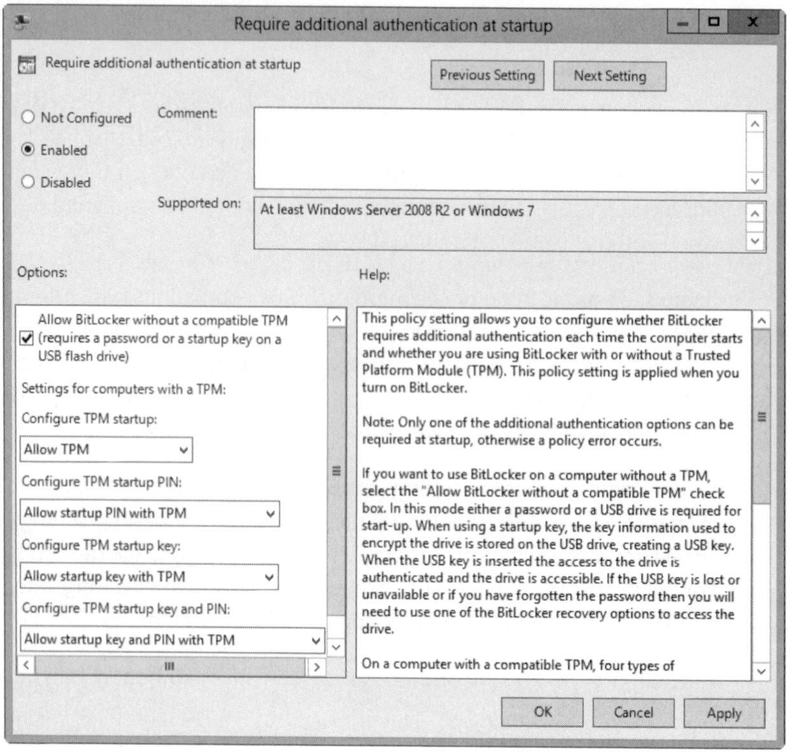

**Figure 13-16** Choose the advanced startup options.

4. Do one of the following:

   ○ If you want to allow BitLocker to be used without a compatible TPM, select the Allow BitLocker Without A Compatible TPM check box. This changes the policy setting so that you can use BitLocker encryption with a startup key on a computer without a TPM.

   ○ If you want to require BitLocker to be used with a TPM, clear the Allow BitLocker Without A Compatible TPM check box. This changes the policy setting so that you can use BitLocker encryption on a computer with a TPM by using a startup PIN, a startup key, or both.

5. For computers with compatible TPMs, several authentication methods can be used at startup to provide added protection for encrypted data. These authentication methods can be not allowed, allowed, or required. The methods available depend on the specific operating-system version of the policy you are working with.

6. Tap or click OK to save your settings. This policy is enforced the next time Group Policy is applied.

7. Close the Group Policy Object Editor. To force Group Policy to apply immediately to this computer, tap or click Start, type **gpupdate.exe /force** in the Search box, and then press Enter.

Computers that have a startup key or a startup PIN also have a recovery password or certificate. The recovery password or certificate is required in the following circumstances:

- Changes are made to the system startup information.

- The encrypted drive must be moved to another computer.

- The user is unable to provide the appropriate startup key or PIN.

The recovery password or certificate should be managed and stored separately from the startup key or startup PIN. Although users are given the startup key or startup PIN, administrators should be the only ones with the recovery password or certificate. As the administrator, you will need the recovery password or certificate to unlock the encrypted data on the volume if BitLocker enters a locked state. Generally, unless you use a common data-recovery agent, the recovery password or certificate is unique to this particular BitLocker encryption. You cannot use it to recover encrypted data from any other BitLocker-encrypted volume—even from other BitLocker-encrypted volumes on the same computer. To increase security, you should store startup keys and recovery data apart from the computer.

When you install BitLocker Drive Encryption and configure policy (if necessary), the BitLocker Drive Encryption console becomes available in Control Panel. When you are configuring BitLocker encryption, the configuration options you have depend on whether the computer has a TPM, as well as how you configured Group Policy.

## Determining whether a computer has BitLocker-encrypted volumes

You can determine whether a computer has BitLocker-encrypted volumes using Disk Management. In Disk Management, any such encrypted volume is listed as BitLocker Encrypted, as shown in Figure 13-17.

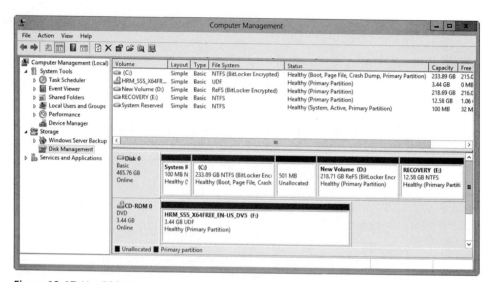

**Figure 13-17** Use Disk Management to check for BitLocker-encrypted volumes.

## Enabling BitLocker on fixed data drives

Encrypting a fixed data drive protects the data stored on the drive. Any drive formatted with FAT, FAT32, exFAT, NTFS, or ReFS can be encrypted with BitLocker. The length of time it takes to encrypt a drive depends on the amount of data to encrypt, the processing power of the computer, and the level of activity on the computer.

Before you enable BitLocker, you should configure the appropriate Fixed Data Drive policies and settings in Group Policy and then either wait for Group Policy to be refreshed or refresh Group Policy manually. If you don't do this and you enable BitLocker, you might need to turn BitLocker off and then turn BitLocker back on because certain state and management flags are set when you turn on BitLocker.

If you dual-boot a computer or move drives between computers, you can use the Allow Access To BitLocker-Protected Fixed Data Drives From Earlier Versions Of Windows setting in Group Policy to ensure that you have access to the volume on other operating systems and computers. Unlocked drives are read-only. To ensure that you can recover an encrypted volume, you should allow data-recovery agents and store recovery information in Active Directory.

You can enable BitLocker encryption on a fixed data drive by following these steps:

1. Open the BitLocker Drive Encryption console. In Control Panel, tap or click System And Security, and then tap or click BitLocker Drive Encryption.

2.  In the BitLocker Drive Encryption console, available drives are listed by category. Under the Fixed Data Drives heading, tap or click Turn On BitLocker for the fixed data drive you want to encrypt. BitLocker verifies that your computer meets its requirements and then initializes the drive. If BitLocker is already enabled on the drive, you have management options instead.

3.  On the Choose How You Want To Unlock This Drive page, shown in Figure 13-18, choose one or more of the following options and then tap or click Next:

    ○  **Use A Password To Unlock The Drive**   Select this option if you want the user to be prompted for a password to unlock the drive. Passwords allow a drive to be unlocked in any location and to be shared with other people.

    ○  **Use My Smart Card To Unlock The Drive**   Select this option if you want the user to use a smart card and enter the smart card PIN to unlock the drive. Because this feature requires a smart card reader, it is normally used to unlock a drive in the workplace and not for drives that might be used outside the workplace.

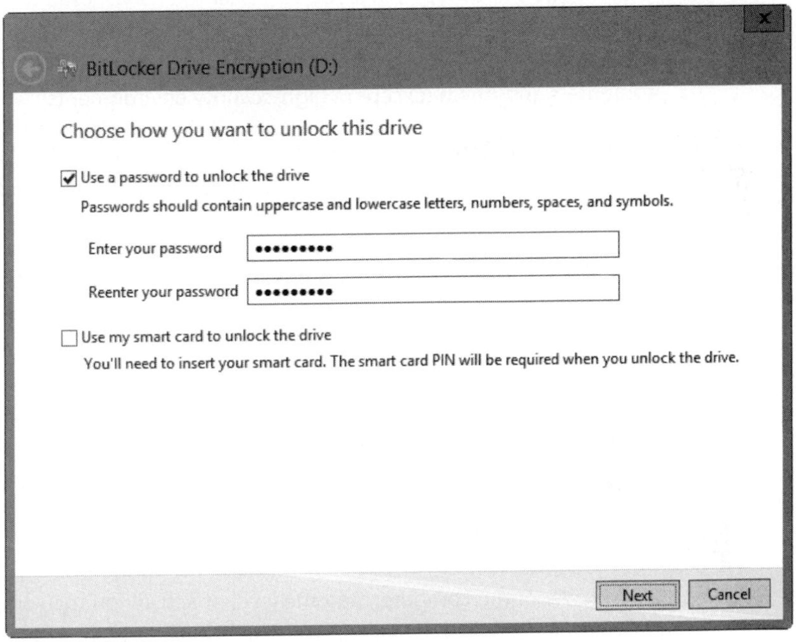

**Figure 13-18** Choose an option for unlocking a drive.

> **Important**
>
> When you tap or click Next, the wizard generates a recovery key. You can use the key to unlock the drive if BitLocker detects a condition that prevents it from unlocking the drive during boot. Note that you should save the key on removable media or on a network share. You can't store the key on the encrypted volume or the root directory of a fixed drive.

4. On the How Do You Want To Back Up Your Recovery Key? page, choose a save location for the recovery key—preferably, a USB flash drive or other removable media.

5. You can now optionally save the recovery key to another folder, print the recovery key, or both. For each option, tap or click the option and then follow the wizard's steps to set the location for saving or printing the recovery key. When you finish, tap or click Next.

6. If it is allowed in Group Policy, you can elect to encrypt used disk space only or the entire drive and then tap or click Next. Encrypting the used disk space only is faster than encrypting an entire volume. It is also the recommended option for newer computers and drives (except in high-security environments).

7. On the Are You Ready To Encrypt This Drive? page, tap or click Start Encrypting. How long the encryption process takes depends on the amount of data being encrypted and other factors.

8. Because the encryption process can be paused and resumed, you can shut down the computer before the drive is completely encrypted and the encryption of the drive will resume when you restart the computer. The encryption state is maintained in the event of a power loss as well.

## Enabling BitLocker on removable data drives

Encrypting removable data drives protects the data stored on the volume. Any removable data drive formatted with FAT, FAT32, exFAT, NTFS, or ReFS can be encrypted with BitLocker. The length of time it takes to encrypt a drive depends on the size of the drive, the processing power of the computer, and the level of activity on the computer.

Before you enable BitLocker, you should configure the appropriate Removable Data Drives policies and settings in Group Policy and then wait for Group Policy to be refreshed. If you don't do this and you enable BitLocker, you might need to turn BitLocker off and then turn BitLocker back on because certain state and management flags are set when you turn on BitLocker.

To be sure that you can recover an encrypted volume, you should allow data-recovery agents and store recovery information in Active Directory. If you use a flash drive with earlier versions of Windows, you can use the Allow Access To BitLocker-Protected Removable Data Drives From Earlier Versions Of Windows policy to ensure that you have access to the removable data drive on other operating systems and computers. Unlocked drives are read-only.

You can enable BitLocker encryption on a removable data drive by following these steps:

1. After you connect the removable data drive, open the BitLocker Drive Encryption console. In Control Panel, tap or click System And Security, and then tap or click BitLocker Drive Encryption.

2. In the BitLocker Drive Encryption console, available drives are listed by category. Under the Removable Data Drives heading, tap or click Turn On BitLocker for the removable data drive you want to encrypt. BitLocker verifies that your computer meets its requirements and then initializes the drive. If BitLocker is already enabled on the drive, you have management options instead.

3. On the Choose How You Want To Unlock This Drive page, choose one or more of the following options and then tap or click Next:

   ○ **Use A Password To Unlock This Drive**   Select this option if you want the user to be prompted for a password to unlock the drive. Passwords allow a drive to be unlocked in any location and to be shared with other people.

   ○ **Use My Smart Card To Unlock The Drive**   Select this option if you want the user to use a smart card and enter the smart card PIN to unlock the drive. Because this feature requires a smart card reader, it is normally used to unlock a drive in the workplace and not for drives that might be used outside the workplace.

4. On the How Do You Want To Back Up Your Recovery Key? page, tap or click Save The Recovery Key To A File.

5. In the Save BitLocker Recovery Key As dialog box, choose a save location and then tap or click Save.

6. You can now print the recovery key if you want to. When you finish, tap or click Next.

7. If it is allowed in Group Policy, you can elect to encrypt used disk space only or the entire drive and then tap or click Next. Encrypting the used disk space only is faster

Chapter 13

than encrypting an entire volume. It is also the recommended option for newer computers and drives (except in high-security environments).

8. On the Are You Ready To Encrypt This Drive? page, tap or click Start Encrypting. Be sure to pause encryption before removing the drive and then resume the process to complete the encryption. Do not otherwise remove the USB flash drive until the encryption process is complete. How long the encryption process takes depends on the amount of data to encrypt and other factors.

The encryption process does the following:

1. It adds an Autorun.inf file, the BitLocker To Go reader, and a Read Me.txt file to the removable data drive.

2. It creates a virtual volume with the encrypted contents of the drive.

3. It encrypts the virtual volume to protect it. Removable data drive encryption takes approximately 6 to 10 minutes per gigabyte to complete. The encryption process can be paused and resumed, as long as you don't remove the drive.

   When you connect an encrypted drive, Windows displays a notification on the secure desktop, as shown in Figure 13-19. If the notification disappears before you can tap or click it, simply remove and then reinsert the encrypted drive.

**Figure 13-19** Tap or click the notification.

4. Tap or click the notification to display the BitLocker dialog box. This dialog box also is displayed on the secure desktop.

5. When you are prompted, enter the password. Optionally, tap or click More Options to expand the dialog box so that you select Automatically Unlock On This Computer to save the password in an encrypted file on the computer's system volume. Finally, tap or click Unlock to unlock the drive so that you can use it.

6. If you forget or lose the password for the drive but have the recovery key, tap or click More Options and then tap or click Enter Recovery Key. Enter the 48-digit recovery key and then tap or click Unlock. This key is stored in the XML-formatted recovery key file as plain text.

## Enabling BitLocker on operating-system volumes

Before you can encrypt a system volume, you must remove all bootable media from a computer's CD/DVD drives, as well as all USB flash drives. You can then enable BitLocker encryption on the system volume by completing the following steps:

1. Open the BitLocker Drive Encryption console. In Control Panel, tap or click System And Security, and then tap or click BitLocker Drive Encryption.

2. In the BitLocker Drive Encryption console, available drives are listed by category. Under the Operating System Drives heading, tap or click Turn On BitLocker for the operating-system drive you want to encrypt. BitLocker verifies that your computer meets its requirements and then initializes the drive. If BitLocker is already enabled on the drive, you have management options instead.

> ### Note
>
> As part of the setup, Windows prepares the required BitLocker partition, if necessary. If Windows RE is in this partition, Windows moves Windows RE to the system volume and then uses this additional partition for BitLocker.
>
> Note also that if the computer doesn't have a TPM, the Allow BitLocker Without A Compatible TPM option must be enabled for operating-system volumes in the Require Additional Authentication At Startup policy.

3. As Figure 13-20 shows, you can now configure BitLocker startup preferences. Continue as discussed in the separate procedures that follow. If the computer doesn't have a TPM, your options will be different. You'll be able to create a password to unlock the drive, or you can insert a USB flash drive and store the startup key on the flash drive.

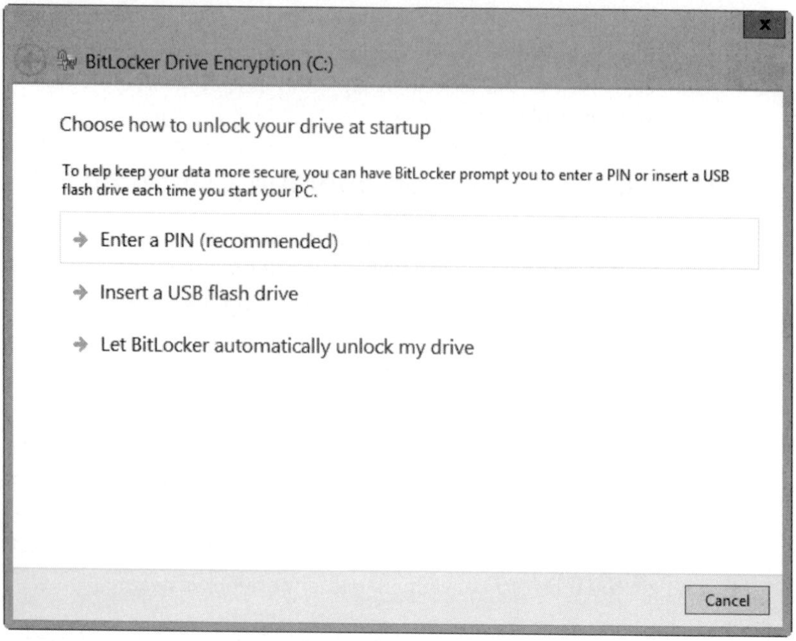

**Figure 13-20** Configure BitLocker startup preferences.

When a computer has a TPM, you can use BitLocker to provide basic integrity checks of the volume without requiring any additional keys. In this configuration, BitLocker protects the system volume by encrypting it. This configuration does the following:

- Grants access to the volume to users who can log on to the operating system

- Prevents those who have physical access to the computer from booting to an alternative operating system to gain access to the data on the volume

- Allows the computer to be used with or without a TPM for additional boot security

- Does not require a password or a smart card with a PIN

To use BitLocker without any additional keys, follow these steps:

1. On the Choose How To Unlock Your Drive At Startup page, tap or click Let BitLocker Automatically Unlock My Drive.

2. On the How Do You Want To Back Up Your Recovery Key page, tap or click Save To A File.

3.  In the Save BitLocker Recovery Key As dialog box, choose the location of your USB flash drive or an appropriate network share and then tap or click Save. Do not use a USB flash drive that is BitLocker-encrypted.

4.  You can now optionally save the recovery key to another location, print the recovery key, or both. Tap or click an option, and then follow the wizard steps to set the location for saving or printing the recovery key. When you finish, tap or click Next.

5.  If it is allowed in Group Policy, you can elect to encrypt used disk space only or the entire drive and then tap or click Next. Encrypting the used disk space only is faster than encrypting an entire volume. It is also the recommended option for newer computers and drives (except in high-security environments).

6.  On the Encrypt The Drive page, tap or click Start Encrypting. How long the encryption process takes depends on the amount of data to encrypt and other factors.

To enhance security, you can require additional authentication at startup. This configuration does the following:

●  Grants access to the volume only to users who can provide a valid key

●  Prevents those who have physical access to the computer from booting to an alternative operating system to gain access to the data on the volume

●  Allows the computer to be used with or without a TPM for additional boot security

●  Requires a password or a smart card with a PIN

●  Optionally, uses Network Unlock to unlock the volume when the computer is joined to and connected to the domain.

A startup key is different from a recovery key. If you create a startup key, this key is required to start the computer. The recovery key is required to unlock the computer if BitLocker enters Recovery mode, which might happen if BitLocker suspects the computer has been tampered with while the computer was offline.

You can enable BitLocker encryption for use with a startup key by following these steps:

1.  Insert a USB flash drive in the computer (if one is not already there). Do not use a USB flash drive that is BitLocker-encrypted.

2.  On the Choose How To Unlock Your Drive At Startup page, tap or click the Insert A USB Flash Drive option.

3. On the Back Up Your Startup Key page, tap or click the USB flash drive and then tap or click Save. Next, you need to save the recovery key. Because you should not store the recovery key and the startup key on the same medium, remove the USB flash drive and insert a second USB flash drive.

4. On the How Do You Want To Back Up Your Recovery Key page, tap or click Save To A File. In the Save BitLocker Recovery Key As dialog box, choose the location of your USB flash drive and then tap or click Save. Do not remove the USB drive with the recovery key.

5. You can now optionally save the recovery key to a network folder, print the recovery key, or both. Tap or click an option, and then follow the wizard's steps to set the location for saving or printing the recovery key. When you finish, tap or click Next.

6. If it is allowed in Group Policy, you can elect to encrypt used disk space only or the entire drive and then tap or click Next. Encrypting the used disk space only is faster than encrypting an entire volume. It is also the recommended option for newer computers and drives (except in high-security environments).

7. On the Encrypt The Volume page, confirm that Run BitLocker System Check is selected and then tap or click Continue. Confirm that you want to restart the computer by tapping or clicking Restart Now.

The computer restarts, and BitLocker ensures that the computer is BitLocker-compatible and ready for encryption. If the computer is not ready for encryption, you will see an error and need to resolve the error status before you can complete this procedure. If the computer is ready for encryption, the Encryption In Progress status bar is displayed. You can monitor the status of the disk-volume encryption by pointing to the BitLocker Drive Encryption icon in the notification area. By double-tapping or double-clicking this icon, you can open the Encrypting dialog box and monitor the encryption process more closely. You also have the option to pause the encryption process. Volume encryption takes approximately one minute per gigabyte to complete.

By completing this procedure, you have encrypted the operating-system volume and created a recovery key unique to that volume. The next time you turn on your computer, either the USB flash drive with the startup key must be plugged into a USB port on the computer or the computer must be connected to the domain network and using Network Unlock. If the USB flash drive is required for startup and you do not have the USB flash drive containing your startup key, you need to use Recovery mode and supply the recovery key to gain access to the data.

You can enable BitLocker encryption for use with a startup PIN by following these steps:

1.  On the Choose How To Unlock Your Drive At Startup page, select the Enter A PIN option.

2.  On the Enter A PIN page, type and confirm the PIN. The PIN can be any number you choose and must be 4 to 20 digits in length. The PIN is stored on the computer.

3.  Insert a USB flash drive on which you want to save the recovery key, and then tap or click Set PIN. Do not use a USB flash drive that is BitLocker-encrypted.

    Continue with Steps 4 through 9 in the previous procedure.

When the encryption process is complete, you have encrypted the entire volume and created a recovery key unique to this volume. If you created a PIN or a startup key, you are required to use the PIN or startup key to start the computer (or the computer must be connected to the domain network and using Network Unlock). Otherwise, you will see no change to the computer unless the TPM changes, the TPM cannot be accessed, or someone tries to modify the disk while the operating system is offline. In these cases, the computer enters Recovery mode, and you need to enter the recovery key to unlock the computer.

## Managing and troubleshooting BitLocker

You can determine whether a system volume, data volume, or inserted removable drive uses BitLocker by tapping or clicking System And Security in Control Panel and then double-tapping or double-clicking BitLocker Drive Encryption. You'll see the status of BitLocker on each volume, as shown in Figure 13-21.

The BitLocker Drive Encryption service must be started for BitLocker to work properly. Normally, this service is configured for manual startup and runs under the LocalSystem account.

To use smart cards with BitLocker, the Smart Card service must be started. Normally, this service is configured for manual startup and runs under the LocalService account.

After you create a startup key or PIN and a recovery key for a computer, you can create duplicates of the startup key, startup PIN, or recovery key as necessary for backup or replacement purposes using the options on the BitLocker Drive Encryption page in Control Panel.

With fixed-data and operating-system drives, another way to access this page is to press and hold or right-click the volume in File Explorer and then tap or click Manage BitLocker. If BitLocker is turned off, the Turn On BitLocker option is displayed instead.

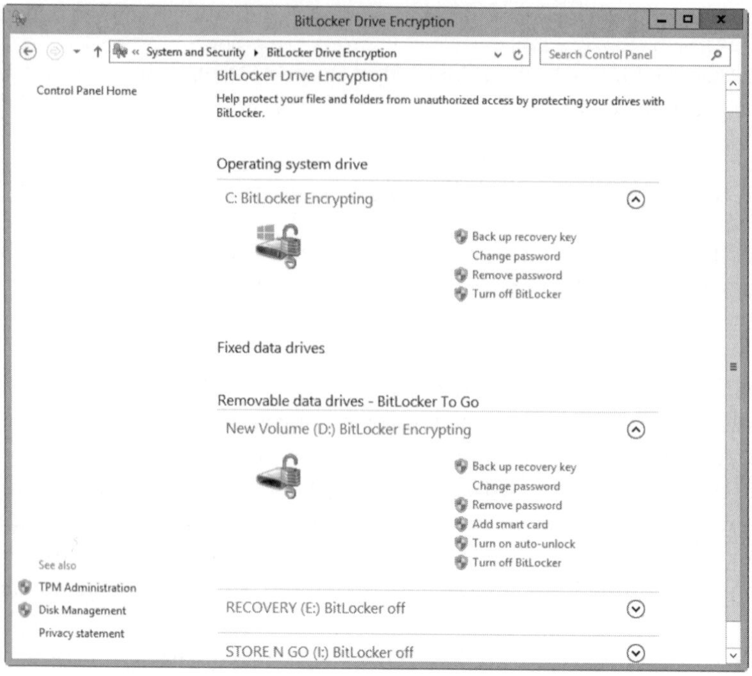

**Figure 13-21** Review the current status of BitLocker for each volume.

The management options provided depend on the type of volume you are working with and the encryption settings you choose. The available options include the following:

- **Back Up Recovery Key** Allows you to save or print the recovery key. Tap or click this option, and then follow the prompts.

- **Change Password** Allows you to change the encryption password. Tap or click this option, enter the old password, and then type and confirm the new password. Tap or click Change Password.

- **Remove Password** Tap or click this option to remove the encryption password requirement for unlocking the drive. You can do this only if another unlocking method is configured first.

- **Add Smart Card** Allows you to add a smart card for unlocking the drive. Tap or click this option, and then follow the prompts.

- **Remove Smart Card** Tap or click this option to remove the smart card requirement for unlocking the drive.

● **Change Smart Card**    Allows you to change the smart card used to unlock the drive. Tap or click this option, and then follow the prompts.

● **Turn On Auto-Unlock**    Tap or click this option to turn on automatic unlocking of the drive.

● **Turn Off Auto-Unlock**    Tap or click this option to turn off automatic unlocking of the drive.

● **Turn Off BitLocker**    Tap or click this option to turn off BitLocker and decrypt the drive.

# INSIDE OUT    Managing BitLocker in large enterprises

Large enterprises might want to use Microsoft BitLocker Administration and Monitoring (MBAM) to simplify BitLocker provisioning and deployment, as well as to improve compliance and reporting on BitLocker. MBAM is included in the Microsoft Desktop Optimization Pack (MDOP), and version 2.0 is recommended for Windows 8 and Windows Server 2012 deployments. MBAM has client components and a multi-tiered server architecture. The MBAM client must be installed on clients throughout the enterprise. The server architecture uses web portals, web services, SQL databases, and SQL Server Reporting Services.

MBAM 2.0 supports a standalone deployment model and a System Center–integrated model. The key difference between the models is how compliance data and reports are collected and stored. The System Center–integrated model moves compliance data and reporting to System Center Configuration Manager, rather than a standalone website.

Once deployed, the administration and monitoring server hosts the HelpDesk Portal and the Self Service Portal. Administrators can use the HelpDesk Portal to view reports, audit activities, and access recovery data. End users can log on to the self-service portal to look up their own recovery keys without requiring help desk support.

## Recovering data protected by BitLocker Drive Encryption

If you configure BitLocker Drive Encryption and the computer enters Recovery mode, you need to unlock the computer. To unlock the computer using a recovery key stored on a USB flash drive, follow these steps:

1. Turn on the computer. If the computer is locked, the computer opens the BitLocker Drive Encryption Recovery console.

2.  When you are prompted, insert the USB flash drive that contains the recovery key, and then press Enter.

3.  The computer will unlock and reboot automatically. You do not need to enter the recovery key manually.

If you saved the recovery key file in a folder on another computer or on removable media, you can use another computer to open and validate the recovery key file. To locate the correct file, find Password ID on the recovery console displayed on the locked computer and write down this number. The file containing the recovery key uses this Password ID as the file name. Open the file and locate the recovery key.

To unlock the computer by typing the recovery key, follow these steps:

1.  Turn on the computer. If the computer is locked, the computer opens the BitLocker Drive Encryption Recovery console.

2.  Type the recovery key, and then press Enter. The computer will unlock and reboot automatically.

A computer can become locked if a user tries to enter the recovery key but is repeatedly unsuccessful. In the recovery console, you can press Esc twice to exit the recovery prompt and turn off the computer. A computer might also become locked if an error related to TPM occurs or boot data is modified. In this case, the computer halts very early in the boot process, before the operating system starts. At this point, the locked computer might not be able to accept standard keyboard numbers. If that is the case, you must use the function keys to enter the recovery password. Here, the function keys F1–F9 represent the digits 1 through 9, and the F10 function key represents 0.

## Disabling or turning off BitLocker Drive Encryption

When you need to make changes to TPM or make other changes to the system, you might first need to temporarily turn off BitLocker encryption on the system volume. You cannot temporarily turn off BitLocker encryption on data volumes; you can only decrypt data volumes.

To temporarily turn off BitLocker encryption on the system volume, follow these steps:

1.  In Control Panel, tap or click System And Security, and then double-tap or double-click BitLocker Drive Encryption.

2.  For the system volume, tap or click Turn Off BitLocker Drive Encryption.

3. In the What Level Of Decryption Do You Want? dialog box, tap or click Disable BitLocker Drive Encryption.

   By completing this procedure, you temporarily disable BitLocker on the operating-system volume.

To turn off BitLocker Drive Encryption and decrypt a data volume, follow these steps:

1. In Control Panel, tap or click System And Security, and then double-tap or double-click BitLocker Drive Encryption.

2. For the appropriate volume, tap or click Turn Off BitLocker Drive Encryption.

3. In the What Level Of Decryption Do You Want? dialog box, tap or click Decrypt The Volume.

To turn off BitLocker Drive Encryption and decrypt a USB flash drive, follow these steps:

1. In Control Panel, tap or click System And Security, and then double-tap or double-click BitLocker Drive Encryption.

2. For the appropriate volume, tap or click Turn Off BitLocker Drive Encryption.

3. In the What Level Of Decryption Do You Want? dialog box, tap or click Decrypt The Volume.

# Managing file systems and storage

CHAPTER 12, "Storage management," discussed storage management, which primarily focuses on storage technologies and techniques for configuring storage. As discussed in that chapter, disks can be apportioned in many ways but ultimately must be formatted with a particular file system. The file system provides the environment for working with files and folders. Windows Server 2012 provides file allocation table (FAT) and NT file system (NTFS) as the basic file-system types. These file systems and their various extensions, which include the Resilient File System (ReFS), are discussed in this chapter.

## Understanding the disk and file-system structure

The basic unit of storage is a *disk*. Regardless of the partition style or disk type, Windows Server 2012 reads data from disks and writes data to disks using the disk input/output (I/O) subsystem. The I/O subsystem understands the physical and logical structures of disks, which allows it to perform read and write operations. The basic physical structure of a hard disk drive (HDD) includes the following items:

- Platters

- Cylinders

- Tracks

- Clusters

- Sectors

Each hard disk drive has one or more platters. Platters are the physical media from which data is read and to which data is written. The disk head travels in a circular path over the platter. This circular path is called a *track*. Tracks are magnetically encoded when you format a disk. Tracks that reside in the same location on each platter form a *cylinder*. For example, if a hard disk drive has four platters, Cylinder 1 consists of Track 1 from all four platters.

Tracks are divided into *sectors*. Sectors represent a subsection within a track and are made up of individual bytes. The number of sectors in a track depends on the hard disk drive type and the location of the track on the platter. Tracks closer to the outside of the platter can have more sectors than tracks near the center of the platter.

In contrast, solid-state drives (SSDs) have no moving parts. This is because solid-state drives use flash memory modules rather than platters, and there are no disk heads that need to travel over platters to read data. With solid-state drives, data is accessed directly from the flash memory over multiple internal flash buses. Typically, solid-state drives use NAND flash memory modules that have either multilevel cells (MLCs) storing two bits per cell or single-level cells (SLCs) storing one bit per cell.

Although solid-state drives that use multilevel cells might be cheaper than those with single-level cells, solid-state drives with single-level cells typically provide better reliability and performance. That said, the endurance of both types of solid-states drives isn't as robust as hard-disk drives but is improving thanks to wear-leveling algorithms and other techniques that distribute writes more evenly across memory modules, provide enhanced error correction, and might also compress data.

As with hard disks, solid-state drives rely on I/O subsystems that understand their physical and logical structure to perform read and write operations. Overall performance of solid-state drives depends on their controllers, firmware, and caching. Typically, solid-state drives are much faster than hard drives, especially for small block I/O with less than 32-kilobyte (KB) reads.

# INSIDE OUT When using SSDs makes sense

As solid-state drive capacities improve and prices come down, using solid-state drives in the enterprise makes more and more sense. Many solid-state-drive solutions are available for enterprise servers and enterprise workstations, including those with their own data protection similar to RAID systems. Applications that require high performance for reads and have heavy read access can benefit from using solid-state drives. For example, you might want to use enterprise SSDs with applications for media streaming, web accelerators, video-on-demand, and frequently accessed data-storage warehouses. Solid-state drives might also make sense in storage-tiering scenarios. For example, you could use Tier 1 storage with solid-state drives for hot data and Tier 2 storage with capacity-optimized drives for cool data.

Solid-state hybrid drives bridge the gap between hard disk drives and solid-state drives. A typical hybrid drive combines a small solid-state drive with a large hard disk drive. The flash memory is used for critical operations, such as boot and initial application load, and the hard disk drive is used for all other operations. Special algorithms can be used to capture boot files and place them on the flash to ensure that the hybrid drive always boots from flash memory rather than the spinning disk. Other algorithms can be used to move applications and data that are initially loaded or frequently used with the system into the flash memory as well. The result is a drive that has some of the speed benefits of solid-state drives with a cost that is closer to that of a traditional hard disk drive.

## INSIDE OUT  When using hybrid drives makes sense

Hybrid drives are ideal for scenarios where you want to reduce boot and initial application load times but don't want to equip your enterprise workstations with more expensive solid-state drives. As such, you could use the hybrid drives as system boot drives and not necessarily as data drives. Keep in mind that it can take several boots for a hybrid drive to normalize the startup process and achieve the best efficiencies. The same is true for normalizing the startup of frequently used applications.

When you format a disk with a file system, the file system structures the disk using *clusters*, which are logical groupings of sectors. Both FAT and NTFS use the fixed sector size of the underlying disk (which can be either 512 bytes per physical sector with 512b disks or 4096 bytes per physical sector with 512e disks) but allow the cluster size to be variable. For example, the cluster size might be 4096 bytes, and if there are 512 bytes per sector, each cluster is made up of eight sectors. ReFS is an exception. In current implementations, as of this writing, ReFS has a fixed cluster size of 64 KBs.

Table 14-1 provides a summary of the default cluster sizes for FAT, FAT32, exFAT, NTFS, and ReFS. You have the option of specifying the cluster size when you create a file system on a disk, or you can accept the default cluster size setting. Either way, the cluster sizes available depend on the type of file system you are using.

## Four different FAT file systems

There are actually four FAT file systems used by Windows platforms: FAT12, FAT16, FAT32, and exFAT (FAT64). The difference among FAT12, FAT16, FAT32, and FAT64 is the number of bits used for entries in their file allocation tables—namely, 12, 16, 32, or 64 bits. From a user's perspective, the main difference in these file systems is the theoretical maximum volume size, which is 16 megabytes (MBs) for a FAT12 volume, 4 gigabytes (GBs) for FAT16, 2 terabytes (TBs) for FAT32, and 256 TBs for FAT64. When the term FAT is used without an appended number, however, it always refers to FAT16.

**TABLE 14-1** Default cluster sizes for Windows Server

| Volume Size | Cluster Size | | | | |
|---|---|---|---|---|---|
| | FAT16 | FAT32 | exFAT | NTFS | ReFS |
| 7 MBs to 16 MBs | 512 bytes | N/A | 4 KBs | 512 bytes | N/A |
| 17 MBs to 32 MBs | 512 bytes | N/A | 4 KBs | 512 bytes | N/A |
| 33 MBs to 64 MBs | 1 KB | 512 bytes | 4 KBs | 512 bytes | N/A |
| 65 MBs to 128 MBs | 2 KBs | 1 KB | 4 KBs | 512 bytes | N/A |
| 129 MBs to 256 MBs | 4 KBs | 2 KBs | 4 KBs | 512 bytes | N/A |
| 257 MBs to 512 MBs | 8 KBs | 4 KBs | 32 KBs | 512 bytes | N/A |
| 513 MBs to 1024 MBs | 16 KBs | 4 KBs | 32 KBs | 1 KB | 64 KBs |
| 1025 MBs to 2 GBs | 32 KBs | 4 KBs | 32 KBs | 4 KBs | 64 KBs |
| 2 GBs to 4 GBs | 64 KBs | 4 KBs | 32 KBs | 4 KBs | 64 KBs |
| 4 GBs to 8 GBs | N/A | 4 KBs | 32 KBs | 4 KBs | 64 KBs |
| 8 GBs to 16 GBs | N/A | 8 KBs | 32 KBs | 4 KBs | 64 KBs |
| 16 GBs to 32 GBs | N/A | 16 KBs | 32 KBs | 4 KBs | 64 KBs |
| 32 GBs to 2 TBs | N/A | * | 128 KBs | 4 KBs | 64 KBs |
| 2 TBs to 16 TBs | N/A | * | 128 KBs | 4 KBs | 64 KBs |
| 16 TBs to 32 TBs | N/A | * | 128 KBs | 8 KBs | 64 KBs |
| 32 TBs to 64 TBs | N/A | * | 128 KBs | 16 KBs | 64 KBs |
| 64 TBs to 128 TBs | N/A | * | 128 KBs | 32 KBs | 64 KBs |
| 128 TBs to 256 TBs | N/A | * | 128 KBs | 64 KBs | 64 KBs |

The important thing to know about clusters is that they are the smallest unit in which disk space is allocated. Each cluster can hold one file at most. So, if you create a 1-KB file and the cluster size is 4 KBs, there will be 3 KBs of empty space in the cluster that isn't available to other files. That's just the way it is. If a single cluster isn't big enough to hold an entire file, the remaining file data will go into the next available cluster and the next until the file is completely stored.

Although the disk I/O subsystem manages the physical structure of disks, Windows Server 2012 manages the logical disk structure at the file-system level. The logical structure of a disk relates to the basic or dynamic volumes you create on a disk and the file systems with which those volumes are formatted. You can format both basic volumes and dynamic volumes using FAT or NTFS. As discussed in the next section, each file system type has a different structure, and there are advantages and disadvantages of each as well.

# Using FAT

FAT volumes use an allocation table to store information about disk space allocation. FAT can be used with both fixed disks and removable media. For both fixed disks and removable media, FAT is available in 16-bit and 32-bit versions, which are referred to as FAT16 and FAT32. For removable media, you can also use extended FAT (exFAT). The advantage of using exFAT with removable media instead of FAT is that exFAT can be used with any operating system or device that supports this file-system type.

## File allocation table structure

Disks formatted using FAT are organized as shown in Figure 14-1. They have a boot sector that stores information about the disk type, starting and ending sectors, the active partition, and a bootstrap program that executes at startup and boots the operating system. This is followed by a reserve area that can be one or more sectors in length.

| Boot Sector | Reserved Sector | FAT 1 (Primary) | FAT 2 (Duplicate) | Root Table | Data area for all other files and folders |
|---|---|---|---|---|---|

Figure 14-1  An overview of the FAT16 volume structure.

The reserve area is followed by the primary file allocation table, which provides a reference table for the clusters on the volume. Each reference in the table relates to a specific cluster and defines the cluster's status as follows:

- Available (unused)

- In use (meaning it is being used by a file)

- Bad (meaning it is marked as bad and won't be written to)

- Reserved (meaning it is reserved for the operating system)

If a cluster is in use, the cluster entry identifies the number of the next cluster in the file or indicates that it is the last cluster of a file—in which case, the end of the file has been reached.

FAT volumes also have the following features:

- Duplicate file allocation table, which provides a backup of the primary file allocation table and can be used to restore the file system if the primary file allocation table gets corrupted

Chapter 14

- Root directory table, which defines the starting cluster of each file in the root directory of the file system

- Data area, which stores the actual data for user files and folders

When an application attempts to read a file, the operating system looks up the starting cluster of the file in the file allocation table and then uses the file allocation table to find and read all the clusters in the file.

## FAT features

Although FAT supports basic file and folder operations, its features are rather limited. By using FAT, you have the following capabilities:

- You can use Windows file sharing and the share permissions you assign completely control remote access to files.

- You can use long file names, meaning file and folder names containing up to 255 characters.

- You can use FAT with floppy disks and removable disks.

- You can use Unicode characters in file and folder names.

- You can use uppercase and lowercase letters in file and folder names.

However, FAT has the following disadvantages:

- You can't control local access to files and folders using Microsoft Windows file and folder access permissions.

- You can't use any advanced file-system features of NTFS, including compression, encryption, disk quotas, and remote storage.

In addition, although FAT16 and FAT32 support small cluster sizes, exFAT does not. Table 14-2 provides a summary of FAT16, FAT32, and exFAT.

> **Note**
> Although Windows Server 2012 can read to or write from FAT32 volumes as large as 2 TBs, the operating system can only format FAT32 volumes up to 32 GBs in size.

**TABLE 14-2 Comparison of FAT16, FAT32, and exFAT features**

| Feature | FAT16 | FAT32 | exFAT |
|---|---|---|---|
| File allocation table size | 16-bit | 32-bit | 64-bit |
| Minimum volume size | See the following Inside Out tip | 33 MBs | 33 MBs |
| Maximum volume size | 4 GBs; best at 2 GBs or less | 2 TBs; limited in Windows Server to 32 GBs | 256 TBs |
| Maximum file size | 2 GBs | 4 GBs | Same as volume size |
| Supports small cluster size | Yes | Yes | No |
| Supports NTFS features | No | No | No |
| Use on fixed disks | Yes | Yes | Yes |
| Use on removable disks | Yes | Yes | Yes |
| Supports network file sharing | Yes | Yes | Yes |
| Supports customized disk and folder views | Yes | Yes | Yes |

Chapter 14

# INSIDE OUT   FAT on very small media

Note that FAT volumes are structured differently depending on the volume size. When you format a volume that is less than 32,680 sectors (16 MBs), the format program uses 12 bits for FAT12. This means less space is reserved for each entry in the table and more space is made available for data. This technique is meant to be used with very small media, such as legacy floppy disks.

By default, Windows Server sets the size of clusters and the number of sectors per cluster based on the size of the volume. Disk geometry also is a factor in determining cluster size because the number of clusters on the volume must fit into the number of bits used by the file system. The actual amount of data you can store on a single FAT volume is a factor of the maximum cluster size and the maximum number of clusters you can use per volume. This can be written out as a formula:

```
ClusterSize x MaximumNumberOfClusters = MaximumVolumeSize
```

FAT16 supports a maximum of 65,526 clusters and a maximum cluster size of 64 KBs. This is where the limitation of 4 GBs for volume size comes from. With disks less than 32 MBs but more than 16 MBs in size, the cluster size is 512 bytes and there is one sector per cluster with 512b disks. This changes as the volume size increases, up to the largest cluster size of 64 KBs with 128 sectors per cluster on 2-GB to 4-GB volumes.

FAT32 volumes using 512-byte sectors on 512b disks can be up to 2 TBs in size and can use clusters of up to 64 KBs. To control the maximum number of clusters allowed, the Windows operating system reserves the upper 4 bits, however, limiting FAT32 to a maximum 28 bits worth of clusters. With a maximum recommended cluster size of 32 KBs (instead of the maximum allowable 64 KBs), this means a FAT32 volume on the Windows operating system can be up to 32 GBs in size. Because the smallest cluster size allowed for FAT32 volumes is 512 bytes, the smallest FAT32 volume you can create is 33 MBs.

## FAT32 volumes of any size can be mounted

Windows Server 2012 does support mounting FAT32 volumes of up to the theoretical limit of 2 TBs. This allows you to mount volumes larger than 32 GBs that were created on other operating systems or by using third-party utilities.

## INSIDE OUT Getting volume format and feature information

A quick way to check the file system type and available features of a volume is to type **fsutil fsinfo volumeinfo** *DriveDesignator* at the command prompt, where *DriveDesignator* is the drive letter of the volume followed by a colon, such as C:. For a FAT or FAT32 volume, you'll see output similar to the following:

```
Volume Name : LogData
Volume Serial Number : 0x70692a2e
Max Component Length : 255
File System Name : FAT32
Preserves Case of filenames
Supports Unicode in filenames
```

# Using NTFS

NTFS is an extensible and recoverable file system that offers many advantages over FAT, FAT32, and exFAT. Because it is extensible, the file system can be extended over time with various revisions. As you'll learn shortly, the version of NTFS that ships with Windows Server 2008 and Windows Server 2008 R2 was extended with new features, as was the version of NTFS that ships with Windows Server 2012, but all are designated as having the same internal version as the revision of the NTFS version that shipped with Microsoft Windows Server 2003. Because it is recoverable, volumes formatted with NTFS can be reconstructed if they contain structure errors. Typically, restructuring NTFS volumes is a task performed at startup.

# NTFS structure

NTFS volumes have a very different structure and feature set than FAT volumes. The first area of the volume is the boot sector, which is located at sector 0 on the volume. The boot sector stores information about the disk layout, and a bootstrap program executes at startup and boots the operating system. A backup boot sector is placed at the end of the volume for redundancy and fault tolerance.

Instead of a file allocation table, NTFS uses a relational database to store information about files. This database is called the master file table (MFT). The MFT stores a file record of each file and folder on the volume, pertinent volume information, and details on the MFT itself. The first 16 records in the MFT store NTFS metadata as summarized in Table 14-3.

**TABLE 14-3** NTFS metadata

| MFT Record | Record Type | File Name | Description |
|---|---|---|---|
| 0 | MFT | $Mft | Stores the base file record of each file and folder on the volume. As the number of files and folders grows, additional records are used as necessary. |
| 1 | MFT mirror | $MftMirr | Stores a partial duplicate of the MFT used for failure recovery. It's also referred to as MFT2. |
| 2 | Log file | $LogFile | Stores a persistent history of all changes made to files on the volume, which can be used to recover files. |
| 3 | Volume | $Volume | Stores volume attributes, including the volume serial number, version, and number of sectors. |
| 4 | Attribute definitions | $AttrDef | Stores a table of attribute names, numbers, and descriptions. |
| 5 | Root file name index | $ | Stores the details on the volume's root directory. |
| 6 | Cluster bitmap | $Bitmap | Stores a table that details the clusters in use. |
| 7 | Boot sector | $Boot | Stores the bootstrap program on bootable volumes. Also includes the locations of the MFT and MFT mirror. |
| 8 | Bad cluster file | $BadClus | Stores a table mapping bad clusters. |
| 9 | Security file | $Secure | Stores the unique security descriptor for all files and folders on the volume. |
| 10 | Upcase table | $Upcase | Stores a table used to convert lowercase to matching uppercase Unicode characters. |
| 11 | NTFS extension file | $Extend | Stores information on enabled file-system extensions. |
| 12–15 | To be determined | To be determined | Reserved records for future use. |

Chapter 14

The MFT mirror stores a partial duplicate of the MFT that can be used to recover the MFT. If any of the records in the primary mirror become corrupted or are otherwise unreadable and there's a duplicate record in the MFT mirror, NTFS uses the data in the MFT mirror and, if possible, uses this data to recover the records in the primary MFT. It is also important to note that the NTFS version that ships with Windows Server 2003 and later (NTFS 5.1) has a slightly different metadata mapping than the version that originally shipped with Windows 2000 (NTFS 5.0). In the current version, the $LogFile and $Bitmap metadata files are located on a different position on disk than they were in Windows 2000. This gives a performance advantage of 5 to 8 percent to disks that are formatted under NTFS 5.1 and comes close to approximating the performance of FAT.

> ## Note
> For NTFS, you typically refer to major version numbers rather than the major version and the revision number. Technically, however, Shadow Copy is a feature of NTFS 5.1 or later. NTFS 5.1 is the version of NTFS that was first included in Windows XP and Windows Server 2003 (and was available with Windows 2000 Server Service Pack 4 or later). With NTFS 5.1, you gain some additional enhancements, primarily the ability to use shadow copies.

The rest of the records in the MFT store file and folder information. Each of these regular entries includes the file or folder name, security descriptor, and other attributes, including file data or pointers to file data. The MFT record size is set when a volume is formatted and can be 1024 bytes, 2048 bytes, or 4096 bytes, depending on the volume size. If a file is very small, all of its contents might be able to fit in the data field of its record in the MFT. When all of a file's attributes, including its data, can be stored in the MFT record, the attributes are called *resident attributes*. Figure 14-2 shows an example of a small file with resident attributes.

If a file is larger than a single record, it has what are called *nonresident attributes*. Here, the file has a base record in the MFT that details where to find the file data. NTFS creates additional areas called *runs* on the disk to store the additional file data. The size of data runs is dependent on the cluster size of the volume. If the cluster size is 2 KBs or less, data runs are 2 KBs. If the cluster size is larger than 2 KBs, data runs are 4 KBs.

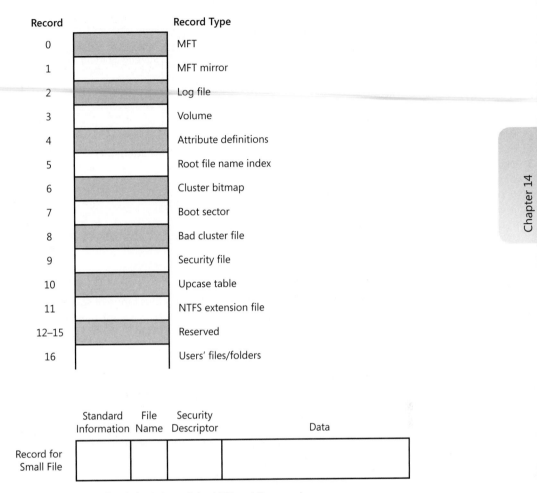

| Record | Record Type |
|--------|-------------|
| 0 | MFT |
| 1 | MFT mirror |
| 2 | Log file |
| 3 | Volume |
| 4 | Attribute definitions |
| 5 | Root file name index |
| 6 | Cluster bitmap |
| 7 | Boot sector |
| 8 | Bad cluster file |
| 9 | Security file |
| 10 | Upcase table |
| 11 | NTFS extension file |
| 12–15 | Reserved |
| 16 | Users' files/folders |

Record for Small File: Standard Information | File Name | Security Descriptor | Data

**Figure 14-2** A graphical depiction of the MFT and its records.

As Figure 14-3 shows, clusters belonging to the file are referenced in the MFT using virtual cluster numbers (VCNs). VCNs are numbered sequentially starting with VCN 0. The Data field in the file's MFT record maps the VCNs to a starting logical cluster number (LCN) on the disk and details the number of clusters to read for that VCN. When these mappings use up all the available space in a record, additional MFT records are created to store the additional mappings.

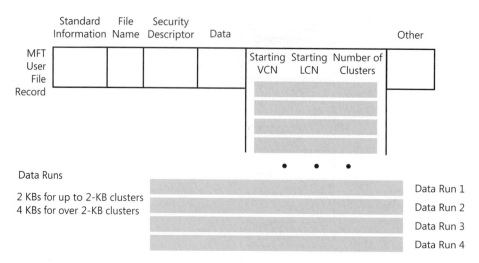

**Figure 14-3** A graphical depiction of a user file record with data runs.

In addition to the MFT, NTFS reserves a contiguous range of space past the end of the MFT called the *MFT zone*. By default, the MFT zone is approximately 12.5 percent of the total volume space. The MFT zone is used to allow the MFT to grow without becoming fragmented. Typically, the MFT zone shrinks as the MFT grows.

The MFT zone is not used to store user data unless the remainder of the volume becomes full. Fragmentation can and still does occur, however. On volumes with lots of small files, the MFT zone can get used up by the MFT, and as additional files are added, the MFT has to grow into unreserved areas of the volume. On volumes with but a few large files, the unreserved space on a volume can get used up before the MFT, and in this case, the files start using the MFT zone space.

# INSIDE OUT   The MFT zone can be optimized

By default, the MFT is optimized for environments that have a mix of large and small files. This setting works well if the average file size is 8 KBs or larger. It doesn't work so well if a volume has many very small files, such as when the average size of files is less than 2 KBs or between 2 KBs and 7 KBs. Here, you might want to configure the volume so that it has a larger MFT zone than normal to help prevent the MFT from becoming fragmented. The MFT zone size is set as eighths of the disk.

You can determine the current MFT zone setting by typing the following command at the command prompt: **fsutil behavior query mftzone**. If this command returns "mftzone=0," the MFT zone is using the default setting. The default setting, 0, specifies that the MFT zone should use one-eighth (12.5 percent) of the total volume space.

This is the same as a setting of 1. You can also use a setting of 2, 3, or 4 to set the MFT zone to use two-eighths (25 percent), three-eighths (37.5 percent), or four-eighths (50 percent) of the total volume space.

You can configure the MFT zone by typing the command **fsutil behavior set mftzone** *Value*, where *Value* is the relative size setting to use, such as 2.

## NTFS features

Several versions of NTFS are available. NTFS 5 was first implemented in Windows 2000. NTFS 5.1 is the version of NTFS that was first included in Windows XP and Windows Server 2003. NTFS 5.1 with Local File System (LFS) 2.0 was first included with Windows 8 and Windows Server 2012.

You have the following capabilities when you use NTFS 5:

- Advanced file and folder access permissions

- Data streams and change journals

- Encrypting File System (EFS)

- File sharing and full-control remote access to files and folders

- Long file names, meaning file and folder names can contain up to 255 characters

- Reparse points, remote storage, and shadow copies

- Sparse files, disk quotas, and object identifiers

- Unicode characters in file and folder names

- Uppercase and lowercase letters in file and folder names

NTFS 5.1 provides some additional enhancements, primarily the ability to use shadow copies. Similarly NTFS 5.1 with Local File System (LFS) 2.0 also provides some additional enhancements, primarily related to self-healing technology used with Check Disk (Chkdsk .exe) and the USN change journal. Specifically, NTFS and ReFS use version 2.0 change-journal records by default, which contain 64-bit identifiers. ReFS also implements version 3.0 records, which contain 128-bit identifiers.

Windows Server automatically sets the size of clusters and the number of sectors per cluster based on the size of the volume. Cluster sizes range from 512 bytes to 64 KBs. As with FAT, NTFS has the following characteristics:

- Disk geometry also is a factor in determining cluster size because the number of clusters on the volume must fit into the number of bits used by the file system.

- The actual amount of data you can store on a single NTFS volume is a factor of the maximum cluster size and the maximum number of clusters you can use per volume.

Thus, although volumes have a specific maximum size, the cluster size used on a volume can be a limiting factor. For example, a dynamic volume with a 4-KB cluster size can have dynamic volumes up to 16 TBs, which is different from the maximum allowed dynamic volume size on NTFS.

## Analyzing the NTFS structure

If you want to examine the structure of a volume formatted using NTFS, you can use the FSUtil FSinfo command to do this. Type **fsutil fsinfo ntfsinfo *DriveDesignator*** at the command prompt, where *DriveDesignator* is the drive letter of the volume followed by a colon. For example, if you want to obtain information on the C drive, you type

```
fsutil fsinfo ntfsinfo c:
```

The output would be similar to the following:

```
NTFS Volume Serial Number :        0xbcf4c873f4c82125
NTFS Version    :                  3.1
LFS Version     :                  2.0
Number Sectors :                   0x000000001d3c57ff
Total Clusters :                   0x0000000003a78aff
Free Clusters   :                  0x00000000035e477d
Total Reserved :                   0x000000000001e2b0
Bytes Per Sector   :               512
Bytes Per Physical Sector :        512
Bytes Per Cluster :                4096
Bytes Per FileRecord Segment    : 1024
Clusters Per FileRecord Segment : 0
Mft Valid Data Length :            0x0000000004e00000
Mft Start Lcn   :                  0x00000000000c0000
Mft2 Start Lcn :                   0x0000000000000002
Mft Zone Start :                   0x00000000000c4e00
Mft Zone End    :                  0x00000000000cc820
Resource Manager Identifier :      CBDD98AD-E33F-11E1-95F2-C407271F80D4
```

As Table 14-4 shows, FSUtil FSinfo provides detailed information on the NTFS volume structure, including space usage and configuration.

**TABLE 14-4  Details from FSUtil FSinfo**

| Field | Description |
|---|---|
| NTFS Volume Serial Number | The unique serial number of the selected NTFS volume. |
| NTFS Version | The internal NTFS version. Here, 3.1 refers to NTFS 5.1. |
| Number Sectors | The total number of sectors on the volume in hexadecimal. |
| Total Clusters | The total number of clusters on the volume in hexadecimal. |
| Free Clusters | The number of unused clusters on the volume in hexadecimal. |
| Total Reserved | The total number of clusters reserved for NTFS metadata. |
| Bytes Per Sector | The number of bytes per sector. |
| Bytes Per Cluster | The number of bytes per cluster. |
| Bytes Per FileRecord Segment | The size of MFT file records. |
| Clusters Per FileRecord Segment | The number of clusters per file-record segment, which is valid only if the file-record size is as large as or larger than the volume cluster size. |
| Mft Valid Data Length | The current size of the MFT. |
| Mft Start Lcn | The location of the first LCN on the disk used by the MFT. |
| Mft2 Start Lcn | The location of the first LCN on the disk used by the MFT mirror. |
| Mft Zone Start | The cluster number that marks the start of the region on the disk reserved by the MFT. |
| Mft Zone End | The cluster number that marks the end of the region on the disk reserved by the MFT. |

Using FSUtil, you can also obtain detailed statistics on NTFS metadata and user file usage since a system was started. To view this information, type **fsutil fsinfo statistics** *DriveDesignator* at the command prompt, where *DriveDesignator* is the drive letter of the volume followed by a colon. For example, if you want to obtain information on the C drive, you type

```
fsutil fsinfo statistics c:
```

The output is shown in two sections. The first section of the statistics details user file and disk activity as well as the overall usage of NTFS metadata. As shown in this example, the output shows the number of reads and writes as well as the number of bytes read or written:

```
File System Type :      NTFS
UserFileReads :         31441
UserFileReadBytes :     857374720
UserDiskReads :         31584
UserFileWrites :        6302
UserFileWriteBytes :    197198336
UserDiskWrites :        6505
MetaDataReads :         3168
MetaDataReadBytes :     21770240
MetaDataDiskReads :     4165
MetaDataWrites :        3883
MetaDataWriteBytes :    16805888
MetaDataDiskWrites :    4644
```

The second section of the statistics details usage of individual NTFS metadata files. As shown in this example, the output details the number of reads and writes as well as the number of bytes read or written for each NTFS metadata file:

```
MftReads :              2962
MftReadBytes :          12132352
MftWrites :             2460
MftWriteBytes :         10465280
Mft2Writes :            0
Mft2WriteBytes :        0
RootIndexReads :        0
RootIndexReadBytes :    0
RootIndexWrites :       0
RootIndexWriteBytes :   0
BitmapReads :           8
BitmapReadBytes :       8388608
BitmapWrites :          847
BitmapWriteBytes :      3796992
MftBitmapReads :        1
MftBitmapReadBytes :    65536
MftBitmapWrites :       107
MftBitmapWriteBytes :   442368
UserIndexReads :        1086
UserIndexReadBytes :    4448256
UserIndexWrites :       711
UserIndexWriteBytes :   3153920
LogFileReads :          8
LogFileReadBytes :      32768
LogFileWrites :         5895
LogFileWriteBytes :     36777984
LogFileFull :           0
```

# Advanced NTFS features

NTFS has many advanced features that administrators should know about and understand. These features include the following:

- Hard links

- Data streams

- Change journals

- Object identifiers

- Reparse points

- Sparse files

- Transactions

Each of these features is discussed in the sections that follow.

## Hard links

Every file created on a volume has a hard link. The hard link is the directory entry for the file, and it is what allows the operating system to find files within folders. On NTFS volumes, files can have multiple hard links. This allows a single file to appear in the same directory with multiple names or to appear in multiple directories with the same name or different names. As with file copies, applications can open a file using any of the hard links you've created and modify the file. If you use another hard link to open the file in another application, the application can detect the changes.

Wondering why you'd want to use hard links? Hard links are useful when you want the same file to appear in several locations. For example, you might want a document to appear in a folder of a network share that is available to all users but have an application that requires the document to be in another directory so that it can be read and processed on a daily basis. Rather than moving the file to the application directory and giving every user in the company access to this protected directory, you decide to create a hard link to the document so that it can be accessed separately by both users and the application.

Regardless of how many hard links a file has, however, the related directory entries all point to the single file that exists in one location on the volume—and this is how hard links differ from copies. With a copy of a file, the file data exists in multiple locations. With a hard link, the file appears in multiple locations but exists in only one location. Thus, if you modify a file using one of its hard links and save, and then someone opens the file using a different hard link, the changes are shown.

> **Note**
>
> Hard links have advantages and disadvantages. Hard links are not meant for environments where multiple users can modify a file simultaneously. If Sandra opens a file using one hard link and is working on the file at the same time Bob is working on the file, there can be problems if they both try to save changes. Although this is a disadvantage of hard links, the really big advantage of hard links shouldn't be overlooked: If a file has multiple hard links, the file will not be deleted from the volume until all hard links are deleted. This means that if someone were to accidentally delete a file that had multiple hard links, the file wouldn't actually be deleted. Instead, only the affected hard link would be deleted and any other hard links and the file itself would remain.

Because there is only one physical copy of a file with multiple hard links, the hard links do not have separate security descriptors. Only the source file has security descriptors. Thus, if you were to change the access permissions of a file using any of its hard links, you would actually change the security of the source file and all hard links that point to this file would have these security settings.

You can create hard links by using the FSUtil Hardlink command. Use the following syntax:

```
fsutil hardlink create NewFilePath CurrentFilePath
```

Here, *NewFilePath* is the file path for the hard link you want to create and *CurrentFilePath* is the name of the existing file to which you are linking. For example, if the file ChangeLog.doc is found in the file path C:\CorpDocs and you want to create a new hard link to this file with the file path C:\UserData\Logs\CurrentLog.doc, you would type

```
fsutil hardlink create C:\UserData\Logs\CurrentLog.doc C:\CorpDocs\ChangeLog.doc
```

Hard links can be created only on NTFS volumes, and you cannot create a hard link on one volume that refers to another volume. Following this, you couldn't create a hard link to the D drive for a file created on the C drive.

## Data streams

Every file created on a volume has a data stream associated with it. A data stream is a sequence of bytes that contains the contents of the file. The main data stream for a file is unnamed and is visible to all file systems. On NTFS volumes, files can also have named data streams associated with them. Named data streams contain additional information about a file, such as custom properties or summary details. This allows you to associate additional information with a file but still be able to manage the file as a single unit.

After you create a named data stream and associate it with a file, any applications that know how to work with named data streams can access the streams by their names and read the additional details. Many applications support named data streams, including Microsoft Office, Adobe Acrobat, and other productivity applications. This is how you can set summary properties for a Microsoft Word document—such as Title, Subject, and Author—and save that information with the file.

In fact, if you were to press and hold or right-click any file on an NTFS volume and select Properties and then tap or click on the Details tab, you can see information that is associated with the file using a data stream, as shown in Figure 14-4.

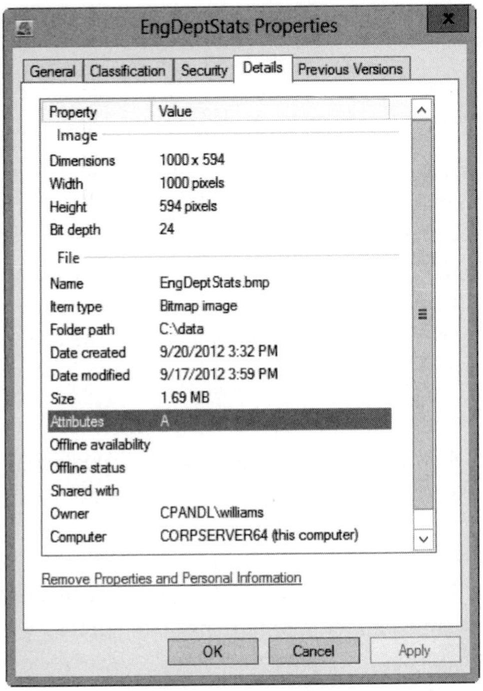

**Figure 14-4**  Information entered on the Details tab is saved to a named data stream.

Generally speaking, the named data streams associated with a file are used to set the names of its property tabs and to populate the fields of those tabs. This is how some document types can have other tabs associated with them and how the Windows operating system can store a thumbnail image within an NTFS file containing an image.

The most important thing to know about streams is that they aren't supported on FAT. If you move or copy a file containing named streams to a FAT volume, you might see the warning prompt labeled "Confirm Stream Loss" telling you the file has additional information associated with it and asking you to confirm that it's okay that the file is saved without this information. If you tap or click Yes, only the contents of the file are copied or moved to the FAT volume—and not the contents of the associated data streams. If you tap or click No, the copy or save operation is canceled.

In a file's Properties dialog box on the Details tab, you also have the option of removing properties and personal information associated with a file. You do this by tapping or clicking the Remove Properties And Personal Information link and then selecting a Remove Properties method. Windows accomplishes this task by removing the values from the related data streams associated with the file.

## Change journals

An NTFS volume can use an update sequence number (USN) change journal. A change journal provides a complete log of all changes made to the volume. It records additions, deletions, and modifications regardless of who made them or how the additions, deletions, and modifications occurred. As with system logs, the change log is persistent, so it isn't reset if you shut down and restart the operating system. The operating system writes records to the NTFS change log when an NTFS checkpoint occurs. The checkpoint tells the operating system to write changes that would allow NTFS to recover from failure to a particular point in time.

The change journal is enabled when you install certain services, including Distributed File System Service. Domain controllers and any other computer in the domain that uses these services rely heavily on the change journal. The change journal allows these services to be very efficient at determining when files, folders, and other NTFS objects have been modified. Rather than checking time stamps and registering for file notifications, these services perform direct lookups in the change journal to determine all the modifications made to a set of files. Not only is this faster, it uses system resources more efficiently as well.

You can gather summary statistics about the change journal by typing **fsutil usn queryjournal** *DriveDesignator* at the command prompt, where *DriveDesignator* is the drive letter of the volume followed by a colon. For example, if you want to obtain change journal statistics on the C drive, you type

```
fsutil usn queryjournal c:
```

The output is similar to the following:

```
Usn Journal ID    : 0x01cd77459da4462a
First Usn         : 0x0000000000000000
Next Usn          : 0x0000000002573bf8
Lowest Valid Usn  : 0x0000000000000000
Max Usn           : 0x7fffffffffff0000
Maximum Size      : 0x0000000020000000
Allocation Delta  : 0x0000000000400000
Minimum record version supported : 2
Maximum record version supported : 2
```

The details show the following information:

- **Usn Journal ID**  The unique identifier of the current change journal. A journal is assigned an identifier on creation and can also be stamped with a new ID. NTFS and ReFS use this identifier for an integrity check.

- **First Usn**  The number of the first record that can be read from the journal.

- **Next Usn**  The number of the next record to be written to the journal.

- **Lowest Valid Usn**  The first record that was written into this journal instance. If a journal has a First Usn value lower than the Lowest Valid Usn, the journal has been stamped with a new identifier since the last USN was written (and this could indicate a discontinuity where changes to some or all files or directories on the volume might have occurred but are not recorded in the change journal).

- **Max Usn**  The highest USN that can be assigned.

- **Maximum Size**  The maximum size in bytes that the change journal can use. On NTFS, if the change journal exceeds this value, older entries are overwritten by truncating the journal at the next NTFS checkpoint.

- **Allocation Delta**  On NTFS, the size in bytes of disk memory that is added to the end and removed from the beginning of the change journal when it becomes full. This is not used with ReFS.

- **Minimum Record Version Supported**  The minimum supported version of USN records, as supported by the file system.

- **Maximum Record Version Supported**  The maximum supported version of USN records, as supported by the file system.

Chapter 14

Individual records written to the change journal look like this:

```
File Ref#          :                          0x18e90000000018e9
ParentFile Ref# :                             0x17c00000000017c0
Usn                :                          0x0000000000000000
SecurityId         :                          0x00000119
Reason             :                          0x00000000
Name (024)         :                          ocmanage.dll
```

The most important information here is the name of the affected file and the security identifier of the object that made the change. You can get the most recent change journal entry
for a file by typing **fsutil usn readdata** *FilePath*, where *FilePath* is the name of the file for
which you want to retrieve change information. For example, if you want to obtain the
most recent change journal information on a file with the path C:\DomainComputers
.txt, you type

```
fsutil usn readdata c:\domaincomputers.txt
```

The output is similar to the following:

```
Major Version      :                          0x2
Minor Version      :                          0x0
FileRef#           :                          0x000800000001c306
Parent FileRef#    :                          0x0005000000000005
Usn                :                          0x00000000237cf7f0
Time Stamp         :                          0x0000000000000000
Reason             :                          0x0
Source Info        :                          0x0
Security Id        :                          0x45e
File Attributes    :                          0x20
File Name Length :                            0x26
File Name Offset :                            0x3c
FileName           :                          domaincomputers.txt
```

This data shows the file's reference number in the root file index and that of its parent. It
also shows the current USN associated with the file and the file attributes flag. The File
Name Length element shows the total length in characters of the file's long and short file
names together. This particular file has a file name length of 38 (0 × 26). That's because the
file name has more than eight characters followed by a dot and a three-letter extension.
This means the file is represented by NTFS using long and short file names. The long file
name is domaincomputers.txt. This is followed by an offset pointer that indicates where the
short file name, domain~1.txt, can be looked up, which is where the total file name length
of 38 characters comes from.

> **Note**
> You can examine a file's short file name by typing **dir /x *FilePath*** at the command
> prompt, where *FilePath* is the path to the file you want to examine, such as:
> **dir /x c:\domaincomputers.txt**.

> **Important**
> Version 2 records will have a 64-bit FileReferenceNumber and a 64-bit
> ParentFileReferenceNumber. Version 3 records will have a 128-bit FileReferenceNumber
> and a 128-bit ParentFileReferenceNumber.

## Object identifiers

Another feature of NTFS is the ability to use object identifiers. Object identifiers are 16
bytes in length and are unique on a per-volume basis. Any file that has an object identifier
also has the following:

- Birth volume identifier (BirthVolumeID), which is the object identifier for the volume
  in which the file was originally created

- Birth object identifier (BirthObjectID), which is the object identifier assigned to the
  file when it was created

- Domain identifier (DomainID), which is the object identifier for the domain in which
  the file was created

These values are also 16 bytes in length. If a file is moved within a volume or moved to a
new volume, it is assigned a new object identifier, but information about the original object
identifier assigned when the object was created can be retained using the birth object
identifier.

Object identifiers are used by several system services to uniquely identify files and the
volumes with which they are associated. The Distributed Link Tracking (DLT) Client service uses object identifiers to track linked files that are moved within an NTFS volume, to
another NTFS volume on the same computer, or to an NTFS volume on another computer.

Chapter 14

Any file used by the DLT Client service has an object identifier field set containing values for the object ID, birth volume ID, birth object ID, and domain ID. The actual field set looks like this:

```
Object ID :                         52eac013e3d34445334345453533ab3d
BirthVolume ID :                    a23bc3243a5a3452d32424332c32343d
BirthObject ID :                    52eac013e3d34445334345453533ab3d
Domain ID :                         00000000000000000000000000000000
```

Here, the file has a specific object ID, birth volume ID, and birth object ID. The domain ID isn't assigned, however, because this is not currently used. You can tell that the file is used by the DLT Client service because the birth volume ID and birth object ID have been assigned and these identifiers are used only by this service. Because the birth volume ID and birth object ID remain the same even if a file is moved, the DLT Client service uses these identifiers to find files no matter where they have been moved.

If you are trying to determine whether a file is used by the DLT Client service, you could use the FSUtil ObjectID command to see if the file has an object identifier field set. Type **fsutil objectid query** *FilePath* at the command prompt, where *FilePath* is the path to the file or folder you want to examine. If the file has an object identifier field set, it is displayed. If a file doesn't have an object identifier field set, an error message is displayed stating "The specified file has no object ID."

## Reparse points

On NTFS volumes, a file or folder can contain a reparse point. Reparse points are file system objects with special attribute tags that are used to extend the functionality in the I/O subsystem. When a program sets a reparse point, it stores an attribute tag as well as a data segment. The attribute tag identifies the purpose of the reparse point and details how the reparse point is to be used. The data segment provides any additional data needed during reparsing.

Reparse points are used for directory junction points and volume mount points. Directory junctions enable you to create a single local namespace using local folders, local volumes, and network shares. Mount points enable you to mount a local volume to an empty NTFS folder. Both directory junction points and volume mount points use reparse points to mark NTFS folders with surrogate names.

When a file or folder containing a reparse point used for a directory junction point or a volume mount point is read, the reparse point causes the path to be reparsed and a surrogate name to be substituted for the original name. For example, if you were to create a mount point with the file path C:\Data that is used to mount a hard disk drive, the reparse point is triggered whenever the file system opens C:\Data and points the file system to the volume you mounted in that folder. The actual attribute tag and data for the reparse point would look similar to the following:

```
Reparse Tag Value :   0xa0000003
Tag value: Microsoft
Tag value: Name Surrogate
Tag value: Mount Point
Substitute Name offset:    0
Substitute Name length:    98
Print Name offset:  100
Print Name Length:  0
Substitute Name:   \??\Volume{3796c3c1-5106-11d7-911c-806d6172696f}\

Reparse Data Length: 0x0000006e
Reparse Data:
0000: 00 00 62 00 64 00 00 00   5c 00 3f 00 3f 00 5c 00   ..b.d...\.?.?.\.
0010: 56 00 6f 00 6c 00 75 00   6d 00 65 00 7b 00 33 00   V.o.l.u.m.e.{.3.
0020: 37 00 39 00 36 00 63 00   33 00 63 00 31 00 2d 00   7.9.6.c.3.c.1.-.
0030: 35 00 31 00 30 00 36 00   2d 00 31 00 31 00 64 00   5.1.0.6.-.1.1.d.
0040: 37 00 2d 00 39 00 31 00   31 00 63 00 2d 00 38 00   7.-.9.1.1.c.-.8.
0050: 30 00 36 00 64 00 36 00   31 00 37 00 32 00 36 00   0.6.d.6.1.7.2.6.
0060: 39 00 36 00 66 00 7d 00   5c 00 00 00 00 00         9.6.f.}.\.....
```

The reparse attribute tag is defined by the first series of values, which identifies the reparse point as a Microsoft Name Surrogate Mount Point and specifies the surrogate name to be substituted for the original name. The reparse data follows the attribute tag values and, in this case, provides the fully expressed surrogate name.

### Examine reparse points

Using the FSUtil ReparsePoint command, you can examine reparse information associated with a file or folder. Type **fsutil reparsepoint query** *FilePath* at the command prompt, where *FilePath* is the path to the file or folder you want to examine.

Reparse points are also used by file-system filter drivers to mark files so that they are used with that driver. When NTFS opens a file associated with a file-system filter driver, it locates the driver and uses the filter to process the file as directed by the reparse information. Reparse points are used in this way to implement Remote Storage, which is discussed in the next section.

## Sparse files

Often scientific or other data collected through sampling is stored in large files that are primarily empty except for sparsely populated sections that contain the actual data. For example, a broad-spectrum signal recorded digitally from space might have only several minutes of audio for each hour of actual recording. In this case, a multiple-gigabyte audio file such as the one depicted in Figure 14-5 might have only a few gigabytes of meaningful information. Because there are large sections of empty space and limited areas of meaningful data, the file is said to be sparsely populated and can also be referred to as a *sparse file*.

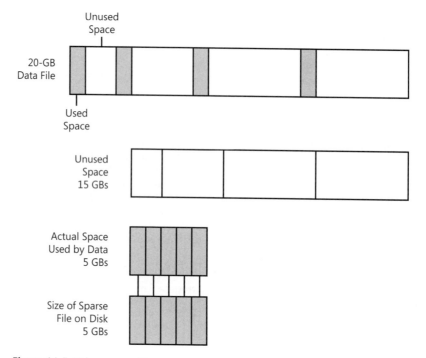

**Figure 14-5**  Using sparse files.

Stored normally, the file would use 20 GBs of space on the volume. If you mark the file as sparse, however, NTFS allocates space only for actual data and marks empty space as nonallocated. In other words, any meaningful or nonzero data is marked as allocated and written to disk, and any data composed of zeros is marked as nonallocated and is not explicitly written to disk. In this example, this means the file uses only 5 GBs of space, which is marked as allocated, and has nonallocated space of 15 GBs.

For nonallocated space, NTFS records only information about how much nonallocated space there is, and when you try to read data in this space, it returns zeros. This allows NTFS to store the file in the smallest amount of disk space possible while still being able to reconstruct the file's allocated and nonallocated space.

In theory, all this works great, but it is up to the actual program working with the sparse file to determine which data is meaningful and which isn't. Programs do this by explicitly specifying the data for which space should be allocated. In Windows Server 2012, several services use sparse files. One of these is the Indexing Service, which stores its catalogs as sparse files.

Using the FSUtil Sparse command, you can easily determine whether a file has the sparse attribute set. Type **fsutil sparse queryflag** *FilePath* at the command prompt, where *FilePath* is the path to the file you want to examine, such as

```
fsutil sparse queryflag c:\data\catalog.wci\00010002.ci
```

If the file has the sparse attribute, this command returns

```
This file is set as sparse
```

You can examine sparse files to determine where the byte ranges that contain meaningful (nonzero) data are located by using FSUtil Sparse as well. Type **fsutil sparse queryrange** *FilePath* at the command prompt, where *FilePath* is the path to the file you want to examine, such as

```
fsutil sparse queryrange c:\data\catalog.wci\00010002.ci
```

The output is the byte ranges of meaningful data within the file, such as

```
sparse range [0] [28672]
```

In this particular case, the output specifies that there's meaningful data at the start of the file to byte 28672. You can mark files as sparse as well. Type **fsutil sparse setflag** *FilePath* at the command prompt, where *FilePath* is the path to the file you want to mark as sparse.

## Transactional NTFS

Windows Server 2012 supports transactional NTFS and Self-Healing NTFS. Transactional NTFS allows file operations on an NTFS volume to be performed transactionally. This means programs can use a transaction to group sets of file and registry operations so that all of them succeed or none of them succeed. While a transaction is active, changes are not visible outside of the transaction. Changes are committed and written fully to disk only when a transaction is completed successfully. If a transaction fails or is incomplete, the program rolls back the transactional work to restore the file system to the state it was in prior to the transaction.

Transactions that span multiple volumes are coordinated by the Kernel Transaction Manager (KTM). The KTM supports the independent recovery of volumes if a transaction fails. The local resource manager for a volume maintains a separate transaction log and is responsible for maintaining threads for transactions separate from threads that perform the file work.

Chapter 14

Using the FSUtil Transaction command, you can easily determine transactional information. You can list currently running transactions by typing **fsutil transaction list** at the command prompt. You can display transactional information for a specific file by typing **fsutil transaction fileinfo *FilePath*** at the command prompt, where *FilePath* is the path to the file you want to examine, such as

```
fsutil transaction fileinfo c:\journal\ls-dts.mdb
```

Traditionally, you had to use the Check Disk tool to fix errors and inconsistencies in NTFS volumes on a disk. Because this process can disrupt the availability of Windows systems, Windows Server 2012 uses Self-Healing NTFS to protect file systems without having to use separate maintenance tools to fix problems. Because much of the self-healing process is enabled and performed automatically, you might need to manually perform volume maintenance only when you are notified by the operating system that a problem cannot be corrected automatically. If such an error occurs, Windows Server 2012 will notify you about the problem and provide possible solutions.

That said, with Windows 8 and Windows Server 2012 self-healing has been enhanced and extended to better work with Check Disk. These improvements allow you to use Check Disk to correct many types of inconsistencies and errors on live (online) volumes where Check Disk previously could perform these types of corrections only with offline volumes.

By using Self-Healing NTFS, the file system is always available and does not need to be corrected offline (in most cases). Self-Healing NTFS does the following:

- Attempts to preserve as much data as possible if corruption occurs, and reduces failed file-system mounting that previously could occur if a volume was known to have errors or inconsistencies. Self-Healing NTFS can repair a volume immediately so that it can be mounted.

- Reports changes made to the volume during repair through existing Chkdsk.exe mechanisms, directory notifications, and update sequence number (USN) journal entries. This feature also allows authorized users and administrators to monitor repair operations through status messages.

- Can recover a volume if the boot sector is readable but does not identify an NTFS volume. In this case, you must run an offline tool that repairs the boot sector and then allow Self-Healing NTFS to initiate recovery.

Although Self-Healing NTFS can correct many types of inconsistencies and errors automatically, some issues can be resolved only by running Check Disk (Chkdsk.exe) and allowing Check Disk to work with NTFS to resolve the problems, as discussed later in this chapter under "Automated disk maintenance."

# INSIDE OUT Understanding journaling and torn writes

NTFS relies on a journal of transactions to ensure consistency. NTFS updates metadata in place on the disk and uses a journal to track changes, which allows rollback to occur on errors and during recovery. Maintaining metadata in place offers advantages for read performance but can cause writes that are randomized. Updates to a disk can corrupt previously written metadata if power is lost at the time of the write. This is also known as a *torn write*.

# Using ReFS

Resilient File System (ReFS), the next-generation file system available with Windows Server 2012, is built on the foundations of NTFS and designed specifically for storage technologies. As such, many of its best features are available only when the file system is used with Microsoft's new storage technology called Storage Spaces. Although ReFS is not available for Windows desktop operating systems, at the time of this writing, Windows desktop operating systems can access data stored on ReFS volumes just as they do with data shared from NTFS volumes.

## ReFS features

As Table 14-5 shows, ReFS maintains compatibility with key aspects of NTFS, particularly when it comes to security features, such as access permissions and share permissions. However, ReFS diverges when it comes to extended features, including support for compression, encryption, and disk quotas. Additionally, you cannot boot from ReFS or use ReFS with removable media.

**TABLE 14-5  Comparing NTFS and ReFS**

| Feature | NTFS | ReFS |
| --- | --- | --- |
| Preserves and enforces access control lists (ACLs) | Yes | Yes |
| Preserves the case of file names | Yes | Yes |
| Supports ACLs | Yes | Yes |
| Supports BitLocker encryption | Yes | Yes |
| Supports booting from the file system | Yes | No |
| Supports case-sensitive file names | Yes | Yes |
| Supports disk quotas | Yes | No |
| Supports Encrypted File System | Yes | No |

| Feature | NTFS | ReFS |
|---|---|---|
| Supports extended attributes | Yes | No |
| Supports file-based compression | Yes | No |
| Supports hard links | Yes | No |
| Supports named streams | Yes | No |
| Supports object identifiers | Yes | No |
| Supports opening by FileID | Yes | Yes |
| Supports removable media | Yes | No |
| Supports reparse points | Yes | Yes |
| Supports shadow copies | Yes | Yes |
| Supports short names | Yes | No |
| Supports sparse files | Yes | Yes |
| Supports Unicode in file names | Yes | Yes |
| Supports user data transactions | Yes | No |
| Supports USN journal | Yes | Yes |
| Supports volume snapshots | Yes | Yes |

Not only are the transactional and self-healing features of NTFS important components of ReFS, but ReFS extends these features in several ways to allow for the automatic verification and online correction of data. ReFS avoids the possibility of torn writes by not writing metadata in place and optimizes for extreme scale by using scalable structures. To provide full end-to-end resilience, ReFS integrates fully with Storage Spaces. This integration does the following:

- Allows for large volume, file, and directory sizes.

- Provides data striping for performance and redundancy for fault tolerance.

- Provides disk scrubbing and salvage to provide online protection against latent disk errors.

- Ensures metadata integrity with checksums.

- Provides pooling and virtualizing storage with load balancing and sharing across servers.

- Provides optional user data integrity using integrity streams.

- Uses copy on write for improved disk update performance.

ReFS reuses the code that implements the file-system semantics of NTFS to ensure compatibility with existing file-system APIs. This ensures that the core of the file-system interface is the same and file operations—including read, write, open, change notification, and close—work in the exact same way. When working with ReFS, Windows maintains the in-memory file and volume state, enforces security, and maintains memory caching and the synchronization of file data in the exact same way as with NTFS.

## ReFS structures

Where NTFS and ReFS differ greatly is in the on-disk store engine underneath the file-system interface. The on-disk store engine is what implements the on-disk structures, such as the master file table (MFT). As discussed earlier in the chapter, the MFT represents files and directories by storing a file record of each file and folder on the volume along with pertinent volume information and details on the MFT itself.

The on-disk store engine for NTFS is NTFS.SYS. The on-disk store engine for ReFS is REFS .SYS. REFS.SYS was architected specifically for ReFS.

ReFS uses B+ tree structures to represent all information on the disk. B+ trees scale well from very small, compact structures to very large, multilevel structures, and using B+ trees simplifies the architecture and reduces the size of the code base.

The on-disk store engine uses enumerable tables with sets of key-value pairs. Access into most tables is provided by a unique object identifier, which is stored in a special object table that forms the base of the B+ tree.

The object table at the base of the B+ tree contains a disk offset and checksum for each unique object ID. This makes the object table the root of all structures within the file system. The entries in the object table refer to directories as well as global system metadata.

As shown in Figure 14-6, directories are represented as tables rooted within the object table. Each directory has an object identifier that acts as a key in the object table, and it has a corresponding value that provides a disk offset for where the table is found on the volume along with a checksum. The directory table contains rows that identify the files in the directory by file name and metadata. File metadata, in turn, identifies file attributes and their actual values. Among these values is a table of offset mappings to file extents. This table contains rows identifying file extents, paired with values that provide the disk offset location for each file extent and an optional checksum. Each file extent contains a section of the data for the parent file.

Chapter 14

# INSIDE OUT   Metadata checksums in ReFS

To ensure data integrity, checksums are used with all ReFS metadata. The checksum is stored at the level of a B+ tree page and stored independently of the page itself. Storing the checksum in this way ensures just about every form of disk corruption can be detected. Additionally, using optional integrity streams, checksums can be added to ensure the integrity of file contents. When integrity streams are enabled, ReFS uses an allocate-on-write approach, where file changes are always written to a location different from the original one. Allocate-on-write ensures pre-existing data is not lost due to a new write. The checksum is updated with the data write to ensure a consistently verifiable version of a file is always available, also ensuring errors and disk corruption can be detected. Because integrity streams reallocate blocks every time file content is changed, they're not appropriate for some applications, such as database systems. Why? Some applications maintain their own checksums of file content and are able to independently verify and correct data using the APIs available for Storage Spaces.

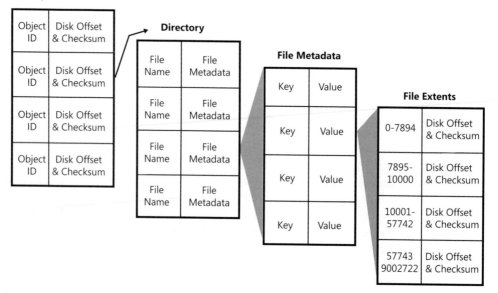

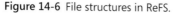

**Figure 14-6**  File structures in ReFS.

Put another way, directories are represented as tables in the file structure. Files are embedded within rows of a directory table and are themselves tables containing rows of file metadata. The file metadata also represented as a table has a row for each file attribute paired with the related value. Within the file metadata is an embedded table containing rows that identify file extents and provide offset locations to the extents on the volume along with optional checksums.

Other global structures are represented within the file system as tables as well. As an example, access control lists (ACLs) are represented as tables rooted within the object table.

## ReFS advantages

ReFS supports file sizes up to $2^{64}-1$ bytes, $2^{64}$ files in a directory, and $2^{64}$ directories on a volume, as well as volume sizes up to $2^{78}$ bytes using 16-KB cluster sizes (while Windows stack addressing allows $2^{64}$ bytes). As B+ trees scale with extreme efficiency, ReFS volumes can perform well whether they contain very large directories, very large files, or both. Disk space allocation is managed using a hierarchical allocator. This allocator represents free space as tables of free-space ranges. Each table has a different level of granularity so that large free-space ranges can be allocated as easily as medium or small free-space ranges, and all are relative to the volume size and available free space.

> ## Note
> ReFS supports large numbers of files and directories using 128-bit file identifiers. ReFS returns a 128-bit file identifier associated with an opened handle along with the 64-bit volume identifier. For backward compatibility, a 64-bit file identifier can be obtained from the API, but applications making incorrect calls into this API might crash.

> ## Important
> ReFS uses hierarchical allocators to find optimal allocation quickly. Having a hierarchical allocation system allows related metadata blocks to be placed closer to each other naturally. By consulting the proper layer of the allocator hierarchy, ReFS can quickly determine the best possible placement for small, medium, or large allocations.

One of the disadvantages of NTFS is that metadata is maintained in place, and this can result in writes that are randomized as well as torn writes. ReFS improves reliability and eliminates torn writes by using an allocate-on-write approach. Here, rather than updating metadata in-place, the file system writes it to a different location. This technique sometimes is also referred to as *shadow paging*. The transaction architecture, derived from NTFS, is built on top of the allocate-on-write framework to provide failure recovery.

ReFS allocates metadata using B+ tree structures that allow for fewer, larger reads and writes. It does this by combining related data, such as stream allocations, file attributes, file names, and directory pages. The approach offers read-write efficiencies whether hard disk drives or solid-state drives are used.

ReFS and Storage Spaces were architected to work together. Using mirroring or disk striping with parity, Storage Spaces can safeguard data against disk failures by maintaining copies of data on multiple disks. Whether you are using NTFS or ReFS, these multiple copies of data allow Storage Spaces to correct read failures by reading alternate copies of data, to correct write failures by reallocating data transparently, and to correct complete media loss on read/write as well. Where Storage Spaces gain efficiencies with ReFS is when it comes to detecting data corruption and lost and misdirected writes. Here, ReFS can detect metadata corruption and lost and misdirected writes using its checksums and then interface with Storage Spaces to read all the available copies of metadata and choose the correct one by validating the checksum. Next, ReFS instructs Storage Spaces to fix the bad metadata using the good copies of the metadata. The error detection and correction happens transparently. When integrity streams are enabled for files, this automatic error detection and correction process is applied to each individual extent of a file as well.

> ### Important
>
> There is a small CPU overhead for computing checksums and a small additional overhead for storing updated checksums with new data. That said, ReFS uses checksums to detect data corruption and log related events that can help you identify the corruption. Redundant Storage Spaces can correct corruption detected by ReFS by using good copies of data to repair bad copies of data.

## ReFS integrity streams, data scrubbing, and salvage

ReFS supports two types of data streams: conventional streams and integrity streams. Conventional streams behave identically to NTFS streams but might have metadata associated with them that is integrity protected. Integrity streams are streams that are integrity protected, meaning data is checksummed and updates to data are handled using copy-on-write.

With ReFS, you need to keep in mind that integrity is an attribute that can be applied to files and directories. When a file or directory has the integrity attribute (FILE_ATTRIBUTE_INTEGRITY_STREAM), it uses integrity streams to protect against data corruption. Only Storage Spaces with redundancy have integrity streams enabled by default.

The integrity attribute is inheritable. When you enable the integrity attribute on a directory, the attribute is inherited by all files and directories created in the directory. Because of this, if you enable the integrity attribute on the root directory of a volume, you can ensure every file and directory on the volume uses integrity streams by default.

You can enable integrity streams on the root directory of a volume when you format it. Use the following command syntax:

```
format /fs:refs /i:enable Volume
```

Here, *Volume* is the drive designator for the volume to format, such as

```
format /fs:refs /i:enable m:
```

For empty files, the integrity attribute can be set and unset. For nonempty files, the integrity attribute can be removed only by moving the file to a file system that doesn't support integrity, such as NTFS.

ReFS safeguards against data loss due to parts of a volume becoming corrupted over time by periodically scrubbing all metadata and integrity stream data. Data is scrubbed by reading all the redundant copies and validating their corrections using checksums. If checksums do not match, bad copies are repaired using good copies. Typically, this automatic process occurs only with Storage Spaces that have redundancy enabled.

In the event that metadata or data corruption cannot be automatically repaired, ReFS performs a salvage operation to remove the corrupt metadata or data from the namespace. The salvage operation ensures nonrepairable corruption cannot adversely affect noncorrupt data. As an example, a corrupt file or directory cannot be opened or deleted by the file system. By removing the corrupt file or directory, ReFS ensures that an administrator can recover the file or directory from backup or have an application re-create it. When ReFS is running on top of redundant Storage Spaces with integrity streams, an automatic error-detection and correction process, applied to each individual extent of a file, can recover file and directory data.

Chapter 14

# INSIDE OUT ReFS and Storage Spaces

Note that when ReFS is running on top of Storage Spaces, bad sectors detected by the disk subsystem are corrected by Storage Spaces. When ReFS is running on top of redundant Storage Spaces, other types of data corruption get detected by ReFS and corrected by Storage Spaces. With parity spaces, parity is used to recompute original data. With mirrored spaces, the mirror is used to recover the data. The entire process, from marking bad sectors (which are not used again) to allocating new blocks and copying the reconstructed data to these new blocks happens transparently and automatically.

ReFS can heal B+ trees using its data-scrubbing processes. Here, it scavenges for bad elements in the B+ trees. ReFS also stores a copy of the boot block that can help a system recover from a corrupt boot block.

Integrity can be enabled when the system is not running on Storage Spaces. When integrity is enabled and ReFS detects a checksum mismatch, ReFS logs an event and fails the read operation by default. If you don't want the read operation to fail, you can configure ReFS to continue with the read operation. A related event will be logged regardless.

# Using file-based compression

You can use file-based compression to reduce the number of bits and bytes in files so that they use less space on a disk. The Windows operating system supports two types of compression: NTFS compression, which is a built-in feature of NTFS, and compressed (zipped) folders, which is an additional feature of Windows available on any type of volume. ReFS does not support NTFS compression.

## NTFS compression

Windows allows you to enable compression when you format a volume using NTFS. When a drive is compressed, all files and folders stored on the drive are automatically compressed when they are created. This compression is transparent to users, who can open and work with compressed files and folders just as they do with regular files and folders. Behind the scenes, Windows decompresses the file or folder when it is opened and compresses it again when it is closed. Although this can decrease a computer's performance, it saves space on the disk because compressed files and folders use less space.

You can turn on compression after formatting volumes as well or, if desired, turn on compression only for specific files and folders. After you compress a folder, any new files added or copied to the folder are compressed automatically. If you move a compressed file to a folder on the same volume, it remains compressed. If you move a compressed file to a folder on a different volume, it inherits the compression attribute of the folder.

Moving uncompressed files to compressed folders affects their compression attribute as well. If you move an uncompressed file from a different drive to a compressed drive or folder, the file is compressed. However, if you move an uncompressed file to a compressed folder on the same NTFS drive, the file isn't compressed. Finally, if you move a compressed file to a FAT16, FAT32, exFAT, or ReFS volume, the file is uncompressed because NTFS compression is not supported.

To compress or uncompress a drive, follow these steps:

1.  Press and hold or right-click the drive that you want to compress or uncompress in File Explorer or in the Disk Management Volume List view, and then select Properties. This displays the disk's Properties dialog box, as shown in Figure 14-7.

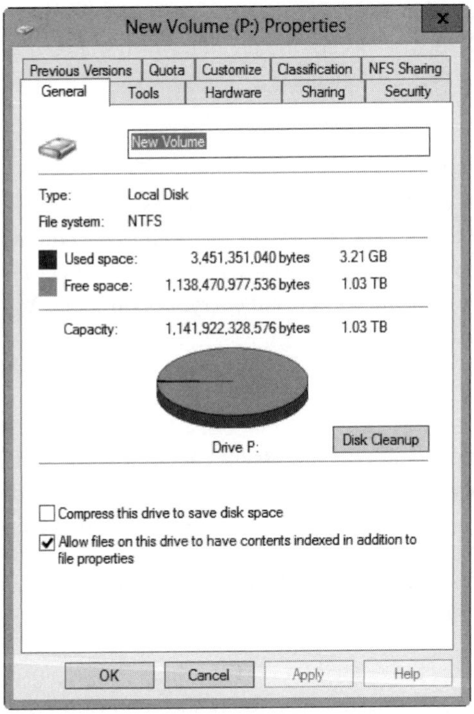

**Figure 14-7**  You can compress entire volumes or perform selective compression for specific files and folders.

2.  Select or clear the Compress This Drive To Save Disk Space check box as appropriate. When you tap or click OK, the Confirm Attribute Changes dialog box shown in Figure 14-8 is displayed.

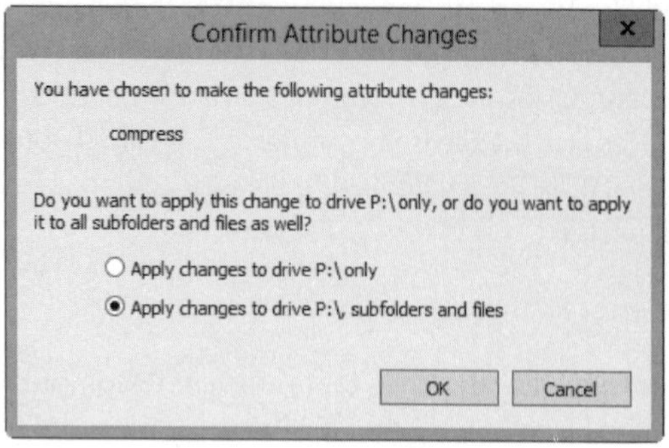

**Confirm Attribute Changes** ✕

You have chosen to make the following attribute changes:

compress

Do you want to apply this change to drive P:\ only, or do you want to apply it to all subfolders and files as well?

○ Apply changes to drive P:\ only

⦿ Apply changes to drive P:\, subfolders and files

OK       Cancel

**Figure 14-8**  Choose a compression option.

3.  If you want to apply changes only to the root folder of the disk, select Apply Changes To Drive *X* Only. Otherwise, accept the default, which will compress the entire contents of the disk. Tap or click OK.

## CAUTION

Although Windows Server 2012 will let you compress system volumes, this is not recommended because the operating system will need to decompress and compress system files each time they are opened, which can seriously affect server performance. Additionally, you can't use compression and encryption together. You can use one feature or the other, but not both.

You can selectively compress and uncompress files and folders as well. The advantage here is that this affects only a part of a disk, such as a folder and its subfolders, rather than the entire disk. To compress or uncompress a file or folder, follow these steps:

1.  In File Explorer, press and hold or right-click the file or folder that you want to compress or uncompress, and then select Properties.

2.  On the General tab of the related Properties dialog box, tap or click Advanced. This displays the Advanced Attributes dialog box shown in Figure 14-9. Select or clear the Compress Contents To Save Disk Space check box as appropriate. Tap or click OK twice.

**Figure 14-9** Use the Advanced Attributes dialog box to compress the file or folder.

3. If you are changing the compression attributes of a folder with subfolders, the Confirm Attribute Changes dialog box is displayed. If you want to apply the changes only to the files in the folder and not files in subfolders of the folder, select Apply Changes To *X* Only. Otherwise, accept the default, which will apply the changes to the folder, its subfolders, and files. Tap or click OK.

Windows Server 2012 also provides command-line utilities for compressing and uncompressing your data. The compression utility is called Compact (Compact.exe). The decompression utility is called Expand (Expand.exe).

You can use Compact to quickly determine whether files in a directory are compressed. At the command line, change to the directory you want to examine and enter **compact** without any additional parameters. If you want to check the directory and all subdirectories, enter **compact /s**. The output will list the compression status and compression ratio on every file, and the final summary details will tell you exactly how many files and directories were examined and found to be compressed, such as

```
Of 15435 files within 822 directories
0 are compressed and 15435 are no compressed.
2,411,539,448 total bytes of data are stored in 2,411,539,448 bytes.
The compression ratio is 1.0 to 1.
```

## Compressed (zipped) folders

Compressed (zipped) folders are another option for compressing files and folders. When you compress data using this technique, you use zip compression technology to reduce the number of bits and bytes in files and folders so that they use less space on a disk.

Compressed (zipped) folders are identified with a zipper on the folder icon and are saved with the .zip file extension.

Compressed (zipped) folders have several advantages over NTFS compression. Because zip technology is an extension of the operating system rather than the file system, compressed (zipped) folders can be used on any type of volume. Zipped folders can be password protected to safeguard their contents and can be sent by email. They can also be transferred using File Transfer Protocol (FTP), Hypertext Transfer Protocol (HTTP), or other protocols. An added benefit of zipped folders is that some programs can be run directly from compressed folders without having to be decompressed. You can also open files directly from zipped folders.

You can create a zipped folder by selecting a file, folder, or a group of files and folders in File Explorer, pressing and holding or right-clicking, pointing to Send To, and tapping or clicking Compressed (Zipped) Folder. The zipped folder is named automatically by using the file name of the last item selected and adding the .zip extension. If you double-tap or double-click a zipped folder in File Explorer, you can access and work with its contents. As shown in Figure 14-10, the zipped folder's contents are listed according to file name, type, and date. The file information also shows the packed file size, original file size, and compression ratio. Double-tapping or double-clicking a program in a zipped folder runs it (as long as it doesn't require access to other files). Double-tapping or double-clicking a file in a zipped folder opens it for viewing or editing.

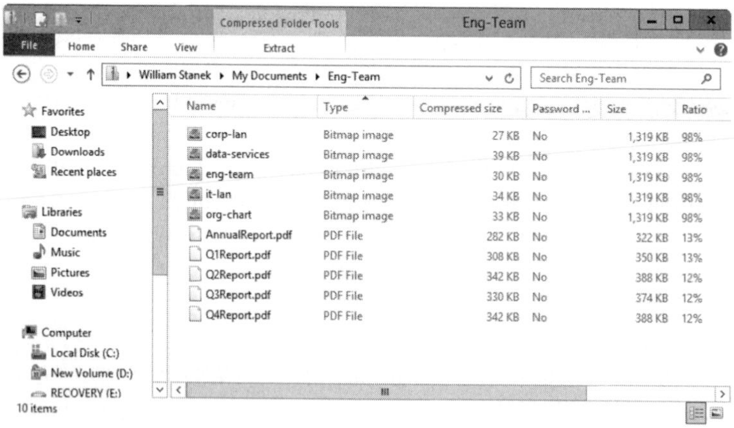

**Figure 14-10** Compressed (zipped) folders can be accessed and used like other folders.

While you're working with a zipped folder, you can perform tasks similar to those you can do with regular folders. You can do the following:

- Add other files, programs, or folders to the zipped folder by dragging them to it.

- Copy a file in the zipped folder, and paste it into a different folder.

- Remove a file from the zipped folder using the Cut command so that you can paste it into a different folder.

- Delete a file or folder by selecting it and tapping or clicking Delete.

You also have the option to perform additional tasks, which are unique to zipped folders. Press and hold or right-click and then choose Extract All to start the Extraction Wizard, which can be used to extract all the files in the zipped folder and copy them to a new location.

# Managing disk quotas

Even with the large disk drives available today, you'll often find that hard-disk space is at a premium, and this is where disk quotas come in handy. Disk quotas are a built-in feature of NTFS that help you manage and limit disk-space usage.

## How quota management works

Using disk quotas, you can monitor and control the amount of disk space people who access folders and disks can use. Without quota management, it is hard to monitor the amount of space being used by individual users and even harder to control the total amount of space they can use. I refer to monitoring and controlling separately because there's a very important difference between monitoring disk-space usage and controlling it—and the disk quota system allows you to perform these tasks separately or together. You can, in fact, do the following:

- Configure the disk quota system to monitor disk-space usage only, allowing administrators to check disk-space usage manually

- Configure the disk quota system to monitor disk-space usage and generate warnings when users exceed predefined usage levels

- Configure the disk quota system to monitor disk-space usage, generate warnings when users exceed predefined usage levels, and enforce the limits by denying disk space to users who exceed the quota limit

Your organization's culture will probably play a major role in the disk quota technique you use. In some organizations, the culture is such that it is acceptable to monitor space usage and periodically notify users that they are over recommended limits, but it wouldn't be well received if administrators enforced controls that limited disk-space usage to specific amounts. In other organizations, especially larger organizations where there might be hundreds or thousands of employees on the network, it can make sense to have some controls in place and users might be more understanding of specific controls. Controls at some point become a matter of necessity to help ensure that the administrative staff can keep up with the disk-space needs of the organization.

Disk quotas are configured on a per-volume basis. When you enable disk quotas, all users who store data on a volume will be affected by the quota. You can set exceptions for individual users as well that either set new limits or remove the limits all together. As users create files and folders on a volume, an ownership flag is applied that says that this particular user owns the file or folder. Thus, if a user creates a file or folder on a volume that user is the owner of, the file or folder and the space used count toward the user's quota limit. However, because each volume is managed separately, there is no way to set a specific limit for all volumes on a server or across the enterprise.

> **Note**
> For NTFS compressed files and sparse files, the space usage reported can reflect the total space of files rather than the actual space the files use. This happens because the quota system reads the total space used by the file rather than its reduced file size.

Ownership of files and folders can change in several scenarios. If a user creates a copy of a file owned by someone else, the copy is owned by the user who created it. This occurs because a file is created when the copy is made. File and folder ownership can also change when files are restored from backup. This can happen if you restore the files to a volume other than the one the files were created on and copy the files over to the original volume. Here, during the copy operation, the administrator becomes the owner of the files. A workaround for this is to restore files and folders to a different location on the same volume and then move the files and folders rather than copying them. When you move files and folders from one location to another on the same volume, the original ownership information is retained.

Administrators can be designated as the owner of files in other ways as well, such as when they install the operating system or application software. To ensure that administrators can always install programs, restore data, and perform other administrative tasks, members of the Administrators group don't have a quota limit as a general rule. This is true even when you enforce disk quotas for all users. In fact, for the Administrators group, the only type of quota you can set is a warning level that warns administrators when they've used more than a set amount of space on a volume. When you think about it, this makes a lot of sense—you don't want to get into a situation where administrators can't recover the system because of space limitations.

That said, you can apply quotas to individual users—even those who are members of the Administrators group. You do this by creating a separate quota entry for each user. The only account that cannot be restricted in this way is the built-in Administrator account. If you try to set a limit on the Administrator account, the limit is not applied.

Finally, note that all space used on a volume counts toward the disk quota—even space used in the Recycle Bin. Thus, if a user who is over the limit deletes files to get under the limit, the disk quota might still give warnings or, if quotas are enforced, the user still might not be able to write files to the volume. To resolve this issue, the user would need to delete files and then empty the Recycle Bin.

## Configuring disk quotas

By default, disk quotas are disabled. If you want to use disk quotas, you must enable quota management for each volume on which you want to use disk quotas. You can enable disk quotas on any NTFS volume that has a drive letter or a mount point. Before you config- ure disk quotas, think carefully about the limit and warning levels. Set values that make the most sense given the number of users that store data on the volume and the size of the volume. For optimal performance of the volume, you won't want to get in a situation where all or nearly all of the disk space is allocated. For optimal user happiness, you want to ensure the warning and limit levels are adequate so that the average user can store the necessary data to perform job duties. Quota limits and warning levels aren't "one size fits all" solutions either. Engineers and graphic designers can have very different space needs from a typical user. In the best situations, you configure network shares so that different groups of users have access to different volumes, and these volumes are sized to meet the typical requirements of a particular group.

In some organizations, I've seen administrators set very low quota limits and warning levels on data shares. The idea behind this was that the administrators wanted users to save most of their data on their workstations and put only files that needed to be shared on the data shares. I discourage this approach for two reasons. Low quota limits and warning levels frustrate users—you don't want frustrated users; you want happy users. Second, you should be encouraging users to store more of their important files on central file servers, not less. Central file servers should be a part of regular enterprisewide backup routines, and backing up data safeguards it from loss. In addition, with the Volume Shadow Copy Service, shadow copies of files on shared folders can be created automatically, allowing users to perform point-in-time file recovery without needing help from administrators.

> **Note**
> If you used the DirQuota command-line utility previously for managing disk quotas, note that this tool has been deprecated in Windows Server 2012 and is subject to removal in subsequent releases of the operating system.

Chapter 14

To enable disk quotas on an NTFS volume, follow these steps:

1. In Computer Management, expand Storage and then select Disk Management. In the details pane, press and hold or right-click the volume on which you want to enable quotas and then select Properties.

2. On the Quota tab, tap or click Show Quota Settings. In the Quota Settings dialog box, select the Enable Quota Management check box, as shown in Figure 14-11.

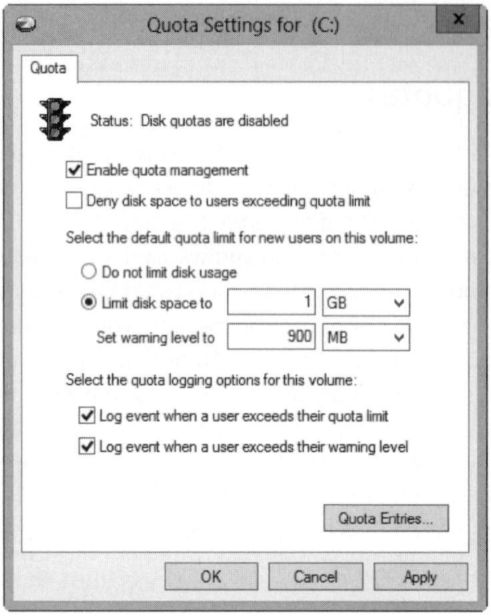

**Figure 14-11** Enable quota management on the volume, and then configure the disk quota settings.

3. Define a default disk quota limit for all users by choosing Limit Disk Space To and then using the fields provided to set a limit in KB, MB, GB, TB, PB, or EB. Afterward, use the Set Warning Level To field to set the default warning limit. In most cases, you'll want the disk quota warning limit to be 90 to 95 percent of the disk quota limit. This should create good separation between when warnings occur and when the limit is reached.

4. To prevent users from going over the disk quota limit, select the Deny Disk Space To Users Exceeding Quota Limit check box. This sets a physical limitation for users that will prevent them from writing to the volume after the limit is reached.

5. NTFS sends warnings to users when they reach a warning level or limit. To ensure that you have a record of these warnings, you can configure quota-logging options. Select the Log Event check boxes as appropriate.

6. Tap or click OK. If the quota system isn't currently enabled, you'll see a prompt asking you to enable the quota system. Tap or click OK to allow Windows Server 2012 to rescan the volume and update the disk usage statistics. Keep in mind that actions might be taken against users who exceed the current limit or warning levels, which can include preventing additional writing to the volume, notifying users the next time they try to access the volume that they've exceeded a warning level or have reached a limit, and logging applicable events in the Application log.

## Customizing quota entries for individual users

After you enable disk quotas, the configuration is set for and applies to all users who store data on the volume. The only exception, as noted previously, is for members of the Administrators group. The default disk quotas don't apply to these users. If you want to set a specific quota limit or warning level for a member of the Administrators group, you can do this by creating a custom quota entry for that particular user account. You can also create custom quota entries for users who have special requirements or special limitations.

To view and work with quota entries access Disk Management, press and hold or right-click the volume on which you enabled quotas, and then select Properties. In the Properties dialog box for the disk, tap or click the Quota tab and then tap or click Quota Entries. You'll then see a list of quota entries for everyone who has ever stored data on the volume, as shown in Figure 14-12. The entries show the following information:

- **Status**  The status of the disk entries. Normal status is OK. If a user has reached a warning level, the status is Warning. If a user is at or above the quota limit, the status is Above Limit.

- **Name**  The display name of the user account.

- **Logon Name**  The logon name and domain (if applicable).

- **Amount Used**  The amount of disk space used by the user.

- **Quota Limit**  The quota limit set for the user.

- **Warning Level**  The warning level set for the user.

- **Percent Used**  The percentage of disk space used toward the limit.

Chapter 14

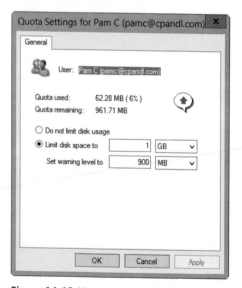

**Figure 14-12** Any existing quota entries are shown.

Quota entries get on the list in one of two ways: either automatically if a user has ever stored data on the volume or by an administrator creating a custom entry for a user. You can customize any of these entries—even the ones automatically created—by double-tapping or double-clicking them, which displays the Quota Settings dialog box shown in Figure 14-13, and selecting the appropriate options either to remove the disk quota limits or set new ones.

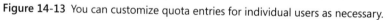

**Figure 14-13** You can customize quota entries for individual users as necessary.

> **Note**
>
> You can't create quota entries for groups. The only group entry that is allowed is the one for the Administrators account, which is created automatically.

If a user doesn't have an entry in the Quota Entries dialog box, it means that user has not yet saved files to the volume. You can still create a custom entry for the user if you want. To do this, choose Quota, New Quota Entry. This displays the Select Users dialog box shown in Figure 14-14. Use this dialog box to find the user account you want to work with. Type the name of the user account or part of the name, and tap or click Check Names. If multiple names match the value you entered, you'll see a list of names and will be able to choose the one you want to use. Otherwise, the name will be filled in for you, and you can tap or click OK to display the Add New Quota Entry dialog box, which has the same options as the Quota Settings dialog box shown in Figure 14-13.

## Use locations to access user accounts from other domains

**B**y default, the Select Users dialog box is set to work with users from your logon domain. If you want to add a user account from another domain, tap or click Locations to display the Locations dialog box. Then either select the entire directory or the specific domain in which the account is located, and tap or click OK.

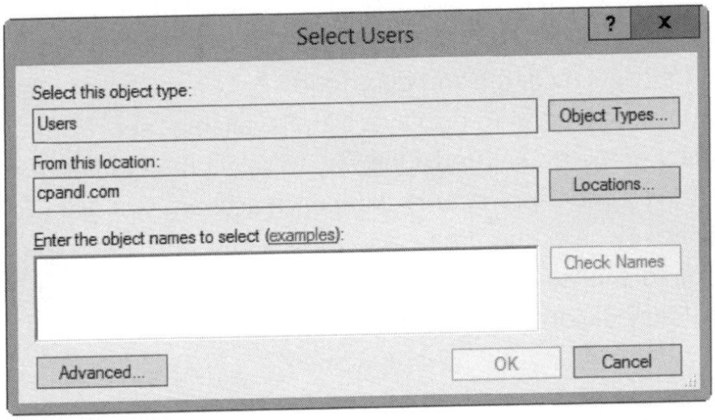

**Figure 14-14** Type the name of the user account or part of the name, and tap or click Check Names.

In the Quota Entries dialog box, there are a couple of tricks you can use to add or manage multiple quota entries at once. If you want to add identical quota entries for multiple users, you can do this by choosing Quota, New Quota Entry. This displays the Select Users dialog box. Tap or click Advanced to display the advanced Select Users dialog box, as shown in Figure 14-15.

Chapter 14

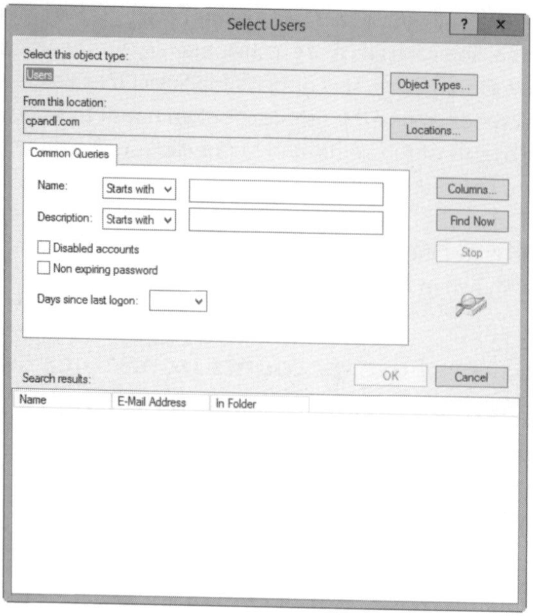

**Figure 14-15** The advanced Select Users dialog box has additional options.

You can now search for users by name and description or by tapping or clicking Find Now without entering any search criteria to display a list of available users from the current location. You can select any of the users listed. One way to select multiple user accounts is by holding down the Ctrl key and tapping or clicking each account you want to select or by holding down the Shift key, selecting the first account name, and then tapping or clicking the last account name to choose a range of accounts. Tap or click OK twice, and then use the Add New Quota Entry dialog box to configure the quota options for all the selected users.

To manage multiple quota entries simultaneously, access the Quota Entries dialog box and then select the entries by holding down the Ctrl key and tapping or clicking each entry you want to select or by holding down the Shift key, selecting the first entry, and then tapping or clicking the last entry to choose a range of entries. Afterward, press and hold or right-click one of the selected entries, and then choose Properties. You'll then be able to configure quota options for all the selected entries at once.

## Managing disk quotas after configuration

Users are notified that they have reached a warning level or quota limit when they access the volume on which you configured disk quotas. As an administrator, you'll want to check for quota violations periodically, and there are several ways you can do this. One way is to access Disk Management, press and hold or right-click the volume that you want to check on, and then select Properties. In the Properties dialog box for the disk, tap or click the Quota tab and then tap or click the Quota Entries button. You can then check the current disk usage of users and see whether there are any quota violations. You can also copy selected entries to the Clipboard by pressing Ctrl+C and then pasting them into other applications, such as Microsoft Excel, using Ctrl+V to help you create reports or lists of disk-space usage.

You can check quota entries from the command line as well. Type **fsutil quota query** *DriveDesignator* at the command prompt, where *DriveDesignator* is the drive letter of the volume followed by a colon, such as D:. If disk quotas are enabled on the volume, you'll then get a summary of the disk quota settings on the volume, as follows:

```
FileSystemControlFlags          =      0x00000031
    Quotas are tracked and enforced on this volume
    Logging enable for quota limits and threshold
    The quota values are up to date

Default Quota Threshold         =      0x0000000038400000
Default Quota Limit             =      0x0000000040000000

SID Name                        =      CPANDL\edwardh (User)
Change time                     =      Saturday, April 26, 2014
Quota Used                      =      528164252
Quota Threshold                 =      943718400
Quota Limit                     =      1073741824

SID Name                        =      CPANDL\mollyp (User)
Change time                     =      Monday, April 28, 2014
Quota Used                      =      627384965
Quota Threshold                 =      943718400
Quota Limit                     =      1073741824
```

In this example, disk quotas are tracked and enforced on the volume, logging is enabled for both quota limits, and the warning levels and the disk quota values are current. In addition, the default warning limit (listed as the quota threshold) is set to 900 MBs (0 × 038400000 bytes) and the default quota limit is set to 1 GB (0 × 040000000 bytes).

The disk quota summary is followed by the individual disk quota entries for each user who has stored data on the volume or has a custom entry regardless of whether the user has ever written data to the volume. The entries show the following information:

- **SID Name**   The logon name and domain of user accounts, or the name of a built-in or well-known group that has a quota entry

- **Change Time**   The last time the quota entry was changed or updated

- **Quota Used**   The amount of space used in bytes

- **Quota Threshold**   The current warning level set for the user in bytes

- **Quota Limit**   The current quota limit set for the user in bytes

When you configure disk quotas, you also have the option of logging two types of events in the system logs: one for when a user exceeds the quota limit, and another for when a user exceeds the warning level. By default, quota violations are written to the system log once an hour, so if you check the logs periodically, you can see events related to any users who have disk quota violations. It's much easier to check for quota violations from the command line, however. Simply type **fsutil quota violations** at the command prompt, and the FSUtil Quota command checks the system and application event logs for quota violations.

> **Note**
>
> Wondering why FSUtil Quota Violations checks the system and application logs? Well, in some cases, quota violations for programs running under user accounts are logged in the application log rather than the system log. To ensure all quota violations are checked for, FSUtil Quota Violations checks both logs.

If there are no quota violations found, the output is similar to the following:

```
Searching in System Event Log...
Searching in Application Event Log...
No quota violations detected
```

If there are quota violations, the output shows the event information related to each violation. In the following example, a user reached the warning level (listed as the quota threshold):

```
Searching in System Event Log...
**** A user hit their quota threshold ! ****
    Event ID : 0x40040024
    EventType : Information
    Event Category : 2
    Source : Ntfs
    User: CPANDL\harryt (User)
    Data: D:
Searching in Application Event Log...
```

As you can see, the output shows you the event ID, type, category, and source. It also shows the user who violated the disk quota settings and the volume on which the violation occurred.

# INSIDE OUT  You can change the notification interval for quota violations

As mentioned previously, quota violations are written to the event logs once an hour by default. You can check or change this behavior using the FSUtil Behavior command. Keep in mind, however, that any changes you make apply to all volumes on the system that use disk quotas. To check the notification interval, type **fsutil behavior query quotanotify**. If the notification interval has been set by you or another administrator, the notification interval is shown in seconds. To set the notification interval, type **fsutil behavior set quotanotify** *Interval*, where *Interval* is the notification interval you want to set expressed as the number of seconds. For example, if you want to receive less-frequent notifications, you might want to set the notification interval to 7200 seconds (2 hours), and you would do this by typing **fsutil behavior set quotanotify 7200**.

## Exporting and importing quota entries

If you want to use the same quotas on more than one NTFS volume, you can do this by exporting the quota entries from one volume and importing them on another volume. When you import quota entries, if there isn't a quota entry for the user already, a quota entry will be created. If a user already has a quota entry on the volume, you'll be asked if you want to overwrite it.

To export and import quota entries, access Disk Management, press and hold or right-click the volume on which you want to enable quotas, and then select Properties. In the Properties dialog box for the disk, tap or click the Quota tab and then tap or click the Quota Entries button. You'll then see the Quota Entries dialog box. Select Export from the Quota menu. This displays the Export Quota Settings dialog box.

Use the Save In selection list to choose the save location for the file containing the quota settings, and then set a name for the file using the File Name field. Afterward, tap or click Save.

Next, access the Quota Entries dialog box for the drive on which you want to import settings. Select Import on the Quota menu. Then, in the Import Quota Settings dialog box, select the quota settings file that you saved previously. Tap or click Open.

If prompted about whether you want to overwrite an existing entry, tap or click Yes to replace an existing entry or tap or click No to keep the existing entry. Select Do This For All Quota Entries prior to tapping or clicking Yes or No to use the same option for all existing entries.

# Automated disk maintenance

Windows Server 2012 performs periodic maintenance daily. Automated maintenance is built on the Windows Diagnostics framework. Windows Server 2012 performs periodic routine maintenance daily at 3:00 A.M. By default, as long as the computer is running on AC power and the operating system is idle, this maintenance is performed in the background. If the computer isn't idle or is running on battery, maintenance starts the next time the computer is running on AC power and the operating system is idle. Because maintenance runs only when the operating system is idle, maintenance is allowed to run in the background for up to three days. This allows Windows to complete complex maintenance tasks automatically.

Maintenance tasks include software updates, security scanning, system diagnostics, Check Disk activity, and disk optimization. File data is stored in clusters, and the Windows operating system uses a file table to determine where a file begins and on which clusters it is stored. With FAT, the file-allocation table defines the starting cluster of each file in the file system and has pointers to each cluster used by a file. With NTFS, an MFT is used. If a file's data can't fit within a single record in this table, clusters belonging to the file are referenced using VCNs that map to starting LCNs on the disk. If a file's pointer or mapping is lost, you might not be able to access the file. Errors can also occur for pointers or mappings that relate to the file tables themselves and to the pointers or mappings for folders.

## Preventing disk-integrity problems

FAT tries to prevent disk-integrity problems by maintaining a duplicate file allocation table that can be used to recover the primary file allocation table if it becomes corrupted. Beyond this, however, FAT doesn't do much else to ensure disk integrity. NTFS, on the other hand, has several mechanisms for preventing and correcting disk-integrity problems automatically. NTFS stores a partial duplicate of the MFT, which can be used for failure recovery. NTFS also stores a persistent history of all changes made to files on the volume in a log file, and the log file can be used to recover NTFS metadata files, regular data files, and folders. What these file-structure recovery mechanisms all have in common is that they are automatic and you, as an administrator, don't need to do anything to ensure that these disk housekeeping tasks are performed. These mechanisms aren't perfect, however, and errors can occur.

The most common errors relate to the following areas:

- Internal errors in a file's structure

- Free space being marked as allocated

- Allocated space being marked as free

- Partially or improperly written security descriptors

- Unreadable disk sectors not marked as bad

Windows Server 2012 proactively scans volumes for these types of errors as part of automated maintenance. Windows does this using Check Disk. Although automated maintenance triggers the disk scan, the process of calling and managing Check Disk is handled by a separate task. In Task Scheduler, you'll find the ProactiveScan task in the scheduler library under Microsoft\Windows\Chkdsk, and you can get detailed run information on the task's History tab.

## INSIDE OUT   How automated maintenance works

On servers running Windows Server 2012, automated maintenance runs daily at 3:00 A.M. You can manage the maintenance schedule in Action Center. One way to open Action Center is to type **action center** in the Settings Search box and then press Enter.

In Action Center, expand the Maintenance panel to view related details and options, including the last run time. In Task Scheduler, the following tasks are triggered by automated maintenance:

- **Microsoft\Windows\Application Experience**   Collects and uploads Application Telemetry information, if opted in to the Microsoft Customer Experience Improvement Program (CEIP)

- **Microsoft\Windows\ChkDsk**   Performs a proactive scan of disks

- **Microsoft\Windows\Defrag**   Performs a scan and fragmentation analysis of disks

- **Microsoft\Windows\Device Setup**   Performs metadata refresh of devices

- **Microsoft\Windows\PI**   Updates secure boot variables

- **Microsoft\Windows\Power Efficiency Diagnostics**   Analyzes power usage

- **Microsoft\Windows\Registry**   Performs a backup of the registry

- **Microsoft\Windows\Servicing**   Cleans up components

- **Microsoft\Windows\Shell**   Keeps the search index up to date

- **Microsoft\Windows\Time Synchronization**   Maintains date and time synchronization

- **Microsoft\Windows\Windows Error Reporting**   Processes queued error reports

Chapter 14

Although automated maintenance is scheduled to run daily at 3:00 A.M., maintenance runs only when the server is on AC power and the operating system is idle. Because of that, you might find that the maintenance ran at a different time. If automated maintenance hasn't run for a while, you can tap or click Start Maintenance to manually start the automated maintenance (with the same requirements regarding being idle and on AC power apply). You can change the daily run time for automated maintenance by tapping or clicking Change Maintenance Settings, selecting a new run hour, such as 12:00 A.M., and then tapping or clicking OK.

Check Disk works on FAT, FAT32, and NTFS volumes and primarily looks for inconsistencies in the file system and its related metadata. It locates errors by comparing the volume bitmap to the disk sectors assigned to files. For files, Check Disk looks at structural integrity, but it won't check for or attempt to repair corrupted data within files that appear to be structurally intact.

However, the way Check Disk performs scan, analysis, and repair has changed. With Windows Server 2012, Check Disk performs either enhanced scan and repair automatically or the legacy scan and repair available with earlier releases of Windows. Whether an enhanced scan and repair is used or a legacy scan and repair depends on the type of volume:

- When you use Check Disk with NTFS volumes, Check Disk performs the enhanced online scan and analysis. This means the scan and analysis process typically does not require taking the volume offline or prevent the volume from being used until a repair is required.

- When you use Check Disk with FAT, FAT32, or exFAT, Windows Server 2012 uses the legacy scan and repair process. This means the scan and repair process typically requires taking an active volume offline, which prevents the volume from being used.

Because the enhanced approach is new, that's what I'll focus on. When you use Check Disk with NTFS volumes, Check Disk performs an online scan and analysis of the volumes. Check Disk writes information about any detected corruptions in the $corrupt system file. When the scan and analysis process is complete, Check Disk can repair detected corruptions by taking the volume offline temporarily and fixing them.

Storing the corruption information and then repairing the volume while it is dismounted allows Windows to rapidly repair volumes. It also allows users to keep using the disk while a scan is being performed. Typically, offline repair takes only a few seconds, compared to what otherwise would have been hours for very large volumes using the legacy scan and repair technique.

Keep in mind that unmounting a volume for repair invalidates all open file handles. With the boot/system volume, the repairs are performed the next time you start the computer. As with other volumes, Check Disk uses the detected corruptions, already stored in the $corrupt system file, to rapidly repair the boot/system volume during startup. Keep in mind that Check Disk isn't needed on ReFS volumes (and won't run on ReFS volumes either).

## Running Check Disk interactively

You can run Check Disk interactively as well. With NTFS volumes, one way to do this is to use Server Manager. In Server Manager, select the File And Storage Services node and then select the related Volumes subnode. As shown in Figure 14-16, you'll then see the available volumes for each server added for management. Next, press and hold or right-click a volume and then select Scan File System For Errors. In the Scan File System For Errors dialog box, tap or click Scan Now. Server Manager displays the percentage of scanning completed. If errors are found, you're notified and can press and hold or right-click the volume and then select Repair File System Errors to resolve them. As discussed earlier, the way the repair process works depends on whether you are working with a boot/system volume or a nonsystem volume.

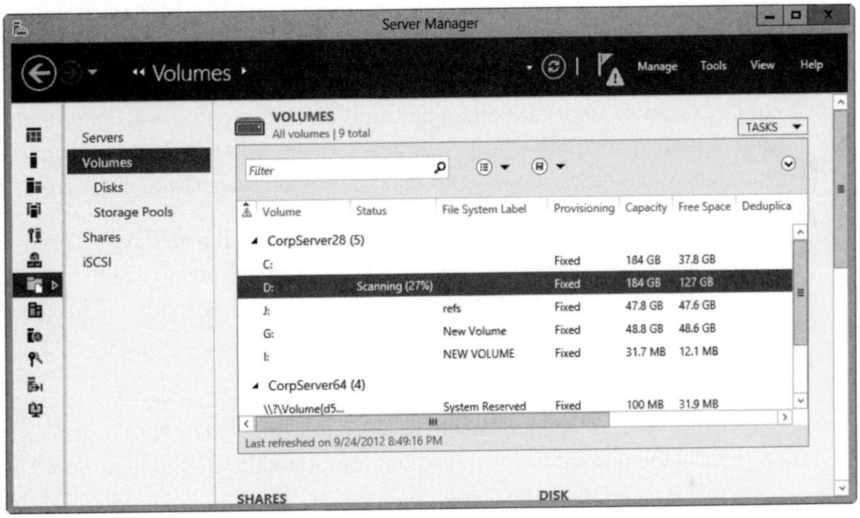

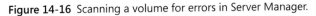

**Figure 14-16** Scanning a volume for errors in Server Manager.

Another way to check NTFS volumes is to start Check Disk by using either File Explorer or Disk Management. Press and hold or right-click the volume, and choose Properties. On the Tools tab of the Properties dialog box, tap or click Check to display the Error Checking dialog box. When you tap or click Scan Drive, the Error Checking dialog box displays the approximate scan and analysis time remaining, as shown in Figure 14-17. If errors are found, you're notified with additional options for repairing them.

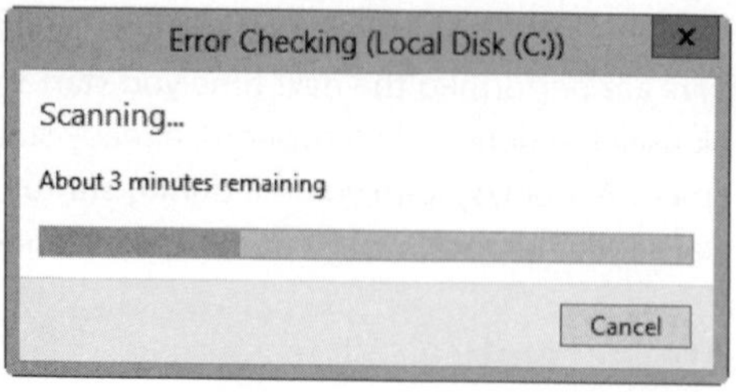

**Figure 14-17**  Check a disk for errors.

With FAT, FAT32, and exFAT volumes, Windows uses the legacy Check Disk, which might require offline scan and repair. Start Check Disk by using either File Explorer or Disk Management. Press and hold or right-click the volume, and choose Properties. On the Tools tab of the Properties dialog box, tap or click Check to display the Error Checking dialog box. When you tap or click Scan And Repair Drive, Check Disk begins scanning the volume.

Check Disk can also be run at the command line using ChkDsk (Chkdsk.exe). The key advantage of using the command-line version is that you get a detailed report of the analysis and repair operations as detailed in "Analyzing FAT volumes by using ChkDsk" and "Analyzing NTFS volumes by using ChkDsk" later in this chapter.

You can run ChkDsk in analysis mode at the command line by entering **chkdsk /scan** followed by the drive designator. For example, if you want to analyze the D drive, you enter **chkdsk /scan d:**. Check Disk then performs an analysis of the disk and returns a status message regarding any problems it encounters. Unless you specify further options, Check Disk won't repair problems, however. To repair errors on drive E, you enter **chkdsk /spotfix d:**.

Because fixing the volume requires exclusive access to the volume, you can't repair an active volume. For system volumes, you'll see a prompt asking whether you would like to schedule the volume for the repair the next time the computer is started. Type **Y** to schedule the repair or **N** to cancel the repair.

For nonsystem volumes, you'll see a prompt asking whether you would like to force a dismount of the volume for the repair. Type **Y** to proceed or **N** to cancel the dismount. If you cancel the dismount, you'll see the prompt asking whether you would like to schedule the repair the next time the computer is started. Here, type **Y** to schedule the repair or **N** to cancel the repair.

You can't run Check Disk with both the *scan* and *spotfix* options. The reason for this is that the scan and repair tasks are now independent of each other.

The complete syntax for ChkDsk is as follows:

```
CHKDSK [volume[[path]filename]] [/F] [/V] [/R] [/X] [/I] [/C] [/B]
    [/L[:size]] [/scan] [/forceofflinefix] [/perf] [/spotfix]
    [/sdcleanup] [/offlinescanandfix]
```

Table 14-6 summarizes the options and parameters available and their uses.

**TABLE 14-6 Command-line parameters for ChkDsk**

| Option/ Parameter | Description |
| --- | --- |
| *Volume* | Sets the volume to work with. |
| *[path]/Filename* | On FAT/FAT32, specifies files to check for fragmentation. |
| **Legacy Check Disk Options** | |
| */B* | Tells ChkDsk to re-evaluate any clusters marked as bad on the volume. (*/R* is implied when you use this parameter.) |
| */C* | On NTFS only, tells ChkDsk not to check for cycles within the folder structure. A cycle is a very rarely occurring type of error in which a directory contains a pointer to itself, causing an infinite loop. |
| */F* | Tells ChkDsk to analyze the disk and fix any errors noted. |
| */I* | On NTFS only, tells ChkDsk to perform a minimum check of indexes. |
| */L[:Size]* | On NTFS only, changes the transaction log file size. The default size is 4096 KBs, which is sufficient most of the time. |
| */R* | Tells ChkDsk to analyze the disk and fix any errors noted and also to check for bad sectors. Any bad sectors found are marked as bad. (*/F* is implied when you use this parameter.) |
| */V* | On FAT/FAT32, lists the full path of every file on the volume. On NTFS, displays cleanup messages related to fixing file-system errors or other discrepancies. |
| */X* | Forces the volume to dismount if necessary. All open file handles to the volume would then be invalid. (*/F* is implied when you use this parameter.) |
| **Enhanced Check Disk Options** | |
| */forceofflinefix* | Bypasses all online repair, and queues errors for offline repair. It must be used with */scan*. |
| */offlinescanandfix* | Performs an offline scan and fix of the volume. |
| */perf* | Performs the scan as fast as possible by using more system resources. |
| */scan* | Performs an online scan of the volume (the default). Errors detected during the scan are added to the $corrupt system file. |
| */sdcleanup* | Cleans up unneeded security descriptor data. It implies */F* (with legacy scan and repair). |
| */spotfix* | Allows certain types of errors to be repaired online (the default). |

Chapter 14

## Analyzing FAT volumes by using ChkDsk

When you run ChkDsk, you can get an analysis report. For FAT volumes, a disk analysis report looks like this:

```
The type of the file system is FAT32.
Volume NEW VOLUME created 9/24/2014 9:10 PM
Volume Serial Number is AAAD-2188
Windows is verifying files and folders...
File and folder verification is complete.

Windows has scanned the file system and found no problems.
No further action is required.
    5,107,712 KB total disk space.
           64 KB in 16 hidden files.
          168 KB in 42 folders.
    1,026,340 KB in 145 files.
    4,081,136 KB are available.

        4,096 bytes in each allocation unit.
    1,276,928 total allocation units on disk.
    1,020,284 allocation units available on disk.
```

Here, ChkDsk examines each record in the file allocation table for consistency. It lists all the file and folder records in use and determines the starting cluster for each using the file allocation table. It checks each file and notes any discrepancies in the output. Any clusters that were marked as in use by files or folders but that weren't actually in use are noted, and during repair the clusters can be marked as available. Other discrepancies noted in the output can be fixed during repair as well.

## Analyzing NTFS volumes by using ChkDsk

Disk analysis for NTFS volumes is performed in three stages, and ChkDsk reports its progress during each stage as shown in this sample report:

```
The type of the file system is NTFS.

Stage 1: Examining basic file system structure ...

Stage 2: Examining file name linkage ...

Stage 3: Examining security descriptors ...

Windows has scanned the file system and found no problems.
No further action is required.
```

During the first stage of analysis, ChkDsk verifies file structures. This means ChkDsk examines each file's record in the MFT for consistency. It examines all the file records in use and determines which clusters the file records are stored in, and then it compares this with the volume's cluster bitmap stored in the $Bitmap metadata file. Any discrepancies are tracked. For example, any clusters that were marked as in use by files but that weren't actually in use are tracked, and during repair the clusters can be marked as available.

During the second stage of analysis, ChkDsk verifies directory structure by examining file-name linking, starting with the volume's root directory index, which is stored in the $Metadata file. ChkDsk examines index records, making sure that each index record corresponds to an actual directory on the disk and that each file that is supposed to be in a directory is in the directory. It also checks to see whether there are files that have an MFT record but that don't actually exist in any directory, and during repair these lost files can be recovered.

During the third stage of the analysis, ChkDsk verifies the consistency of security descriptors for each file and directory object on the volume using the $Secure metadata file. It does this by validating that the security descriptors work. It doesn't actually check to see if the users or groups assigned in the security descriptors exist.

## Repairing volumes and marking bad sectors by using ChkDsk

Running ChkDsk with the /scan option performs an analysis of the volume only. If problems are found, ChkDsk will repair them only if you run ChkDsk again using the /spotfix option.

That said, you can scan a volume and force offline repair using /scan and /forceofflinefix, as shown in this example:

```
chkdsk /scan /forceofflinefix
```

You can use /perf with /scan to perform a scan faster. The /perf option allocates more system resources to the scan, which could possibly affect server performance but allows a scan to be completed more quickly.

Legacy repair options remain available as well, but they might require offline scan as well as offline repair in some instances. You can use the /X parameter to force a volume to dismount if necessary or the /R parameter to locate bad sectors, and each implies the /F parameter. If you use the /R parameter, ChkDsk will perform an additional step in the analysis and repair that involves checking each sector on the disk to make sure it can be read from and written to correctly. If it finds a bad sector, ChkDsk will mark it so that data won't be written to that sector. If the sector was part of a cluster that was being used, ChkDsk will move the good data in that cluster to a new cluster.

The data in the bad sector can be recovered only if there's redundant data from which to copy it. The bad sector won't be used again, so at least it won't cause problems in the future. Checking each sector on a disk is a time-intensive process—and one that you won't perform often. More typically, you'll use **ChkDsk /F** to check for and repair common errors.

> **Note**
>
> With legacy scan and repair, you can force ChkDsk to reevaluate clusters it has marked as bad using the /B parameter. This parameter implies the /R parameter. Here, ChkDsk will again attempt to determine whether it can read from and write to the cluster correctly. If the cluster can be read from and written to correctly, ChkDsk marks the cluster as good so that it can be used by the disk subsystem.

# Automated optimization of disks

As files are created, modified, and moved, fragmentation can occur both within the volume's allocation table and on the volume itself. This happens because files are written to clusters on disk as they are used. The file system uses the first clusters available when writing new data, so as you modify files, different parts of files can end up in different areas of the disk. If you delete a file, an area of the disk is made available, but it might not be big enough to store the next file that is created and, as a result, part of a new file might get written to this newly freed area and part of it might get written somewhere else on the disk.

Although the file system doesn't care if the file data is on contiguous clusters or spread out across the disk, the fact that data is in different areas of the disk can slow down read/write operations. This means it will take longer than usual to open and save files. It also makes it more difficult to recover files in case of serious disk error. Windows Server 2012 provides a tool for defragmenting volumes called the Optimize Drives utility. Unlike Check Disk, which cannot check and repair the operating system volume while it is in use, Optimize Drives can, in most cases, perform online defragmentation of any volume, including the operating-system volume.

## Preventing fragmentation of disks

Windows Server 2012 analyzes fragmentation and optimizes volumes as part of automated maintenance. Windows does this using the Optimize Drives utility. Although automated maintenance triggers the disk analysis, the process of calling and managing Optimize Drives is handled by a separate task. In Task Scheduler, you'll find the ScheduledDefrag task in the scheduler library under Microsoft\Windows\Defrag, and you can get detailed run information on the task's History tab.

Automatic analysis and optimization of disks can occur while the disks are online, so long as the computer is on AC power and the operating system is running but otherwise idle. By default, disk optimization is a weekly task rather than a daily task—and there's a good reason for this. Normally, you need only to periodically optimize a server's disks, and optimization once a week is sufficient in most cases. That said, the more frequently data is updated on drives, the more often disks should be optimized.

Windows automatically performs cyclic pickup defragmentation. With this feature, when a scheduled defragmentation pass is stopped and rerun, the computer automatically picks up the next unfinished volume in line to be defragmented. Although nonsystem disks can be rapidly analyzed and optimized, it can take significantly longer to optimize system disks online.

You can control the approximate start time for the analysis and optimization of disks by changing the automated maintenance start time. Windows Server also notifies you if three consecutive runs are missed. All internal drives and certain external drives are optimized automatically as part of the regular schedule, as are new drives you connect to the server.

With manual optimization, Optimize Drives performs an online analysis of volumes and then reports the percentage of fragmentation. If defragmentation is needed, you can then elect to perform online defragmentation. System and boot volumes can be defragmented online as well, and Optimize Drives can be used with FAT, FAT32, exFAT, NTFS, and ReFS volumes.

You can configure and manage automated defragmentation by following these steps:

1. In Computer Management, select the Storage node and then the Disk Management node. Press and hold or right-click a drive, and then tap or click Properties.

2. On the Tools tab, tap or click Optimize. In the Optimize Drives dialog box, shown in Figure 14-18, note the last run time and status of each volume. The status shows the percentage of fragmentation. A volume that needs optimization is listed as "Needs Optimization." Otherwise, the volume status is listed as OK.

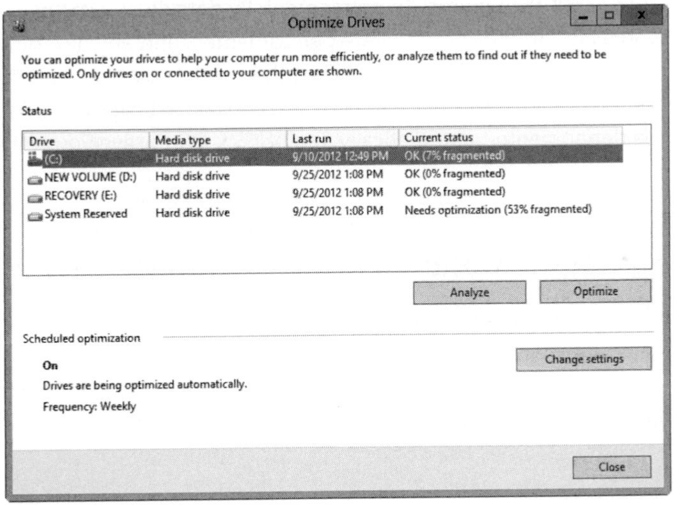

**Figure 14-18** Review the status of each volume.

3. Under Scheduled Optimization, note the scheduled optimization settings, which indicate whether automated optimization is enabled and provide the run frequency. If you want to change how optimization works, tap or click Change Settings. This displays the dialog box shown in Figure 14-19. To cancel automated defragmentation, clear the Run On A Schedule check box. To enable automated defragmentation, select Run On A Schedule.

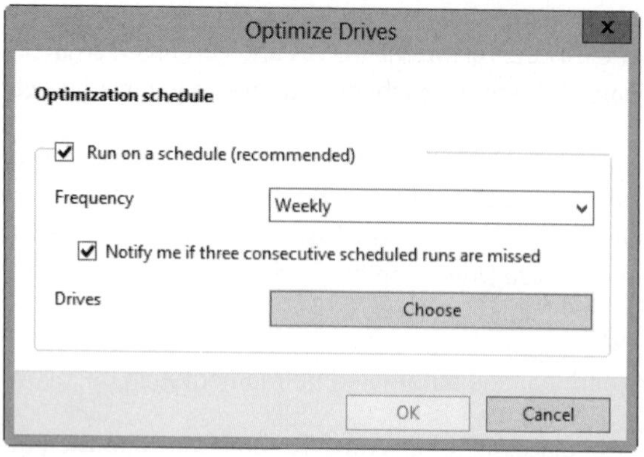

**Figure 14-19**  Set the schedule for automated optimization of volumes.

4. The default run frequency is set as shown. In the Frequency list, you can choose Daily, Weekly, or Monthly as the run schedule. If you don't want to be notified about missed runs, clear the Notify Me check box.

5. If you want to manage which disks are defragmented, tap or click Choose and then select the volumes to defragment. By default, all disks installed within or connected to the computer are defragmented, and any new disks are defrag-mented automatically as well. Select the check boxes for disks that should be defragmented automatically, and clear the check boxes for disks that should not be defragmented automatically. Tap or click OK to save your settings.

6. Tap or click OK, and then tap or click Close.

## Fixing fragmentation by using Optimize Drives

Using Optimize Drives, you can check for and correct volume fragmentation problems on FAT, FAT32, and NTFS volumes. The areas checked for fragmentation include the volume, files, folders, page file (if one exists on the volume), and the MFT. You also can defragment volumes with cluster sizes greater than 4 KBs.

You can run the graphical version of Optimize Drives using either File Explorer or Computer Management. In File Explorer, press and hold or right-click the volume and choose Properties. On the Tools tab of the Properties dialog box, tap or click Optimize to display the Optimize Drives dialog box. In Computer Management, select the Storage node and then the Disk Management node. Press and hold or right-click a drive and then select Properties. On the Tools tab, tap or click Optimize.

In the Optimize Drives dialog box, select a disk and then tap or click Analyze. Optimize Drives then analyzes the disk to determine whether it needs to be defragmented. If so, it recommends that you defragment at this point. If a disk needs to be defragmented, select the disk and then tap or click Optimize. Depending on the size of the disk, defragmentation can take several hours. You can tap or click Stop Operation at any time to stop defragmentation.

> **Note**
>
> Optimize Drives needs 10 to 15 percent free space to defragment a disk completely. Optimize Drives uses this space as a sorting area for file fragments. If a volume has less free space, Optimize Drives will only partially defragment it. By default, Optimize Drives performs partial defragmentation by attempting to consolidate only fragments smaller than 64 MBs.

Optimize Drives can also be run at the command line using Defrag (Defrag.exe). You can run Optimize Drives in analysis mode at the command line by typing **defrag /a** followed by the drive designator. For example, if you want to analyze the fragmentation of the D drive, you type **defrag /a d:**. To analyze and then defragment a volume if defragmentation is necessary, type **defrag** followed by the drive designator, such as **defrag d:**. No parameters are necessary (because the /d parameter is implied, which performs a traditional defrag).

You defrag multiple drives by providing the designator of each drive you want to defrag, such as

```
defrag /a c: d: g:
```

This specifies that you want to defrag C, D, and G drives. By default, Defrag runs with low priority and defrags each volume in turn. Here, that would mean the utility would defrag the C drive, then the D drive, and finally the G drive.

Defrag has several syntaxes. The syntax for analyzing volumes without defragmentation is

```
defrag volume(s) /a [/h] [/m] | [/u] [/v]
```

Chapter 14

Here, when you use /h or /m or both, you cannot use /u, /v, or both. The /h parameter allows you to run the defrag with normal priority, which gives the defrag task the same priority as most other processes and should speed up the defrag. The /m parameter allows Windows to defrag multiple volumes at the same time, in parallel rather than in a series. The /u parameter displays the defrag progress, and the /v parameter displays verbose output, which includes fragmentation statistics. Following this, you could defrag the C, D, and G drives in parallel at normal priority by entering

```
defrag c: d: g: /a /h /m
```

Analyze (/a) is one of several independent tasks that you can perform. Other independent tasks you can perform include traditional defrag (/d), optimization (/o), and free-space consolidation (/x). The syntax for all three variations is the same except for the primary task being performed. As an example, if defrag specifies that drives need to be optimized to reduce fragmentation, you use /o to do this. The syntax for optimizing fragmented drives is

```
defrag volume(s) /o [/h] [/m] | [/u] [/v]
```

The optimization process focuses on reduced file fragmentation. Over time, free space on a drive also can become fragmented. You can use the /x parameter to consolidate the free-space fragments, and the syntax is

```
defrag volume(s) /x [/h] [/m] | [/u] [/v]
```

> **Note**
> Thinly provisioned virtual disks (Storage Spaces, dynamic VHDs, SAN virtual disk) are the only type of disk that have their free space consolidated when optimized.

Rather than trying to remember all these syntaxes separately, I recommend focusing on the primary tasks you can perform: analysis (/a), traditional defrag (/d), optimization (/o), and free-space consolidation (/x). Then consider the additional options you might want to use, including either higher priority (/h) and multitasking (/m) or progress updates (/u) and verbose output (/v).

# INSIDE OUT Optimizing virtual disks

You optimize the internal structures of virtual disks using the standard optimization tasks, including analysis (/a), traditional defrag (/d), optimization (/o), and free-space consolidation (/x). That doesn't necessarily optimize the external structures from which virtual disks are constructed, however, and fragmentation in these external structures can affect virtual disk performance as much as fragmentation of internal structures.

The external structures from which virtual disks are constructed are referred to as *slabs*. A slab is simply an allocation unit or, put another way, a contiguous block of allocated space on the underlying physical disk. The performance of a virtual disk can be affected when there are too many small slabs, too many slabs spread out across the underlying physical disk, or both. You can attempt to consolidate slabs using the /k parameter. The syntax is

```
defrag volume(s) /k [/h] [/m] | [/u] [/v]
```

When you use the /k parameter, the /l parameter is implied. The /l parameter generates trim and unmap hints for sectors that were previously allocated to the virtual disk but are no longer used by the virtual disk. The trim and unmap hints are used by the underlying physical disk to recover unused space.

You can retrim a virtual disk without performing a slab consolidation. The syntax is

```
defrag volume(s) /l [/h] [/m] | [/u] [/v]
```

That said, when you optimize standard virtual disks (.vhd), Defrag will perform slab consolidation automatically as well but won't retrim automatically. When you optimize differential virtual disks or thinly provisioned virtual disks (Storage Spaces, dynamic VHDs, SAN virtual disk), Defrag doesn't perform slab consolidation automatically but does retrim automatically.

Table 14-7 summarizes Defrag options and parameters available and their uses. Note the /C and /E parameters. You use the /C parameter when you want to defrag all available volumes (and don't want to specify the volumes individually by drive designator). You use the /E parameter when you want to defrag all available volumes except those specified after the /E parameter. For example, if you wanted to defrag all available volumes except the D and G drives, you enter

```
defrag /d /e d: g:
```

**TABLE 14-7** **Command-line parameters for Defrag**

| Option/Parameter | Description |
| --- | --- |
| *Volume(s)* | Sets the volume or volumes to work with. |
| /A | Performs an analysis only of the specified volume or volumes. |
| /C | Used instead of a drive letter, telling Defrag to optimize all disks. |
| /D | Performs an analysis of the specified volume or volumes, followed by optimization, if required. |
| /E | Tells Defrag to optimize all disks except those specified after the parameter. |
| /H | Runs Defrag with higher priority, meaning normal priority instead of low priority. |
| /K | Performs slab consolidation and retrim of virtual disks. This applies to virtual disks only. |
| /L | Performs retrim of virtual disks. This applies to virtual disks only. |
| /M | Multitasks the optimization by running Defrag in parallel on each volume specified. |
| /O | Performs optimization of the specified volume or volumes, if fragmented. |
| /T | Tracks in-progress tasks on the specified volume or volumes. |
| /U | Provides progress updates on the screen. |
| /V | Displays verbose output containing fragmentation statistics. |
| /X | Performs free-space consolidation on the specified volume or volumes. |

## Understanding the fragmentation analysis

You can perform fragmentation analysis at the command line using the /a and /v parameters. The command-line report shows the summary of fragmentation. The summary looks like this:

```
Invoking analysis on (C:)...

Post Defragmentation Report:

        Volume Information:
                Volume size          = 183.99 GB
                Cluster size         = 4 KB
                Used space           = 146.14 GB
                Free space           = 37.85 GB

        Fragmentation:
                Total fragmented space   = 7%
                Average fragments per file = 1.09
```

```
        Movable files and folders   = 716750
        Unmovable files and folders = 20

    Files:
        Fragmented files            = 8265
        Total file fragments        = 61643

    Folders:
        Total folders               = 32654
        Fragmented folders          = 2274
        Total folder fragments      = 9690

    Free space:
        Free space count            = 2470
        Average free space size     = 15.64 MB
        Largest free space size     = 7.24 GB

    Master File Table (MFT):
        MFT size                    = 921.25 MB
        MFT record count            = 943359
        MFT usage                   = 100%
        Total MFT fragments         = 7

    Note: File fragments larger than 64MB are not included in the
fragmentation statistics.

    You do not need to defragment this volume.
```

The summary of the volume's configuration and space usage reports on the following areas:

- **Overall fragmentation**   Gives an overview of fragmentation showing the percentage of used space that is fragmented, the average number of fragments per file, the total number of files on the volume that are movable, and the total number of unmovable files. Ideally, you want the percentage of fragmentation to be 10 percent or less and the number of fragments per file to be as close to 1.00 as possible.

- **File fragmentation**   Gives an overview of file-level fragmentation showing how many files are fragmented and the total number of excess fragments.

- **Folder fragmentation**   Gives an overview of folder-level fragmentation showing the total number of folders on the volume, how many folders are fragmented, and the total number of excess fragments.

- **Free space fragmentation**   Gives an overview of fragmentation on a volume's unused space showing how much free space is available on the volume, the number of extents on which free space is located, the average amount of free space per extent, and the largest free-space extent.

Chapter 14

- **Master File Table (MFT) fragmentation**    For NTFS volumes only, gives an overview of fragmentation in the MFT, showing the current size of the MFT, the number of records it contains, the percentage of the MFT in use, and the total number of fragments in the MFT. In this example, the MFT has some fragmentation. But the real concern is that it is at 100 percent of its maximum size. Because of this, the MFT could become more fragmented over time—there is still 37.85 GBs of free space on the volume, and if it needs to grow it will grow into the free space.

If you run Defrag again using /o, Optimize Drives will set about cleaning up the drive to give optimal space usage. This won't clear up all fragmentation, but it will help so that disk space is used more efficiently. On a volume like the one shown with very little fragmentation, you won't really see performance improvements after defragmentation. However, if the fragmentation percentage were higher, performance improvements could be considerable.

With virtual disks, slab consolidation and retrim are used to optimize external structures. You can perform these tasks at the command line using the /k and /v parameters. The command-line report shows the summary of optimization. The summary looks like this:

```
Invoking slab consolidation on New Volume (I:)...

        Retrim:  100% complete.

        Slab consolidation: 100% complete.


The operation completed successfully.

Post Defragmentation Report:

        Volume Information:
                Volume size           = 126.99 GB
                Cluster size          = 4 KB
                Used space            = 102.06 GB
                Free space            = 24.93 GB

        Allocation Units:
                Slab count            = 4063
                Slab size             = 32 MB
                Slab alignment        = 31.00 MB
                In-use slabs          = 3266

        Slab Consolidation:
                Space efficiency      = 92%
                Potential purgable slabs  = 48
                Slabs pinned unmovable    = 704
                Successfully purged slabs = 36
                Recovered space           = 1152 MB
```

```
Retrim:
        Backed allocations          = 68
        Allocations trimmed         = 18
        Total space trimmed         = 539.82 MB
```

The summary reports on the following areas:

- **Volume Information**   Gives an overview of the volume showing its maximum volume size, cluster size, used space, and free space. Because you are optimizing external structures, free space in the volume doesn't affect whether you can consolidate slabs and retrim.

- **Allocation Units**   Gives an overview of the volume's allocation units showing the total number of slabs allocated to the volume, the size of the slabs, the slab alignment offset, and the number of in-use slabs. The difference between the total slab count and the in-use slab count represents the number of available slabs.

- **Slab Consolidation**   Gives an overview of the slab consolidation, showing how efficiently space is being used, the potentially purgable slabs remaining, the number of unmovable slabs, the number of successfully purged slabs, and then total space recovered. Ideally, after consolidating slabs, there will be a high level of space efficiency and relatively few potentially purgable slabs remaining.

- **Retrim**   Gives an overview of the underlying physical disk space recovered by trimming sectors that were previously allocated to the virtual disk but are no longer used by the virtual disk. It shows the number of allocations trimmed and the total space recovered.

# Managing storage spaces

Storage management abstracts storage volumes from the underlying physical layout, resulting in what can be considered as a three-layered architecture. In Layer 1, the layout of the physical disks is controlled by the storage subsystem with hardware-based RAID controlled by the storage subsystem to ensure data is redundant and recoverable in case of failure. In Layer 2, virtual disks created by the storage arrays are made available for allocation and servers can apply software-level RAID or other redundancy approaches to help protect against failure at the operating-system level. In Layer 3, the server creates volumes on the virtual disks and these volumes provide the usable file systems for file and data storage.

Put another way, storage-management hardware handles the architecture particulars for data redundancy and the portions of disks that are presented as usable disks. This means the layout of the physical disks is controlled by the storage subsystem instead of by the operating system. With the physical layout of disks (spindles) abstracted, a "disk" can be a

Chapter 14

logical reference to a portion of a storage subsystem (a virtual disk) or an actual physical disk. This means a disk simply becomes a unit of storage and volumes can be created to allocate space within disks for file systems.

Windows Server 2012 takes typical storage management a few steps further, allowing you to pool available space on disks so that units of storage (virtual disks) can be allocated from this pool on an as-needed basis. These units of storage, in turn, are apportioned with volumes to allocate space and create usable file systems. This pooled storage is referred to as *storage pools*, and the virtual disks created within a pool are referred to as *storage spaces*. Given a set of "disks" from the storage subsystem, you can create a single storage pool by allocating all the disks to the pool or create multiple storage pools by allocating disks separately to each pool.

In Windows Server 2012, the primary storage-management functions are enabled by the Storage Services role service, which is part of the File And Storage Services role. The core components of the Storage Services role service, which is installed by default on all servers, are what allow you to manage storage spaces and work with storage pools. They include

- Extensions for Server Manager that allow you to manage storage

- Windows Storage Management APIs for Windows PowerShell and Windows Management Instrumentation (WMI)

- Storage Management Provider (SMP) interfaces for Storage Spaces

- Pass-through API for extensibility, based on WMI

Together, these features allow you to use Server Manager and other compatible management applications, such as System Center 2012 Virtual Machine Manager with Service Pack 1 or later, to connect to and manage Serial Attached SCSI (SAS), USB, and Serial ATA (SATA) disks. These features also allow Server Manager and other compatible management applications to connect to and manage storage arrays and their RAID controllers using vendor-provided WMI-based provider transports, protocols, or both.

To add support for standards-based storage management, you'll want to add the Windows Standards-Based Storage Management feature to your file servers. This adds components and updates for working with standards-based volumes as implemented in the Storage Management Initiative Specification (SMI-S). Server Manager and other compatible management applications will then be able to connect to and manage storage arrays and their RAID controllers using vendor-provided SMI-S providers.

Seamless integration of storage-management applications with devices ensures flexibility and uniform management for

- Discovery and replication

- Thin provisioning

- Snapshot management

- Masking and unmasking

- Enumerating HBA ports

- Creating pools, virtual disks, and volumes

You can extend these storage-management capabilities in several ways. Cmdlets for Windows PowerShell enable scriptable management. Add the Data Deduplication role service if you want to enable data deduplication. Add the iSCSI Target Server and iSCSI Target Storage Provider role services if you want the server to host iSCSI virtual disks. Add the Data Center Bridging feature if you want to enforce bandwidth allocation for offloaded storage traffic.

> **Note**
> Virtual disks created as part of a storage pool are separate and distinct from iSCSI virtual disks. iSCSI virtual disks can be created on a server using Storage Spaces; they cannot, however, be used in a storage space.

## Using and configuring offloaded transfers

Windows Offloaded Data Transfer (ODX), included in Windows Server 2012, allows direct data transfer within or between data-storage devices. Bypassing host computers and transferring data within or between storage arrays ensures maximum efficiency. Not only does it maximize array throughput, it reduces resource usage on the host computers.

## Important

For an offloaded transfer within an array, the array's copy manager must support ODX. For transfers between arrays, the copy managers for both storage arrays must support cross-storage ODX and be from the same vendor. Storage arrays must be connected using either Internet Small Computer System Interface (iSCSI), Fibre Channel, Fibre Channel over Ethernet, or SAS. As you set out to use ODX, you should also note the default inactive timer value, the maximum token capacity, and the optimal transfer size of the copy managers used by storage arrays. The default inactive timer value specifies how long the copy manager waits to invalidate the idle token after the timer expiration. The maximum token capacity determines how many offload transfers can run simultaneously. The optimal transfer size tells Windows how to send Read/Write commands that are optimally sized for the storage arrays.

With traditional data transfers, data to be transferred is read from the storage through the source server and transferred over the network to the destination server before being written back to the storage through the destination server. This is very inefficient whether servers share storage or use storage from different storage arrays. ODX eliminates this inefficiency.

To see how ODX works at a high level, consider the following scenarios:

- FileServer1 and FileServer2 are running Windows Server 2008 R2, and they are connected to the same storage array from which the servers get their logical unit numbers (LUNs) for storage. You want to move a 2-TB data share from FileServer1 to FileServer2 and initiate the move on FileServer1, which handles the file transfer. Both FileServer1 and FileServer2 use system resources to manage the transfer, which takes several hours and uses a fair amount of CPU and memory resources.

- FileServer1 and FileServer2 are running Windows Server 2012, and they are connected to the same storage array from which the servers get their LUNs for storage. You want to move a 2-TB data share from FileServer1 to FileServer2 and initiate the move on FileServer1. FileServer1 offloads the data transfer to the storage array. Because you are moving data within the same array, the transfer is accomplished rapidly. Because the transfer is offloaded to the array, few CPU or memory resources are used on either FileServer1 or FileServer2.

- FileServer1 and FileServer2 are running Windows Server 2012, and they are connected to different storage arrays from which the servers get their LUNs for storage. You want to move a 2-TB data share from FileServer1 to FileServer2 and initiate the move on FileServer1. FileServer1 offloads the data transfer to its storage array, Array A, which handles the transfer to Array B. Because you are moving data between arrays, the transfer takes longer than moving data within an array. Because the transfer is offloaded, few CPU or memory resources are used on either FileServer1 or FileServer2.

Okay, so that's the top-level view of ODX. To dig deeper into how ODX actually works, let's look at how tokens are used. When an offload transfer is initiated, Windows uses tokens as point-in-time representations of the data being transferred. Instead of routing data through the host, the token is copied between the source server and the destination server. The source server then delivers the token to the source storage array, which performs the actual copy or move while providing status updates regarding the transfer. Step by step, the process looks like this:

1.  An application, user, or the operating system itself copies or moves data stored on an array. This initiates a transfer, which the operating system sees as a transfer request.

2.  The operating system translates this transfer request into an offloaded transfer and receives a token representing the data.

3.  After the token is copied between the source server and the destination server, the source server delivers the token to the source storage array.

4.  The source storage array performs the actual copy or move while providing status updates regarding the transfer.

5.  With MPIO, path failover is handled automatically. Here, Windows retries the offloaded transfer. If the retry also fails, Windows can initiate a cluster failover, if the server is part of a cluster.

6.  With clustering, cluster failover is handled automatically as well. Here, if the transfer was initiated by a cluster-aware application, the application can resume the offloaded transfer after failover.

7.  If the transfer can't be resumed or restarted after Multipath I/O (MPIO) path or cluster failover, Windows issues a LUN reset to the storage array. This ends the transfer and all related operations. Windows then returns an I/O failure.

With ODX, data transfers are offloaded when you copy or move data stored on an array and does so whether you use graphical tools, such as File Explorer, or command-line tools, such as XCOPY. You can verify ODX support by examining the file-system filter drivers that are attached to volumes. For each filter driver, query the registry to determine whether the filter driver has opted in to ODX support.

List the filter-system drivers for a particular volume by entering the following at an elevated PowerShell prompt:

```
fltmc instances -v Volume
```

Here, *Volume* is the drive designator of the volume to examine, such as

```
fltmc instances -v i:
```

Each filter is listed by name and should have a *SprtFtrs* value as well. If the supported features value is 3, the filter driver supports ODX. If this value is not 3, the filter driver doesn't support ODX and you need to obtain a different driver from the vendor.

If the *SprtFtrs* value isn't as expected, you also can go into the registry to confirm support. At an elevated PowerShell prompt, enter

```
get-itemproperty hklm:\system\currentcontrolset\services\filtername
-name "SupportedFeatures"
```

Here, *FilterName* is the name of the filter, as listed by Fltmc. Again, if the supported features value is 3, the filter driver supports ODX. If this value is not 3, the filter driver doesn't support ODX and you need to obtain a different driver from the vendor.

You can enable ODX support by entering the following at an elevated PowerShell prompt:

```
set-itemproperty hklm:\system\currentcontrolset\control\filesystem
-name "FilterSupportedFeaturesMode" -value 0
```

Disable ODX support by entering

```
set-itemproperty hklm:\system\currentcontrolset\control\filesystem
-name "FilterSupportedFeaturesMode" -value 1
```

## Working with available storage

In Server Manager, you select the File And Storage Services node to view and work with your storage volumes. As Figure 14-20 shows, the File And Storage Services node has multiple subnodes. The Volumes subnode lists allocated storage on each server according to how volumes are provisioned and how much free space each volume has. Volumes are listed regardless of whether the underlying disks are physical or virtual.

Press and hold or right-click a volume to display management options, including the following:

- **Configure Data Deduplication**   Allows you to enable and configure data deduplication for NTFS volumes. If the feature is enabled, you can then use this option to disable data deduplication as well.

- **Delete Volume**   Allows you to delete the volume. The space that was used is then marked as unallocated on the related disk.

- **Extend Volume**   Allows you to extend the volume to unallocated space of the related disk.

- **Format**   Allows you to create a new file system on the volume that overwrites the existing volume.

- **Manage Drive Letter And Access Paths**   Allows you to change the drive letter or access path associated with the volume.

- **New iSCSI Virtual Disk**   Allows you to create a new iSCSI virtual disk that is stored on the volume.

- **New Share**   Allows you to create new Server Message Block (SMB) or Network File System (NFS) shares on the volume.

- **Properties**   Displays information about the volume type, file system, health, capacity, used space, and free space. You also can use this option to set the volume label.rft.

- **Repair File System Errors**   Allows you to repair errors detected during an online scan of the file system.

- **Scan File System For Errors**   Allows you to perform an online scan of the file system. Although Windows attempts to repair any errors that are found, some errors can be corrected only by using a repair procedure.

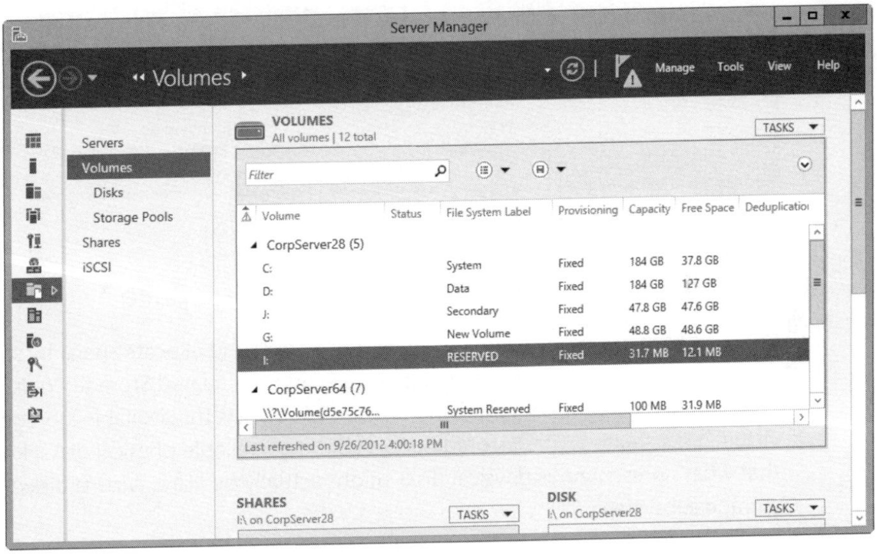

**Figure 14-20**  Viewing available storage volumes.

The Disks subnode, shown in Figure 14-21, lists the disks available to each server according to total capacity, unallocated space, partition style, subsystem, and bus type. Server Manager attempts to differentiate between physical disks and virtual disks by showing the virtual disk label (if one was provided) and the originating storage subsystem. Press and hold or right-click a disk to display management options, including the following:

- **Bring Online**   Allows you to take an offline disk and make it available for use.

- **Take Offline**   Allows you to take a disk offline so that it can no longer be used.

- **Reset Disk**   Allows you to completely reset the disk, which deletes all volumes on the disk and removes all available data on the disk.

- **New Volume**   Allows you to create a new volume on the disk.

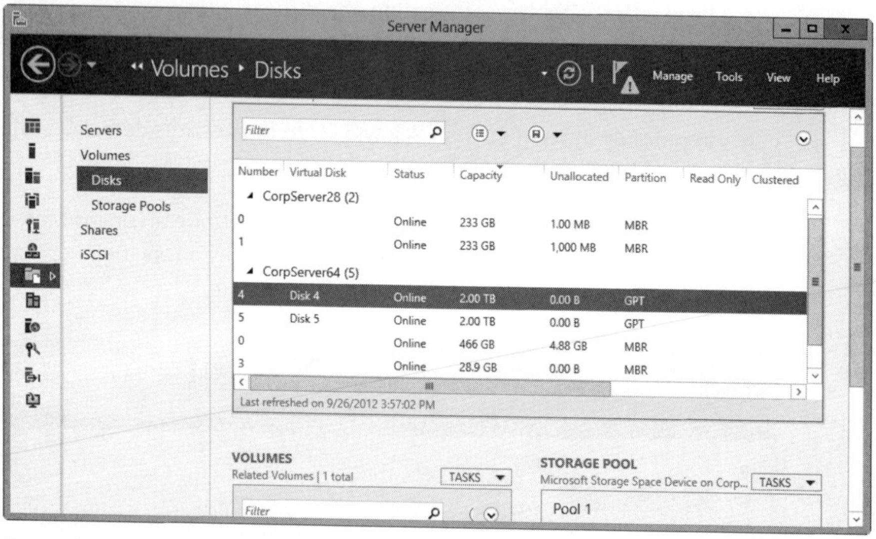

**Figure 14-21**  Viewing available disks and storage allocation.

## Creating storage pools and allocating space

In Server Manager, you can work with storage pools and allocate space by selecting the File And Storage Services node and then selecting the related Storage Pools subnode. The Storage Pools subnode, shown in Figure 14-22, lists the available storage pools, the virtual disks created within storage pools, and the available physical disks. Keep in mind that what's presented as physical disks might actually be LUNs (virtual disks) from a storage subsystem.

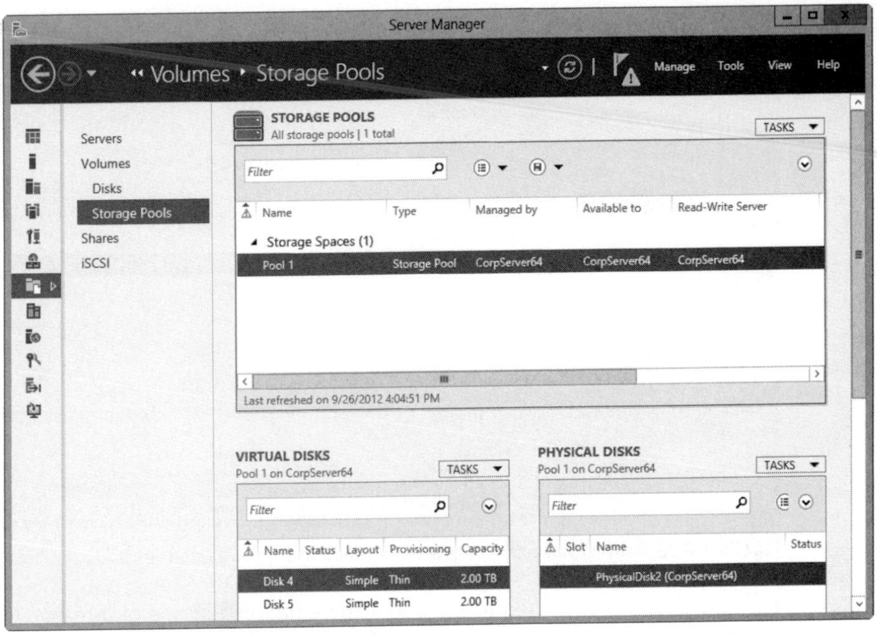

**Figure 14-22** Viewing available storage pools.

Working with storage pools is a multistep process:

1. You create storage pools to pool available space on one or more disks.

2. You allocate space from this pool to create one or more virtual disks.

3. You create one or more volumes on each virtual disk to allocate storage for file systems.

The sections that follow examine procedures related to each of these steps.

## Creating storage spaces

You can use storage pools to pool available space on disks so that units of storage (virtual disks) can be allocated from this pool. To create a storage pool, you must have at least one unused disk and a storage subsystem to manage it. This storage subsystem can be the one included with the Storage Spaces feature or a subsystem associated with attached storage.

As shown in Figure 14-23, each server that has disks that are unallocated but available to be assigned to a storage pool is listed as having a *primordial pool*. A primordial pool is simply a group of disks managed by and available to a specific server via a storage subsystem. A server must have a primordial pool from which disks can be allocated to create a new storage pool.

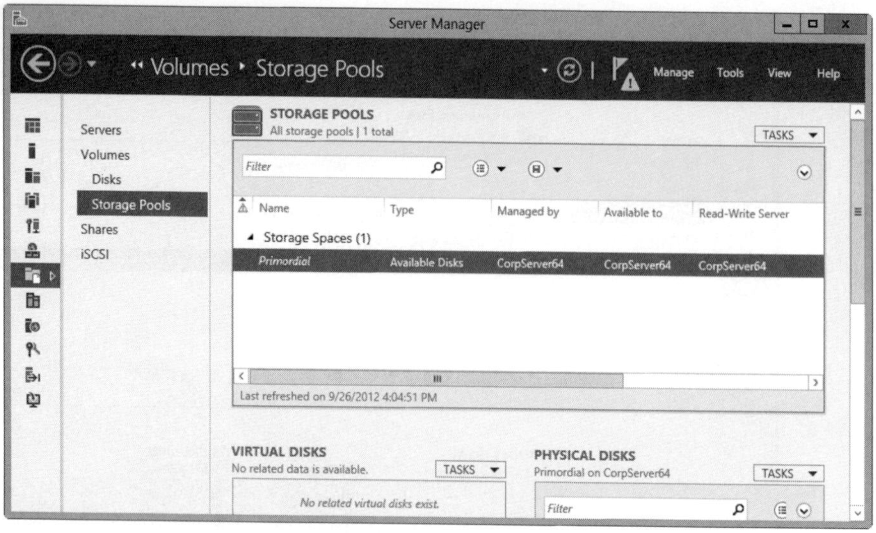

**Figure 14-23** Primordial pools represent unallocated but available disks.

Each physical disk allocated to the pool can be handled in one of three ways:

- As a data store that is available for use

- As a data store that can be manually allocated for use

- As a hot spare in case a disk in the pool fails or is removed from the subsystem

If a server has a primordial pool, you can create a storage pool from its unallocated but available disks by completing the following steps:

1. With the Storage Pools subnode selected in Server Manager, tap or click Tasks on the Storage Pools panel, and then tap or click New Storage Pool. This starts the New Storage Pool Wizard. If the wizard displays the Before You Begin page, read the Welcome text and then tap or click Next.

2. On the Specify A Storage Pool Name And Subsystem page, shown in Figure 14-24, type a name and description for the storage pool. Select the primordial pool for the server you want to associate the pool with and allocate storage for. For example, if you are configuring storage for CorpServer64, select the primordial pool that is available to CorpServer64. Tap or click Next.

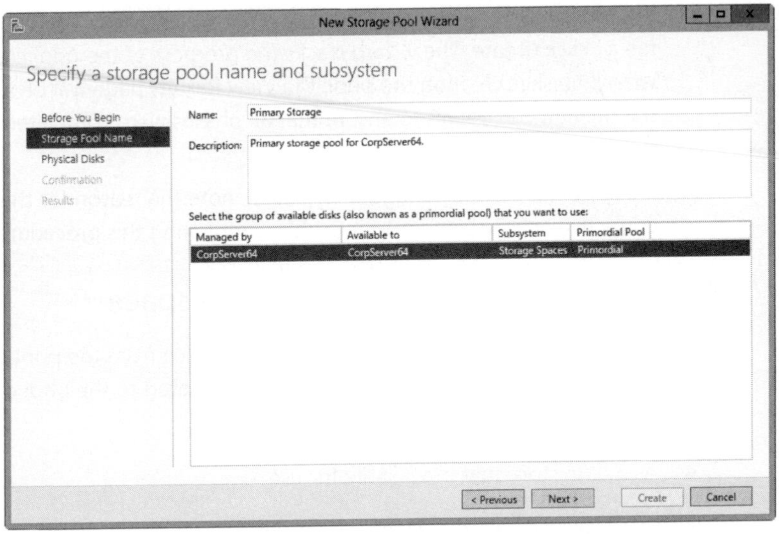

**Figure 14-24**  Select a primordial pool available to the server.

3. On the Select Physical Disks For The Storage Pool page, shown in Figure 14-25, select the unused physical disks that should be part of the storage pool and then specify the type of allocation for each disk. A storage pool must have two or more disks to use the mirroring and parity features available to protect data in case of error or failure. When setting the Allocation value, choose Automatic to allocate the disk to the pool and make it available for use or Hot Spare to allocate the disk to the pool as a spare disk that is made available for use if another disk in the pool fails or is removed from the subsystem.

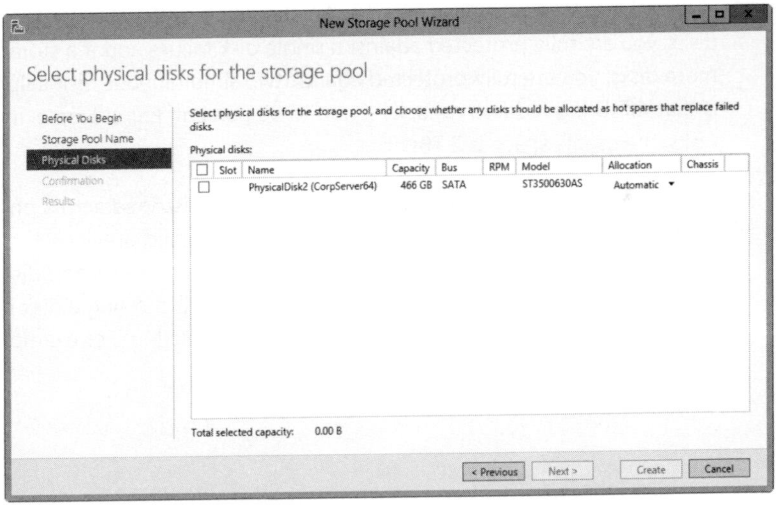

**Figure 14-25**  Specify the disks for the storage pool.

Chapter 14

4.  When you are ready to continue, tap or click Next. After you confirm your selections, tap or click Create. The wizard tracks the progress of the pool creation. When the wizard finishes creating the pool, the View Results page will be updated to reflect this. Review the details to ensure that all phases were completed successfully, and then tap or click Close.

    If any portion of the configuration failed, note the reason for the failure and take corrective actions as appropriate before repeating this procedure.

## Creating a virtual disk in a storage space

After you create a storage pool, you can allocate space from the pool to virtual disks that are available to your servers. Each physical disk allocated to the pool can be handled in one of three ways:

- As a data store that is available for use

- As a data store that can be manually allocated for use

- As a hot spare in case a disk in the pool fails or is removed from the subsystem

When a storage pool has a single disk, your only option for allocating space on that disk is to create virtual disks with a simple layout. A simple layout does not protect against disk failure. If a storage pool has multiple disks, you use mirroring or parity to protect data in case of error or failure.

With a mirror layout, data is duplicated on disks using a mirroring technique similar to what I discussed previously in this chapter. However, the mirroring technique is more sophisticated in that data is mirrored onto two or three disks at a time. Like standard mirroring, this approach has its advantages and disadvantages. Here, if a storage space has two or three disks, you are fully protected against a single disk failure and if a storage space has five or more disks, you are fully protected against two simultaneous disk failures. The disadvantage is that mirroring reduces capacity by up to 50 percent. For example, if you mirror two 2-TB disks, the usable space is 2 TBs.

With a parity layout, data and parity information are striped across physical disks using a striping-with-parity technique similar to what I discussed previously in this chapter. Like standard striping with parity, this approach has its advantages and disadvantages. You need at least three disks to fully protect yourself against a single disk failure. You lose some capacity to the striping, but not as much as with mirroring. For example, if you enable parity on three 2-TB disks, the usable space is 4 TBs.

You can create a virtual disk in a storage pool by completing the following steps:

1. With the Storage Pools subnode selected in Server Manager, tap or click Tasks on the Virtual Disks panel, and then tap or click New Virtual Disk to start the New Virtual Disk Wizard. If the wizard displays the Before You Begin page, read the Welcome text and then tap or click Next.

2. On the Storage Pool page, select the storage pool for the server you want to associate the virtual disk with and allocate storage from. Each available storage pool is listed according to the server it is managed by and available to. Make sure the pool has enough free space to create the virtual disk. Tap or click Next.

3. On the Specify The Virtual Disk Name page, type a name and description for the virtual disk. Tap or click Next.

4. On the Select The Storage Layout page, select the storage layout as appropriate for your reliability and redundancy requirements. The simple layout is the only option for storage pools that contain a single disk. If the underlying storage pool has multiple disks, you can choose a simple layout, mirror layout, or parity layout, as shown in Figure 14-26. Tap or click Next.

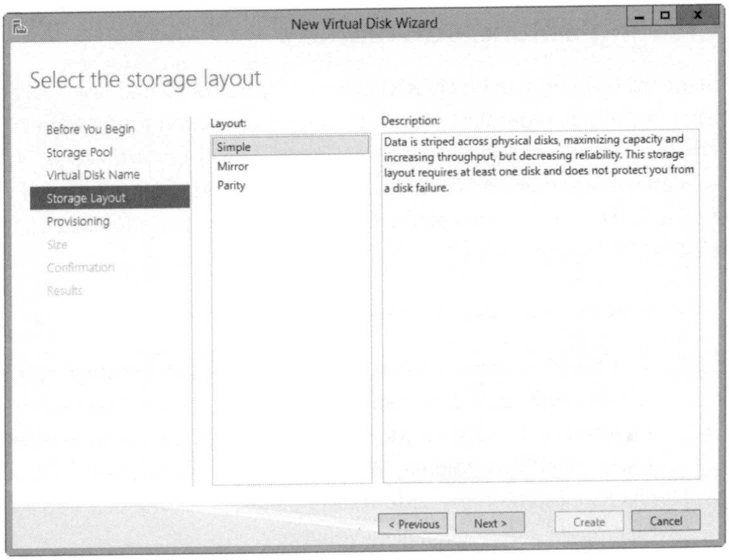

**Figure 14-26**  Specify the layout for the virtual disk.

5. On the Specify The Provisioning Type page, select the provisioning type. Storage can by provisioned in a thin disk or a fixed disk. With thin-disk provisioning, the volume uses space from the storage pool as needed, up to the volume size. With fixed

provisioning, the volume has a fixed size and uses space from the storage pool equal to the volume size. Tap or click Next.

6. On the Specify The Size Of The Virtual Disk page, use the options provided to set the size of the virtual disk. By selecting the Create The Largest Virtual Disk Possible check box, you ensure that the disk is created and sized within the available space. For example, if you are trying to create a 2-TB fixed disk with a simple layout and only 1 TB of space is available, a 1-TB fixed disk will be created. Keep in mind that if a disk is mirrored or striped, it will use more free space than you specify.

7. When you are ready to continue, tap or click Next. After you confirm your selections, tap or click Create. The wizard tracks the progress of the disk creation. When the wizard finishes creating the disk, the View Results page will be updated to reflect this. Review the details to ensure that all phases were completed successfully. If any portion of the configuration failed, note the reason for the failure and take corrective actions as appropriate before repeating this procedure.

8. When you tap or click Close, the New Volume Wizard should start automatically. Use the wizard to create a volume on the disk as discussed in "Creating a standard volume."

## Creating a standard volume

Standard volumes can be created on any physical or virtual disk available. You use the same technique regardless of how the disk is presented to the server. This allows you to create standard volumes on a server's internal disks, on virtual disks in a storage subsystem available to a server, and on virtual iSCSI disks available to a server. If you add the data deduplication feature to a server, you can enable data deduplication for standard volumes created for that server.

You can create a standard volume by completing the following steps:

1. Start the New Volume Wizard. If you just created a storage space, the New Volume Wizard might start automatically. Otherwise, on the Disks subnode, all available disks are listed on the Disks panel. Select the disk you want to work with, and then under Tasks, select New Volume. Similarly, on the Storage Pools subnode, all available virtual disks are listed on the Virtual Disks panel. Select the disk you want to work with, and then under Tasks, select New Volume.

2. On the Select The Server And Disk page, shown in Figure 14-27, select the server for which you are provisioning storage, select the disk where the volume should be created, and then tap or click Next. If you just created a storage space and then New Volume Wizard started automatically, the related server and disk are selected automatically and you simply need to tap or click Next.

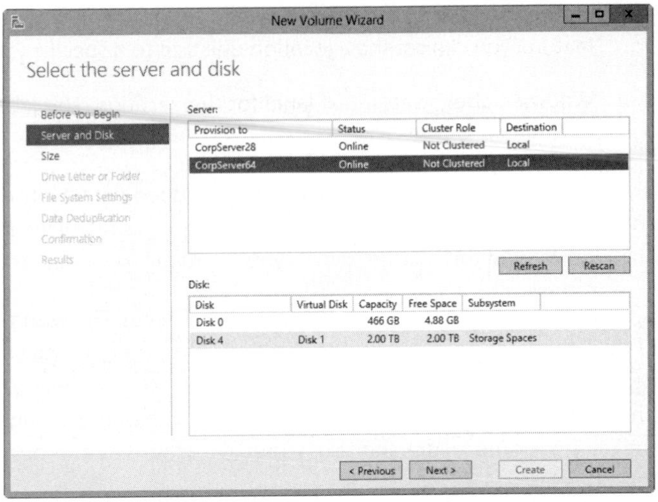

**Figure 14-27** Select the server and disk on which the volume should be created.

3. On the Specify The Size Of The Volume page, use the options provided to set the volume size. By default, the volume size is set to the maximum available on the related disk. Tap or click Next.

4. On the Assign To A Drive Letter Or Folder page, specify whether you want to assign a drive letter or path to the volume and then tap or click Next. You use these options as follows:

   o **Drive Letter**  To assign a drive letter, choose this option and then select an available drive letter in the list provided.

   o **The Following Folder**  To assign a drive path, choose this option and then type the path to an existing folder on an NTFS drive, or tap or click Browse to search for or create a folder.

   o **Don't Assign To A Drive Letter Or Drive Path**  To create the volume without assigning a drive letter or path, choose this option. You can assign a drive letter or path later if necessary.

5. On the Select File System Settings page, specify how the volume should be formatted using the following options:

   o **File System**  Sets the file system type, such as NTFS or ReFS.

   o **Allocation Unit Size**  Sets the cluster size for the file system. This is the basic unit in which disk space is allocated. The default allocation unit size is based on the volume's size and is set dynamically prior to formatting. To override this feature, you can set the allocation unit size to a specific value.

○ **Volume Label**   Sets a text label for the partition. This label is the partition's volume name.

6. If you elected to create an NTFS volume and added data deduplication to the server, you can enable and configure data deduplication, as discussed in "Deduplicating volumes" later in this chapter. When you are ready to continue, tap or click Next.

7. After you confirm your selections, tap or click Create. The wizard tracks the progress of the volume creation. When the wizard finishes creating the volume, the View Results page will be updated to reflect this. Review the details to ensure that all phases were completed successfully. If any portion of the configuration failed, note the reason for the failure and take corrective actions as appropriate before repeating this procedure.

8. When you tap or click Close, the New Volume Wizard should start automatically. Use the wizard to create a volume on the disk as discussed earlier in this section.

9. On the Storage Pool page, tap or click the storage pool in which you want to create the virtual disk and then tap or click Next. Each available storage pool is listed according to the server it is managed by and available to.

## Configuring data deduplication

Windows Server 2012 can use data deduplication to find and remove duplication within data while ensuring its integrity and fidelity. When a volume is deduplicated, the data it contains is transformed and the result includes

- Optimized files

- Unoptimized files

- A chunk store

- Additional free space

### Understanding data deduplication

File optimization is a key part of data deduplication. Optimization involves

1. Segmenting files into 32-KB to 128-KB chunks.

2. Identifying duplicate chunks.

3.  Replacing the duplicates with references to a single copy.

4.  Compressing chunks.

5.  Organizing chunks into special container files.

6.  Placing organized chunks in the chunk store.

The organized chunks are placed in special container files within the chunk store, which is in the System Volume Information folder. Optimized files on the volume are no longer stored as independent streams. Instead, they are replaced with stubs that point to data blocks within a common chunk store. Because duplicate blocks of data are stored only once within the chunk store, optimized files are transparently assembled during file access, ensuring users and applications see the correct blocks without any impact or apparent change in behavior.

> **Important**
>
> A deduplicated volume might contain unoptimized files as well. Files can be omitted from the deduplication process for a variety of reasons. Files smaller than 32 KBs are not deduplicated. Neither are system-state files, encrypted files, or files with extended attributes.

The integrity of deduplicated data is maintained using checksum validation on data and metadata. As a further safeguard against corruption, Windows maintains redundant copies of all metadata as well as the most frequently referenced data. With these safeguards included, the result of optimization is up to 2:1 storage savings for standard data and up to 20:1 storage savings for VHD data.

Data deduplication is for primary data volumes and not for boot, system, or other specialized types of volumes. Ideally, you'll use data deduplication for primary data volumes that have

- File shares for user documents, with space savings of 30–50 percent on average.

- Software deployment shares, with space savings of 70–80 percent on average.

- VHD file storage, with space savings of 80–95 percent on average.

- Mixed use storage, with space savings of 50–60 percent on average.

As part of deduplication, the chunk store is optimized periodically. The default optimization occurs in the background. In addition to periodic optimization, Windows performs garbage collection and data scrubbing periodically. By default, garbage collection and data scrubbing occur weekly at a specified time. Use the Get-DedupSchedule cmdlet to determine the specific times.

# INSIDE OUT    Evaluate space savings from deduplication

You can use the Deduplication Evaluation tool (DDPEval.exe) to determine the expected space savings from deduplication. Run DDPEval.exe at a command-line using the syntax

```
ddpeval VolumeOrPath
```

Here, *VolumeOrPath* is the drive designator of the volume to evaluate, such as D:, a local file path, such as D:\Data, or a UNC path to a shared folder, such as \\Server15\CorpData.

## Selecting data for deduplication

Data chunks in the chunk store are compressed for most file types by default. File types that aren't compressed in the chunk store include those that are already compressed and those that chunk compression might adversely affect, such as audio and video files. There might be file types that you don't want deduplicated as well, and you can specify these file types as exclusions. To exclude specific types of files, you need to specify that they shouldn't be included.

Files that are exclusively open for write operations, updated frequently, or heavily accessed aren't good candidates for deduplication because the frequent updates and high access levels cancel the optimization gains. Instead, use deduplication on volumes with files that aren't constantly being updated or accessed. You'll have better results with these less utilized volumes.

File age policies can be used to control when files are deduplicated, and this will help to reduce early or frequent deduplication of files that are modified regularly. That said, you can configure deduplication to process files that are 0 days old. Deduplication will continue, but it still won't optimize files that are heavily accessed or exclusively open for write operations. Files must be closed when optimization tasks run.

You can enable deduplication on empty volumes and volumes that already contain data. Windows Server 2012 deduplicates data on a single volume at a rate of approximately 10 to 40 MBs per second, depending on server activity levels and capacity, which is approximately 50 GBs to 200 GBs per hour. To ensure the server doesn't run out of resources, the operating system will pause deduplication if available CPU and memory resources run low.

> **Note**
>
> Before you begin deduplication, you should ensure that a volume has ample free space. I recommend that there be free space of at least 2 to 5 percent of total capacity. For optimal operation, I recommend that volumes continue to have free space of 2 to 5 percent of total capacity as well.

## Interoperability with data deduplication

Deduplication works with BranchCache, DFS replication, and failover clusters, but it doesn't work with hard quotas on volume root folders. In Windows Server 2012, BranchCache and deduplication are designed to work together. Deduplicated files are indexed and hashed, so requests for data can be quickly computed and deduplicated data can be more quickly transferred over the network.

Similarly, with DFS replication, there are performance gains and benefits from interoperability. When files are optimized or unoptimized, replication isn't triggered because the files themselves do not change. Although DFS continues to use Remote Differential Compression (RDC) rather than the chunks in the chunk store for network transfer optimization, files on the DFS replica also can be optimized by using deduplication, as long as the replica is running Windows Server 2012.

With failover clusters, each node that accesses deduplicated volumes must have the feature enabled. If so, deduplicated volumes fail over gracefully like any other volume. Additionally, when a cluster is formed, deduplication schedules are put into the schedule for the cluster. As a result, if a deduplicated volume fails over to another node, the scheduled deduplication task runs as expected at the next scheduled run time.

When you are using File Server Resource Manager quotas, you can't create hard quotas on the root folder of a volume that is deduplicated. If a volume has a hard quota on its root folder, the actual free space and the quota restricted space won't match and this might cause deduplication optimization jobs to fail. You can, however, create soft quotas on the root folder of a volume. With soft quotas, File Server Resource Manager (FSRM) uses the logical size of files for enforcing quotas. As a result, quota usage and any quota thresholds are based on the original size of files rather than the optimized size.

> **Note**
>
> Windows Storage Server supports Single Instance Storage (SIS), which is a deduplication technology. As you might expect, you can't use SIS with data deduplication. Because of this, prior to migrating Windows Storage Server to Windows Server 2012, you should remove SIS using either SISAdmin.exe within Storage Server or by moving the data to a volume that is not using SIS.

When backing up deduplicated volumes, keep in mind that the technology is supported by block-based backup applications, such as Windows Server Backup. These applications should be able to back up deduplicated data and maintain the optimization in the backup media.

On the other hand, file-based backup operations might not support deduplication. As a result, file-based backup operations, such as XCOPY, typically copy files in their original form. Files are transparently assembled in memory during the backup copy operation. Because the deduplication is not retained, the backup target must be large enough to hold the full, original size of the entire dataset.

You'll learn more about backing up and restoring deduplicated volumes in Chapter 17, "Backup and recovery."

## Deduplicating volumes

Before you enable data deduplication on volumes, you should consider the types of files that you don't want compressed as part of data deduplication. Typically, this includes file types that are already compressed. Because data deduplication can be applied using background optimization, throughput optimization, or both, you should consider how and when you want servers to deduplicate volumes.

Servers perform background optimization when they're otherwise idle. Background optimization runs at low priority and is paused whenever the server isn't idle. This pause and resume behavior continues until volumes are fully optimized.

Servers perform throughput optimization according to a specific schedule, such as every day at 1:45 A.M. for 6 hours. Throughput optimization runs at normal priority and uses system resources to maximize the optimization process. Once started, optimization continues until it completes or reaches the specified duration value.

> ### Important
> When you are configuring deduplication settings, be sure to note the difference between per-volume settings and per-server settings. For each volume, you can enable or disable deduplication. You also can set the file age policy and the file extensions to exclude. For each server, you can enable or disable background optimization, and enable or disable throughput optimization. The schedule set for throughput optimization is per-server as well.

You can enable and configure data deduplication as part of the volume-creation process by completing the following steps:

1. On the Enable Data Deduplication page in the New Volume Wizard, select Enable Data Deduplication On This Volume, as shown in Figure 14-28.

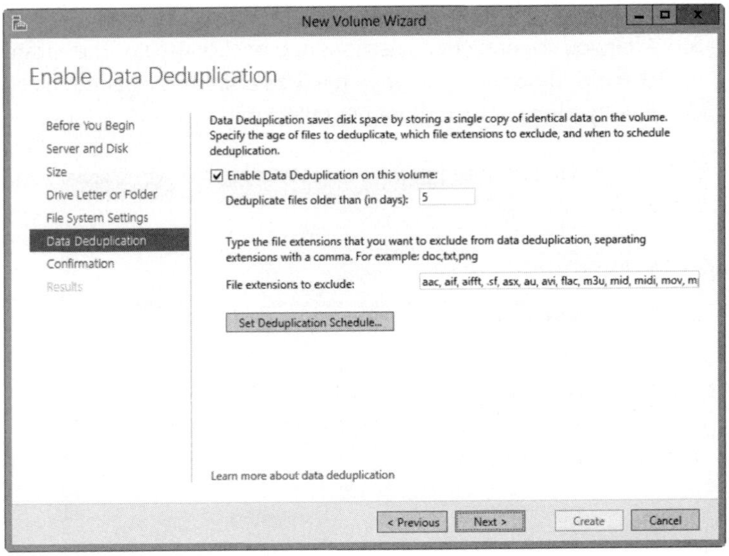

**Figure 14-28** Enable deduplication on the volume.

> **Note**
> The options shown in Figure 14-28 are per-volume.

2. File age policies control when files are deduplicated. In the Deduplicate Files Older Than box, configure deduplication to process files that are a specific number of days old, such as 5 or 10. If you enter 0, files are available for deduplication immediately but must be closed when optimization tasks run.

3. If you want to exclude specific types of files, enter the extensions of those files, separated by a comma.

4. Tap or click Set Deduplication Schedule to display the Deduplication Schedule dialog box shown in Figure 14-29. When you enable deduplication, background optimization is enabled by default. In addition or instead of background optimization, you also can enable and configure throughput optimization.

Throughput optimization follows a primary schedule by default, such as every day of the week at 1:45 A.M. for 6 hours. You can add a secondary schedule as well to help ensure that volumes are fully deduplicated as appropriate. For example, you might want to allow deduplication Monday to Friday at 1:00 A.M. for 3 hours and also allow deduplication on Saturday and Sunday for 6 hours. Tap or click OK, and then tap or click Next.

5.  After you confirm your selections, tap or click Create. The wizard tracks the progress of the volume creation. When the wizard finishes creating the volume, the View Results page will be updated to reflect this. Tap or click Close.

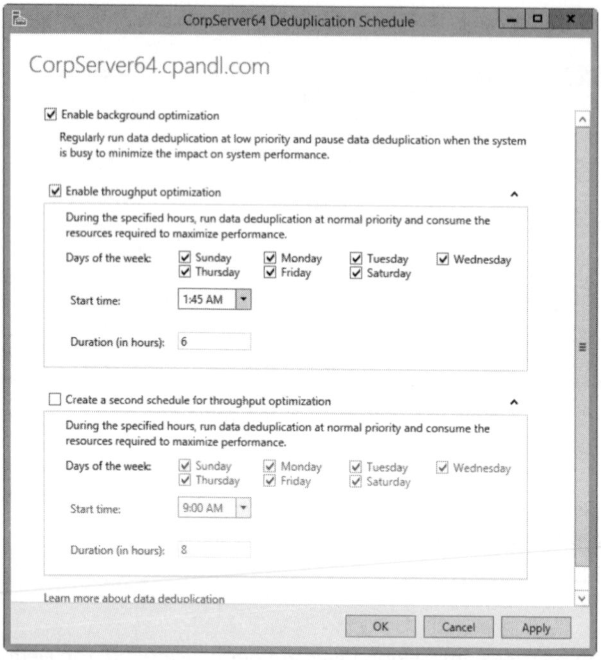

**Figure 14-29** Set the deduplication type and schedule.

> **Note**
>
> The options shown in Figure 14-29 are per-server.

You don't have to enable deduplication when you create volumes. You can enable and manage data deduplication at any time. With the Volumes subnode selected in Server Manager, press and hold or right-click the volume that you want to manage and then select Configure Data Deduplication. As Figure 14-30 shows, the configuration options available are nearly identical to those discussed previously. The exception is that you now can specify folders to exclude. When you exclude a folder, all contents of the folder are excluded from deduplication, including both files and subfolders and their contents. Specify a folder to exclude by tapping or clicking Add, using the dialog box provided to choose a folder to exclude, and then tapping or clicking Select Folder.

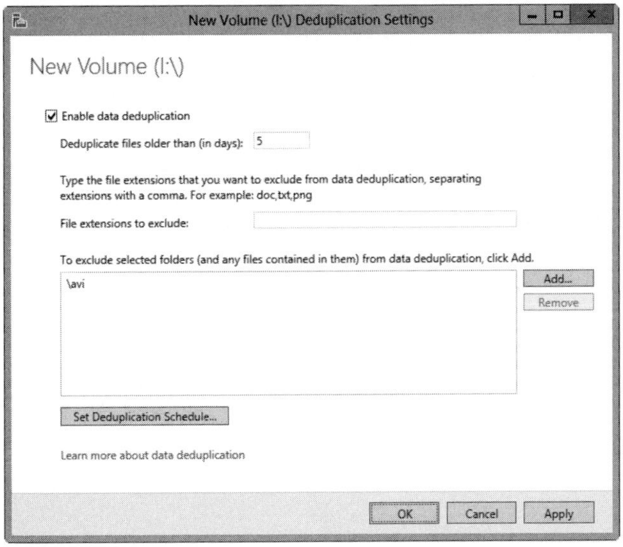

**Figure 14-30**  Configure deduplication settings for the volume.

## Monitoring deduplication

When you add the Data Deduplication role service to a server, related PowerShell cmdlets are installed as well. You can use these cmdlets to track the status of deduplication, determine space savings on volumes, and more. You need to use an elevated PowerShell prompt.

Use Get-DedupStatus to display the status of deduplication for each enabled volume. In the following example, you check deduplication on FileServer28 and FileServer32:

```
Invoke-command -computername fileserver28, fileserver32
-scriptblock {Get-DedupStatus}
```

As shown here, the output shows how much free space is available, how much space was saved using deduplication, the number of optimized files, and the number of in-policy files:

| FreeSpace | SavedSpace | OptimizedFiles | InPolicyFiles | Volume | PSComputerName |
| --------- | ---------- | -------------- | ------------- | ------ | -------------- |
| | | | | | FileServer28 |
| 325.55 GB | 402.22 GB | 32581 | 32588 | I: - | FileServer28 |
| 98.82 GB | 118.75 GB | 29812 | 28714 | K: - | FileServer32 |

You can get more detailed information by formatting the output as a list, as shown here:

```
Get-DedupStatus | fl
```

The information provided for each volume is then much more detailed, as shown in this example for the I volume:

```
Volume                               : I:
VolumeId                             : \\?\Volume{}\
Capacity                             : 466 GB
FreeSpace                            : 325.55 GB
UsedSpace                            : 220.62 GB
UnoptimizedSize                      : 722.68 GB
SavedSpace                           : 502.22 GB
SavingsRate                          : 73 %
OptimizedFilesCount                  : 32581
OptimizedFilesSize                   : 685.32 GB
OptimizedFilesSavingsRate            : 78 %
InPolicyFilesCount                   : 32588
InPolicyFilesSize                    : 699.87 GB
LastOptimizationTime                 : 9/26/2014 5:32:31 AM
LastOptimizationResult               : 0x00000000
LastOptimizationResultMessage        : The operation completed successfully.
LastGarbageCollectionTime            : 9/26/2014 5:33:01 PM
LastGarbageCollectionResult          : 0x00000000
LastGarbageCollectionResultMessage   : The operation completed successfully.
LastScrubbingTime                    : 9/26/2014 6:33:01 AM
LastScrubbingResult                  : 0x00000000
LastScrubbingResultMessage           : The operation completed successfully.
```

Use Get-DedupVolume to examine volume-level deduplication. In the following example, you check volume-level deduplication on FileServer28 and FileServer32:

```
Invoke-command -computername fileserver28, fileserver32
-scriptblock {Get-DedupVolume}
```

As shown here, the output shows the status of deduplication on volumes, how much space was saved using deduplication, and the savings rate:

```
Enabled   SavedSpace    SavingsRate     Volume    PSComputer
-------   ----------    -----------     ------    ----------
True      502.22 GB     73 %            I:        FileServer28
True      118.75 GB     58 %            K:        FileServer32
```

You can get more detailed information by formatting the output as a list, as shown here:

```
Get-DedupVolume | fl
```

The information provided for volume-level deduplication is then much more detailed, as shown in this example for the I volume:

```
Volume                         : I:
VolumeId                       : \\?\Volume{}\
Enabled                        : True
DataAccessEnabled              : True
Capacity                       : 466 GB
FreeSpace                      : 325.55 GB
UsedSpace                      : 220.62 GB
UnoptimizedSize                : 722.68 GB
SavedSpace                     : 502.22 GB
SavingsRate                    : 73 %
MinimuFileAgeDays              : 5
MinimumFileSize                : 32768
NoCompress                     : False
ExcludeFolder                  : {\avi}
ExcludeFileType                :
NoCompressionFileType          : {aac, aif, aiff, asf...}
ChunkRedundancyThreshold       : 100
Verify                         : False
```

Using Get-DedupMetadata, you can get detailed information about how deduplication processed files, which includes the number of chunks in the chunk store, the number of StreamMaps, and the number of hotspots. Hotspots are the most frequently referenced chunks. Enter the following command:

```
Get-DedupMetadata | fl
```

You will see output similar to the following for each volume that uses deduplication:

```
Volume                            : I:
VolumeId                          : \\?\Volume{}\
StoreId                           : { }
DataChunkCount                    : 4082133
DataContainerCount                : 192
DataChunkAverageSize              : 58.21 KB
DataChunkMedianSize               : 0 B
DataStoreUncompactedFreespace     : 0 B
StreamMapChunkCount               : 36424
StreamMapContainerCount           : 18
StreamMapAverageDataChunkCount    :
StreamMapMedianDataChunkCount     :
StreamMapMaxDataChunkCount        :
HotspotChunkCount                 : 12422
HotspotContainerCount             : 1
HotspotMedianReferenceCount       :
CorruptionLogEntryCount           : 0
TotalChunkStoreSize               : 182.5 GB
```

Finally, you can use Get-DedupSchedule to examine the deduplication schedule. As shown here, the output depicts the start time of regular optimization tasks as well as garbage collection and scrubbing:

```
Enabled  Type              StartTime   Days        Name
-------  ----              ---------   ----        ----
True     Optimization                              BackgroundOptimization
True     Optimization      1:45 AM     {Sunday, Monday... ThroughputOptimization
True     Optimization      9:00 AM     {Sunday, Monday... ThroughputOptimization-2
True     GarbageCollection 2:45 AM     Saturday    WeeklyGarbageCollection
True     Scrubbing         3:45 AM     Saturday    WeeklyScrubbing
```

# File sharing and security

S HARING files means that you allow users to access files from across the network. The most basic way to share files is to create a shared folder and make it accessible to users through a mapped network drive. In most cases, you don't want everyone with access to the network to be able to read, modify, or delete the shared files. So, when you share files, the share permissions on the shared folder and the local access permissions are very important in helping to grant access as appropriate and to restrict access to files when necessary. File sharing and file security go hand in hand. You don't want to share files indiscriminately, and to help safeguard important data you can configure auditing. Auditing allows you to track who accessed files and what they did.

Typically, you will use file sharing with Volume Shadow Copy Service (VSS). This service offers two important features:

- **Shadow copying of files in shared folders**   You use this feature to configure volumes so that shadow copies of files in shared folders are created automatically at specific intervals during the day. This allows you to go back and look at earlier versions of files stored in shared folders. You can use these earlier versions to recover deleted, incorrectly modified, or overwritten files. You can also compare versions of files to see what changes were made over time.

- **Shadow copying of open or locked files for backups**   With this feature, you can use backup programs, such as Windows Backup, to back up files that are open or locked. This means you can perform a backup when applications are using the files and do not have to worry about backups failing because files are in use. Backup programs must implement the VSS application programming interface (API).

Both features are independent of each other. You do not need to enable shadow copying of a volume to be able to back up open or locked files on a volume. Although Resilient File System (ReFS) provides a highly reliable file system, only NTFS volumes support shadow copies. Therefore, if you create shares on ReFS volumes, users won't be able to go back to previous versions of files and folders stored in shares.

# File-sharing essentials

File sharing is one of the most fundamental features of a file server, and file servers running Microsoft Windows Server 2012 have many file-sharing features. The basic component that makes file sharing possible is the Server service, which is responsible for sharing file and printer resources over the network.

## Understanding file-sharing models

Windows Server 2012 supports two file-sharing models: standard file sharing and public folder sharing. Standard file sharing allows remote users to access network resources, such as files, folders, and drives. When you share a folder or a drive, you make all its files and subfolders available to a specified set of users. Standard file sharing also is referred to as *in-place file sharing* because you don't need to move files from their current location.

You can enable standard file sharing on disks formatted with extended FAT (exFAT), FAT, FAT32, NTFS, or ReFS. One set of permissions apply to disks formatted with exFAT, FAT, or FAT32. These permissions are called *share permissions*. Two sets of permissions apply to disks formatted with NTFS or ReFS: *NTFS permissions* (also referred to as *access permissions*) and *share permissions*. Having two sets of permissions allows you to determine precisely who has access to shared files and the level of access assigned. With either access permissions or share permissions, you do not need to move the files you are sharing.

With public folder sharing, you share files simply by copying or moving files to a computer's folder. Public files are available to anyone who logs on to a computer locally regardless of whether that person has a standard user account or an administrator user account on the computer. You can also grant network access to the Public folder. If you do this, however, there are no access restrictions. The Public folder and its contents are open to everyone who can access the computer over the local network.

When you copy or move files to the Public folder, access permissions are changed to match that of the Public folder. Some additional permissions are added as well. When a computer is part of a workgroup, you can add password protection to the Public folder. Separate password protection isn't needed in a domain. In a domain, only domain users can access Public folder data.

# INSIDE OUT   Public folder sharing

Public folder sharing allows users with network access to view and manage public files. When you enable public folder sharing without password protection, the implicit group Everyone is granted Full Control permissions to public files and public folders. This allows anyone, including network users, to open, change, create, and delete public files.

When you enable public folder sharing with password protection, the implicit group Interactive is granted Read, Read & Execute, Write, and Modify permissions to public files and public folders. This allows anyone logged on locally to open, change, create, and delete public files. Users with network access who have the password can do the same.

Windows Server 2012 can use either or both sharing models at any time. However, standard file sharing offers more security and better protection than public folder sharing, and increasing security is essential to protecting your organization's data.

Compound identities, claims-based access controls, and central access policies provide additional layers of security. Windows Server 2012 allows administrators to assign claims-based access controls to file and folder resources on NTFS and ReFS volumes. Users are granted access to files and folder resources, either directly with access permissions and share permissions or indirectly with claims-based access controls and central access policies.

## Enabling file sharing

You can configure the basic file-sharing settings for a server using Advanced Sharing Settings. Separate options are provided for public folder sharing on the All Networks panel, and the status of public folder sharing is listed as On or Off, as shown in Figure 15-1.

Chapter 15

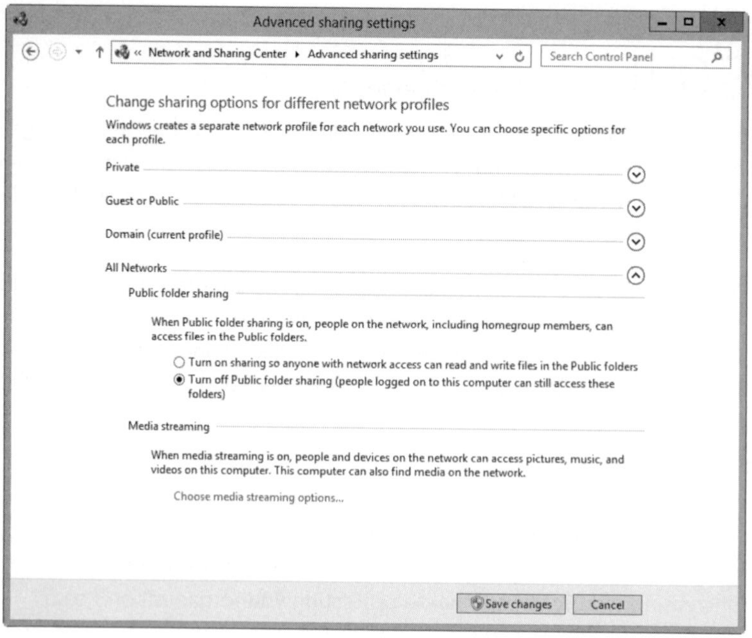

**Figure 15-1** Configure basic file-sharing options.

To open the Advanced Sharing Settings page in Control Panel, tap or click View Network Status And Tasks under the Network And Internet heading and then tap or click Change Advanced Sharing Settings. Public folder sharing options control access to a computer's Public folder. To configure public folder sharing, expand the All Networks panel by tapping or clicking the related Expand button. Choose one of the following options, and then tap or click Save Changes:

- **Turn On Sharing So Anyone With Network Access Can Read And Write Files**   Enables public folder sharing by granting access to the Public folder and all public data to anyone who can access the computer over the network. Keep in mind, however, that Windows Firewall settings might prevent external access.

- **Turn Off Public Folder Sharing**   Disables public folder sharing, preventing network access to the Public folder. Anyone who logs on locally to your computer can still access the Public folder and its files.

In a workgroup setting, you'll be able to manage password-protected sharing on the All Networks panel. You use password-protected sharing to restrict access so that only people with a user account and password on your computer can access shared resources. Select either Turn On Password Protected Sharing to enable password-protected sharing or Turn Off Password Protected Sharing to disable password-protected sharing, and then tap or click Save Changes.

# Using and finding shares

You share file resources over the network by creating a shared folder that users can map to as a network drive. For example, if the D:\Data directory on a computer is used to store user data, you might want to share this folder as UserData. This would allow users to map to it using a drive letter on their machines, such as X. After the drive is mapped, users can access it in File Explorer or by using other tools just like they would a local drive on their computer.

All shared folders have a share name and a folder path. The share name is the name of the shared folder. The folder path is the complete path to the folder on the server. In the previous example, the share name is UserData and the associated folder path is D:\Data. After you share a folder, it is available to users automatically. All they have to know to map to the shared folder is the name of the server on which the folder is located and the share name.

Whether you are working with Windows 8 or Windows Server 2012, you can map network drives in the same way. In File Explorer, tap or click the leftmost option button in the address list, and then tap or click Computer. Next, tap or click the Map Network Drive button on the Computer panel and then tap or click Map Network Drive. This displays the Map Network Drive dialog box shown in Figure 15-2.

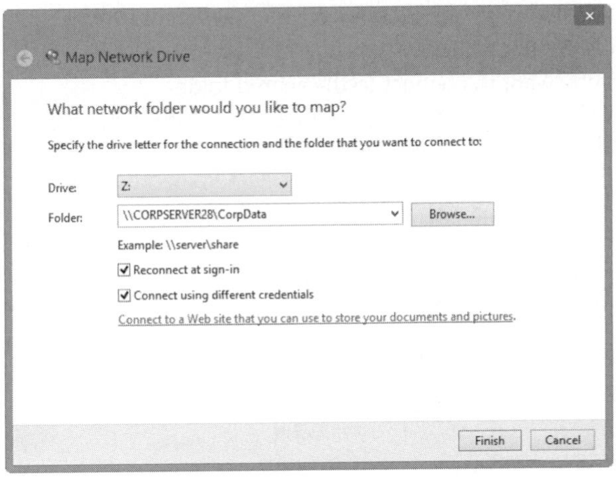

**Figure 15-2**  The Map Network Drive dialog box.

You use the Drive field to select a free drive letter to use and the Folder field to enter the path to the network share. You use the Universal Naming Convention (UNC) path to the share. For example, to access a server called CORPSVR02 and a shared folder called CorpData, you type **\\CorpSvr02\CorpData**. If you don't know the name of the share, you can tap or click the Browse button to the right of the Folder list. In the Browse For Folder dialog box, computers with shared folders are listed by name. When you expand the name of a computer in a workgroup or a domain, as shown in Figure 15-3, you'll see a list of shared folders. Select the shared folder you want to work with, and then tap or click OK.

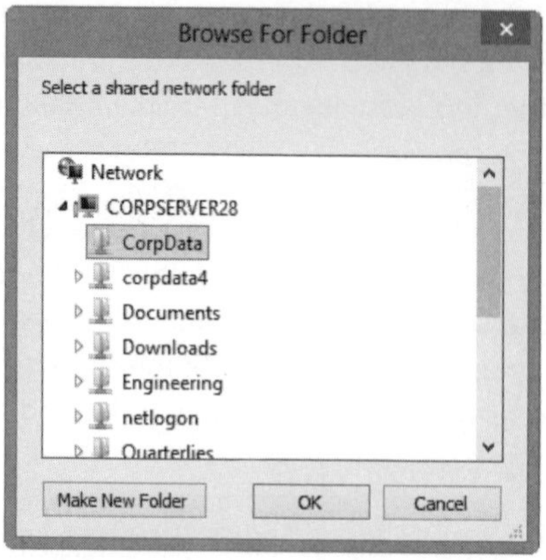

**Figure 15-3**   The Browse For Folder dialog box.

By default, Windows automatically reconnects mapped network drives at logon. Clear the Reconnect At Logon check box if you only want to map the network drive for the current user session. Tap or click Finish. If the currently logged-on user doesn't have appropriate access permissions for the share, select Connect Using Different Credentials and then tap or click Finish. After you tap or click Finish, you can enter the user name and password of the account with which you want to connect to the shared folder.

As shown in Figure 15-4, enter the user name in Domain\Username format, such as **Cpandl\Williams**. Before tapping or clicking OK, select Remember My Credentials if you want the credentials to be saved. Otherwise, you need to provide credentials in the future.

**Figure 15-4**   The Windows Security dialog box.

Domain users can browse the network using Network Explorer to find shares that have been made available, as shown in Figure 15-5. You can open Network Explorer from File Explorer. In File Explorer, tap or click the location path selection button, and then tap or click Network. You now see a list of computers on the network for which Network Discovery is enabled. When you double-tap or double-click a computer entry, any publicly shared resources on that computer are listed and can be connected to simply by double-tapping or double-clicking the associated folder.

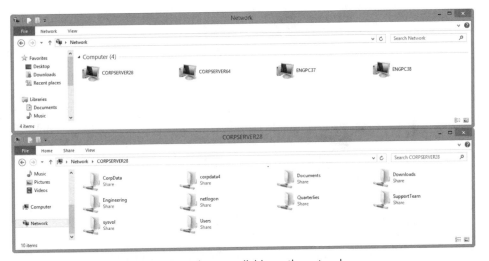

**Figure 15-5** Network Explorer shows shares available on the network.

To make it easier for users to find shared folders, you can also publish information about shares in Active Directory.

When you publish shared resources, users can use Network Explorer to find them, and administrators can find them using Active Directory Users And Computers. The procedures are similar regardless of which tool you are using. An example of how you can find shared folders follows:

1. In Network Explorer, tap or click Search Active Directory on the Network panel. Or in Active Directory Users And Computers, press and hold or right-click the domain name in the left pane, and tap or click Find.

2. As shown in Figure 15-6, in the Find list, choose Shared Folders.

Chapter 15

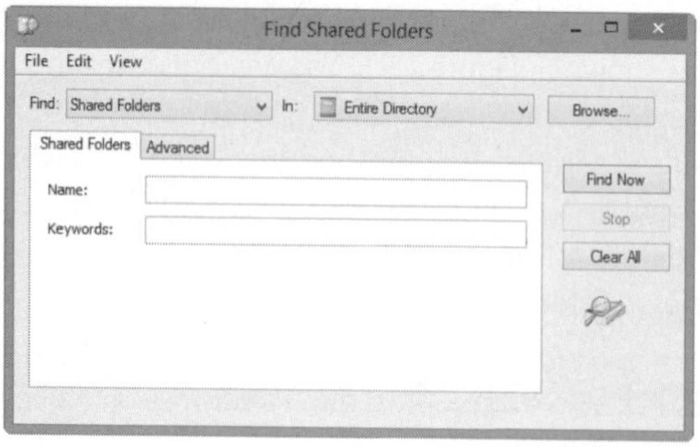

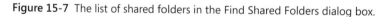

**Figure 15-6** Using the Find Shared Folders dialog box to find shared resources, such as folders and printers.

3.  In the Name field, type the name of the folder you want to find, and then tap or click Find Now. If you know part of the folder name, you can use the asterisk (*) to match partial names. For example, if you know that the folder name ends with the word "data," you could type **\*data** to search for all folders that end with the word "data."

4.  In the Search Results area, you'll see a list of shared folders that match your search criteria, as shown in Figure 15-7. Press and hold or right-click any of the shared folders to display a shortcut menu. You will then be able to open the shared folder, map a network drive to the folder, and access the share's properties.

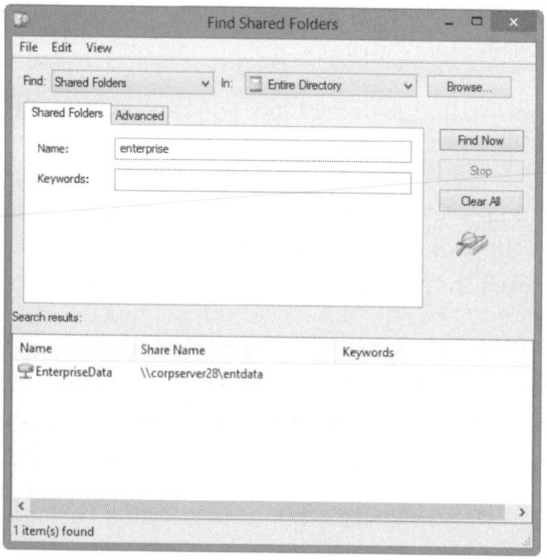

**Figure 15-7** The list of shared folders in the Find Shared Folders dialog box.

## Use keywords for searches

Shared folders can have associated keywords, and you can use these keywords instead of name values. Unlike names, partial keyword values are matched automatically. For example, if you know that the folder has the keyword "Engineering" associated with it, you could enter **eng** in the Keyword box and then tap or click Find Now.

You can use keywords to refine searches as well. For example, if you know that the folder name ends with data and has the keyword "Engineering" associated with it, you could enter **\*data** as the name and **eng** as the keyword for your search.

As an administrator, you can use Computer Management and Server Manager to work with shares. You also can view current shares on a computer by typing **net share** at a command prompt or by typing **get-smbshare** at a Windows PowerShell prompt. Computer Management, net share, and get-smbshare display information about Server Message Block (SMB)–based shares, including standard SMB folder shares, hidden SMB folder shares (those ending with the $ suffix), and SMB folders shared using Distributed File System (DFS). Server Manager displays information about standard SMB folder shares, SMB folders shared using DFS, and folders shared using NFS. Server Manager does not display information about hidden SMB folder shares.

## Hiding and controlling share access

Because there are times when you don't want everyone to see or know about a share, Windows Server also allows you to create hidden shares. Hidden shares are shares that are made available to users but that are not listed in the normal file share lists or published in Active Directory. You can create hidden shares by adding the dollar sign ($) to the end of the share name. For example, if you want to share E:\DataDumps but don't want it to be displayed in the normal file share lists, you could name it Backup$ rather than Backup.

Hiding a share doesn't control access to the share, however. Access to shares is controlled using permissions. Two permission sets apply to shared folders: share permissions and local access permissions. Share permissions set the maximum allowable actions available within a shared folder. Access permissions assigned to the share's contents further constrain the actions users can perform. For example, share permissions can allow a user to access a folder, but access permissions might not allow a user to view or modify files.

Keep in mind that by default, when you create a share, everyone with access to the network has Read access to the share's contents.

> **Note**
>
> You also can hide shares using access-based enumeration. This feature displays only the files and folders that a user has permissions to access. For more information, see "Creating shared folders in Server Manager" later in this chapter.

## Special and administrative shares

In Windows Server 2012, you'll find that several shares are created automatically. These shares are referred to as *special shares* or *default shares*. Most special shares are hidden because they are created for administrative purposes. Thus, they are also referred to as *administrative shares*.

The special shares that are available on a system depend on its configuration. This means a domain controller might have more special shares than a member server. Or that a server that handles network faxing might have shares that other systems don't.

### C$, D$, E$, and other drive shares

All drives, except USB drives and CD/DVD-ROM drives, have special shares with access to the root of the drive. These shares are known as C$, D$, E$, and so on, and they are created to allow administrators to connect to a drive's root folder and perform administrative tasks. For example, if you map to C$, you are connecting to C:\ and have full access to this drive.

On workstations and servers, members of the Administrators or Backup Operators group can access drive shares. On domain controllers, members of the Server Operators group can also access drive shares.

> **Note**
>
> Windows allows you to delete drive shares. However, the next time you restart the computer or the Server service, the drive shares will be re-created.

### ADMIN$

The ADMIN$ share is an administrative share for accessing the %SystemRoot% folder in which the operating-system files reside. It is meant to be used for remote administration. For administrators working remotely with systems, it is a handy shortcut for directly accessing the operating-system folder. Thus, rather than having to connect to C$ or D$ and then look for the operating-system folder, which could be named Windows, Winnt, or just about anything else, you can connect directly to the right folder every time.

On workstations and servers, members of the Administrators or Backup Operators groups can access the ADMIN$ share. On domain controllers, members of the Server Operators group can also access the ADMIN$ share.

### FAX$

The FAX$ share is used to support network faxes. By default, the special group Everyone has Read permissions on these shared folders. This means that anyone with access to the network can access this folder.

### IPC$

The IPC$ share is an administrative share used to support named pipes. Named pipes are used for interprocess (or process-to-process) communications. Because named pipes can be redirected over the network to connect local and remote systems, they also enable remote administration and are what allow you to manage resources remotely.

### NETLOGON

The NETLOGON share is used by domain controllers. It supports the Netlogon service and is used by this service during the processing of logon requests. After users log on, Windows accesses their user profiles and, if applicable, any related logon scripts. Logon scripts contain actions that should be run automatically when users log on to help set up the work environment, perform housekeeping tasks, or complete any other task that must be routinely performed every time users log on.

### PRINT$

The PRINT$ share supports printer sharing by providing access to printer drivers. Any time you share a printer, the system puts the printer drivers in this share so that other computers can access them as needed.

### SYSVOL

The SYSVOL share is used to support Active Directory. Domain controllers have this share and use it to store Active Directory data, including policies and scripts.

## Accessing shares for administration

As Figure 15-8 shows, administrators can view information about existing shares on a
computer, including the special shares, by using Computer Management. In Computer
Management, expand System Tools, Shared Folders, and then select Shares.

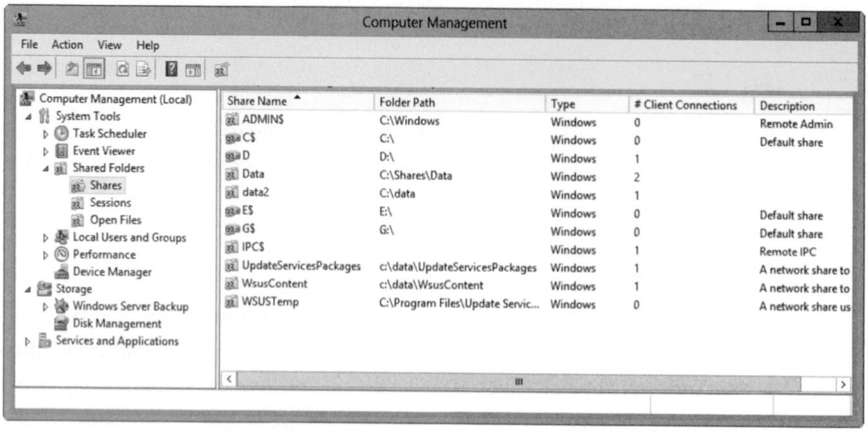

**Figure 15-8**  Use Computer Management to access shared folders.

If you want to work with shares on a remote computer, press and hold or right-click the
Computer Management node in the left pane and select Connect To Another Computer.
This displays the Select Computer dialog box. Select Another Computer, and then type
the computer name or Internet Protocol (IP) address of the computer you want to use. If
you don't know the computer name or IP address, tap or click Browse to search for the
computer you want to work with.

# Creating and publishing shared folders

To create shares on a server running Windows Server 2012, you must be a member of
the Administrators or Server Operators group. You can create shares using File Explorer,
Computer Management, Server Manager, New-SmbShare, or Net Share from the command
line. When deciding which option to use, keep the following in mind:

- File Explorer works well when you want to share folders on computers to which you
  are logged on. Because nonadministrators typically share folders using File Explorer,
  it's important to understand the quirks that come with this approach (and this also
  might help you more easily resolve related access issues).

- Using Computer Management, you can share the folders on the local computer
  and on any computer to which you can connect. You'll be able to configure share
  permissions and offline settings as well.

- Server Manager allows you to manage shared folders on any server added for management. You'll be able to provision all aspects of sharing, including access permissions, share permissions, encrypted data access, and offline settings for caching.

- With New-SmbShare, you can create shares using Windows PowerShell. Type **get-help new-smbshare** at the PowerShell prompt for details on using this cmdlet.

- Using Net Share, you can create shares from the command line or in scripts. Type **net share /?** at the command prompt for details on using this command.

After you create a share, you might want to publish it in Active Directory so that it is easier to find.

## Creating shares by using File Explorer

By using File Explorer, you can share folders on the computer to which you are logged on. In File Explorer, press and hold or right-click the folder you want to share and then select Properties. In the folder's Properties dialog box, tap or click the Sharing tab to view the current sharing configuration (if any), as shown in Figure 15-9.

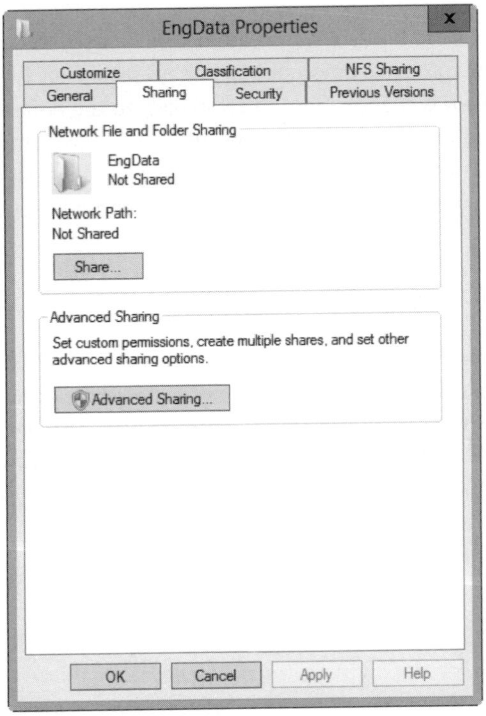

Figure 15-9  View the current sharing configuration.

Tap or click Share to display the File Sharing dialog box, as shown in Figure 15-10. Tap or click the selection button (the down arrow) to the right of the text-entry field provided and then select Find People.

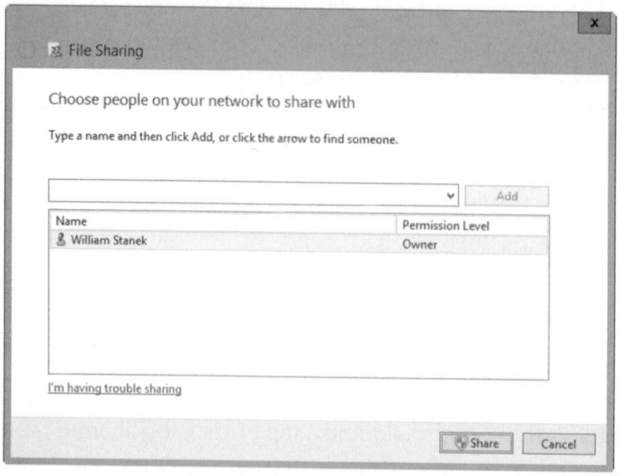

**Figure 15-10**  Configure sharing access and permissions.

In the Select Users Or Groups dialog box, shown in Figure 15-11, check the value of the From This Location field. In workgroups, computers will always show only local accounts and groups. In domains, this field is changeable and set initially to the default (logon) domain of the currently logged-on user. If this isn't the location you want to use for selecting user and group accounts to work with, tap or click Locations to see a list of locations you can search, including the current domain, trusted domains, and other resources that you can access.

> ## Important
>
> Another way to open the File Sharing dialog box is to press and hold or right-click a folder in File Explorer, tap or click Share With, and then tap or click Specific People. Contrary to what you might think, when you set permissions using the File Sharing dialog box, you are configuring the underlying access permissions rather than share permissions. When you assign a user or group the Read permission level, the user or group is granted Read & Execute permissions on the folder. When you assign a user or group the Read/Write permission level, the user or group is granted Full Control permissions on the folder. The share permissions on the folder are set so that the Everyone and Administrators groups have Full Control.

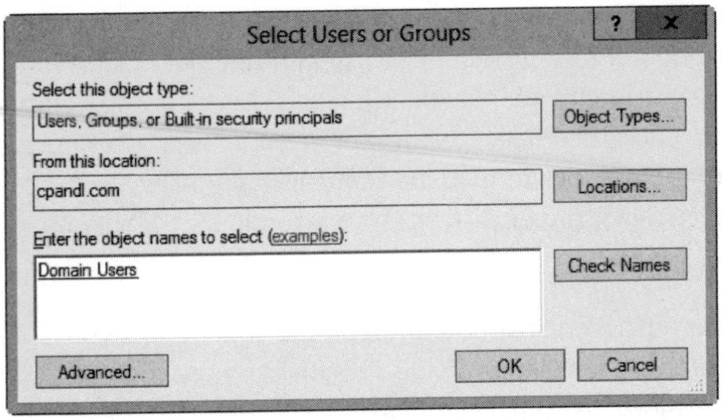

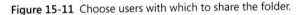

**Figure 15-11**  Choose users with which to share the folder.

In the Enter The Object Names To Select field, type the name of a user or a group account previously defined in the selected or default domain. Be sure to reference the user account name rather than a user's full name. When entering multiple names, separate them with semicolons.

Tap or click Check Names. If a single match is found for each of your entries, the dialog box is automatically updated as appropriate and the entry is underlined. Otherwise, you'll see an additional dialog box. When no matches are found, you've either entered an incorrect name part or you're working with an incorrect location. Modify the name in the Name Not Found dialog box and try again, or tap or click Locations to select a new location. When multiple matches are found, select the name or names you want to use in the Multiple Names Found dialog box, and then tap or click OK.

When you tap or click OK, the users and groups are added to the Name list. You can then configure permissions for each user and group added by tapping or clicking an account name to display the Permission Level options and then choosing the appropriate permission level. The options for permission levels are

- **Read**  Grants the user or group Read & Execute permissions. These are access permissions.

- **Read/Write**  Grants the user or group Full Control permissions. These are access permissions.

Finally, tap or click Share to create the share. The top-level share permissions are set so that the Everyone and Administrators groups have Full Control. After Windows creates the share and makes it available for use, note the share name. This is the name by which the shared resource can be accessed. If you want to email a link to the shared resource to someone, tap or click E-mail. If you want to copy a link to the shared resource to the Clipboard, tap or click Copy. Tap or click Done when you are finished. The share is immediately available for use.

If you tap or click the Share button on the Sharing tab when sharing is already configured, you can change sharing permissions. Grant access to additional users and groups as discussed previously. To change the permission level for a user or group, select the user or group in the Name list and then select the new permission level. To remove access for a user or group, select the user or group in the Name list and then select Remove. When you are finished making changes, tap or click Share to reconfigure the sharing options and then tap or click Done.

If you tap or click the Advanced Sharing button on the Sharing tab, you'll see the Advanced Sharing dialog box, as shown in Figure 15-12. This dialog box allows you to configure top-level share permissions and offline caching.

**Figure 15-12** You can configure different shares of the same folder with different names and permissions as well.

Options in the Advanced Sharing dialog box are used as follows:

- Tap or click Add to share the folder again using a different name and a different set of access permissions. When you create multiple shares for the same folder, the Share Name box of the Sharing tab becomes a selection list that you use to select a share to work with and configure. After you select a share to work with, the options in the Sharing tab apply to that share only. You'll also have a Remove option, which you can use to remove the additional share.

- Tap or click Permissions to view and set the share permissions as discussed in "Managing share permissions" later in this chapter. Share permissions provide the top-level access controls to the share. By default, only users you specify have access to the share. This important security feature is designed to help ensure that permissions aren't given to users unless you grant them.

# INSIDE OUT   Additional sharing options

If a folder hasn't been shared previously, you can use options in the Advanced Sharing dialog box to share it. To do so, select Share This Folder and then enter the Share Name or accept the default value (which is the name of the folder). At this point, you could tap or click OK to create the share. However, when you create a share in this way, the only group granted access by default is the Everyone group, which is granted Read access by default. Thus, instead of tapping or clicking OK at this point, tap or click Permissions and then use the options provided to set additional top-level share permissions.

After you set share permissions, you might want to configure the share for offline use. By default, the share is configured so that only files and programs that users specify are available for offline use. If the BranchCache For Network Files role service is installed on the file server, you might want to keep this setting but also enable BranchCache. To do this, tap or click Caching, and then select Enable BranchCache to enable computers in a branch office to cache files that are downloaded from the shared folder and then securely share the files to other computers in the branch office.

## Creating shares by using Computer Management

By using Computer Management, you can share the folders of any computer to which you can connect on the network. This is handy for when you are sitting at your desk and don't want to have to log on locally to share a server's folders. After you start Computer Management, you can connect to the computer you want to work with by pressing and holding or right-clicking Computer Management in the console tree and then selecting Connect To Another Computer. Use the Select Computer dialog box to choose the computer you want to work with. When you are finished, expand System Tools, Shared Folders, and then select Shares to display the current shares on the system you are working with.

You can then create a shared folder by pressing and holding or right-clicking Shares and then selecting New Share. This starts the Create A Shared Folder Wizard. Tap or click Next to display the Folder Path page as shown in Figure 15-13. In the Folder Path field, type the full path to the folder you want to share. If you don't know the full path or you want to share a new folder, tap or click Browse. You can now

- Use the Browse For Folder dialog box to locate and select the folder you want to share.

- Select the location where you want to create a new folder, tap or click Make New Folder, type a name for the folder, and then press Enter.

> **Note**
> You can start the Create A Shared Folder Wizard by typing **shrpubw** in the App Search box and pressing Enter.

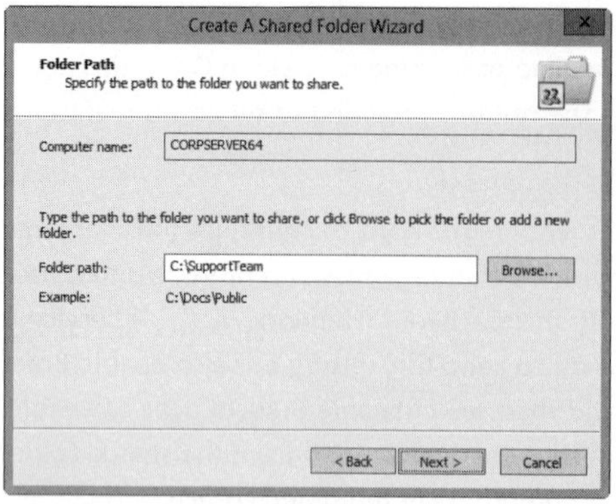

**Figure 15-13** Specify the folder path, or tap or click Browse to search for a folder to use.

Tap or click Next when you are ready to continue. In the Share Name field, type a name for the share, as shown in Figure 15-14. This is the name of the folder to which users will connect, and it must be unique on the computer you are working with. Share names can be up to 80 characters in length and can contain spaces. If you want to provide support for early Windows-operating-system clients, you should limit the share name to eight characters with a three-letter extension. If you want to hide the share from users (which means that they won't be able to see the shared resource when they try to browse to it in File Explorer or at the command line), type **$** as the last character of the share name. Keep in mind that you can hide shares only from normal users. If users have Administrator privileges, they can get a list of the shares.

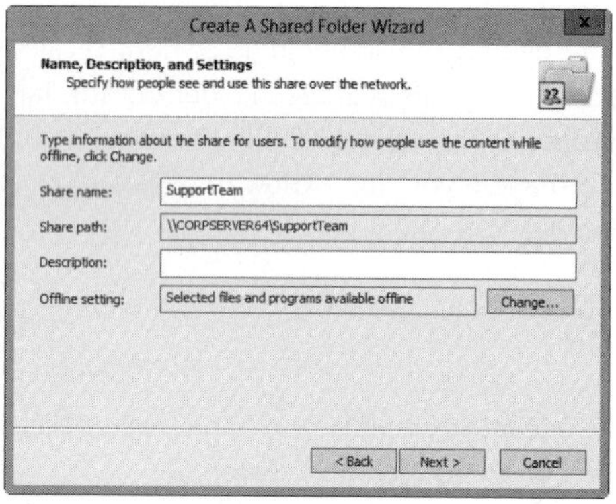

**Figure 15-14** Set the share name and description.

Optionally, type a description of the share in the Description field. The description is displayed as comments when you view shares in Network Explorer and other Windows dialog boxes. Next configure offline settings as appropriate.

By default, the share is configured so that only files and programs that users specify are available for offline use. Normally, this is the option you want to use because this option also allows users to take advantage of the new Always Offline feature. However, if you use this setting, you also might want to enable BranchCache. To do this, tap or click Change, select Enable BranchCache, as shown in Figure 15-15, and then tap or click OK. When the BranchCache For Network Files role service is installed on the file server, enabling BranchCache allows computers in a branch office to cache files that are downloaded from the shared folder and then securely share the files with other computers in the branch office.

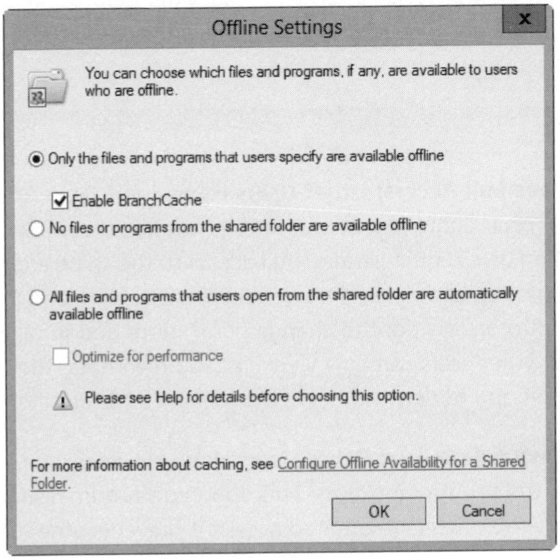

**Figure 15-15**  Configure the offline settings.

Alternatively, tap or click Change and then select All Files And Programs That Users Open From The Shared Folder Are Automatically Available Offline. With this setting, client computers automatically cache all files and programs that users open from the share. You can then also select Optimize For Performance to run cached program files from the local cache instead of the shared folder on the server.

When you are ready to continue, tap or click Next to display the Shared Folder Permissions page shown in Figure 15-16. The available options are as follows:

- **All Users Have Read-Only Access**   Grants the share permission Read to the Everyone group. Because of this, all users have access to the share. The underlying access permissions determine permitted actions.

> **Note**
>
> Granting Read access instead of Full Control by default is designed to help ensure permissions aren't given to users unless you specifically grant them. Although it is a start on better controls, it isn't perfect because this permission is assigned to the special group Everyone, which means anyone with access to the network— even Guests—have Read access to the share.

- **Administrators Have Full Access; Other Users Have Read-Only Access**   Grants the share permission Full Control to Administrators and the share permission Read to Everyone. This option gives administrators full access to the share and allows administrators to create, modify, and delete files and folders. On NTFS and ReFS volumes, it also gives administrators the right to change permissions and to take ownership of files and folders. Other users can only view files and read data. They can't create, modify, or delete files and folders.

- **Administrators Have Full Access; Other Users Have No Access**   Grants the share permission Full Control to Administrators. This option gives administrators full access to the share. Because no others are granted access, it prevents other users from accessing the share.

- **Customize Permissions**   This option allows you to configure access for specific users and groups, which is usually the best technique to use. Setting share permissions is discussed fully in "Managing share permissions" later in this chapter.

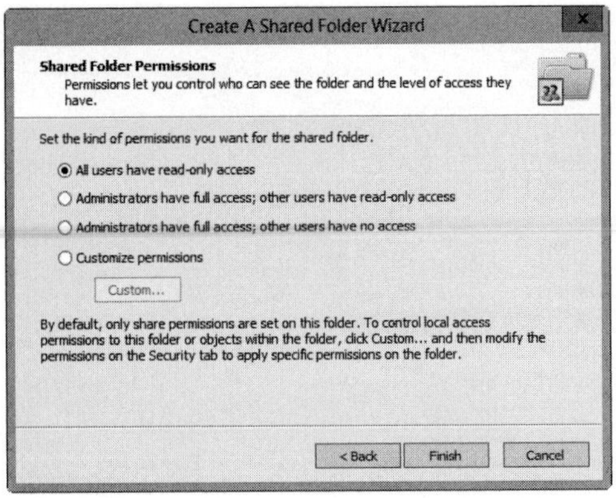

**Figure 15-16**  Set the share permissions.

After you set up permissions on the share, tap or click Finish. The wizard displays a status report, which should state "Sharing Was Successful." If you want to create another share, select the related check box before you tap or click Finish. This will run the Create A Shared Folder Wizard again.

## Creating shared folders in Server Manager

In Server Manager, the Shares subnode of the File And Storage Services node shows existing shares for file servers that have been added for management. I recommend getting to know the options here and using Server Manager for creating and managing shares whenever possible.

As shown in Figure 15-17, the shares are listed in alphabetical order for each server. If you select a share, the Volume panel provides information about the underlying volume and the Quota panel displays information about File Server Resource Manager (FSRM) quotas.

Chapter 15

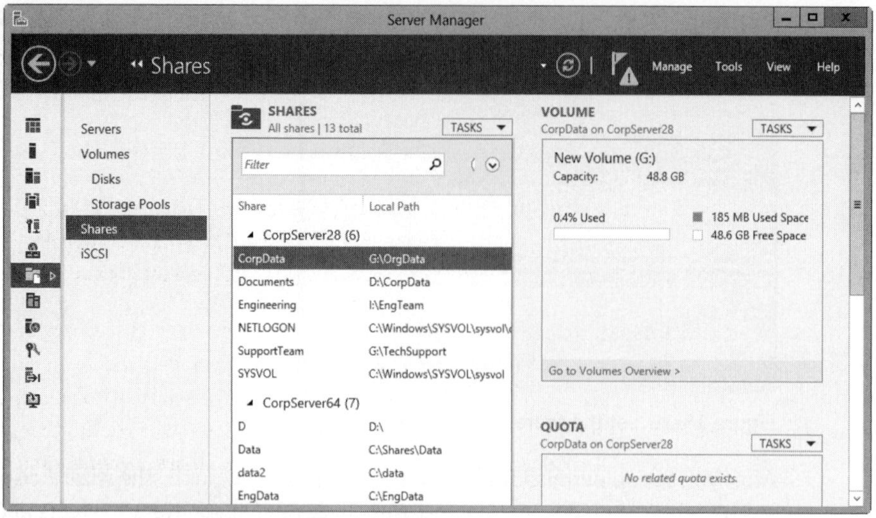

**Figure 15-17** View currently configured shares.

On the Shares panel, tap or click Tasks and then tap or click New Share to start the New Share Wizard. The New Share Wizard has several file-share profiles:

- **SMB Share - Quick** A basic profile for creating SMB file shares that you can use to configure their settings and permissions.

- **SMB Share - Advanced** An advanced profile for creating SMB file shares that you can use to configure their settings, permissions, management properties, and FSRM quota profile (if applicable).

- **SMB Share - Applications** A custom profile for creating SMB file shares with settings appropriate for Hyper-V, certain databases, and other server applications. It's essentially the same as the quick profile, but it doesn't allow you to enable access-based enumeration or offline caching. If the share will be used for Hyper-V, you also might need to enable constrained delegation for remote management of the Hyper-V host.

- **NFS Share - Quick** A basic profile for creating NFS file shares that you can use to configure their authentication settings, manage permissions for hosts, and manage permissions for users.

- **NFS Share - Advanced** An advanced profile for creating NFS file shares that you can use to configure their authentication settings, manage permissions for hosts and users, add management properties, and assign an FSRM quota profile (if applicable).

**Note**

The differences between the file-share profiles are fundamental. Whether you are working with SMB or NFS, the Advanced profiles allow you to add management properties and assign FSRM quota profiles and the Quick profiles don't. The Applications profile is the same as the Quick profile except that it disables access-based enumeration and offline caching in the wizard UI because you don't want to use these settings with server applications and certain databases. If you later edit the properties of a share created with the Applications profile, these properties are configurable.

**Important**

SMB 3.0 includes enhancements that improve performance for small random reads and writes, which are common with server-based applications, such as Microsoft SQL Server OLTP. Packets use large maximum transmission units (MTUs) as well to enhance performance for large, sequential data transfers, such as those used for deploying and copying virtual hard disks (VHDs) over the network, database backup and restore over the network, and SQL Server data-warehouse transactions over the network.

Choose one of the available SMB share profiles, and then tap or click Next. On the Select The Server And Path For This Share page, shown in Figure 15-18, select the server and volume on which you want the share to be created. Only file servers you've added for management are available.

**Note**

Server Manager creates the file share as a new folder in the \Shares directory on the selected volume by default. To change this, choose the Type A Custom Path option and then either type the desired share path, such as **D:\Data**, or click Browse to use the Select Folder dialog box to select the share path. If the folder path doesn't exist, the wizard will create folders as necessary.

Chapter 15

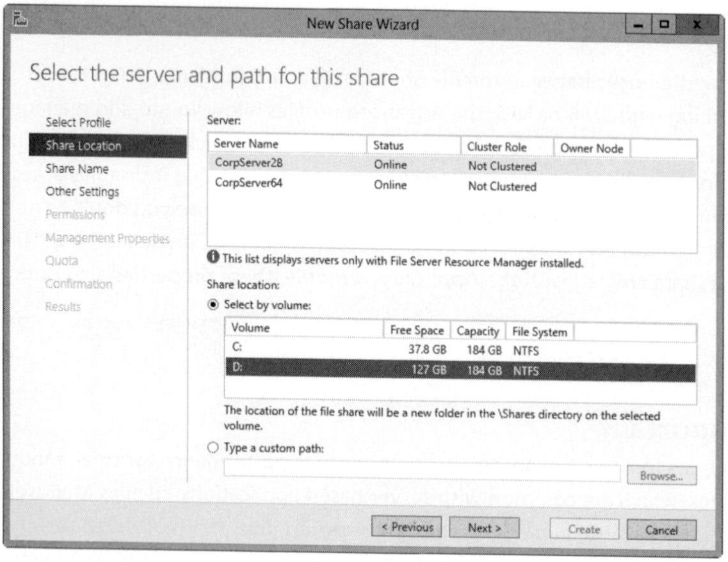

**Figure 15-18** Set the location of the share.

Tap or click Next when you are ready to continue. On the Specify Share Name page, type a name for the share, as shown in Figure 15-19. This is the name of the folder to which users will connect. Note the local and remote paths to the share. These paths are set based on the share location and share name you specified. Keep in mind that share names must be unique for each system and that the wizard creates folders as necessary. For example, if the path is D:\Shares\EngData and neither the Shares folder nor the EngData subfolder have been created, the wizard will create both folders to ensure the share path is valid.

Optionally, type a description of the share in the Share Description text box. When you view shares on a particular computer, the description is displayed in Computer Management. When you are ready to continue, tap or click Next.

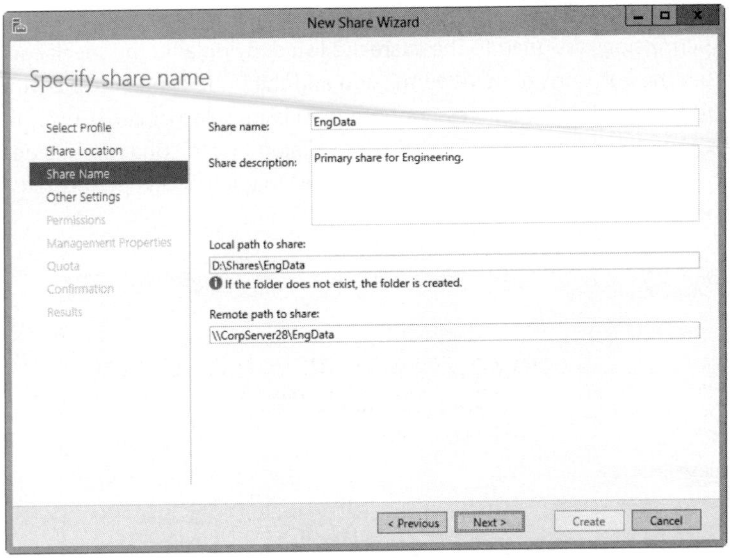

**Figure 15-19**  Set the name and description for the share.

On the Configure Share Settings page, use the following options to configure the way the share is used:

- **Enable Access-Based Enumeration**   With this setting, the wizard configures permissions so that when users browse the folder, only files and folders a user has been granted at least Read access to are displayed. If a user doesn't have at least Read (or equivalent) permission for a file or folder within the shared folder, that file or folder is hidden from view. (This option is dimmed if you are creating an SMB share optimized for applications.)

- **Allow Caching Of Share**   With this setting, the wizard configures the share to cache only the files and programs that users specify for offline use. Although you can later edit the share properties and change the offline files' availability settings, you normally want to select this option because it allows users to take advantage of the new Always Offline feature. Optionally, if the BranchCache For Network Files role service is installed on the file server, select Enable BranchCache to enable computers in a branch office to cache files that are downloaded from the shared folder and then securely share the files to other computers in the branch office. (This option is dimmed if you are creating an SMB share optimized for applications.)

- **Encrypt Data Access**   With this setting, the wizard configures the share to use SMB encryption, which protects file data from eavesdropping while it is being transferred over the network. This option is useful on untrusted networks.

On the Specify Permissions To Control Access page, shown in Figure 15-20, the default access permissions assigned to the share are listed. By default, the special group Everyone is granted the Full Control share permission and the underlying access permissions are as listed. To change the share, access, or both permissions, tap or click Customize Permissions and then use the Advanced Security Settings dialog box to configure the desired permissions. See "Managing share permissions" and "Managing access permissions" later in the chapter for more information on setting permissions.

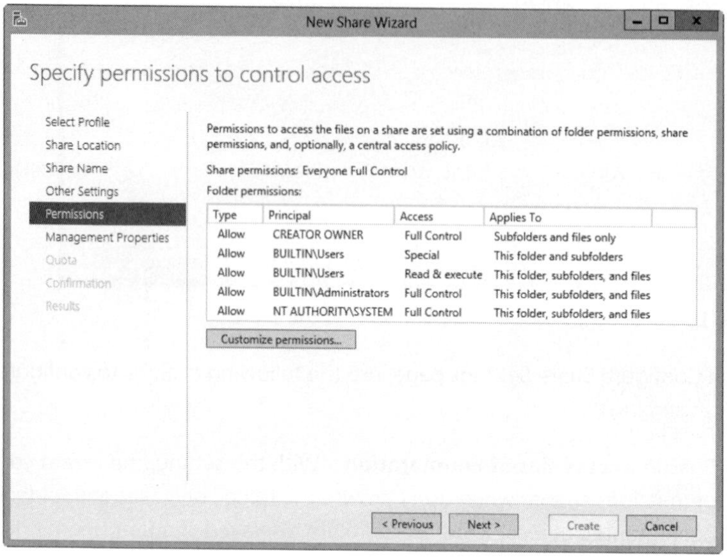

**Figure 15-20** Review the default permissions, and set other permissions as appropriate.

If you are using the advanced profile, do the following:

- Optionally, set the folder management properties and then tap or click Next. These properties specify the purpose of the folder and the type of data stored in it so that data-management policies, such as classification rules, can then use these properties.

- Optionally, apply a quota based on a template to the folder and then tap or click Next. You can select only quota templates that have already been created. For more information, see "Managing file-screen templates" in Chapter 16, "Managing file screening and storage reporting."

On the Confirm Selections page, review your selections. When you tap or click Create, the wizard creates the share, configures it, and sets permissions. The status should state, "The share was successfully created." If an error is displayed instead, note the error and take corrective action as appropriate before repeating this procedure to create the share. Tap or click Close.

# Changing shared folder settings

When you create a share, you can configure many basic and advanced settings, including those for access-based enumeration, encrypted data access, offline settings for caching, and management properties. In Server Manager, the Shares subnode of the File And Storage Services node shows existing shares for file servers that have been added for management. You can modify share settings by pressing and holding or right-clicking the share you want to work with, and then tapping or clicking Properties.

In the Properties dialog box, shown in Figure 15-21, you have several option panels that can be accessed using controls in the left pane. Although you can expand the panels one by one, tap or click Show All instead to expand all the panels at the same time, and then simply scroll through the properties to review the settings. The options available are the same whether you used the basic, advanced, or applications profile to create the shared folder.

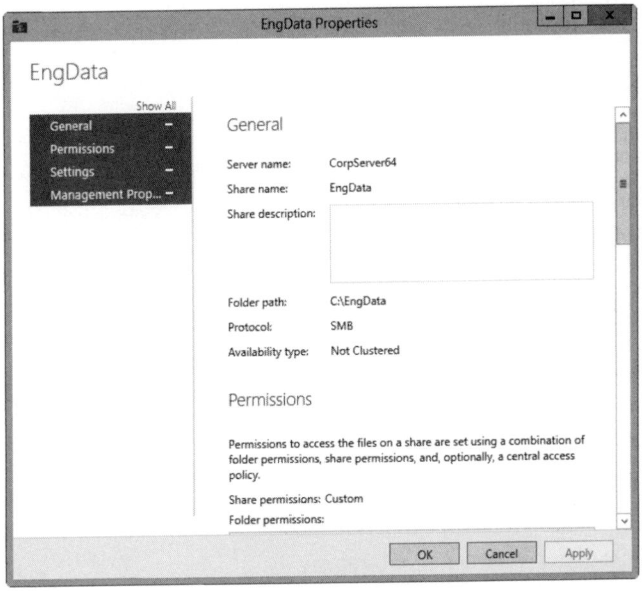

**Figure 15-21**  Review and modify the share settings.

# Publishing shares in Active Directory

Sometimes, you'll also want to publish shares in Active Directory to make them easier to find. The quickest way to do this is to use Computer Management. After you start Computer Management and connect to the computer you want to work with, expand System Tools, Shared Folders, and then select Shares to display the current shares on the system you are working with.

You can then publish a shared folder by pressing and holding or right-clicking the share in the details pane and then selecting Properties. In the share's Properties dialog box, tap or click the Publish tab as shown in Figure 15-22. Finally, select the Publish This Share In Active Directory check box and then tap or click OK.

---

**Note**

As discussed earlier in the chapter in "Using and finding shares," search keywords can help users find shares. To add search keywords, tap or click Edit. In the Edit Keywords dialog box, enter a keyword and then tap or click Add. Repeat as necessary to add additional keywords.

---

**Figure 15-22**  Publish the share in Active Directory.

# Managing share permissions

As discussed previously, Windows Server 2012 has two levels of permissions for shared folders: share permissions and access permissions. Share permissions are applied any time you access a file or folder over the network. These top-level permissions set the maximum allowable actions available within a shared folder. Although share permissions can get you in the door when you work remotely, the access permissions can further constrain access and the allowable actions.

When accessing files locally, only the access permissions are applied. However, when accessing files remotely, first the share permissions are applied and then the access permissions. In the case of file allocation table (FAT) volumes, the share permissions are the only permissions, and if a user has local access to the folder, the user can perform any action.

## Understanding share permissions

With shared folders, you use share permissions to set the maximum allowed access level. Share permissions are applied only when you access a folder remotely, and they can be used to grant access directly to users or implicitly through the groups to which users belong.

The share permissions available are as follows:

- **Full Control**   By granting this permission, users have Read and Change permissions, as well as the following additional capabilities to change access permissions and take ownership of files and folders.

- **Change**   By granting this permission, users have Read permissions and the additional capability to create files and subfolders, modify files, change attributes on files and subfolders, and delete files and subfolders.

- **Read**   By granting this permission, you allow users to view file and subfolder names, access the subfolders of the share, read file data and attributes, and run program files.

If you have Read permissions on a share, the most you can do is perform read operations. If you have Change permissions on a share, the most you can do is perform read operations and change operations. If you have Full Control, you have full access. However, in any case, access permissions can further constrain access.

Permissions assigned to groups work like this: If a user is a member of a group that is granted share permissions, the user also has those permissions. If a user is a member of multiple groups, the permissions are cumulative. This means that if one group of which the user is a member has Read access and another has additional access, the user has additional access as well.

Chapter 15

# INSIDE OUT Changes might be needed to enhance security

When you create a shared folder, default access permissions are assigned. Watch out, though, because the default in most cases is to either give Read access or Full Control to the special group Everyone, and both configurations allows Guests to access shares. This doesn't mean Guests can read files, however, because this is determined by the base-level access permissions. In most cases, it is more prudent to lock down access and grant permissions only to users who truly need access to a shared folder. If you really want to grant wide access to a shared folder, you might want to use the Domain Users group to do this rather than the Everyone group. In this case, you remove the Everyone group and add the Domain Users group. By using Domain Users, you require users to have a logon account to access the shared folder, which excludes Guests.

To override this behavior, you must specifically deny an access permission. Denying permission is the trump card—it takes precedence and overrides permissions that have been granted. When you want to single out a user or group and not let it have a permission, configure the share permissions to specifically deny that permission to the user or group. For example, if a user is a member of a group that has been granted Full Control over a share, but the user should have only Read permissions, configure the share to deny Change permissions to that user.

## Configuring share permissions

The easiest way to configure share permissions is to use Computer Management. After you start Computer Management, connect to the computer you want to work with by pressing and holding or right-clicking Computer Management in the console tree and then selecting Connect To Another Computer. Then use the Select Computer dialog box to choose the computer you want to work with. When you are finished, expand System Tools, Shared Folders, and then select Shares to display the current shares on the system you are working with.

To view or manage the permissions of a share, press and hold or right-click the share and then select Properties. In the share Properties dialog box, tap or click the Share Permissions tab, as shown in Figure 15-23. You can now view the users and groups that have access to the share and the type of access they have.

In this example, members of the Domain Admins group have Full Control over the share and members of the Domain Users group have Change access. The group Everyone was removed to enhance security as discussed in the Inside Out "Changes might be needed to enhance security" earlier in the chapter.

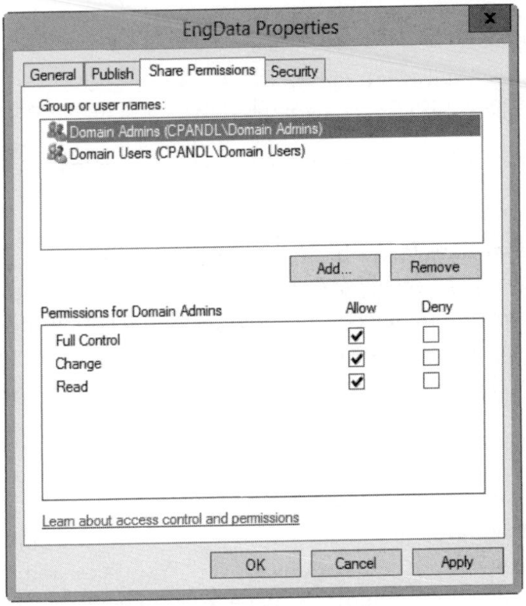

**Figure 15-23**  View or set share permissions.

You can grant or deny permission to access a share by following these steps:

1.  In Computer Management, press and hold or right-click the share and then select Properties. In the share Properties dialog box, tap or click the Share Permissions tab.

2.  On the Share Permissions tab, tap or click Add. This opens the Select Users, Computers, Or Groups dialog box.

3.  The Locations button allows you to access account names from other domains. Tap or click Locations to see a list of the current domains, trusted domains, and other resources that you can access. Because of transitive trusts, you can usually access all the domains in the domain tree or forest.

4.  Type the name of a user or group account in the selected or default domain, and then tap or click Check Names. The options available depend on the number of matches found, as follows:

    ○  When a single match is found, the dialog box is automatically updated as appropriate and the entry is underlined.

    ○  When no matches are found, you've either entered an incorrect name part or you're working with an incorrect location. Modify the name and try again, or tap or click Locations to select a new location.

    o   If multiple matches are found, select the name or names you want to use, and then tap or click OK.

5. To add additional users or groups, type a semicolon (;), and then repeat this process.

6. When you tap or click OK, the users and groups are added to the Name list for the share.

7. Configure access permissions for each user and group added by selecting an account name and then allowing or denying access permissions. If a user or group should be granted access permissions, select the check box for the permission in the Allow column. If a user or group should be denied access permissions, select the check box for the permission in the Deny column.

8. When you're finished, tap or click OK.

In Server Manager, the Shares subnode of the File And Storage Services node shows existing shares for file servers that have been added for management. Press and hold or right-click the share you want to work with, and then tap or click Properties. In the Properties dialog box, tap or click the Permissions in the left pane. You can now view the users and groups that have access to the share and the type of access they have.

To change share, folder, or both permissions, tap or click Customize Permissions and then select the Share tab in the Advanced Security Settings dialog box, as shown in Figure 15-24. Users or groups that already have access to the share are listed in the Permission Entries list. You can remove permissions for these users and groups by selecting the user or group you want to remove and then tapping or clicking Remove.

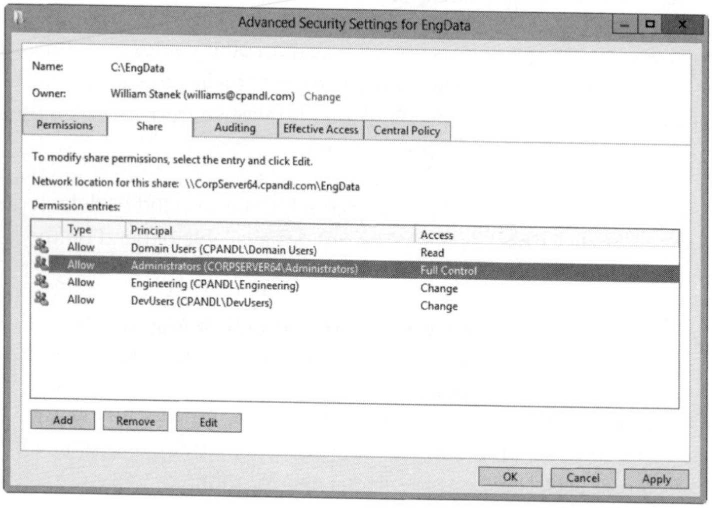

**Figure 15-24** Use the Advanced Security Settings dialog box to manage share permissions.

You can change permissions for these users and groups by doing the following:

1. Select the user or group you want to change, and then select Edit.

2. Allow or deny access permissions in the Permissions list box, and then tap or click OK.

To add permissions for another user or group, follow these steps:

1. Tap or click Add to open the Permission Entry dialog box, shown in Figure 15-25. Next, tap or click Select A Principal to display the Select User, Computer, Service Account Or Group dialog box. Type the name of a user or a group account, and then tap or click Check Names. Only one name can be entered at a time. Be sure to reference the user account name rather than the user's full name.

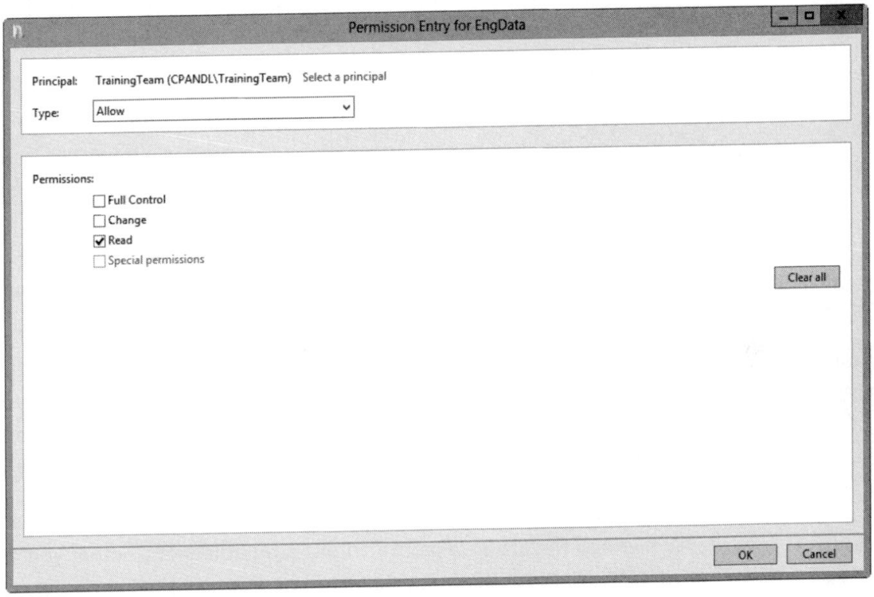

**Figure 15-25**  Add permissions entries to allow or deny access.

2. If a single match is found for each entry, the dialog box is automatically updated, and the entry is underlined. Otherwise, you'll see an additional dialog box. If no matches are found, you either entered the name incorrectly or you're working with an incorrect location. Modify the name in the Name Not Found dialog box and try again, or tap or click Locations to select a new location. When multiple matches are found, in the Multiple Names Found dialog box, select the name you want to use and then tap or click OK.

3. When you tap or click OK, the user and group is added as the Principal, and the Permission Entry dialog box is updated to show this.

4. Use the Type list to specify whether you are configuring allowed or denied permissions, and then select the permissions you want to allow or deny.

5. Tap or click OK to return to the Advanced Security Settings dialog box. To assign additional security permissions for controlling access, see "Managing access permissions."

# Managing access permissions

You can think of access permissions as the base-level permissions—the permissions that are applied no matter what. For NTFS and ReFS volumes, you use access permissions and ownership to further constrain actions within the share as well as share permissions. For FAT volumes, share permissions provide the only access controls. The reason for this is that FAT volumes have no file and folder permission capabilities.

Access permissions are much more complex than share permissions, and to really understand how they can be used and applied, you must understand ownership and inheritance as well as the permissions that are available. Because Windows Server 2012 adds new layers of security, access permissions now include basic permissions, claims-based permissions, and special permissions.

## INSIDE OUT  Changes to basic file and folder attributes are sometimes necessary

As administrators, we often forget about the basic file and folder attributes that can be assigned. However, basic file and folder attributes can affect access, so let's look at these attributes first and then at the access permissions you can apply to NTFS and ReFS volumes.

All files and folders have basic attributes regardless of whether you are working with FAT, NTFS, or ReFS. These attributes can be examined in File Explorer by pressing and holding or right-clicking the file or folder icon and then selecting Properties. Folder and file attributes include Hidden and Read-Only. Hidden determines whether the file is displayed in file listings. You can override this by telling File Explorer to display hidden files. On NTFS and ReFS volumes, the Read-Only attribute for folders is initially shown as unavailable. Here, this means the attribute is in a mixed state regardless of the current state of files in the folder. If you override the mixed state by selecting the Read-Only check box for a folder, all files in the folder will be read-only. If you override the mixed state and clear the Read-Only check box for a folder, all files in the folder will be writable.

# File and folder ownership

Before working with access permissions, you should understand the concept of ownership as it applies to files and folders. In Windows Server, the file or folder owner isn't necessarily the file's or folder's creator. Instead, the file or folder owner is the person who has direct control over the file or folder. File or folder owners can grant access permissions and give other users permission to take ownership of a file or folder.

The way ownership is assigned initially depends on where the file or folder is being created. By default, the user who created the file or folder is listed as the current owner. Ownership can be taken or transferred in several ways. Any administrator can take ownership. Any user or group with the Take Ownership permission can take ownership. Any user who has the right to Restore Files And Directories, such as a member of the Backup Operators group, can take ownership as well. Any current owner can transfer ownership to another user as well.

You can take ownership using File Explorer or Server Manager. In File Explorer, press and hold or right-click the file or folder, and then select Properties. On the Security tab of the Properties dialog box, display the Advanced Security Settings dialog box by tapping or clicking Advanced.

If a folder has been shared, you can change its ownership using Server Manager. In Server Manager, the Shares subnode of the File And Storage Services node shows existing shares for file servers that have been added for management. Press and hold or right-click the share you want to work with, and then tap or click Properties. In the Properties dialog box, tap or click the Permissions in the left pane. Tap or click Customize Permissions to display the Advanced Security Settings dialog box.

As shown in Figure 15-26, the current owner is listed on the Permissions tab. Tap or click Change. Use the options in the Select User, Computer, Service Account, Or Group dialog box to select the new owner. If you're taking ownership of a folder, you can take ownership of all subfolders and files within the folder by selecting the Replace Owner On Subcontainers And Objects option. Tap or click OK twice when you are finished.

Chapter 15

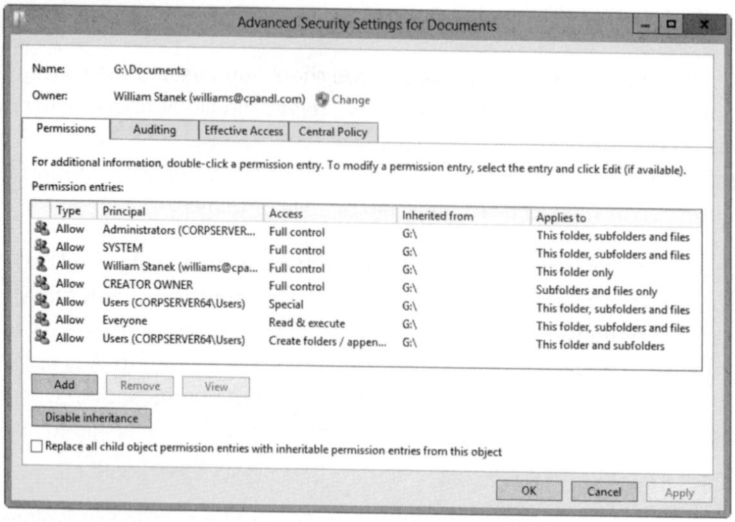

**Figure 15-26**  Taking ownership is done by using the Permissions tab.

# Permission inheritance for files and folders

By default, when you add a folder or file to an existing folder, the folder or file inherits the permissions of the existing folder. For example, if the Domain Users group has access to a folder and you add a file to this folder, members of the Domain Users group will be able to access the file. Inherited permissions are automatically assigned when files and folders are created.

When you assign new permissions to a folder, the permissions propagate down and are inherited by all subfolders and files in the folder and supplement or replace existing permissions. If you add permissions on a folder to allow a new group to access a folder, these permissions are applied to all subfolders and files in the folder, meaning the additional group is granted access. On the other hand, if you were to change the permissions on the folder so that, for instance, only members of the Engineering group could access the folder, these permissions would be applied to all subfolders and files in the folder—meaning only members of the Engineering group would have access to the folder, its subfolders, and its files.

Inheritance is automatic. If you do not want the permissions of subfolders and files within folders to supplement or replace existing permissions, you must override inheritance starting with the top-level folder from which the permissions are inherited. A top-level folder is referred to as a *parent folder*. Files and folders below the parent folder are referred to as *child files and folders*. This is identical to the parent/child structure of objects in Active Directory.

## Changing shaded permissions and stopping inheritance

If a permission you want to change is shaded, the file or folder is inheriting the permission from a parent folder. To change the permission, you must do one of the following:

- Access the parent folder, and make the desired changes. These changes will then be inherited by child folders and files.

- Select the opposite permission to override the inherited permission if possible. In most cases, Deny overrides Allow, so if you explicitly deny permission to a user or group for a child folder or file, this permission should be denied to that user or group of users.

- Stop inheriting permissions from the parent folder, and then copy or remove existing permissions as appropriate.

To stop inheriting permissions from a parent folder, press and hold or right-click the file or folder in File Explorer and then select Properties. On the Security tab of the Properties dialog box, tap or click Advanced to display the Advanced Security Settings dialog box. On the Permissions tab, you'll see a Disable Inheritance button if inheritance currently is enabled. When you tap or click Disable Inheritance, you can either convert the inherited permissions to explicit permissions or remove all inherited permissions and apply only the permissions that you explicitly set on the folder or file. (See Figure 15-27.)

> **Important**
>
> If you remove the inherited permissions and no other permissions are assigned, everyone but the owner of the resource is denied access. This effectively locks out everyone except the owner of a folder or file. However, administrators still have the right to take ownership of the resource regardless of the permissions. Thus, if an administrator is locked out of a file or a folder and truly needs access, she can take ownership and then have unrestricted access.

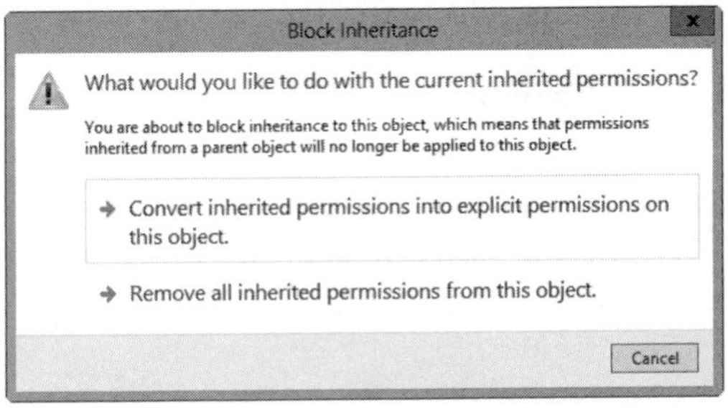

**Figure 15-27** Block inheritance by converting or removing the inherited permissions.

Chapter 15

If a folder has been shared, you can change its inheritance settings using Server Manager. In Server Manager, the Shares subnode of the File And Storage Services node shows existing shares for file servers that have been added for management. Press and hold or right-click the share you want to work with, and then tap or click Properties. In the Properties dialog box, tap or click the Permissions in the left pane. Tap or click Customize Permissions to display the Advanced Security Settings dialog box. After you tap or click Disable Inheritance, you can elect to either convert the inherited permissions to explicit permissions or remove all inherited permissions and apply only the permissions that you explicitly set on the folder or file. (See Figure 15-27.)

## Resetting and replacing permissions

Another way to manage permissions is to reset the permissions of subfolders and files within a folder, replacing their permissions with the current permissions assigned to the folder you are working with. In this way, subfolders and files get all inheritable permissions from the parent folder and all other explicitly defined permissions on the individual subfolders and files are removed.

To reset permissions for subfolders and files of a folder, access the Advanced Settings dialog box, as discussed previously. Next, select Enable Inheritance. Optionally, before you tap or click OK, you can remove all explicitly defined permissions and enable propagation of inheritable permissions to any file or subfolder of the folder. To do this, select the Replace All Child Object Permission Entries check box and then tap or click Yes when prompted to confirm. (See Figure 15-28.)

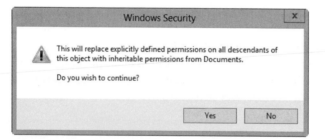

**Figure 15-28** Confirm that you want to replace the existing permissions on subfolders and files.

## Configuring access permissions

On NTFS and ReFS volumes, you can assign access permissions to files and folders. These permissions grant or deny access to users and groups.

## Basic permissions

In File Explorer, you can view basic permissions by pressing and holding or right-clicking the file or folder you want to work with, selecting Properties on the shortcut menu, and then in the Properties dialog box selecting the Security tab, as shown in Figure 15-29. The Group Or User Names list shows groups and users with assigned permissions. If you select a group or user in this list, the applicable permissions are shown in the Permissions For list. If permissions are unavailable, it means the permissions are inherited from a parent folder as discussed previously.

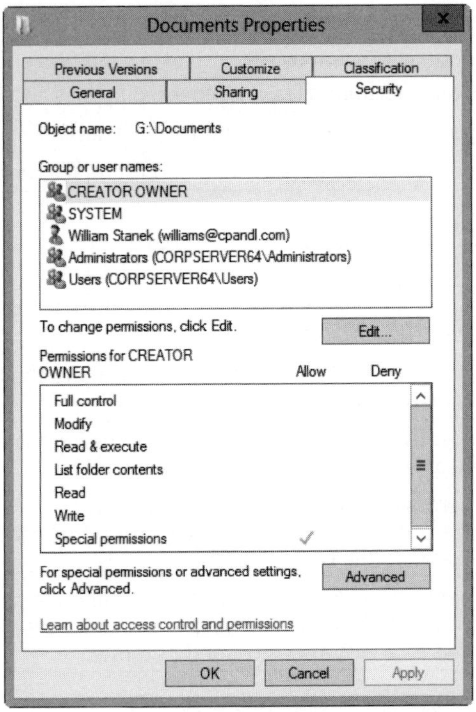

**Figure 15-29**  The Security tab shows the basic permissions assigned to each user or group.

The basic permissions you can assign to folders and files are shown in Table 15-1 and Table 15-2. These permissions are made up of multiple special permissions.

**TABLE 15-1 Basic folder permissions**

| Permission | Description |
|---|---|
| Full Control | This permission permits reading, writing to, changing, and deleting files and subfolders. If a user has Full Control over a folder, she can delete files in the folder regardless of the permission on the files. |
| Modify | This permission permits reading and writing to files and subfolders, and it allows deletion of the folder. |
| List Folder Contents | This permission permits viewing and listing files and subfolders, as well as executing files; it is inherited by folders only. |
| Read & Execute | This permission permits viewing and listing files and subfolders, as well as executing files; it is inherited by files and folders. |
| Write | This permission permits adding files and subfolders. |
| Read | This permission permits viewing and listing files and subfolders. |

**TABLE 15-2 Basic file permissions**

| Permission | Description |
|---|---|
| Full Control | This permission permits reading, writing to, changing, and deleting the file. |
| Modify | This permission permits reading and writing to the file, and it allows deletion of the file. |
| Read & Execute | This permission permits viewing and accessing the file's contents, as well as executing the file. |
| Write | This permission permits writing to a file. Giving a user permission to write to a file but not to delete it doesn't prevent the user from deleting the file's contents. |
| Read | This permission permits viewing or accessing the file's contents. Read is the only permission needed to run scripts. Read access is required to access a shortcut and its target. |

You can set basic permissions for files and folders by following these steps:

1. In File Explorer, press and hold or right-click the file or folder you want to work with, and select Properties. In the Properties dialog box, select the Security tab, shown previously in Figure 15-29.

2. Tap or click Edit to display an editable version of the Security tab. Users or groups that already have access to the file or folder are listed in the Groups Or User Names list box. You can change permissions for these users and groups by selecting the user or group you want to change and then using the Permissions list box to grant or deny access permissions.

3. To set access permissions for additional users, computers, or groups, tap or click Add. This displays the Select Users, Computers, Or Groups dialog box.

**4.** The Locations button allows you to access account names from other domains. Tap or click Locations to see a list of the current domain, trusted domains, and other resources that you can access. Because of transitive trusts, you can usually access all the domains in the domain tree or forest.

**5.** Type the name of a user or group account in the selected or default domain, and then tap or click Check Names. The options available depend on the number of matches found as follows:

  ○ When a single match is found, the dialog box is automatically updated as appropriate and the entry is underlined.

  ○ When no matches are found, you've either entered an incorrect name part or you're working with an incorrect location. Modify the name and try again, or tap or click Locations to select a new location.

  ○ If multiple matches are found, select the name or names you want to use and then tap or click OK.

**6.** To add additional users or groups, type a semicolon (;), and then repeat this process.

**7.** When you tap or click OK, the users and groups are added to the Name list for the share. Configure access permissions for each user and group added by selecting an account name and then allowing or denying access permissions. If a user or group should be granted access permissions, select the check box for the permission in the Allow column. If a user or group should be denied access permissions, select the check box for the permission in the Deny column.

**8.** When you're finished, tap or click OK.

Shared folders also have NTFS permissions. Using Server Manager, you can set basic NTFS permissions for shared folders by following these steps:

**1.** Press and hold or right-click the folder you want to work with, and then tap or click Properties. This displays a Properties dialog box.

**2.** When you tap or click Permissions in the left pane, the current share permissions and NTFS permissions are shown in the main pane.

**3.** Tap or click Customize Permissions to open the Advanced Security Settings dialog box with the Permissions tab selected. The options available include the following:

  ○ **Add**  Adds a user or group. Tap or click Add to display the Permission Entry dialog box, shown in Figure 15-30. Tap or click Select A Principal to display the Select User, Computer, Service Account, Or Group dialog box. Type the name of a user or a group account, and then tap or click Check Names. Be sure to reference the user account name rather than the user's full name. Only one name can be entered at a time.

Chapter 15

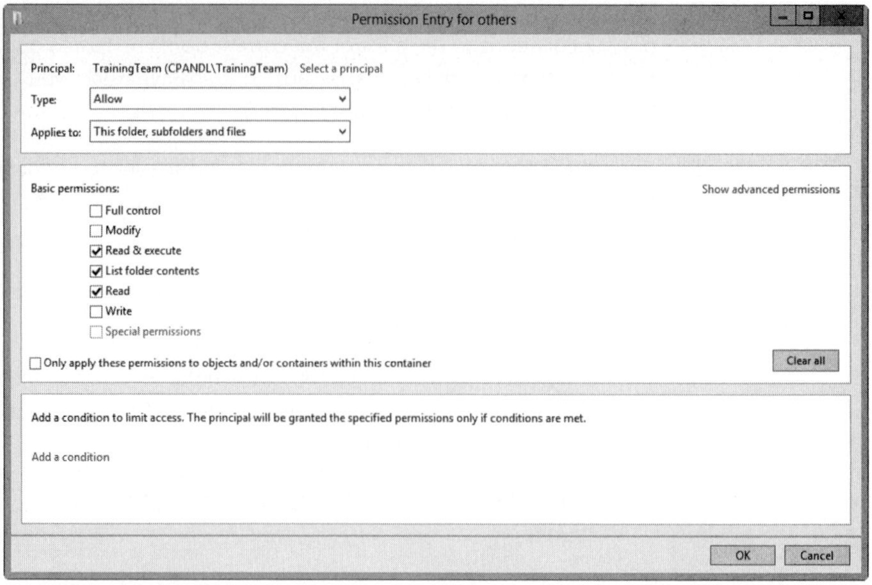

**Figure 15-30** Use the Permission Entry dialog box to set basic permissions.

○ **Edit** Edits an existing user or group entry. Select the user or group whose permissions you want to modify, and then tap or click Edit. The Permissions Entry dialog box shown in Figure 15-30 is displayed.

○ **Remove** Removes an existing user or group entry. Select the user or group whose permissions you want to remove, and then tap or click Remove.

4. When you are editing permissions, you allow and deny special permissions separately. Therefore, if you want to both allow and deny special permissions, you need to configure the allowed permissions and then repeat this procedure starting with step 1 to configure the denied permissions.

5. When finished, use the Apply Onto options shown in Table 15-3 to determine how and where these permissions are applied. If you want to prevent subfolders and files from inheriting these permissions, select Only Apply These Permissions To Objects And/Or Containers Within This Container. When you do this, all the related entries in Table 15-3 are No. This means the settings no longer apply to subsequent subfolders or to files in subsequent subfolders.

**TABLE 15-3 Permissions Apply Onto options**

| Apply Onto | Applies to Current Folder | Applies to Subfolders in the Current Folder | Applies to File in the Current Folder | Applies to Subsequent Subfolders | Applies to Files in Subsequent Subfolders |
|---|---|---|---|---|---|
| This folder only | Yes | No | No | No | No |
| This folder, subfolders, and files | Yes | Yes | Yes | Yes | Yes |
| This folder and subfolders | Yes | Yes | No | Yes | No |
| This folder and files | Yes | No | Yes | No | Yes |
| Subfolders and files only | No | Yes | Yes | Yes | Yes |
| Subfolders only | No | Yes | No | Yes | No |
| Files only | No | No | Yes | No | Yes |

> **Note**
> When Only Apply These Permissions To Objects And/Or Containers Within This Container is selected, all the values under Applies To Subsequent Subfolders and Applies To Files In Subsequent Subfolders are No. The settings no longer apply to subsequent subfolders or to files in subsequent subfolders.

## Special permissions

You can use either File Explorer or Server Manager to view special permissions. In Server Manager, press and hold or right-click the share you want to work with, and then tap or click Properties. In the Properties dialog box, tap or click the Permissions in the left pane. Tap or click Customize Permissions to display the Advanced Security Settings dialog box.

In File Explorer, you can view special permissions by pressing and holding or right-clicking the file or folder you want to work with and selecting Properties on the shortcut menu. In the Properties dialog box, select the Security tab, and then tap or click Advanced to display the Advanced Security Settings dialog box.

The special permissions available are as follows:

- **Traverse Folder/Execute File**   Traverse Folder lets you directly access a folder even if you don't have explicit access to read the data it contains. Execute File lets you run an executable file.

- **List Folder/Read Data**   List Folder lets you view file and folder names. Read Data lets you view the contents of a file.

- **Read Attributes**   Lets you read the basic attributes of a file or folder. These attributes include Read-Only, Hidden, System, and Archive.

- **Read Extended Attributes**   Lets you view the extended attributes (named data streams) associated with a file. As discussed in Chapter 14, "Managing file systems and storage," these include Summary fields—such as Title, Subject, and Author—as well as other types of data.

- **Create Files/Write Data**   Create Files lets you put new files in a folder. Write Data allows you to overwrite existing data in a file (but not add new data to an existing file because this is covered by Append Data).

- **Create Folders/Append Data**   Create Folders lets you create subfolders within folders. Append Data allows you to add data to the end of an existing file (but not to overwrite existing data because this is covered by Write Data).

- **Write Attributes**   Lets you change the basic attributes of a file or folder. These attributes include Read-Only, Hidden, System, and Archive.

- **Write Extended Attributes**   Lets you change the extended attributes (named data streams) associated with a file. As discussed in Chapter 14, these include Summary fields—such as Title, Subject, and Author—as well as other types of data.

- **Delete Subfolders And Files**   Lets you delete the contents of a folder. If you have this permission, you can delete the subfolders and files in a folder even if you don't specifically have Delete permission on the subfolder or file.

- **Delete**   Lets you delete a file or folder. If a folder isn't empty and you don't have Delete permission for one of its files or subfolders, you won't be able to delete it. You can do this only if you have the Delete Subfolders And Files permission.

- **Read Permissions**   Lets you read all basic and special permissions assigned to a file or folder.

- **Change Permissions**   Lets you change basic and special permissions assigned to a file or folder.

- **Take Ownership**   Lets you take ownership of a file or folder. By default, administrators can always take ownership of a file or folder and can also grant this permission to others.

Tables 15-4 and 15-5 show how special permissions are combined to make the basic permissions for files and folders. Because special permissions are combined to make the basic permissions, they are also referred to as *atomic permissions*.

**TABLE 15-4 Special permissions for folders**

| Special Permissions | Full Control | Modify | Read & Execute | List Folder Contents | Read | Write |
|---|---|---|---|---|---|---|
| Traverse Folder/Execute File | X | X | X | X | | |
| List Folder/Read Data | X | X | X | X | X | |
| Read Attributes | X | X | X | X | X | |
| Read Extended Attributes | X | X | X | X | X | |
| Create Files/Write Data | X | X | | | | X |
| Create Folders/Append Data | X | X | | | | X |
| Write Attributes | X | X | | | | X |
| Write Extended Attributes | X | X | | | | X |
| Delete Subfolders And Files | X | | | | | |
| Delete | X | X | | | | |
| Read Permissions | X | X | X | X | X | X |
| Change Permissions | X | | | | | |
| Take Ownership | X | | | | | |

**TABLE 15-5 Special permissions for files**

| Special Permissions | Full Control | Modify | Read & Execute | Read | Write |
|---|---|---|---|---|---|
| Traverse Folder/Execute File | X | X | X | | |
| List Folder/Read Data | X | X | X | X | |
| Read Attributes | X | X | X | X | |
| Read Extended Attributes | X | X | X | X | |
| Create Files/Write Data | X | X | | | X |
| Create Folders/Append Data | X | X | | | X |
| Write Attributes | X | X | | | X |
| Write Extended Attributes | X | X | | | X |
| Delete Subfolders And Files | X | | | | |
| Delete | X | X | | | |
| Read Permissions | X | X | X | X | X |
| Change Permissions | X | | | | |
| Take Ownership | X | | | | |

You set special permissions for files and folders using the Advanced Security Settings dialog box with the Permissions tab selected.

Chapter 15

The options available include

- **Add**   Adds a user or group. Tap or click Add to display the Permission Entry dialog box. Tap or click Select A Principal to display the Select User, Computer, Service Account, Or Group dialog box. Type the name of a user or a group account, and then tap or click Check Names. Be sure to reference the user account name rather than the user's full name. Only one name can be entered at a time.

- **Edit**   Edits an existing user or group entry. Select the user or group whose permissions you want to modify, and then tap or click Edit. This displays the Permissions Entry dialog box.

- **Remove**   Removes an existing user or group entry. Select the user or group whose permissions you want to remove, and then tap or click Remove.

When you are editing permissions, only basic permissions are listed by default. Tap or click Show Advanced Permissions to display the special permissions, as shown in Figure 15-31. Use the Type list to specify whether you are configuring allowed or denied permissions, and then select the permissions you want to allow or deny. If any permissions are dimmed (unavailable), they are inherited from a parent folder.

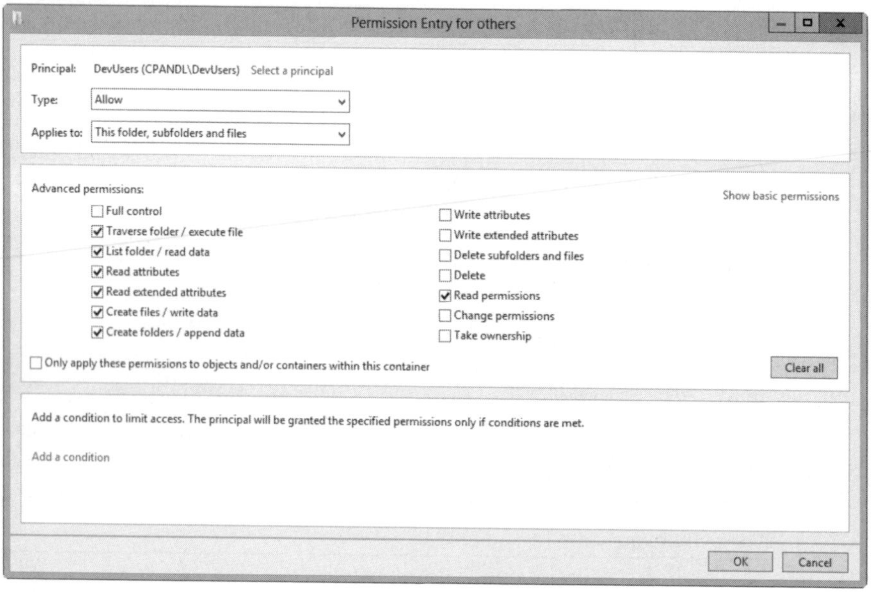

**Figure 15-31**  Use the Permission Entry dialog box to set special permissions.

When finished, use the Apply Onto options shown in Table 15-3 to determine how and where these permissions are applied. If you want to prevent subfolders and files from inheriting these permissions, select Only Apply These Permissions To Objects And/Or Containers Within This Container. When you do this, all the related entries in Table 15-3 are No. This means the settings no longer apply to subsequent subfolders or to files in subsequent subfolders.

## Troubleshooting permissions

Navigating the complex maze of permissions can be daunting even for the best administrators. Sometimes it won't be clear how a particular permission set will be applied to a particular user or group. Sometimes even a minor change in permissions can have unintended consequences. Either way, you have a problem, and one of your first steps to resolving it should be to determine the effective permissions for the files or folders in question.

The effective permissions tell you exactly which permissions are in effect. For a user, the effective permissions are based on all the permissions the user has been granted or denied, no matter whether the permissions are applied explicitly or obtained from groups of which the user is a member. Similarly, for a group, the effective permissions are based on all the permissions the group has been granted or denied, no matter whether the permissions are applied explicitly or obtained from groups of which the group is a member.

> ### Important
> You must have appropriate permissions to view the effective permissions of any user or group. You also should remember that you cannot determine the effective permissions for implicit groups or special identities, such as Authenticated Users or Everyone. Furthermore, the effective permissions do not take into account permissions granted to a user because he is the Creator Owner.

Cumulative permissions can be difficult to navigate because deny entries have precedence over allow entries. For example, if DevonP is a member of the Users, Engineering, DevUsers, and Managers groups, the effective permissions with respect to a particular file or folder are the cumulative set of permissions that DevonP has been explicitly assigned and the permissions assigned to the Users, Engineering, DevUsers, and Managers groups. If DevonP is a member of a group that is specifically denied a permission, DevonP will be denied that permission as well, even if another group is allowed that permission.

User and device claims also have precedence. If you've configured claims-based policies and added a user claim that specifies that a user must or must not be a member of a particular group, that user claim can prevent access. Similarly, if there's a device claim that specifies that a user's computer must or must not be a member of a particular group, that device claim can prevent access.

You can use the Effective Access tab in the Advanced Security Settings dialog box to determine the effective permissions with regard to the related file or folder. On the Effective Access tab, use the options provided to determine the effective permissions for users, groups, and devices. Before you tap or click View Effective Access, keep the following in mind:

- If you only want to determine access for a particular user or user group, tap or click Select A User, type the name of the user or group, and then tap or click OK.

- If you only want to determine access for a particular device or device group, tap or click Select A Device, type the name of the device or the device group, and then tap or click OK.

- If you want to determine access for a particular user or user group on a particular device or in a device group, specify both a user/user group and a device/device group.

As Figure 15-32 shows, the effective permissions for the specified user or group are displayed using the complete set of special permissions. If a user has full control over the selected resource, she will have all the permissions. Otherwise, a subset of the permissions is selected, and you have to carefully consider whether the user or group has the appropriate permissions. Use Table 15-4, earlier in the chapter, to help you interpret the permissions. Any checked permissions have been granted to the user or group.

Chapter 15

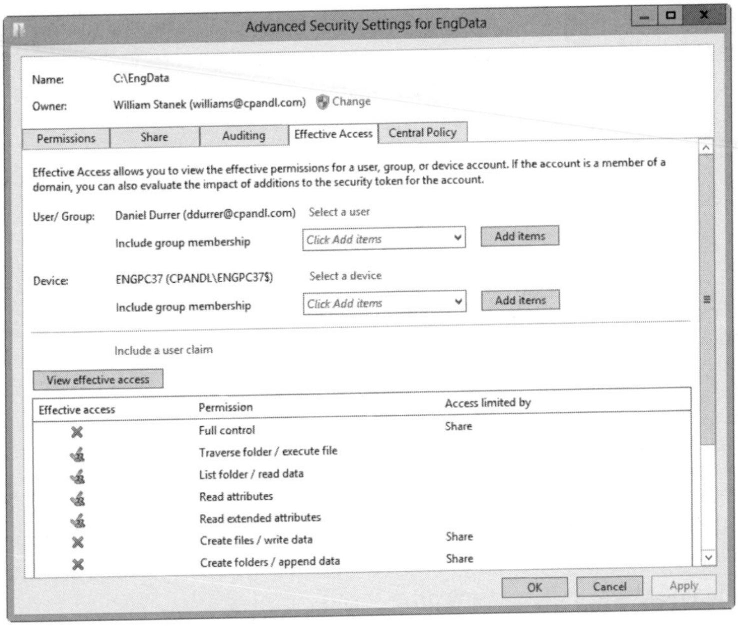

**Figure 15-32** Determine effective access.

# Managing file shares after configuration

Configuring shares can be a time-consuming process, especially if you are trying to troubleshoot why a particular user doesn't have access or set up a new server with the same file shares as a server you are decommissioning. Fortunately, there are some techniques you can use to help you better manage file shares and the way they are implemented.

Net Share is a handy command-line tool for helping you track file-share and print-share permissions. You can use it to display a list of shares and who has access to them. If you redirect the output of Net Share, you can save the share-configuration and access information to a file, and this file can become a log that helps you track share changes over time.

To view a list of configured shares, type **net share** at the command prompt or **get-smbshare** at a PowerShell prompt. The output of Net Share shows you the name of each share on the server, the location of the actual folder being shared, and any descriptions you've added. Here is an example of output from running the net share command:

```
Share name    Resource                      Remark

----------------------------------------------------------
ADMIN$        C:\Windows                    Remote Admin
C$            C:\                           Default share
F$            F:\                           Default share
IPC$                                        Remote IPC
CorpData      C:\CorpData
CorpTech      F:\CorpTech
DevData       F:\DevData
EngData       C:\EngData
HRData        F:\HRData
Public        C:\Users\Public
UserData      C:\UserData
The command completed successfully.
```

The list of shares shown includes the file shares CorpData, CorpTech, EngData, Public, and others. Administrative shares created and managed by Windows are shown as well, including ADMIN$, IPC$, and any drive shares.

If you want to redirect the output to a file, you can do this by typing **net share > FileName.txt**, where *FileName.txt* is the name of the file to create and to which you want to write, such as:

```
net share > C:\logs\fileshares.txt
```

You can redirect the output from get-smbshare to a file as well:

```
get-smbshare > C:\logs\fileshares.txt
```

If you follow the Net Share command with the name of a configured share, you'll see the complete configuration details for the share as shown in the following example:

```
Share name        EngData
Path              C:\EngData
Remark
Maximum users     No limit
Users
Caching           Manual caching of documents
Permission        CPANDL\Domain Admins, FULL
                  CPANDL\Domain Users, READ
                  CPANDL\EngineeringUsers, READ

The command completed successfully.
```

You can append the share configuration details to the previously created log file by using the append symbol (>>) instead of the standard redirect symbol (>), as shown in the following example:

```
net share corpdata >> C:\logs\fileshares.txt
```

Listing 15-1 shows the source of a command-line script that you could use to create a configuration log for the key shares on the computer. Although the path in the example is set to c:\logs\fileshares.txt, you can set any log path you want.

**LISTING 15-1 A sample share logging script**

```
net share > C:\logs\fileshares.txt
net share c$ >> C:\logs\fileshares.txt
net share f$ >> C:\logs\fileshares.txt
net share corpdata >> C:\logs\fileshares.txt
net share corptech >> C:\logs\fileshares.txt
net share devdata >> C:\logs\fileshares.txt
net share engdata >> C:\logs\fileshares.txt
net share hrdata >> C:\logs\fileshares.txt
net share public >> C:\logs\fileshares.txt
net share userdata >> C:\logs\fileshares.txt
```

# Managing claims-based access controls

Windows Server 2012 adds Kerberos armoring, compound identities, and claims-based access controls to the standard access controls. Kerberos with Armoring improves domain security by allowing domain-joined clients and domain controllers to communicate over secure, encrypted channels. Compound identities incorporate not only the groups a user is a member of but also user claims, device claims, and resource properties.

At their most basic, claims-based access controls allow you to define conditions that limit access as part of a resource's advanced security permissions. Typically, these conditions add device claims or user claims to the access controls. User claims identify users; device claims identify devices. For example, to access the CorpTech share, you might want to add a device claim to ensure that the computer being used to access a resource is a member of Tech Computers, and add a user claim that ensures the user is a member of the CorpUsers group.

Kerberos armoring, compound identities, and claims-based access controls can also work together as part of the extended authorization platform in Windows Server. This platform allows dynamic access to resources using central access policies.

Chapter 15

# Understanding central access policies

With central access policies, you define central access rules in Active Directory and those rules are applied dynamically throughout the enterprise. Central access rules use conditional expressions that require you to determine the resource properties required for the policy, the claim types and security groups required for the policy, and the servers where the policy should be applied.

Configuring central access policies is a multistep process that usually begins with defining the resource properties and claim types you'll use as part of your policies. Afterward, you create access rules based on the claim types and then you establish dynamic controls by adding the rules to the appropriate group policies. Thus, the process typically looks like this:

- First, you create resource properties. Resource properties create property definitions for resources. For example, you might want to add Department and Country/Region properties to files so that you can dynamically control access by department and country/region.

- Next, you create claim types that use those properties. Claim types create claim definitions for resources. For example, you might want to create a user claim to add Department and Country/Region properties to User objects so that you can dynamically control access by department and country/region.

- After you create resource properties and claim types and determine where the policy should be applied, you create an access rule and then add it to a central access policy. Adding the rule to a policy makes it available for dynamic control.

- Last, you apply the policy across file servers using Group Policy.

# Enabling dynamic controls and claims-based policy

Servers that you want to apply dynamic controls to must have the File And Storage Services role with the File Server, Storage Services, and File Server Resource Manager role services at a minimum. You need the File Server Resource Manager role service and the related tools to apply classification property definitions to folders.

Claims-based policy should be enabled for all domain controllers in a domain to ensure consistent application. A domain must have at least one Windows Server 2012 domain controller, and file servers must run Windows Server 2012. By default, domain controllers are placed in the Domain Controllers organizational unit (OU) and the Default Domain Controllers policy has the highest precedence among Group Policy Objects (GPOs) linked to the Domain Controllers OU.

If your organization uses this approach, claims-based policy must be enabled for the Default Domain Controllers policy. If your organization uses a different approach, you need to ensure the GPO with the highest precedence for the appropriate OU has claims-based policy enabled and configured properly.

You enable claims-based policy using the KDC Support For Claims, Compound Authentication Dynamic Access Control And Kerberos Arming policy in the Administrative Templates policies for Computer Configuration under System\KDC. The policy must be configured to use a specific mode. The available modes are

- **Supported**   Domain controllers support claims, compound identities, and Kerberos armoring. Client computers that don't support Kerberos armoring can be authenticated.

- **Always Provide Claims**   Same as Supported, but domain controllers always return claims for accounts.

- **Fail Unarmored Authentication**   Specifies that Kerberos armoring is mandatory. Client computers that don't support Kerberos armoring cannot be authenticated.

You'll then be able to work with dynamic access controls in Active Directory Administrative Center. When you are working with the Dynamic Access Controls node, I recommend using Tree View as shown in Figure 15-33, rather than the List View. With Tree View, you'll see related subnodes in the left pane, and this will make it easier to configure central access policy.

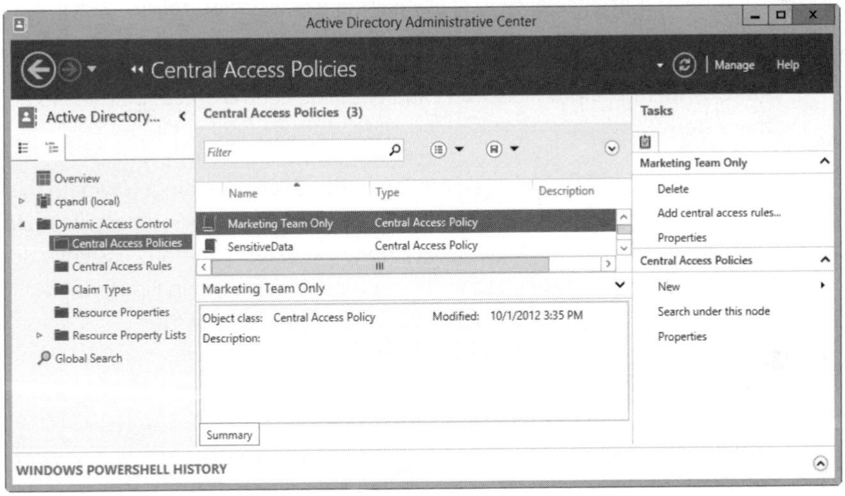

**Figure 15-33** Use Active Directory Administrative Center to create and configure central access policies.

# Defining central access policies

Central access policies don't replace traditional access controls. Instead, you use central access policies to enhance existing access controls by defining very precisely the specific attributes users and devices must have to access resources.

Before you can deploy central access policies, you need to perform the following tasks in Active Directory Administrative Center:

- Use the Claim Types node to create and manage claim types. For example, right-click in the Claim Types pane, click New, and then select Claim Type to start creating a new claim type.

- Use the Resource Properties node to create and manage resource properties. For example, right-click in the Resource Properties pane, click New, and then select Resource Property to start creating a new resource property. Resource properties are added as classification definition properties on file servers as well.

- Use the Central Access Rules node to create and manage central access rules. For example, right-click in the Central Access Rules pane, click New, and then select Central Access Rule to start creating a new access rule.

- Use the Central Access Policies node to create and manage central access policies. For example, right-click in the Central Access Policies pane, click New, and then select Central Access Policy to start creating a new access policy.

You can then complete the deployment by editing the highest-precedence GPO linked to the OU where you put file servers and enabling central access policies. To do this, follow these steps:

1. In Group Policy Management, open the GPO for editing. Navigate the Computer Configuration policies to Windows Settings\Security Settings\File System. When you select the Central Access Policy node in the left pane, any currently deployed central access policies are listed in the right pane, as shown in Figure 15-34.

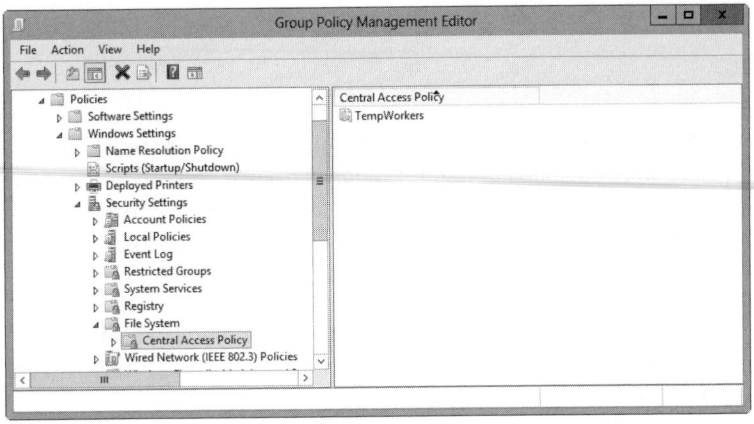

**Figure 15-34** Access the policies in Group Policy.

2. Press and hold or right-click Central Access Policy, and then tap or click Manage Central Access Policies. This opens the Central Access Policies Configuration dialog box.

3. In the Central Access Policies Configuration dialog box, shown in Figure 15-35, available policies are listed in the left pane and currently applied policies are listed in the right pane.

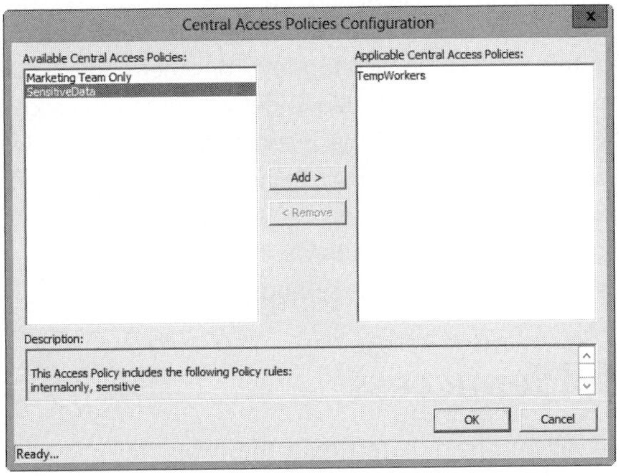

**Figure 15-35** Use the Central Access Policies Configuration dialog box to add or remove policies.

4. To apply a policy, tap or click it in the left pane and then click Add. To remove a policy, tap or click it in the right pane and then click Remove.

5. Tap or click OK to apply any changes.

The dynamic controls are available as soon as the Group Policy changes take effect on your servers. You can speed the refresh along by entering **gpupdate /force** at an elevated, command prompt.

After you enable central access policy and any time you update your classification property definitions, you need to wait for Global Resource Properties from Active Directory to refresh on your file servers as well. You can speed this along by opening an elevated PowerShell prompt and entering **update-fsrmclassificationpropertydefinition**. Do this on each file server where you want to configure central access policies.

The deployment of central access policies isn't completed yet. You still need to edit the properties of each folder where you want a central access policy to apply and do the following:

1.  Add the appropriate classification definitions on the folder's Classification tab. On the Classification tab, each resource property you created will be listed. Select each property in turn, and then set its value as appropriate.

2.  Enable the appropriate policy using advanced security settings for the folder. On the Security tab, tap or click Advanced and then select the Central Policy tab. Any currently selected or applied policy is listed along with a description you can use to review the rules of that policy. When you tap or click Change, you can use the selection list provided to select a policy to apply or you can choose No Central Access Policy to stop using policy. Tap or click OK.

You need to repeat this process for each top-level or other folder where you want to limit access. Files and folders within the selected folder will inherit the access rule automatically unless you specify otherwise. For example, if you create an access rule called "US Marketing Only" and define Department and Country/Region resource definitions, you could edit a folder's properties, select the Classification tab, and use the options available to set Department to Marketing and Country/Region to US. Then you could apply the "US Marketing Only" policy using the advanced security settings for the folder.

# Auditing file and folder access

Access permissions will only help protect data; they won't tell you who deleted important data or who was trying to access files and folders inappropriately. To track who accessed files and folders and what they did, you must configure auditing for file and folder access. Every comprehensive security strategy should include auditing. Auditing settings you configure are applied to specific computers through local computer policy and to multiple computers through Group Policy.

Because auditing policies are applied as part of computer configuration rather than user configuration, they must be applied through GPOs that are applied to computer OUs. Following this, if you want an auditing setting to be applied to specific file servers, you configure the auditing setting in a Group Policy Object linked to the appropriate resource OUs. If you want an auditing setting to be applied throughout a domain, you configure the auditing setting in a Group Policy Object linked to the domain and the setting will apply to all computers in the domain.

Generally, when you want auditing settings to apply only to specified resources and groups of users, you modify the security settings of the relevant objects so that auditing is enabled for the security groups the users are members of. For example, you could configure auditing on the CurrentProjects folder to track changes and deletions made by members of the TempWorkers group.

Windows Server supports basic auditing and advanced auditing. Basic auditing includes the settings under Windows Settings\Security Settings\Local Policies\Audit Policy. Advanced auditing includes the settings under Windows Settings\Security Settings\Advanced Audit Policy Configuration\Audit Policies. When you configure auditing, you use either basic or advanced auditing, not both. Advanced auditing can be applied to computers running Windows 7 or later and Windows Server 2008 R2 or later (as well as Windows Server 2008 and Windows Vista when logon scripts are used to apply advanced audit policy).

To track file and folder access, you must do the following:

- Enable either basic or advanced auditing.
- Specify which files and folders to audit, or enable global object access auditing.
- Track audit events by monitoring the security logs or using a collection tool, such as Audit Collection Services in System Center Operations Manager.

Keep in mind that global object access policy is designed to be used with advanced auditing. If you choose to use advanced auditing rather than basic auditing, you can prevent conflicts between basic and advanced settings by forcing Windows to ignore basic auditing settings. To do this, enable the Audit: Force Audit Policy security setting as appropriate in Group Policy. This security setting is under Windows Settings\Security Settings\Local Policies\Security Options.

## Enabling basic auditing for files and folders

You configure basic auditing policies by using Group Policy or local security policy. Group Policy is used when you want to set auditing policies for an entire site, domain, or organizational unit, and it is used as discussed in Part 5 of this book, "Managing Active Directory and Security." Local security policy settings apply to an individual workstation or server and can be overridden by Group Policy.

To enable basic auditing of files and folders for multiple computers through Group Policy, select Group Policy Management on the Tools menu in Server Manager. Next, press and hold or right-click the GPO you want to work with and then select Edit. In Group Policy Management Editor, expand Policies, Windows Settings, Security Settings, Local Policies and then select Audit Policy, as shown in Figure 15-36.

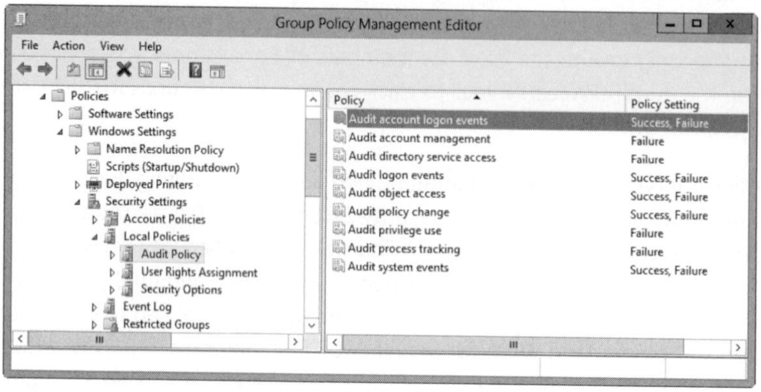

**Figure 15-36** Access the basic auditing settings.

To enable basic auditing of files and folders for a specific computer, start the Local Security Policy tool by selecting the related option on the Tools menu in Server Manager. Expand Local Policies, and then select Audit Policy.

Next, double-tap or double-click Audit Object Access. This displays the Audit Object Access Properties dialog box shown in Figure 15-37. In a domain, enable the policy for configuration by selecting Define These Policy Settings. Under Audit These Attempts, select the Success check box to log successful access attempts, the Failure check box to log failed access attempts, or both check boxes, and then tap or click OK. This enables auditing, but it doesn't specify which objects should be audited. You do that by editing the properties of each object that you want to track, which can include files and folders as well as registry settings and more.

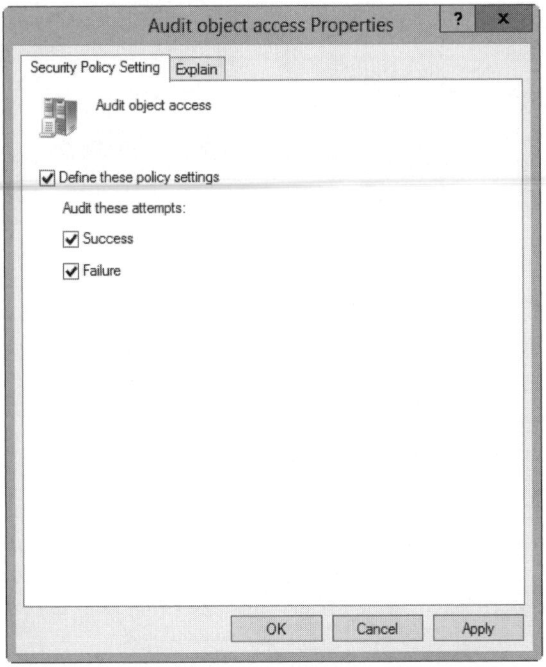

**Figure 15-37**  Configure auditing for object access.

## Enabling advanced auditing

As with basic auditing, you configure advanced auditing policies by using Group Policy or local security policy. To enable advanced auditing of files and folders for multiple computers through Group Policy, select Group Policy Management on the Tools menu in Server Manager. Next, press and hold or right-click the GPO you want to work with and then select Edit. In Group Policy Management Editor, expand Policies, Windows Settings, Security Settings, Advanced Audit Policy Configuration, Audit Policies and then select Object Access, as shown in Figure 15-38.

Chapter 15

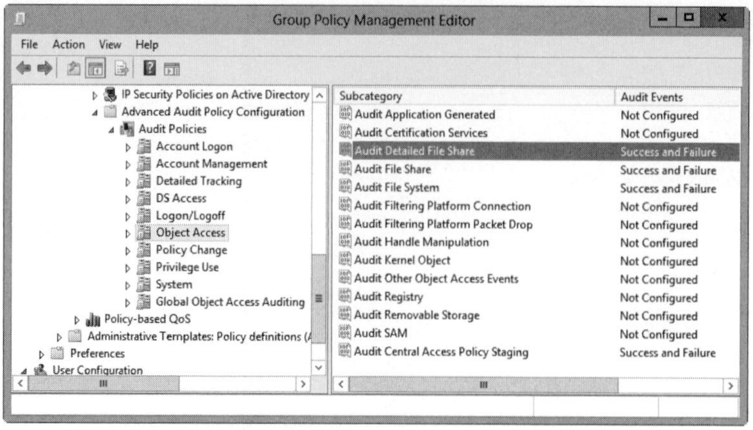

**Figure 15-38** Access the advanced auditing settings.

To enable auditing of files and folders for a specific computer, start the Local Security Policy tool by selecting the related option on the Tools menu in Server Manager. Expand Advanced Audit Policy Configuration, System Audit Policies - Local Group Policy Object, and then select Object Access.

With advanced auditing, you identify specific types of object access to track using the available options, which include

- **Audit File Share**   Generates audit events whenever an attempt is made to access a shared folder. Because shared folders don't have system access control lists (SACLs), access to all shares on the system is audited (which includes network access to the SYSVOL on domain controllers). Only one audit event is recorded for any connection established between a client and a file share. To record events every time a file or folder on a share is accessed, use the Audit Detailed File Share policy.

- **Audit File System**   Generates audit events for objects when the type of access requested and the account making the request match the settings in SACLs set on the objects. For example, if a user tries to modify a file and is a member of a group for which you enabled auditing of success and failure Modify events, related audit events will be generated and recorded in the security log. An audit event is generated each time an account accesses a file system object with a matching SACL.

- **Audit Detailed File Share**   Generates audit events whenever an attempt is made to access a file or folder on a share. Because shared folders don't have SACLs, access to all shared files and folders on the system is audited. An audit event is recorded every time a file or folder on a share is accessed.

To configure these policies, double-tap or double-click a policy to display its Properties dialog box. As shown in Figure 15-39, select Configure The Following Audit Events and then select the Success check box to log successful access attempts, the Failure check box to log failed access attempts, or both check boxes, and then tap or click OK. This enables auditing, but it doesn't specify which files and folders should be audited.

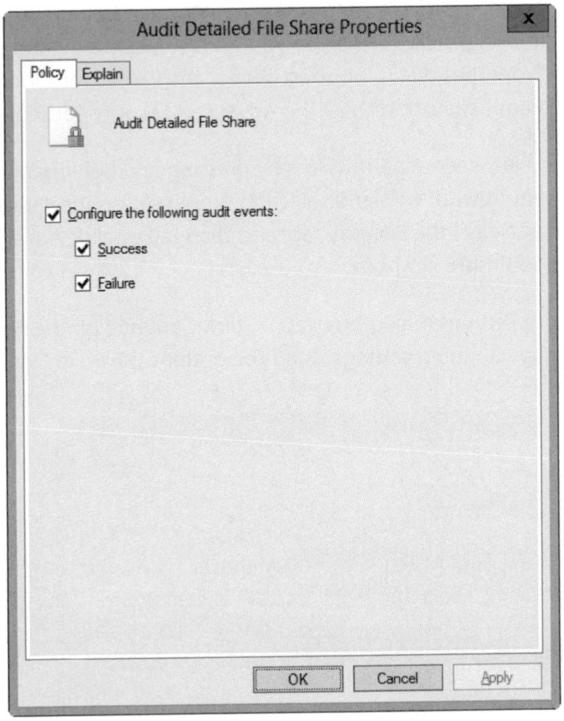

**Figure 15-39** Configure auditing for a specific type of object access.

Next, ensure advanced audit policy overrides basic audit policy. To do this, whenever you edit the Group Policy Objects and enable advanced audit policy, you must also enable the Audit: Force Audit Policy Subcategory Settings security setting. This security setting is under Windows Settings\Security Settings\Local Policies\Security Options.

In the Group Policy editor, double-tap or double-click the Audit: Force Audit Policy security setting to display its Properties dialog box. Select Define This Policy Setting and then select Enabled. Finally, tap or click OK.

## Specifying files and folders to audit

After you enable the auditing of object access, you can set the level of auditing by either specifying which files and folders to audit or enabling global object access auditing.

Auditing of individual folders and files allows you to control whether and how folder and file usage is tracked. Keep in mind auditing is available only on NTFS and ReFS volumes. In addition, everything discussed about inheritance applies to files and folders as well—and this is a good thing. This allows you, for example, to audit access to every file or folder on a volume simply by specifying that you want to audit the root folder of the volume.

You can use either File Explorer or Server Manager to view and configure auditing. In Server Manager, press and hold or right-click the share you want to work with, and then tap or click Properties. In the Properties dialog box, tap or click the Permissions in the left pane. Tap or click Customize Permissions to display the Advanced Security Settings dialog box.

In File Explorer, you can view special permissions by pressing and holding or right-clicking the file or folder you want to work with and selecting Properties on the shortcut menu. In the Properties dialog box, select the Security tab, and then tap or click Advanced to display the Advanced Security Settings dialog box.

In the Advanced Security Settings dialog box, tap or click Continue on the Auditing tab. You can now view and manage auditing settings using the options shown in Figure 15-40.

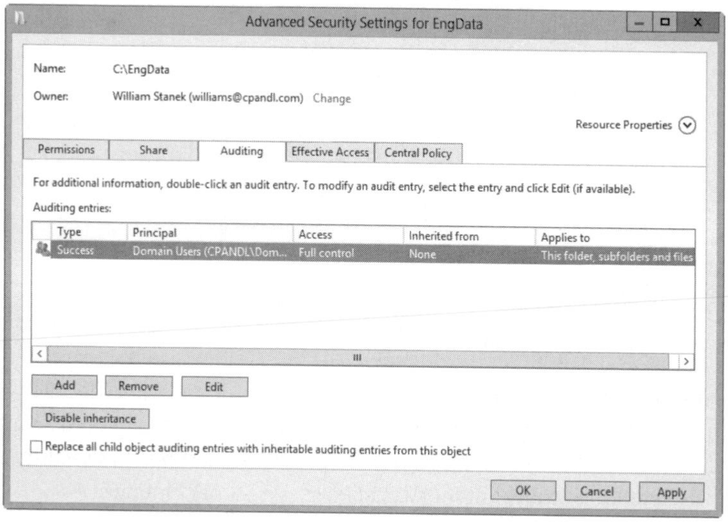

**Figure 15-40** Specify to which users and groups auditing should apply.

The Auditing Entries list shows the users, groups, or computers whose actions you want to audit. To remove an account, select the account in the Auditing Entries list and then tap or click Remove.

You can audit access related to basic permissions and special permissions as listed in Tables 15-4 and 15-5, respectively. Keep in mind basic permissions include multiple special permissions. Therefore, when you audit the Modify permission, this tracks access related to Traverse Folder/Execute File, List Folder/Read Data, Read Attributes, Read Extended Attributes, Create Files/Write Data, Create Folders/Append Data, Write Attributes, Write Extended Attributes, Delete, and Read permissions.

You can configure auditing for additional users, computers, or groups, by following these steps:

1. Tap or click Add to display the Select Users, Computers, Service Accounts, Or Groups dialog box.

2. Type the name of a user, computer, or group in the current domain, and then tap or click Check Names. Be sure to reference the user account name rather than the user's full name. Only one name can be entered at a time. If you want to audit actions for all users, use the special group Everyone. Otherwise, select the specific user groups, users, or both that you want to audit.

3. Tap or click OK. The user and group are added, and the Principal and the Auditing Entry dialog box are updated to show this. Only basic permissions are listed by default. If you want to work with advanced permissions, tap or click Show Advanced Permissions to display the special permissions.

4. Optionally, use the Applies To list to specify where objects are audited. If you are working with a folder and want to replace the auditing entries on all child objects of this folder (and not on the folder itself), select Only Apply These Settings To Objects And/Or Containers Within This Container.

> **Note**
> The Applies To list lets you specify the locations where you want the auditing settings to apply. The Only Apply These Settings To Objects And/Or Containers Within This Container check box controls how auditing settings are applied. When this check box is selected, auditing settings on the parent object replace settings on child objects. When this check box is cleared, auditing settings on the parent are merged with existing settings on child objects.

5. Use the Type list to specify whether you are configuring auditing for success, failure, or both, and then specify which actions should be audited. Success logs successful events, such as successful file reads. Failure logs failed events, such as failed file deletions. The events you can audit are the same as the special permissions discussed previously, except that you can't audit the synchronizing of offline files and folders.

**6.** If you're using claims-based policies and want to limit the scope of the auditing entry, you can add claims-based conditions to the auditing entry. For example, if all corporate computers are members of the Approved Computers group, you might want to closely audit access by devices that aren't members of this group.

**7.** Tap or click OK. Repeat this process to audit other users, groups, or computers.

> ## Note
> Often you'll want to track only failed actions. This way, you know if someone was trying to perform an action and failed. Keep in mind a failed attempt doesn't always mean someone is trying to break into a file or folder. A user simply might have double-tapped or double-clicked a folder or file to which he didn't have access. In addition, some types of actions can cause multiple failed attempts to be logged even when the user performed the action only once. Regardless, as an administrator, you should check multiple failed attempts because of the possibility that someone is attempting to breach your system's defenses.

Instead of tracking access to specific files and folders, your business or compliance policies might require you to track specific types of access on sensitive computers. For example, you might need to track all access activity on servers containing sensitive data. To do this without having to configure SACLs, you can use global object access policy.

Global object access policy is designed to be used with advanced auditing and two object access areas specifically:

- Audit File System, which must be enabled to track global access to files and folders

- Audit Registry, which must be enabled to track global access to the registry

After you enable file system auditing, registry auditing, or both, you can enable global access policy. Global access policy generates audit events for objects when the type of access requested and the account making the request match the settings in SACLs configured in the global access policy.

You configure global access policy by using Group Policy or local security policy. Follow these steps:

**1.** Open the GPO you want to work with for editing. Next, in Group Policy Management Editor, expand Policies, Windows Settings, Security Settings, Advanced Audit Policy Configuration, Audit Policies and then select Global Object Access Auditing.

2.  Double-tap or double-click the File System setting to display its Properties dialog box. Select Define This Policy Setting, and then tap or click Configure. This opens the Advanced Security Settings For Global File SACL dialog box, shown in Figure 15-41.

3.  In the Advanced Security Settings For Global File SACL dialog box, tap or click Add. Next, in the Auditing Entry dialog box, tap or click Select A Principal to display the Select User, Computer, Service Account Or Group dialog box. Type the name of the user, group, or computer to audit and then tap or click Check Names. Only one name can be entered at a time. Be sure to reference the user account name rather than the user's full name.

4.  Use the Type list to specify whether you are tracking successful or failed access, and then select the permissions you want to audit. If you want to track both successful and failed access, choose All as the type.

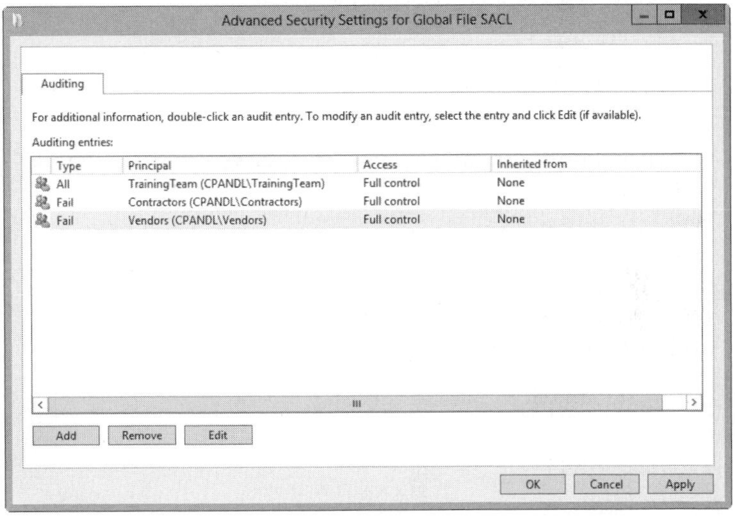

**Figure 15-41**  Specify to which users and groups global auditing should apply.

# Extending access policies to auditing

With Windows Server 2012, you can extend claims-based access controls to auditing. Here, you create central audit policies that use claims and resource properties. The result is more targeted and easier-to-manage auditing policy that can help you meet business and compliance requirements, such as policies that do the following:

●   Audit everyone who tries to access sensitive or confidential data but doesn't have a security clearance that would allow this.

● Audit contractors and vendors when they try to access documents that aren't related to projects they are working on.

Precise targeting helps to limit the volume of collected data while focusing on the most relevant data. Although the auditing events are generated on a per-server basis, event collection and analysis tools, such as the Audit Collection Services in System Center Operations Manager, make it possible to centrally collect the events and search through them in new ways.

The easiest way to extend claims-based access controls to auditing is to follow these steps:

1. Enable and configure central access policies as discussed in "Managing claims-based access controls" earlier in the chapter.

2. Enable either object access or global object access auditing as discussed in "Enabling advanced auditing" earlier in the chapter.

3. Use the claim types and resource properties you defined to help you fine-tune audit policy.

An example of extending claims-based access controls to auditing is shown in Figure 15-42. Here, you limit the auditing to members of the Contractors group who are outside a specified country/region and who don't have their Company property set as City Power.

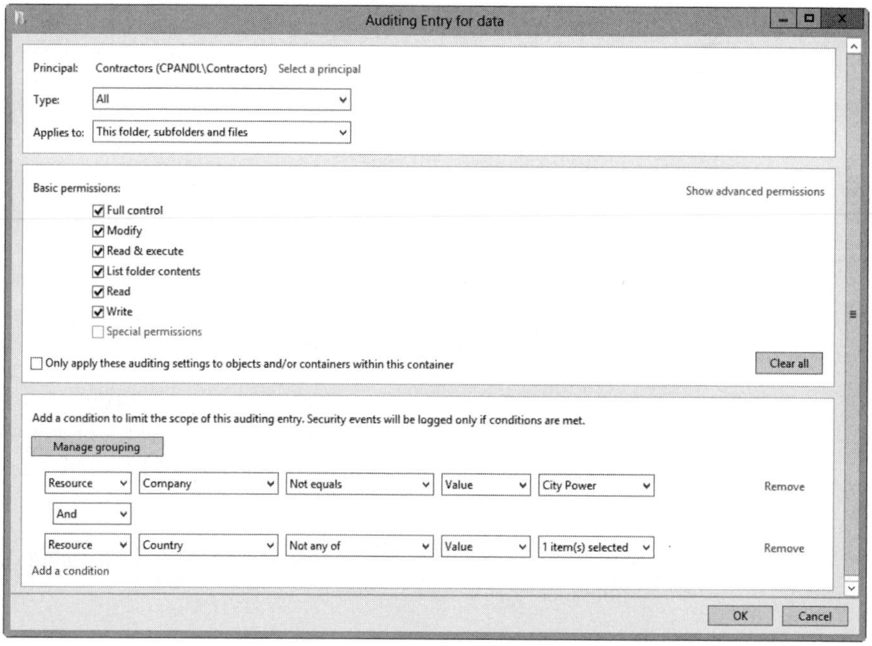

**Figure 15-42** Use claims-based access controls to fine-tune auditing.

## Monitoring the security logs

Any time files and folders that you've configured for auditing are accessed, the action is written to the system's Security log, where it's stored for your review. The Security log is accessible from Event Viewer. Successful actions can cause successful events, such as successful file reads, to be recorded. Failed actions can cause failed events, such as failed file deletions, to be recorded.

# Shadow copy essentials

Shadow copying of files in shared folders is a feature administrators can use to create backup copies of files on designated volumes automatically. You can think of these backup copies as point-in-time snapshots that can be used to recover previous versions of files. Normally, when a user deletes a file from a shared folder, it is immediately deleted and doesn't go to the local Recycle Bin. This means the only way to recover it is from backup. The reason for this is that when you delete files over the network, the files are permanently deleted on the remote server and never make it to the Recycle Bin. This changes with shadow copying. If a user deletes a file from a network share, she can go back to a previous version and recover it—and she can do this without needing assistance from an administrator.

## Using shadow copies of shared folders

Shadow copies of shared folders are designed to help recover files that were accidentally deleted, corrupted, or inappropriately edited. After you configure shadow copies on a server, the server creates and maintains previous versions of all files and folders created on the volumes you specified. It does this by creating snapshots of shared folders at predetermined intervals and storing these images in shadow-copy storage in such a way that users and administrators can easily access the data to recover previous versions of files and folders. Windows Server 2012 also allows you to revert an entire volume to a previous shadow-copy state.

Ideally, after you implement shadow copies throughout the organization and show users how to use the feature, users will be able to recover files and folders without needing assistance. This allows users to manage their own files, resolve problems, and fix mistakes. It also saves time and money because previous versions can be recovered quickly and easily, and resources that would have been used to recover files and perform related tasks can be used elsewhere.

When planning to deploy shadow copies in your organization, look at the shared folders that are in use. When you identify the ones that would benefit from this feature, note the volumes on which those shares are located. Those are the volumes for which you will need

Chapter 15

to configure shadow copying. You might also want to consider changing the way users' personal data is stored. Windows Server enables you to centrally manage user data folders through file shares, and then if you configure shadow copies on these file shares, users will have access to previous versions of all their data files and folders. For Windows Vista and later releases of Windows, the special folders you can manage include AppData(Roaming), Desktop, Documents, Pictures, Music, Videos, Favorites, Contacts, Downloads, Links, Searches, and Saved Games.

You configure central management of these folders through Group Policy. When you do this, you want to redirect the root path for these folders to a file share.

## How shadow copies work

Shadow Copies for Shared Folders is made possible through the Shadow Copy API. The shadow copy driver (Volsnap.sys) and the Volume Shadow Copy service executable (Vssvc.exe) are key components used by this API. When you enable shadow copies on a server, the server is configured to be a client-accessible shadow-copy service provider. The default provider is the Microsoft Software Shadow Copy Provider, and it is responsible for providing the necessary interface between clients that want to access shadow copies and clients that write shadow copies or information pertaining to shadow copies, called *volume shadow copy service writers*.

A number of shadow copy service writers are installed by default and other writers can be installed when you install other programs, such as third-party backup software. The default writers installed depend on the system configuration and include the following:

- **BITS Writer**   A shadow copies writer used to make backups of files in use by the Background Intelligent Transfer Service (BITS).

- **COM+ REGDB Writer**   A shadow copies writer used by COM+ and the Windows internal database so that in-use files can be backed up.

- **Dedup Writer**   A shadow copies writer used by Data Deduplication so that in-use files can be backed up, primarily on file servers.

- **DHCP Jet Writer**   A shadow copies writer used to make backups of files in use by the Dynamic Host Configuration Protocol (DHCP).

- **Distributed File System (DFS) Service Writer**   A shadow copies writer used by DFS so that in-use files can be backed up, primarily on domain controllers.

- **IIS Config Writer**   A shadow copies writer used to make backups of Microsoft Internet Information Services (IIS) configuration files.

- **MSSearch Service Writer**   A shadow copies writer used to make backups of files in use by the Microsoft Search Service.

- **NT Directory Service (NTDS) Writer**   A shadow copies writer used to make backups of files in use by NTDS.

- **Registry Writer**   A shadow copies writer used by other writers to make registry changes.

- **System Writer**   The standard shadow copies writer used by the operating system.

> **Note**
> You can list available shadow copy providers by typing **vssadmin list providers** at the command line. To list shadow copy writers, type **vssadmin list writers**.

To create copies of previous versions of files, Shadow Copies for Shared Folders uses a differential copy procedure. With this technique, only copies of files that have changed since the last copy are marked for copying. During the copy procedure, Shadow Copies for Shared Folders creates the previous version data in one of two ways:

- If the application used to change a file stored details of the changes, Shadow Copies for Shared Folders performs a block-level copy of any changes that have been made to files since the last save. Thus, only changes are copied, not the entire file.

- If the application used to change a file rewrote the entire file to disk, Shadow Copies for Shared Folders saves the entire file as it exists at that point in time.

If you're wondering exactly how this works, I did, too, at first. Then I started experimenting. An example of an application that can save changes or full copies is Microsoft Word. If you enable Fast Saves in Word, only changes to a file are written to disk. If you clear the Allow Fast Saves check box, Word writes a complete copy of the file when you save it.

As mentioned previously, Shadow Copies for Shared Folders runs at predefined intervals. These predefined intervals are set as the run schedule when you configure shadow copying of a volume. As with other processes that have a run schedule, a scheduled task is created that is used to trigger shadow copying at the specified times. Because of this, Shadow Copies for Shared Folders is dependent on the Task Scheduler service. If this service is stopped or improperly configured, shadow copying will not work.

Chapter 15

## Implementing Shadow Copies for Shared Folders

Implementing Shadow Copies for Shared Folders isn't something you should do haphazardly. You should take the time to plan out the implementation. Key issues that you should consider include the following:

- **Copy volumes**   For which volumes should shadow copying be configured?

- **Disk space**   How much disk space will be needed for shadow copying, and is there enough available space on existing volumes?

- **Shadow storage**   Where should the shadow copies be stored and on which volumes?

- **Run schedule**   How often should shadow copies be made?

Start your planning by considering for which volumes you want to configure shadow copies. After you configure this feature, shadow copies will be created of files in the shared folders on these volumes. To implement shadow copying of files of shared folders, you enable shadow copying of the volume in which the shared folders are located. The initial shadow copy requires at least 300 megabytes (MBs) of free space to create, regardless of how much data is stored in the volume's shared folders. The disk space used by Shadow Copies of Shared Folders is referred to as *shadow storage*. Shadow Copies of Shared Folders uses this space to store previous versions of files and as a work area when it is taking snapshots. Because of this, the actual amount of space used for shadow storage is different from the amount of space allocated for shadow storage.

The amount of disk space available shouldn't be overlooked. The Shadow Copy service will save up to 64 versions of each file in shared folders, and the total disk space used depends on the amount of data in the volume's shared folders. You can restrict the total amount of disk space used by Shadow Copy by setting the allowable maximum size of the point-in-time backups. By default, the Shadow Copy service will configure a maximum space usage that typically is about 10 percent of the volume. The service won't, however, reexamine free space later to determine if this maximum value should be changed. If a volume runs out of space, shadow copying will fail and errors will be generated in the event logs.

When you plan your shadow copies implementation, you should think carefully about where shadow storage will be located. Shadow storage can be created on the volumes for which you are creating shadow copies or on different volumes. If you have busy file servers or you must scale this feature to serve many users or an increasing number of users, it might be best to use a separate volume on a separate drive for shadow storage.

## Use the command-line tools to examine shadow storage

You can determine how much space is allocated to and used by shadow storage by using the **vssadmin list shadowstorage** command. Working with this command is discussed in "Configuring shadow copies at the command line" later in this chapter.

Shadow copying is a resource-intensive process. By default, when you configure shadow copying on a volume, copies are made twice each weekday (Monday–Friday): once in the morning at 7:00 A.M. and once at midday at 12:00 P.M. The morning copy allows you to save the work from the previous day and is meant to occur before users come in to work in the morning. The midday copy allows you to save work up to that point in the day and is meant to occur when users are taking a break for lunch. In this way, a user would lose, at most, a half day's work and the resource impact caused by creating shadow copies is minimized.

When you configure the shadow copy schedule for your organization, you should take these same issues into consideration. Start by determining the best times of the day to create shadow copies. Ideally, this is when the server's resources are being used the least. Then determine how much potential data loss is acceptable given the resources, the type of data stored, and the available disk space.

## Plan shadow copies around backups

When planning the run schedule for shadow copies, be sure to take into account the backup schedule for the related volumes. If you schedule shadow copies during backup, the shadow copy service writers might experience time-out errors, and any shadow copies that should have been created at that time could be lost. If you suspect a scheduling conflict, you can use the **vssadmin list writers** command to check the last error status of the shadow copy writers.

You can change the default shadow copy times, add new scheduled run times, and schedule recurring tasks that create copies at specific time intervals during the day. However, it is recommended that you avoid creating shadow copies more frequently than once per hour. When configuring run schedules, keep in mind how much work is saved and how long users will have to retrieve versions of files. If you save changes twice a day during weekdays, the maximum of 64 shadow copies means that users have about 32 working days during which they could retrieve the oldest version of a file before it is automatically deleted.

Users can access shadows copies by pressing and holding or right-clicking a shared file or folder, selecting Properties, and then tapping or clicking the Previous Versions tab. Users will then be able to view a version of a file, save a version of a file to a new location, or restore a previous version of a file.

# Managing shadow copies in Computer Management

Shadow copies are configured on a per-volume basis. Each volume on a server that has shared folders must be configured separately for shadow copying.

## Defragment volumes before enabling shadow copies

Shadow copies can become corrupted on volumes that are heavily fragmented. It is recommended that you defragment volumes before enabling shadow copies.

**TROUBLESHOOTING**

**Be careful when defragmenting**

If you defragment a volume while shadow copies are enabled, the oldest shadow copies can be lost. Shadow copy loss can occur because the shadow copy provider uses a copy-on-write approach that uses a 16-kilobyte (KB) block level. If the volume's cluster size is smaller than 16 KBs, the shadow copy provider cannot distinguish disk defragmentation I/O and normal write I/O operations and, as a result, can create an extra shadow copy. If there are already 64 copies of a file, the oldest file is then deleted, which is how the oldest shadow copy gets deleted accidentally. To prevent this, it is recommended that the cluster size of volumes that use shadow copies be set to 16 KBs or larger.

## Configuring shadow copies in Computer Management

The easiest way to configure shadow copies is to use Computer Management. Start Computer Management, expand Storage, and select Disk Management. Press and hold or right-click a volume in the Disk Management Volume List or Graphical View, and select Properties. In the Properties dialog box, tap or click the Shadow Copies tab.

As shown in Figure 15-43, you'll then see a list of all Shadow Copy–configurable volumes on the computer and can configure shadow copies. However, although you can configure shadow copies for both NTFS and ReFS volumes, only NTFS volumes have a Shadow Copies tab. Because of this, you should be sure to select an NTFS volume in Disk Management. Alternatively, press and hold or right-click Shared Folders, select All Tasks, and then select Configure Shadow Copies.

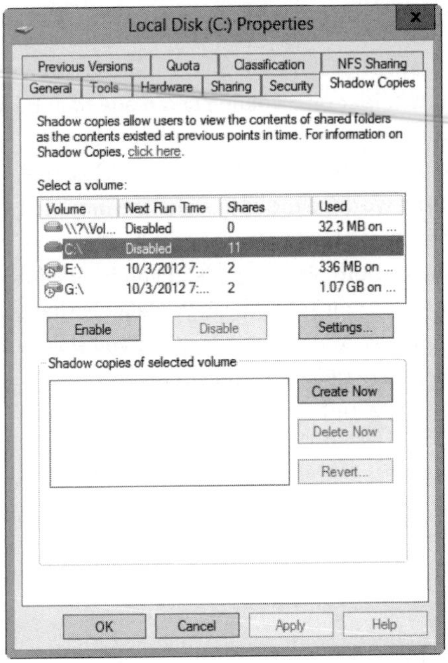

**Figure 15-43** Enable shadow copies on a per-volume basis.

You can configure shadow copies by doing the following:

1. Select the volume for which you want to configure shadow copies, and then tap or click Settings. This displays the Settings dialog box shown in Figure 15-44.

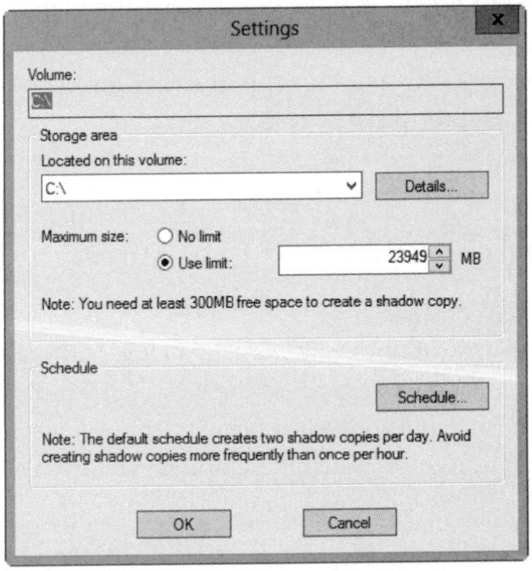

**Figure 15-44** Set storage limits for shadow copies.

## Configure mount points separately

There's a limitation for volumes that have mount points. With a mount point, a volume is attached to an empty folder on a volume and made to appear as part of that volume. If you enable shadow copies on a volume with mounted drives, the mounted drives are not included and users will not be able to access previous versions of files on the mounted volume. The workaround is to share the mounted volume and enable shadow copies for this share. Users then must access the share path to the mounted volume to view previous versions. For example, if you have a folder named F:\Eng\Data, and the Data folder is a mount point for G, you enable shadow copies on both drives F and G. You share F:\Eng as \\CorpSvr01\Eng, and you share F:\Eng\Data as \\CorpSvr01\Data. In this example, users can access previous versions of \\CorpSvr01\Eng and \\CorpSvr01\Data, but not \\CorpSvr01\Eng\Data.

2. Use the Located On This Volume selection list to specify where the shadow copies should be created. Shadow copies can be created on the volume you are configuring or any other volume available on the computer.

3. Tap or click Details to see the free space and total available disk space on the selected volume, and then tap or click OK.

4. Use the Maximum Size options to set the maximum size that shadow copies for this volume can use.

5. Tap or click Schedule to display the dialog box shown in Figure 15-45. Two run schedules are set automatically. Use the selection list to view these schedules. If you don't want to use a scheduled run time, select it and then tap or click Delete. To add a run schedule, configure the run times using the Schedule Task, Start Time, and Schedule Task Weekly options, and then tap or click New. When you are finished configuring run times, tap or click OK twice to return to the volume's Properties dialog box.

## Check the cluster configuration to ensure scheduling can work after failover

To ensure the VolumeShadowCopy task runs after failover on a clustered file server, the %SystemRoot% should be the same on the cluster to which the service is failed over. If it isn't in the same location and failover occurs, the VolumeShadowCopy task might not run. For example, if the %SystemRoot% on node 1 is C:\Windows and the %SystemRoot% on node 2 is C:\Win, the task might not run when the service fails over from node 1 to node 2. This is because the task runs in the %SystemRoot%\System32 folder and the Start In property setting for the task changes the environment variable to the actual folder location rather than using the environment variable once the task is set.

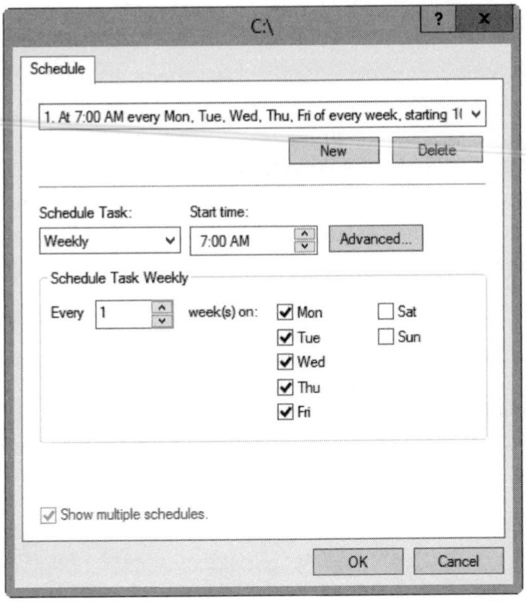

**Figure 15-45**  Set the schedule for when shadow copies are made.

**6.** Select the volume on which you want to enable shadow copies, and tap or click Enable. When prompted, tap or click Yes to confirm the action. Windows will then create a snapshot of the volume.

**7.** Configure any additional volumes for shadow copying by repeating steps 2 through 7. Tap or click OK when you are finished.

## TROUBLESHOOTING

### Shadow copies rely on the Task Scheduler

The schedule you set for shadow copies is set as a scheduled task on the server. Scheduled tasks are run by the Task Scheduler service and can be viewed in the Scheduled Tasks folder as discussed in Chapter 4, "Managing Windows Server 2012." The Task Scheduler service must be running and properly configured for shadow copying to work correctly. In addition, you should not modify ShadowCopyVolume tasks using the Scheduled Tasks folder. Instead, configure the run schedule only by using a volume's Properties dialog box.

# Maintaining shadow copies after configuration

After you configure shadow copying, snapshots are made according to the schedule you've set. Keep the following in mind:

- Individual snapshots taken of a volume can be deleted. On the Shadow Copies tab, tap or click the volume you want to work with. Its snapshots are listed in the Shadow Copies Of Selected Volume list. To delete a specific snapshot, select it in the list and then tap or click Delete Now.

- If you ever want to make a snapshot manually, you can do this by tapping or clicking Create Now on the Shadow Copies tab.

- You can change the settings and run schedule at a later date as well. Access the Shadow Copies tab, select the volume you want to change, and then tap or click Settings. Make the necessary changes, and then tap or click OK.

**CAUTION !**

Changing the maximum allowed size can cause existing shadow copies to disappear. This could happen if you set the maximum allowed size smaller than the amount of space currently in use.

- To delete a shadow copy of a volume, select the shadow copy in the bottom panel of the Shadow Copies tab and then tap or click Delete Now. When prompted to confirm the action, tap or click Yes.

- To disable shadow copies for a volume, select the volume in the top panel of the Shadow Copies tab, and then tap or click Disable. When prompted to confirm the action, tap or click Yes.

**CAUTION !**

Disabling shadow copies deletes all previously saved snapshot images. Because of this, disable snapshots only when you are sure previously saved snapshot images are no longer needed.

> ## Disable shadow copies before removing the associated volume
>
> If you want to remove a volume on which shadow copies have been enabled, you should first disable shadow copies or delete all scheduled tasks that create the shadow copies for the volume. This ensures error events aren't written to the system logs when the Scheduled Task service can't create the snapshot images.

## Reverting an entire volume

Windows Server 2012 allows you to revert an entire volume to the state it was in when a particular shadow copy was created. This capability comes with several caveats: The volume you want to revert must not contain operating-system files or reside on a cluster shared disk. The revert operation cannot be undone. Once you start the revert operation, you cannot cancel it.

You can revert an entire volume to a previous state by following these steps:

1.  On the Shadow Copies tab, select the volume you want to work with in the Select A Volume list.

2.  Individual shadow copies of the currently selected volume are listed in the Shadow Copies Of Selected Volume panel by date and time. Select the shadow copy with the date and timestamp to which you want to revert, and then tap or click Revert.

3.  To confirm this action, select the Check Here If You Want To Revert This Volume check box, as shown in Figure 15-46 and then tap or click Revert Now. Tap or click OK to close the Shadow Copies dialog box.

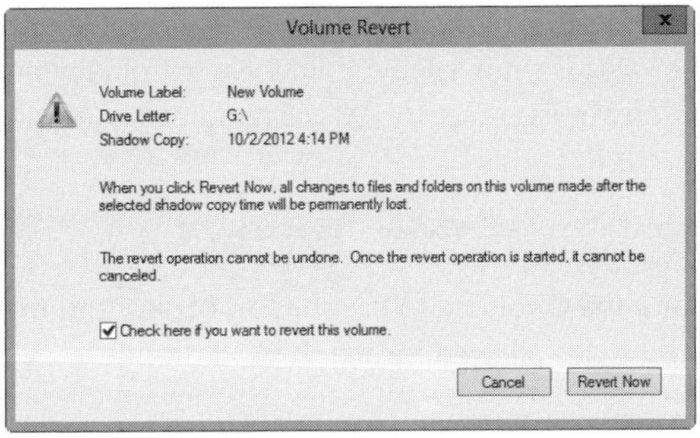

**Figure 15-46**  Confirm that you want to revert the volume.

# Configuring shadow copies at the command line

The command-line tool for configuring shadow copies is VSSAdmin. Using VSSAdmin, you can configure shadow copying of volumes on the computer you're logged on to locally or remotely through Remote Desktop. As with Computer Management, each volume on a server that has shared folders must be configured separately for shadow copying.

## Enabling shadow copying from the command line

To enable shadow copying of a volume, you use the Add ShadowStorage command. The syntax is as follows:

```
vssadmin add shadowstorage /for=ForVolumeSpec / on=OnVolumeSpec
```

Here, /for=*ForVolumeSpec* is used to specify the local volume for which you are configuring or managing shadow copies and /on=*OnVolumeSpec* is used to specify the volume on which the shadow copy data will be stored.

Consider the following example:

```
vssadmin add shadowstorage /for=c: /on=d:
```

Here, you are configuring the C volume to use shadow copies, and the shadow copy data is stored on D. Both values can be set to the same volume as well, such as

```
vssadmin add shadowstorage /for=e: /on=e:
```

Here, you are configuring the E volume to use shadow copies, and the shadow copy data is stored on that same volume.

With VSSAdmin, shadow copying is configured by default so that there is no maximum size limit for shadow storage. To set a specific limit, you can use the */MaxSize* parameter. This parameter expects to be passed a numeric value with a suffix of KB, MB, GB, TB, PB, or EB to indicate whether the value is set in kilobytes, megabytes, gigabytes, terabytes, petabytes, or exabytes. This parameter must be set to 100 MBs or greater. Consider the following example:

```
vssadmin add shadowstorage /for=c: /on=d: /maxsize=2GB
```

Here, you are configuring the C volume to use shadow copies, and the shadow copy data is stored on D. The maximum size allowed for the shadow storage is 2 GBs.

The most common errors that occur when you are configuring shadow copies from the command line relate to improper syntax. If you enter the wrong syntax, VSSAdmin shows the error message "Error: Invalid command" and will display the command syntax. If shadow copying is already configured for a volume, the error message states "Error: The specified shadow copy storage association already exists."

After you configure shadow storage, you can use the Resize Shadow command to resize the shadow storage. The command accepts the same parameters as the Add command and must be entered using the same storage association. Thus, if shadow storage for C is on D, you can resize shadow storage using the following command:

```
vssadmin add shadowstorage /for=c: /on=d: /maxsize=5GB
```

## Create manual snapshots from the command line

When you enable shadow copying, snapshots of shared folders are created automatically according to the default run schedule. If you ever want to make a snapshot manually, you can do this using the Create Shadow command. Type **vssadmin create shadow /for=ForVolumeSpec**, where *ForVolumeSpec* is the local volume for which you are creating the snapshot. Consider the following example:

```
vssadmin create shadow /for=e:
```

Here, you create a snapshot of shared folders on the E volume.

### Set the AutoRetry interval to retry creation automatically

Occasionally, the Shadow Copy service is busy, typically because it is creating a snapshot of this or another volume. Here, you can try again in a few minutes, or, by using the */AutoRetry* parameter, you can specifically set the length of time during which Create Shadow should continue to try to create the snapshot. For example, if you want to retry automatically for 15 minutes, you use */AutoRetry=15*.

## Viewing shadow copy information

VSSAdmin provides several utility commands for viewing shadow copy information. The most useful are List Shadows and List ShadowStorage.

List Shadows lists the existing shadow copies on a volume. By default, all shadow copies on all volumes are displayed. The command accepts /for=*ForVolumeSpec* to list only the information for a particular volume and /shadow=*ShadowId* to list only the information for a particular shadow copy. However, it is much easier just to type **vssadmin list shadows** and go through the information to find what you are looking for.

Chapter 15

The output from List Shadows shows summary information for each snapshot created according to its shadow copy identifier, such as

```
Contents of shadow copy set ID: {ff70e4e6-4117-446a-8ffe-1708632664ff}
   Contained 1 shadow copies at creation time: 2/22/2014 5:34:02 AM
      Shadow Copy ID: {5ba0f3d3-afa8-4e4e-a00e-64a44e11bf81}
         Original Volume: (C:)\\?\Volume{3796c3c0-5106-11d7-911c-806d6172696f}\
            Shadow Copy Volume: \\?\GLOBALROOT\Device\HarddiskVolumeShadowCopy3
            Originating Machine: corpsvr02.cpandl.com
            Service Machine: corpsvr02.cpandl.com
            Provider: 'Microsoft Software Shadow Copy provider 1.0'
            Type: ClientAccessible
         Attributes: Persistent, Client-accessible, No auto release, No writers,
Differential

Contents of shadow copy set ID: {6cb7fba8-afbb-415f-b47a-6800b332af9a}
   Contained 1 shadow copies at creation time: 2/21/2014 5:32:43 AM
      Shadow Copy ID: {3f44a086-2034-4c6b-bf3f-3489a5e98bd8}
         Original Volume: (C:)\\?\Volume{3796c3c0-5106-11d7-911c-806d6172696f}\
            Shadow Copy Volume: \\?\GLOBALROOT\Device\HarddiskVolumeShadowCopy4
            Originating Machine: corpsvr02.cpandl.com
            Service Machine: corpsvr02.cpandl.com
            Provider: 'Microsoft Software Shadow Copy provider 1.0'
            Type: ClientAccessible
         Attributes: Persistent, Client-accessible, No auto release, No writers,
Differential
```

Here, there is a data set for each snapshot that has been created. The most important information is the following:

- **Shadow Copy ID**  The unique identifier for the snapshot image. This identifier can be copied and used to delete a particular snapshot if desired.

- **Original Volume**  The volume for which shadow copies are configured.

- **Originating Machine**  The name of the computer you are working with.

List ShadowStorage displays all shadow copy storage associations on the system. The command accepts the /for=*ForVolumeSpec* and /on=*OnVolumeSpec* parameters to limit the output. But again, it is much easier just to type **vssadmin list shadowstorage** and go through the information to find what you are looking for. Here is an example of the output from this command:

```
Shadow Copy Storage association
   For volume: (C:)\\?\Volume{3796c3c0-5106-11d7-911c-806d6172696f}\
   Shadow Copy Storage volume:

   (C:)\\?\Volume{3796c3c0-5106-11d7-911c-806d6172696f}\
   Used Shadow Copy Storage space: 1.07 GB
   Allocated Shadow Copy Storage space: 10.24 GB
   Maximum Shadow Copy Storage space: 22.206 GB
```

Here, the output shows you the following information:

- **For Volume**   The volume for which shadow copies are configured

- **Shadow Copy Storage Volume**   The volume on which shadow copy data is stored

- **Used Shadow Copy Storage Space**   The actual amount of disk space used on the storage volume

- **Allocated Shadow Copy Storage Space**   The amount of disk space allocated on the storage volume for shadow copies

- **Maximum Shadow Copy Storage Space**   The maximum size allowed for shadow copies on the storage volume

## Deleting snapshot images from the command line

If you want to delete individual snapshots on a volume, you can use the Delete Shadows command to do this. You can delete the oldest snapshot on the specified volume by typing **vssadmin delete shadows /for=*ForVolumeSpec* /oldest**, where /for=*ForVolumeSpec* specifies the local volume for which the snapshot is used. For example, if you configured shadow copying on the C volume and want to delete the oldest snapshot on this volume, you enter the following command:

```
vssadmin delete shadows /for=c: /oldest
```

When prompted to confirm that you really want to delete the snapshot, press Y. VSSAdmin should then report "Successfully deleted 1 shadow copies."

To delete a snapshot by its shadow identifier, use the /Shadow=*ShadowID* parameter instead of the /For=*ForVolumeSpec* and /Oldest parameters. Here, *ShadowID* is the globally unique identifier for the snapshot image, including the brackets ({}). For example, if you want to delete the snapshot image with the ID {f3899e11-613a-4a7d-95de-cb264d1d-bb7b}, you use the following command:

```
vssadmin delete shadows /shadow={f3899e11-613a-4a7d-95de-cb264d1dbb7b}
```

Again, when prompted to confirm that you really want to delete the snapshot, press Y. VSSAdmin doesn't actually check to see if the snapshot exists until you confirm that you want to delete the snapshot. In this case, if the shadow copy ID is invalid or the snapshot has already been deleted, VSSAdmin reports a "not found" error, such as

```
Error: Shadow Copy ID: {f3899e11-613a-4a7d-95de-cb264d1dbb7b} not found.
```

Delete Shadows also lets you delete all snapshots on all volumes configured for shadow copy on the computer. To do this, type **delete shadows /all**. When prompted to confirm

Chapter 15

that you really want to delete all snapshots, press Y. VSSAdmin should then report, "Successfully deleted N shadow copies." Deleting all the shadow copies doesn't disable shadow copy on the volumes, however. To do this, you must use the Delete ShadowStorage command.

## Disabling shadow copies from the command line

To disable shadow copies on a volume, you can use the Delete ShadowStorage command. However, unlike the graphical user interface (GUI), you cannot disable shadow copying until all previously saved snapshot images on the affected volume are deleted. Because of this, you must first delete all the snapshots on the volume and then disable shadow copying. Type the command **vssadmin delete shadowstorage /for=*ForVolumeSpec***, where */for=ForVolumeSpec* is used to specify the local volume for which you are disabling shadow copying. For example, if you want to disable shadow copying of the C volume, you use the following command:

```
vssadmin delete shadowstorage /for=c:
```

As long as the shadow storage isn't in use, you will be able to delete and VSSAdmin will report, "Successfully deleted the shadow copy storage association(s)."

## Reverting volumes from the command line

If you want to revert an entire volume to an earlier snapshot, you can use the Revert Shadow command to do this. You revert to a snapshot using its shadow identifier. Use the */Shadow=ShadowID* parameter, where *ShadowID* is the globally unique identifier for the snapshot image, including the brackets ({}). For example, if you want to revert to the snapshot image with the ID {f3899e11-613a-4a7d-95de-cb264d1dbb7b}, which is associated with the C volume, you use the following command:

```
vssadmin revert shadow /shadow={f3899e11-613a-4a7d-95de-cb264d1dbb7b}
```

If the shadow copy ID is invalid, VSSAdmin reports a "not found" error, such as

```
Error: Shadow Copy ID: {f3899e11-613a-4a7d-95de-cb264d1dbb7b} not found.
```

Otherwise, VSSAdmin prompts you to confirm that you really want to revert to this snapshot. If you do, press Y. After VSSAdmin has started the revert operation, you cannot cancel it. Keep in mind that VSSAdmin will be unable to revert the volume if there are any open file handles. In this case, you can force VSSAdmin to revert the volume using the */ForceDismount* parameter. However, forcing dismount invalidates open handles and, as a result, any unsaved data in open files might be lost.

You can check on the status of revert operations by typing

```
vssadmin query reverts
```

CHAPTER 16

# Managing file screening and storage reporting

T HE Windows Server 2012 operating system provides a robust environment for working with files and folders. For maximum control and flexibility, you'll usually format volumes with the NTFS file system. NTFS gives you many advanced options, including the option to configure file screening and storage reporting. File screening and storage reporting are available when you add the File Server Resource Manager role service to a server as part of the File Services role.

## Understanding file screening and storage reporting

When you work with NTFS volumes, file screening is another tool you can use in your effort to keep networks safe from malicious programs and to block unauthorized types of content. You can use file screening in conjunction with quotas and storage reports as discussed in Chapter 14, "Managing file systems and storage." Using file screening, you can monitor and block the use of certain types of files. You can configure file screening in one of two modes:

- **Active screening**  Does not allow users to save unauthorized files.

- **Passive screening**  Allows users to save unauthorized files, but monitors or warns about using the files (or both).

You actively or passively screen files by defining a file screen. All file screens have a *file-screen path*, which is a folder that defines the base file path to which the screen is applied. Screening applies to the designated folder and all subfolders of the designated folder. The particulars of how screening works and what is screened are derived from a source template that defines the file screen's properties.

Windows Server 2012 includes the file-screen templates listed in Table 16-1. Using the File Server Resource Manager, you can easily define additional templates to use when you define file screens, or you can set single-user, custom file-screen properties when defining the file screen.

**TABLE 16-1 File-screen templates**

| File-Screen Template Name | Screening Type | File-Group Action |
|---|---|---|
| Block Audio And Video Files | Active | Block: Audio and Video Files |
| Block E-Mail Files | Active | Block: E-Mail Files |
| Block Executable Files | Active | Block: Executable Files |
| Block Image Files | Active | Block: Image Files |
| Monitor Executable And System Files | Passive | Warn: Executable Files, System Files |

File-screen templates or custom properties define the following:

- Screening type, active or passive

- File groups to which screening is applied

- Notifications using email, an event log, a command, a report, or any combination of these

Table 16-2 lists the standard file groups for screening. Each file group has a predefined set of files to which it applies. You can modify the included file types and create additional file groups by using File Server Resource Manager.

**TABLE 16-2 File-screen groups and the file types to which they apply**

| File Group | Applies To |
|---|---|
| Audio and video files | .aac, .aif, .aiff, .asf, .asx, .au, .avi, .flac, .m3u, .mid, .midi, .mov, .mp1, .mp2, .mp3, .mp4, .mpa, .mpe, .mpeg, .mpeg2, .mpeg3, .mpg, .ogg, .qt, .qtw, .ram, .rm, .rmi, .rmvb, .snd, .swf, .vob, .wav, .wax, .wma, .wmv, .wvx |
| Backup files | .bak, .bck, .bkf, .old |
| Compressed files | .ace, .arc, .arj, .bhx, .bz2, .cab, .gz, .gzip, .hpk, .hqx, .jar, .lha, .lzh, .lzx, .pak, .pit, .rar, .sea, .sit, .sqz, .tgz, .uu, .uue, .z, .zip, .zoo |
| Email files | .eml, .idx, .mbox, .mbx, .msg, .ost, .oft, .pab, .pst |
| Executable files | .bat, .cmd, .com, .cpl, .exe, .inf, .js, .jse, .msh, .msi, .msp, .ocx, .pif, .pl, .ps1, .scr, .vb, .vbs, .wsf, .wsh |
| Image files | .bmp, .dib, .eps, .gif, .img, .jfif, .jpe, .jpeg, .jpg, .pcx, .png, .ps, .psd, .raw, .rif, .spiff, .tif, .tiff |

| File Group | Applies To |
|---|---|
| Office files | .accdb, .accde, .accdr, .accdt, .adn, .adp, .doc, .docm, .docx, .dot, .dotm, .dotx, .grv, .gsa, .gta, .mad, .maf, .mda, .mdb, .mde, .mdf, .mdm, .mdt, .mdw, .mdz, .mpd, .mpp, .mpt, .obt, .odb, .one, .onepkg, .pot, .potm, .potx, .ppa, .ppam, .pps, .ppsm, .ppsx, .ppt, .pptn, .pptx, .pub, .pwz, .rqy, .rtf, .rwz, .sldm, .sldx, .slk, .thmx, .vdx, .vsd, .vsl, .vss, .vst, .vsu, .vsw, .vsx, .vtx, .wbk, .wri, .xla, .xlam, .xlb, .xlc, .xld, .xlk, .xll, .xlm, .xls, .xlsb, .xlsm, .xlsx, .xlt, .xltm, .xltx, .xlv, .xlw, .xsf, .xsn |
| System files | .acm, .dll, .ocx, .sys, .vxd |
| Temporary files | .temp, .tmp, ~* |
| Text files | .asc, .text, .txt |
| Webpage files | .asp, .aspx, .cgi, .css, .dhtml, .hta, .htm, .html, .mht, .php, .php3, .shtml, .url |

## INSIDE OUT  Exception paths

You can configure exception paths as well to designate specifically allowed locations for saving blocked file types. You can use this feature to allow specific users to save blocked file types to designated locations or to allow all users to save blocked file types to designated locations. As an example, you might want to deter illegal downloading of music and movies within the organization by preventing users from saving audio and video files. However, if your organization has an audio/video department that needs to be able to save audio and video files, you can configure an exception to allow files to be saved on a folder accessible only to members of this department.

Chapter 16

You can generate storage reports as part of quota and file-screening management. Table 16-3 provides a summary of the standard storage reports and their purposes. Using one of the standard storage reports, you can generate three general types of storage reports:

- **Incident reports**   Generated automatically when a user tries to save an unauthorized file or when a user exceeds a quota

- **Scheduled reports**   Generated periodically based on a scheduled report task

- **On-demand reports**   Generated manually upon request

**TABLE 16-3  Standard storage reports**

| Report Name | Description |
| --- | --- |
| Duplicate Files | Lists files that appear to be duplicates based on the file size and last modification time. It helps reclaim wasted space resulting from duplication. |
| File Screening Audit | Lists file-screening audit events on the server for a specified period. It helps identify users and applications that violate screening policies. You can set report parameters to filter events based on the minimum days since the screening event occurred and the user. |
| Files By File Group | Lists files by file group, such as Compressed Files, Executable Files, or Office Files. It helps identify usage patterns and types of files that are using large amounts of disk space. You can set report parameters to include or exclude specific file groups. |
| Files By Owner | Lists files by users who own them. It helps identify users who use large amounts of disk space. You can set report parameters to include or exclude specific users as well as specific files by name pattern. |
| Files By Property | Lists files by a particular classification property. It helps track classification patterns and general usage of classification properties. |
| Folders By Property | Lists folders by a particular classification property. It helps track classification patterns and general usage of classification properties. |
| Large Files | Lists files that are of a specified size or larger. It helps identify file-classification usage patterns. You can set report parameters to generate a report about a specified classification property. You can include and exclude files only by name pattern. |
| Least Recently Accessed Files | Lists files that haven't been accessed recently. It helps identify files that you might be able to delete or archive. You can set report parameters to define what constitutes a least recently used file. By default, any file that hasn't been accessed in the last 90 days is considered to be a least recently used file. You can also include or exclude specific files by name pattern. |
| Most Recently Accessed Files | Lists files that have been accessed recently. It helps identify frequently used files. You can set report parameters to define what constitutes a most recently used file. By default, any file that has been accessed within the last seven days is considered to be a most recently used file. You can also include or exclude specific files by name pattern. |

Chapter 16

| Report Name | Description |
| --- | --- |
| Quota Usage | Lists the quotas that exceed a minimum quota usage value. It helps identify file usage according to quotas. You can set report parameters to define the quotas that should be included according to the percentage of the quota limit used. For example, you might want to report when 75 percent of the quota limit has been reached. |

You manage file screening and storage reporting using the File Server Resource Manager console. This console is installed and available on the Tools menu in Server Manager when you add the File Server Resource Manager role service to the server as part of the File And Storage Services role. When you select the File Server Resource Manager node in the console, you'll see five additional nodes (as shown in Figure 16-1):

- **Quota Management**    Used to manage the quota features of Windows Server 2012 and discussed in Chapter 14

- **File Screening Management**    Used to manage the file-screening features of Windows Server 2012 and discussed in this chapter

- **Storage Reports Management**    Used to manage the storage-reporting features of Windows Server 2012 and discussed in this chapter

- **Classification Management**    Used to manage the file-classification features of Windows Server 2012

- **File Management Tasks**    Used to find subsets of files and then manage the files in some way

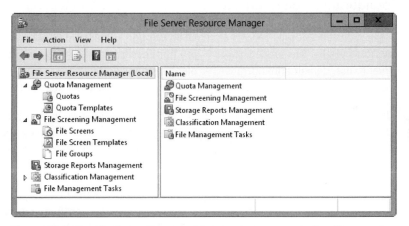

**Figure 16-1** Use File Server Resource Manager to manage quotas, file screening, and storage reports.

Chapter 16

# Managing file screening and storage reporting

File-screening and storage-reporting management can be divided into the following key areas:

- **Global options**  Control global settings for file-server resources, including email notification, storage-report default parameters, report locations, file-screen auditing, and access-denied assistance.

- **File groups**  Control the types of files to which screens are applied

- **File-screen templates**  Control screening properties (screening type: active or passive, file groups to which screening is applied; notifications: email, event log, or both)

- **File screens**  Control file paths that are screened

- **File-screen exceptions**  Control file paths that are screening exceptions

- **Report generation**  Controls whether and how storage reports are generated

The following sections discuss each of these management areas.

## Managing global file-resource settings

You use global file-resource options to configure email notification, storage-report default parameters, report locations, and file-screen auditing. You should configure these global settings prior to configuring quotas, file screens, and storage reporting.

### Configuring email notifications

Notifications and storage reports are emailed through a Simple Mail Transfer Protocol (SMTP) server. For this process to work, you must designate which organizational SMTP server to use, default administrative recipients, and the From address to be used in mailing notifications and reports. To configure these settings, follow these steps:

1. Open File Server Resource Manager. On the Action menu or in the Actions pane, tap or click Configure Options. This displays the File Server Resource Manager Options dialog box with the Email Notifications tab selected by default, as shown in Figure 16-2.

2. In the SMTP Server Name Or IP Address text box, type the fully qualified domain name of the organization's mail server, such as **MailServer48.cpandl.com**, or type the IP address of this server, such as **192.168.10.52**.

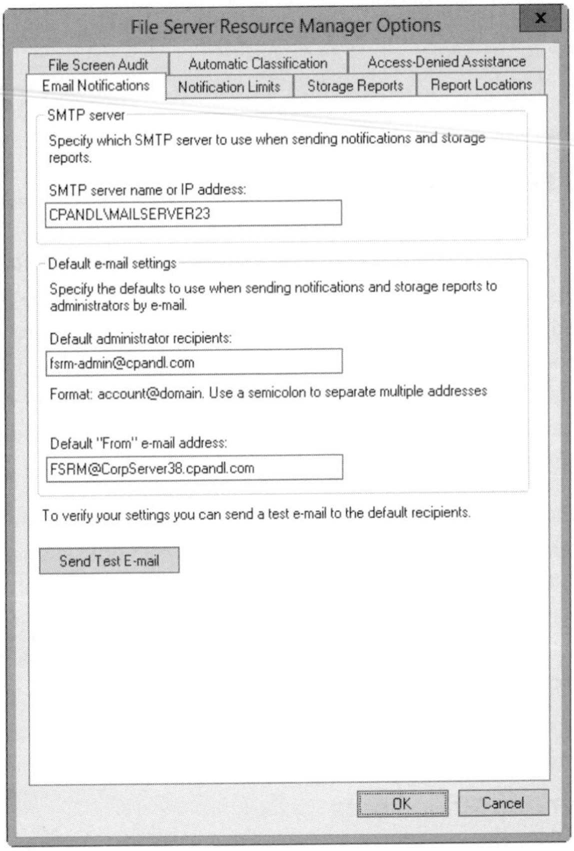

**Figure 16-2** Set email notification and other global file resource settings on the Email Notifications tab.

3.  In the Default Administrator Recipients field, type the email address of the default administrator for notification, such as **filescreens@cpandl.com**. Typically, you'll want this to be a separate mailbox that is monitored by an administrator or a distribution group that goes to the specific administrators responsible for file-server resource management. You can also enter multiple email addresses. Be sure to separate each email address with a semicolon.

4.  In the Default "From" E-Mail Address field, type the email address you want the server to use in the From field of notification messages. Remember, users as well as administrators can receive notifications.

5.  To test the settings, tap or click Send Test E-Mail. The test email message should be delivered to the default administrator recipients almost immediately. If it isn't, check

to be sure that the email addresses used are valid and that the From email address is acceptable to the SMTP server as a valid sender.

**6.**   Tap or click OK.

## TROUBLESHOOTING

### Resolving email notification problems

If you suspect there's a problem with notifications from File Server Resource Manager, the event logs are one of the first places you should look to resolve the problem. Events related to File Server Resource Manager can be found in the Application event log under the source SRMSVC. You'll also want to verify that the email options have been properly configured. Ensure that the SMTP server and default email recipients are valid. Next, send a test email message to confirm the email addresses and verify that the SMTP server is working as expected.

If email notifications are being sent, but you aren't receiving as many notifications as you think you should, check the configuration of email notifications as discussed in the next section "Configuring notification limits." Keep in mind that only one email notification is generated within the interval specified. Thus, whether a user attempts to save a blocked file or a file that exceeds a quota threshold one time or a hundred times in this interval, only one email message is generated.

## Configuring notification limits

When a quota is exceeded or an unauthorized file is detected, File Server Resource Manager sends a notification to administrators by performing one or more of the following actions:

- Sending an email message to the user who attempted to save an unauthorized file, a designated list of administrators, or both

- Recording a warning message in the event logs

- Executing a command that performs administrative tasks under the LocalService, NetworkService, or LocalSystem account

- Generating one or more notification reports and optionally sending those reports to an authorized list of recipients

To reduce the number of notifications, you can set notification limits that specify a period of time that must elapse before a subsequent notification of the same type is raised for the same issue. The default notification limit for email notification, event log notification, command notification, and report notification is 60 minutes.

You can configure notification limits by following these steps:

1.  Open File Server Resource Manager. On the Action menu or in the Actions pane, tap or click Configure Options.

2.  In the File Server Resource Manager Options dialog box, tap or click the Notification Limits tab.

3.  You can now configure limits for the following types of notifications:

    ○  **Email Notification**   Sets the interval between email notifications

    ○  **Event Log Notification**   Sets the interval between event-log notifications

    ○  **Command Notification**   Sets the interval between command notifications

    ○  **Report Notification**   Sets the interval between report notifications

4.  Tap or click OK to save your settings.

## Reviewing reports and configuring storage report parameters

Each storage report has a default configuration you can review and modify using File Server Resource Manager Options. Default parameter changes apply to all future incident reports and any existing report tasks that use the default configuration. You're able to override the default settings as necessary if you subsequently schedule a report task or generate a report on demand.

You can access the standard storage reports and change their default parameters by following these steps:

1.  Open File Server Resource Manager. On the Action menu or in the Actions pane, tap or click Configure Options.

2.  In the File Server Resource Manager Options dialog box, tap or click the Storage Reports tab.

3.  To review a report's current settings, select the report name in the Reports list and then tap or click Review Reports.

4.  To modify a report's default parameters, select the report name in the Reports list and then tap or click Edit Parameters. You can then modify the report parameters as necessary.

5.  When you finish, tap or click Close or OK as appropriate.

Chapter 16

## Configuring report locations

By default, incident, scheduled, and on-demand reports are stored on the server on which notification is triggered in separate subfolders under %SystemDrive%\StorageReports. You can review or modify this configuration by following these steps:

1. Open File Server Resource Manager. On the Action menu or in the Actions pane, tap or click Configure Options.

2. In the File Server Resource Manager Options dialog box, tap or click the Report Locations tab.

3. The report folders currently in use are listed under Report Locations. To specify a different local folder for a particular report type, type a new folder path, or tap or click Browse to search for the folder path you want to use.

4. Tap or click OK.

> **Note**
> You can use only local paths for report storage. Nonlocal folder paths are considered invalid.

**TROUBLESHOOTING**

**Resolving problems with report generation**

Occasionally, you might find that File Server Resource Manager fails to generate reports entirely and that the Application event logs contain little or no information that can help you resolve the problem. Here, errors or corruption on the volume where storage reports are being saved might be causing problems generating reports. If so, you can resolve the problem by running Chkdsk on the volume and then trying to generate the reports again.

## Configuring file-screen auditing

By running a File Screen Auditing Report, you can record file-screening activity in an auditing database for later review. This auditing data is tracked on a per-server basis, so the server on which the activity occurs is the one where the activity is audited. To enable or disable file-screen auditing, follow these steps:

1. Open File Server Resource Manager. On the Action menu or in the Actions pane, tap or click Configure Options.

2.  In the File Server Resource Manager Options dialog box, tap or click the File Screen Audit tab.

3.  To enable auditing, select the Record File Screening Activity In Auditing Database check box.

4.  To disable auditing, clear the Record File Screening Activity In Auditing Database check box.

5.  Tap or click OK to save your settings.

## Configuring classification

You use the classification rules and properties to classify files based on location, type, and content. Classification properties are values that you want to assign to files and folders. Classification rules assign classification properties to files. Each classification rule is used to assign a specific classification property to designated folders and their contents. Two types of properties can be created:

● **Local properties**   Properties defined on a specific server using File Server Resource Manager

● **Global properties**   Properties defined in Active Directory using Active Directory Administrative Center

Each classification rule you define has a specific scope. By default, classification rules apply to all files of any type within designated folders and their subfolders. You can limit the rule by assigning the rule to the lowest-level folders where the rule should be applied. For example, rather than assigning the rule to a drive root, such as C:\, you would set the rule on the C:\Data, C:\Shares\Engineering, and C:\Reports folders. You can further limit the scope of the rule by applying it only to specific types of files, such as only user and group files.

The classification methods you can use include the following:

● **Folder Classifier**   Classifies files according to folder. When you use this classifier, every file in the designated folder (as well as in its subfolders) are assigned the classification property associated with the rule.

● **Content Classifier**   Classifies files according to search strings and regular expression patterns. When you use this classifier, any file containing all specified search strings and matching all specified regular expression patterns are assigned the classification property associated with the rule. The more complex your content classifier, the longer it takes to parse and assign the classification.

- **Windows PowerShell Classifier**   Classifies files using Windows PowerShell scripts. Because scripts are entered directly as part of the classification parameters, you should test the scripts on a subset of data or a specific test set before applying.

Generally, classification rules are applied to files only when applications or file management tasks query their classification properties. Because processing classification rules at the time of a request might slow down performance, you typically want to automatically classify files beforehand. To do this, you create a schedule for automatic classification using File Server Resource Manager.

Automatic classification can be scheduled to run weekly at a specific day and time, such as Sunday at 3:30 AM, or monthly on a specific day of the month, such as the fifth day of every month.

Following this, you can configure classification by doing the following:

1. Create classification properties that you want to assign to files using either File Server Resource Manager or Active Directory Administrative Center.

   ○ Create local properties in File Server Resource Manager. Under Classification Management, select Classification Properties to view currently defined properties. To create a local property, press and hold or right-click Classification Properties in the left pane, select Create Local Property, and then use the options provided to set the property type and value.

   ○ Create global properties in Active Directory Administrative Center. Under Dynamic Access Controls, select Resource Properties to view currently defined global properties and their enabled or disabled status. To create a global property, under Tasks, select New, select Resource Property, and then use the options provided to set the property type and value.

2. In File Server Resource Manager, create one or more classification rules for each classification property. Under Classification Management, select Classification Rules to view currently defined rules. To create a rule, press and hold or right-click Classification Rules in the left pane, select Create Classification Rule, and then use the options provided to define the rule.

3. In File Server Resource Manager, schedule automatic classification to pre-assign classification properties as appropriate. Under Classification Management, select Classification Rules and then select Configure Classification Run Schedule. You can now view the current classification schedule or define a new one.

## Enabling access-denied assistance

In Group Policy, you can configure Access-Denied Assistance policies to help users determine who to contact if they have trouble accessing files. When you enable and configure Access-Denied Assistance policies, you can customize Access Denied errors with additional help text, links to help pages or documents, and an email address for requesting help.

To enable Access-Denied Assistance for all file types, configure Enable Access-Denied Assistance On Client For All File Types as Enabled and then customize Access Denied errors by enabling and configuring Customize Message For Access Denied Errors. As discussed in Chapter 15, "File sharing and security," these policies are found in the Administrative Templates policies for Computer Configuration under System\Access-Denied Assistance.

When you add the File Server Resource Manager role to a file server, you can configure Access-Denied Assistance through File Server Resource Manager and then you can use its standard-message and request-assistance options to quickly configure Access-Denied Assistance. The standard assistance message is similar to the one shown in Figure 16-3. The standard message includes a clickable link to Microsoft Support. You can easily modify the standard message.

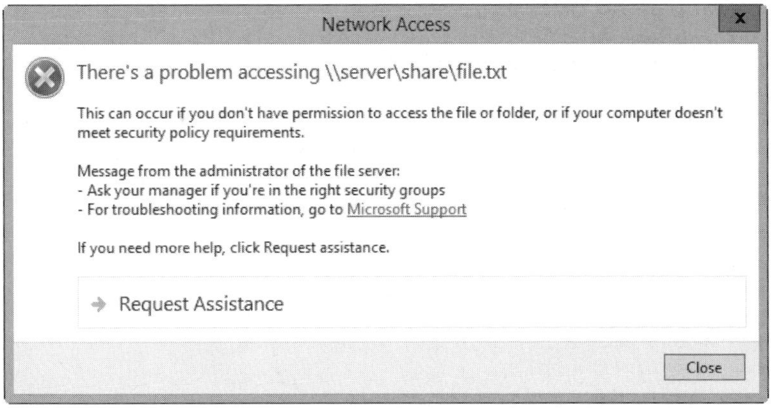

**Figure 16-3** The default assistance message set when using File Server Resource Manager.

To configure Access-Denied Assistance using File Server Resource Manager, follow these steps:

1. Open File Server Resource Manager. On the Action menu or in the Actions pane, tap or click Configure Options.

2. In the File Server Resource Manager Options dialog box, tap or click the Access-Denied Assistance tab, as shown in Figure 16-4.

Chapter 16

**3.** Select the Enable Access-Denied Assistance check box. You can modify the standard message by typing directly into the editable box provided on the Access-Denied Assistance tab. For example, you might want to replace the link to Microsoft Support with a link to your organization's help desk, as I've done here. When creating your message, keep the following in mind:

  ○ The message is standard text except for the *<a> </a>* tags. The begin and end anchor tags are the only acceptable HTML.

  ○ You can enter multiple anchor tags. Each *<a>* tag can have its own hypertext reference, and any text placed between the *<a>* tag and the *</a>* tag becomes a clickable hypertext link.

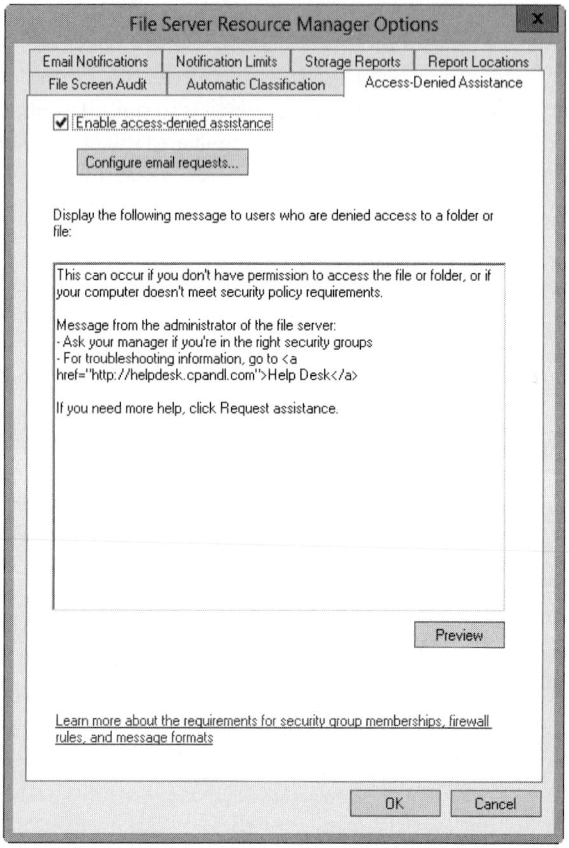

---

**File Server Resource Manager Options**    ✕

| Email Notifications | Notification Limits | Storage Reports | Report Locations |
| File Screen Audit | Automatic Classification | Access-Denied Assistance | |

☑ Enable access-denied assistance

  [ Configure email requests... ]

Display the following message to users who are denied access to a folder or file:

> This can occur if you don't have permission to access the file or folder, or if your computer doesn't meet security policy requirements.
>
> Message from the administrator of the file server:
> - Ask your manager if you're in the right security groups
> - For troubleshooting information, go to <a href="http://helpdesk.cpandl.com">Help Desk</a>
>
> If you need more help, click Request assistance.

  [ Preview ]

Learn more about the requirements for security group memberships, firewall rules, and message formats

  [ OK ]   [ Cancel ]

**Figure 16-4** Customize the Access-Denied Assistance message for your organization.

**4.** If you want users to be able to request assistance by sending an email message to a predesignated administrator, tap or click Configure Email Requests and then select

Enable Users To Request Assistance, as shown in Figure 16-5. Typically, you'll want to include user information (including user claims) and device state information (including device claims), which is why these options are selected by default.

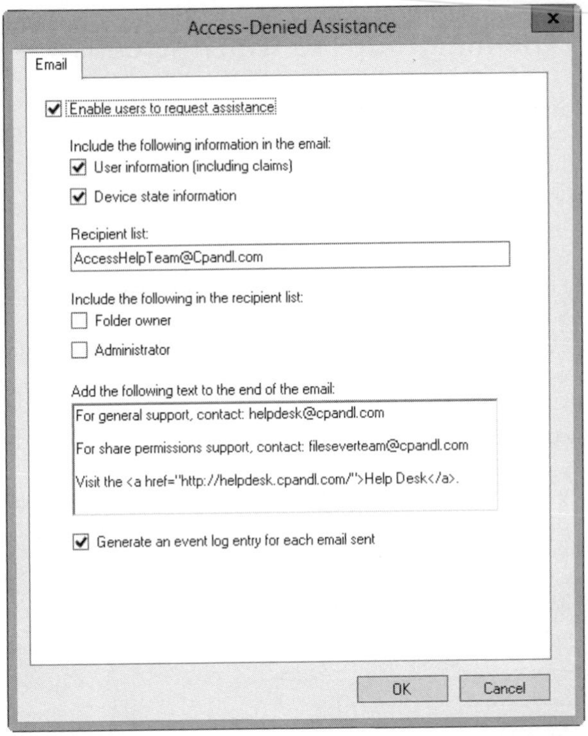

**Figure 16-5** Customize the request assistance email requests.

5. In the Recipient List, enter a semicolon-separated list of recipients for the email request. However, rather than entering the email addresses of specific people, you might want to enter the email address for a distribution group. In this way, you can manage recipients by adding or removing group members rather than editing the Access-Denied Assistance configuration.

6. By default, the email request also is sent to the folder owner and the Administrator account. If you have a specific team handling access assistance and you already provided the email address in the Recipient list, you might want to clear these options. Otherwise, accept the default selections.

7. Next, use the text box provided to customize the text added to the end of the email message. As before, this is standard text that can be modified as necessary and also can include hypertext links.

8. By default, email requests are logged in the Application event log. If you don't want related events to be logged, clear Generate An Event Log Entry For Each Email Sent.

9. Tap or click OK.

## Managing the file groups to which screens are applied

You use file groups to designate sets of similar file types to which screening can be applied. In File Server Resource Manager, you can view the currently defined file-screening groups by expanding the File Server Resource Manager and File Screening Management nodes and then selecting File Groups. Table 16-2, shown previously, lists the default file groups and the included file types.

You can modify existing file groups by following these steps:

1. Open File Server Resource Manager. Expand the File Server Resource Manager and File Screening Management nodes, and then select File Groups.

2. Currently defined file groups are listed along with included and excluded files.

3. To modify file-group properties, double-tap or double-click the file-group name. This displays a Properties dialog box similar to the one shown in Figure 16-6.

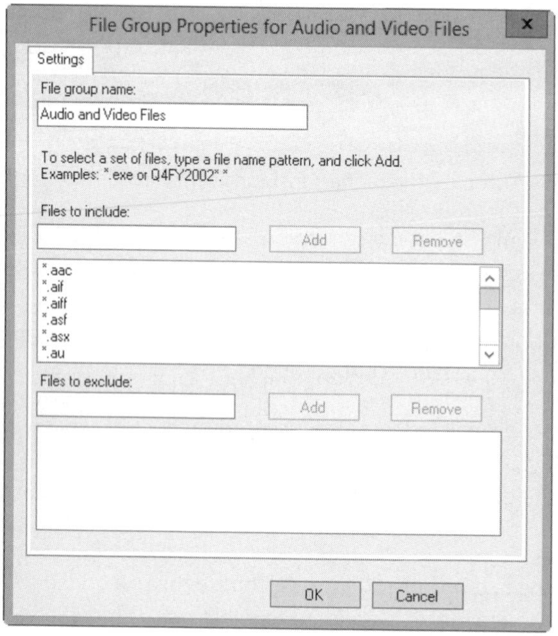

**Figure 16-6** Include and exclude file types by modifying file-group properties.

4. In the Files To Include text box, type the file name extension of an additional file type to screen, such as **.pdf**, or the file name pattern, such as **Archive\*.\***. Tap or click Add. Repeat this step to specify other file types to screen.

5. In the Files To Exclude text box, type the file name extension of a file type to exclude from screening, such as **.doc**, or the file name pattern, such as **Report\*.\***. Tap or click Add. Repeat this step to specify other file types to exclude from screening.

6. Tap or click OK to save the changes.

You can specify additional file groups to screen by following these steps:

1. Open File Server Resource Manager. Expand the File Server Resource Manager and File Screening Management nodes, and then select File Groups.

2. On the Action menu or in the Actions pane, tap or click Create File Group. This displays the Create File Group Properties dialog box.

3. In the File Group Name text box, type the name of the file group you're creating.

4. In the Files To Include field, type the file name extension to screen, such as **.pdf**, or the file name pattern, such as **Archive\*.\***. Tap or click Add. Repeat this step to specify other file types to screen.

5. In the Files To Exclude text box, type the file name extension to exclude from screening, such as **.doc**, or the file name pattern, such as **Report\*.\***. Tap or click Add. Repeat this step to specify other file types to exclude from screening.

6. Tap or click OK to create the file group.

## Managing file-screen templates

You use file-screen templates to define screening properties, including the screening type, the file groups to which a screen is applied, and notification. In File Server Resource Manager, you can view the currently defined file-screen templates by expanding the File Server Resource Manager and File Screening Management nodes and then selecting File Screen Templates. Table 16-1, shown previously, provides a summary of the default file-screen templates.

You can modify existing file-screen templates by following these steps:

1. Open File Server Resource Manager. Expand the File Server Resource Manager and File Screening Management nodes, and then select File Screen Templates.

Chapter 16

2. Currently defined file-screen templates are listed by name, screening type, and file groups affected.

3. To modify file screen template properties, double-tap or double-click the file-screen template name. This displays a Properties dialog box (shown in Figure 16-7).

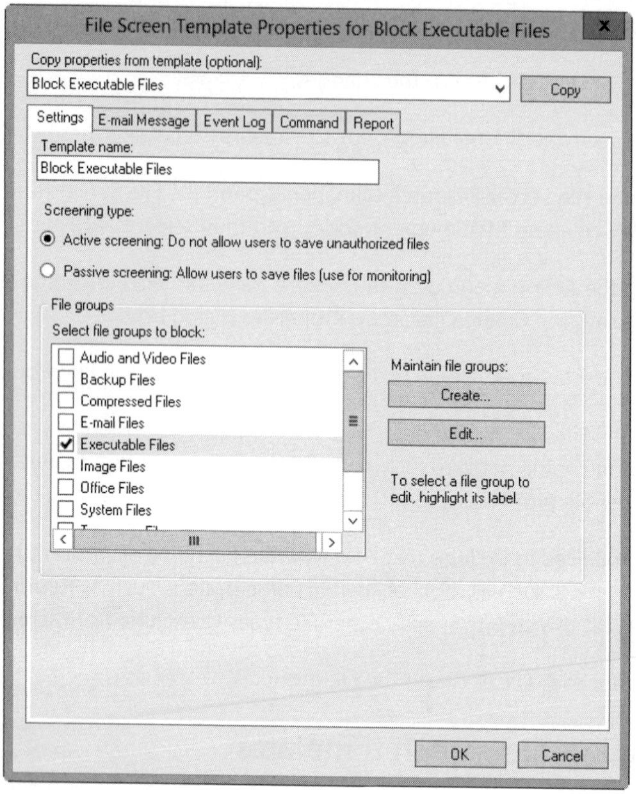

**Figure 16-7** Use file-screen properties to configure the screening type, the file groups to which a screen is applied, and notification.

4. On the Settings tab, you can set the template name, screen type, and file groups affected using the controls provided.

5. On the E-Mail Message tab, you can configure the following notifications:

   ○ To notify an administrator when the file screen is triggered, select the Send E-Mail To The Following Administrators check box and then type the email address or addresses to use. Be sure to separate multiple email addresses with a semicolon. Use the value **[Admin Email]** to specify the default administrator as configured previously under the global options.

  ○  To notify users, select the Send E-Mail To The User Who Attempted To Save An Unauthorized File check box. In the Subject and Message Body text boxes, specify the contents of the user notification message. Table 16-4 lists available variables and their meanings.

**6.** On the Event Log tab, you can configure event logging. Select Send Warning To Event Log to enable logging, and then specify the text of the log entry in the Log Entry field. Table 16-4 lists available variables and their meanings.

**7.** On the Report tab, select the Generate Reports check box to enable incident reporting, and then select the check boxes for the types of reports you want to generate. Incident reports are stored under %SystemDrive%\StorageReports\Incident by default and can also be sent to designated administrators as well as to the user who attempted to save an unauthorized file. Use the value **[Admin Email]** to specify the default administrator as configured previously under the global options.

**8.** Tap or click OK when you have finished modifying the template.

You can create a new file-screen template by following these steps:

**1.** Open File Server Resource Manager. Expand the File Screening Management node, and then select File Screen Templates.

**2.** On the Action menu or in the Actions pane, tap or click Create File Screen Template. This displays the Create File Screen Template dialog box.

**3.** Follow steps 4–8 of the previous procedure.

**TABLE 16-4 File-screen variables**

| Variable Name | Description |
|---|---|
| [Admin Email] | Inserts the email addresses of the administrators defined under the global options |
| [File Screen Path] | Inserts the local file path where the user attempted to save the file, such as C:\Data |
| [File Screen Remote Path] | Inserts the remote file path where the user attempted to save the file, such as \\server\share |
| [File Screen System Path] | Inserts the canonical file path where the user attempted to save the file, such as \\?\VolumeGUID |
| [Server Domain] | Inserts the domain of the server on which the notification occurred |
| [Server] | Inserts the server on which the notification occurred |
| [Source File Owner] | Inserts the user name of the owner of the unauthorized file |

Chapter 16

| Variable Name | Description |
|---|---|
| [Source File Owner Email] | Inserts the email address of the owner of the unauthorized file |
| [Source File Path] | Inserts the source path of the unauthorized file |
| [Source File Remote Paths] | For shared folders, inserts the source path in UNC format, such as \\FileServer15\Data. |
| [Source Io Owner Email] | Inserts the email address of the user who caused the notification |
| [Source Io Owner] | Inserts the name of the user who caused the notification |
| [Source Process Id] | Inserts the process ID (PID) of the process that caused the notification |
| [Source Process Image] | Inserts the executable for the process that caused the notification |
| [Violated File Group] | Inserts the name of the file group in which the file type is defined as unauthorized |

## Creating file screens

You use file screens to designate file paths that are screened. In File Server Resource Manager, you can view current file screens by expanding the File Server Resource Manager and File Screening Management nodes and then selecting File Screens. Before you define file screens, you should specify file-screening groups and file-screen templates that you will use, as discussed in "Managing the file groups to which screens are applied" and "Managing file-screen templates."

After you define the necessary file groups and file-screen templates, you can create a file screen by following these steps:

1.  Open File Server Resource Manager. Expand the File Server Resource Manager and File Screening Management nodes, and then select File Screens.

2.  Tap or click Create File Screen on the Action menu or in the Actions pane.

3.  In the Create File Screen dialog box, set the local computer path to screen by tapping or clicking Browse. In the Browse For Folder dialog box, select the path to screen, such as C:\Data.

4.  In the Derive Properties selection list, choose the file-screen template that defines the screening properties you want to use.

5.  Tap or click Create.

## Defining file-screening exceptions

You use exception paths to designate folder locations where it's permitted to save blocked file types. Based on the NTFS permissions on the excepted file path, you can use this feature to allow specific users to save blocked file types to designated locations or to allow all users to save blocked file types to designated locations.

You can create a file-screen exception by following these steps:

1.  Open File Server Resource Manager. Expand the File Server Resource Manager and File Screening Management nodes, and then select File Screens.

2.  Tap or click Create File Screen Exception on the Action menu or in the Actions pane.

3.  In the Create File Screen Exception dialog box, set the local path to exclude from screening by tapping or clicking Browse. Then, in the Browse For Folder dialog box, select the path to exclude from screening, such as C:\Data\Images.

4.  Select the file groups to exclude from screening on the designated path.

5.  Tap or click OK.

## Scheduling and generating storage reports

Incident reports are generated automatically when triggered, as defined in the Reports tab properties of a file-screen template. (For details, see "Understanding File Screening and Storage Reporting.") Scheduled and on-demand reports are configured separately. In File Server Resource Manager, you can view currently scheduled reports by expanding the File Server Resource Manager node and then selecting Storage Reports Management.

You can schedule reports on a per-volume or per-folder basis by following these steps:

1.  Open File Server Resource Manager. Expand the File Server Resource Manager node, and then select Storage Reports Management.

2.  On the Action menu or in the Actions pane, tap or click Schedule A New Report Task. This displays the Storage Reports Task Properties dialog box, shown in Figure 16-8.

Chapter 16

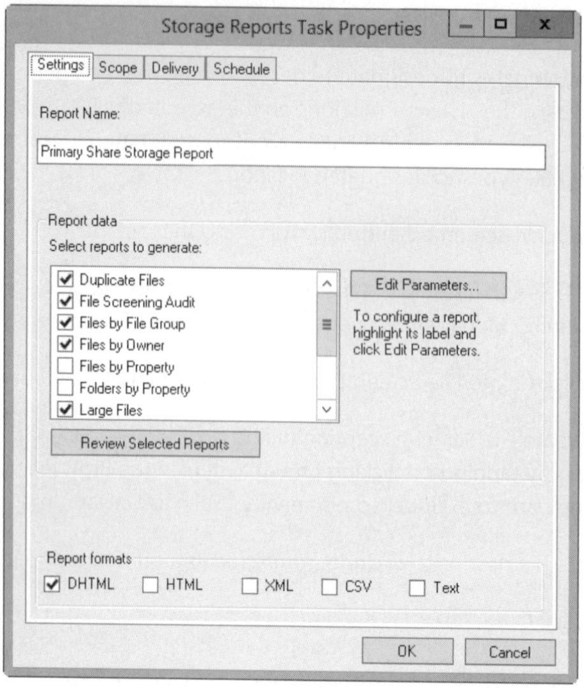

**Figure 16-8** Schedule reports for delivery on a per-volume or per-folder basis.

3. On the Settings tab, type a descriptive name for the report, such as **Primary Data Share Storage Report**.

4. Under Report Data, select the types of reports to generate. Some of the reports have configurable parameters. If a report does have configurable parameters, when you select the report under Report Data and then tap or click Edit Parameters, you'll be able to customize the report.

5. Under Report Formats, select the format for the report, such as Dynamic HTML (DHTML).

6. On the Scope tab, specify the general kinds of data to include by selecting the appropriate check boxes for:

   ○ **Application Files** Data created by applications

   ○ **Backup And Archival Files** Data created for backups and file archives

   ○ **Group Files** Data created and modified by multiple people rather than a particular user

   ○ **User Files** Data created by specific users

7. Next, on the Scope tab, tap or click Add. In the Browse For Folder dialog box, select the volume or folder on which you want to generate scheduled storage reports. Repeat these actions to add other volumes or folders.

> **Note**
> On clustered file servers, you can report only on volumes that belong to the same cluster resource group.

8. By default, Windows Server 2012 stores scheduled storage reports as they're generated in the %SystemDrive%\StorageReports\Scheduled folder. If you also want to deliver reports by email to administrators, tap or click the Delivery tab and then select the Send Reports To The Following Administrators check box. Enter the email address or addresses to which reports should be delivered, being sure to separate each email address with a semicolon.

9. On the Schedule tab, use the options provided to define the run schedule for reporting. For example, you can run the reports weekly on a Monday at 4:30:00 AM or monthly on the last day of the month at 3:00:00 AM.

10. Tap or click OK to schedule the report task.

You can generate an on-demand report by following these steps:

1. Open File Server Resource Manager. Expand the File Server Resource Manager node, and then select Storage Reports Management.

2. On the Action menu or in the Actions pane, tap or click Generate Reports Now. This displays the Storage Reports Task Properties dialog box.

3. On the Settings tab, under Report Data, select the types of reports to generate.

4. Under Report Formats, select the format for the report, such as DHTML.

5. On the Scope tab, specify the general kinds of data to include by selecting the appropriate check boxes for Application Files, Group Files, Backup And Archival Files, and User Files.

6. Next, on the Scope tab, tap or click Add. In the Browse For Folder dialog box, select the volume or folder on which you want to generate the on-demand storage reports. Repeat to add other volumes or folders.

Chapter 16

7. Windows Server 2012 stores on-demand storage reports in the %SystemDrive%\StorageReports\Interactive folder. If you also want to deliver reports by email to administrators, tap or click the Delivery tab and then select the Send Reports To The Following Administrators check box. Enter the email address or addresses to which reports should be delivered, being sure to separate each email address with a semicolon.

8. Tap or click OK. When prompted, specify whether to wait for the reports to be generated and then display them or to generate the reports in the background for later access. Tap or click OK.

# Backup and recovery

EVERY Windows Server system on your network represents a major investment in time, resources, and money. It requires a great deal of planning and effort to deploy a new server successfully. It requires just as much planning and effort—if not more—to ensure that you can restore a server when disaster strikes. Why? Because you not only need to plan and implement a backup for each and every server on your network, but you need to perform backups regularly and you need to test the backup process and procedures to ensure that when disaster strikes you are prepared.

## Disaster-planning strategies

Ask three different people what their idea of a disaster is and you'll probably get three different answers. For most administrators, the term "disaster" probably means any scenario in which one or more essential system services cannot operate and the prospects for quick recovery are less than hopeful—that is, a disaster is something a service reset or system reboot won't fix.

To ensure that operations can be restored as quickly as possible in a given situation, every network needs a clear disaster recovery plan. Many of the same concepts go into disaster planning as when you are planning for highly available, scalable, and manageable systems. Why? Because, at the end of the day, disaster planning involves implementing plans that ensure the availability of systems and services. Remember that part of disaster planning is applying some level of contingency planning to every essential network service and system. You need to implement problem escalation and response procedures. You also need a standing problem-resolution document that describes in great detail what to do when disaster strikes.

# Developing contingency procedures

You should identify the services and systems that are essential to network operations. Typically, this list will include the following components:

- Network infrastructure servers running Active Directory, Domain Name System (DNS), Dynamic Host Configuration Protocol (DHCP), Remote Desktop Services, and Routing and Remote Access Service (RRAS)

- File, database, and application servers, such as servers with essential file shares or those that provide database or email services

- Networking hardware, including switches, routers, and firewalls

Combine your availability, scalability, and manageability plans with plans for contingency procedures in the following areas:

- **Physical security**   Place network hardware and servers in a locked, secure access facility. This could be an office that is kept locked or a server room that requires a passkey to enter. When physical access to network hardware and servers requires special access privileges, you prevent many problems and ensure that only authorized personnel can get access to systems from the console.

- **Data backup**   Implement a regular backup plan that ensures that multiple datasets are available for all essential systems, and that these backups are stored in more than one location. For example, if you keep the most current backup sets on-site in the server room, you should rotate another backup set to off-site storage. In this way, if disaster strikes, you will be more likely to be able to recover operations.

- **Fault tolerance**   Build redundancy into the network and system architecture. At the server level, you can protect data using a redundant array of independent disks (RAID) and guard against component failure by having spare parts on hand. These precautions protect servers at a very basic level. For essential services such as Active Directory, DNS, and DHCP, you can build in fault tolerance by deploying redundant systems using techniques discussed throughout this book. These same concepts can be applied to network hardware components such as routers and switches.

- **Recovery**   Every essential server and network device should have a written recovery plan that details step by step what to do to rebuild and recover it. Be as detailed and explicit as possible, and don't assume that the readers know anything about the system or device they are recovering. Do this even if you are sure that you'll be the one performing the recovery—you'll be thankful for it, trust me. Things can and do go wrong at the worst times, and sometimes, under pressure, you might forget some important detail in the recovery process—not to mention that you might be unavailable to recover the system for some reason.

- **Power protection**    Power-protect servers and network hardware using an uninterruptible power supply (UPS) system. Power protection will help safeguard servers and network hardware from power surges and dirty power. Power protection will also help prevent data loss and allow you to power down servers in an appropriate fashion through manual or automatic shutdown.

## INSIDE OUT    Using and configuring UPS

Putting in a UPS requires a bit of planning, because you need to look not only at servers but also at everything in the server room that requires power. If the power goes out, you want to have ample time for systems to shut down in an orderly fashion. You might also have some systems that you do not want to be shut down, such as routers or servers required for security key cards. In most cases, rather than using individual UPS devices, you should install enterprise UPS solutions that can be connected to several servers or components.

After you install a UPS, you can configure servers to take advantage of UPS using the management software included with the UPS. You can then configure the way a server reacts when it switches to battery power. Typically, you'll want servers to start an orderly shutdown within a few minutes of switching to battery power.

In your planning, remember that 90 percent of power outages last less than 5 minutes and 99 percent of power outages last less than 60 minutes. With this in mind, you might want to plan your UPS implementation so that you can maintain 7 to 10 minutes of power for all server and network components and 60 to 70 minutes for critical systems. You would then configure all noncritical systems to shut down automatically after 5 minutes and configure critical systems to shut down after 60 minutes.

## Implementing problem-escalation and response procedures

As part of planning, you need to develop well-defined problem-escalation procedures that document how to handle problems and emergency changes that might be needed. You need to designate an incident response team and an emergency response team. Although the two teams could consist of the same team members, the teams differ in fundamental ways:

- **Incident response team**   The incident response team's role is to respond to security incidents, such as the suspected cracking of a database server. This team is concerned with responding to an intrusion, taking immediate action to safeguard the organization's information, documenting the security issue thoroughly in an after-action report, and then fixing the security problem so that the same type of incident cannot recur. Your organization's security administrator or network security expert should have a key role in this team.

- **Emergency response team**   The emergency response team's role is to respond to service and system outages, such as the failure of a database server. This team is concerned with recovering the service or system as quickly as possible and allowing normal operations to resume. Like the incident response team, the emergency response team needs to document the outage thoroughly in an after-action report, and then, if applicable, propose changes to improve the recovery process. Your organization's system administrators should have key roles in this team.

## Creating a problem-resolution policy document

Over the years, I've worked with and consulted for many organizations, and I've often been asked to help implement information technology (IT) policies and procedures. In the area of disaster and recovery planning, there's one policy document that I always use, regardless of the size of the company I am working with. I call it the *problem-resolution policy document*.

The problem-resolution policy document has the following six sections:

- **Responsibilities**   The overall responsibilities of IT and engineering staff during and after normal business hours should be detailed in this section. For an organization with 24/7 operations, such as a company with a public World Wide Web site maintained by internal staff, the after-hours responsibilities section should be very detailed and let individuals know exactly what their responsibilities are. Most organizations with 24/7 operations will designate individuals as being "on call" 7 days a week, 365 days a year, and in that case, this section should detail what being "on call" means and what the general responsibilities are for an individual on call.

- **Phone roster**   Every system and service you identify in your planning as essential should have a point of contact. For some systems, you'll have several points of contact. Consider, for example, a database server. You might have a system administrator who is responsible for the server itself, a database administrator who is responsible for the database running on the server, and an integration specialist responsible for any integration components running on the server.

> **Important**
>
> The phone roster should include both on-site and off-site contact numbers. Ideally, this means that you'll have the work phone number, cell phone number, and pager number of each contact. It should be the responsibility of every individual on the phone roster to ensure that contact information is up to date.

- **Key contact information**   In addition to a phone roster, you should have contact numbers for facilities and vendors. The key contacts list should include the main office phone numbers at branch offices and data centers and contact numbers for the various vendors that installed infrastructure at each office, such as the building manager, Internet service provider (ISP), electrician, and network wiring specialist. It should also include the support phone numbers for hardware and software vendors and the information you'll be required to give in order to get service, such as customer identification number and service contract information.

- **Notification procedures**   The way problems get resolved is through notification. This section should outline the notification procedures and the primary point of contact in case of outage. If many systems and services are involved, notification and primary contacts can be divided into categories. For example, you might have an external systems-notification process for your public Internet servers and an internal systems-notification process for your intranet services.

- **Escalation**   When problems aren't resolved within a specific timeframe, there should be clear escalation procedures that detail whom to contact and when. For example, you might have level 1, level 2, and level 3 points of contact, with level 1 contacts being called immediately, level 2 contacts being called when issues aren't resolved in 30 minutes, and level 3 contacts being called when issues aren't resolved in 60 minutes.

> **Important**
>
> You should also have a priority system in place that dictates what types of incidents or outages take precedence over others. For example, you could specify that service-level outages, such as those that involve the complete system, have priority over an isolated outage involving a single server or application, but that suspected security incidents have priority over all other issues.

Chapter 17

- **Post-action reporting**   Every individual involved in a major outage or incident should be expected to write a post-action report. This section details what should be in that report. For example, you would want to track the notification time, actions taken after notification, escalation attempts, and other items that are important to improving the process or preventing the problem from recurring.

Every IT group should have a general policy with regard to problem-resolution procedures, and this policy should be detailed in a problem-resolution policy document or one like it. The document should be distributed to all relevant personnel throughout the organization so that every person who has some level of responsibility for ensuring system and service availability knows what to do in the case of an emergency. After you implement the policy, you should test it to help refine it so that the policy will work as expected in an actual disaster.

# Disaster preparedness procedures

Just as you need to perform planning before disaster strikes, you also need to perform certain predisaster preparation procedures. These procedures ensure that you are able to recover systems as quickly as possible when a disaster strikes and include the following:

- Backups

- Startup repair

- Recovery disks

- Startup and recovery options

- Recovery Console

## Performing backups

You should perform regular backups of every server. Backups can be performed using several techniques. Most organizations choose a combination of dedicated backup servers and per-server backups. If you use professional backup software, you can use one or more dedicated backup servers to create backups of other servers on the network, and then write the backups to media on centralized backup devices. If you use per-server backups, you run backup software on each server that you want to back up and store the backup media on a local backup device. By combining the techniques, you get the best of both worlds.

With dedicated backup servers, you purchase professional backup software, a backup server, and a scalable backup device. The initial costs for purchasing the required equipment and the time required to set up the backup environment can be substantial. However, after the backup environment is configured, it is rather easy to maintain. Centralized backups also offer substantial time savings for administrators because the backup process itself can be fully automated.

With per-server backups, you use a backup utility to perform manual backups of individual systems. The primary tool for performing per-server backups is the Windows Server Backup utility, which is discussed later in this chapter in "Backing up and recovering your data." Because this tool is included with Windows Server 2012, there is no initial cost for implementation. However, because the backup options are limited, the process might require more time than using centralized backup servers.

## Repairing startup

Like its predecessors, Windows Server 2012 has several automatic repair features. If the boot manager or corrupted system file is preventing startup, the Startup Repair tool is started automatically and will initiate the repair of the server. The Startup Repair tool can be helpful if one or more of the following problems are preventing startup:

- A virus infection in the master boot record

- A missing or corrupt boot manager

- A boot configuration data store with bad entries

- A corrupted system file

Although Startup Repair typically runs automatically, you can manually initiate this feature by completing the following steps:

1.  If the computer won't start normally, you'll see a Windows Boot Manager error screen stating that Windows failed to start. Press Enter.

2.  On the OS Selection screen, press F8.

3.  On the Advanced Boot Options screen, choose an appropriate safe mode or other alternate mode to try to start the server so that you can log in to diagnose and resolve the problem.

You also can use the installation disc to initiate recovery. To do so, follow these steps:

1.  Insert the Windows Installation disc, and then boot from the installation disc by pressing a key when prompted during startup. If the server does not allow you to boot from the installation disc, you might need to change firmware options to allow booting from a CD/DVD-ROM drive.

Chapter 17

2. Windows Setup should start automatically. On the Install Windows page, select the language, time, and keyboard layout options that you want to use. Tap or click Next.

3. When prompted, do not tap or click Install Now. Instead, tap or click the Repair Your Computer link in the lower left corner of the Install Windows page.

4. On the Recovery screen, tap or click Troubleshoot. Then, on the Advanced Options screen, tap or click Command Prompt to access the MINWINPC environment. As discussed in Chapter 2, "Deploying Windows Server 2012," the mini Windows PC environment gives you access to the command-line tools listed in Table 2-2.

5. Change directories to x:\sources\recovery by typing **cd recovery**.

6. Run the Startup Repair Wizard by typing **startrep**.

You can recover a server's operating system or perform a full system recovery by using a Windows installation disc and a backup that you created earlier with Windows Server Backup. To initiate a recovery, on the Recovery screen, tap or click Troubleshoot. Then, on the Advanced Options screen, tap or click System Image Recovery.

With an operating system recovery, you recover all critical volumes but do not recover nonsystem volumes. If you recover a full system, Windows Server Backup reformats and repartitions all disks that are attached to the server. Because of this, you should use this method only when you want to recover the server data onto separate hardware or when all other attempts to recover the server on the existing hardware have failed.

## Setting startup and recovery options

As part of planning for the worst-case scenarios, you need to consider how you want systems to start up and recover if a stop error is encountered. The options you choose can add to the boot time or they can specify that if a system encounters a stop error it does not reboot.

You can configure startup and recovery options by completing the following steps:

1. In the Control Panel, tap or click System And Security\System to start the System utility.

2. Tap or click Advanced System Settings. This opens the System Properties dialog box.

3. On the Advanced tab, tap or click Settings in the Startup And Recovery panel. This displays the dialog box shown in Figure 17-1.

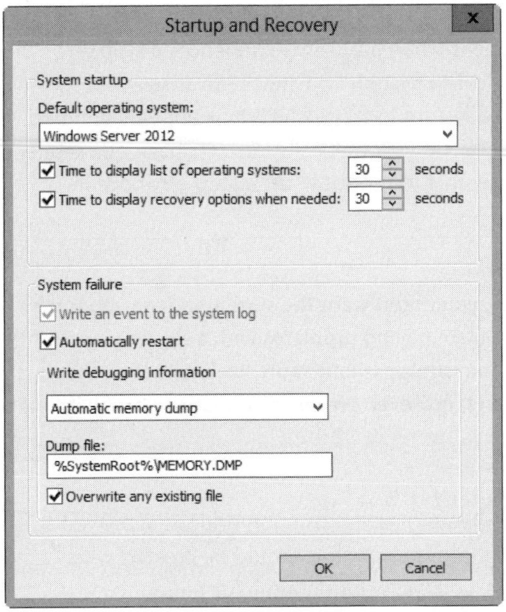

**Figure 17-1** Configuring startup and recovery options.

**4.** In the Startup And Recovery dialog box, you configure the settings as follows:

○ If a server has multiple operating systems, you can set the default operating system by selecting one of the operating systems in the Default Operating System list. These options are obtained from the boot manager.

○ When multiple operating systems are installed, the Time To Display List Of Operating Systems option controls how long the system waits before booting to the default operating system. In most cases, you won't need more than a few seconds to make a choice, so reduce this wait time to perhaps 5 or 10 seconds. Alternatively, you can have the system automatically choose the default operating system by clearing this option.

○ When you want to display recovery options, the operating system uses the Time To Display Recovery Options When Needed setting to determine how long to wait for you to choose a recovery option. The default wait time is 30 seconds. If you don't choose a recovery option in that time, the system boots normally without recovery. As with operating systems, you won't need more than a few seconds to make a choice, so reduce this wait time to perhaps 5 or 10 seconds.

○ Under System Failure, you have several important options for determining what happens when a system experiences a stop error. By default, the Write An Event To The System Log check box is selected so that the system logs an error in the system log. The check box appears dimmed, so it cannot normally be changed. The Automatically Restart check box is selected to ensure that the system attempts to reboot when a stop error occurs.

> ## Important
>
> In some cases, you might want the system to halt rather than reboot. For example, if you are having problems with a server, you might want it to halt so that an administrator will be more likely to notice that it is experiencing problems. Don't, however, prevent automatic reboot without a specific reason.

○ The Write Debugging Information options allow you to choose the type of debugging information that should be created when a stop error occurs. In most cases, you will want debug information to be dumped so that you can use it to determine the cause of a crash.

> ## Important
>
> If you choose a kernel memory dump, you dump all physical memory being used at the time of the failure. You can create the dump file only if the system is properly configured. The system drive must have a paging file at least as large as RAM and adequate disk space to write the dump file.

○ By default, dump files are written to the %SystemRoot% folder. If you want to write the dump file to a different location, type the file path in the Dump File box. Select the Overwrite Any Existing File option to ensure that only one dump file is maintained.

5. Tap or click OK twice to close all open dialog boxes.

# Developing backup strategies

Backups are insurance plans, plain and simple—and every administrator should see them that way. When disaster strikes, your backup implementation will either leave you out of harm's way or drowning without a life preserver. Trust me: You don't want to be drowning when it should be your moment to shine. After all, if you've implemented a well-thought-out backup plan and practiced the necessary recovery procedures until they are second nature, a server that has stopped working is nothing more than a bump in the road that you can smooth out even if you have to rebuild a server from scratch to do it.

## Creating your backup strategy

So, where to start? Start by outlining a backup and recovery plan that describes the servers and the data that need to be backed up. Ask yourself the following questions:

- How important is the role that the server is performing?

- How important is the data stored on the server?

- Is the data unique, or are there multiple masters available?

- How often does the data change?

- How much data in total is there to back up?

- How long does each backup take?

- How quickly do you need to recover the data?

- How much historical data do you need to store?

- Do you have the equipment needed to perform backups?

- Do you need to store backups off site?

- Who will be responsible for performing backups?

The answers to these questions will help you develop your backup and recovery plan. Often you'll find that your current resources aren't enough and that you need to obtain additional backup equipment. It might be one of the ultimate ironies in administration, but you often need more justification for backup equipment than for any other type of equipment. Fight to get the backup resources you need, and do so without reservation. If you have to make incremental purchases over a period of several months to get the backup equipment and supplies, do so without hesitation.

## Backup strategy considerations

In most cases, your backup strategy should involve performing some type of backup of every server daily and full backups of these servers at least once a week. You should also regularly inspect the backup log files and periodically perform test restores of the data to ensure that data is being properly written to the backup media.

Chapter 17

## It's all about the data

**M**uch of your backup strategy depends on the importance of the data, the frequency of changes to it, and the total amount of data to back up. Data that is of higher importance or that frequently changes needs to be backed up more often than other types of data. As the amount of data you are backing up increases, you need to be able to scale your backup implementation. If you are starting out with a large amount of data, you need to consider how much time a complete backup of the data set will take. To ensure that backups can be performed in a timely manner, you might have to purchase faster equipment or purchase backup devices with multiple tape drives.

Plan separate backup strategies for system files and data files.

- *System files* are used by the operating system and applications. These files change when you install new components, service packs, or patches. They include system state data.

### Note

For systems that aren't domain controllers, the system-state data includes essential boot files, key system files, and the COM+ class registration database, as well as the registry data. For domain controllers, the Active Directory database and System Volume (Sysvol) files are included as well, and this data typically changes on a daily basis.

- *Data files* are created by applications and users. Application files contain configuration settings and data. User files contain the daily work of users and can include documents, spreadsheets, media files, and so on. These files change every day.

Administrators often back up an entire machine and dump all the data into a single backup. There are several problems with this strategy. First, on non–domain controllers, system files don't change that often, but data files change frequently. Second, you typically need to recover data files more frequently than system files. You recover data files when documents are corrupted, lost, or accidentally deleted and can't be recovered using other means, such as Previous Versions. You recover system files when you have serious problems with a system and typically are trying to restore the whole machine. Sometimes, however, rather than restore a failed server, it might be faster and easier to set up a new server that provides the same services. For example, with a domain controller that doesn't perform any operations master roles, you might be able to set up a new domain controller from media faster than you can restore the original failed domain controller.

Look at the timing of backups as well. With earlier releases of Windows, you are often concerned about the time that backups are performed. You want backups to be performed when the system's usage is low, so that more resources are available and few files are locked and in use. With the advances in backup technology made possible by the Shadow Copy API built into Windows Server, the backup time is less of a concern than it was previously. Any backup programs that implement the Shadow Copy API allow you to back up files that are open or locked. This means that you can perform backups when applications are using files and no longer have to worry about backups failing because files are being used.

## Selecting the optimal backup techniques

When it comes to backup, there is no such thing as a one-size-fits-all solution. Often you'll implement one backup strategy for one system and a different backup strategy for a differ-ent system. It all comes down to the importance of the data, the frequency of changes to it, and how much data there is to back up on each server. But don't overlook the importance of recovery speed. Different backup strategies take longer to recover than others, and there might be differing levels of urgency involved in getting a system or service back online. Because of this, I recommend a multipronged backup strategy that is optimized on a per-server basis.

Key services running on a system have backup functions that are unique. Implement and use those backup mechanisms as your first line of defense against failure. Remember that a backup of the system state includes a full backup of a server's registry, and that system configuration includes the configuration of all services running on a system. However, if a specific service fails, it is much easier and faster to recover that specific service than to try to recover the whole server. You'll have fewer problems, and it is less likely that something will go wrong.

Specific backup and recovery techniques for key services are as follows:

- With Dynamic Host Configuration Protocol (DHCP), you should periodically back up the DHCP configuration and the DHCP database as discussed in the "Saving and restoring the DHCP configuration" and "Managing and maintaining the DHCP database" sections of Chapter 20, "Managing DHCP."

- With the Windows Internet Naming Service (WINS), you should periodically back up the WINS database as discussed in the "Maintaining the WINS database" section of Chapter 23, "Implementing and maintaining WINS."

- With Domain Name System (DNS), your backup strategy depends on whether you are using Active Directory–integrated zones, standard zones, or both. When you are

Chapter 17

using Active Directory–integrated zones, DNS configuration data is stored in Active Directory. By default, when you are using standard zones, DNS configuration data is stored in the %SystemRoot%\System32\DNS folder and backups of zone data are stored in the %SystemRoot%\System32\DNS\Backup folder.

- With Group Policy, you should periodically back up the Group Policy Object (GPO) configuration as discussed in the "Maintaining and troubleshooting Group Policy" section of Chapter 31, "Managing Group Policy."

- With file servers, you should implement the Volume Shadow Copy Service (VSS) for all network file shares, as discussed in the "Implementing shadow copies for shared folders" section of Chapter 15, "File sharing and security." This makes it easier to restore previous versions of files. In addition, you should back up all user data files on the file server regularly.

The availability, scalability, and manageability techniques discussed in Chapter 1, "Introducing Windows Server 2012," are your next line of defense. Take the time to develop plans and procedures that can help you through everything from a power outage to the worst-case scenario. Don't forget that when you use BitLocker without Network Unlock, protected computers are locked until you provide the necessary recovery password. When a computer is locked, you must use the recovery password from a USB flash drive, or use the function keys to enter the recovery password. F1 through F9 represent the digits 1 through 9, and F10 represents 0.

Finally, you also need to perform regular backups of both system and user data. Most backup programs, including Windows Backup, which is included in Windows Server 2012, support several types of backup jobs. The type of backup job determines how much data is backed up and what the backup program does when it performs a backup.

# INSIDE OUT  How backup programs use the archive bit

Most backup operations make use of the archive attribute that can be set on files. The archive attribute, a bit included in the directory entry of each file, can be turned on or off. In most cases, a backup program will turn off (clear) the archive attribute when it backs up a file. The archive bit is turned on (set) again when a user or the operating system later modifies a file. When the backup program runs again, it knows that only the files with the archive attribute set must be backed up—because these are the only files that have changed since the last backup.

# Understanding backup types

The basic types of backups include the following:

- **Normal**   A normal backup is a full backup of all the files and folders you select, regardless of the archive attribute's setting. When a file is backed up, the archive attribute is turned off.

- **Copy**   A copy backup is a full backup of all files and folders you select, regardless of the archive attribute's setting. Unlike a normal backup, the archive attribute on files isn't turned off by the backup. This means that you can use a copy backup to create an additional or supplemental backup of a system without interfering with the existing backup strategy.

- **Incremental**   An incremental backup is used to create a backup of all files that have changed since the last normal or incremental backup. As such, an incremental backup is a partial backup. The backup program uses the archive attribute to determine which files should be backed up and turns off the archive attribute after backing up a file. This means that each incremental backup contains only the most recent changes.

- **Differential**   A differential backup is used to create a backup of all files that have changed since the last normal backup. Like an incremental backup, in a differential backup, the backup program uses the archive attribute to determine which files should be backed up. However, the backup program does not change the archive attribute. This means that each differential backup contains all changes.

- **Daily**   A daily backup uses the modification date on a file rather than the archive attribute. If a file has been changed on the day the backup is performed, the file will be backed up. This technique doesn't change the archive attributes of files and is useful when you want to perform an extra backup without interfering with the existing backup strategy.

As part of your backup strategy, you'll probably want to perform normal backups on a weekly basis and supplement this with daily, differential, or incremental backups. The advantage of normal backups is that they are a complete record of the files you select. The disadvantage of normal backups is that they take longer to make and use more storage space than other types of backups. Incremental and differential backups, on the other hand, use less space and are faster because they are partial backups. The disadvantage is that the recovery of systems and files using incremental and differential backups is slower than

**Chapter 17**

when you only have to perform a recovery from a normal backup. To see why, consider the following backup and recovery examples:

- **Normal backup with daily incremental backups** You perform a normal backup every Sunday and incremental backups Monday through Saturday. Monday's incremental backup contains changes since Sunday. Tuesday's incremental backup contains changes since Monday, and so on. If a server malfunctions on Thursday and you need to restore the server from backup, you do this by restoring the normal backup from Sunday, the incremental backup from Monday, the incremental backup from Tuesday, and the incremental backup from Wednesday—in that order.

- **Normal backup with daily differential backups** You perform a normal backup every Sunday and differential backups Monday through Saturday. Monday's differential backup contains changes since Sunday, as does Tuesday's differential backup, Wednesday's differential backup, and so on. If a server malfunctions on Thursday and you need to restore the server from backup, you do this by restoring the normal backup from Sunday and then the differential backup from Wednesday.

## Using media rotation and maintaining additional media sets

As part of your backup strategy, you might also want to use copy backups to create extended backup sets for monthly and quarterly use. You might also want to use a media rotation scheme to ensure that you always have a current copy of your data as well as several previous data sets. Although tapes traditionally have been used for backups, more and more organizations have been using disk backup instead of tape backup as disk drives have become more affordable. With disks, you can use a rotation schedule similar to the one you use with tapes.

The point of a media rotation scheme is to reuse media in a consistent and organized manner. If you use a media rotation scheme, monthly and quarterly media sets can simply be media sets that you are rotating to off-site storage. Consider the following media rotation scenarios:

- **Media rotation with three weekly media sets and one monthly media set** In a 24/7 environment, you use a total of 14 tapes or disks as a media set. Seven of those tapes or disks contain your normal weekly backups for a set of servers. The other seven tapes or disks contain your daily incremental backups for that set of servers— one tape or disk for each day of the week. Three weekly media sets are maintained on site. Once a month, you rotate the previous week's media set to offsite storage.

- **Media rotation with three weekly media sets, one monthly media set, and one quarterly media set**    In a 9-to-5 environment, you use a total of 14 tapes or disks as a media set. Nine of those tapes or disks contain your normal weekly backups for a set of servers. The other five tapes or disks contain your daily incremental backups for that set of servers—one tape or disk for each workday. Three weekly media sets are maintained on site. Once a month, you rotate the previous week's media set to off-site storage. Once a quarter, you rotate the previous week's media set to off-site storage.

# Backing up and recovering your data

Many backup and recovery solutions are available for use with Windows Server 2012. When selecting a backup utility, you need to keep in mind the types of backups you want to perform and the types of data you are backing up.

Windows Server 2012 includes Windows Server Backup and backup command-line tools. Windows Server Backup is a basic and easy-to-use backup and recovery utility. When the related feature is installed on a server, you'll find a related option on the Administrative Tools menu. The utility is also added to Server Manager. A set of backup and recovery commands is accessible through the Wbadmin command-line tool. You run and use Wbadmin from an elevated, administrator command prompt. Type **wbadmin /?** for a full list of supported commands.

You can use Windows Server Backup to perform full, copy, and incremental backups on the local system. You cannot use Windows Server Backup to perform differential backups. Windows Server Backup uses the Volume Shadow Copy Service (VSS) to create fast, block-level backups of the operating system, files and folders, and disk volumes. After you create the first full backup, you can configure Windows Server Backup to perform either full or incremental backups on a recurring, scheduled basis automatically.

When you use Windows Server Backup, you need separate, dedicated media for storing archives of scheduled backups. Although you cannot back up to tapes, you can back up to external and internal disks, DVDs, and shared folders. Although you can recover full volumes from DVD backups, you cannot recover individual files, folders, or application data from DVD backups.

Windows Server Backup automatically manages backup disks for you. You can run backups to multiple disks in rotation simply by adding each disk as a scheduled backup location. After you configure a disk as a scheduled backup location, Windows Server Backup automatically manages the disk storage, ensuring that you no longer need to worry about

Chapter 17

a disk running out of space. Windows Server Backup automatically reuses the space of older backups when creating newer backups. To help ensure that you can plan for additional storage needs, Windows Server Backup displays the backups that are available and the current disk usage information.

You can use Windows Server Backup for recovery in several ways. Rather than having to manually restore files from multiple backups if the files are stored in incremental backups, you can recover folders and files by choosing the date on which you backed up the version of the item or items you want to restore. You can recover data to the same server hardware or to new server hardware that has no operating system.

## Using the backup utility

To perform backup and recovery operations, you must use an account that is a member of the Administrators or Backup Operators group. Only members of these groups have authority to back up and restore files regardless of ownership and permissions. File owners and those who have been given control over files can also back up files, but only the files that they own or the files that they have permission to access.

The Windows Server backup and recovery tools are available for all editions of Windows Server 2012. Although you cannot install the graphical components of these utilities on core installations, you can use the command line or manage backups remotely from another computer.

You install the Windows backup and recovery tools using Server Manager. In Server Manager, select Manage and then tap or click Add Roles And Features. This starts the Add Roles And Features Wizard. After you select the server where these tools should be installed continue through the wizard pages until you get to the Select Features page. On this page, select Windows Server Backup. Tap or click Next, and then tap or click Install.

When the wizard finishes installing the selected backup and recovery tools, tap or click Close. From now on, Windows Server Backup will be available as an option on the Tools menu in Server Manager.

The first time you use Windows Server Backup, you'll see a warning that no backup has been configured for the computer, as shown in Figure 17-2. You clear this warning by creating a backup using the Back Up Once feature or by scheduling backups to run automatically using the Backup Schedule feature.

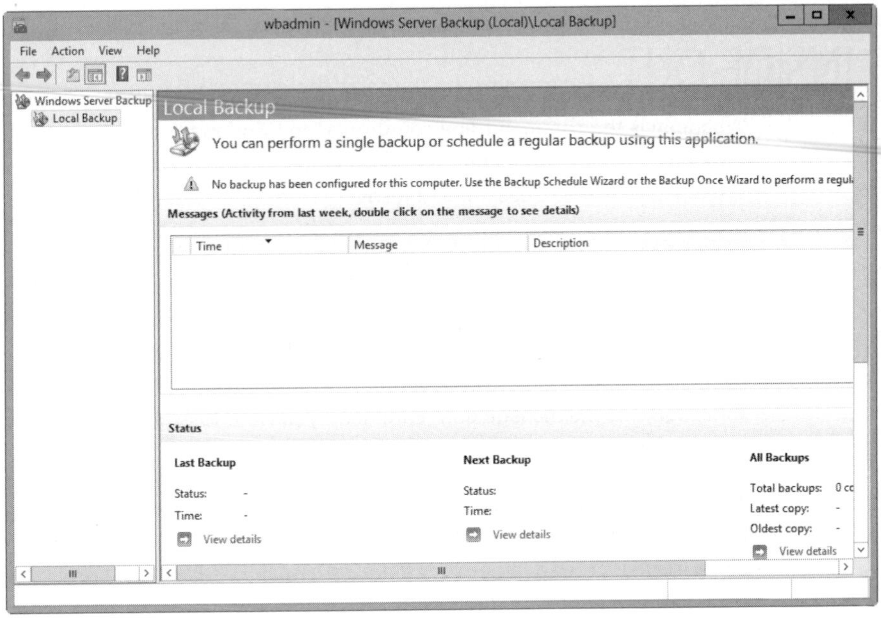

**Figure 17-2**  Getting started with Windows Server Backup.

When you use Windows Server Backup, the first backup of a server is always a full backup. This is because the full backup process clears the archive bits on files so that Windows Server Backup can track which files are updated subsequently. Whether Windows Server Backup performs subsequent full or incremental backups depends on the default performance settings that you configure. When the Local Backup node is selected, you can configure the default performance settings by tapping or clicking Configure Performance Settings in the actions pane or on the Action menu, you can do one of the following and then tap or click OK:

- Select Normal Backup Performance to perform full backups of all attached drives.

- Select Faster Backup Performance to perform incremental backups of all attached drives.

- Select Custom and then, from the option lists provided, select whether to perform full or incremental backups for individual attached drives.

After you configure the default performance settings, you can start a full or copy backup by selecting Backup Once on the Action menu or in the actions pane. You can configure a backup schedule by tapping or clicking Backup Schedule on the Action menu or in the actions pane. These options are available only when the Local Backup node is selected.

Chapter 17

# INSIDE OUT   Performing backups at the command line

Wbadmin is the command-line counterpart to Windows Server Backup. After you install the Backup Command-Line Tools feature as discussed previously, you can use Wbadmin to manage backup and recovery from an elevated, administrator command prompt.

Wbadmin is located in the %SystemRoot%\system32\ directory. When you are working with Wbadmin, you can get help on available commands. To view a list of management commands, type **wbadmin /?** at the command prompt. To view the syntax for a specific management command, type **wbadmin CommandName /?**, where *CommandName* is the name of the management command you want to examine, such as **wbadmin enable backup /?**.

Most Wbadmin commands use the –*backupTarget* parameter. The backup target is the storage location you want to work with, and it can be expressed as a local volume name, such as D:, or as a network share path, such as \\BackupServer05\backups\ Server24.

Windows Backup has several improvements for Windows Server 2012. Previously, you could not back up volumes larger than 2 terabytes (TBs) and volumes had to have 512-byte sectors. Now you can back up volumes larger than 2 TBs and volumes can use sector sizes other than 512 bytes. Previously, when you backed up virtual machines as part of a volume backup, the virtual machines could not be backed up or restored separately. Now you can select individual virtual machines to include in a backup and restore individual virtual machines from a recovery point. Additionally, when you are backing up a volume, you can specify a deletion policy to determine whether backups should be deleted after a certain number of backups have elapsed or whether they should be deleted only when space is needed for additional backups.

## Backing up your data

As part of your planning for each server you plan to back up, you should consider which volumes you want to back up and whether backups will include system-state recovery data, application data, or both. As part of the backup process, you also need to specify a storage location for backups. Keep the following in mind when you are choosing storage locations:

- When you use an internal hard disk for storing backups, you are limited in how you can recover your system. You can recover the data from a volume, but you cannot rebuild the entire disk structure.

- When you use an external hard disk for storing backups, the disk will be dedicated for storing your backups and will not be visible in File Explorer. Choosing this option will format the selected disk or disks, removing any existing data.

- When you use a remote shared folder for storing backups, your backup will be over-written each time you create a new backup. Do not choose this option if you want to store multiple backups for each server.

- When you use removable media or DVDs for storing backups, you can recover only entire volumes, not applications or individual files. The media you use must be at least 1 gigabyte (GB) in size.

When you create or schedule backups, you need to specify the volumes that you want to include, and this will affect the ways you can recover your servers and your data. Back up just critical volumes if you want to be able to recover only the operating system. Back up just individual volumes if you want to be able to recover only files, applications, or data from those volumes.

Back up all volumes with application data if you want to be able to recover a server fully, along with its system state and application data. Because you are backing up all files, the system state, and application data, you should be able to fully restore your server using only the Windows backup tools.

Back up all volumes without application data if you want to be able to restore a server and its applications separately. With this technique, you back up the server using the Windows tools and then back up applications using third-party tools or tools built into the applications. You can recover a server fully using the Windows backup utilities and then use a third-party utility to restore backups of application data.

## Scheduling backups

To automate the backup process, you can create a scheduled task that runs Windows Server Backup for you. Task creation and scheduling processes are integrated into Windows Server Backup. You can schedule automated backups using Windows Server Backup. Select the Local Backup node and then tap or click Backup Schedule on the Action menu or in the actions pane to start the Backup Schedule Wizard. After scanning the available disks, Windows Server Backup starts the Backup Schedule Wizard. Tap or click Next.

On the Select Backup Configuration page, shown in Figure 17-3, note the backup size listed under the Full Server option. This is the storage space required to back up the server data, applications, and the system state. To back up all volumes on the server, choose the Full Server option and then tap or click Next. To back up selected volumes on the server, choose Custom and then tap or click Next.

Chapter 17

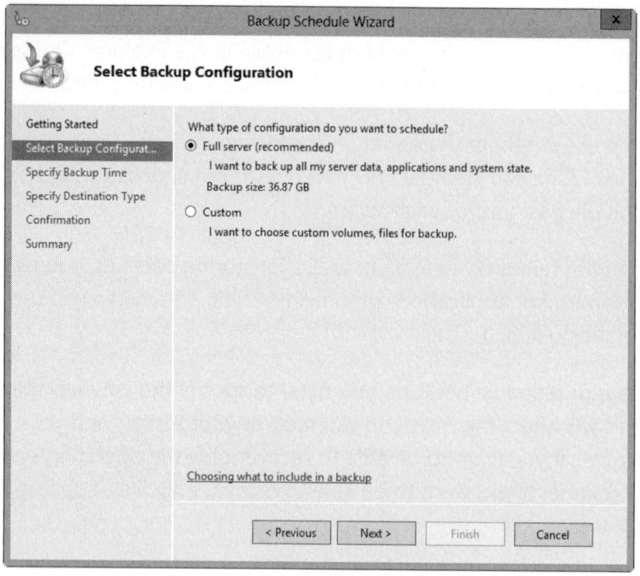

**Figure 17-3** Select data to be included in the backup.

If you chose Custom, the Select Items For Backup page is displayed. Tap or click Add Items. As shown in Figure 17-4, select the check boxes for the volumes that you want to back up and clear the check boxes for the volumes that you want to exclude. Only locally attached disks can be included in scheduled backups. Volumes that contain boot files, operating system files, or applications are included in the backup by default and cannot be excluded. Choose the Bare Metal Recovery option if you want to be able to fully recover the operating system. If the server is a Hyper-V host, you can select individual virtual servers to back up using their saved state as well as the host component.

Next, tap or click Advanced Settings to display the Advanced Settings dialog box. You can now do the following:

- Use the options on the Exclusions tab to exclude files by folder and type. To define an exclusion, tap or click Add Exclusion, use the Select Items To Exclude dialog box to select a folder that should be excluded, and then tap or click OK. This adds the folder to the Excluded File Types list in the Advanced Settings dialog box. By default, all files and subfolders in the specified folder are excluded. To exclude specific types of files in the selected folder, tap or click in the File Type column and enter the file types to exclude in a comma-separated list, such as .tmp, .temp, .htm, and .html. To include only the selected folder and not its subfolders, tap or click in the Subfolders column and then select No.

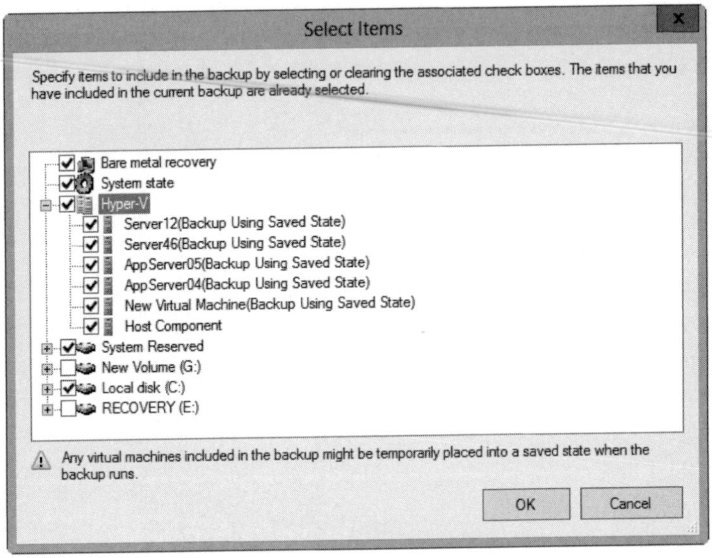

**Figure 17-4**  Select items to include in the backup.

- Use the options on the VSS Settings tab to specify the type of backup to create. The default backup type is a copy backup, which retains application log files and doesn't clear the archive attribute on file to maintain compatibility with other products you might use to back up applications that are on volumes included in the backup. If you don't use other products to back up applications, you can use a full backup instead, which clears the archive attribute and doesn't retain application logs.

On the Specify Backup Time page, shown in Figure 17-5, you can specify how often and when you want to run backups. To perform backups daily at a specific time, choose Once A Day and then select the time to start running the daily backup. To perform backups multiple times each day, choose More Than Once A Day. Next, tap or click a start time under Available Time and then tap or click Add to move the time under Scheduled Time. Repeat for each start time that you want to add. Tap or click Next when you are ready to continue.

Chapter 17

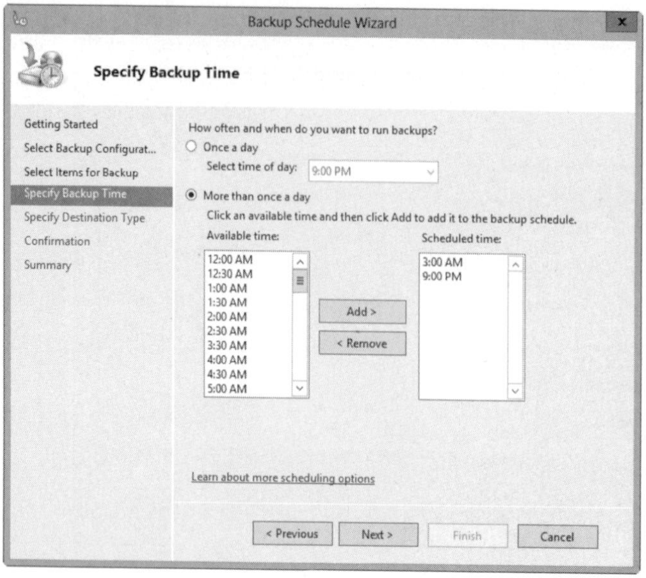

**Figure 17-5** Schedule when backups occur.

On the Specify Destination Type page, shown in Figure 17-6, you have these options:

- **Back Up To A Hard Disk That Is Dedicated For Backups**   Use this option to specify a dedicated hard disk for backups. Each external disk can store up to 512 backups, depending on the amount of data contained in each backup. If you select multiple disks, Windows Server Backup will rotate between them. Any selected disks will be formatted and then dedicated only to backups. This option is recommended because you'll get the best performance. If you choose this option, tap or click Next, select the disk or disks to use, and then tap or click Next again.

- **Back Up To A Volume**   Use this option to write backups to individual volumes on a hard disk. Because any volume you select is not dedicated to backups, it can be used for other purposes. However, the performance of any of the selected volumes is reduced while backups are being written. If you choose this option, tap or click Next, use the Add and Remove options to select the volumes to use, and then tap or click Next again.

- **Back Up To A Shared Network Folder**   Use this option to specify a shared network folder for backups. With this option, you can have only one backup at a time because each new backup overwrites the previous backup. If you choose this option, tap or click Next. When prompted, tap or click OK. Type the UNC path to the network share, such as **\\DataServer18\Backups\Servers**. If you want the backup to be accessible to everyone who has access to the shared folder, select Inherit under Access Control.

If you want to restrict access to the shared folder to the current user and members of the Administrators and Backup Operators groups, select Do Not Inherit under Access Control. Tap or click Next. When prompted to provide access credentials, type the user name and password for an account authorized to access and write to the shared folder. This account should also be an administrator or backup operator on the server you are backing up.

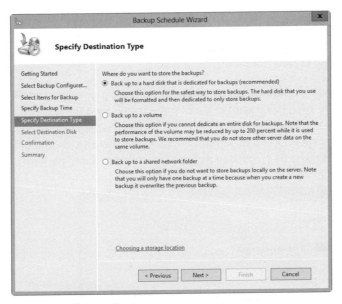

**Figure 17-6**  Select a backup target.

On the Confirmation page, review the details and then tap or click Finish. With dedicated backup disks, the wizard will then format the disks. The formatting process might take several minutes or considerably longer, depending on the size of the disk. When this process finishes, the Summary page should show that you successfully created the backup schedule. Tap or click Close. Your backups are now scheduled for the selected server. You need to check periodically to ensure that backups are being performed as expected and that the backup schedule meets current needs.

After you configure scheduled backups on a server, you can modify or stop the scheduled backups using the Backup Schedule Wizard. Select Backup Schedule on the Action menu or in the Actions pane. On the Modify Scheduled Backup Settings page, Modify Backup is selected by default. Use this option if you want to add or remove backup items, times, or targets.

If you want to stop the scheduled backups from running, select Stop Backup instead, tap or click Next, and then tap or click Finish. When prompted to confirm, tap or click Yes and

Chapter 17

then tap or click Close. Keep in mind that stopping backups releases dedicated backup disks for normal use. Backup archives are not deleted from the backup disks and remain available for use in recovery.

## Performing a one-time backup

Regardless of whether you want to back up data using a recurring schedule or perform a manual backup, the techniques are similar. In this section, I am going to discuss manual backups so that you know how to perform backups manually. You can perform a manual backup using Windows Server Backup. Tap or click Backup Once on the Action menu or in the actions pane to start the Backup Once Wizard.

After scanning the available disks, Windows Server Backup gives you the backup options shown in Figure 17-7. If you want to back up the server using the same options that you use for the Backup Schedule Wizard, choose Scheduled Backup Options, tap or click Next, and then tap or click Backup to perform the backup. Otherwise, choose Different Options, tap or click Next, and then continue through the wizard pages to perform the backup.

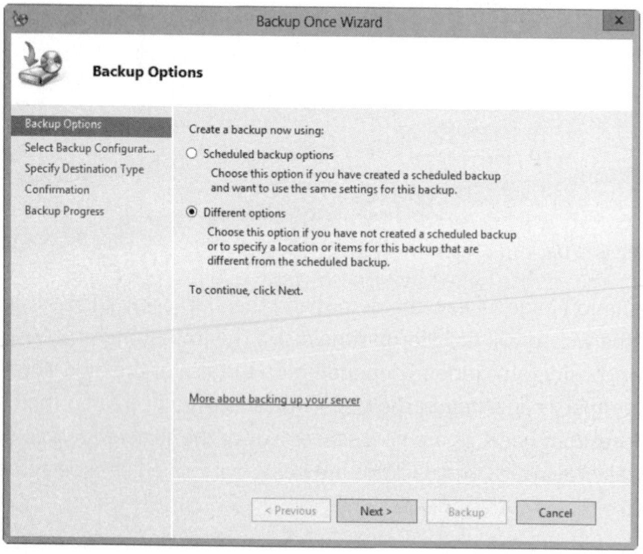

**Figure 17-7**  Choose Different Options to manually configure volumes to back up.

On the Select Backup Configuration page, shown in Figure 17-8, note the backup size listed under the Full Server option. This is the storage space required to back up the server data, applications, and system state. To back up all volumes on the server, choose the Full Server option and then tap or click Next. To back up selected volumes on the server, choose Custom and then tap or click Next.

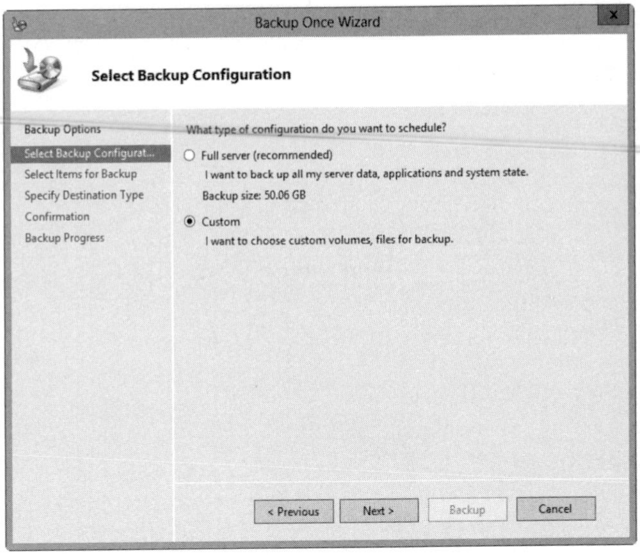

**Figure 17-8** Choose the backup configuration.

If you chose Custom, the Select Items For Backup page is displayed. Tap or click Add Items. Select the check boxes for the volumes that you want to back up, and clear the check boxes for the volumes that you want to exclude. If you want to be able to fully recover the operating system, choose the Bare Metal Recovery option. If the server is a Hyper-V host, you can select individual virtual servers to back up using their saved state and also back up the host component. Tap or click OK, and then tap or click Next.

On the Specify Destination Type page, do one of the following:

- If you want to back up to local drives, select Local Drives and then tap or click Next. On the Select Backup Destination page, shown in Figure 17-9, select the internal or DVD drive to use as the backup target. If you select a volume that is being used for scheduled backups, you can continue only if you used the same settings as with scheduled backups. Backups are compressed when stored on a DVD. As a result, the size of the backup on a DVD might be smaller than the volume on the server and you will be able to recover only full volumes. Additionally, you cannot perform a partial backup of volumes or component files to a DVD. Tap or click Next.

Chapter 17

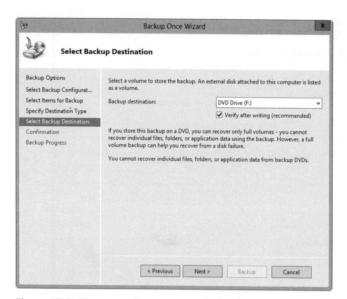

**Figure 17-9** Choose a volume to store the backup.

- If you want to back up to a remote shared folder, select Remote Shared Folder and then tap or click Next. On the Specify Remote Folder page, shown in Figure 17-10, type the UNC path to the remote folder, such as **\\BackupServer06\backups\Server21**. If you want the backup to be accessible to everyone who has access to the shared folder, choose Inherit under Access Control. If you want to restrict access to the shared folder to the current user, administrators, and backup operators, choose Do Not Inherit under Access Control. Tap or click Next. When prompted to provide access credentials, type the user name and password for an account authorized to access and write to the shared folder.

Afterward, tap or click Next and then tap or click Backup. The wizard starts by creating a shadow copy of the selected volumes. When this process finishes, the wizard will then try to write to the media you selected. If you are backing up to DVD, note the disc label in the prompt to insert a disc. As shown in Figure 17-11, the prompt includes a time and date stamp as well as a unique identifier for each disc in the backup set in sequential order. To help you keep track of your disc, you should write the label on the disc before inserting it in the DVD drive.

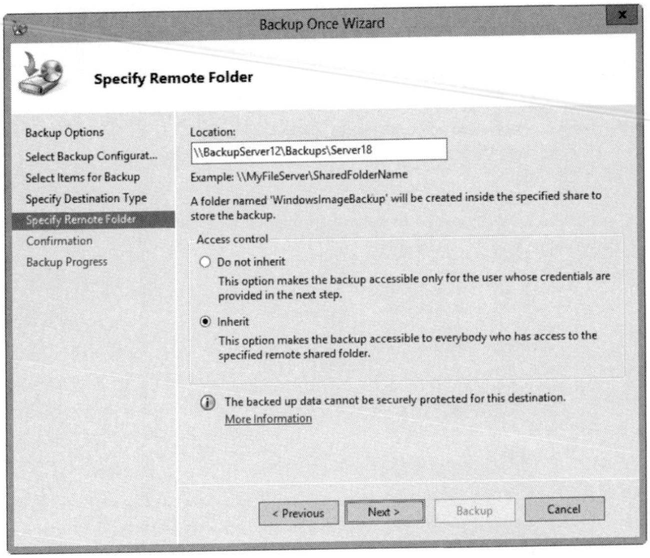

**Figure 17-10**  Restrict or allow user access using inheriting options.

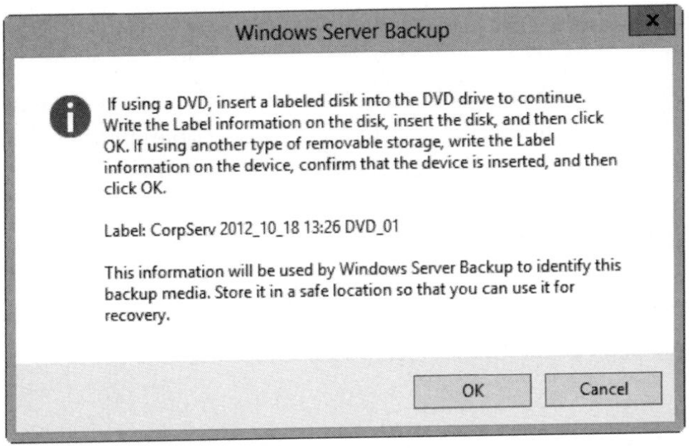

**Figure 17-11**  Insert a disc into the DVD drive to continue the backup.

The wizard displays the progress of the backup in the Backup Progress dialog box, as shown in Figure 17-12. You'll see the status of the backup process for each disk drive that you are backing up. If you tap or click Close, the backup will continue to run in the background.

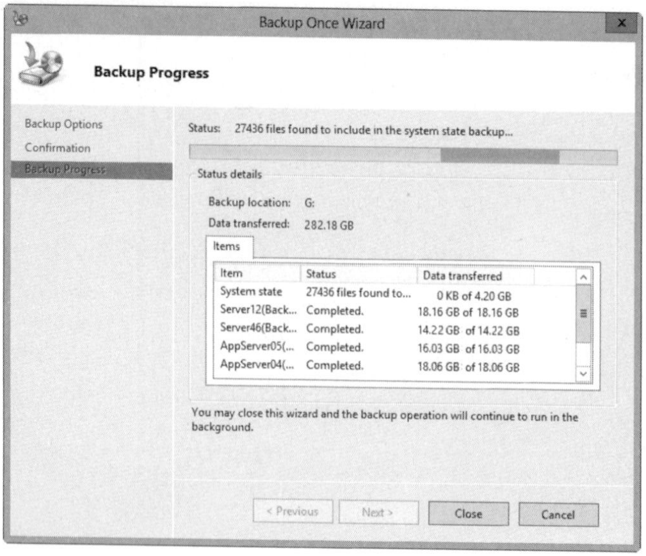

**Figure 17-12** The Backup Once Wizard will display the progress of the backup.

## Tracking scheduled and manual backups

Whenever Windows Server Backup backs up a server, it writes events related to the Windows event logs. You'll find events related to shadow copies in the Application log and all other backup events in the Microsoft\Windows\Backup\Operational log, as shown in Figure 17-13. By looking through the Operational log, you can quickly determine when backups were started, when they were completed, and reasons for failure, such as when backups were canceled by another administrator or there was not enough space on the backup target. By looking at the time difference between when a backup started and when it completed, you can also determine how long backups are taking.

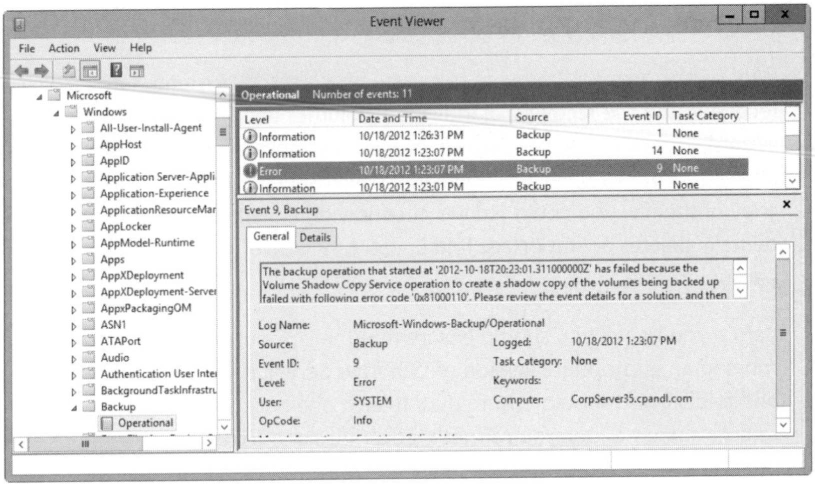

**Figure 17-13** Windows Server Backup writes backup events in the event logs.

As shown in Figure 17-14, Windows Server Backup provides summary details regarding backups as well. In the Messages pane, you'll find information regarding completed, failed, and currently running backups. In the Status pane, you'll find details on the last backup, the next scheduled backup, and all available backups. Tap or click the View Details links to determine what volumes were backed up, the backup type, and more. In the Details dialog box, you can track errors that occurred during the backup on the Errors tab.

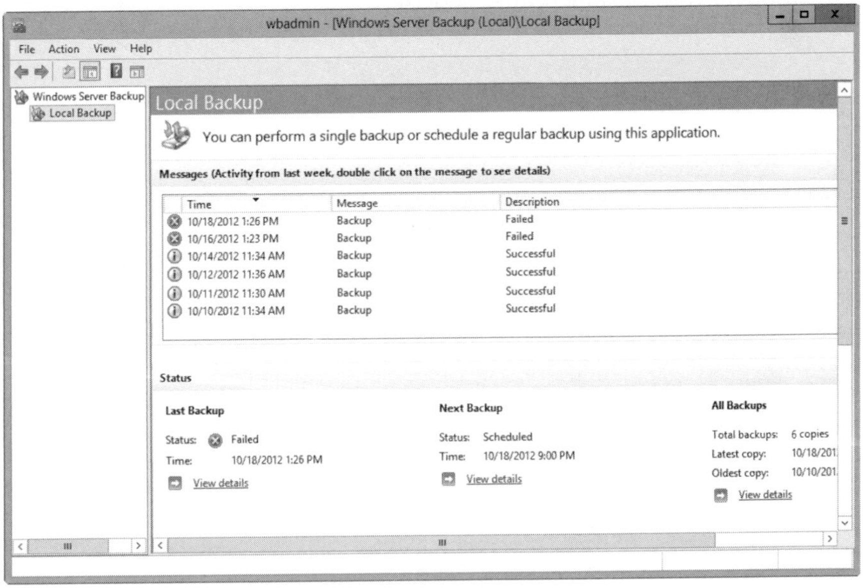

**Figure 17-14** Review the backup status in Windows Server Backup.

Chapter 17

# Recovering your data

Windows Server 2012 provides separate processes for system-state recovery, full-server recovery, and the recovery of individual volumes and files and folders. You use the Recovery Wizard in Windows Server Backup to recover nonsystem volumes and files and folders from a backup. For example, if Mary loses a spreadsheet and there isn't an available shadow copy of the file, you could recover the individual file from the backup archive. If John accidentally deletes an important folder, you can recover the folder and all its contents from a backup archive.

Before you begin, you should ensure that the computer you are recovering files to is running an appropriate version of Windows Server. If you want to recover individual files and folders, you should ensure that at least one backup exists on an external disk or in a remote shared folder. You cannot recover files and folders from backups saved to DVDs.

You can recover data in two ways. You can recover data stored on the server to which you are currently logged on. Or you can recover data stored on another server. Because these are different procedures, I'll discuss them in different sections.

## Recovering data stored on the current server

To recover nonsystem volumes, files and folders, or application data, start Windows Server Backup. Tap or click Recover in the actions pane or on the Action menu to start the Recovery Wizard. On the Getting Started page, choose This Server, as shown in Figure 17-15, and then tap or click Next.

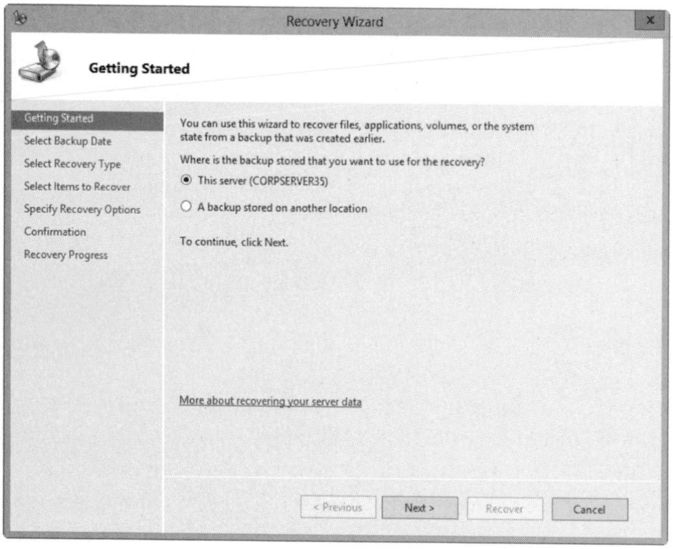

**Figure 17-15**   Select a server to recover data from.

On the Select Backup Date page, shown in Figure 17-16, select the date and time of the backup you want to restore using the calendar and the time list. Backups are available for dates shown in bold. Tap or click Next.

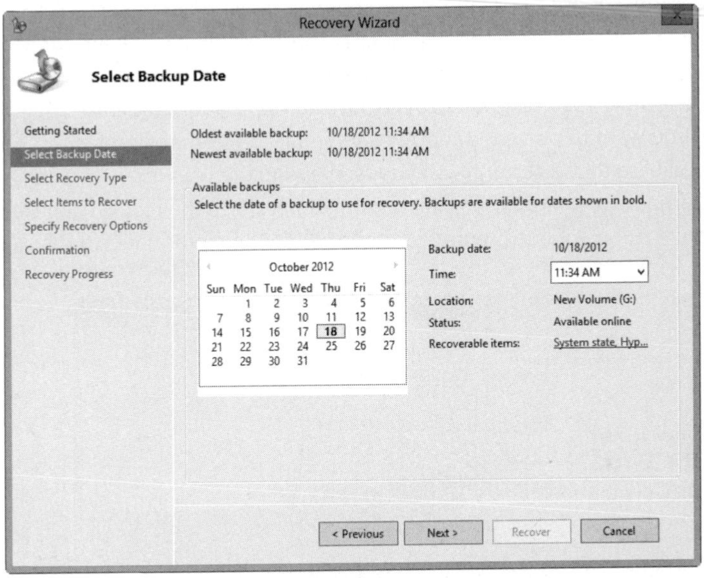

**Figure 17-16** Select the date and time of the backup you want to restore.

On the Select Recovery Type page, shown in Figure 17-17, do one of the following:

- To restore individual files and folders, choose Files And Folders and then tap or click Next. On the Select Items To Recover page, under Available Items, tap or click the plus sign (+) to expand the list until the folder you want is visible. Tap or click a folder to display the contents of the folder in the adjacent pane, tap or click each item you want to restore, and then tap or click Next.

- To restore virtual machines, choose Hyper-V and then tap or click Next. On the Select Items To Recover page, under Hyper-V Items, tap or click the virtual machines and components that you want to recover. Tap or click Next. Because virtual machines might not start if their network settings are different after recovery, verify the network settings in Hyper-V Manager before starting the virtual machines.

- To restore noncritical, non–operating system volumes, choose Volumes and then tap or click Next. On the Select Volumes page, you'll see a list of source and destination volumes. Select the check boxes associated with the source volumes you want to recover, and then select the location to which you want to recover the volume

Chapter 17

by using the Destination Volume lists. Tap or click Next. If prompted to confirm the recovery operation, tap or click Yes.

- To restore data from applications that have been registered with Windows Server Backup, choose Applications and then tap or click Next. On the Select Application page, under Applications, tap or click the application you want to recover. If the backup you are using is the most recent, you might see a check box labeled Do Not Perform A Roll-Forward Recovery Of The Application Databases. Select this check box if you want to prevent Windows Server Backup from rolling forward the application database that is currently on your server. Tap or click Next. Because any data on the destination volume will be lost when you perform the recovery, make sure that the destination volume is empty or does not contain information you will need later.

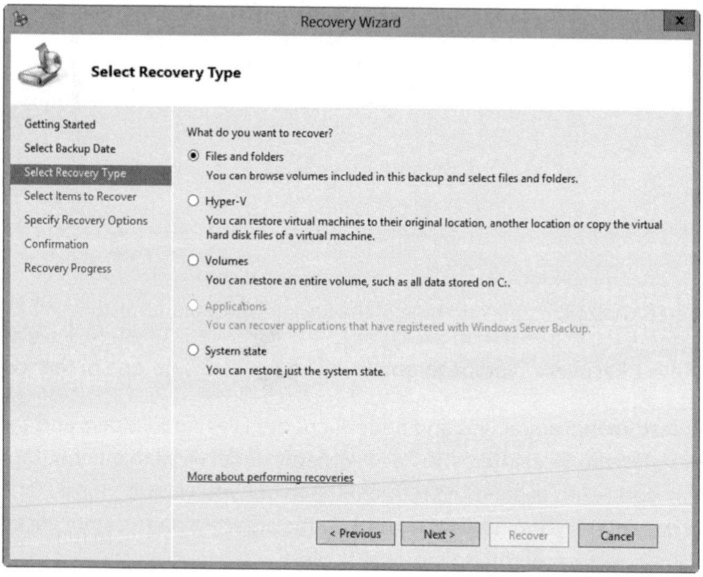

**Figure 17-17** Specify the type of data to recover.

On the Specify Recovery Options page, shown in Figure 17-18, specify whether you want to restore data to its original location (nonsystem files only) or an alternate location. For an alternate location, type the path to the location or tap or click Browse to select it. With applications, you can copy application data to an alternate location. You cannot, however, recover applications to a different location or computer.

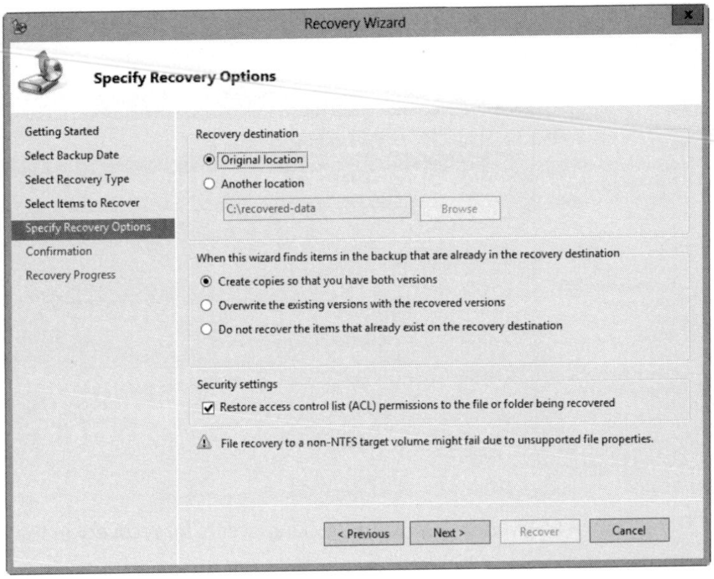

**Figure 17-18** Specify the location to which you want to restore the backup.

For file and folder recovery, choose a recovery technique to apply when files and folders already exist in the recovery location. You can create copies so that you have both versions of the file or folder, overwrite existing files with recovered files, or skip duplicate files and folders to preserve existing files. By default, the Recovery Wizard restores the security settings. In most cases, you'll want to use this option. Tap or click Next when you are ready to continue.

On the Confirmation page, review the details and then tap or click Recover to restore the specified items. The wizard displays the progress of the recovery in the Recovery Progress dialog box. If you tap or click Close, the recovery will continue to run in the background.

Windows Server Backup provides summary details regarding recovery in the Messages pane. You'll find information regarding completed, failed, and currently running recovery operations. Windows Server Backup also writes recovery events related to the Windows event logs. You'll find events related to shadow copies in the Application log and all other recovery events in the Microsoft\Windows\Backup\Operational log. By looking through the Operational log, you can quickly determine when recovery operations were started, when they were completed, and reasons for failure. By navigating through the recovery-related events, you can also find an event that provides the location of a log file that lists all files restored in the recovery operation. Figure 17-19 shows an example.

Chapter 17

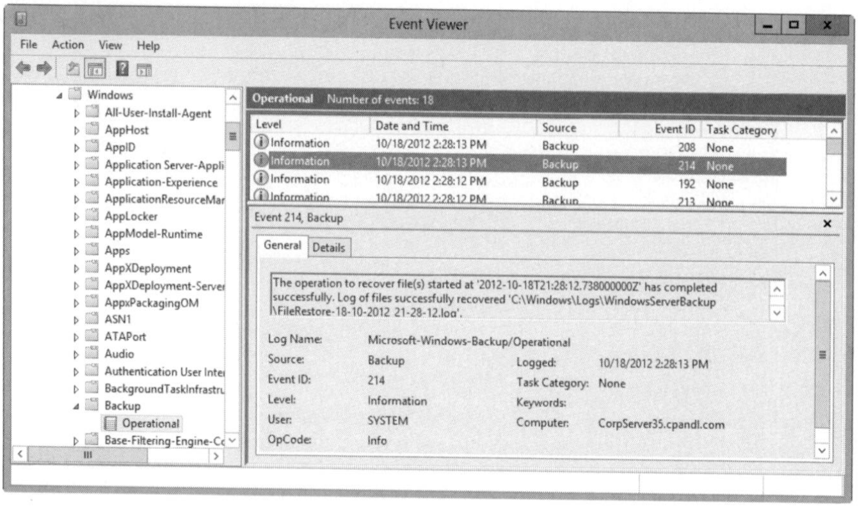

**Figure 17-19** Windows Server Backup writes tracking events for recovery in the event logs.

## Recovering data stored on another server

To recover nonsystem volumes, files and folders, or application data, start Windows Server Backup. Tap or click Recover in the actions pane or on the Action menu to start the Recovery Wizard. On the Getting Started page, choose A Backup Stored On Another Location, as shown in Figure 17-20, and then tap or click Next.

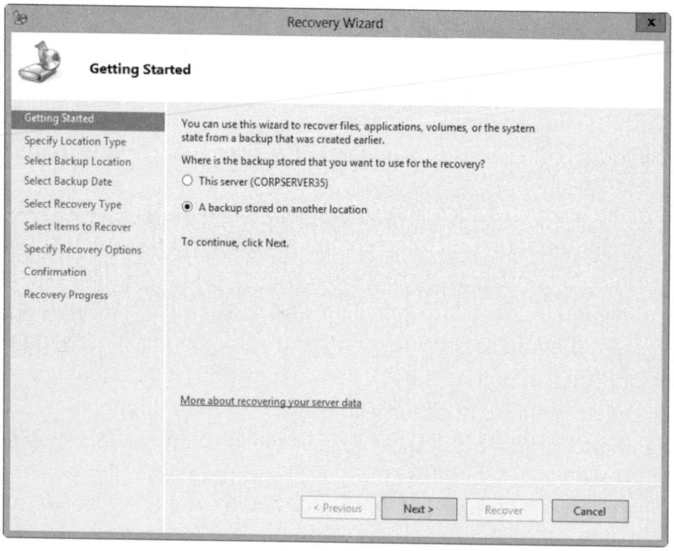

**Figure 17-20** Recover data stored on another server.

On the Specify Location Type page, select Remote Shared Folder and then tap or click Next. On the Specify Remote Folder page, type the path to the folder that contains the backup, such as **\\FileServer07\Servers\Server18Backup**. If you are prompted to provide your logon credentials, enter the user name and password for an account with owner or co-owner permissions on the shared folder.

The rest of the recovery operation is the same as discussed previously, starting with the Select Backup Date page.

## Recovering the system state

There are over 50,000 system-state files, and these files use 4 to 7 GBs of disk space. The fastest and easiest way to back up and restore a server's system state is to use Wbadmin. With Wbadmin, you can use the Start SystemStateBackup command to create a backup of the system state for a computer and the Start SystemStateRecovery command to restore a computer's system state.

> **Note**
> When you select a system-state restore on a domain controller, you have to be in the Directory Services Restore mode. To learn how to restore Active Directory, see "Backing up and restoring Active Directory" later in this chapter.

You can back up a server's system state by typing the following at an elevated command prompt:

```
wbadmin start systemstatebackup -backupTarget:VolumeName
```

Here, *VolumeName* is the storage location for the backup, such as G:.

You can restore a server's system state by typing the following at an elevated command prompt:

```
wbadmin start systemstaterecovery -backupTarget:VolumeName
```

Here, *VolumeName* is the storage location that contains the backup you want to recover, such as G:.

You can use other parameters for recovery operations as well. Use the –*recoveryTarget* parameter to restore to an alternate location. Use the –*machine* parameter to specify the name of the computer to recover if the original backup location contains backups for multiple computers. Use the –*authorsysvol* parameter to perform an authoritative restore of the Sysvol.

Chapter 17

# Restoring the operating system and the full system

As discussed previously, Windows Server 2012 includes startup repair features that can recover a server in the case of corrupted or missing system files. These features can also recover from some types of boot failures involving the boot manager. If these processes fail and the boot manager is the reason you cannot start the server, you can use the Windows Server 2012 installation disc to restore the boot manager and enable startup.

When the automated recovery features fail to recover normal operations, you can recover a server's operating system or perform a full system recovery by using a Windows installation disc and a backup that you created earlier with Windows Server Backup. These two operations differ in fundamental ways:

- With an operating system recovery, you recover all critical volumes but do not recover nonsystem volumes. A critical volume is a volume that has files the operating system needs during startup and normal operations and includes both the boot volume and the system volume (which might or might not be the same volume). You should use this method only when you cannot recover the operating system using other means.

- With a full system recovery, Windows Server Backup reformats and repartitions all disks that are attached to the server and then sets about recovering the server's volumes. Data that was not included in the original backup will be deleted when you recover the system, which includes any volumes that are currently used by the server but were not included in the backup. You should use this method only when you want to recover the server data onto separate hardware or when all other attempts to recover the server on the existing hardware have failed.

Before you begin, you should ensure that your backup data is available. You can recover a server's operating system or perform a full system recovery by inserting the Windows installation disc into the DVD drive and turning on the computer. If needed, press the required key to boot from the disc. Windows Setup should start automatically. On the Install Windows page, select the language, time, and keyboard layout options that you want to use. Tap or click Next.

Don't click Install Now. Instead, tap or click Repair Your Computer. On the Recovery screen, tap or click Troubleshoot. On the Advanced Options screen, tap or click System Image Recovery and then tap or click Windows Server 2012 to select it as your target operating system. On the Select A System Image Backup page, tap or click Use The Latest Available System Image (Recommended) and then tap or click Next. Or tap or click Select A System Image, and then tap or click Next.

If you select an image to restore, do one of the following on the Select The Location Of The Backup page:

- Tap or click the location that contains the system image you want to use, and then tap or click Next. Afterward, tap or click the system image you want to use, and then tap or click Next.

- To browse for a system image on the network, tap or click Advanced and then tap or click Search For A System Image On The Network. When you are prompted to confirm that you want to connect to the network, tap or click Yes. In the Network Folder text box, specify the location of the server and shared folder in which the system image is stored, such as \\BackupServer15\Backups, and then tap or click OK.

- To install a driver for a backup device that doesn't show up in the location list, tap or click Advanced and then tap or click Install A Driver. Insert the installation media for the device, and then tap or click OK. After Windows installs the device driver, the backup device should be listed in the location list.

On the Choose Additional Restore Options page, do the following optional tasks and then tap or click Next:

- Select the Format And Repartition Disks check box to delete existing partitions and reformat the destination disks to be the same as the backup.

- Select Only Restore System Drives to restore only the drives from the backup that are required to run Windows: the boot, system, and recovery volumes. If the server has data drives, they will not be restored.

- Tap or click Install Drivers to install device drivers for the hardware you are recovering.

- Tap or click Advanced to specify whether the computer is restarted and the disks are checked for errors immediately after the recovery operation is completed.

On the Confirmation page, review the details for the restoration and then tap or click Finish. The wizard then restores the operating system or the full server as appropriate for the options you selected.

# Backing up and restoring Active Directory

Backing up Active Directory is easy. Recovery of Active Directory itself, however, is different from recovery for other types of network services. A key reason for this involves the way Active Directory data is replicated and restored. Because of this, let's look at backup and recovery strategies for Active Directory, and then look at various restore techniques.

# Backup and recovery strategies for Active Directory

Domain controllers have replication partners with whom they share information. When you have multiple domain controllers in a domain and one fails, the other domain controllers automatically detect the failure and change their replication topology accordingly. You can repair or replace the failed domain controller from backup. However, the restore doesn't recover Active Directory information stored on the domain controller.

To restore Active Directory on the failed domain controller, you use either a nonauthoritative or authoritative approach. A nonauthoritative restore allows the domain controller to come back online and then get replication updates from other domain controllers. An authoritative restore makes the restored domain controller the authority in the domain, and its data is replicated to other domain controllers.

In most cases, you'll have multiple domain controllers in a domain, giving you flexibility in your disaster recovery plan. If one of the domain controllers fails, you can install a new domain controller, clone an existing domain controller, or promote an existing member server so that it can be a domain controller. The directory on the new domain controller is updated automatically through replication. You could also recover the failed domain controller, and then perform a nonauthoritative restore. In this case, you would restore Active Directory on the domain controller and obtain directory updates from other domain controllers in the domain.

In some cases, you might need to perform an authoritative restore of Active Directory. For example, if a large number of objects were deleted from Active Directory and you are not using Active Directory Recycle Bin as discussed in the "Extensible Storage Engine" section of Chapter 24, "Active Directory architecture," the only way to recover those objects would be to use an authoritative restore. In this case, you would restore Active Directory on a domain controller and use the recovered data as the master copy of the directory database. This data is then replicated to all other domain controllers.

The disaster recovery strategy you choose for Active Directory might depend on whether you have dedicated or nondedicated domain controllers, for the following reasons:

- When you have dedicated domain controllers that perform no other domain services, you can implement a very simple disaster recovery procedure for domain controllers. As long as you have multiple domain controllers in each domain, you can restore a failed domain controller by installing a new domain controller or cloning an existing domain controller and then populating the directory on this new domain controller. You can do so through replication or by recovering the domain controller using a nonauthoritative restore. You should always back up one or more of the domain controllers and their system state as well so that you always have a current snapshot of Active Directory in the backup archives. If you need to recover from a disaster that has caused all your domain controllers to fail or Active Directory has been corrupted, you can recover using an authoritative restore in the Directory Services Restore mode.

- When you have nondedicated domain controllers, you should back up the system state whenever you perform a full backup of a domain controller. This stores a snapshot of Active Directory along with the other pertinent system information that can be used to fully recover the domain controller. If a domain controller fails, you can recover the server the way you recover any server. You then have the option of restoring the system state data and Active Directory to allow the server to resume operating as a domain controller by using a nonauthoritative restore in the Directory Services Restore mode. If you need to recover from a disaster that has caused all your domain controllers to fail or Active Directory has been corrupted, you also have the option of using an authoritative restore in the Directory Services Restore mode.

When planning backups of Active Directory, you should also remember the tombstone lifetime. In Chapter 24, I discuss how Active Directory doesn't actually delete objects when you remove them from the directory. Instead, objects are either logically deleted or *tombstoned* (marked for deletion) and this state is replicated to all the other domain controllers. By default, the deleted object lifetime and the tombstone lifetime are 60 days, meaning that a deleted object will remain in the directory for at least 60 days. To ensure that you don't accidentally restore objects that have actually been removed from Active Directory, you are prevented from restoring Active Directory if the backup archive is older than the tombstone lifetime. This means that, by default, you cannot restore a backup of Active Directory that is older than 60 days.

Other system information is contained in the system state besides Active Directory. So, any restore of Active Directory includes all that information, and that information will be restored to its previous state as well. If a server's configuration changed since the backup, the configuration changes will be lost.

## Performing a nonauthoritative restore of Active Directory

When a domain controller fails, you can restore it the way you restore any other server except when it comes to Active Directory. With this in mind, first fix the problem that caused the server to fail. After you restore the server, you can then work to restore Active Directory.

You recover Active Directory by restoring the system state on the domain controller, using a special recovery mode called Directory Services Restore mode. If you made changes to Active Directory since the backup, the system-state backup will not contain those changes. However, other domain controllers in the domain will have the most recent changes, and

Chapter 17

the domain controller will be able to obtain those changes through the normal replication process.

When you want to restore Active Directory on a domain controller and have the domain controller get directory updates from other domain controllers, you perform a nonauthoritative restore. A nonauthoritative restore allows the domain controller to come back online and then get replication updates from other domain controllers.

Schedule a full server backup of a domain controller to ensure the recovery of the server operating system and application data in the event of a hardware failure. Schedule a separate backup of critical volumes to ensure timely recovery of Active Directory. To guard against unforeseen issues, schedule backups on at least two different domain controllers for each domain and schedule additional backups on any domain controller with a unique application partition.

A full server backup is a backup of every volume on the server. You can use this type of backup to recover a domain controller onto new hardware. On a domain controller, critical volumes include the boot volume and the volumes that contain the following data:

- Operating-system files

- The registry

- The Active Directory database and log files

- SYSVOL folders

You can use critical-volume backups to restore Active Directory on a domain controller. Critical-volume backups can also be restored and copied to transferrable media to install a new domain controller in the same domain.

The procedure to perform a full server or critical-volume recovery of a domain controller is the same as for any server. When you do this, you will also be performing a nonauthoritative restore of Active Directory. After the recovery is complete, restart the domain controller in the standard operations mode and then verify the installation. When you restart the domain controller, Active Directory automatically detects that it has been recovered from a backup. Active Directory will then perform an integrity check and re-index the database. From that point on, the server can then act as a domain controller and it has a directory database that is current as of the date of the backup. The domain controller then connects to its replication partners and begins updating the database so that any changes since the backup are reflected.

After you log on to the server, check Active Directory and verify that all of the objects that were present in the directory at the time of the backup are restored. The easiest way to confirm this is to browse Active Directory Users And Computers, Active Directory Domains And Trusts, and Active Directory Sites And Services.

# Performing an authoritative restore of Active Directory

An authoritative restore is used when you need to recover Active Directory to a specific point in time and then replicate the restored data to all other domain controllers. Consider the following example: John accidentally deleted the Marketing organizational unit (OU) and all the objects it contained. Because the changes have already been replicated to all domain controllers in the domain and Recycle Bin is not enabled, the only way to fully restore the OU and the related objects would be to use an authoritative restore. Similarly, if Active Directory were somehow corrupted, the only way to recover Active Directory fully would be to use an authoritative restore.

When performing authoritative restores, there are several significant issues that you should consider. The first and most important issue has to do with passwords used for computers and Windows NT LAN Manager (NTLM) trusts. These passwords are changed automatically every seven days. If you perform an authoritative restore of Active Directory, the restored data will contain the passwords that were in use when the backup archive was made. If you monitor the event logs after the restore, you might see related events or you might hear from users who are experiencing problems accessing resources in the domain.

Computer account passwords allow computers to authenticate themselves in a domain using a computer trust. If a computer password has changed, the computer might not be able to reauthenticate itself in the domain. In this case, you might need to reset the computer account password by pressing and holding or right-clicking on the computer account in Active Directory Users And Computers, and then selecting Reset Account. If the reset of the password doesn't work, you might need to remove the computer account from the domain, and then add it back.

NTLM trusts are trusts between Active Directory domains and Microsoft Windows NT domains. If a trust password has changed, the trust between the domains might fail. In this case, you might need to delete the trust, and then re-create it as discussed in "Establishing external, shortcut, realm, and cross-forest trusts" in Chapter 25, "Designing and managing the domain environment."

Another significant issue when performing an authoritative restore has to do with group membership. Problems with group membership can occur after an authoritative restore for several reasons.

In the first case, an administrator has updated a group object's membership on a domain controller that has not yet received the restored data. In this case, the domain controller might replicate the changes to other domain controllers, causing a temporary

Chapter 17

inconsistency. The changes shouldn't be permanent, however, because when you perform an authoritative restore, the update sequence number (USN) of all restored objects is incremented by 100,000. This ensures that the restored data is authoritative and overwrites any existing data.

Another problem with group membership can occur if group objects contain user accounts that do not currently exist in the domain. In this case, if group objects are replicated before these user objects are, the user accounts that do not currently exist in the domain will be seen as invalid user accounts. As a result, the user accounts will be deleted as group members. When the user accounts are later replicated, the user accounts will not be added back to the groups.

Although there is no way to control which objects are replicated first, there is a way to correct this problem. You must force the domain controller to replicate the group membership list with the group object. You can do this by creating a temporary user account and adding it to each group that contains user accounts that are currently not valid in the domain. Here's how this would work: You authoritatively restore and then restart the domain controller. The domain controller begins replicating its data to other domain controllers. When this initial replication process finishes, you create a temporary user account and add it to the requisite groups. The group membership list will then be replicated. If any domain controller has removed previously invalid user accounts as members of these groups, the domain controller will then return the user accounts to the group.

You can perform an authoritative restore by completing the following steps:

1.  Perform a full server or critical-volume recovery of the domain controller. After you repair or rebuild the server, restart the server and access the Advanced Boot Options menu. Typically, to do this you must press F8 before the Windows splash screen appears.

2.  On the Advanced Boot Options menu, select Directory Services Repair Mode. Windows will then restart in Safe Mode without loading Active Directory components.

3.  You will next need to choose the operating system you want to start.

4.  Log on to the server using the Administrator account with the Directory Services Repair Mode password that was configured on the domain controller when Active Directory was installed.

5.  The Desktop prompt warns you that you are running in Safe Mode, which allows you to fix problems with the server but makes some of your devices unavailable. Tap or click OK.

6. At an elevated command prompt, type **ntdsutil**. This starts the Directory Services Management Tool.

7. At the Ntdsutil prompt, type **authoritative restore**. You should now be at the Authoritative Restore prompt, where you have the following options:

   ○ You can authoritatively restore the entire Active Directory database by typing **restore database**. If you restore the entire Active Directory database, there will be a significant amount of replication traffic generated throughout the domain and the forest. You should restore the entire database only if Active Directory has been corrupted or there is some other significant reason for doing so.

   ○ You can authoritatively restore a container and all its related objects (referred to as a *subtree*) by typing **restore subtree *ObjectDN***, where *ObjectDN* is the distinguished name of the container to restore. For example, if someone accidentally deleted the Marketing OU in the cpandl.com domain, you could restore the OU and all the objects it contained by typing the command **restore subtree ou=marketing,dc=cpandl,dc=com**.

   ○ You can authoritatively restore an individual object by typing **restore object *ObjectDN***, where *ObjectDN* is the distinguished name of the object to restore. For example, if someone accidentally deleted the Sales group from the default container for users and groups (cn=users) in the cpandl.com domain, you could restore the group by typing the command **restore object cn=sales, cn=users,dc=cpandl,dc=com**.

8. When you type a restore command and press Enter, the Authoritative Restore Confirmation dialog box appears, which prompts you to tap or click Yes if you're sure you want to perform the restore action. Tap or click Yes to perform the restore operation.

9. Type **quit** twice to exit Ntdsutil, and then restart the server.

> **Note**
> Every object that is restored will have its USN incremented by 100,000. When you are restoring the entire database, you cannot override this behavior, which is necessary to ensure that the data is properly replicated. For subtree and object restores, you can override this behavior by setting a different version increment value using the Verinc option. For example, if you want to restore the Sales group in the cpandl.com domain and increment the USN by 500 rather than 100,000, you could do this by typing the command **restore object cn=sales,cn=users,dc=cpandl,dc=comverinc 500**.

## Restoring Sysvol data

The Sysvol folder is backed up as part of the system-state information and contains critical domain information, including GPOs, Group Policy templates, and scripts used for startup, shutdown, logging on, and logging off. If you restore a domain controller, the Sysvol data will be replicated from other domain controllers. Unlike Active Directory data, Sysvol data is replicated using the File Replication Service (FRS).

When you perform a nonauthoritative restore of a domain controller, the domain controller's Sysvol data is not set as the primary data. This means that the restored Sysvol would not be replicated and could instead be overwritten by Sysvol data from other domain controllers.

When you perform an authoritative restore of a domain controller, the domain controller's Sysvol data is set as the primary data for the domain. This means that the restored Sysvol would be replicated to all other domain controllers. For example, if someone deleted several scripts used for startup or logon and there were no backups of these scripts, these could be restored by performing an authoritative restore and allowing the restored, authoritative domain controller's Sysvol data to be replicated.

You can prevent a restored, authoritative domain controller's Sysvol data from overwriting the Sysvol on other domain controllers. To do this, you should back up the Sysvol in the desired state on another domain controller prior to performing the authoritative restore. After you complete the authoritative restore, you can then restore the Sysvol in the desired state to the authoritative domain controller.

## Restoring a failed domain controller by installing a new domain controller

Sometimes you won't be able to or won't want to repair a failed domain controller and might instead elect to install a new domain controller. You can install a new domain controller by promoting an existing member server so that it is a domain controller, or by installing a new computer and then promoting it. Either way, the domain controller will get its directory information from another domain controller.

Installing a new domain controller is the easy part. When you've finished that, you need to clean up references to the old domain controller so that other computers in the domain don't try to connect to it anymore. You need to remove references to the server in DNS, and you need to examine any roles that the failed server played. If the failed server was a global catalog server, you should designate another domain controller as a global catalog server. If the failed server held an operations master role, you need to seize the role and give it to another domain controller. Let's start with DNS and roles:

- To clean up DNS, you need to remove all records for the server in DNS. This includes SRV records that designate the computer as a domain controller and any additional records that designate the computer as a global catalog server or PDC emulator if applicable.

- To designate another server as a global catalog server, see "Designating global catalog servers" in Chapter 25.

- To transfer operations master roles, see "Design considerations for Active Directory operations masters" in Chapter 25.

To clean up references to the failed domain controller in Active Directory, you are going to need to use Ntdsutil. You must use an account with Administrator privileges in the domain and should run Ntdsutil on your Windows Server. The cleanup process is as follows:

1. At an elevated command prompt, type **ntdsutil**. This starts the Directory Services Management Tool.

2. At the Ntdsutil prompt, type **metadata cleanup**. You should now be at the Metadata Cleanup prompt.

3. Access the Server Connections prompt so that you can connect to a domain controller. To do this, type **connections** and then type **connect to server *DCName***, where *DCName* is the name of a working domain controller in the same domain as the failed domain controller.

4. Exit the Server Connections prompt by typing **quit**. You should now be back at the Metadata Cleanup prompt.

5. Access the Select Operation Target prompt so that you can work your way through Active Directory from a target domain to a target site to the actual domain controller you want to remove. Type **select operation target**.

6. List all the sites in the forest by typing **list sites** and then type **select site *Number***, where *Number* is the number of the site containing the failed domain controller.

7. List all the domains in the site by typing **list domains in site** and then type **select domain *Number***, where *Number* is the number of the domain containing the failed domain controller.

8. List all the domain controllers in the selected domain and site by typing **list servers in site** and then type **select server *Number***, where *Number* is the number of the server that failed.

Chapter 17

9. Exit the Select Operation Target prompt by typing **quit**. You should now be back at the Metadata Cleanup prompt.

10. Remove the selected server from the directory by typing **remove selected server**. When prompted, confirm that you want to remove the selected server.

11. Type **quit** twice to exit Ntdsutil. Next, remove the related computer object from the Domain Controllers OU in Active Directory Users And Computers. Finally, remove the computer object from the Servers container for the site in which the domain controller was located, using Active Directory Sites And Services.

# Troubleshooting startup and shutdown

Troubleshooting startup and shutdown are also part of system recovery. When problems occur, you need to be able to resolve them, and the key techniques are discussed in this part of the chapter. As part of your troubleshooting, you might need to refer to the extensive startup troubleshooting techniques discussed in the "Managing startup and boot configuration" section of Chapter 3, "Boot configuration," as well as the "Troubleshooting hardware" section of Chapter 7, "Managing and troubleshooting hardware."

## Resolving startup issues

When you have problems starting a system, think about what has changed recently. If you and other administrators keep a change log, access the log to see what has changed on the system recently. A new device driver might have been installed or an application might have been installed that incorrectly modified the system configuration.

Often you can resolve startup issues using Safe Mode to recover or troubleshoot system problems. In Safe Mode, Windows Server loads only basic files, services, and drivers. Because Safe Mode loads a limited set of configuration information, it can help you troubleshoot problems. You start a system in Safe Mode by completing the following steps:

1. If the system is currently running and you want to troubleshoot startup, shut down the server, and then start it again. If the system is already powered down or has previously failed to start, start the server again.

2. If you see a Windows Boot Manager error screen stating that Windows failed to start, press Enter to continue.

3. Press F8 during startup to access the Windows Advanced Options menu. You must press F8 before the Windows splash screen appears.

4.  In the Windows Advanced Options menu, select a startup mode. The key options are as follows:

- **Safe Mode**   Starts the computer, and loads only basic files, services, and drivers during the initialization sequence. The drivers loaded include the mouse, monitor, keyboard, mass storage, and base video. No networking services or drivers are started.

- **Safe Mode With Command Prompt**   Starts the computer, and loads only basic files, services, and drivers, and then starts a command prompt instead of the graphical interface. No networking services or drivers are started.

- **Safe Mode With Networking**   Starts the computer, and loads only basic files, services, drivers, and the services and drivers needed to start networking.

- **Enable Boot Logging**   Starts the computer with boot logging enabled, which enables you to create a record of all startup events in a boot log.

- **Enable Low Resolution Video**   Starts the computer in low-resolution 640x480 display mode, which is useful if the system display is set to a mode that can't be used with the current monitor.

- **Last Known Good Configuration**   Starts the computer normally using registry information that the operating system saved at the last working configuration.

- **Debugging Mode**   Starts the system in debugging mode, which is useful only for troubleshooting operating system bugs.

- **Directory Services Recovery Mode**   Starts the system in safe mode, and allows you to restore the directory service. This option is available on domain controllers.

- **Disable Automatic Restart On System Failure**   Prevents the operating system from automatically restarting after an operating system crash.

- **Disable Driver Signature Enforcement**   Starts the computer in safe mode without enforcing digital signature policy settings for drivers. If a driver with an invalid or missing digital signature is causing startup failure, this will resolve the problem temporarily so that you can start the computer and resolve the problem by either getting a new driver or changing the driver signature enforcement settings.

- **Disable Early Launch Anti-Malware Driver**   Starts the computer in safe mode without initiating an anti-malware driver. This prevents an anti-malware driver from blocking a critical driver that might be needed for startup.

Chapter 17

5. If a problem doesn't reappear when you start in Safe mode, you can eliminate the default settings and basic device drivers as possible causes. If a newly added device or updated driver is causing problems, you can use Safe mode to remove the device or roll back the update.

6. Make other changes as necessary to resolve startup problems. If you are still having a problem starting the system, you might need to uninstall recently installed applications or devices to try to correct the problem.

## Repairing missing or corrupted system files

Windows Server 2012 enters Windows Error Recovery mode automatically if Windows fails to start. In this mode, you have options similar to those you have when working with the Advanced Boot menu. For troubleshooting, you can choose from the following options to boot the system: Safe Mode, Safe Mode With Networking, or Safe Mode With Command Prompt. You can also choose to use the Last Known Good Configuration or to start Windows normally.

If you can't start or recover a system in Safe mode, you can manually run Startup Repair to try to force Windows Server 2012 to resolve the problem. To do this, complete the following steps:

1. Insert the Windows installation or Windows Recovery disc for the hardware architecture, and then boot from the installation disc by pressing a key when prompted. If the server does not allow you to boot from the installation disc, you might need to change firmware options to allow booting from a CD/DVD-ROM drive.

2. With a Windows Recovery disc, select Windows Setup (EMS Enabled) on the Windows Boot Manager menu to start Windows Setup. With a Windows installation disc, Windows Setup should start automatically.

3. On the Install Windows page, select the language, time, and keyboard layout options that you want to use. Tap or click Next.

4. When prompted, do not tap or click Install Now. Instead, tap or click the Repair Your Computer link in the lower left corner of the Install Windows page.

5. On the Recovery screen, tap or click Troubleshoot. Then, on the Advanced Options screen, tap or click Command Prompt to access the MINWINPC environment. As discussed in Chapter 2, the mini Windows PC environment gives you access to the command-line tools listed in Table 2-2.

6. At the command prompt, change directories to x:\sources\recovery by typing **cd recovery**.

7. Run the Startup Repair Wizard by typing **startrep**.

## Resolving restart or shutdown issues

Normally, you can shut down or restart Windows Server 2012 by tapping or clicking the Power Options button on the Charms bar and then selecting Shut Down or Restart as appropriate. Sometimes, however, Windows Server 2012 won't shut down or restart normally and you are forced to take additional actions, such as stopping programs that have stopped responding when prompted. Telling Windows Server to stop programs that aren't responding to the shutdown event won't always resolve your problem, however. In these cases, follow these steps:

1. Press Ctrl+Alt+Delete. The Windows Security screen should be displayed. If the Windows Security screen doesn't appear, skip to step 4.

2. Tap or click Task Manager, and then look for an application that is not responding. If all programs appear to be running normally, skip to step 4.

3. Select the application that is not responding, and then tap or click End Task. If the application fails to respond to the request, you'll see a prompt you can use to end the application immediately or cancel the end task request. Tap or click End Now.

4. Try shutting down or restarting the computer. Press Ctrl+Alt+Delete, tap or click the Power Options button, and then tap or click Shut Down. As a last resort, you might be forced to perform a hard shutdown by holding down the physical power button or unplugging the computer. If you do this, run Check Disk the next time you start the computer to check for errors and problems that might have been caused by the hard shutdown.

# Networking with TCP/IP

TCP/IP is a protocol suite consisting of Transmission Control Protocol (TCP) and Internet Protocol (IP). TCP is a connection-oriented protocol designed for reliable end-to-end communications. IP is an internetworking protocol that is used to route packets of data called *datagrams* over a network. An IP datagram consists of an IP header and an IP payload. The IP header contains information about routing the datagram, including source and destination IP addresses. The IP payload contains the actual data being sent over the network.

TCP/IP is the backbone for Microsoft Windows networks. It is required for internetwork communications and for accessing the Internet. Before you can implement TCP/IP networking, you should understand IP addressing conventions, subnetting options, and name-resolution techniques—all of which are covered in this chapter.

## Navigating networking in Windows Server 2012

The networking features in Windows Server 2012 are different from those in early releases of Windows. Windows Server 2012 has a suite of networking tools, including the following:

- **Network Explorer**  Provides a central console for browsing computers and devices on the network

- **Network And Sharing Center**  Provides a central console for viewing and managing a computer's networking and sharing configuration

- **Windows Network Diagnostics**  Provides automated diagnostics to help diagnose and resolve networking problems

Before discussing how these networking tools are used, we must first look at the features on which these tools rely:

- **Network Discovery**   Controls the ability to see other computers and devices

- **Network Location Awareness**   Reports changes in network connectivity and configuration

> ## Important
> Network Location Awareness also allows a computer with multiple network interfaces to select the best route for a particular data transfer. As part of selecting the best route, Windows chooses the best interface (either wired or wireless) for the transfer. This mechanism improves the selection of wireless over wired networks when both interfaces are present.

The network discovery settings of the computer you are working with determine the computers and devices you can browse or view in networking tools. Discovery settings work in conjunction with a computer's Windows Firewall to either block or allow the following:

- Discovery of network computers and devices

- Discovery of your computer by others

Network discovery settings are meant to provide the appropriate level of security for each of the various categories of networks to which a computer can connect. Three categories of networks are defined for servers:

- **Domain Network**   Intended as a designation for a network in which computers are connected to the corporate domain to which they are joined

- **Private Network**   Intended as a designation for a network in which computers are configured as members of a homegroup or workgroup and are not connected directly to the public Internet

- **Public Network**   Intended as a designation for a guest network in a public place, such as a coffee shop or airport, rather than for an internal network

In domains, you can enable discovery on domain controllers to view member computers. On member computers, you can enable discovery to see other member computers. With computers running nonserver versions of Windows, both homegroups and workgroups are available on private networks. Homegroups have special sharing settings that are not available in workgroups.

## TROUBLESHOOTING

**Correcting the network category**

If Windows detects the wrong type of network, you should check the TCP/IP configuration settings for the related network adapter. If the public category is incorrectly assigned and the TCP/IP settings are correct, you can change the network category to private (or domain, if appropriate) using Network Explorer. Open Network Explorer, tap or click the warning message in the notification area and then tap or click Turn On Network Discovery And File Sharing. In the dialog box provided, tap or click No, Make The Network That I Am Connected To A Private Network. This sets the network category as private while leaving network discovery disabled.

Because a computer saves settings separately for each category of network, different block and allow settings can be used for each network category. When you connect to a network for the first time, Windows automatically sets the network category based on the computer's network settings. If the computer has multiple network adapters, the adapters can be connected to different networks and, therefore, can be assigned different network categories.

Based on the network category, Windows Server 2012 automatically configures settings that turn discovery either on or off. You can manage these settings as well. Regardless of whether network discovery was managed automatically and configured manually, the On (Enabled) state means

- The computer can discover other computers and devices on the network.

- Other computers on the network can discover the computer.

The Off (Disabled) state means

- The computer cannot discover other computers and devices on the network.

- Other computers on the network cannot discover the computer.

Network Explorer, shown in Figure 18-1, displays a list of discovered computers and devices on the network. In any File Explorer view, you can access Network Explorer by tapping or clicking the leftmost option button in the address list and then tapping or clicking Network. The computers and devices listed in Network Explorer depend on the network discovery settings of the computer.

If discovery is blocked, you'll see a note about this. When you tap or click the warning message, you can enable network discovery by selecting Turn On Network Discovery And File Sharing. This opens the appropriate Windows Firewall ports so that network discovery

Chapter 18

is allowed. If no other changes have been made with regard to network discovery, the computer will be in the discovery-only state. You will need to manually configure the sharing of printers, files, and media, as discussed in Chapter 15, "File sharing and security."

When you attempt to enable network discovery for a network identified as public, you'll see an additional prompt with options for making the network a private network or turning on network discovery and file sharing for all public networks. Generally, you don't want to turn on network discovery and file sharing on public networks because this can open the computer to attack. Therefore, if the computer is actually connected to a public (open) network, click Cancel and do not turn on network discovery. Otherwise, if the computer is connected to an unidentified private network, select the option for making the network a private network.

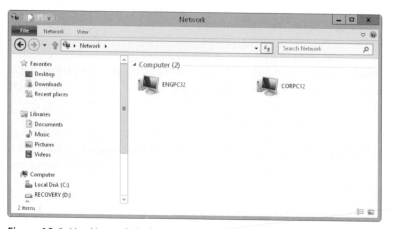

**Figure 18-1**  Use Network Explorer to browse network resources.

Network And Sharing Center, shown in Figure 18-2, provides the current network status, as well as an overview of the current network configuration. In Control Panel, you can access Network And Sharing Center by tapping or clicking View Network Status And Tasks under the Network And Internet heading. In Network Explorer, tap or click Network on the toolbar and then tap or click Network And Sharing Center.

Network And Sharing Center lists the current network by name and provides an overview of the network, including the category of the current network as Domain Network, Private Network, or Public Network. The Access Type field specifies whether and how the computer is connected to its current network as No Internet Access or Internet Access. The Connections field shows the name of the Local Area Connection being used to connect to the current network. If you tap or click connection, you can view the connection status in the related Status dialog box.

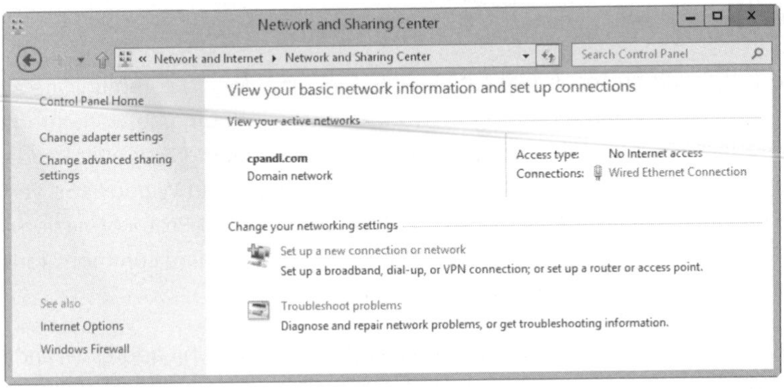

**Figure 18-2** View and manage network settings with Network And Sharing Center.

Windows assigns the public category to any unidentified network, even on domain-joined computers. In Network And Sharing Center, the network adapter used to connect to the domain should identify the domain and show the network category as Domain Network. However, if a computer's TCP/IP settings aren't set correctly, Windows might misidentify a network as public or private rather than as a domain network. To resolve this, change the network adapter's TCP/IP settings. When you enter the correct TCP/IP settings, Windows will attempt to identify the network again and should set the network category correctly.

Occasionally, Windows might identify multiple networks on a computer with only one network adapter. Often the quickest solution for this mixed-state problem is to disable and then enable the network adapter. In Network And Sharing Center, click Change Adapter Settings. Next, tap or click the network adapter and then tap or click Disable This Network Device. Finally, tap or click Enable This Network Device.

If a computer has multiple network adapters connected to different networks, Windows Server might incorrectly identify the connected networks as either public or private instead of domain as well. Often the quickest solution for this mixed-state problem is to disable the network adapter that isn't connected to the corporate network. For example, during development testing, I often run Windows Server on laptops with both wired and wireless connections. To get Windows Server to correctly identify the domain-connected adapter, I disable the wireless adapter.

Windows Server does allow multiple network adapters to be used. You can aggregate bandwidth using network adapter teaming. Up to 32 network adapters can be configured to work together.

Chapter 18

# Using TCP/IP

The TCP and IP protocols make it possible for computers to communicate across various networks and the Internet using network adapters, including network-interface cards, USB-attachable network adapters, PC Card network adapters, or built-in adapters on the motherboard. Since the introduction of Windows Vista and Windows Server 2008, Windows has had a dual IP layer architecture in which both Internet Protocol version 4 (IPv4) and Internet Protocol version 6 (IPv6) are implemented and share common Transport and Frame layers.

IPv4 and IPv6 are used in very different ways. IPv4 has 32-bit addresses and is the primary version of IP used on most networks, including the Internet. IPv6 has 128-bit addresses and is the next-generation version of IP.

When networking hardware is detected during installation of the operating system, both IPv4 and IPv6 are enabled by default in Windows Vista and later and you don't need to install a separate component to enable support for IPv6. The modified IP architecture is referred to as the Next Generation TCP/IP stack. Table 18-1 summarizes the key TCP/IP enhancements implemented in the Next Generation TCP/IP stack. Table 18-2 summarizes the key TCP/IP enhancements that are specific to IPv6.

**TABLE 18-1  Key TCP/IP enhancements in the Next Generation TCP/IP stack**

| Feature Supported | Description |
| --- | --- |
| Automatic Black Hole Router Detection | Prevents TCP connections from terminating due to intermediate routers silently discarding large TCP segments, retransmissions, or error messages. |
| Automatic Dead Gateway Retry | Ensures that an unreachable gateway is checked periodically to determine whether it has become available. |
| Compound TCP | Optimizes TCP transfers for the sending host by increasing the amount of data sent in a connection while ensuring that other TCP connections are not affected. |
| Extended Selective Acknowledgments | Extends the way Selective Acknowledgments (SACKs) are used, enabling a receiver to indicate up to four noncontiguous blocks of received data and to acknowledge duplicate packets. This helps the receiver determine when it has retransmitted a segment unnecessarily and adjust its behavior to prevent future retransmissions. |
| Modified Fast Recovery Algorithm | Provides faster throughput by altering the way that a sender can increase the sending rate if multiple segments in a window of data are lost and the sender receives an acknowledgment stating only part of the data has been successfully received. |

| Feature Supported | Description |
| --- | --- |
| Neighbor Unreachability Detection for IPv4 | Determines when neighboring nodes and routers are no longer reachable and reports the condition. |
| Network Diagnostics Framework | Provides an extensible framework that helps users recover from and troubleshoot problems with network connections. |
| Receive Window Auto Tuning | Optimizes TCP transfers for the host receiving data by automatically managing the size of the memory buffer (the receive windows) to use for storing incoming data based on the current network conditions. |
| Routing Compartments | Prevents unwanted forwarding of traffic between interfaces by associating an interface or a set of interfaces with a login session that has its own routing tables. |
| SACK-Based Loss Recovery | Makes it possible to use SACK information to perform loss recovery when duplicate acknowledgments have been received and to more quickly recover when multiple segments are not received at the destination. |
| Spurious Retransmission Timeout Detection | Provides correction for sudden, temporary increases in retransmission timeouts, and prevents unnecessary retransmission of segments. |
| TCP Extended Statistics | Helps determine whether a performance bottleneck for a connection is the sending application, receiving application, or network. |
| Windows Filtering Platform | Provides application programming interfaces (APIs) for extending the TCP/IP filtering architecture so that it can support additional features. |

**TABLE 18-2  Key TCP/IP enhancements for IPv6**

| Feature Supported | Description |
| --- | --- |
| DHCPv6-Capable DHCP client | Extends the Dynamic Host Configuration Protocol (DHCP) client to support IPv6 and allows stateful address autoconfiguration with a DHCPv6 server. |
| IP Security | Allows use of Internet Key Exchange (IKE) and data encryption for IPv6. |
| IPv6 over Point-to-Point Protocol (PPPv6) | Allows native IPv6 traffic to be sent over PPP-based connections, which in turn allows remote-access clients to connect with an IPv6-based Internet service provider (ISP) through dial-up or PPP over Ethernet (PPPoE)–based connections. |
| Link-Local Multicast Name Resolution (LLMNR) | Allows IPv6 hosts on a single subnet without a Domain Name System (DNS) server to resolve each other's names. |

Chapter 18

| Feature Supported | Description |
|---|---|
| Multicast Listener Discovery version 2 (MLDv2) | Provides support for source-specific multicast traffic and is equivalent to Internet Group Management Protocol version 3 (IGMPv3) for IPv4. |
| Random Interface IDs | Prevents address scanning of IPv6 addresses based on the known company IDs of network-adapter manufacturers. By default, Windows Vista and later generate random interface IDs for nontemporary autoconfigured IPv6 addresses, including public and link-local addresses. |
| Symmetric Network Address Translators | Maps the internal (private) address and port number to different external (public) addresses and ports, depending on the external destination address. |

Windows PowerShell 3.0 includes the NetTCPIP module for working with TCP/IP from the command line and in scripts. This module is imported automatically when you open a PowerShell prompt. Cmdlets you might want to use for TCP/IP troubleshooting include the following:

- **Get-NetIPAddress**   Lists information about IP address configuration

- **Get-NetIPInterface**   Provides summary information about IP interface properties

- **Get-NetIPv4Protocol**   Provides summary information about the IPv4 protocol configuration

- **Get-NetIPv6Protocol**   Provides summary information about the IPv6 protocol configuration

- **Get-NetNeighbor**   Displays information about the neighbor cache for IPv4 and IPv6

- **Get-NetOffloadGlobalSetting**   Lists the status of the global TCP/IP offload settings, including receive-side scaling, receive-segment coalescing, and TCP/IP chimney

- **Get-NetRoute**   Lists the IP routing table

- **Get-NetTCPConnection**   Lists details about current TCP connection statistics

- **Get-NetTCPSetting**   Displays TCP settings and configuration

To list all of the available NetTCPIP cmdlets, type **Get-Command –Module NetTCPIP** at a PowerShell prompt.

# Understanding IPv4 addressing

The most important thing IPv4 gives you is the IPv4 address. It is the existence of IPv4 addresses that allows information to be routed from point A to point B over a network. An IPv4 address is a 32-bit logical address that has two components: a network address and a node address. Typically, IPv4 addresses are divided into four 8-bit values called *octets* and are written as four separate decimal values delimited by a period (referred to as a *dot*). The binary values are converted to decimal equivalents by adding the numbers represented by the bit positions that are set to 1. The general way to write this value is in the form *w.x.y.z*, where each letter represents one of the four octets.

IPv4 addresses can be used in three ways:

- **Unicast**   Unicast IPv4 addresses are assigned to individual network interfaces that are attached to an IPv4 network and are used in one-to-one communications.

- **Multicast**   Multicast IPv4 addresses are addresses for which one or multiple IPv4 nodes can listen on the same or different network segments and are used in one-to-many communications.

- **Broadcast**   Broadcast IPv4 addresses are designed to be used by every IPv4 node on a particular network segment and are used for one-to-everyone communications.

Each of these IPv4 addressing techniques is discussed in the sections that follow.

## Unicast IPv4 addresses

Unicast IPv4 addresses are the ones you'll work with the most. These are the IPv4 addresses that are assigned to individual network interfaces. In fact, each network interface that uses TCP/IPv4 must have a unique unicast IPv4 address. A unicast IPv4 address consists of two components:

- **A network ID**   The network ID or address identifies a specific logical network and must be unique within its boundaries. Typically, IPv4 routers set the boundaries for a logical network, and this boundary is the same as the physical network defined by the routers. All nodes that are on the same logical network must share the same network ID. If they don't, routing or delivery problems occur.

- **A host ID**   The host ID or address identifies a specific node on a network, such as a router interface or server. As with a network ID, it must be unique within a particular network segment.

Chapter 18

Address classes are used to create subdivisions of the IPv4 address space. With unicast IPv4 addresses, the classes A, B, and C can be applied. Each describes a different way of dividing a subset of the 32-bit IPv4 address space into network addresses and host addresses.

> ## Note
>
> Classes D and E are defined as well. Class D addresses are used for multicast, as discussed in the next section of this chapter. Class E addresses are reserved for experimental use. Class D addresses begin with a number between 224 and 239 for the first octet. Class E addresses begin with a number between 240 and 255 for the first octet. Although Windows Server 2012 supports the use of Class D addresses, it does not support Class E addresses.

## Class A networks

Class A networks are designed for when you need a large number of hosts but only a few network segments, and they have addresses that begin with a number between 1 and 127 for the first octet. As shown in Figure 18-3, the first octet (the first 8 bits of the address) defines the network ID, and the last three octets (the last 24 bits of the address) define the host ID. As you'll learn shortly, the Class A address 127 has a special meaning and isn't available for your use. This means that there are 126 possible Class A networks and each network can have 16,277,214 nodes. For example, a Class A network with the network address 100 contains all IPv4 addresses from 100.0.0.0 to 100.255.255.255.

Network ID                         Host ID

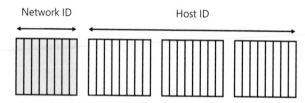

**Figure 18-3**  IPv4 addressing on Class A networks.

## Class B networks

Class B networks are designed for when you need a moderate number of networks and hosts, and they have addresses that begin with a number between 128 and 191 for the first octet. As shown in Figure 18-4, the first two octets (the first 16 bits of the address) define the network ID, and the last two octets (the last 16 bits of the address) define the host ID. This means that there are 16,384 Class B networks and each network can have 65,534 nodes.

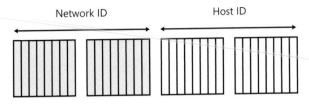

**Figure 18-4**  IPv4 addressing on Class B networks.

## Class C networks

Class C networks are designed for when you need a large number of networks and relatively few hosts, and they have addresses that begin with a number between 192 and 223 for the first octet. As shown in Figure 18-5, the first three octets (the first 24 bits of the address) define the network ID, and the last octet (the last 8 bits of the address) defines the host ID. This means that there are 2,097,152 Class C networks and each network can have 254 nodes.

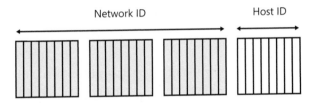

**Figure 18-5**  IPv4 addressing on Class C networks.

## Loopback, public, and private addresses

When using any of the IPv4 address classifications, certain rules must be followed. The network ID cannot begin with 127 as the first octet. All IPv4 addresses that begin with 127 are reserved as loopback addresses. Any packets sent to an IPv4 address beginning with 127 are handled as if they've already been routed and have reached their destination, which is the local network interface. This means any packets addressed to an IPv4 address of 127.0.0.0 to 127.255.255.255 are addressed to and received by the local network interface.

In addition, some addresses in the ranges are defined as public and others as private. Public IPv4 addresses are assigned by Internet service providers (ISPs). ISPs obtain allocations of IPv4 addresses from a local Internet registry (LIR) or national Internet registry (NIR), or from their appropriate regional Internet registry (RIR). Private addresses are addresses reserved for organizations to use on internal networks. Because they are nonroutable, meaning they are not reachable on the Internet, they do not affect the public Internet and do not have to be assigned by an addressing authority.

The private IPv4 addresses defined are as follows:

- **Class A private IPv4 addresses**   10.0.0.0 through 10.255.255.255

- **Class B private IPv4 addresses**   172.16.0.0 through 172.31.255.255

- **Class C private IPv4 addresses**   192.168.0.0 through 192.168.255.255

Because you shouldn't connect hosts on an organization's private network directly to the Internet, you should indirectly connect them using the Network Address Translation (NAT) protocol or a gateway program such as a proxy. When NAT is configured on the organization's network, a device, such as a router, is responsible for translating private addresses to public addresses, allowing nodes on the internal network to communicate with the nodes on the public Internet. When proxies are configured on the organization's network, the proxy acts as the go-between. It receives requests from nodes on the internal network and sends the requests to the public Internet. When the response is returned, the proxy sends the response to the node that made the original request. In both cases, the device providing NAT or proxy services has a private IP address on its internal network interface and a public address on its Internet interface.

## Multicast IPv4 addresses

Multicast IPv4 addresses are used only as destination IPv4 addresses and allow multiple nodes to listen for packets sent by a single originating node. In this way, a single packet can be delivered to and received by many hosts. Here's how it works: A sending node addresses a packet using a multicast IPv4 address. If the packet is addressed to the sending node's network, nodes on the network that are listening for multicast traffic receive and process the packet. If the packet is addressed to another network, a router on the sending node's network forwards the packet as it would any other packet. When it is received on the destination network, any nodes on the network that are listening for multicast traffic receive and process the packet.

The nodes listening for multicast packets on a particular IPv4 address are referred to as the *host group*. Members of the host group can be located anywhere—as long as the organization's routers know where members of the host group are located so that the routers can forward packets as appropriate.

One address class is reserved for multicast: Class D. Class D addresses begin with a number between 224 and 239 for the first octet.

Multicast IPv4 addresses in the range of 224.0.0.0 through 224.0.0.255 are reserved for local subnet traffic. For example, the address 224.0.0.1 is an all-hosts multicast address and is designed for multicasting to all hosts on a subnet. The address 224.0.0.2 is an all-routers multicast address and is designed for multicasting to all routers on a subnet. Other addresses in this range are used as specified by the Internet Assigned Numbers Authority (IANA), which is a function of the Internet Corporation for Assigned Names and Numbers (ICANN). For details, see the IANA website at *http://www.iana.org/assignments/ multicast-addresses/multicast-addresses.xml.*

## Broadcast IPv4 addresses

Broadcast IPv4 addresses are used only as destination IPv4 addresses and allow a single node to direct packets to every node on the local network segment. When a sending node addresses a packet using a broadcast address, every node on that network segment receives and processes the packet.

To understand how broadcasts are used, you must understand the difference between classful networks and nonclassful networks. A *classful network* is a network that follows the class rules as defined, meaning a Class A, B, or C network is configured with network addresses and host addresses as described previously. A *nonclassful network* is a network that doesn't strictly follow the class rules. Nonclassful networks might have subnets that don't follow the normal rules for network and host IDs. You'll learn more about subnets in "Using subnets and subnet masks," later in this chapter.

> ### Note
> A nonclassful network can also be referred to as a *classless network*. However, classless inter-domain routing (CIDR) and all it implies are specifically spelled out in Request For Comments (RFCs), such as RFC 1812. RFC 1812 provides rules that supersede those of some previous RFCs, such as RFC 950, which prohibited the use of all-zeros subnets.

All nodes listen for and process broadcasts. Because IPv4 routers usually do not forward broadcast packets, broadcasts are generally limited by router boundaries. The broadcast address is obtained by setting all the host bits in the IPv4 address to 1 as appropriate for the broadcast type. Three types of broadcasts are used:

- **Network broadcasts**   Network broadcasts are used to send packets to all nodes on a classful network. For network broadcasts, the host ID bits are set to 1. For a nonclassful network, there is no network broadcast address, only a subnet broadcast address.

- **Subnet broadcasts**   Subnet broadcasts are used to send packets to all nodes on nonclassful networks. For subnet broadcasts, the host ID bits are set to 1. For a classful network, there is no subnet broadcast address, only a network broadcast address.

- **Limited broadcasts**   Limited broadcasts are used to send packets to all nodes when the network ID is unknown. For a limited broadcast, all network ID and host ID bits are set to 1.

---

### DHCP uses limited broadcasts

Limited broadcasts are sent by nodes that have their IPv4 address automatically configured, as is the case with Dynamic Host Configuration Protocol (DHCP). With DHCP, clients use a limited broadcast to advertise that they need to obtain an IPv4 address. A DHCP server on the network acknowledges the request by assigning the node an IPv4 address, which the client then uses for normal network communications.

---

### Note

Previously, a fourth type of broadcast was available, called an *all-subnets-directed broadcast*. This broadcast type was used to send packets to all nodes on all the subnets of a nonclassful network. Because of the changes specified in RFC 1812, all-subnets-directed broadcasts have been deprecated, meaning they are no longer to be supported.

---

# Special IPv4 addressing rules

As you've seen, certain IPv4 addresses and address ranges have special uses:

- The addresses 127.0.0.0 through 127.255.255.255 are reserved for local loopback.

- The addresses 10.0.0.0 through 10.255.255.255, 172.16.0.0 through 172.31.255.255, and 192.168.0.0 through 192.168.255.255 are designated as private and, as such, are nonroutable.

- On classful networks, the Class A addresses w.255.255.255, Class B addresses w.x.255.255, and Class C addresses w.x.y.255 are reserved for broadcasts.

- On nonclassful networks, the broadcast address is the last IPv4 address in the range of IPv4 addresses for the associated subnet.

> **Note**
>
> Certain IPv4 addresses are also reserved for other purposes as well. For example, the IPv4 addresses 169.254.0.1 to 169.254.255.254 are used for Automatic Private IPv4 Addressing (APIPA) as discussed in "Configuring TCP/IP networking" in Chapter 20, "Managing DHCP."

On classful networks, all the bits in the network ID cannot be set to 0 because this expression is reserved to indicate a host on a local network. Similarly, on a classful network all the bits in the host ID cannot be set to 0 because this is reserved to indicate the IPv4 network number.

Table 18-3 lists the ranges of network numbers based on address classes. You cannot assign the network number to a network interface. The network number is common for all network interfaces attached to the same logical network. On a nonclassful network, the network number is the first IPv4 address in the range of IPv4 addresses for the associated subnet—as specified in RFC 1812.

**TABLE 18-3 Network IDs for classful networks**

| Address Class | First Network Number | Last Network Number |
| --- | --- | --- |
| Class A | 1.0.0.0 | 126.0.0.0 |
| Class B | 128.0.0.0 | 191.255.0.0 |
| Class C | 192.0.0.0 | 223.255.255.0 |

When you apply all the rules for IPv4 addresses, you find that many IPv4 addresses cannot be used by hosts on a network. This means the first available host ID and last available host ID are different from the range of available IPv4 addresses. Table 18-4 shows how these rules apply to classful networks. On a nonclassful network, the same rules apply—you lose the first and last available host IDs from the range of available IPv4 addresses.

**TABLE 18-4 Available host IDs on classful networks**

| Address Class | First Host ID | Last Host ID |
| --- | --- | --- |
| Class A | w.0.0.1 | w.255.255.254 |
| Class B | w.x.0.1 | w.x.255.254 |
| Class C | w.x.y.1 | w.x.y.254 |

# INSIDE OUT Routers, gateways, and bridges connect networks

A router is needed for hosts on a network to communicate with hosts on other networks. It is standard convention for the network router to be assigned the first available host ID. On Windows systems, you identify the address for the router as the gateway IPv4 address for the network. Although the terms "gateways" and "routers" are often used interchangeably, technically the two are different. A *router* is a device that sends packets between network segments. A *gateway* is a device that performs the necessary translation so that communication between networks with different architectures is possible. When working with networks, you might also hear the term "bridge." A *bridge* is a device that directs traffic between two network segments using physical machine addresses (Media Access Control, or MAC, addresses). Routers, gateways, and bridges can be implemented in hardware as separate devices or in software so that a system on the network can handle the role as a network router, gateway, or bridge as necessary.

# Using subnets and subnet masks

Anyone who works with computers should learn about subnetting and what it means. A *subnet* is a portion of a network that operates as a separate network. Logically, it exists separately from other networks, even if hosts on those other networks share the same network ID. Typically, such networks are also physically separated by a router. This ensures the subnet is isolated and doesn't affect other subnets.

Subnetting is designed to make more efficient use of the IPv4 address space. Thus, rather than having networks with hundreds, thousands, or millions of nodes, you have a subnet that is sized appropriately for the number of nodes you use. This is important, especially for the crowded public IPv4 address space, where it doesn't make sense to assign the complete IPv4 address range for a network to an individual organization. Thus, instead of getting a complete network address for the public Internet, your organization is more likely to get a block of consecutive IPv4 addresses to use.

## Subnet masks

You use a 32-bit value known as a subnet mask to configure nodes in a subnet to communicate only with other nodes on the same subnet. The mask works by blocking areas outside the subnet so that they aren't visible from within the subnet. Because they are 32-bit values, subnet masks can be expressed as an address for which each 8-bit value (octet) is written as four separate decimal values delimited by a period (dot). As with IPv4 addresses, the basic form is *w.x.y.z.*

The subnet mask identifies which bits of the IPv4 address belong to the network ID and which bits belong to the host ID. Nodes can see only the portions of the IPv4 address space that aren't masked by a bit with a value of 1. If a bit is set to 1, it corresponds to a bit in the network ID. If a bit is set to 0, it corresponds to a bit in the host ID.

Because a subnet mask must be configured for each IPv4 address, nodes on both classful and nonclassful networks have subnet masks. On a classful network, all the bits in the network ID portion of the IPv4 address are set to 1 and can be presented in dotted decimal as shown in Table 18-5.

**TABLE 18-5 Standard subnet masks for classful networks**

| Address Class | Bits for Subnet Mask | Subnet Mask |
| --- | --- | --- |
| Class A | 11111111 00000000 00000000 00000000 | 255.0.0.0 |
| Class B | 11111111 11111111 00000000 00000000 | 255.255.0.0 |
| Class C | 11111111 11111111 11111111 00000000 | 255.255.255.0 |

# INSIDE OUT   Blocks of IPv4 addresses on the public Internet

For internal networks that use private IPv4 addresses, you'll often be able to use the standard subnet masks. This isn't true, however, when you need public IPv4 addresses. Most of the time, you'll be assigned a small block of public IPv4 addresses to work with. For example, you might be assigned a block of eight (six usable) addresses. In this case, you must create a subnet that uses the subnet mask to isolate your nodes as appropriate for the number of nodes you've been assigned. I say there are six usable addresses out of eight because the lowest address is reserved as the network number and the highest address is reserved as the broadcast address for the network. This is always the case, as any good Cisco Certified Network Associate (CCNA) will tell you.

## Network prefix notation

With subnetting, an IPv4 address alone doesn't help you understand how the address can be used. To be sure, you must know the number of bits in the network ID. As discussed, the subnet mask provides one way to determine which bits in the IPv4 address belong to the network ID and which bits belong to the host ID. If you have a block of IPv4 addresses, writing out each IPv4 address and the subnet mask is rather tedious. A shorthand way to do this is to use network prefix notation, which is also referred to as the classless inter-domain routing (CIDR) notation.

Chapter 18

In network prefix notation, the network ID is seen as the prefix of an IPv4 address and the host ID as the suffix. To write a block of IPv4 addresses and specify which bits are used for the network ID, you write the network number followed by a forward slash and the number of bits in the network ID, as in

`NetworkNumber/# of bits in the network ID`

The slash and the number of bits in the network ID are referred to as the *network prefix*. Following this, you could rewrite Table 18-5 as shown in Table 18-6.

**TABLE 18-6  Standard network prefixes for classful networks**

| Address Class | Bits for Subnet Mask | Network Prefix |
|---|---|---|
| Class A | 11111111 00000000 00000000 00000000 | /8 |
| Class B | 11111111 11111111 00000000 00000000 | /16 |
| Class C | 11111111 11111111 11111111 00000000 | /24 |

You now have two ways of detailing which bits are used for the network ID and which bits are used for the host ID. With the network number 192.168.1.0, you could use either of the following to specify that the first 24 bits identify the network ID:

- 192.168.1.0, 255.255.255.0

- 192.168.1.0/24

With either entry, you know that the first 24 bits identify the network ID and the last 8 bits identify the host ID. This, in turn, means the usable IPv4 addresses are 192.168.1.1 through 192.168.1.254.

## Subnetting

When you use subnetting, nodes no longer follow the class rules for determining which bits in the IPv4 address are used for the network ID and which bits are used for the host ID. Instead, you set the 32 bits of the IPv4 address as appropriate to be either network ID bits or host ID bits based on the number of subnets you need and then number nodes for each subnet. There is an inverse relationship between the number of subnets and the number of nodes per subnet that can be supported. As the number of subnets goes up by a factor of 2, the number of hosts per subnet goes down by a factor of 2.

Because Class A, B, and C networks have a different number of host ID bits to start with, borrowing bits from the host ID yields different numbers of subnets and hosts. The technique is the same, however. Each bit represented as a 1 in the subnet mask corresponds to a bit that belongs to the network ID. This means the value of each bit can be represented as shown in Figure 18-6.

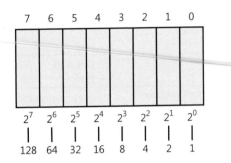

**Figure 18-6** Represents the value of each bit when it is set to 1.

You start with the high-order bits and work your way to the low-order bits. When you borrow 1 bit of the host ID, you raise the number of possible subnets by a factor of 2 and reduce the number of possible hosts by a factor of 2.

## Subnetting Class A networks

The network entry mask for a standard Class A network can be defined as follows:

| Address Class | Bits for Subnet Mask | Network Prefix | Decimal |
|---|---|---|---|
| Class A | 11111111 00000000 00000000 00000000 | /8 | 255.0.0.0 |

If you want to divide a Class A network into two separate subnets, you can borrow the high-order bit from the host ID in the second octet and add this bit to the network ID. Because the value of this bit taken from the host ID is 128, the corresponding subnet mask is 255.128.0.0. Thus, the network entry for the subnetted Class A network can be defined as follows:

| Address Class | Bits for Subnet Mask | Network Prefix | Decimal |
|---|---|---|---|
| Class A | 11111111 10000000 00000000 00000000 | /9 | 255.128.0.0 |

> **Note**
> Each time you borrow a bit from the host ID, the network prefix bits go up by 1.

If you take an additional bit from the host ID bits, you allow the Class A network to be divided into up to four subnets. The value of this bit taken from the host ID is 64. When you add this value to the value of the previous bit taken from the host ID, the sum is 192 (128 + 64) and the corresponding subnet mask is 255.192.0.0. This means the network

Chapter 18

entry for a subnetted Class A network that can be divided into up to four subnets can be defined as follows:

| Address Class | Bits for Subnet Mask | Network Prefix | Decimal |
|---|---|---|---|
| Class A | 11111111 11000000 00000000 00000000 | /10 | 255.192.0.0 |

Table 18-7 shows how Class A networks can be subnetted and how this affects the number of possible subnets and hosts per subnet.

**TABLE 18-7  Subnetting Class A networks**

| Maximum Subnets | Bits for Subnet Mask | Network Prefix | Decimal | Maximum Nodes |
|---|---|---|---|---|
| 1 | 11111111 00000000 00000000 00000000 | /8 | 255.0.0.0 | 16,777,214 |
| 2 | 11111111 10000000 00000000 00000000 | /9 | 255.128.0.0 | 8,388,606 |
| 4 | 11111111 11000000 00000000 00000000 | /10 | 255.192.0.0 | 4,194,302 |
| 8 | 11111111 11100000 00000000 00000000 | /11 | 255.224.0.0 | 2,097,150 |
| 16 | 11111111 11110000 00000000 00000000 | /12 | 255.240.0.0 | 1,048,574 |
| 32 | 11111111 11111000 00000000 00000000 | /13 | 255.248.0.0 | 524,286 |
| 64 | 11111111 11111100 00000000 00000000 | /14 | 255.252.0.0 | 262,142 |
| 128 | 11111111 11111110 00000000 00000000 | /15 | 255.254.0.0 | 131,070 |
| 256 | 11111111 11111111 00000000 00000000 | /16 | 255.255.0.0 | 65,534 |
| 512 | 11111111 11111111 10000000 00000000 | /17 | 255.255.128.0 | 32,766 |
| 1,024 | 11111111 11111111 11000000 00000000 | /18 | 255.255.192.0 | 16,382 |
| 2,048 | 11111111 11111111 11100000 00000000 | /19 | 255.255.224.0 | 8,190 |
| 4,096 | 11111111 11111111 11110000 00000000 | /20 | 255.255.240.0 | 4,094 |
| 8,192 | 11111111 11111111 11111000 00000000 | /21 | 255.255.248.0 | 2,046 |
| 16,384 | 11111111 11111111 11111100 00000000 | /22 | 255.255.252.0 | 1,022 |
| 32,768 | 11111111 11111111 11111110 00000000 | /23 | 255.255.254.0 | 510 |
| 65,536 | 11111111 11111111 11111111 00000000 | /24 | 255.255.255.0 | 254 |
| 131,072 | 11111111 11111111 11111111 10000000 | /25 | 255.255.255.128 | 126 |
| 262,144 | 11111111 11111111 11111111 11000000 | /26 | 255.255.255.192 | 62 |
| 524,288 | 11111111 11111111 11111111 11100000 | /27 | 255.255.255.224 | 30 |
| 1,048,576 | 11111111 11111111 11111111 11110000 | /28 | 255.255.255.240 | 14 |
| 2,097,152 | 11111111 11111111 11111111 11111000 | /29 | 255.255.255.248 | 6 |
| 4,194,304 | 11111111 11111111 11111111 11111100 | /30 | 255.255.255.252 | 2 |

## Subnetting Class B networks

The network entry mask for a standard Class B network can be defined as follows:

| Address Class | Bits for Subnet Mask | Network Prefix | Decimal |
|---|---|---|---|
| Class B | 11111111 11111111 00000000 00000000 | /16 | 255.255.0.0 |

A standard Class B network can have up to 65,534 hosts. If you want to divide a Class B network into two separate subnets, you can borrow the high-order bit from the host ID in the third octet and add this bit to the network ID. Because the value of this bit taken from the host ID is 128, the corresponding subnet mask is 255.255.128.0. Thus, the network entry for the subnetted Class B network can be defined as follows:

| Address Class | Bits for Subnet Mask | Network Prefix | Decimal |
|---|---|---|---|
| Class B | 11111111 11111111 10000000 00000000 | /17 | 255.255.128. 0 |

If you take an additional bit from the host ID bits, you allow the Class B network to be divided into up to four subnets. The value of this bit taken from the host ID is 64. When you add this value to the value of the previous bit taken from the host ID, the sum is 192 (128 + 64) and the corresponding subnet mask is 255.255.192.0. This means the network entry for a subnetted Class B network that can be divided into up to four subnets can be defined as follows:

| Address Class | Bits for Subnet Mask | Network Prefix | Decimal |
|---|---|---|---|
| Class B | 11111111 11111111 11000000 00000000 | /18 | 255.255.192.0 |

Table 18-8 shows how Class B networks can be subnetted and how this affects the number of possible subnets and hosts per subnet.

**TABLE 18-8  Subnetting Class B networks**

| Maximum Subnets | Bits for Subnet Mask | Network Prefix | Decimal | Maximum Nodes |
|---|---|---|---|---|
| 1 | 11111111 11111111 00000000 00000000 | /16 | 255.255.0.0 | 65,534 |
| 2 | 11111111 11111111 10000000 00000000 | /17 | 255.255.128.0 | 32,766 |
| 4 | 11111111 11111111 11000000 00000000 | /18 | 255.255.192.0 | 16,382 |
| 8 | 11111111 11111111 11100000 00000000 | /19 | 255.255.224.0 | 8,190 |
| 16 | 11111111 11111111 11110000 00000000 | /20 | 255.255.240.0 | 4,094 |
| 32 | 11111111 11111111 11111000 00000000 | /21 | 255.255.248.0 | 2,046 |
| 64 | 11111111 11111111 11111100 00000000 | /22 | 255.255.252.0 | 1,022 |
| 128 | 11111111 11111111 11111110 00000000 | /23 | 255.255.254.0 | 510 |
| 256 | 11111111 11111111 11111111 00000000 | /24 | 255.255.255.0 | 254 |
| 512 | 11111111 11111111 11111111 10000000 | /25 | 255.255.255.128 | 126 |

| Maximum Subnets | Bits for Subnet Mask | Network Prefix | Decimal | Maximum Nodes |
|---|---|---|---|---|
| 1,024 | 11111111 11111111 11111111 11000000 | /26 | 255.255.255.192 | 62 |
| 2,048 | 11111111 11111111 11111111 11100000 | /27 | 255.255.255.224 | 30 |
| 4,096 | 11111111 11111111 11111111 11110000 | /28 | 255.255.255.240 | 14 |
| 8,192 | 11111111 11111111 11111111 11111000 | /29 | 255.255.255.248 | 6 |
| 16,384 | 11111111 11111111 11111111 11111100 | /30 | 255.255.255.252 | 2 |

## Subnetting Class C networks

The network entry mask for a standard Class C network can be defined as follows:

| Address Class | Bits for Subnet Mask | Network Prefix | Decimal |
|---|---|---|---|
| Class C | 11111111 11111111 11111111 00000000 | /24 | 255.255.255.0 |

A standard Class C network can have up to 254 hosts. If you want to divide a Class C network into two separate subnets, you can borrow the high-order bit from the host ID in the fourth octet and add this bit to the network ID. Because the value of this bit taken from the host ID is 128, the corresponding subnet mask is 255.255.255.128. Thus, the network entry for the subnetted Class C network can be defined as follows:

| Address Class | Bits for Subnet Mask | Network Prefix | Decimal |
|---|---|---|---|
| Class C | 11111111 11111111 11111111 10000000 | /25 | 255.255.255.128 |

If you take an additional bit from the host ID bits, you allow the Class C network to be divided into up to four subnets. The value of this bit taken from the host ID is 64. When you add this value to the value of the previous bit taken from the host ID, the sum is 192 (128 + 64) and the corresponding subnet mask is 255.255.255.192. This means the network entry for a subnetted Class C network that can be divided into up to four subnets can be defined as follows:

| Address Class | Bits for Subnet Mask | Network Prefix | Decimal |
|---|---|---|---|
| Class C | 11111111 11111111 11111111 11000000 | /26 | 255.255.255.192 |

Table 18-9 shows how Class C networks can be subnetted and how this affects the number of possible subnets and hosts per subnet.

**TABLE 18-9  Subnetting Class C networks**

| Maximum Subnets | Bits for Subnet Mask | Network Prefix | Decimal | Maximum Nodes |
|---|---|---|---|---|
| 1 | 11111111 11111111 11111111 00000000 | /24 | 255.255.255.0 | 254 |
| 2 | 11111111 11111111 11111111 10000000 | /25 | 255.255.255.128 | 126 |
| 4 | 11111111 11111111 11111111 11000000 | /26 | 255.255.255.192 | 62 |
| 8 | 11111111 11111111 11111111 11100000 | /27 | 255.255.255.224 | 30 |
| 16 | 11111111 11111111 11111111 11110000 | /28 | 255.255.255.240 | 14 |
| 32 | 11111111 11111111 11111111 11111000 | /29 | 255.255.255.248 | 6 |
| 64 | 11111111 11111111 11111111 11111100 | /30 | 255.255.255.252 | 2 |

# Understanding IP data packets

With IPv4, computers send data in discrete packets of information with a header and a payload. IPv4 headers are variable in size, between 20 and 60 bytes, in 4-byte increments. Each bit range is broken into different sections, and each section corresponds to the range of a related field in a packet. Header bit ranges consist of 0–3, 4–7, 8–15, 16–18, and 15–31. These correspond to the values 0, 32, 64, 96, 128, 160, and 160/152+ for data.

For examples of the ranges and their use, refer to Table 18-10. The IP payload is of variable size as well, ranging from 8 bytes to 65,515 bytes. Although most people will never use this information on a regular basis, it is very useful for understanding how to troubleshoot network problems.

**TABLE 18-10  IPv4 packets**

| + | Bits 0–3 | 4–7 | 8–15 | 16–18 | 15–31 |
|---|---|---|---|---|---|
| 0 | Version | Header length | Type of service | Total length | |
| 32 | Identification | | | Flags | Fragment offset |
| 64 | Time to Live (TTL) | | Protocol | Header checksum | |
| 96 | Source address information | | | | |
| 128 | Destination address information | | | | |
| 160 | Optional information | | | | |
| 160/152+ | Data transmitted | | | | |

# Getting and using IPv4 addresses

As discussed previously, there are two categories of IPv4 addresses:

- **Public**   Public addresses are assigned by Network Solutions (formerly this was InterNIC) and can be purchased as well from IANA/ICANN. Most organizations don't need to purchase their IPv4 addresses directly, however. Instead, they get the IPv4 addresses they need from their Internet service provider (ISP).

- **Private**   Private addresses are reserved for Class A, B, and C networks and can be used without specific assignment. Most organizations follow the private addressing scheme as determined by their Information Technology (IT) department; in this case, they request IPv4 addresses from the IT department.

> ## Important
>
> Technically, if your organization doesn't plan to connect to the Internet, you can use any IPv4 address. However, I still recommend using private IPv4 addresses in this case and taking the time to plan out the IPv4 address space carefully. If you do this and you later must connect the organization to the Internet, you won't have to change the IPv4 address of every node on the network. Instead, you'll need to reconfigure only the network's Internet-facing nodes, such as a proxy server or NAT router, to connect your organization to the Internet.

## INSIDE OUT   Public IPv4 address space

The public IPv4 address space is running out of new addresses that can be assigned to public devices (and might have already run out completely by the time you read this). Whether public IPv4 addresses are exhausted for you depends on where your company is located, what regional Internet registry (RIR) is responsible for allocating IP addresses in your area of the world, and whether your Internet service provider (ISP) has any IPv4 addresses left from those it obtained from an RIR. As of February 2011, the IANA/ICANN, the global authority coordinating IP addresses, ran out of new IPv4 address blocks to allocate to RIRs. Now, the RIRs themselves are running out (or have already run out) of new IPv4 addresses to assign. Because of this, if your company needs public IPv4 addresses, you might not be able to get them. In this case, you need to use IPv6 for your company's public Internet communications.

If you are planning your organization's network infrastructure, you must determine how you want to structure the network. In many cases, you'll want to isolate the internal systems from the public Internet and place them on their own private network. An example of this is shown in Figure 18-7.

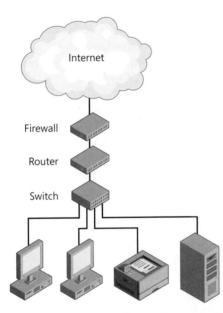

**Figure 18-7** Overview diagram for connecting a private network to the Internet.

In this example, hosts on the internal network connect to a switch. The switch, in turn, connects to a router, which performs the necessary internal-to-external IPv4 address translation using NAT. The NAT router, in turn, is connected to a firewall, and the firewall connects to the Internet. If the internal network ID is 192.168.1.0/24, the internal IPv4 addresses range from 192.168.1.1 to 192.168.1.254 and all hosts use the network mask 255.255.255.0. After this occurs, the hosts might include the following:

- A router with IPv4 address 192.168.1.1 on the interface facing the internal network

- A manageable switch with IPv4 address 192.168.1.2

- Computers with IPv4 addresses 192.168.1.20 to 192.168.149

- Servers with IPv4 addresses 192.168.1.150 to 192.168.199

- A network printer with the IPv4 address 192.168.1.200

Chapter 18

### Follow an IPv4 addressing plan

Notice how the IPv4 addresses are assigned. I generally recommend reserving blocks of IPv4 addresses for the various types of hosts you'll have on a network. On an internal network with the ID 192.168.1.0/24, you might designate that IPv4 addresses 192.168.1.1 to 192.168.1.19 are reserved for network hardware, IPv4 addresses 192.168.1.20 to 192.168.1.149 are reserved for workstations, IPv4 addresses 192.168.1.150 to 192.168.1.199 are reserved for servers, and IPv4 addresses above 192.168.1.200 are reserved for other types of network hardware, such as printers.

You can then determine the number of public IPv4 addresses you need by assessing the number of public Internet-facing nodes you need. In this example, the NAT router needs a public IPv4 address as does the external firewall. To be able to send and receive email, you'll need an IPv4 address for the organization's email server. To set up a public website, you'll need an IPv4 address for the organization's web server.

That's a total of four IPv4 addresses (six, including the network ID address and the broadcast address). In this case, your ISP might assign you a /29 subnet, giving you a total of six usable addresses. If you think you might need more than this, you could ask for a /28 subnet. However, keep in mind that you might have to pay a per–IPv4 address leasing fee.

## Understanding IPv6

As with IPv4, the most important thing IPv6 gives you is the IPv6 address. Although IPv4 allows for more than four billion networked devices, the world is running out of available IPv4 addresses. To resolve this problem, IPv6 uses 128-bit addresses, and this allows for 340,282,237,000,000,000,000,000,000,000,000,000,000 addresses—give or take a few hundred million quadrillion addresses. Or put another way, IPv6 makes available enough IP addresses so that every person on 100 billion worlds of 100 billion people could have 34 quadrillion IP addresses (and there would still be 2.8236 x 10^33 IP addresses left over).

### Note

Okay, so 128 bits might seem like overkill. However, the abundance of IPv6 addresses makes it possible to allocate addresses in large blocks. Not only does this help simplify administration, it avoids fragmentation of the address space, which in turn leads to smaller routing tables. One reason for selecting 128 bits for the address length is the increasing prevalence of 64-bit processors over 32-bit processors. 64-bit processors can efficiently work with 128-bit addresses. As we look to the future, the next logical step is 128-bit computing, and 128-bit addresses will already be in place by that time. A key advantage of IPv6's larger address space is that it makes scanning certain IP blocks for vulnerabilities significantly more difficult than in IPv4, which makes IPv6 more resistant to malicious attacks by hackers looking for vulnerable computers.

Keeping track of so many IPv6 addresses using the numbering scheme used with IPv4 is impractical, and this is why IPv6 uses hexadecimal numbers rather than decimal numbers to define the address space. This means that instead of allowing only the numbers 0 through 9 for each position in the IP address, IPv6 allows the values 0 through 9 and A through F, with A representing 10, B representing 11, and so on, up to F representing 15. Therefore, the values 0 through 15 can be represented using the values 0 through F.

IPv6's 128-bit addresses are divided into eight 16-bit blocks delimited by colons. Each 16-bit block is expressed in hexadecimal form. With standard unicast IPv6 addresses, the first 64 bits represent the network ID and the last 64 bits represent the network interface. An example of an IPv6 address follows:

FE80:0:0:02BC:00FF:BECB:FE4F:961D

Because many IPv6 address blocks are set to 0, a contiguous set of 0 blocks can be expressed as "::", a notation referred to as the *double-colon notation*. Using double-colon notation, the two 0 blocks in the previous address are compressed as follows:

FE80::02BC:00FF:BECB:FE4F:961D

Three or more 0 blocks would be compressed in the same way. For example, FFE8:0:0:0:0:0:0:1 becomes FFE8::1. However, more than one double-colon abbreviation in an address is invalid because it makes the notation ambiguous. Additionally, leading zeros in a group can be omitted. Thus, FE80::02BC:00FF:BECB:FE4F:961D can be shortened to FE80::2BC:FF:BECB:FE4F:961D. Following this, the addresses shown next are all valid and equivalent:

- FE80:0000:0000:02BC:00FF:BECB:FE4F:961D

- FE80:0:0:02BC:00FF:BECB:FE4F:961D

- FE80::02BC:00FF:BECB:FE4F:961D

- FE80::2BC:FF:BECB:FE4F:961D

Finally, you can write a sequence of 4 bytes at the end of an IPv6 address in decimal, using dots as separators. You can use this notation with IPv4 compatibility addresses, such as FE80::192.168.10.52.

As with IPv4 addresses, there are different types of IPv6 addresses. As Table 18-11 shows, the type of an IPv6 address is identified by the high-order bits of the address. Link-local unicast IPv6 addresses are the equivalent of IPv4 private addresses because they are not globally reachable on the Internet. Global unicast IPv6 addresses are the equivalent of IPv4 public addresses because they are globally reachable on the Internet and must be assigned by an IP address authority.

Chapter 18

**TABLE 18-11  IPv6 address types**

| Address Type | Binary Prefix | IPv6 Notation | Description |
|---|---|---|---|
| Unspecified | 000000 | ::/128 | The IPv6 address 0:0:0:0:0:0:0:0 is an unspecified address and should be used only in software. |
| Loopback | 0000000001 | ::1/128 | The IPv6 address 0:0:0:0:0:0:0:1 is used for local loopback. If an application sends packets to this address, the IPv6 stack will loop these packets back to the same host (corresponding to 127.0.0.1 in IPv4). |
| Multicast | 1111111100 | FF00::/8 | IPv6 addresses beginning with FF00 are used for multicast transmissions (both link local and across routers). There are no address ranges reserved for broadcast in IPv6—the same effect can be achieved by multicasting to the all-hosts group with a hop count of one. |
| Link-Local unicast | 1111111010 | FE80::/10 | IPv6 addresses beginning with FE80 are used for link-local unicast transmissions and are valid only in the local physical link (similar to the autoconfiguration IP address 169.254.x.x in IPv4). |
| Global unicast | All other addresses | | All other IP addresses are used for global unicast transmissions and are valid on the public Internet. |

IPv6 doesn't use subnet masks to identify which bits belong to the network ID and which bits belong to the host ID. Instead, each IPv6 address is assigned a subnet prefix length that specifies how the bits in the network ID are used. The subnet prefix length is represented in decimal form. Therefore, if 48 bits in the network ID are used, the subnet prefix length is written as shown in the following example:

| | |
|---|---|
| FE01:1234:5678::/48 | FE01:1234:5678:: through address FE01:1234:5678::FFFF:FFFF:FFFF:FFFF |

As with IPv4, IPv6 packets are composed of two parts: a header and a payload. Unlike IPv4, IPv6 allows for sending *jumbograms*. A *jumbogram* is an IP datagram containing a payload larger than 64 KBs. IPv4 does not support this type of transmission, and it has a 64-KB payload limit.

Jumbograms greatly increase the throughput of high-performance networks. The first 40 octets of an IPv6 packet contain the header (composed of the source and destination addresses, including an IPv4 version where necessary), a traffic class section, a flow label (for packet priority information), the payload length, the next header addressing section, and the hop limit. The payload section consists of the actual data sent during transmission. The payload section can contain either 64 KBs of information, as with IPv4 packets, or a jumbogram for true IPv6 networking architectures.

Another major difference between IPv4 and IPv6 is that IP security (IPsec) is implemented within the IPv6 protocol. IPsec lies within the IP network layer and encrypts and authenticates as an integrated part of the protocol by default. This eliminates additional overhead in encoding and decoding packets using separate IPsec functionality.

# Understanding name resolution

Although IP addressing works well for computer-to-computer communications, it doesn't work so well when you want to access resources. Could you imagine having to remember the IP address of every computer you work with? That would be difficult, and it would make working with computers on networks a chore. This is why computers are assigned names. Names are easier to remember than numbers—at least for most people.

When a computer has a name, you can type that name rather than its IP address to access it. This name resolution doesn't happen automatically. In the background, a computer process translates the computer name you type into an IP address that computers can understand. Windows Vista and later versions natively support three name-resolution systems:

- Domain Name System (DNS)

- Windows Internet Naming Service (WINS)

- Link-Local Multicast Name Resolution (LLMNR)

The sections that follow examine these services.

## Domain Name System

DNS provides a distributed database that enables computer names to be resolved to their corresponding IP addresses. When working with DNS, you need to understand what is meant by the terms "host name," "domain name," "fully qualified domain name," and "name resolution."

### Host names

A *host name* identifies an individual host in DNS. Ordinarily, you might call this a computer name. The difference, however, is that there is an actual record in the DNS database called a *host record* that corresponds to the computer name and details how the computer name is used on the network. Host names can be assigned by administrators and other members of the organization.

### Domain names

A *domain name* is the logical identity of a network in DNS. Domain names follow a specific naming scheme that is organized in a tree-like structure. Periods (dots) are used to separate the name components or levels within the domain name.

The first level of the tree is where you'll find the top-level domains. *Top-level domains* describe the kinds of networks that are within their domain. For example, the .edu top-level domain is for educational domains, the .gov top-level domain is for U.S. government domains, and .com is for commercial domains. As you can see, top-level domains generally are organized by category. There are also top-level domains organized geographically, such as .ca for Canada and .uk for United Kingdom.

The second level of the tree is where you'll find parent domains. *Parent domains* are the primary domain names of organizations. For example, City Power & Light's domain name is cpandl.com. The domain name cpandl.com identifies a specific network in the .com domain. No parent domain can be used on the public Internet without being reserved and registered. Name registrars, such as Network Solutions, charge a fee for this service.

Additional levels of the tree belong to individual hosts or subsequent levels in the organization's domain structure. These subsequent levels are referred to as *child domains*. For example, City Power & Light might have Tech, Support, and Sales child domains, which are named tech.cpandl.com, support.cpandl.com, and sales.cpandl.com, respectively.

## INSIDE OUT  Connect the network to the Internet

If your organization's network must be connected to the Internet, you should obtain a public domain name from a name registrar or use a similar service as provided by an ISP. Because many domain names have already been taken, you should have several previously agreed-upon alternative names in mind when you go to register. After you obtain a domain name, you must configure DNS hosting for that domain. You do this by specifying the addresses of two or more DNS servers that will handle DNS services for this domain. Typically, these DNS servers belong to your ISP.

# INSIDE OUT    Additional top-level domains

Although top-level domains generally are organized by category and country/region, new top-level domains are introduced periodically, after approval by the ICANN. Additional top-level domains that have been approved include .Aero for the air-transport industry, .Asia for the Asia-Pacific region, .Biz for businesses, .Info for information, .Jobs for companies with jobs to advertise, .Mobi for mobile-compatible sites, .Museum for museums, and .Travel for the travel and tourism industry.

## Fully qualified domain names

All hosts on a TCP/IP network have what is called a *fully qualified domain name (FQDN)*. The FQDN combines the host name and the domain name and serves to uniquely identify the host. For a host named CPL05 in the cpandl.com domain, the FQDN would be cpl05.cpandl.com. For a host named CORPSVR17 in the tech.cpandl.com domain, the FQDN would be corpsvr17.tech.cpandl.com.

## Name resolution

*Name resolution* is the process by which host names are resolved to IP addresses and vice versa. When a TCP/IP application wants to communicate with another host on a network, it needs the IP address of that host. Typically, the application knows only the name of the host it is looking for, so it has to resolve that name to an IP address.

To do this, the application first looks in its local DNS cache of names that it has previously looked up. If the name is in this cache, the IP address is found without having to look elsewhere and the application can connect to the remote host. If the name isn't in the cache, the application must ask the network's DNS server or servers to help resolve the name. These servers perform a similar lookup. If the name is in their database or cache, the IP address for the name is returned. Otherwise, the DNS server has to request this information from another DNS server.

That's the way it works—the simplified version at least. Most of the time, a TCP/IP application has the host name and needs to find the corresponding IP address. Occasionally, a TCP/IP application will have an IP address and needs the corresponding host name. To do this, the application must perform a reverse lookup, so instead of requesting an IP address, the application requests a host name using the IP address.

The application first looks in its local cache of information that has been previously looked up. If the IP address is in this cache, the name is found without having to look elsewhere and the application can perform whichever tasks are necessary. If the IP address isn't in the

Chapter 18

cache, the application must ask the network's DNS server or servers to help resolve the IP address. These servers perform a similar lookup. If the IP address is in their reverse lookup database or cache, the name for the IP address is returned. Otherwise, the DNS server has to request this information from another DNS server.

## Windows Internet Naming Service

Windows Internet Naming Service (WINS) is a name-resolution service that resolves computer names to IP addresses. Using WINS, the computer name COMPUTER84, for example, could be resolved to an IP address that enables computers on a Microsoft network to find one another and transfer information. WINS is needed to support applications that use Network Basic Input/Output System (NetBIOS) over TCP/IP, such as Exchange Server 2003, the .NET command-line utilities, and network browsing for users in pre–Windows Server 2008 environments. If you don't have NetBIOS applications on the network or pre–Windows Server 2008 infrastructure, you don't need to use WINS.

WINS is designed for client/server environments where WINS clients send queries to WINS servers for name resolution and WINS servers resolve the queries and respond. To transmit WINS queries and other information, computers use NetBIOS. NetBIOS is an interface developed to allow applications to perform basic network operations, such as sending data, connecting to remote hosts, and accessing network resources.

NetBIOS computer names can be up to 15 characters long. They must be unique on the network and can be looked up on a server called a WINS server. WINS supports both forward lookups (NetBIOS computer name to IP address) and reverse lookups (IP address to NetBIOS computer name).

NetBIOS applications rely on WINS or the local LMHOSTS file to resolve computer names to IP addresses. On early Windows networks, WINS was the primary name-resolution service available. On current Windows networks, DNS is the primary name-resolution service and WINS has a different function. This function is to allow applications written to the NetBIOS interface to browse lists of resources on the network and to allow systems to locate NetBIOS resources. To enable WINS name resolution on a network, you need to configure WINS clients and servers. When you configure WINS clients, you tell the clients the IP addresses of WINS servers on the network. Using the IP address, clients can communicate with WINS servers anywhere on the network, even if the servers are on different subnets. WINS clients can also communicate using a broadcast method in which clients broadcast messages to other computers on the local network segment requesting their IP addresses. Because messages are broadcast, the WINS server isn't used. Any non-WINS clients that support this type of message broadcasting can also use this method to resolve computer names to IP addresses.

Your organization must set up WINS if you are using applications that rely on NetBIOS over TCP/IP. If you are currently using WINS and don't have applications that rely on NetBIOS over TCP/IP, you can eliminate the need for this service by moving workstations and servers to currently supported versions of Windows.

> ## Important
>
> Where legacy systems have been upgraded to current Windows Server versions, WINS might be needed to establish or re-establish trust relationships in Active Directory. The only way to be sure WINS is not needed for trusts is to ensure there are no legacy references within Active Directory, and that means performing a bare-metal install of Windows Server 2003 with forest and domain operations in Windows Server 2003 Native Mode or higher. NetBIOS names are still used under the hood for trust relationships in Active Directory with current Windows Server operating systems.

## Link-Local Multicast Name Resolution

Link-Local Multicast Name Resolution (LLMNR) fills a need for peer-to-peer name-resolution services for devices with IPv4, IPv6, or both addresses, allowing IPv4 and IPv6 devices on a single subnet without a WINS or DNS server to resolve each other's names—a service that neither WINS nor DNS can fully provide. Although WINS can provide NetBIOS name-resolution services for IPv4, it does not support IPv6 addresses. DNS, on the other hand, supports IPv4 and IPv6 addresses, but it depends on designated servers to provide name-resolution services.

Windows Vista and later support LLMNR. LLMNR is designed for both IPv4 and IPv6 clients when other name-resolution systems are not available, such as on a small-office or ad hoc network. LLMNR can also be used on corporate networks where DNS services are not available.

LLMNR is designed to complement DNS by enabling name resolution in scenarios in which conventional DNS name resolution is not possible. Although LLMNR can replace the need for WINS in cases where NetBIOS is not required, LLMNR is not a substitute for DNS because it operates only on the local subnet. Because LLMNR traffic is prevented from propagating across routers, it cannot accidentally flood the network.

As with WINS, you use LLMNR to resolve a host name, such as COMPUTER84, to an IP address. By default, LLMNR is enabled on all computers running Windows Vista and later, and these computers use LLMNR only when all attempts to look up a host name through DNS fail. As a result, name resolution works like this for Windows Vista and later:

1.  A host computer looks up the name in its internal name cache. If the name is not found in the cache, the host sends a query to its configured primary DNS server. If the host computer does not receive a response or receives an error, it tries each configured alternate DNS server in turn. If the host has no configured DNS servers or fails to connect to a DNS server without errors, name resolution fails over to LLMNR.

2.  The host computer sends a multicast query over User Datagram Protocol (UDP) requesting the IP address for the name being looked up. This query is restricted to the local subnet (also referred to as the *local link*).

3.  Each computer on the local link that supports LLMNR and is configured to respond to incoming queries receives the query and compares the name to its own host name. If the host name is not a match, the computer discards the query. If the host name is a match, the computer transmits a unicast message containing its IP address to the originating host.

You can also use LLMNR for reverse mapping. With a reverse mapping, a computer sends a unicast query to a specific IP address, requesting the host name of the target computer. An LLMNR-enabled computer that receives the request sends a unicast reply containing its host name to the originating host.

LLMNR-enabled computers are required to ensure that their names are unique on the local subnet. In most cases, a computer checks for uniqueness when it starts, when it resumes from a suspended state, and when you change its network-interface settings. If a computer has not yet determined that its name is unique, it must indicate this condition when responding to a name query.

By default, LLMNR is automatically enabled on computers running Windows Vista and later. You can disable LLMNR through registry settings. To disable LLMNR for all network interfaces, create and set the following DWORD value to 0 (zero): HKLM/SYSTEM/ CurrentControlSet/Services/Dnscache/Parameters/EnableMulticast. To disable LLMNR for a specific network interface, create and set the following DWORD value to 0 (zero): HKLM/SYSTEM/CurrentControlSet/Services/Tcpip/Parameters/Interfaces/AdapterGUID/ EnableMulticast, where *AdapterGUID* is the globally unique identifier (GUID) of the network interface adapter for which you want to disable LLMNR.

You can re-enable LLMNR at any time by setting these DWORD values to 1. You also can manage LLMNR through Group Policy.

# Managing TCP/IP networking

A s an administrator, you enable networked computers to communicate by using the basic networking protocols built into Microsoft Windows Server 2012. The key protocol you'll use is Transmission Control Protocol/Internet Protocol (TCP/IP). TCP/IP is actually a collection of protocols and services used for communicating over a network. It's the primary protocol used for internetwork communications. Compared to configuring other networking protocols, configuring TCP/IP communications is fairly complicated, but TCP/IP is the most versatile protocol available.

> **Note**
>
> Group Policy settings can affect your ability to install and manage TCP/IP networking. The key policies you'll want to examine are in User Configuration\Administrative Templates\Network\Network Connections and Computer Configuration\Administrative Templates\System\Group Policy. Group Policy is discussed in Chapter 31, "Managing Group Policy."

## Installing TCP/IP networking

If you want to install networking on a computer, you must install TCP/IP networking and a network adapter. Windows Server 2012 uses TCP/IP as its networking protocol. Normally, networking is installed during setup of the operating system. You can also install TCP/IP networking through network connection properties. Although name resolution can be performed using Domain Name System (DNS), Windows Internet Naming Service (WINS), or Link-Local Multicast Name Resolution (LLNMR), the preferred technique on Windows Server domains is DNS.

# Preparing for installation of TCP/IP networking

Before you can configure TCP/IP networking on individual computers, you need the following information:

- **Domain name**   The name of the domain in which the computer will be located. This can be a parent or child domain.

- **IP address type, value, or both**   The IP address information to assign to the computer, which can include both Internet Protocol version 4 (IPv4) and Internet Protocol version 6 (IPv6) addressing details.

- **Subnet mask**   The subnet mask for the IPv4 network to which the computer is attached.

- **Subnet prefix length**   The subnet prefix length for the IPv6 network to which the computer is attached.

- **Default gateway address**   The address of the router or routers that will function as the computer's gateway.

- **DNS server address**   The address of the DNS server or servers that provide DNS name-resolution services on the network.

- **WINS server address**   The address of the WINS server or servers that provide WINS name-resolution services on the network.

If you are unsure of any of this information, you should ask the IT staff. In many cases, even if you are an administrator, there is a specific person you must ask for the IP address setup that should be used. Typically, this is your organization's network administrator, and it is that person's job to maintain the spreadsheet or database that shows how IP addresses are assigned within the organization.

If no one in your organization has this role yet, this role should be assigned to someone or jointly managed to ensure that IP addresses are assigned following a specific plan. The plan should detail the following information:

- The address ranges that are reserved for network equipment and hardware and which individual IP addresses in this range are currently in use

- The address ranges that are reserved for DHCP and, as such, cannot be assigned using a static IP address

- The address ranges that are for static IP addresses and which individual IP addresses in this range are currently in use

## Installing network adapters

Network adapters are hardware devices that are used to communicate on networks. You can install and configure network adapters by following these steps:

1. Configure the network adapter following the manufacturer's instructions. For example, you might need to use the software provided by the manufacturer to modify the Interrupt setting or the Port setting of the adapter.

2. If you're installing an internal network interface card, shut down the computer, unplug it, and install the adapter card in the appropriate slot on the computer. When you're finished, plug the computer in and start it.

3. Windows Server should detect the new adapter during startup. If you have a separate driver disk for the adapter, insert it now. Otherwise, you might be prompted to insert a driver disk.

4. If Windows Server doesn't detect the adapter automatically, follow the installation instructions in Chapter 7, "Managing and troubleshooting hardware."

5. If networking services aren't installed on the system, install them as described in the next section.

## Installing networking services (TCP/IP)

If you're installing TCP/IP after installing Windows Server 2012, log on to the computer using an account with Administrator privileges and then follow these steps:

1. In Control Panel, tap or click View Network Status And Tasks under the Network And Internet heading.

2. In Network And Sharing Center, tap or click Change Adapter Settings.

3. In Network Connections, press and hold or right-click the connection you want to work with and then select Properties.

4. This displays the Properties dialog box for the connection, shown in Figure 19-1.

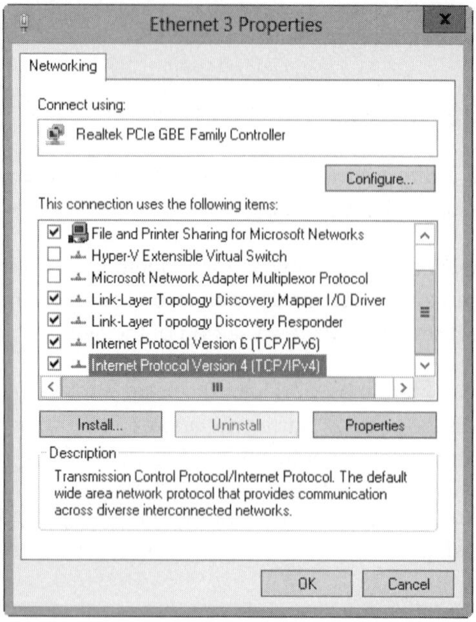

**Figure 19-1** Install and configure TCP/IP in the Properties dialog box for the connection.

5. If Internet Protocol Version 6 (TCP/IPv6), Internet Protocol Version 4 (TCP/IPv4), or both aren't shown in the list of installed components, you need to install them. Tap or click Install. Select Protocol, and then tap or click Add. In the Select Network Protocol dialog box, select the protocol to install and then tap or click OK. If you are installing both TCP/IPv6 and TCP/IPv4, repeat this procedure for each protocol.

6. In the Properties dialog box for the connection, make sure that the following are selected as appropriate: Internet Protocol Version 6 (TCP/IPv6), Internet Protocol Version 4 (TCP/IPv4), or both. Then tap or click OK.

7. As necessary, follow the instructions in the next section for configuring network connections for the computer.

# Configuring TCP/IP networking

A network connection is created automatically if a computer has a network adapter and is connected to a network. If a computer has multiple network adapters and is connected to a network, you'll have one network connection for each adapter. If no network connection is available, you should connect the computer to the network or create a different type of connection, as explained in "Managing network connections" later in this chapter.

Computers use IP addresses to communicate over TCP/IP. Windows Server provides the following ways to configure IP addressing:

- **Manually**   IP addresses that are assigned manually are called *static IP addresses*. Static IP addresses are fixed and don't change unless you change them. You'll usually assign static IP addresses to Windows servers, and when you do this, you'll need to configure additional information to help the server navigate the network.

- **Dynamically**   A Dynamic Host Configuration Protocol (DHCP) server (if one is installed on the network) assigns dynamic IP addresses at startup, and the addresses might change over time. Dynamic IP addressing is the default configuration.

- **Alternatively (IPv4 only)**   When a computer is configured to use DHCPv4 and no DHCPv4 server is available, Windows Server assigns an alternate private IP address automatically. By default, the alternate IPv4 address is in the range from 169.254.0.1 to 169.254.255.254 with a subnet mask of 255.255.0.0. You can also specify a user-configured alternate IPv4 address, which is particularly useful for laptop users.

> **Important**
> Unless an IP address is specifically reserved, DHCP servers assign IP addresses for a specific period of time, known as an *IP address lease*. If this lease expires and cannot be renewed, the client assigns itself an automatic private IP address.

## Configuring static IP addresses

When you assign a static IP address, you need to tell the computer the IP address you want to use, the subnet mask for this IP address, and, if necessary, the default gateway to use for internetwork communications. An IP address is a numeric identifier for a computer. IP addressing schemes vary according to how your network is configured, but they're normally assigned based on a particular network segment.

IPv6 addresses and IPv4 addresses are very different. With IPv6, the first 64 bits represent the network ID and the remaining 64 bits represent the network interface. With IPv4, a variable number of the initial bits represent the network ID and the rest of the bits represent the host ID. For example, if you're working with IPv4 and a computer on the network segment 192.168.10.0 with a subnet mask of 255.255.255.0, the first 24 bits represent the network ID and the address range you have available for computer hosts is from 192.168.10.1 to 192.168.10.254. In this range, the address 192.168.10.255 is reserved for network broadcasts.

If you're on a private network that is indirectly connected to the Internet, you should use private IPv6 addresses. Link-local unicast addresses are private IPv6 addresses. All link-local unicast addresses begin with FE80.

If you're on a private network that is indirectly connected to the Internet, you should use private IPv4 addresses. Table 19-1 summarizes private network IPv4 addresses.

**TABLE 19-1  Private IPv4 network addressing**

| Private Network ID | Subnet Mask | Network Address Range |
|---|---|---|
| 10.0.0.0 | 255.0.0.0 | 10.0.0.0–10.255.255.255 |
| 172.16.0.0 | 255.240.0.0 | 172.16.0.0–172.31.255.255 |
| 192.168.0.0 | 255.255.0.0 | 192.168.0.0–192.168.255.255 |

All other IPv4 network addresses are public and must be leased or purchased. If the network is connected directly to the Internet and you've obtained a range of IPv4 addresses from your Internet service provider, you can use the IPv4 addresses you've been assigned.

## Testing an IP address

Before you assign a static IP address, you should make sure that the address isn't already in use or reserved for use with DHCP. You can do this with the PING command and with the Test-Connection cmdlet.

### TROUBLESHOOTING

**Blocked pings**
Windows Firewall (and other firewalls) can be configured to block pings. If a firewall is configured in this way, ping tests will fail, as will connection tests using Test-Connection. The reason Test-Connection fails if pings are blocked is because the cmdlet uses Get-WMIObject Win32_PingStatus to test connections.

With the PING command, you can check to see whether an address is in use. Open a command prompt and type **ping**, followed by the IP address you want to check.

To test the IPv4 address 10.0.10.12, you would use the following command:

```
ping 10.0.10.12
```

To test the IPv6 address FEC0::02BC:FF:BECB:FE4F:961D, you would use the following command:

```
ping FEC0::02BC:FF:BECB:FE4F:961D
```

If you receive a successful reply from the PING test, the IP address is in use and you should try another one. If no current host on the network uses this IP address, the PING command output should be similar to the following:

```
Pinging 192.168.1.100 with 32 bytes of data:

Request timed out.
Request timed out.
Request timed out.
Request timed out.

Ping statistics for 192.168.1.100:
Packets: Sent = 4, Received = 0, Lost = 4 (100% loss)
```

You can then use the IP address.

> ## Important
> Pinging an IP address will work as long as all the hosts are active and reachable on the network at the time you ping the address. However, a firewall could be blocking your PING request. More important is to plan the assignment of static addresses to machines on your network carefully.

You also can use the Test-Connection cmdlet to check whether an IP address is in use. The cmdlet's basic syntax is this:

```
test-connection [-count Count] IPAddressOrServerName
```

Here, you can optionally use the –*Count* parameter to specify the number of times to test a connection and *IPAddressOrServerName* is the IP address or server name you want to check. If you don't specify a count, Windows PowerShell only tries to connect to a server or IP address once. In the following example, you try to connect five times to 192.168.10.24:

```
test-connection -count 5 192.168.10.24
```

If the IP address is in use, the test results will look similar to the following:

| Source | Destination | IPV4Address | IPV6Address | Bytes | Time(ms) |
|--------|-------------|-------------|-------------|-------|----------|
| CORPSERVER64 | 192.168.10.42 | 192.168.10.42 | | 32 | 0 |
| CORPSERVER64 | 192.168.10.42 | 192.168.10.42 | | 32 | 0 |
| CORPSERVER64 | 192.168.10.42 | 192.168.10.42 | | 32 | 0 |
| CORPSERVER64 | 192.168.10.42 | 192.168.10.42 | | 32 | 0 |
| CORPSERVER64 | 192.168.10.42 | 192.168.10.42 | | 32 | 0 |

As with PING, a successful reply from the test means the IP address is in use and you should try another one. If no current host on the network uses this IP address, the output should be similar to the following:

```
test-connection : Testing connection to computer '192.168.10.42' failed:
A non-recoverable error occurred
At line:1 char:1
+ test-connection -count 5 192.168.10.42
+ ~~~~~~~~~~~~~~~~~~~~~~~~~~~~~~~~~~~~~~
    + CategoryInfo          : ResourceUnavailable: (192.168.10.42:String)
[Test-Connection], PingException
```

## Configuring a static IPv4 or IPv6 address

One local area network (LAN) connection is available for each network adapter installed. These connections are created automatically. To configure static IP addresses for a particular connection, follow these steps:

1.  In Control Panel, tap or click View Network Status And Tasks under the Network And Internet heading.

2.  In Network And Sharing Center, tap or click Change Adapter Settings. In Network Connections, press and hold or right-click the connection you want to work with and then select Properties.

3.  Double-tap or double-click Internet Protocol Version 6 (TCP/IPv6) or Internet Protocol Version 4 (TCP/IPv4) as appropriate for the type of IP address you are configuring.

4.  For an IPv6 address, do the following:

    ○   Select Use The Following IPv6 Address, and then type the IPv6 address in the IPv6 Address text box. The IPv6 address you assign to the computer must not be used anywhere else on the network.

    ○   Press the Tab key. The Subnet Prefix Length field ensures that the computer communicates over the network properly. Windows Server should insert a default value for the subnet prefix into the Subnet Prefix Length text box. If the network doesn't use variable-length subnetting, the default value should suffice. If your network does use variable-length subnets, you need to change this value as appropriate for your network.

5. For an IPv4 address, do the following:

   ○ Select Use The Following IP Address, and then type the IPv4 address in the IP Address text box. The IPv4 address you assign to the computer must not be used anywhere else on the network.

   ○ Press the Tab key. The Subnet Mask field ensures that the computer communicates over the network properly. Windows Server should insert a default value for the subnet prefix into the Subnet Mask text box. If the network doesn't use variable-length subnetting, the default value should suffice. If your network does use variable-length subnets, you need to change this value as appropriate for your network.

6. If the computer needs to access other TCP/IP networks, the Internet, or other subnets, you must specify a default gateway. Type the IP address of the network's default router in the Default Gateway text box.

7. DNS is needed for domain-name resolution. Select Use The Following DNS Server Addresses, and then type a preferred address and an alternate DNS server address in the text boxes provided.

8. When you're finished, tap or click OK three times to save your changes. Repeat this process for other network adapters and IP protocols you want to configure.

9. With IPv4 addressing, configure WINS as necessary, following the technique outlined in "Configuring WINS resolution" later in this chapter.

## Configuring dynamic IP addresses and alternate IP addressing

Many organizations use DHCP servers to dynamically assign IPv4 and IPv6 addresses. To receive an IPv4 or IPv6 address, client computers use a limited broadcast to advertise that they need to obtain an IP address. DHCP servers on the network acknowledge the request by offering the client an IP address. The client acknowledges the first offer it receives, and the DHCP server in turn tells the client that it has succeeded in leasing the IP address for a specified amount of time.

The message from the DHCP server can, and typically does, include the IP addresses of the default gateway, the preferred and alternate DNS servers, and the preferred and alternate WINS servers. This means these settings don't need to be manually configured on the client computer.

Chapter 19

## INSIDE OUT  DHCP is primarily for clients

Dynamic IP addresses aren't for all hosts on the network, however. Typically, you'll want to assign dynamic IP addresses to workstations and, in some instances, member servers that perform noncritical roles on the network. But if you use dynamic IP addressing for member servers, these servers should have reservations for their IP addresses. For any server that has a critical network role or provides a key service, you definitely want to use static IP addresses. Finally, with domain controllers and DHCP servers, you must use static IP addresses, so don't try to assign dynamic IP addresses to these servers.

Although you can use static IP addresses with workstations, most workstations use dynamic addressing, alternative IP addressing, or both. You configure dynamic and alternative addressing by following these steps:

1. In Control Panel, tap or click View Network Status And Tasks under the Network And Internet heading.

2. In Network And Sharing Center, tap or click Change Adapter Settings. In Network Connections, one LAN connection is shown for each network adapter installed. These connections are created automatically. If you don't see a LAN connection for an installed adapter, check the driver for the adapter. It might be installed incorrectly. Press and hold or right-click the connection you want to work with and then select Properties.

3. Double-tap or double-click Internet Protocol Version 6 (TCP/IPv6) or Internet Protocol Version 4 (TCP/IPv4) as appropriate for the type of IP address you are configuring.

4. Select Obtain An IPv6 Address Automatically or Obtain An IP Address Automatically as appropriate for the type of IP address you are configuring. If desired, select Obtain DNS Server Address Automatically. Or select Use The Following DNS Server Addresses, and then type preferred and alternate DNS server addresses in the text boxes provided.

5. When you use dynamic IPv4 addressing with desktop computers, you should configure an automatic alternative address. To use this configuration, on the Alternate Configuration tab, select Automatic Private IP Address. Tap or click OK, tap or click Close, and then skip the remaining steps.

6. When you use dynamic IPv4 addressing with mobile computers, you'll usually want to configure the alternative address manually. To use this configuration, on the Alternate

Configuration tab, select User Configured and then type the IP address you want to use in the IP Address text box. The IP address you assign to the computer should be a private IP address, as shown in Table 19-1, and it must not be in use anywhere else when the settings are applied.

7.  With dynamic IPv4 addressing, complete the alternate configuration by entering a subnet mask, default gateway, DNS, and WINS settings. When you're finished, tap or click OK and then tap or click OK again.

## INSIDE OUT  Disabling APIPA

Whenever DHCP is used, Automatic Private IP Addressing (APIPA) is enabled by default. If you don't want a computer to use APIPA, you can either assign a static TCP/IP address or disable APIPA. For example, if your network uses routers or your network is connected to the Internet without a Network Address Translation (NAT) or proxy server, you might not want to use APIPA. You can disable APIPA in the registry.

You can disable APIPA by creating *IPAutoconfigurationEnabled* as a DWORD value in the registry under HKEY_LOCAL_MACHINE\SYSTEM\CurrentControlSet\Services\ Tcpip\Parameters\Interfaces\*AdapterGUID*, where *AdapterGUID* is the globally unique identifier (GUID) for the computer's network adapter. Set the value to 0×0.

If you create *IPAutoconfigurationEnabled* as a DWORD value entry, you can enable APIPA at any time by changing the value to 0×1.

For more information about disabling APIPA, see Microsoft Knowledge Base article 220874 at *http://support.microsoft.com/kb/220874*.

## Configuring multiple IP addresses and gateways

Using advanced TCP/IP settings, you can configure a single network interface on a computer to use multiple IP addresses and multiple gateways. This allows a computer to appear to be several computers and to access multiple logical subnets to route information or to provide internetworking services.

To provide fault tolerance in case of a router outage, you can choose to configure Windows servers so that they use multiple default gateways. When you assign multiple gateways, Windows Server uses the gateway metric to determine which gateway is used and at what time. The gateway metric indicates the routing cost of using a gateway. The gateway with the lowest routing cost, or metric, is used first. If the computer can't communicate with this gateway, Windows Server tries to use the gateway with the next lowest metric.

The best way to configure multiple gateways depends on the configuration of your network. If your organization's computers use DHCP, you'll probably want to configure the additional gateways through settings on the DHCP server. If computers use static IP addresses or you want to set gateways specifically, assign them by following these steps:

1. In Control Panel, tap or click View Network Status And Tasks under the Network And Internet heading.

2. In Network And Sharing Center, tap or click Change Adapter Settings. In Network Connections, press and hold or right-click the connection you want to work with and then select Properties.

3. Double-tap or double-click Internet Protocol Version 6 (TCP/IPv6) or Internet Protocol Version 4 (TCP/IPv4) as appropriate for the type of IP address you are configuring.

4. Tap or click Advanced to open the Advanced TCP/IP Settings dialog box. Figure 19-2 shows advanced settings for IPv4. The dialog box for IPv6 is similar.

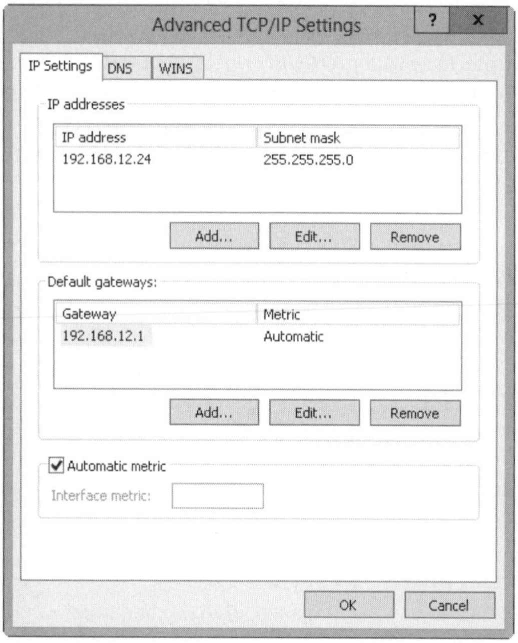

**Figure 19-2** Configure multiple IP addresses and gateways in the Advanced TCP/IP Settings dialog box.

5.  To add an IP address, tap or click Add below IP Address to display the TCP/IP Address dialog box. After you type the IP address in the IP Address field, enter the subnet mask in the Subnet Mask field for IPv4 addresses or the subnet prefix length in the Subnet Prefix Length field for IPv6 addresses. Tap or click Add to return to the Advanced TCP/IP Settings dialog box. Repeat this step for each IP address you want to add.

6.  The Default Gateways panel shows the current gateways that have been manually configured (if any). To add a default gateway, tap or click Add below Default Gateways to display the TCP/IP Gateway Address dialog box. Type the gateway address in the Gateway field. By default, Windows Server automatically assigns a metric to the gateway, which determines in which order the gateway is used. To assign the metric manually, clear the Automatic Metric check box and then enter a metric in the field provided. Tap or click Add, and then repeat this step for each gateway you want to add.

7.  Tap or click OK three times to close the open dialog boxes.

## Configuring DNS resolution

DNS is a host-name resolution service you can use to determine the IP address of a computer from its host name. This lets users work with host names, such as fileserver18 .cpandl.com or www.microsoft.com, rather than an IP address, such as 192.168.5.102 or 192.168.12.68. DNS is the primary name service for Windows Server and the Internet.

As with gateways, the best way to configure DNS depends on the configuration of your network. If computers use DHCP, you'll probably want to configure DNS through settings on the DHCP server. If computers use static IP addresses or you want to configure DNS specifically for a particular computer, you'll want to configure DNS manually.

### Basic DNS settings

You can configure basic DNS settings by following these steps:

1.  In Control Panel, tap or click View Network Status And Tasks under the Network And Internet heading.

2.  In Network And Sharing Center, tap or click Change Adapter Settings. In Network Connections, press and hold or right-click the connection you want to work with and then select Properties.

3.  Double-tap or double-click Internet Protocol Version 6 (TCP/IPv6) or Internet Protocol Version 4 (TCP/IPv4) as appropriate for the type of IP address you are configuring.

4.  If the computer is using DHCP and you want DHCP to specify the DNS server address, select Obtain DNS Server Address Automatically. Otherwise, select Use The Following DNS Server Addresses and then type primary and alternate DNS server addresses in the text boxes provided.

5.  Tap or click OK three times to save your changes.

## Advanced DNS settings

You configure advanced DNS settings on the DNS tab of the Advanced TCP/IP Settings dialog box, shown in Figure 19-3. You use the fields of the DNS tab as follows:

- **DNS Server Addresses, In Order Of Use**   Use this area to specify the IP address of each DNS server that is used for domain-name resolution. Tap or click Add if you want to add a server IP address to the list. Tap or click Remove to remove a selected server address from the list. Tap or click Edit to edit the selected entry. You can specify multiple servers for DNS resolution. Their priority is determined by the order. If the first server isn't available to respond to a host-name resolution request, the next DNS server on the list is accessed, and so on. To change the position of a server in the list box, select it and then tap or click the Up or Down arrow button.

- **Append Primary And Connection Specific DNS Suffixes**   Normally, this option is selected by default. Select this option to resolve unqualified computer names in the primary domain. For example, if the computer name Gandolf is used and the parent domain is microsoft.com, the computer name resolves to gandolf.microsoft.com. If the fully qualified computer name doesn't exist in the parent domain, the query fails. The parent domain used is the one set in the System Properties dialog box on the Computer Name tab. (Tap or click System And Security\System in Control Panel, and then tap or click Change Settings and view the Computer Name tab to check the settings.)

- **Append Parent Suffixes Of The Primary DNS Suffix**   This option is selected by default. Select this check box to resolve unqualified computer names using the parent/child domain hierarchy. If a query fails in the immediate parent domain, the suffix for the parent of the parent domain is used to try to resolve the query. This process continues until the top of the DNS domain hierarchy is reached. For example, if the computer name Gandolf is used in the dev.microsoft.com domain, DNS attempts to resolve the computer name to gandolf.dev.microsoft.com. If this doesn't work, DNS attempts to resolve the computer name to gandolf.microsoft.com.

- **Append These DNS Suffixes (In Order)**   Select this option to set specific DNS suffixes to use rather than resolving through the parent domain. Tap or click Add if you want to add a domain suffix to the list. Tap or click Remove to remove a selected domain suffix from the list. Tap or click Edit to edit the selected entry. You can specify multiple domain suffixes, which are used in order. If the first suffix doesn't resolve properly, DNS attempts to use the next suffix in the list. If this fails, the next suffix is used, and so on. To change the order of the domain suffixes, select the suffix and then tap or click the Up or Down arrow button to change its position.

- **DNS Suffix For This Connection**   This option sets a specific DNS suffix for the connection that overrides DNS names already configured for use on this connection. You'll usually set the DNS domain name through the System Properties dialog box on the Computer Name tab.

- **Register This Connection's Addresses In DNS**   Select this option if you want all IP addresses for this connection to be registered in DNS under the computer's fully qualified domain name. This option is selected by default.

> **Note**
> Dynamic DNS updates are used in conjunction with DHCP to enable a client to update its A (Host Address) record if its IP address changes, and to enable the DHCP server to update the PTR (Pointer) record for the client on the DNS server. You can also configure DHCP servers to update both the A and PTR records on the client's behalf. Dynamic DNS updates are supported only by BIND 8.2.1 or higher DNS servers as well as server editions of Microsoft Windows.

- **Use This Connection's DNS Suffix In DNS Registration**   Select this check box if you want all IP addresses for this connection to be registered in DNS under the parent domain.

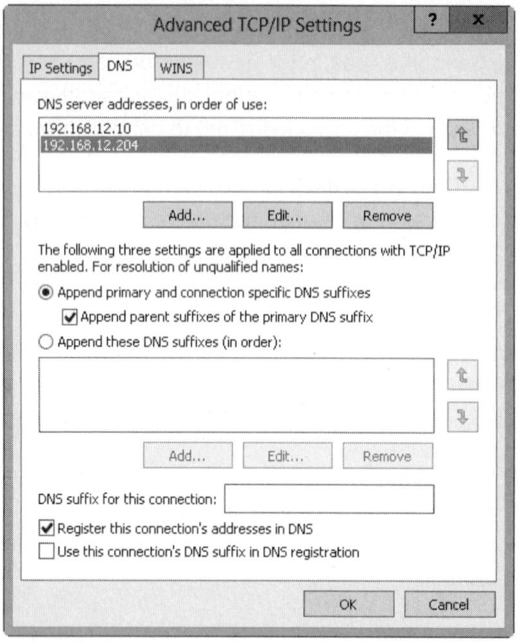

**Figure 19-3** Configure advanced DNS settings on the DNS tab of the Advanced TCP/IP Settings dialog box.

## Configuring WINS resolution

You use WINS to resolve Network Basic Input/Output System (NetBIOS) computer names to IPv4 addresses. You can use WINS to help computers on a network determine the address of other computers on the network. If a WINS server is installed on the network, you can use the server to resolve computer names. Although WINS is supported on all versions of Windows, Windows Server 2012 primarily uses WINS for backward compatibility.

You can also configure Windows Server 2012 computers to use the local file LMHOSTS to resolve NetBIOS computer names. However, LMHOSTS is consulted only if normal name resolution methods fail. In a properly configured network, these files are rarely used. Thus, the preferred method of NetBIOS computer name resolution is WINS in conjunction with a WINS server.

As with gateways and DNS, the best way to configure WINS depends on the configuration of your network. If computers use DHCP, you'll probably want to configure WINS through settings on the DHCP server. If computers use static IPv4 addresses or you want to configure WINS specifically for a particular computer, you'll want to configure WINS manually.

You can manually configure WINS by following these steps:

1. Access the Advanced TCP/IP Settings dialog box for IPv4, and tap or click the WINS tab as shown in Figure 19-4. In the WINS Addresses, In Order Of Use panel, you can specify the IPv4 addresses of each WINS server that is used for NetBIOS name resolution. Tap or click Add if you want to add a server IPv4 address to the list. Tap or click Remove to remove a selected server from the list. Tap or click Edit to edit the selected entry.

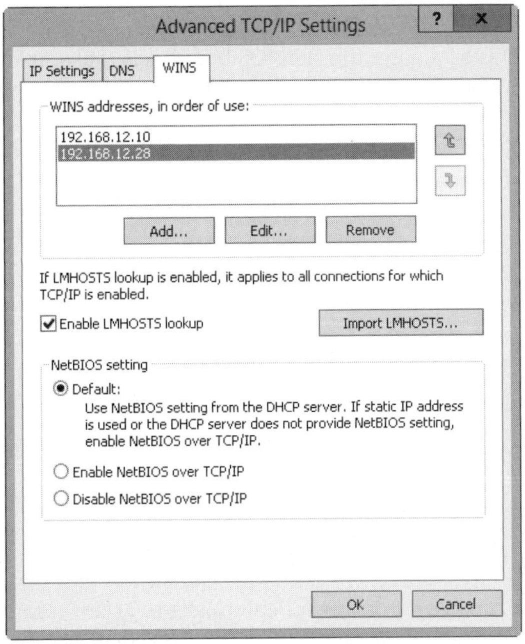

**Figure 19-4** Configure WINS resolution for NetBIOS computer names on the WINS tab of the Advanced TCP/IP Settings dialog box.

2. You can specify multiple servers, which are used in order, for WINS resolution. If the first server isn't available to respond to a NetBIOS name-resolution request, the next WINS server on the list is accessed, and so on. To change the position of a server in the list box, select it and then tap or click the Up or Down arrow button.

3. To enable LMHOSTS lookups, select the Enable LMHOSTS Lookup check box. If you want the computer to use an existing LMHOSTS file defined somewhere on the network, retrieve this file by tapping or clicking Import LMHOSTS. You generally will use LMHOSTS only when other name-resolution methods fail.

4.  WINS name resolution requires NetBIOS Over TCP/IP services. Select one of the following options to configure WINS name resolution using NetBIOS:

    ○  If you use DHCP and dynamic addressing, you can get the NetBIOS setting from the DHCP server. Select Default: Use NetBIOS Setting From The DHCP Server.

    ○  If you use a static IP address or the DHCP server does not provide NetBIOS settings, select Enable NetBIOS Over TCP/IP.

    ○  If WINS and NetBIOS are not used on the network, select Disable NetBIOS Over TCP/IP. This eliminates the NetBIOS broadcasts that would otherwise be sent by the computer.

5.  Tap or click OK two times, and then tap or click OK. As necessary, repeat this process for other network adapters.

> **Note**
>
> LMHOSTS files are maintained locally on a computer-by-computer basis, which can eventually make them unreliable. Rather than relying on LMHOSTS, ensure that your DNS and WINS servers are configured properly and are accessible to the network for centralized administration of name-resolution services.

# Managing network connections

Local area connections make it possible for computers to access resources on the network and the Internet. One network connection is created automatically for each network adapter installed on a computer. This section examines techniques you can use to manage these connections.

## Checking the status, speed, and activity for network connections

To check the status of a network connection, follow these steps:

1.  In Control Panel, tap or click View Network Status And Tasks under the Network And Internet heading.

2. In Network And Sharing Center, tap or click Change Adapter Settings. In Network Connections, press and hold or right-click the connection you want to work with and then tap or click Status.

3. This displays the Status dialog box for the connection. If the connection is disabled or the media is unplugged, you won't be able to access this dialog box. Enable the connection or connect the network cable to resolve the problem, and then try to display the status dialog box again.

The General tab of this dialog box, shown in Figure 19-5, provides useful information regarding the following:

- **IPv4 Connectivity**   The current IPv4 connection state and type. You'll typically see the status as Local when connected to an internal network or Not Connected when not connected to a network.

- **IPv6 Connectivity**   The current IPv6 connection state and type. You'll typically see the status as Local when connected to an internal network or Not Connected when not connected to a network.

- **Media State**   The state of the media. Because the Status dialog box is available only when the connection is enabled, you'll typically see this as Enabled.

- **Duration**   The amount of time the connection has been established. If the duration is fairly short, the user either recently connected to the network or the connection was recently reset.

- **Speed**   The speed of the connection. This should read 100.0 Mbps for 100-Mbps connections, 1 gigabit per second (Gbps) for 1-gigabit connections, and 10 Gbps for a 10-gigabyte connection. An incorrect setting can affect the computer's performance.

- **Bytes**   The number of bytes sent and the number received by the connection. As the computer sends or receives packets, you'll see the computer icons light up to indicate the flow of traffic.

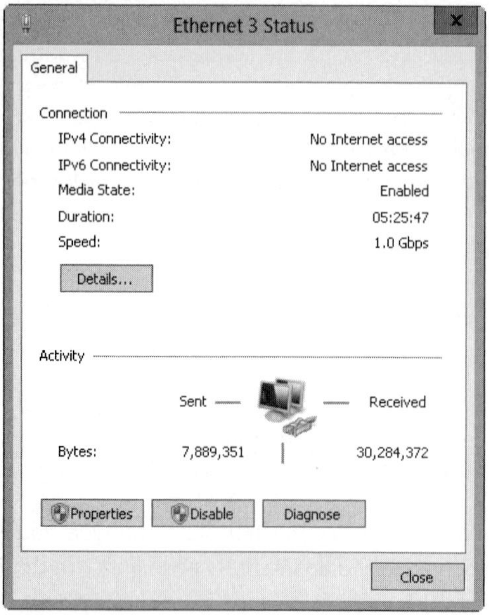

**Figure 19-5** The General tab of the Status dialog box for the connection provides access to summary information regarding connections, properties, and support.

## Viewing network configuration information

You can view the current configuration for network adapters in several ways. To view configuration settings using the Status dialog box for the connection, follow these steps:

1. In Control Panel, tap or click View Network Status And Tasks under the Network And Internet heading.

2. In Network And Sharing Center, tap or click Change Adapter Settings. In Network Connections, press and hold or right-click the connection you want to work with and then tap or click Status. This displays the Status dialog box for the connection. If the connection is disabled or the media is unplugged, you won't be able to access this dialog box. Enable the connection or connect the network cable to resolve the problem, and then try to display the status dialog box again.

3. Tap or click Details to view the following detailed information about the IP address configuration:

   ○ **Connection-Specific DNS Suffix**   The DNS suffix used to resolve unqualified computer names (if any) for this connection.

   ○ **Description**   Normally, shows the descriptive name of the network adapter.

○ **Physical Address**    The machine or Media Access Control (MAC) address of the network adapter. This address is unique for each network adapter.

○ **IPv4 IP Address**    The IPv4 address assigned for IPv4 networking.

○ **IPv4 Subnet Mask**    The subnet mask used for IPv4 networking.

○ **IPv4 Default Gateway**    The IPv4 address of the default gateway used for IPv4 networking.

○ **IPv4 DNS Servers**    IPv4 addresses for DNS servers used with IPv4 networking.

○ **IPv4 WINS Servers**    IPv4 addresses for WINS servers used with IPv4 networking.

○ **IPv4 DHCP Server**    The IPv4 address of the DHCPv4 server from which the current lease was obtained (DHCPv4 only).

○ **Lease Obtained**    A date and time stamp for when the DHCPv4 lease was obtained (DHCPv4 only, when enabled).

○ **Lease Expires**    A date and time stamp for when the DHCPv4 lease expires (DHCPv4 only, when enabled).

○ **NetBIOS Over Tcpip Enabled**    Shows whether NetBIOS over TCP/IP is enabled.

○ **Link-Local IPv6 Address**    Shows the computer's link-local IPv6 address.

○ **IPv6 Default Gateway**    The IPv6 address of the default gateway used for IPv6 networking.

○ **IPv6 DNS Servers**    The IPv6 address of the DNS servers used with IPv6 networking.

You can also use the IPCONFIG command to view advanced configuration settings. To do so, follow these steps:

1. Type **cmd** in the Apps Search field, and press Enter.

2. At the command line, type **ipconfig /all** to see detailed configuration information for all network adapters configured on the computer.

> **Note**
> The command prompt is started in standard user mode. You also can enter the command at the PowerShell prompt.

INSIDE OUT Getting IP configuration in Windows PowerShell

Although you can use Windows PowerShell to obtain similar information, there really is no single-command substitute for **ipconfig /all**. That said, you can enter **Get-NetIPAddress –AddressState Preferred** to view information about all valid and active IP addresses a computer is using. You also can enter **Get-NetIPInterface –ConnectionState Connected | FL –Property \*** to get detailed information about each active and connected interface.

## Enabling and disabling network connections

Local area connections are created and connected automatically. If you want to disable a connection so that it cannot be used, follow these steps:

1.  In Control Panel, tap or click View Network Status And Tasks under the Network And Internet heading.

2.  In Network And Sharing Center, tap or click Change Adapter Settings. In Network Connections, press and hold or right-click the connection and select Disable to deactivate the connection and disable it.

3.  If you want to enable the connection later, press and hold or right-click the connection in Network Connections and select Enable.

If you want to disconnect from a network or start another connection, follow these steps:

1.  In Control Panel, tap or click View Network Status And Tasks under the Network And Internet heading.

2.  In Network And Sharing Center, tap or click Change Adapter Settings. In Network Connections, press and hold or right-click the connection and select Disconnect. Typically, only remote access or wireless connections have a Disconnect option.

3.  If you want to activate the connection later, press and hold or right-click the connection in Network Connections and select Connect.

## Renaming network connections

Windows Server 2012 initially assigns default names for network connections. In Network Connections, you can rename the connections at any time by pressing and holding or right-clicking the connection, selecting Rename, and then typing a new connection name. If a computer has multiple network connections, proper naming can help you and others better understand the uses of a particular connection.

# Troubleshooting and testing network settings

Windows Server 2012 includes many tools for troubleshooting and testing TCP/IP connectivity. This section looks at automated diagnostics, basic tests that you should perform whenever you install or modify a computer's network settings, and techniques for resolving difficult networking problems involving DHCP and DNS. The final section shows you how to perform detailed network diagnostics testing.

## Diagnosing and resolving network connection problems

Occasionally, network cables can get unplugged or the network adapter might experience a problem that temporarily prevents it from working. After you plug the cable back in or solve the adapter problem, the connection should automatically reconnect. To diagnose network connection problems, follow these steps:

1. In Control Panel, tap or click View Network Status And Tasks under the Network And Internet heading.

2. In Network And Sharing Center, tap or click Change Adapter Settings.

3. Press and hold or right-click the connection you want to work with, and select Diagnose.

Windows Network Diagnostics will then try to identify the problem. A list of possible solutions is provided for identifiable configuration problems. Some solutions provide automated fixes you can execute by tapping or clicking the solution. Other solutions require manual fixes, such as might be required if you need to reset a network router or broadband modem. If your actions don't fix the problem, refer to other appropriate parts of this troubleshooting section.

## Diagnosing and resolving Internet connection problems

Because of the many interdependencies between services, protocols, and configuration settings, troubleshooting network problems can be difficult. Fortunately, Windows Server 2012 includes a powerful network diagnostics tool for pinpointing problems that relate to the following:

- General network connectivity problems

- Internet service settings for email, newsgroups, and proxies

- Settings for modems, network clients, and network adapters

- DNS, DHCP, and WINS configuration

- Default gateways and IP addresses

To diagnose Internet connection problems, follow these steps:

1. In Control Panel, tap or click View Network Status And Tasks under the Network And Internet heading.

2. Tap or click Troubleshoot Problems, and then tap or click a troubleshooter to run, such as Incoming Connections or Network Adapter.

3. When the troubleshooter starts, tap or click Next.

Windows Network Diagnostics will then try to identify the problem. If identifiable configuration problems exist, a list of possible solutions is provided. Some solutions provide automated fixes you can execute by tapping or clicking the solution. Other solutions require manual fixes, such as might be required if you need to reset a network router or broadband modem. If your actions don't fix the problem, refer to other appropriate parts of this troubleshooting section.

## Performing basic network tests

Whenever you install a new computer or make configuration changes to the computer's network settings, you should test the configuration. The most basic TCP/IP test is to use the PING command or the Test-Connection cmdlet to test the computer's connection to the network. PING is a command-line command. To use it, type **ping <*host*>** at the command prompt or **Test-Connection <*host*>** at a PowerShell prompt, where <*host*> is either the computer name or the IP address of the host computer you're trying to reach. Keep in mind that Test-Connection is a wrapper for Get-WMIObject Win32_PingStatus, so whether you type **Ping** at a command prompt or Test-Connection at a PowerShell prompt, you are using PING.

You can use the following methods to test the configuration using PING:

- **Try to PING IP addresses**   If the computer is configured correctly and the host you're trying to reach is accessible to the network, PING should receive a reply, as long as pinging is allowed by the computer's firewall. If ping can't reach the host or is blocked by a firewall, PING times out.

- **On domains that use WINS, try to PING NetBIOS computer names**   If NetBIOS computer names are resolved correctly by PING, the NetBIOS facilities, such as WINS, are correctly configured for the computer.

- **On domains that use DNS, try to PING DNS host names**    If fully qualified DNS host names are resolved correctly by PING, DNS name resolution is configured properly.

You might also want to test network browsing for the computer. If the computer is a member of a domain and computer browsing is enabled throughout the domain, log on to the computer and then use File Explorer or Network Explorer to browse other computers in the domain. Afterward, log on to a different computer in the domain and try to browse the computer you just configured. These tests tell you if the DNS resolution is being handled properly in the local environment. If you can't browse, check the configuration of the DNS services and protocols.

In some cases, discovering and sharing might be set to block discovery. You'll need to allow discovery to resolve this by following these steps:

1. In Control Panel, tap or click View Network Status And Tasks under the Network And Internet heading.

2. In Network And Sharing Center, in the left pane, tap or click Change Advanced Sharing Settings.

3. You'll then see options for configuring the computer's sharing and discovery settings for each network profile. Manage the settings for each profile as appropriate. For example, if network discovery is disabled for a profile and should be enabled, tap or click the related Turn On Network Discovery option.

4. Tap or click Save Changes.

## Diagnosing and resolving IP addressing problems

The current IP address settings of a computer can be obtained as discussed in "Viewing network configuration information" earlier in this chapter. If a computer is having problems accessing network resources or communicating with other computers, an IP addressing problem might exist. Take a close look at the IP address currently assigned, as well as other IP address settings, and use the following tips to help in your troubleshooting:

- If the IPv4 address currently assigned to the computer is in the range 169.254.0.1 to 169.254.255.254, the computer is using Automatic Private IP Addressing (APIPA). An automatic private IP address is assigned to a computer when it is configured to use DHCP and its DHCP client cannot reach a DHCP server. When using APIPA, Windows Server will automatically periodically check for a DHCP server to become available. If a computer doesn't eventually obtain a dynamic IP address, the network connection usually has a problem. Check the network cable, and if necessary trace the cable back to the switch or hub into which it connects.

Chapter 19

- If the IPv4 address and the subnet mask of the computer are currently set as 0.0.0.0, the network is either disconnected or someone attempted to use a static IP address that duplicated another IP address already in use on the network. In this case, you should access Network Connections and determine the state of the connection. If the connection is disabled or disconnected, this should be shown. Press and hold or right-click the connection, and select Enable or Diagnose as appropriate. If the connection is already enabled, you need to modify the IP address settings for the connection.

- If the IP address is dynamically assigned, make sure that another computer on the network isn't using the same IP address. You can do this by disconnecting the network cable for the computer you are working with and pinging the IP address in question. If you receive a response from the PING test, you know that another computer is using the IP address. This computer probably has an improper static IP address or a reservation that isn't set up properly.

- If the IP address appears to be set correctly, check the subnet mask, gateway, DNS, and WINS settings by comparing the network settings of the computer you are troubleshooting with those of a computer that is known to have a good network configuration. One of the biggest problem areas is the subnet mask. When subnetting is used, the subnet mask used in one area of the network might look very similar to that of another area of the network. For example, the subnet mask in one IPv4 area might be 255.255.255.240, and it might be 255.255.255.248 in another IPv4 area.

When you are using static IP addressing, you can check the current IPv4 or IPv6 settings by typing **ipconfig /all** at a command prompt. The display of the *ipconfig /all* command includes IPv4/IPv6 addresses, default routers, and DNS servers for all interfaces. You can also check IPv4 and IPv6 addressing separately. To check the IPv4 addressing configuration, type **netsh interface ipv4 show address**. To check IPv6 addressing, type **netsh interface ipv6 show address**. To use Netsh to show the configuration of a remote computer, use the **–r** *RemoteComputerName* command-line option. For example, to display the configuration of the remote computer named CORPSERVER26, you would type **netsh –r corpserver26 interface ipv4 show address**.

To make changes to the configuration of IP interfaces, use the **netsh interface ipv4 set interface** and **netsh interface ipv6 set interface** commands. To add the IP addresses of DNS servers, use the **netsh interface ipv4 add dns** and **netsh interface ipv6 add dns** commands.

## Diagnosing and resolving routing problems

As part of troubleshooting, you can verify the reachability of local and remote destinations. You can ping your default router by its IPv4 or IPv6 address. You can obtain the local IPv4 address of your default router by typing **netsh interface ipv4 show route** at a command prompt or **get-netroute –addressfamily ipv4** at a PowerShell prompt. You can obtain the link-local IPv6 address of your default router by typing **netsh interface ipv6 show route** at a command prompt or **get-netroute –addressfamily ipv6** at a PowerShell prompt. Ping-ing the default router tests whether you can reach local nodes and whether you can reach the default router, which forwards IP packets to remote nodes.

When you ping the default IPv6 router, you must specify the zone identifier (ID) for the interface on which you want the ICMPv6 Echo Request messages to be sent. The zone ID for the default router is listed when you enter the **ipconfig /all** command.

If you are able to ping your default router, ping a remote destination by its IPv4 or IPv6 address. If you are unable to ping a remote destination by its IP address, there might be a routing problem between your node and the destination node. Type **tracert –d *IPAddress*** to trace the routing path to the remote destination You use the **–d** command-line option to speed up the response by preventing Tracert from performing a reverse DNS query on every near-side router interface in the routing path.

The inability to reach a local or remote destination might be due to incorrect or missing routes in the local IP routing table. To view the local IP routing table, type the **netsh interface ipv4 show route** or **netsh interface ipv6 show route** command. Use the command output to verify that you have a route corresponding to your local subnet. The route with the lowest metric is used first. If you have multiple default routes with the same lowest metric, you might need to modify your IP router configuration so that the default route with the lowest metric uses the interface that connects to the correct network.

You can add a route to the IP routing table by using the **netsh interface ipv4 add route** or **netsh interface ipv6 add route** command. To modify an existing route, use the **netsh interface ipv4 set route** or **netsh interface ipv6 set route** command. To remove an existing route, use the **netsh interface ipv6 delete route** or **netsh interface ipv6 delete route** command.

If you suspect a problem with router performance, use the **pathping –d *IPAddress*** command to trace the path to a destination and display information on packet losses for each router in the path. You use the **–d** command-line option to speed up the response by preventing Pathping from performing a reverse DNS query on every near-side router interface in the routing path.

# INSIDE OUT  Checking IPsec policies and Windows Firewall

The problem with reaching a destination node might be due to the configuration of Internet Protocol security (IPsec) or packet filtering. Check for IPsec policies that have been configured on the computer having the problem, on intermediate IPv6 routers, and on the destination computer. On computers running Windows Vista or later, connection security rules are configured using Windows Firewall With Advanced Security and IPsec policies are configured using the IP Security Policy Management snap-in for MMC.

In many cases, packet filtering is configured to allow specific types of traffic and discard all others, or to discard specific types of traffic and accept all others. Because of this, you might be able to view webpages on a web server but not ping the web server by its host name or IP address.

Each network connection configured on a computer can be enabled or disabled in Windows Firewall. When enabled, IPv4 and IPv6 drop incoming requests. During troubleshooting, you can disable Windows Firewall for a specific IPv4 or IPv6 interface with the **netsh interface ipv4 set interface interface=NameOrIndex firewall=disabled** and **netsh interface ipv6 set interface interface=NameOrIndex firewall=disabled** commands. You can also completely turn off Windows Firewall with the **netsh firewall set opmode disable** command. Don't forget to re-enable the firewall when you are done troubleshooting.

## Releasing and renewing DHCP settings

DHCP servers can assign many network configuration settings automatically, including IP addresses, default gateways, primary and secondary DNS servers, primary and secondary WINS servers, and more. When computers use dynamic addressing, they are assigned a lease on a specific IP address. This lease is good for a specific time period and must be renewed periodically. When the lease needs to be renewed, the computer contacts the DHCP server that provided the lease. If the server is available, the lease is renewed and a new lease period is granted. You can also renew leases manually as necessary on individual computers or by using the DHCP server itself.

Problems that prevent network communications can occur during the lease assignment and renewal process. If the server isn't available and cannot be reached before a lease expires, the IP address can become invalid. If this happens, the computer might use the alternate IP address configuration to set an alternate address, which in most cases has settings that are inappropriate and prevent proper communications. To resolve this problem, you need to release and then renew the DHCP lease.

Another type of problem occurs when users move around to various offices and subnets within the organization. While users are moving from location to location, their laptop or tablet might obtain DHCP settings from the wrong server. When the users return to their offices, the laptop or tablet might seem sluggish or perform incorrectly because of the settings assigned by the DHCP server at another location. If this happens, you need to release and then renew the DHCP lease. (Alternatively, because computers don't retain their dynamically assigned settings, you can simply restart the computer.)

You can use the graphical interface to release and renew DHCP leases by following these steps:

1.  In Control Panel, tap or click View Network Status And Tasks under the Network And Internet heading.

2.  In Network And Sharing Center, tap or click Change Adapter Settings. In Network Connections, press and hold or right-click the connection you want to work with and then select Diagnose.

3.  After Windows Network Diagnostics tries to identify the problem, a list of possible solutions is provided. If the computer has one or more dynamically assigned IP addresses, one of the solutions should be Automatically Get New IP Settings. Tap or click this option.

You can also follow these steps to use the IPCONFIG command to renew and release settings:

1.  Open an elevated command prompt.

2.  To release the current settings for all network adapters, type **ipconfig /release** at the command line. Then renew the lease by typing **ipconfig /renew**.

3.  To renew a DHCP lease for all network adapters, type **ipconfig /renew** at the command line.

4.  You can check the updated settings by typing **ipconfig /all** at the command line.

Chapter 19

**TROUBLESHOOTING**

Identifying a specific interface

If a computer has multiple network adapters and you only want to work with one or a subset of the adapters, specify all or part of the connection name after the **ipconfig /renew** or **ipconfig /release** command. Use the asterisk as a wildcard to match any characters in a connection's name. For example, if you want to renew the lease for all connections with names starting with *Loc*, type the command **ipconfig /renew Loc***. If you want to release the settings for all connections containing the word *Network*, type the command **ipconfig /release *Network***.

## Diagnosing and fixing name-resolution issues

When you can reach a destination using an IP address but not reach a host using a host name, you might have a problem with host-name resolution. Typically, name-resolution issues have to do with improper configuration of the DNS client or problems with DNS registration. You can use the following tasks to troubleshoot problems with DNS name resolution:

- Verify DNS configuration.

- Test DNS name resolution with the Ping tool.

- Use the Nslookup tool to view DNS server responses.

- Display and flush the DNS client resolver cache.

On the computer having DNS name-resolution problems, verify the following information:

- Host name

- The primary DNS suffix

- DNS suffix search list

- Connection-specific DNS suffixes

- DNS servers

You can obtain this information by typing **ipconfig /all** at a command prompt. To obtain information about which DNS names should be registered in DNS, type **netsh interface ip show dns**.

Computers running Windows Vista and later support DNS traffic over IPv6. By default, IPv6 configures the well-known, site-local addresses of DNS servers at FEC0:0:0:FFFF::1, FEC0:0:0:FFFF::2, and FEC0:0:0:FFFF::3. To add the IPv6 addresses of your DNS servers, use the properties of the Internet Protocol Version 6 (TCP/IPv6) component in Network Connections or the **netsh interface ipv6 add dns** command. To register the appropriate DNS names as IP address resource records with DNS dynamic update, use the **ipconfig /registerdns** command. Computers running Windows XP or Windows Server 2003 do not support DNS traffic over IPv6.

TCP/IP checks the DNS client resolver cache before sending DNS name queries. The DNS resolver cache maintains a history of DNS lookups that have been performed when a user accesses network resources using TCP/IP. This cache contains forward lookups, which provide host name–to–IP address resolution, and reverse lookups, which provide IP address–to–host name resolution. After a DNS entry is stored in the resolver cache for a particular DNS host, the local computer no longer has to query external servers for DNS information on that host. This enables the computer to resolve DNS requests locally, providing a quicker response.

How long entries are stored in the resolver cache depends on the Time to Live (TTL) value assigned to the record by the originating server. To view current records and see the remaining TTL value for each record, type **ipconfig /displaydns** in an elevated command prompt. These values are given as the number of seconds that a particular record can remain in the cache before it expires. These values are continually being counted down by the local computer. When the TTL value reaches zero, the record expires and is removed from the resolver cache.

Occasionally, you'll find that you need to clear out the resolver cache to remove old entries and enable computers to check for updated DNS entries before the normal expiration and purging process takes place. Typically, this happens because server IP addresses have changed and the current entries in the resolver cache point to the old addresses rather than the new ones. Sometimes the resolver cache itself can get out of sync, particularly when DHCP has been misconfigured.

# INSIDE OUT  Decreasing TTLs for important DNS records

Skilled administrators know that several weeks in advance of the actual change, they should start to decrease the TTL values for important DNS records that are going to be changed. Typically, this means reducing the TTL from a number of days (or weeks) to a number of hours, which allows for quicker propagation of the changes to computers that have cached the related DNS records. After the change is completed, administrators should restore the original TTL value to reduce renewal requests.

In most cases, you can resolve problems with the DNS resolver cache by either flushing the cache or reregistering DNS. When you flush the resolver cache, all DNS entries are cleared out of the cache and new entries are not created until the next time the computer performs a DNS lookup on a particular host or IP address. When you reregister DNS, Windows Server attempts to refresh all current DHCP leases and then performs a lookup on each DNS entry in the resolver cache. By looking up each host or IP address again, the entries are renewed and reregistered in the resolver cache. You'll generally want to flush the cache completely and allow the computer to perform lookups as needed. Reregister DNS only when you suspect problems with DHCP and the DNS resolver cache.

You can test DNS name resolution by pinging a destination using its host name or fully qualified domain name (FQDN). If an incorrect IP address is shown, you can flush the DNS resolver cache and use the Nslookup tool to determine the set of addresses returned in the DNS Name Query Response message.

You can use the IPCONFIG command to flush and reregister entries in the DNS resolver cache by following these steps:

1. Start an elevated command prompt.

2. To clear out the resolver cache, type **ipconfig /flushdns** at the command line.

3. To renew DHCP leases and reregister DNS entries, type **ipconfig /registerdns** at the command line.

4. When the tasks are complete, you can check your work by typing **ipconfig /displaydns** at the command line.

To start Nslookup, type **Nslookup** at a command prompt. At the *Nslookup* > prompt, use the **set d2** command to get detailed information about DNS response messages. Then use Nslookup to look up the desired FQDN. Look for A and AAAA records in the detailed display of the DNS response messages.

With IPv6, the DNS client maintains a neighbor's cache of recently resolved link-layer addresses as well as a standard resolver cache. To display the current contents of the neighbor cache, enter **netsh interface ipv6 show neighbors**. To flush the neighbor's cache, enter **netsh interface ipv6 delete neighbors**.

For IPv6, the DNS client also maintains a destination cache. The destination cache stores next-hop IPv6 addresses for destinations. To display the current contents of the destination cache, type **netsh interface ipv6 show destinationcache** command. To flush the destination cache, type **netsh interface ipv6 delete destinationcache**.

# Managing DHCP

M OST Microsoft Windows networks should be configured to use Dynamic Host Configuration Protocol (DHCP). DHCP simplifies administration and makes it easier for users to get their computer on the organization's network. How does DHCP do this? DHCP is a protocol that allows client computers to start up and automatically receive an Internet Protocol (IP) address and other related Transmission Control Protocol/Internet Protocol (TCP/IP) settings such as the subnet mask, default gateway, Domain Name System (DNS) server addresses, and Windows Internet Naming Service (WINS) server addresses. DHCP servers can assign a dynamic IP version 4 (IPv4), IP version 6 (IPv6), or both addresses to any of the network interface cards (NICs) on a computer.

## DHCP essentials

DHCP is a standards-based protocol that was originally defined by the Internet Engineering Task Force (IETF) and based on the Bootstrap Protocol (BOOTP). It has been implemented on a variety of operating systems, including UNIX and Windows. Because DHCP is a client/server protocol, a server component and a client component are necessary to implement the protocol on a network. To make it easier to deploy DHCP in the enterprise, all server editions of Windows Server 2012 include the DHCP Server service, which can be installed to support DHCP, and all current versions of the Windows operating system automatically install the DHCP Client service as part of TCP/IP.

A computer that uses dynamic IP addressing and configuration is called a *DHCP client*. When you boot a DHCP client, a 32-bit IPv4 address, a 128-bit IPv6 address, or both can be retrieved from a pool of IP addresses defined for the network's DHCP server. It's the job of the DHCP server to maintain a database about the IP addresses that are available and the related configuration information. When an IP address is given out to a client, the client is said to have a *lease* on the IP address. The term "lease" is used because the assignment generally is not permanent. The DHCP server sets the duration of the lease when the lease is granted and can also change it later as necessary, such as when the lease is renewed.

DHCP also provides a way to assign a lease on an address permanently. To do this, you can create a reservation by specifying the IP address to reserve and the unique identifier of the computer that will hold the IP address. The reservation thereafter ensures that the client computer with the specified device address always gets the designated IP address. With IPv4, you specify the necessary unique identifier using the Media Access Control (MAC) address of the network card. With IPv6, you specify the DHCP unique identifier for the DHCPv6 client and the identity association identifier (IAID) being used by the DHCPv6 client.

### Note

MAC addresses are tied to the network interface card (NIC) of a computer. If you remove a NIC or install an additional NIC on a computer, the MAC address of the new or additional card will be different from the address of the original NIC.

## Consider DHCP for non-DHCP member servers

You'll find that configuring member servers to use DHCP and then assigning them a reservation is an easy way to ensure that member servers have a fixed IP address while maintaining the flexibility provided by DHCP. After the member servers are configured for DHCP, they get all of their TCP/IP options from DHCP, including their IP addresses. If you ever need to change their addressing, you can do this from within DHCP rather than on each member server—and changing IP addressing and other TCP/IP options in one location is much easier than having to do so in multiple locations. Keep in mind that some server applications or roles might require a static IP address in order to work properly.

Microsoft recommends that a single DHCP server service no more than 10,000 clients. You define a set of IP addresses that can be assigned to clients using a *scope*. A scope is a pool of IPv4 or IPv6 addresses and related configuration options. The IP addresses set in a scope are contiguous and are associated with a specific subnet mask or network prefix length. To define a subset of IP addresses within a scope that should not be used, you can specify an *exclusion*. An exclusion defines a range of IP addresses that you can exclude so that it isn't assigned to client computers.

All current releases of Windows Server support integration of DHCP with dynamic DNS. When configured, this ensures that the client's DNS record is updated when it receives a new IP address. To ensure that client names can be resolved to IP addresses, you should configure the integration of DHCP and DNS.

DHCP can be integrated with the Routing and Remote Access Service (RRAS). When configured, dial-up networking clients or virtual private network (VPN) clients can log on to the network remotely and use DHCP to configure their IP address and TCP/IP options. The server managing their connection to the network is called a *remote access server*, and it is the responsibility of this server to obtain blocks of IP addresses from a DHCP server for use by remote clients. If a DHCP server is not available when the remote access server requests IP addresses, the remote clients are configured with Automatic Private IP Addressing (APIPA). APIPA works differently for IPv4 and IPv6.

## DHCPv4 and autoconfiguration

The availability of a DHCP server doesn't affect startup or logon (in most cases). DHCP clients can start and users can log on to the local machine even if a DHCP server isn't available. During startup, the DHCP client looks for a DHCP server. If a DHCP server is available, the client gets its configuration information from the server. If a DHCP server isn't available and the client's previous lease is still valid, the client pings the default gateway listed in the lease.

A successful ping tells the client that it's probably on the same network it was on when it was issued the lease, and the client will continue to use the lease as described previously. A failed ping tells the client that it might be on a different network. In this case, the client uses IP autoconfiguration. The client also uses IP autoconfiguration if a DHCP server isn't available and the previous lease has expired.

IPv4 autoconfiguration works like this:

1. The client computer selects an IP address from the Microsoft-reserved Class B subnet 169.254.0.0 and uses the subnet mask 255.255.0.0. Before using the IPv4 address, the client performs an Address Resolution Protocol (ARP) test to make sure that no other client is using this IPv4 address.

2. If the IPv4 address is in use, the client repeats step 1, testing up to 10 IPv4 addresses before reporting failure. When a client is disconnected from the network, the ARP test always succeeds. As a result, the client uses the first IPv4 address it selects.

3. If the IPv4 address is available, the client configures the NIC with this address. The client then attempts to contact a DHCP server, sending out a broadcast every five minutes to the network. When the client successfully contacts a server, the client obtains a lease and reconfigures the network interface.

# DHCPv6 and autoconfiguration

You can use DHCP to configure IPv6 addressing in two key ways: DHCPv6 stateful mode and DHCPv6 stateless mode. In DHCPv6 stateful mode, clients acquire their IPv6 address as well as their network-configuration parameters through DHCPv6. In DHCPv6 stateless mode, clients use autoconfiguration to acquire their IP address and acquire their network-configuration parameters through DHCPv6. You also can use a combination of both stateful and stateless address autoconfiguration.

A computer that uses dynamic IPv6 addressing, configuration, or both is called a *DHCPv6 client*. Windows Vista and later include a DHCPv6 client. Like DHCPv4, the components of a DHCPv6 infrastructure consist of DHCPv6 clients that request configuration, DHCPv6 servers that provide configuration, and DHCPv6 relay agents that convey messages between clients and servers when clients are on subnets that do not have a DHCPv6 server.

Unlike DHCPv4, you must also configure your IPv6 routers to support DHCPv6. A DHCPv6 client performs autoconfiguration based on the M and O flags in the Router Advertisement message sent by a neighboring router. When the Managed Address Configuration, or M, flag is set to 1, the client uses a configuration protocol to obtain stateful addresses. When the Other Stateful Configuration, or O, flag is set to 1, the client uses a configuration protocol to obtain other configuration settings.

Windows Vista and later obtain dynamic IPv6 addresses using a process similar to that used for dynamic IPv4 addresses. Typically, IPv6 autoconfiguration for DHCPv6 clients in stateful mode works like this:

1. The client computer selects a link-local unicast IPv6 address. Before using the IPv6 address, the client performs an ARP test to make sure that no other client is using this IPv6 address.

2. If the IPv6 address is in use, the client repeats step 1. Note that when a client is disconnected from the network, the ARP test always succeeds. As a result, the client uses the first IPv6 address it selects.

3. If the IPv6 address is available, the client configures the NIC with this address. The client then attempts to contact a DHCP server, sending out a broadcast every five minutes to the network. When the client successfully contacts a server, the client obtains a lease and reconfigures the network interface.

This is not how IPv6 autoconfiguration works for DHCPv6 clients in stateless mode. In stateless mode, DHCPv6 clients configure both link-local addresses and additional non-link-local addresses by exchanging Router Solicitation and Router Advertisement messages with neighboring routers. Although stateless address autoconfiguration is convenient, one reason for deploying a DHCPv6 server on an IPv6 network is because Windows does not support stateless address autoconfiguration of DNS server settings using Router Advertisement messages. Because of this, a DHCPv6 server is required if your Windows computers need to be able to perform DNS name resolution using IPv6. Additionally, keep in mind that link-local IPv6 addresses are always autoconfigured regardless of whether DHCPv6 is being used.

# DHCP security considerations

DHCP is inherently insecure. Anyone with access to the network can perform malicious actions that could cause problems for other clients trying to obtain IP addresses. A user could take the following actions:

- Initiate a denial of service (DoS) attack by requesting all available IP addresses or by using large numbers of IP addresses, either of which could make it impossible for other users to obtain IP addresses.

- Initiate an attack on DNS by performing a large number of dynamic updates through DHCP.

- Use the information provided by DHCP to set up rogue services on the network, such as using a non-Microsoft DHCP server to provide incorrect IP address information.

To reduce the risk of attacks, you should limit physical access to the network. Don't make it easy for unauthorized users to connect to the network. If you use wireless technologies, configure the network so that it doesn't broadcast the service set identifier (SSID) or use protected-access encryption, which prohibits wireless users from obtaining a DHCP lease until they provide an appropriate encryption key using strong data encryption. Wi-Fi Protected Access (WPA) and Wi-Fi Protected Access Version 2 (WPA2) are the preferred strong-data-encryption techniques.

To reduce the risk of a rogue DHCP server, configure the Active Directory on the network and use it to determine which DHCP servers are authorized to provide services and which aren't. By using Active Directory, any computer running a current Windows operating system must be authorized to provide DHCP services. After a server is authorized, it is available for clients to use. This, unfortunately, doesn't restrict the use of unauthorized servers running DHCP, but it is a start.

Unauthorized DHCP servers are detected by the DHCP Server service running on authorized DHCP servers, and they are tracked in the event logs with the event source Microsoft-Windows-DHCP-Server and the event ID 1042. Look also for event IDs 1098, 1100, 1101, 1103, 1105, 1107, 1109, 1110, and 1111. Tracking these events can help you prevent most of the accidental damage caused by either misconfigured DHCP servers or correctly configured DHCP servers running on the wrong network.

Chapter 20

In addition, the DHCP Server service should not be placed on an Active Directory domain controller if this can be avoided. The reason for this is because this changes security related to service locator (SRV) records, which domain controllers are responsible for publishing. SRV records detail the location of domain controllers, Kerberos servers, and other servers, and the changes to the security of these records when you install DHCP means that the records could be altered by any client on the network.

The reason this happens is because DHCP servers must be able to update client records dynamically if a client's IP address changes. Because of this, they are made members of the DNSUpdateProxy group, and members of this group do not have any security applied to objects they create in the DNS database. If you can't avoid placing DHCP on a domain controller, it is recommended that you remove the DHCP server from the DNSUpdateProxy group. This should help you avoid the security problem outlined here, but it will also prevent the DHCP server from dynamically updating client records in DNS when the client IP addresses change.

# DHCP and IPAM

When you want to manage your IP address space and track IP address usage trends, you can deploy IP Address Management (IPAM) servers. You can use IPAM to automatically discover DHCP and DNS servers, and then you can manage these servers using IPAM. Because auditing, reporting, and monitoring capabilities are key components of IPAM, you can more easily maintain the IP address space across the enterprise.

You deploy IPAM servers using a distributed approach, with an IPAM server deployed at every site in an enterprise, or a centralized model, with only a central IPAM server in an enterprise. Each IPAM server can have a secondary configured as a backup. Because there is no communication or database sharing between IPAM servers, you must customize the scope of discovery for each distributed IPAM server or filter the list of managed servers for each location.

IP Address Management (IPAM) Server is a feature that you can add using the Add Roles And Features Wizard. Several security groups are created when you install IPAM:

- **IPAM Users**   Members can view all information in server discovery, IP address space, operational events, and server management, but they cannot view IP address tracking information.

- **IPAM MSM Administrators**   IPAM Multi-Server Management (MSM) administrators have the privileges of IPAM Users and can also perform most IPAM management tasks.

- **IPAM ASM Administrators**   IPAM Address Space Management (ASM) administrators have the privileges of IPAM Users, can perform IPAM common management tasks, and can manage the IP address space.

- **IPAM IP Audit Administrators**   Members of this group have the privileges of IPAM Users, can perform IPAM common management tasks, and can view IP address-tracking information.

- **IPAM Administrators**   IPAM Administrators view all IPAM information and perform all IPAM tasks.

Each IPAM server periodically attempts to locate other servers within its scope of management. When new servers are discovered, you must choose whether these servers are managed and monitored by IPAM. With DHCP servers, IPAM allows you to monitor DHCP and configure certain server and scope properties. With DNS servers, IPAM allows you to monitor zone status and configure some properties. In addition to detecting DHCP and DNS servers, IPAM discovers domain controllers for monitoring purposes and Network Policy Servers for IP address tracking purposes.

These discovery tasks run daily as a scheduled task called DiscoveryTask, which is under Microsoft\Windows\IPAM in Task Scheduler. Other scheduled tasks for IPAM are

- **AddressUtilizationCollectionTask**   Runs every two hours, and collects address space utilization data from the DHCP servers

- **AuditTask**   Runs daily, and collects auditing information from DHCP and IPAM servers, as well as IP Lease Audit logs from domain controllers and Network Policy Servers

- **ConfigurationTask**   Runs every six hours, and collects configuration information from DHCP and DNS servers for ASM and MSM

- **ServerAvailabilityTask**   Runs every 15 minutes, and collects the service availability status for DHCP and DNS servers

After you install IPAM Server, you must provision IPAM to sets its scope of management. When you add the IPAM Server as a managed server or log on locally to the IPAM server, you can select the IPAM node in Server Manager and then tap or click Provision The IPAM Server to start the Provision IPAM Wizard. By default, IPAM is provisioned using Group Policy, which will be applied to managed servers by linking Group Policy Objects (GPOs) at the appropriate levels in Active Directory. One GPO is created for DHCP servers, another for DNS servers, and a third for domain controllers and Network Policy Servers. Follow the wizard steps, wait for provisioning to complete, and then, on the Completion page, verify that IPAM provisioning was successful. If it was, tap or click Close.

Chapter 20

In Server Manager, with the IPAM node selected, you can then do the following:

1.   Configure discovery settings.

2.   Start server discovery.

3.   Select or add servers to manage, and verify IPAM access to those servers.

4.   Use the Invoke-IpamGpoProvisioning cmdlet to create and link the GPOs.

# Planning DHCPv4 and DHCPv6 implementations

Planning a new DHCP implementation or revamping your existing DHCP implementation requires a good understanding of how DHCP works. You need to know the following information:

● How DHCP messages are sent and received

● How DHCP relay agents are used

● How multiple servers should be configured

These processes are essentially the same whether you are working with IPv4 or IPv6.

## DHCPv4 messages and relay agents

When a DHCP client is started, it uses network broadcasts to obtain or renew a lease from a DHCP server. These broadcasts are in the form of DHCP messages. A client obtains its initial lease as shown in Figure 20-1. Here, the client broadcasts a DHCP Discover message. All DHCP servers on the network respond to the broadcast with a DHCP Offer message, which offers the client an IP lease. The client accepts the first offer received by sending a DHCP Request message back to the server. The server accepts the request by sending the client a DHCP Acknowledgment message.

DHCP clients must renew their leases periodically, either at each restart or when 50 percent of the lease time has passed. If the renewal process fails, the client tries to renew the lease again when 87.5 percent of the lease time has passed. Renewing the lease involves the client sending the DHCP server a DHCP Request and the server accepting the request by sending a DHCP Acknowledgment. This streamlined communication process is shown in Figure 20-2.

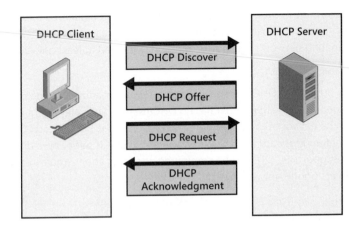

**Figure 20-1** Obtaining an initial lease.

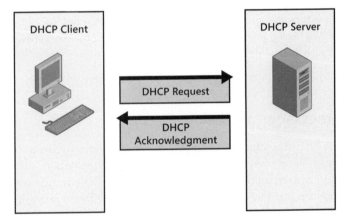

**Figure 20-2** Renewing a lease.

If a DHCP client is unable to reach a DHCP server at startup or to renew its lease, it pings the default gateway that was previously assigned. If the default gateway responds, the client assumes it is on the subnet from which the lease was originally obtained and continues to use the lease. If the default gateway doesn't respond, the client assumes it has been moved to a new subnet and that there is no DHCP server on this subnet. It then autoconfigures itself. The client will continue to check for a DHCP server when it is autoconfigured. By default, it does this by sending a DHCP Discover message every five minutes. If the client gets a DHCP Offer back from a DHCP server, it sends a DHCP Request to the server. When it gets back a DHCP Acknowledgment, it abandons its autoconfiguration and uses the address and other configuration settings sent by the DHCP server.

Typically, the messages sent by DHCP clients and servers are limited by the physical boundaries of the network. As a result, DHCP client broadcasts aren't routed and stay on only the originating network. In this configuration, you need at least one DHCP server per subnet.

To reduce the number of DHCP servers needed for your organization, you can configure a DHCP relay agent on any subnet that has no DHCP server. This relay agent is a router or a computer on the network that is configured to listen for DHCP broadcasts from clients on the local subnet and forward them as appropriate to a DHCP server on a different subnet. A router that supports BOOTP can be configured as a relay agent. You can also configure Windows servers on the network to act as DHCP relay agents.

### Relay agents are best for LANs

Relay agents work best in local area network (LAN) environments, where subnets are all in the same geographic location. In a wide area network (WAN) environment, where you are forwarding broadcasts across links, you might not want to use relay agents. If a WAN link goes down, clients won't be able to obtain or renew leases, and this could cause the clients to autoconfigure themselves.

## DHCPv6 messages and relay agents

The way a DHCPv6 client attempts DHCPv6-based configuration depends on the values of the M and O flags in received Router Advertisement messages. If there are multiple advertising routers for a given subnet, they should be configured to advertise the same stateless address prefixes and values of the M and O flags. IPv6 clients running Windows XP or Windows Server 2003 do not include a DHCPv6 client and therefore ignore the values of the M and O flags in received router advertisements.

You can configure an IPv6 router that is running Windows Vista or later to set the M flag to 1 in router advertisements with the **netsh interface ipv6 set interface** *InterfaceName* **managedaddress=enabled** command. Similarly, you can set the O flag to 1 in router advertisements with the **netsh interface ipv6 set interface** *InterfaceName* **otherstateful=enabled** command.

When you are working with the M and O flags, keep the following in mind:

- If both the M and O flags are set to 0, the network is considered not to have DHCPv6 infrastructure. Clients use router advertisements for non-link-local addresses and manual configuration to configure other settings.

- If both the M and O flags are set to 1, DHCPv6 is used for both IP addressing and other configuration settings. This combination is known as *DHCPv6 stateful mode*, in which DHCPv6 is assigning stateful addresses to IPv6 clients.

- If the M flag is set to 0 and the O flag is set to 1, DHCPv6 is used only to assign other configuration settings. Neighboring routers are configured to advertise non-link-local address prefixes from which IPv6 clients derive stateless addresses. This combination is known as *DHCPv6 stateless mode*.

- If the M flag is set to 1 and the O flag is set to 0, DHCPv6 is used for IP address configuration but not for other settings. Because IPv6 clients typically need to be configured with other settings, such as the IPv6 addresses of DNS servers, this combination typically is not used.

As with DHCPv4, DHCPv6 uses User Datagram Protocol (UDP) messages. DHCPv6 clients listen for DHCP messages on UDP port 546. DHCPv6 servers and relay agents listen for DHCPv6 messages on UDP port 547. The structure for DHCPv6 messages is much simpler than for DHCPv4, which had its origins in the BOOTP protocol to support diskless workstations.

DHCPv6 messages start with a 1-byte Msg-Type field that indicates the type of DHCPv6 message. This is followed by a 3-byte Transaction-ID field that is determined by a client and used to group the messages of a DHCPv6 message exchange together. Following the Transaction-ID field, DHCPv6 options are used to indicate client and server identification, addresses, and other configuration settings. Three fields are associated with each DHCPv6 option:

- A 2-byte Option-Code field indicates a specific option.

- A 2-byte Option-Len field indicates the length of the Option-Data field in bytes.

- An Option-Data field contains the data for the option.

Messages exchanged between relay agents and servers use a different message structure to transfer additional information. A 1-byte Hop-Count field indicates the number of relay agents that have received the message. A receiving relay agent can discard the message if it exceeds a configured maximum hop count. A 16-byte Link-Address field contains a non-link-local address that is assigned to an interface connected to the subnet on which the client is located. Based on the Link-Address field, the server can determine the correct address scope from which to assign an address. A 16-byte Peer-Address field contains the IPv6 address of the client that originally sent the message or the previous relay agent that relayed the message. Following the Peer-Address field are DHCPv6 options. A key option is the Relay Message option. This option provides an encapsulation of the messages being exchanged between the client and the server.

IPv6 does not have broadcast addresses. Because of this, the use of the limited broadcast address for some DHCPv4 messages has been replaced with the use of the All_DHCP_ Relay_Agents_and_Servers address of FF02::1:2 for DHCPv6. A DHCPv6 client attempting to discover the location of the DHCPv6 server on the network sends a Solicit message from its link-local address to FF02::1:2. If there is a DHCPv6 server on the client's subnet, it receives the Solicit message and sends an appropriate reply. If the client and server are on differ- ent subnets, a DHCPv6 relay agent on the client's subnet receiving the Solicit message will forward it to a DHCPv6 server.

## DHCP availability and fault tolerance

As part of planning, you must consider how many DHCP servers should be made available on the network. In most cases, you'll want to configure at least two DHCP servers. If they are configured properly, having multiple DHCP servers increases reliability and allows for load balancing and fault tolerance.

In a large enterprise, a server cluster can be your primary technique for ensuring DHCP availability and providing for fault tolerance. Here, if a DHCP server fails, the DHCP Server service can be failed over to another server in the cluster, allowing for the seamless transi- tion of DHCP services. Clustering uses a shared storage and is fairly complex to set up.

Although you can configure the DHCP Server service for failover on a cluster, much simpler fault-tolerance implementations are now available natively in the DHCP Server service on Windows Server 2012, and these implementations work with large networks as well as small and medium networks. The implementations use failover scopes that are shared between two DHCP servers to increase fault tolerance, provide redundancy over using a single DHCP server, and enable load balancing.

The way scopes are shared depends on the failover-scope configuration settings. You can optimize the shared scope for either load sharing using the Load Balancing setting or fault tolerance using the Hot Standby setting. Whether you optimize a failover scope for load balancing or fault tolerance, the DHCP servers involved replicate lease information between them to maintain the scope state. The key difference being how the member servers are used.

In a load-balancing configuration, the two servers simultaneously serve IP addresses and options to clients in the scope. The client requests are load balanced and shared between the two servers. More specifically, a failover scope optimized for load balancing has little or no time delay configured in its scope properties. With no time delay, both the primary and the secondary servers can respond to DHCP DISCOVER requests from DHCP clients. This allows the fastest server to respond to and accept a DHCPOFFER first. Fault tolerance con- tinues to be a part of the scope. If one of the servers becomes unavailable or overloaded and is unable to respond to requests, the other server handles requests and continues distributing addresses until the normal process is restored.

In a fault-tolerance configuration, there is an active partner and a standby partner for the scope. The active server is responsible for leasing IP addresses and options to all clients in the scope. The standby, also referred to as the *passive server*, assumes this responsibility if the active server becomes unavailable or doesn't respond in a timely manner. More specifically, a failover scope optimized for fault tolerance can have an extended time delay configured in its scope properties. This time delay causes the standby server to respond with a delay to DHCP DISCOVER requests from DHCP clients. The delay on the standby server allows the active server to respond to and accept the DHCPOFFER first. However, if the active server becomes unavailable or overloaded and is unable to respond to requests, the standby server handles requests and continues distributing addresses until the active server is available to service clients again. Because failover scopes are a server-side enhancement, no additional configuration is required for DHCP clients. Because scope state and lease information are automatically replicated between the active and passive servers, the state of the scope is always maintained.

> ## Important
>
> For failover scopes to work properly, time must be kept synchronized between the two servers in the failover relationship. If the time difference between the servers is greater than 60 seconds, you won't be able to complete the failover setup process. If the time doesn't remain synchronized, workloads might not be properly balanced between servers in failover scopes. Replication and other errors might occur as well.

> # INSIDE OUT   IPv6 doesn't use or require failover scopes
>
> Failover scopes apply only to IPv4 addresses. IPv6 clients typically determine their own IPv6 address using stateless IP autoconfiguration. In this mode, DHCP servers deliver only the DHCP option configuration and don't maintain lease state information. Further, you can ensure high availability for stateless DHCPv6 simply by setting up two servers with identical DHCPv6 option configurations.

## Failover scope: Load sharing

Whether you are configuring a failover scope for load sharing or fault tolerance, the scope you are configuring is shared between two servers, with each server having a relative weighting preference assigned as a load-balancing percentage. For load balancing, you'll typically want to use a weighting between 50/50 and 60/40. By configuring load sharing in this way, each DHCP server has an equal or nearly equal workload. To see how this would be implemented, consider the following example. The organization has two DHCP servers. Scope 1 is configured to use the IPv4 address range 192.168.10.1 to 192.168.10.254 and is 60/40 load balanced between Server A and Server B.

Here, 254 IP addresses are available, which could be used to service 200 or more clients. When a client starts up on the network, both DHCP servers respond. The client accepts the first IP address offered, which could be on either Server A or Server B and which is often the server that is closest to the client. Because both servers are configured to use the same IP address range, both servers can service clients on that subnet.

The way the workload is load balanced is through a small time delay configured in the scope properties for Server B. This small time delay ensures that Server A has a 60/40 preference over Server B for responding to DHCP DISCOVER requests from DHCP clients and accepting DHCPOFFER requests.

Keep in mind the length of the time delay is relative to the weighting for load balancing. The higher percentage of workload that one server has over the other, the stronger the preference for one server over the other. If one of the servers fails, lease information is maintained. Why? Lease information was replicated between both DHCP servers, and the remaining server has all the lease information.

As you can see, the load-sharing approach is designed to provide load balancing but also has some redundancy and fault tolerance built in. Because the lease information is replicated between the servers, the DHCP servers share a common pool of IP addresses and it doesn't matter whether one of the servers actually assigns more IP addresses than the other. The common IP address pool ensures that as long as there are available addresses, the addresses are available to be assigned by either server. Keep in mind that once all IP addresses in the pool have been allocated, no IP addresses are available to clients seeking new leases and they are configured to use automatic private IP addressing.

## Failover scope: Fault tolerance

As stated previously, whether you are configuring a failover scope for load sharing or fault tolerance, the scope you are configuring is shared between two servers, with each server having a relative weighting preference assigned as a load-balancing percentage. For fault tolerance, you'll typically want to use a weighting between 80/20 and 90/10. By configuring fault tolerance in this way, you ensure that one server handles most of the workload. Here, you have a primary DHCP server that assigns most of the IP addresses to clients and a backup DHCP server that assigns few or no IP addresses to clients. This situation is ideal when the DHCP servers are separated from each other, such as when the primary DHCP server is on the primary subnet and the backup DHCP server is on a centralized site.

To see how this would be implemented, consider the following example. The organization has two DHCP servers. Scope 1 is configured to use the IPv4 address range 192.168.10.1 to 192.168.10.254 and is 90/10 load balanced between Server A and Server B. Here, 254 IP addresses are again available, which could be used to service 200 or more clients—the bulk of which are located on the primary subnet. You are using a DHCP server in a central site as a backup for this scope. If the primary server goes down, the backup can respond to client requests and handle their leases. When the primary comes back online, it handles the majority of client leases because it is located on the primary subnet closer to the bulk of the client computers. Again, you achieve basic fault tolerance and availability.

The way the workload is load balanced is through an extended time delay configured in the scope properties for Server B. This extended time delay ensures Server A has a 90/10 preference over Server B for responding to DHCP DISCOVER requests from DHCP clients and accepting DHCPOFFER requests. As you can see, the fault-tolerance approach is designed to provide redundancy and ensure availability. Because the lease information is replicated between the servers, the DHCP servers share a common pool of IP addresses and it doesn't matter which server actually assigns the IP address to a client. The common IP address pool ensures that as long as there are available addresses, the addresses are available to be assigned by either server. Keep in mind that once all IP addresses in the pool have been allocated, no IP addresses are available to clients seeking new leases and they are configured to use automatic private IP addressing.

## Traditional split scopes

In addition to failover scopes, which are managed automatically by the DHCP Server service and share their entire pool of leasable addresses, you can continue to use existing split scopes, which don't share their pool of leasable addresses and generally require closer monitoring to ensure proper operations. You won't, however, be able to create new split scopes once you create a failover scope on a server. Why? Failover scopes are designed to replace split scopes.

With split scopes, you use two DHCP servers to make a specific percentage of a scope's IP addresses available on one server and the rest of the IP addresses available on another server. Here, each DHCP server is configured with an identical scope range but with different exclusions within that range. The first server gets the first portion of the scope's IP address range and excludes the rest. The second server gets the rest of the scope's IP address range and excludes the first portion.

As with failover scopes, you split scopes between two servers with one of two goals:

- Load balancing

- Fault tolerance

For load balancing, you split the scope equally or nearly so between the two servers. For fault tolerance, you assign most of the available IP addresses to the primary server and few IP addresses to the backup server. To see how split scopes could be implemented, consider the following example. The organization has two DHCP servers configured as follows:

- Server A's primary scope is configured to use the IPv4 address range 192.168.10.1 to 192.168.10.254 and has an exclusion range of 192.168.10.203 to 192.168.10.254.

- Server B's primary scope is configured to use the IPv4 address range 192.168.10.1 to 192.168.10.254 and has an exclusion range of 192.168.10.1 to 192.168.10.202.

Here, 254 IP addresses are available, which could be used to service 200 or more clients—the bulk of which are located on the primary subnet. You are using a DHCP server on a central site as a backup. If the primary server goes down, the backup can respond to client requests and handle their leases. When the primary comes back online, it handles the majority of client leases because it is located on the primary subnet closer to the bulk of the client computers. Thus, you achieve basic fault tolerance and availability.

Although this approach is designed to provide some redundancy and fault tolerance, it is possible that the primary would be offline too long and the backup DHCP server would run out of available IP addresses. If this were to happen, no IP addresses would be available to clients seeking new leases, and they would be configured to use APIPA.

Keep in mind that split scopes don't share their lease information. As a result, each server can assign only a subset of the available IP addresses. In this example, the primary server has 80 percent of the assignable IP addresses, while the backup server has only 20 percent. As a result, if the primary is offline too long, the backup could run out of assignable IP addresses much more quickly than it would if the entire pool of IP addresses was shared.

Because split scopes don't share their address pool, you might want to use a 100/100 failover technique. Here, you make twice as many IP addresses available as are needed. Thus, if you must provide DHCP services for 200 clients, you make at least 400 IP addresses available to those clients. As before, each DHCP server is configured with an identical scope range, but with different exclusions within that range. The first server gets the first half of the scope's IP address range and excludes the second half. The second server gets the second half of the scope's IP address range and excludes the first half.

To make twice as many IP addresses available as are needed, you must think carefully about the IP address class you use and would most likely want to use a Class A or Class B network. With this in mind, the organization's two DHCP servers might be configured as follows:

- Server A's primary scope is configured to use the IPv4 address range 10.0.1.1 to 10.0.10.254 and has an exclusion range of 10.0.6.1 to 10.0.10.254. You also must block the potential broadcast addresses in the nonexcluded range, so you also exclude 10.0.1.255, 10.0.2.255, 10.0.3.255, 10.0.4.255, and 10.0.5.255.

- Server B's primary scope is configured to use the IPv4 address range 10.0.1.1 to 10.0.10.254 and has an exclusion range of 10.0.1.1 to 10.0.5.254. You also must block the potential broadcast addresses in the nonexcluded range, so you also exclude 10.0.6.255, 10.0.7.255, 10.0.8.255, 10.0.9.255, and 10.0.10.255.

Here, more than 2500 IP addresses are available, which is more than two times what is needed to service the network's 1000 clients. When a client starts up on the network, both DHCP servers respond. The client accepts the first IP address offered, which could be on either Server A or Server B and which is often the server that is closest to the client. Because both servers are configured to use the same IP address range, both servers can service clients on that subnet. If one of the servers fails, a client using an IP address in the excluded range of the remaining server would be allowed to obtain a new lease.

Because more than two times as many IP addresses are available, every client on the network can obtain a lease even if one of the DHCP servers goes offline. Not only does this approach offer availability and fault tolerance, it gives you flexibility. You are able to take one of the DHCP servers offline and perform maintenance or upgrades without worrying about running out of available IP addresses. That said, split scopes are not as dynamic as failover scopes and failover scopes are the preferred technique to use for availability and fault tolerance.

> **Note**
>
> Split scopes apply only to IPv4 addresses. You cannot split a superscope or a scope that is part of a superscope. You create a split scope on the DHCP server that you want to act as the primary server by splitting an existing scope. During the split-scope creation process, you need to specify the DHCP server with which you want to split the primary server's scope. This additional server acts as the secondary server for the scope. Because split scopes are a server-side enhancement, no additional configuration is required for DHCP clients.

# Setting up DHCP servers

The approach you use to set up DHCP servers depends on many factors, including the number of clients on the network, the network configuration, and the Windows domain implementation you are using. From a physical-server perspective, the DHCP Server service doesn't use a lot of system resources and can run on just about any system configured with Windows Server 2012. The DHCP Server service is, in fact, often installed as an additional service on an existing infrastructure server or on an older server that isn't robust enough to offer other types of services. Either approach is fine as long as you remember the security precaution discussed previously about not installing DHCP on a domain controller if possible. However, I prefer to install the DHCP Server service on hardware that I know and trust. Rather than installing it on an older system that might fail, I install it on either a workstation-class system running Windows Server 2012 or an existing infrastructure server that can handle the additional load.

Speaking of server load, a single DHCP server can handle about 10000 clients and about 1000 scopes. This is, of course, if the system is a dedicated DHCP server with adequate processing power and memory. Because DHCP is so important for client startup and network access, I don't trust the service to a single server, and you shouldn't either. In most cases, you'll want to have at least two DHCP servers on the network. If you have multiple subnets, you might want two DHCP servers per subnet. However, configuring routers to forward DHCP broadcasts or having DHCP relay agents reduces the need for additional servers.

Many organizations have standby DHCP servers available as well. A standby DHCP server is a server that has the DHCP Server service fully configured but has its scopes deactivated. Then, if a primary DHCP server fails and can't be recovered immediately, the scopes can be activated to service clients on the network as necessary.

After you select the server hardware, you should plan the IP address ranges and exclusions you want to use. "Planning DHCPv4 and DHCPv6 implementations" earlier in this chapter should have given you some good ideas on how to configure IP address ranges and exclusions for availability and fault tolerance. At the implementation stage, don't forget about IP addresses that might have been or will be assigned to computers using static IP addresses. You should either specifically exclude these IP address ranges or simply not include them in the scopes you configure.

The way you set up DHCP services depends on whether the network in which the DHCP server will be placed is using Active Directory domains or workgroups. With Active Directory domains, you set up DHCP services by completing the following steps:

1. Installing the DHCP Server service

2. Authorizing the DHCP server in Active Directory

3. Configuring the DHCP server with the appropriate scopes, exclusions, reservations, and options

4. Activating the DHCP server's scopes

With workgroups, you don't need to authorize the DHCP server in Active Directory. This means the steps for setting up DHCP services look like this:

1. Installing the DHCP Server service

2. Configuring the DHCP server with the appropriate scopes, exclusions, reservations, and options

3. Activating the DHCP server's scopes

The sections that follow examine the related procedures in detail.

## Installing the DHCP Server service

You install the DHCP Server service as a server role. To install the DHCP Server service using the Add Roles and Features Wizard, follow these steps:

1. DHCP servers should be assigned a static IPv4 and IPv6 address on each subnet they will service and to which they are connected. Ensure the server has static IPv4 and IPv6 addresses.

2. In Server Manager, tap or click Manage and then tap or click Add Roles And Features, or select Add Roles And Features in the Quick Start pane. This starts the Add Roles And Features Wizard. If the wizard displays the Before You Begin page, read the Welcome text and then tap or click Next.

3. On the Installation Type page, Role-Based Or Feature-Based Installation is selected by default. Tap or click Next.

4. On the Server Selection page, you can choose to install roles and features on running servers or virtual hard disks. Only servers running Windows Server 2012 and that have been added for management in Server Manager are listed. Either select a server from the server pool or select a server from the server pool on which to mount a virtual hard disk (VHD). If you are adding roles and features to a VHD, tap or click Browse and then use the Browse For Virtual Hard Disks dialog box to locate the VHD. When you are ready to continue, tap or click Next.

5. On the Select Roles page, select DHCP Server. If additional features are required to install a role, you'll see an additional dialog box. Tap or click Add Features to close the dialog box, and add the required features to the server installation. When you are ready to continue, tap or click Next three times.

6. If the server on which you want to install the DHCP Server role doesn't have all the required binary source files, the server gets the files via Windows Update by default or from a location specified in Group Policy. To specify an alternate path for

the required source files, click the Specify An Alternate Source Path link, type that alternate path in the box provided, and then tap or click OK. For network shares, type the UNC path to the share, such as **\\CorpServer65\WinServer2012\**. For mounted Windows images, type the WIM path prefixed with *WIM:* and including the index of the image to use, such as **WIM:\\CorpServer65\WinServer2012\ install.wim:4**.

7. After you review the installation options and save them as necessary, tap or click Install to begin the installation process. The Installation Progress page tracks the progress of the installation. If you close the wizard, tap or click the Notifications icon in Server Manager and then tap or click the link provided to re-open the wizard. When Setup finishes installing the DHCP Server role, the Installation Progress page will be updated to reflect this. Review the installation details to ensure that all phases of the installation were completed successfully.

8. As stated in the Post-Deployment Configuration task panel, additional configuration is required for DHCP servers. Tap or click the Complete DHCP Configuration link. This starts the DHCP Post-Install Configuration Wizard.

9. The Description page states the DHCP Administrators and DHCP Users groups will be created in the domain for delegation of DHCP Server administration. Additionally, if the DHCP server is joined to a domain, the server will be authorized in Active Directory. Tap or click Next.

10. On the Authorization page, do one of the following to specify the credentials to use to authorize the DHCP server in Active Directory:

   ○ Your current user name is shown in the User Name text box. If you have administrator privileges in the domain that the DHCP server is a member of and you want to use your current credentials, tap or click Commit to attempt to authorize the server using these credentials.

   ○ If you want to use alternate credentials or if you are unable to authorize the server using your current credentials, select Use Alternate Credentials and then tap or click Specify. In the Windows Security dialog box, enter the user name and password for the authorized account and then tap or click OK. Tap or click Commit to attempt to authorize the server using these credentials.

   ○ If you want to authorize the DHCP server later, select Skip AD Authorization and then tap or click Commit. Keep in mind that in domains, only authorized DHCP servers can provide dynamic IP addresses to clients.

11. When the wizard finishes the post-install configuration, review the installation details to ensure tasks were completed successfully and then tap or click Close. Next, you

need to restart the DHCP Server service on the DHCP server so that the DHCP Administrators and DHCP Users groups can be used. To do this, tap or click DHCP in the left pane of Server Manager. Next, in the main pane, on the Servers panel, select the DHCP server. Finally, on the Services panel, press and hold or right-click the entry for the DHCP server and then tap or click Restart Service.

12. To complete the installation, you need to do the following:

   ○ If the server has multiple network cards, review the server bindings and specify the connections that the DHCP server supports for servicing clients. See "Binding the DHCP Server service to a network interface" later in this chapter.

   ○ Configure server options to assign common configuration settings for DHCP clients, including 003 Router, 006 DNS Servers, 015 DNS Domain Name, and 044 WINS/NBNS Servers. See "Configuring TCP/IP options" later in the chapter.

   ○ Create and activate any DHCP scopes that the server will use, as discussed in "Creating and configuring scopes" later in the chapter.

After you install the DHCP Server service, the DHCP console is available. In Server Manager, tap or click Tools and then tap or click DHCP to open the DHCP console, shown in Figure 20-3. The main window is divided into two panes. The left pane lists the DHCP servers in the domain according to their fully qualified domain name (FQDN). You can expand a server listing to show subnodes for IPv4 and IPv6. If you expand the IP nodes, you'll see the scopes and options defined for the related IP version. The right pane shows the expanded view of the current selection.

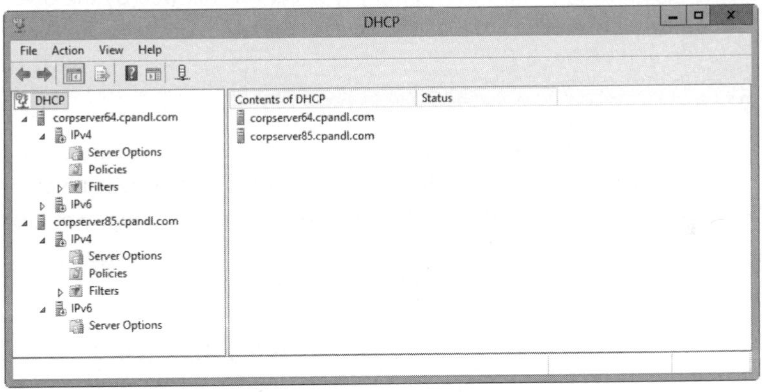

**Figure 20-3** The DHCP console.

When you start the DHCP console, you are connected directly to a local DHCP server, but you won't see entries for remote DHCP servers. You can connect to remote servers by pressing and holding or right-clicking DHCP in the console tree, and then tapping or clicking Add Server. In the Add Server dialog box, select This Server, type the IP address or computer name of the DHCP server you want to manage, and then tap or click OK. An entry for the DHCP server is added to the console tree.

The command-line counterpart to the DHCP console is the Netsh DHCP command. From the command prompt on a computer running Windows Server 2012, you can use Netsh DHCP to perform all the tasks available in the DHCP console as well as to perform some additional tasks that can't be performed in the DHCP console. To start Netsh DHCP and access a particular DHCP server, follow these steps:

1.  Start a command prompt, and then type **netsh** to start Netsh. The command prompt changes to netsh>.

2.  Access the DHCP context within Netsh by typing **dhcp**. The command prompt changes to netsh dhcp>.

3.  Type **server** followed by the Universal Naming Convention (UNC) name or IP address of the DHCP server, such as **\\corpsvr02** or **\\192.168.1.50**. If the DHCP server is in a different domain from your logon domain, you should type the fully qualified domain name (FQDN) of the server, such as **\\corpsvr02.cpandl.com**.

4.  The command prompt changes to netsh dhcp server>. You can now work with the selected server. If you later want to work with a different server, you can do this without having to start over. Simply type **server** followed by the UNC name or IP address of that server.

> **Note**
>
> Technically, you don't need to type \\ when you specify an IP address. You must, however, type \\ when you specify a server's name or FQDN. Because of this discrepancy, you might want to use \\ all the time so that you remember that it is needed.

## Authorizing DHCP servers in Active Directory

Before you can use a DHCP server in an Active Directory domain, you must authorize the server in Active Directory. In the DHCP console, any unauthorized DHCP server to which you connect will have an icon showing a red down arrow. Authorized DHCP servers have an icon showing a green up arrow.

New DHCP servers are not authorized automatically. In the DHCP console, you can authorize a DHCP server by pressing and holding or right-clicking the server entry in the console tree and selecting Authorize. To remove the authorization later, press and hold or right-click the server entry in the console tree and select Unauthorize.

In Netsh, you can authorize a server by typing the following command:

```
netsh dhcp server ServerID initiate auth
```

Here, *ServerID* is the UNC name or IP address of the DHCP server on which you want to create the scope, such as \\CORPSVR03 or \\192.168.1.1. Keep in mind that if you are already at the netsh dhcp server prompt, you only need to type **initiate auth**.

## Creating and configuring scopes

After you install the DHCP Server service, the next thing you must do is create the scopes that will provide the range of IP addresses and TCP/IP options for clients. With IPv4, the DHCP Server service supports four types of scopes:

- **Normal scope**   A normal scope is used to assign IPv4 address pools for Class A, B, and C networks. Normal scopes have an IP address range assignment that includes the subnet mask and can also have exclusions and reservations as well as TCP/IP options that are specific to the scope. When you create normal scopes, each scope must be in its own subnet. This means if you add a normal scope, it must be on a different subnet than any of the existing scopes configured on the server.

- **Multicast scope**   A multicast scope is used to assign IP address pools for IPv4 Class D networks. Multicast scopes are created in the same way as normal scopes except that they do not have an associated subnet mask, reservations, or related TCP/IP options. This means there is no specific subnet association for multicast scopes. Instead of a subnet mask, you assign the scope a Time to Live (TTL) value that specifies the maximum number of routers the messages sent to computers over multicast can go through. The default TTL is 32. Additionally, because multicast IP addresses are used for destination addresses only, they have a longer lease duration than unicast IP addresses—typically, from 30 to 60 days.

- **Superscope**   A superscope is a container for IPv4 scopes and also can be used to distribute IP addresses from multiple logical IP networks to the same physical network segment. If you configure multiple scopes on a server and want to be able to activate or deactivate them as a unit or view the usage statistics for all the scopes at once, you can use a superscope to do this. Create the superscope and then add to it the scopes you want to manage as a group.

Chapter 20

- **Failover scopes**   These are scopes split between two DHCP servers to increase fault tolerance, provide redundancy, and enable load balancing.

Before you create a normal scope, you should plan the IP address range you want to use as well as any necessary exclusions and reservations. You must know the IP address of the default gateway and any DNS or WINS servers that should be used. You must also configure DHCPv4 and DHCPv6 relays to relay DHCPv4 and DHCPv6 broadcast requests between network segments.

> **Note**
> You can configure relay agents with the RRAS and the DHCP Relay Agent Service. You can configure some routers as relay agents as well.

## Creating normal scopes for IPv4 addresses

In the DHCP console, you can create a normal scope for IPv4 addresses by expanding the node for the server you want to work with, selecting the IPv4 node and then pressing and holding or right-clicking the IPv4 node. Next, from the shortcut menu, select New Scope.

In the New Scope Wizard, tap or click Next to display the Scope Name page, as shown in Figure 20-4. Type a descriptive name for the scope and a description that will be used as a comment.

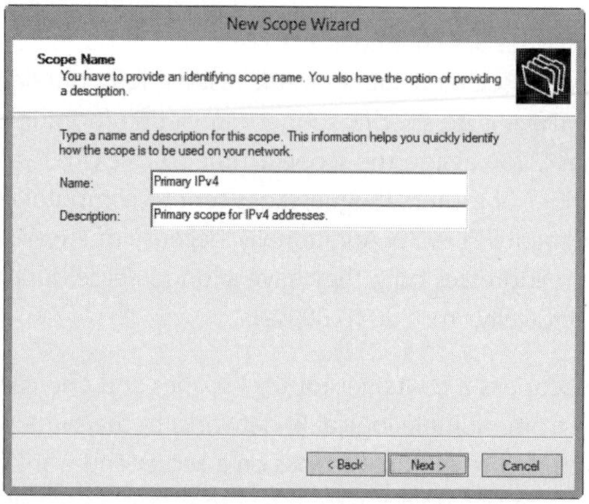

**Figure 20-4** Set the scope name and description.

Tap or click Next to display the IP Address Range page, as shown in Figure 20-5. Enter the start and end IP addresses to use for the scope in the Start IP Address and End IP Address boxes. Be sure to specify the first and last usable IP address only, which means you shouldn't include the *x.x.x*.0 and *x.x.x*.255 addresses. When you enter an IP address range, the bit length and subnet mask are filled in automatically for you. Change the default values if you use subnets.

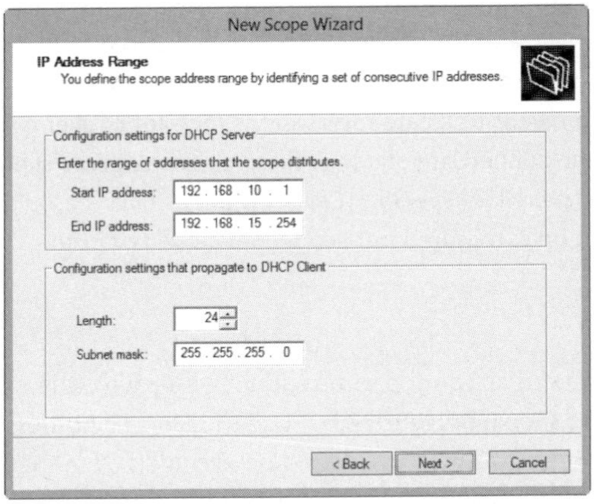

**Figure 20-5** Set the IP address range and subnet information.

Tap or click Next. If the IP address range you entered is on multiple subnets, you'll see a Create Superscope page as shown in Figure 20-6 instead of the Add Exclusions page. This page gives you the opportunity to create a superscope that contains separate scopes for each subnet. Tap or click Yes and then tap or click Next to continue to the Lease Duration page.

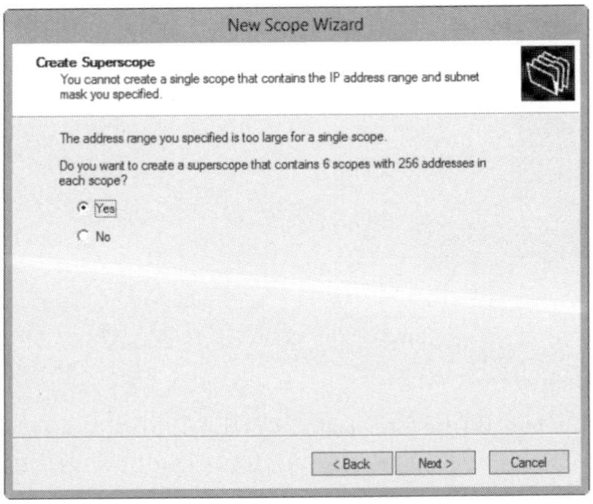

**Figure 20-6** The New Scope Wizard knows when you cross subnet boundaries and will let you create a superscope with multiple scopes automatically.

# INSIDE OUT Multiple subnets on the same physical network

If you're wondering how it would work to have multiple subnets on the same network segment, it should work just fine, and it generally won't matter to which subnet a client connects as long as you've set up DHCP to give clients the appropriate TCP/IP options. The physical network provides the boundaries for these subnets unless you've configured routers or DHCP relay agents to forward DHCP broadcasts. Incidentally, if you want to be sure that clients use a specific subnet, there is a way to do that using reservations. However, you don't want to create reservations for a lot of clients. Instead, you might want to create a user-defined or vendor-defined class and allow clients to connect to any subnet to get their class-specific TCP/IP options. Policy-based assignment also is available, and it can be configured per-scope, per-server, or both.

If all the IP addresses you entered are on the same subnet, you'll have the opportunity to specify an exclusion range, as shown in Figure 20-7. Use the Start IP Address and End IP Address boxes to define IP address ranges that are to be excluded from the scope, such as servers that have static IP addresses assigned to them. After you enter the Start IP Address and End IP Address for the exclusion range, tap or click Add. You can then add additional exclusion ranges as necessary.

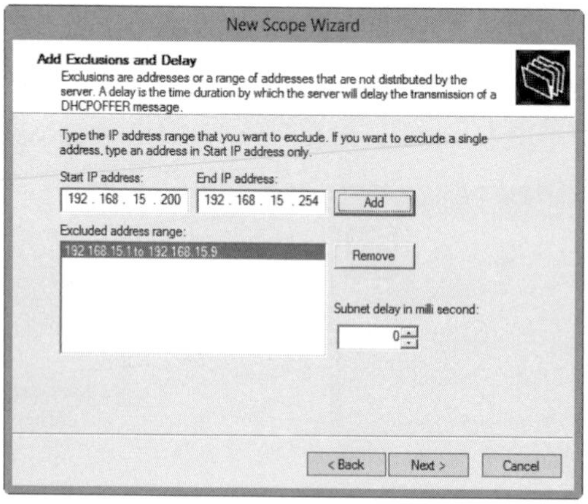

**Figure 20-7** Set exclusion ranges.

Tap or click Next to display the Lease Duration page, as shown in Figure 20-8. Specify the duration of leases for the scope. The default lease duration is eight days, but don't accept the default without first giving some thought to how leases will be used. A lease duration that's too long or too short can reduce the effectiveness of DHCP. If a lease is too long, you could run out of IP addresses because the DHCP server is holding IP addresses for computers that are no longer on the network, such as when there are a lot of mobile users who connect and disconnect their portable computers. If a lease is too short, this could generate a lot of unnecessary broadcast traffic on the network as clients attempt to renew leases.

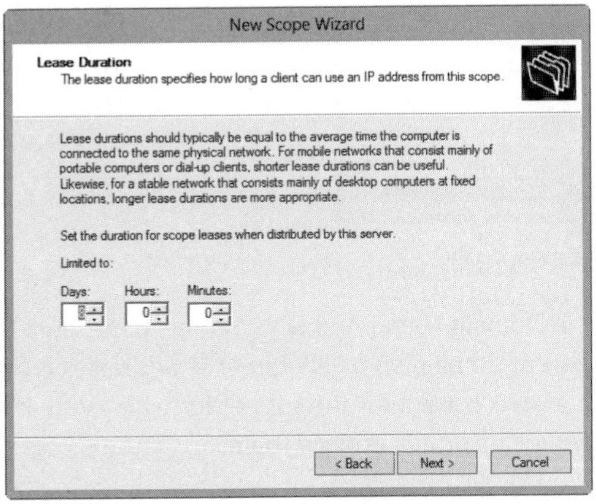

**Figure 20-8**  Set the lease duration.

By default, clients try to renew leases when 50 percent of the lease time has passed and then again when 87.5 percent of the lease time has passed if the first attempt fails. With this in mind, you generally want to find a balance in the lease time that serves the type of clients on the subnet. If there are only fixed desktops and servers, you could use a longer lease duration of 14 to 21 days. If there are only mobile users with portable computers, you could shorten the lease duration to 2 to 3 days. If there's a mix of fixed systems and mobile systems, a lease duration of 5 to 7 days might be more appropriate.

Tap or click Next to display the Configure DHCP Options page. If you want to set TCP/IP options now, select Yes and then tap or click Next to continue to the Router (Default Gateway) page, as shown in Figure 20-9. If you don't want to set TCP/IP options now, select No, tap or click Next, and then tap or click Finish to create the scope and exit the wizard.

On the Router (Default Gateway) page, in the IP Address box enter the IP address of the primary default gateway, and then tap or click Add. You can repeat this process to specify other default gateways. Keep in mind clients try to use gateways in the order they are listed, and you can use the Up and Down buttons to change the order of the gateways, as necessary.

Chapter 20

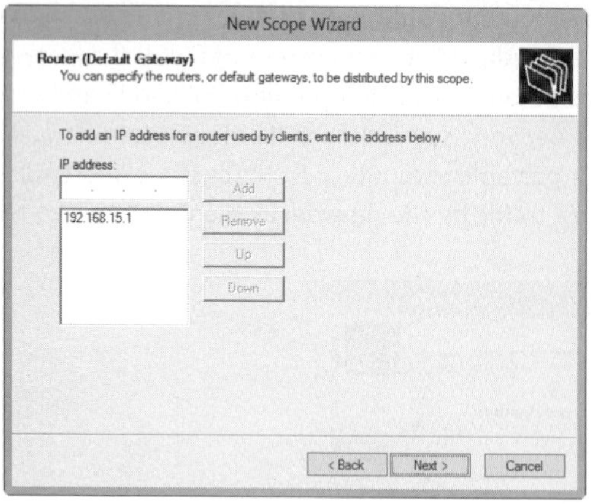

**Figure 20-9**  Set the default gateways.

Tap or click Next to display the Domain Name And DNS Servers page, as shown in Figure 20-10. Although the parent domain and DNS server IP addresses typically are filled in for you, ensure this information is correct for the subnet for which you are configuring the scope. If the default values are incorrect, replace them.

In the Parent Domain box, enter the name of the parent domain to use for DNS resolution of computer names that aren't fully qualified. In the IP Address box, remove any invalid entries. Next, as necessary, type the IP address of the primary DNS server, and then tap or click Add. As necessary, repeat this process to specify the IP addresses of additional DNS servers. As with gateways, the order of the entries determines which DNS server is used first, and you can change the order as necessary using the Up and Down buttons.

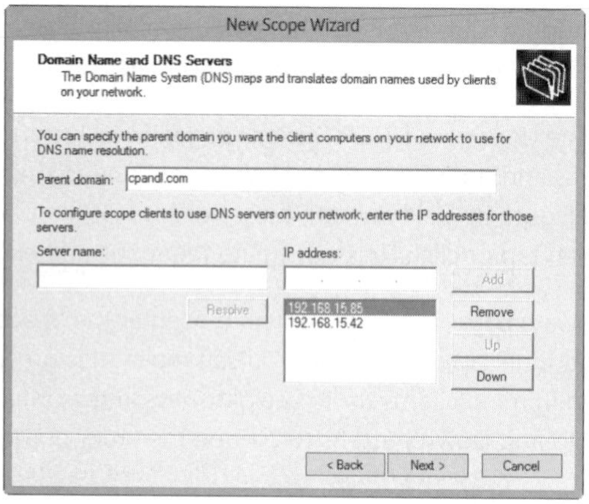

**Figure 20-10**  Set the DNS servers to use.

Tap or click Next to display the WINS Servers page, as shown in Figure 20-11. If WINS servers aren't used on your network, continue without entering any information. Otherwise, in the IP Address box, type the IP address of the primary WINS server and then tap or click Add. You can repeat this process to specify additional WINS servers. As with gateways, the order of the entries determines which WINS server is used first, and you can change the order as necessary using the Up and Down buttons.

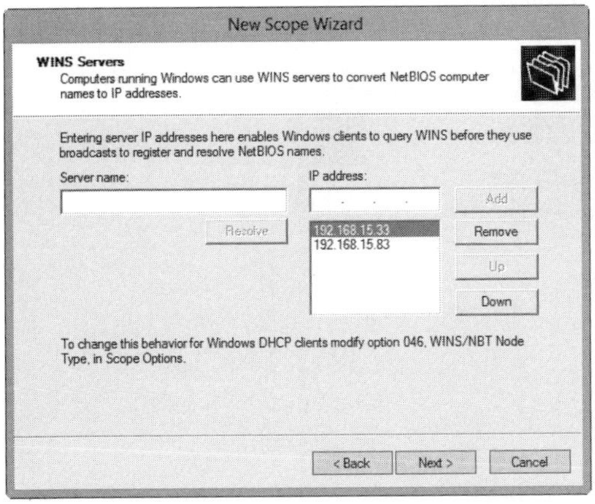

**Figure 20-11**  Set the WINS servers to use.

Tap or click Next to display the Activate Scope page. If you want to activate the scope, select Yes, I Want To Activate This Scope Now. Otherwise, select No, I Will Activate This Scope Later. Tap or click Next, and then tap or click Finish to create the scope and exit the wizard.

## Creating normal scopes for IPv6 addresses

Normal scopes, multicast scopes, and superscopes are all available with IPv4 addresses. With IPv6 addresses, only normal scopes are available. Your IPv6 scopes will use either link-local unicast addresses beginning with FE80 or multicast IPv6 addresses beginning with FF00.

You create normal scopes for IPv6 addresses using the New Scope Wizard. When you are configuring DHCP for IPv6 addresses, you must enter the network ID and a preference value. Typically, the first 64-bits of an IPv6 address identify the network and a 64-bit value is what the New Scope Wizard expects you to enter. The preference value sets the priority of the scope relative to other scopes. The scope with the lowest preference value will be used first. The scope with the second lowest preference will be used second, and so on.

In the DHCP console, you create a normal scope for IPv6 addresses by expanding the node for the server you want to work with, selecting the IPv6 node, and then pressing and holding or right-clicking the IPv6 node. Next, from the shortcut menu, select New Scope.

In the New Scope Wizard, tap or click Next to display the Scope Name page. Type a name and description for the scope that will be used as a comment. Tap or click Next to display the Scope Prefix page, shown in Figure 20-12. Enter the 64-bit network prefix, and then set a preference value. Tap or click Next.

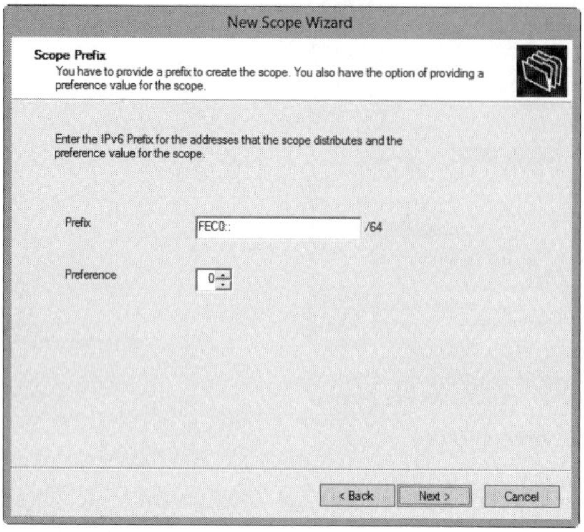

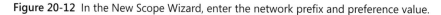

**Figure 20-12** In the New Scope Wizard, enter the network prefix and preference value.

On the Add Exclusions page, shown in Figure 20-13, use the Start IPv6 Address and End IPv6 Address fields to define IPv6 address ranges that are to be excluded from the scope. You can exclude addresses as follows:

- To define an exclusion range, type a start address and an end address in the Exclusion Range's Start IPv6 Address and End IPv6 Address fields, respectively, and then tap or click Add.

- To exclude a single IPv6 address, use that address as the start IPv6 address and then tap or click Add.

- To track which address ranges are excluded, use the Excluded Address Range list box.

- To delete an exclusion range, select the range in the Excluded Address Range list box and tap or click Remove.

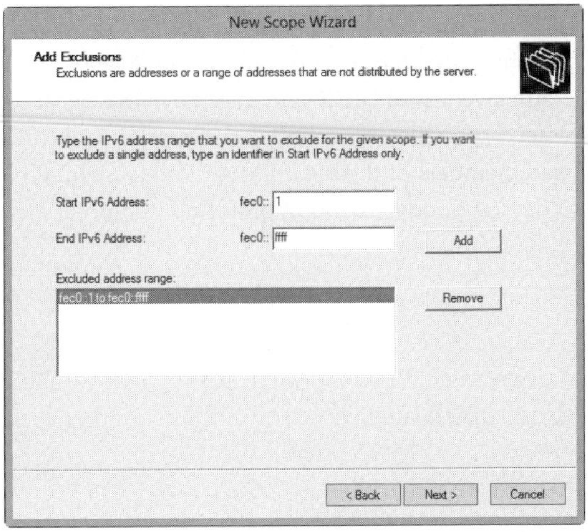

**Figure 20-13**  Set the exclusions for IPv6 addresses.

Tap or click Next to display the Scope Lease page, shown in Figure 20-14. Dynamic IPv6 addresses can be temporary or nontemporary. A nontemporary address is similar to a reservation. Specify the duration of leases for temporary and nontemporary addresses using the Day(s), Hour(s), and Minutes fields under Preferred Life Time and Valid Life Time. The preferred lifetime is the preferred amount of time the lease should be valid. The valid lifetime is the maximum amount of time the lease is valid. Tap or click Next.

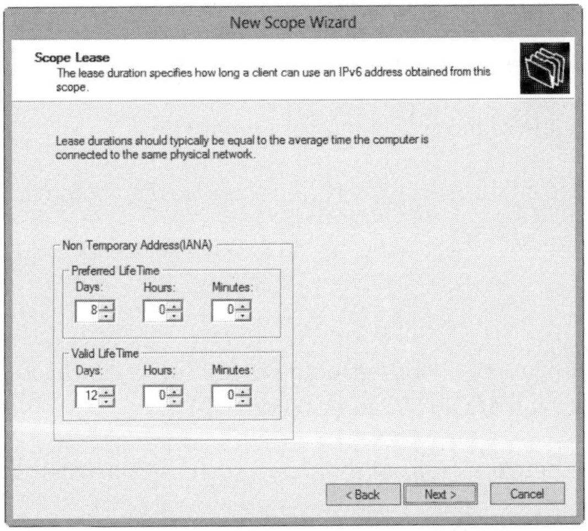

**Figure 20-14**  Specify the duration of temporary and nontemporary leases.

> **Note**
>
> Take a few minutes to plan the lease lifetime you want to use. A lease lifetime that's set too long can reduce the effectiveness of DHCP and might eventually cause you to run out of available IP addresses, especially on networks with mobile users or other types of computers that aren't fixed members of the network. A good lease lifetime for temporary leases is from 1 to 3 days. A good lease duration for nontemporary leases is from 8 to 30 days.

If you want to activate the scope, select Yes under Activate Scope Now and then tap or click Finish. Otherwise, select No under Activate Scope Now and then tap or click Finish.

## Creating normal scopes using Netsh

Using Netsh, you can create an IPv4 scope by typing the following command at an elevated command prompt:

```
netsh dhcp server ServerID add scope NetworkID SubnetMask ScopeName
```

Here, the following is true:

- *ServerID* is the UNC name or IP address of the DHCP server on which you want to create the scope, such as \\CORPSVR03 or \\192.168.1.1.

- *NetworkID* is the network ID of the scope, such as 192.168.1.0.

- *SubnetMask* is the subnet mask of the scope, such as 255.255.255.0.

- *ScopeName* is the name of the scope, such as Primary IPv4.

Using Netsh, you can create an IPv6 scope by typing the following command:

```
netsh dhcp server ServerID add scope NetworkPrefix PrefValue ScopeName
```

Here, the following is true:

- *ServerID* is the UNC name or IP address of the DHCP server on which you want to create the scope, such as \\CORPSVR03 or \\192.168.1.1.

- *NetworkPrefix* is the network prefix of the scope, such as FE80:0:0:0.

- *PrefValue* is the preference value of the scope, such as 1.

- *ScopeName* is the name of the scope, such as Primary IPv6.

After you create the scope, you must use separate commands to set the scope's IP address, exclusions, reservations/lease permanence, and options. You can add an IP range to the scope using the add iprange command for the NETSH DHCP SERVER SCOPE context. Type the following:

```
netsh dhcp server ServerID scope NetworkID add iprange StartIP EndIP
```

Here, the following is true:

- *ServerID* is the UNC name or IP address of the DHCP server on which the scope resides, such as \\CORPSVR03 or \\192.168.1.1.

- *NetworkID* is the network ID of the scope, such as 192.168.1.0.

- *StartIP* is the first IP address in the range, such as 192.168.1.1.

- *EndIP* is the last IP address in the range, such as 192.168.1.254.

Other commands available when you are working with the Netsh DHCP server scope context include the following:

- **add excluderange *StartIP EndIP***   Adds a range of excluded IP addresses to the scope

- **delete iprange *StartIP EndIP***   Deletes an IP address range from the scope

- **delete excluderange *StartIP EndIP***   Deletes an exclusion range from the scope

- **show iprange**   Shows currently configured IP address ranges for the scope

- **show excluderange**   Shows currently configured exclusion ranges for the scope

- **show clients**   Lists clients using the scope

- **show state**   Shows the state of the scope as active or inactive

## Activating scopes

Scopes are available only when they are activated. If you want to make a scope available to clients, you must press and hold or right-click it in the DHCP console and then select Activate. Activating a scope won't make clients switch to that scope. If you want to force clients to switch to a different scope or to use a different DHCP server, you can terminate the client leases in the DHCP console and then deactivate the scope the clients are currently using.

To terminate a lease, you expand the scope you want to work with in the DHCP console and then select Address Leases. You will then see a list of current leases, and you can terminate a lease by pressing and holding or right-clicking it and selecting Delete. The next time the client goes to renew its lease, the DHCP server will tell the client the lease is no longer valid and that a new one must be obtained.

To prevent clients from reusing the original scope, you can deactivate that scope by pressing and holding or right-clicking it in the DHCP console and then selecting Deactivate.

You can perform these same actions using Netsh. To terminate a lease, type the following command:

```
netsh dhcp server ServerID scope NetworkID delete lease IPAddress
```

Here, the following is true:

- *ServerID* is the UNC name or IP address of the DHCP server on which the scope resides, such as \\CORPSVR03 or \\192.168.1.1.

- *NetworkID* is the network ID of the scope, such as 192.168.1.0.

- *IPAddress* is the IP address for the lease you want to remove, such as 192.168.1.8.

To activate or deactivate a scope, type the following:

```
netsh dhcp server ServerID scope NetworkID state StateVal
```

Here, the following is true:

- *ServerID* is the UNC name or IP address of the DHCP server on which the scope resides, such as \\CORPSVR03 or \\192.168.1.1.

- *NetworkID* is the network ID of the scope, such as 192.168.1.0.

- *StateVal* is set to 0 to deactivate the scope and 1 to activate it. If you are using a switched network where multiple logical networks are hosted on a single physical network, use 2 to deactivate the scope and 3 to activate the scope.

## Scope exclusions

To exclude IPv4 or IPv6 addresses from a scope, you can define an exclusion range. Typically, you exclude IP addresses from a scope when they are otherwise assigned. For example, if you assign static IP addresses to certain computers on the network and they are within the range of addresses used by a particular scope, you should define exclusions for those IP addresses to ensure that DHCP doesn't try to use them.

In the DHCP console, any existing exclusions for a scope can be displayed by expanding the scope and selecting Address Pool, as shown in Figure 20-15. To list exclusions at the command line, type the following:

```
netsh dhcp server ServerID scope NetworkID show excluderange
```

Here, *ServerID* is the UNC name or IP address of the DHCP server on which the scope resides, such as \\CORPSVR03 or \\192.168.1.1, and *NetworkID* is the network ID of the scope, such as 192.168.1.0.

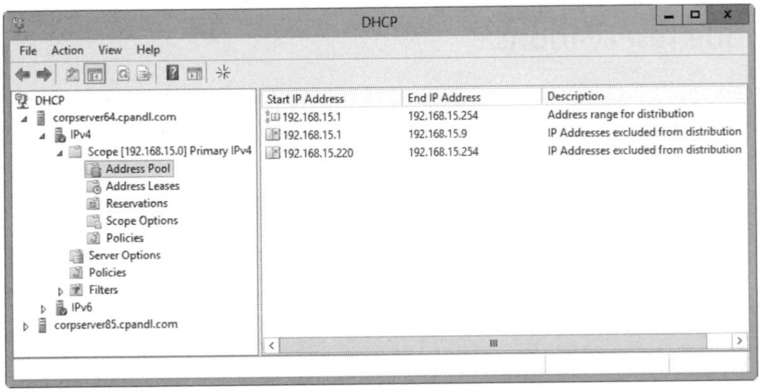

**Figure 20-15**  Exclusions are listed under the Address Pool node.

In the DHCP console, you can define an exclusion range by pressing and holding or right-clicking Address Pool within the scope you want to work with and choosing New Exclusion Range. In the Add Exclusion dialog box, enter a start address and an end address for the exclusion range, as shown in Figure 20-16, and then tap or click Add. Keep in mind the range excluded must be a subset of the scope's range and must not currently be in use by DHCP clients.

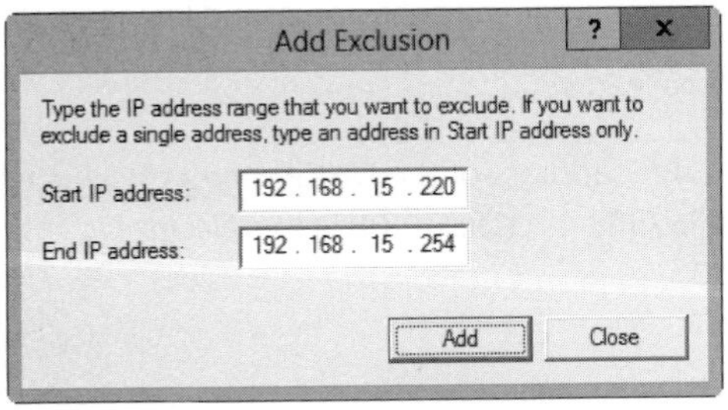

**Figure 20-16**  Set the exclusion range.

Using Netsh, you can add an exclusion range in much the same way. Type the following:

```
netsh dhcp server ServerID scope NetworkID add excluderange StartIP EndIP
```

Here, the following is true:

- *ServerID* is the UNC name or IP address of the DHCP server on which the scope resides, such as \\CORPSVR03 or \\192.168.1.1.

- *NetworkID* is the network ID of the scope, such as 192.168.1.0.

- *StartIP* is the first IP address in the exclusion range, such as 192.168.1.200.

- *EndIP* is the last IP address in the exclusion range, such as 192.168.1.219.

## Scope reservations

Reservations provide a way to assign a permanent lease on an IPv4 address to a client. In this way, the client has a fixed IP address, but you retain flexibility in that you could change the IPv4 address at any time if necessary through DHCP rather than having to do so on the client.

Reservations also are used to show clients with static IP addresses. Here, you create reservations to display these clients, not assign IP addresses to them.

> **Important**
>
> Reserved IP addresses are not static IP addresses. Reserved IP addresses can be leased from DHCP. Static IP addresses must be manually assigned on the client.

In the DHCP console, any existing reservations for a scope can be displayed by expanding the scope and selecting Reservations. As shown in Figure 20-17, existing reservations are shown according to the reservation name and IP address reserved. You can press and hold or right-click a reservation and select Properties to see the associated MAC address. To list reservations by IPv4 address and MAC address at the command line, type the following:

```
netsh dhcp server ServerID scope NetworkID show reservedip
```

Here, *ServerID* is the UNC name or IP address of the DHCP server on which you want to create the scope, such as \\CORPSVR03 or \\192.168.1.1, and *NetworkID* is the network ID of the scope, such as 192.168.1.0.

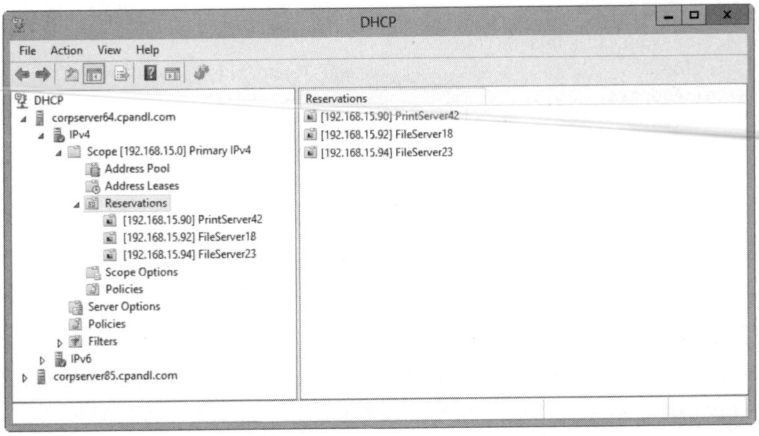

**Figure 20-17** Current reservations are listed by reservation name and IP address.

To create a reservation, you need to know the MAC or device unique identifier (DUID) address of the computer that will hold the IP address. MAC and DUID addresses are specific to an individual network interface configured on the client. You can view the MAC address of an interface by typing **ipconfig /all** at the command prompt. The output will list the MAC address as the physical address of the network interface, as it does under Physical Address in the following example:

```
Windows IP Configuration
Host Name . . . . . . . . . . . . : corpserver64
Primary Dns Suffix  . . . . . . . : cpandl.com
Node Type . . . . . . . . . . . . : Hybrid
IP Routing Enabled. . . . . . . . : No
WINS Proxy Enabled. . . . . . . . : No
DNS Suffix Search List. . . . . . : cpandl.com

Ethernet adapter Local Area Connection:
Connection-specific DNS Suffix  . : cpandl.com
Description . . . . . . . . . . . : Intel(R) PRO/1000 PM Network Connection
Physical Address. . . . . . . . . : 23-24-AE-67-B4-E8
DHCP Enabled. . . . . . . . . . . : Yes
Autoconfiguration Enabled . . . . : Yes
IPv4 Address. . . . . . . . . . . : 192.168.15.124(Preferred)
Subnet Mask . . . . . . . . . . . : 255.255.255.0
Lease Obtained. . . . . . . . . . : Sunday, Feb 21, 2014 5:25:14 AM
Lease Expires . . . . . . . . . . : Sunday, Feb 28, 2014 3:28:56 PM
Default Gateway . . . . . . . . . : 192.168.15.1
DHCP Server . . . . . . . . . . . : 192.168.15.1
DNS Servers . . . . . . . . . . . : 192.168.15.1
NetBIOS over Tcpip. . . . . . . . : Enabled
```

Chapter 20

```
Tunnel adapter Local Area Connection* 6:
Connection-specific DNS Suffix  . :
Description . . . . . . . . . . . : Teredo Tunneling Pseudo-Interface
Physical Address. . . . . . . . . : 23-24-AE-67-B4-E8
DHCP Enabled. . . . . . . . . . . : No
Autoconfiguration Enabled . . . . : Yes
IPv6 Address. . . . . . . . . . . : fe80::fd1b:2778:f7e1:67d2%10(Preferred)
Link-local IPv6 Address . . . . . : fe80::2beb:f99:fe57:f87b%10(Preferred)
Default Gateway . . . . . . . . . : ::
NetBIOS over Tcpip. . . . . . . . : Disabled
```

> **Note**
> You create IPv6 reservations in much the same way as you create IPv4 reservations. When you create the reservation, you enter the DUID and the IAID for the DHCPv6 client instead of a MAC address.

In the DHCP console, you can reserve a DHCPv4 address for a client as follows:

1. After you expand the scope you want to work with, press and hold or right-click the Reservations folder and choose New Reservation. This opens the New Reservation dialog box, as shown in Figure 20-18.

2. In the Reservation Name box, type a descriptive name for the reservation. This doesn't have to be the name of the computer to which the reservation belongs, but that does help simplify administration.

3. In the IP Address box, enter the IP address you want to reserve for the client. This IP address must be valid for the currently selected scope.

4. In the MAC address text box, type the MAC address in the text box provided and as previously obtained using the **ipconfig /all** command.

5. If desired, enter an optional comment in the Description box.

6. By default, the reservation is configured to accept both DHCP and BOOTP clients. Change the default only if you want to exclude a particular type of client. DHCP clients include computers running the standard version of the DHCP client as with most Windows operating systems. BOOTP clients are clients running other operating systems and could also include devices such as printers that can use dynamic IP addressing.

7. Tap or click Add to create the address reservation.

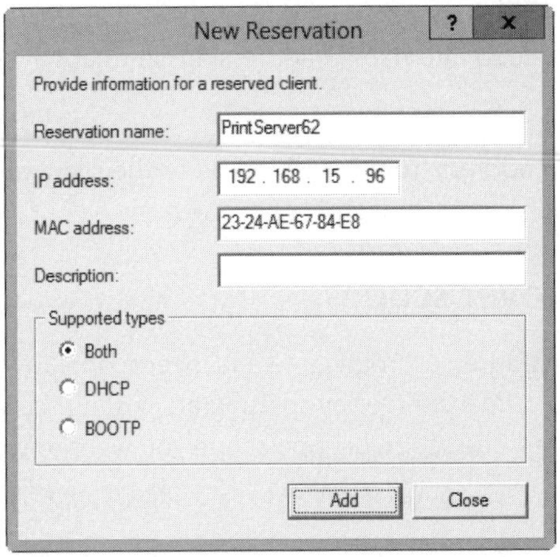

**Figure 20-18** Create a reservation for an IP address using the MAC address of the client.

In Netsh, you can create a reservation by typing the following command:

```
netsh dhcp server ServerID scope NetworkID add reservedip ReservedIP MacAddress Name
Comment
```

Here, the following is true:

- *ServerID* is the UNC name or IP address of the DHCP server on which the scope resides, such as \\CORPSVR03 or \\192.168.1.1.

- *NetworkID* is the network ID of the scope, such as 192.168.1.0.

- *ReservedIP* is the IP address you are reserving, such as 192.168.1.20.

- *MacAddress* is the MAC address of the client (excluding the dashes), such as 2324AE67B4E8.

- *Name* is the descriptive name of the reservation.

- *Comment* is the optional comment describing the reservation.

When you assign reservations, keep in mind that a client with an existing lease won't automatically use the reservation. If a client has a current lease, you must force the client to release that lease and then request a new one. If a client has an existing address and you want to force it to start using DHCP, you must force the client to stop using its current IP address and request a new IP address from DHCP.

To force a client to release an existing lease or drop its current IP address, log on to the client and type **ipconfig /release** at the command prompt. Next, if the client isn't already configured to use DHCP, you must configure the client to use DHCP as discussed in "Configuring dynamic IP addresses and alternate IP addressing" in Chapter 19, "Managing TCP/IP networking."

To get a client to request a new IP address from DHCP, log on to the client and type **ipconfig /renew** at the command prompt.

## Creating and using failover scopes

Failover scopes apply only to IPv4 addresses. You create a failover scope on the DHCP server that you want to act as the primary server by splitting an existing scope or a super-scope that contains multiple scopes. The scope or superscope you want to work with must already be defined.

During the failover-scope creation process, you need to specify the partner server with which you want to split the primary server's scope. This additional server acts as the secondary server for the scope. Because failover scopes are a server-side enhancement, no additional configuration is required for DHCP clients.

Time synchronization is essential for failover scopes to function correctly. Partner servers must have their time synchronized. You can synchronize time on servers using Network Time Protocol (NTP) or other techniques. When you are creating failover scopes, the time difference between the servers cannot be significant (usually this means greater than one minute). If it is significant, setup will fail and you see an error telling you to synchronize the time on the partner servers.

To create a failover scope, complete the following steps:

1.  In the DHCP console, connect to the primary DHCP server for the failover scope. Expand the entry for the primary server, and then expand its IPv4 folder in the tree view.

2.  Press and hold or right-click the scope or superscope that you want to configure for failover, and then tap or click Configure Failover to open the Configure Failover Wizard. The wizard shows the scope or scopes that will be included. Tap or click Next to continue.

> **Note**
> With superscopes, child scopes that are already configured for availability are not listed and all other child scopes are shown and selected by default. If you'd rather select the child scopes to include individually, clear Select All and then select the individual scopes to include.

> **Important**
>
> The scope you are configuring for failover cannot already exist on the partner server. If the scope is on the partner server already, you need to delete it before configuring failover. However, don't delete scopes on partner servers without first determining how the scopes are being used. For example, if a scope has been split between two servers, you might be deleting part of a split scope.

**3.** As shown in Figure 20-19, you can now specify the partner server to use for failover. You can select from a list of servers that were previously or are currently used as failover partners, or you can select other authorized DHCP servers. Tap or click Add Server to browse a list of authorized servers. In the Add Server dialog box, select the partner server for the failover scope and then tap or click OK.

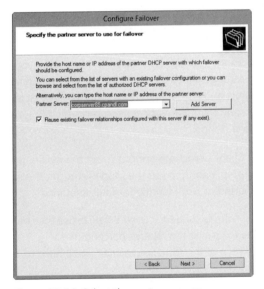

**Figure 20-19**  Select the partner server.

# INSIDE OUT Reusing failover relationships

By default, if you configured failover previously, the wizard will reuse the configuration. Because you can't edit the failover settings after creating a failover scope, you'll usually want to clear the Reuse Existing Failover Relationships Configured With This Server check box and manually configure the failover scope to ensure you can optimize each failover scope as appropriate. That said, if you don't clear this check box and decide to reuse settings, the next page will display the settings that will be used. When there are multiple existing failover relationships, you'll be able to select the failover relationship to use and the settings for the selected relationship will be displayed. When you are ready to continue, tap or click Next and then skip ahead to step 8.

4.  On the Create A New Failover Relationship page, shown in Figure 20-20, a default relationship name is set based on the names of the partner servers. Rather than use the default value, I recommend entering a relationship name that helps you uniquely identify each failover relationship. The reason for this is that you cannot edit the active relationship settings directly. Instead, you edit them indirectly according to the relationship name, and it's difficult to distinguish between a relationship that's actively being used and one that was created previously but is no longer associated with a specific failover scope.

5.  Use the Maximum Client Lead Time options to set the maximum client lead time for the failover relationship, and then use the Mode list to set the failover mode as Load Balance for load sharing or Hot Standby for fault tolerance.

    ○ If you set the failover mode for Load Balance, use the Load Balance Percentage combo boxes to specify the relative percentage for how to allocate the IP addresses to each of the servers. Typically, you'll want to use an equal or nearly equal split, such as 50/50 or 60/40.

    ○ If you set the failover mode to Hot Standby, set the role of the partner as either Active or Standby and then specify the relative percentage of IP addresses to reserve. Typically, you'll want the primary to have most of the available IP addresses and the backup DHCP server to have relatively few of the available IP addresses. Here, you might want to use a split such as 90/10 or 80/20.

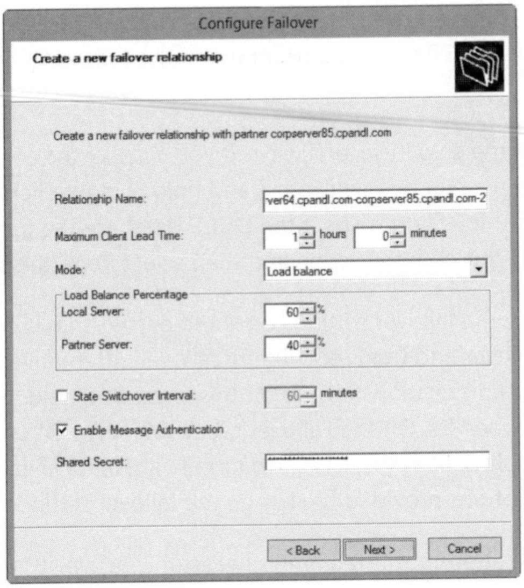

**Figure 20-20**  Set the mode and address space split.

6.  By default, the switchover interval is disabled, which allows for an immediate switchover to the Partner Down state. Any other value sets the timer for automatic state transition.

> **Important**
>
> When you enable failover scopes, the member servers track their own state as well as the state of their partner. The state switchover interval sets the time interval for which the DHCP Server service should continue operating in the Communication Interrupted state before transitioning to the Partner Down state. When the Partner Down state is reached, the partner takes over responsibility for the scope.

7.  Type a shared secret for the partners. The shared secret is a password that the partners use when synchronizing the DHCP database and performing other tasks related to maintaining the DHCP failover partnership. When you are ready to continue, tap or click Next.

8.  Tap or click Finish. Review the summary of the failover scope configuration. If any errors were encountered, you might need to take corrective action. Tap or click Close.

Failover scopes are not identified as such in the DHCP console. You can identify a failover scope by its network ID and IP address pool. Generally, you'll find a scope with the same network ID on two DHCP servers, and the scope properties will include information about the failover partnership. You'll find this information on the Failover tab in the Properties dialog box.

You can manage the partnership in several ways. If you suspect the configuration details related to the partnership are out of sync, press and hold or right-click the scope and then select Replicate Relationship. If you suspect the DHCP database the partners share is out of sync, press and hold or right-click the scope and then select Replicate Scope.

You can't directly modify the failover settings once the partnership is established. However, you can deconfigure failover and then reconfigure failover. Alternatively, you use the IPv4 Properties dialog box to edit relationships. To do this, press and hold or right-click the IPv4 node and then select Properties. On the Failover tab, you'll see a list of every failover relationship created and applicable to the server. To modify a relationship, select, tap, or click Edit, and then use the options provided to change the failover settings.

However, because the relationships listed aren't necessarily active, it's not easy to differentiate between a live, active relationship and a previously created but no longer active relationship. If you have many active and inactive relationships, one way to specifically identify an active relationship, meaning one associated with a scope, is to try to delete a relationship. When you select a relationship and then tap or click Delete, the Delete Failover Relationship dialog box is displayed. If the relationship is active, the actual scope or scopes with which it is associated are listed on the Scopes panel. Otherwise, the Scopes panel will be blank.

If you no longer want the scope to fail over, you access the scope on the server where the original scope should be maintained. Next, you press and hold or right-click the scope and then select Deconfigure Failover. This removes the scope from the partner, while leaving the scope on the server you are working with.

# Configuring TCP/IP options

The messages clients and servers broadcast to each other allow you to set TCP/IP options that clients can obtain by default when they obtain a lease or can request if they need additional information. Note, however, that the types of information you can add to DHCP messages are limited in several ways:

- DHCP messages are transmitted using User Datagram Protocol (UDP), and the entire DHCP message must fit into the UDP datagram. On Ethernet with 1500-byte datagrams, this leaves 1236 bytes for the body of the message (which contains the TCP/IP options).

- BOOTP messages have a fixed size of 300 bytes as set by the original BOOTP standard. Any clients using BOOTP are likely to have their TCP/IP options truncated.

- Although there are many options that you can set, clients understand only certain TCP/IP options. Thus, the set of options available to you is dependent on the client's implementation of DHCP.

With that in mind, let's look at the levels at which options can be assigned and the options that Windows clients understand.

## Levels of options and their uses

Each individual TCP/IP option, such as a default gateway, is configured separately. There are different scope options for IPv4 and IPv6. DHCP administrators can manage options at five levels within the DHCP server configuration:

- **Predefined options**   DHCP administrators can use these options to specify the way in which options are used and to create new option types for use on a server. In the DHCP console, you can view and set predefined options by pressing and holding or right-clicking the IPv4 or IPv6 node in the console tree and selecting Set Predefined Options.

- **Server options**   DHCP administrators can use these options to configure options that are assigned to all scopes created on the DHCP server. Think of server options as global options that are assigned to all clients. Server options can be overridden by scope, class, and client-assigned options. In the DHCP console, you can view and set server options by expanding the entry for the server you want to work with, pressing and holding or right-clicking Server Options, and then choosing Configure Options.

- **Scope options**   DHCP administrators can use these options to configure options that are assigned to all clients that use a particular scope. Scope options are assigned only to normal scopes and can be overridden by class and client-assigned options. In the DHCP console, you can view and set scope options by expanding the scope you want to work with, pressing and holding or right-clicking Scope Options, and then choosing Configure Options.

- **Class options**   DHCP administrators can use these options to configure options that are assigned to all clients of a particular class. Client classes can be user defined or vendor defined. Class options can be overridden by client-assigned options. You define new user and vendor classes by pressing and holding or right-clicking the IPv4 or IPv6 entry and selecting either Define User Classes or Define Vendor Classes as appropriate. When defined, class options can be configured on the Advanced tab of the Server Options, Scope Options, and Reservation Options dialog boxes.

- **Reservation options** Administrators can use these options to set options for an individual client that uses a reservation. These options are also referred to as *client-specific options*. After you create a reservation for a client, you can configure reservation options by expanding the scope, expanding Reservations, pressing and holding or right-clicking the reservation, and selecting Configure Options. Only TCP/IP options manually configured on a client can override client-assigned options.

## Policy-based assignment

To the complex maze of option levels, Windows Server 2012 adds a policy-based assignment of options. Here, IP addresses and options are assigned based on fields contained in the DHCP client request packet, allowing for the targeted application of options.

Policy-based options can be configured at the server level and at the scope level. Server-level policies specify options that you want to assign. Scope-level policies specify IP addresses and options that you want to assign. Policies applicable for a particular scope can be inherited from the server level, assigned at the scope level, or both, with the DHCP server processing all matching policies sequentially according to a defined processing order.

At the server level and at the scope level, each policy has a defined precedence order, as shown in Figure 20-21. If you create policies at both the server and scope levels, the server applies both sets of policies and evaluates the scope policies before the server policies.

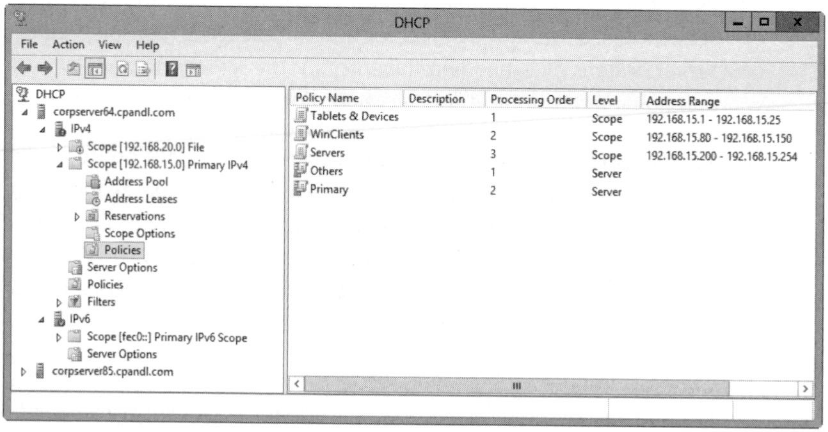

**Figure 20-21** Each policy has a defined precedence order.

The DHCP server determines the scope to which a DHCP client belongs based on the gateway IP address of the relay agent or the interface of the DHCP server on which it receives the DHCP client packet. Once the server determines the client scope, the server evaluates the DHCP packet against the policies applicable for the scope according to the processing order. The policies applicable for a scope are those configured at the scope and those inherited from the server.

A single client request can match the targeting parameters of multiple policies. These policy matches determine how the server assigns IP addresses and options. DHCP servers process policies in two phases:

1. The DHCP server tries to assign an IP address.

   The DHCP server evaluates the fields in the client request against each policy applicable for the scope using the defined processing order. If a client request matches the conditions of a policy with an IP address range, the server assigns the first free IP address from the range. If a policy is associated with multiple address ranges, the server attempts to assign an IP address from the lowest address range.

   If no IP addresses are available in this address range, the server then looks for a free IP address from the next higher address range, and so on. If no IP addresses are free in any of the address ranges associated with the policy, the server attempts to assign an IP address from the next matched policy, as determined by the processing order. If none of the matched policies has a free IP address, the server drops the client packet and logs an event.

   If a DHCP client packet does not match any of the policies applicable for the scope, or none of the matched policies is associated with an IP address range, the server leases the client an IP address from the IP address range configured for the scope exclusive of any policy-specific IP address ranges.

2. The DHCP server tries to assign options.

   A DHCP client uses the parameter request list field in a DHCP packet to request a list of standard options from the DHCP server. Option assignment processing for a client is similar to that for IP address assignment. The DHCP server evaluates the fields in the client request against each policy applicable for the scope using the defined processing order. If the client request matches the conditions of an applicable policy, and the policy includes specific options, the server returns these options to the client. If multiple policies match the client request, the server returns the sum of the options specified for each of the matched policies.

## Options used by Windows clients

RFC 3442 defines many TCP/IP options that you can set in DHCP messages. Although you can set all of these options on a DHCP server, the set of options available is dependent on the client's implementation of DHCP.

Table 20-1 shows the options that can be configured by administrators and used by Windows computers running the DHCP Client service. Each option has an associated option code, which is used to identify it in a DHCP message, and a data entry, which contains the value setting of the option. These options are requested by clients to set their TCP/IP configuration.

**TABLE 20-1 Standard TCP/IP options that administrators can configure**

| Option Name | Option Code | Description |
| --- | --- | --- |
| Router | 003 | Sets a list of IP addresses for the default gateways that should be used by the client. IP addresses are listed in order of preference. |
| DNS Servers | 006 | Sets a list of IP addresses for the DNS servers that should be used by the client. IP addresses are listed in order of preference. |
| DNS Domain Name | 015 | Sets the DNS domain name that clients should use when resolving host names using DNS. |
| WINS/NBNS Servers | 044 | Sets a list of IP addresses for the WINS servers that should be used by the client. IP addresses are listed in order of preference. |
| WINS/NBT Node Type | 046 | Sets the method to use when resolving NetBIOS names. The acceptable values are the following: 0x1 for B-node (broadcast), 0x2 for P-node (peer-to-peer), 0x4 for M-node (mixed), and 0x8 for H-node (hybrid). See "NetBIOS node types" in Chapter 23, "Implementing and maintaining WINS." |
| NetBIOS Scope ID | 047 | Sets the NetBIOS scope for the client. |

## Using user-specific and vendor-specific TCP/IP options

DHCP uses classes to determine which options are sent to clients. The user classes let you assign TCP/IP options according to the type of user the client represents on the network. The default user classes include the following:

- **Default User Class**  An all-inclusive class that includes clients that don't fit into the other user classes. Any computer on the network is in this class, regardless of whether it is directly connected, subject to NAP, or remotely connected.

- **Default BOOTP Class**  Any computer directly connected to the local network has this class. Any settings applied to this class are used by directly connected clients.

- **Default Routing And Remote Access Class**  Any computer that connects to the network using RRAS has this class. Any settings applied to this class are used by dial-in and VPN users, which allows you to set different TCP/IP options for these users.

- **Default Network Access Protection Class**  Any computer that connects to the network and is subject to the Network Access Protection (NAP) policy has this class. Any settings applied to this class are used by restricted-access clients, which allows you to set different TCP/IP options for these users.

Clients can be members of multiple user classes, and you can view the user class memberships for each network interface by typing **ipconfig /showclassid *** at the command prompt. (The asterisk tells the command that you want to see all the network interfaces.) The output you'll see on a computer running Windows will be similar to the following:

```
Windows IP Configuration
DHCP Classes for Adapter "Local Area Connection":

    DHCP ClassID Name            :      Default Routing and Remote Access Class
    DHCP ClassID Description     :      User class for remote access clients

    DHCP ClassID Name            :      Default BOOTP Class
    DHCP ClassID Description     :      User class for BOOTP Clients
```

Here, the client is a member of the Default Routing And Remote Access Class and the Default BOOTP Class. The client, however, doesn't get its options from both classes. Rather the class from which the client gets its options depends on its connection state. If the client is connected directly to the network, it uses the Default BOOTP Class. If the client is connected by Routing and Remote Access, it uses the Default Routing And Remote Access Class.

Vendor classes work a bit differently because they define the set of options available to and used by the various user classes. The default vendor class, DHCP Standard Options, is used to set the standard TCP/IP options, and the various user classes all have access to these options so that they can be implemented in a user-specific way. Additional vendor classes beyond the default define extensions or additional options that can be implemented in a user-specific way. This means that the vendor class defines the options and makes them available, while the user class settings determine which of these additional options (if any) are used by clients.

The default vendor classes that you'll likely use are as follows:

- **Microsoft Options**    Add-on options available to any client running any version of Windows

- **Microsoft Windows 2000 Options**    Add-on options available to any client running Windows 2000 or later

When it comes to these classes, a client applies the options from the most specific add-on vendor class. Thus, if both Microsoft Options and Microsoft Windows 2000 Options are configured, a Windows 2000 or later client would apply the Microsoft Windows 2000 Options vendor class. Again, these options are in addition to the standard options provided through the DHCP Standard Options vendor class and can be implemented in a manner specific to a user class. This means you can have one set of add-on options for

Chapter 20

directly connected clients (Default BOOTP Class) and one set for remotely connected clients (Default Routing And Remote Access Class).

The add-on options that can be set are listed in Table 20-2.

**TABLE 20-2 Additional TCP/IP options that administrators can configure**

| Option Name | Option Code | Description |
|---|---|---|
| Microsoft Disable NetBIOS Option | 001 | Disables NetBIOS if selected as an option with a value of 0x1. |
| Microsoft Release DHCP Lease On Shutdown Option | 002 | Specifies that a client should release its DHCP lease on shutdown if selected as an option with a value of 0x1. |
| Microsoft Default Router Metric Base | 003 | Specifies that the default router metric base should be used if selected as an option with a value of 0x1. |

## Setting options for all clients

On the DHCP server, you can set IPv4 and IPv6 options at several levels. You can set standard options for the following components:

- **All scopes on a server**   In the DHCP console, expand the entry for the server and IP protocol you want to work with, press and hold or right-click Server Options, and then choose Configure Options.

- **A specific scope**   In the DHCP console, expand the scope you want to work with, press and hold or right-click Scope Options, and then choose Configure Options.

- **A single reserved IP address**   In the DHCP console, expand the scope, expand Reservations, press and hold or right-click the reservation you want to work with, and select Configure Options.

Regardless of the level at which you are setting IPv4 and IPv6 options, the dialog box displayed has the exact same set of choices as that shown in Figure 20-22. You can now select each standard TCP/IP option you want to use in turn—such as Router, DNS Servers, DNS Domain Name, WINS/NBNS Servers, and WINS/NBT Node Type—and configure the appropriate values. Tap or click OK when you are finished.

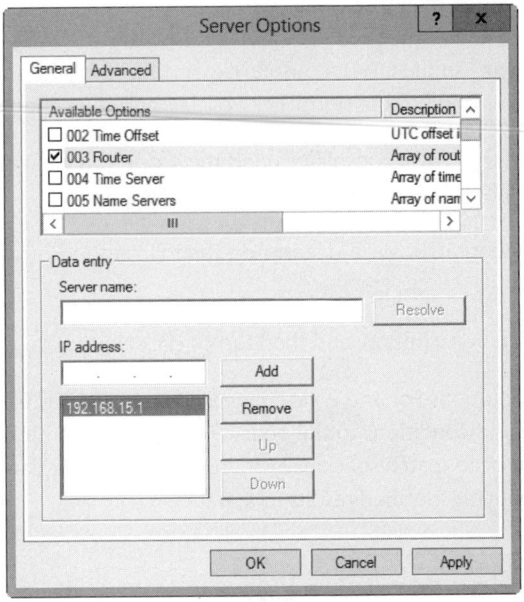

**Figure 20-22** Set class-specific options using the General tab.

Instead of or in addition to standard options, you can set policy-based options that will be applied to clients matching specific criteria, which can include the following:

- User and vendor classes

- The MAC addresses of a client's primary network adapter

- Custom Client Identifiers defined in the registry of client machines

- Relay agent information

# INSIDE OUT    Setting custom client identifiers

You set a client identifier by adding the DhcpClientIdentifier key to the HKEY_LOCAL_ MACHINE\SYSTEM\CurrentControlSet\Services\\*AdapterName*\Parameters\Tcpip key, where *AdapterName* is the actual name of the client's primary network adapter. The DhcpClientIdentifier key must be set as a REG_DWORD with a value range of 0x0 to 0xFFFFFFFF.

Chapter 20

You can create policies for the following components:

- **All scopes on a server** In the DHCP console, expand the entry for the server and the IPv4 protocol, press and hold or right-click Policies, and then choose New Policy.

- **A specific scope** In the DHCP console, expand the scope you want to work with, press and hold or right-click Policies, and then choose New Policy.

When the DHCP Policy Configuration Wizard starts, do the following to configure the policy:

1. Type a policy name and description, and then tap or click Next.

2. On the Configure Conditions For The Policy page, shown in Figure 20-23, use the options provided to add conditions to the policy. The default operator is Equals. You use the Equals operator to match specifically. If you use the Not Equals operator, any value other than what you specified results in a match.

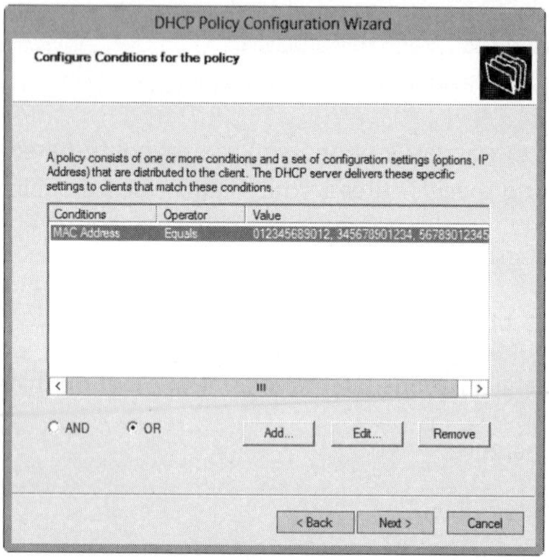

**Figure 20-23** Define the conditions for the policy.

3. Conditions can be joined with AND clauses or OR clauses. Use AND clauses when a client must match each condition. Use OR clauses when a client can match either condition. Select AND or OR as appropriate.

4. When you are ready to continue, tap or click Next. If you are assigning the policy at the scope level, you can next define the IP ranges that should be associated with this policy. You divide a scope into multiple IP address ranges for easier management. For example, you could have a specific range for printers, a different range for clients, and yet another range for servers.

5.  Tap or click Next, and then select the check box for each standard TCP/IP option you want to use in turn—such as Router, DNS Servers, DNS Domain Name, WINS/NBNS Servers, and WINS/NBT Node Type—and configure the appropriate values.

6.  Select each add-on TCP/IP option you want to use in turn—such as Microsoft Disable NetBIOS Option and Microsoft Release DHCP Lease On Shutdown Option—and accept the default value (0x1) to turn on the option.

7.  Tap or click OK.

## Setting options for RRAS and NAP clients

On the DHCP server, you can set IPv4 options for specific clients using a policy-based assignment. IPv4 options for RRAS and NAP clients can be set at several levels, and you can create one policy for both RRAS and NAP clients or separate policies for each.

With DHCPv4, you can set client options for the following components:

*   **All scopes on a server**   In the DHCP console, expand the entry for the server and the IPv4 protocol, press and hold or right-click Policies, and then choose New Policy.

*   **A specific scope**   In the DHCP console, expand the scope you want to work with, press and hold or right-click Policies, and then choose New Policy.

When the DHCP Policy Configuration Wizard starts, do the following to configure the policy:

1.  Type a policy name and description. For example, you might want to name the policy **RRAS** or **NAP Client Policy**. When you are ready to continue, tap or click Next.

2.  On the Configure Conditions For Policy page, use the options provided to add conditions to the policy. As an example, if you want the policy to apply to both RRAS and NAP clients, you do the following:

    a.  Add the RRAS client condition by tapping or clicking Add. Next, in the Add/Edit Condition dialog box, select User Class as the Criteria and then select Default Routing And Remote Access Class as the Value. Tap or click Add, and then tap or click OK. The default operator is Equals. You use the Equals operator to match the class specifically. If you use the Not Equals operator, any class other than the Default Routing And Remote Access Class results in a match.

    b.  Conditions can be joined with AND clauses or OR clauses. Use AND clauses when a client must match each condition. Use OR clauses when a client can match either condition. Select AND or OR as appropriate.

c. Add the NAP client condition by tapping or clicking Add. Next, in the Add/Edit Condition dialog box, select User Class as the Criteria and then select Default Network Access Protection Class as the Value. Tap or click Add and then tap or click OK. Again, the default operator is Equals because you want to match the NAP class specifically.

3. When you are ready to continue, tap or click Next. If you are assigning policy at the scope level, you can next define the IP ranges that should be associated with this policy. You divide a scope into multiple IP address ranges for easier management. For example, you could have a specific range for printers, a different range for clients, and yet another range for servers.

4. Tap or click Next, and then select the check box for each standard TCP/IP option you want to use in turn—such as Router, DNS Servers, DNS Domain Name, WINS/NBNS Servers, and WINS/NBT Node Type—and configure the appropriate values.

5. Select each add-on TCP/IP option you want to use in turn—such as Microsoft Disable NetBIOS Option and Microsoft Release DHCP Lease On Shutdown Option—and accept the default value (0x1) to turn on the option.

6. Tap or click OK.

## Setting add-on options for directly connected clients

You can set add-on options for directly connected clients that are different from those of RRAS and NAP clients. For policy-based assignment, start the DHCP Policy Configuration Wizard at the appropriate level and then do the following to configure the policy:

1. Type a policy name and description. For example, you might want to name the policy **Directly Connected Client Policy**. When you are ready to continue, tap or click Next.

2. On the Configure Conditions For Policy page, use the options provided to add conditions to the policy. As you are configuring options for directly connected clients, tap or click Add. Then, in the Add/Edit Condition dialog box, select Vendor Class as the Criteria. Select Microsoft Windows 2000 Options as the vendor class. Tap or click Add, and then tap or click OK. The default operator is Equals. You use the Equals operator to match the class specifically.

3. Next, add the Default BOOTP Class as the user class. Add this client condition by tapping or clicking Add. Next, in the Add/Edit Condition dialog box, select User Class as the Criteria, and then select Default BOOTP Class as the Value. Tap or click Add, and then tap or click OK. Again, the default operator is Equals because you want to match the Default BOOTP class specifically.

4.  When you are ready to continue, tap or click Next. If you are assigning policy at the scope level, you can next define the IP ranges that should be associated with this policy. You divide a scope into multiple IP address ranges for easier management. For example, you could have a specific range for printers, a different range for clients, and yet another range for servers.

5.  Tap or click Next, and then select the check box for each standard TCP/IP option you want to use in turn—such as Router, DNS Servers, DNS Domain Name, WINS/NBNS Servers, and WINS/NBT Node Type—and configure the appropriate values.

6.  Select each add-on TCP/IP option you want to use in turn—such as Microsoft Disable NetBIOS Option and Microsoft Release DHCP Lease On Shutdown Option—and accept the default value (0x1) to turn on the option.

7.  Tap or click OK.

## Defining classes to get different option sets

If you want a group of DHCP clients to use a set of options different from other computers, you can use classes to do this. It is a two-part process. First, create your own user-defined class on each DHCP server to which the clients might connect. Then configure the network interfaces on the clients to use the new class.

### Creating the class

In the DHCP console, you can define the new user class by pressing and holding or right-clicking the IP protocol you want to work with and selecting Define User Classes. In the DHCP User Classes dialog box, shown in Figure 20-24, the existing classes are listed, except for the Default User Class because it is the base user class.

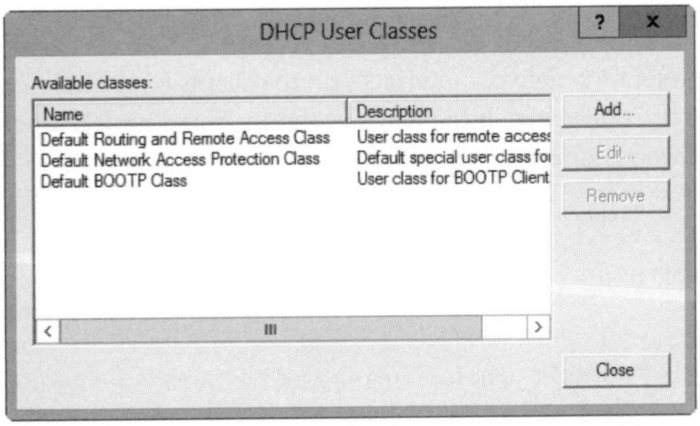

Figure 20-24  User classes in addition to the base class.

Tap or click Add to display the New Class dialog box shown in Figure 20-25. In the Display Name box, type the name of the class you are defining. The name is arbitrary, and it should be short but descriptive enough so that you know what that class is used for by seeing its name. You can also type a description in the Description box. Afterward, tap or click in the empty area below the word ASCII. In this space, type the class identifier, which is used by DHCP to identify the class. The class identifier cannot have spaces. Tap or click OK to close the New Class dialog box, and then tap or click Close to return to the DHCP console.

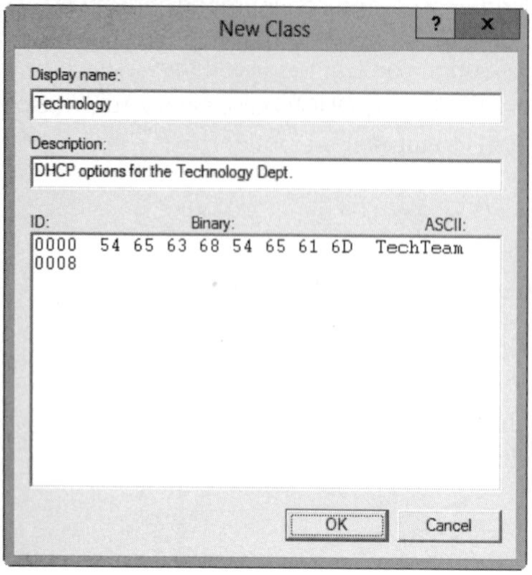

**Figure 20-25**  Set the class name, description, and class ID.

Next, you must configure the TCP/IP options that should be used by this class using policy-based assignment.

## Configuring clients to use the class

Now you must configure the network interfaces on the clients to use the new class. Assuming "Local Area Connection" is the name of the network interface on the client, you would type the following command to do this:

```
ipconfig /setclassid "Ethernet" ClassID
```

Here, *ClassID* is the ID of the user class to use. For example, if the class ID is Engineering, you would type

```
ipconfig /setclassid "Ethernet" Engineering
```

In these examples, I use "Ethernet" as the network interface name because that is the default connection created by Windows. If a client has multiple network interfaces or a user has changed the name of the default network interface, you must use the name of the appropriate interface. You can get a list of all network interfaces on a client by typing **ipconfig /all** at the command prompt.

After you set the class ID, type **ipconfig /renew** at the command prompt. This tells the client to renew the lease, and because the client has a new class ID, it also forces the client to request new TCP/IP options. The output should be similar to the following:

```
Windows IP Configuration
Ethernet adapter Ethernet:

    Connection-specific DNS Suffix    :
    IP Address                        :    192.168.1.22
    Subnet Mask                       :    255.255.255.0
    Default Gateway                   :    192.168.1.1
    DHCP Class ID                     :    Technology
```

That's it. Because the class ID is persistent, you need to set it only once. So, if the client is restarted, the class ID will remain. To remove the class ID and use the defaults again, type the following command:

```
ipconfig /setclassid "Ethernet"
```

## TROUBLESHOOTING

**Class ID problems**
Sometimes the network interface won't report that it has the new class ID. If this happens, try releasing the DHCP lease first by typing **ipconfig /release** and then obtaining a new lease by typing **ipconfig /renew**.

# Advanced DHCP configuration and maintenance

You manage DHCP servers through the DHCP Server service. As with any other service, you can start, stop, pause, and resume the DHCP Server service in the Services node of Computer Management or from the command line. You can also manage the DHCP Server service in the DHCP console. Press and hold or right-click the server you want to manage in the DHCP console, point to All Tasks, and then tap or click Start, Stop, Pause, Resume, or Restart, as appropriate.

> **Note**
>
> You also can use Server Manager to start and stop a DHCP server. Tap or click DHCP in the left pane of Server Manager. Next, in the main pane, on the Servers panel, select the DHCP server. Finally, on the Services panel, press and hold or right-click the entry for the DHCP Server and then tap or click Start Services, Stop Services, Pause Services, Resume Services, or Restart Service, as appropriate.

When you install the DHCP Server service, many advanced features are configured for you automatically, including audit logging, network bindings, integration with DNS, integration with NAP, and DHCP database backups. All of these features can be fine-tuned to optimize performance, and many of these features—such as auditing, logging, and backups—should be periodically monitored.

## Monitoring DHCP audit logging

Audit logging is enabled by default for the DHCP Server service and is used to track DHCP processes and requests in log files. Although you can enable and configure logging separately for IPv4 and IPv6, by default, the two protocols use the same log files. The DHCP logs are stored in the %SystemRoot%\System32\DHCP folder by default. In this folder, you'll find a different log file for each day of the week. For example, the log file for Monday is named DhcpSrvLog-Mon.log. When you start the DHCP Server service or a new day arrives, a header message is written to the log file. As shown in Listing 20-1, the header provides a summary of DHCP events and their meanings. The header is followed by the actual events logged by the DHCP Server service. The event IDs and descriptions are entered because different versions of the DHCP Server service can have different events.

**Listing 20-1** DHCP Server Log File

```
Microsoft DHCP Service Activity Log
Event ID  Meaning
00  The log was started.
01  The log was stopped.
02  The log was temporarily paused due to low disk space.
10  A new IP address was leased to a client.
11  A lease was renewed by a client.
12  A lease was released by a client.
13  An IP address was found to be in use on the network.
14  A lease request could not be satisfied because address pool was exhausted.
15  A lease was denied.
16  A lease was deleted.
17  A lease was expired and DNS records for an expired leases have not been deleted.
18  A lease was expired and DNS records were deleted.
20  A BOOTP address was leased to a client.
21  A dynamic BOOTP address was leased to a client.
```

22  A BOOTP request could not be satisfied, the address pool for BOOTP was exhausted.
23  A BOOTP IP address was deleted after checking to see it was not in use.
24  IP address cleanup operation has begun.
25  IP address cleanup statistics.
30  DNS update request to the named DNS server.
31  DNS update failed.
32  DNS update successful.
33  Packet dropped due to NAP policy.
34  DNS update request failed as the DNS update request queue limit exceeded.
35  DNS update request failed.
50+ Codes above 50 are used for Rogue Server Detection information.

QResult: 0: NoQuarantine, 1:Quarantine, 2:Drop Packet, 3:Probation,6:No Quarantine
Information ProbationTime:Year-Month-Day Hour:Minute:Second:MilliSecond.

ID,Date,Time,Description,IP Address,Host Name,MAC Address,User Name, TransactionID,
QResult,Probationtime, CorrelationID,Dhcid,VendorClass(Hex),VendorClass(ASCII),
UserClass(Hex),UserClass(ASCII),RelayAgentInformation.
00,10/02/12,09:18:27,Started,,,,,0,6,,,,,,,,
50,10/02/12,09:19:27,Unreachable Domain,,cpandl.com,,,0,6,,,,,,,,
56,10/02/12,09:19:27,Authorization failure, stopped servicing,,cpandl.
com,,,0,6,,,,,,,,
24,10/02/12,10:18:27,Database Cleanup Begin,,,,,0,6,,,,,,,,
25,10/02/12,10:18:27,0 leases expired and 0 leases deleted,,,,,0,6,,,,,,,,,
25,10/02/12,10:18:27,0 leases expired and 0 leases deleted,,,,,0,6,,,,,,,,,
24,10/02/12,11:18:27,Database Cleanup Begin,,,,,0,6,,,,,,,,

The events in the audit logs can help you troubleshoot problems with a DHCP server. As
you examine Listing 20-1, you see that the first event entry with ID 00 tells you the DHCP
Server service was started. The second event entry with ID 50 tells you there's a problem
reaching the cpandl.com domain. The third event entry with ID 56 tells you the DHCP
Server hasn't been properly authorized to service the cpandl.com domain. Resolving this
problem is fairly easy but not as straightforward as you might think.

As stated earlier, in a domain, each DHCP server must be authorized in Active Directory and
you can authorize a server in the DHCP console simply by pressing and holding or right-
clicking the server entry and then selecting Authorize. However, if the post-installation
setup tasks in steps 7 through 11 in "Installing the DHCP Server service" earlier in the
chapter haven't been performed, authorization will fail as well. The reason for this is that
you must specify the credentials to use to authorize the DHCP server in Active Directory
as part of the deployment. Resolve the problem by completing the post-installation tasks
as discussed previously. Display notifications by tapping the Notifications icon in Server
Manager or the warning link in the main pane when you select the DHCP node in the left
pane.

Every hour that the service is running, it also performs cleanup operations. Database
cleanup is used to check for expired leases and leases that no longer apply.

Chapter 20

The audit logs also serve as a record of all DHCP connection requests by clients on the network. Events related to lease assignment, renewal, and release are recorded according to the IP address assigned, the client's FQDN, the client's MAC address, vendor class, user class, and more.

Quarantine results, shown in the QResult column, apply when you've configured Network Access Protection. The QResult can be 0 for no quarantine, 1 for quarantine, 2 for drop packet, 3 for probation, or 6 for no quarantine information.

Declined leases are listed with the event ID 13, and the description of the event is DECLINE. A DHCP client can decline a lease if it detects that the IP address is already in use. The primary reason this happens is that a system somewhere on the network is using a static IP address in the DHCP range or has leased it from another DHCP server during a network glitch. When the server receives the decline, it marks the address as bad in the DHCP database. See "Enabling conflict detection on DHCP servers" later in the chapter for details on how IP address conflicts can be avoided.

Denied leases are listed with the event ID 15, and the description of the event is NACK. DHCP can deny a lease to a client that is requesting an address that cannot be provided. This could happen if an administrator terminated the lease or if the client moved to a different subnet where the original IP address held is no longer valid. When a client receives a NACK, the client releases the denied IP address and requests a new one.

As discussed previously, audit logging is enabled by default. If you want to check or change the logging setting, you can do this in the DHCP console. Expand the node for the server you want to work with, press and hold or right-click IPv4 or IPv6 as appropriate for the type of binding you want to work with, and then select Properties. This displays the dialog box shown in Figure 20-26.

On the General tab, select or clear the Enable DHCP Audit Logging check box as necessary. Afterward, select the Advanced tab. The Audit Log File Path box shows the current folder location for log files. Enter a new folder location or tap or click Browse to find a new location. Tap or click OK. If you change the audit log location, Windows Server will need to restart the DHCP Server service. When prompted to confirm that this is OK, tap or click Yes.

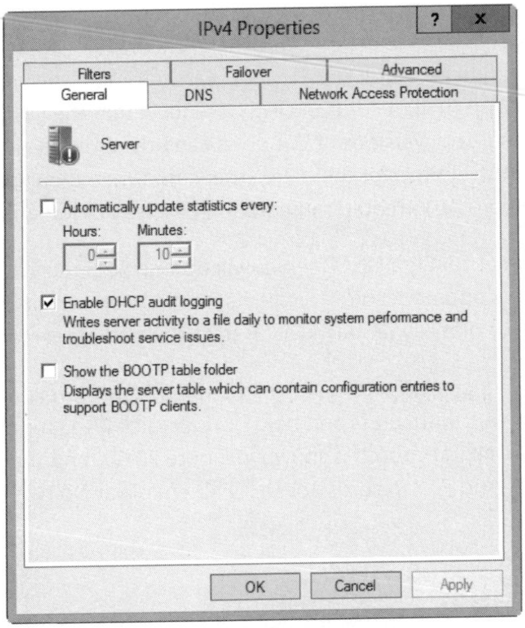

Figure 20-26  Audit logging is enabled by default.

## Binding the DHCP Server service to a network interface

The DHCP Server service should bind automatically to the first NIC on the server. This means that the DHCP Server service should use the IP address and TCP/IP configuration of this network interface to communicate with clients. In some instances, the DHCP Server service might not bind to any available network interface or it might bind to a network interface that you don't want it to use. To resolve this problem, you must bind the DHCP Server service to a specific network interface by following these steps:

1.  In the DHCP console, expand the node for the server you want to work with, press and hold or right-click IPv4 or IPv6 as appropriate for the type of binding you want to work with, and then select Properties.

2.  In the Advanced tab of the IPv4 or IPv6 Properties dialog box, tap or click Bindings to display the Bindings dialog box. This dialog box displays a list of available network connections for the DHCP server.

3.  If you want the DHCP Server service to use a connection to service clients, select the option for the connection. If you don't want the service to use a connection, clear the related option.

4.  Tap or click OK twice when you are finished.

Chapter 20

# Integrating DHCP and DNS

Using the DNS Dynamic Update protocol, DHCP clients can automatically update their forward (A) and reverse lookup (PTR) records in DNS or request that the DHCP server do this for them. Clients running early versions of Windows can't dynamically update any of their records, so DHCP must do this for them. In either case, when the DHCP server is required to update DNS records, this requires integration between DHCP and DNS.

In the default configuration of DHCP, a DHCP server will update DNS records for clients only if requested but will not update records for clients running early versions of Windows. You can modify this behavior globally for each DHCP server or on a per-scope basis.

To change the global DNS integration settings, start the DHCP console, expand the node for the server you want to work with, press and hold or right-click IPv4, and then select Properties. Tap or click the DNS tab, which is shown in Figure 20-27, and then select the Dynamically Update DNS A And PTR Records For DHCP Clients That Do Not Request Updates check box.

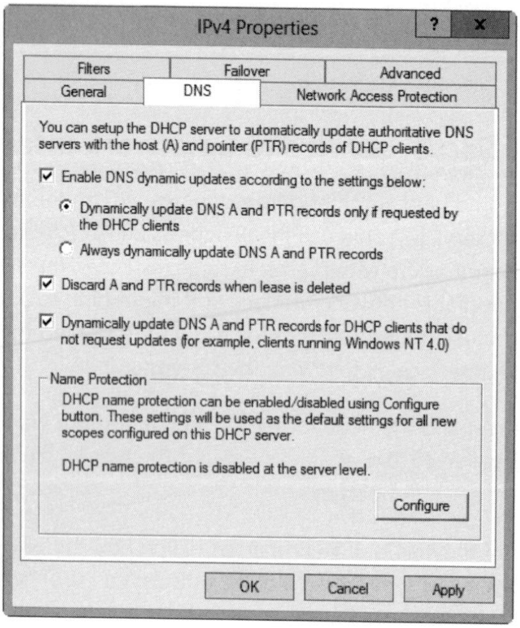

Figure 20-27 DHCP and DNS integration.

If you are using secure dynamic updates and have enabled DNSSEC, you can enable name protection. Name protection secures names so that other clients can't use them. Tap or click Configure on the Name Protection panel, select Enable Name Protection, and then tap or click OK.

Don't change the other settings. These settings are configured by default, and you don't need to modify the configuration in most cases.

To change scope-specific settings, expand the node for the server you want to work with and then expand IPv4. Press and hold or right-click the scope you want to work with and then select Properties. Tap or click the DNS tab. The options available are the same as those shown in Figure 20-27. Because these settings are configured by default, you usually don't need to modify the configuration.

## Integrating DHCP and NAP

Network Access Protection (NAP) is designed to protect the network from clients that do not have the appropriate security measures in place. The easiest way to enable NAP with DHCP is to set up the DHCP server as a Network Policy Server. To do this, you need to install the Network Policy console, configure a compliant policy for NAP and DHCP integration on the server, and then enable NAP for DHCP. This process enables NAP for network computers that use DHCP; it does not fully configure NAP for use.

You can create an NAP and DHCP integration policy by completing the following steps:

1. On the server that you want to act as the Network Policy Server, install the Network Policy And Access Services role using the Add Roles And Features Wizard. During setup, choose Network Policy Server as a role service.

2. After you install Network Policy Server, the Network Policy console will be available in Server Manager as an option in the Tools menu. In the Network Policy console, select the NPS (Local) node in the console tree and then tap or click Configure NAP in the main pane. This starts the Configure NAP Wizard.

3. On the Network Connection Method list, choose Dynamic Host Configuration Protocol (DHCP) as the connection method that you want to deploy on your network for NAP-capable clients. As shown in Figure 20-28, the policy name is set to NAP DHCP by default. Tap or click Next.

Chapter 20

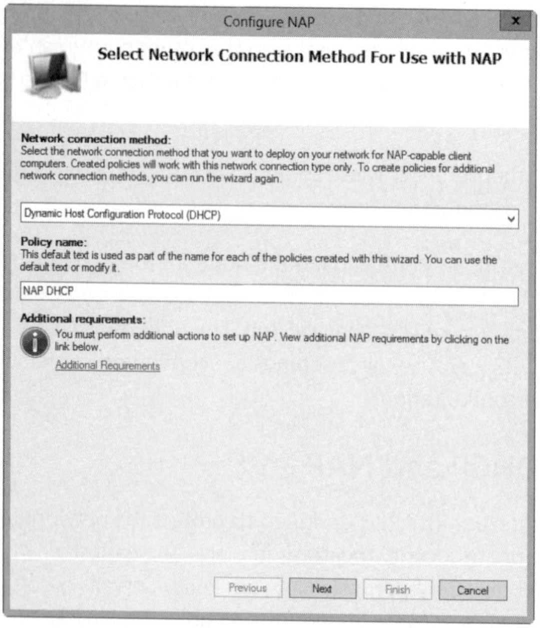

**Figure 20-28** Configure the Network Access Protection policy for the local DHCP server.

4. On the Specify NAP Enforcement Servers Running DHCP Server page, you need to identify all remote DHCP servers on your network by doing the following and then tapping or clicking Next:

   ○ Tap or click Add. In the Add RADIUS Client dialog box, type a friendly name for the remote server in the Friendly Name text box. Then type the DNS name of the remote DHCP server in the Address text box. To validate the name and resolve it to its IP address, tap or click Verify. In the Verify dialog box, tap or click Resolve and then tap or click OK.

   ○ On the Shared Secret panel, select Generate and then tap or click Generate to create a long shared-secret keyphrase. You need to enter this keyphrase in the NAP DHCP policy on all remote DHCP servers. Be sure to write down this keyphrase. Alternatively, copy the keyphrase to Notepad and then save it in a file stored in a secure location. Tap or click OK.

5. On the Specify DHCP Scopes page, you can identify the DHCP scopes to which this policy should apply. If you do not specify any scopes, the policy applies to all NAP-enabled scopes on the selected DHCP servers. Tap or click Next twice to skip the Configure Machine Groups page.

6. On the Specify A NAP Remediation Server Group And URL page, select a Remediation Server or tap or click New Group to define a remediation group and specify servers to handle remediation. Remediation servers store software updates for NAP clients that need them. In the text box provided, type a URL to a webpage that provides users with instructions on how to bring their computers into compliance with the NAP health policy. Ensure that all DHCP clients can access this URL. Tap or click Next.

7. On the Define NAP Health Policy page, use the options provided to determine how NAP health policy works. In most cases, the default settings work fine. With the default settings, NAP-ineligible clients are denied access to the network; NAP-capable clients are checked for compliance and automatically remediated, which allows them to get needed software updates that you've made available. Tap or click Next, and then tap or click Finish.

You can modify NAP settings globally for each DHCP server or on a per-scope basis. To view or change the global NAP settings, complete the following steps:

1. In the DHCP console, expand the node for the server you want to work with, press and hold or right-click IPv4, and then select Properties.

2. On the Network Access Protection tab, shown in Figure 20-29, tap or click Enable On All Scopes or Disable On All Scopes to enable or disable NAP for all scopes on the server.

> **Note**
> When the local DHCP server is also a Network Policy Server, the Network Policy Server should always be reachable. If you haven't configured the server as a Network Policy Server or the DHCP server is unable to contact the designated Network Policy Server, you'll see an error stating this on the Network Access Protection tab.

Chapter 20

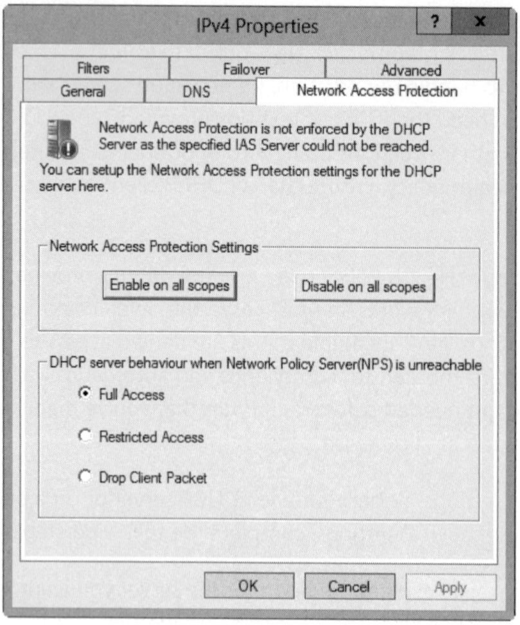

Figure 20-29  The Network Access Protection tab controls the protection options for DHCP.

3.  Choose one of the following options to specify how the DHCP server behaves if the Network Policy Server is unreachable, and then tap or click OK to save your settings:

    ○ **Full Access**   Gives DHCP clients full (unrestricted) access to the network. This means clients can perform any permitted actions.

    ○ **Restricted Access**   Gives DHCP clients restricted access to the network. This means clients can work with access only on the server to which they are connected.

    ○ **Drop Client Packet**   Blocks client requests, and prevents the clients from accessing the network. This means clients have no access to resources on the network.

You can view and change the NAP settings for individual scopes by completing the following steps:

1.  In the DHCP console, expand the node for the server you want to work with and then expand IPv4.

2.  Press and hold or right-click the scope you want to work with, and then select Properties.

3. On the Network Access Protection tab, tap or click Enable For This Scope or Disable For This Scope to enable or disable NAP for this scope.

4. If you're enabling NAP and want to use an NAP profile other than the default, tap or click Use Custom Profile and then type the name of the profile, such as **Alternate NAP DHCP**.

5. Tap or click OK to save your settings.

## Enabling conflict detection on DHCP servers

No two computers on the network can have the same unicast IP address. If a computer is assigned the same unicast IP address as another, one of the computers will be disconnected from the network. Generally, the computer that caused the conflict (meaning the second or later computer to use the IP address) is the one that is disconnected.

To prevent IP address conflicts, DHCP has built-in conflict detection that enables clients to check the IP address they've been assigned by pinging the address on the network. If a client detects that an IP address it has been assigned is in use, it sends the DHCP server a Decline message telling the server that it is declining the lease because the IP address is in use. When this happens, the server marks the IP address as bad in the DHCP database, and then the client requests a new lease. This process works fairly well but requires additional time because the client is responsible for checking the IP address, declining a lease, and requesting a new one.

To speed up the process, you can configure DHCP servers to check for conflicts before assigning an IP address to a client. When conflict detection is enabled, the process works in much the same way as before, except the server checks the IP address to see if it is in use. If the address is in use, the server marks it as bad without interaction with the client. You can configure conflict detection on a DHCP server by specifying the number of conflict-detection attempts that the DHCP server will make before it leases an IP address to a client. The DHCP server checks IP addresses by sending a ping request over the network.

You can configure conflict detection in the DHCP console by expanding the node for the server you want to work with, pressing and holding or right-clicking IPv4, and then selecting Properties. On the Advanced tab, set Conflict Detection Attempts to a value other than zero. At the command line, type the following command:

```
netsh dhcp server ServerID set detectconflictretry Attempts
```

Here, *ServerID* is the name or IP address of the DHCP server and *Attempts* is the number of conflict-detection attempts the server should use. You can confirm the setting by typing the following:

```
netsh dhcp server ServerID show detectconflictretry
```

Chapter 20

# Saving and restoring the DHCP configuration

After you finish configuring a DHCP server, you should save the configuration settings so that you can easily restore the server to a known state or use the same settings on another server. To do this, type the following command at the command prompt:

```
netsh dhcp server dump ServerID > SaveFile
```

Here, *ServerID* is the name or IP address of the DHCP server and *SaveFile* is the name of the file in which you want to store the configuration settings. Here is an example:

```
netsh dhcp server dump > dhcpconfig.dmp
```

If you examine the file Netsh creates, you'll find that it is a Netsh configuration script. To restore the configuration, run the script by typing the following command:

```
netsh exec SaveFile
```

Here, *SaveFile* is the name of the file in which you stored the configuration settings. Here is an example:

```
netsh exec dhcpconfig.dmp
```

## Copy to a new DHCP server

You can run the script on a different DHCP server to configure it the same as the original DHCP server whose configuration you saved. Copy the configuration script to a folder on the destination computer, and then run it. The DHCP server will be configured like the original server.

# Managing and maintaining the DHCP database

Information about leases and reservations used by clients is stored in database files on the DHCP server. Like any other data set, the DHCP database has properties that you can set and techniques you can use to maintain it.

## Setting DHCP database properties

In the default configuration, these files are stored in the %SystemRoot%\System32\ Dhcp folder, and automatically created backups of the files are stored in %SystemRoot%\ System32\Dhcp\Backup. The DHCP Server service performs two routine actions to maintain the database:

- Database cleanup, during which the DHCP Server service checks for expired leases and leases that no longer apply

- Database backup, during which the DHCP Server service backs up the database files

By default, both maintenance tasks are performed every 60 minutes, and you can confirm this as well as the current DHCP folders being used by typing the following command at the command prompt:

```
netsh dhcp server ServerID show dbproperties
```

Here, *ServerID* is the name or IP address of the DHCP server, such as

```
netsh dhcp server 192.168.1.50 show dbproperties
```

The output of this command shows you the current database properties for the DHCP server:

```
Server Database Properties:

    DatabaseName           =    dhcp.mdb
    DatabasePath           =    C:\WINDOWS\System32\dhcp
    DatabaseBackupPath     =    C:\WINDOWS\System32\dhcp\backup
    DatabaseBackupInterval  =    60 mins.
    DatabaseLoggingFlag    =    1
    DatabaseRestoreFlag    =    0
    DatabaseCleanupInterval =    60 mins.
```

Note the *DatabaseLoggingFlag* and *DatabaseRestoreFlag* properties. *DatabaseLoggingFlag* tracks whether audit logging is enabled. If the flag is set to 0, audit logging is disabled. If the flag is set to 1, audit logging is enabled. *DatabaseRestoreFlag* is a special flag that tracks whether the DHCP Server service should restore the DHCP database from backup the next time it starts. If the flag is set to 0, the main database is used. If the flag is set to 1, the DHCP Server service restores the database from backup, overwriting the existing database.

You can use the following commands to set these properties:

- **Netsh dhcp server** *ServerID* **set databasename** *NewFileName* Sets the new file name for the database, such as Dhcp1.mdb.

- **Netsh dhcp server** *ServerID* **set databasepath** *NewPath* Sets the new path for the database files, such as C:\Dhcp\Dbfiles.

- **Netsh dhcp server** *ServerID* **set databasebackupinterval** *NewIntervalMinutes* Sets the database backup interval in minutes, such as 120.

- **Netsh dhcp server** *ServerID* **set databasebackuppathname** *NewPath* Sets the new path for the database backup files, such as C:\Dhcp\Dbbackup.

- **Netsh dhcp server** *ServerID* **set databaseloggingflag** *FlagValue* Enables or disables audit logging. Set this to 0 to disable or 1 to enable.

- **Netsh dhcp server** *ServerID* **set databaserestoreflag** *FlagValue* Forces DHCP to restore the database from backup when it is started. Set this to 1 to restore.

- **Netsh dhcp server** *ServerID* **set databasecleanupinterval** *NewIntervalMinutes* Sets the database backup interval in minutes, such as 120.

> **Note**
> If you change the database name or folder locations, you must stop the DHCP server and then start it again for the changes to take effect. To do this, type **net stop "dhcp server"** to stop the server and then type **net start "dhcp server"** to start the server again.

## Backing up and restoring the database

The DHCP database is backed up automatically. You can manually back it up as well at any time. In the DHCP console, press and hold or right-click the server you want to back up and then choose Backup. In the Browse For Folder dialog box, select the backup folder and then tap or click OK.

If a server crash corrupts the database, you might need to restore and then reconcile the database. Start by restoring a good copy of the contents of the backup folder from tape or other archive source. Afterward, start the DHCP console, press and hold or right-click the server you want to restore, and then choose Restore. In the Browse For Folder dialog box, select the folder that contains the backup you want to restore and then tap or click OK.

During restoration of the database, the DHCP Server service is stopped and then started automatically.

Chapter 20

# INSIDE OUT  Moving the DHCP database to a new server

You can use the backup and restore procedure to move the DHCP database to a new server. For example, before upgrading a DHCP server or decommissioning it, you could configure a new DHCP server and move the current DHCP database from the old server to the new server. Start by installing the DHCP Server service on the destination server and then restart the server. When the server restarts, log on, and at the command prompt type **net stop "dhcp server"** to stop the DHCP Server service. Remove the contents of the %SystemRoot%\System32\Dhcp folder on this server.

Afterward, log on to the original (source) server, and at the command prompt type **net stop "dhcp server"** to stop the DHCP Server service. In the Services node of Computer Management, disable the DHCP Server service so that it can no longer be started, and then copy the entire contents of the %SystemRoot%\System32\Dhcp folder to the %SystemRoot%\System32\Dhcp folder on the destination server. After all the necessary files are on the destination server, type **net start "dhcp server"** to start the DHCP Server service on the destination server, which completes the migration.

# Setting up DHCP relay agents

In an ideal configuration, you have multiple DHCP servers on each subnet. However, because this isn't always possible, you can configure your routers to forward DHCP broadcasts or configure a computer on the network to act as a relay agent. Any computer running Windows Server 2012 can act as a relay agent. Doing so requires that Routing And Remote Access be configured and enabled on the computer first, and then you can configure the computer as a relay agent using the Routing And Remote Access console.

## Configuring and enabling Routing And Remote Access

Routing And Remote Access Services can be installed as part of the Remote Access role. On a server with no other policy and access role services configured, you can install Routing And Remote Access using the Add Roles And Features Wizard. During setup, choose Direct Access And VPN and Routing as the role services to install.

You'll then be able to work with Routing And Remote Access Services in Computer Management. Under Services And Applications, press and hold or right-click the Routing And Remote Access node in the left pane and then Configure And Enable Routing And

Remote Access. This starts the Routing And Remote Access Setup Wizard. Tap or click Next. Choose Custom Configuration, as shown in Figure 20-30, and then tap or click Next again. On the Custom Configuration page, select LAN Routing. Tap or click Next, and then tap or click Finish.

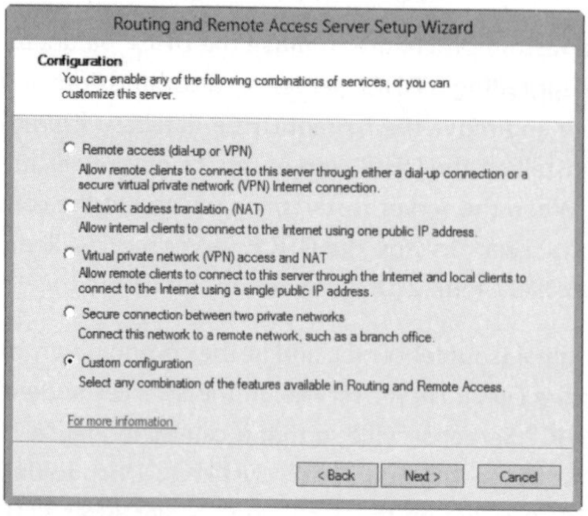

**Figure 20-30** Configure and enable Routing And Remote Access.

The wizard then creates a default Network Policy Server connection request policy on your organization's Network Access Policy server. You need to review this policy in the Network Policy console to ensure that it is configured properly and does not conflict with existing policies. Tap or click OK. Finally, when prompted to start the Routing And Remote Access Service, tap or click Start Service.

## Adding and configuring the DHCP relay agent

You can configure DHCP relay agents for IPv4 and IPv6. To configure a relay agent for IPv4 follow these steps:

1. In Computer Management, expand the Routing And Remote Access node and then expand IPv4.

2. Press and hold or right-click the General node, and then choose New Routing Protocol.

3. In the New Routing Protocol dialog box, select DHCP Relay Agent and then tap or click OK. This adds an entry under IPv4 labeled DHCP Relay Agent.

4.  Press and hold or right-click the DHCP Relay Agent entry, and choose New Interface.

5.  The New Interface For DHCP Relay Agent dialog box is displayed, as shown in Figure 20-31, showing the currently configured network interfaces on the computer. Select the network interface that is connected to the same network as the DHCP clients whose DHCP broadcasts need forwarding, and then tap or click OK.

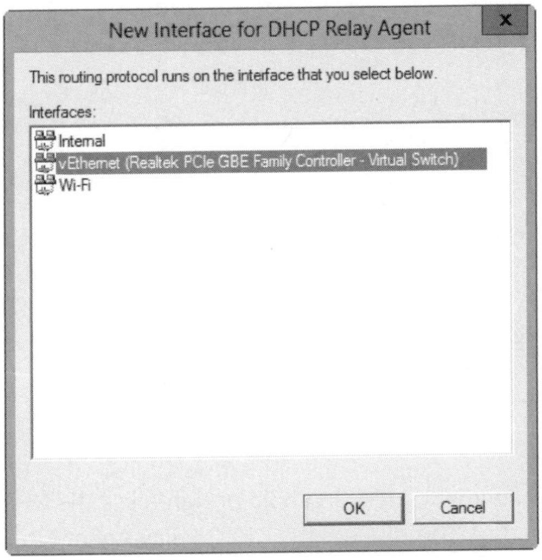

**Figure 20-31** Select the network interface on the same network as the DHCP clients.

6.  The DHCP Relay Properties dialog box is displayed automatically, as shown in Figure 20-32. After you set the following relay options, tap or click OK:

    ○ **Relay DHCP Packets** When selected, this option ensures that DHCP packets are relayed.

    ○ **Hop-Count Threshold** Determines the maximum number of relay agents a DHCP request can pass through. The default is 4. The maximum is 16.

    ○ **Boot Threshold (Seconds)** Determines the number of seconds the relay agent waits before forwarding DHCP packets. The delay is designed so that local DHCP servers will be the first to respond if they are available. The default delay is four seconds.

Chapter 20

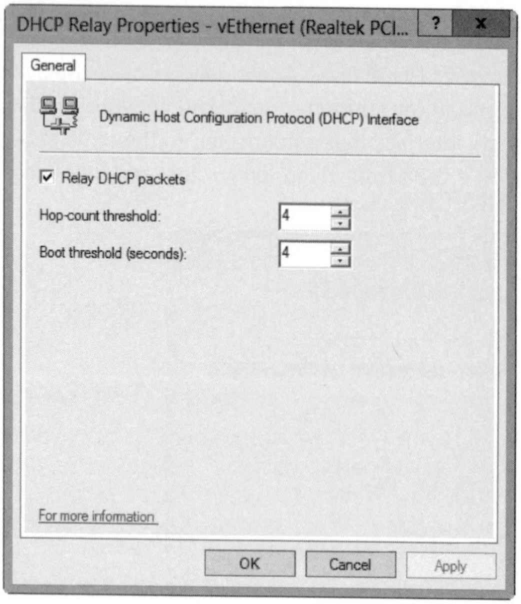

**Figure 20-32** Set the relay options.

7. In Computer Management, press and hold or right-click the DHCP Relay Agent entry and choose Properties. This displays the DHCP Relay Agent Properties dialog box.

8. Type the IP address of the DHCP server to which DHCP packets should be forwarded, and then tap or click Add. Tap or click OK. The computer is then configured as a DHCPv4 relay agent.

To configure a relay agent for IPv6 follow these steps:

1. In Computer Management, expand the Routing And Remote Access node and then expand IPv6.

2. Press and hold or right-click the General node, and then choose New Routing Protocol.

3. In the New Routing Protocol dialog box, select DHCPv6 Relay Agent and then tap or click OK. This adds an entry under IPv6 labeled DHCPv6 Relay Agent.

4. In Computer Management, press and hold or right-click the DHCPv6 Relay Agent entry and choose New Interface.

5. The New Interface For DHCPv6 Relay Agent dialog box is displayed. Select the network interface that is connected to the same network as the DHCPv6 clients whose DHCPv6 broadcasts need forwarding, and then tap or click OK.

6.   The DHCP Relay Properties dialog box is displayed automatically. After you set the following relay options, tap or click OK:

   ○   **Relay DHCP Packets**   When selected, this option ensures that DHCPv6 packets are relayed.

   ○   **Hop-Count Threshold**   Determines the maximum number of relay agents a DHCPv6 request can pass through. The default is 4. The maximum is 16.

   ○   **Elapsed-Time Threshold (Centi-Seconds)**   Determines the number of seconds the relay agent waits before forwarding DHCPv6 packets. The delay is designed so that local DHCPv6 servers will be the first to respond if they are available. The default delay is 32 seconds (3200 centi-seconds).

7.   In Computer Management, press and hold or right-click the DHCP Relay Agent entry and choose Properties. This displays the DHCP Relay Agent Properties dialog box.

8.   On the Servers tab, type the IPv6 address of the DHCPv6 server to which DHCPv6 packets should be forwarded and then tap or click Add. Tap or click OK. The computer is then configured as a DHCPv6 relay agent.

Chapter 20

# Architecting DNS infrastructure

T HE Domain Name System (DNS) is an Internet Engineering Task Force (IETF) standard name service. Its basic design is described in Requests for Comments (RFCs) 1034 and 1035, and it has been implemented on many operating systems, including UNIX and Microsoft Windows. All versions of Windows automatically install a DNS client as part of Transmission Control Protocol/Internet Protocol (TCP/IP). To get the server component, you must install the DNS Server service. All editions of Microsoft Windows Server 2012 include the DNS Server service. Because DNS is the name-resolution service for Active Directory, DNS is installed automatically if you install Active Directory on a network.

## DNS essentials

Like Dynamic Host Configuration Protocol (DHCP), DNS is a client/server protocol. This means a client component and a server component are necessary to successfully implement DNS. Because of the client/server model, any computer seeking DNS information is referred to as a *DNS client*, and the computer that provides the information to the client is referred to as a *DNS server*. It's the job of a DNS server to store a database containing DNS information, to respond to DNS queries from clients, and to replicate DNS information to other DNS servers as necessary.

DNS provides for several types of queries, including forward-lookup queries and reverse-lookup queries. Forward-lookup queries allow a client to resolve a host name to an Internet Protocol (IP) address. A DNS client makes a forward lookup using a name query message that asks the DNS server for the host address record of a specific host. The response to this query is sent as a name query response message. If there's a host address record for the specified host, the name server returns this. If the host name is an alias, the name server returns the record for the alias (CNAME) as well as the host address record to which the alias points.

Reverse-lookup queries allow a client to resolve an IP address to a host name, as Figure 21-1 shows. The DNS Server service supports IPv4 and IPv6 for reverse lookups.

Reverse lookups are primarily used by computers to verify the identity of a remote computer. A DNS client makes a reverse lookup using a reverse name query message. The response to the query is sent as a reverse name query response message. This message contains the reverse address record (PTR) for the specified host.

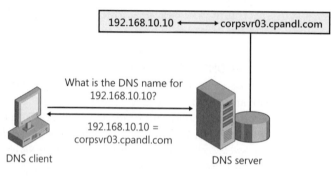

**Figure 21-1** A reverse lookup query.

DNS also provides a way to cache DNS information to reduce the number of queries that are required. So, instead of having to send a query to a name server each time the host wants to resolve a particular name, the DNS client checks its local cache for the information first. All queries into the DNS cache are asynchronous and, as such, are processed one at a time in sequence.

DNS information in the cache is held for a set amount of time, referred to as the Time to Live (TTL) value of a record. When a record exists in cache and its TTL has not expired, it is used to answer subsequent queries. Not only does this reduce traffic on the network, it also speeds up the name-resolution process. A record's TTL is set in the query response from a name server.

When a recursive DNS server responds to a query, the server caches the results obtained so that it can respond quickly if it receives another query requesting the same information. The TTL determines how long the DNS server will cache a resource record. During this time, the cache might be overwritten if updated information about a cached record is received. However, Windows Server 2008 R2 and later use DNS cache locking to ensure cached records can't be overwritten until their TTL expires.

# INSIDE OUT DNS cache locking

Although cache locking is designed to enhance security and prevent cache poisoning attacks, there might be instances where you want to allow cached records to be updated sooner. The registry key CacheLockingPercent under HKEY_LOCAL_MACHINE\ SYSTEM\CurrentControlSet\services\DNS\Parameters controls how cache locking works. This key sets the percentage of the TTL duration that must be reached before a cached record can be overwritten.

By default, CacheLockingPercent is set to 100, meaning the TTL has to fully expire before a cached record can be overwritten. If you want to allow cached records to be overwritten after 50 percent or more of their TTL duration has been reached, you set CacheLockingPercent to 50. To configure cache locking, type **dnscmd /config /cachelockingpercent** *Percent* at an elevated command prompt, where *Percent* is the percentage of the TTL duration that must be reached for a cached record to be overwritten. If you change the cache locking percentage, you must restart the DNS Server service for the change to take effect. To do this, type **net stop dns** at an elevated command prompt. Then, after the service stops, type **net start dns**.

# Planning DNS implementations

Creating a new DNS implementation or revamping your existing DNS implementation requires good planning. You need a solid understanding of how DNS works, and the areas you should know about include the following:

- How DNS namespaces are assigned and used

- How DNS name resolution works and can be modified

- How DNS devolution works and can be configured

- What resource records are available and how they are used

- How DNS zones and zone transfers can be used

- How internal and external servers can be used

- How DNS is integrated with other technologies

# Public and private namespaces

The DNS domain namespace is a hierarchical tree in which each node and leaf in the tree represents a named domain. Each level of the domain namespace tree is separated by a period (called a "dot"). As discussed in "Understanding name resolution" in Chapter 18, "Networking with TCP/IP," the first level of the tree is where you'll find the top-level domains, and these top-level domains form the base of the DNS namespace. The second level of the tree is for second-level or parent domains, and subsequent levels of the tree are for subdomains. For example, cpandl.com is the parent domain of the child domains sales .cpandl.com and tech.cpandl.com.

> **Note**
>
> Although the actual root of the DNS namespace is represented by "." and doesn't have a name, each level in the tree has a name, which is referred to as its label. The fully qualified domain name (FQDN) of a node in the DNS namespace is the list of all the labels in the path from the node to the root of the namespace. For example, the FQDN for the host named CORPSVR02 in the cpandl.com domain is corpsvr02.cpandl.com.

To divide public and private namespaces, the top-level domains are established and maintained by select organizations. The top authority, Internet Corporation for Assigned Names and Numbers (ICANN), is responsible for defining and delegating control over the top-level domains to individual organizations. Top-level domains are organized functionally and geographically. Table 21-1 lists the functions of key generic top-level domains; the list can be extended to include other generic top-level domains. (See *http://www.iana.org/domains/root/db/* for the most current list.) The geographically organized top-level domains are identified by two-level country/region codes. These country/region codes are based on the International Organization for Standardization (ISO) country/region name and are used primarily by organizations outside the United States.

> **Note**
>
> The United Kingdom is the exception to the ISO naming rule. Although the ISO country/region code for the United Kingdom is GB (Great Britain), its two-letter designator is UK.

**TABLE 21-1** Top-level domain names for the Internet

| Domain | Purpose |
|--------|---------|
| .aero | For aerospace firms, including airlines |
| .asia | For the Asia-Pacific region |
| .biz | For businesses; extends the .com area |
| .com | For commercial organizations |
| .coop | For business cooperatives |
| .edu | For educational institutions |
| .gov | For U.S. government agencies |
| .info | For information sources |
| .int | For organizations established by international treaties |
| .mil | For U.S. military departments and agencies |
| .mobi | For mobile-compatible sites |
| .museum | For museums |
| .name | For use by individuals |
| .net | For use by network providers |
| .org | For use by organizations, such as those that are nongovernmental or nonprofit |
| .pro | For professional groups, such as doctors and lawyers |
| .travel | For the travel and tourism industry |

After ICANN delegates control over a top-level domain, it is the responsibility of the designated organization to maintain the domain and handle registrations. After an organization registers a domain name with one of these authorities, the organization controls the domain and can create subdomains within this domain without having to make a formal request. For example, if you register the domain cpandl.com, you can create the subdomains seattle.cpandl.com, portland.cpandl.com, and sf.cpandl.com without having to ask the registration authority for permission.

Private namespaces aren't controlled by ICANN. You can create your own private namespace for use within your company. For example, you could use .local for your top-level domain. This keeps your internal network separate from the public Internet. You would then need to rely on Network Address Translation (NAT) or proxy servers to access the public Internet.

## Name resolution using DNS

In DNS, name resolution is made possible using a distributed database. The resource records in this database detail host name and IP address information relating to domains.

It is the job of DNS name servers to store the DNS database and respond to queries from clients about the information the database contains. A portion of the DNS namespace that is controlled by a DNS name server or a group of name servers is referred to as a *zone*.

Zones establish the boundaries within which a particular name server can resolve requests. On clients, it is the job of DNS resolvers to contact name servers and perform queries about resource records. Thus, the three main components of DNS are as follows:

- Resource records stored in a distributed database

- DNS name servers that are responsible for maintaining specific zones

- DNS resolvers running on clients

These key components are used to perform DNS operations, which can consist of query operations, query replies, and DNS update operations. A basic query and reply work as shown in Figure 21-2. Here, a DNS client wants information from a DNS name server, so it sends a DNS query. The DNS server to which the query is sent checks its local database and forwards the request to an authoritative server. The authoritative server sends back a response to the local DNS server, and that response is forwarded to the client.

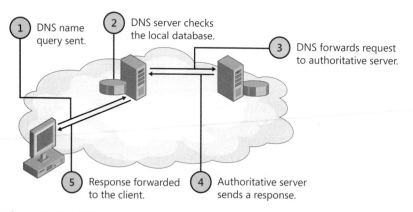

**Figure 21-2**  A DNS query and reply.

As Figure 21-3 shows, things get a bit more complicated when a client requests the name of an external resource, such as a website. If you were on an internal domain and requested a resource on the public Internet, such as the IP address for the www.cpandl.com server, the DNS client on your computer queries the local name server as specified in its TCP/IP configuration. The local name server forwards the request to the root server for the external resource domain. This domain contacts the name server for the related top-level domain, which in turn contacts the name server for the cpandl.com domain. This authoritative server sends a response, which is forwarded to the client, who can then access the external resource.

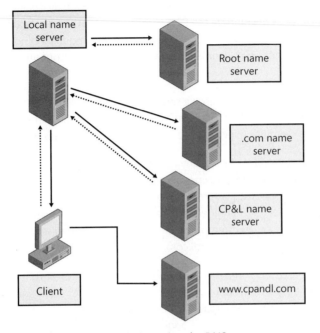

**Figure 21-3** Name resolution using the DNS tree.

As you can see, in a normal DNS configuration, if your DNS name server can't resolve a request, it simply forwards the request to another name server for resolution. This allows your organization's name servers to get internal DNS information and external DNS information on the public Internet. However, what if the domain you were trying to reach was a resource in another one of your own internal domains? In this case, you wouldn't want requests to be forwarded to a public DNS name server for resolution. The public DNS server would have no idea how to resolve the request.

There are several ways to resolve this problem, and one of these ways is to use conditional forwarding. By using conditional forwarding, you can tell your DNS name servers that if you see a request for domain XYZ, don't forward it to the public DNS name servers for resolution. Instead, forward the request directly to the XYZ name server—which is the authoritative name server for the domain being looked up. This name server will then be able to reply to the query, and the DNS lookup will be resolved. For more information on resolving name-resolution problems and conditional forwarding, see "Secondary zones, stub zones, and conditional forwarding" later in this chapter.

# Understanding DNS devolution

DNS devolution allows client devices that are members of child namespaces to access resources in parent namespaces without explicitly specifying the fully qualified domain name of a resource. With devolution, the DNS resolver creates the fully qualified domain name of a resource by adding parent suffixes to single-label, unqualified domain names. However, devolution is not used when a global suffix search list is configured in Group Policy.

With devolution, DNS clients try to resolve single-label names using the parent suffix of the primary DNS suffix, the parent of that suffix, and so on until the name is successfully resolved or until the devolution level allowed by devolution settings is reached.

The devolution level determines how many levels of antecedents are used. For example, if the primary DNS suffix is engineering.cpandl.com and devolution is enabled with a devolution level of two, an application attempting to query the host name mailserver23 will attempt to resolve mailserver23.engineering.cpandl.com and mailserver23.cpandl.com. If the devolution level is three, an attempt will be made to resolve mailserver23.engineering .cpandl.com, but not mailserver23.cpandl.com.

However, if the primary DNS suffix is not a trailing subset of the forest root domain, the DNS resolver doesn't perform devolution. Why? The primary DNS suffix and the forest root domain don't share the same namespace. For example, if the primary DNS suffix is tech .cpandl.com but the forest root domain is engineering.cpandl.com, the resolver doesn't perform devolution. This is because tech.cpandl.com is not a trailing subset of engineering.cpandl.com.

More specifically, the DNS resolver first determines the primary DNS suffix and forest root domain of the client. If the number of labels for the primary DNS suffix is one, the DNS resolver doesn't perform devolution. Otherwise, if the primary DNS suffix is a trailing subset of the forest root domain, the devolution level is set to the number of labels in the forest root domain. Here are some examples:

- If the primary DNS suffix is cpandl.com and the forest root domain is cpandl, no devolution is performed. Why? The forest root domain is single-labeled.

- If the primary DNS suffix is cpandl.com and the forest root domain is cpandl.com, the devolution level is 2. Why? The forest root domain has two labels, and the primary DNS suffix is a trailing subset of the forest root domain.

- If the primary DNS suffix is tech.cpandl.com and the forest root domain is cpandl.com, the devolution level is 2. Why? The forest root domain has two labels.

- If the primary DNS suffix is tech.cpandl.com and the forest root domain is tech .cpandl.com, the devolution level is 3. Why? The forest root domain has three labels.

- If the primary DNS suffix is tech.cpandl.com and the forest root domain is eng.cpandl.com, no devolution is performed. Why? The primary DNS suffix is not a trailing subset of the forest root domain.

DNS devolution is enabled by default. Prior to Windows 7 and Windows Server 2008 R2, the effective devolution level was two. With current and updated DNS clients and servers, however, the devolution level is used to precisely control how clients resolve resource names within a domain.

> **Note**
>
> You can control devolution using Group Policy. If you don't want DNS clients to resolve names using devolution, disable the Primary DNS Suffix Devolution setting in the Administrative Templates for Computer Configuration under Network\DNS Client. To set a specific devolution level, enable and configure the Primary DNS Suffix Devolution Level policy in the Administrative Templates for Computer Configuration under Network\DNS Client.

## DNS resource records

Resource records are used to store domain information. DNS name servers contain resource records for those portions of the DNS namespace for which they are authoritative. It is the job of administrators who maintain an authoritative DNS name server to maintain the resource records and ensure that they are accurate. DNS name servers can also cache resource records for those areas for which they can answer queries sent by hosts. This means DNS name servers can cache resource records relating to any part of the domain tree.

Although many types of resource records are defined and supported by DNS servers, only a few record types are actually used on a Windows Server network. With that in mind, take a look at Table 21-2, which provides an overview of the resource records that you'll use.

**TABLE 21-2 Common resource records used on Windows Server networks**

| Record Type | Common Name | Description |
| --- | --- | --- |
| A | Host address | Contains the name of a host and its Internet Protocol version 4 (IPv4) address. Any computer that has multiple network interfaces or IP addresses should have multiple address records. |
| AAAA | IPv6 host address | Contains the name of a host and its Internet Protocol version 6 (IPv6) address. |
| CNAME | Canonical name | Creates an alias for a host name. This allows a host to be referred to by multiple names in DNS. The most common use is when a host provides a common service, such as World Wide Web (WWW) or File Transfer Protocol (FTP), and you want it to have a friendly name rather than a complex name. For example, you might want www.cpandl.com to be an alias for the host dc06.cpandl.com. |
| MX | Mail exchanger | Indicates a mail exchange server for the domain, which allows mail to be delivered to the correct mail servers in the domain. For example, if an MX record is set for the domain cpandl.com, all mail sent to username@cpandl.com will be directed to the server specified in the MX record. |
| NS | Name server | Provides a list of authoritative servers for a domain, which allows DNS lookups within various zones. Each primary and secondary name server in a domain should be declared through this record. |
| PTR | Pointer | Enables reverse lookups by creating a pointer that maps an IP address to a host name. |
| SOA | Start of authority | Indicates the authoritative name server for a particular zone. The authoritative server is the best source of DNS information for a zone. Because each zone must have an SOA record, the record is created automatically when you add a zone. The SOA record also contains information about how resource records in the zone should be used and cached. This includes refresh, retry, and expiration intervals as well as the maximum time that a record is considered valid. |
| SRV | Service location | Makes it possible to find a server providing a specific service. Active Directory uses SRV records to locate domain controllers, global catalog servers, Lightweight Directory Access Protocol (LDAP) servers, and Kerberos servers. SRV records are created automatically. For example, Active Directory creates an SRV record when you set a domain controller as a global catalog. LDAP servers can add an SRV to indicate they are available to handle LDAP requests in a particular zone. All domains have SRV records associated with them. SRV records are created in the forest root zone, domain zones, and tree zones, as discussed in "Using DNS with Active Directory" in Chapter 22, "Implementing and managing DNS." |

# DNS zones and zone transfers

DNS name servers that have complete information for a part of the DNS namespace are said to be *authoritative*. As mentioned earlier, a portion of the namespace over which an authoritative name server has control is referred to as a zone. Zones establish the boundaries within which a particular name server can resolve requests and are the main replication units in DNS. Zones can contain resource records for one or more related DNS domains.

Windows Server 2012 supports four types of zones:

- **Standard primary**   Stores a writable master copy of a zone as a text file. All changes to a zone are made in the primary zone. The information in, as well as changes to, a primary zone can be replicated to secondary zones.

- **Standard secondary**   Stores a read-only copy of a zone as a text file. It is used to provide redundancy and load balancing for a primary zone. The information in, and changes to, a primary zone are replicated to a secondary zone using zone transfers.

- **Active Directory–integrated**   Integrates zone information in Active Directory Domain Services, and uses Active Directory Domain Services to replicate zone information. This is a proprietary zone type that is only possible when you deploy Active Directory Domain Services on the network. Windows Server can selectively replicate DNS information.

## Active Directory–integrated zones are only on domain controllers

Designating a zone as Active Directory–integrated means that only domain controllers can be primary name servers for the zone. These domain controllers can accept dynamic updates, and Active Directory security is used automatically to restrict dynamic updates to domain members. Any DNS servers in the zone that aren't domain controllers can act only as secondary name servers. These secondary name servers cannot accept dynamic updates.

- **Stub**   Stores a partial zone that can be used to identify the authoritative DNS servers for a zone. A stub zone has no information about the hosts in a zone. Instead, it has information only about the authoritative name servers in a zone so that queries can be forwarded directly to those name servers.

Each of these four DNS zone types can be created for forward or reverse lookups. A forward-lookup zone is used to resolve DNS names into IP addresses and provide information about available network services. A reverse-lookup zone is used to resolve IP addresses to DNS names.

## Zones that aren't integrated with Active Directory

With standard zones that aren't integrated with Active Directory, a master copy of the zone is stored in a primary zone on a single DNS server, called a *primary DNS server*. This server's SOA record indicates that it is the primary zone for the related domain. Secondary zones are used to improve performance and provide redundancy. A server storing a copy of a secondary zone is referred to as a *secondary DNS server*.

A primary DNS server automatically replicates a copy of the primary zone to any designated secondary servers. The transfer of zone information is handled by a zone-replication process and is referred to as a *zone transfer*. Although the initial zone transfer after configuring a new secondary server represents a full transfer of the zone information, subsequent transfers are made incrementally as changes occur. Here's how it works: When changes are made to a primary zone, the changes are made first to the primary zone and then transferred to the secondary zone on the secondary servers. Because only changes are transferred, rather than a complete copy of the zone, the amount of traffic required to keep a secondary zone current is significantly reduced.

You can implement DNS zones in many ways. One way to do this is to mimic your organization's domain structure. Figure 21-4 shows an example of how zones and zone transfers could be configured for child domains of a parent domain. Here, you have separate zones that handle name services for the cpandl.com, tech.cpandl.com, and sales.cpandl.com domains. Zone transfers are configured so that copies of the primary zone on cpandl.com are transferred to the name servers for the tech.cpandl.com and sales.cpandl.com domains. The reason for this is that users in these zones routinely work with servers in the cpandl.com zone. This makes lookups faster and reduces the amount of DNS traffic as well.

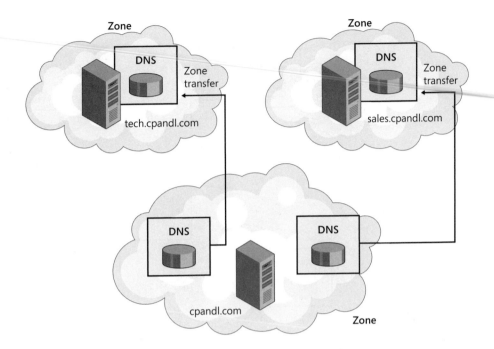

**Figure 21-4** DNS zones on separate servers.

Although you can configure DNS services in this way, your organization's domain structure is separate from its zone configuration. If you create subdomains of a parent domain, they can either be part of the same zone or belong to another zone, and these zones can be on separate DNS servers or the same DNS servers.

The example in Figure 21-5 shows a wide area network (WAN) configuration. The branch offices in Seattle and New York are separate from the company headquarters, and key zones are organized geographically. At company headquarters, there's an additional zone running on the same DNS name server as the zone for the cpandl.com domain. This zone handles services.cpandl.com, tech.cpandl.com, and sales.cpandl.com.

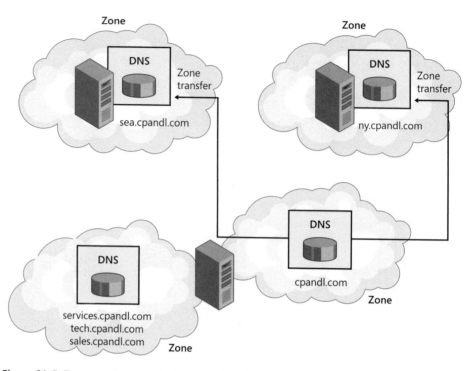

**Figure 21-5**  Zones can be separate from the domain structure.

## Zones that are integrated with Active Directory

Using Active Directory–integrated zones, you can store DNS zone information within Active Directory. This gives you several advantages. Any primary zone or stub zone integrated with Active Directory is automatically replicated to other domain controllers using Active Directory replication. Because Active Directory can compress replication data between sites, you can more efficiently replicate DNS information, and this is especially important over slow WAN links.

Figure 21-6 shows an example of Active Directory–integrated zones and replication. Here, zone information for cpandl.com, seattle.cpandl.com, portland.cpandl.com, and sf.cpandl.com has been integrated with Active Directory. This allows any DNS changes made at branch offices or at company headquarters to be replicated throughout the organization to all the available name servers. Because the decision to integrate zones with Active Directory isn't an all-or-nothing approach, there are also standard primary and secondary zones, and standard DNS zone transfers are used to maintain these zones.

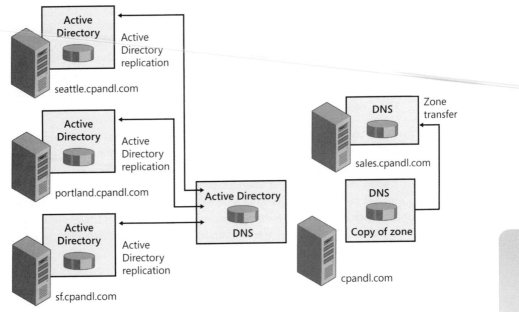

**Figure 21-6** Active Directory–integrated zones.

# INSIDE OUT Multimaster replication for DNS changes

By using Active Directory integration, copies of zone information are maintained on all domain controllers that are also configured as DNS servers. This is different from standard DNS zones. When you use standard zones, there's a single authoritative DNS server for a zone, and it maintains a master copy of the zone. All updates to the primary zone must be made on the primary server. With Active Directory–integrated zones, each domain controller configured as a DNS server in a domain is an authoritative server for that domain. This means clients can make updates to DNS records on any of these servers and the changes will be automatically replicated.

With Active Directory–integrated zones, default application partitions are used to ensure that DNS information is replicated only to domain controllers that are also configured as DNS servers. Here's how it works: For every domain in an Active Directory forest, a separate application partition is created and used to store all records in each Active Directory–integrated zone configured for that domain. Because the application partition context is outside that of other Active Directory information, DNS information is not replicated with other Active Directory information. There's also a default application partition that stores DNS information and replicates that information to all DNS servers in an Active Directory forest. This simplifies DNS replication for organizations with multiple domains.

Another benefit of Active Directory integration is the ability to perform conditional forwarding. By using conditional forwarding, you can eliminate the split-brain syndrome when internal requests get incorrectly forwarded to external DNS servers. Finally, with dynamic updates using DHCP, clients gain the ability to use secure dynamic updates. Secure dynamic updates ensure that only clients that created a record can subsequently update the record. You'll find more on secure dynamic updates in "Security considerations" later in this chapter.

When you are working with early releases of a DNS server for Windows Server, restarting a DNS server could take a long time in very large organizations with extremely large Active Directory Domain Services–integrated zones. The reason for this was that the zone data was loaded in the foreground while the server was starting the DNS service. To ensure that DNS servers can be responsive after a restart, current releases of Windows Server load zone data from Active Directory Domain Services in the background while it restarts. This ensures that the DNS server is responsive and can handle requests for data from other zones.

DNS servers perform the following tasks at startup:

- Enumerate all zones to be loaded.

- Load root hints from files or Active Directory Domain Services storage.

- Load all zones that are stored in files rather than in Active Directory Domain Services.

- Begin responding to queries and remote procedure calls (RPCs).

- Create one or more threads to load the zones that are stored in Active Directory Domain Services.

Because separate threads load zone data, the DNS server is able to respond to queries while zone loading is in progress. If a DNS client performs a query for a host in a zone that has already been loaded, the DNS server responds appropriately. If the query is for a host that has not yet been loaded into memory, the DNS server reads the host's data from Active Directory Domain Services and updates its record list accordingly.

## Secondary zones, stub zones, and conditional forwarding

Secondary zones, stub zones, and conditional forwarding can all be used to resolve name-resolution problems—chiefly the split-brain scenario in which internal DNS servers blindly forward any requests that they can't resolve to external servers. Rather than blindly forwarding requests, you can configure internal servers so that they know about certain DNS domains. This ensures that name resolution works for domains that aren't known on the public Internet and can also be used to speed up name resolution for known domains, which makes users much happier than if name resolution fails or they have to wait all the time for name requests to be resolved.

By using a secondary zone, you create a complete copy of a zone on a DNS server that can be used to resolve DNS queries without having to go to the authoritative name server for that domain. Not only can this be used for subdomains of a parent domain that exists in different zones, but for different parent domains as well. For example, on the name servers for cpandl.com you could create secondary zones for a partner company, such as The Phone Company whose domain is thephone-company.com. In this way, DNS clients in the cpandl.com domain can perform fast lookups for hosts in thephone-company.com domain.

The downside is that you must replicate DNS information between the domains. If this replication takes place over the public Internet, the administrators at The Phone Company would need to configure firewalls on their network to allow this and make other security changes as well, which might not be acceptable. Because you are maintaining a full copy of the zone, any change generates replication traffic.

With a stub zone, you create a partial copy of a zone that has information about only the authoritative name servers in a zone. As Figure 21-7 shows, this allows a DNS server to forward queries directly to a name server for a particular domain and bypass the normal name-server hierarchy. This speeds up the lookup because you don't have to go through multiple name servers to find the authoritative name server for a domain.

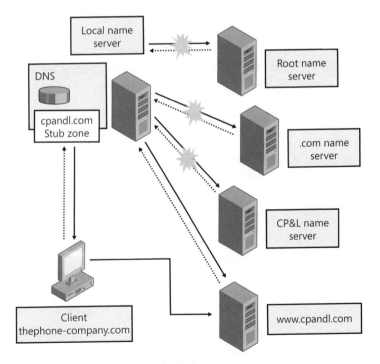

**Figure 21-7** Using stub zones for lookups.

Stub zones work like this: When you set up a stub zone for a domain, only the resource records needed to identify the authoritative name servers for the related domain are transferred to the name server. These records include the SOA and NS records as well as the related A records for these servers (referred to as *glue records*). These records can be maintained in one of two ways. If you use Active Directory integration, the normal Active Directory replication process can be used to maintain the stub zone. If you use a standard stub zone, standard zone transfers are used to maintain the stub zone. Both techniques require access to the domain specified in the stub zone, which can be a security issue. Replication traffic isn't an issue, however, because you are maintaining a very small amount of data.

Conditional forwarding is very similar to stub zones except that you don't need to transfer any information from the domain to which you want to forward requests. Instead, you configure name servers in domain A so that they know the IP address of the authoritative name servers in domain B, allowing these name servers to be used as forwarders. There's no access requirement, so you don't need permission to do this, and there's no bandwidth requirement, so you don't need to worry about extra replication traffic.

By using conditional forwarding, there are some trade-offs to be made, however. If the authoritative name servers change, the IP addresses aren't updated automatically as they are with stub zones or secondary zones. This means you would have to reconfigure name servers manually in domain A with the new IP addresses of the authoritative name servers in domain B. When you configure conditional forwarders on a name server, the name server has to check the forwarders list each time it resolves a name. As the list grows, it requires more and more time to work through the list of potential forwarders.

## Integration with other technologies

The DNS client built into computers running Windows Vista and later supports DNS traffic over IPv4 and IPv6. By default, IPv6 configures the well-known site-local addresses of DNS servers at FEC0:0:0:FFFF::1, FEC0:0:0:FFFF::2, and FEC0:0:0:FFFF::3. To add the IPv6 addresses of your DNS servers, use the properties of the Internet Protocol Version 6 (TCP/IPv6) component in Network Connections or the **netsh interface ipv6 set dns** command.

When the network uses DHCP, you should configure DHCP to work with DNS. DHCP clients can register IPv4 and IPv6 addresses. To ensure proper integration of DHCP and DNS, you need to set the appropriate DHCP scope options. For IPv4, you should set the 006 DNS Servers and 015 DNS Domain Name scope options. For IPv6, you should set the 00023 DNS Recursive Name Server IPV6 Address and 00024 Domain Search List scope options.

DNS client computers running Windows Vista and later can use Link-Local Multicast Name Resolution (LLMNR) to resolve names on a local network segment when a DNS server is not available. They also periodically search for a domain controller in the domain to which they belong and can be configured to locate the nearest domain controller instead of searching randomly. This functionality helps avoid performance problems that might occur if a DNS client creates an association with a distant domain controller located on a slow link rather than a local domain controller because of a network or server failure. Previously, this association continued until the client was forced to seek a new domain controller, such as when the client computer was disconnected from the network for a long period of time. By periodically renewing its association with a domain controller, a DNS client can reduce the probability that it will be associated with an inappropriate domain controller.

DNS clients for Windows 8 and Windows Server 2012 have significant changes. You can control the way these changes work using Group Policy settings found in the Administrative Templates for Computer Configuration under Network\DNS Client.

By default, these clients do not send outbound LLMNR queries to mobile broadband or virtual private network (VPN) interfaces, nor do they send outbound NetBIOS queries to mobile broadband interfaces. These clients issue LLMNR and NetBIOS queries in parallel with DNS queries, optimized for IPv4 and IPv6 with a binding order preference. Interfaces are divided into networks to send parallel queries, and responses are preferred in binding order as well.

You can control whether queries are optimized and issued in parallel using the Turn Off Smart Multi-Home Name Resolution setting. When you enable this setting, parallel queries are not used. Instead, DNS queries are issued first across all networks. If DNS queries fail, LLMNR queries are issued. If LLMNR queries fail, NetBIOS queries are used.

By default, LLMNR and NetBIOS responses are preferred over DNS responses if the LLMNR and NetBIOS responses are from a network with a higher binding order. You can control the way binding order preference works using the Prefer Link Local Responses Over DNS setting. When you enable this setting, LLMNR and NetBIOS responses are preferred over DNS responses if the LLMNR and NetBIOS responses are from a network with a higher binding order.

To resolve a problem with computers in power-saving mode, the LLMNR query timeout has been increased to 410 milliseconds (ms) for the first retry and 410 ms for the second retry, giving a total timeout value of 820 ms instead of 300 ms. Additionally, if a specific interface is hijacking DNS names, these clients send LLMNR and NetBIOS queries in parallel with DNS queries on those networks and the LLMNR or NetBIOS response is preferred.

You can control LLMNR in several ways. To disable LLMNR, enable the Turn Off Multicast Name Resolution setting. To ensure DNS clients on nondomain networks always prefer DNS responses, enable the Turn Off Smart Protocol Reordering setting. When this setting is enabled, DNS clients on nondomain networks will prefer DNS responses to LLMNR responses and LLMNR responses to NetBIOS responses.

# Security considerations

DNS security is an important issue, and this discussion focuses on three areas:

- DNS queries from clients

- DNS dynamic updates

- External DNS name resolution

## DNS queries and security

A client that makes a query trusts that an authoritative DNS name server gives it the right information. In most environments, this works fine. Users or administrators specify the initial DNS name servers to which DNS queries should be forwarded in a computer's TCP/IP configuration. In some environments where security is a major concern, administrators might be worried about DNS clients getting invalid information from DNS name servers. Here, administrators might want to look at the DNS Security (DNSSEC) protocol. DNSSEC is especially useful for companies that have many branch locations and DNS information is transferred over the public Internet using zone transfers.

DNSSEC provides authentication of DNS information. Using DNSSEC, you can digitally sign zone files so that they can be authenticated. These digital signatures can be sent to DNS clients as resource records from DNS servers hosting signed zones. The client can then verify that the DNS information sent from the DNS server is authentic.

When you use DNS Server for Windows Server 2012, there are some added benefits. Active Directory–integrated zones support dynamic updates in DNSSEC signed zones. DNS Server supports automated trust anchor distribution through Active Directory and automated trust anchor rollover. DNS Server also supports the validation of records with updated DNSSEC standards, including NSEC3 and RSA/SHA-2.

DNSSEC digital signatures are encrypted using private key encryption on a per-zone basis. In private key encryption, there is a public key and a private key. A zone's public key is used to validate a digital signature. Like the digital signature itself, the public key is stored in a signed zone in the form of a resource record. A zone's private key is not stored in the zone; it is private and used only by the name server to sign the related zone or parts of the zone. The records used with DNSSEC are summarized in Table 21-3.

**TABLE 21-3 DNSSEC resource records**

| Record Type | Common Name | Description |
| --- | --- | --- |
| KEY | Public Key | Contains the public key that is related to a DNS domain name. The public key can be for a zone, host, or other entity. KEY records are authenticated by SIG records. |
| NXT | Next | Indicates the next record in a digitally signed zone and states which records exist in a zone. It can be used to validate that a particular record doesn't exist in the zone. For example, if there's a record for corpsvr07.cpandl.com and the Next record points to corpsvr09.cpandl.com, there isn't a record for corpsvr08 .cpandl.com, so that server doesn't exist in the zone. |
| SIG | Signature | Contains the digital signature for a zone or part of a zone and is used to authenticate a resource record set of a particular type. |

## DNS dynamic updates and security

Windows Server 2003 and later fully support DNS dynamic updates. Dynamic updates are defined in RFC 2136 and are used in conjunction with DHCP to allow a client to update its A record if its IP address changes and allow the DHCP server to update the PTR record for the client on the DNS server. DHCP servers can also be configured to update both the A and PTR records on the client's behalf. Dynamic DNS is also supported for IPv6 AAAA records, which allows for dynamic updating of host addresses on systems that use IPv6 and DHCP.

If dynamic updates are enabled, the DNS name server trusts the client to update its own DNS record and trusts the DHCP server to make updates on behalf of the client. There are two types of dynamic updates:

- **Secure dynamic updates**  You can use secure dynamic updates to put security mechanisms in place to ensure that only a client that created a record can update a record.

- **Nonsecure dynamic updates**  By using nonsecure dynamic updates, there is no way to ensure that only a client that created a record can update a record.

Secure dynamic updates are the default setting for Active Directory–integrated zones. By using secure updates, known clients that have DNS records in Active Directory can update their records dynamically and unknown clients are prevented from adding their records to a zone.

Any client capable of using secure dynamic updates can update their records. This means clients running any current version of Windows can update their own records. DHCP servers can be configured to make updates on behalf of these clients. For more information on this, see "Integrating DHCP and DNS" in Chapter 20, "Managing DHCP."

Chapter 21

With standard zones, the default setting is to allow both secure and nonsecure dynamic updates. The reason standard zones are configured for both secure and nonsecure dynamic updates is that this allows clients running current Windows operating systems as well as clients running early Windows operating systems to update records dynamically. Although it seems to imply that security is involved, in fact, it is not. Here, allowing secure updates simply means that the dynamic update process won't break when a secure update is made. By default, DNS doesn't validate updates, and this means dynamic updates are accepted from any client. This creates a significant security vulnerability because updates can be accepted from untrusted sources.

You can eliminate this security vulnerability using name protection. With name protection, which is a feature that you can enable on DHCP servers running Windows Server 2012, the DHCP server registers records on behalf of the client only if no other client with this DNS information is already registered. On a DHCP server, you can configure name protection for IPv4 and IPv6 at the protocol level or at the scope level. Name protection settings configured at the scope level take precedence over the setting at the IPv4 or IPv6 level.

Name protection is designed to prevent name squatting. Name squatting occurs when a non-Windows-based computer registers a name in DNS that is already registered to a computer running a Windows operating system. By enabling name protection, you can prevent name squatting by non-Windows-based computers. Although name squatting generally does not present a problem when you use Active Directory to reserve a name for a single user or computer, it usually is a good idea to enable name protection on all Windows networks.

Name protection is based on the Dynamic Host Configuration Identifier (DHCID) and support for the DHCID RR (resource record) in DNS. DHCID is a resource record stored in DNS that maps names to prevent duplicate registration. DHCP uses the DHCID resource record to store an identifier for a computer along with related information for the name, such as the A and AAAA records of the computer. The DHCP server can request a DHCID record match and then refuse the registration of a computer with a different address attempting to register a name with an existing DHCID record.

## External DNS name resolution and security

Typically, as part of a standard DNS configuration, you'll configure DNS servers on your internal network to forward queries that they can't resolve to DNS servers outside the organization. Normally, these servers are the name servers for the Internet service provider (ISP) that provides your organization's Internet connection. In this configuration, you know that internal servers forward to designated external servers. However, if those servers don't respond, the internal servers typically will forward requests directly to the root name servers, and this is where security problems can be introduced.

By default, DNS servers include a list of root servers that can be used for name resolution to the top-level domains. This list is maintained in what is called a *root hints file*. If this file is not updated regularly, your organization's internal name servers could point to invalid root servers, and this leaves a hole in your security that could be exploited. To prevent this, periodically update the root hints file.

On a DNS server that doesn't use Active Directory, the root hints are read from the %SystemRoot%\System32\DNS\Cache.dns file. You can obtain an update for this file from *http://www.internic.net/zones/named.root*. To determine whether an update is needed, compare the version information in your current root hints file with that of the published version. Within the root hints file, you'll find a section of comments like this:

```
;    This file holds the information on root name servers needed to
;         initialize cache of Internet domain name servers
;         (e.g. reference this file in the "cache  .  <file>"
;         configuration file of BIND domain name servers).
;
;    This file is made available by InterNIC
;    under anonymous FTP as
;         file                          /domain/named.root
;         on server                     FTP.INTERNIC.NET
;
;         last update:                  Jun 8, 2012
;         related version of root zone: 2012060800
```

Here, the version information is in the last two lines of the comments. If you changed the root hints file, you must stop and then start the DNS Server service so that the root hints file is reloaded. In the DNS console, you can do this by pressing and holding or right-clicking the server entry, pointing to All Tasks, and selecting Restart.

On a DNS server that uses Active Directory Domain Services–integrated zones, the root hints are read from Active Directory and the registry at startup. You can view and modify the root hints in the DNS console. To do this, press and hold or right-click the DNS server entry and then select Properties. In the Properties dialog box, tap or click the Root Hints tab. You can then manage each of the individual root hint entries using Add, Edit, or Remove as necessary. To update the entire root hints using a known good DNS server, tap or click Copy From Server, type the IP address of the DNS server, and then tap or click OK. If you suspect the root hints file is corrupted, you might need to reload the file into Active Directory using the %SystemRoot%\System32\DNS\Cache.dns file. To do this, follow these steps:

1. At an elevated command prompt, type **net stop dns** to stop the DNS Server service. When the DNS Server service stops, type **copy %systemroot%\system32\ dns\samples\cache.dns %systemroot%\system32\dns**. If you are prompted to overwrite the existing file, type **Y** for yes.

2. In Active Directory Users And Computers, make sure Advanced Features is selected on the View menu, and then expand System MicrosoftDNS. Next, press and hold or right-click RootDNSServers and then tap or click Delete.

3. When you are prompted to delete this object, tap or click Yes. When you are prompted to delete this object as well as the objects it contains, tap or click Yes.

4. At the elevated command prompt, type **net start dns** to start the DNS Server service.

5. In the DNS console, press and hold or right-click the server entry and then select Properties. In the Properties dialog box, verify that the root servers appear on the Root Hints tab.

6. In Active Directory Users And Computers, verify that the RootDNSServers container has been re-created and contains the root servers. The new root hints are automatically replicated as necessary.

## INSIDE OUT  Consider whether external root servers should be used

In some instances, you might not want to use a root hint file, or you might want to bypass using root servers. Here are two scenarios to consider:

- If your organization isn't connected to the Internet, your name servers don't need pointers to the public root servers. Instead, you should remove the entries in the Cache.dns file and replace them with NS and A records for the DNS server authoritative for the root domain at your site. For example, if you use a private top-level domain, such as .local, you must set up a root name server for the .local domain, and the Cache.dns file should point to these root name servers. You must then restart the DNS Server service so that the root hints file is reloaded. In the DNS console, you can do this by pressing and holding or right-clicking the server entry, pointing to All Tasks, and selecting Restart.

- Making a connection to the root name servers exposes your internal name servers. The internal name server must connect through your organization's firewall to the root name server. While this connection is open and your name server is waiting for a response, there is a potential vulnerability that could be exploited. Here, someone could have set up a fake name server that is waiting for such connections and then could use this server to perform malicious activity on your DNS servers. To prevent this, you can configure forwarding to specific external name servers and tell your name servers not to use the root name servers. You do this by configuring the Do Not Use Recursion For This Domain option when you set up forwarding.

For more information, see "Configuring forwarders and conditional forwarding" in Chapter 22.

# Architecting a DNS design

After you complete your initial planning, you should consider an overall design architecture. There are two primary DNS designs used:

- Split-brain design

- Separate-name design

Although the split-brain design is less common these days, both are valid approaches.

## Split-brain design: Same internal and external names

What a split-brain design means is that your organization uses the same domain name internally as it does externally, and DNS is designed so that the name services for your organization's internal network are separate from that used for the organization's external network. Put another way, an organization's private network should be private and separate from its presence on the public Internet, so your internal name servers should be separate from your external name servers. You don't want a situation in which you have one set of name servers and they are used for both users within the organization and users outside the organization. That's a security no-no that could open your internal network to attack.

The concern with this design—and this is why it is called split-brain—is that if your internal network uses the same domain namespace as that of your public Internet presence, you can get in a situation in which users within the organization can't look up information related to the organization's public Internet presence and users outside the organization can't look up information for the organization's private network.

From an internal user perspective, it is a bad thing that users can't access the organization's public Internet resources. There's an easy fix, however. You simply create records on the authoritative name server for the internal network that specify the IP address for the organization's public Internet resources. For example, to allow users on the internal cpandl.com domain to access www.cpandl.com on the public Internet, you create a host record on the internal DNS server for www in the cpandl.com domain that specifies its IP address.

From a security perspective, it is a good thing that outside users can't look up information for the organization's private network—you don't want them to be able to do this. If you have business partners at other locations that need access to the internal network, you should set up a secure link between your organizations or make other arrangements, such as using an extranet.

To implement split-brain design, you should do the following:

- **Complete your planning**  Complete your planning, and decide how many DNS servers you are going to use on the internal network. Decide on the host names and

IP addresses these servers will use. In most cases, you'll need only two DNS servers for a domain. It is a standard convention to set the host names of DNS servers as Primary and Secondary if there are two servers and as NS01, NS02, and so on if there are more than two servers. You can use this naming convention or adopt a different one.

- **Install and configure the DNS Server service**  Install the DNS Server service on each of the designated DNS servers. If you are using Active Directory, DNS is already implemented on some servers because it is required. With Active Directory Domain Services–integrated zones, every DNS server in a domain that is also configured as a domain controller is a primary name server—and any DNS server not configured as a domain controller can be only a secondary in that zone. With standard primary and secondary zones, you can have only one primary server for a zone—and every other DNS server in that zone must be a secondary.

- **Create records on internal name servers for your public resources**  For each of the organization's public Internet resources to which internal users need access, you must create records on the internal name servers. This allows the internal users to access and work with these resources. This includes the organization's WWW, FTP, and mail servers.

- **Configure forwarding to your ISP's name servers**  The ISP that provides your connection to the Internet should provide you with the host names and IP addresses of name servers to which internal users can forward DNS queries. Configure your internal name servers so that they forward to your ISP's name servers DNS queries that they cannot resolve. As necessary, configure secondary zones, stub zones, or conditional forwarding to any domains for which you desire direct lookups.

- **Configure internal systems to use your internal DNS servers**  Every workstation and server on your internal network should be configured with the IP address of your primary and secondary DNS name servers. If you have more than two name servers, set the name servers that should be used as appropriate. Normally, you'll point a system to only one or two internal name servers. Don't point internal systems to external name servers—you don't want internal systems trying to resolve requests on these name servers.

- **Configure external name servers for internal resources as necessary**  Consider whether you need to create resource records on your ISP's external name servers for servers on your internal network that need to be resolvable from the Internet, such as by mobile users. If you do, provide the necessary information to your ISP to set up these resource records.

# Separate-name design: Different internal and external names

Another approach to DNS design is to use separate-name design in which your internal network uses different domain names than that of your organization's public Internet presence. This creates actual physical separation between your organization's internal and external namespaces by placing them in different parent domains. For example, your organization could use cohovineyard.com for its internal network and cohowinery.com for its external network. Now you have a situation in which completely different namespaces are used to create separation.

As with split-brain design, you have different internal name servers and different external name servers. Unlike split-brain design, internal users should be able to look up information related to the organization's public Internet presence, and you won't need to create additional records to do this. Here, it is only a matter of ensuring the internal name servers forward to external name servers, which can perform the necessary lookups.

If you use different names that are in the public domain hierarchy, you should register all the internal and external domain names you use. In the previous example, you would register cohovineyard.com and cohowinery.com. This ensures someone else can't register one of the domain names you use internally, which could mess up name resolution in some instances. You wouldn't need to register a domain name, such as cohowinery.local, however, because .local is not a public top-level domain.

Rather than using two completely different names, a more common separate-name design is to register a domain name for the company's public Internet presence and then use a child domain of that domain for the internal domain. For example, you could register cpandl.com for the company's external domain name and then use corp.cpandl.com as the internal domain name.

To implement separate-name design, you should do the following:

- **Complete your planning**   Complete your planning, and decide how many DNS servers you are going to use on the internal network. Decide on the host names and IP addresses these servers will use. In most cases, you'll need only two DNS servers for a domain. It is a standard convention to set the host names of DNS servers as Primary and Secondary if there are two servers and as NS01, NS02, and so on if there are more than two servers. You can use this naming convention or adopt a different one.

- **Install and configure the DNS Server service**   Install the DNS Server service on each of the designated DNS servers. If you are using Active Directory, DNS is already implemented on some servers because it is required. With Active Directory Domain

Services–integrated zones, every DNS server in a domain that is also configured as a domain controller is a primary name server—and any DNS server not configured as a domain controller can be only a secondary in that zone. With standard primary and secondary zones, you can have only one primary server for a zone—and every other DNS server in that zone must be a secondary.

- **Configure forwarding to your ISP's name servers**   The ISP that provides your connection to the Internet should provide you with the host names and IP addresses of name servers to which internal users can forward DNS queries. Configure your internal name servers so that they forward DNS queries that they cannot resolve to your ISP's name servers. As necessary, configure secondary zones, stub zones, or conditional forwarding to any domains for which you desire direct lookups.

- **Configure internal systems to use your internal DNS servers**   Every workstation and server on your internal network should be configured with the IP address of your primary and secondary DNS name servers. If you have more than two name servers, set the name servers that should be used as appropriate. Normally, you'll point a system to only one or two internal name servers. Don't point internal systems to external name servers—you don't want internal systems trying to resolve requests on these name servers.

- **Configure external name servers for internal resources as necessary**   Consider whether you need to create resource records on your ISP's external name servers for servers on your internal network that need to be resolvable from the Internet, such as by mobile users. If you do, provide the necessary information to your ISP to set up these resource records.

## Securing DNS from attacks

When you are planning your DNS infrastructure, you should be aware of the common security threats and how those threats are commonly mitigated. DNS infrastructure can be threatened by attackers in many ways. Often DNS domain names and computer names indicate the function or location of a domain or computer to help users identify domains and computers more easily. If so, an attacker can try to diagram your network by using his or her knowledge or your naming scheme to try to learn about other domains and computers on your network.

Once an attacker has a footprint of your network, the attacker can use this knowledge to generate IP packets containing valid IP addresses. This approach, called *IP spoofing*, makes it seem as if the packets are coming from a valid IP address in your network and allows the attacker to gain access to the network.

Attackers might attempt to redirect queries. One way of doing this is to pollute the DNS cache of a DNS server with DNS data that directs future queries to servers that are under the control of the attackers. This type of redirection attack can occur whenever attackers have writable access to DNS data. For example, if your network uses dynamic updates that are not secure, the attackers might be able to insert bad data during a dynamic update.

Attackers also might attempt to deny the availability of network services by flooding your DNS servers with recursive queries. The goal is to overwhelm your DNS servers until the DNS Server service becomes unavailable. When that happens, network services that use DNS will be unavailable to network users.

The way you mitigate DNS security threats is to increase the DNS security on your network as much as possible. There are three basic security configurations that you can implement for DNS:

- **Low**  A DNS deployment without any security precautions. Deploy this level of DNS security only in a private network where there is no threat from external sources or when you have no concern about the integrity of your DNS data. With this security level, the DNS infrastructure is fully exposed to the Internet.

- **Medium**  A DNS deployment with standard security precautions. Your DNS servers use available DNS security features. You might or might not run DNS servers on domain controllers and you might or might not store DNS zones in Active Directory. With this security level, the DNS infrastructure has limited exposure to the Internet.

- **High**  A DNS deployment with standard and additional security precautions. Your DNS servers use available DNS security features. You run DNS servers on domain controllers and store DNS zones in Active Directory. Your DNS infrastructure has no Internet communication by means of internal DNS servers. With this security level, the DNS infrastructure has no direct exposure to the Internet.

Table 21-4 compares the configuration settings for low-security, medium-security, and high-security DNS deployments. To help safeguard the network, most organizations will want to implement at least a medium security environment for DNS.

Chapter 21

**TABLE 21-4 Comparing low-, medium-, and high-security configurations for DNS servers**

| Low Security | Medium Security | High Security |
| --- | --- | --- |
| DNS resolution is performed by all DNS servers in your network. DNS servers use root hints pointing to Internet root servers. | DNS servers that are configured with forwarders point to specific internal DNS servers when they cannot resolve names locally. | Same as medium. Also, root hints point to internal DNS servers that host the root zone for your internal namespace. |
| DNS servers permit zone transfers to any server. | DNS servers limit zone transfers to servers that are listed in (NS) records in their zones. | DNS servers limit zone transfers to specific IP addresses. |
| DNS servers listen on all of their IP addresses. | DNS servers listen on specific IP addresses. | DNS servers listen on specific IP addresses. |
| Cache pollution prevention is disabled. | Cache pollution prevention is enabled. | Cache pollution prevention is enabled. |
| Dynamic update is allowed for all DNS zones. | Only secure dynamic updates are allowed. | Uses secure dynamic updates, except for top-level and root zones, which disable dynamic updates. |
| UDP and TCP port 53 is open on the network firewall for both source and destination addresses. | Firewalls use the allowed source and destination address list. Perimeter network DNS servers are configured with root hints that point to Internet root servers. Proxy servers and gateways perform Internet name resolution. | Permissions restrict who can configure DNS servers and who can create, modify, or delete DNS zones and resource records. |

**CHAPTER 22**

# Implementing and managing DNS

N AME services are essential for communications for Transmission Control
Protocol/Internet Protocol (TCP/IP) networking. Windows Server uses the Domain
Name System (DNS) as its primary method of name resolution. DNS enables
computers to register and resolve DNS domain names. DNS defines the rules under
which computers are named and how names are resolved to IP addresses.

## Installing the DNS Server service

The way you install the DNS Server service depends on whether you plan to use DNS with
Active Directory or without Active Directory. After you make that decision, you can install
DNS as necessary.

### Using DNS with Active Directory

On a domain with Active Directory, DNS is required. You can install DNS as part of the
setup of the first domain controller in a domain or you can install DNS after installing the
first domain controller. Active Directory doesn't require Windows DNS, however. Active
Directory is designed to work with any DNS server that supports dynamic updates and
service locator (SRV) records. This means Active Directory can work with any DNS server
running Berkeley Internet Name Domain (BIND) version 8.1.2 or later. If you have DNS servers that use BIND version 8.1.2 or later, you can use those servers. If you don't already have
BIND servers, you probably won't want to set these up because there are many benefits to
using the Microsoft DNS Server service. It's also important to point out that only Microsoft
DNS servers can automatically create the delegation records required by Active Directory.

When you install the DNS Server service as part of the Active Directory installation process,
you can use Active Directory–integrated zones and take advantage of the many replication
and security benefits of Active Directory. Here, any server configured as a domain controller with DNS and using Active Directory–integrated zones is an Active Directory primary
name server.

Here's how installation of DNS on the first domain controller in a forest works:

1. You use the Active Directory Domain Services Configuration Wizard to install the first domain controller. During the installation process, you specify that you are installing a new forest and then specify the Active Directory domain name, as shown in Figure 22-1. This sets the DNS name for the domain as well.

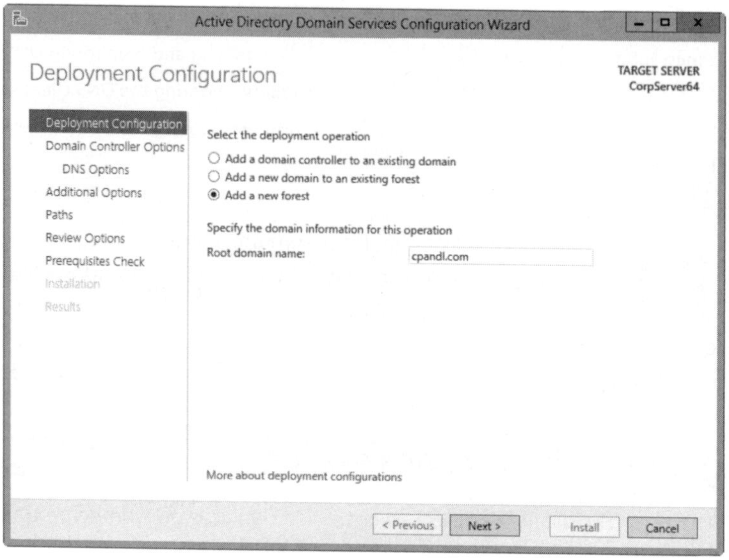

**Figure 22-1** Specify the Active Directory domain name.

> **Note**
>
> For more information about promoting domain controllers, see "Installing Active Directory Domain Services" in Chapter 28, "Implementing Active Directory Domain Services."

2. When the Active Directory installation process begins, the Active Directory Domain Services Configuration Wizard will check the current DNS configuration. If no authoritative DNS servers are available for the domain, the wizard selects Domain Name System DNS Server as an additional installation option, as shown in Figure 22-2.

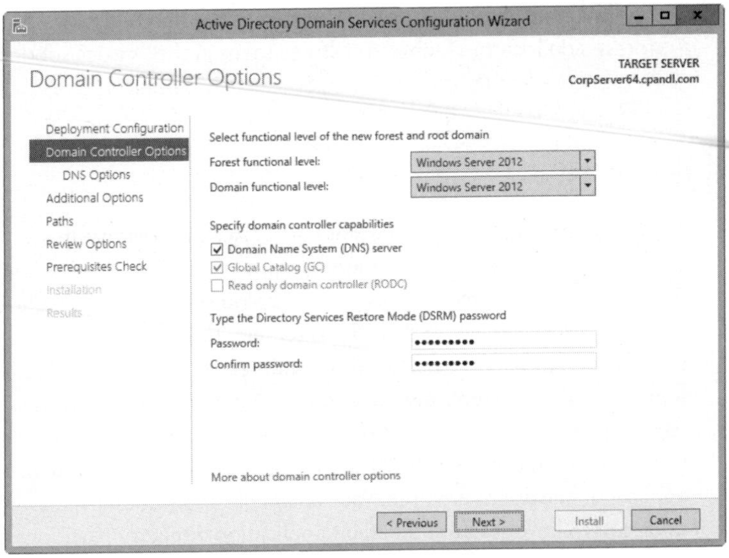

**Figure 22-2** The wizard selects the DNS server when no authoritative DNS servers are available.

3. In most cases, you'll want to install DNS. If you install DNS, the Active Directory Domain Services Configuration Wizard installs DNS, and then you can use the Configure A DNS Server Wizard to complete the initial setup. As Figure 22-3 shows, typically this means a forward lookup zone will be created for the domain. The forward lookup zone will have the Start of Authority (SOA), Name Server (NS), and Host Address (A) records for the server you are working with. This designates it as the authoritative name server for the domain. If you want to, you can also create reverse lookup zones to allow for IP-address-to-host-name lookups. DNS servers support IPv4 and IPv6 for reverse lookups.

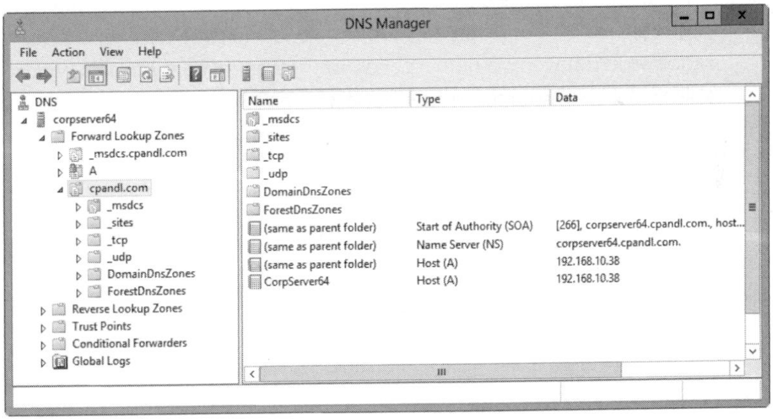

**Figure 22-3** A forward lookup zone is created for the domain.

4. For the first DNS server in a forest, the installation and setup process creates the forest-side locator records and stores them in the _msdcs subdomain. Windows Server creates this as a separate zone, which is referred to as the *forest root zone*.

# INSIDE OUT   Forest root zones

The forest root zone is an important part of Active Directory. It is in this zone that Active Directory creates SRV resource records that are used when clients are looking for a particular resource, such as global catalog servers, Lightweight Directory Access Protocol (LDAP) servers, and Kerberos servers. The _msdcs subdomain is created as its own zone to improve performance with remote sites. With early implementations, remote sites had to replicate the entire DNS database to access forest root records, which meant increased replication and bandwidth usage. As a separate zone, only the zone will be replicated to the DNS servers in remote sites as long as Active Directory application partitions are used. You can enable application partitions for use with DNS as discussed in "Configuring default application directory partitions and replication scope" later in this chapter.

When you install additional domain controllers in a domain, the DNS Server service will be selected for installation by default. If you want the domain controller to also act as a DNS server, you should keep this selection.

In an Active Directory domain, secondary and stub zones can also be useful, as discussed in "DNS zones and zone transfers" in Chapter 21, "Architecting DNS infrastructure." In fact, in certain situations you might have to use a secondary or stub zone for name resolution to work properly. Consider the case when you have multiple trees in a forest, each in their own namespace. For instance, City Power & Light and The Phone Company are both part of one company and use the domains cpandl.com and thephone-company.com, respectively. If the namespaces for these domains are set up as separate trees of the same forest, your organization would have two namespaces. In the cpandl.com domain, you might want users to be able to access resources in thephone-company.com domain and vice versa. To do this, you would configure DNS as shown in Figure 22-4.

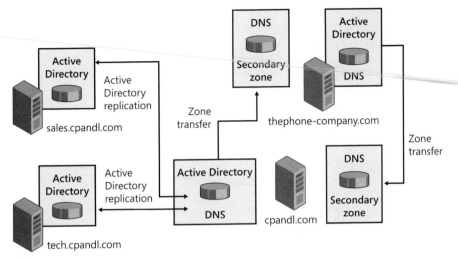

**Figure 22-4** Using secondary zones with Active Directory.

The implementation steps for this example are as follows:

1. Set up a secondary or stub zone for thephone-company.com on the authoritative name server for cpandl.com.

2. Set up a secondary or stub zone for cpandl.com on the authoritative name server for thephone-company.com.

3. Configure zone transfers between cpandl.com and thephone-company.com.

4. Configure zone transfers between thephone-company.com and cpandl.com.

## Using DNS without Active Directory

On a domain without Active Directory, DNS servers act as standard primary or standard secondary name servers. You must install the DNS Server service on each primary or secondary server. You do this using the Add Roles And Features Wizard as detailed in the next section, "DNS setup."

On primary name servers, you configure primary zones for forward lookups and as necessary for reverse lookups. The forward lookup zone will have SOA, NS, and A records for the server you are working with. This designates it as the authoritative name server for the domain. You can also create reverse lookup zones to allow for IP-address-to-host-name lookups.

Chapter 22

On secondary name servers, you configure secondary zones to store copies of the records on the primary name server. You can create secondary zones for the forward lookup zones as well as the reverse lookup zones configured on the primary.

Stub zones and forwarders are also options for these DNS servers.

## DNS setup

You can install the DNS Server service by completing the following steps:

1. Start the Add Roles And Features Wizard. In Server Manager, tap or click Manage and then tap or click Add Roles And Features.

2. If the wizard displays the Before You Begin page, read the Welcome text and then tap or click Next.

3. On the Installation Type page, Role-Based Or Feature-Based Installation is selected by default. Tap or click Next.

4. On the Server Selection page, you can choose to install roles and features on running servers or virtual hard disks. Only servers running Windows Server 2012 and that have been added for management in Server Manager are listed. Either select a server from the server pool or select a server from the server pool on which to mount a virtual hard disk (VHD). If you are adding roles and features to a VHD, tap or click Browse and then use the Browse For Virtual Hard Disks dialog box to locate the VHD. When you are ready to continue, tap or click Next.

5. On the Select Server Roles page, select DNS Server. If additional features are required to install a role, you'll see an additional dialog box. Tap or click Add Features to close the dialog box, and add the required features to the server installation. When you are ready to continue, tap or click Next three times.

6. If the server on which you want to install the DNS Server role doesn't have all the required binary source files, the server gets the files via Windows Update by default or from a location specified in Group Policy. To specify an alternate path for the required source files, click the Specify An Alternate Source Path link, type that alternate path in the box provided, and then tap or click OK. For network shares, enter the UNC path to the share, such as **\\CorpServer24\WinServer2012\**. For mounted Windows images, enter the WIM path prefixed with *WIM:* and including the index of the image to use, such as **WIM:\\CorpServer24\WinServer2012\ install.wim:4**.

7. Tap or click Install to begin the installation process. The Installation Progress page tracks the progress of the installation. If you close the wizard, tap or click the

Notifications icon in Server Manager and then tap or click the link provided to re-open the wizard.

**8.** When Setup finishes installing the DNS Server role, the Installation Progress page will be updated to reflect this. Review the installation details to ensure that the installation was successful.

After you install the DNS Server service, DNS Manager is available. The DNS Server service should start automatically each time you reboot the server. If it doesn't start, you need to start it manually.

In Server Manager, tap or click Tools and then tap or click DNS to open DNS Manager, shown in Figure 22-5. When you start DNS Manager, you are connected directly to a local DNS server, but you won't see entries for remote DNS servers. You can connect to remote servers by pressing and holding or right-clicking DNS in the console tree and then select-ing Connect To DNS Server. In the Connect To DNS Server dialog box, select The Following Computer, type the name or IP address of the DNS server, and then tap or click OK. In DNS Manager, host addresses are displayed as IPv4 or IPv6 addresses as appropriate.

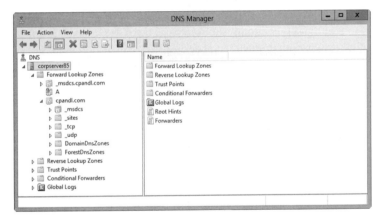

**Figure 22-5**  DNS Manager.

The command-line counterpart to DNS Manager is Dnscmd. The Dnscmd command-line tool accepts addresses in IPv4 and IPv6 formats. You can use Dnscmd to perform most of the tasks available in DNS Manager as well as to perform many troubleshooting tasks that are specific to Dnscmd. Unlike Netsh, Dnscmd doesn't offer internal command prompts. You can specify only the server you want to work with followed by the command and the command-line options to use for that command. Thus, the syntax is as follows:

```
dnscmd ServerName Command CommandOptions
```

Here

- *ServerName* is the name or IP address of the DNS server you want to work with, such as CORPSVR03 or 192.168.10.15.

- *Command* is the command to use.

- *CommandOptions* are the options for the command.

> **Note**
> If you are working on the server you want to configure, you don't have to type the server name or IP address.

You also can use the DnsServer module in Windows PowerShell to manage DNS servers. To list all the cmdlets available with this module, type the following at the PowerShell prompt: **Get-Command –Module DnsServer**.

After you set up a DNS server, the setup process should configure the server's TCP/IP settings so that the server attempts to resolve its own DNS queries. Setup does this by setting the server's primary DNS server address to its own address for both IPv4 and IPv6. You can confirm this by entering **ipconfig /all** at a command prompt. In the output of the command, you should see that the DNS servers are set as follows:

- ::1

- 127.0.0.1

Here, ::1 is the local loopback address for IPv6, and 127.0.0.1 is the local loopback address for IPv4. If necessary, you can modify the DNS server entries as discussed in Chapter 19, "Managing TCP/IP networking." For Preferred DNS Server, type the computer's own IP address. Set an alternate DNS server as necessary.

You can also set the preferred DNS server IP address from the command line. Type the following command:

```
netsh interface ip set dns ConnectionName static ServerIPAddress
```

Here, *ConnectionName* is the name of the local area connection and *ServerIPAddress* is the IP address of the server.

Consider the following example:

```
netsh interface ip set dns "Local Area Connection" static 192.168.1.100
```

Here, you set the preferred DNS server address for the network connection named Local Area Connection to 192.168.1.100. The Static option says that you want to use the local setting for DNS rather than the Dynamic Host Configuration Protocol (DHCP) setting when applicable.

You can confirm the new setting by typing **ipconfig /all** at the command prompt and checking for the DNS server entry. The server should have the same setting for the IP address and primary DNS server.

## INSIDE OUT Dynamic port ranges for IPv4 and IPv6 with TCP and UDP

To enhance security and guard against some types of cache-poisoning attacks, the DNS Server service uses the socket pool to randomize the source port when issuing DNS queries. Randomization ensures the server randomly picks a source point from a pool of available sockets that it opens when the DNS Server service starts. This makes it more difficult for an attacker to poison the DNS cache, because the attacker would need to correctly guess the source port of a query as well as the query's random transaction ID. By default, the dynamic port range is 49152 to 65535. Some server applications, such as Exchange Server, might change this range. You also can modify the port range used by a server. One way to do this is to use Netsh. You configure the port range separately for TCP and UDP with regard to either IPv4 or IPv6.

The basic syntax for viewing the dynamic port range for either the IPv4 or IPv6 stack and either the TCP or UDP protocol follows:

```
netsh int [ipv4|ipv6] show dynamicport [tcp|udp]
```

Here, you specify that you want to work with either the IPv4 or IPv6 stack and either the TCP or UDP protocol.

When working with Netsh at an elevated command prompt, the basic syntax for changing the port range is

```
netsh int [ipv4|ipv6] set dynamic [tcp|udp] start=StartPort num=NumPorts
```

Here, you specify that you want to work with either the IPv4 or IPv6 stack and either the TCP or UDP protocol, and then you set the start port of the range (*StartPort*) and the number of ports in the range (*NumPorts*). The minimum starting port is 1025. The maximum end port is 65535. The minimum number of ports is 255.

## Configuring DNS using the wizard

From DNS Manager, you can start the Configure A DNS Server Wizard and use it to help you set up a DNS server. This wizard is useful for helping you configure small networks that work with Internet service providers (ISPs) and large networks that use forwarding.

INSIDE OUT  Are reverse lookups needed?

For small networks, the Configure A DNS Server Wizard creates only a forward lookup zone. For large networks, the Configure A DNS Server Wizard creates a forward lookup zone and a reverse lookup zone. This might get you to thinking whether reverse lookup zones are needed on your network. Computers use reverse lookups to find out who is contacting them. Often this is so that they can display a host name to users rather than an IP address. So, although a reverse lookup zone isn't created by the Configure A DNS Server Wizard for small networks, you might still want to create one. If so, follow the procedure discussed in "Creating reverse lookup zones" later in this chapter.

## Configuring a small network using the Configure A DNS Server Wizard

For a small network, you can use the wizard to set up your forward lookup zone and query forwarding to your ISP or other DNS servers. You can also choose to configure this zone as a primary or secondary zone. You use the primary zone option if your organization maintains its own zone. You use the secondary zone if your ISP maintains your zone. This gives you a read-only copy of the zone that can be used by internal clients. Because small networks don't normally need reverse lookup zones, these are not created. You can, of course, create these zones later if needed.

To configure a small network using the Configure A DNS Server Wizard, follow these steps:

1. Press and hold or right-click the server entry in DNS Manager, and select Configure A DNS Server. Then, when the wizard starts, tap or click Next.

   **Note**

   If the server you want to work with isn't shown, press and hold or right-click the DNS node in the left pane and select Connect To DNS Server. In the Connect To DNS Server dialog box, select The Following Computer, type the name or IP address of the DNS server, and then tap or click OK.

**2.** Choose Create A Forward Lookup Zone (Recommended For Small Networks), as shown in Figure 22-6, and then tap or click Next.

> ### Note
> If Active Directory is installed on the network, this zone will be automatically integrated with Active Directory. To avoid this, you can choose the second option, Create Forward And Reverse Lookup Zones (Recommended For Large Networks), and then proceed as discussed in "Configuring a large network using the Configure A DNS Server Wizard" later in this chapter. When the wizard gets to the reverse lookup zone configuration part, you can skip this if you don't want to create a reverse lookup zone.

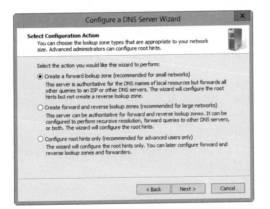

**Figure 22-6**  Select the first option to configure DNS for a small network.

**3.** As shown in Figure 22-7, you can now choose whether the DNS server or your ISP maintains the zone and then tap or click Next. Keep the following in mind:

- ○ If the DNS server maintains the zone, the wizard configures a primary zone that you control. This allows you to create and manage the DNS records for the organization.

- ○ If your ISP maintains the zone, the wizard configures a secondary zone that will get its information from your ISP. This means the staff at the ISP will need to create and manage the DNS records for the organization—and you will need to pay them to do so.

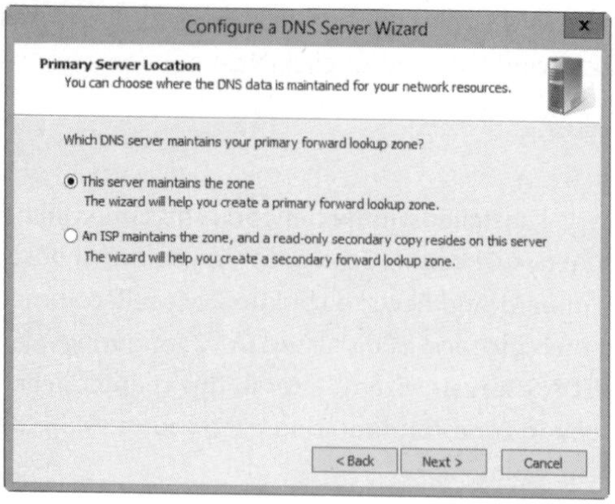

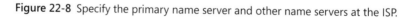

**Figure 22-7** Specify whether the zone will be maintained on the server or by your ISP.

4. On the Zone Name page, type the full DNS name for the zone. The zone name should help determine how the zone fits into the DNS domain hierarchy. For example, if you're creating the primary server for the cpandl.com domain, you should type **cpandl.com** as the zone name. Tap or click Next.

5. If your ISP maintains the zone, you see the Master DNS Servers page, as shown in Figure 22-8. Type the IP address of the primary DNS server that's maintaining the zone for you, and then press Enter. Repeat this step to specify additional name servers at your ISP. The wizard automatically validates the IP address or addresses you enter. Zone transfers will be configured to copy the zone information from these DNS servers.

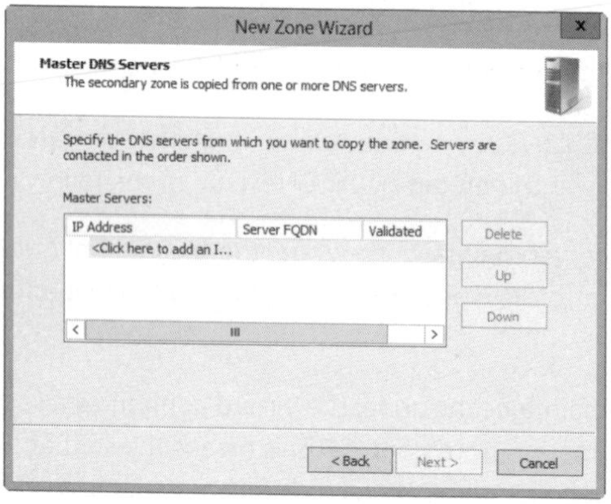

**Figure 22-8** Specify the primary name server and other name servers at the ISP.

**6.** If you choose to maintain the zone, you see the Dynamic Update page, as shown in Figure 22-9. Choose how you want to configure dynamic updates, and then tap or click Next. You can use one of these options:

○ **Allow Only Secure Dynamic Updates**   This option is available only on domain controllers and when Active Directory is deployed. It provides for the best security possible by restricting which clients can perform dynamic updates.

○ **Allow Both Nonsecure And Secure Dynamic Updates**   This option allows any client to update resource records in DNS. Although it allows both secure and nonsecure updates, it doesn't validate updates, which means dynamic updates are accepted from any client.

○ **Do Not Allow Dynamic Updates**   This option disables dynamic updates in DNS. You should use this option only when the zone isn't integrated with Active Directory.

**7.** You can use the Forwarders page to configure the forwarding of DNS queries. If you want internal DNS servers to forward queries that they can't resolve to another server, type the IP address for that server. You can optionally include the IP address for a second forwarder as well. If you don't want to use forwarders, select No, It Should Not Forward Queries.

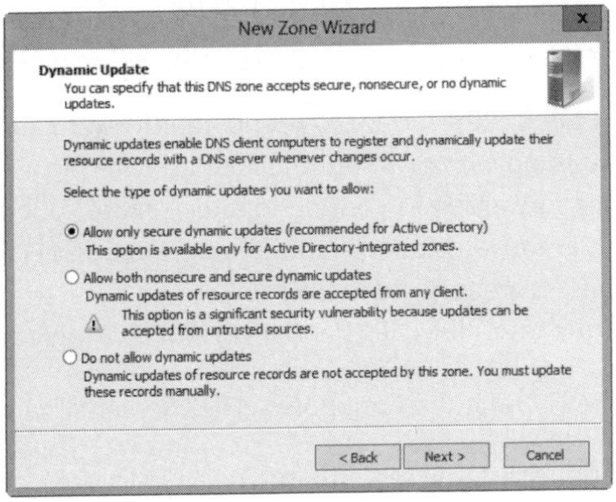

**Figure 22-9** Set the dynamic updates options.

Chapter 22

> **Important**
>
> Selecting the No, It Should Not Forward Queries option won't prevent internal name servers from forwarding queries altogether. A root hints file will still be created, which lists the root name servers on the public Internet. Thus, if you don't designate forwarders, such as the primary and secondary name servers of your ISP, the internal name servers will still forward queries. To prevent this, you must modify the root hints file as discussed in "Security considerations" in Chapter 21.

8. When you tap or click Next, the wizard searches for and retrieves the current root hints. Tap or click Finish to complete the configuration and exit the wizard. If there is a problem configuring the root hints, you need to configure the root hints manually or copy them from another server. For more information, see "External DNS name resolution and security" in Chapter 21. Keep in mind, a default set of root hints is included with the DNS Server service, and these root hints should be added automatically. To confirm, press and hold or right-click the server entry in DNS Manager and then select Properties. In the Properties dialog box, the currently configured root hints are shown on the Root Hints tab.

## Configuring a large network using the Configure A DNS Server Wizard

For a large network, you can use the wizard to set up your forward and reverse lookup zones and to set up forwarding with or without recursion. With recursion, queries for external resources are first forwarded to your designated servers, but if those servers are unavailable, the DNS server forwards queries to the root name servers. Without recursion, queries for external resources are forwarded only to your designated servers. The DNS Server service can send queries to IPv4, IPv4 and IPv6, and IPv6-only servers.

To configure a large network using the Configure A DNS Server Wizard, follow these steps:

1. Press and hold or right-click the server entry in DNS Manager, and select Configure A Server. When the wizard starts, tap or click Next.

> **Note**
>
> If the server you want to work with isn't shown, press and hold or right-click the DNS node in the left pane and select Connect To DNS Server. In the Connect To DNS Server dialog box, select The Following Computer, type the name or IP address of the DNS server, and then tap or click OK.

2. Choose Create Forward And Reverse Lookup Zones (Recommended For Large Networks), as shown in Figure 22-10, and then tap or click Next.

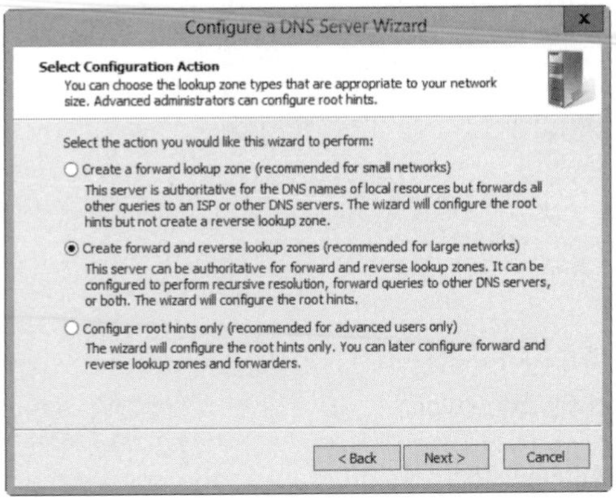

**Figure 22-10** Select the second option to configure DNS for a large network.

3. To create a forward lookup zone, accept the default option on the Forward Lookup Zone page and then tap or click Next. Otherwise, tap or click No, and skip to step 10.

4. As Figure 22-11 shows, you can now select the zone type. Choose one of the following options, and then tap or click Next:

   ○ **Primary Zone**   Use this option to create a primary zone and designate this server to be authoritative for the zone. Ensure that the Store The Zone In Active Directory check box is selected if you want to integrate DNS with Active Directory. Otherwise, clear this check box so that a standard primary zone is created.

   ○ **Secondary Zone**   Use this option to create a secondary zone. This means the server will have a read-only copy of the zone and must use zone transfers to get updates.

   ○ **Stub Zone**   Use this option to create a stub zone. This creates only the necessary glue records for the zone. Optionally, specify that this zone should be integrated with Active Directory. This means the zone will be stored in Active Directory and updated using Active Directory replication.

Chapter 22

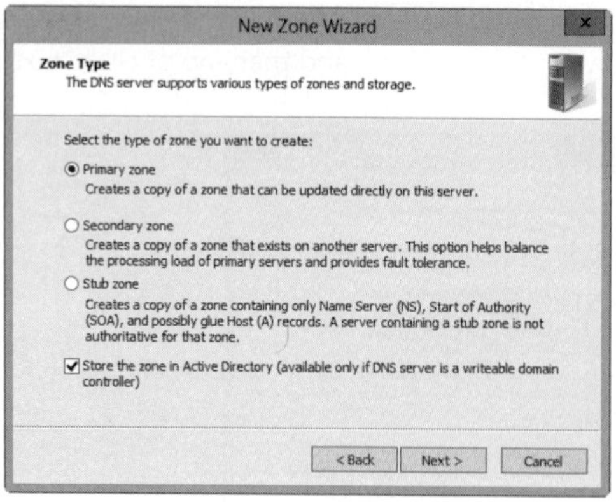

**Figure 22-11**  Select the zone type.

5.  If you created an Active Directory–integrated zone, specify the replication scope and then tap or click Next. As Figure 22-12 shows, you have the following options:

○ **To All DNS Servers Running On Domain Controllers In This Forest**   Enables replication of the zone information to all domains in the Active Directory forest. Each DNS server in the forest will receive a copy of the zone information and get updates through replication.

○ **To All DNS Servers Running On Domain Controllers In This Domain**   Enables replication of the zone information in the current domain. Each DNS server in the domain will receive a copy of the zone information and get updates through replication.

○ **To All Domain Controllers In This Domain**   Replicates zone information to all domain controllers in the Active Directory domain. All domain controllers will get a copy of the zone information and get updates through replication regardless of whether they are also running the DNS Server service.

○ **To All Domain Controllers Specified In The Scope Of This Directory Partition**   If you configured application partitions other than the default partitions, you can limit the scope of replication to a designated application partition. Any domain controllers configured with the application partition will get a copy of the zone information and get updates through replication regardless of whether they are also running the DNS Server service.

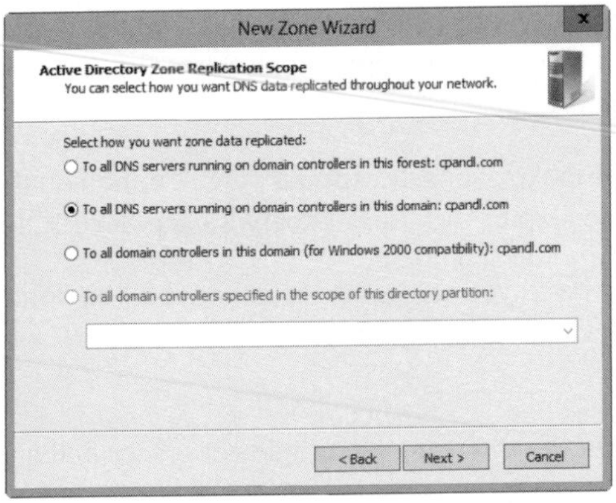

**Figure 22-12** Select the replication scope if you are using Active Directory integration.

6. On the Zone Name page, type the full DNS name for the zone. The zone name should help determine how the zone fits into the DNS domain hierarchy. For example, if you're creating the primary server for the cpandl.com domain, you should type **cpandl.com** as the zone name. Tap or click Next.

7. If you're creating a standard primary zone, you see the Zone File page. This page allows you to create a new zone file or use an existing zone file. In most cases, you'll simply accept the default name and allow the wizard to create the file for you in the %SystemRoot%\System32\Dns folder. If you are migrating from a BIND DNS server or have a preexisting zone file, you can select Use This Existing File and then type the name of the file that you copied to the %SystemRoot%\System32\Dns folder. Tap or click Next when you are ready to continue.

8. If you're creating a secondary zone, you see the Master DNS Servers page. Type the IP address of the primary DNS server that's maintaining the zone, and then tap or click Add. Repeat this step to specify additional name servers. Zone transfers will be configured to copy the zone information from these DNS servers.

9. On the Dynamic Update page, choose how you want to configure dynamic updates and then tap or click Next. You can use one of the following options:

   ○ **Allow Only Secure Dynamic Updates**   This option is available only on domain controllers and when Active Directory is deployed. It provides for the best security possible by restricting which clients can perform dynamic updates.

   ○ **Allow Both Nonsecure And Secure Dynamic Updates**   This option allows any client to update resource records in DNS. Although it allows both secure and nonsecure updates, it doesn't validate updates, which means dynamic updates are accepted from any client.

Chapter 22

- ○ **Do Not Allow Dynamic Updates** This option disables dynamic updates in DNS. You should use this option only when the zone isn't integrated with Active Directory.

10. To create a reverse lookup zone, accept the default option on the Reverse Lookup Zone page and then tap or click Next. Otherwise, tap or click No, and skip to step 16.

11. On the Zone Type page, you can select the zone type. The options available are the same as when creating a forward lookup zone. Tap or click Next after making a selection.

12. If you created an Active Directory–integrated zone, specify the replication scope and then tap or click Next.

13. Specify whether you are creating an IPv4 reverse lookup zone or an IPv6 reverse lookup zone, and then tap or click Next. Do one of the following:

- ○ If you are configuring a reverse lookup zone for IPv4, type the network ID for the reverse lookup zone as shown in Figure 22-13 and then tap or click Next. The values you enter set the default name for the reverse lookup zone. If you have multiple subnets on the same network—such as 192.168.1, 192.168.2, and 192.168.3—you should enter only the network portion for the zone name, such as **192.168**, rather than the complete network ID. The DNS Server service will then fill in the necessary subnet zones as you use IP addresses on a particular subnet.

- ○ If you are configuring a reverse lookup zone for IPv6, type the network prefix for the reverse lookup zone and then tap or click Next. The values you enter are used to automatically generate the related zone names. Depending on the prefix you enter, up to eight zones might be created.

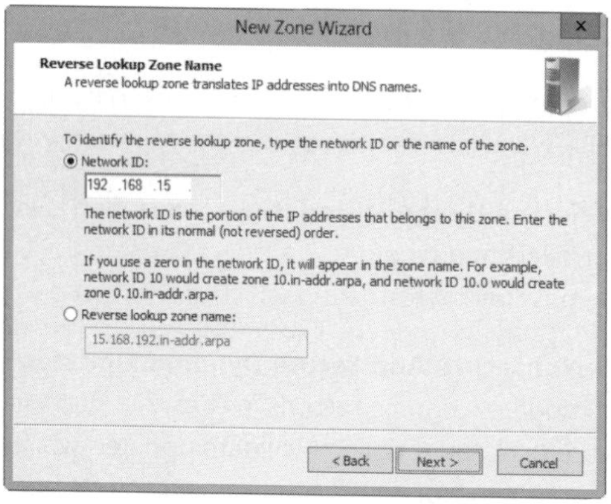

**Figure 22-13** Set the network ID for the reverse lookup zone.

**14.** If you're creating a standard secondary zone, you see the Zone File page. This page allows you to create a new zone file or use an existing zone file.

**15.** On the Dynamic Update page, choose how you want to configure dynamic updates and then tap or click Next.

**16.** You can use the Forwarders page to configure forwarding of DNS queries. If you want internal DNS servers to forward queries that they can't resolve to another server, type the IP address of that server. You can optionally include the IP address for a second forwarder as well. If you don't want to use forwarders, select No, It Should Not Forward Queries.

> **Important**
>
> Selecting the No, It Should Not Forward Queries option won't prevent internal name servers from forwarding queries altogether. A root hints file will still be created, which lists the root name servers on the public Internet. Thus, if you don't designate forwarders, such as the primary and secondary name servers of your ISP, the internal name servers will still forward queries. To prevent this, you must modify the root hints file as discussed in "Security considerations" in Chapter 21.

**17.** When you tap or click Next, the wizard searches for and retrieves the current root hints. Tap or click Finish to complete the configuration and exit the wizard. If there is a problem configuring the root hints, you need to configure the root hints manually or copy them from another server. For more information, see "External DNS name resolution and security" in Chapter 21. Keep in mind, a default set of root hints is included with the DNS Server service, and these root hints should be added automatically. To confirm, press and hold or right-click the server entry in DNS Manager and then select Properties. In the Properties dialog box, the currently configured root hints are shown on the Root Hints tab.

# Configuring DNS zones, subdomains, forwarders, and zone transfers

Windows Server 2012 supports primary, secondary, Active Directory–integrated, and stub zones, each of which can be created to support either forward lookups or reverse lookups. Forward lookup queries allow a client to resolve a host name to an IP address. Reverse lookups allow a client to resolve an IP address to a host name. At times, you might also need to configure subdomains, forwarders, and zone transfers. All of these topics are discussed in this section.

# Creating forward lookup zones

To create the initial forward lookup zone or additional forward lookup zones on a server, follow these steps:

1. In DNS Manager, expand the node for the server you want to work with. Press and hold or right-click the Forward Lookup Zones entry, and then choose New Zone. Afterward, in the New Zone Wizard, tap or click Next.

2. Select the zone type. Choose one of the following options, and then tap or click Next:

   ○ **Primary Zone**  Use this option to create a primary zone and designate this server to be authoritative for the zone. Ensure that the Store The Zone In Active Directory check box is selected if you want to integrate DNS with Active Directory. Otherwise, clear this check box so that a standard primary zone is created.

   ○ **Secondary Zone**  Use this option to create a secondary zone. This means the server will have a read-only copy of the zone and will need to use zone transfers to get updates.

   ○ **Stub Zone**  Use this option to create a stub zone. This creates only the necessary glue records for the zone. Optionally, specify that this zone should be integrated with Active Directory. This means the zone will be stored in Active Directory and updated using Active Directory replication.

3. If you created an Active Directory–integrated zone, specify the replication scope and then tap or click Next. You have the following options:

   ○ **To All DNS Servers In This Forest**  Enables replication of the zone information to all domains in the Active Directory forest. Each DNS server in the forest will receive a copy of the zone information and get updates through replication.

   ○ **To All DNS Servers In This Domain**  Enables replication of the zone information in the current domain. Each DNS server in the domain will receive a copy of the zone information and get updates through replication.

   ○ **To All Domain Controllers In This Domain**  Replicates zone information to all domain controllers in the Active Directory domain. All domain controllers will get a copy of the zone information and get updates through replication regardless of whether they are also running the DNS Server service.

&#9675; **To All Domain Controllers Specified In The Scope Of This Directory Partition**   If you configured application partitions, you can limit the scope of replication to a designated application partition. Any domain controllers configured with the application partition will get a copy of the zone information and get updates through replication regardless of whether they are also running the DNS Server service.

4. On the Zone Name page, type the full DNS name for the zone. The zone name should help determine how the zone fits into the DNS domain hierarchy. For example, if you're creating the primary server for the cpandl.com domain, you should type **cpandl.com** as the zone name. Tap or click Next.

5. If you're creating a standard primary zone, you see the Zone File page. This page allows you to create a new zone file or use an existing zone file. In most cases, you'll simply accept the default name and allow the wizard to create the file for you in the %SystemRoot%\System32\Dns folder. If you are migrating from a BIND DNS server or have a preexisting zone file, you can select Use This Existing File and then type the name of the file that you copied to the %SystemRoot%\System32\Dns folder. Tap or click Next when you are ready to continue.

6. If you're creating a secondary zone, you see the Master DNS Servers page. Type the IP address of the primary DNS server that's maintaining the zone, and then tap or click Add. Repeat this step to specify additional name servers. Zone transfers will be configured to copy the zone information from these DNS servers.

7. On the Dynamic Update page, choose how you want to configure dynamic updates, and then tap or click Next. You can use one of these options:

   &#9675; **Allow Only Secure Dynamic Updates**   This option is available only on domain controllers and when Active Directory is deployed. It provides for the best security possible by restricting which clients can perform dynamic updates.

   &#9675; **Allow Both Nonsecure And Secure Dynamic Updates**   This option allows any client to update resource records in DNS. Although it allows both secure and nonsecure updates, it doesn't validate updates, which means dynamic updates are accepted from any client.

   &#9675; **Do Not Allow Dynamic Updates**   This option disables dynamic updates in DNS. You should use this option only when the zone isn't integrated with Active Directory.

8. Tap or click Next, and then tap or click Finish to complete the configuration and exit the wizard.

Chapter 22

# Creating reverse lookup zones

To create the initial reverse lookup zone or additional reverse lookup zones on a server, follow these steps:

1. In DNS Manager, expand the node for the server you want to work with. Press and hold or right-click the Reverse Lookup Zones entry, and choose New Zone. Afterward, in the New Zone Wizard, tap or click Next.

2. On the Zone Type page, you can select the zone type. The options available are the same as for forward lookup zones. Tap or click Next after making a selection.

3. If you created an Active Directory–integrated zone, specify the replication scope and then tap or click Next.

4. Specify whether you are creating an IPv4 reverse lookup zone or an IPv6 reverse lookup zone, and then tap or click Next. Do one of the following:

   ○ If you are configuring a reverse lookup zone for IPv4, type the network ID for the reverse lookup zone and then tap or click Next. The values you enter set the default name for the reverse lookup zone. If you have multiple subnets on the same network—such as 192.168.1, 192.168.2, and 192.168.3—you should enter only the network portion for the zone name, such as **192.168**, rather than the complete network ID. The DNS Server service will then fill in the necessary subnet zones as you use IP addresses on a particular subnet.

   ○ If you are configuring a reverse lookup zone for IPv6, type the network prefix for the reverse lookup zone and then tap or click Next. The values you enter are used to automatically generate the related zone names. Depending on the prefix you enter, up to eight zones might be created.

5. If you're creating a standard secondary zone, you see the Zone File page. This page allows you to create a new zone file or use an existing zone file.

6. On the Dynamic Update page, choose how you want to configure dynamic updates, and then tap or click Next.

7. Tap or click Next, and then tap or click Finish to complete the configuration and exit the wizard.

# Configuring forwarders and conditional forwarding

In a normal configuration, if a DNS name server can't resolve a request, it forwards the request for resolution. A server to which DNS queries are forwarded is referred to as a *forwarder*. You can specifically designate forwarders that should be used by your internal

DNS servers. For example, if you designate your ISP's primary and secondary name servers as forwarders, queries that your internal name servers can't resolve will be forwarded to these servers. Forwarding can still take place, however, even if you don't specifically designate forwarders. The reason for this is that the root hints file specifies the root name servers for the public Internet and these servers can be used as forwarders.

Any time forwarders are not specified or available, requests can be forwarded to the root name servers. The root name servers then forward the requests to the appropriate top-level domain name server, which forwards them to the next level domain server, and so on. This process is referred to as *recursion*, and, as you can see, this involves a number of forwarding actions. DNS servers can send recursive queries to IPv4, IPv4 and IPv6, and IPv6-only servers.

Another forwarding option is to configure what is called a *conditional forwarder*. When using conditional forwarding, you can tell your DNS name servers that if they see a request for domain XYZ, they should not forward it to the public DNS name servers for resolution. Instead, the name servers should forward the request directly to the authoritative name server for the XYZ domain.

You can configure forwarding options by following these steps:

1. In DNS Manager, press and hold or right-click the server you want to work with and select Properties. In the Properties dialog box, tap or click the Forwarders tab, as shown in Figure 22-14.

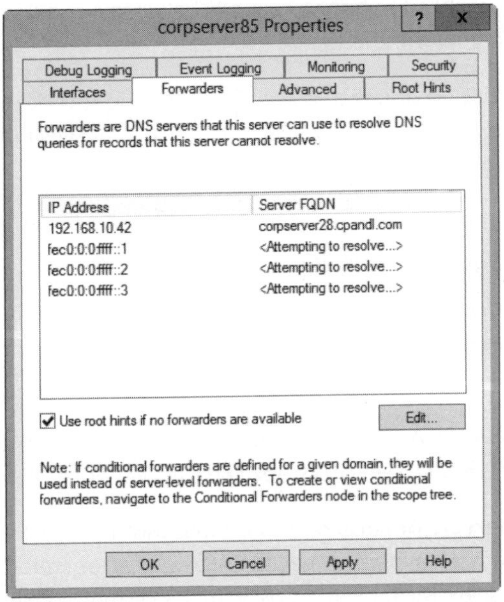

**Figure 22-14** The Forwarders tab.

2.  To allow forwarding to root name servers when configured forwarders are not available, select the Use Root Hints If No Forwarders Are Available check box.

3.  Display the Edit Forwarders dialog box by tapping or clicking Edit. To forward queries that internal servers can't resolve to another server, type the IP address or DNS name for the other server and then press Enter. Repeat this process to add other forwarders. You can organize the forwarders in priority order by selecting each in turn and tapping or clicking the Up or Down buttons as appropriate.

4.  Use the Number Of Seconds Before Forward Queries Time Out to set the query timeout in seconds. By default, a DNS server will continue to attempt to contact and use a listed forwarder for three seconds. When the timeout expires, the server moves to the next forwarder on the list and does the same. When there are no additional forwarders, the server uses the root hints to locate a root server to which the query can be forwarded.

5.  Tap or click OK to close the Edit Forwarders dialog box.

6.  In the Properties dialog box, tap or click the Advanced tab. Ensure that the Disable Recursion check box is cleared, and then tap or click OK to close the Properties dialog box.

If you have multiple internal domains, you might want to consider configuring conditional forwarding, which allows you to direct requests for specific domains to specific DNS servers for resolution. Conditional forwarding is useful if your organization has multiple internal domains and you need to resolve requests between these domains. To configure conditional forwarding, follow these steps:

1.  In DNS Manager, select and then press and hold or right-click the Conditional Forwarders folder for the server you want to work with. Select New Conditional Forwarder on the shortcut menu.

2.  In the New Conditional Forwarder dialog box, enter the name of the domain to which queries should be forwarded, such as **adatum.com**.

3.  Tap or click in the IP address list, type the IP address of an authoritative DNS server in the specified domain, and then press Enter. Repeat this process to specify additional IP addresses.

4.  If you're integrating DNS with Active Directory, select the Store This Conditional Forwarder In Active Directory check box and then choose a replication strategy:

    ○  **All DNS Servers In This Forest**   Choose this strategy if you want the widest replication strategy. Remember, the Active Directory forest includes all domain trees that share the directory data with the current domain.

○ **All DNS Servers In This Domain**   Choose this strategy if you want to replicate forwarder information within the current domain and child domains of the current domain.

○ **All Domain Controllers In This Domain**   Choose this strategy if you want to replicate forwarder information to all domain controllers within the current domain and child domains of the current domain. Although this strategy gives wider replication for forwarder information within the domain, not every domain controller is a DNS server as well (and you don't need to configure every domain controller as a DNS server either).

5. Set the Number Of Seconds Before Forward Queries Time Out value. This value controls how long the server tries to query the forwarder if it gets no response. When the Number Of Seconds Before Forward Queries Time Out interval passes, the server tries the next authoritative server on the list. The default is five seconds. Tap or click OK.

6. Repeat this procedure to configure conditional forwarding for other domains.

You can disable recursion and forwarders using DNS Manager. In DNS Manager, press and hold or right-click the server you want to work with and select Properties. In the Properties dialog box, tap or click the Advanced tab. Disable recursion and forwarders by selecting the Disable Recursion check box and tapping or clicking OK.

## Configuring subdomains and delegating authority

Your organization's domain structure is separate from its zone configuration. If you create subdomains of a parent domain, you can add these subdomains to the parent domain's zone or create separate zones for the subdomains. When you create separate zones, you must tell DNS about the other servers that have authority over a particular subdomain. You do this by telling the primary name server for the parent domain that you delegated authority for a subdomain.

When you add subdomains of a parent domain to the same zone as the parent domain, you have a single large namespace hosted by primary servers. This gives you a single unit to manage, which is good when you want centralized control over DNS in the domain. The disadvantage is that as the number of subdomains in the zone grows, there's more and more to manage and, at some point you might want to partition the management of the DNS system—especially if dynamic updates are allowed and there are many thousands of host records.

When you create a separate zone for a subdomain, you have an additional unit of management that can be placed on the same DNS server or on a different DNS server. This means that you can delegate control over the zone to someone else, which would allow

Chapter 22

branch offices or other departments within the organization to manage their own DNS services. If the zone is on another DNS server, you shift the load associated with that zone to another server. The disadvantage is that you lose centralized control over DNS.

> **Note**
> It isn't possible to combine domains from different branches of the namespace and place them in a single zone. As a result, domains that are part of the same Active Directory forest but on different trees must be in separate zones. Thus, you would need separate zones for cohowinery.com and cohovineyards.com.

To create subdomains in separate zones on the same server as the parent domain, complete the following steps:

1.  Create the necessary forward and reverse lookup zones for the subdomains as described earlier in this chapter in "Creating forward lookup zones" and "Creating reverse lookup zones."

2.  You don't need to delegate authority because these subdomains are on the primary name server for the parent domain. This server automatically has control over the zones.

To create subdomains in separate zones and on separate servers, complete the following steps:

1.  Install a DNS server in each subdomain, and then create the necessary forward and reverse lookup zones for the subdomains as described earlier in "Creating forward lookup zones" and "Creating reverse lookup zones."

2.  On the primary DNS server for the parent domain, you must delegate authority to each subdomain. In DNS Manager, expand the node for the server on which the parent domain is located, and then expand the related Forward Lookup Zones folder.

3.  Press and hold or right-click the parent domain entry, and then select New Delegation. This starts the New Delegation Wizard. Tap or click Next.

4.  As shown in Figure 22-15, type the name of the subdomain, such as **ny**. Check the fully qualified domain name (FQDN) to ensure that it is correct, and then tap or click Next.

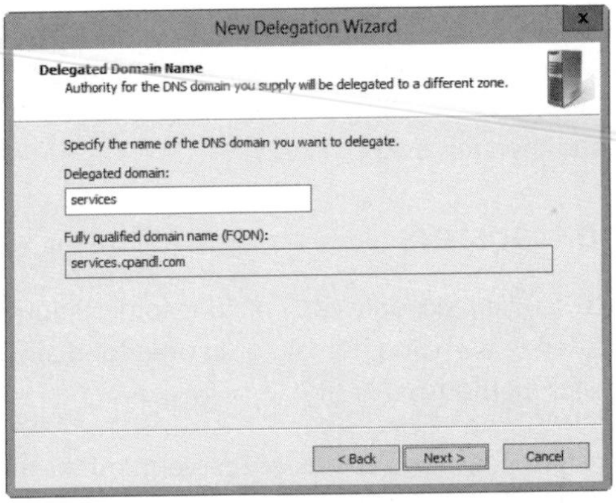

**Figure 22-15** Specify the subdomain name.

5.  On the Name Servers page, tap or click Add. As shown in Figure 22-16, the New Name Server Record dialog box is displayed.

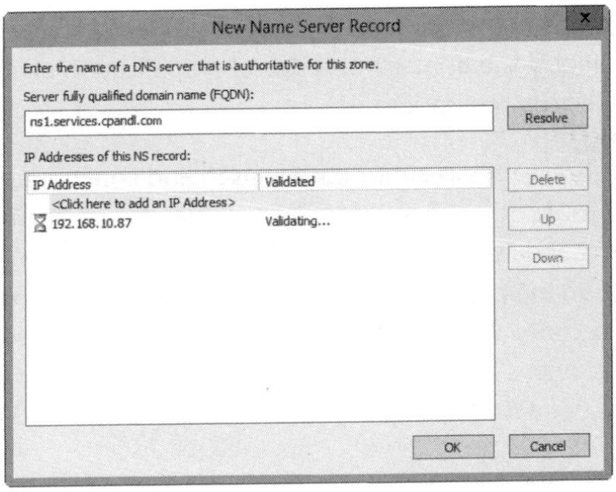

**Figure 22-16** Specify the server name and IP address.

6.  In the Server Fully Qualified Domain Name (FQDN) box, type the fully qualified host name of a DNS server for the subdomain, such as **ns1.ny.cpandl.com**, and then tap or click Resolve. The wizard then validates the name server and fills in its IP address. You can add additional IP addresses for the name server by tapping or clicking in the IP Address list, typing the IP address, and pressing Enter.

> **Note**
> You must specify the server name and at least one IP address. The order of the entries determines which IP address is used first. You can change the order as necessary using the Up and Down buttons.

Chapter 22

7. Tap or click OK to close the New Name Server Record dialog box. Repeat steps 5 and 6 to specify other authoritative DNS servers for the subdomain.

8. Tap or click Next, and then tap or click Finish.

## Configuring zone transfers

Zone transfers are used to send a read-only copy of zone information to secondary DNS servers, which can be located in the same domain or in other domains. Windows Server supports three zone transfer methods:

- Standard zone transfers, in which a secondary server requests a full copy of a zone from a primary server

- Incremental zone transfers, in which a secondary server requests only the changes that it needs to synchronize its copy of the zone information with the primary server's copy

- Active Directory zone replication, in which changes to zones are replicated to all domain controllers in the domain (or a subset if application partitions are configured) using Active Directory replication

Active Directory zone replication is automatically used and configured when you use Active Directory–integrated zones. If you have secondary name servers, these name servers can't automatically request standard or incremental zone transfers. To allow this, you must first enable zone transfers on the primary name server. Zone transfers are disabled by default to enhance DNS server security. Speaking of security, although you can allow zone transfers to any DNS server, this opens the server to possible attack. It is better to designate specific name servers that are permitted to request zone transfers.

Zone transfers can be enabled for domains and subdomains in forward lookup zones and subnets in reverse lookup zones. You enable zone transfers on primary name servers. If a server is a secondary name server, it is already configured to perform zone transfers with the primary name server in the zone.

## INSIDE OUT    Incremental zone transfers

To manage incremental zone transfers, DNS servers track changes that have been made to a zone between each increment of a zone's serial number. Secondary servers use the zone's serial number to determine whether changes have been made to the zone. If the serial number matches what the secondary server has for the zone, no changes have been made and an incremental transfer isn't necessary. If the serial number doesn't match, the secondary server's copy of the zone isn't current and the secondary server then requests only the changes that have occurred since the last time the secondary zone was updated.

Using DNS Manager, you can enable zone transfers on a primary name server and restrict the secondary name servers that can request zone transfers. In DNS Manager, expand the node for the primary name server, and then expand the related Forward Lookup Zones or Reverse Lookup Zones folder as appropriate. Press and hold or right-click the domain or subnet you want to configure, and then choose Properties. In the Properties dialog box, tap or click the Zone Transfers tab, as shown in Figure 22-17.

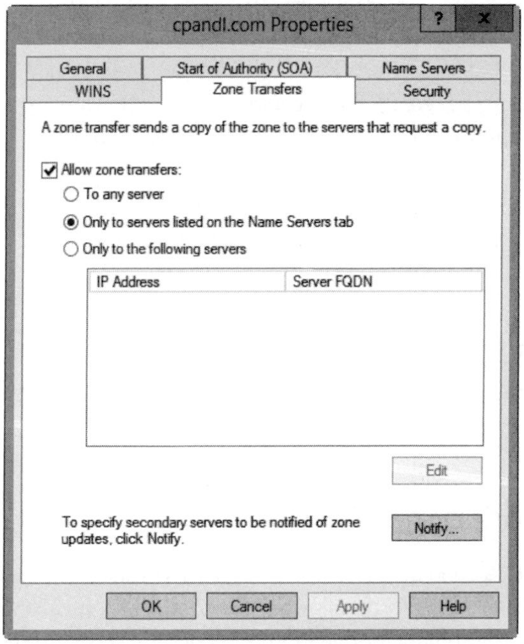

Figure 22-17  Configure zone transfers for a domain or subnet.

Chapter 22

Select the Allow Zone Transfers check box. You have three zone transfer options:

- **To Any Server**   Choose To Any Server to allow any DNS server to request zone transfers.

- **Only To Servers Listed On The Name Servers Tab**   Choose Only To Servers Listed On The Name Servers Tab to restrict transfers to name servers listed on the Name Servers tab, and then tap or click the Name Servers tab. Then complete these steps:

    1. The Name Servers list shows the DNS servers currently configured to be authoritative for the zone and includes DNS servers that host secondary zones. If a secondary server isn't listed and you want to authorize the server to request zone transfers, tap or click Add. This displays the New Name Server Record dialog box.

        a. In the Server Fully Qualified Domain Name (FQDN) field, type the fully qualified host name of a secondary server for the domain and then tap or click Resolve. The wizard then validates the name server and fills in its IP address. You can add additional IP addresses for the name server by tapping or clicking in the IP Address list, typing the IP address, and pressing Enter.

        b. Tap or click OK to close the New Name Server Record dialog box. Repeat this process to specify other secondary DNS servers for the domain or subnet.

- **Only To The Following Servers**   Choose Only To The Following Servers to restrict transfers to a list of approved servers. Then complete these steps:

    1. Tap or click Edit to display the Allow Zone Transfers dialog box.

        a. Type the IP address of a secondary server that should receive zone transfers, and then press Enter.

        b. Repeat this process to specify other secondary DNS servers for the domain or subnet.

        c. Tap or click OK to close the Allow Zone Transfers dialog box.

When you are finished, tap or click OK to close the Properties dialog box.

## Configuring secondary notification

When changes are made to a zone on the primary server, secondary servers can be automatically notified of the changes. This allows the secondary servers to request zone transfers. You can configure automatic notification of secondary servers using DNS Manager.

In DNS Manager, expand the node for the primary name server, and then expand the related Forward Lookup Zones or Reverse Lookup Zones folder as appropriate. Press and hold or right-click the domain or subnet you want to configure, and then choose Properties. In the Properties dialog box, tap or click the Zone Transfers tab. Tap or click Notify in the bottom right corner of the Zone Transfers tab. This displays the Notify dialog box, as shown in Figure 22-18.

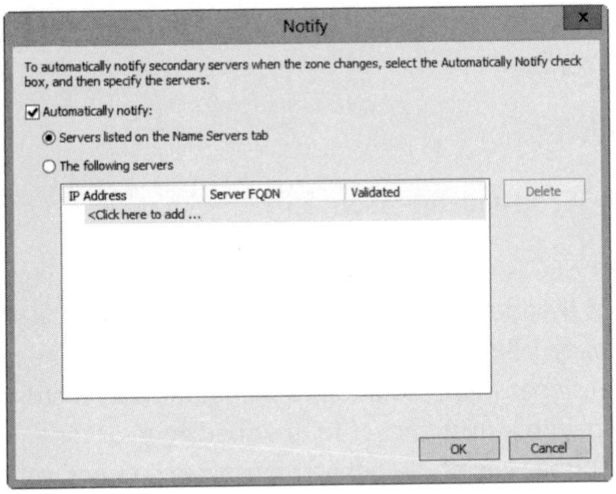

**Figure 22-18** Configure secondary notification.

Select the Automatically Notify check box. You have two notification options:

- **Servers Listed On The Name Servers Tab** Choose this option to notify only the name servers listed in the Name Servers tab.

- **The Following Servers** Choose this option to specify the name servers that should be notified. Then complete these steps:

  1. Type the IP address of a secondary server that should receive notification, and then press Enter.

     a. Repeat this process to notify other secondary DNS servers for the domain or subnet.

     b. When you are finished, tap or click OK twice.

# Deploying DNSSEC

You sign zones using DNS Security Extensions (DNSSEC). DNSSEC is supported by Windows 7 or later, as well as Windows Server 2008 R2 or later, and it is defined in several Request For Comments (RFCs), including RFCs 4033, 4034, and 4035. These RFCs add origin authority, data integrity, and authenticated denial of existence to DNS.

## DNSSEC essentials

The DNS clients running on current Windows operating systems can send queries that indicate support for DNSSEC, process related records, and determine whether a DNS server has validated records on its behalf. On Windows servers, DNSSEC allows your DNS servers to

- Securely sign zones

- Host DNSSEC-signed zones

- Process related records

- Perform both validation and authentication

The way DNS clients use DNSSEC is configurable through the Name Resolution Policy Table (NRPT), which stores settings that define the DNS client's behavior. Normally, you manage the NRPT through Group Policy. When a DNS server hosting a signed zone receives a query, the server returns the digital signatures in addition to the requested records. A resolver or another server configured with a trust anchor for a signed zone or for a parent of a signed zone can obtain the public key of the public/private key pair and validate that the responses are authentic and have not been tampered with.

Before you deploy DNSSEC, you need to identify the DNS zones that you want to secure with digital signatures. Zones signed with DNSSEC have several additional resource records. These include

- DNSKEY (Domain Name System Key)

- RRSIG (Resource Record Signature)

- NSEC (NextSECure)

- DS (Domain Services)

When you install DNS Server service on Windows Server 2012, support for DNSSEC is enabled by default. In DNS Manager, you can confirm whether DNSSEC support is enabled or disabled by pressing and holding or right-clicking the server entry and then selecting Properties. In the Properties dialog box, click the Advanced tab. If you want to use DNSSEC, the Enable DNSSEC Validation For Remote Responses setting should be enabled.

DNS Server for Windows Server 2012 has several significant enhancements for DNSSEC. Windows Server 2012 supports secure dynamic updates in Active Directory–integrated zones. Previously, if an Active Directory domain zone was signed, you needed to manually update all SRV records and other resource records. This is no longer required because DNS Server now does this automatically.

Windows Server 2012 also supports online signing, automated key management, and automated trust anchor distribution. Previously, you needed to configure and manage signings, keys, and trust anchors. This is no longer required because DNS Server now does this automatically.

Finally, Windows Server 2012 supports validations of records signed with updated DNSSEC standards (NSEC3 and RSA/SHA-2 standards). Previously, you could not sign records with NSEC3 and RSA/SHA-2.

## Securing zones with digital signatures

To secure DNS zones with digital signatures, you need to designate a key master. Any authoritative server that hosts a primary copy of a zone can act as the key master. Next, you need to generate a key signing key and a zone signing key. A key signing key (KSK) that is an authentication key has a private key and a public key associated with it. The private key is used for signing all of the DNSKEY records at the root of the zone. The public key is used as a trust anchor for validating DNS responses. A zone signing key (ZSK) is used for signing zone records.

After you generate keys, you create resource records for authenticated denial of existence using either the more secure NSEC3 standard or the less secure NSEC standard. Because trust anchors are used to validate DNS responses, you also need to specify how trust anchors are updated and distributed. Typically, you'll want to automatically update and distribute trust anchors. By default, records are signed with SHA-1 and SHA-256 encryption. You can select other encryption algorithms as well.

You don't need to go through the configuration process each time you sign a zone. The signing keys and other signing parameters are available for re-use. Additionally, keep the following in mind:

- For file-backed zones, the primary server and all secondary servers hosting the zone must be a Windows Server 2008 R2 or later DNS server or a DNSSEC-aware server that is running an operating system other than Windows.

- For Active Directory–integrated zones, every domain controller that is a DNS server in the domain must be running Windows Server 2008 R2 or later if the signed zone is set to replicate to all DNS servers in the domain. Every domain controller that is a DNS server in the forest must be running Windows Server 2008 R2 or later if the signed zone is set to replicate to all DNS servers in the forest.

- For mixed environments, all servers that are authoritative for a DNSSEC-signed zone must be DNSSEC-aware servers. DNSSEC-aware Windows clients that request

Chapter 22

DNSSEC data and validation must be configured to issue DNS queries to a DNSSEC-aware server. Non-DNSSEC-aware Windows clients can be configured to issue DNS queries to DNSSEC-aware servers. DNSSEC-aware servers can be configured to recursively send queries to a non-DNSSEC-aware DNS server.

## Signing a zone

In DNS Manager, press and hold or right-click the zone you want to secure. On the shortcut menu, select DNSSEC and then select Sign The Zone. This starts the Zone Signing Wizard. If the wizard displays a welcome page, read the Welcome text and then tap or click Next. On the Signing Options page, choose how to sign the zone. Here, you can

- Use the default settings.

- Use settings of an existing signed zone.

- Use custom settings.

If you want to use the default signing settings, choose Use Default Settings To Sign The Zone as the signing option. (See Figure 22-19.) When you use the default settings, the wizard sets the options for the key signing key, zone signing key, trusted anchors, polling, and authenticated denial of existence. KSK and ZSK rollover will be enabled, and trust anchors will update automatically on key rollover as per RFC 5011. Click Next twice, and then click Finish.

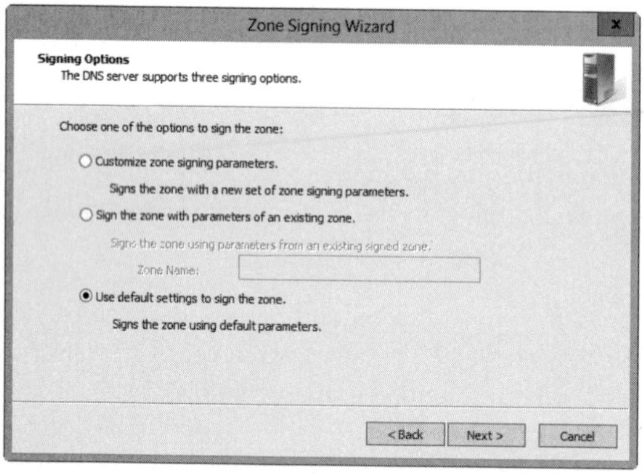

**Figure 22-19** Use the default signing options to configure signing automatically.

If you signed other zones previously, you can use the settings of one of the signed zones. To do this, choose Sign The Zone With Parameters Of An Existing Zone as the signing option and then type the name of the zone. (See Figure 22-20.) When you tap or click Next, you can elect to use the same key master as the existing zone or you can select another primary server as the key master. When you are ready to continue, tap or click Next twice and then click Finish.

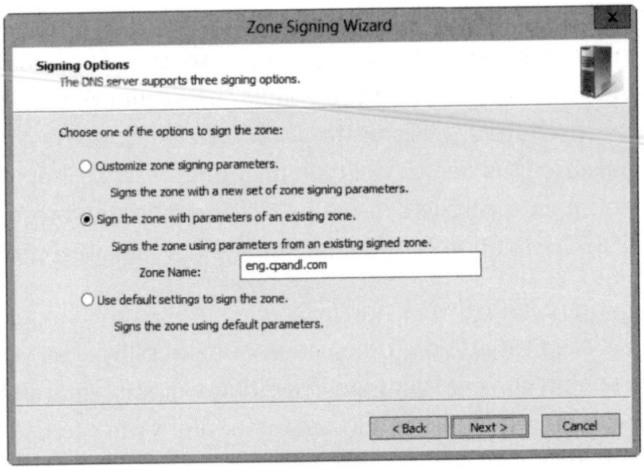

**Figure 22-20** Use the settings of another signed zone to quickly set up a new zone.

If you want to use custom settings, sign the zone by completing the following steps:

1.  Select Customize Zone Signing Parameters as the signing option, and then tap or click Next.

2.  Select a key master for the zone. Any authoritative server that hosts a primary copy of a zone can act as the key master. When you are ready to continue, tap or click Next until you see the Key Signing Key page that allows you to configure a KSK.

3.  Configure a KSK by tapping or clicking Add, accepting or changing the default values for key properties and the key rollover frequency, and then tapping or clicking OK. When you are ready to continue, tap or click Next until you see the Zone Signing Key page that allows you to configure a ZSK.

4.  Configure a ZSK by tapping or clicking Add, accepting or changing the default values for key properties and the key rollover frequency, and then tapping or clicking OK.

5.  When you are ready, continue through the remaining pages, which allow you to configure next the secure resource records, trust anchors, signing, and polling parameters. Keep the following in mind:

    ○ Typically, you'll want to use the more current NSEC3 resource record rather than the older NSEC resource record for authenticated denial of existence. If you allow unsigned delegations in the zone, select Use Opt-Out To Cover Unsigned Delegations.

Chapter 22

○ By default, trust anchors are updated automatically on key rollover. Generally, you want this to happen. Otherwise, you need to manually update trust anchors on key rollover. You also can enable the distribution of trust anchors for the zone. This option works best with DNS Server running on a domain controller because DNS Server will then distribute trust anchors for the zone to all other domain controllers running DNS Server in the forest, which in turn enables DNSSEC validation for the zone on all the domain controllers.

○ For signing and polling, SHA-1 and SHA-256 are the default algorithms used. This option is used for attaining the widest compatibility. If all your servers and clients are running current Windows operating systems, you might not want to use the weaker SHA-1 algorithm; instead you might want to use only SHA-256, SHA-256 with SHA-384, or only SHA-384.

**6.** Tap or click Next twice. After the wizard signs the zone, click Finish.

After you sign a zone, you can manage the signing properties by pressing and holding or right-clicking the zone, selecting DNSSEC, and then selecting Properties. To remove zone signing, press and hold or right-click a signed zone, select DNSSEC, and then select Unsign The Zone. In the Unsign Zone Wizard, tap or click Next and then tap or click Finish.

# Adding resource records

When you create a zone in Windows Server, several records are created automatically:

- For a forward lookup zone, these records include an SOA record, an NS record, and an A record. The SOA record contains information about how resource records in the zone should be used and cached. The NS record contains the name of the authoritative name server, which is the server on which the zone was configured. The A record is the Host Address record for the name server.

- For a reverse lookup zone, these records include an SOA record, an NS record, and a PTR record. The SOA record contains information about how resource records in the zone should be used and cached. The NS record contains the name of the authoritative name server, which is the server on which the zone was configured. The PTR record is the Pointer record for the name server that allows reverse lookups on the server's IP address.

- When you use Active Directory, SRV records are automatically created as well for domain controllers, global catalog servers, and PDC emulators.

- When you allow dynamic updates, A, AAAA, and PTR records for clients are automatically created for any computer using DHCP.

Any other records that you need must be created manually. The technique you use to create additional records depends on the type of record.

## Create and change records on primary servers

When you create records or make changes to records, you should do so on a primary server. For Active Directory–integrated zones, this means any domain controller running the DNS Server service. For standard zones, this means the primary name server only. After you make changes to standard zones, press and hold or right-click the server entry in DNS Manager and select Update Server Data Files. This increments the serial number for zones as necessary to ensure secondary name servers know changes have been made. You do not need to do this for Active Directory– integrated zones because Active Directory replicates changes automatically.

## Host Address (A and AAAA) and Pointer (PTR) records

Host Address (A) records contain the name of a host and its IPv4 address, and Host Address (AAAA) records contain the name of a host and its IPv6 address. Any computer that has multiple network interfaces or IP addresses should have multiple address records. Pointer (PTR) records enable reverse lookups by creating a pointer that maps an IP address to a host name.

You do not need to create A, AAAA, and PTR records for hosts that use dynamic DNS. These records are created automatically. For hosts that don't use dynamic DNS, you can create a new host entry with A and PTR records by completing the following steps:

1. In DNS Manager, expand the node for the primary name server, and then expand the related Forward Lookup Zones folder. Press and hold or right-click the domain to which you want to add the records, and then choose New Host (A or AAAA). This displays the dialog box shown in Figure 22-21.

Chapter 22

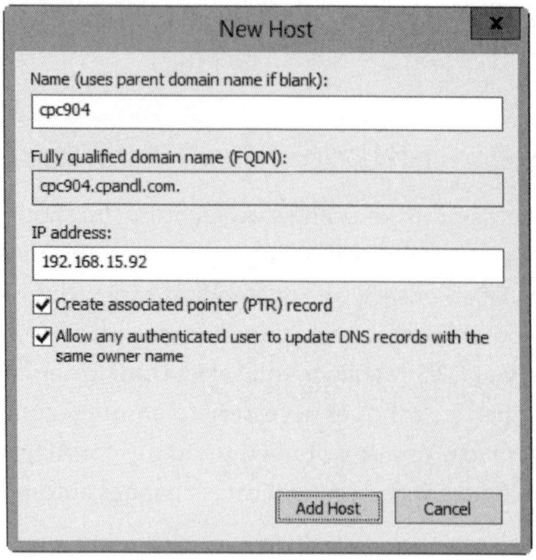

**Figure 22-21** Create a host record.

2. Type the host name, such as **cpc904**, and then type the IP address, such as **192.168.15.92**.

3. If a reverse lookup zone has been created for the domain and you want to create a PTR record for this host, select the Create Associated Pointer (PTR) Record check box.

> **Note**
>
> If you are working with an Active Directory–integrated zone, you have the option of allowing any authenticated client with the designated host name to update the record. To enable this, select Allow Any Authenticated User To Update DNS Records With The Same Owner Name. This is a nonsecure dynamic update where only the client host name is checked.

4. Tap or click Add Host. Repeat this process as necessary to add other hosts.

5. Tap or click Done when you're finished.

If you opt not to create a PTR record when you create an A record, you can create the PTR later as necessary. In DNS Manager, expand the node for the primary name server, and then expand the related Reverse Lookup Zones folder. Press and hold or right-click the subnet to which you want to add the record, and then choose New Pointer (PTR). This displays the dialog box shown in Figure 22-22. Type the Host ID part of the IP address, such as **49**, and then type the host name, such as **corpsvr05**. Tap or click OK.

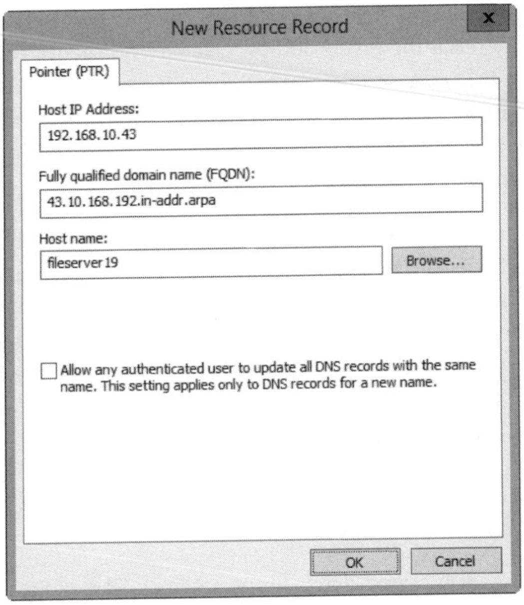

**Figure 22-22** Create a PTR record.

# INSIDE OUT    Using round robin for load balancing

If a host name has multiple A records associated with it, the DNS Server service uses round robin for load balancing. With round robin, the DNS server cycles between the A records so that queries are routed proportionally to the various IP addresses that are configured. Here's how round robin works: Say that your organization's web server gets a ton of hits—so much that the single web server you set up can't handle the load anymore.

To spread the workload, you configure three machines: one with the IP address 192.168.12.18, one with the IP address 192.168.12.19, and one with the IP address 192.168.12.20. On the DNS server, you configure a separate A record for each IP address, but you use the same host name: www.cpandl.com. This tells the DNS server to use round robin to balance the incoming requests proportionally. As requests come in, DNS will respond in a fixed circular fashion with the IP addresses. Although the DNS server gives clients all three IP addresses for the web server, the IP addresses are given in a changing order. For a series of requests, the first user might be directed to 192.168.12.18 (because this is the first IP address given to this client), the next user to 192.168.12.19 (because this is the first IP address given to this client), and the next user

Chapter 22

to 192.168.12.20 (because this is the first IP address given to this client). The next time around, the order will be the same, so the fourth user is directed to 192.168.12.18, the next user to 192.168.12.19, and the next user to 192.168.12.20. As you can see, with three servers, each server will get approximately one-third of the incoming requests and, ideally, about one-third of the workload as well.

Round robin isn't meant to be a replacement for clustering technologies, but it is an easy and fast way to get basic load balancing. Support for round robin is enabled by default. If you have to disable round robin, type **dnscmd ServerName /config /roundrobin 0**. To enable round robin again later, type **dnscmd ServerName /config /roundrobin 1**. In both cases, *ServerName* is the name or IP address of the DNS server you want to configure.

## Canonical Name (CNAME) records

Canonical Name (CNAME) records create aliases for host names. This allows a host to be referred to by multiple names in DNS. The most common use is when a host provides a common service, such as World Wide Web (WWW) or File Transfer Protocol (FTP) service, and you want it to have a friendly name rather than a complex name. For example, you might want www.cpandl.com to be an alias for the host dc06.cpandl.com.

To create an alias for a host name in DNS Manager, expand the node for the primary name server, and then expand the related Forward Lookup Zones folder. Press and hold or right-click the domain to which you want to add the record, and then choose New Alias (CNAME). This displays the dialog box shown in Figure 22-23. Type the alias for the host name, such as **www**, and then type the FQDN for the host, such as **corpsvr17.cpandl.com**. Tap or click OK.

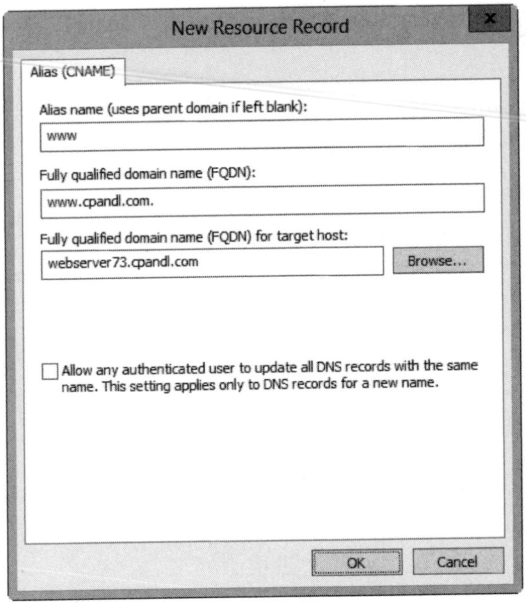

Figure 22-23  Create a new alias.

## Mail Exchanger (MX) records

Mail Exchanger (MX) records designate a mail exchange server for the domain, which allows mail to be delivered to the correct mail servers in the domain. For example, if an MX record is set for the domain cpandl.com, all mail sent to Username@cpandl.com will be directed to the server specified in the MX record.

You can create an MX record by completing the following steps:

1. In DNS Manager, expand the node for the primary name server, and then expand the related Forward Lookup Zones folder. Press and hold or right-click the domain to which you want to add the record, and then choose New Mail Exchanger (MX). This displays the dialog box shown in Figure 22-24.

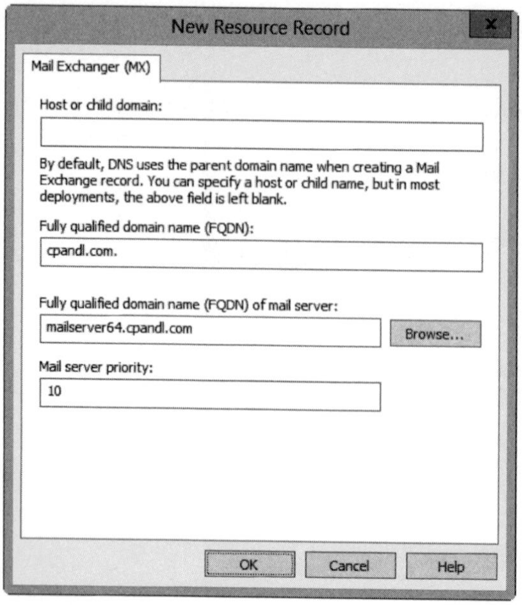

**Figure 22-24** Create an MX record.

2. Consider leaving the Host Or Child Domain box blank. A blank entry specifies the mail exchanger is responsible for the parent domain, not for a child domain under the parent domain.

3. Type the FQDN of the mail exchange server in the Fully Qualified Domain Name (FQDN) Of Mail Server box, such as **exchange.cpandl.com**. This is the name used to route mail for delivery.

4. Specify the priority of the mail server relative to other mail servers in the domain. The mail server with the lowest priority is the mail server that is tried first when mail must be routed to a mail server in the domain.

5. Tap or click OK.

## Name Server (NS) records

Name Server (NS) records provide a list of authoritative servers for a domain, which allows DNS lookups within various zones. Each primary and secondary name server in a domain should be declared through these records. These records are created automatically when Active Directory–integrated zones are used. For standard zones, you can create an NS record by doing the following:

1. In DNS Manager, expand the node for the primary name server, and then expand the related Forward Lookup Zones or Reverse Lookup Zones folder as appropriate.

2. Press and hold or right-click the domain of the subnet for which you want to create name servers, and then select Properties. In the Properties dialog box, tap or click the Name Servers tab, as shown in Figure 22-25.

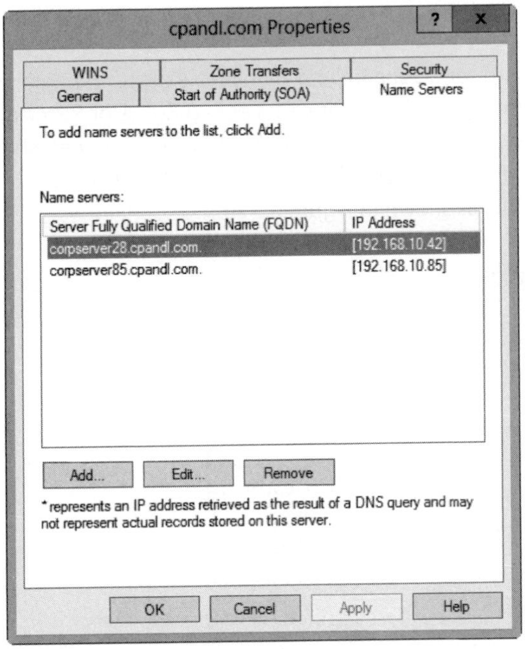

**Figure 22-25** The Name Servers tab lists current name servers for the domain or subnet.

3. The Name Servers list shows the DNS servers currently configured to be authoritative for the zone and includes DNS servers that host secondary zones. If a name server isn't listed and you want to add it, tap or click Add. This displays the New Name Server Record dialog box.

4. In the Server Fully Qualified Domain Name (FQDN) field, type the fully qualified host name of a secondary server for the domain, and tap or click Resolve. If the IP address of the name server is filled in for you, tap or click Add, and then add other IP addresses for this name server as necessary.

5. Tap or click OK to close the New Name Server Record dialog box. Repeat this process to specify other name servers for the domain.

Chapter 22

# Start of Authority (SOA) records

Start of Authority (SOA) records indicate the authoritative name server for a particular zone. The authoritative server is the best source of DNS information for a zone. Because each zone must have an SOA record, the record is created automatically when you add a zone. The SOA record also contains information about how resource records in the zone should be used and cached. This includes refresh, retry, and expiration intervals as well as the maximum time that a record is considered valid.

To view the SOA record for a zone in DNS Manager, expand the node for the primary name server, and then expand the related Forward Lookup Zones or Reverse Lookup Zones folder as appropriate. Press and hold or right-click the domain or subnet whose SOA record you want to view, and then select Properties. In the Properties dialog box, tap or click the Start Of Authority (SOA) tab, as shown in Figure 22-26.

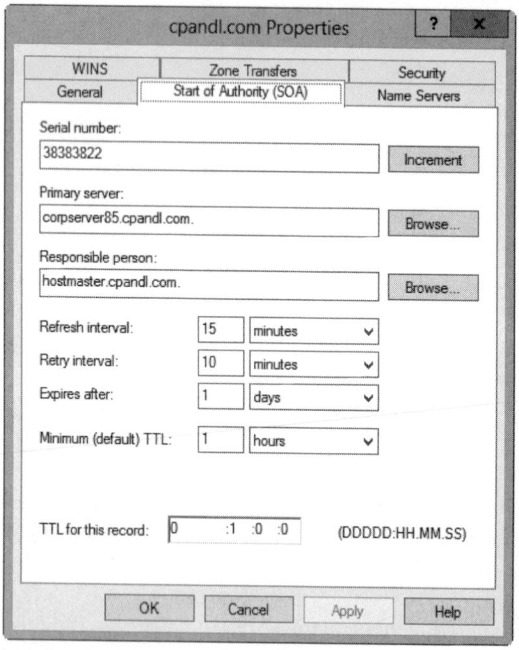

**Figure 22-26** The Start Of Authority (SOA) tab for a domain or subnet.

The key field here is the Serial Number field. Whenever you make changes manually to records in standard zones, the serial number in the related zone or zones is updated to show that changes have been made. You can manually increment the serial number as well. In DNS Manager, press and hold or right-click the server entry and then choose Update Server Data Files. As discussed previously, you do not need to do this with Active Directory–integrated zones because changes are replicated automatically.

## Service Location (SRV) records

Service Location (SRV) records make it possible to find a server providing a specific service. Active Directory uses SRV records to locate domain controllers, global catalog servers, LDAP servers, and Kerberos servers. SRV records are created automatically. For example, Active Directory creates an SRV record when you promote a domain controller. LDAP servers can add an SRV record to indicate they are available to handle LDAP requests in a particular zone.

In the forest root zone, SOA, NS, CNAME, and SRV records are created. The SOA record contains information about the forest root zone. The NS records indicate the primary DNS servers for the forest root zone. The CNAME records are used to designate aliases that allow Active Directory to use the globally unique identifier (GUID) of a domain to find the forest root name servers for that domain. The SRV records used to locate Active Directory resources are organized by function as follows:

- **DC**   Contains SRV records for domain controllers. These records are organized according to the Active Directory site in which domain controllers are located.

- **Domains**   Contains SRV records for domain controllers listed by domain. Folders for each domain in the forest are organized by the domain's GUID.

- **GC**   Contains SRV records for global catalog servers in the forest. These records are primarily organized according to the Active Directory site in which domain controllers are located.

- **PDC**   Contains SRV records for PDC emulators in the forest.

In the forward lookup zone for a domain, you'll find similar SRV records used to locate Active Directory resources. These records are organized by the following criteria:

- Active Directory site

- The Internet protocol used by the resource, either TCP or User Datagram Protocol (UDP)

- Zone, either DomainDnsZones or ForestDnsZones

As Figure 22-27 shows, each record entry identifies a server that provides a particular service according to the following:

- **Domain**   The DNS domain in which the record is stored.

- **Service**   The service being made available. LDAP is for directory services on a domain controller. Kerberos indicates a Kerberos server that enables Kerberos

Chapter 22

authentication. GC indicates a global catalog server. KPasswd indicates Kerberos password service.

- **Protocol**   The protocol the service uses, either TCP or UDP.

- **Priority**   The priority or level of preference given to the server providing the service. The highest priority is 0. If multiple servers have the same priority, clients can use the weight to load balance between available servers.

- **Weight**   The relative weight given to the server for load balancing when multiple servers have the same priority level.

- **Port Number**   The TCP/IP port used by the server to provide the service.

- **Host Offering This Service**   The FQDN of the host providing the service.

**Figure 22-27**  An SRV record.

# Deploying global names

The GlobalNames zone is a specially named forward lookup zone that is available when all the DNS servers for your zones are running Windows Server 2008 or later. Deploying a GlobalNames zone creates static, global records with single-label names without relying on Windows Internet Naming Service (WINS). This allows users to access hosts using single-label names rather than fully qualified domain names (FQDNs).

You'll want to use the GlobalNames zone when name resolution depends on DNS, such as when your organization is no longer using WINS and you are planning to deploy only IPv6. When you are using global names, an authoritative DNS server will try to resolve queries in the following order:

1. Using local zone data

2. Using the GlobalNames zone

3. Using DNS suffixes

4. Using WINS

The GlobalNames zone should be created as an Active Directory–integrated zone. Because dynamic updates cannot be used to register updates in the GlobalNames zone, you should configure single-label name resolution only for your primary servers. An authoritative DNS server will first check the GlobalNames zone before checking the local zone data. If you want DNS clients in another forest to use the GlobalNames zone for resolving names, you need to add an SRV resource record with the service name _globalnames._msdcs to that forest's forestwide DNS partition. The record must specify the FQDN of the DNS server that hosts the GlobalNames zone.

You can deploy a GlobalNames zone by completing the following steps:

1. In DNS Manager, press and hold or right-click the Forward Lookup Zones node and then select New Zone. In the New Zone Wizard, tap or click Next twice to accept the defaults to create a primary zone integrated with Active Directory Domain Services.

2. On the Active Directory Zone Replication Scope page, choose to replicate the zone throughout the forest and then tap or click Next.

3. On the Zone Name page, enter **GlobalNames** as the zone name. Tap or click Next twice, and then tap or click Finish.

4. On every authoritative DNS server on the forest now and in the future, you need to type the following at an elevated command prompt:

   ```
   dnscmd ServerName /enableglobalnamessupport 1
   ```

   Here, *ServerName* is the name of the DNS server that hosts the GlobalNames zone. To specify the local computer, use a period (.) instead of the server name, such as

   ```
   dnscmd . /enableglobalnamessupport 1
   ```

5. For each server that you want users to be able to access using a single-label name, add an alias (CNAME) record to the GlobalNames zone. In DNS Manager, press and hold or right-click the GlobalZones node, select New Alias (CNAME), and then use the dialog box provided to create the new resource record.

Chapter 22

# Maintaining and monitoring DNS

When using DNS, you can perform many routine tasks to maintain and monitor domain name-resolution services. Key tasks you might need to perform include the following:

- Configuring default application directory partitions and replication scope

- Setting aging and scavenging

- Configuring logging and checking event logs

## Configuring default application directory partitions and replication scope

When the domain controllers running DNS in all the domains of your forest are using Windows Server 2008 or later, you can create default application directory partitions for DNS. This reduces DNS replication traffic because DNS changes are replicated only to domain controllers also configured as DNS servers. There are two ways to configure default application directory partitions:

- **Forestwide**   Creates a single application directory partition that stores DNS zone data and replicates that data to all DNS servers in the forest. The default partition name is ForestDnsZones.*DnsForestName*, where *DnsForestName* is the domain name of the forest.

- **Domainwide**   Creates a single application directory partition that stores DNS zone data and replicates that data to all DNS servers in a designated domain. The default partition name is DomainDnsZones.*DnsDomainName*, where *DnsDomainName* is the domain name of the domain.

### Check the DNS configuration fast

A fast way to check for the default application partitions and other DNS server configuration settings is to use Dnscmd. At a command prompt, type **dnscmd ServerName /info**, where *ServerName* is the name or IP address of a DNS server, such as CORPSVR03 or 192.168.10.15.

By default, the DNS Server service will try to create the default application directory partitions when you install it. You can verify this by connecting to the primary DNS server in the forest root domain and looking for subdomains of the forest root domain named DomainDnsZones and ForestDnsZones. Figure 22-28 shows an example in which these partitions have been created.

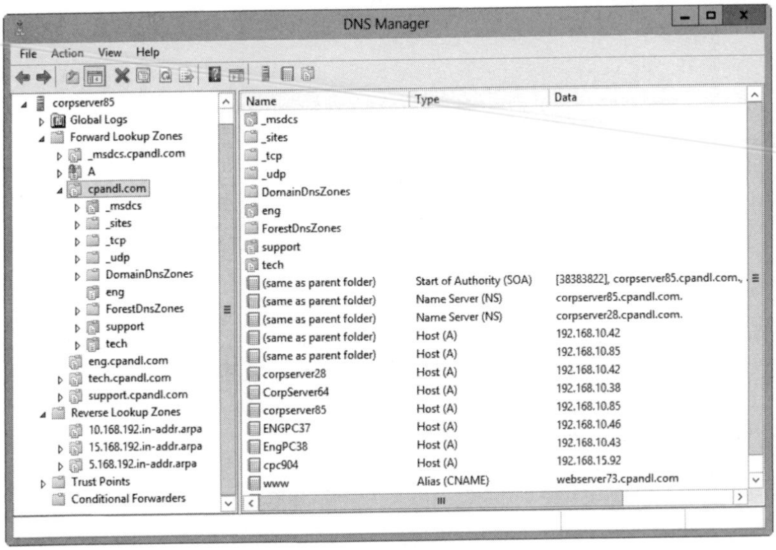

**Figure 22-28** The default application partitions.

If the DNS Server service is unable to create these partitions, you need to create the partitions manually. To do so, you must use an account that is a member of the Enterprise Admins group. If the default application partitions are currently available, the option to create them should not be available in DNS Manager.

If the default application partitions have not yet been created, you can create them in DNS Manager by following these steps:

1. In DNS Manager, connect to the DNS server handling the zone for the parent domain of your forest root, such as cpandl.com rather than tech.cpandl.com.

2. Press and hold or right-click the server entry, and select Create Default Application Directory Partitions.

3. The first prompt, shown in Figure 22-29, asks Would You Like To Create A Single Partition That Stores DNS Zone Data And Replicates That Data To All DNS Servers That Are Domain Controllers In The Active Directory Domain *DomainName*? Tap or click Yes if you want to create the DomainDnsZones.Dns-DomainName default partition.

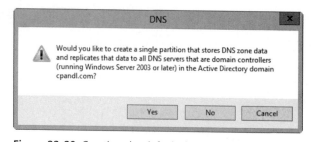

**Figure 22-29** Creating the default domain partition.

4. The next prompt states: Would You Like To Create A Single Partition That Stores DNS Zone Data And Replicates That Data To All DNS Servers In The Active Directory Forest *ForestName*? Tap or click Yes if you want to create the ForestDnsZones .DnsForestName default partition.

When you create Active Directory–integrated zones, you have the option of setting the replication scope. Four replication scopes are available:

- To All DNS Servers In The Active Directory Forest

- To All DNS Servers In The Active Directory Domain

- To All Domain Controllers In The Active Directory Domain

- To All Domain Controllers Specified In The Scope Of This Directory Partition

To check or change the replication scope for a zone in DNS Manager, press and hold or right-click the related domain or subnet entry and select Properties. In the Properties dialog box, the current replication scope is listed to the right of the Replication entry. If you tap or click the related Change button, you can change the replication scope using the dialog box shown in Figure 22-30.

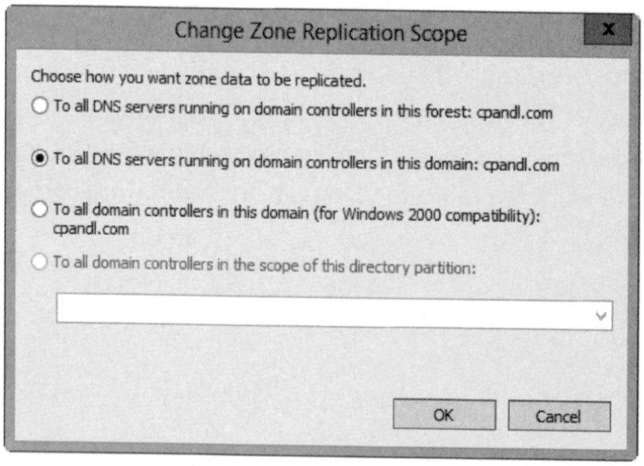

**Figure 22-30** Change the replication scope as necessary.

## Setting the aging and scavenging rules

By default, the DNS Server service doesn't clean out old records. In some ways, this is a good thing because you don't want records you created manually to be deleted. However, for records created automatically through dynamic DNS, you might want to clear out old records periodically. Why? Consider the case of systems that register with DNS and then are removed from the network. Records for these systems will not be cleared automatically, which means the DNS database might contain records for systems that are no longer in use.

DNS can help you clear out old records by using aging and scavenging. These rules determine how long a record created through a dynamic DNS update is valid and, if a record isn't reregistered within the allotted time, whether it can be cleared out. Aging and scavenging rules are set at two levels:

- **Zone**   Zone aging/scavenging properties apply to an individual zone on a DNS server. To set zone-level options, press and hold or right-click a zone entry and select Properties. In the Properties dialog box, tap or click Aging on the General tab. After you enable and configure aging/scavenging, tap or click OK.

- **Server**   Server aging/scavenging properties apply to all zones on a DNS server. To set server-level options in DNS Manager, press and hold or right-click a server entry and select Set Aging/Scavenging For All Zones. After you enable and configure aging/scavenging, tap or click OK. You'll see a prompt telling you these settings will be applied to new Active Directory–integrated zones created on the server. To apply these settings to existing zones, select Apply These Settings To The Existing Active Directory–Integrated Zones before you tap or click OK.

In either case, the dialog box you see is similar to the one shown in Figure 22-31. To enable aging/scavenging, select the Scavenge Stale Resource Records check box and then set these intervals:

- **No-Refresh Interval**   Sets a period of time during which a DNS client cannot reregister its DNS records. When aging/scavenging is enabled, the default interval is 7 days. This means that if a DNS client attempts to reregister its record within 7 days of creating it, the DNS server will ignore the request. Generally, this is what you'll want to use because each time a record is reregistered this is seen as a change that must be replicated. The No-Refresh Interval option doesn't affect clients whose IP address has changed and who therefore need to reregister their DNS records. The reason for this is that the previous records are actually deleted and new records are then created.

- **Refresh Interval**   Sets the extent of the refresh window. Records can be scavenged only when they are older than the combined extent of the No-Refresh Interval and the Refresh interval. When aging/scavenging is enabled, the default No-Refresh

Interval is 7 days and the default Refresh interval is 7 days. This means their combined extent is 14 days, and the DNS server cannot scavenge records until they are older than 14 days.

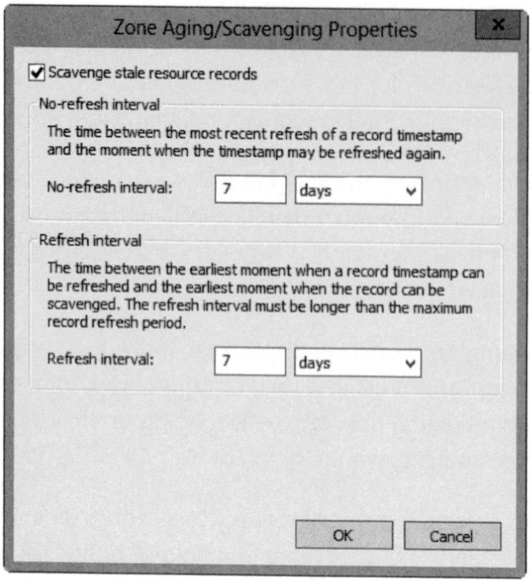

**Figure 22-31** Set scavenging/aging options.

## Scavenge stale records manually

In addition to configuring automatic aging/scavenging, you can manually scavenge for stale (old) records. To do this in DNS Manager, press and hold or right-click a server entry and select Scavenge Stale Resource Records. When prompted to confirm the action, tap or click Yes. You can start scavenging at the command prompt by typing **dnscmd ServerName /startscavenging**, where *ServerName* is the name or IP address of the DNS server to work with, such as NS1 or 10.10.1.52.

## Configuring logging and checking DNS Server logs

By default, the DNS Server service is configured to record all types of events (error, warning, and informational events) in the DNS Server log. You change this behavior in DNS Manager; press and hold or right-click a server entry, and then select Properties. In the Properties dialog box, tap or click the Event Logging tab. Select the appropriate logging option so that no events, errors only, or errors and warnings are logged, and then tap or click OK.

Using DNS Manager, you can view only DNS-related events that have been logged in the system log by expanding the Global Logs node in the left pane and selecting DNS Events. As Figure 22-32 shows, you'll then see the current DNS events for the server. The primary events you will want to examine are error and warning events.

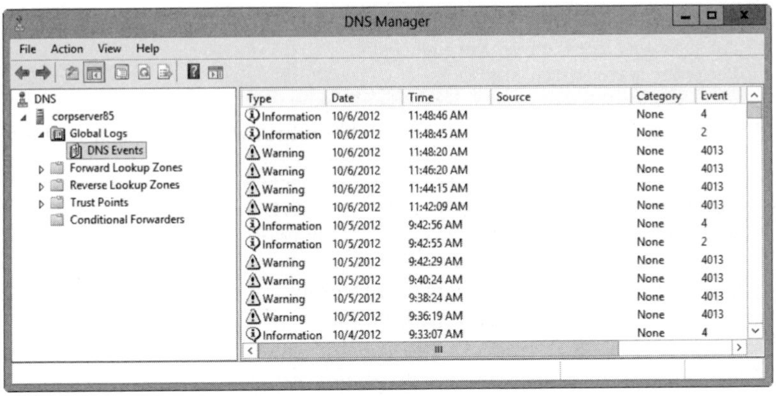

**Figure 22-32**  Check the event logs for warnings and errors.

# Troubleshooting the DNS client service

Frequently, when you are trying to troubleshoot DNS problems, you will want to start on the client that is experiencing the problem. If you don't find a problem on the client, try troubleshooting the DNS Server service.

## Try reregistering the client

If the problem has to do with a client not showing up in DNS, force the client to reregister itself in DNS by typing **ipconfig /registerdns**. A client's A and PTR records must exist, however, for this to work. Although the necessary A and PTR records will be created automatically for a client using dynamically configured DNS records, you must manually create and update the A and PTR records for clients using statically configured records.

## Check the client's TCP/IP configuration

If the problem has to do with the client making lookups, start by checking the DNS servers configured for the client to use.

## Checking IPv4

You can display IPv4 information by typing **netsh interface ipv4 show dnsserver**. The output will show you the DNS servers for the client. If the DNS servers are configured through DHCPv4, the output will look similar to the following:

```
Configuration for interface "Local Area Connection"
    DNS servers configured through DHCP:  192.168.20.21
    Register with which suffix:           Primary only
```

If the DNS servers are configured locally, the output will look similar to the following:

```
Configuration for interface "Local Area Connection"
    Statically Configured DNS Servers:   192.168.20.11
    Register with which suffix:           Primary only
```

If you see a problem with the client's DNS configuration, you can change a locally assigned DNS server IP address by typing the following command:

```
netsh interface ipv4 set dns ConnectionName static ServerIPAddress
```

Here, *ConnectionName* is the name of the local area connection and *ServerIPAddress* is the IP address of the server, such as

```
netsh interface ipv4 set dns "Local Area Connection" static 192.168.0.1
```

If you see a problem with a DHCP-assigned DNS server IP address, try renewing the client's IP address lease by typing **ipconfig /renew**.

## Checking IPv6

You can display IPv6 information by typing **netsh interface ipv6 show dnsserver**. The output will show you the DNS servers for the client. If the DNS servers are configured through DHCPv6, the output will look similar to the following:

```
Configuration for interface "Local Area Connection"
    DNS servers configured through DHCP: fec0:0:0:ffff::1%1
                                         fec0:0:0:ffff::2%1
                                         fec0:0:0:ffff::3%1
        Register with which suffix:      Primary only
```

If the DNS servers are configured locally, the output will look similar to the following:

```
Configuration for interface "Local Area Connection"
    Statically Configured DNS Servers: fec0:0:0:ffff::1%1
                                       fec0:0:0:ffff::2%1
                                       fec0:0:0:ffff::3%1
        Register with which suffix:        Primary only
```

If you see a problem with the client's DNS configuration, you can change a locally assigned DNS server IP address by typing the following command:

```
netsh interface ipv6 set dns ConnectionName static ServerIPAddress
```

Here, *ConnectionName* is the name of the local area connection and *ServerIPAddress* is the IP address of the server, such as

```
netsh interface ipv6 set dns "Local Area Connection" static fe80::fdc2:3222:ab7e:23b1
```

If you see a problem with a DHCP-assigned DNS server IP address, try renewing the client's IP address lease by typing **ipconfig /renew**.

## Check the client's resolver cache

If you don't see a problem with the client's DNS configuration, you will want to check the client's DNS resolver cache. All current Windows operating systems have a built-in DNS resolver cache that caches resource records from query responses that the DNS Client service receives. When performing lookups, the DNS client first looks in the cache. Records remain in the cache until one of the following events occurs:

- Their Time to Live (TTL) expires.

- The system or the DNS Client service is restarted.

- The cache is flushed.

You can display the records in a cache by typing **ipconfig /displaydns** at the command prompt. Records in the cache look like this:

```
Windows IP Configuration

    1.0.0.127.in-addr.arpa
    ----------------------------------------
    Record Name.......... : 1.0.0.127.in-addr.arpa.
    Record Type.......... : 12
    Time To Live......... : 573686
    Data Length.......... : 4
    Section.............. : Answer
    PTR Record........... : localhost

    www.williamstanek.com
    ----------------------------------------
    Record Name.......... : www.williamstanek.com
    Record Type.......... : 5
    Time To Live......... : 12599
    Data Length.......... : 4
    Section.............. : Answer
    CNAME Record ........ : williamstanek.com
```

If you suspect a client has stale records in its cache, you can force it to flush the cache. To do so, type **ipconfig /flushdns** at the command prompt.

## Perform lookups for troubleshooting

Another useful command to use when troubleshooting DNS is NSLookup. You can use NSLookup to query the default DNS server of a client and check to see the actual records it is using. To perform a basic lookup simply type **NSLookup** followed by the FQDN of the host to look up. Consider the following example:

```
nslookup www.microsoft.com
```

The response shows the information that the default DNS server has on that host, such as

```
C:\Documents and Settings\WS>nslookup www.microsoft.com
DNS request timed out.
    timeout was 2 seconds.
Non-authoritative answer:
Name:  www2.microsoft.akadns.net
Addresses:  207.46.244.188, 207.46.156.252, 207.46.144.222, 207.46.245.92
            207.46.134.221, 207.46.245.156, 207.46.249.252, 207.46.156.220
Aliases:  www.microsoft.com, www.microsoft.akadns.net
```

If you want to look up a particular type of record, follow these steps:

1. Type **nslookup** at the command prompt. The prompt changes to >.

2. Type **set query=*RecordType***, where *RecordType* is the type of record, such as **set query=mx**, **set query=soa**, or **set query=ns**.

3. Type the FQDN for the domain in which you want to search, such as **microsoft.com**.

The output shows you matching records in the specified domain, such as

```
microsoft.com    MX preference = 10, mail exchanger = mailb.microsoft.com

microsoft.com    nameserver = dns1.cp.msft.net
microsoft.com    nameserver = dns1.dc.msft.net
mailb.microsoft.com internet address = 131.107.3.122
mailb.microsoft.com internet address = 131.107.3.123
```

# Troubleshooting the DNS Server service

If you suspect the DNS problem is on the server itself, you can begin troubleshooting on the server. There are, of course, many troubleshooting techniques. This section covers the key ones you'll want to use.

## Check the server's TCP/IP configuration

When you are troubleshooting DNS on a DNS server, start with the server's TCP/IP configuration. After you verify or modify the TCP/IP configuration as necessary, you can continue to troubleshoot. DNS servers maintain a cache memory of resource records for the zones they are configured to work with.

## Check the server's cache

If the problem with DNS is that you think the server has stale records, you can check the zone information on the DNS server by using the following command:

dnscmd *ServerName* /zoneprint .

Here, *ServerName* is the name or IP address of the DNS server and "." indicates that you want to examine the root hints. This list includes the root name servers being used by the server. You also can specify the name of a specific zone to examine, such as

dnscmd *ServerName* /zoneprint eng.cpand1.com

If necessary, you can force a server to clear out its cache memory of resource records. To do so, in DNS Manager, press and hold or right-click the server entry and select Clear Cache. You can clear the cache at the command prompt by typing the following:

dnscmd *ServerName* /clearcache

Here, *ServerName* is the name or IP address of the DNS server whose cache you want to clear.

## Check replication to other name servers

Active Directory replication of changes to DNS zones is automatic. By default, Active Directory checks for changes to zones every 180 seconds. This interval is called the *directory service polling interval*. For advanced configuration needs, you can set the directory service polling interval using Dnscmd. Type **dnscmd *ServerName* /config /dspollinginterval *Interval***, where *ServerName* is the name or IP address of the DNS server you want to configure and *Interval* is the polling interval in seconds.

If the problem has to do with failure to replicate changes to secondary servers, start by ensuring that zone transfers are enabled as discussed in "Configuring zone transfers" earlier in this chapter. If zone transfers are properly configured, try updating the serial number on the zone records on the primary server. In DNS Manager, press and hold or right-click the server entry in DNS Manager and select Update Server Data Files. This increments the serial number for zones as necessary, which should trigger zone transfers if they are necessary.

Chapter 22

# Examine the configuration of the DNS server

Frequently, DNS problems have to do with a DNS server's configuration. Rather than trying to navigate multiple tabs and dialog boxes to find the configuration details, you can
use Dnscmd to help you out. You can view a DNS server's configuration by typing **dnscmd**
**ServerName /info** at the command prompt, where *ServerName* is the name or IP address
of the DNS server you want to check, such as Primary or 10.10.1.52. The output looks like
this:

```
Query result:
Server info
    server name              = CorpServer28.cpandl.com
    version                  = 23F00206 (6.2 build 9200)
    DS container             = cn=MicrosoftDNS,cn=System,DC=cpandl,DC=com
    forest name              = cpandl.com
    domain name              = cpandl.com
    builtin forest partition = ForestDnsZones.cpandl.com
    builtin domain partition = DomainDnsZones.cpandl.com
    read only DC             = 0
    last scavenge cycle      = not since restart (0)
Configuration:
    dwLogLevel               = 00000000
    dwDebugLevel             = 00000000
    dwRpcProtocol            = 00000005
    dwNameCheckFlag          = 00000002
    cAddressAnswerLimit      = 0
    dwRecursionRetry         = 3
    dwRecursionTimeout       = 8
    dwDsPollingInterval      = 180
Configuration Flags:
    fBootMethod                  = 3
    fAdminConfigured             = 1
    fAllowUpdate                 = 1
    fDsAvailable                 = 1
    fAutoReverseZones            = 1
    fAutoCacheUpdate             = 0
    fSlave                       = 1
    fNoRecursion                 = 0
    fRoundRobin                  = 1
    fStrictFileParsing           = 0
    fLooseWildcarding            = 0
    fBindSecondaries             = 0
    fWriteAuthorityNs            = 0
    fLocalNetPriority            = 1
Aging Configuration:
    ScavengingInterval           = 0
    DefaultAgingState            = 0
    DefaultRefreshInterval       = 168
    DefaultNoRefreshInterval     = 168
ServerAddresses:
```

```
Ptr          = 000000AE3189DF10
MaxCount   = 2
AddrCount  = 2
Addr[0] => af=23, salen=28, [sub=0, flag=00000000] p=13568,
            addr=fe80::81ff:7053:92ab:bc14
Addr[1] => af=2, salen=16, [sub=0, flag=00000000] p=13568, addr=192.168.10.42

ListenAddresses:
  NULL IP Array.
Forwarders:

Ptr          = 000000AE3188EBF0
MaxCount   = 3
AddrCount  = 3
Addr[0] => af=23, salen=28, [sub=0, flag=00000000] p=13568, addr=fec0:0:0:ffff::1
Addr[1] => af=23, salen=28, [sub=0, flag=00000000] p=13568, addr=fec0:0:0:ffff::2
Addr[2] => af=23, salen=28, [sub=0, flag=00000000] p=13568, addr=fec0:0:0:ffff::3

forward timeout  = 3
slave            = 1

Command completed successfully.
```

Table 22-1 summarizes section by section the output from Dnscmd /Info. Using Dnscmd /Config, you can configure most of these options. The actual subcommand to use is indicated in parentheses in the first column, and examples of acceptable values are indicated in the final column. For example, if you want to set the fBindSecondaries configuration setting to allow maximum compression and efficiency (assuming you are using Microsoft DNS servers or BIND 4.9.4 or later), you type **dnscmd *ServerName* /config /bindsecondaries 0**, where *ServerName* is the name or IP address of the DNS server you want to configure. This overrides the default setting to support other DNS servers.

**TABLE 22-1** DNS server configuration parameters

| Section/Entry (Command) | Description | Example/Accepted Values |
|---|---|---|
| **SERVER INFO** | | |
| Server name | The FQDN of the DNS server. | Corpsvr28.cpandl.com |
| Version | The operating system version and build. Version 6.2 is Windows Server 2012. | 23F00206 (6.2 build 9200) |
| DS container | The directory services container for a DNS server that uses Active Directory–integrated zones. | cn=MicrosoftDNS, cn=System, DC=cpandl,DC=com |
| Forest name | The name of the Active Directory forest in which the server is located. | cpandl.com |
| Domain name | The name of the Active Directory domain in which the server is located. | cpandl.com |

| Section/Entry (Command) | Description | Example/Accepted Values |
|---|---|---|
| Builtin domain partition | The default application partition for the domain. | DomainDnsZones.cpandl.com |
| Builtin forest partition | The default application partition for the forest. | ForestDnsZones.cpandl.com |
| Read Only DC | The domain controller is read only. | 0, false; 1, true |
| Last scavenge cycle | The last time records were aged/scavenged. | not since restart (0) |
| **CONFIGURATION** | | |
| dwLogLevel (/loglevel) | Indicates whether debug logging is enabled. A value other than zeros means it is enabled. | 0x0; default, no logging. |
| dwDebugLevel | The debug logging level, not used. dwLogLevel is used instead. | 00000000 |
| dwRpcProtocol (/rpcprotocol) | The RPC protocol used. 5 = 0x1+0x4, meaning TCP/IP and LPC. | 0x0; disables remote procedure call (RPC) for DNS. 0x1; default, uses TCP/IP. 0x2; uses named pipes. 0x4; uses LPC. |
| dwNameCheckFlag (/namecheckflag) | The name-checking flag. By default, DNS names can be in multibyte Unicode format as indicated by the example entry. | 0; Strict RFC (ANSI). 1; Non RFC (ANSI). 2; Multibyte (UTF8). 3; All Names. |
| cAddressAnswerLimit (/addressanswerlimit) | The maximum number of records the server can send in response to a query. | 0; default with no maximum. [5–28]; sets a maximum. |
| dwRecursionRetry (/recursionretry) | The number of seconds the server waits before trying to contact a remote server again. | 3 |
| dwRecursionTimeout (/recursiontimeout) | The number of seconds the server waits before stopping contact attempts. | 8 |

| Section/Entry (Command) | Description | Example/Accepted Values |
|---|---|---|
| dwDsPollingInterval (/dspollinginterval) | How often, in seconds, Active Directory polls for changes in Active Directory–integrated zones. | 180 |

**CONFIGURATION FLAGS**

| Section/Entry (Command) | Description | Example/Accepted Values |
|---|---|---|
| fBootMethod (/bootmethod) | The source from which the server gets its configuration information. | 1; loads from the BIND file. 2; loads from the registry. 3; loads from Active Directory and the registry. |
| fAdminConfigured | Indicates whether the settings are administrator-configured. | 1; default for yes. |
| fAllowUpdate | Indicates whether dynamic updates are allowed. | 1; default dynamic updates are allowed. 0; dynamic updates are not allowed. |
| fDsAvailable | Indicates whether Active Directory directory services are available. | 1; Active Directory is available. 0; Active Directory isn't available. |
| fAutoReverseZones (/disableauto reversezone) | Indicates whether automatic creation of reverse lookup zones is enabled. | 1; default enabled. 0; disabled. |
| fAutoCacheUpdate (/secureresponses) | Indicates how server caching works. | 0; default, saves all responses to name queries to cache. 1; saves only records in same DNS subtree to cache. |
| fSlave (/isslave) | Determines how the DNS server responds when forwarded queries receive no response. | 0; default, recursion is enabled. If the forwarder does not respond, the server attempts to resolve the query itself using recursion. 1; recursion is disabled. If the forwarder does not respond, the server terminates the search and sends a failure message to the resolver. |

Chapter 22

| Section/Entry (Command) | Description | Example/Accepted Values |
|---|---|---|
| fNoRecursion (/norecursion) | Indicates whether the server performs recursive name resolution. | 0; default, DNS server performs recursion if requested. 1; DNS server doesn't perform recursion. |
| fRoundRobin (/roundrobin) | Indicates whether the server allows round-robin load balancing when there are multiple A records for hosts. | 1; default, automatically load balances using round robin for any hosts with multiple A records. 0; disables round robin. |
| fStrictFileParsing (/strictfileparsing) | Indicates server behavior when it encounters bad records. | 0; default, continues to load, logs error. 1; stops loading DNS file and logs error. |
| fBindSecondaries (/bindsecondaries) | Indicates the zone transfer format for secondaries. By default, DNS server is configured for compatibility with other DNS server types. | 1; for pre-BIND 4.9.4 compatibility. 0; default, enables compression and multiple transfers on Windows secondaries and others with BIND 4.9.4 or later. |
| fWriteAuthorityNs (/writeauthorityns) | Indicates whether the server writes NS records in the authority section of a response. | 0; default, writes for referrals only. 1; writes for all successful authoritative responses. |
| fLocalNetPriority (/localnetpriority) | Determines the order in which host records are returned when there are multiple host records for the same name. | 1; returns records with similar IP addresses first. 0; returns records in the order in which they are in DNS. |
| **AGING CONFIGURATION** | | |
| ScavengingInterval (/scavenginginterval) | Indicates the number of hours between scavenging intervals. | 0x0; scavenging is disabled. |
| DefaultAgingState (/defaultagingstate) | Indicates whether scavenging is enabled by default in new zones. | 0; default, scavenging is disabled. 1; scavenging is enabled. |
| DefaultRefresh Interval (/defaultrefresh interval) | Indicates the default refresh interval in hours. | 168 (set in hexadecimal). |
| DefaultNo RefreshInterval (/defaultno refreshinterval) | Indicates the default no-refresh interval in hours. | 168 (set in hexadecimal). |

| Section/Entry (Command) | Description | Example/Accepted Values |
|---|---|---|
| **SERVERADDRESSES** | | |
| Addr Count | The number of IP addresses configured on the server and the IP address used. | 2<br>Addr[0]dr=fe80::81ff:7053: 92ab:bc14<br>Addr[1] addr=192.168.10.42 |
| **LISTENADDRESSES** | | |
| Addr Count | The number and value of IP addresses configured for listening for requests from clients. NULL IP Array when there are no specific IP addresses are designated for listening for requests from clients. | NULL IP Array |
| **FORWARDERS** | | |
| Addr Count | The number and value of IP addresses of servers configured as forwarders. NULL IP Array when there are no forwarders. | 3<br>Addr[0] addr=fec0:0:0:ffff::1<br>Addr[1] addr=fec0:0:0:ffff::2<br>Addr[2] addr=fec0:0:0:ffff::3 |
| Forward timeout (/forwardingtimeout) | Timeout for queries to forwarders in seconds. | 3 |
| Slave | Indicates whether recursion is enabled. | 0; recursion is enabled.<br>1; recursion is disabled. |

Another useful command for troubleshooting DNS Server is Dnscmd /Statistics. This command shows you the following information:

- DNS server time statistics, including server start time, seconds since start, and stats of last cleared date and time

- Details on queries and responses, including total queries received, total responses sent; the number of UDP queries received and sent, UDP responses received and sent; and the number of TCP queries received and sent, TCP responses received and sent

- Details on queries by record, including the exact number of each type of record sent

- Details on failures and where they occurred, including recursion failures, retry limits reached, and partial answers received

- Details on the total number of dynamic updates, the status for each update type; later breakdowns on the number and status of secure updates, the number of updates that were forwarded, and the types of records updated

Chapter 22

- Details on the amount of memory used by DNS, including the total amount of memory used, standard allocations, and allocations from standard to the heap

### Save the stats to a file

Write the output of Dnscmd /Statistics to a file so that you don't overflow the history buffer in the command prompt. This also allows you to go through the stats at your leisure. Enter **dnscmd *ServerName* /statistics > *FileName***, where *ServerName* is the name or IP address of the DNS server and *FileName* is the name of the file to use, such as **dnscmd corpsvr02 /statistics > dns-stats.txt**.

## Examine zones and zone records

Dnscmd provides several useful commands for helping you pinpoint problems with records. To get started, list the available zones by typing **dnscmd *ServerName* /enumzones**, where *ServerName* is the name or IP address of the DNS server you want to check. The output shows a list of the zones that are configured as follows:

```
Enumerated zone list: Zone count = 11
  Zone name                 Type        Storage       Properties
  .                         Cache       AD-Domain
  _msdcs.cpandl.com         Primary     AD-Forest     Secure
  10.168.192.in-addr.arpa   Primary     AD-Domain     Secure Rev
  15.168.192.in-addr.arpa   Primary     AD-Domain     Secure Rev
  5.168.192.in-addr.arpa    Primary     AD-Domain     Secure Rev
  A                         Primary     AD-Domain     Secure
  cpandl.com                Primary     AD-Domain     Secure Aging
  eng.cpandl.com            Primary     AD-Domain     Secure
  support.cpandl.com        Primary     AD-Domain     Secure
  tech.cpandl.com           Primary     AD-Domain     Secure
  TrustAnchors              Primary     AD-Forest
```

The zone names you can work with are listed in the first column. The other values tell you the type of zone and the way it is configured as summarized in Table 22-2.

**TABLE 22-2  Zone entries and their meanings**

| Column/Entry | Description |
| --- | --- |
| **TYPE** | |
| Cache | A *cache zone (server cache)*. |
| Primary | A primary zone. |
| Secondary | A secondary zone. |
| Stub | A stub zone. |

| Column/Entry | Description |
|---|---|
| **FILE** | |
| AD-Forest | Active Directory–integrated with a forestwide replication scope. |
| AD-Legacy | Active Directory–integrated with a legacy replication scope to all domain controllers in the domain. |
| AD-Domain | Active Directory–integrated with a domainwide replication scope. |
| File | Indicates the zone data is stored in a file. |
| **PROPERTIES** | |
| Secure | Zone allows secure dynamic updates only and is a forward lookup zone. |
| Secure Rev | Zone allows secure dynamic updates only and is a reverse lookup zone. |
| Secure Aging | Zone allows secure dynamic updates only and is configured for scavenging/aging. |
| Aging | Zone is configured for scavenging/aging but isn't configured for dynamic updates. |
| Update | Zone is a forward lookup zone configured to allow both secure and nonsecure dynamic updates. |
| Update Rev | Zone is a reverse lookup zone configured to allow both secure and nonsecure dynamic updates. |
| Down | Secondary or stub zone hasn't received a zone transfer since startup. |

After you examine the settings for zones on the server, you can print out the zone records of a suspect zone by typing **dnscmd *ServerName* /zoneprint *ZoneName*** at the command prompt, where *ServerName* is the name or IP address of the DNS server and *ZoneName* is the name of the zone as reported previously.

Consider the following example:

```
dnscmd corpsvr02 /zoneprint cpandl.com
```

Here, you want to examine the cpandl.com zone records on the CORPSVR02 server. The output from this command shows the records in this zone and their settings. Here is a partial listing:

```
;
;  Zone:     cpandl.com
;  Server:   corpserver28
;  Time:     Sat Oct 06 22:32:15 2012 UTC
;
```

```
@ [Aging:3609354] 600 A  192.168.10.85
[Aging:3609352] 600 A  192.168.10.42
3600 NS  corpserver28.cpand1.com.
3600 NS  corpserver85.cpand1.com.
3600 SOA  corpserver28.cpand1.com. hostmaster.cpand1.com. 38383822 900 600 86400 3600
3600 MX  10 mailserver64.cpand1.com.
_msdcs 3600 NS  corpserver28.cpand1.com.

CorpServer28 3600 A  192.168.10.42
CorpServer64 [Aging:3608421] 1200 A  192.168.10.38
CorpServer85 3600 A  192.168.10.85

;
;  Finished zone: 212 nodes and 137 records in 0 seconds

;
```

The Dnscmd /Zoneprint shows all the records, even the ones created by Active Directory. This is particularly useful because it means you don't have to try to navigate the many subfolders in which these SRV records are stored.

# CHAPTER 23

# Implementing and maintaining WINS

WINDOWS Internet Naming Service (WINS) enables computers to register and resolve Network Basic Input/Output System (NetBIOS) names on Internet Protocol version 4 (IPv4) networks. WINS is not used with IPv6 networks. WINS is maintained primarily for backward support and compatibility with legacy applications and early versions of Microsoft Windows that used WINS for computer name resolution; or for networks running pre–Windows Server 2008 versions of Windows Server that don't have Active Directory deployed and thus don't require Domain Name System (DNS). On most large networks, WINS is needed to support legacy applications and legacy hooks into Active Directory from upgrades that proceeded from early versions of Windows Server to current versions.

If you are setting up a new network and there are no legacy operating systems, you probably don't need WINS. Here, only DNS is needed because these computers rely exclusively on DNS for name resolution if Active Directory is deployed. Because WINS is not required, WINS support could be removed from the network. Doing so, however, means that legacy applications and services that rely on NetBIOS, such as the computer Browser service, would no longer function.

# WINS essentials

Like DNS, WINS is a client/server protocol. All Windows servers have a WINS service that can be installed to provide WINS services on the network. All Windows computers have a WINS client that is installed automatically. The Workstation and Server services on computers are used to specify resources that are available, such as file shares. These resources have NetBIOS names as well.

## NetBIOS namespace and scope

WINS architecture is very different from DNS. Unlike DNS, WINS has a flat namespace and doesn't use a hierarchy or tree. Each computer or resource on a Windows network has a NetBIOS name, which can be up to 15 characters long. This name must be unique on the network—no other computer or resource can have the same name. Although there are no extensions to this name per se that indicate a domain, a NetBIOS scope can be set in Dynamic Host Configuration Protocol (DHCP).

The NetBIOS scope is a hidden 16th character (suffix) for the NetBIOS name. It is used to limit the scope of communications for WINS clients. Only WINS clients with the same Net-BIOS scope can communicate with each other. See "Configuring TCP/IP options" in Chapter 20, "Managing DHCP," for details on setting the NetBIOS scope for computers that use DHCP.

# INSIDE OUT Decommissioning WINS

WINS is needed to support legacy applications written to the NetBIOS over TCP/IP interface and to support network browsing for users in pre–Windows Server 2008 environments. If you don't have NetBIOS applications on the network or pre–Windows Server 2008 infrastructure, you don't need to use WINS. That said, before you decommission existing WINS infrastructure, you should ensure that your Active Directory domains and forests don't have legacy hooks that use the NetBIOS over TCP/IP interface. Your network might have legacy hooks that use NetBIOS if trusts were established in your domains and forests under early Windows Server releases and you subsequently upgraded to later releases of Windows Server. If so, you might need WINS to get the trusts verified and re-established. The only way to be certain that you don't need WINS in this situation where legacy hooks might exist is to perform a fresh install of the network environment with Windows Server 2003 or later and Active Directory operations in Windows Server 2003 Native Mode or higher.

If WINS is no longer needed on your network, you can look to decommission WINS. The best approach to decommissioning WINS is a methodical one that includes clear communication of your plan to decommission WINS throughout the organization as appropriate for IT guidelines. Start by examining the applications and server products in use throughout the organization that use or rely on network connections, such as Exchange Server, Systems Management Server, and Microsoft BackOffice Server. If the product version was developed and released prior to the release of Windows Vista and Windows Server 2008, the product might require NetBIOS naming. After you upgrade or replace applications and server products as appropriate, you can then enter the next phase of the transition where you stop and then disable the WINS service on your organization's WINS servers. This stops NetBIOS name resolution, without uninstalling your WINS servers. During this phase, you might find that some applications require WINS for name resolution. If so, you can enable WINS and then make plans to phase out those applications. Once you are certain there is no need for WINS, you can completely decommission WINS by removing the WINS Server feature from your servers.

# NetBIOS node types

The way WINS works on a network is determined by the node type set for a client. The node type defines how name services work. WINS clients can be one of four node types:

- **B-Node (Broadcast Node)**    Broadcast messages are used to register and resolve names. Computers that need to resolve a name broadcast a message to every host on the local network, requesting the IP address for a computer name. This node type is best for small networks.

- **P-Node (Peer-to-Peer Node)**    WINS servers are used to register and resolve computer names to Internet Protocol (IP) addresses. Computers that need to resolve a name send a query message to the server and the server responds. This node type is best if you want to eliminate broadcasts. In some cases, however, resources might not be seen as available if the WINS server isn't updated by the computer providing the resources.

- **M-Node (Mixed Node)**    A combination of B-Node and P-Node. WINS clients first try to use broadcasts for name resolution. If this fails, the clients then try using a WINS server. Using this node type still results in a lot of broadcast traffic.

- **H-Node (Hybrid Node)**    A combination of B-Node and P-Node. WINS clients first try to use a WINS server for name resolution. If this fails, the clients then try broadcasts for name resolution. This node type is best for most networks that use WINS servers because it reduces broadcast traffic.

## Small networks might not need a WINS server

WINS resolves NetBIOS computer names to IP addresses. Using WINS, the computer name DESKTOP12, for example, could be resolved to an IP address that enables computers on a Microsoft network to find one another and transfer information. On a small network without subnets and a limited number of computers, WINS clients can rely on broadcasts for name resolution. In this case, it isn't necessary to set up a WINS server.

# WINS name registration and cache

WINS maintains a database of name-to-IP-address mappings automatically. Whenever a computer or resource becomes available, it registers itself with the WINS server to tell the server the name and IP address it is using. As long as no other computer or resource on the network is using that name, the WINS server accepts the request and registers the computer or resource in its database.

Name registration isn't permanent. Each name that is registered has a lease period associated with it, which is called its Time to Live (TTL). A WINS client must reregister its name before the lease expires, and it attempts to do so when 50 percent of the lease period has elapsed or when it is restarted. If a WINS client doesn't reregister its name, the lease expires and is marked for deletion from the WINS database. During normal shutdown, a WINS client sends a message to the WINS server requesting the release of the registration. The WINS server then marks the record for deletion. Whenever records are marked for deletion, they are said to be *tombstoned*.

As with DNS clients, WINS clients maintain a cache of NetBIOS names that have been looked up. The WINS cache, however, is designed to hold only names looked up recently. By default, names are cached for up to 10 minutes and the cache is limited to 16 names. You can view entries in the NetBIOS cache by typing **nbtstat –c** at the command prompt.

## WINS implementation details

On most networks that use WINS, you'll want to configure at least two WINS servers for name resolution. When there are multiple WINS servers, you can configure replication of database entries between the servers. Replication allows for fault tolerance and load balancing by ensuring that entries in one server's database are replicated to its replication partners. These replication partners can then handle renewal and release requests from clients as if they held the primary registration in the first place.

WINS supports the following:

- **Persistent connections**   In a standard configuration, replication partners establish and release connections each time they replicate WINS database changes. With persistent connections, replication partners can be configured to maintain a persistent connection. This reduces the overhead associated with opening and closing connections and speeds up the replication process.

- **Automatic replication partners**   Using automatic replication partners, WINS can automatically configure itself for replication with other WINS servers. To do this, WINS sends periodic multicast messages to announce its availability. These messages are addressed to the WINS multicast group address (224.0.1.24), and any other WINS servers on the network that are listening for datagrams sent on this group address can receive and process the automatic replication request. After replication is set up with multicast partners, the partners use standard replication with either persistent or nonpersistent connections.

- **Manual tombstoning**   Manual tombstoning allows administrators to mark records for deletion. A record marked for deletion is said to be tombstoned. This state is then replicated to a WINS server's replication partners, which prevents the record from being re-created on a replication partner and then being replicated back to the original server on which it was marked for deletion.

- **Record export**   The record export feature allows administrators to export the entries in the WINS database to a file that can be used for tracking or reporting on which clients are using WINS.

# Setting up WINS servers

To make a computer running Windows Server into a WINS server, you must install the WINS service. This service doesn't require a dedicated server and uses limited resources in most cases. This means you can install the WINS service on a DNS server, DHCP server, or domain controller. The only key requirement is that the WINS service can be installed only on a computer with a static IPv4 address. Although you can install WINS on a server with multiple IPv4 addresses or multiple network interfaces, this isn't recommended because the server might not be able to replicate properly with its replication partners. In most cases, you won't want to configure a domain controller as a WINS server.

You can install the WINS service by following these steps:

1. In Server Manager, select Add Roles And Features on the Manage menu. This starts the Add Roles And Features Wizard. If the wizard displays the Before You Begin page, read the introductory text and then tap or click Next.

2. On the Installation Type page, Role-Based Or Feature-Based Installation is selected by default. Tap or click Next.

3. On the Server Selection page, you can choose to install roles and features on running servers or virtual hard disks. Either select a server from the server pool or select a server from the server pool on which to mount a virtual hard disk (VHD). If you are adding roles and features to a VHD, tap or click Browse and then use the Browse For Virtual Hard Disks dialog box to locate the VHD. When you are ready to continue, tap or click Next twice.

4. On the Features page, select WINS Server. Tap or click Next. If additional features are required, you'll see an additional dialog box. Tap or click Add Features to close the dialog box, and add the required features to the server installation. When you are ready to continue, tap or click Next.

5. Tap or click Install. When the wizard finishes installing the selected features, tap or click Close.

Chapter 23

After you install WINS Server, the WINS console is available on the Tools menu in Server Manager. After you open the WINS console, select the WINS server you are working with to see its entries, as shown in Figure 23-1.

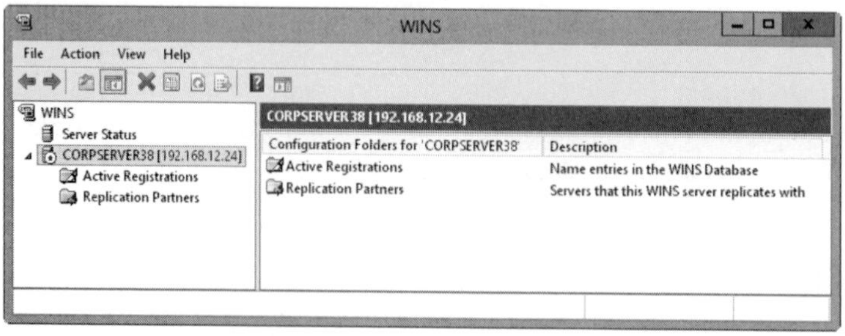

**Figure 23-1** The WINS console.

The only key postinstallation task for the WINS service is to configure replication partners. However, you should check the Transmission Control Protocol/Internet Protocol (TCP/IP) configuration of the WINS server. It should have only itself listed as the WINS server to use and shouldn't have a secondary WINS server. This prevents the WINS client on the server from registering itself with a different WINS database, which can cause problems.

To set the server's primary WINS server address to its own IP address and clear out any secondaries from the list, open Network And Sharing Center. In Network And Sharing Center, tap or click Change Adapter Settings. In Network Connections, press and hold or right-click the connection you want to work with and then select Properties. In the Properties dialog box, open the Internet Protocol (TCP/IP) Properties dialog box by double-tapping or double-clicking Internet Protocol Version 4 (TCP/IPv4). Tap or click Advanced to display the Advanced TCP/IP Settings dialog box, and then tap or click the WINS tab. Set the WINS server's IP address as the WINS server to use, and remove any additional WINS server addresses. When you're finished, tap or click OK twice and then Close.

You can remotely manage and configure WINS. Simply start the WINS console, press and hold or right-click the WINS node in the left pane, and select Add Server. In the Add Server dialog box, select WINS Server, type the name or IP address of the WINS server, and then tap or click OK.

The command-line counterpart to the WINS console is *Netsh WINS*. From the command prompt on a computer running Windows Server, you can use Netsh WINS to perform all the tasks available in the WINS console as well as to perform some additional tasks that can't be performed in the WINS console. To start Netsh WINS and access a particular WINS server, follow these steps:

1. Start a command prompt, and then type **netsh** to start Netsh. The command prompt changes to *netsh>*.

2. Access the WINS context within Netsh by typing **wins**. The command prompt changes to *netsh wins>*.

3. Type **server** followed by the Universal Naming Convention (UNC) name or IP address of the WINS server, such as **\\wins2** or **\\10.10.15.2**. If the WINS server is in a different domain from your logon domain, you should type the fully qualified domain name (FQDN) of the server, such as **\\wins2.cpandl.com**.

4. The command prompt changes to *netsh wins server>*. You can now work with the selected server. If you later want to work with a different server, you can do this without having to start over. Simply type **server** followed by the UNC name or IP address of that server.

> **Note**
> Technically, you don't need to type the double backslashes (\\) when you specify an IP address. You must, however, type \\ when you specify a server's name or FQDN. Because of this discrepancy, you might want to use \\ all the time so that you won't leave it out by accident when you need it.

## TROUBLESHOOTING

**Resolving WINS replication errors**
Most WINS replication errors involve incorrectly configured WINS servers. If you see replication errors in the event logs, check the TCP/IP configuration of your WINS servers. Every WINS server in the organization should be configured as its own primary WINS server, and you should delete any secondary WINS server addresses. This ensures that WINS servers register their NetBIOS names only in their own WINS databases. If you don't configure WINS in this way, WINS servers might register their names with other WINS servers. This can result in different WINS servers owning the NetBIOS names that a particular WINS server registers and, ultimately, to problems with WINS itself. For more information on this issue, see Microsoft Knowledge Base article 321208 (*http://support.microsoft.com/default.aspx?scid=kb;en-us;321208*).

# Configuring replication partners

When you have two or more WINS servers on a network, you should configure replication between them. When servers replicate database entries with each other, they are said to be *replication partners*.

## Replication essentials

There are two replication roles for WINS servers:

- **Push partner**  A push partner is a replication partner that notifies other WINS servers that updates are available.

- **Pull partner**  A pull partner is a replication partner that requests updates.

By default, all WINS servers have replication enabled and replication partners are configured to use both push and pull replication. After a replication partner notifies a partner that there are changes using push replication, the partner can request the changes using pull replication. This pulls the changes down to its WINS database. In addition, all replication is done using persistent connections by default to increase efficiency.

Because replication is automatically enabled and configured, all you have to do to start replication is tell each WINS server about the other WINS servers that are available. On a small network, you can do this using the automatic replication partners feature. Because this can cause a lot of broadcast traffic on medium or large networks that contain many clients and servers, you'll probably want to designate specific replication partners to reduce broadcast traffic.

## Configuring automatic replication partners

To configure automatic replication partners, follow these steps:

1. Start the WINS console. If the server you want to configure as a partner isn't listed in the console, press and hold or right-click the WINS node in the left pane and select Add Server. In the Add Server dialog box, select WINS Server, type the name or IP address of the WINS server, and then tap or click OK.

2. Expand the server entry, press and hold or right-click the Replication Partners entry in the left pane, and then select Properties. In the Replication Partners Properties dialog box, tap or click the Advanced tab, as shown in Figure 23-2.

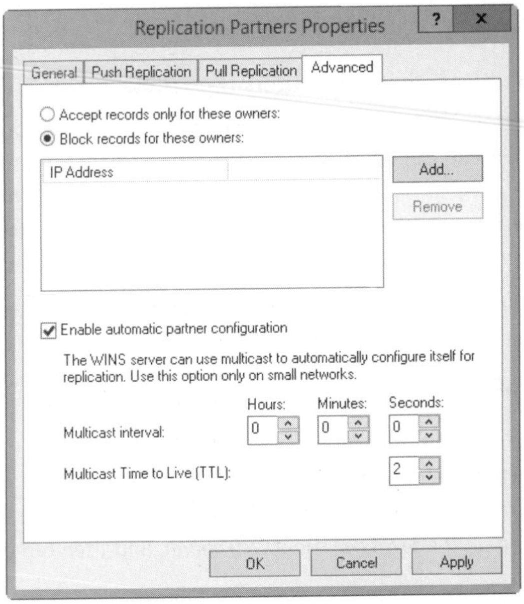

**Figure 23-2** Enable automatic replication.

3. Select the Enable Automatic Partner Configuration check box.

4. Use the Multicast Interval options to set the interval between multicast broadcasts to the WINS server group address. These broadcasts are used to tell other WINS servers about the availability of the server you are configuring. The default interval is 0 minutes, which disables WINS broadcasts.

## INSIDE OUT  Registrations remain until restart

After a server is discovered and added as a partner through multicasting, the server remains as a configured partner until you restart the WINS service or until you restart the server. When WINS is shut down properly, part of the shutdown process is to send messages to current replication partners and remove its registration.

5. Use the Multicast Time To Live (TTL) combo box to specify how many links multicast broadcasts can go through before being discarded. The default is 2, which allows the broadcasts to be relayed through two routers.

6. Tap or click OK.

Chapter 23

INSIDE OUT  Multicast through routers is possible

The Multicast TTL is used to allow the discovery broadcasts to be routed between subnets. This means you can use automatic replication partners on networks with subnets. However, routing isn't automatic just because a datagram has a TTL. You must configure the routers on each subnet to forward multicast traffic received from the WINS multicast group address (224.0.1.24).

## Using designated replication partners

To designate specific replication partners, start the WINS console. If the server you want to configure as a partner isn't listed in the console, press and hold or right-click the WINS node in the left pane and select Add Server. In the Add Server dialog box, select WINS Server, type the name or IP address of the WINS server, and then tap or click OK.

Next, expand the server entry, press and hold or right-click the Replication Partners entry in the left pane, and select New Replication Partners. In the New Replication Partner dialog box, type the name or IP address of the WINS server that should be used as a replication partner and then tap or click OK. The replication partner is added and listed as available in the WINS console. As shown in Figure 23-3, replication partners are listed by server name, IP address, and replication type.

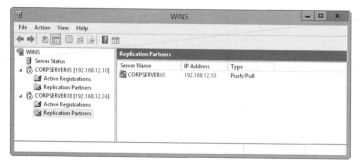

**Figure 23-3** View replication partners in the WINS console.

By default, the replication partner is configured to use both push and pull replication as well as persistent connections. After you configure a replication partner, the configuration is permanent. If you restart a server, you do not need to reconfigure replication partners.

To view or change the replication settings for a replication partner, start the WINS console. Expand the server entry for the server you want to work with, and then select the Replication Partners entry in the left pane. Double-tap or double-click the replication partner in the details pane. This displays the replication partner's Properties dialog box. Tap or click the Advanced tab, as shown in Figure 23-4.

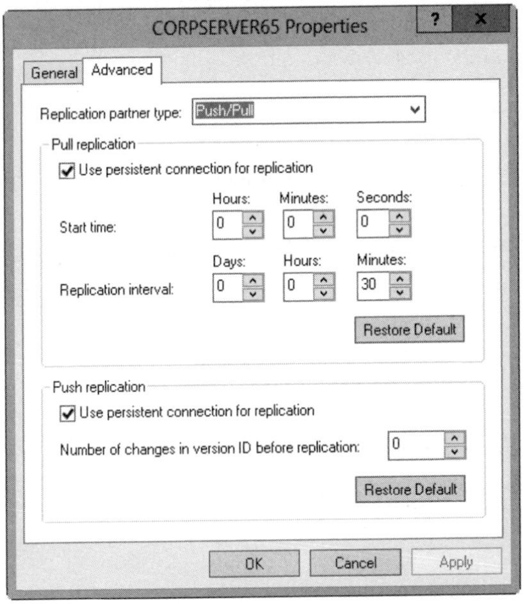

**Figure 23-4** Configure replication partner settings.

The configuration options are used as follows:

- Replication Partner Type   Sets the replication type as push, pull, or push/pull.

- Pull Replication

  ○ *Use Persistent Connection For Replication*   Configures pull replication so that a persistent connection is used. This reduces the time spent opening and closing connections and improves performance.

  ○ *Start Time*   Sets the hour of the day when replication should begin using a 24-hour clock.

  ○ *Replication Interval*   Sets the frequency of replication. The default is every 30 minutes.

Chapter 23

- Push Replication

  ○ *Use Persistent Connection For Replication*   Configures push replication so that a persistent connection is used. This reduces the time spent opening and closing connections and improves performance.

  ○ *Number Of Changes In Version ID Before Replication*   Can be used to limit replication by allowing replication to occur only when a set number of changes have occurred in the local WINS database.

> **Note**
> By default, Number Of Changes In Version ID Before Replication is set to 0, which allows replication at the designated interval whenever there are changes. If you set a specific value, that many changes must occur before replication takes place.

# Configuring and maintaining WINS

WINS is fairly easy to configure and maintain after you set it up and replication partners are configured. The key configuration and maintenance tasks are related to the following issues:

- Configuring burst handling as the network grows

- Checking server status and configuration

- Checking active registrations, and scavenging records if necessary

- Maintaining the WINS database

## Configuring burst handling

If you configured the WINS server on a network with more than 100 clients, you should enable burst handling of registrations. As your network grows, you should change the burst-handling sessions as appropriate for the number of clients on the network. To configure burst handling of registration and name refresh requests, start the WINS console. Press and hold or right-click the server entry in the WINS console, and then select Properties. In the Properties dialog box, tap or click the Advanced tab, as shown in Figure 23-5.

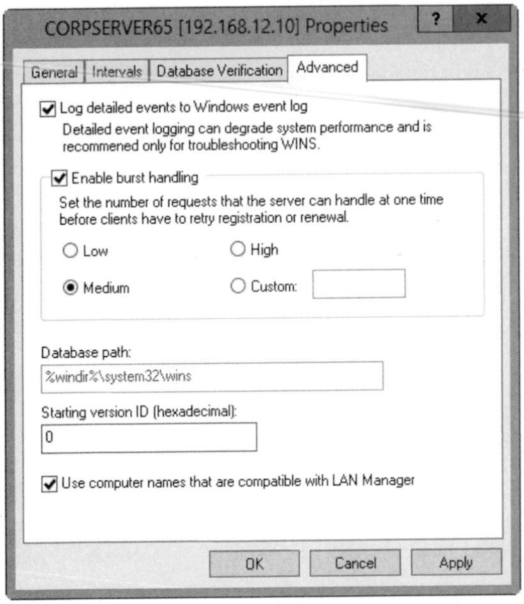

**Figure 23-5** Set burst handling for medium and large networks.

Select the Enable Burst Handling check box, and then select one of the following burst-handling settings:

- Low, for handling up to 300 registration and name refresh requests

- Medium, for handling up to 500 registration and name refresh requests

- High, for handling up to 1000 registration and name refresh requests

# INSIDE OUT Set a custom threshold for burst handling

You can also set a custom threshold value for burst handling. To do this, select Custom and then enter a threshold value between 50 and 5000. For example, if you set the threshold to 5000, up to 5000 requests can be queued at once. Keep in mind that you would do this only if your network environment needs this setting. If you set the value to 5000 but only need a queue that allows up to 100 name registration requests, you would waste a lot of server resources maintaining a very large queue that you don't need.

# Checking server status and configuration

Using the WINS console, you can do the following:

- View the status of all WINS servers on the network by tapping or clicking the Server Status entry in the left pane. The status of the servers is then displayed in the right pane.

- View the current replication partners for a server by expanding the server entry and selecting Replication Partners in the left pane. The replication partners for that server are displayed in the right pane.

- View server statistics for startup, replication, queries, releases, registrations, and replication partners by pressing and holding or right-clicking the server entry in the left pane and selecting Display Server Statistics.

Using Netsh WINS, you can view server statistics by typing the command

```
netsh wins server ServerName show statistics
```

Here *ServerName* is the name or IP address of the WINS server you want to work with, such as \\WINS02 or 10.10.12.15. An example of the statistics follows:

```
***You have Read and Write access to the server corpsvr02.cpandl.com***

        WINS Started                          : 8/11/2014 at 12:25:11
        Last initialization                   : 8/13/2014 at 03:12:12
        Last planned scavenging               : 8/20/2014 at 11:22:24
        Last admin triggered scavenging       : 8/10/2014 at 18:41:31
        Last replicas tombstones scavenging   : 8/22/2014 at 10:31:44
        Last replicas verification scavenging : 8/24/2014 at 13:42:12
        Last planned replication              : 8/10/2014 at 17:30:59
        Last admin triggered replication      : 8/27/2014 at 09:32:45
        Last reset of counter                 : 9/01/2014 at 19:33:21

Counter Information :
        No of U and G Registration requests = (250 222)
        No of Successful/Failed Queries = (812/67)
        No of U and G Refreshes = (213 144)
        No of Successful/Failed Releases = (68/12)
        No of U. and G. Conflicts = (12 10)

~~~~~~~~~~~~~~~~~~~~~~~~~~~~~~~~~~~~~~~~~~~~~~~~~~~~~~~~~~~~~~~~~~~~~~~~~~~~~~~~
WINS Partner IP Address    -No. of Replication    -No. of Comm Failure
~~~~~~~~~~~~~~~~~~~~~~~~~~~~~~~~~~~~~~~~~~~~~~~~~~~~~~~~~~~~~~~~~~~~~~~~~~~~~~~~
        192.168.15.18      -    153      -    2
```

These statistics are useful for troubleshooting registration and replication problems. Scavenging and replication are automatic once configured. Problems to look for include the following:

- **Replication**   If there are problems with replication, you should see a high number of communication failures relative to the number of replications. Check the links over which replication is occurring to see if there are intermittent failures or times when links aren't available.

- **Name resolution**   If WINS clients are having problems with name resolution, you'll see a high number of failed queries. You might need to scavenge the database for old records more frequently. Check the server statistics for the renew interval, extinction interval, extinction timeout, and verification interval on the Intervals tab in the server's Properties dialog box.

- **Registration release**   If WINS clients aren't releasing registrations properly, you'll see a high number of failed releases. Clients might not be getting shut down properly.

You can view the configuration details for a WINS server by typing the command

```
netsh wins server ServerName show info
```

Here *ServerName* is the name or IP address of the WINS server. The output looks like this:

```
WINS Database backup parameter
~~~~~~~~~~~~~~~~~~~~~~~~~~~~~~~~~~~~~~~~~~~~~~~~~~~~~~~~~~~~~~~~
Backup Dir          :
Backup on Shutdown  : Disabled

Name Record Settings(day:hour:minute)
~~~~~~~~~~~~~~~~~~~~~~~~~~~~~~~~~~~~~~~~~~~~~~~~~~~~~~~~~~~~~~~~
Refresh Interval               : 006:00:00
Extinction(Tombstone) Interval : 004:00:00
Extinction(Tombstone) TimeOut  : 006:00:00
Verification Interval          : 024:00:00

Database consistency checking parameters :
~~~~~~~~~~~~~~~~~~~~~~~~~~~~~~~~~~~~~~~~~~~~~~~~~~~~~~~~~~~~~~~~
Periodic Checking              : Disabled

WINS Logging Parameters:
~~~~~~~~~~~~~~~~~~~~~~~~~~~~~~~~~~~~~~~~~~~~~~~~~~~~~~~~~~~~~~~~

Log Database changes to JET log files    : Enabled
Log details events to System Event Log   : Enabled
```

```
Burst Handling Parameters :
~~~~~~~~~~~~~~~~~~~~~~~~~~~~~~~~~~~~~~~~~~~~~~~~~~~~~~~~~~

Burst Handling State             : Enabled
Burst handling queue size        : 500
```

# Checking active registrations and scavenging records

Using the WINS console, you can view the active registrations in the WINS database by expanding the server entry, pressing and holding or right-clicking Active Registrations, and choosing Display Records. In the Display Records dialog box, tap or click Find Now without making any selections to see all the available records or use the filter options to specify the types of records you want to view, and then tap or click Find Now. To tombstone a record manually, press and hold or right-click it and then select Delete. This deletes it from the current server, and this deletion is then replicated to other WINS servers; that is, the record will be replicated marked as Tombstoned.

Netsh provides many ways to examine records in the WINS database. Because this is something you won't use that frequently, the easiest way to do it is to list all available records and write the information to a file you can search. To do this, type the command

```
netsh wins server ServerName show database Servers={}
```

Here *ServerName* is the name or IP address of the WINS server. The output shows you the registration entries in the database as follows:

```
~~~~~~~~~~~~~~~~~~~~~~~~~~~~~~~~~~~~~~~~~~~~~~~~~~~~~~~~~~~~~~~~~~~~~~~~~~~~
    NAME  -T-S-VERSION  -G-  IPADDRESS  -   EXPIRATION DATE
~~~~~~~~~~~~~~~~~~~~~~~~~~~~~~~~~~~~~~~~~~~~~~~~~~~~~~~~~~~~~~~~~~~~~~~~~~~~
Retrieving database from the Wins server 192.168.1.50
CPANDL     [1Bh]-D-A- 2  -U- 192.168.1.50  -7/30/2014 13:18:01 PM
CORPSVR02  [00h]-D-A- 7  -U- 192.168.1.50  -7/30/2014 13:18:01 PM
CORPSVR02  [20h]-D-A- 6  -U- 192.168.1.50  -7/30/2014 13:18:01 PM
CPANDL     [00h]-D-A- 4  -N- 192.168.1.50  -7/30/2014 13:18:01 PM
CPANDL     [1Ch]-D-A- 3  -I- 192.168.1.50  -7/30/2014 13:18:01 PM
CPANDL     [1Eh]-D-A- 1  -N- 192.168.1.50  -7/30/2014 13:18:01 PM
```

WINS automatically scavenges the database to mark old records for deletion. To see when this is done, check the server statistics for the renew interval, extinction interval, extinction timeout, and verification interval on the Intervals tab in the server's Properties dialog box.

You can initiate scavenging (referred to as an *admin-triggered scavenging* in the server statistics) by pressing and holding or right-clicking the server entry in the WINS console and selecting Scavenge Database. To initiate scavenging at the command prompt, type **netsh wins server *ServerName* init scavenge**, where *ServerName* is the name or IP address of the WINS server.

After scavenging, the renew interval, extinction interval, extinction timeout, and verification interval are used to mark each record as follows:

- If the renew interval has not expired, the record remains marked as Active.

- If the renew interval has expired, the record is marked as Released.

- If the extinction interval has expired, the record is marked as Tombstoned.

If the record was tombstoned, it is deleted from the database. If the record is active and was replicated from another server but the verification interval has expired, the record is revalidated.

## Maintaining the WINS database

The WINS database, like any database, should be maintained. You should routinely perform the following maintenance operations:

- Verify the database consistency

- Compact the database

- Back up the database

### Verifying the WINS database consistency

WINS can be configured to verify the database consistency automatically. This operation checks and verifies the registered names. To configure automatic database consistency checks, follow these steps:

1. Start the WINS console. Press and hold or right-click the WINS node in the left pane, and select Add Server. In the Add Server dialog box, select WINS Server, type the name or IP address of the WINS server, and then tap or click OK.

2. Press and hold or right-click the server entry in the WINS console, and select Properties. In the Properties dialog box, tap or click the Database Verification tab, as shown in Figure 23-6.

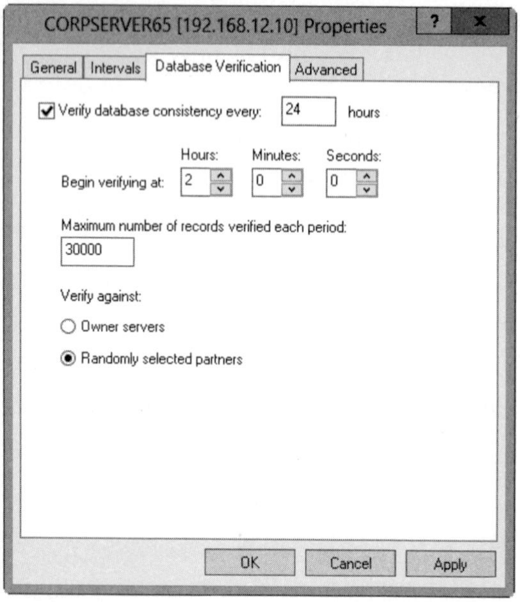

**Figure 23-6** Set automatic verification of the WINS database.

3. Select the Verify Database Consistency Every check box, and then set a check interval. Typically, you'll want to perform this operation no more frequently than once every 24 hours.

4. Use the Begin Verifying At section to set the time at which verification checks are started. This time is on a 24-hour clock, and the default time is 2 hours, 0 minutes, and 0 seconds, meaning 2:00 A.M. If you want verification checks to begin at 2:00 P.M. instead, you set the time to 14 hours, 0 minutes, and 0 seconds.

5. Set other options as necessary, and then tap or click OK.

## Compacting the WINS database

The WINS database should be compacted periodically—at least once a month or once every other month, depending on how often computers are added to or removed from your network. In addition to reducing the size of the database by squeezing out unneeded space that has been allocated and is no longer needed, compacting the database can improve performance and make the database more reliable.

At the command prompt, you can compact the WINS database by following these steps:

1. Change to the WINS directory by typing **cd %SystemRoot%\System32\Wins**.

2. Stop the WINS service by typing **net stop wins**.

3.  Compact the WINS database by typing **jetpack wins.mdb winstemp.mdb**.

4.  Start the WINS service by typing **net start wins**.

## Backing up the WINS database

By default, the WINS database is not backed up—but it should be. You can perform manual or automatic backups. To back up the WINS database manually, follow these steps:

1.  Start the WINS console. Press and hold or right-click the server entry, and then select Back Up Database.

2.  In the Browse For Folder dialog box, select the folder where the WINS server should store the database backup files and then tap or click OK.

3.  The WINS server then writes the backup files to a subfolder of the designated folder called Wins_bak. When it finishes, tap or click OK.

To configure automatic backups of the WINS database, follow these steps:

1.  Start the WINS console. Press and hold or right-click the server entry, and then select Properties.

2.  In the Properties dialog box, tap or click Browse in the General tab.

3.  Use the Browse For Folder dialog box to select the folder where the WINS server should store the database backup files, and then tap or click OK. The WINS server will write backup files to a subfolder of the designated folder called Wins_bak.

4.  Select Back Up Database During Shutdown.

5.  Tap or click OK. Now whenever you shut down the server or the WINS service on the server, the WINS service will back up the database to the designated folder.

## Restoring the WINS database

If something happens to the WINS database, you can use the backup files to recover it to the state it was in prior to the problem. To restore the WINS database from backup, follow these steps:

1.  Start the WINS console. Press and hold or right-click the server entry, point to All Tasks, and then select Stop. This stops the WINS service.

2.  Press and hold or right-click the server entry again, and select Restore Database.

3. In the Browse For Folder dialog box, select the parent folder of the Wins_bak folder created during backup (not the Wins_bak folder itself) and tap or click OK.

4. The WINS server then restores the database from backup. When it finishes, tap or click OK.

5. The WINS service will be restarted automatically.

# Enabling WINS lookups through DNS

You can enable WINS lookups through DNS. This integration of WINS and DNS provides for an additional opportunity to resolve an IP address to a host name when normal DNS lookups fail. Typically, this might be necessary for clients that can't register their IP addresses in DNS using dynamic updates.

You enable WINS name resolution on a zone-by-zone basis from within the DNS console. Follow these steps:

1. In the DNS console, press and hold or right-click the zone you want to work with and then select Properties.

2. In the Properties dialog box, tap or click the WINS or WINS-R tab as appropriate for the type of zone. The WINS tab is used with forward lookup zones, and the WINS-R tab is used with reverse lookup zones.

3. Select Use WINS Forward Lookup or Use WINS Reverse Lookup as appropriate.

4. If you're not using DNS servers running on Windows Server, select Do Not Replicate This Record. This ensures the WINS record that is created during this configuration won't be replicated to servers that don't support this feature.

5. Type the IP address of a WINS server you want to use for name resolution, and tap or click Add. Repeat this step for other WINS servers that should be used.

6. Tap or click OK.

# Active Directory architecture

A CTIVE Directory is an extensible directory service that enables you to manage network resources efficiently. A directory service does this by storing detailed information about each network resource, which makes it easier to provide basic lookup and authentication. Being able to store large amounts of information is a key objective of a directory service, but the information must also be organized so that it is easily searched and retrieved.

Active Directory provides for authenticated search and retrieval of information by dividing the physical and logical structures of the directory into separate layers. Understanding the physical structure of Active Directory is important for understanding how a directory service works. Understanding the logical structure of Active Directory is important for implementing and managing a directory service.

## Active Directory physical architecture

The physical layer of Active Directory controls the following features:

- How directory information is accessed

- How directory information is stored on the hard disk of a server

### Active Directory physical architecture: A top-level view

From a physical or machine perspective, Active Directory is part of the security subsystem. (See Figure 24-1.) The security subsystem runs in user mode. User-mode applications do not have direct access to the operating system or hardware. This means that requests from user-mode applications have to pass through the executive services layer and must be validated before being executed.

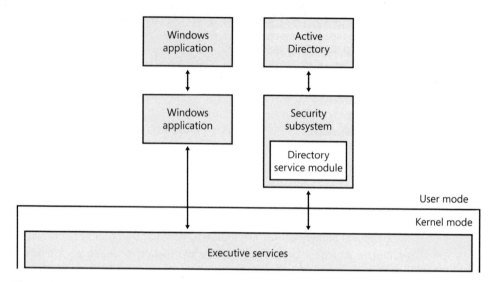

**Figure 24-1** Top-level overview of the Active Directory architecture.

> **Note**
>
> Being part of the security subsystem makes Active Directory an integrated part of the access-control and authentication mechanism built into Windows Server. Access control and authentication protect the resources in the directory.

Each resource in Active Directory is represented as an object. Anyone who tries to gain access to an object must be granted permission. Lists of permissions that describe who or what can access an object are referred to as *access control lists (ACLs)*. Each object in the directory has an associated ACL.

You can restrict permissions across a broader scope by using Group Policy. The security infrastructure of Active Directory uses policy to enforce security models on several objects that are grouped logically. Trust relationships between groups of objects can also be set up to allow for an even broader scope for security controls between trusted groups of objects that need to interact. From a top-level perspective, that's how Active Directory works, but to really understand Active Directory, you need to delve into the security subsystem.

## Active Directory within the Local Security Authority

Within the security subsystem, Active Directory is a subcomponent of the Local Security Authority (LSA). As shown in Figure 24-2, the LSA consists of many components that provide the security features of Windows Server and ensure that access control and authentication function as they should. Not only does the LSA manage local security policy, it also performs the following functions:

- Generates security identifiers

- Provides the interactive process for logon

- Manages auditing

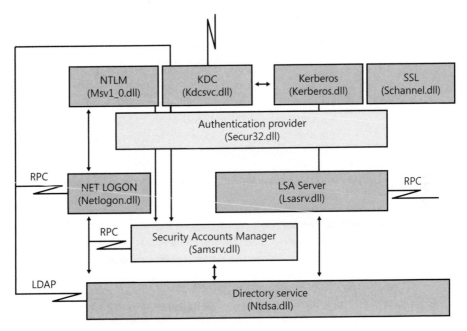

**Figure 24-2** Windows Server security subsystem using Active Directory.

When you work through the security subsystem as it is used with Active Directory, you'll find the three following key areas:

- Authentication mechanisms

  ○ NTLM (Msv1_0.dll) used for Windows NT LAN Manager (NTLM) authentication

  ○ Kerberos (Kerberos.dll) and Key Distribution Center (Kdcsvc.dll) used for Kerberos V5 authentication

  ○ SSL (Schannel.dll) used for Secure Sockets Layer (SSL) authentication

  ○ Authentication provider (Secur32.dll) used to manage authentication

- Logon/access-control mechanisms

  ○ NET LOGON (Netlogon.dll) used for interactive logon via NTLM. For NTLM authentication, NET LOGON passes logon credentials to the directory service module and returns the security identifiers for objects to clients making requests.

  ○ LSA Server (Lsasrv.dll) used to enforce security policies for Kerberos and SSL. For Kerberos and SSL authentication, LSA Server passes logon credentials to the directory service module and returns the security identifiers for objects to clients making requests.

  ○ Security Accounts Manager (Samsrv.dll) used to enforce security policies for NTLM.

- Directory service component: Directory service (Ntdsa.dll) used to provide directory services for Windows Server. This is the actual module that allows you to perform authenticated searches and retrieval of information.

As you can see, users are authenticated before they can work with the directory service component. Authentication is handled by passing a user's security credentials to a domain controller. After the user is authenticated on the network, she can work with resources and perform actions according to the permissions and rights she has been granted in the directory. At least, this is how the Windows Server security subsystem works with Active Directory.

When you are on a network that doesn't use Active Directory or when you log on locally to a machine other than a domain controller, the security subsystem works as shown in Figure 24-3. Here, the directory service is not used. Instead, authentication and access control are handled through the Security Accounts Manager (SAM). Here, information about resources is stored in the SAM, which itself is stored in the registry.

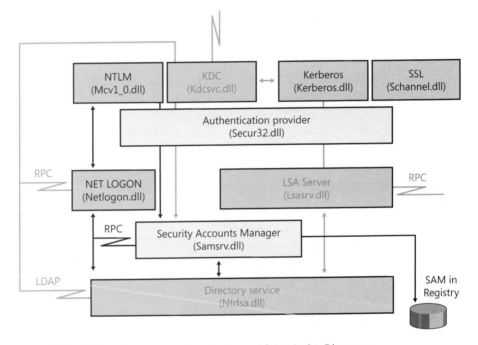

**Figure 24-3** Windows Server security subsystem without Active Directory.

## Directory service architecture

As you've seen, incoming requests are passed through the security subsystem to the directory service component. The directory service component is designed to accept requests from many different kinds of clients. As shown in Figure 24-4, these clients use specific protocols to interact with Active Directory.

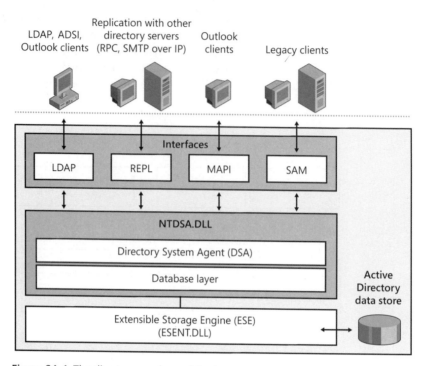

**Figure 24-4** The directory service architecture.

## Protocols and client interfaces

The primary protocol for Active Directory access is Lightweight Directory Access Protocol (LDAP). LDAP is an industry-standard protocol for directory access that runs over Transmission Control Protocol/Internet Protocol (TCP/IP). Active Directory supports LDAP versions 2 and 3. Clients can use LDAP to query and manage directory information, depending on the level of permissions they have been granted, by establishing a TCP connection to a domain controller. The default TCP port used by LDAP clients is 389 for standard communications and 636 for SSL.

Active Directory supports intersite and intrasite replication through the REPL interface, which uses either remote procedure calls (RPCs) or Simple Mail Transfer Protocol over Internet Protocol (SMTP over IP), depending on how replication is configured. Each domain controller is responsible for replicating changes to the directory to other domain controllers, using a multimaster approach. The multimaster approach used in Active Directory allows updates to be made to the directory by any domain controller and then replicated to other domain controllers.

For older messaging clients, Active Directory supports the Messaging Application Programming Interface (MAPI). MAPI allows messaging clients to access Active Directory (which is used by Microsoft Exchange for storing information), primarily for address-book lookups. Messaging clients use RPCs to establish a connection with the directory service. UDP port 135 and TCP port 135 are used by the RPC Endpoint Mapper. Current messaging clients use LDAP instead of RPC.

For legacy clients, Active Directory supports the SAM interface, which also uses RPCs. This allows legacy clients to access the Active Directory data store the same way they would access the SAM database. The SAM interface is also used during certain replication activities.

## Directory System Agent and database layer

Clients and other servers use the LDAP, REPL, MAPI, and SAM interfaces to communicate with the directory service component (Ntdsa.dll) on a domain controller. From an abstract perspective, the directory service component consists of the following:

- Directory System Agent (DSA), which provides the interfaces through which clients and other servers connect

- Database layer, which provides an application programming interface (API) for working with the Active Directory data store

From a physical perspective, the DSA is really the directory-service component, and the database layer resides within it. The reason for separating the two is that the database layer performs a vital abstraction. Without this abstraction, the physical database on the disk would not be protected from the applications the DSA interacts with. Furthermore, the object-based hierarchy used by Active Directory would not be possible. Why? Because the data store is in a single data file using a flat (record-based) structure, while the database layer is used to represent the flat file records as objects within a hierarchy of containers. Like a folder that can contain files as well as other folders, a container is simply a type of object that can contain other objects as well as other containers.

Each object in the data store has a name relative to the container in which it is stored. This name is aptly called the object's *relative distinguished name (RDN)*. An object's full name, also referred to as an object's *distinguished name (DN)*, describes the series of containers, from the highest to the lowest, of which the object is a part.

To make sure every object stored in Active Directory is truly unique, each object also has a globally unique identifier (GUID), which is generated when the object is created. Unlike an object's RDN or DN, which can be changed by renaming an object or moving it to another container, the GUID can never be changed. It is assigned to an object by the DSA, and it never changes.

Chapter 24

The DSA is responsible for ensuring that the type of information associated with an object adheres to a specific set of rules. This set of rules is referred to as the *schema*. The schema is stored in the directory and contains the definitions of all object classes and describes their attributes. In Active Directory, the schema is the set of rules that determine the kind of data that can be stored in the database, the type of information that can be associated with a particular object, the naming conventions for objects, and so on.

## INSIDE OUT The schema saves space and helps validate attributes

The schema serves to separate an object's definition from its actual values. Thanks to the schema, Active Directory doesn't have to write information about all of an object's possible attributes when it creates the object. When you create an object, only the defined attributes are stored in the object's record. This saves a lot of space in the database. Furthermore, because the schema not only specifies the valid attributes but also the valid values for those attributes, Active Directory uses the schema both to validate the attributes that have been set on an object and to keep track of what other possible attributes are available.

The DSA is also responsible for enforcing security limitations. It does this by reading the security identifiers (SIDs) on a client's access token and comparing them to the SIDs for an object. If a client has appropriate access permissions, it is granted access to an object. If a client doesn't have appropriate access permissions, it is denied access.

Finally, the DSA is used to initiate replication. Replication is the essential functionality that ensures that the information stored on domain controllers is accurate and consistent with changes that have been made. Without proper replication, the data on servers would become stale and outdated.

### Extensible Storage Engine

The Extensible Storage Engine (ESE) is used by Active Directory to retrieve information from and write information to the data store. The ESE uses indexed and sequential storage with transactional processing, as follows:

- **Indexed storage**   Indexing the data store allows the ESE to access data quickly without having to search the entire database. In this way, the ESE can rapidly retrieve, write, and update data.

- **Sequential storage**   Sequentially storing data means that the ESE writes data as a stream of bits and bytes. This allows data to be read from and written to specific locations.

- **Transactional processing**  Transactional processing ensures that changes to the database are applied as discrete operations that can be rolled back if necessary.

Any data that is modified in a transaction is copied to a temporary database file. This gives two views of the data that is being changed: one view for the process changing the data, and one view of the original data that is available to other processes until the transaction is finalized. A transaction remains open as long as changes are being processed. If an error occurs during processing, the transaction can be rolled back to return the object being modified to its original state. If Active Directory finishes processing changes without errors occurring, the transaction can be committed.

As with most databases that use transactional processing, Active Directory maintains a transaction log. A record of the transaction is written first to an in-memory copy of an object, then to the transaction log, and finally to the database. The in-memory copy of an object is stored in the *version store*. The version store is an area of physical memory (RAM) used for processing changes. Typically, the version store is 25 percent of the physical RAM.

The transaction log serves as a record of all changes that have yet to be committed to the database file. The transaction is written first to the transaction log to ensure that even if the database shuts down immediately afterward, the change is not lost and can take effect. To ensure this, Active Directory uses a checkpoint file to track the point up to which transactions in the log file have been committed to the database file. After a transaction is committed to the database file, it can be cleared out of the transaction log.

The actual update of the database is written from the in-memory copy of the object in the version store and not from the transaction log. This reduces the number of disk I/O operations and helps ensure that updates can keep pace with changes. When many updates are made, however, the version store can reach a point where it is overwhelmed. This happens when the version store reaches 90 percent of its maximum size. When this happens, the ESE temporarily stops processing cleanup operations that are used to return space after an object is modified or deleted from the database.

Although index creation could affect domain controller performance in earlier releases of Windows Server, Windows Server 2012 allows you to defer index creation to a time when it is more convenient. By deferring index creation to a designated point in time, rather than creating indexes as needed, you can ensure that domain controllers can perform related tasks during off-peak hours, thereby reducing the impact of index creation. Any attribute that is in a deferred index state will be logged in the Event log every 24 hours. Look for event IDs 2944 and 2945. When indexes are created, event ID 1137 is logged.

In large Active Directory environments, deferring index creation is useful to prevent domain controllers from becoming unavailable due to building indexes after schema updates. Before you can use deferred index creation, you must enable the feature in the forest root domain. You do this using the *DSHeuristics* attribute of the Directory Services object for the domain. Set the 18th bit of this attribute to 1. Because the 10th bit of this attribute typically also is set to 1 (if the attribute is set to a value), the attribute normally is set to the following: 000000000100000001. You can modify the *DSHeuristics* attribute using ADSI Edit or Ldp.exe:

- ADSI Edit is a snap-in you can add to any Microsoft Management Console (MMC). Open a new MMC by entering **MMC** at a prompt, and then use the Add/Remove Snap-in option on the File menu to add the ADSI Edit snap-in to the MMC. In ADSI Edit, press and hold or right-click the root node and then select Connect To. In the Connection Settings dialog box, choose the Select A Well Known Naming Context option. On the related selection list, select Configuration (because you want to connect to the Configuration naming context for the domain) and then tap or click OK. In ADSI Edit, work your way down to the CN=Directory Service container by expanding the Configuration naming context, the CN=Configuration container, the CN=Services container, and the CN=Windows NT container. Next, press and hold or right-click CN=Directory Service and then select Properties. In the Properties dialog box, select the dsHeuristics properties and then tap or click Edit. In the String Attribute Editor dialog box, type the desired value, such as **000000000100000001**, and then tap or click OK twice.

- Ldp is a graphical utility. Open Ldp by typing **ldp** in the Apps Search box or at a prompt. In Ldp, select Connect on the Connection menu and then connect to a domain controller in the forest root domain. After you connect to a domain controller, select Bind on the Connection menu to bind to the forest root domain using an account with enterprise administrator privileges. Next, select Tree on the View menu to open the Tree View dialog box. In the Tree View dialog box, choose CN=Configuration container as the base distinguished name to work with. In the CN=Configuration container, expand the CN=Services container, expand the CN=Windows NT container, and then select the CN=Directory Service container. Next, press and hold or right-click CN=Directory Service and then select Modify. In the Modify dialog box, type the attribute name as **dsHeuristics** and the value as **000000000100000001**. If the attribute already exists, set the Operation as Replace. Otherwise, set the Operation as Add. Tap or click Enter to create an LDAP transaction for this update, and then tap or click Run to apply the change.

> **Note**
> The value 000000000100000001 is nine zeros with a 1 in the 10th position followed by seven zeros with a 1 in the 18th position.

Once the change is replicated to all domain controllers in the forest, they will defer index creation automatically. You must then trigger index creation manually by either restarting domain controllers, which rebuilds the schema cache and deferred indexes, or by triggering a schema update for the RootDSE. In ADSI Edit, you can initiate an update by connecting to the RootDSE. To do this, press and hold or right-click the root node and then select Connect To. In the Connection Settings dialog box, choose the Select A Well Known Naming Context option. On the related selection list, select RootDSE and then tap or click OK. In ADSI Edit, press and hold or right-click the RootDSE node and then select Update Schema Now.

To allow for object recovery and for the replication of object deletions, an object that is deleted from the database is logically removed rather than being physically deleted. The way deletion works depends on whether Active Directory Recycle Bin is enabled or disabled.

**Deletion without Recycle Bin**   When Active Directory Recycle Bin is disabled, as with standard deployments prior to Windows Server 2008 R2, most of the object's attributes are removed and the object's *Deleted* attribute is set to TRUE to indicate that it has been deleted. The object is then moved to a hidden Deleted Objects container where its deletion can be replicated to other domain controllers. (See Figure 24-5.) In this state, the object is said to be *tombstoned*. To allow the tombstoned state to be replicated to all domain controllers, and thus removed from all copies of the database, an attribute called *tombstoneLifetime* is also set on the object. The *tombstoneLifetime* attribute specifies how long the tombstoned object should remain in the Deleted Objects container. The default lifetime is 180 days.

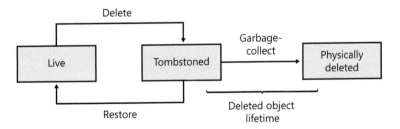

**Figure 24-5**  Active Directory object life cycle without Recycle Bin.

# INSIDE OUT  The tombstone process

When an object is tombstoned, Active Directory changes the distinguished name so that the object name cannot be recognized. Next, Active Directory deletes all of the object's link-valued attributes, and most of the object's non-link-valued attributes are cleared. Finally, the object is moved to the Deleted Objects container.

You can recover tombstoned objects using tombstone reanimation. However, attribute values that were removed are not recovered. This means the link-valued attributes, which include group memberships of user accounts, and the non-link-valued attributes are not recovered.

The ESE uses a garbage-collection process to clear out tombstoned objects after the tombstone lifetime has expired, and it performs automatic online defragmentation of the database after garbage collection. The interval at which garbage collection occurs is a factor of the value set for the *garbageCollPeriod* attribute and the tombstone lifetime. By default, garbage collection occurs every 12 hours. When there are more than 5000 tombstoned objects to be garbage-collected, the ESE removes the first 5000 tombstoned objects, and then uses the CPU availability to determine if garbage collection can continue. If no other process is waiting for the CPU, garbage collection continues for up to the next 5000 tombstoned objects whose tombstone lifetime has expired, and the CPU availability is again checked to determine if garbage collection can continue. This process continues until all the tombstoned objects whose tombstone lifetime has expired are deleted or another process needs access to the CPU.

**Deletion with Recycle Bin**   When Active Directory Recycle Bin is enabled as an option with Windows Server 2008 R2 and Windows Server 2012, objects aren't tombstoned when they are initially deleted, nor are their attributes removed. Instead, the deletion process occurs in stages.

In the first stage of the deletion, the object is said to be *logically deleted*. Here, the object's *Deleted* attribute is set to TRUE to indicate that it has been deleted. The object is then moved, with its attributes and name preserved, to a hidden Deleted Objects container where its deletion can be replicated to other domain controllers. (See Figure 24-6.) To allow the logically deleted state to be replicated to all domain controllers, and thus removed from all copies of the database, an attribute called *ms-DeletedObjectLifetime* is also set on the object. The *ms-DeletedObjectLifetime* attribute specifies how long the logically deleted object should remain in the Deleted Objects container. The default deleted-object lifetime is 180 days.

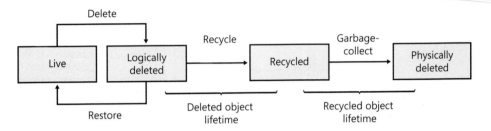

**Figure 24-6** Active Directory object life cycle with Recycle Bin.

When the deleted object lifetime expires, Active Directory removes most of the object's attributes, changes the distinguished name so that the object name cannot be recognized, and sets the object's *tombstoneLifetime* attribute. This effectively tombstones the object (and the process is the same as the legacy tombstone process).

The recycled object remains in the Deleted Objects container until the recycled object lifetime expires and is said to be in the *recycled* state. The default tombstone lifetime is 180 days.

As with deletion without the Recycle Bin, the ESE uses a garbage-collection process to clear out tombstoned objects after the tombstone lifetime has expired. This garbage-collection process is the same as discussed previously.

## Data store architecture

After you examine the operating-system components that support Active Directory, the next step is to see how directory data is stored on a domain controller's hard disks. As Figure 24-7 shows, the data store has a primary data file and several other types of related files, including working files and transaction logs.

Chapter 24

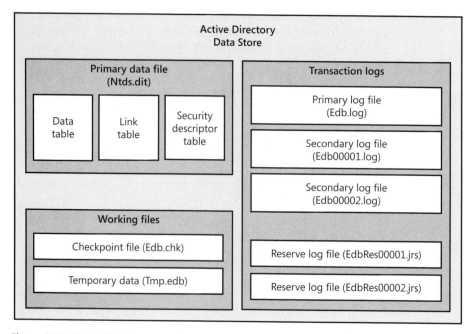

**Figure 24-7** The Active Directory data store.

These files are used as follows:

- **Primary data file (Ntds.dit)**  Physical database file that holds the contents of the Active Directory data store

- **Checkpoint file (Edb.chk)**  Checkpoint file that tracks the point up to which the transactions in the log file have been committed to the database file

- **Temporary data (Tmp.edb)**  Temporary workspace for processing transactions

- **Primary log file (Edb.log)**  Primary log file that contains a record of all changes that have yet to be committed to the database file

- **Secondary log files (Edb00001.log, Edb00002.log, ...)**  Additional logs files that are used as needed

- **Reserve log files (EdbRes00001.jrs, EdbRes00002.jrs, ...)**  Files that are used to reserve space for additional log files if the primary log file becomes full

The primary data file contains three indexed tables:

- **Active Directory data table**   The data table contains a record for each object in the data store, which can include object containers, the objects themselves, and any other type of data that is stored in Active Directory.

- **Active Directory link table**   The link table is used to represent linked attributes. A linked attribute is an attribute that refers to other objects in Active Directory. For example, if an object contains other objects (that is, it is a container), attribute links are used to point to the objects in the container.

- **Active Directory security descriptor table**   The security descriptor table contains the inherited security descriptors for each object in the data store. Windows Server uses this table so that inherited security descriptors no longer have to be duplicated on each object. Instead, inherited security descriptors are stored in this table and linked to the appropriate objects. This makes Active Directory authentication and control mechanisms very efficient.

Think of the data table as having rows and columns; the intersection of a row and a column is a *field*. The table's rows correspond to individual instances of an object. The table's columns correspond to attributes defined in the schema. The table's fields are populated only if an attribute contains a value. Fields can be a fixed or a variable length. If you create an object and define only 10 attributes, only these 10 attributes will contain values. Although some of those values might be fixed length, others might be variable length.

Records in the data table are stored in data pages that have a fixed size of 8 kilobytes (KBs, or 8192 bytes). Each data page has a page header, data rows, and free space that can contain row offsets. The page header uses the first 96 bytes of each page, leaving 8096 bytes for data and row offsets. Row offsets indicate the logical order of rows on a page, which means that offset 0 refers to the first row in the index, offset 1 refers to the second row, and so on. If a row contains long, variable-length data, the data might not be stored with the rest of the data for that row. Instead, Active Directory can store an 8-byte pointer to the actual data, which is stored in a collection of 8-KB pages that aren't necessarily written contiguously. In this way, an object and all its attribute values can be much larger than 8 KBs.

The primary log file has a fixed size of 10 megabytes (MBs). When this log fills up, Active Directory creates additional (secondary) log files as necessary. The secondary log files are also limited to a fixed size of 10 MBs. Active Directory uses the reserve log files to reserve space on disk for log files that might need to be created. Because several reserve files are already created, this speeds up the transactional logging process when additional logs are needed.

By default, the primary data file, working files, and transaction logs are all stored in the same location. On a domain controller's system volume, you'll find these files in the

Chapter 24

%SystemRoot%\NTDS folder. Although these are the only files used for the data store, there are other files used by Active Directory. For example, policy files and other files, such as startup and shutdown scripts used by the DSA, are stored in the %SystemRoot%\Sysvol folder.

> **Note**
>
> A distribution copy of Ntds.dit is also placed in the %SystemRoot%\System32 folder. This is used to create a domain controller when you install Active Directory on a server running Windows Server. If the file doesn't exist, the Active Directory Installation Wizard will need the installation media to promote a member server to be a domain controller.

## INSIDE OUT   The log files have attributes you can examine

When you stop Active Directory Domain Services, you can use the Extensible Storage Engine Utility (esentutl.exe) to examine log file properties. At an elevated command prompt, type **esentutl.exe –ml LogName**, where *LogName* is the name of the log file to examine, such as edb.log, to obtain detailed information on the log file, including the base name, creation time, format version, log sector sizes, and logging parameters. While Active Directory Domain Services is offline, you can also use esentutl.exe to perform defragmentation, integrity checks, and copy, repair, and recovery operations. To learn more about this utility, type **esentutl.exe** at an elevated command prompt. Following the prompts, you can then type the letter corresponding to the operation you want to learn more about. For example, type **esentutl.exe** and then press the D key to learn the defragmentation options.

# Active Directory logical architecture

The logical layer of Active Directory determines how you see the information contained in the data store and also controls access to that information. The logical layer does this by defining the namespaces and naming schemes used to access resources stored in the directory. This provides a consistent way to access directory-stored information regardless of type. For example, you can obtain information about a printer resource stored in the directory in much the same way that you can obtain information about a user resource.

To better understand the logical architecture of Active Directory, you need to understand the following topics:

- Active Directory objects

- Active Directory domains, trees, and forests

- Active Directory trusts

- Active Directory namespaces and partitions

- Active Directory data distribution

## Active Directory objects

Because so many types of resources can be stored in the directory, a standard storage mechanism was needed and Microsoft developers decided to use the LDAP model for organizing data. In this model, each resource that you want to represent in the directory is created as an object with attributes that define information you want to store about the resource. For example, the user object in Active Directory has attributes for a user's first name, middle initial, last name, and logon name.

An object that holds other objects is referred to as a *container object* or simply a *container*. The data store itself is a container that contains other containers and objects. An object that can't contain other objects is a *leaf object*. Each object created within the directory is of a particular type or class. The object classes are defined in the schema and include the following types:

- User

- Group

- Computer

- Printer

When you create an object in the directory, you must comply with the schema rules for that object class. Not only do the schema rules dictate the available attributes for an object class, they also dictate which attributes are mandatory and which attributes are optional. When you create an object, mandatory attributes must be defined. For example, you can't create a user object without specifying the user's full name and logon name. The reason is that these attributes are mandatory.

Some rules for attributes are defined in policy as well. For example, the default security policy for Windows Server specifies that a user account must have a password and the password must meet certain complexity requirements. If you try to create a user account without a password or with a password that doesn't meet these complexity requirements, the account creation will fail because of the security policy.

The schema can be extended or changed as well. This allows administrators to define new object classes, add attributes to existing objects, and change the way attributes are used. However, you need special access permissions and privileges to work directly with the schema.

## Active Directory domains, trees, and forests

Within the directory, objects are organized using a hierarchical tree structure called a *directory tree*. The structure of the hierarchy is derived from the schema and is used to define the parent–child relationships of objects stored in the directory.

A logical grouping of objects that allows central management of those objects is called a *domain*. In the directory tree, a domain is itself represented as an object. In fact, it is the parent object of all the objects it contains. An Active Directory domain can contain millions of objects. You can create a single domain that contains all the resources you want to manage centrally. In Figure 24-8, a domain object is represented by a large triangle and the objects it contains are as shown.

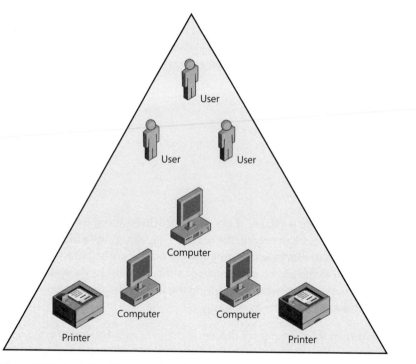

**Figure 24-8** An Active Directory domain.

Domains are only one of several building blocks for implementing Active Directory structures. Other building blocks include the following:

- Active Directory trees, which are logical groupings of domains

- Active Directory forests, which are logical groupings of domain trees

As described, a directory tree is used to represent a hierarchy of objects, showing the parent–child relationships between those objects. Thus, when we're talking about a domain tree, we're looking at the relationship between parent and child domains. The domain at the top of the domain tree is referred to as the *root domain* (think of this as an upside-down tree). More specifically, the root domain is the first domain created in a new tree within Active Directory. When talking about forests and domains, there is an important distinction made between the first domain created in a new forest—a forest root domain—and the first domain created in each additional tree within a forest—a root domain.

In the example shown in Figure 24-9, cohovineyard.com is the root domain in an Active Directory forest with a single tree—that is, it is the forest root domain. As such, cohovineyard.com is the parent of the sales.cohovineyard.com domain and the mf.cohovineyard.com domain. The mf.cohovineyard.com domain itself has a related subdomain: bottling.mf.cohovineyard.com. This makes mf.cohovineyard.com the parent of the child domain bottling.mf.cohovineyard.com.

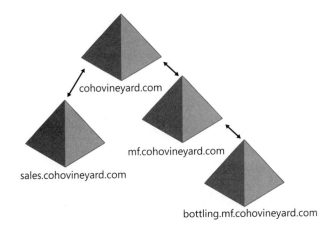

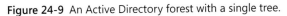

**Figure 24-9** An Active Directory forest with a single tree.

The most important thing to note about this and all domain trees is that the namespace is contiguous. Here, all the domains are part of the cohovineyard.com namespace. If a domain is a part of a different namespace, it can be added as part of a new tree in the forest. In the example shown in Figure 24-10, a second tree is added to the forest. The root domain of the second tree is cohowinery.com, and this domain has cs.cohowinery.com as a child domain.

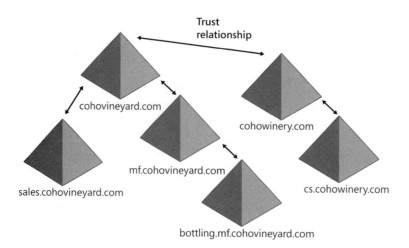

**Figure 24-10** An Active Directory forest with multiple trees.

You create a forest root domain by installing Active Directory on a standalone server and establishing the server as the first domain controller in a new forest. To add an additional tree to an existing forest, you install Active Directory on a standalone server and configure the server as a member of the forest, but with a domain name that is not part of the current namespace being used. You make the new domain part of the same forest to allow associations called *trusts* to be made between domains that belong to different namespaces.

## Active Directory trusts

In Active Directory, two-way transitive trusts are established automatically between domains that are members of the same forest. Trusts join parent and child domains in the same domain tree and join the roots of domain trees. Trusts are transitive, which means that if domain A trusts domain B and domain B trusts domain C, domain A trusts domain C as well. Because all trusts in Active Directory are two-way and transitive, by default every domain in a forest implicitly trusts every other domain. It also means that resources in any domain are available to users in every domain in the forest. For example, with the trust relationships in place, a user in the sales.cohovineyard.com domain could access a printer or other resources in the cohovineyard.com domain or even the cs.cohowinery.com domain.

However, the creation of a trust doesn't imply any specific permission. Instead, it implies only the ability to grant permissions. No privileges are automatically implied or inherited by the establishment of a trust relationship. The trust doesn't grant or deny any permission. It exists only to allow administrators to be able to grant permissions.

There are several key terms used to describe trusts, including the following:

- **Trusting domain**   A domain that establishes a trust is referred to as a *trusting domain*. Trusting domains allow access by users from another domain (the trusted domain).

- **Trusted domain**   A domain that trusts another domain is referred to as a *trusted domain*. Users in trusted domains have access to another domain (the trusting domain).

To make it easier for administrators to grant access throughout a forest, Active Directory allows you to designate two types of administrators:

- **Enterprise administrators**   These are the designated administrators of the enterprise. Enterprise administrators can manage and grant access to resources in any domain in the Active Directory forest.

- **Domain administrators**   These are the designated administrators of a particular domain. Domain administrators in a trusting domain can access user accounts in a trusted domain and set permissions that grant access to resources in the trusting domain.

Going back to the example, an enterprise administrator in this forest could grant access to resources in any domain in the forest. If Jim, in the sales.cohovineyard.com domain, needed access to a printer in the cs.cohowinery.com domain, an enterprise administrator could grant this access. Because cs.cohowinery.com is the trusting domain and sales .cohovineyard.com is the trusted domain in this example, a domain administrator in the cs.cohowinery.com domain could grant permission to use the printer as well. A domain administrator for sales.cohovineyard.com could not grant such permissions, however, because the printer resource exists in a domain other than the one the administrator controls.

To continue working with Figure 24-10, take a look at the arrows that designate the trust relationships. For a user in the sales.cohovineyard.com domain to access a printer in the cs.cohowinery.com domain, the request must pass through the following series of trust relationships:

1. The trust between sales.cohovineyard.com and cohovineyard.com

2. The trust between cohovineyard.com and cohowinery.com

3. The trust between cohowinery.com and cs.cohowinery.com

Chapter 24

The *trust path* defines the path that an authentication request must take between the two domains. Here, a domain controller in the user's local domain (sales.cohovineyard .com) would pass the request to a domain controller in the cohovineyard.com domain. This domain controller, in turn, would pass the request to a domain controller in the cohowinery.com domain. Finally, the request would be passed to a domain controller in the cs.cohowinery.com domain, which would ultimately grant or deny access.

In all, the user's request has to pass through four domain controllers—one for each domain between the user and the resource. Because the domain structure is separate from your network's physical structure, the printer could actually be located right beside the user's desk and the user would still have to go through this process. If you expand this scenario to include all the users in the sales.cohovineyard.com domain, you could potentially have hundreds of users whose requests have to go through a similar process to access resources in the cs.cohowinery.com domain.

Omitting the fact that the domain design in this scenario is very poor—because if many users are working with resources, those resources are ideally in their own domain or a domain closer in the tree—one solution for this problem would be to establish a *shortcut trust* between the user's domain and the resource's domain. With a shortcut trust, you could specify that cs.cohowinery.com explicitly trusts sales.cohovineyard.com. Now when a user in the sales.cohovineyard.com requests a resource in the cs.cohowinery.com domain, the local domain controller knows about cs.cohowinery.com and can directly submit the request for authentication. This means that the sales.cohovineyard.com domain controller sends the request directly to a cs.cohowinery.com domain controller.

Shortcut trusts are meant to help make more efficient use of resources on a busy network. On a network with a lot of activity, the explicit trust can reduce the overhead on servers and on the network as a whole. Shortcut trusts shouldn't be implemented without careful planning. They should be used only when resources in one domain will be accessed by users in another domain on a regular basis. They don't need to be used between two domains that have a parent–child relationship because a default trust already exists explicitly between a parent domain and a child domain.

With Active Directory, you can also make use of *external trusts*. External trusts are manually configured and are always nontransitive. External trusts can be either one-way or two-way. When you establish a trust between a domain in one forest and a domain in another forest, security principals from the external domain can access resources in the internal domain. In the internal domain, Active Directory creates a foreign security principal to represent each security principal in the external domain. Foreign security principals can be added to domain local groups in the internal domain.

## Active Directory namespaces and partitions

Any data stored in the Active Directory database is represented logically as an object. Every object in the directory has a relative distinguished name (RDN). That is, every object has a name relative to the parent container in which it is stored. The relative name is the name of the object itself and is also referred to as an object's *common name*. This relative name is stored as an attribute of the object and must be unique for the container in which it is located. Following this, no two objects in a container can have the same common name, but two objects in different containers could have the same name.

In addition to an RDN, objects also have a distinguished name (DN). An object's DN describes the object's place in the directory tree and is logically the series of containers from the highest to the lowest of which the object is a part. It is called a distinguished name because it serves to distinguish like-named objects and, as such, must be unique in the directory. No two objects in the directory will have the same distinguished name.

Every object in the directory has a parent, except the root of the directory tree, which is referred to as the rootDSE. The rootDSE represents the top of the logical namespace for a directory. It has no name *per se*. Although there is only one rootDSE, the information stored in the rootDSE specifically relates to the domain controller on which the directory is stored. In a domain with multiple domain controllers, the rootDSE will have a slightly different representation on each domain controller. The representation relates to the capability and configuration of the domain controller in question. In this way, Active Directory clients can determine the capabilities and configuration of a particular domain controller.

Below the rootDSE, every directory tree has a root domain. The root domain is the first domain created in an Active Directory forest and is also referred to as the forest root domain. After it is established, the forest root domain never changes, even if you add new trees to the forest. The LDAP distinguished name of the forest root domain is DC=*ForestRootDomainName*, where DC is an LDAP identifier for a domain component and *ForestRootDomainName* is the actual name of the forest root domain. Each level within the domain tree is broken out as a separate domain component. For example, if the forest root domain is cohovineyard.com, the domain's distinguished name is DC=cohovineyard,DC=com.

When Active Directory is installed on the first domain controller in a new forest, three containers are created below the rootDSE:

- The Forest Root Domain container, which is the container for the objects in the forest root domain

- The Configuration container, which is the container for the default configuration and all policy information

- The Schema container, which is the container for all objects, classes, attributes, and syntaxes

From a logical perspective, these containers are organized as shown in Figure 24-11. The LDAP identifier for an object's common name is CN. The DN for the Configuration container is CN=configuration,DC=*ForestRootDomainName*, and the DN for the Schema container is CN=schema,CN=configuration,DC=*ForestRootDomainName*. In the cohovineyard.com domain, the DNs for the Configuration and Schema containers are CN=configuration,DC=cohovineyard,DC=com and CN=schema,CN=configuration, DC=cohovineyard,DC=com, respectively. As you can see, the distinguished name allows you to walk the directory tree from the relative name of the object you are working with to the forest root.

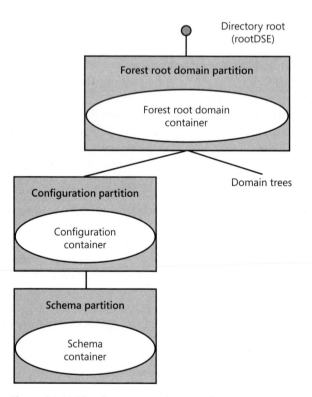

**Figure 24-11** The directory tree in a new forest.

As shown in the figure, the forest root domain and the Configuration and Schema containers exist within their own individual partitions. Active Directory uses partitions to logically apportion the directory so that each domain controller does not have to store a complete copy of the entire directory. To do this, object names are used to group objects into logical categories so that the objects can be managed and replicated as appropriate. The largest logical category is a directory partition. All directory partitions are created as instances of the domainDNS object class.

As far as Active Directory is concerned, a domain is a container of objects that is logically partitioned from other container objects. When you create a new domain in Active Directory, you create a new container object in the directory tree, and that container, in turn, is contained by a domain directory partition for the purposes of management and replication.

## Active Directory data distribution

Active Directory uses partitions to help distribute three general types of data:

- Domainwide data, which is data replicated to every domain controller in a domain

- Forestwide data, which is data replicated to every domain controller in a forest

- Application data, which is data replicated to an arbitrary set of domain controllers

Every domain controller stores at least one domain directory partition, as well as two forestwide data partitions: the schema partition and the configuration partition. Data in a domain directory partition is replicated to every domain controller in the domain as a writeable replica.

Forestwide data partitions are replicated to every domain controller in the forest. The configuration partition is replicated as a writeable replica. The schema partition is replicated as a read-only replica, and the only writeable replica is stored on a domain controller that is designated as having the schema operations master role. Other operations master roles are defined as well.

Active Directory can replicate application-specific data that is stored in an application partition such as the default application partitions used with zones in Domain Name System (DNS) that are integrated with Active Directory. Application partition data is replicated on a forestwide, domainwide, or other basis to domain controllers that have a particular application partition. If a domain controller doesn't have an application partition, it doesn't receive a replica of the application partition.

In addition to full replicas that are distributed for domains, Active Directory distributes partial replicas of every domain in the forest to special domain controllers designated as global catalog servers. The partial replicas stored on global catalog servers contain information on every object in the forest and are used to facilitate searches and queries for

Chapter 24

objects in the forest. Because only a subset of an object's attributes is stored, the amount of data replicated to and maintained by a global catalog server is significantly smaller than the total size of all object data stored in all the domains in the forest.

Every domain must have at least one global catalog server. By default, the first domain controller installed in a domain is set as that domain's global catalog server. You can change the global catalog server, and you can designate additional servers as global catalog servers as necessary.

# Designing and managing the domain environment

As you learned in the previous chapter, the physical structure of Active Directory is tightly integrated with the security architecture of the Microsoft Windows operating system. At a high level, Active Directory provides interfaces to which clients can connect, and the directory physically exists on disk in a database file called Ntds.dit. When you install Active Directory on a computer, the computer becomes a domain controller. When you implement Active Directory, you can have as many domain controllers as are needed to support the directory service needs of the organization.

Before you implement or modify the Active Directory domain environment, you need to consider the limitations and architecture requirements for the following processes:

- Replication

- Search and global catalogs

- Compatibility and functional levels

- Authentication and trusts

- Delegated authentication

- Operations masters

Remember that planning for Active Directory is an ongoing process that you should think about whether you are planning to deploy Active Directory for the first time or have already deployed Active Directory in your organization. Why? Because every time you consider making changes to your organizational structure or network infrastructure, you should consider how this affects Active Directory and plan accordingly.

In planning for Active Directory, few things are outside the scope of the design. When you initially deploy Active Directory, you need to develop an Active Directory design and implementation plan that involves every level of your organization and your network infrastructure. After you deploy Active Directory, any time you plan to change your organizational structure or network infrastructure, you should determine the impact on Active Directory. You then need to plan for and implement any changes to Active Directory that are required.

# Design considerations for Active Directory replication

Because Active Directory uses a multimaster replication model, there are no primary or backup domain controllers. Every domain controller deployed in the organization is autonomous, with its own copy of the directory. When you need to make changes to standard directory data, you can do so on any domain controller and you can rely on Active Directory's built-in replication engine to replicate the changes to other domain controllers in the organization as appropriate.

As shown in Figure 25-1, the actual mechanics of replication depend on the level and role of a domain controller in the organization. To help manage replication, Active Directory uses partitions in the following ways:

- Forestwide data is replicated to every domain controller in the forest and includes the configuration and schema partitions for the forest. A domain controller designated as the schema master maintains the only writeable copy of the schema data. Every domain controller maintains a writeable copy of the configuration data.

- Domainwide data is replicated to every domain controller in a domain and includes only the data for a particular domain. Every domain controller in a domain has a writeable copy of the data for that domain.

> **Note**
>
> Domain controllers designated as Domain Name System (DNS) servers also replicate directory partitions for DNS. Every domain controller that is designated as a DNS server has a copy of the ForestDNSZones and DomainDNSZones partitions. Windows Server 2008 and later support two different types of domain controllers: writeable domain controllers and read-only domain controllers. Writeable domain controllers are the standard type of domain controller. Writeable domain controllers are the only type of domain controller with writeable directory partitions. Read-only domain controllers, on the other hand, only have read-only directory partitions. To help make the architecture and design discussions easier to follow, I discuss architecture and design considerations for read-only domain controllers separately, and you'll find a complete discussion in Chapter 29, "Deploying read-only domain controllers."

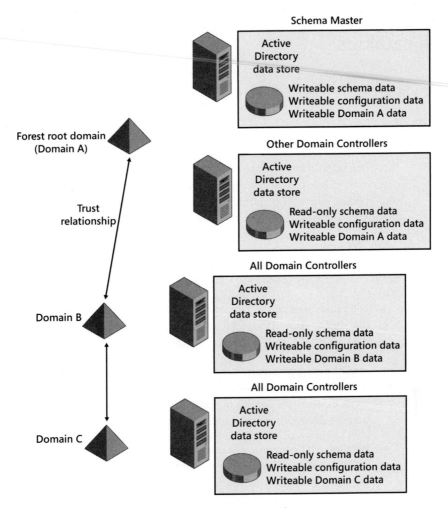

**Figure 25-1** Replication of data in the Active Directory data store.

# Design considerations for Active Directory search and global catalogs

Active Directory uses the Lightweight Directory Access Protocol (LDAP) model to query and manage directory information. Objects in the directory can be located using an LDAP query.

## Searching the tree

Every object has a name relative to its location in the directory and a distinguished name that points to its exact location in relation to the root of the directory tree. The relative distinguished name (RDN) is the actual name of the object. The distinguished name (DN) is the complete object name as seen by Active Directory.

When you work your way down the tree, you add a naming component for each successive level. In Figure 25-2, the relative names of several objects are shown on the left and the distinguished names of those objects are shown on the right.

- **cohovineyards.com**   The cohovineyards.com domain object is near the top of the tree. In Active Directory, its relative distinguished name is DC=cohovineyards and its distinguished name is DC=cohovineyards,DC=com.

- **mf.Cohovineyards.com**   The mf.cohovineyards.com domain object is at the next level of the tree. In Active Directory, its relative name is DC=mf and its distinguished name includes the path to the previous level as well as its relative name. This means that the DN is DC=mf,DC=cohovineyards,DC=com.

- **Bottling.Mf.Cohovineyards.com**   The bottling.mf.cohovineyards.com domain object is below the mf.cohovineyards.com domain in the directory tree. In Active Directory, its relative distinguished name is DC=bottling and its distinguished name includes the path to all the previous levels as well as its relative name. This means the DN is DC=bottling,DC=mf,DC=cohovineyards,DC=com.

Being able to find objects in the directory efficiently regardless of their location in the directory tree is extremely important. If objects can't be easily located, users won't be able to find resources that are available and administrators won't be able to manage the available resources either. To make it easier to find resources, Active Directory uses special-purpose domain controllers that function as global catalog servers.

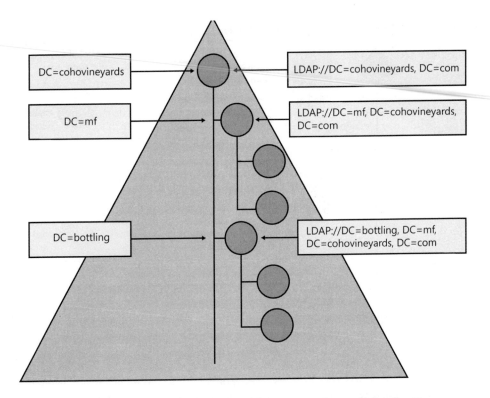

**Figure 25-2** Active Directory uses the LDAP model to query and manage the directory.

## Accessing the global catalog

A domain controller designated as a global catalog server contains an additional data store called the *global catalog*, as shown in Figure 25-3. The global catalog contains a partial, read-only replica of all the domains in the Active Directory forest. Although the catalog is a partial replica, it does contain a copy of every object in the directory, but only the base attributes of those objects. Queries to global catalog servers are made over TCP port 3268 for standard communications and TCP port 3269 for secure communications.

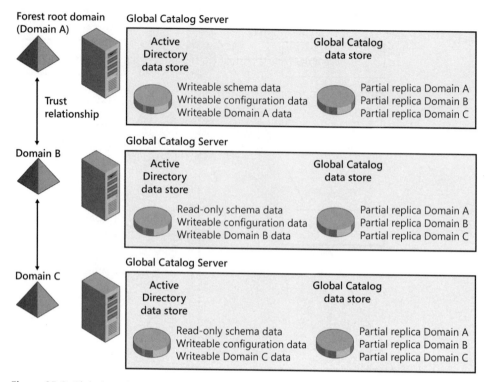

**Figure 25-3** Global catalog servers in an Active Directory forest.

Global catalog data is replicated to global catalog servers using the normal Active Directory replication process. In an Active Directory forest with domains A, B, and C, this means that any domain controller designated as a global catalog server has a partial replica of all three domains. If a user in domain C searches for a resource located in domain A, the global catalog server in domain C can respond to the query using an attribute that has been repli-cated to the global catalog without needing to refer to another domain controller. Without a global catalog server, a domain controller in domain C would need to forward the query to a domain controller in domain A.

## Designating global catalog servers

The first domain controller installed in a domain is automatically designated as a global catalog server. You can designate additional domain controllers to be global catalog servers as well. To do this, you use the Active Directory Sites And Services tool to set the Global Catalog Server option for the domain controller you want to be a global catalog server.

Start Active Directory Sites And Services by selecting the related option on the Tools menu in Server Manager. Expand the site you want to work with, such as Default-First-Site-Name, expand the related Servers node, and then select the server you want to designate as a global catalog, as shown in Figure 25-4.

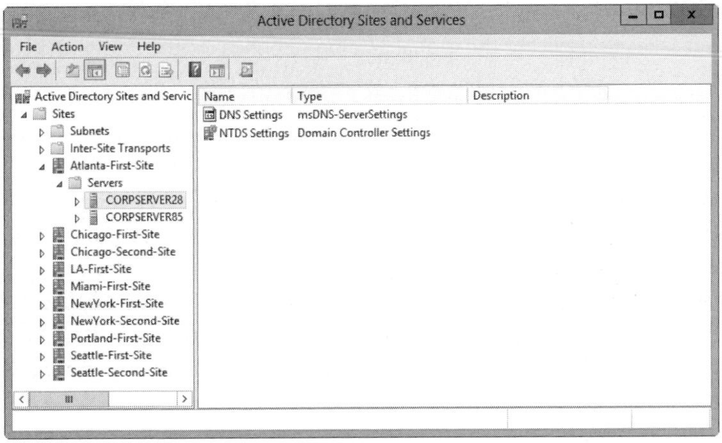

**Figure 25-4**  Select the server to designate as a global catalog.

In the right pane, press and hold or right-click NTDS Settings, and then select Properties. This displays the NTDS Settings Properties dialog box, as shown in Figure 25-5.

**Figure 25-5**  Configure NTDS settings.

If you want the selected server to be a global catalog, select the Global Catalog check box. If you want the selected server to stop being a global catalog, clear the Global Catalog check box. When you designate a new global catalog server, the server will request a copy of the global catalog from an existing global catalog server in the domain. The amount of time it takes to replicate the global catalog depends on the size of the catalog and the network configuration.

> ### Note
> Exchange Server is tightly integrated with Active Directory. Exchange Server stores schema data, configuration data, domain data, and application data in the directory. It also uses Active Directory replication topology to determine how to route messages within the organization. You must install Exchange Server 2010 with Service Pack 3 or later to run Exchange Server 2010 on Windows Server 2012. To learn more about Exchange Server and Active Directory, refer to *Microsoft Exchange Server 2010 Administrator's Pocket Consultant* (Microsoft Press, 2009).

## Designating replication attributes

The contents of the global catalog are determined by the attributes that are replicated for each object class. Common object classes you'll work with include the following:

- **Computer**  Represents a computer account in the domain or forest

- **Contact**  Represents a contact in the domain or forest

- **Domain**  Represents a domain

- **Group**  Represents a group account in the domain or forest

- **InetOrgPerson**  Represents a special type of user account, which typically has been migrated from another directory service

- **PrintQueue**  Represents a logical printer (print queue) in the domain or forest

- **Server**  Represents a server account in the domain or forest

- **Site**  Represents an Active Directory site

- **Subnet**  Represents an Active Directory subnet

- **User**  Represents a user account in the domain or forest

Schema administrators can configure additional attributes to be replicated by global catalog servers. The primary reason for replicating additional attributes is to add attributes for which users routinely search. You shouldn't add attributes for which users search infrequently. You should rarely, if ever, remove attributes that are being replicated.

If you are a member of the Schema Admins group, you can manage the attributes that are replicated through the global catalog by using the Active Directory Schema snap-in for the Microsoft Management Console (MMC). When you start this snap-in, it makes a direct connection to the schema master for the forest.

The Active Directory Schema snap-in is not available by default. You must install this tool by registering its dynamic-link library (DLL). To do this, type the following at an elevated command prompt:

```
regsvr32 schmmgmt.dll
```

After you install this tool, you can add the Active Directory Schema snap-in to a custom console by following these steps:

1.  Open a blank MMC in Author mode. Type **mmc** in the Apps Search box. Next, tap or click mmc and then press Enter.

2.  In your MMC, choose Add/Remove Snap-in from the File menu in the main window. This displays the Add Or Remove Snap-ins dialog box.

3.  The Available Snap-ins list shows all the snap-ins that are available. Select Active Directory Schema, and then tap or click Add. The Active Directory Schema snap-in is added to the Selected Snap-ins list.

4.  Now close the Add Or Remove Snap-ins dialog box by tapping or clicking OK and return to the console you are creating.

After you add the snap-in to a custom console, you can edit the schema for the object whose attribute you want to replicate in the global catalog. In Active Directory Schema, expand the Active Directory Schema node, and then select the Attributes node. A list of the attributes for all objects in the directory appears in the right pane, as shown in Figure 25-6.

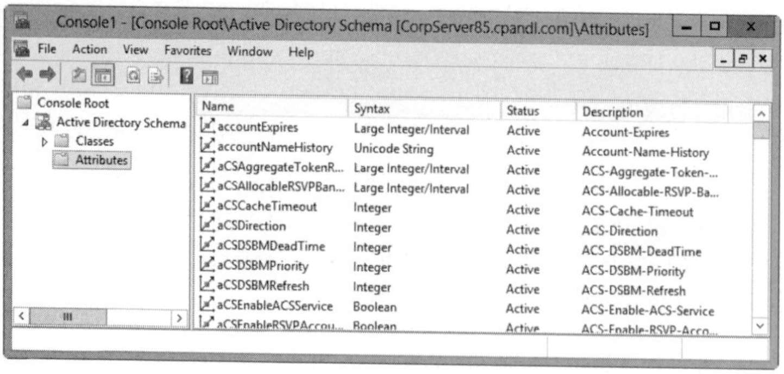

**Figure 25-6** View a list of attributes for all objects in the directory.

Double-tap or double-click the attribute you want to replicate to the global catalog. In the attribute's Properties dialog box, mark the attribute to be replicated by selecting the Replicate This Attribute To The Global Catalog check box, as shown in Figure 25-7. If you want the attribute to be indexed in the database for faster search and retrieval, select the Index This Attribute check box. Although indexing an attribute allows it to be found more quickly, each index you create slightly increases the size of the Active Directory database.

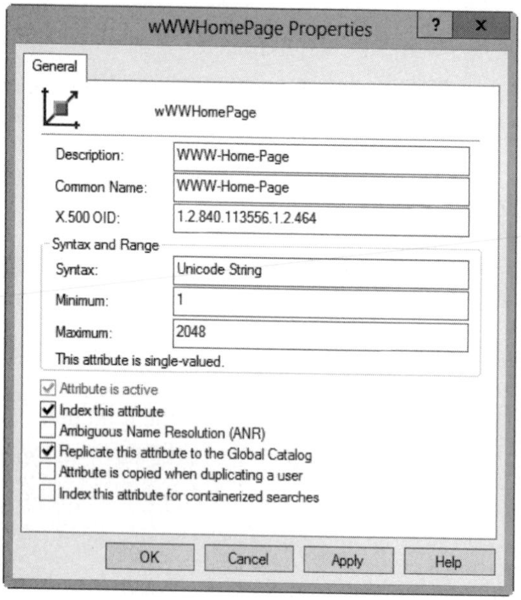

**Figure 25-7** Replicate an attribute to the global catalog.

**TROUBLESHOOTING**

**You cannot change an attribute even though you are a member of the Administrators group**

As a member of the Administrators group, you can view Active Directory schema. To change schema, you must be a member of the Schema Admins group. The Active Directory Schema snap-in doesn't check to ensure that you are a member of the Schema Admins group until you try to change attribute settings. If you aren't a member of the group, it states that you have insufficient permissions.

# Design considerations for compatibility

Each forest and each domain within a forest can be assigned a functional level. The functional level for a forest is referred to as the *forest functional level*. The functional level for a domain within a forest is referred to as the *domain functional level*. Functional levels affect the inner workings of Active Directory and are used to enable features that are compatible with the installed server versions of the Windows operating system.

## Understanding domain functional level

When you set a functional level for a domain, the level of functionality applies only to that domain. This means that other domains in the forest can have different functional levels.

As shown in Table 25-1, there are several domain functional levels. Changing a functional level changes the operating systems that are supported for domain controllers. For example, in Windows 2008 functional level, the domain can have domain controllers running Microsoft Windows Server 2008 or later.

> **Note**
>
> Generally, you cannot lower the domain functional level once you raise it. However, there are specific exceptions. When you raise the domain functional level to Windows Server 2012, you can lower it to Windows Server 2008 R2. If Active Directory Recycle Bin has not been enabled, you can also lower the domain functional level from Windows Server 2012 to Windows Server 2008 R2 or Windows Server 2008 or from Windows Server 2008 R2 back to Windows Server 2008. You cannot roll the domain functional level back to Windows Server 2003 or lower.

**TABLE 25-1** Domain functional levels

| Domain Functional Level | Supported Domain Controllers |
| --- | --- |
| Windows Server 2003 | Windows Server 2012<br>Windows Server 2008 R2<br>Windows Server 2008<br>Windows Server 2003 |
| Windows Server 2008 | Windows Server 2012<br>Windows Server 2008 R2<br>Windows Server 2008 |
| Windows Server 2008 R2 | Windows Server 2012<br>Windows Server 2008 R2 |
| Windows Server 2012 | Windows Server 2012 |

Domains operating in Windows Server 2003 mode can use group nesting, group type conversion, universal groups, and migration of security principals. They also can use many improved Active Directory features, including group nesting, group type conversion, universal groups, easy domain controller renaming, updating logon timestamps, migration of security principals, and Kerberos KDC key version numbers. Applications can use constrained delegation to take advantage of the secure delegation of user credentials through the Kerberos authentication protocol. You can also redirect the Users and Computers containers to define a new well-known location for user and computer accounts.

The Windows Server 2008 domain functional level adds the following features in addition to those available with Windows Server 2003:

- Distributed File System Replication for SYSVOL, which provides more robust and granular replication of SYSVOL

- Advanced Encryption Standard (AES) support for the Kerberos protocol, allowing user accounts to use AES 128-bit or AES 256-bit encryption

- Last interactive logon information, which displays the time of the last successful interactive logon for a user, the number of failed logon attempts since the last logon, and the time of the last failed logon

- Fine-grained password policies, which make it possible for password and account lockout policy to be specified for user and global security groups in a domain

The Windows Server 2008 R2 forest functional level adds support for Active Directory Recycle Bin, managed service accounts, Authentication Mechanism Assurance, and other important Active Directory enhancements. Although Active Directory for Windows Server 2012 has many enhancements, most of these enhancements require using only Windows Server

2012 domain controllers. That said, Kerberos Armoring requires the Windows Server 2012 domain functional level.

# Understanding forest functional level

The forest functional levels are listed in Table 25-2. Generally, you cannot lower the forest functional level once you raise it. However, there are specific exceptions. When you raise the forest functional level to Windows Server 2012, you can lower it to Windows Server 2008 R2. If Active Directory Recycle Bin has not been enabled, you can also lower the forest functional level from Windows Server 2012 to Windows Server 2008 R2 or Windows Server 2008 or from Windows Server 2008 R2 back to Windows Server 2008. You cannot roll the forest functional level back to Windows Server 2003 or lower.

**TABLE 25-2  Forest functional levels**

| Forest Functional Level | Supported Domain Controllers |
| --- | --- |
| Windows Server 2003 | Windows Server 2012<br>Windows Server 2008 R2<br>Windows Server 2008<br>Windows Server 2003 |
| Windows Server 2008 | Windows Server 2012<br>Windows Server 2008 R2<br>Windows Server 2008 |
| Windows Server 2008 R2 | Windows Server 2012<br>Windows Server 2008 R2 |
| Windows Server 2012 | Windows Server 2012 |

The Windows Server 2003 forest functional level supports linked-value replication to improve the replication of changes to group memberships, domain rename and domain restructure using renaming, and one-way, two-way, and transitive forest trusts. Also supported are dynamic auxiliary classes and the deactivation of schema class objects and attributes.

The Windows Server 2008 forest functional level offers incremental improvements over the Windows Server 2003 forest functional level. When all domains within a forest are operating at this level, you'll see improvements in both intersite and intrasite replication throughout the organization. Domain controllers can use Distributed File System (DFS) replication rather than File Replication Service (FRS) replication as well. In addition, Windows Server 2008 security principals are not created until the primary domain controller (PDC) emulator operations master in the forest root domain is running Windows Server 2008.

The Windows Server 2008 R2 forest functional level adds the Active Directory Recycle Bin, managed service accounts, and Authentication Mechanism Assurance. The Windows

Server 2012 forest functional level adds functionality improvements as well as support for Kerberos Armoring.

## Raising or lowering the domain or forest functional level

You can raise the domain or forest functional level using either Active Directory Domains And Trusts or Active Directory Administrative Center. Generally, you cannot lower the domain or forest functional level once you raise it. However, there are specific exceptions, as discussed previously in this chapter. Keep in mind that if you enabled Active Directory Recycle Bin, you won't be able to lower the forest functional level.

In Active Directory Administrative Center, you can raise the domain functional level by following these steps:

1. The local domain is opened for management by default. If you want to work with a different domain, tap or click Manage and then tap or click Add Navigation Nodes. In the Add Navigation Nodes dialog box, select the domain you want to work with and then tap or click OK.

2. Select the domain you want to work with by tapping or clicking it in the left pane. In the Tasks pane, tap or click Raise Domain Functional Level.

3. The current domain name and functional level are displayed in the Raise Domain Functional Level dialog box.

4. To change the domain functionality, select the new domain functional level by using the list provided and then tap or click Raise.

5. Tap or click OK. The new domain functional level is replicated to each domain controller in the domain. This operation can take some time in a large organization.

To raise the forest functional level using Active Directory Administrative Center, follow these steps:

1. Select the domain you want to work with by tapping or clicking it in the left pane. In the Tasks pane, tap or click Raise Forest Functional Level.

2. The current forest name and functional level are displayed in the Raise Forest Functional Level dialog box.

3. To change the forest functionality, select the new forest functional level by using the list provided and then tap or click Raise.

4. Tap or click OK. The new forest functional level is replicated to each domain controller in each domain in the forest. This operation can take some time in a large organization.

In Active Directory Domains And Trusts, you can raise the domain functional level by following these steps:

1. Press and hold or right-click the domain you want to work with, and then select Raise Domain Functional Level. The current domain name and functional level appear in the Raise Domain Functional Level dialog box.

2. To change the domain functionality, select the new domain functional level using the selection list provided and then tap or click Raise.

3. When you tap or click OK, the new domain functional level is replicated to each domain controller in the domain. This operation can take some several minutes or longer in a large organization.

To raise the forest level functionality using Active Directory Domains And Trusts, complete the following steps:

1. Press and hold or right-click the Active Directory Domains And Trusts node in the console tree, and then select Raise Forest Functional Level. The current forest name and functional level appear in the Raise Forest Functional Level dialog box.

2. To change the forest functionality, select the new forest functional level using the selection list provided and then tap or click Raise.

3. When you tap or click OK, the new forest functional level is replicated to each domain controller in each domain in the forest. This operation can take several minutes or longer in a large organization.

# Design considerations for Active Directory authentication and trusts

Authentication and trusts are integral parts of Active Directory. Before you implement any Active Directory design or try to modify your existing Active Directory infrastructure, you should have a firm understanding of how both authentication and trusts work in an Active Directory environment.

## Universal groups and authentication

When a user logs on to a domain, Active Directory looks up information about the groups of which the user is a member to generate a security token for the user. The security token is needed as part of the normal authentication process and is used whenever a user accesses resources on the network.

## Understanding security tokens and universal group membership caching

To generate the security token, Active Directory checks the domain local and global group memberships for the user. All the supported domain functional levels support a special type of group called a *universal group*. Universal groups can contain user and group accounts from any domain in the forest. Because global catalog servers are the only servers in a domain with forestwide domain data, the global catalog is essential for logon.

Because of problems authenticating users when global catalog servers are not available, Windows Server 2003 introduced a technique for caching universal group membership. In a domain with domain controllers running Windows Server 2003 or later, universal group membership caching can be enabled. After you enable caching, the cache is where domain controllers store universal group membership information that they have previously looked up. Domain controllers can then use this cache for authentication the next time the user logs on to the domain. The cache is maintained indefinitely and updated periodically to ensure that it is current. By default, domain controllers check the consistency of the cache every eight hours.

Thanks to universal group membership caching, remote sites running Windows Server 2003 or later domain controllers don't necessarily have to have global catalog servers configured as well. This gives you additional options when configuring the Active Directory forest. The assignment of security tokens is only part of the logon process. The logon process also includes authentication and the assignment of a User Principal Name (UPN) to the user.

## INSIDE OUT  The User Principal Name (UPN) suffix can be changed

Every user account has a User Principal Name (UPN), which consists of the User Logon Name combined with the at symbol (@) and a UPN suffix. The names of the current domain and the root domain are set as the default UPN suffix. You can specify an alternate UPN suffix to use to simplify logon or provide additional logon security. This name is used only within the forest and does not have to be a valid DNS name. For example, if the UPN suffix for a domain is it.seattle.cpandl.local, you could use an alternate UPN suffix to simplify this to cpandl.local. This would allow the user Williams to log on using williams@cpandl.local rather than williams@it.seattle.cpandl.local.

You can add or remove UPN suffixes for an Active Directory forest and all domains within that forest by completing the following steps:

1. Start Active Directory Domains And Trusts from the Administrative Tools menu.

2. Press and hold or right-click the Active Directory Domains And Trusts node, and then tap or click Properties.

3. To add a UPN suffix, type the alternate suffix in the box provided and then tap or click Add.

4. To remove a UPN suffix, tap or click the suffix to remove in the list provided and then tap or click Remove.

5. Tap or click OK.

## Enabling universal group membership caching

In a domain with domain controllers, you use the Active Directory Sites And Services tool to configure universal group membership caching. You enable caching on a per-site basis. Start Active Directory Sites And Services by selecting the related option on the Tools menu in Server Manager. Expand and then select the site in which you want to enable universal group membership caching, as shown in Figure 25-8.

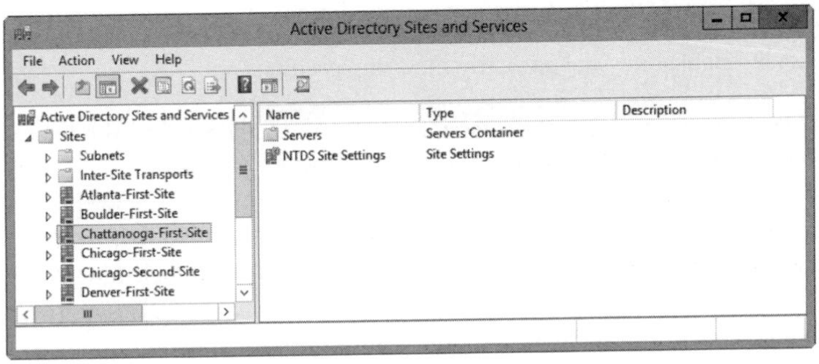

**Figure 25-8** Enable caching on a per-site basis.

In the right pane, press and hold or right-click NTDS Site Settings, and then select Properties. This displays the NTDS Site Settings Properties dialog box, as shown in Figure 25-9.

**Figure 25-9** Enable universal group membership caching.

To enable universal group membership caching for the site, select the Enable Universal Group Membership Caching check box and continue as follows:

- If the directory has multiple sites, you can replicate existing universal group membership information from a specific site's cache by selecting the site on the Refresh Cache From list. With this option, universal group membership information doesn't need to be generated and then replicated; it is simply replicated from the other site's cache.

- If the directory has only one site or you'd rather get the information from a global catalog server in the nearest site, accept the default setting <Default>. With this option, universal group membership information is generated and then replicated.

When you are finished configuring universal group membership caching, tap or click OK.

## NTLM and Kerberos authentication

Windows operating systems use either NT LAN Manager (NTLM) or Kerberos for authentication. With NTLM, an encrypted challenge/response is used to authenticate a user without sending the user's password over the network. The system requesting authentication must perform a calculation that proves it has access to the secured NTLM credentials. It does this by sending a one-way hash of the user's password that can be verified.

NTLM authentication has interactive and noninteractive authentication processes. Interactive NTLM authentication over a network typically involves a client system from which a user is requesting authentication and a domain controller on which the user's password is stored. As the user accesses other resources on the network, noninteractive authentication might take place as well to permit an already logged-on user to access network resources. Typically, noninteractive authentication involves a client, a server, and a domain controller that manages the authentication.

To see how NTLM authentication works, consider the situation that occurs when a user tries to access a resource on the network and she is prompted for her user name and password. Assuming the resource is on a server that is not also a domain controller, the authentication process is similar to the following:

1. When prompted, the user provides a domain name, user name, and password. The client computer generates a cryptographic hash of the user's password, discards the actual password, and then sends the user name to the server as unencrypted text.

2. The server generates a 16-byte random number, called a *challenge*, and sends it to the client.

3. The client encrypts the challenge with the hash of the user's password and returns the result, called a *response*, to the server. The server then sends the domain controller the user name, the challenge sent to the client, and the response from the client.

4. The domain controller uses the user name to retrieve the hash of the user's password from the Security Accounts Manager (SAM) database. The domain controller uses this password hash to encrypt the challenge and then compares the encrypted challenge it computed to the response computed by the client. If they are identical, the authentication is successful.

Active Directory uses Kerberos as the default authentication protocol, and NTLM authentication is maintained only for backward compatibility with legacy clients. Whenever a current client tries to authenticate with Active Directory, the client tries to use Kerberos. Kerberos has a number of advantages over NTLM authentication, including the use of mutual authentication. Mutual authentication in Kerberos allows for two-way authentication so that not only can a server authenticate a client, but a client can also authenticate a server. Thus, mutual authentication ensures that not only is an authorized client trying to access the network, but also that an authorized server is the one responding to the client request.

Kerberos uses the following three main components:

- A client that needs access to resources

- A server that manages access to resources and ensures that only authenticated users can gain access to resources

- A Key Distribution Center (KDC) that acts as a central clearinghouse

## Establishing the initial authentication

All domain controllers run the Kerberos Key Distribution Center service to act as KDCs. With Kerberos authentication, a user password is never sent over the network. Instead, Kerberos authentication uses a shared-secret authentication model. In most cases, the client and the server use the user's password as the shared secret. With this technique, authentication works as shown in Figure 25-10.

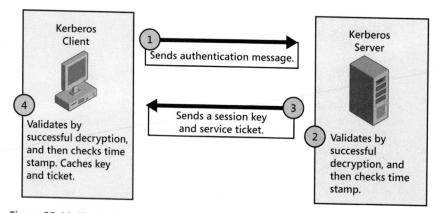

**Figure 25-10** The Kerberos authentication process.

The details of the initial authentication of a user in the domain are as follows:

1. When a user logs on to the network, the client sends the KDC server a message containing the user name, domain name, and a request for access to the network. In the message is a packet of information that has been encrypted using the shared-secret information (the user's password), which includes a time stamp.

2. When the KDC server receives the message, the server reads the user name, and then it checks the directory database for its copy of the shared-secret information (the user's password). The KDC server then decrypts the secret part of the message and checks the message time stamp. As long as the message time stamp is within five minutes of the current time on the server, the server can then authenticate the user. If the decryption fails or the message time stamp is more than five minutes off the current time, the authentication fails. Five minutes is the default value; the allowable time difference can be configured through domain security policy, using the Kerberos policy Maximum Tolerance For Computer Clock Synchronization.

3. After the user is authenticated, the KDC server sends the client a message that is encrypted with the shared-secret information (the user's password). The message includes a session key that the client will use when communicating with the KDC server from now on and a session ticket that grants the user access to the domain controller. The ticket is encrypted with the KDC server's key, which makes it valid only for that domain controller.

4. When the client receives the message, the client decrypts the message and checks the message time stamp. As long as the message time stamp is within five minutes of the current time on the server, the client can then authenticate the server and assume that the server is valid. The client then caches the session key so that it can be used for all future connections with the KDC server. The session key is valid until it expires or the user logs off. The session ticket is cached as well, but it isn't decrypted.

## Accessing resources after authentication

After initial authentication, the user is granted access to the domain. The only resource to which the user has been granted access is the domain controller. When the user wants to access another resource on the network, the client must request access through the KDC. An overview of the process for authenticating access to network resources is shown in Figure 25-11.

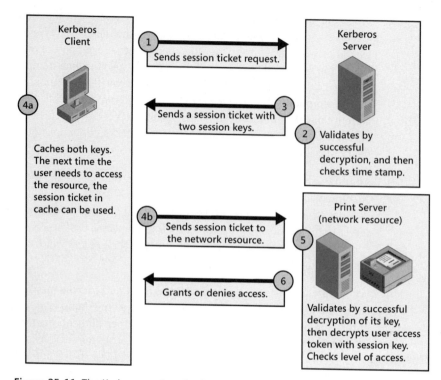

**Figure 25-11** The Kerberos authentication process.

The details of an access request for a network resource are as follows:

1. When a user tries to access a resource on the network, the client sends the KDC server a session ticket request. The message contains the user's name, the session ticket the client was previously granted, the name of the network resource the client is trying to access, and a time stamp that is encrypted with the session key.

2. When the KDC server receives the message, the server decrypts the session ticket using its key. Afterward, it extracts the original session key from the session ticket and uses it to decrypt the time stamp, which is then validated. The validation process is designed to ensure that the client is using the correct session key and that the time stamp is valid.

3. If all is acceptable, the KDC server sends a session ticket to the client. The session ticket includes two copies of a session key that the client will use to access the requested resource. The first copy of the session key is encrypted using the client's session key. The second copy of the session key contains the user's access information and is encrypted with the resource's secret key known only by the KDC server and the network resource.

4. The client caches the session ticket, and then it sends the session ticket to the network resource to gain access. This request also contains an encrypted time stamp.

5. The network resource decrypts the second session key in the session ticket, using the secret key it shares with the KDC server. If this is successful, the network resource has validated that the session ticket came from a trusted KDC. It then decrypts the user's access information, using the session key, and checks the user's access permissions. The time stamp sent from the client is also decrypted and validated by the network resource.

6. If the authentication and authorization are successful (meaning that the client has the appropriate access permissions), the user is granted the type of access to the network resource that the particular permissions allow. The next time the user needs to access the resource, the session ticket in cache is used, as long as it hasn't expired. Using a cached session ticket allows the client to send a request directly to the network resource. If the ticket has expired, however, the client must start over and get a new ticket.

## Authentication and trusts across domain boundaries

Active Directory uses Kerberos security for server-to-server authentication and the establishment of trusts, while allowing legacy clients and servers on the network to use NTLM if necessary. Figure 25-12 shows a one-way trust in which one domain is the trusted domain and the other domain is the trusting domain. Typically, you implement one-way trusts when you have separate account and resource domains. The establishment of the trust allows users in the account domain to access resources in the resource domain.

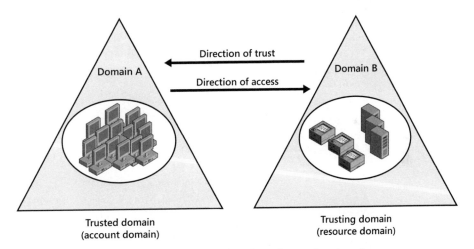

**Figure 25-12** One-way trust with a trusted domain and a trusting domain.

## Two-way transitive trusts

With Active Directory, trusts are automatically configured between all the domains in a forest and are implemented as two-way, transitive trusts. As a result, if the domains shown in Figure 25-12 were domains in the same forest, users in domain A can automatically access resources in domain B and users in domain B can automatically access resources in domain A. Because the trusts are automatically established between all domains in the forest, no setup is involved and there are many more design options for implementing Active Directory domains.

As trusts join parent and child domains in the same domain tree and join the roots of domain trees, the structure of trusts in a forest can be referred to as a *trust tree*. When a user tries to access a resource in another domain, the trust tree is used, and the user's request has to pass through one domain controller for each domain between the user and the resource. This type of authentication takes place across domain boundaries. Authentication across domain boundaries also applies when a user with an account in one domain visits another domain in the forest and tries to log on to the network from that domain.

Consider the example shown in Figure 25-13. If a user from domain G visits domain K and tries to log on to the network, the user's computer must be able to connect to a domain controller in domain K. Here, the user's computer sends the initial logon request to the domain K domain controller. When the domain controller receives the logon request, it determines that the user is located in domain G. The domain controller refers the request to a domain controller in the next domain in its trust tree, which in this case is domain J. A domain controller in domain J refers the request to domain I. A domain controller in domain I refers the request to domain H. This process continues through domains A, E, and F until the request finally gets to domain G.

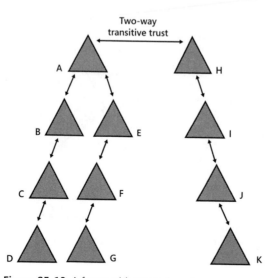

**Figure 25-13** A forest with many domains.

## Shortcut trusts

This rather lengthy referral process can be avoided if you establish an explicit trust between domain G and domain K as shown in Figure 25-14. Technically, explicit trusts are one-way transitive trusts, but you can establish a two-way explicit trust by creating two one-way trusts. Thus, unlike standard trusts within the trust tree, which are inherently two-way and transitive, explicit trusts can be made to be two-way if desired. Because they can be used to establish authentication shortcuts between domains, they are also referred to as *short-cut trusts*. In this example, it was decided to create two one-way trusts: one from domain G to domain K, and one from domain K to domain G. With these shortcut trusts in place, users in domain G could visit domain K and be rapidly authenticated and users in domain K could visit domain G and be rapidly authenticated.

If you examine the figure closely, you'll see that several other shortcut trusts were added to the forest as well. Shortcut trusts have been established between B and E and between E and I. Establishing the shortcut trusts in both directions allows for easy access to resources and rapid authentication in several combinations, such as the following:

- Using the B to E shortcut trust, users in domain B can rapidly access resources in domain E.

- Using the B to E and E to I shortcut trusts, users in domain B can also rapidly access resources in domain I.

- Using the B to E shortcut trust, users in domain B can visit domain E and be rapidly authenticated.

- Using the B to E and E to I shortcut trusts, users in domain B can visit domain I and be rapidly authenticated.

The trusts work similarly for users in domain E. Users in domain E have direct access to both domain B and domain I. Imagine that domain B is sales.cohovineyard.com, domain E is mf.cohovineyard.com, and domain I is cs.cohowinery.com, and you might be able to better picture how the shortcut trusts allow users to cut across trees in the Active Directory forest. I hope that you can also imagine how much planning should go into deciding your domain structure, especially when it comes to access to resources and authentication.

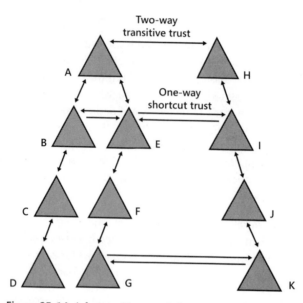

**Figure 25-14** A forest with several shortcut trusts.

# Authentication and trusts across forest boundaries

You can establish authentication and trusts across forest boundaries as well. One-way external trusts, such as the one depicted in Figure 25-15, are nontransitive. This means that if, as in the example, a trust is established between domain H and domain L only, a user in any domain in forest 1 could access a resource in domain L but not in any other domain in forest 2. The reason for this limitation is that the trust doesn't continue past domain L and it does not matter that a two-way transitive trust does exist between domain L and domain M or that a two-way trust also exists between domain L and domain O.

Windows Server supports cross-forest transitive trusts, also referred to simply as *forest trusts*. With this type of trust, you can establish a one-way or two-way transitive trust between forests to share resources and to authenticate users. With a two-way trust, as shown Figure 25-16, you enable cross-forest authentication and cross-forest authorization. Cross-forest trusts are supported when all domain controllers in all domains of both forests are running Windows Server 2003 or higher, and the forest is operating at the Windows Server 2003 or higher functional level.

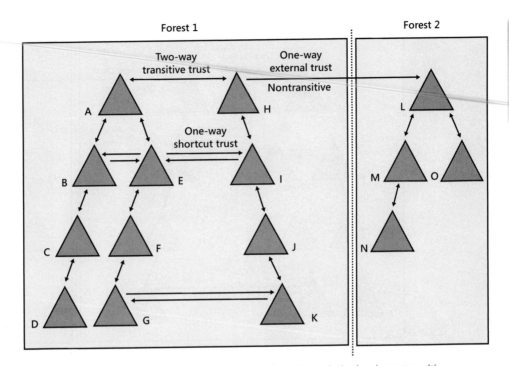

**Figure 25-15**  A one-way external trust that crosses forest boundaries but is nontransitive.

As discussed in "NTLM and Kerberos authentication" earlier in the chapter, Kerberos is the default authentication protocol, but NTLM can also be used. This allows current clients and servers as well as older clients and servers to be authenticated. After you establish a two-way cross-forest trust, users get all the benefits of Active Directory regardless of where they sign on to the network. With cross-forest authentication, you ensure secure access to resources when the user account is in one forest and the computer account is in another forest, and when the user in one forest needs access to network resources in another trusted forest. As part of cross-forest authorization, administrators can select users and global groups from trusted forests for inclusion in local groups. This ensures the integrity of the forest security boundary while allowing trust between forests.

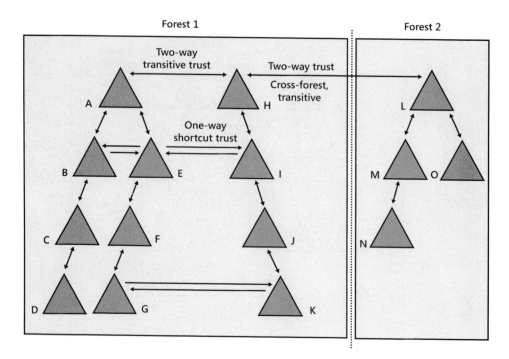

**Figure 25-16** A two-way transitive trust between forests.

When you connect two or more forests using cross-forest trusts, the implementation is referred to as a *federated forest design*. The federated forest design is most useful when you need to join two separate Active Directory structures—for example, when two companies merge, when one company acquires another, or when an organization has a major restructuring. Consider the case in which two companies merge and, rather than migrate their separate Active Directory structures into a single directory tree, the staff decides to link the two forests using cross-forest trusts. As long as the trusts are two-way, users in forest 1 can access resources in forest 2 and users in forest 2 can access resources in forest 1.

Having separate forests with cross-forest trusts between them is also useful when you want a division or group within the organization to have more autonomy but still have a link to the other divisions or groups. By placing the division or group in a separate forest, you ensure strict security and give that division or group ownership of the Active Directory structure. If users in the forest needed access to resources in another forest, you could establish a one-way cross-forest trust between the forests. This would allow users in the secured forest to gain access to resources in the second forest, but it would not allow users in the second forest to gain access to the secure forest.

Organizations that contain groups or divisions with high security requirements could use this approach. For example, consider Figure 25-17.

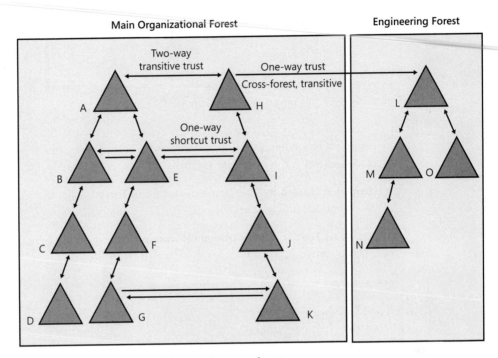

**Figure 25-17** A one-way transitive trust between forests.

In this situation, the users in the organization's Engineering department need access to resources in other departments, but for security reasons they should be isolated from the rest of the organization. Here, the organization has implemented two forests: a main organizational forest and a separate Engineering forest. Using a one-way, cross-forest trust from the main forest to the Engineering department forest, the organization allows Engineering users to access other resources, but it ensures that the Engineering department is secure and isolated.

## Examining domain and forest trusts

You can examine existing trusts using Active Directory Domains And Trusts. Start Active Directory Domains And Trusts by selecting the related option on the Tools menu in Server Manager. As shown in Figure 25-18, you see a list of available domains.

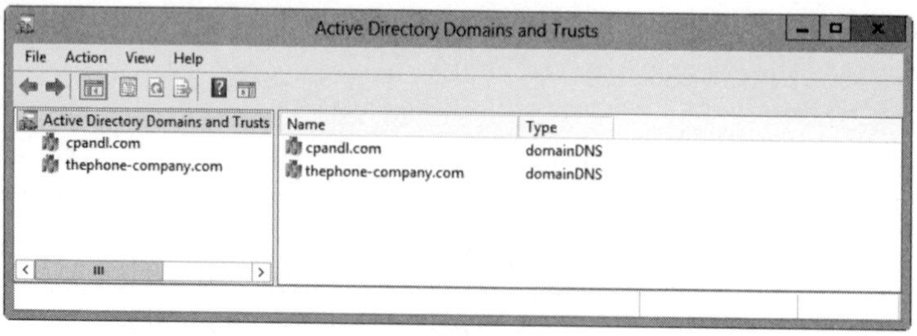

**Figure 25-18** Examine trusts in available domains.

To examine the existing trusts for a domain, press and hold or right-click the domain entry and then select Properties. Then, in the domain's Properties dialog box, tap or click the Trusts tab as shown in Figure 25-19. The Trusts tab is organized into two panels:

- **Domains Trusted By This Domain (Outgoing Trusts)**  Lists the domains that this domain trusts (the trusted domains)

- **Domains That Trust This Domain (Incoming Trusts)**  Lists the domains that trust this domain (the trusting domains)

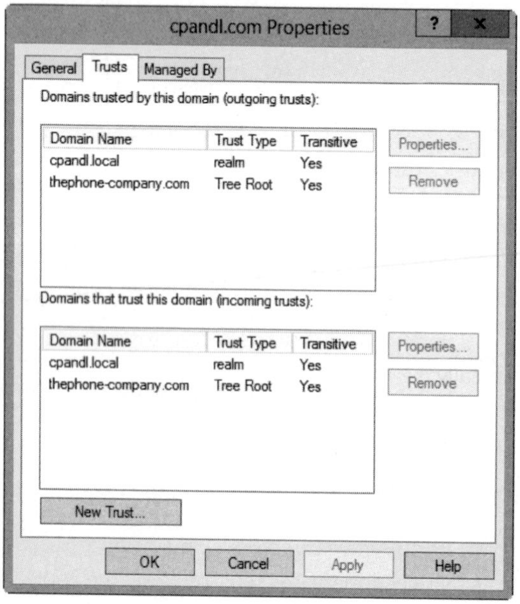

**Figure 25-19** Examine the existing trusts of a domain.

To view the details of a particular trust, select it and then tap or click Properties. Figure 25-20 shows the trust's Properties dialog box.

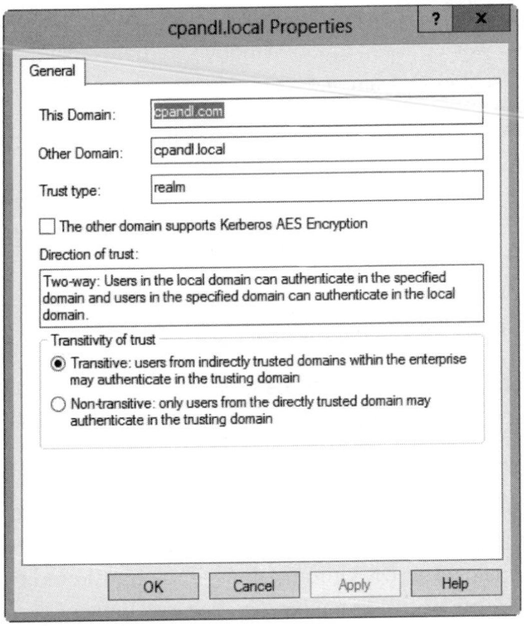

**Figure 25-20** Examine the details of an existing trust.

The Properties dialog box contains the following information:

- **This Domain**   The domain you are working with.

- **Other Domain**   The domain with which the trust is established.

- **Trust Type**   The type of trust. By default, two-way transitive trusts are created automatically when a new domain is added to a new domain tree within the forest or a subdomain of a root domain. There are two default trust types: Tree Root and Parent And Child. When a new domain tree is added to the forest, the default trust that is established automatically is a tree-root trust. When a new domain is a subdomain of a root domain, the default trust that is established automatically is a parent and child trust. Other trust types that might appear include the following:

  - External, which is a one-way or two-way nontransitive trust used to provide access to resources in a domain or to a domain in a separate forest that is not joined by a forest trust

  - Forest, which is a one-way or two-way transitive trust used to share resources between forests

○ Realm, which is a transitive or nontransitive trust that can be established as one way or two way between a non-Windows Kerberos realm and a Windows Server 2008 or higher domain

○ Shortcut, which is a one-way or two-way transitive trust used to speed up authentication and resource access between domain trees

- **Direction Of Trust**   The direction of the trust. All default trusts are established as two-way trusts. This means that users in the domain you are working with can authenticate in the other domain and users from the other domain can authenticate in the domain you are working with.

- **Transitivity Of Trust**   The transitivity of the trust. All default trusts are transitive, which means that users from indirectly trusted domains can authenticate in the other domain.

When setting up trusts, don't forget about the role of DNS in the trusts. The domain controllers in the domains must have access to DNS information about the domain controllers in the other domains. This DNS information can be transferred to the domain's DNS server as a secondary zone, or conditional forwarding can be configured.

## Establishing external, shortcut, realm, and cross-forest trusts

All trusts, regardless of type, are established in the same way. For all trusts, there are two sides: an incoming trust and an outgoing trust. To configure both sides of the trust, keep the following in mind:

- For domain trusts, you need to use two accounts: one that is a member of the Domain Admins group in the first domain and one that is a member of the Domain Admins group in the second domain. If you don't have appropriate accounts in both domains, you can establish one side of the trust and allow another administrator in the other domain to establish the other side of the trust.

- For forest trusts, you need to use two accounts: one that is a member of the Enterprise Admins group in the first forest and one that is a member of the Enterprise Admins group in the second forest. If you don't have appropriate accounts in both forests, you can establish one side of the two-way trust and allow another administrator in the other forest to establish the other side of the trust.

- For realm trusts, you need to establish the trust separately for the Windows domain and for the Kerberos realm. If you don't have appropriate administrative access to both the Windows domain and the Kerberos realm, you can establish one side of the trust and allow another administrator to establish the other side of the trust.

To establish a trust, follow these steps:

1. In Active Directory Domains And Trusts, press and hold or right-click the domain for which you want to establish a one-way incoming trust, one-way outgoing trust, or two-way trust and then choose Properties. For a cross-forest trust, this must be the forest root domain in one of the participating forests.

2. In the domain Properties dialog box, tap or click the Trusts tab, and then tap or click the New Trust button. This starts the New Trust Wizard. Tap or click Next to skip the welcome page.

3. On the Trust Name page, specify the domain name of the other domain, as shown in Figure 25-21. For a cross-forest trust, this must be the name of the forest root domain in the other forest.

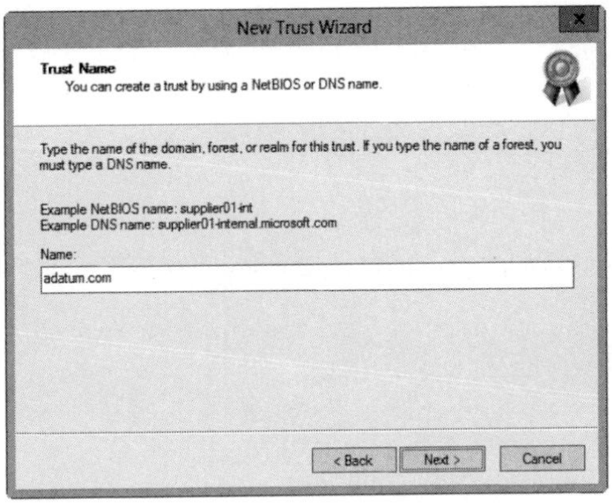

**Figure 25-21** Specify the name of the other domain.

4. When you tap or click Next, the wizard tries to establish a connection to the other domain. The options on the next page depend on whether you are connecting to a Windows domain, a Windows forest, or a non-Windows forest:

   ○ If the domain is determined to be a Windows forest, you have the option of creating an external trust that is nontransitive or a forest trust that is transitive. Choose either External Trust or Forest Trust, and then tap or click Next.

   ○ If the domain is determined to be a Windows domain, it is assumed that you are creating a shortcut trust, and the wizard goes directly to the Direction Of Trust page.

   ○ If the domain is determined to be a non-Windows domain, you have the option of creating a realm trust with a Kerberos version 5 realm. Select Realm Trust, and then, on the Transitivity Of Trust page, select either Nontransitive or Transitive and then tap or click Next.

5.  On the Direction Of Trust page, shown in Figure 25-22, choose the direction of the trust and then tap or click Next. The following options are available:

     ○ **Two-Way**   Users in the domain initially selected and in the designated domain can access resources in either domain or realm.

     ○ **One-Way: Incoming**   Users in the domain initially selected will be able to access resources in the designated domain. Users in the designated domain will not be able to access resources in the domain initially selected.

     ○ **One-Way: Outgoing**   Users in the designated domain will be able to access resources in the domain initially selected. Users in the domain initially selected will not be able to access resources in the designated domain.

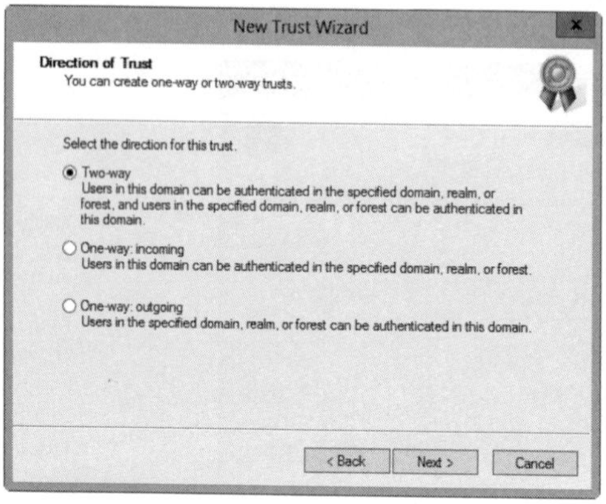

**Figure 25-22**  Choose the direction of trust.

6.  For shortcut or forest trusts, the next page you see is the Sides Of Trust page. To begin using a trust, you must create both sides of the trust. You have the option of setting the sides of the trust for This Domain Only or for Both This Domain And The Specified Domain:

     ○ If you are creating only one side of the trust, select This Domain Only and then tap or click Next.

     ○ If you are setting both sides of the trust or the administrator from the other domain is at your desk, select Both This Domain And The Specified Domain and then tap or click Next. When prompted, type (or let the other administrator type) the name and password of an appropriate account in the other domain or forest, and then tap or click OK.

7.  On the Trust Password page, shown in Figure 25-23, type and then confirm the initial password you want to use for the trust. The password is arbitrary but must follow the

strong security rules, meaning that it must have at least eight characters, contain a combination of uppercase and lowercase characters, and contain either numerals or special characters.

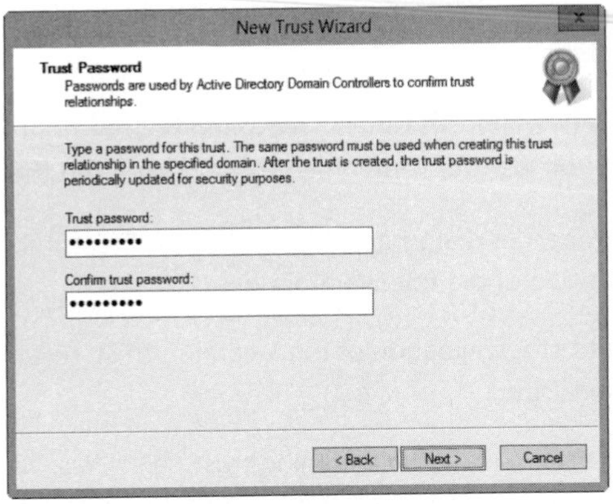

**Figure 25-23** Set the initial password for the trust.

---

## INSIDE OUT You might need the password

The trust password you use must be the same for both the domain initially selected and the specified domain, so be sure to write down the password so that you can use it when configuring the other side of the trust. After you create the trust, Active Directory periodically updates the password, using an automatic password reset. This helps safeguard the integrity of the trust.

---

8. For domain or realm trusts, tap or click Next twice to begin the trust creation process.

9. For forest trusts, you can set the outgoing trust authentication level as either Domain-Wide Authentication or Selective Authentication. With domain-wide authentication, users in the trusted domain can be authenticated to use all the resources in the trusting domain (and any trusted domains). This means that authentication is automatic for all users. With Selective Authentication, only the users or groups to which you explicitly grant permission can access resources in the trusting domain. This means that authentication is not automatic and you will need to grant individual access to each server that you want to make available to users in the trusting domain. Tap or click Next twice.

10. After the trust is created, you are given the opportunity to verify the trust.

## Verifying and troubleshooting trusts

By default, Windows validates all incoming trusts automatically. If the credentials used to establish the trust are no longer valid, the trust fails verification. If you want to revalidate a trust by providing new credentials or to specify that incoming trusts should not be validated, follow these steps:

1.  In Active Directory Domains And Trusts, press and hold or right-click the trusted domain for which you want to verify the incoming trust and then select Properties.

2.  In the domain's Properties dialog box, tap or click the Trusts tab, and then tap or click Validate and select one of the following options:

    ○ If you want to stop validation of the incoming trust, select No, Do Not Validate The Incoming Trust.

    ○ If you want to revalidate the incoming trust, select Yes, Validate The Incoming Trust and then type the user account and password for an administrator account in the other (trusting) domain.

3.  Tap or click OK. For a two-way trust, repeat this procedure for the other (trusting) domain.

You might want to revalidate trusts or specify that incoming trusts should not be validated for the following reasons:

● If clients are unable to access resources in a domain outside the forest, the external trust between the domains might have failed. In this case, you should verify the trust for the trusted domain. Note that a primary domain controller (PDC) emulator must be available to reset and verify the external trust.

● If clients or servers get trust errors within an Active Directory forest, there could be several causes. The time on the clients or servers trying to authenticate might be more than five minutes off, which is the default maximum time difference allowed for Kerberos authentication. In this case, synchronize the time on the clients and servers. The problem could also be that the domain controller might be down or the trust relationship could be broken. For the latter case, you can run NETDOM to verify or reset the trust.

# Delegating authentication

The delegation of authentication is often a requirement when a network service is distributed across several servers, such as when the organization uses web-based application services with front-end and back-end servers. In this environment, a client connects to the front-end servers and the user's credentials might need to be passed to back-end servers to ensure that the user gets access only to information to which she has been granted access.

## Delegated authentication essentials

Delegated authentication is provided via Kerberos using either proxy tickets or forwarded tickets:

- With proxy tickets, the client sends a session ticket request to a domain controller acting as a KDC, asking for access to the back-end server. The KDC grants the session ticket request and sends the client a session ticket with a PROXIABLE flag set. The client can then send this ticket to the front-end server, and the front-end server, in turn, uses this ticket to access information on the back-end server. In this configuration, the client needs to know the name of the back-end server, which in some cases is problematic—particularly if you need to maintain strict security for the back-end databases and don't want their integrity to be compromised.

- With forwarding tickets, the client sends an initial authorization request to the KDC, requesting a session ticket that the front-end server will be able to use to access the back-end servers. The KDC grants the session ticket request and sends it to the client. The client can then send the ticket to the front-end server, which then uses the session ticket to make a network resource request on behalf of the client. The front-end server then gets a session ticket to access the back-end server using the client's credentials.

You also can use *constrained delegation*. Constrained delegation allows you to configure accounts so that they are delegated only for specific purposes. This kind of delegation is based on service principal names, and a front-end server can access only network resources for which delegation has been granted.

## Configuring delegated authentication

To use delegated authentication, the user account (as well as the service or computer account acting on the user's behalf) must be configured to support delegated authentication.

### Configuring the delegated user account

For the user account, you must ensure that the account option Account Is Sensitive And Cannot Be Delegated is not selected, which by default it isn't. If you want to check this option, use Active Directory Users And Computers, as shown in Figure 25-24. Double-tap or double-click the user's account entry in Active Directory Users And Computers, and then tap or click the Account tab. You'll find the Account Is Sensitive And Cannot Be Delegated check box under Account Options. Scroll through the list until you find it.

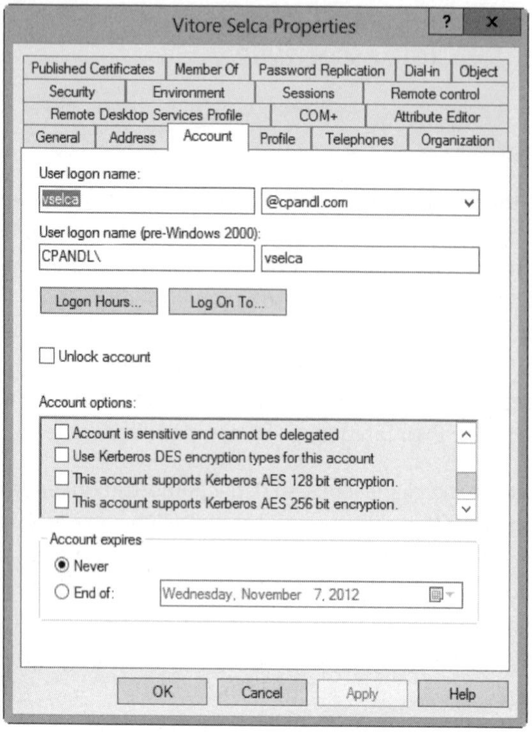

**Figure 25-24**  Configure delegated authentication.

## Configuring the delegated service or computer account

For the service acting on the user's behalf, you must first determine if the service is running under a normal user account or under a special identity, such as LocalSystem. If the service runs under a normal user account, check the account in Active Directory Users And Computers and ensure that the Account Is Sensitive And Cannot Be Delegated check box is not selected. If the service runs under a special identity, you need to configure delegation for the computer account of the front-end server.

In Active Directory Users And Computers, double-tap or double-click the computer account to display its Properties dialog box, and then tap or click the Delegation tab, as shown in Figure 25-25.

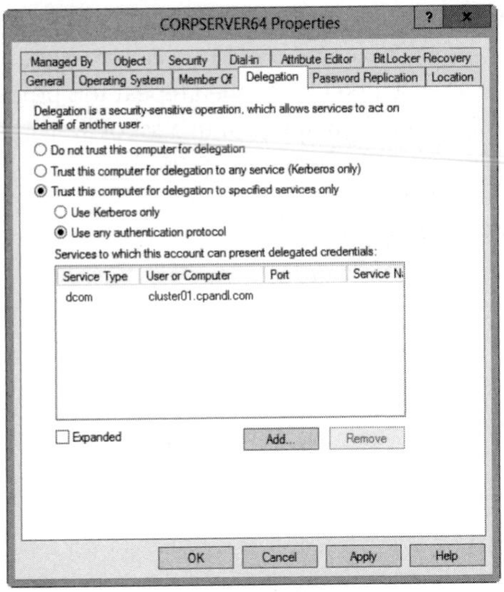

**Figure 25-25**  Configure the delegated service.

You have the following options for configuring a computer for delegation:

- **Do Not Trust This Computer For Delegation**   Select this option if you don't want the computer to be trusted for delegation.

- **Trust This Computer For Delegation To Any Service (Kerberos Only)**   Select this option to use the legacy client level of authentication, which allows the service to make requests for any network resources on the client's behalf.

- **Trust This Computer For Delegation To Specified Services Only**   Select this option to use the Windows Server 2008 and higher levels of authentication, which allows the service to make requests only for specified services. You can then specify whether the client must authenticate using Kerberos only or can use any authentication protocol.

When you are using the Windows Server 2008 and higher levels of authentication, you must next specify the services to which the front-end server can present a client's delegated credentials. To do this, you need to know the name of the computers running the services and the types of services you are authorizing. Tap or click Add to display the Add Services dialog box, and then tap or click Users Or Computers to display the Select Users Or Computers dialog box.

In the Select Users Or Computers dialog box, type the name of the computer providing the service, such as **CORPSVR02**, and then tap or click Check Names. If multiple matches are found, select the name or names you want to use and then tap or click OK. If no matches are found, you either entered an incorrect name or you're working with an incorrect location. Modify the name and try again, or tap or click Locations to select a new location. To add additional computers, type a semicolon (;), and then repeat this process. When you tap or click OK, the Add Services dialog box is updated with a list of available services on the selected computer or computers, as shown in Figure 25-26.

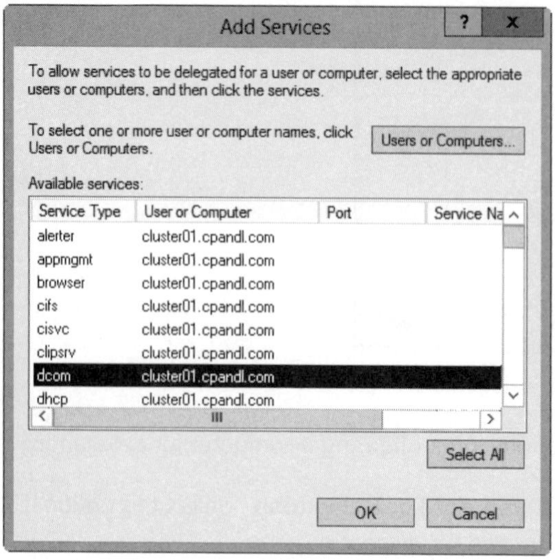

**Figure 25-26** The Add Services dialog box will update with a list of available services for the selected computer or computers.

Use the Add Services dialog box to select the services for which you are authorizing delegated authentication. You can use Shift+click or Ctrl+click to select multiple services. After you select the appropriate services, tap or click OK. The selected services are added to the Services To Which This Account Can Present Delegated Credentials list. Tap or click OK to close the computer's Properties dialog box and save the delegation changes.

# Design considerations for Active Directory operations masters

The multimaster replication model of Active Directory creates a distributed environment that allows any domain controller to be used for authentication and allows you to make changes to standard directory information without regard to which domain controller you use. The approach works well for most Active Directory operations—but not all. Some Active Directory operations can be performed only by a single authoritative domain controller called an *operations master*.

# Operations master roles

A designated operations master has a flexible single-master operations (FSMO) role. The five designated roles are

- Schema master

- Domain naming master

- Relative ID (RID) master

- PDC emulator

- Infrastructure master

As depicted in Figure 25-27, two of the roles—schema master and domain naming master—are assigned on a per-forest basis. This means that there is only one schema master and only one domain naming master in a forest. The other three roles—RID master, PDC emulator, and infrastructure master—are assigned on a per-domain basis. For each domain in the forest, there is only one of these operations master roles.

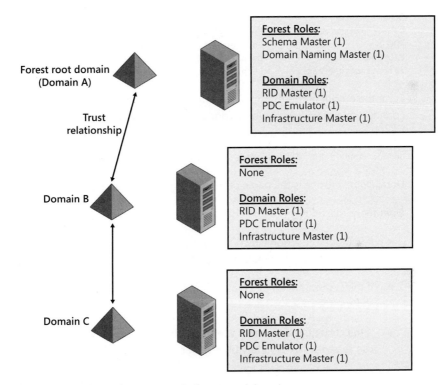

**Figure 25-27** Operations masters in forests and domains.

When you install Active Directory and create the first domain controller in a new forest, all five roles are assigned to that domain controller. As you add domains, the first domain controller you install in a domain is automatically designated the RID master, infrastructure master, and PDC emulator for that domain.

As part of domain design, you should consider how many domain controllers you need per domain, and whether you need to transfer operations master roles after you install new domain controllers. In all cases, you'll want to have at least two domain controllers in each domain in the forest. The reasons for transferring the operations master roles depend on several factors. First, you might want to transfer an operations master role to improve performance, as you might do when a server has too heavy a workload and you need to distribute some of the load. Second, you might need to transfer an operations master role if you plan to take the server with that role offline for maintenance or if the server fails.

You can determine the current operations masters for your logon domain by typing the following at a command prompt:

```
netdom query fsmo
```

As shown here, the output lists each role owner by its fully qualified domain name:

```
Schema master            CorpServer26.cpandl.com
Domain naming master     CorpServer26.cpandl.com
PDC                      CorpServer32.tech.cpandl.com
RID pool manager         CorpServer32.tech.cpandl.com
Infrastructure master    CorpServer41.tech.cpandl.com
```

From the output in this example, you can also determine that the forest root domain is cpandl.com and the current logon domain is tech.cpandl.com. If you want to determine the operations masters for a specific domain, use the following command:

```
netdom query fsmo /d:DomainName
```

Here, *DomainName* is the name of the domain, such as eng.cpandl.com.

Operations master roles can be changed in several ways:

- If you demote a domain controller acting as an operations master, any operations master roles are automatically transferred to other domain controllers.

- If the current operations master is online, you can perform a role transfer, gracefully shifting the role from one domain controller to another.

- If the current operations master has failed and will not be coming back online, you can seize the role and forcibly transfer it to another domain controller.

# INSIDE OUT  Recommended placement of operations master roles

Microsoft recommends the following configuration:

- Ideally, you should place the forestwide roles, schema master and domain naming master, on the same domain controller. There is very little overhead associated with these roles, so placement on the same server adds very little load overall. However, you must safeguard this server because these are critical roles in the forest. In addition, the server acting as the domain naming master should also be a global catalog server.

- Ideally, you should place the relative ID master and PDC emulator roles on the same domain controller. The reason for this is that the PDC emulator uses more relative IDs than most other domain controllers. If the relative ID master and PDC emulator roles aren't on the same domain controller, the domain controllers on which they are placed should be in the same Active Directory site, and the domain controllers should have a reliable connection between them.

- Ideally, you should not place the infrastructure master on a domain controller that is also a global catalog server. The reason for this is a bit complicated, and there are some important exceptions to note.

The infrastructure master is responsible for updating cross-domain group membership, and it determines whether its information is current or out of date by checking a global catalog and then replicating changes to other domain controllers as necessary. If the infrastructure master and the global catalog are on the same server, the infrastructure master doesn't see that changes have been made and thus doesn't replicate them.

The exceptions are for a single-domain forest or a multidomain forest where all domain controllers are global catalog servers. In the case of a single domain forest, there are no cross-group references to update, so it doesn't matter where the infrastructure master is located. In the case of a multidomain forest where all domain controllers are global catalog servers, all the domain controllers know about all the objects in the forest already, so the infrastructure master doesn't really have to make updates.

## Using, locating, and transferring the schema master role

The schema master is the only domain controller in the forest with a writeable copy of the schema container. This means that it is the only domain controller in the forest on which you can make changes to the schema. You make changes to the schema using the Active Directory Schema snap-in. When you start the Active Directory Schema snap-in, it makes a direct connection to the schema master, allowing you to view the schema for the directory.

To make changes to the schema, however, you must use an account that is a member of the Schema Admins group.

By default, the schema master is the first domain controller installed in the forest root domain. You can transfer this role using the Active Directory Schema snap-in or the NTDSUTIL command-line utility.

To locate the schema master, open the Active Directory Schema snap-in in a custom console. Press and hold or right-click the Active Directory Schema node, and then select Operations Master. The Change Schema Master dialog box, shown in Figure 25-28, shows the current schema master.

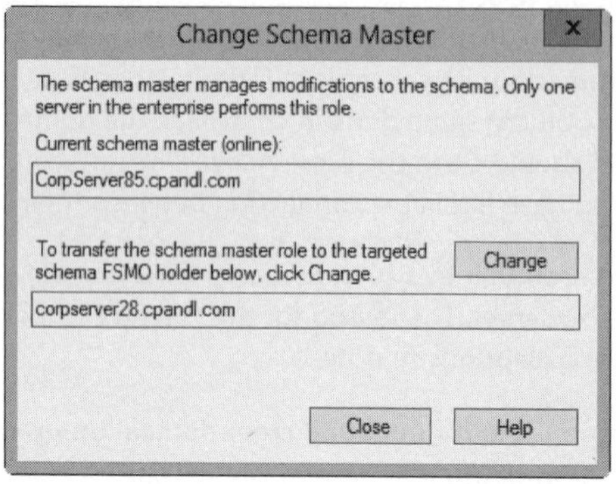

**Figure 25-28** View the current schema master.

To transfer the schema master role to another server, follow these steps:

1. Open the Active Directory Schema snap-in in a custom console. Press and hold or right-click the Active Directory Schema node, and then select Change Active Directory Domain Controller.

2. In the Change Directory Server dialog box, select This Domain Controller and then select the forest root domain name in the Look In This Domain list. Next, select an available domain controller to which you want to transfer the role, and then tap or click OK.

3. In the Change Directory Server dialog box, select This Domain Controller. Next, tap or click the domain controller to which you want to transfer the schema master role, and then tap or click OK.

4. Press and hold or right-click the Active Directory Schema node, and then select Operations Master. In the Change Schema Master dialog box, tap or click Change. When prompted to confirm, tap or click Yes, and then tap or click Close.

# Using, locating, and transferring the domain naming master role

The domain naming master is responsible for adding or removing domains from the forest. Any time you create a domain, a remote procedure call (RPC) connection is made to the domain naming master, which assigns the domain a globally unique identifier (GUID). Any time you remove a domain, an RPC connection is made to the domain naming master and the previously assigned GUID reference is removed. If you cannot connect to the domain naming master when you are trying to add or remove a domain, you will not be able to create or remove the domain.

To locate the domain naming master, start Active Directory Domains And Trusts. Press and hold or right-click the Active Directory Domains And Trusts node, and then select Operations Master. The Operations Master dialog box, shown in Figure 25-29, shows the current domain naming master:

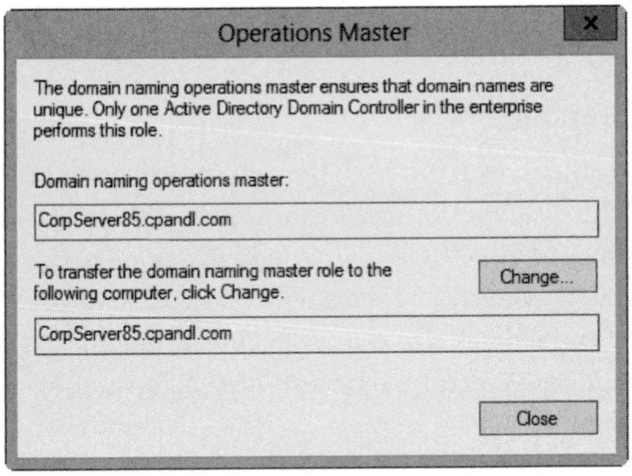

**Figure 25-29** View the current domain naming operations master.

To transfer the domain naming master role to another server, follow these steps:

1.  In Active Directory Domains And Trusts, press and hold or right-click the Active Directory Domains And Trusts node and then select Change Active Directory Domain Controller.

2.  In the Change Directory Server dialog box, select This Domain Controller and then select the forest root domain name in the Look In This Domain list. Next, select an available domain controller to which you want to transfer the role, and then tap or click OK.

3.  Press and hold or right-click the Active Directory Domains And Trusts node, and then select Operations Master. In the Change Operations Master dialog box, tap or click Change. When prompted to confirm, tap or click Yes, and then tap or click Close.

## Using, locating, and transferring the relative ID master role

The relative ID (RID) master controls the creation of new security principals—such as users, groups, and computers—throughout its related domain. Every domain controller in a domain is issued a block of relative IDs by the RID master. These relative IDs are used to build the security IDs that uniquely identify security principals in the domain. The actual security ID generated by a domain controller consists of a domain identifier, which is the same for every object in a domain, and a unique relative ID that differentiates the object from any other objects in the domain. The block of relative IDs issued to a domain controller is called a *RID pool*. Typically, blocks of relative IDs are issued in lots of 500. When the RID pool on a domain controller is nearly exhausted, the domain controller requests a new block of 500 RIDs. It is the job of the RID master to issue blocks of RIDs, and it does so as long as it is up and running. If a domain controller cannot connect to the RID master and for any reason runs outs of RIDs, no new objects can be created on the domain controller and object creation will fail. To resolve this problem, the RID master must be made available or the RID master role must be transferred to another server.

## INSIDE OUT  Size the RID pool

Size the RID pool by editing the registry on each domain controller and changing the REG_DWORD value of the RID Block Size value located in HKLM\System\ CurrentControlSet\Services\NTDS\RID Values. For Windows Server 2012, the maximum RID pool block size is 15,000. Previously, the maximum was 10,000. If you enter a value greater than 15,000, the RID pool block size will be 15,000. Additionally, an error with event ID 16653 and the source as Directory-Services-SAM will be logged each time you start the domain controller.

Because relative IDs are not re-used and there is a finite number of them available for assignment throughout the lifetime of a domain, older enterprise environments could run out of relative IDs. RID pool exhaustion can seriously affect the domain because no new objects can be created. In an Active Directory domain, $2^{30} - 1$ (1,073,741,823) RIDs are available. Although approximately 1 billion objects sounds like a lot, RIDs could be leaked and lost in earlier releases of Windows Server. If an RID was taken from an RID pool to create an object but the object creation failed, the RID was not available for re-use. If a deleted Domain Controller computer object was restored, the domain controller could repeatedly request a new RID pool block because of a missing *rIDSetReference* attribute and, by itself, could use up the RID pool in about 24 months. Windows Server 2012 resolves these and other identified problems that could lead to faster-than-normal depletion of the RID pool.

Some of these problems are resolved with the newly implemented RID Reuse pool. When object creation fails, the RID, instead of being leaked and lost, is placed in the Reuse pool. Because a domain controller checks the Reuse pool prior for available RIDs before taking an RID from the primary pool, the RID can be assigned to the next object created on that domain controller. Keep in mind, however, that rebooting a domain controller clears its RID Reuse pool.

Because the RID master can run out of assigned addresses in its global RID pool space, Windows Server 2012 issues periodic RID consumption warnings and also has a soft ceiling for the RID pool. When 10 percent of the global address space is used, the RID master logs an informational event with an RID consumption warning. The RID master logs another RID consumption warning when 10 percent of the remainder is used, and so on so that the RID consumption warnings become more frequent as more and more of the global space is depleted. The soft ceiling is reached when 90 percent of the available address space is used. As a result, the RID master will not allocate any additional blocks of RIDs until the soft ceiling is removed.

Using Dcdiag, you can check the number of RIDs available by entering the following at a command prompt on the RID master for the domain:

```
dcdiag /test:ridmanager /v | find /i "Available RID Pool"
```

The output will show the available RIDs and be similar to the following:

```
* Available RID Pool for the Domain is 480678 to 1073741823
```

From this output, you know the number of available RIDs and can infer the number of RIDs that have been used. Here, 480,677 RIDs have been used and 1,073,261,146 RIDs are available. That's 480,678 minus 1 to determine the number of RIDs that have been used and 1,073,741,823 minus 480,677 to determine the number of RIDs available.

If a domain's RID master is running Windows Server 2012, you can double the size of the RID pool by enabling SID compatibility. Enabling SID compatibility unlocks the 31st bit of the RID pool, which effectively raises the total number of RIDs available for a domain to $2^{31} - 1$ (2,147,483,647) or approximately 2 billion objects. Set the *sidCompatibilityVersion* property on the RID master to 1 to unlock the 31st bit and enable SID compatibility. However, before you implement this change, you must ensure that all other domain controllers in the domain are also running Windows Server 2012 or that domain controllers running earlier versions of Windows Server have updates applied to ensure compatibility with this change.

# INSIDE OUT Removing the soft ceiling on the RID pool

Active Directory blocks further allocations from the global RID pool by setting the *msDS-RIDPoolAllocationEnabled* attribute of the RID *Manager$* object to FALSE. To enable the RID master to allocate blocks of RIDs from the global space, you must set the *msDS-RIDPoolAllocationEnabled* attribute to TRUE.

You can modify the *msDS-RIDPoolAllocationEnabled* attribute using ADSI Edit or Ldp .exe. This value is set on a per-domain basis. ADSI Edit is a snap-in for MMC. Open a new MMC by typing **MMC** at a prompt and then use the Add/Remove Snap-in option on the File menu to add the ADSI Edit snap-in to the MMC. In ADSI Edit, press and hold or right-click the root node and then select Connect To. In the Connection Settings dialog box, choose the Select A Well Known Naming Context option. On the related selection list, select Default Naming Context and then tap or click OK. In ADSI Edit, work your way down to the CN=System container by expanding the Default naming context and the domain container. With the CN=System container selected in the left pane, press and hold or right-click CN=RID Manager$ and then select Properties. In the Properties dialog box, select the *msDS-RIDPoolAllocationEnabled* property and then tap or click Edit. In the Boolean Attribute Editor dialog box, select True, and then tap or click OK twice.

Ldp is a graphical utility. Open Ldp by typing **ldp** in the Apps Search box or at a prompt. In Ldp, select Connect on the Connection menu to connect to a domain controller in the domain you want to work with. After you connect to a domain controller, select Bind on the Connection menu to bind to the domain using an account with domain administrator privileges. Next, select Tree on the View menu to open the Tree View dialog box. In the Tree View dialog box, use domain container as the base distinguished name to work with. In the domain container, expand the CN=System container. Next, press and hold or right-click CN=RID Manager$ and then select Modify. In the Modify dialog box, type **msDS-RIDPoolAllocationEnabled** in the Edit Entry Attribute box and then type **True** in the Values box. Because the attribute should already exist, set the Operation value as Replace. Tap or click Enter to create an LDAP transaction for this update, and then tap or click Run to apply the change.

In Ldp, select Connect on the Connection menu to connect to the RID master for the domain you want to work with. After you connect to the RID master, select Bind on the Connection menu to bind to the domain using an account with domain administrator privileges. Next, select Modify on the Browse menu to open the Modify dialog box. Type **sidCompatibilityVersion** in the Edit Entry Attribute box. Type **1** in the Values box. Because the attribute shouldn't already exist set the Operation value as Add. Tap or click Enter to create an LDAP transaction for this update. Ensure Synchronous is selected as an option, and then tap or click Run to apply the change.

To locate the RID master, start Active Directory Users And Computers. Press and hold or right-click the domain you want to work with, and then select Operations Masters. The Operations Masters dialog box, shown in Figure 25-30, shows the current RID master on the RID tab.

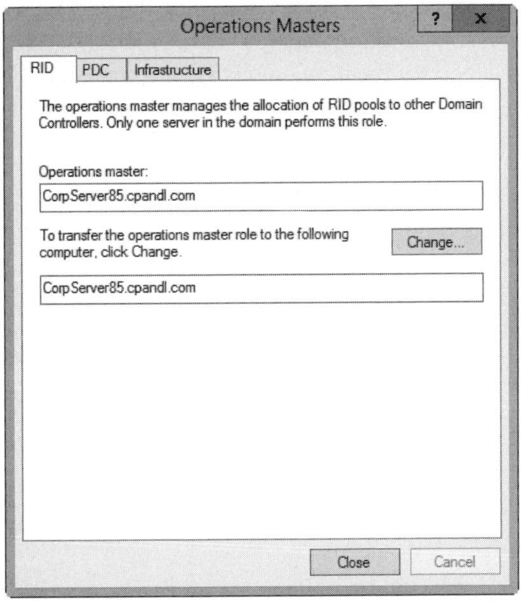

**Figure 25-30** View the current RID master.

To transfer the RID master role to another server, follow these steps:

1.  In Active Directory Users And Computers, press and hold or right-click the domain node and then select Change Domain Controller. In the Change Directory Server dialog box, select This Domain Controller, select an available domain controller to which you want to transfer the role, and then tap or click OK.

2.  Press and hold or right-click the domain node again, and then select Operations Masters. In the Operations Masters dialog box, the RID tab is selected by default. Tap or click Change. When prompted to confirm, tap or click Yes, and then tap or click Close.

# Using, locating, and transferring the PDC emulator role

The PDC emulator role is responsible for processing password changes and also is the default authoritative time server in the forest. All domain controllers in a domain know which server has the PDC emulator role.

When a user changes a password, the change is first sent to the PDC emulator, which in turn replicates the change to all the other domain controllers in the domain. If a user tries to log on to the network but provides an incorrect password, the domain controller checks the PDC emulator to see that it has a recent password change for this account. If so, the domain controller retries the logon authentication on the PDC emulator. This approach is designed to ensure that if a user has recently changed a password, he is not denied logon with the new password.

Because the PDC emulator is the default time server for the forest, other computers on the network rely on the PDC emulator for time synchronization. To ensure that time synchronization is accurate in the Active Directory forest, you should configure the PDC emulator to synchronize time with a reliable external time source, a reliable internal time source, or a hardware clock. If you want the PDC emulator to use a Network Time Protocol (NTP) time source, type the following at an elevated command prompt:

```
w32tm /config /computer:PDCName /manualpeerlist:time.windows.com
/syncfromflags:manual /update
```

Here, *PDCName* is the fully qualified domain name of the PDC emulator and the */ManualPeerList* option configures the PDC emulator to get its time from *time.windows .com*. Here is an example:

```
w32tm /config /computer:dc05.cpandl.com /manualpeerlist:time.windows.com
/syncfromflags:manual /update
```

If you configured a reliable time server in the forest root domain, you can configure the PDC emulator master to synchronize with this server instead by typing

```
w32tm /config /computer:PDCName /syncfromflags:domhier /update
```

Here, the */SyncFromFlags* option configures the PDC emulator to get its time synchronization information from the forest root domain hierarchy.

> **Important**
>
> The first domain controller to hold the PDC emulator role is the default authoritative time server for the forest. If the PDC emulator role is moved to a new domain controller, the time server role doesn't move automatically to the new domain controller. In this case, you must configure the Windows Time service for the new PDC emulator master role holder and reconfigure the original PDC emulator master role holder to synchronize from the domain and not from an external or internal time source.

Domain computers on the network don't necessarily get their time directly from the PDC emulator. Generally, domain computers follow the directory hierarchy and synchronize time with a domain controller in their local domains. Domain controllers synchronize their time using a series of queries that help them determine the best time source. A domain controller will make up to six queries:

1. The domain controller queries for parent domain controllers in the same site.

2. The domain controller queries for other domain controllers in the same site.

3. The domain controller queries for a same-site PDC emulator.

4. The domain controller queries for parent domain controllers in other sites.

5. The domain controller queries for other domain controllers in other sites.

6. The domain controller queries for a PDC emulator in other sites.

> **Note**
>
> Parent domain controllers prefer reliable time sources but can also synchronize with nonreliable time sources if that is all that is available. Local domain controllers synchronize only with reliable time sources. Reliable time sources can synchronize only with domain controllers in the parent domain. The PDC emulator can synchronize with a reliable time source in its own domain or any domain controller in the parent domain.

Each query returns a list of domain controllers that can be used as a time source and a relative weighting for each based on reliability and location. A score of 8 is assigned to a domain controller in the same site. A score of 4 is assigned to a domain controller configured as a reliable time source. A score for 2 is assigned to a domain controller in a parent domain. A score of 1 is used for a domain controller that is the PDC emulator. Because the weighting scores are cumulative, a same-site PDC emulator would have a score of 9 (8 + 1).

To locate the PDC emulator, start Active Directory Users And Computers. Press and hold or right-click the domain you want to work with, and then select Operations Masters. The Operations Masters dialog box shows the current PDC emulator on the PDC tab.

To transfer the PDC emulator role to another server, follow these steps:

1. In Active Directory Users And Computers, press and hold or right-click the domain node and then select Change Domain Controller. In the Change Directory Server dialog box, select This Domain Controller, select an available domain controller to which you want to transfer the role, and then tap or click OK.

2. Press and hold or right-click the domain node again, and then select Operations Master. In the Operations Masters dialog box, click the PDC tab. Tap or click Change. When prompted to confirm, tap or click Yes, and then tap or click Close.

## Using, locating, and transferring the infrastructure master role

The infrastructure master is responsible for updating cross-domain, group-to-user references. This means that the infrastructure master is responsible for ensuring that changes to the common name of a user account are correctly reflected in the group membership information for groups in other domains in the forest. The infrastructure master does this by comparing its directory data to that of a global catalog. If the data is outdated, it updates the data and replicates the changes to other domain controllers in the domain. If for some reason the infrastructure master is unavailable, group-to-user name references will not be updated, and cross-domain group membership might not accurately reflect the actual names of user objects.

To locate the infrastructure master, start Active Directory Users And Computers. Press and hold or right-click the domain you want to work with, and then select Operations Masters. The Operations Masters dialog box shows the current infrastructure master on the Infrastructure tab.

To transfer the infrastructure master role to another server, follow these steps:

1. In Active Directory Users And Computers, press and hold or right-click the domain node and then select Change Domain Controller. In the Change Directory Server dialog box, select This Domain Controller, select an available domain controller to which you want to transfer the role, and then tap or click OK.

2. Press and hold or right-click the domain node again, and then select Operations Masters. In the Operations Masters dialog box, click the Infrastructure tab. Tap or click Change. When prompted to confirm, tap or click Yes, and then tap or click Close.

## Seizing operations master roles

When an operations master fails and is not coming back online, you need to seize the role to forcibly transfer it to another domain controller. Seizing a role is a drastic step that you should perform only when the previous role owner will never be available again. Don't seize an operations master role when you can transfer it gracefully using the normal transfer procedure. Only seize a role as a last resort.

Before you seize a role and forcibly transfer it, you should determine how up to date the domain controller that will take over the role is with respect to the previous role owner.

Active Directory tracks replication changes using update sequence numbers (USNs). Because of replication latency, domain controllers might not all be up to date. If you compare a domain controller's USN to that of other servers in the domain, you can determine whether the domain controller is the most up to date with respect to changes from the previous role owner. If the domain controller is up to date, you can transfer the role safely. If the domain controller isn't up to date, you can wait for replication to occur and then transfer the role to the domain controller.

For working with Active Directory replication, Windows Server includes Repadmin and Windows PowerShell cmdlets. To display the highest sequence number for a specified naming context on each replication partner of a designated domain controller, type the following at a command prompt:

```
repadmin /showutdvec DomainControllerName NamingContext
```

Here, *DomainControllerName* is the fully qualified domain name of the domain controller and *NamingContext* is the distinguished name of the domain in which the server is located, such as

```
repadmin /showutdvec corpserver52 dc=cpandl,dc=com
```

The output shows the highest USN on replication partners for the domain partition:

```
Main-Site\corpserver31    @ USN    678321 @ Time 2014-05-12 04:32:45
Main-Site\corpserver26    @ USN    681525 @ Time 2014-05-12 04:32:45
```

In this example, if CorpServer31 was the previous role owner and the domain controller you are examining has an equal or larger USN for CorpServer31, the domain controller is up to date. However, if CorpServer31 was the previous role owner and the domain controller you are examining has a lower USN for CorpServer31, the domain controller is not up to date and you should wait for replication to occur before seizing the role. You could also use **Repadmin /Syncall** to force the domain controller that is the most up to date with respect to the previous role owner to replicate with all of its replication partners. Note that you can use **Repadmin /Replsingleobject** to replicate a specific object using its distinguished name.

With PowerShell, you can use the Get-AdReplicationUpToDatenessVectorTable cmdlet to display similar information about USNs. Simply follow the cmdlet name with the name of the domain controller to examine, such as

```
get-adreplicationuptodatenessvectortable corpserver85.cpandl.com
```

The output shows a list of the highest USNs seen by the specified domain controller for every domain controller in the forest. You also can use Sync-ADObject to replicate a specific object.

To seize an operations master role, follow these steps:

1. Open a command prompt on the console of the server you want to assign as the new operations master locally or via Remote Desktop.

2. List current operations masters by typing **netdom query fsmo**.

3. Type **ntdsutil**. At the ntdsutil prompt, type **roles**.

4. At the fsmo maintenance prompt, type **connections**.

5. At the server connections prompt, type **connect to server** followed by the fully qualified domain name of the domain controller to which you want to assign the operations master role.

6. After you establish a connection to the domain controller, type **quit** to exit the server connections prompt.

7. At the fsmo maintenance prompt, type one of the following:

   ○ seize pdc

   ○ seize rid master

   ○ seize infrastructure master

   ○ seize schema master

   ○ seize domain naming master

8. At the fsmo maintenance prompt, type **quit**.

9. At the ntdsutil prompt, type **quit**.

# Organizing Active Directory

WHETHER you are implementing a new Active Directory environment or updating your existing environment, there's a lot to think about when it comes to design. Every Active Directory design is built from the same basic building blocks. These basic building blocks include the following:

- **Domains**   A domain is a logical grouping of objects that allows for central management and control over the replication of those objects. Every organization has at least one domain, which is implemented when Active Directory is installed on the first domain controller.

- **Domain Trees**   A domain tree is a single domain in a unique namespace or a group of domains that share the same namespace. The domain at the top of a domain tree is referred to as the *root domain*. Two-way transitive trusts join parent and child domains in the same domain tree.

- **Forests**   A forest is a single domain tree or a group of domain trees that are grouped together to share resources. The first domain created in a new forest is referred to as the *forest root domain*. Domain trees in a forest have two-way transitive trusts between their root domains.

Many organizations have only one domain, and although I'll discuss reasons why you might want to have additional domains, domain trees, and forests in this chapter, you might also want to add structure to a domain. The building block you use to add structure to a domain is the organizational unit (OU), which I'll discuss in depth in this chapter.

# Creating an Active Directory implementation or update plan

Creating or modifying an existing domain and forest plan is the single most important design decision you make when implementing Active Directory. As such, this isn't a decision you should make alone. When you design Active Directory for an organization of any size, you should get the organization's management involved in the high-level design process.

*Involvement* doesn't mean letting other groups decide on all aspects of the design. There are many complex components that all have to fit together, and the actual implementation of Active Directory should be the responsibility of the IT group. Involvement means getting feedback from and working with the business managers of other groups to ensure that the high-level design meets their business requirements.

In addition, you almost certainly need to get approval for the high-level design goals with regard to security, access, usability, and manageability. Keep this in mind as you are developing the initial implementation plan. Your plan should start with the highest-level objects and work toward the lowest-level objects. This means that you must do the following:

1. Develop a forest plan.

2. Develop a domain plan that supports the forest plan.

3. Develop an organizational unit plan that supports the domain and forest plans.

The sections that follow discuss how to develop the necessary plans. After you have completed the planning and the plans are approved, you can implement the plans.

As part of your Active Directory planning, you should keep in mind the planning strategies discussed in Chapter 1, "Introducing Windows Server 2012." This means your plan should meet or exceed your organization's service-level agreements (SLAs) and include the necessary hardware and network plans to make sure your implementation or upgrade is a success. For remote locations, such as branch offices, you should also determine whether read-only domain controllers (RODCs) are appropriate. RODCs are discussed in Chapter 29, "Deploying read-only domain controllers."

## Developing a forest plan

Forest planning involves developing a plan for the namespace and administration needs of the organization as a whole. As part of this planning, you should decide who are the owners of the forest or forests you intend to implement. From an administration standpoint, the owners of a forest are the users who are the members of the Schema Admins and Enterprise Admins groups of the forest, as well as users who are members of the Domain

Admins group in the root domain of the forest. Although these users have direct control over the forest structure, they typically don't make the final decisions when it comes to implementing forestwide changes. Typically, the final authority for making forestwide changes is an IT or business manager who is requesting changes based on a specific business need or requirement and acting after coordinating with business managers from other groups as necessary.

## Forest namespace

The top structure in any Active Directory implementation is the forest root domain. The forest root domain is established when you install Active Directory on the first domain controller in a new forest. Any time you add a new domain that is part of a different namespace to an existing forest, you establish a root domain for a new tree. The name given to a root domain—either the forest root domain itself or the root domain of a new tree in a forest—acts as the base name for all domains later created in that tree. As you add subsequent domains, the domains are added below an established root domain. This makes the domains child domains of a root domain. (See Figure 26-1.)

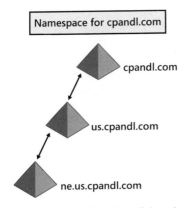

**Figure 26-1** A hierarchy of domains.

Regardless of whether your forest uses a single namespace or multiple namespaces, additional domains in the same forest have the following characteristics:

- **Share a common schema**   All domain controllers in the forest have the same schema, and a single schema master is designated for the forest.

- **Share a common configuration directory partition**   All domain controllers share the same configuration container, and it stores the default configuration and policy information.

Chapter 26

- **Share a common trust configuration**   All domains in the forest are configured to trust all the other domains in the forest, and the trust is two-way and transitive.

- **Share a common global catalog**   All domains in the forest have the same global catalog, and it stores a partial replica of all objects in the forest.

- **Share common forestwide administrators**   All domains in the forest have the same top-level administrators: Enterprise Admins and Schema Admins, who have the following roles:

  - Enterprise Admins are the only administrators with forest-level privileges, which let them add or remove domains. The Enterprise Admins group is also a member of the local Administrators group of each domain, so, by default, these users can manage any domain in the forest.

  - Schema Admins are the only administrators who have the right to modify the schema.

## A single forest vs. multiple forests

Part of creating a forest plan is deciding how many forests you need or whether you need additional forests. This isn't an easy decision or a decision that should be made lightly. With a single forest, you have a single top-level unit for sharing and managing resources. You can share information across all domains in the forest. However, this requires a great deal of trust and cooperation among all the groups in the organization.

With multiple forests, you change the dynamic considerably. You no longer have a single top-level unit for sharing and managing resources. You have separate structures that are fully autonomous and isolated from one another. The forests do not share schema, configuration information, trusts, global catalogs, or forestwide administrators. If you want to, you can join the forests with a cross-forest trust.

If you decide to implement a cross-forest trust between the forests, you can control whether a trust is one-way or two-way and the trust authentication level. Unlike interforest trusts, which are two-way and transitive by default, cross-forest trusts are either two-way or one-way. With a two-way trust, users in either forest have access to resources in the other forest. With a one-way trust, users in one forest have access to resources in the other forest but not vice versa.

The trust authentication level is set on outgoing trusts and is either domainwide or selective. Domainwide authentication is open and implies a certain level of trust because users in the trusted forest can be authenticated to use all of the resources in the trusting forest. Selective authentication is closed and more secure because only the users or groups to which you explicitly grant permission can access resources in the trusting domain.

INSIDE OUT Consider the size of the organization

You should consider the size of the organization when deciding on a forest structure. However, the size of an organization alone is not a reason for deploying multiple forests. A forest can contain multiple domains. The domains can be deployed in multiple namespaces. Each domain is a separate unit of administration, and each domain can have millions of objects.

INSIDE OUT Geographically separated sites

Geographically separated business units might want completely separate forests or domains. Although there might be business reasons for this, you should not make the decision based on perceived limitations in Active Directory. As long as a connection can be made between locations, there is no need for separate forests or domains. Active Directory sites provide the solution for connecting across limited bandwidth links. With the automatic compression feature for site bridgehead servers, replication traffic is compressed 85 to 90 percent, meaning that it is 10 to 15 percent of its noncompressed size. This means that even low-bandwidth links can often be used effectively for replication. For more information on sites, see Chapter 32, "Active Directory site administration."

## Forest administration

Most companies opt to deploy a single forest, and it is only through merger or acquisition that additional forests enter the picture. In part, this is because there is no easy way to merge multiple forests into a single forest if you decide to do so later. To merge forests, you must migrate objects from one forest to the other using the Active Directory Migration Tool (ADMT), which can be a very long process. For this and other reasons, you should decide from the start how many forests are going to be implemented and you should justify the need for each additional forest. Sometimes additional forests are deployed because of organizational politics or the inability of business units to decide how to manage the top-level forest functions. At other times, additional forests are deployed to isolate business units or give complete control of the directory to a business unit.

The organization should consider the following factors before creating additional forests:

- Additional forests make it more difficult for users to collaborate and share information. For example, users have direct access to the global catalog and can search for resources easily only for their own forest. You must configure access to resources in other forests, and the users cannot directly search for available resources in other forests.

- Additional forests mean additional administrative overheard and duplication of infrastructure. Each forest has its own forest-level configuration and one or more additional domain-level configurations that need to be managed. The ability to share resources and synchronize information across forests must be specifically configured rather than implemented by using built-in trusts and synchronization.

Sometimes, however, you need the additional controls put in place with additional forests to be reasonably sure that administrators from other domains in a forest do not make harmful changes to the directory, which are then replicated throughout the organization. All the domain controllers in a forest are tightly integrated. A change made on one domain controller is replicated to all other domain controllers. Replication is automatic, and there are no security checks other than the fact that the person making the change must have the appropriate permissions in the first place; that is, the person must be a member of the appropriate administrator group for the type of change being made. If such an administrator is acting maliciously in making changes, those changes will be replicated regardless of the effect on the organization.

That said, reasonable assurance about administrative access can be addressed by putting strict administration rules and procedures in place. With strict rules and procedures, the organization has the following multiple levels of administrators:

- Top-level administrators with enterprisewide privileges who are trusted with forestwide administration. These administrators are members of the Enterprise Admins group.

- High-level administrators with domainwide privileges who are trusted with domainwide administration. These administrators are members of the Domain Admins, Administrators, Server Operators, or Backup Operators group.

- Administrators who are delegated responsibilities for specific tasks, which might include being a member of the Server Operators, Backup Operators, or a similar group.

To have reasonable assurance that the level of administrative access is appropriate, the organization also needs to physically secure domain controllers, set policies about how administrators use their accounts (such as running tasks as an administrator only when needed for administration), and configure auditing of all actions performed by both users and administrators.

# Developing a domain plan

After you determine how many forests are needed based on the current namespace and administration needs of the organization as a whole, you next need to determine the domain structure that needs to be implemented. Whether your organization has an existing Active Directory structure or is implementing Active Directory for the first time, this means assessing the current environment and determining what changes are needed.

You need to thoroughly document the existing infrastructure and determine what—if anything—needs to be restructured, replaced, or upgraded. You also need to determine if it is even possible or practical to update the existing infrastructure as proposed. In some cases, you might find that current design is not ideal for updating as proposed and you might need to revise your plans.

That's all acceptable because design is usually an iterative process in which you go from the theoretical to the practical during successive revisions. Just remember that it is difficult to change the domain namespace as well as the number of forests and domains after you've started implementing the design. Other parts of a design, such as the OU and site structure, are easier to change after implementation.

> **Note**
>
> For tips and techniques on naming domains and establishing a naming hierarchy, see Chapter 21, "Architecting DNS infrastructure." You'll also find detailed information on using DNS (Domain Name System) with Active Directory in Chapter 22, "Implementing and managing DNS."

## Domain design considerations

Domains allow you to logically group objects for central management and control over the replication of those objects. You use domains to partition a forest into smaller components. As part of domain design, you should consider the following:

- **Replication**  Domains set the replication boundary for the domain directory partition and for domain policy information stored in the Sysvol folder on every domain controller in the domain. Any changes made to the domain directory partition or domain policy information on one of the domain controllers are

Chapter 26

replicated automatically to the other domain controllers in the domain. Although other directory partitions, such as the schema and configuration, are replicated throughout a forest, the domain information is replicated only within a particular domain, and the more objects in the domain container, the more data that potentially needs to be replicated.

- **Resource access**   The trusts between and among domains in a forest do not by themselves grant permission to access resources. A user must be specifically given permission to access a resource in another domain. By default, an administrator of a domain can manage only resources in that domain and cannot manage resources in another domain. This means that domain boundaries are also boundaries for resource access and administration.

- **Policy**   The policies that apply to one domain are independent from those applied to other domains. This means that policies for user and computer configuration and security can be applied differently in different domains. Certain policies can be applied only at the domain level. These policies, referred to as *domain security policies*, include password policies, account lockout policies, and Kerberos policies and are applied to all domain accounts.

- **Language**   For organizations in which multiple languages are used, you might want to configure servers within a domain with the same additional languages. This is a consideration for administration purposes but not a requirement.

## A single domain vs. multiple domains

With domain design, part of the decision involves the number of domains that are needed. You might need to implement additional domains or continue using a single domain. A single domain is the easiest to manage. It is also the ideal environment for users because it is easier for users to locate resources in a single domain environment than in a multidomain or multitree forest.

Beyond simplicity, there are several other reasons for implementing or keeping to a single-domain design, such as the following:

- You do not need to create additional domains to limit administrative access, delegate control, or create a hierarchical structure. In Active Directory, you can use OUs for these purposes.

- You might want to make authentication and resource access easier to configure and less prone to problems. A single domain doesn't have to rely on trusts or the assignment of resource access in other domains.

- You might want to make domain structure easier to manage. A single domain has only one set of domain administrators and one set of domain policy. A single domain doesn't need duplicate domainwide infrastructure for domain controllers.

- Your organization might frequently restructure its business units. It is easy to rename OUs, but it's very difficult to rename domains. It is easy to move accounts and resources between OUs, but it's much more difficult to move accounts and resources between domains.

With Active Directory, you can have millions of objects in a single domain, so the reason for using multiple domains should not be based solely on the number of objects—although the number of objects is certainly still a factor to consider from a manageability standpoint. That said, using multiple domains sometimes makes sense, particularly if your organization has loosely connected business divisions or business locations with wide geographic separation. For example, if City Power & Light and The Phone Company are two divisions of one company, it might make sense to have a cpandl.com domain and a thephone-company.com domain within the same forest. If City Power & Light has Canadian and USA operations, it might make sense to have can.cpandl.com and us.cpandl.com domains.

Restricting access to resources and the need to enforce different sets of security policies are also reasons for using multiple domains. Using multiple domains creates boundaries for resource access and administration. It also creates boundaries for security policy. So, if you need to limit resource access or tighten security controls for both users and administrators, you will probably want to use multiple domains.

Like additional forests, multiple domains require additional administrative and infrastructure overhead. Each domain has its own domain-level configuration, which requires server hardware and administrators to manage that hardware. Because users might be accessing and authenticating resources across trusts, there is more complexity and there are more points of failure.

## Forest root domain design configurations

The forest root domain can be either a dedicated root or a nondedicated root. A dedicated root, also referred to as an *empty root*, is used as a placeholder to start the directory. No user or group accounts are associated with it other than accounts created when the forest root is installed and accounts that are needed to manage the forest. Because no additional user or group accounts are associated with it, a dedicated root domain is not used to assign access to resources. This approach also would let you use cpandl.com as your external DNS name and corp.cpandl.com as your internal DNS name. A nondedicated root is used as a normal part of the directory. It has user and group accounts associated with it and is used to assign access to resources.

For an organization that is going to use multiple domains anyway, using a dedicated root domain makes a lot of sense. The forest root domain contains the forestwide administrator accounts (Enterprise Admins and Schema Admins) and the forestwide operations masters (domain naming master and schema master). It must be available when users log on to domains other than their home domain and when users access resources in other domains.

A dedicated root domain is easier to manage than a root domain that contains accounts. It allows you to separate the root domain from the rest of the forest. The separation also helps safeguard the entire directory, which is important because the forest root domain cannot be replaced. If the root domain is destroyed and cannot be recovered, you must re-create the entire forest.

## Changing domain design

Ideally, after you implement a domain structure, the domain names never need to change. In the real world, however, things change. Organizations change their names, merge with other companies, are acquired, or restructure more often than we'd like. With Active Directory, you have several options for changing structure. If you find that you need to move a large number of objects from one domain to another, you can use the Active Directory Migration Tool (ADMT). You can rename domains as long as the forest is running at the Microsoft Windows Server 2003 or higher functional level. Changing the domain design after implementation is difficult, however, and involves using the Domain Rename utility (Rendom.exe) and other tools, which are built into Windows Server 2008 and later.

> **Note**
> You cannot change domain names if you have deployed Exchange Server 2007 or Exchange Server 2010. For a complete list of Microsoft applications and servers that do not support Domain Rename, see Microsoft Knowledge Base article 300684 (*http://support.microsoft.com/kb/300684/en-us*).

You can rename domains in the following key ways:

- Rename domains to move them within a domain tree. For example, you could rename a child domain from eng.it.cohowinery.com to eng.cohowinery.com.

- Rename domains so that a new tree is created. For example, you could change the name of a child domain from vineyard.cohowinery.com to cohovineyard.com.

- Rename domains to move them to a new tree. For example, you could change the name of a child domain from it.cohowinery.com to it.cohovineyard.com.

- Rename domains to set new domain names without changing the parent–child structure. For example, if the company name changes from Coho Vineyard to Coho Winery, you could change the existing domain names to use cohowinery.com instead of cohovineyard.com.

You cannot use the Domain Rename utility to change which domain is the forest root domain. Although you can change the name of the forest root domain so that it is no longer the forest root logically, the domain remains the forest root domain physically in Active Directory. It still contains the forestwide administrator accounts (Enterprise Admins and Schema Admins) and the forestwide operations masters (domain naming master and schema master). This occurs because there is no way to change the forest root domain assignment within Active Directory after the forest root has been established.

As you might imagine, renaming a domain in a single-domain forest is the easiest renaming operation. As you increase the number of domains within a forest, you increase the complexity of the Domain Rename operation. Regardless of how many domains you are working with, you should always plan the project completely from start to finish and back up the entire domain infrastructure before trying to implement Domain Rename.

The reason for this planning and backup is that when you rename domains, even if you rename only one domain in a forest of many domains, you must make a change to every domain controller in the forest so that it recognizes the renamed domain. When you are finished, you must reboot each domain controller. If you don't perform the rename change on every domain controller, you must remove from service the domain controllers that did not get the updates. Furthermore, from the time you start the rename operation to the time you reboot domain controllers, the forest is out of service.

To complete the process after renaming a domain and updating domain controllers, you must reboot each workstation or member server in the renamed domain twice. While you are working with domain controllers and other computers that don't use Dynamic Host Configuration Protocol (DHCP) in the renamed domain, you should rename the computer so that the DNS name is correct and make other DNS name changes as appropriate.

# Developing an organizational unit plan

So far in this book, I've discussed domains, domain trees, and forests. These are the components of Active Directory that can help you scale the directory to meet the needs of any organization regardless of its size. Sometimes, however, what you want to do is not scale the directory but create hierarchical structures that represent parts of the organization or limit or delegate administrative access for a part of the organization. This is where OUs come in handy.

# Using organizational units

An *organizational unit* (OU) is a logical administrative unit that is used to group objects within a domain. Within a domain, you can use OUs to delegate administrator privileges while limiting administrative access and to create a hierarchy that mirrors the business's structure or functions. So, rather than having multiple domains to represent the structure of the organization or its business functions, you can create OUs within a domain to do this.

At its most basic level, an OU is a container for objects that can contain other OUs as well as the following objects:

- Computers

- Contacts

- Groups

- inetOrgPerson

- Printers

- Shared Folders

- Users

> **Note**
>
> OUs are used to contain objects within a domain. They cannot, however, contain objects from other domains.

> **Note**
>
> An inetOrgPerson object is used for LDAP compatibility and is defined in Request For Comments (RFC) 2798. Except for having a different object name, you manage inetOrgPerson objects the same way as user objects.

For administrative purposes, OUs can be used in two key ways. First, you can use OUs to delegate administrative rights. You can use this approach to give someone limited or full administrative control over only a part of a domain. For example, if you have a branch office, you could create an OU for all the accounts and resources at that office, and then delegate administration of that OU to the local administrator.

Second, you can use OUs to manage a group of objects as a single unit. Unlike domains, OUs are not a part of DNS structure. Within Active Directory, OUs are seen as container objects that are part of a domain. In the directory tree, they are referenced with the OU= identifier, such as OU=Sales for an OU named Sales. The distinguished name (DN) of an OU includes the path to its parent as well as its relative name. As you might recall, the DC= identifier is used to reference domain components. This means that the Sales OU in the cpandl.com domain has a DN of OU=Sales,DC=cpandl,DC=com.

Because OUs can contain other OUs, you can have multiple levels of OUs. For example, if you had a USA OU and a Europe OU within the Sales OU, the DNs of these OUs would be OU=USA,OU=Sales,DC=cpandl,DC=com and OU=Europe,OU=Sales,DC=cpandl,DC=com, respectively. When you nest OUs in this way, the nested OUs inherit the Group Policy set- tings of the top-level OUs by default, but you can override inheritance if you want to use unique Group Policy settings for a particular OU.

From a user perspective, OUs are fairly transparent. Because OUs aren't a part of the DNS structure, users don't have to reference OUs when they log on, during authentication, or when they perform searches of Active Directory. This makes multiple OUs much easier to work with than multiple domains. Also, it is easy to change the names and structures of OUs, which isn't the case with domains.

## Using OUs for delegation

Although you will want to centrally manage Active Directory structure, many other administrative tasks related to Active Directory can be delegated to specific groups or individuals. Delegating administrative rights allows a user to perform a set of assigned administrative tasks for a specific OU. The tasks allowed depend on the way you configure delegation and include allowing an individual to perform the following actions:

- Create, delete, and manage accounts

- Reset user passwords, and force password changes at next logon

- Read all user information

- Create, delete, and manage groups

- Modify the membership of a group

- Manage Group Policy links

- Generate Resultant Set of Policy

One of the common reasons for delegating administrative rights is to allow an individual in a department or business unit to reset user passwords. When you delegate this right, you allow a trusted person to change someone's password if the need arises. Because the right is delegated to a user within a particular OU, this right is limited to that specific OU. In many organizations, this type of right is granted to Help Desk staff to allow them to reset passwords while preventing the Help Desk staff from changing other account properties.

## Using OUs for Group Policy

Group Policy allows you to specify a set of rules for computer and user configuration settings. These rules control the working environment for computers and users. Although I'll discuss Group Policy in depth in Chapter 31, "Managing Group Policy," the important thing to know about Group Policy is that you can use it to set default options, to limit options, and to prevent changing options in virtually every aspect of computer and user configuration.

Every domain you create has a default Group Policy rule set, referred to as the Default Domain Policy. Group Policy can also be applied to OUs, which makes OUs important in helping administrators manage groups of accounts and resources in a particular way. By default, OUs inherit the Group Policy settings of their parent object. For top-level OUs within a domain, this means that the Default Domain Policy is inherited by default. For lower-level OUs, this means that the OUs inherit the Group Policy of the OUs above them (and if the higher-level OUs inherit Group Policy from the domain, so do the lower-level OUs).

To manage Group Policy, you can use the Group Policy Management Console (GPMC). Group Policy is a very important part of Active Directory. Not only can you use it to manage the functionality available to users, you can also use it to enforce security, standardize desktop configuration, install software, specify scripts that should run when a computer starts or shuts down and when a user logs on or logs off, and so on.

Because Group Policy is so important in Active Directory, you should plan your OU structure with Group Policy in mind. You do this by grouping objects that require the same Group Policy settings. For example, if a group of users requires a specific environment configuration to use an application or if a group of users requires a standard set of mapped drives, you can configure this through Group Policy.

## Creating an OU design

OUs simplify administration by organizing accounts and resources in ways that best fit the organizational structure. When designing an OU structure, you should plan the structure before you try to implement it. Often, you'll find that you need multiple levels of OUs. This is fine. The levels of OUs will form a hierarchy, much like the hierarchy formed when you use multiple levels of domains. The key thing to understand about any OU design is that it is really for administrators. As such, the design needs to be meaningful for your organization's administrators—and ideally, it should help make administration easier.

Creating a good OU design isn't always as easy as it seems. It is a good idea to go through several possible scenarios on paper before trying to implement a design. Through successive revisions on paper, you should be able to improve the design substantially. Common design models for OUs are discussed in the sections that follow.

## OU design: Division or business unit model

With a division or business unit model, you use OUs to reflect the department structure within the organization. The advantage to this model is that users will know and understand it. The disadvantage to this model is that when the company restructures, you might need to redesign the OU structure.

In the example shown in Figure 26-2, OUs are organized by department within the company and, to allow for separate controls for accounts and resources, the related objects are put in second-level OUs. If you want to have only one level of OUs, you could do this by putting all the objects in the top-level OU.

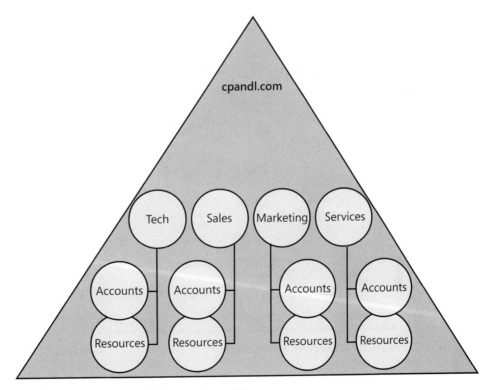

**Figure 26-2** The division or business unit model.

## OU design: Geographic model

With a geographic model, you use OUs to reflect geographic location. In this model, top-level OUs represent the largest geographic units, such as continents, and the lower-level OUs represent successively smaller geographic units, such as countries/regions. (See Figure 26-3.)

There are several advantages to this model. A geographic structure is stable. Many companies reorganize internally frequently, but they only rarely change geographic structure. Additionally, when you use a geographic model, it is easy to determine where accounts and resources are physically located.

The disadvantages to this model have to do with its scope. For a global company, this design would put all accounts and resources in a single domain. As a result, changes made to Active Directory at any location would be replicated to every office location. Additionally, the OU structure doesn't relate to the business structure of the organization.

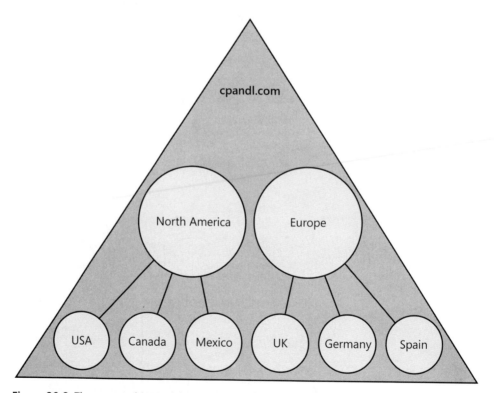

**Figure 26-3** The geographic model.

## OU design: The cost center model

With a cost center model, you use OUs to reflect cost centers. In this model, top-level OUs represent the major cost centers within the organization and the lower-level OUs represent geographic locations, projects, or business structures, as shown in Figure 26-4. In a company where budget is the top priority, the cost center model might be an effective way to reflect this priority. Cost centers could also be independent divisions or business units within the company that have their own management and cost controls.

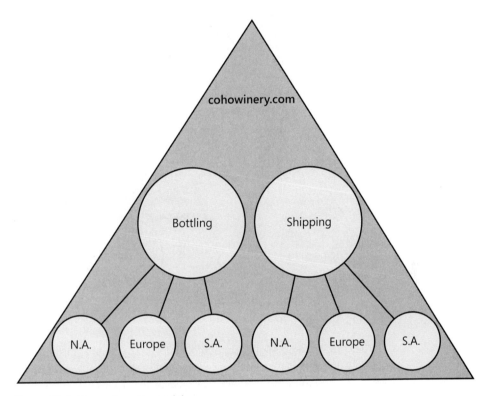

**Figure 26-4** The cost center model.

The ability to represent costs and budgets in this way is a definite advantage but could also be a disadvantage. Cost center structure is not a structure well known to most administrators, and it might be confusing.

## OU design: The administration model

With an administration model, you use OUs to reflect the way resources and accounts are managed. Because this model reflects the business structure of a company, it is very similar to the division or business unit model. The key difference is that the top-level OU is for administrators and second-level OUs are for the business structure. (See Figure 26-5.) If successive levels are needed, they can be organized by resource type, geographic location, project type, or some combination of the three.

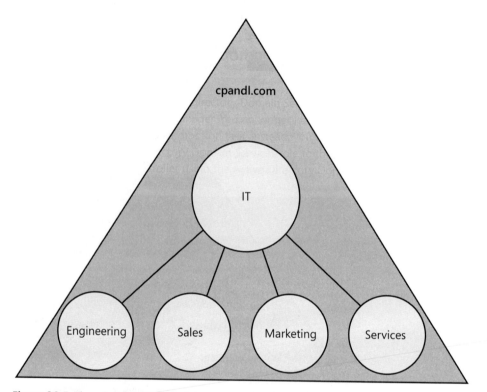

**Figure 26-5**  The administration model.

In a large company, you might use multiple implementations of this model for each division or business unit. In this case, the top-level administrative group would be for the division or business unit and the second-level OUs would be for groups within the division.

The advantage to this model is that it is designed around the way administrators work and represents the business structure of the company. The disadvantage to this model is that when the company or divisions within the company restructure, you might need to redesign the OU structure.

# Configuring Active Directory sites and replication

A s part of the design of Active Directory Domain Service, you should examine the network topology and determine if you need to manage network traffic between subnets or business locations. To manage network traffic related to Active Directory, you use sites, which can be used to reflect the physical topology of your network. Every Active Directory implementation has at least one site. An important part of understanding sites involves understanding Active Directory replication. Active Directory uses two replication models: one model for replication within sites and one model for replication between sites. You need a solid understanding of these replication models to plan your site structure.

## Working with Active Directory sites

A *site* is a group of Transmission Control Protocol/Internet Protocol (TCP/IP) subnets that are implemented to control directory replication traffic and isolate logon authentication traffic between physical network locations. Each subnet that is part of a site should be connected by reliable, high-speed links. Any business location connected over slow or unreliable links should be part of a separate site. Because of this, individual sites typically represent the individual local area networks (LANs) within an organization, and the wide area network (WAN) links between business locations typically mark the boundaries of these sites. However, sites can be used in other ways as well.

Sites do not reflect the Active Directory namespace. Domain and site boundaries are separate. From a network topology perspective, a single site can contain multiple TCP/IP subnets as well. However, a single subnet can be in only one site. This means that the following conditions apply:

- A single site can contain resources from multiple domains.

- A single domain can have resources spread out among multiple sites.

- A single site can have multiple subnets.

As you design the site structure, you have many options. Sites can contain a domain or a portion of a domain. A single site can have one subnet or multiple subnets. Note that replication is handled differently between sites than it is within sites. Replication that occurs within a site is referred to as *intrasite replication*. Replication between sites is referred to as *intersite replication*. Each side of a site connection has one or more designated bridgehead servers.

Figure 27-1 shows an example of an organization that has one domain and two sites at the same physical location. Here, the organization has an East Campus site and a West Campus site. As you can see, the organization has multiple domain controllers at each site. The domain controllers in the East Campus site perform intrasite replication with each other, as do the domain controllers in the West Campus site. Designated servers in each site, referred to as site *bridgehead* servers, perform intersite replication with each other.

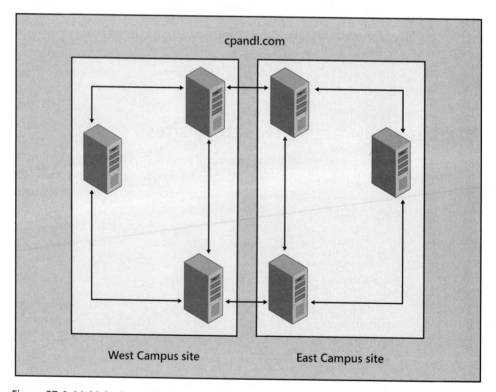

**Figure 27-1** Multiple sites at the same location.

Figure 27-2 shows an example of an organization that has two different physical locations. Here, the organization has decided to use two domains and two sites. The Main site is for the cohowinery.com domain and the Seattle site is for the sea.cohowinery.com domain. Again, replication occurs both within and between the sites.

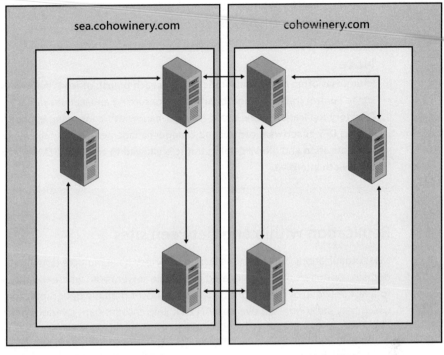

**Seattle site**      **Main site**

**Figure 27-2** Multiple sites at different locations.

## Single site vs. multiple sites

One reason to create additional sites at the same physical location is to control replication traffic. Replication traffic between sites is automatically compressed, reducing the amount of traffic passed between sites by 85 to 90 percent of its original size. Because network clients try to log on to network resources within their local site first, you can use sites to isolate logon traffic as well.

It is recommended that each site have at least one domain controller and one global catalog for client authentication. For name resolution and IP address assignment, it is also recommended that each site have at least one Domain Name System (DNS) server and one Dynamic Host Configuration Protocol (DHCP) server. Then—by creating multiple sites in the same physical location and establishing a domain controller, global catalog, and DNS and DHCP server within each site—you can closely control the logon process.

In the figure labels: **sea.cohowinery.com**      **cohowinery.com**

You should also design sites with other network resources in mind, including Distributed File System (DFS) file shares, certificate authorities, and Microsoft Exchange servers. You want to configure sites so that clients' network queries can be answered within the site. If every client query for a network resource has to be sent to a remote site, there could be substantial network traffic between sites, which could be a problem over slow WAN links.

> **Note**
>
> Enterprises often have branch offices where each branch office is defined as a separate site to control traffic for high-bandwidth–consuming applications rather than Active Directory replication. Here, traffic for high-bandwidth-consuming applications, such as DFS or software control and change management, is carefully managed, but authentication and global catalog traffic is allowed to cross the WAN because it is less bandwidth intensive.

## Replication within and between sites

Most organizations implementing Active Directory have multiple domain controllers. The domain controllers might be located in a single server room where they are all connected to a fast network, or they might be spread out over multiple geographic locations, from which they are connected over a WAN that links the company's various office locations.

All domain controllers in the same forest—regardless of how many domain controllers there are and where domain controllers are located—replicate information with each other. Although more replication is performed within a domain than between domains, replication between domains occurs nonetheless. The same replication model is used in both cases.

When a change is made to a domain partition in Active Directory, the change is replicated to all domain controllers in the domain. If the change is made to an attribute of an object tracked by the global catalog, the change is replicated to all global catalog servers in all domains of the forest. Similarly, if you make a change to the forestwide configuration or schema partitions, these changes are replicated to all domain controllers in all the domains of the forest.

Authentication within and between domains is also handled by domain controllers. If a user logs in to his home domain, the local domain controller authenticates the logon. If a user logs in to a domain other than the home domain, the logon request is forwarded through the trust tree to a domain controller in the user's home domain.

Active Directory's replication model is designed for consistency, but the consistency is loosely defined. By *loosely defined*, I mean that at any given moment the information on one domain controller can be different from the information on a different domain controller. This can happen when Windows Server has not yet replicated the changes on the first domain controller to the other domain controller. Over time, Windows Server replicates the changes made to one domain controller to all domain controllers as necessary.

When multiple sites are involved, the replication model is used to store and then forward changes as necessary between sites. In this case, a domain controller in the site where the changes were originally made forwards the changes to a domain controller in another site. This domain controller, in turn, stores the changes and then forwards the changes to all the domain controllers in the second site. In this way, the domain controller on which a change is made doesn't have to replicate directly with all the other domain controllers. Instead, it can rely on the store-and-forward technique to ensure that the changes are replicated as necessary.

## Determining site boundaries

When trying to determine site boundaries, you should configure sites so that they reflect the physical structure of your network. Use connectivity between network segments to determine where you should locate site boundaries. Areas of the network that are connected with fast connections should all be part of the same site, unless you have specific requirements for controlling replication or the logon process. Areas of the network that are connected with limited bandwidth or unreliable links should be part of different sites.

As you examine each of the organization's business locations, determine whether placing domain controllers and other network resources at that location is necessary. If you elect not to place a domain controller at a remote location, you cannot make the location a part of a separate site. This has the following advantages:

- No Active Directory replication between the business locations

- No remote domain controllers to manage

- No additional site infrastructure to manage

There are also several disadvantages to this approach:

- All logon traffic must cross the link between the business locations.

- Users might experience slow logon and authentication when trying to access network resources.

In the end, the decision to establish a separate site might come down to the user experience and the available bandwidth. If you have fast connections between sites—which should be dedicated and redundant—you might not want to establish a separate site for the remote business location. If you have limited bandwidth between business locations

Chapter 27

and want to maintain the user experience, you might want to establish a separate site and place domain controllers and possibly other network resources at the site. This speeds up the logon and authentication process and allows you to better control the network traffic between sites.

# Understanding Active Directory replication

When you are planning the site structure, you need to understand how replication works. As discussed previously, Active Directory uses two replication models, each of which is handled differently. The intrasite replication model is used for replication within sites and is optimized for high-bandwidth connections. The intersite replication model is used for replication between sites and is optimized for limited-bandwidth connections. Before I get into the specifics of replication and the replication models, let's look at the way replication has changed from its early implementations to present.

## Tracking Active Directory replication changes over time

The replication model used for current Windows Server versions has changed in several important ways from the model first implemented. Understanding these changes can inform the way you deploy and work with Active Directory, and it also can help ensure that outdated guidance isn't driving configuration decisions.

Originally, the smallest unit of replication is an individual attribute. At first examination, this seems to be what is wanted; after all, you don't want to have to replicate an entire object if only an attribute of that object has changed. The problem with this approach is that some attributes are multivalued. That is, they have multiple values. An example is the membership attribute of a universal group. This attribute represents all the members of the universal group.

As a result of this design oversight, when you added or removed a single user from the group, you caused the entire group membership to be replicated. In large organizations, a significant amount of replication traffic was often generated because universal groups might have several thousand members. Current Active Directory architecture resolves this problem by replicating only the attribute's updated value. With universal group membership, this means that only the users you've added or removed are updated, rather than the entire group membership.

Intersite replication has also changed over time. You can turn off compression for intersite replication and enable notification for intersite replication. An improved knowledge consistency checker (KCC) allows Active Directory to support a greater number of sites. These changes affect intersite replication in the following key ways:

- All intersite replication traffic is compressed by default. Although this significantly reduces the amount of traffic between sites, it increases the processing overhead required on the bridgehead servers to replicate traffic between sites. Therefore, if processor utilization on bridgehead servers is a concern, and you have adequate bandwidth connections between sites, you might want to disable compression.

- Replication between sites occurs at scheduled intervals according to the site-link configuration. You can enable notification for intersite replication, which allows the bridgehead server in a site to notify the bridgehead server on the other side of a site link that changes have occurred. This allows the other bridgehead server to pull the changes across the site link and thereby get more frequent updates.

- In early implementations, the maximum number of sites you could have in a forest was greatly influenced by the KCC. As a result, there was a practical limit of about 100 sites per forest. With current implementations, the KCC itself is no longer the limiting factor. This means that you can have many hundreds of sites per forest.

> **Note**
> To turn off compression or enable notification, you need to edit the related site link or connection object. See "Configuring advanced site-link options" in Chapter 32, "Active Directory site administration."

Windows Server 2008 R2 and later support improved load balancing to distribute the workload more evenly among bridgehead servers. Prior to Windows Server 2008 R2 and Windows Server 2012, inbound connections from sites primarily targeted one bridgehead server in a site with requests even if multiple bridgeheads were available. Windows Server 2008 R2 and Windows Server 2012 have load-balancing improvements that help ensure inbound connections are more evenly balanced when there are multiple bridgehead servers.

Because improved load balancing is a feature of the operating system and does not require operating in a Windows Server 2008 R2 or higher forest or domain functional level, you can start taking advantage of the improvements simply by upgrading bridgehead servers. It's important to point out that intrasite replication algorithms have not changed—only intersite replication algorithms have changed. This means that these improvements are specific to intersite replication and do not apply to intrasite replication. Additionally, this load balancing occurs between two sites and doesn't extend outward in a spanning tree. Thus, the KCC doesn't take into account other sites when load-balancing connections between two sites.

The way load balancing works with multiple domains is slightly different from how it works with a single domain environment. This is because an existing connection is always used instead of a new one, even if the connection is for a different naming context. Thus, with multiple domains, it might appear that load balancing isn't working properly when in fact it is.

The KCC can still have unbalanced connections, such as when domain controllers go offline for extended periods. This unbalance can occur because the KCC does not rebalance connections when offline domain controllers come back online. Instead, the KCC prefers to maintain a stable topology, rather than try to rebalance the topology.

## INSIDE OUT  Load balancing manually

You can manually force load balancing. To do this, start by deleting the inbound intersite connections for a domain controller or site. Next, either wait for the KCC to run automatically (which will occur within 15 minutes) or manually run the KCC by entering the following command at an elevated prompt: **repadmin /kcc**.

Don't run the KCC at all your sites simultaneously. If you do this, inbound connections all choose the same bridgehead server. The reason this happens is that the system clock seeds the probabilistic choices for inbound connections. To avoid this problem, ensure there is at least a one-second interval between the times you start the KCC in each site.

## Tracking Active Directory system volume changes over time

As with replication, the Active Directory system volume has changed in several important ways since it was first implemented. Understanding these changes can inform the way you deploy and work with Active Directory, and it also can help ensure outdated guidance isn't driving configuration decisions.

The Active Directory system volume (Sysvol) contains domain policy—as well as scripts used for log on, log off, shutdown, and startup—and other related files as well as files stored within Active Directory. The way domain controllers replicate the Sysvol depends on the domain functional level:

- When a domain is running at the Windows Server 2003 functional level, domain controllers replicate the Sysvol using File Replication Service (FRS).

- When a domain is running at the Windows Server 2008 or higher functional level, domain controllers replicate the Sysvol using Distributed File System (DFS).

FRS and DFS are replication services that use the Active Directory replication topology to replicate files and folders in the Sysvol shared folders on domain controllers. The way this works is that the replication service checks with the KCC to determine the replication topology that has been generated for Active Directory replication, and then it uses this replication topology to replicate Sysvol files to all the domain controllers in a domain. Because DFS has been significantly enhanced, you'll want to use DFS instead of FRS whenever possible.

# INSIDE OUT  Why DFS instead of FRS?

When used with Active Directory, DFS has several advantages over FRS. DFS was enhanced for Windows Server 2003 R2. Not only did these enhancements make DFS easier to manage, they also introduced several additional replication and compression technologies. With Windows Server 2003 R2 and later, DFS Replication (DFS-R) and Remote Differential Compression (RDC) are used instead of Rsync version 2.6.2 to provide up to 300 percent faster replication and 200 to 300 percent faster compression. Operational overhead for managing content and replication also was reduced by 40 percent. Additionally, DFS-R supports automated recovery from database loss or corruption, replication scheduling, and bandwidth throttling. Together, these features make DFS-R significantly more scalable than FRS.

RDC is the secret ingredient associated with enhanced DFS that allows for the granular replication of changes—this is what's referred to when you read a vague statement that says DFS allows for the granular replication of the Sysvol. RDC enables granular replication by accurately identifying changes within and across files and transmitting only those changes to achieve significant bandwidth savings. More specifically, RDC detects insertions, removals, or rearrangements of data in files, enabling DFS-R to replicate only the changed file blocks when files are updated. Changes within or across files are called *file deltas*.

In addition to calculating file deltas and transferring only the differences, RDC also can copy any similar file from any client or server to another using data that is common to both computers. This further reduces the amount of the data sent and the overall bandwidth requirements for file transfers. Local differencing techniques are used to transform the old version into a new version. The differences between two versions of the file are calculated on the source domain controller and then sent to the DFS client on the target domain controller.

The storage techniques and replication architectures for DFS and FRS are decidedly different. Figure 27-3 shows a conceptual view of how File Replication Service is used with

Active Directory on a domain controller. The File Replication Service (Ntfrs.exe) stores FRS topology and schedule information in Active Directory and periodically polls Active Directory to retrieve updated information using Lightweight Directory Access Protocol (LDAP). Most administrator tools that work with FRS use LDAP as well. Internally, FRS makes direct calls to the file system using standard I/O. FRS uses the remote procedure call (RPC) protocol when communicating with remote servers.

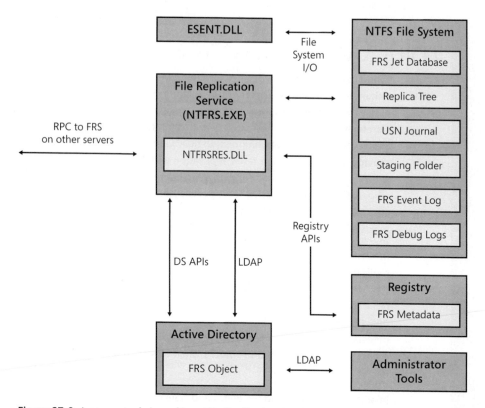

**Figure 27-3** A conceptual view of how File Replication Service works.

FRS stores various types of data in the NTFS file system, including transactions in the FRS Jet database (Ntfrs.jdb), events and error messages in the FRS Event log (NtFrs.evt), and debug logs stored in the debug log folder (%SystemRoot%\Debug). Esent.dll is a dynamic-link library used by the Jet database to store transactions. Ntfrsres.dll is a dynamic-link library used by FRS to store events and error messages.

The contents of the Replica tree determine what FRS replicates. The Replica tree for Active Directory is the Sysvol. The Sysvol contains domain, staging, staging areas, and sysvol folders. The USN journal is a persistent log of changes made to files on an NTFS volume. NTFS uses the USN journal to track information about added, deleted, and modified files. FRS, in turn, uses the USN journal to determine when changes are made to the contents of the Replica tree. FRS then replicates changes according to the schedule in Active Directory. FRS stores configuration data in the registry.

# INSIDE OUT  The replica root

The actual replica root begins at the %SystemRoot%\Sysvol\domain folder, but the folder that is actually shared is the %SystemRoot%\Sysvol\sysvol folder. These folders appear to contain the same content because Sysvol uses *junction points* (also known as *reparse points*). A junction point is a physical location on a hard disk that points to data that is located elsewhere on the hard disk or on another storage device.

The Sysvol\domain folder contains policies and scripts in separate subfolders. The Sysvol\Staging folder acts as a queue for changed files that need to be replicated. Within the Sysvol\Staging Areas folder, the *DomainName* folder is a junction point to the Sysvol\staging\domain folder. Within the Sysvol\sysvol folder, the *DomainName* folder is a junction point to the Sysvol\domain folder.

After a user or the operating system changes a Sysvol file and the file is closed, FRS creates the file in the staging folder using the backup application programming interfaces (APIs) and replicates the file according to the schedule set in Active Directory. FRS uses the same backup APIs used to ensure that Volume Shadow Copy Service–compatible backup programs, such as Windows Backup, can make point-in-time, consistent backups of the replica tree. Before such a program takes a shadow copy of a replica tree, the program instructs FRS to stop requesting new work items. After all currently active items are complete, FRS enters a pause state during which no new items can be processed.

Figure 27-4 shows a conceptual view of how Distributed File System is used with Active Directory on a domain controller. The Distributed File System (Dfssvc.exe) stores information about standalone namespaces in the registry and information about domain-based namespaces in Active Directory.

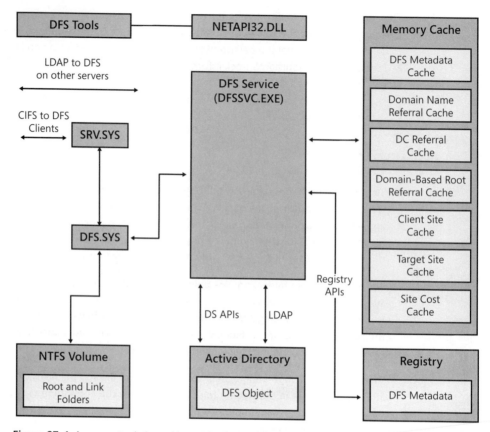

**Figure 27-4** A conceptual view of how Distributed File System works.

The standalone DFS metadata contains information about the root, root target, links, link targets, and configuration settings defined for each standalone namespace. This metadata is maintained in the registry of the root server at HKLM\SOFTWARE\Microsoft\Dfs\Roots\ Standalone.

Domain-based root servers have a registry entry for each root under KEY_LOCAL_ MACHINE\SOFTWARE\Microsoft\Dfs\Roots\Domain, but these entries do not contain the domain-based DFS metadata. When the DFS service starts on a domain controller using Active Directory with DFS, the service checks this path for registry entries that correspond to domain-based roots. If these entries exist, the root server polls the primary domain controller (PDC) emulator master to obtain the DFS metadata for each domain-based namespace and stores the metadata in memory.

In the Active Directory data store, the DFS object stores the DFS metadata for a domain-based namespace. The DFS object is created in Active Directory when you install a domain at or raise a domain to at least the Windows Server 2008 domain functional level. Active Directory replicates the entire DFS object to all domain controllers in a domain.

DFS uses a client/server architecture. A domain controller hosting a DFS namespace has both the client and server components, allowing the domain controller to perform local lookups in its own data store and remote lookups in data stores on other domain controllers. DFS uses the Common Internet File System (CIFS) for communication between DFS clients, root servers, and domain controllers. CIFS is an extension of the Server Message Block (SMB) file-sharing protocol.

When a domain controller receives a CIFS request, the SMB Service server driver (Srv.sys) passes the request to the DFS driver (Dfs.sys) and this driver, in turn, directs the request to the DFS service. Dfs.sys also handles the processing of links when they are encountered during file-system access.

When a client requests a referral for a domain-based namespace, the domain controller first checks its domain-based root referral cache for an existing referral. If the referral cache exists, the domain controller uses the cache to create the referral. If the referral cache does not exist, the domain controller locates the DFS object for that namespace and uses the metadata in the object to create the necessary referral. A referral contains a list of Universal Naming Convention (UNC) paths that the client can use. DFS uses LDAP to retrieve metadata about the domain-based namespace from Active Directory and stores this information in its in-memory cache. Various types of in-memory cache are used:

- Domain Name Referral Cache contains the host names of computers as well as the fully qualified names of the local domain, all trusted domains in the forest, and domains in trusted forests.

- Domain Controller Referral Cache contains the host names of computers as well as the fully qualified names of the domain controllers for the list of domains it has cached.

- Domain-Based Root Referral Cache contains a list of root targets that host a given domain-based namespace.

- Client Site Cache stores information about the site in which a client is located (as determined using a DSAddressToSiteNames lookup).

- Target Site Cache stores information about the site in which a target UNC path is located (as determined using a DSAddressToSiteNames lookup).

- Site Cost Cache contains a mapping of sites to their associated cost information as defined in Active Directory.

Chapter 27

After this information is cached, DFS can provide this to clients that are requesting information about DFS namespaces. The physical structures and caches on a domain controller vary according to the type of namespace the server hosts (domain-based or standalone). Each root and link in a namespace has a physical representation on an NTFS volume on each domain controller. The DFS root for Active Directory corresponds to the Sysvol shared folder. If a domain controller hosts additional namespaces, the domain controller will have additional roots and links.

## Replication architecture: An overview

Active Directory replication is a multipart process that involves a source domain controller and a destination domain controller. From a high level, replication works much as shown in Figure 27-5.

The step-by-step procedure goes like this:

1. When a user or a system process makes a change to the directory, this change is implemented as an LDAP write to the appropriate directory partition.

2. The source domain controller begins by looking up the IP address of a replication partner. For the initial lookup or when the destination DNS record has expired, the source domain controller does this by querying the primary DNS server. Subsequent lookups can be done using the local resolver cache.

3. The source and destination domain controllers use Kerberos to mutually authenticate each other.

4. The source domain controller then sends a change notification to the destination domain controller using RPC over IP.

5. The destination domain controller sends a request for the changes using RPC over IP, including information that allows the source domain controller to determine if those changes are needed.

6. Using the information sent by the destination domain controller, the source domain controller determines what changes (if any) need to be sent to the destination domain controller, and then it sends the required changes using RPC over IP.

7. The destination domain controller then uses the replication subsystem to write the changes to the directory database.

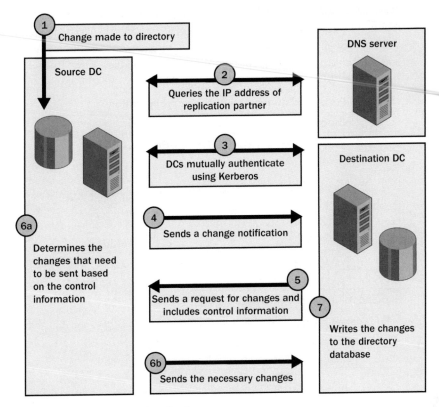

**Figure 27-5**  An overview of replication.

> **Note**
>
> For intersite replication, two transports are available: RPC over IP and Simple Mail Transfer Protocol (SMTP). With this in mind, SMTP could also be used as an alternate transport. SMTP uses TCP port 25.

As you can see from this overview, Active Directory replication depends on the following key services:

- LDAP

- Domain Name System (DNS)

- Kerberos version 5 authentication

- Remote procedure call (RPC)

Chapter 27

These Windows services must be functioning properly to allow directory updates to be replicated. Active Directory also uses either FRS or DFS to replicate files in the System Volume (Sysvol) shared folders on domain controllers. The User Datagram Protocol (UDP) and TCP ports used during replication are similar regardless of whether FRS or DFS is used. Table 27-1 summarizes the ports that are used.

**TABLE 27-1 Ports used during Active Directory replication**

| Service/Component | Port | |
|---|---|---|
| | UDP | TCP |
| LDAP | 389 | 389 |
| LDAP Secure Sockets Layer (SSL) | | 686 |
| Global Catalog (LDAP) | | 3268 |
| Global Catalog (LDAP, SSL) | | 3269 |
| Kerberos version 5 | 88 | 88 |
| DNS | 53 | 53 |
| RPC | | Dynamic |
| RPC endpoint mapper with DFS | | 135 |
| Server Message Block (SMB) over IP | 445 | 445 |
| SMTP | | 25 |
| Kerberos Change/Set Password | 464 | 464 |

# INSIDE OUT  Intrasite replication essentials

The Active Directory replication model is designed to ensure that there is no single point of failure. In this model, every domain controller can access changes to the database and replicate those changes to all other domain controllers. When replication occurs within a domain, the replication follows a specific model that is very different from the replication model used for intersite replication.

With intrasite replication, the focus is on ensuring that changes are rapidly distributed. Intrasite replication traffic is not compressed, and replication is designed so that changes are replicated almost immediately after a change has been made. The main component in Active Directory responsible for the replication structure is the KCC. One of the main responsibilities of the KCC is to generate the replication topology—that is, the way replication is implemented.

As domain controllers are added to a site, the KCC configures a ring topology for intrasite replication with pull replication partners. Why use this model? For the following reasons:

- In a ring topology model, there are always at least two paths between connected network resources to provide redundancy. Creating a ring topology for Active Directory replication ensures that there are at least two paths that changes can follow from one domain controller to another.

- In a pull replication model, two servers are used. One is designated the push partner; the other is the pull partner. It is the responsibility of the push partner to notify the pull partner that changes are available. The pull partner can then request the changes. Creating push and pull replication partners allows for rapid notification of changes and for updating after a request for changes has been made.

The KCC uses these models to create a replication ring. As domain controllers are added to a site, the size and configuration of this ring change. When there are at least three domain controllers in a site, each domain controller is configured with at least two incoming replication connections. As the number of domain controllers changes, the KCC updates the replication topology.

When a domain controller is updated, it waits approximately 15 seconds before initiating replication. This short wait is implemented in case additional changes are made. The domain controller on which the change is made notifies one of its partners, using an RPC, and specifies that changes are available. The partner can then pull the changes. After replication with this partner completes, the domain controller waits approximately 3 seconds and then notifies its second partner of changes. The second partner can then pull the changes. Meanwhile, the first partner is notifying its partners of changes as appropriate. This process continues until all the domain controllers have been updated.

Chapter 27

# INSIDE OUT  Replicating urgent changes

The 15-second delay for replication applies to all current implementations of Active Directory. However, the delay is overridden to allow for the immediate replication of priority changes. Priority (urgent) replication is triggered if you perform one of the following actions:

- Lock out an account, or change the account lockout policy (or if an account is locked out automatically due to failed logon attempts)

- Change the domain password policy

- Change the password on a domain controller computer account

- Change the relative ID master role owner

- Change a shared secret password used by the Local Security Authority (LSA) for Kerberos authentication

Urgent replication means that there is no delay to initiate replication. Note that all other changes to user and computer passwords are handled by the designated primary domain controller (PDC) emulator in a domain. When a user changes a normal user or computer password, the domain controller to which that user is connected immediately sends the change to the PDC emulator. This way, the PDC emulator always has the latest password for a user. This is why the PDC emulator is checked for a new password if a logon fails initially. After the new password is updated on the PDC emulator, the PDC emulator replicates the change using normal replication. The only exception is when a domain controller contacts the PDC emulator requesting a password for a user. In this case, the PDC emulator immediately replicates the current password to the requesting domain controller so that no additional requests are made for that password.

Figure 27-6 shows a ring topology that a KCC would construct if there were three domain controllers in a site.

As you can see from the figure, replication is set up as follows:

- DC1 has incoming replication connections from DC2 and DC3.

- DC2 has incoming replication connections from DC1 and DC3.

- DC3 has incoming replication connections from DC1 and DC2.

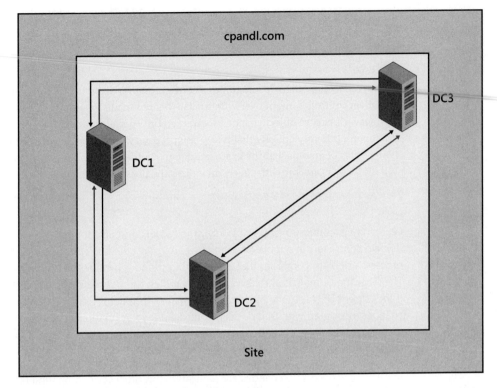

**Figure 27-6** Intrasite replication using a ring topology.

If you make changes to DC1, DC1 notifies DC2 of the changes. DC2 then pulls the changes. After replication completes, DC1 notifies DC3 of the changes. DC3 then pulls the changes. Because all domain controllers in the site have now been notified, no additional replication occurs. However, DC2 still notifies DC3 that changes are available. DC3 does not pull the changes, however, because it already has them.

Domain controllers track directory changes using update sequence numbers (USNs). Any time a change is made to the directory, the domain controller assigns the change a USN. Each domain controller maintains its own local USNs and increments their values each time a change occurs. The domain controller also assigns the local USN to the object attribute that changed. Each object has a related attribute called *uSNChanged*. The *uSNChanged* attribute is stored with the object and identifies the highest USN that has been assigned to any of the object's attributes.

To see how this works, consider the following example. The local USN for DC1 is 125. An administrator connected to DC1 changes the password on a user's account. DC1 registers the change as local USN 126. The local USN value is written to the *uSNChanged* attribute of the user object. If the administrator next edits a group account and changes its

description, DC1 registers the change as local USN 127. The local USN value is written to the *uSNChanged* attribute of the *Group* object.

> **Note**
>
> With replication, there is sometimes a concern that replication changes from one domain controller might overwrite similar changes made to another domain controller. However, because object changes are tracked on a per-attribute basis, this rarely happens. It is very unlikely that two administrators would change the exact same attributes of an object at the exact same time. By tracking changes on a per-attribute basis, Active Directory effectively minimizes the possibility of any conflict.

Each domain controller tracks not only its local USN, but also the local USNs of other domain controllers in a table referred to as an *up-to-dateness vector*. During the replication process, a domain controller that is requesting changes includes its up-to-dateness vector. The receiving domain controller can then compare the USN values to those it has stored. If the current USN value for a particular domain controller is higher than the stored value, changes associated with that domain controller need to be replicated. If the current value for a particular domain controller is the same as the stored value, changes for that domain controller do not need to be replicated.

Because only necessary changes are replicated, this process of comparing up-to-dateness vectors ensures that replication is very efficient and that changes propagate only when necessary. The up-to-dateness vectors are, in fact, the mechanism that enables domain controllers with redundant connections to know that they've already received the necessary 0.

# INSIDE OUT  Schema changes have priority

Several types of replication changes have priority. If you make changes to object attributes in the schema, these changes take precedence over most other changes. In this case, Active Directory blocks the replication of normal changes and replicates the schema changes. Active Directory continues to replicate schema changes until the schema configuration is synchronized on all domain controllers in the forest. This ensures that schema changes are applied rapidly. Still, it's a good idea to make changes to the schema during off-hours because schema changes need to propagate throughout the forest before other changes, such as resetting passwords, can be made to Active Directory.

# Intersite replication essentials

While intrasite replication focuses on speed, intersite replication focuses on efficiency. The primary goal of intersite replication is to transfer replication information between sites while making the most efficient use of the available resources. With efficiency as a goal, intersite replication traffic uses designated bridgehead servers and a default configuration that is scheduled rather than automatic, and compressed rather than uncompressed:

- With designated bridgehead servers, the Inter-Site Topology Generator (ISTG) limits the points of replication between sites. Instead of allowing all the domain controllers in one site to replicate with all the domain controllers in another site, the ISTG designates a limited number of domain controllers as bridgehead servers. These domain controllers are then the only ones used to replicate information between sites.

- With scheduled replication, you can set the valid times during which replication can occur and the replication frequency within this scheduled interval. By default, when you configure intersite replication, replication is scheduled to occur every 180 minutes 24 hours a day. When there's limited bandwidth between sites, you might want to change the default schedule to better accommodate the users who also use the link. For example, you might want to allow replication to occur every 180 minutes 24 hours a day on Saturday and Sunday, but during the week set the schedule to allow more bandwidth during the day. For example, you might set replication to occur every 60 minutes from 6 A.M. to 8 A.M. and from 7 P.M. to 3 A.M. Monday through Friday.

- With compression, replication traffic is compressed 85 to 90 percent, meaning that it is 10 to 15 percent of its uncompressed size. This means that even low-bandwidth links can often be used effectively for replication. Compression is triggered when the replication traffic is more than 32 kilobytes (KBs) in size.

As discussed previously, there are two key ways to change intersite replication:

- Turn off automatic compression if you have sufficient bandwidth on a link and are more concerned about the processing power used for compression.

- Enable automatic notification of changes to allow domain controllers on either side of the link to indicate that changes are available. Automatic notification allows those changes to be requested rather than making domain controllers wait for the next replication interval.

Regardless of the site-link configuration, replication traffic is sent through dedicated bridgehead servers rather than through multiple replication partners. When changes are made to the directory in one site, those changes replicate to the other site via the designated bridgehead servers. The bridgehead servers then initiate the replication of the changes exactly as was discussed in the Inside Out "Intrasite replication essentials" earlier in this chapter, except that the servers can use SMTP instead of RPC over IP if you use SMTP as a transport. Thus, intersite replication is really concerned with getting changes from one site to another across a site link.

Figure 27-7 shows an example of intersite replication using a single dedicated bridgehead server on each side of a site link. In this example, DC3 is the designated bridgehead server for Site 1 and DC4 is the designated bridgehead server for Site 2.

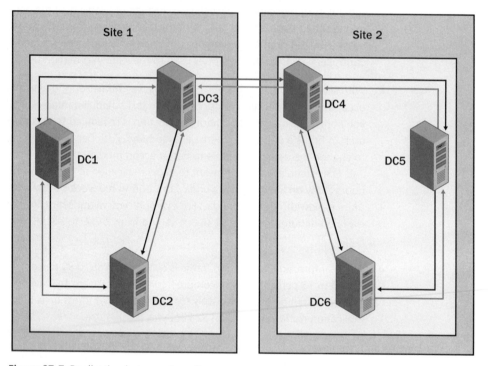

**Figure 27-7**  Replication between two sites.

As you can see from the figure, replication is set up as follows:

- DC1 has incoming replication connections from DC2 and DC3.
- DC2 has incoming replication connections from DC1 and DC3.
- DC3 has incoming replication connections from DC1 and DC2.
- DC4 has incoming replication connections from DC5 and DC6.
- DC5 has incoming replication connections from DC4 and DC6.
- DC6 has incoming replication connections from DC4 and DC5.

If changes are made to DC1 in Site 1, DC1 notifies DC2 of the changes. DC2 then pulls the changes. After replication completes, DC1 notifies DC3 of the changes. DC3 then pulls the changes. Because all domain controllers in Site 1 have now been notified, no additional replication occurs within the site. However, DC2 still notifies DC3 that changes are available. DC3 does not pull the changes, however, because it already has them.

According to the site-link configuration between Site 1 and Site 2, DC3 notifies DC4 that changes are available. DC4 then pulls the changes. Next DC4 notifies DC5 of the changes. DC5 then pulls the changes. After replication completes, DC4 notifies DC6 of the changes. DC6 then pulls the changes. Because all domain controllers in Site 2 have now been notified, no additional replication occurs. However, DC5 still notifies DC6 that changes are available. DC6 does not pull the changes, however, because it already has the changes.

So far, I've talked about designated bridgehead servers but haven't said how bridgehead servers are designated. That's because it is a rather involved process. When you set up a site, the knowledge consistency checker (KCC) on a domain controller that Active Directory has designated the Inter-Site Topology Generator (ISTG) is responsible for generating the intersite topology. Each site has only one ISTG, and its job is to determine the best way to configure replication between sites.

The ISTG does this by identifying the bridgehead servers that are to be used. Replication between sites is always sent from a bridgehead server in one site to a bridgehead server in another site. This ensures that information is replicated only once between sites. As domain controllers are added and removed from sites, the ISTG regenerates the topology automatically.

The ISTG also creates the connection objects that are needed to connect bridgehead servers on either side of a site link. This is how Active Directory logically represents a site link. The ISTG continuously monitors connections and will create new connections when a domain controller acting as a designated bridgehead server is no longer available. In most cases, there will be more than one designated bridgehead server, and I'll discuss why in "Replication rings and directory partitions."

> **Note**
> You can manually configure intersite replication in several ways. In addition to using the techniques discussed previously for scheduling, notification, and compression, you can also configure site link costs, configure connection objects manually, and designate preferred bridgehead servers.

Chapter 27

# Replication rings and directory partitions

The KCC is responsible for generating the intrasite replication topology, and the ISTG uses the KCC to generate the intersite replication topology. The KCC always configures the replication topology so that each domain controller in a site has at least two incoming connections if possible, as already discussed. The KCC also always configures intrasite replication so that each domain controller is no more than three hops from any other domain controller. This also means that *maximum replication latency*, the delay in replicating a change across an entire site, is approximately 45 seconds for normal replication.

When there are two domain controllers in a site, each domain controller is the replication partner of the other. When there are between three and seven domain controllers in the domain, each domain controller has two incoming connections and two replication partners. Figure 27-8 shows the replication topology for City Power & Light's Sacramento campus. Here, the network is spread over two buildings that are connected with high-speed interconnects. Because the buildings are connected over redundant high-speed links, the organization uses a single site with three domain controllers in each building. The replication topology for the six domain controllers as shown ensures that no domain controller is more than three hops from any other domain controller.

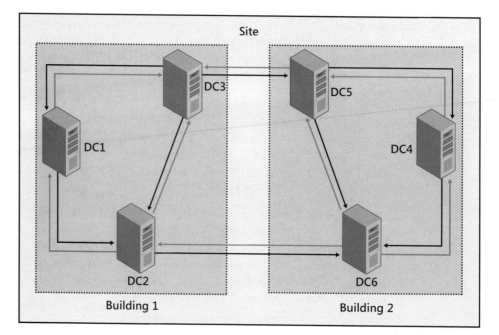

**Figure 27-8** Campus replication with two buildings and three domain controllers in each building.

When the number of domain controllers increases beyond seven, additional connection objects are added to ensure that no domain controller is more than three hops from any other domain controller in the replication topology. To see an example of this, consider Figure 27-9. Here, City Power & Light has built a third building that connects its original buildings to form a U-shaped office complex. The administrators have placed two new domain controllers in building 3. As a result of adding the additional domain controllers, some domain controllers now have three replication partners.

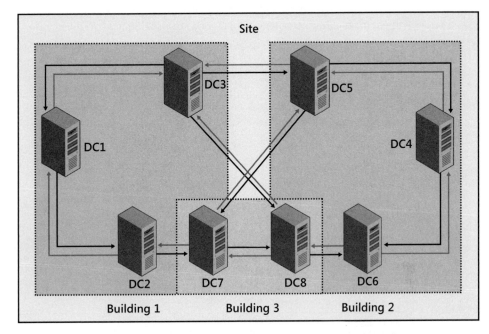

**Figure 27-9** Campus replication with three buildings and eight domain controllers.

At this point, you might be wondering what role, if any, directory partitions play in the replication topology. After all, from previous discussions, you know that Active Directory has multiple directory partitions and that those partitions are replicated in the following ways:

- On a forestwide basis for configuration and schema directory partitions

- On a domainwide basis for the domain directory partition

- On a selective basis for the global catalog partition or other application-specific partitions, which include special application partitions as well as the ForestDnsZones and DomainDnsZones application partitions used by DNS

In previous discussions, I didn't want to complicate things unnecessarily by adding a discussion of partition replication. From a logical perspective, partitions do play an important role in replication. Replication rings, the logical implementation of replication, are based on the types of directory partitions that are available. The KCC generates a replication ring for each kind of directory partition.

Table 27-2 details the replication partners for each kind of directory partition. Replication rings are implemented on a per-directory partition basis. There is one replication ring per directory partition type, and some rings include all the domain controllers in a forest, all the domain controllers in a domain, or only those domain controllers using application partitions.

**TABLE 27-2 Per-directory partition replication rings**

| Directory Partition | Replication Partners |
| --- | --- |
| Configuration directory partition | All the domain controllers in the forest |
| Schema directory partition | All the domain controllers in the forest |
| Domain directory partition | All the domain controllers in a domain |
| Global catalog partition | All domain controllers in the forest that host global catalogs |
| Application directory partition | All the domain controllers using the application partition on a forestwide, domainwide, or selective basis, depending on the configuration of the application partition |
| ForestDnsZones directory partition | All the domain controllers in the forest that host DNS |
| DomainDnsZones directory partition | All the domain controllers that host DNS for that domain |

When replication rings are within a site, the KCC on each domain controller is responsible for generating the replication topology and keeping it consistent. When replication rings go across site boundaries, the ISTG is responsible for generating the replication topology and keeping it consistent. Because replication rings are merely a logical representation of replication, the actual implementation of replication rings is expressed in the replication topology by using connection objects. Regardless of whether you are talking about intrasite or intersite replication, there is one connection object for each incoming connection. The KCC and ISTG do not create additional connection objects for each replication ring. Instead, they reuse connection objects for as many replication rings as possible.

When you extend the reuse of connection objects to the way intersite replication is performed, this is how multiple bridgehead servers might be designated. Typically, each site also has a designated bridgehead server for replicating the domain, schema, and configuration directory partitions. Other types of directory partitions might be replicated between sites by domain controllers that host these partitions. For example, if two sites have multiple domain controllers and only a few have application partitions, a connection object might be created for the intersite replication of the application partition.

Figure 27-10 shows an example of how you might use multiple bridgehead servers. Here, the domain, schema, and configuration partitions replicate from Site 1 to Site 2 and vice versa using the connection objects between DC3 and DC5. A special application partition is replicated from Site 1 to Site 2 and vice versa using the connection objects between DC2 and DC6.

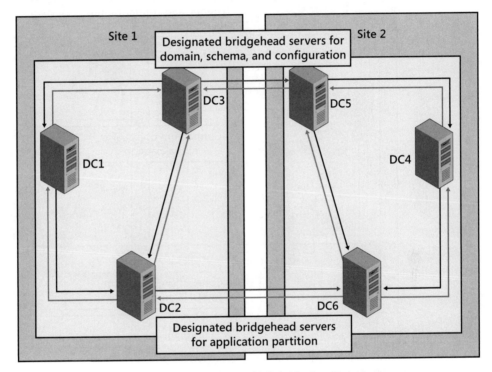

**Figure 27-10**  Replication between sites using multiple bridgehead servers.

The global catalog partition is a special exception. The global catalog is built from all the domain databases in a forest. Each designated global catalog server in a forest must get global catalog information from the domain controllers in all the domains of the forest. This means that a global catalog server must connect to a domain controller in every domain and there must be an associated connection object to do this. Because of this, global catalog servers are another reason for having more than one designated bridgehead server per site.

Figure 27-11 provides an example of how replication might work for a more complex environment that includes domain, configuration, and schema partitions as well as DNS and global catalog partitions. Here, the domain, schema, and configuration partitions replicate from Site 1 to Site 2 and vice versa using the connection objects between DC3 and DC5. The connection objects between DC1 and DC4 replicate the global catalog partition from Site 1 to Site 2 and vice versa. In addition, the connection objects between DC2 and DC6 replicate the DNS partitions from Site 1 to Site 2 and vice versa.

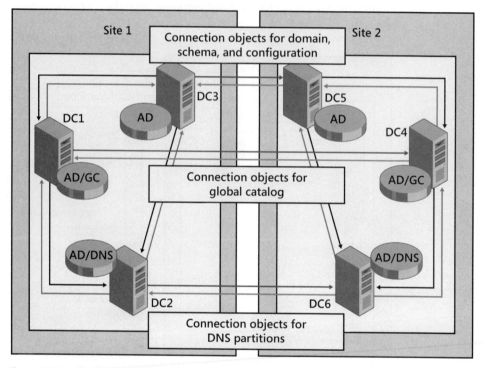

**Figure 27-11**  Replication in a complex environment.

# Developing or revising a site design

Site design depends on the networking infrastructure of your organization. As you set out to implement an initial site design, you must start by mapping your organization's existing network topology. Any time you plan to revise your network infrastructure, you must also plan the necessary revisions to your existing site design.

## Mapping network infrastructure

Although site design is relatively independent from domain structure, the replication topology depends on how available domain controllers are and how they are configured. The KCC running on each domain controller monitors domain controller availability and configuration, and it updates replication topology as changes occur. The ISTG performs similar monitoring to determine the best way to configure intersite replication. This means that as you implement or change the domain controller configuration, you might change the replication topology.

To develop a site design, you should start by mapping your existing network architecture. Be sure to include all the business locations in the organization that are part of the forest or forests for which you are developing a site plan. Document the subnets on each network segment and the connection speed on the links connecting each network segment. Keep the following in mind:

- You need to document the subnets because each site in the organization will have separate subnets. Although a single subnet can exist only in one site, a single site can have multiple subnets associated with it. After you create sites, you will create subnet-to-site associations by adding subnets to these sites.

- You need to document the connection speeds for links because the available bandwidth on a connection affects the way you configure site links. Each site link is assigned a link cost, which determines its priority order for replication. If there are several possible routes to a site, the route with the lowest link cost is used first. In the event that a primary link fails, a secondary link can be used.

Because site design and network infrastructure are so closely linked, you'll want to work closely with your organization's network administrators. If you wear both hats, start mapping the network architecture by listing each network location, the subnets at that location, and the links that connect the location. For an organization with its headquarters in Chicago and four regional offices—in Seattle, New York, Los Angeles (LA), and Miami— this information might come together as shown in Table 27-3. Notice that I start with the hubs and work my way to the central office. This way, the multiple connections to the central office are all accounted for when I finally make this entry.

**TABLE 27-3 Mapping network structure**

| Location | Subnets | Connections |
|---|---|---|
| Seattle | 10.1.11.0/24, 10.1.12.0/24 | 256 kilobits per second (Kbps) Seattle–Chicago, 128 Kbps Seattle–LA |
| LA | 10.1.21.0/24, 10.1.22.0/24 | 512 Kbps LA–Chicago, 128 Kbps LA–Seattle |
| New York | 10.1.31.0/24, 10.1.32.0/24 | 512 Kbps New York–Chicago, 128 Kbps New York–Miami |
| Miami | 10.1.41.0/24, 10.1.42.0/24 | 256 Kbps Miami–Chicago, 128 Kbps Miami–New York |
| Chicago | 10.1.1.0/24, 10.1.2.0/24 | 256 Kbps Seattle–Chicago, 512 Kbps LA–Chicago, 512 Kbps New York–Chicago, 256 Kbps Miami–Chicago |

Chapter 27

I then use the table to create a diagram similar to the one shown in Figure 27-12, in which I depict each network and the connections between them. I also noted the subnets at each location. Although it is also helpful to know the number of users and computers at each location, this information alone isn't enough to help you determine how links connecting sites are used. The only certain way to know that is to monitor the network traffic going over the various links.

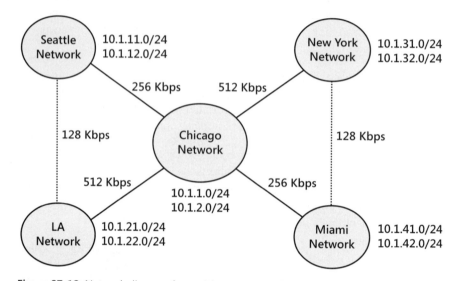

**Figure 27-12** Network diagram for a wide area network (WAN).

## Creating a site design

After you map the network structure, you are ready to create a site design. Creating a site design involves the following steps:

1. Mapping the network structure to site structure

2. Designing each individual site

3. Designing the intersite replication topology

4. Considering the impact of site-link bridging

5. Planning the placement of servers in sites

Each of these steps is examined in the sections that follow.

## Mapping the network structure to the site structure

To map the network structure to the site structure, start by examining each network location and the speed of the connections between those locations. In general, if you want to make separate network locations part of the same site, the sites should have at least 512 Kbps of available bandwidth. If the sites are in separate geographic locations, I also recommend that the network locations have redundant links for fault tolerance.

These recommended speeds are for replication traffic only, not for other user traffic. Smaller organizations with fewer than 100 users at branch locations might be able to scale down to dedicated 128-Kbps or 256-Kbps links. Larger organizations with 250 or more users at branch locations might need to scale up.

Following the previous example, the Chicago-based company would probably be best served by having separate sites at each network location. With this in mind, the site-to-network mapping is as shown in Figure 27-13. By creating the additional sites at the other network locations, you help control replication over the slow links, which can significantly improve the performance of Active Directory. More good news is that sites are relatively low-maintenance sites once you configure them, so you get a significant benefit without a lot of additional administration overhead.

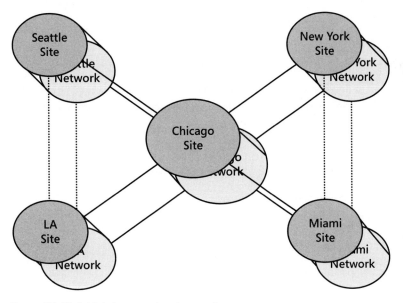

**Figure 27-13** Initial site-to-network mapping.

## Designing each individual site

After you determine how many sites you will have, you next need to consider the design of each site. A key part of the site design has to do with naming the sites and identifying the subnets that are associated with each site. Site names should reflect the physical location of the site. The default site created by Active Directory is Default-First-Site-Name, and most site names should follow a similar naming scheme. Continuing the example, you might use the following site names:

- Seattle-First-Site

- LA-First-Site

- NewYork-First-Site

- Miami-First-Site

- Chicago-First-Site

I used dashes instead of spaces, following the style Active Directory uses for the default first site. I named the sites *City*-First-Site rather than *City*-Site to allow for easy revision of the site architecture to include additional sites at each location. Now, if a location receives additional sites, the naming convention is very clear, and it is also very clear that if you have a Seattle-First-Site, Seattle-Second-Site, and Seattle-Third-Site, these are all different sites at the Seattle location.

To determine the subnets that you should associate with each site, use the network diagram developed in the previous section. It already has a list of the subnets. In your site documentation, simply note the IP subnet associations that are needed and update your site diagram to include the subnets.

## Designing the intersite replication topology

After you name the sites and determine subnet associations, you should design the intersite replication topology. You do this by planning the details of replication over each link designated in the initial site diagram. For each site link, plan the following components:

- Replication schedule

- Replication interval

- Link cost

Typically, you want replication to occur at least every 180 minutes, 24 hours a day, 7 days a week. This is the default replication schedule. If you have limited bandwidth, you might need to alter the schedule to allow user traffic to have priority during peak usage times. If bandwidth isn't a concern or if you have strong concerns about keeping branch locations up to date, you might want to increase the replication frequency. In all cases, if possible you should monitor any existing links to get a sense of the bandwidth utilization and the peak usage periods.

Calculating the link cost can be a bit complicated. When there are multiple links between locations, you need to think carefully about the appropriate cost of each link. Even if there is only one link between all your sites now, you should set an appropriate link cost now to ensure that if links are added between locations, all the links are used in the most efficient way possible.

Valid link costs range from 1, which assigns the highest possible preference to a link, to 99999, which assigns the lowest possible preference to a link. When you create a new link, the default link cost is set to 100. If you set all the links to this cost, all the links have equal preference for replication. But would you really want replication to go over a 128-Kbps link when you have a 512-Kbps link to the same location? Probably not.

In most cases, the best way to set the link cost is to assign a cost based on the available network bandwidth over a link. Table 27-4 provides an example of how this could be done.

**TABLE 27-4 Setting the link cost based on available bandwidth**

| Available Bandwidth | Link Cost | Preference |
|---|---|---|
| 10 gigabits per second (Gbps) to 2 Gbps | 1 | Top |
| 2 Gbps to 1 Gbps | 2 | Extremely high |
| 1 Gbps to 512 megabits per second (Mbps) | 4 | Very high |
| 512 Mbps to 256 Mbps | 10 | Moderately High |
| 100 Mbps to 100 Mbps | 20 | High |
| 100 Mbps to 10 Mbps | 40 | Above Normal |
| 10 Mbps to 1.544 Mbps | 100 | Normal |
| 1.544 Mbps to 512 Kbps | 200 | Below normal |
| 512 Kbps to 256 Kbps | 400 | Moderately Low |
| 256 Kbps to 128 Kbps | 800 | Low |
| 128 Kbps or less | 1600 | Very Low |

You can use the costs in the table to assign costs to each link you identified in your site diagram. After you do this, update your site diagram so that you can determine the route that is used for replication if all the links are working. As Figure 27-14 shows, your site diagram should now show the names of the sites, associated subnets, and cost of each link.

Chapter 27

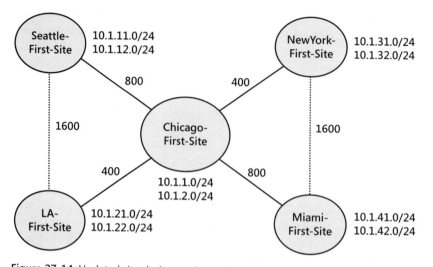

**Figure 27-14** Updated site design to show site names, subnet associations, and link costs.

## Considering the impact of site-link bridging

By default, Active Directory automatically configures site-link bridges, which makes links transitive between sites in much the same way that trusts are transitive between domains. When a site is bridged, any two domain controllers can make a connection across any consecutive series of links. The site-link-bridge cost is the sum of all the costs of the links included in the bridge. Let's calculate the site-link-bridge costs using the links shown in Figure 27-14. Because of site-link bridges, the domain controllers at the Chicago head-quarters have two possible routes for replication to each of the branch office locations. The costs of these routes are summarized in Table 27-5.

**TABLE 27-5 Link and bridge costs**

| Site/Link | Link/Bridge Cost |
| --- | --- |
| **SEATTLE SITE** | |
| Chicago–Seattle | 800 |
| Chicago–LA–Seattle | 2000 |
| **LA SITE** | |
| Chicago–LA | 400 |
| Chicago–Seattle–LA | 2400 |
| **NEW YORK SITE** | |
| Chicago–New York | 400 |
| Chicago–Miami–New York | 2400 |

| Site/Link | Link/Bridge Cost |
|---|---|
| **MIAMI SITE** | |
| Chicago–Miami | 800 |
| Chicago–New York–Miami | 2000 |

Knowing the costs of links and link bridges, you can calculate the effects of a network link failure. In this example, if the primary link between Chicago and Seattle went down, replication would occur over the Chicago–LA–Seattle site-link bridge. It's relatively straight-forward in this example, but if you introduce additional links between network locations, the scenarios become very complicated very quickly.

The network topology used in the previous example is referred to as a *hub-and-spoke* design. The headquarters in Chicago is the hub, and the rest of the offices are spokes. Automatic site-link bridging works well with a hub-and-spoke design. It doesn't work so well when you have multiple hubs. Consider the example shown in Figure 27-15. In this example, Chicago is the main hub, but because Seattle and LA have a spoke, they are also considered hubs.

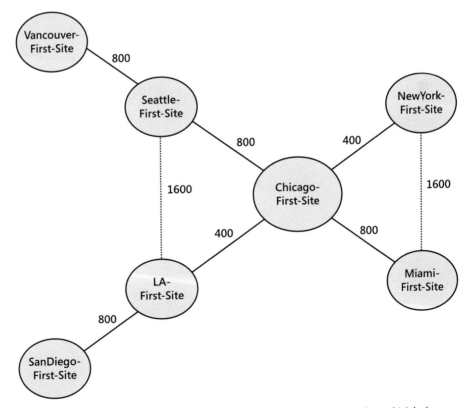

**Figure 27-15** Additional sites added to original site design, making Seattle and LA hubs.

Site-link bridging can have unintended consequences when you have multiple hubs and spokes on each hub. Here, when the bridgehead servers in the Chicago site replicate with other sites, they replicate with Seattle, New York, LA, and Miami bridgehead servers as before, but they also replicate with the Vancouver and San Diego bridgehead servers across the site bridge from Chicago–Seattle–Vancouver and from Chicago–LA–San Diego. This means that the same replication traffic could go over the Chicago–Seattle and Chicago–LA links twice. This can happen because of the rule of three hops for optimizing replication topology.

The repeat replication over the hub links becomes worse as you add additional spokes. Consider Figure 27-16. Here, the LA hub has connections to sites in Sacramento, San Diego, and San Francisco. As a result of site-link bridging, the same replication traffic could go over the Chicago–LA links four times. This happens because of the rule of three hops for optimizing replication topology.

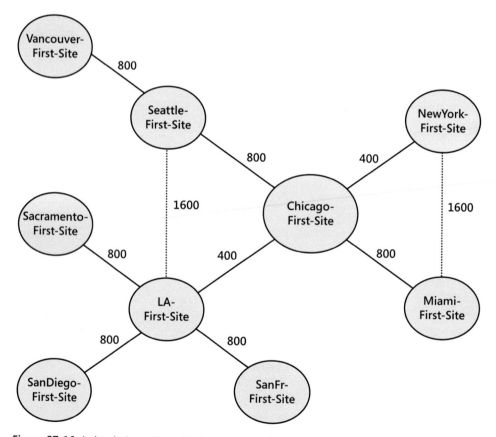

**Figure 27-16** A site design with multiple spokes at hubs.

The solution to the problem of repeat replication traffic is to disable automatic site bridging. Unfortunately, the automatic bridging configuration is all or nothing. This means that if you disable automatic site-link bridging and still want to bridge some site links, you must configure those bridges manually. You can enable, disable, and manually configure site-link bridges as discussed in "Configuring site-link bridges" in Chapter 32.

## Planning the placement of servers in sites

When you finish configuring site links, you should plan the placement of servers in the sites. Think about which types of domain controllers and how many of each will be located in a site. Answer the following questions:

- Will there be domain controllers? If so, how many?

- Will any of the domain controllers host a global catalog? If so, how many?

- Will any of the domain controllers host DNS? If so, how many?

- Will any of the domain controllers have an operations master role? If so, what roles and on which domain controllers?

Think about which Active Directory partitions will be replicated between the sites as a result of the domain controller placement, and about any additional partitions that might need to be replicated to a site. Answer the following questions:

- Will domain, configuration, and schema partitions be replicated to the site?

- Will a global catalog be replicated to the site?

- Will ForestDnsZones and DomainDnsZones partitions be replicated to the site?

- Will any special application partitions be replicated to the site? If so, what partitions, how are they used, and which domain controllers will host them?

By answering all these questions, you know what servers will be placed in each site, as well as what information will be replicated between sites. Don't forget about dependent services for Active Directory. At a minimum, each site should have at least one domain controller, a global catalog, and DNS. This configuration allows intrasite replication to occur without having to go across site links for dependent services. To improve the user experience, keep in mind the following facts:

- Global catalogs are needed for logon (unless universal group membership caching is enabled). If there is a local global catalog, logon can complete without a request having to go across a site link.

- DHCP servers are needed for dynamic IP addressing. If there is a local DHCP server, clients with dynamic IP addressing will be able to start up and get an IP address assignment without having to go across a site link.

- DNS servers are needed for forward and reverse lookups. If there is a local DNS server, clients will be able to perform DNS queries without having to go across a site link.

# CHAPTER 28

# Implementing Active Directory Domain Services

A FTER you've completed planning, the process of implementing Active Directory Domain Services (AD DS) is similar whether you are installing Active Directory for the first time or extending your existing Active Directory infrastructure. In either case, you need to take the following steps:

1. Install the necessary domain controllers, and assign any other needed roles to these servers.

2. Create the necessary organizational units (OUs), and delegate administrative control over these OUs as necessary.

3. Create any necessary user, group, and computer accounts as well as the resources that are required for use in a domain.

4. Use group policy and local security policy to set default settings for user and computer environments in any domains and OUs you created.

5. Create the necessary sites, and configure those sites for use and replication.

In this chapter, I examine the steps for installing domain controllers, creating OUs, and delegating administrative control. Chapter 30, "Managing users, groups, and computers," discusses creating user, group, and computer accounts as well as related Group Policy. Chapter 31, "Managing Group Policy," discusses managing Group Policy and local security policy. Chapter 32, "Active Directory site administration," discusses creating sites and managing replication.

## Preinstallation considerations for Active Directory

Whenever you work with a server role as complex as Active Directory Domain Services, you should take time to carefully consider the physical implementation. As with the installation of Microsoft SQL Server, Microsoft Exchange Server, or Microsoft Internet Information

Services (IIS), you should evaluate hardware requirements, plan for the system's backup needs, and consider how the system will be used.

## Hardware and configuration considerations for domain controllers

Every domain controller is essentially a database server with a complex replication system, and as such, when you select hardware for and configure domain controllers, you should use all the care and attention that you'd give to one of your mainstay database servers. The hardware you choose for the domain controllers should be correctly sized.

The following guidelines should be taken into consideration:

- **Processor**  The CPU for a domain controller needs to be relatively fast. As soon as you install the second domain controller in a forest, a process called the knowledge consistency checker (KCC) begins running on every domain controller. The KCC is responsible for generating the replication topology and dynamically handling changes and failures within the replication topology. By default, the KCC on every domain controller recalculates the replication topology every 15 minutes. The more complex the replication topology, the more processing power it takes to perform this task. In many cases, even in small domain environments, the calculations performed by the KCC considerably increase CPU utilization. This is acceptable for short durations. However, if the domain controller doesn't have a fast enough CPU, generating the replication topology in a complex environment could take several minutes rather than several seconds, which could severely affect the performance of all other processes running on the server.

- **Multiprocessing**  Some installations might benefit from having domain controllers with multiple CPUs. With multiple processors, you might see significant performance improvements. However, rather than having a single beefy domain controller, it is better to have multiple domain controllers placed appropriately.

- **Memory**  Domain controllers might use more memory than other servers. In addition to running standard processes, domain controllers must run special processes, such as storage engine processes, knowledge consistency checking, replication, and garbage collection. Therefore, most domain controllers should have at least 4 gigabytes (GBs) of RAM as a recommended starting point for full server installations and 2 GBs of RAM for core server installations. Be sure to monitor memory usage and upgrade as necessary.

- **Disks**  The data storage capacity you need depends entirely on the number of objects related to users, computers, groups, and resources that are stored in the Active Directory database. The initial installation of Active Directory requires a small amount of available space. By default, the database is stored in the Ntdis.dit database file on the system volume, as are related log files. When the database and log files are stored together, the storage volume should have free disk space of at least 20 percent of the combined size of the database and log files. When the database and log files are stored separately, each storage volume should have free disk space of at least 20 percent of either the database or the log files, as appropriate.

- **Data protection**   Domain controllers should use fault-tolerant drives to protect against hardware failure of the system volume and any other volumes used by Active Directory. I recommend using a redundant array of independent disks (RAID), either RAID 1 or RAID 5. Hardware RAID is preferable to software RAID.

When configuring the hardware, you should consider where you will install the files used by Active Directory. Active Directory database and log files are stored by default in the %SystemRoot%\NTDS folder, although the Active Directory system volume (Sysvol)—which is created as a shared folder and contains policy, scripts, and other related files—is stored by default in the %SystemRoot%\SYSVOL folder. These locations are completely configurable during installation; you should consider whether you want to accept the defaults or store the files elsewhere. You'll get much better scalability and performance if you put the database and log files on different volumes, each on a separate drive. The Active Directory Sysvol can remain in the default location in most cases.

> **Note**
> If you decide to move the Sysvol, you must move it to an NTFS volume. For security reasons, the database and log folders should be on NTFS volumes as well, but this isn't a requirement.

Active Directory is dependent on network connectivity and the Domain Name System (DNS). You should configure domain controllers to use static Internet Protocol (IP) addresses and have the appropriate primary and secondary DNS servers set in their Transmission Control Protocol/Internet Protocol (TCP/IP) configuration, as discussed in Chapter 19, "Managing TCP/IP networking." If DNS isn't available on the network, you have the opportunity to make DNS available during the installation of Active Directory. Implement DNS as discussed in Chapter 21, "Architecting DNS infrastructure," and Chapter 22, "Implementing and managing DNS," and be sure to configure the DNS server to use itself for DNS resolution. If you previously deployed Microsoft DNS, as discussed in Chapters 21 and 22, the DNS environment should already be set to work with Active Directory.

If you are using a DNS server that does not use Microsoft DNS, you can verify that the DNS server will work properly with Active Directory by using the Domain Controller Diagnostic

Utility (Dcdiag.exe). You can run Dcdiag and test the DNS configuration by typing the following command at the command prompt:

```
dcdiag /test:dcpromo /dnsdomain:DomainName /newforest
```

Here, *DomainName* is the name of the DNS domain in which the domain controller is located. Consider the following example:

```
dcdiag /test:dcpromo /dnsdomain:cpandl.com /newforest
```

Here, you run a test of the Active Directory Domain Services Configuration Wizard (Dcpromo.exe) to see if the DNS domain cpandl.com is compatible with creating a new forest. Any errors in the output of the test would need to be examined closely and resolved.

## Configuring Active Directory for fast recovery with storage area networks

Domain controllers are backed up differently than other servers are. To back up Active Directory, you must back up the System State. On Windows Server 2012, there are approximately 50,000 system state files, which use approximately 4 GBs of disc space in the default installation. These files must be backed up as a set and cannot be divided. To keep the System State intact when you place the volumes related to Active Directory on a storage area network (SAN), you must also place the operating system (system and boot volume) on the SAN. This means that you must then boot from the SAN.

Booting from a SAN and configuring Active Directory so that the related volumes are on a SAN enables several fast recovery scenarios—most of which make use of the Volume Shadow Copy Service (VSS). For instance, suppose that a domain controller is using the C, D, and E volumes: C for the operating system and Sysvol, D for the Active Directory database, and E for the Active Directory logs. Using a third-party backup utility that makes use of the Volume Shadow Copy Service, you might be able to use that backup software to create shadow copies of the System State on separate logical unit numbers (LUNs) on the SAN.

On the SAN, let's say that volumes C, D, and E correspond to LUNs 1, 2, and 3 and that the current shadow copy of those volumes is on LUNs 7, 8, and 9. If Active Directory failed at this point, you could recover by performing the following steps:

1. Use the DiskRAID utility to mask the failed LUNs (1, 2, and 3) so that they are no longer accessible.

2. Use the DiskRAID utility to unmask the shadow-copied LUNs (7, 8, and 9) so that they are usable.

> **Note**
>
> The DiskRaid utility is a command-line tool for configuring and managing RAID storage subsystems, such as those associated with network-attached storage (NAS) and SANs. Windows 8 and Windows Server 2012 might be the last versions of Windows to support DiskRaid. Storage technologies are in transition from traditional approaches to standards-based approaches. As a result, several popular tools and favored features are being phased out, including DiskRAID.

3. You then boot the domain controller to firmware, set the boot device to LUN 6, and then reboot.

4. You've now recovered Active Directory. When the domain controller starts, it will recover the Active Directory database and synchronize with the rest of the domain controllers in the organization through regular replication.

# INSIDE OUT   Secure communications for domain controllers

One reason for configuring secure communications by default is to prevent certain types of security attacks. Secure communications specifically thwart man-in-the-middle attacks, among others. In this attack, a third machine gets between the client and the server and pretends to be the other machine to each. This allows the man-in-the-middle machine to intercept and modify data that is transmitted between the client and the server. With that said, if you must disable secure communications, you can do so.

To disable the secure communications requirement, follow these steps:

1. Open the related Group Policy Object (GPO) for editing in the Group Policy Management Editor.

2. Expand Computer Configuration, Windows Settings, Security Settings, Local Policies, and then select Security Options.

3. Under Security Options, press and hold or right-click Domain Member: Digitally Encrypt Or Sign Secure Channel Data (Always), and then select Properties.

4. In the Properties dialog box, select Disabled and then tap or click OK.

Chapter 28

## Connecting clients to Active Directory

Network clients connect to Active Directory for logon and authentication and to perform Lightweight Directory Access Protocol (LDAP) lookups. In a standard configuration of Active Directory, communications between clients and servers are secure and use either Server Message Block (SMB) signing or secure channel encryption and signing. Secure communications are used by default because the default security policy for Windows Server 2008 and later has higher security settings than the security policies for previous versions of Windows. All current Windows clients natively support SMB signing, secure channel encryption and signing, or both.

# Installing Active Directory Domain Services

Any server running Windows Server can act as a domain controller. You configure a server as a domain controller by following a two-part process. You add the Active Directory Domain Services (AD DS) role to the server you want to promote to a domain controller and then configure the services using the Active Directory Domain Services Configuration Wizard.

## Active Directory installation options and issues

You have several options for installing Active Directory binaries:

- Use the Add Roles And Features Wizard in Server Manager to add the Active Directory Domain Services role to the server. On the Select Server Roles page, select Active Directory Domain Services and then tap or click Next twice. Tap or click Install.

- Enter the following command at an elevated Windows PowerShell prompt: **install-windowsfeature ad-domain-services –includemanagementtools**.

Both of these installation techniques do the same thing: They prepare the server by installing the AD DS binaries and the related management tools. The AD DS binaries include the Windows components that enable servers to act as domain controllers. The technique you use depends primarily on your personal preference. However, although any administrator can install the AD DS binaries, you might need additional administrator permissions to fully configure a domain controller.

After you install the binaries, you can configure Active Directory Domain Services and promote the server to a domain controller. In Server Manager, you'll have a Notification task labeled Promote This Server To A Domain Controller. Tapping or clicking the related link starts the Active Directory Domain Services Configuration Wizard. At the PowerShell prompt, you use the following cmdlets in the ADDSDeployment module to configure Active Directory Domain Service:

- **Install-ADDSForest**   Installs a new forest root domain. The *–DomainMode* and *–ForestMode* parameters set the domain and forest functional levels, respectively, which have acceptable values of Win2003, Win2008, Win2008R2, and Win2012. The *–SafeModeAdministratorPassword* parameter sets the recovery password. The *–CreateDNSDelegation* parameter creates a delegation for the domain in DNS, and the *–InstallDNS* parameter installs DNS. The basic syntax and an example follow:

  ```
  install-addsforest –domainname DomainName –DomainMode DomMode
  –ForestMode ForMode
  –CreateDNSDelegation –installdns –SafeModeAdministratorPassword Password

  install-addsforest –domainname cpandl.com –DomainMode Win2012
  –ForestMode Win2012
  –SafeModeAdministratorPassword
  (convertto-securestring "Str!F#789" –asplaintext)
  ```

- **Install-ADDSDomain**   Installs a new child or tree domain. The *–NewDomainName* parameter sets the name of the domain, and the *–ParentDomainName* parameter sets the name of the parent domain. The *–DomainType* parameter sets the domain type as either *ChildDomain* or *TreeDomain*. The basic syntax and an example follow:

  ```
  install-addsdomain –domainname DomainName –parentdomainname ParentDomain
  –SafeModeAdministratorPassword Password –DomainMode DomMode
  –DomainType DomType –installdns –CreateDNSDelegation

  install-addsdomain –domainname eng –parentdomainname cpandl.com
  –SafeModeAdministratorPassword (read-host –prompt "Recovery Password:"
  –assecurestring) –DomainMode Win2012 –installdns –CreateDNSDelegation
  ```

- **Install-ADDSDomainController**   Installs an additional domain controller. The *–InstallationMediaPath* parameter sets the path of the folder to install media from. The *–SiteName* parameter specifies the Active Directory site for the domain controller. The basic syntax and an example follow:

  ```
  install-addsdomaincontroller –domainname DomainName –CreateDNSDelegation
  –installdns –SafeModeAdministratorPassword Password –SiteName Site
  –installfrommedia FolderPath

  install-addsdomaincontroller –domainname cpandl.com –CreateDNSDelegation
  –SafeModeAdministratorPassword (convertto-securestring "Str!F#789"
      –asplaintext)
  –installdns –SiteName Seattle-First-Site –installfrommedia d:\Data\ADDS
  ```

When you configure Active Directory, you are given the option of setting the domain controller type as a domain controller either for a new domain or as an additional domain controller in an existing domain. If you make the domain controller part of a new domain, you can create a new domain in a new forest, a child domain in an existing domain tree, or

Chapter 28

a new domain tree in an existing forest. In fact, this is how you extend the Active Directory structure from the first domain in a new forest to include additional domains and domain trees.

To configure Active Directory, you must use an account with administrator privileges. The administrator privileges and installation requirements are as follows:

- **Creating a domain controller in a new forest**   If you are creating a domain controller in a new forest, you should log on to the local machine using either the local Administrator account or an account that has administrator privileges on the local machine, and then start the installation. Because you are creating the new forest, the server should have a static IP address. After you install DHCP servers in the new forest, you can assign the domain controller a dynamic IP address.

- **Creating a domain controller in a new domain or a domain tree**   If you are creating a domain controller in a new domain or a new domain tree in an existing forest, you should log on to the local machine using either the local Administrator account or an account that has administrator privileges on the local machine, and then start the installation. You will also be required to provide the credentials for an account that is a member of the Enterprise Admins group in the forest of which the domain will be a part.

  Because you are creating a new domain or domain tree, the server should have a static IP address. After you install DHCP servers in the new domain or domain tree, you can assign the domain controller a dynamic IP address.

- **Creating an additional domain controller in an existing domain**   If you are creating an additional domain controller in an existing domain, you should consider whether you want to perform an installation from media rather than creating the domain controller from scratch. With either technique, you need to log on to the local machine using either the local Administrator account or an account that has administrator privileges on the local machine, and then start the installation.

  You will also be required to provide the credentials for an account that is a member of the Domain Admins group in the domain of which the domain controller will be a part. Because you are installing an additional domain controller, the server should already be a member of the domain and must have a valid IP address. The IP address can be a static IP address or a dynamic IP address assigned by a DHCP server.

> **Note**
> Domain controllers that also act as DNS servers should not have dynamic IP addresses. The reason for this is that the IP address of a DNS server should be fixed to ensure reliable DNS operations.

> **Important**
>
> The server you want to promote must have appropriately configured TCP/IP settings. This means the server must have an appropriate IP address, as discussed previously. It also might mean that the server needs to have an appropriate subnet mask and default gateway, as well as preferred and alternate DNS server settings.

Before starting an Active Directory installation, you should examine local accounts and check for encrypted files and folders. Because domain controllers do not have local accounts or separate cryptographic keys, making a server a domain controller deletes all local accounts and all certificates and cryptographic keys from the server. Any encrypted data on the server, including data stored using the Encrypting File System (EFS), must be decrypted before installing Active Directory or it will be permanently inaccessible.

# INSIDE OUT Finding encrypted files

To search an entire volume for encrypted files, change directories to the root directory using the CD command, and then examine the entire contents of the directory by using the EFSInfo utility as follows:

```
efsinfo /s:DriveDesignator /i | find ": Encrypted"
```

Here, *DriveDesignator* is the drive designator of the volume to search, such as C:, as shown in the following example:

```
efsinfo /s:c: /i | find ": Encrypted"
```

Here, *EFSInfo* is used to search the root directory of C and all its subdirectories and display the encryption status of all files and folders. Because you care about only the encrypted files and folders, you pipe the output to the Find utility and search it for the string ": Encrypted", which is a text string that appears only in the output for encrypted files and folders.

To add the first domain controller that runs Windows Server 2012 to an existing Active Directory infrastructure, the Active Directory Domain Services Configuration Wizard automatically runs Adprep.exe as needed for the forest and domain. This is a new feature for Windows Server 2012. Preparing the forest and domain includes updating the Active Directory schema as needed, creating new objects and containers as needed, and modifying security descriptors and access control lists as needed. For forest prep, the account you use must be a member of the Schema Admins group, the Enterprise Admins group, and the

Chapter 28

Domain Admins group of the domain that hosts the schema master, which is, by default, the forest root domain. For domain prep, you use an account that can log on to the infrastructure master and is a member of the Domain Admins group. For read-only domain controller (RODC) prep, you must use an account that is a member of the Enterprise Admins group.

## Using the Active Directory Domain Services Configuration Wizard

With Windows Server 2012, Active Directory Domain Services installation and configuration tasks are performed via Server Manager. You no longer have to run an installation wizard and a separate command-line promotion task. Instead, you use the Add Roles And Features Wizard to add the Active Directory Domain Services role to the server and then promote the server to a domain controller using the Active Directory Domain Services Configuration Wizard. The basic steps are as follows:

1. In Server Manager, tap or click Manage and then tap or click Add Roles And Features. This starts the Add Roles And Features Wizard. If the wizard displays the Before You Begin page, read the Welcome message and then tap or click Next.

2. On the Select Installation Type page, select Role-Based Or Feature-Based Installation and then tap or click Next.

3. On the Select Destination Server page, the server pool shows servers you added for management. Tap or click the server you are configuring, and then tap or click Next.

4. On the Select Server Roles page, select Active Directory Domain Services and then tap or click Next twice. Tap or click Install. This runs the Active Directory Domain Services Configuration Wizard.

5. When the initial installation task completes, you need to tap or click Promote This Server To A Domain Controller to start the Active Directory Domain Services Configuration Wizard. If you closed the Add Roles And Features Wizard window, you need to tap or click the Notifications icon and then tap or click Promote This Server To A Domain Controller.

6. If the computer is currently a member server, the wizard takes you through the steps needed to install Active Directory Domain Services, which might include running Adprep.exe automatically to prepare the directory schema in the forest and domain for Windows Server 2012. Upgrading the forest requires credentials that include

group memberships in Enterprise Admins, Schema Admins and Domain Admins for the forest root domain. Upgrading a domain, other than the forest root domain, requires credentials that include group memberships in Domain Admins.

> **Note**
>
> The Active Directory Domain Services Configuration Wizard does not run GPPREP. You must run Adprep.exe /gpprep manually for all domains that were not previously prepared for Windows Server 2003, Windows Server 2008, or Windows Server 2008 R2. You need to prepare Group Policy only once, not for every upgrade. Group Policy isn't automatically prepared because these preparations can cause all files and folders in the SYSVOL folder to re-replicate on all domain controllers.
>
> Additionally, it's important to point out that the Active Directory Domain Services Configuration Wizard doesn't prepare a domain for RODCs when you install the first writeable Windows Server 2012 domain controller. Instead, domains are prepared for RODCs automatically when you promote the first unstaged RODC in a domain. You also can manually prepare a domain for RODCs by running Adprep.exe /rodcprep.
>
> To automatically create or update a DNS delegation, the account you use must be a member of the DNS Admins group in the domain.

The way you continue depends on whether you are creating an additional domain controller for an existing domain, creating a new domain in a new forest, or creating a new domain tree or domain in an existing forest.

## Creating additional domain controllers for an existing domain

To create an additional domain controller for an existing domain, follow these steps:

1.  Start the Active Directory Domain Services Configuration Wizard as discussed previously. On the Deployment Configuration page, shown in Figure 28-1, choose Add A Domain Controller To An Existing Domain.

Chapter 28

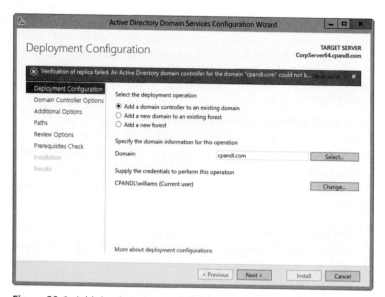

**Figure 28-1** Add the domain controller to an existing domain.

## Important

Note the verification error shown in Figure 28-1. If the server doesn't have appropriate TCP/IP settings, the wizard won't be able to connect to a domain controller in the target domain and the error you'll see is the one shown in the figure. You can see this same verification error for several other reasons as well: if you type an invalid domain name, or if all the domain controllers in the specified domain are offline. You need to correct the issue before you can continue.

A verification error also occurs if you enter the wrong password when setting credentials. Here, the error states: "Verification of replica failed. The wizard cannot access the list of domains in the forest. The user name or password is incorrect." Although the wizard checks the credentials when you enter them to ensure the user name and password are valid, the wizard doesn't verify user credential permissions until just before installation.

2. In the Domain box, type the full DNS name of the domain in the forest where you plan to install the domain controller, such as **cpandl.com**. To select a domain in the forest from a list of available domains, tap or click Select. Next, in the Select A Domain dialog box, tap or click the domain to use and then tap or click OK. (See Figure 28-2.)

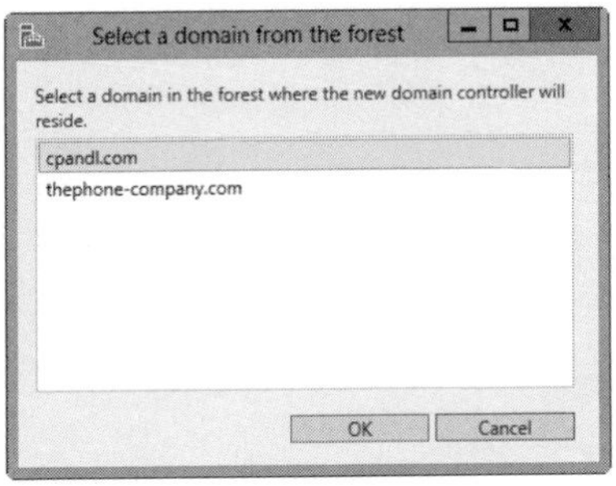

**Figure 28-2** Select the domain where you plan to install the domain controller.

3. If you are logged on to a domain in this forest and have the appropriate permissions, you can use your current logged-on credentials to perform the installation. Otherwise, you need to provide alternate credentials. Tap or click Change. In the Windows Security dialog box, type the user name and password for an enterprise administrator account in the previously specified domain and then tap or click OK.

4. When you tap or click Next, the wizard performs several preliminary checks and then displays the Domain Controller Options page, shown in Figure 28-3. The wizard does the following:

   ○ Checks any user credentials you entered to ensure that the user name and password are valid. The wizard doesn't verify user credential permissions until the Prerequisite Checks, which occur just before installation.

   ○ Determines the available Active Directory sites. The most appropriate site for the server's current subnet is selected by default on the Domain Controller Options page.

Chapter 28

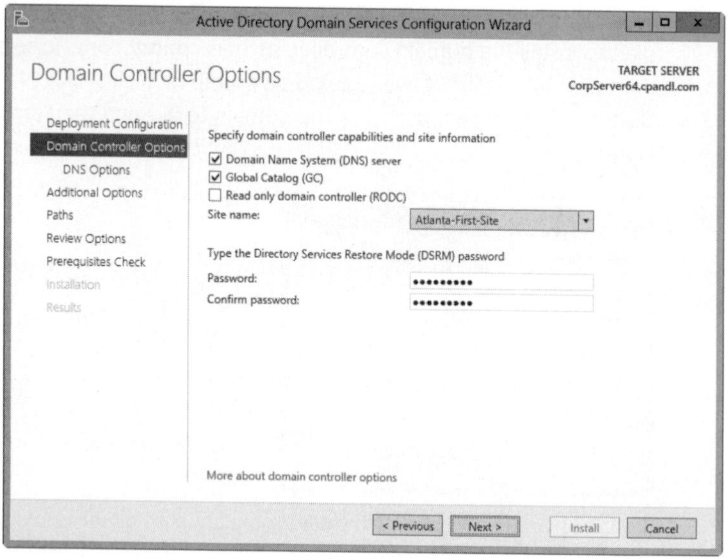

**Figure 28-3** Set primary options for the domain controller.

5. As permitted, select additional installation options. The domain controller can be a DNS server, global catalog server, or both. To ensure high availability of directory services, all domain controllers should provide DNS and global catalog services. DNS Server is selected by default if the current domain hosts DNS already on its domain controllers (based on the Start of Authority query in DNS). Global Catalog is always selected by default.

6. Select the Active Directory site in which you want to locate the domain controller. By default, the wizard selects the site with the most correct subnet. If there is only one site, the wizard selects that site automatically. No automatic selection is made if the server does not belong to an Active Directory subnet and there are multiple sites available.

7. Type and confirm the password that should be used when you want to start the computer in Directory Services Restore Mode. Be sure to track this password carefully. This special password is used only in Restore mode and is different from the Administrator account password. (It is the local Administrator password, which is in the local database of domain controllers; this database normally is hidden.) To continue, tap or click Next.

8. The next page you see depends on whether you are installing DNS Server. If you are installing the DNS Server service as an additional option, the wizard next attempts to register a delegation for the DNS server with an authoritative parent zone. If you are integrating with an existing DNS infrastructure, you should manually create a delegation to the DNS server. Otherwise, you can ignore this warning. Tap or click Next to continue.

> **Note**
>
> Before continuing, make sure you check for encrypted files and folders as discussed in the section "Active Directory installation options and issues" earlier in this chapter. If you don't do this and there are encrypted files and folders present, you will only be able to decrypt them using previously backed-up recovery agent EFS private keys. If you don't have backups of these keys, you won't be able to decrypt previously encrypted files and folders.

9. On the Additional Options page, specify whether to replicate the necessary Active Directory data from media or over the network, as shown in Figure 28-4. When you are installing from media, you must specify the folder location of the media before continuing. This folder must be on the local computer and cannot be a mapped network drive.

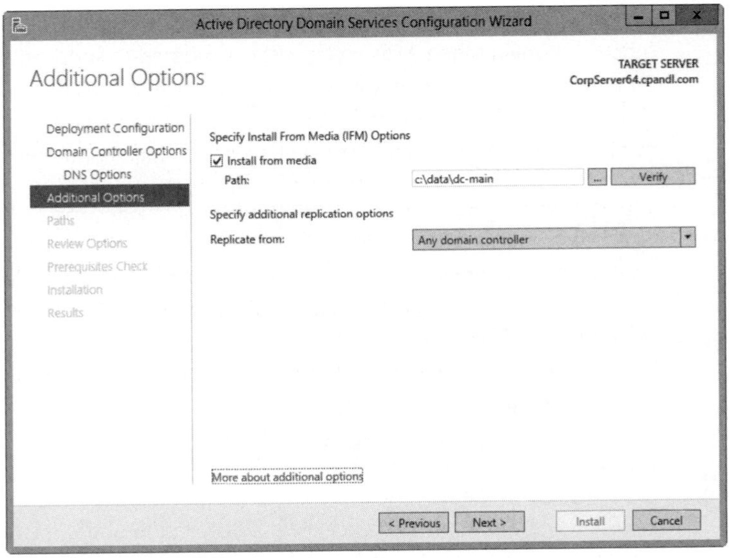

**Figure 28-4** Specify whether to replicate over the network or from media.

10. If you choose to replicate data over the network, you can choose a replication partner for the installation or all replication from any available domain controller. When you install a domain controller and do not use backup media, all directory data is replicated from the replication partner to the domain controller you are installing. Because this can be a considerable amount of data, you typically want to ensure that both domain controllers are located in the same site or connected over reliable, high-speed networks.

Chapter 28

11. On the Paths page, select a location to store the Active Directory database folder, log folder, and SYSVOL. Keep the following in mind when configuring these locations:

    ○ The default location for the database and log folders is a subfolder of %SystemRoot%\NTDS. As discussed in the section "Hardware and configuration considerations for domain controllers" earlier in this chapter, you'll get better performance if these folders are on two separate volumes, each on a separate disk.

    ○ The default location for the SYSVOL folder is %SystemRoot%\Sysvol. In most cases, you'll want to accept the default because the replication services store their database in a subfolder of the %SystemRoot% folder anyway. By keeping the folders on the same volume, you reduce the need to move files between drives.

12. If the Active Directory schema must be updated for Windows Server 2012, you'll see the Preparation Options page. You see this page when you are installing the first Windows Server 2012 domain controller in the forest or domain because the forest schema, domain schema, or both must be updated to support Windows Server 2012. When you tap or click Next to continue, the wizard doesn't use Adprep.exe to extend the schema or update the domain. Instead, the wizard does this during the installation phase, just before promoting the domain controller.

> **Note**
> If the forest, domain, or both must be prepared, the user credentials are checked on the Preparation Options page. If the user isn't a member of the appropriate groups, you'll see an error message. In this case, click Change. In the Windows Security dialog box, provide the user name and password of an account with sufficient permissions.

13. On the Review Options page, review the installation options. Optionally, tap or click View Script to export the settings to a PowerShell script that you can use to perform automated installation of other domain controllers. When you tap or click Next, the wizard performs preliminary checks to verify that the domain and forest are capable of supporting a new Windows Server 2012 domain controller. The wizard also displays information about security changes that could affect older operating systems.

**14.** When you tap or click Install, the wizard will use the options you selected to install and configure Active Directory. This process can take several minutes. Keep the following in mind:

○ If you specified that the DNS Server service should be installed, the server will also be configured as a DNS Server at this time.

○ Because you are installing an additional domain controller in an existing domain, the domain controller needs to obtain updates of all the directory partitions from other domain controllers and will do this by initiating a full synchronization. The only way to avoid this is to make a media backup of Active Directory on an existing domain controller, start the Active Directory Domain Services Configuration Wizard in Advanced mode, and then specify the backup media to use during installation of Active Directory.

**15.** When the wizard finishes configuring Active Directory, you receive a prompt informing you that the computer will be restarted. After the server restarts, Active Directory will be completely configured and the server can then act as a domain controller.

After installing Active Directory, you should verify the installation by doing the following (in no particular order):

● Examine the log of the installation, which is stored in the Dcpromo.log file in the %SystemRoot%\Debug folder. As shown in Figure 28-5, the log is very detailed and takes you through every step of the installation process, including the creation of directory partitions and the securing of the registry for Active Directory.

```
DCPROMO - Notepad
File   Edit   Format   View   Help
10/02/2014 11:53:00 [INFO] Promotion request for replica domain controller
10/02/2014 11:53:00 [INFO] DnsDomainName  cpandl.com
10/02/2014 11:53:00 [INFO]      ReplicaPartner  CorpServer28.cpandl.com
10/02/2014 11:53:00 [INFO]      SiteName  Default-First-Site-Name
10/02/2014 11:53:00 [INFO]      DsDatabasePath  C:\Windows\NTDS, DsLogPath  C:\Windows\NTDS
10/02/2014 11:53:00 [INFO]      SystemVolumeRootPath  C:\Windows\SYSVOL
10/02/2014 11:53:00 [INFO]      Account (NULL)
10/02/2014 11:53:00 [INFO]      Options  1179840
10/02/2014 11:53:00 [INFO] Validate supplied paths
10/02/2014 11:53:00 [INFO] Validating path C:\Windows\NTDS.
10/02/2014 11:53:00 [INFO]      Path is a directory
10/02/2014 11:53:00 [INFO]      Path is on a fixed disk drive.
10/02/2014 11:53:00 [INFO] Validating path C:\Windows\NTDS.
10/02/2014 11:53:00 [INFO]      Path is a directory
10/02/2014 11:53:00 [INFO]      Path is on a fixed disk drive.
10/02/2014 11:53:00 [INFO] Validating path C:\Windows\SYSVOL.
10/02/2014 11:53:00 [INFO]      Path is on a fixed disk drive.
10/02/2014 11:53:00 [INFO]      Path is on an NTFS volume
10/02/2014 11:53:00 [INFO] Start the worker task
10/02/2014 11:53:00 [INFO] Request for promotion returning 0
10/02/2014 11:53:00 [INFO] Forcing time sync
10/02/2014 11:53:00 [INFO] Forcing a time sync with CorpServer28.cpandl.com
10/02/2014 11:53:00 [INFO] Searching for a domain controller for the domain cpandl.com that
contains the account CORPSERVER85$
```

**Figure 28-5** Examine the log of the installation.

Chapter 28

- Check for DNS updates in the DNS console, shown in Figure 28-6. If you added a domain controller to an existing domain, DNS is updated to add SRV records for the server, and these are in the appropriate subfolders of the zone, such as _tcp and _udp. If you created a new domain, DNS is updated to include a forward lookup zone for the domain.

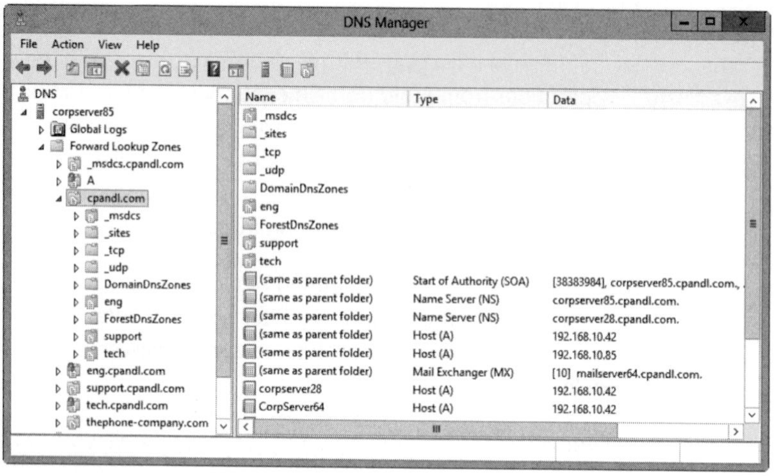

**Figure 28-6**  Check for DNS updates.

- Check for updates in Active Directory Users And Computers. For example, check to make sure the new domain controller is listed in the Domain Controllers OU, as shown in Figure 28-7.

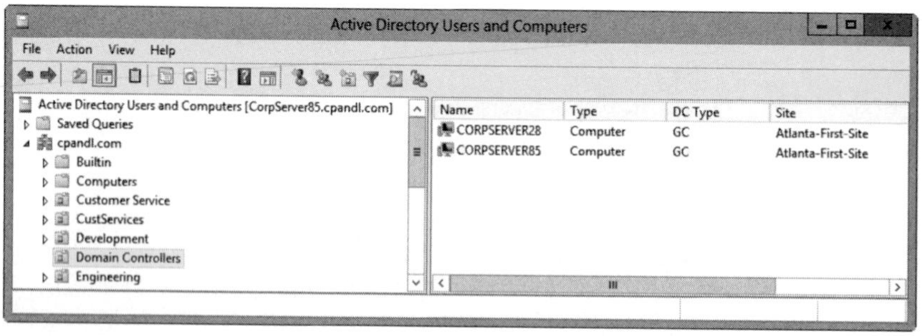

**Figure 28-7**  Check for updates in Active Directory Users And Computers.

If you created a new domain, the following containers are created and populated as appropriate:

- Builtin contains the built-in accounts for administration, including Administrators and Account Operators.

- Computers contains computer accounts for the domain.

- Domain Controllers contains the domain controller accounts and should have an account for the domain controller you installed.

- ForeignSecurityPrincipals is a container for security principals from other domain trees.

- Users is the default container for user accounts in the domain.

## Creating new domains in new forests

To create a new domain in a new forest, follow these steps:

1. Start the Active Directory Domain Services Configuration Wizard as discussed previously. The wizard uses the credentials of the built-in Administrator account to create the forest root.

   > **Note**
   > If the server doesn't have an appropriate IP address, you'll see a warning about the invalid IP address or improper network configuration and you need to correct the issue before you can continue.

2. On the Deployment Configuration page, select Add A New Forest. Type the full DNS name for the new root domain in the new forest. Domain names are not case-sensitive and use the letters A to Z, the numerals 0 to 9, and the hyphen (-) character. The name must have at least two naming components. Each component of the domain name must be separated by a dot (.) and cannot be longer than 63 characters. Following this, thephone-company.com is a valid domain name, but thephone-company is not.

3. When you tap or click Next, the wizard determines whether the name you entered is already in use on your network. If the name is already in use, you need to enter a different name or go back and make a different configuration selection. Keep in mind the domain should not have the same name as an external DNS name. If the external DNS name is thephone-company.com, you should use a different name for your internal forest to avoid compatibility issues.

4. On the Domain Controller Options page, shown in Figure 28-8, choose the desired functional level for the new Active Directory forest. The forest functional level can be set to Windows Server 2003, Windows Server 2008, Windows Server 2008 R2, or Windows Server 2012. See "Domain design considerations" in Chapter 26,

"Organizing Active Directory," and the section of Chapter 25 entitled "Using Forest Functional Levels" for a complete discussion on forest functional levels.

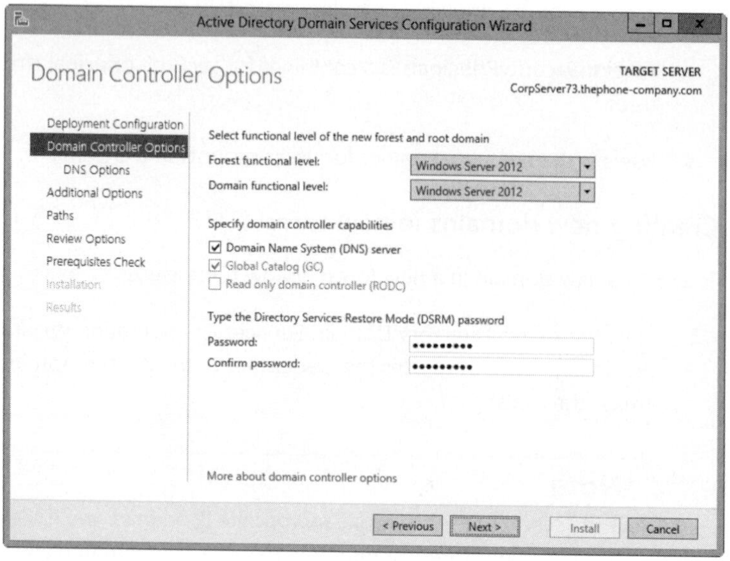

**Figure 28-8**  Choose the functional level and options for the new domain in a new forest.

5.  Next, choose the desired functional level for the new domain. The domain functional level cannot be set lower than the forest functional level. For example, if you set the forest functional level to Windows Server 2008 R2, you can set the domain functional level to Windows Server 2008 R2 or Windows Server 2012 only. See "Domain Design considerations" in Chapter 26 and "Using Domain Functional Levels" in Chapter 25 for a complete discussion on domain functional levels.

6.  As permitted, select additional installation options. When you are creating a new forest root domain, the first domain controller must be a global catalog and cannot be an RODC. The domain controller also can be a DNS server, and the related option is selected by default.

7.  Type and confirm the password that should be used when you want to start the computer in Directory Services Restore Mode. Be sure to track this password carefully. This special password is used only in Restore mode and is different from the Administrator account password. To continue, tap or click Next.

8.  The next page you see depends on whether you are installing DNS Server. If you are installing the DNS Server service as an additional option, the wizard next attempts to register a delegation for the DNS server with an authoritative parent zone. If you are integrating with an existing DNS infrastructure, you should manually create a delegation to the DNS server. Otherwise, you can ignore this warning. Tap or click Next to continue.

> **Note**
>
> If you choose to let the wizard install DNS Server, the DNS Server service will be installed and the domain controller will also act as a DNS server. A primary DNS zone will be created as an Active Directory–integrated zone with the same name as the new domain you are setting up. The wizard will also update the server's TCP/IP configuration so that its primary DNS server is set to itself.

9. When you tap or click Next, the wizard examines the network environment and attempts to register the domain and the domain controller in DNS. When you are installing a new forest root domain and DNS Server, you can't configure DNS options or DNS delegation. When you elect not to install DNS Server and have existing DNS infrastructure, however, you can create a DNS delegation using the related option and you'll also be able to provide alternate credentials. In this case, the credentials you provide must have the right to update the DNS zone.

10. The wizard uses the domain name to generate a default NetBIOS name. You can accept the wizard-generated name or type a new NetBIOS name of up to 15 characters and then tap or click Next to continue.

11. The rest of the installation proceeds as previously discussed. Continue with steps 11–15 and the post-installation checks discussed in the previous section, "Creating additional domain controllers for an existing domain."

## Creating a new domain or domain tree within an existing forest

To create a new domain or domain tree within an existing forest, follow these steps:

1. Start the Active Directory Domain Services Configuration Wizard as discussed previously. If the server doesn't have an appropriate IP address, you'll see a warning about the invalid IP address or improper network configuration and you need to correct the issue before you can continue.

2. On the Deployment Configuration page, you need to choose one of the following:

   ○ **Choose Add A New Domain To An Existing Forest and then choose Child Domain as the domain type**   Choose these options to establish the first domain controller in a domain that is a child domain of an existing domain. By choosing these options, you are specifying that the necessary parent domain already exists. For example, you would choose this option if the parent domain cpandl.com had already been created and you wanted to create the tech .cpandl.com domain as a child of this domain.

For Parent Domain Name, type or select the fully-qualified name of the parent domain, such as **cpandl.com**. Next, type the name of the new child domain in the New Domain Name box. Be sure to provide a valid, single-label name for the child domain, such as **tech** rather than **tech.cpandl.com**. The name must follow DNS domain name requirements. This means the name can use the letters A to Z, the numerals 0 to 9, and the hyphen (-) character. Following this, thephone-company

.com is a valid domain name but thephone-company is not.

○ **Choose Add A New Domain To An Existing Forest and then choose Tree Domain as the domain type**   Choose these options to establish a new domain tree that is separate from any existing trees in the existing Active Directory forest. By choosing these options, you specify that there isn't an existing parent domain with which you want to associate the new domain. For example, you should choose this option if the cohowinery.com domain already exists and you want to establish the cohovineyard.com domain in a new tree in the existing forest.

For Forest Name, type the fully-qualified name of the forest root domain, such as **cpandl.com**. Next, type the fully qualified name of the new tree domain in the New Domain Name box. The name must have at least two naming components. Each component of the domain name must be separated by a dot (.) and cannot be longer than 63 characters. Use only the letters A to Z, the numerals 0 to 9, and the hyphen (-) character.

3.  The rest of the installation proceeds as previously discussed. Continue with steps 3–15 and the post-installation checks discussed in the previous section, "Creating additional domain controllers for an existing domain." Note that you do not have the option to install from media or replicate from an existing domain controller, so the Additional Options page does not appear.

Additionally, if you created a new domain, you also need to configure DNS so that name resolution works appropriately with any existing domains. Normally, when you create a new domain, a DNS delegation is created automatically during the installation process. This delegation, created in the parent Domain Name System (DNS) zone, transfers name-resolution authority and provides an authoritative referral to other DNS servers and clients of the new zone.

Several resource records, which point to the DNS server as authoritative for the zone, are created as well:

- A name server (NS) resource record to establish the delegation and specify that the server is an authoritative server for the delegated subdomain

- A host (A or AAAA) resource record to resolve the name of the server

Creating the delegation ensures that computers in other domains can resolve DNS queries for computers in the subdomain. The wizard can create the delegation records only on Microsoft DNS servers. If the parent DNS domain zone resides on third-party DNS servers, such as Berkeley Internet Name Domain (BIND), you'll see a warning prompt stating the records can't be created and will need to create the records manually.

The wizard creates the required resource records in the parent DNS zone, and then it verifies the records after you click Next on the Domain Controller Options page. If the wizard cannot verify that the records exist in the parent domain, the wizard provides you with the option to either create a new DNS delegation for a new domain or update the existing delegation, and then continue with the new domain controller installation.

Creating a DNS delegation during installation requires credentials that have permissions to update the parent DNS zones. If you don't want to or can't create the delegation during the installation, that's okay as well, because you can manually create and validate the delegation before or after the installation.

## INSIDE OUT  Creating a zone delegation for a subdomain

To create a zone delegation in DNS Manager, press and hold or right-click the parent domain and then click New Delegation. Use the New Delegation Wizard to create the delegation as discussed in "Configuring subdomains and delegating authority" in Chapter 22.

If zone delegation is not possible at all, you can use other methods for providing name resolution from other domains to the hosts in the subdomain. As an example, the DNS administrator of another domain could configure conditional forwarding, stub zones, or secondary zones in order to resolve names in the subdomain. To enable name resolution for computers within the new domain, you typically want to create secondary zones for all existing domains in the new domain and set up zone transfers. To enable name resolution into the new domain from existing domains, you typically want to create a secondary zone in existing domains for the new domain and set up zone transfers.

# Performing an Active Directory installation from media

Whenever you install an additional domain controller in an existing domain, you should consider whether you want to perform an installation from media rather than creating the domain controller from scratch. Doing so allows the Active Directory Domain Services Configuration Wizard to get the initial data for the Configuration, Schema, and Domain directory partitions and, optionally, the SYSVOL from backup media rather than performing a full synchronization over the network.

Not only does this reduce the amount of network traffic, which is especially important when installing domain controllers in remote sites that are connected by low-bandwidth WAN links, it can also greatly speed up the process of installing an additional domain controller and getting the directory partition data synchronized. This means that rather than having to replicate the full data across the network, the domain controller needs to get only the changes made since the backup media was made. This can mean that only several megabytes of replication traffic are generated rather than several gigabytes, and on a busy or low-bandwidth network this can be very important.

> **Note**
>
> Installing Active Directory from media is not designed to be used to restore failed domain controllers. To restore failed domain controllers, you should use System State restore because this ensures that all the data that needs to be restored is recovered as necessary, including registry settings, Sysvol data, and Active Directory data.

In Windows Server 2008 or later, you can create installation media by restoring a System State backup of a domain controller. Windows Server 2008 or later versions also give you the option of performing an installation from media backup. A media backup is preferred to a System State backup because it includes only directory data. On the other hand, a System State backup includes over 50,000 files that require several gigabytes of space, not including the directory data.

Regardless of which technique you want to use, there are a few guidelines you should follow when installing Active Directory from backup media:

- Always try to use the most recent media backup of Active Directory as possible. This reduces the number of updates that must replicate to the domain controller, which in turn minimizes the post-installation replication traffic.

- Always use a backup of a domain controller in the same domain in which the new domain controller is being created, and always use a backup from another domain controller running the same version of Windows Server.

- Always copy the backup to a local drive on the server for which you are installing Active Directory. You cannot use backup media from Universal Naming Convention (UNC) paths or mapped drives.

- Never use backup media that is older than the deleted object lifetime of the domain. The default value is 60 days. If you try to use backup media older than 60 days, the Active Directory installation fails. For more information about the deleted object lifetime and why it is important, see the section "Extensible Storage Engine," in Chapter 24, "Active Directory architecture."

With these guidelines in mind, you can create an additional domain controller from backup media by completing the following steps:

1. Open an elevated command prompt window. At the command prompt, type **ntdsutil**. This starts the Directory Services Management Tool.

2. At the ntdsutil prompt, type **activate instance ntds**. This sets Active Directory as the directory service instance to work with.

3. Type **ifm** to access the install from a media prompt, and then type one of the following commands, where *FolderPath* is the full path to the folder in which to store the Active Directory backup media files:

   ○ **Create Full *FolderPath*** Creates a full writeable installation media backup of Active Directory. You can use the media to install a writeable domain controller or a read-only domain controller.

   ○ **Create RODC *FolderPath*** Creates a read-only installation media backup of Active Directory. You can use the media to install a read-only domain controller. The backup media does not contain security credentials, such as passwords.

   ○ **Create Sysvol Full *FolderPath*** Creates a full writeable installation media backup of Active Directory and the Sysvol. You can use the media to install a writeable domain controller or a read-only domain controller. The Sysvol files include computer and user scripts, as well as Group Policy settings.

   ○ **Create Sysvol RODC *FolderPath*** Creates a read-only installation media backup of Active Directory and the Sysvol. You can use the media to install a read-only domain controller.

4. Ntdsutil then creates snapshots of Active Directory partitions. When it is finished creating the snapshots, Ntdsutil mounts the snapshots as necessary and then defragments the media backup of the Active Directory database. The progress of the defragmentation is shown as a percentage complete.

Chapter 28

5. Next, Ntdsutil copies registry data related to Active Directory. If you are creating backup media for the Sysvol, Ntdsutil also creates backups of all policy settings, scripts, and other data stored on the Sysvol. When it finishes this process, Ntsdsutil unmounts any snapshots it was working with. The backup process should complete successfully. If it doesn't, note and resolve any issues that prevented successful creation of the backup media, such as the target disk running out of space or insufficient permissions to copy to the folder path.

6. Type **quit** at the ifm prompt, and type **quit** at the ntdsutil prompt.

7. Copy the backup media to a local drive on the server for which you are installing Active Directory.

8. On the server you want to make a domain controller, start the Active Directory Domain Services Configuration Wizard. Follow all the same steps as you would if you were adding a domain controller to the domain without media. After you select additional domain controller options and get past any DNS prompts, you see the Additional Options page, shown previously in Figure 28-4. On this page, select Install From Media, and then type the folder location of the backup media files or tap or click the options button to find this location.

9. You can now complete the rest of the installation as discussed in the section "Creating additional domain controllers for an existing domain" earlier in this chapter. Continue with the rest of the steps, and perform the post-installation checks as well.

You can create an additional domain controller using a System State backup media by completing the following steps:

1. Create a System State backup on a domain controller in the domain using Windows Backup or by typing the following at an elevated command prompt:

   ```
   wbadmin start systemstatebackup -backupTarget:VolumeName
   ```

   Here, *VolumeName* is the storage location for the backup, such as F:.

2. Restore the System State backup to an alternate location using Windows Backup or by typing the following at an elevated command prompt:

   ```
   wbadmin start systemstaterecovery -backupTarget:VolumeName
   -recoveryTarget:OtherLocation
   ```

   Here, *VolumeName* is the storage location that contains the System State backup you want to recover, such as F:, and *OtherLocation* is the alternate folder location in which the backup should be restored, such as F:\NTDSRestore.

3. Copy the backup media to a local drive on the server for which you are installing Active Directory.

4. On the server you want to make a domain controller, start the Active Directory Domain Services Configuration Wizard in Advanced Installation mode. Follow all the same steps as you would if you were adding a domain controller to the domain without media. After you select additional domain controller options and get past any DNS prompts, you see the Additional Options page, shown previously in Figure 28-4. On this page, select Install From Media, and then type the folder location of the backup media files or tap or click the options button to find this folder.

5. You can now complete the rest of the installation as discussed in the section "Creating additional domain controllers for an existing domain" earlier in this chapter. Continue with the rest of the steps, and perform the post-installation checks as well.

# Cloning virtualized domain controllers

Windows Server 2012 includes enhancements that ensure virtualized domain controllers work properly. After you virtualize the first domain controller in a domain, you can clone the machine to easily add additional domain controllers to the domain.

## Using clones of virtualized domain controllers

When you clone a domain controller, you make a copy of an existing virtual domain controller's virtual hard disk or virtual machine. The clone domain controller determines that it is a copy because the value of the VM-Generation ID supplied by the virtual machine will be different from the value of the VM-Generation ID stored in the directory.

The clone also looks for a DCCloneConfig.xml file in the directory where the directory resides, %windir%\NTDS, or the root of a removable media drive. This triggers an update whereby the new VM-Generation ID is stored in the directory, the clone's invocationID is reset, and any update sequence numbers (USNs) previously allocated from the RID pool are discarded.

The clone then continues provisioning itself. Using the security context of the domain controller whose copy it represents, the clone contacts the PDC emulator, which also must be running Windows Server 2012 but doesn't have to be running in a virtualized environment. The PDC emulator verifies that the requesting domain controller is authorized for cloning.

Once the PDC emulator verifies the clone, the PDC emulator creates a new machine identity—including a new security identifier, account, and password that identifies the clone as a replica domain controller—and then sends this information back to the clone. The clone uses this information to finalize the configuration of Active Directory Domain Services.

Chapter 28

> **Note**
>
> You can create multiple clones at the same time in batches. Generally, you should not try to create more than 16 clones at the same time. This number is controlled by the maximum number of outbound replication connections, which is 16 by default for Distributed File System Replication.

## Creating a clone virtualized domain controller

Deploying a clone virtualized domain controller is a multistep process that involves the following steps:

1.  Granting the source virtualized domain controller the permission to be cloned. Any virtualized domain controller in the same domain as the domain controller can be prepared for cloning. In Active Directory Administrative Center, press and hold or right-click the source virtualized domain controller and then choose Add To Group. In the Select Groups dialog box, type **Cloneable Domain Controllers** and then click OK. Once the group membership change is replicated to the PDC emulator, you can continue. If the Cloneable Domain Controllers group is not found, the PDC emulator might not be hosted on a domain controller that runs Windows Server 2012, which is a prerequisite.

> **Important**
>
> Don't add servers to the Cloneable Domain Controllers group until you are ready to perform cloning operations. After cloning operations are complete and you verify the operation, remove the servers from the Cloneable Domain Controllers group.

2.  On the source virtualized domain controller, run the Get-ADDCCloningExcludedApplicationList cmdlet at an elevated PowerShell prompt to identify installed applications or services on the source domain controller that have not been evaluated for cloning. Either correct any issues with these applications and services or remove them prior to cloning. For any remaining applications and services that can be safely cloned, run the command again with the –*GenerateXML* parameter. This provisions the applications and programs in the CustomDCCloneAllowList.xml file.

3.  On the source virtualized domain controller, run the New-ADDCCloneConfigFile cmdlet at an elevated PowerShell prompt to generate the configuration file for the

clone. Set the host name, TCP/IP configuration, and optionally, the Active Directory site, as shown in this example:

```
New-ADDCCloneConfigFile -CloneComputerName "VCorpServer18" –Static
-IPv4Address "192.168.10.34" -IPv4SubnetMask "255.255.255.0"
-IPv4DefaultGateway "192.168.10.1" -IPv4DNSResolver "192.168.10.38"
-SiteName "Seattle-First-Site"
```

4. Export a copy of the virtualized domain controller. Before you can copy the virtualized domain controller, you must shut down the source domain controller and then delete any associated snapshots. Deleting snapshots merges any AVHD files into the base VHD, which ensures that you create a clone from the newest directory version and get the correct configuration. To shut down the source domain controller, enter the following at an elevated PowerShell prompt:

```
Stop-VM –Name SourceDC –ComputerName HyperVHost
```

Here, *SourceDC* is the source virtualized domain controller and *HyperVHost* is the server hosting the virtualized domain controller, such as

```
Stop-VM –Name VCorpServer01 –ComputerName VHostServer12
```

To delete snapshots of the source domain controller, enter the following at an elevated PowerShell prompt:

```
Get-VMSnapshot SourceDC | Remove-VMSnapshot -IncludeAllChildSnapshots
```

Here, *SourceDC* is the source virtualized domain controller, such as

```
Get-VMSnapshot VCorpServer01 | Remove-VMSnapshot -IncludeAllChildSnapshots
```

Finally, copy the virtualized domain controller. To do this, enter the following at an elevated PowerShell prompt:

```
Export-VM –Name SourceDC –ComputerName HyperVHost -Path FolderPath
```

Here, *SourceDC* is the source virtualized domain controller, *HyperVHost* is the server hosting the virtualized domain controller, and *FolderPath* sets the save location such as

```
Export-VM –Name VCorpServer01 –ComputerName VHostServer12 -Path d:\VMs\
VServer01
```

5. Import the copy of the virtualized source domain controller, and rename it. If you plan to run the virtualized domain controller on a different Hyper-V host, copy the contents of the save folder to a folder on that host. Import the virtualized source domain controller by entering the following at an elevated PowerShell prompt:

```
Import-VM -Path FolderPath –Copy -GenerateNewId
```

Here, *FolderPath* sets the folder path to the save location such as

```
Import-VM –Name -Path d:\VMs\VServer01
```

Chapter 28

Rename the virtualized source domain controller by entering the following at an elevated PowerShell prompt:

```
Rename-VM -Name OrigDCName -NewName NewDCName
```

Here, *OrigDCName* is the name of the original source domain controller and *NewDCName* is the new name for the new virtualized domain controller, such as

```
Rename-VM -Name VCorpServer01 -NewName VCorpServer02
```

While the source domain controller is offline, you can create multiple clones as well. Simply repeat the import-and-rename process, making sure each clone has a different save location for its required files. You can use the *–VhdDestinationPath* parameter to set the location for virtual hard disks for a virtual machine, the *–SnapshotFilePath* parameter to set the path for the Snapshot store, the *–SmartPagingFilePath* to set the path for the smart paging folder, and the *–VirtualMachinePath* to set the path for the virtual machine configuration folder. These paths all can be set to the same destination.

## Finalizing the clone deployment

After you copy, import, and export the clone or clones, you can finalize the deployment. To do this, follow these steps:

1.  Restart the source domain controller to bring it back online. To start the source domain controller, enter the following at an elevated PowerShell prompt:

    ```
    Start-VM -Name SourceDC -ComputerName HyperVHost
    ```

    Here, *SourceDC* is the source virtualized domain controller and *HyperVHost* is the server hosting the virtualized domain controller, such as

    ```
    Start-VM -Name VCorpServer01 -ComputerName VHostServer12
    ```

2.  Start each clone in turn to bring it online for the first time. To start a clone, enter the following at an elevated PowerShell prompt:

    ```
    Start-VM -Name NewDC -ComputerName HyperVHost
    ```

    Here, *NewDC* is the name of the clone and *HyperVHost* is the server hosting the virtualized domain controller, such as

    ```
    Start-VM -Name VCorpServer02 -ComputerName VHostServer45
    ```

3.  Ensure the cloning completed successfully by logging on to the clone and checking its configuration. If you can't log on normally, the clone might be operating in Directory Services Recovery Mode. At this point, simply restarting the clone might resolve the problem.

# Troubleshooting the clone deployment

If the clone does not return to a normal mode on the next reboot, try logging on using Directory Services Recovery Mode. Type **.\Administrator** as the user and the DSRM password. You'll find errors related to cloning by reviewing the following:

- The System event log

- The Directory Service event log

- The Dcpromo log

In the Dcpromo log, which is stored in the %SystemRoot%/Debug folder, look for entries regarding the state of the directory-cloning process. If the entries state that cloning cannot be retried, the virtual machine could not be set up as a clone virtualized domain controller. Delete the virtual machine on the Hyper-V host and re-create the clone.

If the errors you see relate to cloning and cloning can be retried, you need to remove the DS Restore Mode boot flag so that Active Directory Domain Services can configure itself again. To do this, follow these steps:

1. After you fix the cause of any errors, type **msconfig** in the Apps Search box and then press Enter to start the System Configuration utility. Alternatively, you could press Windows key + R, type **msconfig**, and then press Enter.

2. On the Boot tab, under Boot Options, clear Safe boot and then tap or click OK. When prompted to restart the server, tap or click Yes.

3. When the virtual machine restarts, Active Directory attempts to finalize the cloning and provision itself again. Log on to the clone, and determine whether the issues are resolved.

If entries in the Dcpromo log indicate cloning succeeded, other types of issues might relate to the following items:

- Promotion, the directory configuration, incompatible applications, and services in the allow list (CustomDCCloneAllowList.xml). Incompatible applications and services must be removed.

- Invalid or duplicated IP address or other improper TCP/IP settings or an invalid Active Directory site listed in the config file (Dccloneconfig.xml). TCP/IP and site settings must be corrected as appropriate.

- Invalid or duplicate MAC address. The machine address must be valid and unique.

- An invalid or duplicate host name. The clone cannot have the same host name as the source domain controller.

- The PDC emulator being unavailable. The PDC emulator must be reachable by a remote procedure call (RPC).

- The domain controller not having appropriate permissions. The domain controller must be a member of Cloneable Domain Controllers. The Allow A DC To Create A Clone Of Itself permission must be set on the domain root for the Cloneable Domain Controllers group.

If the domain controller is not advertising itself as available, check the Directory Service, System, Application, and DFS Replication event logs for errors and take corrective action as appropriate. Otherwise, if the domain controller is advertising itself as available, troubleshoot as you would any other newly promoted domain controller.

# Uninstalling Active Directory

When you uninstall Active Directory, you demote the domain controller and make it a workgroup server. You uninstall Active Directory Domain Services by following these steps:

1. In Server Manager, tap or click Manage and then tap or click Remove Roles And Features. This starts the Remove Roles And Features Wizard. If the wizard displays the Before You Begin page, read the Welcome message and then tap or click Next.

2. On the Select Installation Type page, select Role-Based Or Feature-Based Installation and then tap or click Next.

3. On the Select Destination Server page, the server pool shows servers you added for management. Tap or click the server you are configuring, and then tap or click Next.

4. On the Remove Server Roles page, clear Active Directory Domain Services. An additional prompt is displayed warning you about dependent features, such as Group Policy Management and the AD DS management tools. If you tap or click the Remove Features button, the wizard removes the dependent features as well as Active Directory Domain Services. If you want to keep related management tools, clear the Remove Management Tools check box and then click Continue.

5. Next, you see the Validation Results dialog box, shown in Figure 28-9. Tap or click Demote This Domain Controller. This starts the Active Directory Domain Services Wizard.

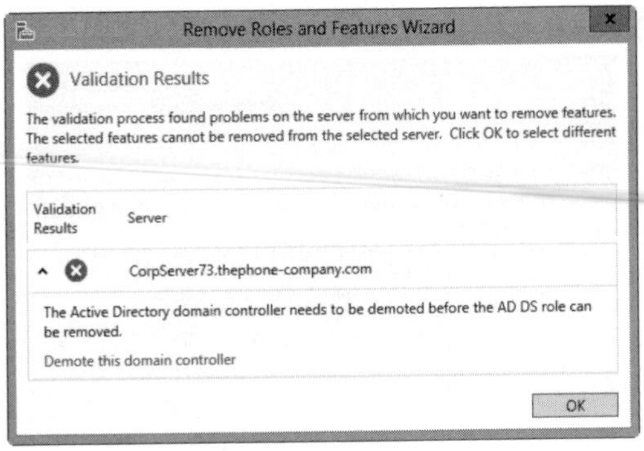

**Figure 28-9** Demote the domain controller.

When the Active Directory Domain Services Configuration Wizard starts, you'll see the Credentials page shown in Figure 28-10. You must be a member of the Domain Admins group to remove an additional domain controller in a domain and a member of the Enterprise Admins group to remove the last domain controller from a domain. If you are logged on with an account that has appropriate permissions for uninstalling Active Directory, you can use your current logged-on credentials. Otherwise, tap or click Change and then use the options in the Windows Security dialog box to enter the user name and password for an account that does have the appropriate permissions.

If this is the last domain controller in the domain and you want to permanently remove the domain from the forest, select the Last Domain Controller In The Domain check box before you continue. After you remove the last domain controller in the domain, you can no longer access any application partition data, domain accounts, or encrypted data. Therefore, before you uninstall the last domain controller in a domain, you should examine domain accounts and look for encrypted files and folders.

> **Note**
>
> Because the deleted domain no longer exists, its accounts and cryptographic keys are no longer applicable, and this results in the deletion of all domain accounts and all certificates and cryptographic keys from the server. You must decrypt any encrypted data on the server, including data stored using the Encrypting File System (EFS), before removing Active Directory or the data will be permanently inaccessible.

Chapter 28

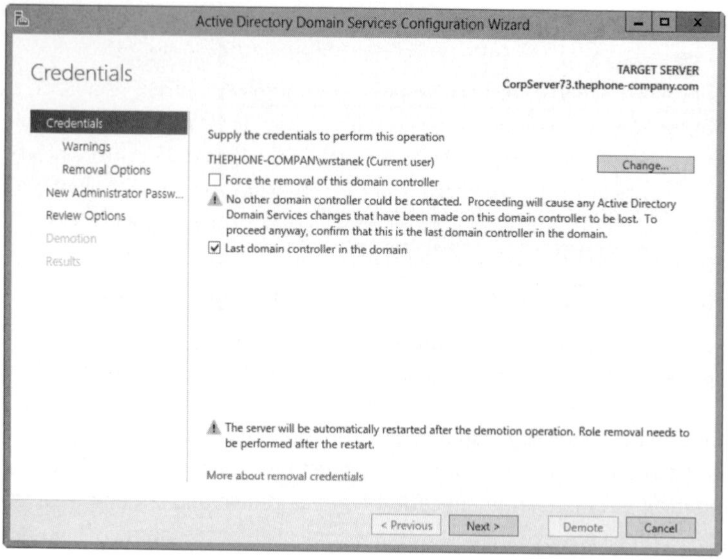

**Figure 28-10**  Removing Active Directory from a server.

# INSIDE OUT  Forcing the removal of a domain controller

You also have the option of forcing the removal of the domain controller. Force a removal only when the domain controller cannot contact other domain controllers and you cannot resolve the network problems that are preventing communications. If you force removal, you need to clean up orphaned metadata from the directory.

Forcing removal demotes the domain controller without removing the domain controller object's metadata from Active Directory. As a result, the metadata remains in Active Directory on other domain controllers in the forest. Any unreplicated changes on the domain controller—such as new user accounts, modified settings, or changed passwords—are lost as well.

When you are ready to continue, tap or click Next. The Active Directory Domain Services Configuration Wizard then examines the Active Directory forest, checking the credentials you provided and attempting to determine related functions that the domain controller performs, such as DNS Server and Global Catalog. If additional functions are found, you must select Proceed With Removal to continue.

# INSIDE OUT   Considerations for removing global catalogs

If you run the Active Directory Domain Services Configuration Wizard on a domain controller that is also a global catalog server, you see a warning prompt about this because you don't want to remove the last global catalog from the domain accidentally. If you remove the last global catalog from the domain, users won't be able to log on to the domain. A quick way to check to determine the global catalog servers in a domain is to type the following command at a command prompt:

```
dsquery server -domain DomainName | dsget server -isgc -dnsname
```

Here, *DomainName* is the name of the domain you want to examine. Consider the following example:

```
dsquery server -domain cpandl.com | dsget server -isgc -dnsname
```

Here, you are examining the cpandl.com domain to obtain a list of the global catalog servers according to their DNS names. The output is shown in two columns, for example:

```
dnsname               isgc
corpsvr15.cpandl.com  no
corpsvr17.cpandl.com  yes
```

The first column is the DNS name of each domain controller in the domain. The second column is a flag that indicates whether the domain controller is also a global catalog. Thus, if the *isgc* value is set to yes for a domain controller, it is also a global catalog server.

On the Removal Options page, you have several additional removal options. If this domain controller also is hosting the last DNS Server for the zone, you can select Remove This DNS Zone to force the removal of DNS Server. You also can elect to remove application partitions. Tap or click View Partitions to confirm which application partitions should be deleted.

Next, you are prompted to type and confirm the password for the local Administrator account on the server. This is necessary because domain controllers don't have local accounts but member or standalone servers do, so this account will be re-created as part of the Active Directory removal process. Tap or click Next.

On the Review Options page, review your selections. Optionally, tap or click Export Settings to export the settings to a PowerShell script that you can use to perform an automated demotion of other domain controllers. When you tap or click Demote, the wizard uses the options you selected to demote the domain controller. This process can take several minutes. Keep the following in mind:

- If there are updates to other domains in the forest that have not been replicated, the domain controller replicates these updates and then the wizard begins the demotion process.

- If the domain controller is also a DNS server, the DNS data in the ForestDnsZones and DomainDnsZones partitions is removed. If the domain controller is the last DNS server in the domain, this results in the last replica of the DNS information being removed from the domain. All associated DNS records are lost and might need to be re-created.

At this point, the actions the Active Directory Domain Services Configuration Wizard performs depend on whether you are removing an additional domain controller or removing the last domain controller from a domain. If you are removing an additional domain controller from a domain, the wizard does the following:

- Removes Active Directory and all related services from the server, and makes it a member server in the domain

- Changes the computer account type, and moves the computer account from the Domain Controllers container in Active Directory to the Computers container

- Transfers any operations master roles from the server to another domain controller in the domain

- Updates DNS to remove the domain controller SRV records

- Creates a local Security Accounts Manager (SAM) account database and a local Administrator account

If you are removing the last domain controller from a domain, the wizard verifies that there are no child domains of the current domain before continuing. If child domains are found, the removal of Active Directory fails with an error telling you that you cannot remove Active Directory. When the domain being removed is a child domain, the wizard notifies a domain controller in the parent domain that the child domain is being removed. For a parent domain in its own tree, a domain controller in the forest root domain is notified. Either way, the domain object is either tombstoned or logically deleted, and this change is then replicated to other domain controllers. The domain object and any related trust objects are also removed from the forest.

As part of removing Active Directory from the last domain controller in a domain, all domain accounts, all certificates, and all cryptographic keys are removed from the server. The wizard creates a local SAM account database and a local Administrator account. It then changes the computer account type to a standalone server and puts the server in a new workgroup.

# Creating and managing organizational units

Organizational units (OUs) are logical administrative units that can help you limit the scope of a domain. They can contain many types of objects, including those for computers, contacts, groups, printers, or users. Because they can also contain other OUs, you can build a hierarchy of OUs within a domain. You can also use OUs to delegate administrator privileges on a limited basis.

## Creating an OU

Several tools are available for creating OUs. Typically, the tool you use depends on what other administrative tasks you might need to perform. For example, if you are creating an OU to add resources to it, you might want to use either Active Directory Users And Computers or Active Directory Administrative Center. If you are creating an OU to apply Group Policy to it, you might want to use Group Policy Management.

As long as you use an account that is a member of the Administrators group, you'll be able to create OUs anywhere in the domain. The only exception is that you cannot create OUs within the default containers created by Active Directory.

> **Note**
> You can create OUs within the Domain Controllers container. This is possible because this container is created as an OU. Creating OUs within Domain Controllers is useful if you want to organize domain controllers.

When you work with Active Directory Users And Computers, you are connected to your login domain by default. If you want to create OUs in a different domain, press and hold or right-click the Active Directory Users And Computers node in the console tree and then select Change Domain. In the Change Domain dialog box, type the name of the domain to which you want to connect and then tap or click OK. Alternatively, in the Change Domain dialog box, you can tap or click Browse to open the Browse For Domain dialog box so that you can find the domain to which you want to connect.

You can now create the OU. If you want to create a top-level OU (that is, an OU that has the domain container as its parent), press and hold or right-click the domain node in the console tree, point to New, and then select Organizational Unit. If you want to create a lower-level OU, press and hold or right-click the OU in which you want to create the new OU, point to New, and then select Organizational Unit.

In the New Object–Organizational Unit dialog box, type a new name for the OU, as shown in Figure 28-11, and then tap or click OK. Although the OU name can be any string of up to 256 characters, the best OU names are short and descriptive.

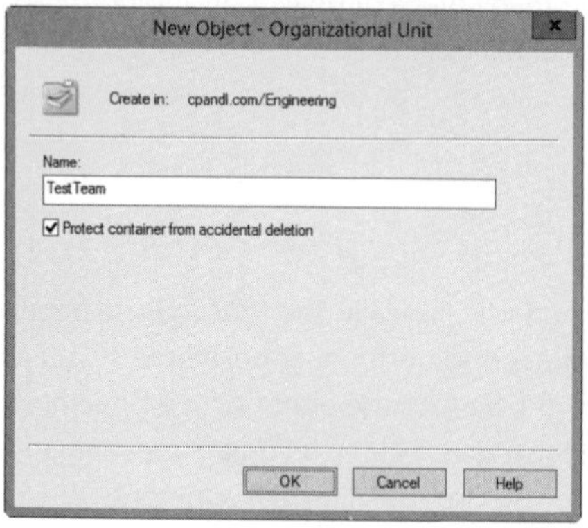

**Figure 28-11** Specify the name of the OU to create.

# INSIDE OUT  Understanding deletion protection for OUs

When you create a new OU, the Protect Container From Accidental Deletion check box is selected automatically. This prevents any user or administrator in the domain from deleting the OU accidentally. Before you can delete a protected OU, you must clear this protection flag. In Active Directory Administrative Center, this is a standard property in the Properties dialog box. In Active Directory Users And Computers, this is an advanced property on the Object tab, and you must enable the Advanced Features view by selecting Advanced Features on the View menu before you can clear or select it. Therefore, to delete an OU, you must complete the following steps:

1. In Active Directory Users And Computers, enable the Advanced Features view by selecting Advanced Features on the View menu.

2. Press and hold or right-click the OU and then select Properties.

3. On the Object tab of the Properties dialog box, clear the Protect Object From Accidental Deletion check box and then tap or click OK.

4. In Active Directory Users And Computers, press and hold or right-click the OU and then select Delete.

5. When prompted to confirm, tap or click Yes.

Creating OUs in Active Directory Administrative Center is similar. When you work with Active Directory Administrative Center, you are connected to your login domain by default. If you want to create OUs in a different domain, tap or click Manage and then select Add Navigation Nodes.

In the Additional Navigation Nodes dialog box, shown in Figure 28-12, you'll see available domains for the forest in the Columns list. To add a node for a listed domain, select it in the Columns list, tap or click the Add (>>) button, and then tap or click OK. To add a node for a domain that isn't listed, click Connect To Another Domain, enter the fully qualified domain name, and then tap or click OK. Either way, a management node for the domain should be added to the console.

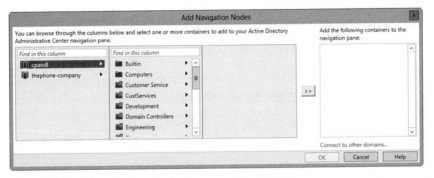

**Figure 28-12**  Select the domain that you want to manage.

If you want to create a top-level OU in Active Directory Administrative Center, press and hold or right-click the domain node in the console tree, point to New, and then select Organizational Unit. If you want to create a lower-level OU, press and hold or right-click the OU in which you want to create the new OU, point to New, and then select Organizational Unit. In the Create Organizational Unit dialog box, type a new name for the OU and then tap or click OK.

## Setting OU properties

OUs have properties that you can set to add descriptive information. This helps other administrators know how the OU is used.

To set the properties of an OU in Active Directory Users And Computers, press and hold or right-click the OU and then select Properties. This displays the OU's Properties dialog box, as shown in Figure 28-13.

Chapter 28

**Figure 28-13** The OU Properties dialog box.

- On the General tab, you can enter descriptive information about the OU, including a text description and address information.

- On the Managed By tab, you can specify the user or contact responsible for managing the OU. This gives a helpful point of contact for questions regarding the OU.

- On the Object tab, you can determine the canonical name of the OU object and specify whether the OU should be protected from accidental deletion.

- On the COM+ tab, you can specify the COM+ partition of which the OU should be a member (if any).

- On the Attribute Editor tab, you can view and set attributes of the OU object.

Similar options for setting the properties of an OU are available in Active Directory Administrative Center. Press and hold or right-click the OU and then select Properties to open the OU's Properties dialog box. COM+ and Attribute Editor options are available on the Extensions panel.

## Creating or moving accounts and resources for use with an OU

After you create an OU, you might want to place accounts and resources in it. In either Active Directory Users And Computers or Active Directory Administrative Center, you follow one of these procedures:

- You create accounts in the OU. To do so, press and hold or right-click the OU, point to New, and then select the type of object to create, such as Computer, Group, or User.

- You move existing accounts or resources to an OU. To do so, select the accounts or resources in their existing container. Using Ctrl+Tap or click or Shift+Tap or click, you can select and move multiple accounts or resources as well. Next, press and hold or right-click on the accounts or resources and then select Move. In the Move dialog box, select the container to which you want to move the accounts or resources and then tap or click OK.

# Delegating the administration of domains and OUs

When you create domains and OUs, you'll often want to be able to delegate control over them to specific individuals. This is useful if you want to give someone limited administrative privileges for a domain or OU. Before you delegate administration, you should carefully plan the permissions to grant. Ideally, you want to delegate the permissions that allow a user to perform necessary tasks, while preventing your delegate from performing tasks he or she should not. Often, figuring out the tasks that a user with limited administrative permissions should be able to perform requires talking to the department or office manager or the individual.

## Understanding delegation of administration

You delegate control of Active Directory objects to grant users permission to manage users, groups, computers, OUs, or other objects stored in Active Directory. You can grant permissions in the following ways:

- **Grant full control over an OU**   Useful when you have local administrators within departments or at branch offices and you want those individuals to be able to manage all objects in the OU. Among other things, this allows local administrators to create and manage accounts in the OU.

- **Grant full control over specific types of objects in an OU**   Useful when you have local administrators who should be able to manage only specific types of objects in an OU. For example, you might want local administrators to be able to manage users and groups but not to be able to manage computer accounts.

- **Grant full control over specific types of objects in a domain**   Useful when you want to allow an individual to be able to manage only specific types of objects in a domain. Rather than adding the user as a member of the Administrators group, you grant the user full control over specific objects. For example, you might allow the user to manage user and group accounts in the domain but not to perform other administrative tasks.

- **Grant rights to perform specific tasks**   Useful when you want to allow an individual to perform a specific task. For example, you might want to allow a department manager to read information related to user accounts in Active Directory Users And Computers, or you might want to allow help desk staff to be able to reset user passwords.

When you delegate permissions, be sure to keep in mind how inheritance works in Active Directory. As you might recall from previous discussions of permissions, lower-level objects inherit permissions from top-level objects. In a domain, the top-level object is the domain object itself. This has the following results:

- Any user designated as an administrator for a domain automatically has full control over the domain.

- If you grant permissions at the domain level, the user has those permissions for all OUs in the domain as well.

- If you grant permissions in a top-level OU, the user has those permissions for all OUs that are created within the top-level OU.

## Delegating administration

To delegate administration of a domain or OU, follow these steps:

1. In Active Directory Users And Computers, press and hold or right-click the domain or OU for which you want to delegate administration and then select Delegate Control. When the Delegation Of Control Wizard starts, tap or click Next.

2. On the Users Or Groups page shown in Figure 28-14, tap or click Add to display the Select Users, Computers, Or Groups dialog box.

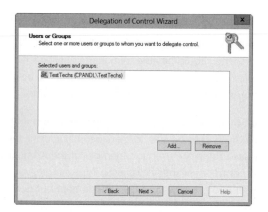

**Figure 28-14** Select the users and groups for which you want to delegate control.

3. The default location is the current domain. Tap or click Locations to see a list of the available domains and other resources that you can access. Because of the built-in transitive trusts, you can usually access all the domains in the domain tree or forest.

4. Type the name of a user or group account in the selected or default domain, and then tap or click Check Names. The options available depend on the number of matches found as follows:

   ○ When a single match is found, the dialog box is automatically updated as appropriate and the entry is underlined.

   ○ When no matches are found, you either entered an incorrect name part or you're working with an incorrect location. Modify the name and try again, or tap or click Locations to select a new location.

   ○ If multiple matches are found, select the name or names you want to use and then tap or click OK.

5. To add additional users or groups, type a semicolon (;), and then repeat this process.

6. When you tap or click OK, the users and groups are added to the Selected Users And Groups list in the Delegation Of Control Wizard. Tap or click Next to continue.

7. On the Tasks To Delegate page, shown in Figure 28-15, a list of common tasks is provided. If you want to delegate any of these common tasks, select the tasks. Afterward, tap or click Next, and then tap or click Finish. Skip the remaining steps that follow.

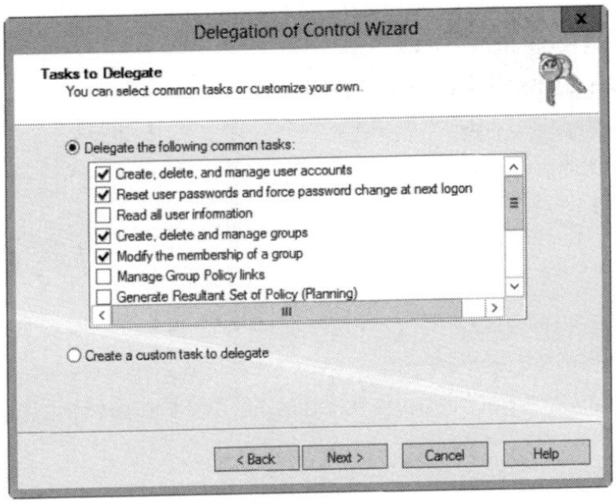

**Figure 28-15** Select the tasks to delegate, or choose to create a custom task.

8. If you want to create a custom task to delegate, choose Create A Custom Task To Delegate and then tap or click Next. On the Active Directory Object Type page, shown in Figure 28-16, you can now choose to delegate management of all objects in the container or limit the delegation to specific types of objects.

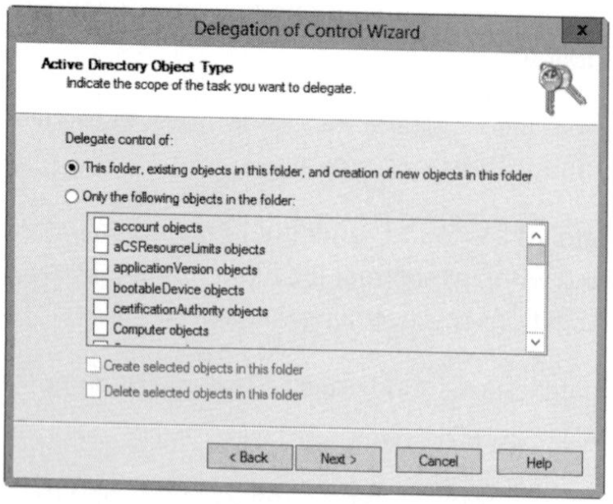

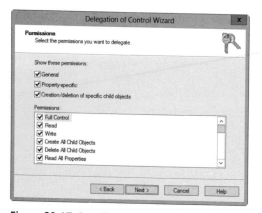

**Figure 28-16** Designate the control of tasks.

9. On the Permissions page, shown in Figure 28-17, you can select the levels of permissions to delegate for the previously selected objects. You can choose to allow Full Control over the object or objects, or you can delegate very specific permissions.

**Figure 28-17** Specify the permissions to delegate for the previously selected objects.

10. Tap or click Next, and then tap or click Finish.

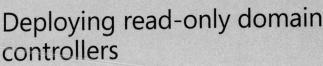

I N the previous chapter, you learned about installing domain controllers using a standard read/writeable installation. That chapter, however, did not discuss read-only domain controllers (RODCs) or detail the differences between read-only domain controllers and read/writeable domain controllers (RWDCs), which is exactly what this chapter is about. After you work with RODCs and RWDCs for a time, you'll understand why it is important to consider them as separate and distinct from each other.

When working with RODCs, you should keep in mind that they represent a paradigm shift. Although many enterprises continue to use writeable domain controllers at all office locations, enterprises will increasingly use read/writeable domain controllers only in their data centers and on trusted networks, and they will deploy only readable domain controllers everywhere else. The primary reason for this paradigm shift is that RODCs offer improved security and reduced risk compared to their RWDC counterparts.

That said, you should also understand that the infrastructure and techniques related to RODCs might change over time. For this reason, I discuss RODCs with a look to the future and also deviate from common terminology in my references to RODCs and RWDCs. My hope is that my many years' experience with RODCs and RWDCs will help you successfully deploy both in your organization and that when you do so, you'll do so by prefacing the installation plans with enough caveats to see you safely through the changes required.

## Introducing read-only domain controllers

When the domain and forest are operating at the Windows Server 2003 functional level or higher, you have the option of deploying read-only domain controllers. A read-only domain controller (RODC) is an additional domain controller that hosts a read-only replica of a domain's Active Directory data store. RODCs are designed to be placed in locations that require fast and reliable authentication services but aren't necessarily secure. This makes RODCs ideally suited to the needs of branch offices where a domain controller's physical security cannot be guaranteed.

Only Windows Server 2008 and later releases of Windows Server can act as read-only domain controllers. Typically, you do not need to make any changes to client computers to allow them to use an RODC.

RODCs support the same features as RWDCs and can be used in both Core Server and Full Server installations. Except for passwords and designated, nonreplicated attributes, RODCs store the same objects and attributes as writeable domain controllers. These objects and attributes are replicated to RODCs using unidirectional replication from a writeable domain controller acting as a replication partner. Because no changes are written directly to RODCs, writeable domain controllers acting as replication partners do not have to pull changes from RODCs. This reduces the workload of bridgehead servers in the hub site and the scope of your replication monitoring efforts. See Figure 29-1 for a top-level overview of how the replication of data works.

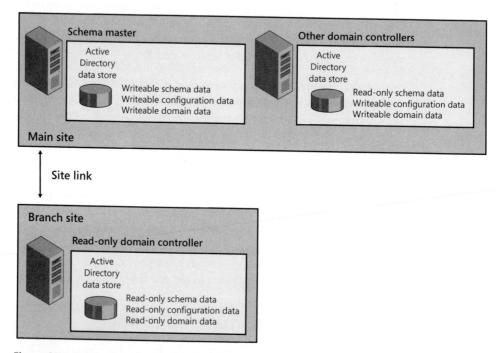

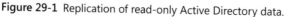

**Figure 29-1** Replication of read-only Active Directory data.

Although Active Directory clients and applications can access the directory to read data, the clients are not able to write changes directly to an RODC. Instead, they are referred to a writeable domain controller in a hub site. This prevents changes made by malicious users at branch locations from corrupting the Active Directory forest.

# INSIDE OUT Test your applications before deploying RODCs

Test all your applications that work with Active Directory before deploying RODCs. Most applications that work with Active Directory are read-intensive and do not require write access. Some applications, however, update information that is stored in Active Directory and expect this capability always to be available. If an application tries to write to an RODC, it is referred to a writeable domain controller (DC) running Windows Server 2008 or later. If the write operation succeeds, subsequent read operations might fail because the application will attempt to read from the RODC, which might not have received the updates through replication yet. To ensure proper operations, you should update applications that require write access to the directory to use binding calls to writeable domain controllers.

You can install the Domain Name System (DNS) Server service on an RODC. When you do this, the RODC receives a read-only replica of all application directory partitions that are used by DNS, including ForestDNSZones and DomainDNSZones. (See Figure 29-2.) Clients can query DNS on the RODC for name resolution as they would query any other DNS server. As with Active Directory data, the DNS server on an RODC does not support client updates directly.

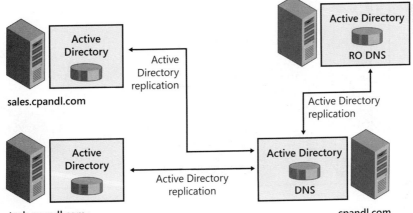

**Figure 29-2** Replication of read-only DNS data.

The RODC does not register name server (NS) resource records for any Active Directory–integrated zone that it hosts. When a client attempts to update its DNS records on an RODC, the RODC returns a referral to another DNS server and the client can then attempt the update with this DNS server. In the background, the DNS server on the RODC then attempts to pull the updated record from the DNS server that made the update. This replication request is only for the updated DNS record. The entire list of changed zone or domain data does not get replicated during this special replication request.

Because RODCs by default do not store passwords or credentials other than for their own computer accounts and the Kerberos Ticket Granting (krbtgt) accounts, RODCs pull user and computer credentials from a writeable domain controller running Windows Server 2008 or later and clients can, in turn, authenticate against an RODC, as shown in Figure 29-3. You must explicitly allow any other credentials to be cached on that RODC using Password Replication Policy. If allowed by a Password Replication Policy that is enforced on the writeable domain controller, an RODC retrieves and then caches credentials as necessary until the credentials change. Because only a subset of credentials is stored on an RODC, the number of credentials that can possibly be compromised is limited.

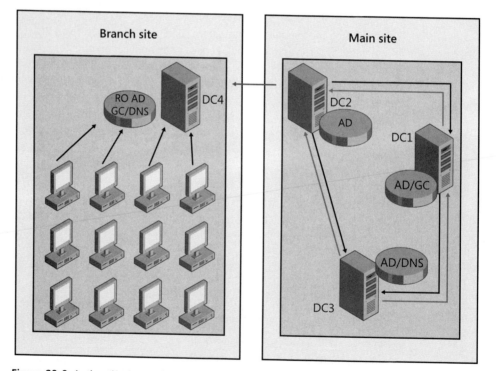

**Figure 29-3**  Authentication and credential caching with an RODC.

The RODC is advertised as the Key Distribution Center (KDC) for the branch office. After an account is successfully authenticated, the RODC attempts to contact and pull the user credentials or computer credentials from a writeable domain controller that is running

Windows Server 2008 or later in the hub site. The hub site can be any Active Directory site with writeable domain controllers running Windows Server 2008 or later.

The writeable domain controller recognizes that the request is coming from an RODC because of the use of the special Kerberos Ticket Granting account of the RODC. The Password Replication Policy that is enforced at the writeable domain controller determines whether a user's credentials or a computer's credentials can be replicated to the RODC. If the Password Replication Policy allows it, the RODC pulls and then caches the credentials from the writeable domain controller. After the credentials are cached on the RODC, the RODC can directly service that user's or computer's logon requests until the credentials change. This limits the exposure of credentials if an RODC is compromised.

> **Note**
>
> The RODC uses a different Kerberos Ticket Granting account and password than the KDC on a writeable domain controller uses when it signs or encrypts Ticket-Granting Ticket (TGT) requests. This provides cryptographic isolation between KDCs in different branches and prevents a compromised RODC from issuing service tickets to resources in other branches or in a hub site.

RODCs reduce the administration burden on the enterprise by allowing any domain user to be delegated as a local administrator without granting any other rights in the domain. This creates a clear separation between domain administrators and delegated administrator users at branch offices. An RODC cannot act as an operations master role holder. Although RODCs can pull information from domain controllers running Windows Server 2003, RODCs can only pull updates of the schema, configuration, and domain partitions from a writeable domain controller running Windows Server 2008 or later in the same domain and a partial attribute set of the other domain partitions in the forest (the global catalog). Although RODCs can host a global catalog, they cannot act as bridgehead servers or hold operations master roles.

# Design considerations for read-only replication

Before you can deploy any RODCs in a domain, the primary domain controller (PDC) emulator operations master role holder for the domain must be running Windows Server 2008 or later and you must ensure there is a bidirectional communications path open between the RODC and the PDC emulator. As necessary to accommodate this requirement, you might need to modify router and firewall configurations.

RODCs are designed to be placed in sites that have no other domain controllers. Consider the example shown in Figure 29-4. Here, the organization has one domain and two sites at the same physical location. Because the East Campus site is used for the organization's primary operations and is more secure from a physical perspective, the administrative staff decided to configure this site with the writeable domain controllers and the operations masters for the domain. Because the West Campus site is less secure from a physical perspective, the administrative staff decided to remove all other domain controllers and place only a read-only domain controller in this site.

> **Note**
>
> You cannot place RODCs from the same domain in the same site. However, you can place an RODC in a site with RWDCs from the same domain or different domains or RODCs from different domains. Doing so has a number of constraints and requires additional planning.

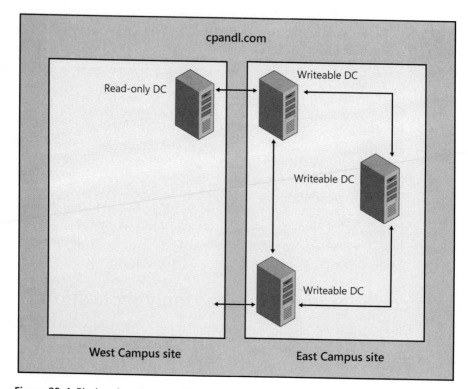

**Figure 29-4** Placing domain controllers within domains.

RODCs perform inbound replication only, by pulling data from a designated replication partner. RODCs cannot perform outbound replication and therefore cannot be a source domain controller for any other domain controller. An RODC can replicate data from a domain controller running Windows Server 2003 or later. However, it can replicate updates of the domain partition only from a domain controller located in the same domain and that is running Windows Server 2008 or later.

Table 29-1 lists the specific partitions that can be replicated and the permitted replication partners. Only an RODC also configured as a DNS server can obtain the application partitions containing DNS data. In contrast, writeable domain controllers running Windows Server 2003 or later can perform inbound and outbound replication of all available partitions.

**TABLE 29-1  Replicating directory partitions with RODCs**

| Directory Partition | Replication Partner |
| --- | --- |
| Schema | DC running Windows Server 2003 or later |
| Configuration | DC running Windows Server 2003 or later |
| Domain | DC running Windows Server 2008 or later |
| Application | DC running Windows Server 2003 or later |
| DNS | DC running Windows Server 2003 or later with Active Directory–integrated DNS zones |
| Global catalog | DC running Windows Server 2003 or later |

Generally speaking, you should place writeable domain controllers in hub sites and read-only domain controllers in spoke sites. This configuration can relieve the inbound replication load on bridgehead servers because RODCs never replicate any changes. Consider the example shown in Figure 29-5. In this example, Main Site is the hub site and there are four branch office sites: Site A, Site B, Site C, and Site D. In this example, sites are connected in several different ways with redundant pathways. However, the site link with the lowest cost is always the link between the Main Site and a particular branch site.

Chapter 29

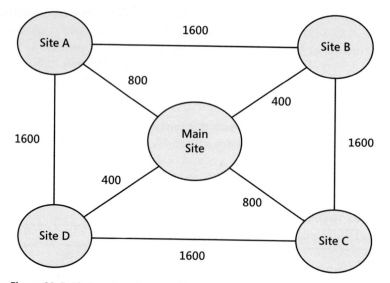

**Figure 29-5** Placing domain controllers within sites.

To put an RODC in any branch site, a domain controller running Windows Server 2008 or later for the same domain should be placed in Main Site to replicate the domain partition to the RODC. Placing only a domain controller running Windows Server 2003 in Main Site permits the RODC in the branch site to replicate the schema, configuration, and application directory partitions, but not the domain partition.

The replication schedule for site links can cause delays in receiving directory updates when replicating to other sites across a wide area network (WAN). To improve replication performance, RODCs refer many types of write operations to a writeable domain controller immediately, and this can cause unscheduled network traffic over WAN links. Additionally, for these select operations, RODCs immediately attempt inbound replication of individual changes:

- Password changes made using the Security Accounts Manager (SAM) interface rather than the Lightweight Directory Access Protocol (LDAP)

- DNS updates where a client attempts to make a DNS update and is then referred to the DNS server where the updates are registered

# Installing RODCs

RODCs can cache passwords for accounts. After an RODC has cached the password for a user, it remains in the Active Directory database until the user changes the password or the Password Replication Policy for the RODC changes such that the user's password should no longer be cached. Accounts that will not have credentials cached on the RODC can still use the RODC for domain logon. The RODC retrieves the credentials from its RWDC replication partner. The credentials, however, will not be cached for subsequent logons using the RODC.

## Preparing for an RODC installation

You can install an RODC only in an existing domain. Before you install RODCs in any domain, you must ensure the following are true:

- Forest functional level is Windows Server 2003 or higher. This ensures that linked-value replication is available to help ensure replication consistency.

- Domain functional level is Windows Server 2003 or higher. This ensures that Kerberos constrained delegation is available so that security calls can be impersonated under the context of the caller.

- The domain in which you are deploying the RODC includes domain controllers running Windows Server 2003 or later.

- The domain controller that holds the PDC emulator operations master role is running Windows Server 2008 or later, and the RODC can communicate over a secure channel with the PDC emulator.

- At least one domain controller running Windows Server 2008 or later for the same domain must be located in the site closest to the site that includes the RODC. To ensure the RODC can replicate all directory partitions, this domain controller must be a global catalog server.

- To run the DNS server on the RODC, another domain controller running Windows Server 2008 or later must be running in the domain and hosting the Active Directory–integrated DNS domain zone. An Active Directory–integrated DNS zone on an RODC is always a read-only copy of the zone file.

- You must run the **adprep /rodcprep** command before installing any RODCs in a domain. You only need to do this once ever for a domain. This ensures that the RODC can replicate DNS partitions. This is not required for new forests with only domain controllers that run Windows Server 2008 or later or when you are not using Active Directory–integrated DNS in the existing forest.

When you install an RODC, you can do the following:

- **Configure the Password Replication Policy**   The Password Replication Policy controls whether user and group passwords are replicated to the RODC. You can configure Denied Accounts for which passwords are never replicated and Allowed

Chapter 29

Accounts for which passwords are always replicated. See "Managing Password Replication Policy" later in this chapter for more information.

- **Delegate administrative permissions**  By delegating administrative permissions, you allow a specified user or group to act as the local administrator of the RODC. Delegating permissions in this way grants the user or group no other administrative permissions in the domain. For ease of administration, you should create a new group for this purpose prior to deploying an RODC. See "Delegating administrative permissions" later in this chapter for more information.

- **Install from media**  When you install from media, the RODC can get the required directory data from a local or shared folder rather than from over the network. Performing an RODC installation from media reduces directory-replication traffic over the network. You must create the media before installing the RODC as discussed in "Installing an RODC from media" later in this chapter.

- **Stage the deployment**  Typically, you use a staged deployment to allow a person who might not otherwise have appropriate permissions to deploy an RODC. You do this by creating the RODC in two phases. First, an administrator prestages the RODC by creating an RODC account in the domain. Then, a server is attached to the account during the installation of Active Directory Domain Services.

## Installing an RODC

You can install an RODC as an additional domain controller in a domain using a standard deployment or a staged deployment. If you haven't run **adprep /rodcprep** in the domain previously, which typically is required except as noted earlier, you must run this command now. The Active Directory Domain Services Configuration Wizard will not prepare a domain for RODCs.

To install an RODC in an existing domain, follow these steps:

1.  In Server Manager, tap or click Manage and then tap or click Add Roles And Features. This starts the Add Roles And Features Wizard. If the wizard displays the Before You Begin page, read the Welcome message and then tap or click Next.

2.  On the Select Installation Type page, select Role-Based Or Feature-Based Installation and then tap or click Next.

3.  On the Select Destination Server page, the server pool shows servers you added for management. Tap or click the server you are configuring, and then tap or click Next.

4. On the Select Server Roles page, select Active Directory Domain Services and then tap or click Next twice. Tap or click Install. This runs the Active Directory Domain Services Configuration Wizard.

5. When the initial installation task completes, you need to tap or click Promote This Server To A Domain Controller to start the Active Directory Domain Services Configuration Wizard. If you closed the Add Roles And Features Wizard window, you need to tap or click the Notifications icon and then tap or click Promote This Server To A Domain Controller.

6. On the Deployment Configuration page, shown in Figure 29-6, select Add A Domain Controller To An Existing Domain.

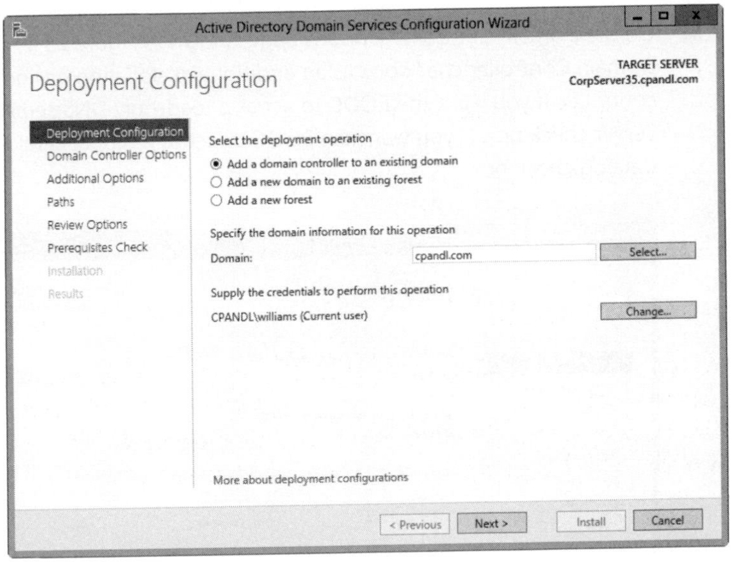

**Figure 29-6** Add the domain controller to an existing domain.

7. In the Domain box, type the full DNS name of the domain in the forest where you plan to install the domain controller, such as **cpandl.com**. To select a domain in the forest from a list of available domains, tap or click Select. Next, in the Select A Domain dialog box, tap or click the domain to use and then tap or click OK.

8. If you are logged on to a domain in this forest and have the appropriate permissions, you can use your current logged-on credentials to perform the installation. Otherwise, you need to provide alternate credentials. Tap or click Change. In the Windows Security dialog box, type the user name and password for an enterprise administrator account in the previously specified domain, and then tap or click OK.

Chapter 29

> **Important**
>
> The wizard performs several preliminary checks on this page when you tap or click Next. If the server doesn't have appropriate TCP/IP settings, the wizard won't be able to connect to a domain controller in the target domain. You'll see an error if the user name and password you entered are invalid. However, the wizard doesn't verify that the account has appropriate permissions until the Prerequisite Checks, which occur just before installation. Finally, you'll also see an error if the domain name you entered is invalid or if the domain cannot be contacted. In each case, before you can continue, you need to correct the problem.

9. On the Domain Controller Options page, shown in Figure 29-7, select the Read-Only Domain Controller check box as an additional installation option for the domain controller. If you want the RODC to act as a read-only DNS server, select the DNS Server check box. If you want the RODC to act as a global catalog, select the Global Catalog check box.

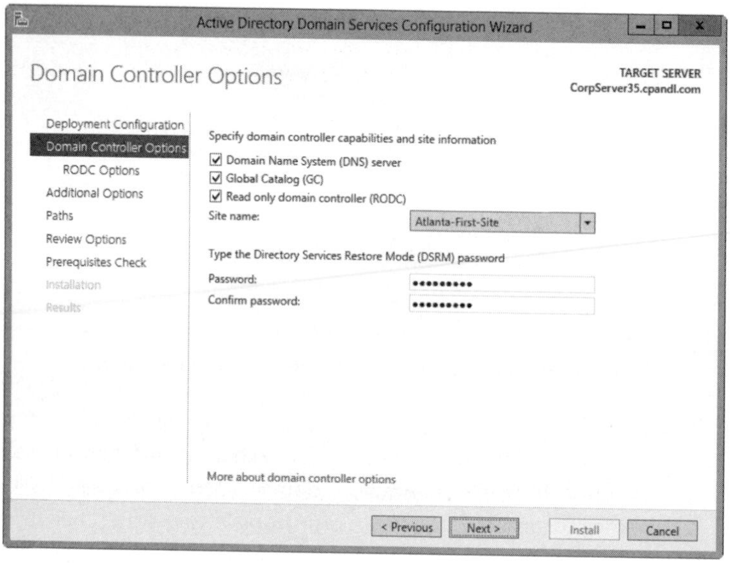

**Figure 29-7** Set options for the RODC.

10. Select the Active Directory site in which you want to locate the domain controller. By default, the wizard selects the site with the most correct subnet. If there is only one site, the wizard selects that site automatically. No automatic selection is made if the

server does not belong to an Active Directory subnet and there are multiple sites available.

11. Type and confirm the password that should be used when you want to start the computer in Directory Services Restore Mode. Be sure to track this password carefully. This special password is used only in Restore mode and is different from the Administrator account password. (It is the local Administrator password, which is in the local database of domain controllers; this database normally is hidden.) To continue tap or click Next.

12. You'll next be able to configure the Password Replication Policy for the RODC. (See Figure 29-8.) Add or remove any users or groups for which you want to allow or deny password replication. See "Allowing or denying accounts in Password Replication Policy" later in this chapter for more information. Tap or click Next to continue.

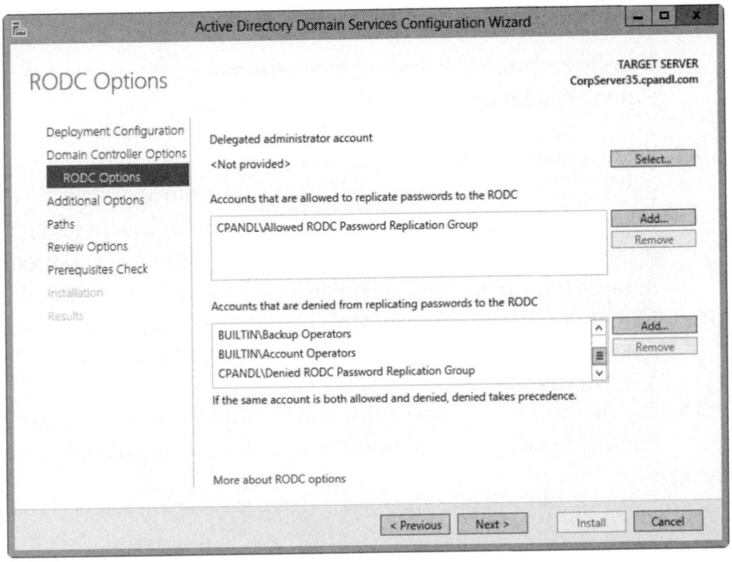

**Figure 29-8** Configure the Password Replication Policy.

13. On the Additional Options page, specify whether to replicate the necessary Active Directory data from media or over the network, as shown in Figure 29-9. When you are installing from media, you must specify the folder location of the media before continuing. This folder must be on the local computer and cannot be a mapped network drive.

Chapter 29

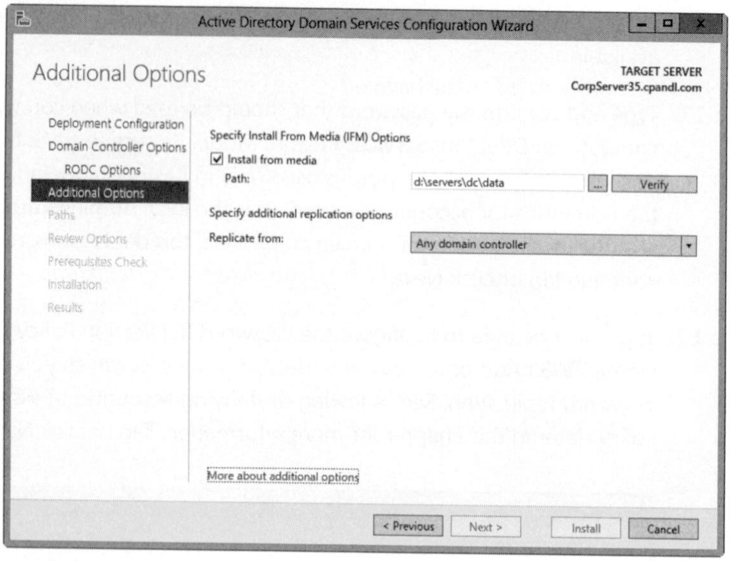

**Figure 29-9** Set the Install From Media options.

14. If you choose to replicate data over the network, you can choose a replication partner for the installation or all replication from any available domain controller. When you install a domain controller and do not use backup media, all directory data is replicated from the replication partner to the domain controller you are installing. Because this can be a considerable amount of data, you typically want to ensure that both domain controllers are located in the same site or connected over reliable, high-speed networks.

15. On the Paths page, select a location to store the Active Directory database folder, log folder, and SYSVOL. Keep the following in mind when configuring these locations:

   ○ The default location for the database and log folders is a subfolder of %SystemRoot%\NTDS. As discussed in the section "Hardware and configuration considerations for domain controllers" in Chapter 28, "Implementing Active Directory Domain Services," you'll get better performance if these folders are on two separate volumes, each on a separate disk.

   ○ The default location for the SYSVOL folder is %SystemRoot%\Sysvol. In most cases, you'll want to accept the default because the replication services store their database in a subfolder of the %SystemRoot% folder anyway. By keeping the folders on the same volume, you reduce the need to move files between drives.

16. On the Review Options page, review the installation options. Optionally, tap or click View Script to export the settings to a Windows PowerShell script that you can use to perform automated installation of other domain controllers. When you tap or click Next, the wizard performs preliminary checks to verify that the domain and forest are capable of supporting a new Windows Server 2012 domain controller. The wizard also displays information about security changes that could affect older operating systems.

17. When you tap or click Install, the wizard uses the options you selected to install and configure Active Directory. This process can take several minutes. Keep the following in mind:

   ○ If you specified that the DNS Server service should be installed, the server will also be configured as a DNS server at this time.

   ○ Because you are installing an additional domain controller in an existing domain, the domain controller needs to obtain updates of all the directory partitions from other domain controllers and will do this by initiating a full synchronization. The only way to avoid this is to make a media backup of Active Directory on an existing domain controller, start the Active Directory Domain Services Configuration Wizard in Advanced mode, and then specify the backup media to use during the installation of Active Directory.

18. When the wizard finishes configuring Active Directory, you are shown a prompt stating that the computer will be restarted. After the server restarts, Active Directory will be completely configured and the server can then act as a domain controller.

Verify the installation by checking the Dcpromo.log file in the %SystemRoot%\Debug folder. Next, check for DNS updates in the DNS console. Because you added a domain controller, DNS should be updated with SRV records for the server, and these are in the appropriate subfolders of the zone, such as _tcp and _udp. In Active Directory Users And Computers, you should see the domain controller listed in the Domain Controllers OU, as shown in Figure 29-10.

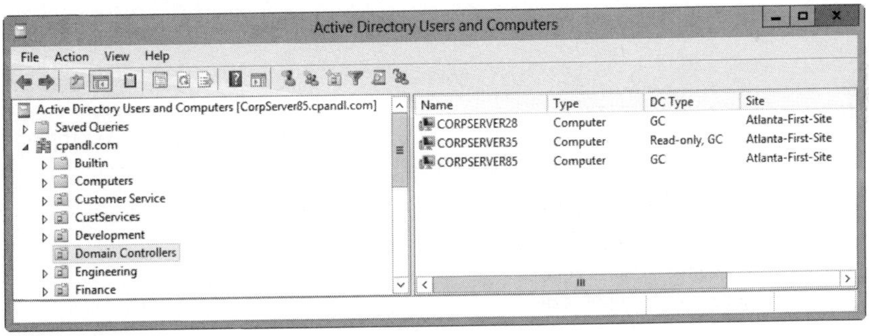

**Figure 29-10** Look for the RODC account in Active Directory Users And Computers.

# Installing an RODC from media

You can create the necessary installation media by completing these steps:

1.  Log on to a domain controller for the domain in which you are creating the RODC.

2.  At an elevated command prompt, type **ntdsutil**.

3.  At the ntdsutil prompt, type **activate instance ntds**.

4.  At the ntdsutil prompt, type **ifm**.

5.  You can now create a copy of the directory data with or without the Sysvol.

    a.  To create a copy of directory data without the Sysvol data, type **create RODC**
        *SaveFolder*, where *SaveFolder* is an empty folder into which you want to
        write the RODC data, such as C:\RODC. Ntdsutil then performs a number of
        housekeeping tasks while creating the snapshot for the RODC media. The
        output while it performs these tasks will look similar to the following:

```
Creating snapshot for RODC media...
Snapshot set {09a1fe9b-4224-4094-a6a9-9f4f49cee068} generated successfully.
Snapshot {de9f9bb6-ebc0-4913-ac8b-3d49f5c32975} mounted as
C:\$SNAP_201210131424_VOLUMEC$\
Initiating DEFRAGMENTATION mode...
    Source Database: C:\$SNAP_201210131424_VOLUMEC$\Windows\NTDS\ntds.dit
    Target Database: c:\rodc\Active Directory\ntds.dit

                Defragmentation  Status (% complete)

    0    10   20   30   40   50   60   70   80   90  100
    |----|----|----|----|----|----|----|----|----|----|
    ..................................................

Converting Full DC IFM media to Read-only DC IFM media...
Records scanned:      4443
Records scanned:       202
Read-only DC IFM media conversion completed successfully.

                Securing   Status (% complete)

    0    10   20   30   40   50   60   70   80   90  100
    |----|----|----|----|----|----|----|----|----|----|
    ..................................................

3328 pages seen
1564 blank pages seen
0 unchanged pages seen
2 unused pages zeroed
1683 used pages seen
```

```
0 pages with unknown objid
82270 nodes seen
16 flag-deleted nodes zeroed
0 flag-deleted nodes not zeroed
0 version bits reset seen
0 orphaned LVs
Snapshot {de9f9bb6-ebc0-4913-ac8b-3d49f5c32975} unmounted.
IFM media created successfully in c:\rodc
```

**b.** To create a copy of directory data with the Sysvol data, type **create sysvol rodc *SaveFolder***, where *SaveFolder* is a different, empty folder into which you want to write Sysvol data for the RODC, such as C:\SysvolSave. Ntdsutil then performs a number of housekeeping tasks while creating the snapshot of the Sysvol. The output while performing these tasks will look similar to the following:

```
Creating snapshot for RODC media...
Snapshot set {510f93b4-d2ef-4800-b4e4-82926bad7c85} generated successfully.
Snapshot {35c61a1b-5072-462f-b2bb-c340799d7094} mounted as
C:\$SNAP_201210131428_VOLUMEC$\
Snapshot {35c61a1b-5072-462f-b2bb-c340799d7094} is already mounted.
Initiating DEFRAGMENTATION mode...
     Source Database: C:\$SNAP_201210131428_VOLUMEC$\Windows\NTDS\ntds.dit
     Target Database: c:\rodc-sysvol\Active Directory\ntds.dit

           Defragmentation  Status (% complete)

       0    10   20   30   40   50   60   70   80   90  100
       |----|----|----|----|----|----|----|----|----|----|
       ...................................................

Converting Full DC IFM media to Read-only DC IFM media...
Records scanned:      4443
Records scanned:       202
Read-only DC IFM media conversion completed successfully.

              Securing  Status (% complete)

       0    10   20   30   40   50   60   70   80   90  100
       |----|----|----|----|----|----|----|----|----|----|
       ...................................................

3328 pages seen
1564 blank pages seen
0 unchanged pages seen
2 unused pages zeroed
1683 used pages seen
0 pages with unknown objid
82270 nodes seen
16 flag-deleted nodes zeroed
0 flag-deleted nodes not zeroed
```

Chapter 29

```
0 version bits reset seen
0 orphaned LVs
Copying SYSVOL...
Copying c:\rodc-sysvol\SYSVOL
Copying c:\rodc-sysvol\SYSVOL\cpandl.com
Copying c:\rodc-sysvol\SYSVOL\cpandl.com\Policies
...
Copying c:\rodc-sysvol\SYSVOL\cpandl.com\scripts
Snapshot {35c61a1b-5072-462f-b2bb-c340799d7094} unmounted.
IFM media created successfully in c:\rodc-sysvol
```

6. Copy the save folder and its entire contents to a local folder on the RODC. The amount of data written to the Save folder will vary depending on the number of objects and the properties those objects contain in the directory.

Because you created installation media for an RODC, passwords are not included in the data. You can use this same technique to create installation media for writeable domain controllers. In step 5, instead of typing **create rodc**, type **create full**. Instead of typing **create sysvol rodc**, type **create sysvol full**. That's it; it's that easy. However, a full copy of the directory data contains passwords and other critically important security data that require additional safeguards.

## Staging an RODC

You stage deployment to allow a person who might not otherwise have appropriate permissions to deploy an RODC. You do this by creating the RODC in two phases. First an administrator prestages the RODC by creating an RODC account in the domain. Then the server you are promoting is attached to the account during the installation of Active Directory Domain Services. To perform either task, you need to use an account that is a member of the Domain Admins group. You also can delegate permission to a user or group that allows attaching the RODC.

You can pre-create the RODC account by following these steps:

1. Start the Active Directory Domain Services Installation Wizard. Do one of the following:

   ○ In Active Directory Users And Computers, connect to the domain where the RODC will be added, press and hold or right-click the related Domain Controllers node, and then select Pre-Create Read-Only Domain Controller Account.

   ○ In Active Directory Administrative Center, connect to the domain where the RODC will be added, select the related Domain Controllers node in the console tree, and then select Pre-Create Read-Only Domain Controller Account under Tasks.

2. By default, the wizard uses Basic Installation mode. Select Use Advanced Mode Installation before tapping or clicking Next to continue.

3. If the server doesn't have an appropriate IP address, you'll see the Configure TCP/IP page. This page displays a warning about the invalid IP address or improper network configuration, and you need to correct the issue before you can continue.

4. When you tap or click Next, you will see the Network Credentials page. If you are logged on to a domain in this forest and have the appropriate permissions, you can use your current logged-on credentials to perform the installation. Otherwise, select Alternate Credentials, tap or click Set, type the user name and password for an enterprise administrator account in the previously specified domain, and then tap or click OK.

5. When you tap or click Next, the wizard examines the Active Directory forest and domain configuration. On the Specify The Computer Name page, shown in Figure 29-11, enter the name of the computer that will be the RODC and confirm that the fully qualified name is the one you expected. If the fully qualified name isn't the one you expected, you might have selected the wrong domain before starting the wizard.

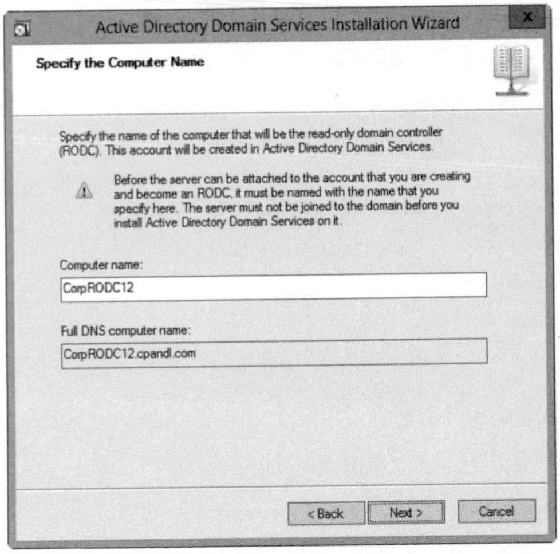

**Figure 29-11** Specify the name of the server that will be promoted.

6. When you tap or click Next, the wizard verifies the source domain and the computer name, and it then loads a list of sites in the Active Directory forest. On the Select A Site page, select the site in which the domain controller should be located and then tap or click Next.

7. When you tap or click Next, the wizard validates the site name, examines the DNS configuration, and attempts to determine whether any authoritative DNS servers are available. If you want the RODC to act as a read-only DNS server, select the DNS Server check box. If you want the RODC to act as a global catalog, select the Global Catalog check box. Tap or click Next when you are ready to continue.

8. If you are installing the DNS Server service as an additional option and the server doesn't have static IP addresses for both Internet Protocol version 4 (IPv4) and Internet Protocol version 6 (IPv6), you'll see a warning prompt regarding the server's dynamic IP address or addresses. Tap or click Yes only if you plan to use the dynamic IP address or addresses, despite the possibility that this could result in an unreliable DNS configuration. Tap or click No if you plan to change the IP configuration before continuing.

9. Next, you configure the Password Replication Policy for the RODC, as shown in Figure 29-12. Add or remove any users or groups for which you want to allow or deny password replication. See "Allowing or denying accounts in Password Replication Policy" later in this chapter for more information. Tap or click Next to continue.

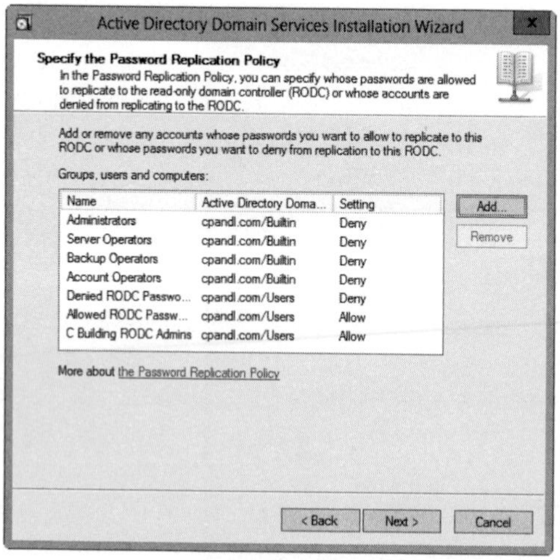

**Figure 29-12**  Configure the Password Replication Policy.

10. Next, you configure delegation. The delegated user or group will be able to attach the RODC and also will have local administrative permissions on the RODC. Tap or click Set, use the Select User Or Group dialog box to specify a delegated user or group, and then tap or click OK.

**11.** Tap or click Next. Review the installation options. Optionally, tap or click Export Settings to save these settings to an answer file that you can use to perform unattended installations of other read-only domain controllers. When you tap or click Next again, the wizard uses the options you selected to configure the account in Active Directory.

**12.** When the wizard finishes configuring Active Directory, tap or click Finish. In the Domain Controllers container, an account is created for the RODC with the type set as Unoccupied DC Account. This indicates the account is staged and ready for a server to be attached to it.

Any user who is a member of Domain Admins can attach a server to the RODC account, as can any user or group that was delegated permission when setting up the RODC account. To attach a server to the account, do the following:

**1.** If a server with the server name specified as the RODC account name isn't already set up, configure this server and add it for management in Server Manager.

**2.** Follow the steps for installing an RODC as listed in "Installing an RODC" earlier in the chapter. In step 3, when you select the destination server, select the server you are promoting to an RODC. In step 8, when you need to confirm permissions, enter the appropriate credentials.

**3.** In step 9, the Domain Controllers Options page will have a notification that states, "A pre-created account that matches the name of the target server exists in the directory." You'll have options for using the existing RODC account (the default) or to reinstall the domain controller. Because you want to attach to the existing account, use the existing account.

**4.** You won't be able to set the domain controller options for DNS or global catalogs because these options are set when the RODC account is prestaged. However, you will be able to install from media or replication. You also will be able to set the directory paths.

You can pre-create an RODC account using the Add-ADDSReadOnlyDomainControllerAccount cmdlet as well. Use the *–DomainControllerAccountName* parameter to specify the name of the account, the *–DomainName* parameter to specify the domain in which to create the account, and the *–SiteName* parameter to specify the Active Directory site for the account. Here is an example:

```
add-addsdomaincontrolleraccount -domaincontrolleraccountname corpserver15
-domainname tech.cpandl.com -sitename chicago-first-site
```

Chapter 29

Once you stage the account, you can use the Install-ADDSDomainController cmdlet to promote the server that you want to be the RODC. Use the *–ExistingAccount* parameter to attach the server to the existing account, as shown in this example:

```
install-addsdomaincontroller -domainname tech.cpand1.com -useexistingaccount
-credential (get-credential)
```

# Managing Password Replication Policy

When you deploy an RODC, you must configure the Password Replication Policy on the writeable domain controller that will be its replication partner. The Password Replication Policy acts as an access control list (ACL) and determines whether an RODC should be permitted to cache a password for a particular user or group. After the RODC receives an authenticated user or computer logon request, it refers to the Password Replication Policy to determine whether it should cache the password for the account.

## Working with Password Replication Policy

You can configure Password Replication Policy in several ways:

- Allow no accounts to be cached for the strictest control, such as when the physical security of the RODC cannot be guaranteed.

- Allow few accounts to be cached for strong control, such as when the physical security of the RODC is good but cannot be reasonably assured at all times.

- Allow many accounts to be cached for less strict control, such as when the physical security of the RODC can be reasonably assured at all times.

> **Note**
> The fewer account passwords replicated to RODCs, the less risk that security could be breached if an RODC is compromised. The more account passwords replicated to RODCs, the greater the risk involved if an RODC is compromised.

Password Replication Policy is managed on a per-computer basis. The computer object for an RODC is updated to include the following multivalued directory attributes that contain security principals (users, computers, and groups):

- *msDS-Reveal-OnDemandGroup*, which defines the Allowed Accounts list

- *msDS-NeverRevealGroup*, which defines the Denied Accounts list

- *msDS-RevealedUsers*, which defines the Revealed Accounts list

- *msDS-AuthenticatedToAccountList*, which defines the Authenticated To list

The RODC uses these attributes together to determine whether an account password can be replicated and cached. The passwords for Denied Accounts are never replicated and cached. The passwords for Allowed Accounts can always be replicated and cached. Whether a password is cached or not doesn't depend on whether a user or computer has logged on to the domain via the RODC. At any time, an RODC can replicate the passwords for Allowed Accounts and administrators can also prepopulate passwords for Allowed Accounts using Active Directory Users And Computers.

During an advanced installation of an RODC, you can configure the initial Password Replication Policy settings. To support RODCs, Windows Server 2008 and later use several built-in groups:

- **Enterprise Read-Only Domain Controllers**   Every RODC in the Active Directory forest is a member of this group automatically. Membership in this group is required for proper operations.

- **Read-Only Domain Controllers**   Every RODC in the Active Directory domain is a member of this group automatically. Membership in this group is required for proper operations.

- **Allowed RODC Password Replication Group**   You can manage Allowed Accounts using the Allowed RODC Password Replication Group. Passwords for members of this group are always replicated to RODCs.

- **Denied RODC Password Replication Group**   You can manage Denied Accounts using the Denied RODC Password Replication Group. Passwords for members of this group are never replicated to RODCs.

By default, the Allowed RODC Password Replication Group has no members. Also by default, Allowed RODC Password Replication Group is the only Allowed Account defined in Password Replication Policy.

By default, the Denied RODC Password Replication Group contains the following members:

- Cert Publishers

- Domain Admins

- Domain Controllers

- Enterprise Admins

Chapter 29

- Group Policy Creator Owners

- Read-Only Domain Controllers

- Schema Admins

- The domainwide krbtgt account

Also by default the Denied Accounts list contains the following security principals, all of which are built-in groups:

- Account Operators

- Administrators

- Backup Operators

- Denied RODC Password Replication Group

- Server Operators

## Allowing or denying accounts in Password Replication Policy

Each RODC has a separate Password Replication Policy. To manage the Password Replication Policy, you must be a member of the Domain Admins group. The easiest way to manage Password Replication Policy is to do the following:

- Add accounts for which passwords should not be replicated to the Denied RODC Password Replication Group.

- Add accounts for which passwords should be replicated to the Allowed RODC Password Replication Group.

You can also edit Password Replication Policy settings directly. To edit the Password Replication Policy for an RODC, follow these steps:

1.  In Active Directory Users And Computers, ensure that Active Directory Users And Computers points to a writeable domain controller that is running Windows Server 2008 or later. Press and hold or right-click the Active Directory Users And Computers node and then select Change Domain Controller. As shown in Figure 29-13, the domain controller to which you are connected should be a writeable domain controller—that is, it should not list RODC under DC Type. If you are connected to an RODC, change to a writeable domain controller. Tap or click Cancel or OK as appropriate.

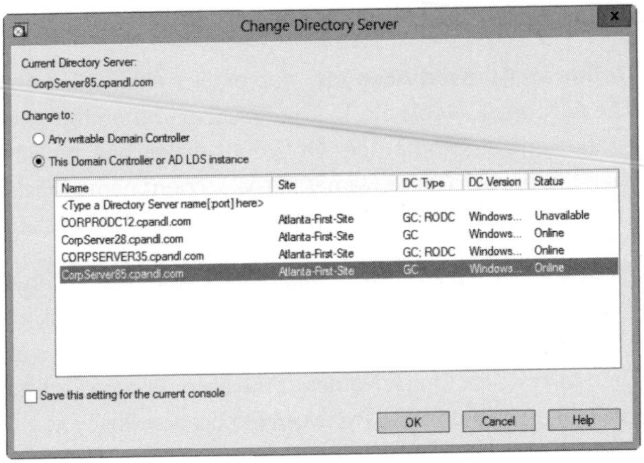

**Figure 29-13**  Make sure you are connected to a writeable domain controller.

2.  In Active Directory Users And Computers, expand the domain node and then select Domain Controllers.

3.  In the details pane, press and hold or right-click the RODC computer account and then choose Properties.

4.  On the Password Replication Policy tab, shown in Figure 29-14, you'll see the current settings for Password Replication Policy on the RODC.

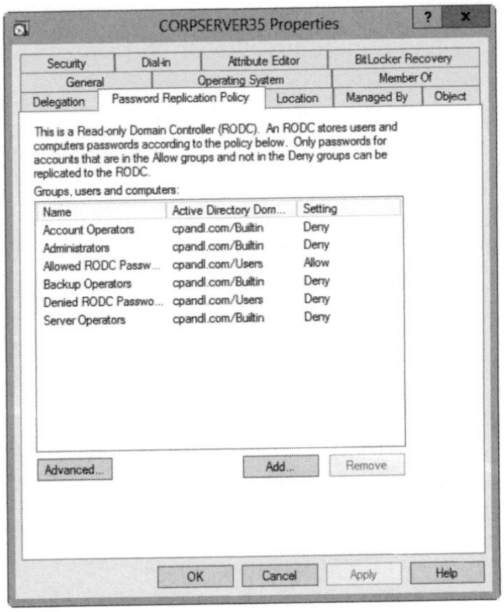

**Figure 29-14**  Review the current Password Replication Policy settings for the RODC.

5. You can now do the following:

   ○ **Define an Allowed Account**   Tap or click Add, select Allow Passwords For The Account To Replicate To This RODC, and then tap or click OK. In the Select Users, Contacts, Computers, Or Groups dialog box, type an account name and then tap or click Check Names. If the account name is listed correctly, tap or click OK to add it to the Password Replication Policy as an Allowed Account.

   ○ **Define a Denied Account**   Tap or click Add, select Deny Passwords For The Account To Replicate To This RODC, and then tap or click OK. In the Select Users, Contacts, Computers, Or Groups dialog box, type an account name and then tap or click Check Names. If the account name is listed correctly, tap or click OK to add it to the Password Replication Policy as a Denied Account.

   ○ **Remove an account from Password Replication Policy**   Select the account name in the Groups, Users And Computers list, and then tap or click Remove. When prompted to confirm, tap or click Yes.

## Viewing and managing credentials on an RODC

You can review cached credentials or prepopulate credentials using the Advanced Password Replication Policy dialog box. When you are prepopulating user accounts, you should also consider prepopulating the passwords of computer accounts that the users will be using.

To view and work with this dialog box, follow these steps:

1. In Active Directory Users And Computers, expand the domain node and then select Domain Controllers.

2. In the details pane, press and hold or right-click the RODC computer account and then choose Properties.

3. On the Password Replication Policy tab, tap or click Advanced to display the Advanced Password Replication Policy dialog box, shown in Figure 29-15.

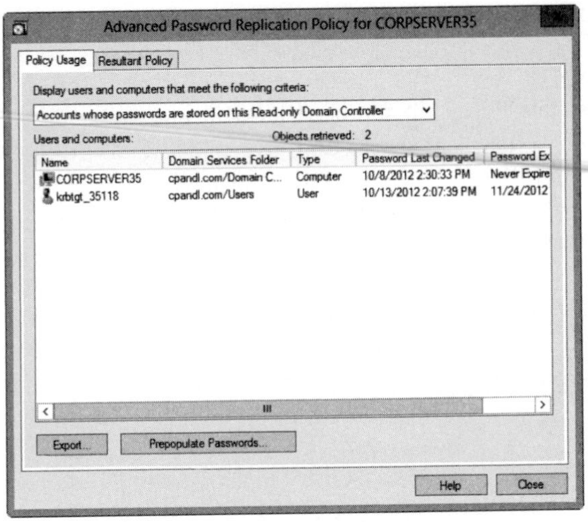

**Figure 29-15** Review stored credentials.

4. You now have the following options:

   ○ Accounts for which passwords are stored on the RODC are displayed by default. To view accounts that have been authenticated to this RODC, select Accounts That Have Been Authenticated To This Read-Only Domain Controller on the Display Users And Computers That Meet The Following Criteria list.

   ○ To prepopulate passwords for an account, tap or click Prepopulate Passwords. In the Select Users Or Computers dialog box, type an account name and then tap or click Check Names. If the account name is listed correctly, tap or click OK to add a request that its password be replicated to the RODC. When prompted to confirm, tap or click Yes. The password is then prepopulated. Tap or click OK.

## Determining whether an account is allowed or denied access

To determine whether an account is allowed or restricted, you can use Resultant Set of Policy (RSoP) to examine all related group memberships and determine exactly what rules apply. Follow these steps:

1. In Active Directory Users And Computers, expand the domain node and then select Domain Controllers.

2. In the details pane, press and hold or right-click the RODC computer account and then choose Properties.

3. On the Password Replication Policy tab, tap or click Advanced to display the Advanced Password Replication Policy dialog box.

4. On the Resultant Policy tab, tap or click Add.

5. In the Select Users Or Computers dialog box, type an account name and then tap or click Check Names. If the account name is listed correctly, tap or click OK to display the RSoP, as shown in Figure 29-16.

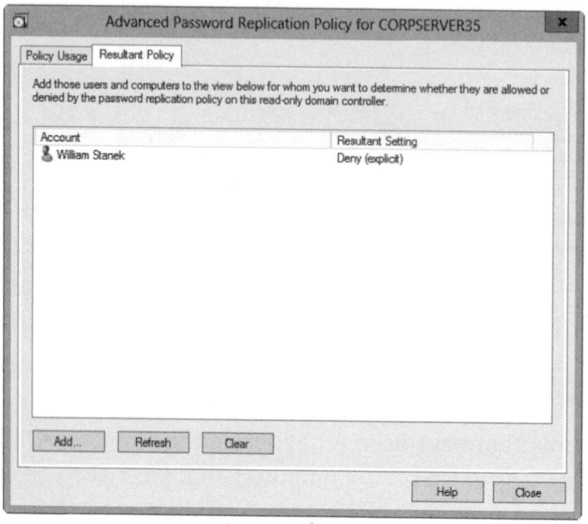

**Figure 29-16** Determine whether an account is allowed or denied access using Resultant Set of Policy.

## Resetting credentials

In the event that an RODC is compromised or stolen, you can reset the passwords for all accounts for which credentials were cached on the RODC by following these steps:

1. In Active Directory Users And Computers, ensure that Active Directory Users And Computers points to the writeable domain controller that is running Windows Server 2008 or later. Press and hold or right-click the Active Directory Users And Computers node and then select Change Domain Controller. The domain controller to which you are connected should be a writeable domain controller—that is, it should not list RODC under DC Type. If you are connected to an RODC, change to a writeable domain controller. Tap or click Cancel or OK as appropriate.

2. In Active Directory Users And Computers, expand the domain node and then select Domain Controllers.

3. In the details pane, press and hold or right-click the RODC computer account and then choose Delete.

4. When prompted to confirm, tap or click Yes.

5. When prompted again, specify whether you want to reset all passwords for user accounts, computer accounts, or both that were cached on this RODC. If you reset user account passwords, the affected users won't be able to log on until they contact you or the help desk to obtain a new password. If you reset computer account passwords, the affected computers will be disjoined from the network and won't be able to connect to the domain until they are rejoined.

6. You want to export the list of cached accounts to a file, and this is the default selection. Tap or click Browse to select a save location and set a file name for the account list. The password for every user whose account is listed in this file has been reset.

7. Tap or click Delete. When prompted, confirm that you really want to delete all metadata for the RODC by tapping or clicking OK.

## Delegating administrative permissions

During the configuration of an RODC, you have an opportunity to specify user or group accounts that should be delegated administrative permissions. After the initial configuration, you can add or remove administrative permissions using Dsmgmt.

To grant administrative permissions to an additional user, follow these steps:

1. At an elevated command prompt, type **dsmgmt**.

2. At the dsmgmt prompt, type **local roles**.

3. At the local roles prompt, type **show roles administrators** to list current administrators. In the default configuration, no users or groups are listed.

4. At the local roles prompt, type **add *Domain\User* administrator** to grant administrative permissions, where *Domain* is the domain in which the user account is located and *User* is the account name, such as **CPANDL\williams**.

5. Confirm the addition by typing **show roles administrators**.

6. Type **quit** twice to exit Dsmgmt.

Chapter 29

To remove administrative permissions, follow these steps:

1.  At an elevated command prompt, type **dsmgmt**.

2.  At the dsmgmt prompt, type **local roles**.

3.  At the local roles prompt, type **show roles administrators** to list current administrators. In the default configuration, no users or groups are listed.

4.  At the local roles prompt, type **remove *Domain\User* administrator** to remove administrative permissions for a specified user, where *Domain* is the domain in which the user account is located and *User* is the account name, such as **CPANDL\williams**.

5.  Confirm the removal by typing **show roles administrators**.

6.  Type **quit** twice to exit Dsmgmt.

# Managing users, groups, and computers

A s an administrator, managing users, groups, and computers will probably be a significant part of your duties and responsibilities. Managing users, groups, and computers encapsulates the important duties of a system administrator because of the way you must balance convenience, performance, fault tolerance, and security.

# Managing domain user accounts

The next part of this chapter is dedicated to helping you plan, manage, and administer user accounts in a secure and efficient manner. Microsoft Windows operating systems have come a long way since the early days of Windows Server, and you now have many options for managing users.

## Configuring user account policies

Because domain controllers share the domain accounts database, user account policies must be consistent across all domain controllers. The way consistency is ensured is by having domain controllers obtain user account policies only from the domain container and allowing only one top-level account policy for domain accounts. The one top-level account policy allowed for domain accounts is determined by the highest precedence Group Policy Object (GPO) linked to the domain container. This top-level account policy is then enforced by the domain controllers in the domain. Domain controllers always obtain the top-level account policy from the highest-precedence GPO linked to the domain container. By default, this is the Default Domain Policy GPO.

When a domain is operating at the Windows Server 2008 or higher functional level, there are two object classes in the Active Directory schema you can use to fine-tune the way account policy is applied:

- Password Settings Container
- Password Settings Object

The default Password Settings Container (PSC) is created under the System container in the domain, and it stores the Password Settings Objects (PSOs) for the domain. Although you cannot rename, move, or delete the default PSC, you can add PSOs to this container that define the various sets of secondary account policy settings you want to use in your domain. You can then apply the desired secondary account policy settings to users, inetOrgPersons, and global security groups, as discussed later in this chapter in the section "Creating password settings objects and applying secondary settings."

## Local account policy is used for local login

Local account policies can be different from the domain account policy, such as when you specifically define an account policy for local accounts in local GPOs (LGPOs). For example, if you configure an account policy for LGPOs, when users log on to Active Directory they'll obtain their account policy from the Default Domain Policy instead of the LGPOs. The only exception is when users log on locally to their machines instead of logging on to Active Directory; in that case, any account policy applied to an applicable local GPO is applied and enforced.

## Some security options are also obtained from the Default Domain Policy GPO

Two policies in Computer Configuration\Windows Settings\Security Settings\ Local Policies\Security Options also behave like account policies. These policies are Network Access: Allow Anonymous SID/NAME Translation and Network Security: Force Logoff When Logon Hours Expire. For domain accounts, the settings for these policies are obtained only from the Default Domain Policy GPO. For local accounts, the settings for these policies can come from a local organizational unit (OU) GPO if one is defined and applicable.

As discussed in Chapter 31, "Managing Group Policy," account policies in a domain are configured through the policy editors accessible from the Group Policy Management Console (GPMC). When you are editing policy settings, you'll find account policies under Computer Configuration\Windows Settings\Security Settings\Account Policies. To change Group Policies, you must be a member of the Administrators, Domain Admins, or Enterprise Admins group in Active Directory. Members of the Group Policy Creator Owners group can also modify Group Policy for the domain.

The account policies for a domain contain three subsets: Password Policy, Account Lockout Policy, and Kerberos Policy. Although secondary account policies include Password Policy and Account Lockout Policy, they do not include Kerberos Policy. Kerberos Policy can be set only at the domain level for the top-level account policy.

## Enforcing Password Policy

Password policies for domain user accounts and local user accounts are very important in preventing unauthorized access. There are six settings for password policies that enable you to control how passwords are managed. When you are setting the top-level account policy for the Default Domain Policy, these policies are located in Computer Configuration\Windows Settings\Security Settings\Account Policies\Password Policy. (See Figure 30-1.) When you are setting the secondary account policy for a PSO, you configure these settings using similarly named object attributes.

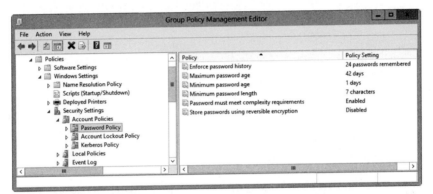

**Figure 30-1** Managing Password Policy in the Default Domain Policy.

The settings are as follows:

- **Enforce Password History**   When users change their passwords, this setting determines how many old passwords will be maintained and associated with each user. The maximum value is 24. If you enter zero (0), a password history is not kept. On a domain controller, the default is 24 passwords; on a standalone server, it is zero passwords.

- **Maximum Password Age**   This determines when users are required to change their passwords. For example, if this is set to 90 days, on the 91st day the user will be required to change her password. The default on domain controllers is 42 days. The minimum number of days is 0, which effectively means that the password never changes. The maximum number of days is 999. In an environment where security is critical, you probably want to set the value low—in contrast, for environments where security is less stringent, you could set the password age high (rarely requiring users to change passwords).

Chapter 30

- **Minimum Password Age**   How long users must use passwords before they are allowed to change the password is determined by this setting. It must be more than zero days for the Enforce Password History policy to be effective. In an environment where security is critical, you should set this to a shorter time, and set it to a longer time where security is not as tight. This setting must be configured to be less than the Maximum Password Age policy. The maximum value is 998. If you enter zero (0), a password can be changed immediately. The default is 1 day on a domain controller and 0 days on standalone servers.

- **Minimum Password Length**   This is the number of characters that sets the minimum requirement for the length of the password. Again, an environment where security is more critical might require longer password lengths than one with reduced security requirements. The maximum value is 14. If you enter zero (0), a password is not required. The default length is seven characters on domain controllers. The default is zero characters on standalone servers.

> **Note**
> If you change the Minimum Password Length setting to less than seven characters (the default), you might not be able to create a new user or change a user's password. To work around this limitation, set the password length to seven characters or more.

- **Password Must Meet Complexity Requirements**   If this policy is defined, passwords can't contain the user account name, must contain at least six characters, and must consist of uppercase letters, lowercase letters, numerals, and special non-alphabetical characters, such as the percentage sign (%) and the asterisk (*). (Complexity requirements are enabled by default on domain controllers and disabled by default on standalone servers.)

- **Store Passwords Using Reversible Encryption**   This is an additional policy that allows for plain text encryption of passwords for applications that might need it. By default, this feature is disabled. Enabling this policy is basically the same as storing passwords as plain text and is used when applications use protocols that need information about the user's password. Because this policy degrades the overall security of the domain, it should be used only when necessary.

## Configuring Account Lockout Policy

Account Lockout Policy is invoked after a local user or a domain user has been locked out of his account. There are three settings for account lockout policies:

- **Account Lockout Duration**   If a user becomes locked out, this setting determines how long the user will be locked out before the user account is unlocked. There is no default setting because this setting is dependent on the account lockout threshold setting. The range is from 0 through 99,999 minutes. The account will be locked out indefinitely when this is set to 0 and, in that case, will require an administrator to unlock it.

- **Account Lockout Threshold**   This setting determines how many failed attempts at logon Windows Server permits before a user will be locked out of the account. The range is from 0 to 999. If this setting is 0, the account will never be locked out and the Account Lockout Duration security setting is disabled. The default setting is 0.

- **Reset Account Lockout Counter After**   This setting is the number of minutes after a failure to log on before the logon counter is reset to zero. This value must be less than or equal to the Account Lockout Duration setting if the Account Lockout Threshold policy is enabled. The valid range is from 1 to 99,999 minutes.

When you are setting the top-level account policy for the Default Domain Policy, these policies are located in Computer Configuration\Windows Settings\Security Settings\ Account Policies\Account Lockout Policy. When you are setting the secondary account policy for a PSO, you configure these settings using similarly named object attributes.

## Setting Kerberos Policy

Kerberos is an authentication system designed to ensure the secure exchange of information, as discussed in the section "NTLM and Kerberos authentication" in Chapter 25, "Designing and managing the domain environment." Windows Server has five settings for Kerberos Policy, which are applied only to domain user accounts. The policies, which are described in the following list, can be set only for the top-level account policy and are located in Computer Configuration\Windows Settings\Security Settings\Account Policies\ Kerberos Policy:

- **Enforce User Logon Restrictions**   If you want to validate every session ticket request against the user rights, keep the default setting enabled.

- **Maximum Lifetime For Service Ticket**   The default is 600 minutes, but this setting must be greater than 10 minutes, and it also must be less than or equal to what is configured for the Maximum Lifetime For User Ticket setting. The setting does not apply to sessions that have already been validated.

- **Maximum Lifetime For User Ticket**   This is different from the Maximum Lifetime For Service Ticket setting. Maximum Lifetime For User Ticket sets the maximum amount of time that a ticket can be used before either a new one must be requested or the existing one is renewed, whereas the Maximum Lifetime For Service Ticket setting is used to access a particular service. The default is 10 hours.

Chapter 30

- **Maximum Lifetime For User Ticket Renewal** This user account security policy object configures the maximum amount of time the ticket can be used. The default is seven days.

- **Maximum Tolerance For Computer Clock Synchronization** Sometimes workstations and servers have different local clock times. You can use this setting to configure a tolerance level (defaults to five minutes) for this possible difference so that Kerberos authentication does not fail.

## Creating Password Settings Objects and applying secondary settings

When you want to fine-tune the way account policy is applied, you need to create a password settings policy and add users, inetOrgPersons, and global security groups as members of the password settings policy. A password settings policy is simply a global security group that applies the desired secondary PSO rather than the default PSO. Afterward, you have to create a Password Settings Object with attributes that define the desired policy settings and then link this object to the password settings policy.

Password settings policies can have attributes for all the settings that can be defined in the Default Domain Policy, except Kerberos settings but including the following settings: Account Lockout Duration, Account Lockout Threshold, Enforce Password History, Maximum Password Age, Minimum Password Age, Minimum Password Length, Passwords Must Meet Complexity Requirements, Reset Account Lockout After, Store Passwords Using Reversible Encryption.

> ### Important
> User objects have three settings that override the settings in a PSO: Reversible Password Encryption Required, Password Not Required, and Password Does Not Expire. You can configure these settings in the *userAccountControl* attribute of a *User* object.

Before you start, you should consider how you will organize your password settings policies. In most cases, you'll want to create password settings policies that closely resemble the OUs in your domain. To do this, you create password settings policies with the same names as your OUs and then add users, inetOrgPersons, and global security groups as members of these groups as appropriate to reflect the organizational structure of your OUs.

You can create the password settings policy and define its members using either Active Directory Users And Computers or Active Directory Administrative Center, as discussed in "Managing groups" later in this chapter. By default, only members of the Administrators, Domain Admins, or Enterprise Admins group can create PSOs. You can create a PSO and set its attributes using Active Directory Administrative Center. At the Windows PowerShell prompt, you can create PSOs using the New-ADFineGrainedPasswordPolicy cmdlet.

# INSIDE OUT Understanding PSO precedence

A user, inetOrgPerson, or global security group can have multiple PSOs linked to it. This can occur either because of membership in multiple groups that each have different PSOs applied to them or because multiple PSOs are applied directly to the object. However, only one PSO is applied as the effective policy, and only the settings from that PSO affect the user, inetOrgPerson, or group. The settings from other PSOs do not apply and cannot be merged in any way.

Active Directory determines the applicable PSO according to the precedence value assigned to its *msDS-PasswordSettingsPrecedence* attribute. This attribute has an integer value of 1 or greater. A lower value for the precedence attribute indicates that the PSO has a higher priority than other PSOs. For example, suppose an object has three PSOs linked to it. One PSO has a precedence value of 5, one has a precedence of 8, and the other PSO has a precedence value of 12. In this case, the PSO that has the precedence value of 5 has the highest priority and is the one applied to the object.

If multiple PSOs are linked to a user or group, the PSO that is applied is determined as follows:

1. A PSO that is linked directly to the user object is applied. If more than one PSO is linked directly to the user object, the PSO with the lowest precedence value is applied.

2. If no PSO is linked directly to the user object, all PSOs that are applicable to the user, based on the user's global group memberships, are compared and the PSO with the lowest precedence value is applied.

3. If no PSO is linked directly or indirectly to the user object, the Default Domain Policy is applied.

Microsoft recommends that you assign each PSO in the domain a unique precedence value. However, you can create multiple PSOs with the same precedence value. If multiple PSOs have the same precedence value, the PSO with the lowest GUID is applied. Typically, this means Active Directory will apply the PSO with the earliest creation date.

The user object has three attributes that override the settings that are present in the applicable PSO: Reversible Password Encryption Required, Password Not Required, and Password Does Not Expire. You can set these attributes in the *userAccountControl* attribute of the user object in Active Directory Users And Computers or Active Directory Administrative Center.

When you work with Active Directory Administrative Center, you are connected to your login domain by default. If you want to work with objects in a different domain, tap or click Manage and then select Add Navigation Nodes. In the Additional Navigation Nodes dialog box, you'll see available domains for the forest in the Columns list. To add a node for a listed domain, select it in the Columns list, tap or click the Add (>>) button, and then tap or click OK. To add a node for a domain that isn't listed, select Connect To Another Domain, enter the fully qualified domain name (FQDN), and then tap or click OK.

To create a password settings policy and define its attributes, follow these steps:

1. In the left pane of Active Directory Administrative Center, you can use the List view or Tree view. Select the Tree view.

2. In the Tree view, expand the System container for the domain you want to work with and then select the Password Settings Container to view any previously created password settings policies in the main pane.

3. Under Tasks, select New and then select Password Settings. This opens the Create Password Settings dialog box, shown in Figure 30-2.

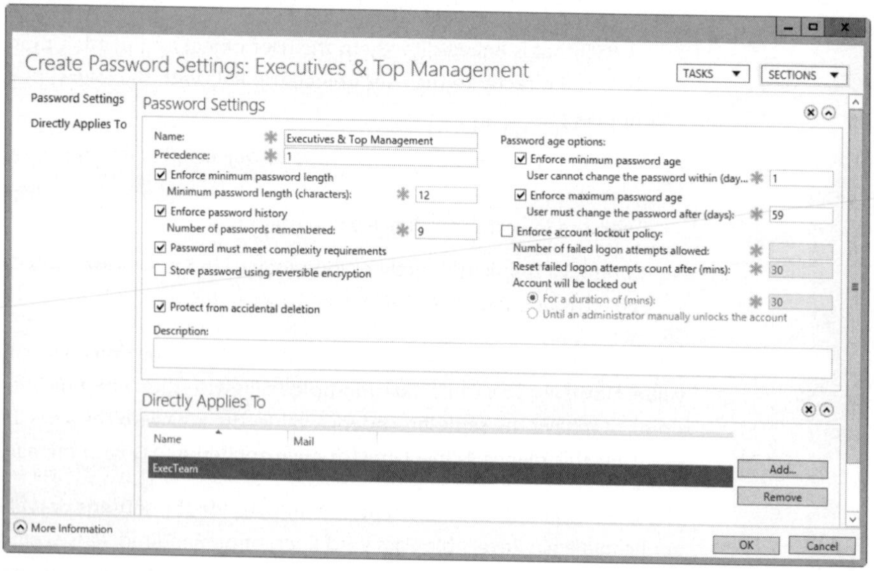

**Figure 30-2** Specify a name for the password settings policy, and then configure its settings.

4. In the Name box, type a descriptive name of the password settings policy.

5. In the Precedence box, type the precedence order for the policy. When multiple password settings policies apply to a user, the precedence of the policy determines which settings are applied. A policy with a precedence of 1 always has precedence over a policy with a lower precedence.

6. As appropriate, use the following options to define the policy settings:

    ○ **Enforce Minimum Password Length**   Sets the minimum password length for user accounts. The maximum value is 14. If you enter zero (0), a password is not required.

    ○ **Enforce Password History**   Sets the password history length. The maximum value is 24. If you enter zero (0), a password history is not kept.

    ○ **Password Must Meet Complexity Requirements**   Sets the password complexity status for passwords as either false or true. In most cases, you'll want to turn this feature on to ensure users enter complex passwords.

    ○ **Store Password Using Reversible Encryption**   Sets the reversible encryption status for passwords as either true or false. In most cases, you'll want to turn this feature off to ensure passwords are stored with strong encryption.

    ○ **Enforce Minimum Password Age**   Sets the minimum password age in days. The maximum value is 998 days. If you enter zero (0), a password can be changed immediately.

    ○ **Enforce Maximum Password Age**   Sets the maximum password age in days. The maximum value is 999 days. If you enter zero (0), passwords never expire.

7. If you also want to enforce lockout policy, select Enforce Account Lockout Policy and then use the following options to configure lockout settings:

    ○ **Number Of Failed Logon Attempts Allowed**   Specifies how many failed attempts at logon are allowed before a user is locked out. The maximum value is 999. If you enter zero (0), accounts will never be locked.

    ○ **Reset Failed Logon Attempts Count After**   Specifies the number of minutes after a logon failure before the logon counter is reset. The valid range is from 1 to 99,999 minutes.

    ○ **Account Will Be Locked Out**   Specifies how long a user will be locked out before the account is unlocked automatically. You can set a specific duration with a valid range from 1 to 99,999 minutes, or you can specify that the account will be locked out until an administrator unlocks it.

Chapter 30

8. Under Directly Applies To, click Add. This displays the Select Users Or Groups dialog box, which you can use to specify an account to which this password settings policy will apply. Repeat this step to apply the policy to multiple accounts.

9. Tap or click OK.

> **Note**
>
> You can link a PSO to other types of groups in addition to global security groups. However, when the Resultant Set of Policy (RSoP) is determined for a user or group, only PSOs that are linked to global security groups, user objects, and inetOrgPerson objects are considered. PSOs that are linked to distribution groups or other types of security groups are ignored.

## Understanding user account capabilities, privileges, and rights

All user accounts have specific capabilities, privileges, and rights. When you create a user account, you can grant the user specific capabilities by making the user a member of one or more groups. This gives the user the capabilities of these groups. You then assign additional capabilities by making a user a member of the appropriate groups or withdraw capabilities by removing a user from a group.

Some capabilities of accounts are built in. The built-in capabilities of accounts are assigned to groups and include the group's automatic capabilities. Although built-in capabilities are predefined and unchangeable, they can be granted to users by making them members of the appropriate group or delegated by specifically granting the capability—for example, the ability to create, delete, and manage user accounts. This capability is assigned to administrators and account operators. Thus, if a user is a member of the Administrators group, the user can create, delete, and manage user accounts.

Other capabilities of accounts—such as permissions, privileges, and logon rights—can be assigned. The access permissions for accounts define the operations that can be performed on network resources. For example, permissions control whether a user can access a particular shared folder. You can assign access permissions to users, computers, and groups as discussed in Chapter 15, "File sharing and security." The privileges of an account grant permissions to perform specific tasks, such as the ability to change the system time. The logon rights of an account grant logon permissions, such as the ability to log on locally to a server.

An important part of an administrator's job is being able to determine and set permissions, privileges, and logon rights as necessary. Although you can't change a group's built-in capabilities, you can change a group's default privileges and logon rights. For example, you could revoke network access to a computer by removing a group's right to access the computer from the network.

# Assigning user rights

The most efficient way to assign user rights is to make the user a member of a group that already has the right. In some cases, however, you might want a user to have a particular right but not have all the other rights of the group. One way to resolve this problem is to give the user the rights directly. Another way to resolve this is to create a special group for users that need the right. This is the approach used with the Remote Desktop Users group, which was created by Microsoft to grant the Allow Logon Through Remote Desktop Services right to groups of users.

You assign user rights through the Local Policies node of Group Policy. Local policies can be set on a per-computer basis using a computer's local security policy or on a domain or OU basis through an existing Group Policy for the related domain or OU. When you do this, the local policies apply to all accounts in the domain or OU.

## Assigning user rights for a domain or OU

You can assign user rights for a domain or OU by completing the following steps:

1. In Group Policy Management Console, select the policy you want to work with and then tap or click Edit. Access the User Rights Assignment node by working your way down the console tree. Expand Computer Configuration, Windows Settings, Security Settings, Local Policies, and User Rights Assignment, as shown in Figure 30-3.

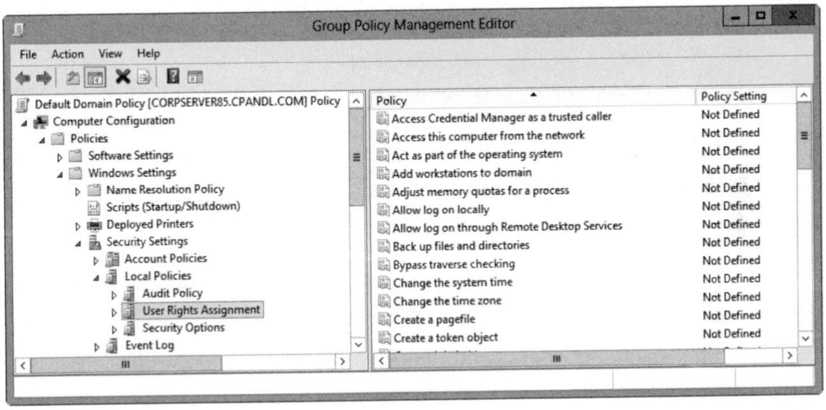

Figure 30-3  Configuring user rights in Group Policy.

2. To configure a user right, double-tap or double-click a user right or press and hold or right-click it and select Properties. This opens a Properties dialog box, as shown in Figure 30-4. If the policy isn't defined, select Define These Policy Settings. To apply the right to a user or group, tap or click Add User Or Group. Then, in the Add User Or Group dialog box, tap or click Browse. This opens the Select Users, Computers, Or Groups dialog box.

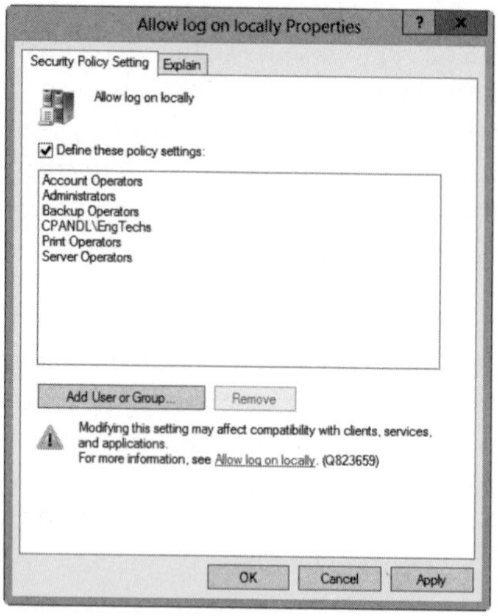

**Figure 30-4** Define the user right, and then assign the right to users and groups.

3. Type the name of the user or group you want to use in the field provided, and then tap or click Check Names. By default, the search is configured to find built-in security principals, groups, and user accounts. After you select the account names or groups to add, tap or click OK. The Add User Or Group dialog box should now show the selected accounts. Tap or click OK again.

4. The Properties dialog box is updated to reflect your selections. If you made a mistake, select a name and remove it by tapping or clicking Remove. When you're finished granting the right to users and groups, tap or click OK.

## Assigning user rights on a specific computer

User rights can also be applied to a specific computer. However, remember that domain and OU policy take precedence over local policy. This means that any settings in these policies will override settings you make on a local computer.

You can apply user rights locally by completing the following steps:

1. Start local security policy by selecting the related option on the Tools menu in Server Manager. All computers, even domain controllers, have local security policy. Settings available in the Local Security Policy console are a subset of the computer's local policy.

2. Under Security Settings, expand Local Policies and then select User Rights Assignment.

3. Double-tap or double-click the user right you want to modify. The Properties dialog box shows current users and groups that have been given the user right.

4. You can apply the user right to additional users and groups by tapping or clicking Add User Or Group. This opens the Select Users, Computers, Or Groups dialog box, which you can use to add users and groups.

5. Tap or click OK twice to close the open dialog boxes.

> **Note**
> If the options in the Properties dialog box are dimmed, it means the policy has been set at a higher level and can't be overridden locally.

## Creating and configuring domain user accounts

As a member of the Administrators, Account Operators, Enterprise Admins, or Domain Admins group, you can use Active Directory Users And Computers or Active Directory Administrative Center to create user accounts. The process is similar regardless of which tool you use.

Follow these steps to create a user account in Active Directory Users And Computers:

1. By default, you are connected to your logon domain. If you want to create accounts in a different domain, press and hold or right-click the Active Directory Users And Computers node in the console tree, and then select Change Domain. In the Change Domain dialog box, type the name of the domain to which you want to connect, and then tap or click OK. Alternatively, you can tap or click Browse to find the domain to which you want to connect in the Browse For Domain dialog box.

Chapter 30

2. You can now create the user account. Press and hold or right-click the container in which you want to create the user, point to New, and then select User. This will start the New Object–User Wizard.

When you create a new user, you're prompted for the first name, initials, last name, full name, and logon name, as shown in Figure 30-5. The pre–Windows 2000 logon name then appears automatically. This logon name is used with early releases of Windows.

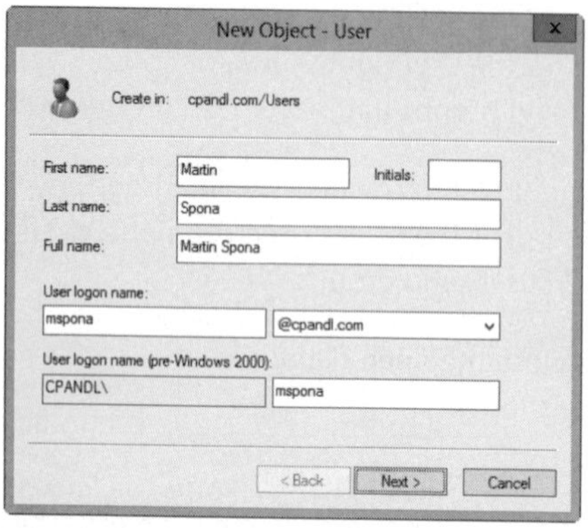

**Figure 30-5** Creating a user account.

3. When you tap or click Next, you can set the user's password and account options. The password must meet the complexity requirements set in the Group Policy. As shown in Figure 30-6, these options are as follows: User Must Change Password At Next Logon, User Cannot Change Password, Password Never Expires, Account Is Disabled.

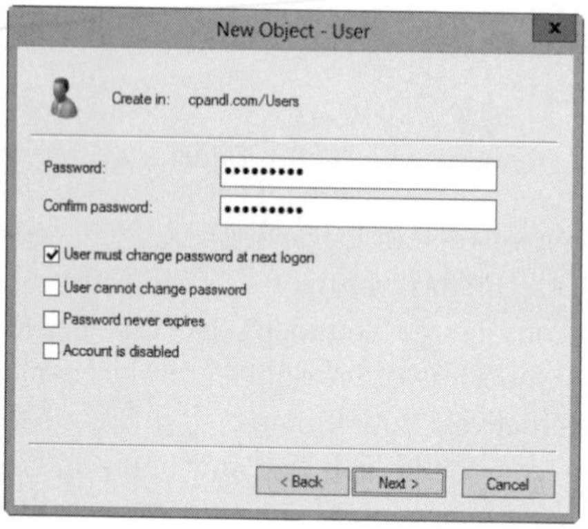

**Figure 30-6** Set the user's password and account options.

4. Tap or click Next, and then tap or click Finish. If you use a password that doesn't meet the complexity requirements of Group Policy, you'll see an error and you'll have to tap or click Back to change the user's password before you can continue.

# INSIDE OUT Creating user accounts using Windows PowerShell

With Windows PowerShell, you can create user accounts with the New-ADUser cmdlet and set account properties using the Set-ADUser, Set-ADAccountPassword, Set-ADAccountControl, and Enable-ADAccount cmdlets. With New-ADUser, use *–DisplayName* to set the display name, *–GivenName* to set the first name, *–Initials* to set the middle initial, *–Surname* to set the last name, and *–Name* to set the full name. You also need to specify the user principal name (UPN), whether the account should be enabled, and the account password. You do this using the *–UserPrincipalName*, *–Enabled*, and *–AccountPassword* parameters, respectively. Here is an example:

```
New-ADUser –DisplayName "William R. Stanek" –GivenName "William" –Initials "R"
–Name "William R. Stanek" –SamAccountName "WilliamS" –Enabled $true
–AccountPassword (ConvertTo-SecureString "ChangePasswordNow!" -AsPlainText
-force) -PassThru
```

To bulk create user accounts, you can import the account details from a text file containing a list of column headings on the first line, followed by the details of each account you want to create on separate lines, as shown in this example:

```
DisplayName,GivenName,FullName,SamName
Peter Brehm,Peter,PeterBrehm,peterb
Oliver Kiel,Oliver,Oliver Kiel,oliverk
```

If you saved this file with the name *newusers.csv* in the c:\scripts\data folder, you could then use the following script to bulk create accounts:

```
$NewUsers = import-csv c:\scripts\data\newusers.csv
ForEach ($User in $NewUsers) { New-ADUser –DisplayName $User.FullName
–GivenName $User.GivenName –Name $User.FullName –SamAccountName
$User.SamName-Enabled $true -ChangePasswordAtLogon $true -AccountPassword
(ConvertTo-SecureString "ChangePasswordNow!" -AsPlainText -force) -PassThru }
```

Or you could use the file to create the accounts directly from the prompt by entering the following command all on one line:

```
import-csv c:\scripts\data\newusers.csv | ForEach { New-ADUser
–DisplayName $_.FullName –GivenName $_.GivenName –Name $_.FullName
–SamAccountName $_.SamName -Enabled $true -ChangePasswordAtLogon $true
-AccountPassword
(ConvertTo-SecureString "ChangePasswordNow!" -AsPlainText -force) -PassThru }
```

Chapter 30

## Obtaining effective access

In Active Directory, user accounts are defined as objects—as are group and computer accounts. This means that user accounts have security descriptors that list the users and groups that are granted access. Security descriptors also define ownership of the object and specify the permissions that those users and groups have been assigned with respect to the object.

Individual entries in the security descriptor are referred to as *access control entries (ACEs)*. Active Directory objects can inherit ACEs from their parent objects. This means that permissions for a parent object can be applied to a child object. For example, all members of the Account Operators group inherit permissions granted to this group.

Because of inheritance, sometimes it isn't clear whether a particular user, group, or computer has permission to work with another object in Active Directory. This is where the Effective Access tool comes in handy. You use this tool to examine the permissions that a user, group, or computer has with respect to another object. For example, if you want to determine what permissions, if any, a user who has received delegated control has over another user or group, you can use Effective Access to do this.

> **Important**
> The Effective Access tool is available in Active Directory Users And Computers—but only if you are in the Advanced Features view. Select Advanced Features from the View menu if necessary.

In Active Directory Users And Computers or Active Directory Administrative Center, double-tap or double-click the user, group, or computer for which you are trying to determine the effective permissions of another user or group. If you are working with Active Directory Administrative Center, open the Extensions panel.

Next, tap or click the Advanced button on the Security tab to open the Advanced Security Settings dialog box. Tap or click the Effective Access tab. Next, tap or click Select A User, type the name of the user or group for which you want to see the effective permissions with regard to the previously selected object, and then tap or click OK.

When you tap or click View Effective Access, the effective permissions for the selected user or group in relation to the previously selected object appear, as shown in Figure 30-7. The Effective Access column has check marks showing which permissions are in effect. If there are no effective permissions, none of the permissions' check boxes are selected.

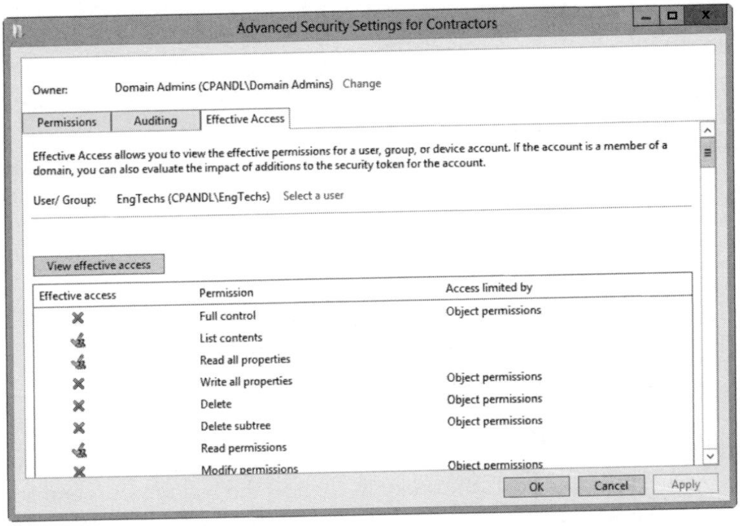

**Figure 30-7** Obtaining effective access for a user, group, or computer.

## Configuring account options

Every user account created in Active Directory has account options that control logon hours, the computers to which a user can log on, account expiration, and so on. To manage these settings for a user, double-tap or double-click the user account in Active Directory Users And Computers or Active Directory Administrative Center. Next, click the Account tab or Account panel as appropriate.

Figure 30-8 shows an account Properties dialog box for Active Directory Users And Computers. You'll find similar options for the Properties dialog box that opens when you are working with Active Directory Administrative Center.

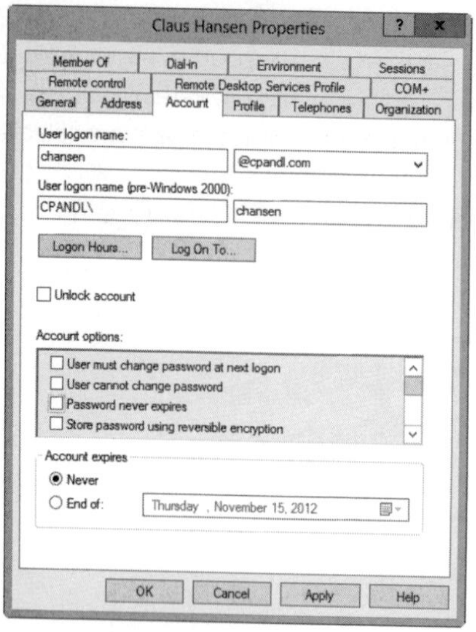

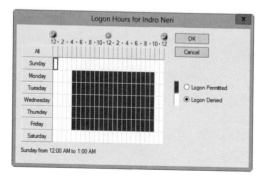

**Figure 30-8** Display of logon settings in the user account Properties dialog box.

Below the general account name fields, the available options are divided into three main areas. The first area that you can configure controls the Logon Hours and Log On To computer options.

- **Setting Logon Hours**   Tap or click Logon Hours to configure when a user can log on to the domain. By default, users can log on 24 hours a day, seven days a week. To deny a user a specific day or time, select the area you want to restrict the user from logging on to, and then select the Logon Denied option, as shown in Figure 30-9. For example, this option can be used to restrict shift workers to certain hours or to restrict working days to weekdays.

**Figure 30-9** Configure logon hours for a specific user.

- **Configuring Logon Computer** When you tap or click Log On To, you can restrict which computers a user can log on from. The default setting allows users to log on from all computers. To restrict which computers a user can log on from, choose The Following Computers, as shown in Figure 30-10. Type a host name or a fully qualified domain name in the Computer Name field, such as **Workstation18** or **Workstation.cpandl.com**. Tap or click Add. Repeat this procedure to set other logon computers.

> **Note**
>
> Earlier releases of Windows required the NetBIOS protocol to restrict which computers a user can log on from. This requirement has been phased out.

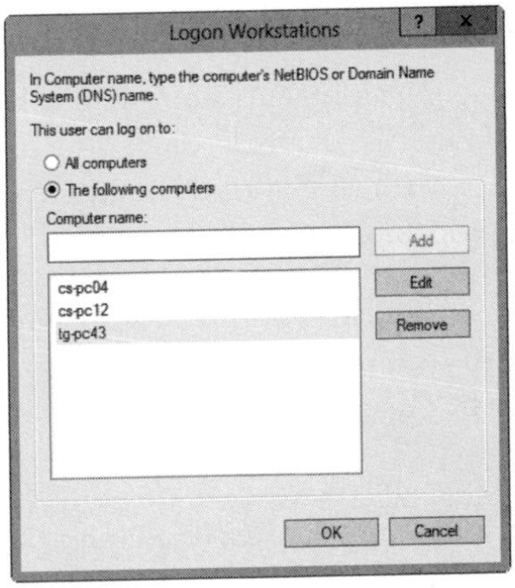

**Figure 30-10** Specify which computers the user can log on to.

Below the Logon Hours and Log On To buttons is the Unlock Account check box. If the user has locked herself out by trying to log on with the wrong password too many times, you can unlock the account by clearing this check box.

Finally, the Account Expires panel is what you use to set expiration options for the account. The default is Never, but you might need to configure this setting for some users. For example, temporary workers, contract workers, summer help, or consultants might be working on your network for only a specified amount of time. If you know how long they need access to resources in your domain, you can use the Account Expires settings to automate the disabling of their account.

Chapter 30

## Disabling accounts

In most network environments, administrators to whom the task of managing users has been delegated will not be able to remove users immediately upon their leaving the company, creating a window of vulnerability. Yet, when accounts have scheduled end points, you can schedule them to be disabled on a specific date. So, it is a good idea to schedule accounts to be disabled if you are sure that the user will no longer be working. If the account is automatically disabled but the user needs access, he will let you know. But, if the account is not disabled automatically, it can represent a big security problem. To handle this on an enterprise level, many businesses are reviewing (or implementing) provisioning applications to automate the process of taking away access to company resources when employees leave the company.

## Configuring profile options

User accounts also can have profiles, logon scripts, and home directories associated with them. To configure these options, double-tap or double-click a user account in Active Directory Users And Computers or Active Directory Administrative Center. Next, click the Profile tab or the Profile panel as appropriate.

Figure 30-11 shows the Profile tab in the Properties dialog box that opens when you are working with Active Directory Users And Computers. Similar options are available on the Profile panel of the Properties dialog box that opens when you are working with Active Directory Administrative Center.

As the figure shows, you can set the following options in the Profile tab:

- **Profile Path** Sets the location of the roaming user profile for the user. Profiles provide the environment settings for users. Each time a user logs on to a computer, that user's profile is used to determine desktop and Control Panel settings, the availability of menu options and applications, and so on. Setting the profile path and working with profiles is covered in "Managing user profiles" later in this chapter.

- **Logon Script** As the name implies, logon scripts are accessed when users log on to their accounts. Logon scripts set commands that should be executed each time a user logs on. One user or many users can use a single logon script, and, as the administrator, you control which users run which scripts. You can specify a logon script to use by typing the path to the logon script in the Logon Script field. Be sure to set the full path to the logon script, such as **\\Corpdc05\LogonScripts\eng.vbs**.

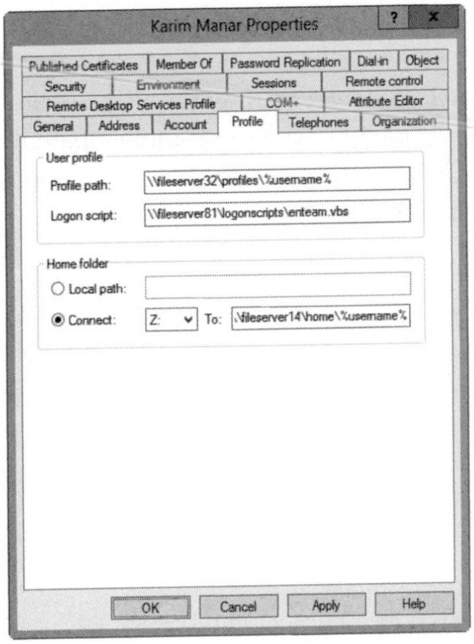

**Figure 30-11** Configure paths for User Profile settings.

> **Note**
> You shouldn't use scripts to set environment variables. Environment settings used by scripts aren't maintained for subsequent user processes.

- **Home Folder**   A home folder can be assigned to each user account. Users can store and retrieve their personal files in this directory. Many applications use the home folder as the default for File Open and Save As operations, helping users find their resources easily. Home directories can be located on a user's local hard drive or on a shared network drive. If you don't assign a home folder, Windows Server uses a default local home folder.

  To specify a home folder, do either of the following:

  - You specify a local home folder by tapping or clicking the Local Path option button and then typing the path to the home folder on the user's computer. Here's an example: **C:\Home\%UserName%**.

  - You specify a network home folder by selecting the Connect option button in the Home Folder section and then selecting a drive letter for the home folder. For consistency, you should use the same drive letter for all users. Also, be sure to select a drive letter that won't conflict with any currently configured physical or mapped drives. To avoid problems, you might want to use Z as the drive letter. After you select the drive letter, type the complete path to the home folder, using the Universal Naming Convention (UNC) notation, such as: **\\Corpdc09\Home\%UserName%**.

> ## Note
>
> %UserName% refers to the *UserName* environment variable. The Windows operating system has many environment variables, which are used to refer to user-specific and system-specific values. In this case, %UserName% is used to dynamically assign the user name as appropriate for the applicable user account.

## Troubleshooting user accounts

When a user logs on to the network using her domain user account, the account credentials are validated by a domain controller. By default, users can log on using their domain user accounts even if the network connection is down or there is no domain controller available to authenticate the user's logon. However, the user must have previously logged on to the computer and have valid, cached credentials. If the user has no cached credentials on the computer and the network connection is down or there is no domain controller available, the user will not be able to log on to the domain.

Each member computer in a domain can cache up to 10 credentials by default. Authentication also can fail if the system time on the member computer deviates from the logon domain controller's system time more than is allowed in the Kerberos Policy: Maximum Tolerance For Computer Clock Synchronization setting. The default tolerance is five minutes for member computers.

Users' accounts can be disabled by administrators or locked out due to Account Lockout Policy. When a user tries to log on using an account that is disabled or locked out, he sees a prompt that notifies him he cannot log on because his account is disabled or locked out. The prompt also tells him to contact an administrator.

Active Directory Users And Computers shows disabled accounts with a red warning icon next to the account name. To enable a disabled account, press and hold or right-click the account in Active Directory Users And Computers and then select Enable Account. You can search the entire domain for users with disabled accounts by typing **dsquery user –disabled** at a command prompt. To enable a disabled account from the command line, type **dsmod user UserDN –disabled no**.

When a user account has been locked out by the Account Lockout Policy, the account cannot be used for logging on until the lockout duration has elapsed or the account is reset by an administrator. If the account lockout duration is indefinite, the only way to unlock the account is to have an administrator reset it. In Active Directory Users And Computers, you can unlock an account by pressing and holding or right-clicking the locked account and then selecting Properties. On the Account tab of the Properties dialog box, select the Unlock Account check box and then tap or click OK.

Additionally, when account logon failure auditing is enabled, logon failure is recorded in the security log on the logon domain controller. Auditing policies for a site, domain, or OU GPO are stored under Computer Configuration\Windows Settings\Security Settings\ Local Policies\Audit Policy.

# Maintaining user accounts

User accounts are easy to maintain after they've been configured. Most of the maintenance tasks you need to perform involve user profiles and group membership, which are covered in separate sections of this chapter. Other than these areas, you might also need to perform the following tasks:

- Delete user accounts

- Disable, enable, or unlock user accounts

- Move user accounts

- Rename user accounts

- Reset a user's domain password

- Set logon scripts and home folders

- Create a local user account password backup

Each of these tasks is examined in the sections that follow.

## Deleting user accounts

Each user account created in the domain has a unique security identifier (SID), and that SID is never reused. If you delete an account, you cannot create an account with the same name and regain all the same permissions and settings of the previously deleted account. The SID for the new account will be different from the old one, and you will have to redefine all the necessary permissions and settings. Because of this, you should delete accounts only when you know they are not going to be used again. If you are unsure, disable the account rather than deleting it.

To delete an account, select the account in either Active Directory Users And Computers or Active Directory Administrative Center and then press Delete. When prompted to confirm the deletion, tap or click Yes and the account is permanently deleted. Deleting a user account doesn't delete a user's on-disk data. It only deletes the user account from Active Directory. This means the user's profile and other personal data will still be available on disk until you manually delete them.

> **CAUTION**!
>
> The permissions on users are internally characterized within Active Directory by unique SIDs that are allocated when the user is created. If you delete a user account and then re-create it, it will have a new SID and thus new permissions.

## Disabling and enabling user accounts

If you need to deactivate a user account temporarily so that it cannot be used for logon or authentication, you can do this by disabling the account. Although disabling an account makes it unusable, you can later enable the account so that it can be used again. To disable an account in Active Directory Users And Computers, press and hold or right-click the account and then select Disable Account. To disable an account in Active Directory Administrative Center, press and hold or right-click the account and then select Disable.

Next, when you are notified by a prompt that the account has been disabled, tap or click OK. A circle with a down arrow is added to the account's icon to show that it is disabled. If you later need to enable the account, you can do so by pressing and holding or right-clicking the account and then selecting either Enable Account or Enable, depending on which management tool you are using.

## Moving user accounts

When there is a reorganization or a user otherwise changes departments, you might need to move the user account to a new container in Active Directory Users And Computers or Active Directory Administrative Center. To move a user account, press and hold or right-click the account and then select Move. The Move dialog box appears, which you can use to select the container to which you want to move the user account. Alternatively, you can drag the user account into a new container. You can also select multiple users to move by using Windows keyboard shortcuts, such as Ctrl, and then selecting multiple users, or using Shift and selecting the first and last users.

# Renaming user accounts

Active Directory tracks objects by their SID. This allows you to safely rename user, computer, and group accounts without worrying about having to change access permissions as well. That said, however, the process of renaming a user account is not as easy as the process of renaming other types of accounts. The reason is that users have several name components that are all related to a user's last name, including a full name, display name, and user logon name. So, when a person's last name changes as the result of a marriage, adoption, or divorce, you not only need to update the user's account name in Active Directory, but you need to update the rest of the related name components as well.

To simplify the process of renaming user accounts, Active Directory Users And Computers provides the Rename User dialog box (shown in Figure 30-12), which you can use to rename a user's account and all the related name components. Active Directory Administrative Center does not have this simple renaming tool.

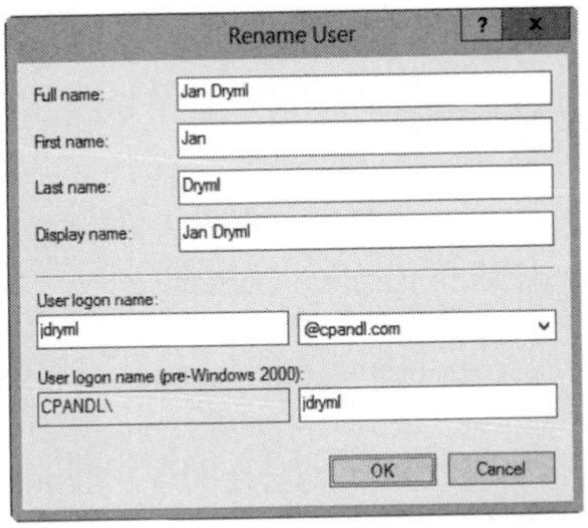

**Figure 30-12** Rename a user account.

With the addition of the Rename User dialog box, the process for renaming user accounts is as follows:

1. Find the user account that you want to rename in Active Directory Users And Computers.

2. Press and hold or right-click the user account, and then select Rename. Active Directory Users And Computers then highlights the account name for editing. Press the Backspace or Delete key to erase the existing name, and then press Enter to open the Rename User dialog box.

3. Make the necessary changes to the user's name information, and then tap or click OK. If the user is logged on, you'll see a warning prompt telling you that the user should log off and then log back on using the new account logon name.

Chapter 30

4. The account is renamed, and the SID for access permissions remains the same. You might still need to modify other data for the user in the account's Properties dialog box, including the following:

○ **User Profile Path** As necessary, change the Profile Path information on the Profile tab, and then rename the corresponding directory on disk.

○ **Logon Script Name** If you use individual logon scripts for each user, change the Logon Script Name value on the Profile tab, and then rename the logon script on disk.

○ **Home Folder** As necessary, change the home folder path on the Profile tab, and then rename the corresponding directory on disk.

## Resetting a user's domain password

One of the good things about using domain policy to require users to change their passwords is that the overall security of the network is improved by doing so. One of the downsides of frequent password changes is that users occasionally forget their password. If this happens, it is easy to fix by doing the following:

1. Find the user account whose password you want to reset in Active Directory Users And Computers or in Active Directory Administrative Center.

2. Press and hold or right-click the user account, and then select Reset Password.

3. In the Reset Password dialog box, shown in Figure 30-13, type the new password and then confirm it for the user by typing it again.

**Figure 30-13** Configure the new password for the selected user.

4. If the account status is listed as locked, select the Unlock The User's Account check box.

5. Tap or click OK.

> **Note**
>
> The password change is immediately replicated to the primary domain controller (PDC) emulator, as discussed in the section "Using, locating, and transferring the PDC emulator role" in Chapter 25, "Designing and managing the domain environment." This makes the password available for the user to log on anywhere in the domain.

## Unlocking user accounts

Whenever users violate Group Policy, such as when they fail to change their passwords before they expire or exceed the limit for bad logon attempts, Active Directory locks their accounts. After an account is locked, the user can no longer log on. Because accounts also can be locked because someone is trying to break into an account, you shouldn't automatically unlock accounts. Instead, either wait until the user asks you to unlock her account or go speak to the user when you notice her account has been locked.

You can unlock accounts by completing the following steps:

1.  In Active Directory Users And Computers, press and hold or right-click the locked account and then select Properties.

2.  In the Properties dialog box, click the Account tab.

3.  Clear the Unlock Account check box, and then tap or click OK.

This option is not available in Active Directory Administrative Center.

## Creating a user account password backup

Sometimes a user (or even an administrator) will forget the local Administrator's password or another user's account password. If you manually reset a user's account password, and the user has encrypted email, files that have been encrypted, or passwords he uses for Internet accounts, that data will be lost or not available with the new or reset password. To prevent this, you can create a password reset disk.

You can make a reset disk for any computer running Windows Vista or later, except for domain controllers. Reset disks can be for both local accounts and domain accounts. Be careful of the following when creating a reset disk:

- You are not allowed to create a reset disk and change your password from the Logon screen simultaneously.

- You do not have to create a new reset disk each time you change a user's password; you need to create the reset disk only once for an account.

- Users should create their own reset disks for each account they use.

Follow these steps to make a password reset disk:

1. Press Ctrl+Alt+Del, and then tap or click the Change A Password option.

2. Tap or click Create A Password Reset Disk to start the Forgotten Password Wizard.

3. In the Forgotten Password Wizard, read the introductory message. Insert the USB flash drive you want to use, and then tap or click Next.

4. Select the USB flash drive you want to use in the drive list. Tap or click Next.

5. Type the current password for the account in the text box provided, and then tap or click Next.

6. After the wizard creates the password reset disk, remove the disk and then tap or click Finish.

Store the USB flash drive in a secure place because now anyone can use it to gain access to the account. If a user is unable to log in because she forgot the password, you can use the password reset disk to create a new password and log in to the account using this password by following these steps:

1. On the Log On screen, tap or click the arrow button without entering a password. The Reset Password option should be displayed. If the user has already entered the wrong password, the Reset Password option might already be displayed.

2. Insert the disk or USB flash device containing the password recovery file, and then tap or click Reset Password to start the Reset Password Wizard.

3. In the Reset Password Wizard, read the introductory message and then tap or click Next.

4. Insert the disk into drive A or insert the USB flash key containing the password recovery file and then tap or click Next.

5. Select the device you want to use in the drive list, and then tap or click Next.

6. On the Reset The User Account Password page, type and confirm a new password for the user.

7. Type a password hint, and then tap or click Next. Tap or click Finish.

INSIDE OUT  How the password reset disk works

The reset disk process generates a public/private key pair. There are no passwords stored on the reset disk. The reset disk contains the private key, and the public key encrypts the account password. When a user forgets the account password, the restore process uses the private key on the reset disk to decrypt the current password and create a new one that is encrypted with the same key. Data is not lost because the same encryption is used for any other encrypted data.

# Managing groups

Active Directory groups are objects that can hold users, contacts, computers, or other groups. When you want to manage users, computers, and other resources—such as files, directories, printers, network shares, and email distribution lists—using groups can decrease administration time and improve network performance.

## Understanding groups

Types of groups and the group scope are essential topics in planning and managing an efficient network. Planning an environment that uses Active Directory and groups is critical—failing to plan or taking shortcuts can negatively affect network traffic and create more administrative work in the long run.

There are two types of groups used in Windows Server: security groups and distribution groups.

- Security groups are used to control access to resources. This is the kind of group you will probably use most often, and it might already be familiar to you. Security groups are listed in discretionary access control lists (DACLs). DACLs are part of an object's descriptor and are used to define permissions on objects and resources.

- Distribution groups are used for unsecured email lists. Distribution lists do not use the functionality of the DACL permissions that security groups do. Distribution groups are not security-enabled but can be used by email servers such as Microsoft Exchange Server.

Windows Server uses three group scopes: domain local, global, and universal. The group scope determines the types of objects that can be included as members of a group and the permissions and rights those objects can be granted. In practice, you will almost always use security groups rather than distribution groups because they include distribution group functionality and are the only types of groups that have DACLs.

Chapter 30

**Domain Local Groups** Consider using domain local groups first when you are giving groups or users access to local domain resources. For instance, if you have a domain named northwind.com and you want users or groups in that local domain to access a shared folder in the northwind.com local domain, you could create a domain local group called SalesPersons, insert in the SalesPersons group the users and global groups to whom you want to give access to the shared folder, and then assign the SalesPersons group permissions on the resource.

Access policies for domain local groups are not stored in Active Directory. This means that they do not get replicated to the global catalog, and thus queries performed on the global catalog will not return results from domain local groups. This is because domain local groups cannot be determined across domains.

**Global Groups** Use global groups to give users or groups access to resources according to how they have been organized. For instance, users from the Marketing and Development departments could be put in separate global groups to simplify the administration of their need to access resources such as printers and network shares. Global groups can be nested to grant access to any domain in the forest.

**Universal Groups** Universal groups have very few fundamental restrictions. Universal groups can be a tempting shortcut for administrators to use because they can be used across domains in the forest. Memberships in universal groups can be drawn from any domain, and permissions can be set within any domain. However, using universal groups as your main method of grouping users, groups, and computers has a significant caveat.

Universal groups are stored in the global catalog, and whenever changes are made to a universal group, the changed properties must be replicated to other domain controllers configured as global catalog servers. The replication of individual property changes rather than entire objects is an improvement for Windows Server that should allow wider use of universal groups without causing network bottlenecks or slowed performance during authentication and global catalog changes.

## Creating a group

You can create groups in the Users container or in a new OU that you created in the domain. Use either Active Directory Users And Computers or Active Directory Administrative Center to create groups. The process is similar regardless of which tool you use.

To create a group, start Active Directory Users And Computers. Press and hold or right-click the Users container or the OU in which you want to place the group, point to New, and then select Group. This displays the New Object–Group dialog box shown in Figure 30-14.

Type a group name, and then choose an option in both the Group Scope and Group Type areas. Afterward, tap or click OK to create the group.

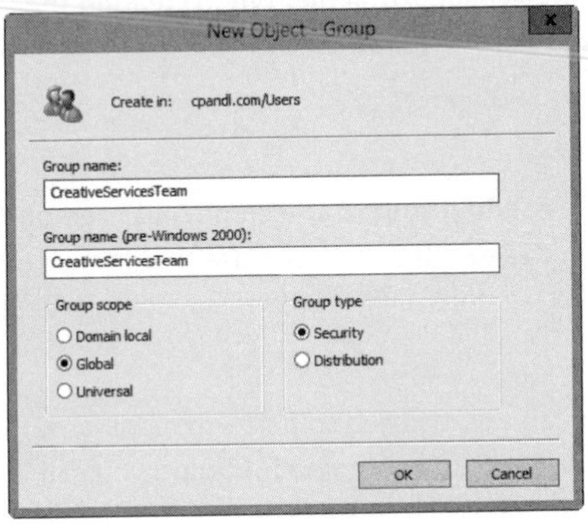

**Figure 30-14** Creating a group.

Windows Server has three group scopes and two group types you can select from. This allows you to create six different combinations of groups. You must be a member of the Account Operators, Domain Admins, or Enterprise Admins group to create new groups.

> **Note**
>
> The built-in accounts for Active Directory in Windows Server are located in two places. The built-in domain local groups—such as Administrators, Account Operators, and Backup Operators—are located in the Builtin container. Built-in global groups—such as Domain Admins and Enterprise Admins—are located in the Users container.

# INSIDE OUT Creating group accounts at the command line

At the command line, you can create groups using DSADD. For groups, AD path strings describe the group's location in the directory, from the group name to the actual containers in which it is stored. You specify whether the group is a security group by typing **–secgrp yes** or that a group is a distribution group by typing **–secgrp no**. You specify the scope of the group by typing **–scope u** for universal, **–scope g** for global, and **–scope l** for domain local.

For example, if you want to create a global security group called SeattleServices in the Services OU for the cpandl.com domain, the full path to this group object is CN=SeattleServices,OU=Services,DC=cpandl,DC=com. When creating the group object using DSADD, you must specify this path as follows:

```
dsadd group "CN=SeattleServices,OU=Services,DC=cpandl,DC=com" –secgrp yes
–scope g
```

For the full syntax and usage, type **dsadd group /?** at a command prompt. Although quotation marks aren't required in this example, I always use them to ensure I don't forget them when they actually are needed, such as when name components contain spaces.

The directory services commands can also be used to perform many group-management tasks. Using DSGET GROUP at a command prompt, you can

- Determine whether a group is a security group by typing **dsget group *GroupDN* –secgrp**.

- Determine group scope by typing **dsget group *GroupDN* –scope**.

- Determine the members of a group by typing **dsget group *GroupDN* –members**, where *GroupDN* is the distinguished name of the group.

- Determine the groups of which a group is a member by typing **dsget group *GroupDN* –memberof**. The **–expand** option can be added to display the recursively expanded list of groups of which a group is a member.

Using DSMOD GROUP at a command prompt, you can

- Change group scope using **dsmod group *GroupDN* –scope u** for universal, **–scope g** for global, and **–scope l** for domain local.

- Add members by typing **dsmod group *GroupDN* –addmbr *MemberDN***, where *GroupDN* is the distinguished name of the group and *MemberDN* is the distin-guished name of the account or group you want to add to the designated group.

- Remove members by typing **dsmod group *GroupDN* –rmmbr *MemberDN***.

- Convert the group to a security group using **dsmod group *GroupDN* –secgrp yes** or to a distribution group using **dsmod group *GroupDN* –secgrp no**.

## Adding members to groups

The easiest way to add users to a group is to press and hold or right-click the user in the details pane of Active Directory Users And Computers, and then select Add To A Group. The Select Groups dialog box appears, and you can select the group of which the user is to become a member. You can also get to the same dialog box by pressing and holding or right-clicking on the user name, selecting Properties, tapping or clicking the Member Of tab, and then tapping or clicking Add. The process is similar for Active Directory Administrative Center.

> **Note**
> To add multiple users to a group, select more than one user, using Shift+click or Ctrl+click, and follow the same steps.

If you want to add both users and groups as members of a group, you can do this by performing the following steps:

1. Double-tap or double-click the group entry in Active Directory Users And Computers. This opens the group's Properties dialog box.

2. On the Members tab, tap or click Add to add accounts to the group.

3. Use the Select Users, Contacts, Computers, Or Groups dialog box to choose users, computers, and groups that should be members of the currently selected group. Tap or click OK.

4. Repeat steps 2 and 3 as necessary to add additional users, computers, and groups as members.

5. Tap or click OK.

## Deleting a group

Deleting a group is as simple as pressing and holding or right-clicking the group name within Active Directory Users And Computers or Active Directory Administrative Center and then selecting Delete. You should be very careful when deleting groups because, though it does not delete the user accounts contained by the group, the permissions you assigned to the group are lost and cannot be recovered by merely re-creating the group with the same name.

Chapter 30

**CAUTION**

The permissions on groups are internally characterized within Active Directory by unique SIDs that are allocated when the group is created. If you delete a group and then re-create it, it will have a new SID and thus new permissions.

# Modifying groups

There are a number of modifications, property changes, and management procedures you might want to apply to groups. You can change the scope, change the members and other groups contained in the group, move a group, delegate the management of a group, and send mail to a group.

## Finding a group

When you have a substantial number of groups, you can use the search function to locate the one you need to manage. In Active Directory Users And Computers, just press and hold or right-click the domain or OU and then select Find. In the Find Users, Contacts, And Groups dialog box, you can specify what type of object to find, change the starting point, or structure a search query from the available tabs. After the query has run, many administrative or management functions can be performed on the objects returned in the results window.

In Active Directory Administrative Center, just press and hold or right-click the domain or OU and then select Search Under This Node. In the main pane under Global Search, type the name of the object to find and then tap or click Search.

**INSIDE OUT** Saved queries in Active Directory

In Active Directory Users And Computers, you can reuse and save queries. This allows you to find groups quickly and repeatedly when you want to manage and modify them. You can locate the Saved Queries folder in the default position at the top of the Active Directory Users And Computers console tree (left pane). You cannot save queries from the Find menu when you press and hold or right-click a group. You can save them only by using the Saved Query procedure that is found in the uppermost part of the tree in Active Directory Users And Computers and creating a new query.

# Managing computer accounts

Computer accounts are managed and configured using Active Directory Users And Computers or Active Directory Administrative Center. The process is similar regardless of which tool you use.

By default, computer accounts are stored in the Computers container and domain controller accounts are stored in the Domain Controllers container. Computer accounts also can be stored in other containers, such as the OUs you created. Computers can be joined and removed from a domain using Computer Management or the System tool in Control Panel.

## Creating a computer account in Active Directory

You can create two types of computer accounts: standard computer accounts and managed computer accounts. Managed computer accounts are available when you install Windows Deployment Services in your domain.

To create a new computer account, start Active Directory Users And Computers. Press and hold or right-click the container in which you want to create the new computer account, point to New, and then select Computer. This starts the New Object–Computer Wizard shown in Figure 30-15.

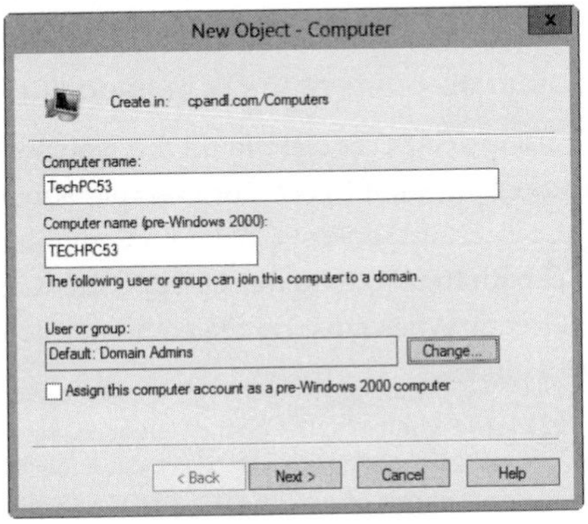

**Figure 30-15**  Creating a computer account.

Type a computer name. By default, only members of the Administrators, Account Operators, Enterprise Admins, or Domain Admins group can join computers to the domain. To allow a different user or group to join the computer to the domain, tap or click Change and then use the Select User Or Group dialog box to select a user or group account that is authorized to join the computer to the domain.

If this account will be used with applications written for legacy operating systems, select Assign This Computer Account As A Pre–Windows 2000 Computer. If Windows Deployment

Chapter 30

Services are not installed, tap or click OK to create the computer account. Otherwise, you can create the account by tapping or clicking Next twice and then tapping or clicking Finish.

Or you can configure the computer as a managed PC. To do this, tap or click Next to display the Managed page. Select the This Is A Managed Computer check box, and then type the computer's globally unique identifier/universally unique identifier (GUID/UUID). On the Host Server page, you have the option to specify which host server to use for remote installation or to allow any available host server to be used for remote installation. To select a host server, select The Following Remote Installation Server. In the Find dialog box, tap or click Find Now to display a list of all remote installation servers in the organization. Tap or click the host server you want to use, and then tap or click OK to close the Find dialog box. Tap or click Next, and then tap or click Finish.

---

## Note

Creating a computer account does not join the computer to the domain. It merely creates the account to simplify the process of joining a domain. You can, however, create a computer account when you join a computer to a domain.

---

## INSIDE OUT    Creating computer accounts at the command line

You can create computer accounts using DSADD as well. To do this, you need to know the Active Directory service path string you want to use. For example, suppose that you want to create a computer account called CustServicePC27 in the Computers container for the cpandl.com domain. The full path to this computer object is CN=CustServiceP C27,CN=Computers,DC=cpandl,DC=com. When creating the computer object using DSADD, you must specify this path as follows:

```
dsadd computer "CN=CustServicePC27,CN=Computers,DC=cpandl,DC=com"
```

Here, CN= is used to specify the common name of an object and DC= is used to specify a domain component. With Active Directory path strings, you will also see OU=, which is used to specify the name of an organizational unit object. For the full syntax and usage, type **dsadd computer /?** at a command prompt. Although quotation marks aren't required in this example, I always use them to ensure I don't forget them when they actually are needed, such as when name components contain spaces.

The directory services commands can also be used to perform many computer management tasks. Use DSMOD COMPUTER to set properties, disable accounts, and reset accounts. Use DSMOVE COMPUTER to move computer accounts to a new container or OU. Use DSRM COMPUTER to remove the computer account.

# Joining computers to a domain

When you join a computer to a domain, you must supply the credentials for creating a new computer account in Active Directory. The new computer will be placed in the default Computers container in Active Directory. You must be a member of the Administrators group on the local computer to join it to the domain. Windows Server allows any authenticated user to join workstations to the domain—up to a total of 10 (by default)—providing that you already created the necessary computer accounts. To join a server to a domain, you must be a member of the Administrators, Account Operators, Domain Admins, or Enterprise Admins group.

To join a server or workstation to a domain, follow these steps:

1. Ensure the client's DNS server settings point to a domain controller or DNS server. Often, these settings are obtained through DHCP.

2. On the Computer Name tab of the System Properties dialog box, tap or click Change. This displays the Computer Name/Domain Changes dialog box.

3. Select the Domain option, type the name of the domain to join, and then tap or click OK.

4. In the Windows Security prompt, type the name and password of an account with permission to add the computer to the specified domain or to remove the computer from a previously specified domain, and then tap or click OK.

5. When prompted that your computer has joined the domain you specified, tap or click OK.

6. You'll see a prompt stating that you need to restart the computer. Tap or click OK.

7. Tap or click Close, and then tap or click Restart Now to restart the computer.

**TROUBLESHOOTING**

**The computer won't join the domain**

If there are problems joining the computer to the domain, there might be an existing computer in the domain with the same name. In this case, you change the computer name and then repeat this procedure. The computer must also have Transmission Control Protocol/Internet Protocol (TCP/IP) properly configured. If you suspect a problem with the TCP/IP configuration, ping the loopback address 127.0.0.1 to ensure TCP/IP is installed correctly and then check the configuration settings by typing **ipconfig /all** at the command prompt.

Chapter 30

## Moving a computer account

A corporation might have organizational changes requiring you to move a computer account. The computer account can be moved from one container to another. Plan and test moving the computer account to ensure that possible conflicts in permissions or rights don't occur. You can use the Effective Permissions tool in planning mode to simulate moving computer accounts and to determine if there could be conflicts.

To move a computer account, you can drag and drop the computer object from one container to another within the details pane of Active Directory Users And Computers. Alternatively, you can press and hold or right-click the computer account name, select Move, and then select the container to which you want to move the account using the Move dialog box. You cannot move computer accounts for domain controllers across domains. You must first demote the domain controller, and then move the computer account.

## Disabling a computer account

Security issues, such as malicious viral attacks or rogue user actions, might require you to temporarily disable a computer account. Perhaps a critical software bug has caused an individual computer to repeatedly try to receive authentication from a domain controller. You disable a computer account to prevent it from authenticating until you fix the problem.

You disable a computer account by pressing and holding or right-clicking it in Active Directory Users And Computers and selecting Disable Account. This prevents the computer from logging on to the domain but does not remove the related account from Active Directory. Active Directory Administrative Center doesn't have an option for disabling computer accounts.

## Deleting a computer account

When you delete a computer account, you cannot just re-create a new computer account with the same name and access. The SID of the original computer account will be different from that of the new account.

To remove a computer account, press and hold or right-click the computer account in either Active Directory Users And Computers or Active Directory Administrative Center, and then select Delete.

## Managing a computer account

Managing a remote computer is a common task when troubleshooting server or workstation problems. You can configure management settings such as shares, system settings, services and applications, and the event log of the remote computer. Care should be taken when changing settings or restarting services on remote machines.

Press and hold or right-click the computer account name in Active Directory Users And Computers, and then select Manage to bring up Computer Management for that computer. This option is not available in Active Directory Administrative Center.

## Resetting a computer account

Computer accounts have passwords, just like user accounts. Unlike user accounts, however, computer account passwords are managed and maintained automatically. To perform this automated management, computers in the domain store a computer account password, which is changed every 30 days by default, and a secure channel password for establishing secure communications with domain controllers.

The secure channel password is also updated by default every 30 days, and both passwords must be synchronized. If the secure channel password and the computer account password get out of sync, the computer won't be allowed to log on to the domain, and a domain authentication error message will be logged for the Netlogon service with an event ID of 3210 or 5722.

If this happens, you need to reset the computer account password. One way to do this is to press and hold or right-click the computer account in Active Directory Users And Computers and select Reset Account. You then need to remove the computer from the domain (by making the computer a member of a workgroup or another domain) and then rejoin the computer to the domain.

## Troubleshooting computer accounts

As an administrator, you might see a variety of problems related to computer accounts. When you are joining a computer to a domain, you might experience problems due to incorrect network settings. The computer joining the domain must be able to communicate with the domain controller in the domain. You can resolve connectivity problems by configuring the computer's Local Area Network connection settings appropriately for the domain to which you are connecting. Be sure to check the IP address, default gateway, and DNS server settings.

Another common problem is related to insufficient permissions. The user joining the computer to the domain must have appropriate permissions in the domain. Be sure to use an account with appropriate permissions to join the domain.

After a computer is joined to a domain, you sometimes might see problems with the computer password or the trust between the computer and the domain. Diagnosing a password/trust problem is straightforward. If you try to access or browse resources in the

Chapter 30

domain and are prompted for a user name and password when you normally are not, you might have a password/trust issue with the computer account. For example, if you are trying to connect to a remote computer in Computer Management, and you are repeatedly prompted for a user name and password where you weren't previously, the computer account password should probably be reset.

You can verify a password/trust problem by checking the System event log. Look for an error with event ID 3210 generated by the NETLOGON service. The related error message should read as follows:

```
This computer could not authenticate with RESOURCENAME, a Windows domain controller
for domain DOMAINNAME, and therefore this computer might deny logon requests. This
inability to authenticate might be caused by another computer on the same network
using the same name or the password for this computer account is not recognized. If
this message appears again, contact your system administrator.
```

As part of the troubleshooting process, you should always check the status of the account in Active Directory Users And Computers. A disabled account has a circle with a down arrow. A deleted account will no longer be listed, and you won't be able to search for and find it in the directory. If a user was trying to connect to a resource on a remote computer, the computer to which the user is connecting should have a related error or warning event in the event logs.

If the related computer account is disabled or deleted, you will be denied access to remote resources when connecting to those resources from this computer. As an example, if you are trying to access FileServer75 from CustServicePC83, you will be denied access if the computer account is disabled or deleted. The system event log on the remote computer (FileServer75) should log related NETLOGON errors specifically related to the computer account, such as the following with event ID 5722:

```
The session setup from the computer CORPPC18 failed to authenticate. The name(s) of
the account(s) referenced in the security database is CORPPC18$. The following error
occurred: Access is denied.
```

With Kerberos authentication, a computer's system time can affect authentication. If a computer's system time deviates outside the permitted norms set in Group Policy, the computer will fail authentication.

If you are still experiencing problems, check the computer's group membership and the container in which it is located in Active Directory. Computer accounts, like user accounts, can be made members of specific groups and are placed in a specific container in Active Directory. The group membership of a computer determines many permissions with regard to security and resource access. Changing a computer's group membership can significantly affect security and resource access. The container in which a computer is placed determines how Group Policy is applied to the computer. Moving a computer to a different container or OU can significantly affect the way policy settings are applied.

# Recovering deleted accounts

Active Directory Recycle Bin allows you to undo the accidental deletion of Active Directory objects in much the same way as you can recover deleted files from the Windows Recycle Bin. Before you can use the recycle bin, you must raise the domain and forest functional levels to the Windows Server 2008 R2 level or higher and then you must enable the feature. Keep in mind that once you enable Active Directory Recycle Bin you will not be able to lower the domain or forest functional level.

## Enabling Active Directory Recycle Bin

When an Active Directory object is deleted and the recycle bin is enabled, the object is put in a state referred to as *logically deleted*. The object's distinguished name is altered, and it is moved to the Deleted Objects container, where it remains for the period of time set in the deleted object lifetime value, which is 180 days by default.

You enable the recycle bin for use by following these steps:

1.  In Active Directory Administrative Center, the local domain is opened for management by default. If you want to work with a different domain, tap or click Manage and then tap or click Add Navigation Nodes. In the Add Navigation Nodes dialog box, select the domain you want to work with and then tap or click OK.

2.  Select the domain you want to work with by tapping or clicking it in the left pane. In the Tasks pane, tap or click Enable Recycle Bin and then tap or click OK in the confirmation dialog box.

> **Important**
> Enabling the recycle bin is a forestwide change. When you enable the recycle bin in one domain of a forest, Active Directory replicates the change to all domain controllers in all domains of the forest. Thus, every domain in the forest will have its own recycle bin.

After you enable the recycle bin, Active Directory will begin replicating the change to all domain controllers in the forest. Once the change is replicated, the recycle bin will be available for use. If you then tap or click Refresh in Active Directory Administrative Center, you'll see that a Deleted Objects container is available for each domain you select.

## Recovering objects from the recycle bin

When Active Directory Recycle Bin is enabled, you can easily recover deleted objects. To do this, you use Active Directory Administrative Center. Domains using the recycle bin will have a Deleted Object container. In this container, you'll see a list of deleted objects, as shown in Figure 30-16.

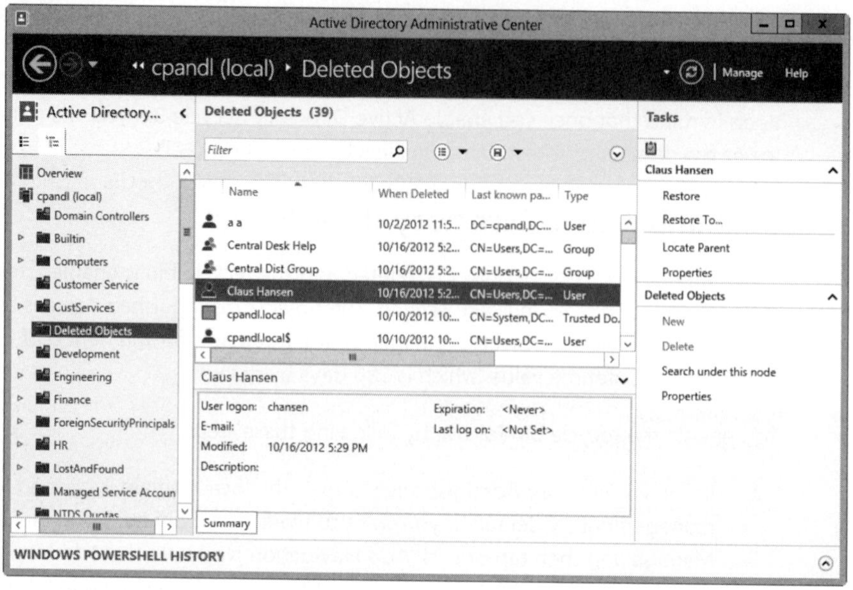

**Figure 30-16** The Deleted Objects container.

As discussed in Chapter 24, "Active Directory architecture," under "Extensible Storage Engine," deleted objects remain in the Deleted Objects container for the deleted object lifetime value, which is 180 days by default. Each deleted object is listed by name, and you can see when it was deleted, the last known parent, and the type. When you select a deleted object by tapping or clicking it, you can use the options in the Tasks pane to work with it. The Restore option restores the object to its original container. For example, if the object was deleted from the Users container, it is restored to this container.

The Restore To option restores the object to an alternate container within its original domain or a different domain within the current forest. Specify the alternate container in the Restore To dialog box. For example, if the object was deleted from the Users container in the eng.cpandl.com domain, you could restore it to the Technology OU in the tech.cpandl.com domain.

# Managing Group Policy

GROUP Policy is designed to simplify administration by allowing administrators to configure user and computer settings in Active Directory Domain Services and then have those policies automatically applied to computers throughout an organization. Not only does this provide for the central management of computers, it also helps to automate key administrative tasks. Using Group Policy, you can accomplish the following tasks:

- Configure security policies for account lockout, passwords, Kerberos, and auditing

- Redirect special folders such as a user's Documents folder to centrally managed network shares

- Lock down computer desktop configurations

- Define logon, logoff, shutdown, and startup scripts

- Automate the installation of application software

- Maintain Internet Explorer, and configure standard settings

Some of these features—such as security policies and folder redirection—have been discussed in previous chapters. Other features are discussed in this chapter. The focus of this chapter, however, is on the management of Group Policy, which is the most challenging aspect of implementing Group Policy in an organization.

> **Note**
> Under the Computer Configuration and User Configuration nodes, you find two nodes: Policies and Preferences. Settings for general policies are listed under the Policies node. Settings for general preferences are listed under the Preferences node. When referencing settings under the Policies node, I'll typically use shortcut references, such as User Configuration\Administrative Templates\Windows Components rather than User Configuration\Policies\Administrative Templates: Policy Definitions\Windows Components. This shortcut reference tells you the policy setting being discussed is under User Configuration rather than Computer Configuration and can be found under Administrative Templates\Windows Components.

# Understanding Group Policy

You can think of Group Policy as a set of rules that help you manage users and computers. Like any set of rules, Group Policy is effective only under certain conditions.

> **Note**
> Like Active Directory, Group Policy has gone through several revisions. As a result of these revisions, some policies work only with a version of the Windows operating system that is compatible with a particular revision. For example, some group policies are compatible with Windows 7, Windows 8, Windows Server 2008, Windows Server 2008 R2, and Windows Server 2012, while others are compatible only with Windows XP Professional and Windows Server 2003 or with Windows Vista and Windows Server 2008.

## Local and Active Directory Group Policy

Two types of group policies are available. The first type is Local Group Policy, which is stored locally on individual computers in the %SystemRoot%\System32\GroupPolicy folder and applies only to a particular computer. Every computer running Windows has one or more local group policies. For a computer in a workgroup, Local Group Policy is the only Group Policy available. A computer in a domain also has a Local Group Policy, but it is not the only Group Policy available, and this is where the second type of Group Policy, called Active Directory Group Policy (or more commonly just "Group Policy"), comes into the picture.

Active Directory Group Policy is stored in the Sysvol folder used by Active Directory for replicating policies and is represented logically as an object called a Group Policy Object (GPO). A GPO is simply a container for the policies you configure and their settings that can be linked to sites, domains, and organizational units (OUs) in your Active Directory structure. You can create multiple GPOs, and by linking those objects to different locations in your Active Directory structure, you can apply the related policy settings to the users and computers in those Active Directory containers.

When you create a domain, two Active Directory group policies are created:

- **Default Domain Controllers Policy GPO**   A default GPO created for the Domain Controllers OU and applicable to all domain controllers in a domain as long as they are members of this OU

- **Default Domain Policy GPO**   A default GPO, which is created for and linked to the domain within Active Directory

You can create additional GPOs as necessary and link them to the sites, domains, and OUs you've created. Linking a GPO to Active Directory structure is how you apply Group Policy. For example, you could create a GPO called Technology Policy and then link it to the Technology OU. The policy then applies to that OU.

## Group Policy settings

Group Policy applies only to users and computers. Although groups can be used to specify to which users a particular policy applies, the actual policies are applied only to member users. Group Policy settings are divided into two categories: Computer Configuration and User Configuration. Computer Configuration contains settings that apply to computers. User Configuration contains settings that apply to user accounts.

Figure 31-1 shows the Default Domain Policy for a computer. As you can see in the figure, both Computer Configuration–related and User Configuration–related settings are divided into three major classes, each of which contains several subclasses of settings:

- **Software Settings**   You use these to install software on computers and then maintain it by installing patches or upgrades. You can also uninstall software.

- **Windows Settings**   You use these to manage key Windows settings for both computers and users, including scripts and security. For users, you can also manage Remote Installation Services, folder redirection, and Internet Explorer maintenance.

- **Administrative Templates** You use these to control registry settings that configure the operating system, Windows components, and applications. Administrative Templates are implemented for specific operating-system versions.

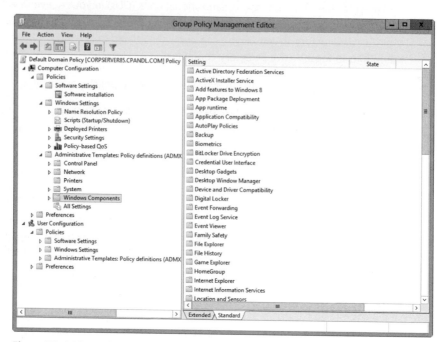

**Figure 31-1** The Default Domain Policy.

## Group Policy architecture

Within the Windows operating system, the components of Group Policy have separate server and client implementations. (See Figure 31-2.) Each Group Policy client has client-side extensions that are used to interpret and apply Group Policy settings. The client-side extensions are implemented as dynamic-link libraries (DLLs) that are installed with the operating system. The main DLL for processing Administrative Templates is Userenv.dll.

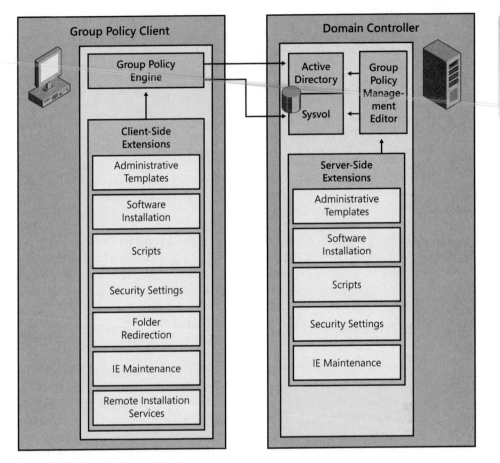

**Figure 31-2** Group Policy architecture.

The Group Policy engine running on a client triggers the processing of policy when one of two events occurs: either the system is started, or a user logs on to the computer. When a system is started and the network connection is initialized, computer policy settings are applied.

Administrators and others who are delegated permissions in Group Policy can use Group Policy Management Editor to manage Group Policy. This snap-in for the Microsoft Management Console (MMC) provides the three top-level classes (Software Settings, Windows Settings, and Administrative Templates) that can be managed and makes use of a number of extensions. These extensions provide the functionality you can use to configure various Group Policy settings. Some client-side extensions don't have specific implementations on the server because they are registry-based and can be configured through Administrative Templates.

Although GPOs are represented logically in Active Directory and replicated through normal replication, most server-side Group Policy components are represented on the Sysvol as physical files. The default location for the Sysvol folder is %SystemRoot%\Sysvol with the subfolder %SystemRoot%\Sysvol\sysvol shared as Sysvol. Within the shared Sysvol folder, you'll find subfolders organized by domain and the globally unique identifier (GUID) of each GPO created in a particular domain.

## Administrative templates

Windows Server displays the registry-based policy settings in the Administrative Templates. Registry-based policy settings are defined using a standards-based, XML file format, called ADMX. This format replaces the ADM format previously used with Windows XP Professional and Windows Server 2003.

You can edit GPOs using ADMX files only on computers running current Windows operating systems. The reason for this is current Windows operating systems have policy editors that have been updated to work with ADMX. With that said, the policy editors automatically read and display Administrative Template policy settings from both the ADMX and ADM files. This means any custom ADM files you created will still be available. However, the policy editors will exclude ADM files that were included by default in earlier releases of Windows because the ADMX files supersede these files.

ADMX files are divided into language-neutral files ending with the .admx file extension and language-specific files ending with the .adml extension. The language-neutral files ensure that a GPO has identical core policies. The language-specific files allow policies to be viewed and edited in multiple languages. Because the language-neutral files store the core settings, policies can be edited in any language for which a computer is configured, thus allowing one user to view and edit policies in English and another to view and edit policies in Spanish, for example. The mechanism that determines the language used is the language pack installed on the computer.

Unlike ADM files, ADMX files are not stored in individual GPOs by default. Language-neutral ADMX files are installed in the %SystemRoot%\PolicyDefinitions folder. Language-specific ADMX files are installed in the %SystemRoot%\PolicyDefinitions\LanguageCulture folder. Each subfolder is named after the appropriate International Organization for Standardization (ISO) language/culture name, such as en-US for US English.

When you start a policy editor, it automatically reads in ADMX files from the policy definitions folders. Because of this, you can copy ADMX files that you want to use to the appropriate policy definitions folder to make them available when you are editing GPOs. If the policy editor is running when you copy the file or files, you must restart the policy editor to force it to read in the file or files.

Because of these changes, only the current state of a setting is stored in the GPO and the details related to the settings are stored in the ADMX files. This reduces the amount of storage space used as the number of GPOs increases and also reduces the amount of data being replicated throughout the enterprise. As long as you edit GPOs using current Windows operating systems, new GPOs will contain neither ADM nor ADMX files inside the GPO.

# Implementing Group Policy

As discussed previously, there are two types of Group Policy: Local Group Policy and Active Directory Group Policy. Local Group Policy applies to a local machine only, and there is only one local GPO per local machine. Active Directory Group Policy, on the other hand, can be implemented separately for sites, domains, and OUs.

In an effort to streamline management of Group Policy, Microsoft removed management features from Active Directory–related tools and moved to a primary console called Group Policy Management Console (GPMC). The GPMC is a feature that you can add to any installation of Windows Server by using the Add Features Wizard. The GPMC is also included with Windows desktop operating systems and available as a download from the Microsoft website. After you add the GPMC to a server, it is available on the Administrative Tools menu.

When you want to edit a GPO in the GPMC, the GPMC opens Group Policy Management Editor, which you use to manage the policy settings. Also available are Group Policy Starter GPO Editor and Local Group Policy Object Editor. You use Group Policy Starter GPO Editor to create and manage Starter Group Policy objects, which are meant to provide a starting point for new policy objects that you use throughout your organization. When you create a new policy object, you can specify a starter GPO as the source or basis of the new object. You use Local Group Policy Object Editor to create and manage policy objects for the local computer rather than using those settings for an entire site, domain, or organizational unit.

When you use any of these tools to create a new GPO or modify an existing GPO in Active Directory (but not with local policy), the related changes are made on the domain controller acting as the PDC emulator if it is available. The reason the PDC emulator is used is so that there is a central point of contact for GPO creation and editing, and this in turn helps to ensure that only one administrator is granted access to edit a particular GPO at a time. This also simplifies replication of the changes because changes are always replicated from the same point of origin—the PDC emulator. However, if the PDC emulator cannot be reached or is otherwise unavailable when you try to work with GPOs, you are given the opportunity to choose to make changes on the domain controller to which you are currently connected or any available domain controller.

# Working with Local Group Policy

Current Windows operating systems support multiple Local Group Policy Objects (LGPOs) on a single computer (as long as the computer is not a domain controller). Previously, computers had only one LGPO. Having multiple LGPOs allows you to

- Have a top-level LGPO, referred to simply as *Local Group Policy*. Local Group Policy is the only LGPO that allows both computer configuration and user configuration settings to be applied to all users of the computer.

- Assign a different LGPO to each general user type. There are two general user types: Administrators, which includes only the user accounts that are members of the local Administrators group, and Non-Administrators, which includes only the user accounts that are not members of the local Administrators group. Administrators and Non-Administrators Local Group Policy contain only user configuration settings.

- Assign a different LGPO to each local user. User-specific Group Policy is applied to a specific user or group and contains only user configuration settings.

These multiple LGPOs act as policy layers and are processed by Windows in the following order:

1. Local Group Policy

2. Administrators and Non-Administrators Group Policy

3. User-specific Local Group Policy

When computers are being used in a standalone configuration rather than a domain configuration, you might find that multiple LGPOs are useful because you no longer have to explicitly disable or remove settings that interfere with your ability to manage a computer before performing administrator tasks. Instead, you can implement one LGPO for administrators and another LGPO for non-administrators. In a domain configuration, however, you might not want to use multiple LGPOs. In domains, most computers and users already have multiple Group Policy Objects applied to them—adding multiple Local Group Policy Objects to this already varied mix can make managing Group Policy confusing. This is especially true when you consider that a setting in one LGPO can possibly conflict with a setting in another LGPO, which, in turn, could conflict with domain GPO settings.

Windows resolves conflicts in settings by overwriting any previous setting with the last-read and most current setting (unless blocking or enforcing is enabled). Regardless, the final setting applied is the one that Windows uses. When Windows resolves conflicts, only the enabled or disabled state of settings matters. If a setting is set as Not Configured, this has no effect on the state of the setting from a previous policy application. You can simplify domain administration by disabling processing of all Local Group Policy Objects. You do this by enabling the Turn Off Local Group Policy Objects Processing policy setting in a domain Group Policy Object. In Group Policy, this setting is located under Computer Configuration\Administrative Templates\System\Group Policy. When this setting is enabled, as shown in Figure 31-3, computers in the domain process only domain-based policy.

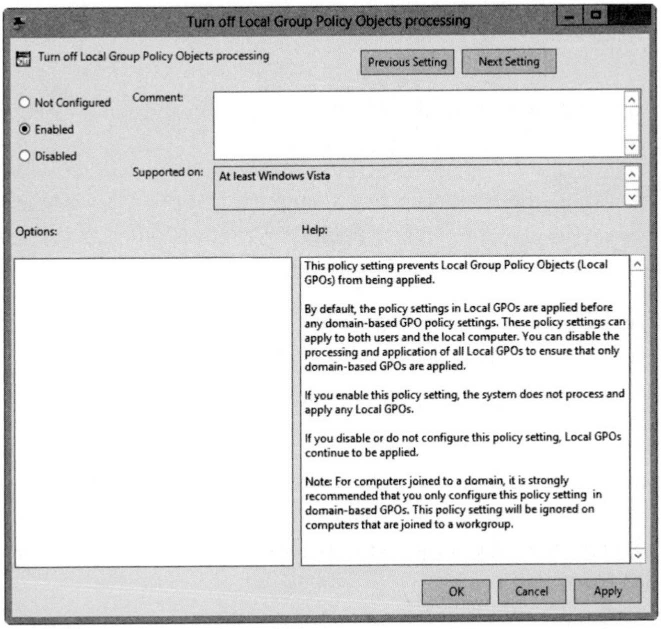

**Figure 31-3** Simplify administration by configuring the processing of only domain policy.

You can access the top-level Local Group Policy Object in several ways. One way is to type the following command at a command prompt:

```
gpedit.msc /gpcomputer:"%computername%"
```

This command starts Group Policy Object Editor in an MMC and tells Group Policy Object Editor to target the local computer. Here, *%ComputerName%* is an environment variable that sets the name of the local computer and must be enclosed in double quotation marks as shown. To access Local Group Policy on a remote computer, type the following command at a command prompt:

```
gpedit.msc /gpcomputer: "RemoteComputer"
```

Here, *RemoteComputer* is the host name or fully qualified domain name (FQDN) of the remote computer, such as

```
gpedit.msc /gpcomputer: "CorpServer08"
```

You can also manage the top-level local policy on a computer by following these steps:

1. Type **mmc** into the Apps Search box, and then press Enter.

2. In the Microsoft Management Console, click File and then select Add/Remove Snap-in.

3. In the Add Or Remove Snap-ins dialog box, select Group Policy Object Editor and then tap or click Add.

4. If you want to work with local policy on the computer, tap or click Finish because local computer is the default object. Tap or click OK.

5. If you want to work with local policy on another computer, tap or click Browse. In the Browse For A Group Policy Object dialog box, on the Computers tab, select Another Computer and then tap or click Browse again.

If you want to work with security settings only in the top-level Local Group Policy Object, you can use the Local Security Policy console. In Server Manager, select Tools and then select Local Security Policy.

In Group Policy Object Editor and Local Security Policy, you can configure security settings that apply to users and the local computer itself. Any policy changes you make are applied to that computer the next time Group Policy is refreshed. The settings you can manage locally depend on whether the computer is a member of a domain or a workgroup, and they include the following:

- Account policies for passwords, account lockout, and Kerberos

- Event logging options for configuring log size, access, and retention options for the application, system, and security logs

- Local policies for auditing, user rights assignment, and security options

- Security restriction settings for groups, system services, registry keys, and the file system

- Security settings for wireless networking, public keys, and Internet Protocol security (IPsec)

- Software restrictions that specify applications that aren't allowed to run on the computer

Figure 31-4 shows the Local Group Policy Editor. You configure Local Group Policy in the same way that you configure Active Directory–based Group Policy. To apply a policy, you enable it and then configure any additional or optional values as necessary. An enabled policy setting is turned on and active. If you don't want a policy to apply, you must disable it. A disabled policy setting is turned off and inactive.

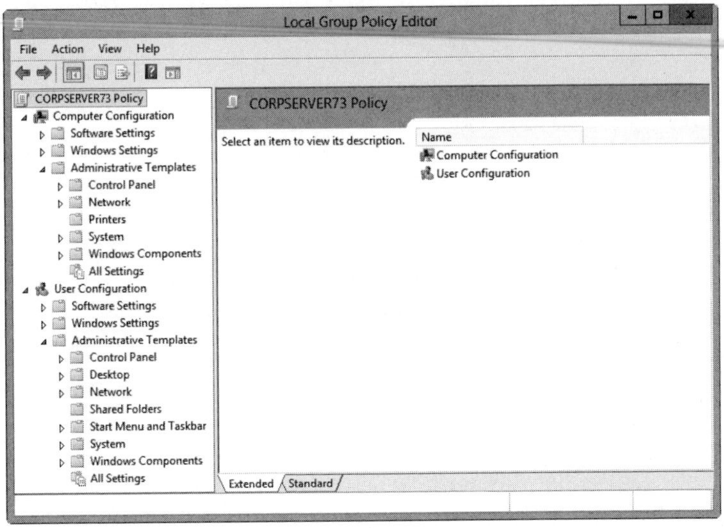

**Figure 31-4** Configure local policy using the Local Group Policy Editor.

# Working with Group Policy Management Console

Group Policy Management Console (GPMC) provides an integrated interface for working with GPOs. You must install GPMC using the Add Roles And Features Wizard. Alternatively, you can install GPMC by entering the following command at an elevated Windows PowerShell prompt: **install-windowsfeature gpmc**. When you install GPMC, several related snap-ins and tools are installed as well. The sections that follow provide an overview of using GPMC.

## Using Group Policy Management Console

You can run Group Policy Management Console from the Tools menu in Server Manager. When you start Group Policy Management Console, the tool connects to Active Directory running on the domain controller acting as the PDC emulator for your logon domain and obtains a list of all GPOs and OUs in that domain. It does this using Lightweight Directory Access Protocol (LDAP) to access the directory store and the Server Message Block (SMB) protocol to access the Sysvol. The result, as shown in Figure 31-5, is that for each domain to which you are connected, you have all the related GPOs and OUs available to work with in one location.

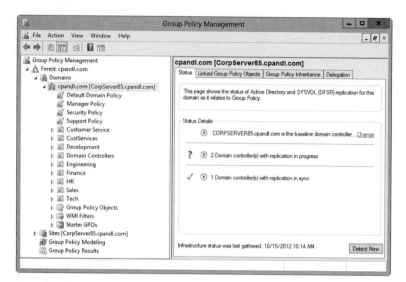

**Figure 31-5** Group Policy Management Console.

In Group Policy Management Console, infrastructure status is displayed on the Status tab when you select a domain, telling you at a glance the status of Active Directory and SYSVOL replication for the domain. The status is gathered from a configurable baseline domain controller. If no status is available, simply tap or click Detect Now. To change the baseline domain controller, tap or click Change, select a new baseline domain controller, and then tap or click OK.

The status details tell you the number of domain controllers that have their GPO information synchronized with the baseline domain controller as well as the number of domain controllers with replication in progress. Domain controllers with replication in progress do not have the same GPO information as the baseline domain controller.

The reason codes for in-progress replication can be related to Active Directory or the SYSVOL. With Active Directory, the reason codes and meaning are as follows:

- **Accessibility**   The Active Directory service cannot be contacted on the specified domain controller.

- **ACLs**   The Active Directory permissions for a specific GPO or GPOs are different from the baseline domain controller.

- **Created Date**   The created date stored in Active Directory for a specific GPO or GPOs is different from the baseline domain controller.

- **GPO Version**   The GPO version information in Active Directory is different from the baseline domain controller.

- **Modified Date**  The modified date stored in Active Directory for a specific GPO or GPOs is different from the baseline domain controller.

- **Number of GPOs**  The total number of GPOs in Active Directory is different from the baseline domain controller.

With the SYSVOL folder, the reason codes and their meaning are as follows:

- **Accessibility**  The SYSVOL folder cannot be contacted on the specified domain controller.

- **ACLs**  The SYSVOL permissions on a specified GPO or GPOs are different from the baseline domain controller.

- **GPO Contents**  The contents of the SYSVOL folder for a specified GPO or GPOs are different from the baseline domain controller.

- **GPO Version**  The GPO version information in the GPT.ini file is different from the baseline domain controller.

- **Number of GPOs**  The total number of GPOs in the SYSVOL folder is different from the baseline domain controller.

Helpful links are provided with each message to get further information for troubleshooting.

## Accessing forests, domains, and sites in Group Policy Management Console

Working with forests, domains, and sites in Group Policy Management Console is fairly straightforward, as the following list describes:

- **Accessing forests**  The forest root is listed for each forest to which you are connected. You can connect to additional forests by pressing and holding or right-clicking the Group Policy Management node in the console tree and selecting Add Forest. In the Add Forest dialog box, shown in Figure 31-6, type the name of a domain in the forest to which you want to connect, and then tap or click OK. As long as there is an external trust to the domain, you can establish the connection and obtain forest information—even if you don't have a forest trust with the entire forest.

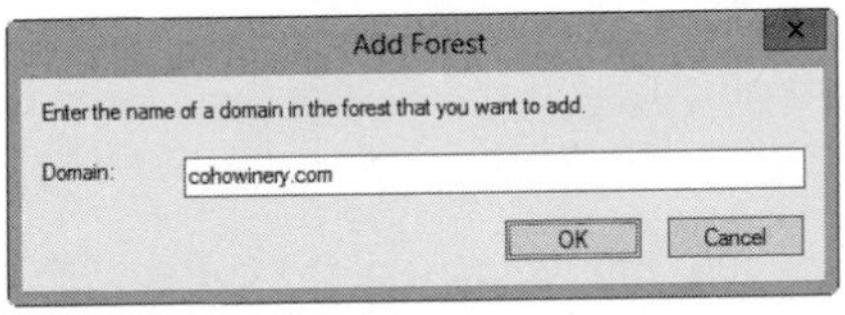

**Figure 31-6** Type the name of the domain to be connected to.

- **Accessing domains** You can view the domain to which you are connected in a forest by expanding the forest node and then expanding the related Domains node. By default, you are connected to your logon domain in the current forest. If you want to work with other domains in a particular forest, press and hold or right-click the Domains node in the designated forest, and then select Show Domains. In the Show Domains dialog box, which has the same options as the Show Sites dialog box, select the options for the domains you want to work with and clear the options for the domains you don't want to work with. Then tap or click OK.

- **Accessing sites** Because Group Policy is primarily configured for domains and OUs, sites are not shown by default in GPMC. If you want to work with the sites in a particular forest, press and hold or right-click the Sites node in the designated forest, and then select Show Sites. In the Show Sites dialog box, shown in Figure 31-7, select the check boxes for the sites you want to work with and clear the check boxes for the domains you don't want to work with. Then tap or click OK.

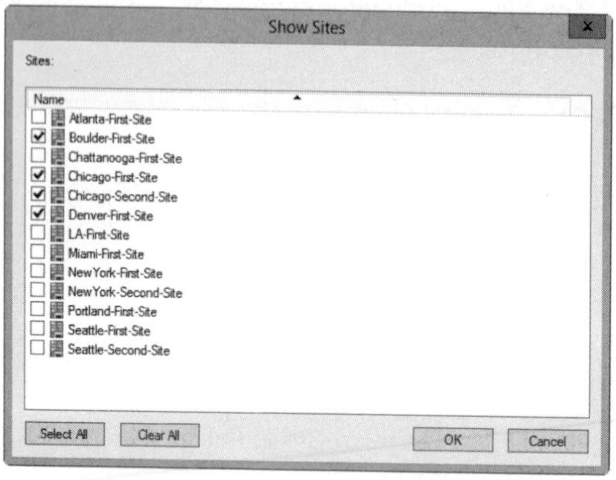

**Figure 31-7** Select the sites you want to work with.

## Creating and linking a new GPO in Group Policy Management Console

In Group Policy Management Console, you can create and link a new GPO by completing the following steps:

1. Access the domain or OU you want to work with in Group Policy Management Console. Do this by expanding the forest node and the related Domains node as necessary, with the following guidelines:

   ○ If you select a domain node, you see a list of the current GPOs and OUs in the domain.

   ○ If you select an OU node, you see a list of the current GPOs for the OU (if any).

2. Press and hold or right-click the domain or OU node, and select Create A GPO In This Domain, And Link It Here.

3. In the New GPO dialog box, type a descriptive name for the GPO, such as **Support Policy**. If you want to use a starter GPO as the source for the initial settings, select the starter GPO to use from the Source Starter GPO drop-down list. Tap or click OK.

> **Note**
>
> Group Policy Management Console doesn't let you create and link a new GPO for sites. You can, however, use Group Policy Management Console to link a site to an existing GPO. For more information, see "Linking to an existing GPO in Group Policy Management Console" later in this chapter.

The new GPO is added to the current list of linked GPOs. If you select the domain or OU node, you can change the preference order of the GPO by selecting it on the Linked Group Policy Objects tab and then tapping or clicking the Move Link Up or Move Link Down button to change the preference order. (See Figure 31-8.)

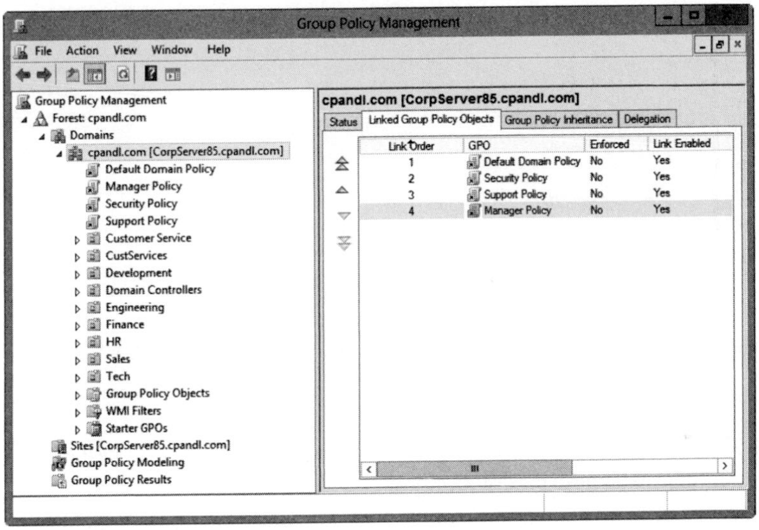

**Figure 31-8** Changing the preference order of a GPO.

## Editing an existing GPO in Group Policy Management Console

In Group Policy Management Console, you can edit an existing GPO linked to the selected container by pressing and holding or right-clicking it and then selecting Edit. This displays the Group Policy Object Editor console. You can then make changes to Group Policy as necessary. The changes will be applied the next time Active Directory is refreshed, according to the inheritance and preference options used by Active Directory.

## Linking to an existing GPO in Group Policy Management Console

Linking a GPO to a container applies the object to the container. In Group Policy Management Console, you can link an existing GPO to a domain, OU, or site by completing the following steps:

1. Access the domain or OU you want to work with in Group Policy Management Console. Do this by expanding the forest node and the related Domains node as necessary.

2. Press and hold or right-click the domain, OU, or site node, and select Link An Existing GPO.

3. In the Select GPO dialog box, shown in Figure 31-9, select the GPO to use and then tap or click OK.

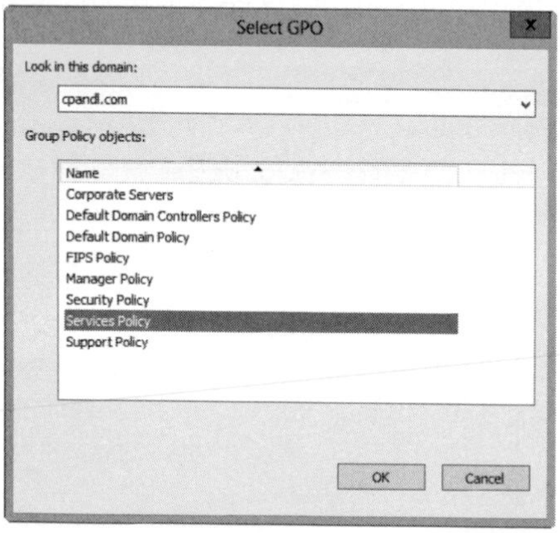

**Figure 31-9** Select the GPO that you want to link to the currently selected container.

4. The linked policy will be applied the next time Active Directory is refreshed, according to the inheritance and preference options used by Active Directory.

## Working with starter GPOs

Any time you create a new GPO in Group Policy Management Console, you can base the new GPO on a starter GPO. Because the settings of the starter GPO are then imported into the new GPO, you can use a starter GPO to define the base configuration settings for a new GPO. In the enterprise, you'll want to create different categories of starter GPOs based on the users and computers they will be used with, or based on the required security configurations.

To create a starter GPO, follow these steps:

1. In Group Policy Management Console, expand the entry for the forest you want to work with, and then double-tap or double-click the related Domains node to expand it.

2. Press and hold or right-click the Starter GPOs node, and then select New. In the New Starter GPO dialog box, type a descriptive name for the new starter GPO, such as **Standard User GPO**. If you want, you can enter comments describing the GPO's purpose. Tap or click OK.

3. Press and hold or right-click the new GPO, and then select Edit. In Group Policy Object Editor, configure policy settings as necessary, and then close Group Policy Object Editor.

### Deleting an existing GPO in Group Policy Management Console

In Group Policy Management Console, you use different techniques to remove GPO links and the GPOs themselves, as follows:

- If you want to remove a link to a GPO, you press and hold or right-click the GPO in the container to which it is linked and then select Delete. When prompted to confirm that you want to remove the link, tap or click OK.

- If you want to remove a GPO and all links to the object, expand the forest, the Domains node, and the Group Policy Objects node. Press and hold or right-click the GPO, and then select Delete. When prompted to confirm that you want to remove the GPO and all links to it, tap or click OK.

## Working with the default Group Policy Objects

When you create a domain, Windows creates the Default Domain Controllers Policy GPO and the Default Domain Policy GPO. These default GPOs are essential to the proper operation and processing of Group Policy. By default, in the precedence order of GPOs, Default Domain Controllers Policy GPO is the highest-precedence GPO linked to the Domain Controllers OU and Default Domain Policy GPO is the highest-precedence GPO linked to the domain.

Although the Default Domain Policy GPO is a complete policy set that includes settings for managing the many policy areas discussed previously, this GPO isn't meant for the general management of Group Policy. You should edit the Default Domain Policy GPO only to manage the default settings for Account Policies (and three specific policies that I'll mention in a moment).

The areas of Account Policy you manage through the Default Domain Policy GPO are as follows:

- **Password Policy**  Determines the default password policies for domain controllers, such as the password history and minimum password length settings.

- **Account Lockout Policy**  Determines the default account lockout policies for domain controllers, such as the account lockout duration and account lockout threshold.

- **Kerberos Policy**  Determines default Kerberos policies for domain controllers, such as the maximum tolerance for computer clock synchronization.

The Default Domain Policy GPO is the only GPO through which Account Policies should be set. To manage other areas of policy, you should create a new GPO and link it to the domain or an appropriate OU within the domain. This is because only the Account Policy settings for the GPO linked to the domain level with the highest precedence in Active Directory are applied, and, by default, this is the Default Domain Policy GPO.

A few additional policy settings should be managed through the GPO linked to the domain level and have the highest precedence as well. These policies—located under Computer Configuration, Windows Settings, Security Settings, Local Policies, Security Options in Group Policy—are as follows:

- **Accounts: Rename Administrator Account**  Configure this policy setting if you want to rename the Administrator account throughout the domain. This sets a new name for the built-in Administrator account so that it is better protected from malicious users. It is important to point out that this specifically affects the logon name of the account and not the display name. The display name will continue to be set to Administrator or whatever else you've set it to. Further, if you or another administrator changes the logon name for this account through Active Directory Users And Computers, the logon name will automatically change back to what is set in policy the next time Group Policy is refreshed.

- **Accounts: Rename Guest Account**  Configure this policy setting if you want to rename the Guest account throughout the domain. This sets a new name for the built-in Guest account so that it is better protected from malicious users. It is important to point out that this specifically affects the logon name of the account and not the display name. The display name will continue to be set to Guest or whatever else you've set it to. Further, if you or another administrator changes the logon name for this account through Active Directory Users And Computers, the logon name will automatically change back to what is set in policy the next time Group Policy is refreshed.

- **Network Access: Allow Anonymous SID/Name Translation** Determines whether an anonymous user can request security identifier (SID) attributes for another user. This setting is disabled by default in most configurations. If this setting is enabled, a malicious user could use the well-known Administrator's SID to obtain the real name of the built-in Administrator account, even if the account has been renamed.

- **Network Security: Force Logoff When Logon Hours Expire** Configure this policy setting if you want to force users to log off from the domain when logon hours expire. For example, if you set the logon hours from 7 A.M. to 7 P.M. for the user, the user will be forced to log off at 8 P.M.

The Default Domain Controllers Policy GPO is designed to ensure that all domain controllers in a specified domain have the same security settings. This is important because all domain controllers in an Active Directory domain are equal. If there were different security settings on each domain controller, different domain controllers might behave differently, and this would be bad, bad, bad. If one domain controller has a specific policy setting, this policy setting should be applied to all domain controllers to ensure consistent behavior across a domain.

Because all domain controllers are placed in the Domain Controllers OU by default, any security setting changes you make apply to all domain controllers by default. You should use the Default Domain Controllers Policy GPO only to set user rights and audit policies. Audit Policy determines default auditing policies for domain controllers, such as logging event success, failure, or both. User Rights Assignment determines the default user rights assignment for domain controllers, such as the Log On As A Service and Allow Log On Locally rights.

**CAUTION**

If you move a domain controller out of the Domain Controllers OU, you could adversely affect domain management, which also could lead to inconsistent behavior during logon and authentication. To prevent problems, any time you move a domain controller out of the Domain Controllers OU you should carefully manage its security settings thereafter. As an example, whenever you make security changes to the Default Domain Controllers Policy GPO, you should ensure those security changes are applied to domain controllers stored in OUs other than the Domain Controllers OU.

# Managing Group Policy through delegation

In Active Directory, administrators are automatically granted permissions for performing different Group Policy management tasks. Other individuals can be granted such permissions through delegation. You delegate to allow a user who is not a member of Enterprise Admins or Domain Admins to perform any management tasks.

## Managing GPO creation rights

In Active Directory, administrators have the ability to create GPOs in a domain, and anyone who has created a GPO in a domain has the right to manage that GPO. You can determine who can create GPOs in a domain by following these steps:

1. In Group Policy Management Console, expand the entry for the forest you want to work with, expand the related Domains node, and then select the Group Policy Objects node.

2. As shown in Figure 31-10, the users and groups who can create GPOs in the selected domain are listed on the Delegation tab.

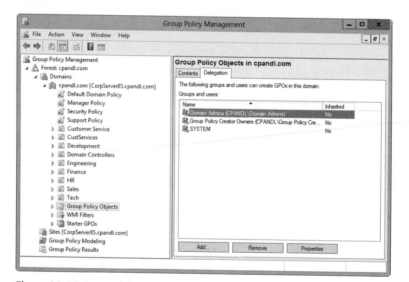

**Figure 31-10**  Determining creation rights for GPOs.

You can delegate the permission to create GPOs (and thus implicitly grant users or groups the ability to manage the GPOs they create). To grant GPO creation permission to a user or group, follow these steps:

1. In Group Policy Management Console, expand the entry for the forest you want to work with, expand the related Domains node, and then select the Group Policy Objects node.

2. In the right pane, select the Delegation tab. The current GPO creation permissions for individual users and groups are listed. To grant the GPO creation permission to another user or group, tap or click Add.

3. In the Select User, Computer, Or Group dialog box, select the user or group and then tap or click OK.

4. The options on the Delegation tab are updated as appropriate. If you later want to remove the GPO creation permission, access the Delegation tab, select the user or group, and then tap or click Remove.

## Reviewing Group Policy management privileges

Group Policy Management Console provides several ways to determine who can manage Group Policy. You can determine Group Policy permissions for a specific site, domain, or OU by following these steps:

1. In Group Policy Management Console, expand the entry for the forest you want to work with, and then expand the related Domains or Sites node as appropriate.

2. When you select the domain, site, or OU you want to work with, the right pane is updated with several tabs. Select the Delegation tab as shown in Figure 31-11.

3. In the Permission list, select the permission you want to check. The options are

   ○ **Link GPOs** The user or group can create and manage links to GPOs in the selected site, domain, or OU.

   ○ **Perform Group Policy Modeling Analyses** The user or group can determine the Resultant Set of Policy (RSoP) for the purposes of planning.

   ○ **Read Group Policy Results Data** The user or group can determine the RSoP that is currently being applied, for the purposes of verification or logging.

4. The individual users or groups with the selected permissions are listed under Groups And Users.

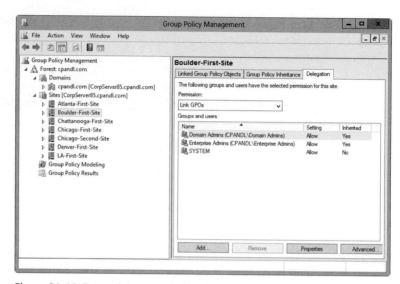

**Figure 31-11**  Determining permissions for a site, domain, or OU.

You can determine which users or groups have access to a particular GPO and what permissions have been granted to them by following these steps:

1. In Group Policy Management Console, expand the entry for the forest you want to work with, expand the related Domains node, and then select the Group Policy Objects node.

2. When you select the GPO whose permissions you want to check, the right pane is updated with several tabs. Select the Delegation tab as shown in Figure 31-12.

3. The permissions for individual users and groups are listed. You'll see three general types of allowed permissions:

   ○ **Read**  Enables the user or group to view the GPO and its settings.

   ○ **Edit Settings**  Enables the user or group to view the GPO and its settings. The user or group can also change settings—but not delete the GPO or modify its security.

   ○ **Edit Settings, Delete, Modify Security**  Enables the user or group to view the GPO and its settings. The user or group can also change settings, delete the GPO, and modify its security.

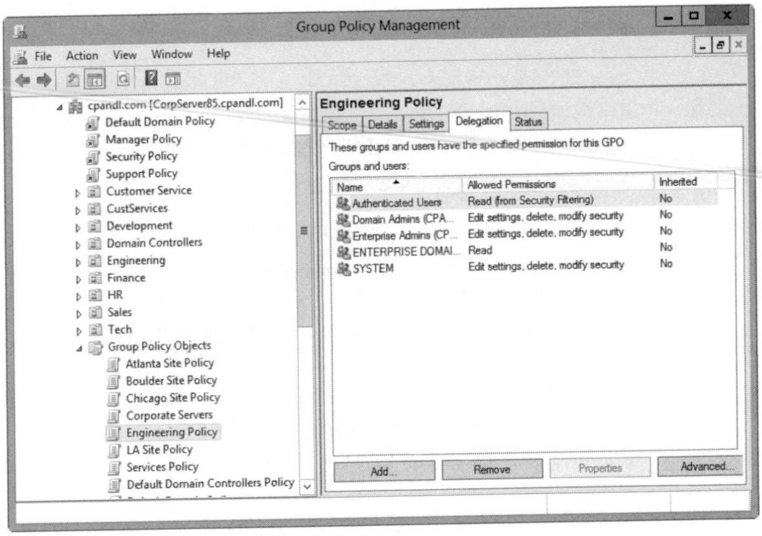

**Figure 31-12** Determining permissions on a GPO.

# Delegating Group Policy management privileges

You can allow a non-administrative user or a group (including users and groups from other domains) to work with a domain, site, or OU GPO by granting one of three specific permissions:

- **Read**   Permits the user or group to view the GPO and its settings.

- **Edit Settings**   Permits the user or group to view the GPO and its settings. The user or group can also change settings—but not delete the GPO or modify its security.

- **Edit Settings, Delete, Modify Security**   Permits the user or group to view the GPO and its settings. The user or group can also change settings, delete the GPO, and modify its security.

You can grant these permissions to a user or group by following these steps:

1. In Group Policy Management Console, expand the entry for the forest you want to work with, expand the related Domains node, and then expand the Group Policy Objects node.

2. Select the GPO you want to work with in the left pane. In the right pane, select the Delegation tab.

3. The current permissions for individual users and groups are listed. To grant permissions to another user or group, tap or click Add.

4.  In the Select User, Computer, Or Group dialog box, select the user or group and then tap or click OK.

5.  In the Add Group Or User dialog box, select the permission to grant: Read, Edit Settings, or Edit Settings, Delete, Modify Security. Tap or click OK.

6.  The options on the Delegation tab are updated to reflect the permissions granted. If you later want to remove this permission, access the Delegation tab, select the user or group, and then tap or click Remove.

## Delegating privileges for links and RSoP

You can allow a non-administrative user or a group (including users and groups from other domains) to manage GPO links and RSoP. The related permissions can be granted in any combination and are defined as follows:

- **Link GPOs**   Permits the user or group to create and manage links to GPOs in the selected site, domain, or OU.

- **Perform Group Policy Modeling Analyses**   Permits the user or group to determine RSoP for the purposes of planning.

- **Read Group Policy Results Data**   Permits the user or group to determine RSoP that is currently being applied, for the purposes of verification or logging.

You can grant these permissions to a user or group by following these steps:

1.  In Group Policy Management Console, expand the entry for the forest you want to work with, and then expand the related Domains or Sites node as appropriate.

2.  In the left pane, select the domain, site, or OU you want to work with. In the right pane, select the Delegation tab.

3.  In the Permission list, select the permission you want to grant. The options are Link GPOs, Perform Group Policy Modeling Analyses, and Read Group Policy Results Data.

4.  The current permissions for individual users and groups are listed. To grant the selected permission to another user or group, tap or click Add.

5.  In the Select User, Computer, Or Group dialog box, select the user or group and then tap or click OK.

6.  In the Add Group Or User dialog box, specify how the permission should be applied. To apply the permission to the current container and all child containers, select This Container And All Child Containers. To apply the permission only to the current container, select This Container Only. Tap or click OK.

7.  The options on the Delegation tab are updated to reflect the permissions granted. If you later want to remove this permission, access the Delegation tab, select the user or group, and then tap or click Remove.

# Managing Group Policy inheritance and processing

GPOs can be linked to sites, domains, and OUs in Active Directory. When you create and link a GPO to one of these containers in Active Directory, the GPO is applied to the user and computer objects in that container according to the inheritance and preference options used by Active Directory. Computer-related policies are processed during startup of the operating system. User-related policies are processed when a user logs on to a computer. After they are applied, Group Policy settings are automatically refreshed at a specific interval to ensure they are current. Group Policy settings can also be refreshed manually.

## Group Policy inheritance

Active Directory uses inheritance to determine how Group Policy is applied. By default, Group Policy settings are inherited from top-level containers by lower level containers. The order of inheritance goes from the site level to the domain level to the OU level. This means the Group Policy settings for a site are passed down to the domains within the site, and the settings for a domain are passed down to the OUs within that domain.

When multiple group policies are in place, the policies are applied in the following order:

- **Local group policies**  Each computer running Windows 2000 or later has Local Group Policy. The local policy is applied first.

- **Site group policies**  Policies linked to sites are processed second. If there are multiple site policies, they are processed synchronously in the listed preference order.

- **Domain group policies**  Policies linked to domains are processed third. If there are multiple domain policies, they are processed synchronously in the listed preference order.

- **OU group policies**  Policies linked to top-level OUs are processed fourth. If there are multiple top-level OU policies, they are processed synchronously in the listed preference order.

- **Child OU group policies**  Policies linked to child OUs are processed fifth. If there are multiple child OU policies, they are processed synchronously in the listed preference order. When there are multiple levels of child OUs, policies for higher level OUs are applied first and policies for the lower level OUs are applied next.

The order in which policies are applied determines which policy settings take effect if multiple policies modify the same settings. Most policies have three configuration options: Not Configured, Enabled, and Disabled. The default state of most policies is Not Configured, meaning the policy setting is not configured and does not apply. If a policy is set to Enabled, the policy is enforced and does apply to users and computers that are subject to the GPO. If a policy is set to Disabled, the policy is not enforced and does not apply to users and computers that are subject to the GPO.

To override a policy that is enabled in a higher level container, you can specifically disable it in a lower level policy. For example, if the user policy Prohibit Access To The Control Panel is enabled for a site, users in the site should not be able to access Control Panel. However, if domain policy specifically disables the user policy Prohibit Access To The Control Panel, users in the domain would be able to access Control Panel. On the other hand, if the domain policy was set to Not Configured, the policy setting would not be modified and would be inherited as normal from the higher level container.

To override a policy that is disabled in a higher level container, you can specifically enable it in a lower level policy. For example, if the user policy Force Classic Control Panel Style is disabled for a domain, users in the domain would be able to choose whether they wanted to use Classic or Simple Control Panel. However, if the Engineering OU policy specifically enables the user policy Force Classic Control Panel Style, users in the Engineering OU would be able to use only the Classic Control Panel style. Again, if the OU policy was set to Not Configured instead, the policy setting would not be modified and would be inherited as normal from the higher level container.

## Changing link order and precedence

The order of inheritance for Group Policy goes from the site level to the domain level and then to each nested OU level. When there are multiple policy objects linked to a particular level, the link order determines the order in which policy settings are applied. Linked policy objects are always applied in link ranking order. Lower ranking policy objects are processed first and then higher ranking policy objects are processed.

In Figure 31-13, these policies will be processed from the lowest link order to the highest. Here the Mobile Devices Policy (with link order 2) will be processed before the Technology Policy (with link order 1). Because Technology Policy settings are processed after Mobile Devices Policy settings, Technology Policy settings have precedence and take priority.

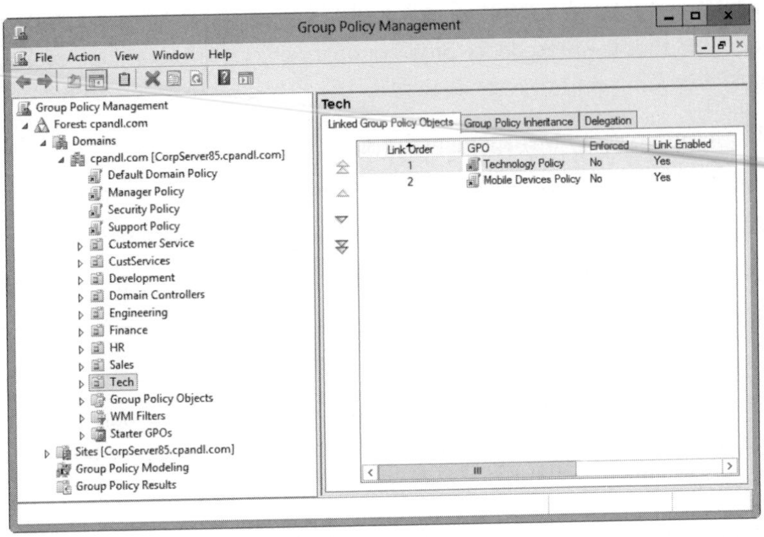

**Figure 31-13**  Determining the policy-processing order.

To view all inherited GPOs, tap or click the Group Policy Inheritance tab as shown in Figure 31-14. The precedence order shows exactly how policy objects are being processed for a site, domain, or OU. As with link order, lower ranking policy objects are processed first and then higher ranking policy objects are processed. Here, the Manager Policy (with precedence 4) will be processed first, and then Support Policy (with precedence 3), and so on. Because Default Domain Policy is processed last, any policy settings configured in this policy object are final and will override those of other policy objects (unless inheritance blocking or enforcing is used).

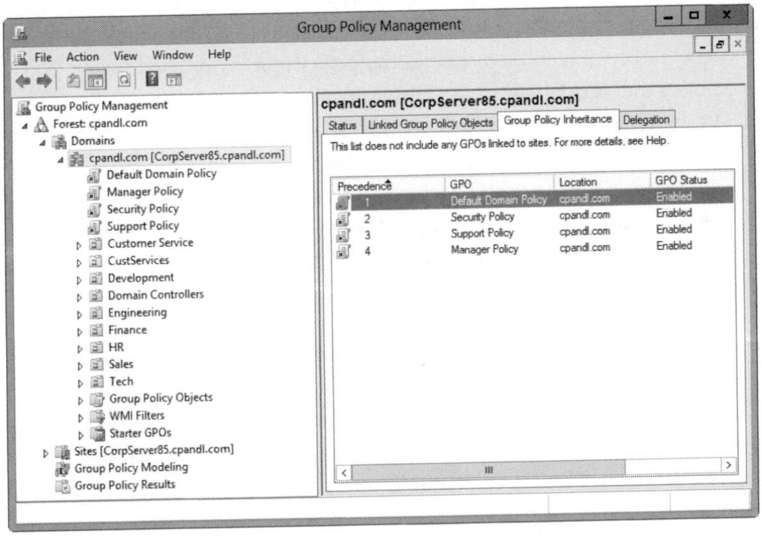

**Figure 31-14**  Determining the order of inheritance.

When multiple policy objects are linked at a specific level, you can easily change the link order (and thus the precedence order) of policy objects linked at that level. Follow these steps:

1. In Group Policy Management Console, select the container for the site, domain, or OU with which you want to work.

2. In the right pane, the Linked Group Policy Objects tab should be selected by default. Select the policy object with which you want to work.

3. Tap or click the Move Link Up or Move Link Down button as appropriate to change the link order of the selected policy object.

4. When you are done changing the link order, confirm that policy objects are being processed in the expected order by checking the precedence order on the Group Policy Inheritance tab.

## Overriding inheritance

As you know, Group Policy settings are inherited from top-level containers by lower level containers. If multiple policy objects modify the same settings, the order in which the policy objects are applied determines which policy settings take effect. Essentially, the order of inheritance goes from the site level to the domain level to the OU level. This means Group Policy settings for a site are passed down to the domains within the site, and the settings for a domain are passed down to the OUs within that domain.

You can override policy in two key ways:

- **Disable an enabled (and inherited) policy**   When a policy is enabled in a higher level policy object, you can override inheritance by disabling the policy in a lower level policy object. By disabling the policy in a lower level policy, you override the policy that is enabled in the higher level container. For example, if the user policy Prohibit Use Of Internet Connection Sharing On Your DNS Domain is enabled for a site, users in the site should not be able to use Internet Connection Sharing. However, if domain policy specifically disables this user policy, users in the domain would be able to use Internet Connection Sharing. On the other hand, if the domain policy was set to Not Configured, the policy setting would not be modified and would be inherited as normal from the higher level container.

- **Enable a disabled (and inherited) policy**   When a policy is disabled in a higher level policy object, you can override inheritance by enabling the policy in a lower level policy object. By enabling the policy in a lower level policy, you override the policy that is disabled in the higher level container. For example, if the user policy Allow Shared Folders To Be Published is disabled for a domain, users in the domain would not be able to publish shared folders in Active Directory. However, if the Support Team OU policy specifically enables this user policy, users in the Support Team OU would be able to publish shared folders in Active Directory. Again, if the OU policy was set to Not Configured instead, the policy setting would not be modified and would be inherited as normal from the higher level container.

Overriding inheritance is a basic technique for changing the way inheritance works. As long as a policy is not blocked or enforced, this technique will achieve the desired effect.

## Blocking inheritance

Sometimes, you will want to block inheritance so that no policy settings from higher level containers are applied to users and computers in a particular container. When inheritance is blocked, only configured policy settings from policy objects linked at that level are applied. This means all GPOs from all high level containers are blocked (as long as there is no policy enforcement).

Domain administrators can use inheritance blocking to block inherited policy settings from the site level. OU administrators can use inheritance blocking to block inherited policy settings from both the domain level and the site level. Here are some examples of inheritance blocking in action:

- You don't want a domain to inherit any site policies, so you configure the domain to block inheritance from higher level containers. Because inheritance is blocked, only the configured policy settings from policy objects linked to the domain are applied. Although blocking inheritance of a site policy doesn't affect the inheritance of the domain policy objects by OUs, it does mean that OUs in that domain will not inherit site policies either.

- You don't want an OU to inherit any site or domain policies, so you configure the OU to block inheritance from higher level containers. Because inheritance is blocked, only the configured policy settings from policy objects linked to the OU are applied. If the OU contains other OUs, inheritance blocking won't affect inheritance of policy objects linked to this OU, but the child OUs will not inherit site or domain policies.

Using Group Policy Management Console, you can block inheritance by pressing and holding or right-clicking the domain or OU that should not inherit settings from higher level containers and selecting Block Inheritance. If Block Inheritance is already selected, selecting it again removes the setting. When you block inheritance in Group Policy Management Console, a blue circle with an exclamation point is added to the container's node in the console tree. The notification icon provides a quick way to tell whether any domain or OU has the Block Inheritance setting enabled.

# Enforcing inheritance

To prevent administrators who have authority over a container from overriding or blocking the inherited Group Policy settings, you can enforce inheritance. When inheritance is enforced, all policy settings from higher level policy objects are inherited and applied regardless of the policy settings in lower level policy objects. Thus, the enforcement of inheritance is used to supersede the overriding and blocking of policy settings.

Forest administrators can use inheritance enforcement to ensure policy settings from the site level are applied and to prevent the overriding or blocking of policy settings by both domain and OU administrators. Domain administrators can use inheritance enforcement to ensure policy settings from the domain level are applied and prevent the overriding or blocking of policy settings by OU administrators. Here are some examples of inheritance enforcement in action:

- As a forest administrator, you want to ensure domains inherit a particular site policy, so you configure the site policy so that inheritance is enforced. Because inheritance is enforced, all policy settings from the site policy are applied regardless of whether domain administrators have tried to override or block policy settings from the site level. The enforcement of the site policy also affects the inheritance for OUs in the affected domains. OUs in the affected domains will inherit the site policy regardless of whether overriding or blocking has been used.

- As a domain administrator, you want to ensure OUs within the domain inherit a particular domain policy, so you configure the domain policy so that inheritance is enforced. Because inheritance is enforced, all policy settings from the domain policy are applied regardless of whether OU administrators have tried to override or block policy settings from the domain level. The enforcement of the domain policy also affects the inheritance for child OUs within the affected OUs. Child OUs within the affected OUs will inherit the domain policy regardless of whether overriding or blocking has been used.

Using Group Policy Management Console, you enforce policy inheritance by expanding the container to which the policy is linked, pressing and holding or right-clicking the policy, and then selecting Enforced. If Enforced is already selected, selecting it again removes the enforcement. In Group Policy Management Console, you can determine which policies are inherited and which policies are enforced in several ways:

- Select a policy object anywhere in Group Policy Management Console and then view the related Scope tab in the right pane. If the policy is enforced, the Enforced column under Links will have a Yes entry. After you select a policy object, you can press and hold or right-click a location entry on the Scope tab to display a shortcut menu. You can use this shortcut menu to manage linking and policy enforcement.

- Select a domain or OU container in Group Policy Management Console and then view the related Group Policy Inheritance tab in the right pane. If the policy is enforced, you'll see an (Enforced) entry in the Precedence column.

## Filtering Group Policy application

By default, GPOs apply to all users and computers in the container to which the GPO is linked. The GPO applies to all users and computers in this way because of the security settings on the GPO, which specify that Authenticated Users have Read permission as well as Apply Group Policy permission. Thus, all users and computers with accounts in the domain are affected by the policy. Permissions are also assigned to administrators and the operating system. All members of the Enterprise Admins and Domain Admins groups, as well as the LocalSystem account, have permission to edit GPOs and manage their security.

You can modify which users and computers are affected by a particular GPO by changing the accounts for which the Apply Group Policy permission is set. In this way, you can selectively apply a GPO, which is known as *filtering* Group Policy. For example, say that you create a Technology OU with separate Group Policy objects for users and managers. You want the user GPO to apply to all users who are members of the TechUsers group and the manager GPO to apply to all users who are members of the TechMgrs group. To do this, you must configure the user policy so that the Read and Apply Group Policy permissions apply to the TechUsers group only, and you must configure the manager policy so that the Read and Apply Group Policy permissions apply to the TechMgrs group only.

Before you selectively apply a GPO, you must carefully consider the types of policies it sets. If the GPO sets computer policies, you must ensure the computer accounts are included so that the computer reads the GPO and applies it at the startup of networking. If the GPO sets user policies, you must ensure the groups in which the users are members or the individual user accounts are included so that the Group Policy engine reads the GPO and applies it when users log on.

Use the following guidelines to help you determine how permissions should be configured:

- **Group Policy should be applied to all members of a group**   Add the group to the access control list (ACL) for the GPO. Set Read to Allow, and set Apply Group Policy to Allow. The Group Policy Object will then be applied to all members of the group except those who are members of another group to which Read or Apply Group Policy is set to Deny.

- **Group Policy should not be applied to members of a group**   Add the group to the ACL for the GPO. Set Read to Deny, and set Apply Group Policy to Deny. The Group Policy Object will not be applied to any members of the group, regardless of which other groups members belong to.

- **Membership in this group should not determine whether Group Policy is applied** Remove the group from the ACL for the GPO. Or clear both the Allow and Deny check boxes for the Read permission as well as the Apply Group Policy permission. After you do this, membership in the group will determine whether the GPO is applied.

You can selectively apply a GPO by completing the following steps:

1. In Group Policy Management Console, select the policy in a container to which the GPO is linked or in the Group Policy Objects node.

2. In the details pane, select the Delegation tab, and then tap or click the Advanced button in the bottom right corner of the dialog box. This displays the policy's Security Settings dialog box, as shown in Figure 31-15.

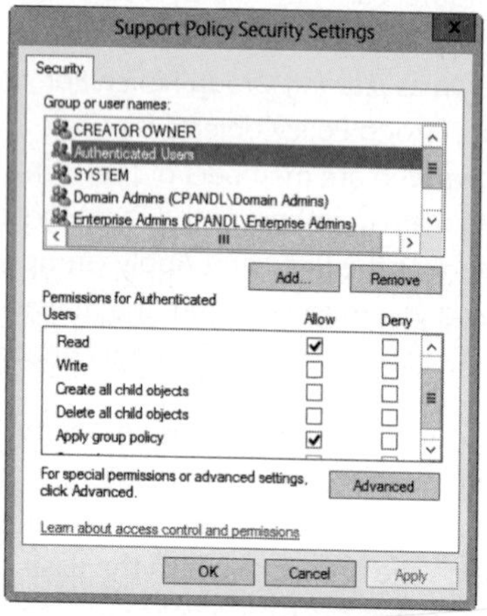

**Figure 31-15** Accessing the security settings for a GPO.

3. You can then add or remove groups as necessary. After a group is added, you can select the Allow or Deny check box for the Read and Apply Group Policy permissions as necessary.

4. When you are finished configuring the ACL for the GPO, tap or click OK until all open dialog boxes are closed.

## Group Policy processing

Group Policy settings are divided into two categories:

- **Computer Configuration settings** Policies that apply to computer accounts only

- **User Configuration settings** Policies that apply to user accounts only

Normally, Computer Configuration settings are applied during the startup of the operating system and User Configuration settings are applied when a user logs on to a computer. The sequence of events is often important in troubleshooting system behavior. The events that take place during startup and logon are as follows:

1.  When the client computer starts, networking is started as part of the normal system startup. The computer reads the registry to determine the Active Directory site in which the computer is located. The computer then sends a query to its primary Domain Name System (DNS) server to determine the Internet Protocol (IP) addresses of domain controllers in the site.

2.  When the DNS server replies to the query, the computer connects to a domain controller in the local site. The client computer and domain controller authenticate each other. The client computer then requests a list of all the GPOs that apply to the computer.

3.  The domain controller sends a list of GPOs that apply to the computer. The computer processes and applies the GPOs, starting with the local policy and continuing as discussed in "Group Policy inheritance" earlier in the chapter. Note that only the Computer Configuration settings are sent at this point.

4.  After processing computer policies, the computer runs any startup scripts. Startup scripts are hidden from view by default, and if there are multiple startup scripts, the scripts run in sequential order by default. Each script must finish running before the next one can be started. The default timeout for scripts is 600 seconds. Both the synchronous processing of scripts and their timeout value can be modified using Group Policy.

5.  When a user logs on to the computer and is validated, the computer loads the user profile and then requests a list of all the GPOs that apply to the user.

6.  The domain controller sends a list of GPOs that apply to the user. The computer processes and applies the GPOs, starting with the local policy and continuing as discussed in "Group Policy inheritance" earlier in the chapter. Although only the User Configuration settings are sent and applied at this point, note that any computer policy settings that overlap with user policy settings are overwritten by default. User policy settings have precedence by default.

7.  After processing user policies, the computer runs any logon scripts. Logon scripts are hidden from view by default, and if there are multiple logon scripts, the scripts run asynchronously by default. Thus, unlike startup scripts for which each script must finish running before the next one can be started, logon scripts are all started and run simultaneously. The default timeout for scripts is 600 seconds.

Chapter 31

8. The user interface, as defined in the user's profile and governed by the policy settings that are in effect, is displayed. If the user logs off the computer, any logoff scripts defined for the user are run. If the user shuts down the computer, logging off is part of the shutdown process, so the user is first logged off and any logoff scripts defined for the user are run. Then the computer runs any shutdown scripts defined for the computer.

## INSIDE OUT All Group Policy processing is handled as a refresh

Technically, all Group Policy processing is handled as a Group Policy refresh. Thus, processing during startup and logon is technically a refresh, which is handled as discussed in "Group Policy refresh" later in the chapter. The most important note about refresh is that if the client computer detects that it is using a slow network connection, only Security Settings and Administrative Templates are processed. Although there is no way to turn off the processing of these extensions, you can configure other extensions so that they are processed even across a slow network connection. For more information, see "Modifying Group Policy refresh" later in the chapter.

## Modifying Group Policy processing

You can modify Group Policy processing by disabling a policy in whole or in part. Disabling a policy is useful if you no longer need a policy but might need to use that policy again in the future. Disabling part of a policy is useful so that the policy applies only to either users or computers, but not both.

In Group Policy Management Console, you can enable and disable policies partially or entirely by completing the following steps:

1. In Group Policy Management Console, select the container for the site, domain, or OU with which you want to work.

2. In the right pane, select the Details tab, and then use the GPO Status selection menu to choose a status as one of the following:

   ○ **Enabled**   Allows the processing of the policy object and all its settings

   ○ **All Settings Disabled**   Disallows the processing of the policy object and all its settings

   ○ **Computer Configuration Settings Disabled**   Disables the processing of Computer Configuration settings, which means only User Configuration settings are processed

○ **User Configuration Settings Disabled**   Disables the processing of User Configuration settings, which means only Computer Configuration settings are processed

3. When prompted to confirm that you want to change the status of this GPO, tap or click OK.

## Modifying user policy preference using loopback processing

When a user logs on, the client computer applies User Configuration settings. Because user policy settings have precedence by default, any computer policy settings that overlap with user policy settings are overwritten. However, for some computers (particularly special-use computers in classrooms, labs, or public places), you might want to restrict the computer to a specific configuration. In this case, you might not want less-restrictive user policy settings to be applied.

To change the default behavior that gives preference to user policy, you can enable the loopback processing policy. By enabling the loopback processing policy, you ensure that the Computer Configuration settings always apply. Loopback processing can be set in one of two ways: either with Replace or Merge. When you use the Replace option, user settings from the computer's GPOs are processed and the user settings in the user's GPOs are not processed. This means the user settings from the computer's GPOs replace the user settings normally applied to the user.

When you use the Merge option, user settings in the computer's GPOs are processed first, then user settings in the user's GPOs are processed, and then user settings in the computer's GPOs are processed again. This processing technique serves to combine the user settings in both the computer and user GPOs. If there are any conflicts, the user settings in the computer's GPOs have preference and overwrite the user settings in the user's GPOs.

To configure loopback processing, follow these steps:

1. Start Group Policy Object Editor. In Group Policy Management Console, press and hold or right-click the Group Policy Object you want to modify, and then select Edit.

2. Double-tap or double-click the Configure User Group Policy Loopback Processing Mode in the Computer Configuration\Administrative Templates\System\Group Policy folder.

3. Define the policy by selecting Enabled, as shown in Figure 31-16 and then use the Mode selection menu to set the processing mode as either Replace or Merge.

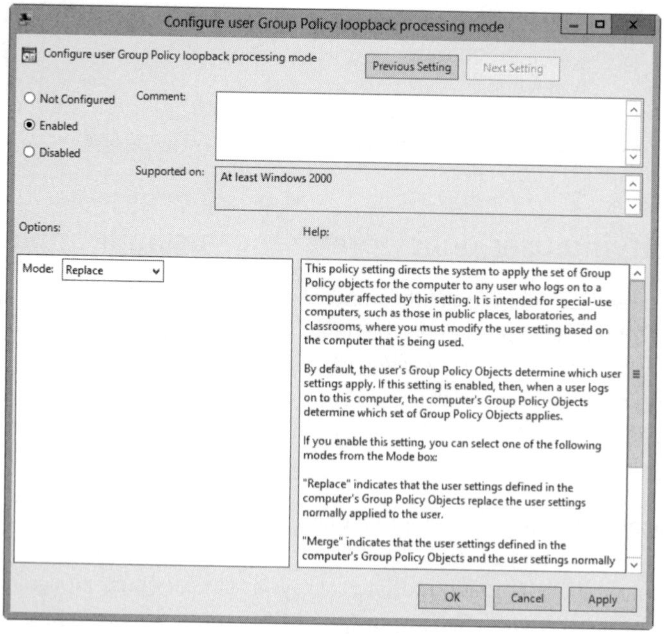

**Figure 31-16** Configure loopback processing to give the Computer Configuration settings preference.

4. Tap or click OK. This policy is supported by all current Windows operating systems.

# Using scripts in Group Policy

You can configure computer startup and shutdown scripts, as well as user logon and logoff scripts. You can write these scripts as command-shell batch scripts ending with the .bat or .cmd extension, as scripts that use the Windows Script Host (WSH), or as scripts that use Windows PowerShell. WSH is a feature of Windows Server that lets you use scripts written in a scripting language, such as Microsoft JScript and Microsoft VBScript.

## Configuring computer startup and shutdown scripts

You can assign computer startup and shutdown scripts as part of a Group Policy Object. In this way, all computers in a site, domain, or OU run scripts automatically when they're started or shut down.

To configure a script that should be used during computer startup or shutdown, follow these steps:

1. For easy management, copy the scripts you want to use to the Machine\Scripts\ Startup or Machine\Scripts\Shutdown folder for the related policy. By default,

policies are stored in the %SystemRoot%\Sysvol\Domain\Policies folder on domain controllers.

2. Start Group Policy Object Editor. In Group Policy Management Console, press and hold or right-click the Group Policy Object you want to modify, and then select Edit.

3. In the Computer Configuration node, double-tap or double-click the Windows Settings folder, and then select Scripts.

4. To work with startup scripts, press and hold or right-click Startup and then select Properties. Or press and hold or right-click Shutdown, and then select Properties to work with shutdown scripts.

5. The Scripts tab is selected by default. If you are working with PowerShell scripts, select the PowerShell Scripts tab.

6. Tap or click Show Files. If you copied the computer script to the correct location in the Policies folder, you should see the script.

7. Tap or click Add to assign a script. This opens the Add A Script dialog box. In the Script Name field, type the name of the script you copied to the Machine\Scripts\Startup or the Machine\Scripts\Shutdown folder for the related policy. Repeat this step to add other scripts.

8. During startup or shutdown, scripts are run in the order in which they're listed in the Properties dialog box. Use the Up or Down button to reposition scripts as necessary.

9. To delete a script, select the script in the Script For list and then tap or click Remove.

10. If you are working with PowerShell scripts, you can elect to run PowerShell scripts before or after other types of scripts. Use the Run Scripts In The Following Order list to specify your preference.

## Configuring user logon and logoff scripts

You can assign logon and logoff scripts as part of a Group Policy Object. In this way, all users in a site, domain, or OU run scripts automatically when they log on or log off.

To configure a script that should be executed when a user logs on or logs off, complete the following steps:

1. For easy management, copy the scripts you want to use to the User\Scripts\Logon or the User\Scripts\Logoff folder for the related policy. By default, policies are stored in the %SystemRoot%\Sysvol\Domain\Policies folder on domain controllers.

2. Start Group Policy Object Editor. In Group Policy Management Console, press and hold or right-click the Group Policy Object you want to modify, and then select Edit.

3. Double-tap or double-click the Windows Settings folder in the User Configuration node, and then tap or click Scripts.

4. To work with logon scripts, press and hold or right-click Logon and then select Properties. Or press and hold or right-click Logoff and then select Properties to work with logoff scripts.

5. The Scripts tab is selected by default. If you are working with PowerShell scripts, select the PowerShell Scripts tab.

6. Tap or click Show Files. If you copied the user script to the correct location in the Policies folder, you should see the script.

7. Tap or click Add to assign a script. This opens the Add A Script dialog box. In the Script Name field, type the name of the script you copied to the User\Scripts\Logon or the User\Scripts\Logoff folder for the related policy. Repeat this step to add other scripts.

8. During logon or logoff, scripts are executed in the order in which they're listed in the Properties dialog box. Use the Up or Down button to reposition scripts as necessary.

9. To delete a script, select the script in the Script For list and then tap or click Remove.

10. If you are working with PowerShell scripts, you can elect to run PowerShell scripts before or after other types of scripts. Use the Run Scripts In The Following Order list to specify your preference.

# Applying Group Policy through security templates

Security templates take the guesswork out of configuring a computer's initial security. You use security templates to apply customized sets of Group Policy definitions that are security related. These policy definitions generally affect the following components:

- Account policy settings that control security for passwords, account lockout, and Kerberos

- Local policy settings that control security for auditing, user rights assignment, and other security options

- Event log policy settings that control security for event logging

- Restricted groups policies that control security for local group membership and administration

- System services policy settings that control the startup mode for local services

- File system policy settings that control security for the local file system

- Registry policy settings that control the values of security-related registry keys

## Working with security templates

Security templates can be imported into any GPO. The templates are stored in the %SystemRoot%\Security\Templates folder by default, and you can access them using the Security Templates snap-in. You can also use the snap-in to create new templates. The standard template for domain controllers is DC Security, which contains the default security settings for a domain controller.

After you select the template that you want to use, you should go through each setting that the template will apply and evaluate how the setting will affect your environment. If a setting doesn't make sense, you should modify or delete it as appropriate.

You use the Security Templates snap-in only for viewing templates. You apply templates using the Security Configuration And Analysis snap-in. You can also use Security Configuration And Analysis to compare the settings in a template to the existing settings on a computer. The results of the analysis will highlight areas in which the current settings don't match those in the template. This is useful to determine whether security settings have changed over time.

You can access the security snap-ins by completing the following steps:

1. Tap or click Start, type **mmc** into the Search box, and then press Enter.

2. In the Microsoft Management Console, click File and then select Add/Remove Snap-in.

3. In the Add Or Remove Snap-ins dialog box, select Security Templates and then tap or click Add.

4. Select Security Configuration And Analysis, and then tap or click Add. Tap or click OK.

5. By default, the Security Templates snap-in looks for security templates in the %SystemDrive%\Users\%UserName%\Documents\Security\Templates folder. To add other search paths, select New Template Search Path on the Action menu.

6.  Select the template location to add from the Browse For Folder dialog box, such as %SystemRoot%\Security\Templates. Tap or click OK.

You can create a new template by following these steps:

1.  In the Security Templates snap-in, press and hold or right-click the search path where the template should be created and then select New Template.

2.  Type a name and description for the template in the text boxes provided.

3.  Tap or click OK to create the template. The template will have no settings configured, so you need to modify the settings carefully before the template is ready for use.

## Applying security templates

You use the Security Templates snap-in to view existing templates or to create new templates. After you create a template or determine that you want to use an existing template, you can then configure and analyze the template by completing the following steps:

1.  Access the Security Configuration And Analysis snap-in. Press and hold or right-click the Security Configuration And Analysis node, and then select Open Database. This displays the Open Database dialog box.

2.  Type a new database name in the File Name field, and then tap or click Open. The Import Template dialog box is displayed next. Select the security template that you want to use, and then tap or click Open.

3.  Press and hold or right-click the Security Configuration And Analysis node, and then select Analyze Computer Now. When prompted to set the error log path, type a new path or tap or click OK to use the default path.

4.  Wait for the snap-in to complete the analysis of the template. Afterward, review the findings and update the template as necessary. You can view the error log by pressing and holding or right-clicking the Security Configuration And Analysis node and choosing View Log File.

5.  When you're ready to apply the template, press and hold or right-click the Security Configuration And Analysis node, and select Configure Computer Now. When prompted to set the error log path, tap or click OK. The default path should be fine.

6.  View the configuration error log by pressing and holding or right-clicking the Security Configuration And Analysis node and choosing View Log File. Note any problems, and take action as necessary.

# Maintaining and troubleshooting Group Policy

Most Group Policy maintenance and troubleshooting tasks are related to determining when a policy is refreshed and applied and then changing the refresh options as appropriate to ensure the policy is applied as expected. Thus, maintaining and troubleshooting Group Policy require a keen understanding of how Group Policy refresh works and how it can be changed to meet your needs. You also need tools for modeling and viewing the GPOs that would be or have been applied to users and computers. Group Policy Management Console provides these tools through the Group Policy Modeling Wizard and Group Policy Results Wizard, both of which can be used instead of running the Resultant Set Of Policy (RSoP) Wizard in logging mode or planning mode.

## Group Policy refresh

Computer policies are applied when a computer starts, and user policies are applied when a user logs on. After the policies are applied, Group Policy settings are automatically refreshed to ensure they are current. The default refresh interval for domain controllers is every 5 minutes. For all other computers, the default refresh interval is every 90 minutes, with up to a 30-minute variation to avoid overloading the domain controller with numerous client requests at the same time.

### Change the refresh interval through Group Policy

You can change the Group Policy refresh interval if desired. The related policies are stored in the Computer Configuration\Administrative Templates\System\Group Policy folder. To set the refresh interval for domain controllers, configure the Set Group Policy Refresh Interval For Domain Controllers policy. Select Enabled, set the refresh interval, and then tap or click OK. To set the refresh interval for all other computers, configure the Group Policy Refresh Interval For Computers policy. Select Enabled, set the refresh interval and random offset, and then tap or click OK.

During Group Policy refresh, the client contacts an available domain controller in its local site. If one or more of the GPOs defined in the domain have changed, the domain controller provides a list of all the GPOs that apply to the computer and to the user who is currently logged on, as appropriate. The domain controller does so regardless of whether the version numbers on all the listed GPOs have changed.

By default, the computer processes the GPOs only if the version number of at least one of the GPOs has changed. If any one of the related policies has changed, all of the policies have to be processed again. This is required because of inheritance and the interdependencies within policies. Security Settings are a noted exception to the processing rule. By default, Security Settings are refreshed every 16 hours (960 minutes) regardless of whether GPOs contain changes. Additionally, if the client computer detects that it is connecting over a slow network connection, it tells the domain controller this and only the Security Settings and Administrative Templates are transferred over the network, which means only the Security Settings and Administrative Templates are applied.

## Modifying Group Policy refresh

Group Policy refresh can be changed in several ways. First, client computers determine that they are using a slow network connection by pinging the domain controller to which they are connected with a zero-byte packet. If the response time from the domain controller is more than 10 milliseconds, the computer then pings the domain controller three times with a 2-kilobyte (KB) message packet to determine if it is on a slow network. The computer uses the average response time to determine the network speed. By default, if the connection speed is determined to be less than 500 kilobits per second (Kbps), the computer interprets that as having a slow network connection—in which case, it notifies the domain controller of this. As a result, only the Security Settings and Administrative Templates in the applicable GPOs are sent by the domain controller.

> **Important**
>
> Windows 8 and Windows Server 2012 support policies related to connections on cellular and broadband networks as well. Because these types of networks can incur usage charges, they are referred to as *costed networks*, and you'll find related policies under Computer Configuration\Administrative Templates\Network. In Group Policy under the Network folder, you also can specify that wireless WAN (WWAN) connections should always be treated as slow links.

You can configure slow-link detection using the Configure Group Policy Slow Link Detection policy, which is stored in the Computer Configuration\Administrative Templates\System\ Group Policy folder. To configure this policy, follow these steps:

1. Start Group Policy Object Editor. In Group Policy Management Console, press and hold or right-click the Group Policy Object you want to modify and then select Edit.

2. Double-tap or double-click the Configure Group Policy Slow Link Detection policy in the Computer Configuration\Administrative Templates\System\Group Policy folder.

3. Define the policy by selecting Enabled, as shown in Figure 31-17, and then use the Connection Speed combo box to specify the speed that should be used to determine whether a computer is on a slow link. For example, if you want connections less than 384 Kbps to be deemed "slow connections," you type **384**. If you want to disable slow-link detection, type **0** (zero) in the Connection Speed box.

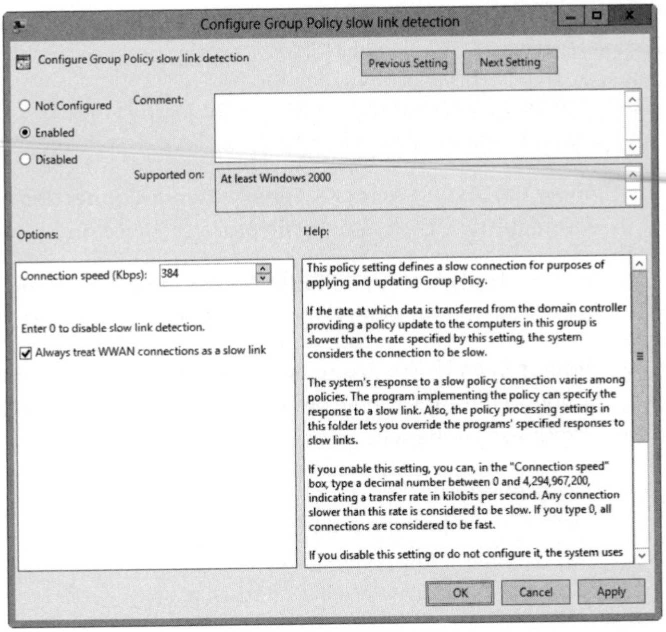

**Figure 31-17**  Configure slow-link detection as necessary.

4.  You also can specify that WWAN connections should always be treated as slow links. Tap or click OK.

If there is any area of Group Policy for which you want to configure refresh, you can do this in Group Policy Object Editor. The related policies are stored in the Computer Configuration\Administrative Templates\System\Group Policy folder and include Applications Policy Processing, Data Sources Policy Processing, Devices Policy Processing, Disk Quota Policy Processing, Drive Maps Policy Processing, EFS Recovery Policy Processing, Environment Policy Processing, and several dozen other specific areas of policy processing.

> **Note**
> You use Registry Policy Processing to control the processing of all other registry-based extensions.

To configure the refresh of an extension, follow these steps:

1.  Start Group Policy Object Editor. In Group Policy Management Console, press and hold or right-click the Group Policy Object you want to modify, and then select Edit.

2. Double-tap or double-click the policy in the Computer Configuration\Administrative Templates\System\Group Policy folder.

3. Define the policy by selecting Enabled, as shown in Figure 31-18. The options you have differ slightly depending on the policy selected and include the following:

   ○ **Allow Processing Across A Slow Network Connection**   Select this option to ensure the extension settings are processed even on a slow network.

   ○ **Do Not Apply During Periodic Background Processing**   Select this option to override refresh when extension settings change after startup or logon.

   ○ **Process Even If The Group Policy Objects Have Not Changed**   Select this option to force the client computer to process the extension settings during refresh even if the settings haven't changed.

   ○ **Background Priority**   Determines when background processing occurs. If you select Idle, the background processing of the related policy occurs only when the computer is idle. Other processing options are for the lowest activity levels, below-normal activity levels, or normal activity levels.

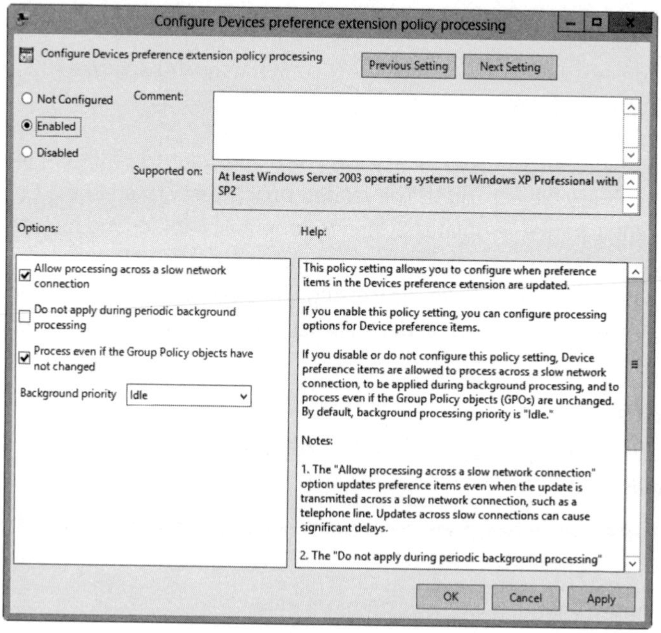

**Figure 31-18** Change the way refresh works as necessary.

4. Tap or click OK.

# Viewing applicable GPOs and the last refresh

In Group Policy Management Console, you can view all of the GPOs that apply to a computer as well as the user logged on to that computer. You can also view the last time the applicable GPOs were processed (refreshed). To do this, you run the Group Policy Results Wizard.

To start the Group Policy Results Wizard and view applicable GPOs and the last refresh, follow these steps:

1. Start Group Policy Management Console. Press and hold or right-click Group Policy Results, and then select Group Policy Results Wizard.

2. When the Group Policy Results Wizard starts, tap or click Next. On the Computer Selection page shown in Figure 31-19, select This Computer to view information for the local computer. If you want to view information for a remote computer, select Another Computer and then tap or click Browse. In the Select Computer dialog box, type the name of the computer and then tap or click Check Names. After the correct computer account is selected, tap or click OK.

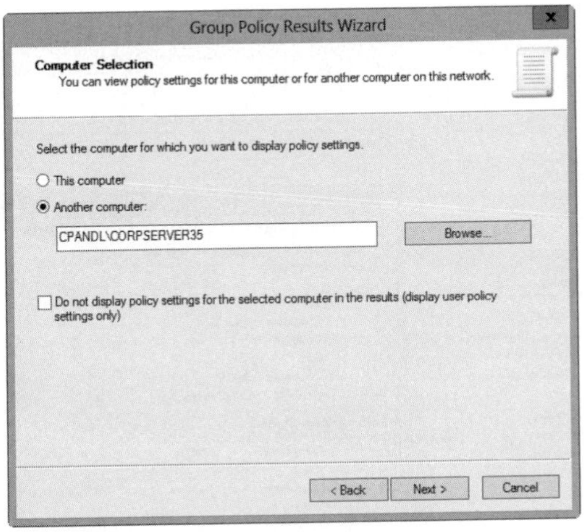

**Figure 31-19** Select the computer to work with.

3. In the Group Policy Results Wizard, tap or click Next. On the User Selection page, shown in Figure 31-20, select the user whose policy information you want to view. You can view policy information for any user who has logged on to the computer.

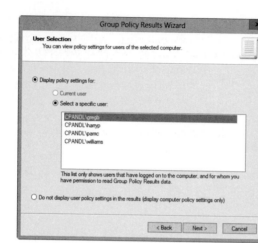

**Figure 31-20**  Select the user whose policy information you want to view.

4.  Tap or click Next twice. After the wizard gathers the policy information, tap or click Finish. The wizard then generates a report, the results of which are displayed in the Details pane as shown in Figure 31-21.

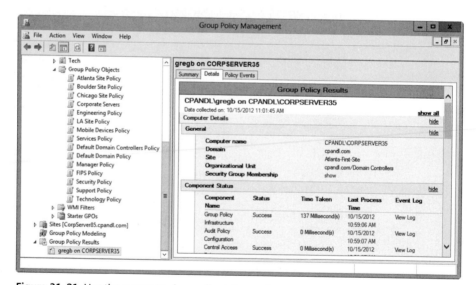

**Figure 31-21**  Use the report to view policy information.

5.  On the report, tap or click Show All to display all of the policy information that was gathered.

Computer and user policy information is listed separately. Information about the last time the computer or user policy was refreshed is listed on the Summary tab. To view all applicable GPOs, look on the Details tab under either Computer Details or User Details as appropriate. You'll see entries under Group Policy Objects for Applied GPOs and Denied GPOs.

The Applied GPOs entry shows all GPOs that have been applied. The Denied GPOs entry shows all GPOs that should have been applied but weren't processed for some reason, such as because they were empty or did not contain any computer policy settings. The GPO also might not have been processed because inheritance was blocked. If so, the Reason Denied is Blocked Scope Of Management (SOM).

## Modeling GPOs for planning

In Group Policy Management Console, you can test different scenarios for modifying Computer Configuration and User Configuration settings. For example, you can model the effect of a slow link or the use of loopback processing. You can also model the effect of moving a user or computer to another container in Active Directory or adding the user or computer to an additional security group. To do this, you run the Group Policy Modeling Wizard.

To start the Group Policy Modeling Wizard and test various scenarios, follow these steps:

1.  Start Group Policy Management Console. Press and hold or right-click Group Policy Modeling, and then select Group Policy Modeling Wizard. If you run the results against a remote client, the following firewall rules must be enabled on that client: Remote Event Log Management (NP-In), Remote Event Log Management (RPC), Remote Event Log Management (RPC_EPMAP), and Windows Management Instrumentation (WMI-In).

2.  When the Group Policy Modeling Wizard starts, tap or click Next. On the Domain Controller Selection page, as shown in Figure 31-22, under Show Domain Controllers In This Domain, select the domain for which you want to model results. Next, select either Any Available Domain Controller or This Domain Controller, and then select a specific domain controller. Tap or click Next.

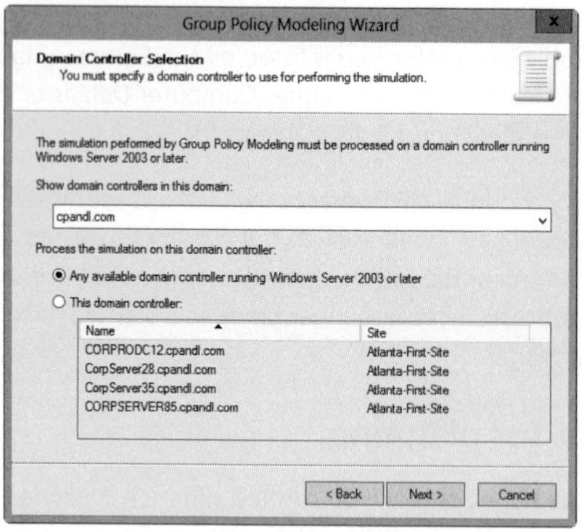

**Figure 31-22** Select the domain controller to work with.

**3.** On the User And Computer Selection page, shown in Figure 31-23, select the modeling options for users and computers.

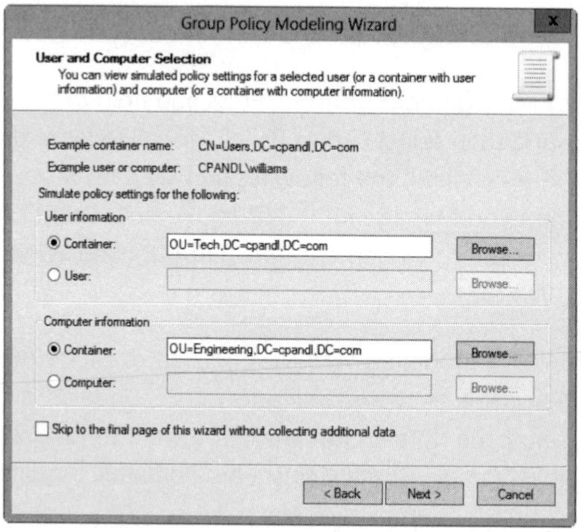

**Figure 31-23** Select the modeling options for users and computers.

Typically, you'll want to model policy for a specific container using user and computer information. In this case, the following instructions apply:

❍ Under User Information, select Container and then tap or click Browse to display the Choose User Container dialog box, which you can use to choose any of the available user containers in the selected domain.

❍ Under Computer Information, select Container and then tap or click Browse to display the Choose Computer Container dialog box, which you can use to choose any of the available computer containers in the selected domain.

4. Tap or click Next. On the Advanced Simulation Options page, shown in Figure 31-24, select any advanced options for slow network connections, loopback processing, and sites as necessary, and then tap or click Next.

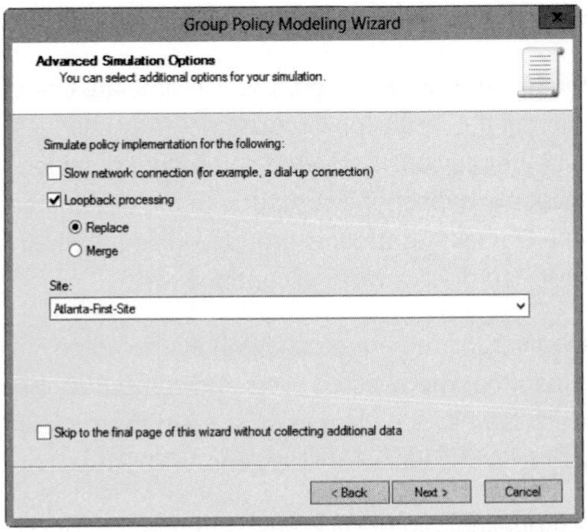

**Figure 31-24** Select advanced options as necessary.

5. On the User Security Groups page, shown in Figure 31-25, you can simulate changes to security group membership to model the results on Group Policy. Any changes you make to group membership affect the previously selected user container. For example, if you want to see what would happen if a user in the designated user container is a member of the Domain Admins group, you could add this group to the Security Groups list. Tap or click Next to continue.

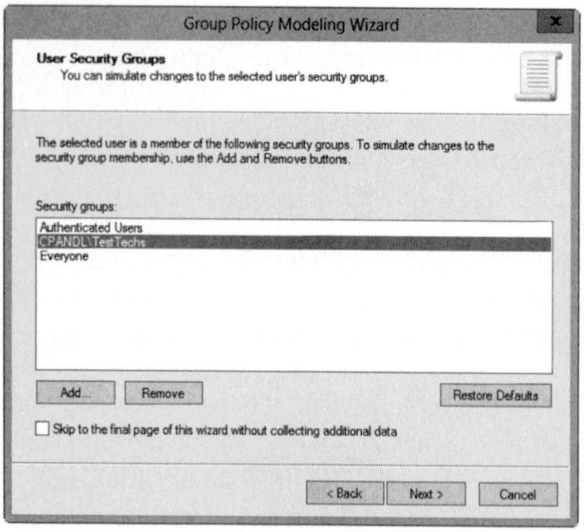

**Figure 31-25**  Simulate changes to security groups for users.

**6.** On the Computer Security Groups page, you can simulate changes to security group membership to model the results on Group Policy. Any changes you make to group membership affect the previously selected computer container. For example, if you want to see what would happen if a computer in the designated computer container is a member of the Domain Controllers group, you could add this group to the Security Groups list. Tap or click Next to continue.

**7.** Windows Management Instrumentation (WMI) filters can be linked to GPOs. By default, it is assumed that the selected users and computers meet all the WMI filter requirements, which is what you want in most cases for modeling, so tap or click Next twice to skip past the WMI Filters For Users and WMI Filters For Computers pages.

**8.** To complete the modeling, tap or click Next and then tap or click Finish. The wizard then generates a report, the results of which are displayed in the details pane.

**9.** The name of the modeling report is generated based on the containers you chose and highlighted for editing. Type a new name as required, and then press the Tab key. On the report, select the Details tab and then tap or click Show All to display all of the policy information that was modeled. Figure 31-26 shows an example. Note that the details show how long client-side extensions took to process, the last time an extension was processed, and where GPOs are linked. Detailed event log information from the latest policy application is available as well.

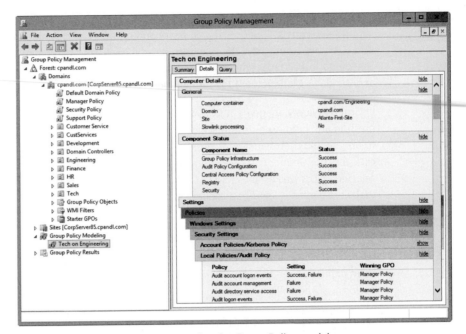

**Figure 31-26** Use the report to examine the Group Policy model.

## Refreshing Group Policy manually

You can refresh Group Policy manually using the Gpupdate command-line utility. If you type **gpupdate** at a command prompt, both the Computer Configuration settings and the User Configuration settings in Group Policy are refreshed on the local computer.

You can also selectively refresh Group Policy. If you want to refresh only Computer Configuration settings, you type **gpupdate /target:computer** at the command prompt. If you want to refresh only User Configuration settings, you type **gpupdate /target:user** at the command prompt. By default, only policy settings that have changed are processed and applied. You can change this behavior using the */Force* parameter. This parameter forces a refresh of all policy settings.

Gpupdate can also be used to log off a user or restart a computer after Group Policy is refreshed. This is useful because some Group Policy Objects are applied only when a user logs on or when a computer starts up. To log off a user after a refresh, add the */Logoff* parameter. To restart a computer after a refresh, add the */Boot* parameter.

For remote computers, you can perform a refresh in several ways using the Gpupdate command. You can use a remote connection, log on locally, or ask a user to perform the refresh. You also can perform a remote update using Group Policy Management Console. Remote update uses a remote connection to create a task in the task scheduler of the remote computers on which you want to refresh Group Policy. The task executes within 10 minutes and runs a *Gpupdate /Force* command on the local machine. Because this feature uses a remote connection, the following firewall rules must be enabled on clients: Remote Scheduled Tasks Management (RPC), Remote Scheduled Tasks Management (RPC-EPMAP), and Windows Management Instrumentation (WMI-In).

In Group Policy Management Console, you can perform remote updates at the OU level by pressing and holding or right-clicking the OU that contains the computer objects you want to update and then selecting Group Policy Update. Next, when prompted to confirm, tap or click Yes. The *Gpupdate /Force* command is then scheduled to run on all computers in the selected OU as well as any child OUs of that OU. A results dialog box identifies computers that were contacted and had the task scheduled.

## Backing up GPOs

In Group Policy Management Console, you can back up GPOs so that you can restore them at a later time to recover Group Policy to the state it was in when the backup was performed. The ability to back up and restore GPOs is one of the reasons why Group Policy Management Console is more useful than the older Group Policy tools that come with Windows Server. Also, be sure to keep in mind that you can back up and restore GPOs only when you have installed Group Policy Management Console.

You can either back up an individual GPO in a domain or all GPOs in a domain by completing the following steps:

1.  Start Group Policy Management Console. Expand the forest, the Domains node, and the Group Policy Objects node.

2.  If you want to back up all GPOs in the domain, press and hold or right-click the Group Policy Objects node and then select Back Up All.

3.  If you want to back up a specific GPO in the domain, press and hold or right-click the GPO and then select Back Up.

4.  In the Back Up Group Policy Object dialog box, shown in Figure 31-27, tap or click Browse, and then use the Browse For Folder dialog box to set the location in which the GPO backup should be stored. This location can be a local folder or a network share.

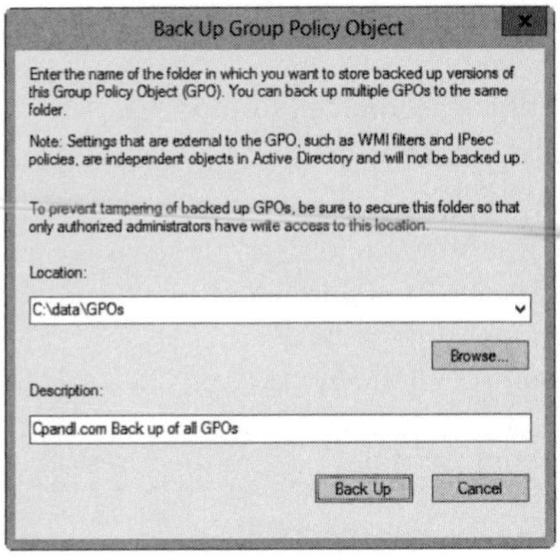

**Figure 31-27** Set the backup location and description.

5. In the Description field, type a clear description of the contents of the backup.

6. Tap or click Back Up to start the back up process. The Backup dialog box, shown in Figure 31-28, shows the progress and status of the backup. If a backup fails, check the permissions on the GPO and the folder to which you are writing the backup. You need Read permission on a GPO and Write permission on the backup folder to create a backup. By default, members of the Domain Admins and Enterprise Admins groups should have these permissions.

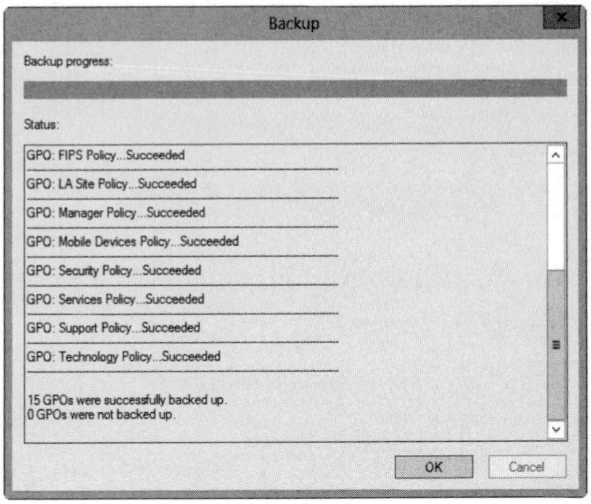

**Figure 31-28** The Backup dialog box shows the backup progress and status.

# Restoring GPOs

Using Group Policy Management Console, you can restore a GPO to the state it was in when it was backed up. Group Policy Management Console tracks the backup of each GPO separately, even if you back up all GPOs at once. Because version information is also tracked according to the backup time stamp and description, you can restore the last version of each GPO or a particular version of any GPO.

You can restore a GPO by completing the following steps:

1.  Start Group Policy Management Console. Expand the forest, the Domains node, and then the Group Policy Objects node.

2.  If you want to back up all GPOs in the domain, press and hold or right-click the Group Policy Objects node and then select Manage Backups. This displays the Manage Backups dialog box. (See Figure 31-29.)

3.  In the Backup Location field, type the folder path to the backup or tap or click Browse to use the Browse For Folder dialog box to find the folder.

4.  All GPO backups in the designated folder are listed under Backed Up GPOs. To show only the latest version of the GPOs according to the time stamp, select the Show Only The Latest Version Of Each GPO check box.

5.  Select the GPO you want to restore. If you want to confirm its settings, tap or click View Settings, and then verify the settings are as expected using Internet Explorer. When you are ready to continue, tap or click Restore. Confirm that you want to restore the selected GPO by tapping or clicking OK.

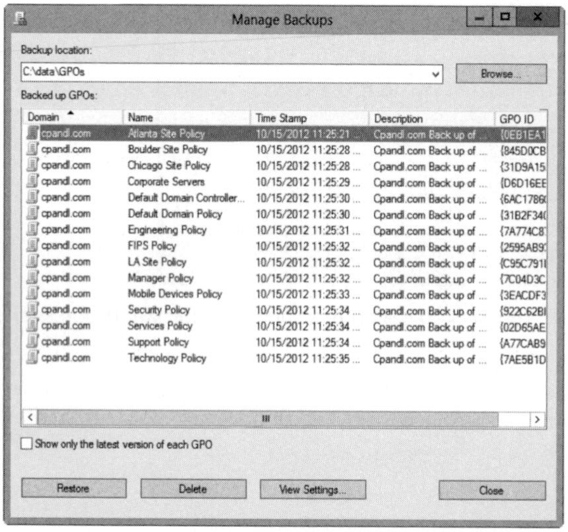

**Figure 31-29** Use the Manage Backups dialog box to restore a GPO.

6. The Restore dialog box, shown in Figure 31-30, shows the progress and status of the restore. If a restore fails, check the permissions on the GPO and the folder from which you are reading the backup. To restore a GPO, you need Edit, Delete, and Modify permissions on the GPO and Read permission on the folder containing the GPO backup. By default, members of the Domain Admins and Enterprise Admins groups should have these permissions.

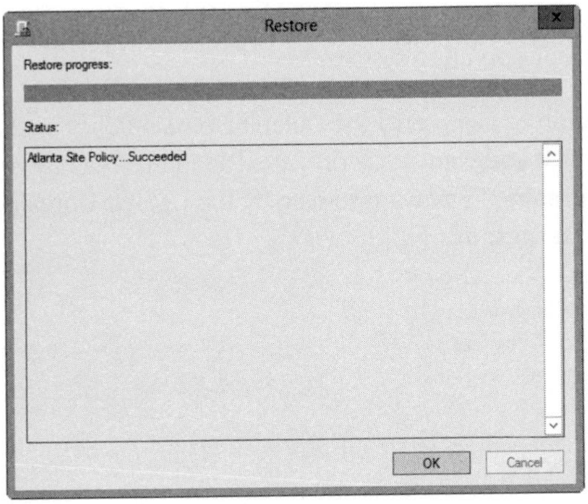

**Figure 31-30**  The Restore dialog box shows the restore progress and status.

7. Tap or click OK, and then either restore additional GPOs as necessary or tap or click Close.

## Fixing default Group Policy

The Default Domain Policy and Default Domain Controllers Policy GPOs are vital to the health of Active Directory in a domain. If for some reason these policies become corrupted, Group Policy will not function properly. To resolve this, you must run the Dcgpofix utility. This utility restores the default GPOs to their original, default state, meaning the state they are in when you first install Active Directory in a new domain. You must be a member of Domain Admins or Enterprise Admins to run Dcgpofix.

By default, when you run Dcgpofix, both the Default Domain Policy and Default Domain Controllers Policy GPOs are restored and you will lose any base changes made to these GPOs. The only exceptions are for the following extension settings: Remote Installation Services (RIS), Security Settings, and Encrypting File System (EFS). These extension settings are maintained separately and will not be lost. Non-default Security Settings are not maintained, however. All other extensions settings are restored to their default post-installation state, and any changes you made are lost.

To run Dcgpofix, log on to a domain controller in the domain in which you want to fix default Group Policy and then type **dcgpofix** at the command prompt. Dcgpofix checks the Active Directory schema version number to ensure compatibility between the version of Dcgpofix you are using and the Active Directory schema configuration. If the versions are not compatible, Dcgpofix exits without fixing the default Group Policy. By specifying the *Ignoreschema* parameter, you can enable Dcgpofix to work with different versions of Active Directory. However, default policy objects might not be restored to their original state. Because of this, you should always be sure to use the version of Dcgpofix that is installed with the current operating system.

You also have the option of fixing only the Default Domain Policy or the Default Domain Controllers Policy GPO. If you want to fix only the Default Domain Policy GPO, type **dcgpofix /target: domain**. If you want to fix only the Default Domain Controllers Policy GPO, type **dcgpofix /target: dc**.

# CHAPTER 32

# Active Directory site administration

IN this chapter, I discuss the administration of sites, subnets, site links, and related components. Active Directory sites are used to control directory replication traffic and isolate logon authentication traffic between physical network locations. Every site has one or more subnets associated with it. Ideally, each subnet that is part of a site should be connected by reliable, high-speed links. Any physical location connected over slow or unreliable links should be part of a separate site, and these individual sites are linked to other sites using site links.

## Managing sites and subnets

When you install Active Directory Domain Services in a new forest, a new site called the Default-First-Site-Name is created. As you add additional domains and domain controllers to the forest, these domains and domain controllers are added to this site as they are installed unless you configured other sites and associated subnets with those sites as necessary.

The administration of sites and subnets involves determining the sites and subnets you need and creating those sites and subnets. All sites have one or more subnets associated with them. It is, in fact, the subnet assignment that tells Active Directory where the site boundaries are established. As you create additional sites, you might also need to specify which domain controllers are a part of the sites. You do this by moving domain controllers to the site containers with which they should be associated. Thus, the most common administrative tasks for sites involve the following:

- Creating sites

- Creating subnets and associating them with sites

- Moving domain controllers between sites

# Creating an Active Directory site

As part of Active Directory design, discussed in Chapter 27, "Configuring Active Directory sites and replication," you must consider whether separate sites are needed. If your organization has multiple locations with limited bandwidth or unreliable connections between locations, you will typically want to create additional sites. In some cases, you might also want to create additional sites to separate network segments even if they are connected with high-speed links; the reason for doing this is to isolate logon authentication traffic between the network segments.

To create an additional site, follow these steps:

1.  Start Active Directory Sites And Services. In Server Manager, select Tools and then select Active Directory Sites And Services.

## Connect to the forest you want to work with

Active Directory Sites And Services is used to view a single forest. If your organization has multiple forests, you might need to connect to another forest. To do this, press and hold or right-click the Active Directory Sites And Services node in the console tree, and then select Change Forest. In the Change Forest dialog box, type the name of the root domain in the forest to which you want to connect and then tap or click OK.

2.  Press and hold or right-click the Sites container in the console tree, and select New Site. This displays the New Object–Site dialog box, as shown in Figure 32-1.

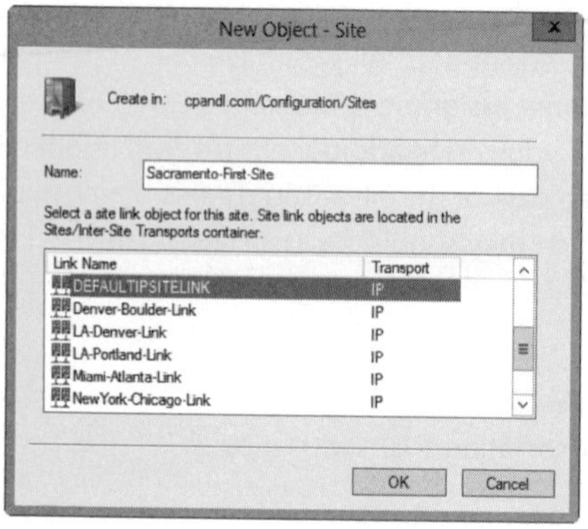

**Figure 32-1** Use the New Object–Site dialog box to create a new site.

3. In the New Object–Site dialog box, type a descriptive name for the site. The site name serves as a point of reference for administrators and should clearly depict the purpose or physical location of the site.

4. Choose which site link will be used to connect this site to other sites. If the site link you want to use doesn't exist, that's okay—the site must exist before you can create links to it. Select the default site link DEFAULTIPSITELINK for now, and change the site-link settings after you create the necessary site link or links.

5. When you are ready to continue, tap or click OK. A prompt is displayed detailing the steps you must complete to finish the site configuration. Tap or click OK again. As the prompt details, you should do the following:

   ○ Ensure the links to this site are appropriate by creating the necessary site links. The catch in this is that both endpoints in a site link—the sites you want to link—must exist before you can create a site link.

   ○ Create subnets and associate them with the site. This tells Active Directory the network addresses that belong to a site.

Each site should have one or more domain controllers. Ideally, this domain controller should also be a global catalog server. Because of this, you should install one or more domain controllers in the site or move existing domain controllers into the site.

## Creating a subnet and associating it with a site

You create subnets and associate them with sites to allow Active Directory to determine the network segments that belong to the site. Any computer with an Internet Protocol (IP) address on a network segment associated with a site is considered to be located in the site. A site can have one or more subnets associated with it. Each subnet, however, can be associated with only one site.

You can create a subnet and associate it with a site by completing the following steps:

1. In Active Directory Sites And Services, press and hold or right-click the Subnets container in the console tree and select New Subnet. This displays the New Object–Subnet dialog box, as shown in Figure 32-2.

2. In the Prefix field, type the address prefix for the subnet. As discussed in "Network prefix notation" in Chapter 18, "Networking with TCP/IP," the address prefix for a network address consists of the network ID address followed by a forward slash followed by the number of bits in the network ID. Typically, the subnet address ends with a 0, such as 192.168.1.0, except when subnetting is used. For example, if the

network address is 192.168.1.0 and the subnet mask is 255.255.255.0, you should enter the address prefix as 192.168.1.0/24.

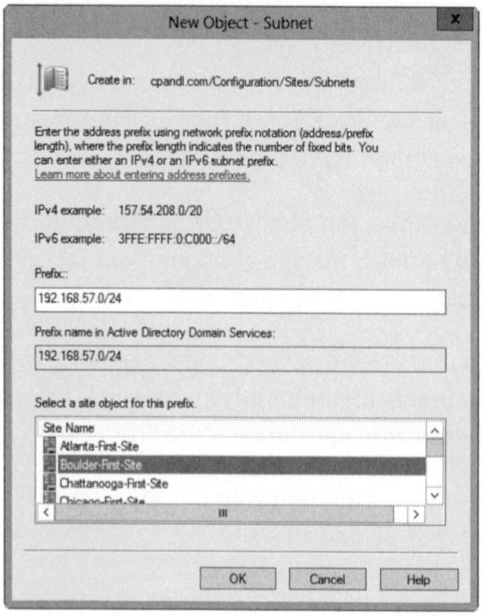

**Figure 32-2** Use the New Object–Subnet dialog box to create a new subnet.

3.  Select the site with which the subnet should be associated, and then tap or click OK. If you ever need to change the site association for the subnet, double-tap or double-click the subnet in the Subnets folder and then, on the General tab, use the Site selection menu to change the site association.

## Associating domain controllers with a site

After you associate subnets with a site, any domain controllers you install will automatically be located in the site where the IP address subnet matches the domain controller's IP address. Any domain controllers installed before you established the site and associated subnets with it will not be moved to the site automatically. You must manually move existing domain controllers if necessary. In addition, if you associate a subnet with a different site, you might need to move domain controllers in that subnet to the new site.

Before you can move a domain controller from one site to another, you must determine in which site the domain controller is currently located. One way to do this is to use the Servers nodes for each site in Active Directory Sites And Services. You can also do this by typing the following command at a command prompt:

```
dsquery server -s DomainControllerName | dsget server -site
```

Here, *DomainControllerName* is the fully qualified domain name of the domain controller, such as

```
dsquery server -s corpserver92.cpand1.com | dsget server -site
```

The output of this command is the name of the site in which the designated domain controller is located.

You can move a domain controller to a site by completing the following steps:

1. Start Active Directory Sites And Services. Domain controllers associated with a site are listed in the site's Servers node. To locate the domain controller that you want to move, expand the site node, and then expand the related Servers node.

2. Press and hold or right-click the domain controller, and then select Move. This displays the Move Server dialog box.

3. In the Move Server dialog box, select the site that should contain the server and then tap or click OK.

Another way to move a domain controller from one site to another is to drag the domain controller from its current site to the new site. But don't move a domain controller to a site arbitrarily. Move a domain controller to a site only if it is on a subnet associated with the site.

# Managing site links and intersite replication

Site links are used to connect two or more sites together for the purpose of replication. When you install Active Directory in a new forest, a new site link called the DEFAULTIPSITELINK is created. As you add additional sites to the forest, these sites are included in the default site link unless you configured other site links. If all of the network connections between sites are the same speed and priority, the default configuration can work. In this case, the intersite replication configuration for all sites will have the same properties. If you were to change these properties, the changes would affect the replication topology for all sites. By creating additional site links, you can configure different replication properties when the network connections between sites have different speeds and priorities.

Creating additional site links helps the designated Inter-Site Topology Generator (ISTG) for a site to prioritize the site links and determine when a site link should be used. It doesn't, however, change the way intersite replication works. Replication traffic between sites is always sent from a bridgehead server in one site to a bridgehead server in another site. Although it is the job of the ISTG to generate the intersite replication topology and designate bridgehead servers, you can manually designate bridgehead servers as well. After you establish site links and designated bridgehead servers as necessary, you might want to change the way replication between sites is handled. For example, you might want to disable compression or enable notification so that changes can be replicated more quickly between sites.

Following this, the most common administrative tasks related to site links involve the following:

- Creating site links

- Configuring site-link bridges

- Determining the ISTG

- Configuring site bridgehead servers

- Setting site-link replication options

Before looking at these administrative tasks, however, let's first look at the available replication transports.

## Understanding IP and SMTP replication transports

When you create a site link, you will have to select a replication transport protocol. Two replication transports are available: IP and Simple Mail Transfer Protocol (SMTP). All replication connections within sites are synchronous and use RPC over IP. In this configuration, domain controllers establish an RPC-over-IP connection with a single replication partner at a time and replicate Active Directory changes. By default, the remote procedure call (RPC) connection uses dynamic port mapping. During replication, a replication client establishes a connection to a server on the RPC endpoint mapper port 135 and determines which port is to be used for replication on the server. Any additional replication traffic is sent over the ports defined in Table 27-1 in Chapter 27. When RPC over IP is used for intersite replication, these same ports are used. If there are firewalls between the sites, the appropriate ports on the firewalls must be opened to allow replication to occur.

Because RPC over IP is synchronous, both replication partners must be available at the time the connection is established. This is important because of the transitive nature of site links. For example, if Site 1 has a link to Site 2, and Site 2 has a link to Site 3, there is an automatic bridge between Site 1 and Site 3 that allows Site 1 to replicate traffic directly to Site 3. Because of this, you must carefully configure site-link schedules so that all potential RPC-over-IP replication partners are available as necessary—more on this in a moment.

Replication between sites also can be configured to use SMTP. By using SMTP as the transport, all replication traffic is converted to email messages that are sent between the sites. Because SMTP replication is asynchronous, it can be a good choice when you do not have a permanent connection between sites or when you have unreliable connections between sites. It is also a good choice when you have to replicate between locations over the public Internet.

Before you use SMTP as the replication protocol, there are several important considerations. First, SMTP can be used only to replicate information between domain controllers in different domains because the domain directory partition cannot be replicated using SMTP—only the configuration, schema, and global catalog directory partitions can be replicated. Second, SMTP messages are digitally signed and encrypted to ensure that replication traffic is secure even if replication traffic is routed over the public Internet. All domain controllers that will use SMTP for replication require additional components to create, digitally sign, and then encrypt email messages. Specifically, you must install the SMTP Server feature on each domain controller and you must install a Microsoft certificate authority (CA) in your organization. The certificates from the CA are used to digitally sign and encrypt the SMTP messages sent between the sites.

## Configure replication through firewalls

If you plan to use SMTP for replication, you must open port 25 on the firewall between sites. Port 25 is the default port used for SMTP. Although SMTP has definite security advantages over standard IP, you can encrypt RPC communications between domain controllers using IP security (IPsec) and then open the appropriate ports on your firewalls for RPC over IP. Encrypting the RPC traffic between domain controllers would then be a viable alternative for replication over the public Internet when you have a dedicated connection between sites.

## Creating a site link

After you create the sites that your organization needs, you can create site links between those sites to better manage intersite replication. Each site link must have at least two sites associated with it. These sites establish the endpoints or transit points for the link. For example, if you create a site link and add Portland-First-Site and LA-First-Site to the link, the Portland and LA sites are the endpoints for the link and the ISTG will use the link to create the connection objects that are required to replicate traffic between these sites.

Before you create a site link, you should determine the transport that you want to use as discussed previously in "Understanding IP and SMTP replication transports." You should also consider the following:

- **Link cost**  The cost for a site link determines the relative priority of the link in relationship to other site links that might be available. If there are multiple possible routes to a site, the route with the lowest link cost is used first. In the event a primary link fails, a secondary link can be used. Typically, the link cost reflects the bandwidth available for a specific connection. It also can reflect the actual cost of sending traffic over a particular link if the organization has to pay a fee based on bandwidth usage.

- **Replication schedule**   The replication schedule determines the times during the day that the site link is available for replication. By default, replication is allowed 24 hours a day. If you have a limited-bandwidth connection or you want user traffic to have priority at certain times of the day, you might want to configure a different availability schedule.

- **Replication interval**   The replication interval determines the intervals at which the bridgehead servers in each site check to see if there are directory updates available. By default, the interval is set to 180 minutes. Following this, if the replication schedule is configured to allow replication from 7 P.M. to 7 A.M. each day, the bridgehead servers will check for updates at 7 P.M., 10 P.M., 1 A.M., 4 A.M., and 7 A.M. daily.

You can create a site link between two or more sites by completing the following steps:

1. Start Active Directory Sites And Services. If your organization has multiple forests, you might need to connect to another forest. To do this, press and hold or right-click the Active Directory Sites And Services node in the console tree and then select Change Forest. In the Change Forest dialog box, type the name of the root domain in the forest to which you want to connect and then tap or click OK.

2. Expand the Sites container, and then expand the Inter-Site Transports container. Press and hold or right-click the container for the transport protocol you want to use, either IP or SMTP, and select New Site Link. This displays the New Object–Site Link dialog box, as shown in Figure 32-3.

3. In the New Object–Site Link dialog box, type a descriptive name for the site link. The site name serves as a point of reference for administrators and should clearly depict the sites the link connects.

**Figure 32-3** Create the site link.

4. In the Sites Not In This Site Link list, select a site that should be included in the link, and then tap or click Add to add the site to the Sites In This Site Link list. Repeat this process for each site you want to add to the link. The link must include at least two sites.

5. Tap or click OK to close the New Object–Site Link dialog box.

6. In Active Directory Sites And Services, the site link is added to the appropriate transport folder (IP or SMTP). Select the transport folder in the console tree, and then double-tap or double-click the site link in the right pane. This displays the Link Properties dialog box, as shown in Figure 32-4.

7. Use the Cost combo box to set the relative cost of the link. The default cost is 100. For pointers on determining what cost to use, see "Mapping network infrastructure" and "Designing the intersite replication topology" in Chapter 27.

**Figure 32-4** Set the site-link properties.

8. Use the Replicate Every combo box to set the replication interval. The default interval is 180 minutes.

9. By default, the site link is available for replication 24 hours a day. To set a different schedule, tap or click Change Schedule and then use the Schedule For dialog box to set the desired replication schedule. When you are finished, tap or click OK.

10. Tap or click OK to close the site link's Properties dialog box.

# INSIDE OUT  The transitive nature of site links

Site links are transitive and follow the "three hops" rules discussed in "Replication rings and directory partitions" in Chapter 27. This means that if Site 1 is linked to Site 2, Site 2 is linked to Site 3, and Site 3 is linked to Site 4, the domain controllers in Site 1 can replicate with Site 2, Site 3, and Site 4. Because of the transitive nature of site links, site-link replication schedules and intervals for each site link are combined to determine the effective replication window and interval. To see the impact of combining replication schedules and intervals, consider the following examples:

- Site 1 to Site 2 link has a replication schedule of 7 P.M. to 7 A.M. and an interval of 60 minutes.

- Site 2 to Site 3 link has a replication schedule of 9 P.M. to 5 A.M. and an interval of 60 minutes.

- Site 3 to Site 4 link has a replication schedule of 1 P.M. to 3 A.M. and an interval of 180 minutes.

Because of the overlapping windows and intervals, replication between Site 1 and Site 2 could occur every 60 minutes from 7 P.M. to 7 A.M. Replication between Site 1 and Site 3 could occur every 60 minutes from 9 P.M. to 5 A.M. Replication between Site 1 and Site 4 could occur every 180 minutes from 9 P.M. to 3 A.M. This occurs because the replication availability window must overlap for replication to occur using transitive links.

If the site-replication schedules do not overlap, replication is still possible between multiple sites. To see how replication would work if schedules do not overlap, consider the following example:

- Site 1 to Site 2 link has a replication schedule of 11 P.M. to 3 A.M. and an interval of 60 minutes.

- Site 2 to Site 3 link has a replication schedule of 6 P.M. to 9 P.M. and an interval of 60 minutes.

- Site 3 to Site 4 link has a replication schedule of 1 A.M. to 5 A.M. and an interval of 180 minutes.

Assuming there are no alternate links between the sites, replication between Site 1 and Site 2 could occur every 60 minutes from 11 P.M. to 3 A.M. Site 1 would not be able to replicate with Site 3 and Site 4, however. Instead, Site 2 would replicate changes to Site 3 every 60 minutes from 6 P.M. to 9 P.M. daily. Site 3, in turn, would replicate changes to Site 4 every 180 minutes from 1 A.M. to 5 A.M. daily. In this configuration, there is significant replication latency (delay). Changes made at 5 P.M. in Site 1 would not be replicated to Site 2 until 11 P.M. The following day, the changes would be replicated to Site 3 at 6 P.M., and then at 1 A.M. on the third day the changes would be replicated to Site 4.

# Configuring replication schedules for site links

You can manage the replication schedule for site links in one of two ways: globally or individually. By default, IP site links use individual replication schedules and replicate within these schedules according to the replication interval. On the other hand, by default, SMTP site links ignore individual replication schedules and replicate only according to the replication interval. You can control whether global or individual schedules are used by following these steps:

1.  Start Active Directory Sites And Services. Expand the Sites container, and then expand the Inter-Site Transports container. Press and hold or right-click the container for the transport protocol you want to work with, either IP or SMTP, and then select Properties. This displays a Properties dialog box. (See Figure 32-5.)

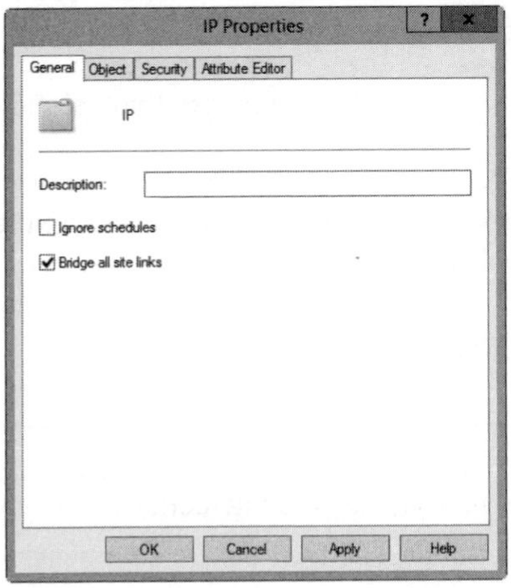

**Figure 32-5** Configuring global replication.

2.  You can now configure global replication for the selected transport. To ignore individual replication schedules on site links, select the Ignore Schedules check box. To use individual schedules, clear the Ignore Schedules check box. Tap or click OK.

When you use individual schedules, you can manage the times when replication is permitted by setting a replication schedule for each site link. By default, replication is available 24 hours a day, 7 days a week. To better manage the traffic flow over intersite links, you might need to change the permitted replication times. For example, if you find that a particular link is too saturated at specific times of the day, you might want to limit replication to ensure users have more bandwidth for collaboration and communication.

When individual schedules are allowed, you can configure a site link's replication schedule by following these steps:

1. Start Active Directory Sites And Services. Expand the Sites container, expand the Inter-Site Transports container, and then select the container for the transport protocol you want to work with, either IP or SMTP.

2. In the details pane, press and hold or right-click the site link you want to configure and then select Properties.

3. Tap or click Change Schedule. You can now set the valid and invalid replication hours using the Schedule For SiteLink dialog box. In this dialog box each hour of the day or night is a field that you can turn on and off.

   ○ Hours that are allowed are filled in with a dark bar—you can think of these hours as being turned on.

   ○ Hours that are disallowed are blank—you can think of these hours as being turned off.

4. To change the setting for an hour, tap or click it. Then select either Replication Not Available or Replication Available.

Scheduling features are listed in Table 32-1.

**TABLE 32-1  Scheduling features**

| Feature | Function |
| --- | --- |
| All | Allows you to select all the time periods |
| Day of week buttons | Allows you to select all the hours in a particular day |
| Hourly buttons | Allows you to select a particular hour for all the days of the week |
| Replication Available | Sets the allowed replication hours |
| Replication Not Available | Sets the disallowed replication hours |

> **Note**
>
> When you set replication hours, you'll save yourself a lot of work in the long run if you consider peak usage times and use a moderately restricted time window. For example, you might be tempted to restrict replication from 8 A.M. to 6 P.M. every weekday on a limited bandwidth link. However, such a wide restriction would not allow replication during the day. Instead, you might want to allow replication from 10 A.M. to 1 P.M. and from 6 P.M. to 6 A.M.

# Configuring site-link bridges

Be default, all site links are transitive, which allows Active Directory to automatically configure site-link bridges between sites. When a site is bridged, any two domain controllers can make a connection across any consecutive series of links as long as the site links are all using the same transport. The site-link-bridge cost is the sum of all the links included in the bridge.

A significant advantage of automatically created site-link bridges is that fault tolerance is built in whenever there are multiple possible routes between sites. Another significant advantage is that Active Directory automatically manages the site-link bridges and the ISTG monitors for changes and reconfigures the replication topology accordingly—and all without any administrator involvement required. Site-link bridges are discussed in more detail in "Considering the impact of site-link bridging" in Chapter 27.

You can enable or disable site-link bridges on a per-transport basis. By default, both the IP and SMTP transports have site-link bridging enabled. If you disable site-link bridging, Active Directory will no longer manage site-link bridges for the transport. You must then create and manage all site-link bridges for that transport. Any sites you add to a site-link bridge are considered to be transitive with each other. Site links that are not included in the site-link bridge are not transitive.

To see how this works, consider the previous example in which Site 1 is linked to Site 2, Site 2 is linked to Site 3, and Site 3 is linked to Site 4. If you disable site-link bridging and then create a site-link bridge that includes Site 1, Site 2, and Site 3, only those sites would have a transitive site link. Site 4 would be excluded. This means Site 1 could replicate changes to Site 2 and Site 1 could replicate changes to Site 3. Site 1 could not, however, replicate changes to Site 4. Only Site 3 would replicate changes to Site 4. This would occur because adjacent sites can always replicate changes with each other.

> **Note**
> One reason to create site-link bridges manually is to reduce the processing overhead on the designated ISTGs in each site. When you disable transitive links, the ISTGs no longer have to create and manage the site-link bridges, and this reduces the number of computations required to create the intersite replication topology.

To turn off transitive site links and manually configure site-link bridges, follow these steps:

1.  Start Active Directory Sites And Services. Expand the Sites container, and then expand the Inter-Site Transports container. Press and hold or right-click the container for the transport protocol you want to work with, either IP or SMTP, and then select Properties. This displays a Properties dialog box, as shown previously in Figure 32-5.

Chapter 32

2. Clear the Bridge All Site Links check box, and then tap or click OK. If you later want to enable transitive links and have Active Directory ignore the site-link bridges you created, you can select the Bridge All Site Links check box.

After you disable transitive links, you can manually create a site-link bridge between two or more sites by completing the following steps:

1. In Active Directory Sites And Services, expand the Sites container, and then expand the Inter-Site Transports container. Press and hold or right-click the container for the transport protocol you want to use, either IP or SMTP, and then select New Site Link Bridge. This displays the New Object–Site Link Bridge dialog box, as shown in Figure 32-6.

2. In the New Object–Site Link Bridge dialog box, type a descriptive name for the site-link bridge. This name serves as a point of reference for administrators and should clearly depict all the site links that are a part of the bridge.

3. In the Site Links Not In This Site Link Bridge list, select a site link that should be included in the bridge and then tap or click Add to add the site link to the Site Links In This Site Link Bridge list. Repeat this process for each site link you want to add to the bridge. The bridge must include at least two site links.

4. Tap or click OK to close the New Object–Site Link Bridge dialog box.

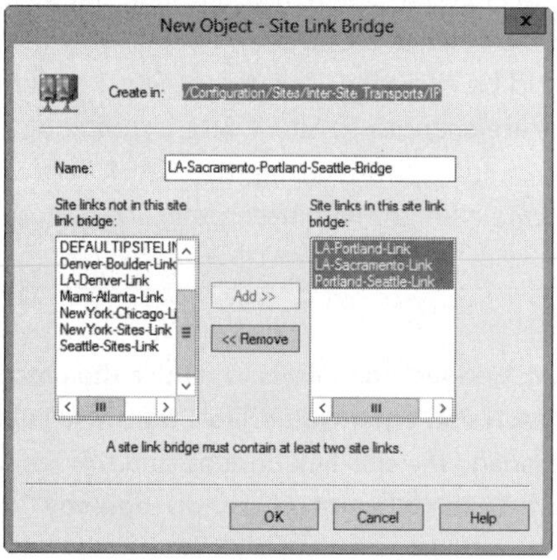

**Figure 32-6**  Create a site-link bridge.

# INSIDE OUT  Intersite transport options

In Active Directory Sites And Services, you can control the way site links work using the Bridge All Site Links and Ignore Schedules check boxes in the IP Properties and SMTP Properties dialog boxes, and as discussed previously in the "Configuring replication schedules for site links" and "Configuring site-link bridges" sections earlier in this chapter.

Selecting or clearing these check boxes modifies the flag values on the *Options* attribute, which you can view on the Attribute Editor tab in the related Properties dialog box. The *Options* attribute has two flags: IGNORE_SCHEDULES with an enabled value of 1, and BRIDGES_REQUIRED with an enabled value of 2.

BRIDGES_REQUIRED enables or disables transitive site links. When you disable transitive site links by clearing the Bridge All Site Links check box, you are setting the BRIDGES_ REQUIRED flag on the *Options* attribute. When you enable transitive site links by selecting the Bridge All Site Links check box, you are clearing the BRIDGES_REQUIRED flag on the *Options* attribute.

IGNORE_SCHEDULES enables or disables the use of individual replication schedules for site links. When you override the replication schedule for individual site links by selecting the Ignore Schedules check box, you are setting the IGNORE_SCHEDULES flag on the *Options* attribute. When you allow each site link to have a replication schedule by clearing the Ignore Schedules check box, you are clearing the IGNORE_SCHEDULES flag on the *Options* attribute.

## Determining the ISTG

Each site has an ISTG that is responsible for generating the intersite replication topology. As your organization grows and you add domain controllers and sites, the load on the ISTG can grow substantially because each addition means the ISTG must perform additional calculations to determine and maintain the optimal topology. When the ISTG is calculating the replication topology, its processor typically will reach 100 percent utilization. As the topology becomes more and more complex, the process will stay at maximum utilization longer and longer.

Because there is the potential for the ISTG to get overloaded, you should monitor the designated ISTG in a site more closely than other domain controllers. At the command line, you can determine the ISTG for a particular site by typing **repadmin /istg "site:***SiteName***"**, where *SiteName* is the name of the site that you want to work with such as **repadmin /istg "site:Denver-First-Site"**. If you want to examine the site in which your computer is located, simply type **repadmin /istg**. You also can determine the ISTG by completing the following steps:

1.  In Active Directory Sites And Services, expand the Sites container and then select the site whose ISTG you want to locate in the console tree.

2.  In the details pane, double-tap or double-click NTDS Site Settings.

3.  In the NTDS Site Settings Properties dialog box, the current ISTG is listed in the Inter-Site Topology Generator panel, as shown in Figure 32-7.

**Figure 32-7**  Locating the ISTG.

## Configuring site bridgehead servers

Replication between sites is performed by bridgehead servers in each site. A bridgehead server is a domain controller designated by the ISTG to perform intersite replication. Bridgehead servers are discussed in detail in Chapter 27 in the "Intersite replication essentials" and "Replication rings and directory partitions" sections.

As with the ISTG role, operating as a bridgehead server can add a significant load to a domain controller. This load increases with the number and frequency of replication changes. Because of this, the designated bridgehead servers should also be closely monitored to make sure they don't become overloaded.

## Determine bridgehead servers

You can list the bridgehead servers in a site by typing the following command at a command prompt: **repadmin /bridgeheads site:*SiteName***, where *SiteName* is the name of the site, such as **repadmin /bridgeheads site:Seattle-First-Site**. If you omit the *site:SiteName* values, the details for the current site are returned.

In situations in which you have domain controllers that are already overloaded or not equipped to possibly handle the additional load of being a bridgehead server, you might want to control which domain controllers operate as bridgehead servers. You do this by designating preferred bridgehead servers in a site.

There are several important considerations for designating bridgehead servers. First, after you designate a preferred bridgehead server, the ISTG will use only the preferred bridgehead server for intersite replication. This means if the domain controller acting as the bridgehead server goes offline or is unable to replicate for any reason, intersite replication will stop until the server is again available for replication or you change the preferred bridgehead server configuration options. In the latter case, you need to do one of the following:

- Remove the server as a preferred bridgehead server, and then specify a different preferred bridgehead server.

- Remove the server as a preferred bridgehead server, and then allow the ISTG to select the bridgehead servers that should be used.

Because you can designate multiple preferred bridgehead servers, you can prevent this situation simply by specifying more than one preferred bridgehead server. When there are multiple preferred bridgehead servers, the ISTG attempts to load-balance connections between the servers you designated as the preferred bridgehead servers. If a server fails, the other preferred bridgehead servers handle the load of the failed server.

An additional consideration to make when designating preferred bridgehead servers is that you must configure a bridgehead server for each partition that needs to be replicated. This means you must configure at least one domain controller with a replica of each directory partition as a bridgehead server. If you don't do this, the replication of the partition will fail and the ISTG will log an event in the Directory Services event log detailing the failure. Consider the example shown in Figure 32-8.

Chapter 32

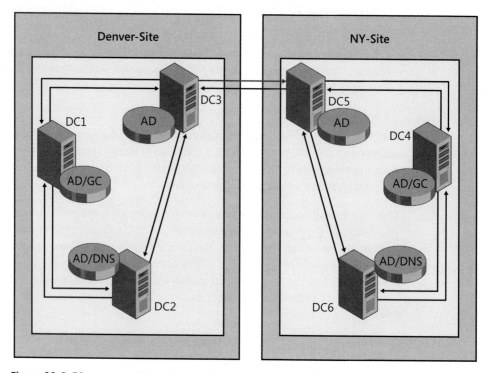

**Figure 32-8** Directory partitions in separate sites must have a designated bridgehead server.

Here, the Denver-Site and the NY-Site are part of the same domain, ThePhone-Company .com. Each site has a global catalog and a DNS server that is integrated with Active Directory. In this configuration, the bridgehead servers must replicate the following directory partitions: domain, configuration, schema, global catalog, and DNS (for the Domain Name System). If you designate DC3 and DC5 as the preferred bridgehead servers, only the domain, configuration, and schema directory partitions are replicated. This means replication for the global catalog and the DNS partition would fail and the ISTG would log an event in the Directory Services event log specifying the reason for the failure. On the other hand, if you designate DC1 and DC2 as the preferred bridgehead servers for the Denver site and DC4 and DC6 as the preferred bridgehead servers for the NY site, all the directory partitions are replicated.

To configure a domain controller as a preferred bridgehead server, complete the following steps:

1. Start Active Directory Sites And Services. Domain controllers associated with a site are listed in the site's Servers node. To locate the domain controller that you want to work with, expand the site node and then expand the related Servers node.

2. Press and hold or right-click the server you want to designate as a preferred bridgehead, and then select Properties.

3. In the Properties dialog box, shown in Figure 32-9, you have the option of configuring the server as a preferred bridgehead server for either IP or SMTP. Select the appropriate transport in the Transports Available For Inter-Site Data Transfer list, and then tap or click Add. If you later want the server to stop being a preferred bridgehead, select the transport in the This Server Is A Preferred Bridgehead Server For The Following Transports list and then tap or click Remove.

**Figure 32-9** Designating a preferred bridgehead server.

4. Tap or click OK.

## Configuring advanced site-link options

After you configure sites and site links, you might want to or need to optimize the configuration options to better suit the needs of your organization. Using site-link options, you can manage compression and notification during replication. You do this by editing the *Options* attribute on either the site-link object or the connection object related to the site link you want to modify. Only members of the Enterprise Admins group can change these options.

You can configure a site-link object's *Options* attribute by following these steps:

1. Start Active Directory Sites And Services. Expand the Sites container, and then expand the Inter-Site Transports container. Select the transport protocol you want to work with, either IP or SMTP. Next, press and hold or right-click the site link you want to modify, and then select Properties.

2.   In the Properties dialog box, tap or click the Attribute Editor tab. Scroll through the list of attributes until you find the *Options* attribute. When you find this attribute, select it and then tap or click Edit.

3.   In the Integer Attribute Editor dialog box, you can now do the following:

○   Type **1** to enable notification for intersite replication. This means the bridgehead servers on either side of the link will no longer use compression. Use this option only when you have sufficient bandwidth for a site connection and are concerned about high processor utilization on the affected bridgehead servers.

○   Type **2** to enable two-way synchronization for intersite replication. This means bridgehead servers on either side of the link can synchronize changes at the same time. This allows simultaneous synchronization in two directions for faster updates. Only use this setting on links with sufficient bandwidth to handle two-way sync traffic.

○   Type **4** to turn off compression for intersite replication. This means the bridgehead servers on either side of the link can notify each other that changes have occurred. This allows the bridgehead server receiving the notification to pull the changes across the site link and thereby get more frequent updates.

○   Use combinations of the flag values to set multiple flags. For example, a value of 5 means compression will be turned off and notification for intersite replication will be enabled.

○   Tap or click Clear to reset the *Options* attribute to its default value of *<not set>*. When the *Options* attribute is not set, notification for intersite replication is disabled and compression is turned on.

4.   Tap or click OK twice.

# Monitoring and troubleshooting replication

When you have problems with replication, you'll find that monitoring is an important part of your diagnostics and troubleshooting process. Several tools are available to help you, including the Replication Administrator (RepAdmin), which is a command-line utility.

## Using the Replication Administrator

You run the Replication Administrator from the command line. Most command-line parameters accept a list of the domain controllers you want to work with (called DCList) and specified as follows:

- * is a wildcard that includes all domain controllers in the enterprise.

- *PartialName** is a partial server name that includes a wildcard to match the remainder of the server name.

- *Site:SiteName* includes only domain controllers in the named site.

- *Gc:* includes all global catalog servers in the enterprise.

Knowing this, there are many tasks you can perform using the Replication Administrator. These tasks are summarized in Table 32-2.

**TABLE 32-2 Key replication administrator commands**

| Command to Type | Description |
|---|---|
| **repadmin /bridgeheads** *DCList* **[/verbose]** | Lists bridgehead servers. |
| **repadmin /failcache** *DCList* | Lists failed replication events that were detected by the knowledge consistency checker (KCC). |
| **repadmin /istg** *DCList* **[/verbose]** | Lists the name of the ISTG for a specified site. |
| **repadmin /kcc** *DCList* **[/async]** | Forces the KCC to recalculate the intrasite replication topology for a specified domain controller. By default, this recalculation occurs every 15 minutes. Use the /Async options to start the KCC and not wait for it to finish the calculation. |
| **repadmin /latency** *DCList* **[/verbose]** | Lists the amount of time between intersite replications using the ISTG Keep Alive time stamp. |
| **repadmin /queue** *DCList* | Lists tasks waiting in the replication queue. |
| **repadmin /replsummary** *DCList* | Displays a summary of the replication state. |
| **repadmin /showcert** *DCList* | Displays the server certificates loaded on the specified domain controllers. |
| **repadmin /showconn** *DCList* | Displays the connection objects for the specified domain controllers. It defaults to the local site. |
| **repadmin /showctx** *DCList* | Lists computers that have opened sessions with a specified domain controller. |
| **repadmin/showoutcalls** *DCList* | Lists calls that were made by the specified server to other servers but that have not yet been answered. |

Chapter 32

| Command to Type | Description |
|---|---|
| **repadmin /showrepl** *DCList* | Lists the replication partners for each directory partition on the specified domain controller. |
| **repadmin /showtrust** *DCList* | Lists all domains trusted by a specified domain. |

## Using PowerShell to monitor and troubleshoot replication

The ActiveDirectory module includes cmdlets for monitoring and troubleshooting replication. Type **Get-Help *–Ad*** to see a complete list of cmdlets for working with Active Directory. The ones you'll use the most for troubleshooting are

- Get-ADReplicationPartnerMetadata

- Get-ADReplicationFailure

- Sync-ADObject

Get-ADReplicationPartnerMetadata returns information about the configuration and state of replication for a domain controller, including the date and time of the last replication attempt and the date and time of the last successful replication. The basic syntax is

```
Get-ADReplicationPartnerMetadata -target ServerName
```

Here, *ServerName* is the name of the domain controller to check, or you can use * to look at all domain controllers in the forest, such as

```
Get-ADReplicationPartnerMetadata -target CorpServer25
```

*or*

```
Get-ADReplicationPartnerMetadata -target *
```

Get-ADReplicationFailure returns information about recent replication errors, including the most recent failures and the partners a domain controller failed to contact. The basic syntax is

```
Get-ADReplicationFailure -target ObjectName -scope [server|site|domain|forest]
```

Here, *ObjectName* is the name of the object to check and *scope* sets the scope of the search. This example checks all domain controllers in the named site:

```
Get-ADReplicationFailure -target Seattle-First-Site -scope site
```

You use Sync-ADObject to perform immediate replication of changes related to a specific object. Typically, you'll use it along with another cmdlet, such as Get-ADDomainController. Consider the following scenario:

> The TestTeam group was deleted accidentally, and you recovered the group from the Active Directory Recycle Bin. Now you want to restore the group throughout the domain. The command you use to do this is as follows:

```
Get-ADDomainController -filter * | foreach {Sync-ADObject -object
"cn=testteam,cn=users,dc=cpandl,dc=com" -source corpserver85
-destination $_.hostname}
```

## Monitoring replication

Using the Performance Monitor, you can perform in-depth monitoring and analysis of Active Directory. You open the Performance Monitor by selecting the related option on the Tools menu in Server Manager. You can track the performance of multiple domain controllers from a single, monitoring server using Performance Monitor's remote monitoring capabilities.

DirectoryServices is the performance object you'll use for monitoring Active Directory. Several hundred performance counters are available for selection. Most counters have a prefix that reflects the aspect of Active Directory to which the counter relates. These prefixes include the following:

- **AB**  AB counters relate to the Address Book in Active Directory.

- **ATQ**  ATQ counters relate to the Asynchronous Thread Queue in Active Directory.

- **DRA**  DRA counters relate to the Directory Replication Agent in Active Directory.

- **DS**  DS counters relate to the Directory Service in Active Directory.

- **LDAP**  LDAP counters relate to the Lightweight Directory Access Protocol in Active Directory.

- **SAM**  SAM counters relate to the Security Accounts Manager in Active Directory.

Depending on the operations mode, either DFS or FRS is used for replication of the Sysvol. When Distributed File System (DFS) is used to replicate the Sysvol files between domain controllers, you can monitor the Distributed File System using the DFS Replicated Folders, DFS Replication Connections, and DFS Replication Service Volumes objects. When File Replication Service (FRS) is used to replicate the Sysvol files between domain controllers, you can monitor File Replication Service using the *FileReplicaConn* and *FileReplicatSet* monitoring objects. Each object has a number of counters that can be used to track the status and health of replication.

Chapter 32

You can specify counters to monitor by following these steps:

1. In the Performance Monitor console, expand the Monitoring Tools node and then select the Performance Monitor node.

2. Tap or click the Add (+) button on the toolbar, or press Ctrl+I. In the Add Counters dialog box, use the Select Counters From Computer list to select the computer to monitor.

3. Double-tap or double-click the object you want to work with on the Available Counters list. Specify counters to track by selecting them in the Select Counters From Computer list and then tapping or clicking Add. You can learn more about counters by selecting the Show Description check box.

4. Tap or click OK when you are finished adding counters.

You also can configure performance logging and performance alerting if desired:

- Events related to Active Directory are also logged in the event logs. Active Directory–related events, including NTDS replication events, are logged in the Directory Service log on the domain controller.

- Events related to DFS are recorded in the DFS Replication log on the domain controller. The primary source for events is DFSR, which is the DFS Service itself.

- Events related to FRS are recorded in the File Replication Service log on the domain controller. The primary source for events is NtFrs, which is the File Replication Service itself.

## Modifying intersite replication for testing

Occasionally, when you are testing or troubleshooting intersite replication, you might need to temporarily modify the way intersite replication works. You can modify the way intersite replication works by editing the *Options* attribute on a bridgehead server's server object. Only members of the Enterprise Admins group can change these options.

You can configure a server object's *Options* attribute by following these steps:

1. Start Active Directory Sites And Services. Domain controllers associated with a site are listed in the site's Servers node. To locate the domain controller that you want to work with, expand the site node and then expand the related Servers node.

2. In the left pane, select the bridgehead server you want to work with. Next, press and hold or right-click the related NTDS Settings node, and then select Properties.

3. In the Properties dialog box, tap or click the Attribute Editor tab. Scroll through the list of attributes until you find the *Options* attribute. When you find this attribute, select it and then tap or click Edit.

4. In the Integer Attribute Editor dialog box, you can now do the following:

   ○ Type **2** to disable inbound replication. This means the bridgehead server will no longer perform inbound replication. The server will still accept replication connections and also perform outbound replication.

   ○ Type **4** to disable outbound replication. This means the bridgehead server will no longer perform outbound replication. The server will still accept replication connections and also perform inbound replication.

   ○ Type **8** to prevent connections from forming replication partnerships. This means the bridgehead servers will not allow connections to be established for inbound or outbound replication. Existing connections will continue, but no new connections will be established.

   ○ Use combinations of the flag values to set multiple flags. For example, a value of *14* means inbound and outbound replication are disabled and that servers are prevented from forming replication partnerships.

   ○ Tap or click Clear to reset the *Options* attribute and undo your changes. When the *Options* attribute is not set, notification for intersite replication is disabled and compression is turned on.

5. Tap or click OK twice.

> **Note**
> When the original value for the *Options* attribute is *1*, the server hosts a global catalog and you must add 1 to all values you enter to ensure the server can continue to act as a global catalog. When you are finished testing, you can restore the original settings by entering a value of *1*.

Chapter 32

**CAUTION**

Setting these options changes the way the KCC works and also might disable the KCC's ability to automatically generate replication topology. Before you make any changes, note the current value of the *Options* attribute. Typically, the attribute has a value of *<not set>* or *1*. When the original value is *<not set>*, you can tap or click Clear to reset the *Options* attribute and undo your changes. Failure to restore your changes after testing or troubleshooting can cause replication failure throughout the enterprise.

# Index to troubleshooting topics

| Topic | Page |
|---|---|
| Several versions of BitLocker | 597 |
| Be careful when defragmenting | 786 |
| Shadow copy relies on the Task Scheduler | 789 |
| Resolving email notification problems | 804 |
| Resolving problems with report generation | 806 |
| Correcting the network category | 877 |
| Blocked pings | 914 |
| Identifying a specific interface | 938 |
| Class ID problems | 997 |
| Resolving WINS replication errors | 1119 |
| You cannot change an attribute even though you are a member of the Administrators group | 1171 |
| The computer won't join the domain | 1381 |

# Index

# About the author

**William R. Stanek** (*http://www.williamrstanek.com/*) has more than 20 years of hands-on experience with advanced programming and development. He is a leading technology expert, an award-winning author, and a pretty-darn-good instructional trainer. Over the years, his practical advice has helped millions of programmers, developers, and network engineers all over the world. His current and books include *Windows 8 Administration Pocket Consultant*, *Windows Server 2012 Pocket Consultant*, and *SQL Server 2012 Pocket Consultant*.

William has been involved in the commercial Internet community since 1991. His core business and technology experience comes from more than 11 years of military service. He has substantial experience in developing server technology, encryption, and Internet solutions. He has written many technical white papers and training courses on a wide variety of topics. He frequently serves as a subject matter expert and consultant.

William has an MS with distinction in information systems and a BS in computer science, magna cum laude. He is proud to have served in the Persian Gulf War as a combat crewmember on an electronic warfare aircraft. He flew on numerous combat missions into Iraq and was awarded nine medals for his wartime service, including one of the United States of America's highest-flying honors, the Air Force Distinguished Flying Cross. Currently, he resides in the Pacific Northwest with his wife and children.

William recently rediscovered his love of the great outdoors. When he's not writing, he can be found hiking, biking, backpacking, traveling, or trekking in search of adventure with his family!

Find William on Twitter at WilliamStanek and on Facebook at *www.facebook.com/William.Stanek.Author.*

# What do you think of this book?

We want to hear from you!

To participate in a brief online survey, please visit:

**microsoft.com/learning/booksurvey**

Tell us how well this book meets your needs—what works effectively, and what we can do better. Your feedback will help us continually improve our books and learning resources for you.

Thank you in advance for your input!